France
touring atlas

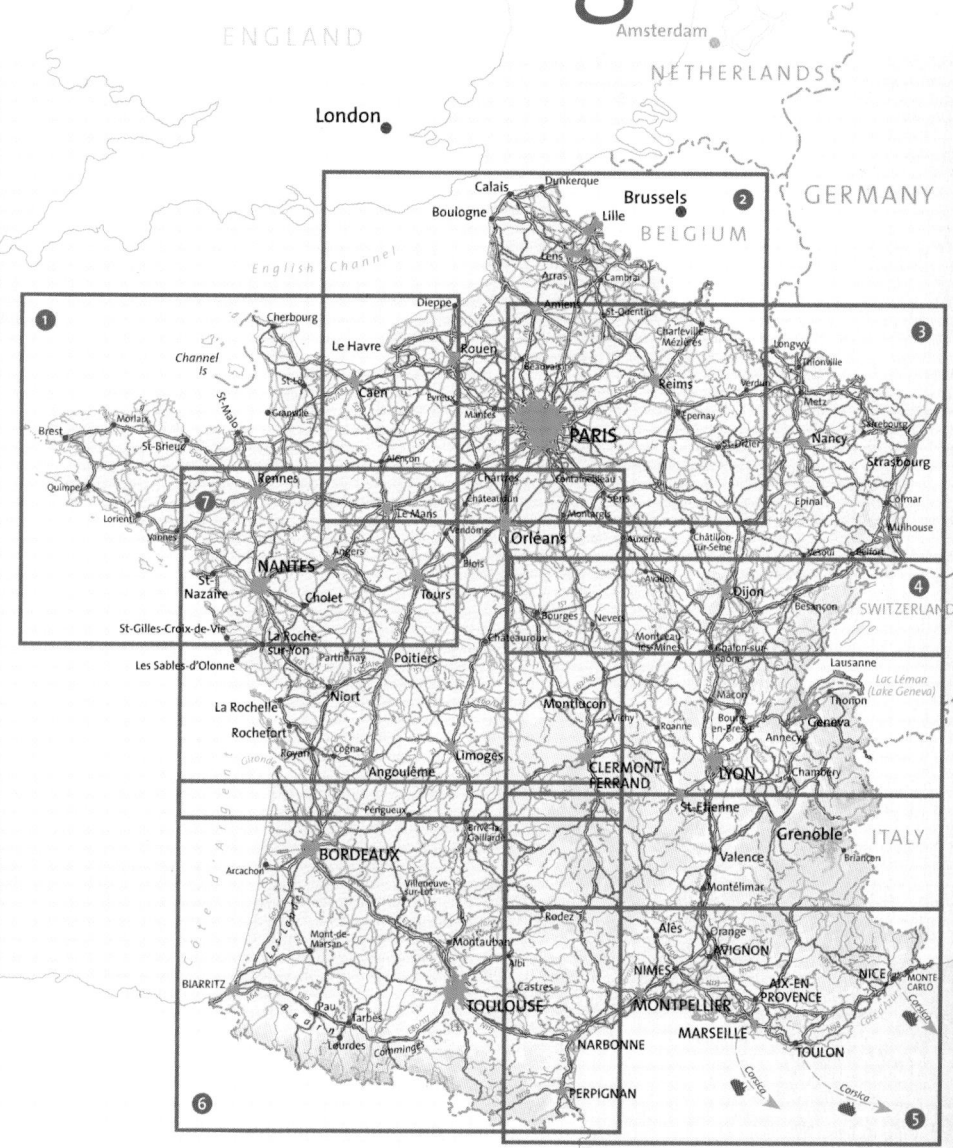

D0634110

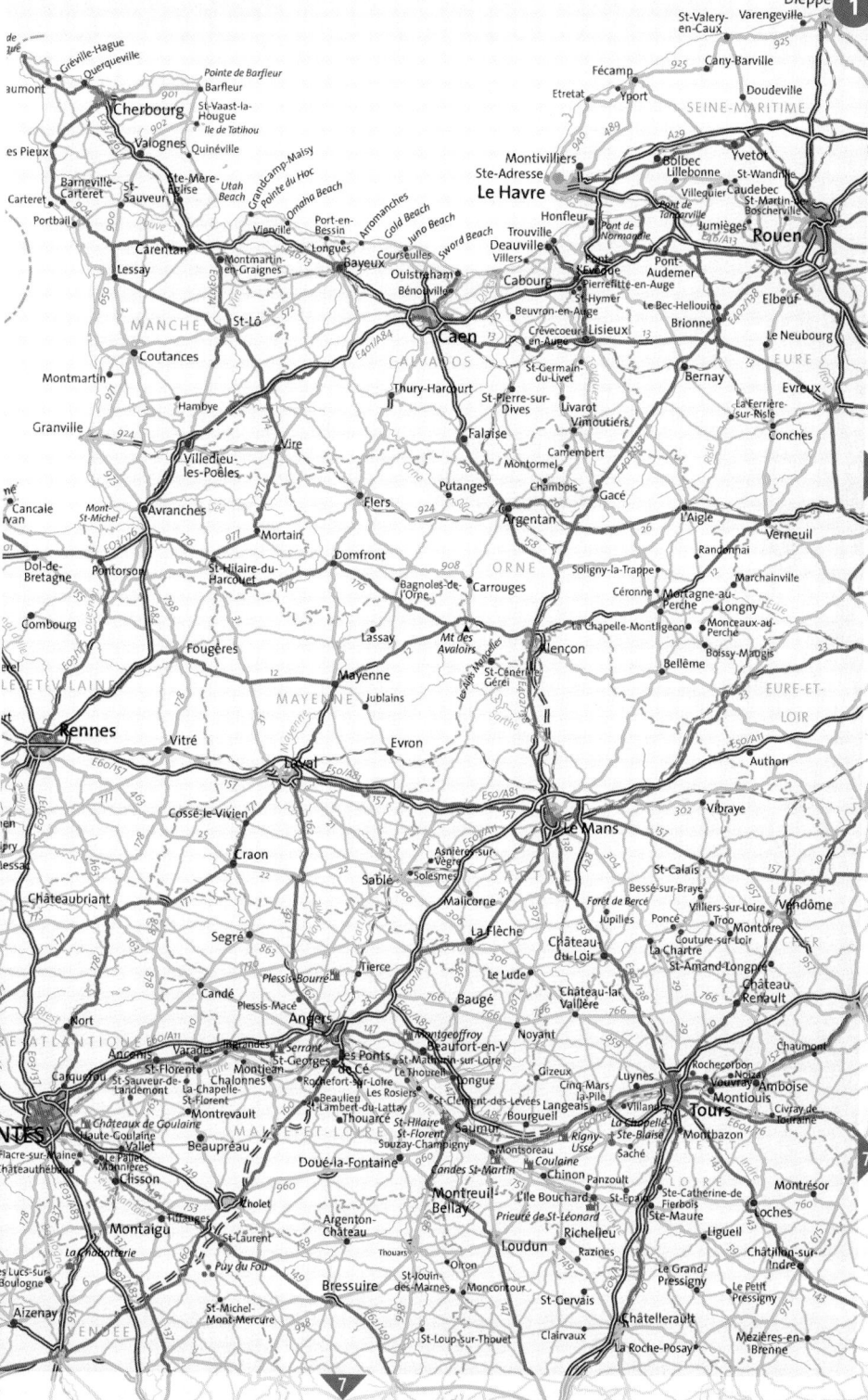

20 km
10 miles

N

BELGIUM

Bray-
Dunes
Leffinckoucke
ergues
Wormhout
assel
Hazebrouck
Armentières
Tourcoing
Roubaix
Bethune
Lille
Carvin
St-Amand-
les-Eaux
Notre-Dame-
de-Lorette
Lens
Hénin-
Beaumont
NORD
Valenciennes
Aubigny
Vimy
Denain
Arras
Douai
Bavay
Maubeuge
Hautmont
Le Quesnoy
Bapaume
Cambrai
Le
Cateau
Caudry
Ors
Avesnes
Givet
Albert
Le Catelet
Bony
Bohain-en-V
Haybes
Fumay
Revin
Corbie
Péronne
St-Quentin
Guise
St-Michel
Rocroi
Monthermé
Vervins
Charleville-
Mézières
Crécy
Sedan
Roye
Tergnier
ARDENNES
Avioth
Montdidier
Noyon
Chauny
Sissonne
Poix-Terron
Mouzon
Montmédy
Maignelay-
Montigny
AISNE
Laon
Blérancourt
Coucy-le-
Château
Fliain
Rethel
Stenay
Compiègne
Forêt de
Compiègne
Pierrefonds
Craonne
Vendresse
Vouziers
Buzancy
Crépy-en-
Valois
Villers-
Cotterêts
Soissons
Creil
Senlis
Nanteuil
Parc Astérix
La Ferté-Milon
Reims
Montfaucon
d'Argonne
Etain
Chantilly
Ermenonville
Marfaux
Pourcy
Verzenay
Verzy
Verdun
N3
Fresnes-
en-W
Hautvillers
Ay
Château-
Thierry
Epernay
Ste-
Menehould
MEUSE
Meaux
La Ferté-s/s-
Jouarre
MARNE
Vertus
Châlons-en-
Champagne
St-Mihiel
Disneyland
Paris
Coulommiers
Mondemont-
Montgivroux
Fère-
Champenoise
Revigny
Bar-le-Duc
Commercy
PARIS
Melun
Sézanne
Vitry-le-
François
St-Dizier
N4
SEINE-ET-
MARNE
Provins
Wassy
Joinville
Corbeil-
Essonnes
Fontainebleau
Forêt de
Fontainebleau
Romilly
Lac de Der
Chantecoq
Grand
Nemours
AUBE
Lac du
Temple
Brienne-
le-Château
Cirey-sur-
Blaise
Sens
Troyes
Lac
d'Orient
Vignory
Colombey-les-
Deux-Églises
Andelot
Montargis
Courtenay
Villeneuve-sur-
Yonne
Joigny
Chaource
Bar-sur-Aube
Clairvaux
Bar-sur-Seine
Essoyes
HAUTE-MARNE
Chaumont
Flogny
Les Riceys
Arc-en-
Barrois

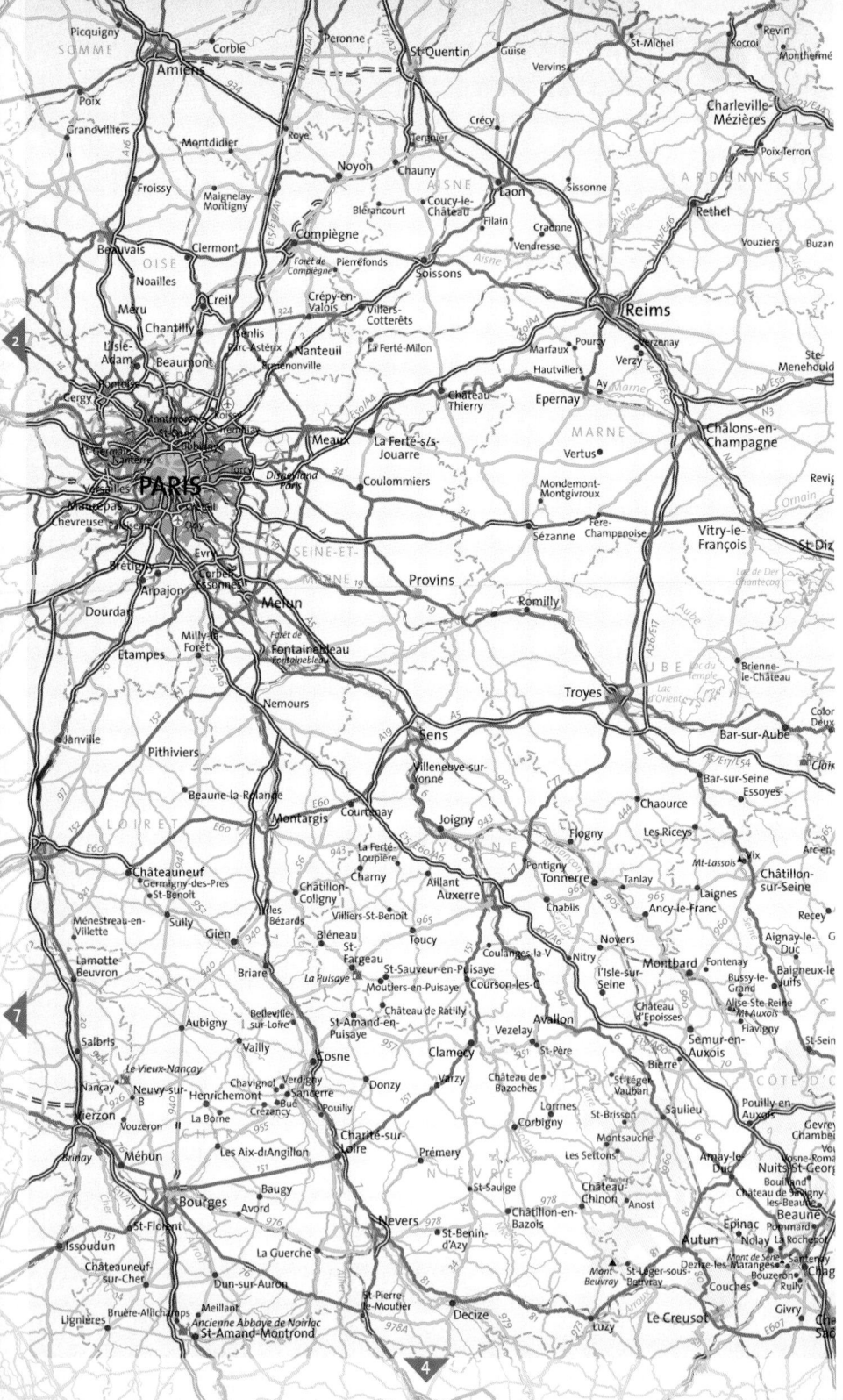

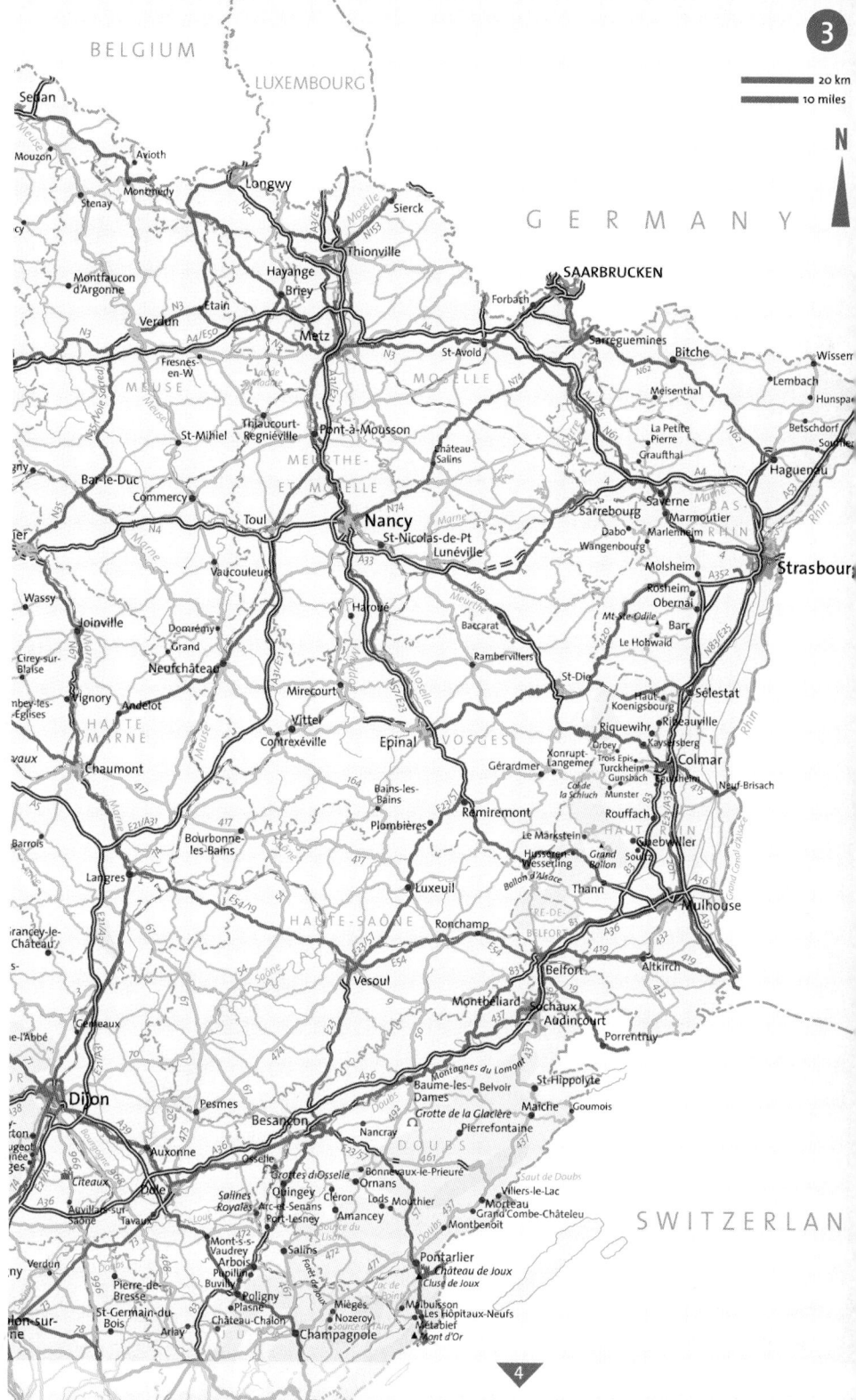

BELGIUM

LUXEMBOURG

GERMANY

20 km
10 miles

N

Sedan
Mouzon
Avioth
Stenay
Montmédy
Longwy
Sierck
cy
Thionville
Montfaucon
d'Argonne
Hayange
Briey
Verdun
Etain
SAARBRUCKEN
Forbach
Fresnes-
en-W
Metz
St-Avold
Sarreguemines
Bitche
Wissem
MEUSE
MOSELLE
Meisenthal
Lembach
Hunspac
St-Mihiel
Thiaucourt-
Regniéville
Pont-à-Mousson
Château-
Salins
La Petite
Pierre
Grauffhal
Betschdorf
Souffler
Bar-le-Duc
MEURTHE-
ET MOSELLE
Haguenau
igny
Commercy
Toul
Nancy
Sarrebourg
Saverne
Marmoutier
Marlenheim
Vaucouleurs
St-Nicolas-de-Pt
Lunéville
Dabo
Wangenbourg
Molsheim
Strasbour
Wassy
Haroué
Baccarat
Rosheim
Obernai
Joinville
Domrémy
Grand
Rambervillers
Mt-Ste-Odile
Barr
Le Hohwald
Cirey-sur-
Blaise
Neufchâteau
St-Dié
mbey-les-
Eglises
Vignory
Andelot
HAUTE
MARNE
Mirecourt
Haut
Koenigsbourg
Sélestat
Vittel
Contrexéville
Epinal
VOSGES
Riquewihr
Ribeauville
Kaysersberg
Chaumont
Gérardmer
Xonrupt-
Langemer
Orbey
Trois Epis
Turckheim
Gunsbach
Col de
la Schluch
Colmar
Munster
Neuf-Brisach
Bains-les-
Bains
Remiremont
Rouffach
Bourbonne-
les-Bains
Plombières
Le Markstein
Guebwiller
HAUT-RHIN
Barrois
Hussoren
Wesserling
Grand
Ballon
Soultz
Langres
Luxeuil
Ballon d'Alsace
Thann
rancey-le-
Château
HAUTE-SAÔNE
Ronchamp
Mulhouse
Belfort
Altkirch
Vesoul
la-l'Abbé
Montbéliard
Sochaux
Audincourt
Porrentruy
Dijon
Pesmes
Montagnes du Lomont
Baume-les-
Dames
Belvoir
St-Hippolyte
ton
ugeot
rnée
ges
Auxonne
Besançon
Nancray
Grotte de la Glacière
Maiche
Goumois
Citeaux
Osselle
DOUBS
Pierrefontaine
Dole
Grottes d'Osselle
Quingey
Ornans
Bonnevaux-le-Prieuré
Cléron
Lods
Mouthier
Saut de Doubs
Villers-le-Lac
Auvillar-sur-
Saône
Tavaux
Salines
Royales
Arc-et-Senans
Port-Lesney
Amancey
Grand-Combe-Châteleu
Montbenoit
ny
Verdun
Mont-s-s-
Vaudrey
Arbois
Salins
Pontarlier
Château de Joux
Cluse de Joux
Pierre-de-
Bresse
St-Germain-du-
Bois
Papillon
Buvilly
Poligny
Plasne
Mieges
Nozeroy
Malbuisson
Les Hôpitaux-Neufs
Metabief
Arlay
Château-Chalon
Champagnole
Mont d'Or

SWITZERLAN

ITALY

20 km
10 miles

N

SPAIN

Grottes de Villars · Thiviers · Champagnac-de-Belair · Excideuil · Sorges · Savignac · Hautefort · Terrasson-la-Villedieu · Brive-la-Gaillarde · Larche · St-Amand-de-Coly · Montignac · Grotte de Lascaux · St-Léon-sur-Vézère · Périgueux · Rouffignac · Les Eyzies-de-Tayac · Le Bugue · Sarlat · Souillac · Gourdon · Martel · Carlux · St-Céré · Bretenoux · Beaulieu-sur-Dordogne · Argentat · Tulle · Uzerche · Corrèze · Bort-les-Orgues · Mauriac · Aurillac · Murat · St-Flour · Langeac · Brioude · Paulhaguet · Laguiole · Figeac · Conques · Espalion · Rodez · Mende · Marvejols · Millau · Montauban · Gaillac · Albi · Carmaux · Castres · Mazamet · TOULOUSE · Muret · Carcassonne · NARBONNE · Béziers · Castelnaudary · Limoux · Quillan · Foix · Tarascon-sur-Ariège · Ax-les-Thermes · Prades · PERPIGNAN · Céret · Le Boulou · Argelès-sur-Mer · Port-Vendres · Banyuls-sur-Mer · Puigcerda · Prats-de-Molo

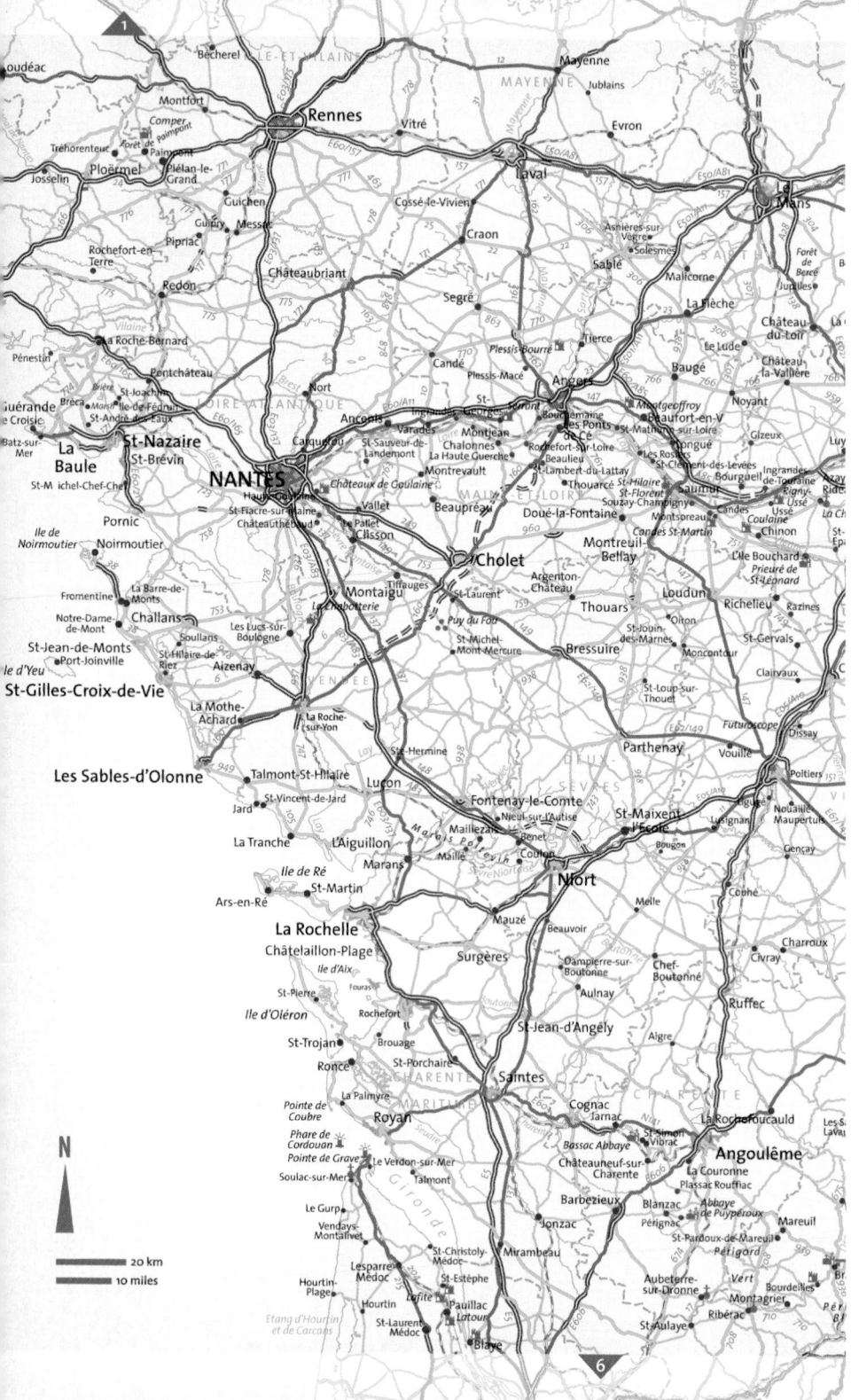

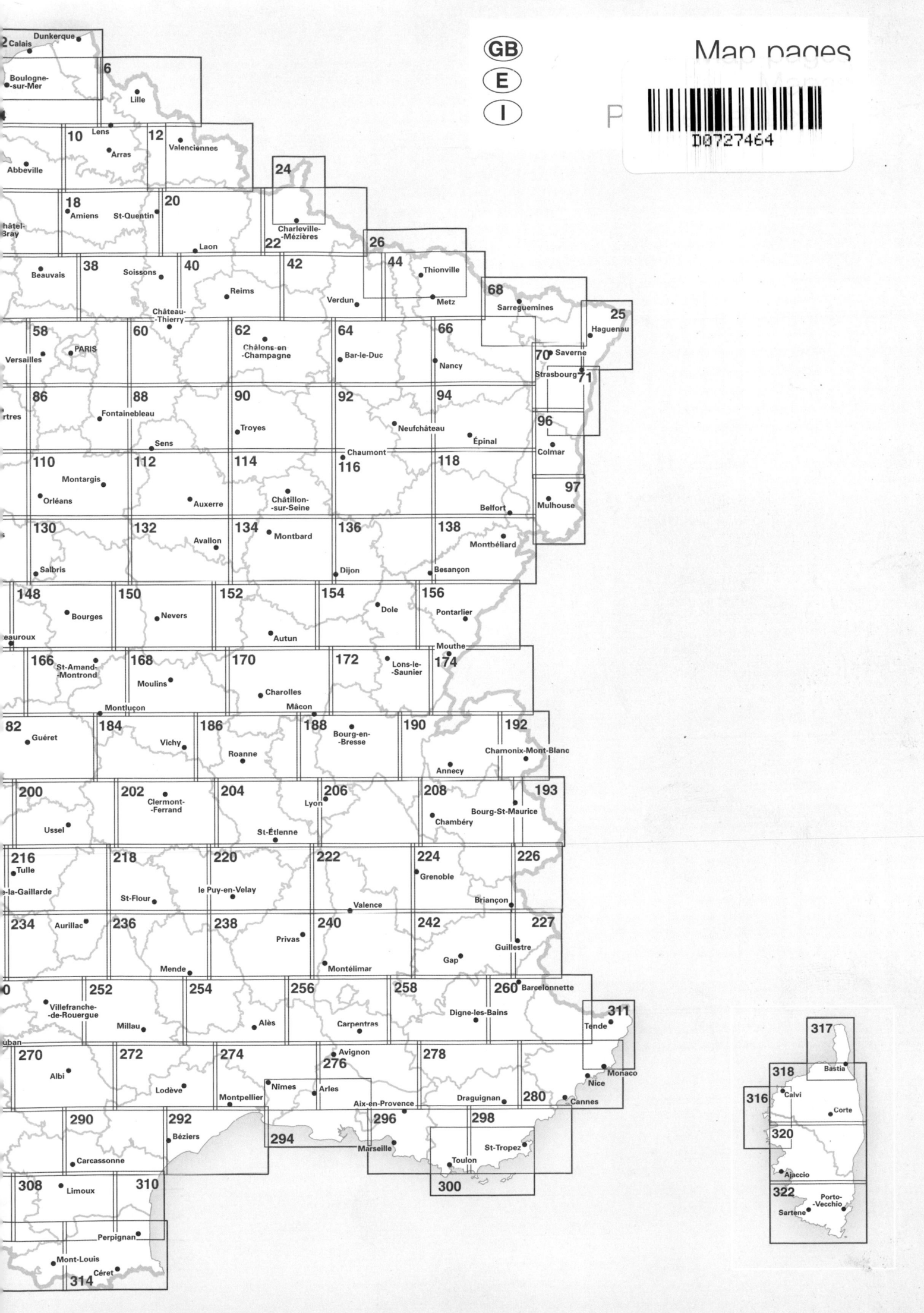

GB
E
I

D0727464

2 Calais Dunkerque
6
Boulogne-sur-Mer
Lille
10 Lens
Arras
12 Valenciennes
Abbeville
24
18 Amiens St-Quentin
20
Châtel-Bray
Charleville-Mézières
22
Laon
26
44 Thionville
38 Beauvais Soissons 40 Reims 42 Verdun Metz
68 Sarreguemines
25 Haguenau
Château-Thierry
58 Versailles PARIS 60 62 Châlons-en-Champagne 64 Bar-le-Duc 66 Nancy 70 Saverne Strasbourg
71
86 88 Fontainebleau 90 Troyes 92 Neufchâteau 94 Épinal 96 Colmar
110 Montargis 112 Sens 114 116 Chaumont 118 97 Mulhouse
Orléans Auxerre Châtillon-sur-Seine Belfort
130 132 134 Montbard 136 138 Montbéliard
Salbris Avallon Dijon Besançon
148 150 152 154 156 Pontarlier
Bourges Nevers Dole
eauroux Autun Mouthe
166 St-Amand-Montrond 168 Moulins 170 Charolles 172 Lons-le-Saunier 174
Montluçon Mâcon
82 184 186 188 Bourg-en-Bresse 190 192
Guéret Vichy Roanne Chamonix-Mont-Blanc
Annecy
200 202 Clermont-Ferrand 204 206 Lyon 208 193
Ussel St-Étienne Chambéry Bourg-St-Maurice
216 Tulle 218 St-Flour 220 le Puy-en-Velay 222 Valence 224 Grenoble 226 Briançon
e-la-Gaillarde
234 Aurillac 236 238 Privas 240 Montélimar 242 Gap 227 Guillestre
Mende
252 Villefranche-de-Rouergue 254 256 Carpentras 258 Digne-les-Bains 260 Barcelonnette 311 Tende
Millau Alès
270 Albi 272 Lodève 274 Montpellier 276 Avignon Nîmes Arles 278 Draguignan 280 Monaco Nice Cannes
uban Aix-en-Provence
290 Béziers 292 294 296 Marseille 298 St-Tropez Toulon 300
Carcassonne
308 Limoux 310
Perpignan
Mont-Louis Céret
314

317
318 Bastia
316 Calvi Corte
320
322 Porto-Vecchio
Ajaccio
Sartène

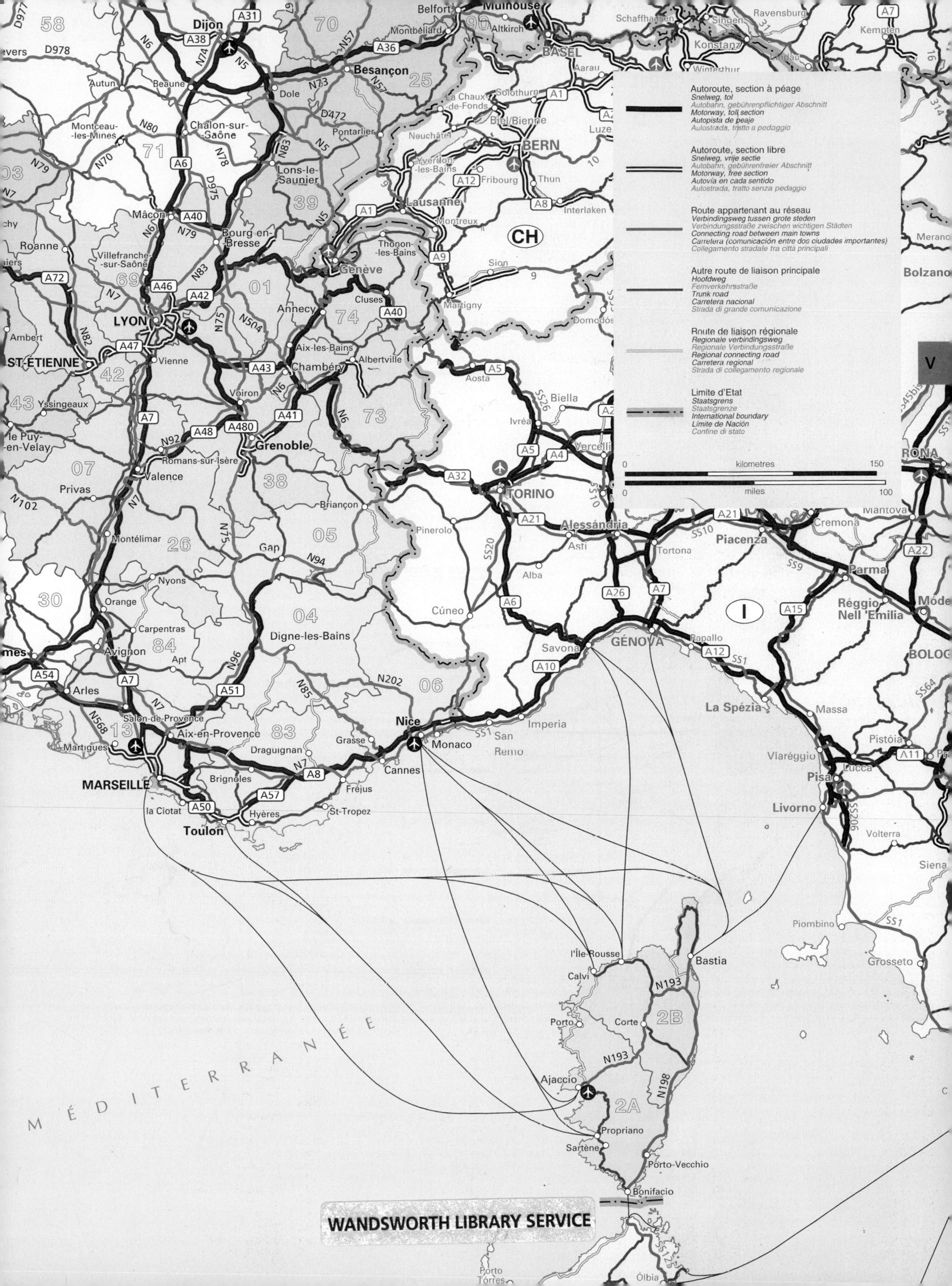

(F) Légende   Legend (GB)
(NL) Legende   Leyenda (E)
(D) Legende   Legenda (I)

Autoroute, section à péage
Autosnelweg, tol
Autobahn, gebührenpflichtiger Abschnitt

Motorway, toll section
Autopista de peaje
Autostrada, tratto a pedaggio

Autoroute, section libre, voie à caractère autoroutier
Autosnelweg, vrije sectie, expressweg
Autobahn, gebührenfreier Abschnitt, Schnellverkehrsstraße

Motorway, free section, dual carriageway with motorway characteristics
Autopista libre, autovía
Autostrada, tratto senza pedaggio, strada con carretterische autostradali

Autoroute en construction
Autosnelweg onder constructie
Autobahn im Bau

Motorway under construction
Autopista en construcción
Autostrada in costruzione

Route appartenant au réseau vert
Verbindingsweg tussen grote steden (groene wegtekens)
Verbindungsstraße zwischen wichtigen Städten (grüne Verkehrsschilder)

Connecting road between main towns (green road sign)
Carretera verde (comunicación entre dos ciudades importantes)
Collegamento stradale tra città principali (cartelli stradali verdi)

Autre route de liaison principale
Hoofdweg
Fernverkehrsstraße

Trunk road
Otra carretera principal
Strada di grande comunicazione

Route de liaison régionale
Regionale verbindingsweg
Regionale Verbindungsstraße

Regional connecting road
Carretera regional
Strada di collegamento regionale

Autre route
Andere weg
Sonstige Straße

Other road
Otra carretera
Altra strada

Route interdite
Verboden weg
Gesperrte Straße

Prohibited road
Carretera prohibida o cortada
Strada vietata

Route à deux chaussées avec ou sans séparation
Dubbele rijbaan met of zonder tussenberm
Zweibahnige Fernstraße mit oder ohne Mittelstreifen

Dual carriageway with or without separator
Carretera de dos carriles con o sin mediana
Doppia carreggiata con o senza spartitraffico

Route à deux voies larges et plus
Weg met twee of meer brede rijstroken
Straße mit zwei breiten Fahrspuren und mehr

Road with two wide lanes or more
Carretera con dos o más carriles anchos
Strada a due o più corsie ampie

Route à une ou deux voies
Weg met één of twee rijstroken
Ein- oder zweispurige Straße

Road with one lane or two lanes
Carretera con uno o dos carriles
Strada a corsia unica o doppia

Échangeur : complet (1), partiel (2), numéro
Knooppunt: volledig (1), gedeeltelijk (2), nummer
Vollanschlußstelle (1), beschränkte Anschlußstelle (2), Nummer

Junction : complete (1), restricted (2), exit number
Accesos: completo (1), parcial (2), número
Svincolo: completo (1), parziale (2), numero

Barrière de péage (1), aire de service (2)
Tol slagboom (1), benzinestation (2)
Mautstelle (1), Tankstelle (2)

Toll gate (1), service area (2)
Punto de peaje (1), área de servicio (2)
Barriera di pedaggio (1), area di servizio (2)

Tunnel routier
Wegtunnel
Straßentunnel

Road tunnel
Túnel
Galleria stradale

Distances kilométriques (km)
Afstanden in kilometers (km)
Entfernungen in Kilometern (km)

Distance in kilometres (km)
Distancia en kilómetros (km)
Distanze in chilometri (km)

Numérotation: Autoroute, type autoroutier
Wegnummers: Autosnelweg
Straßennummerierung : Autobahn

Road numbering: Motorway
Numeración de las carreteras: Autopista
Numerazione stradale: Autostrada

Numération routière: Route nationale, route secondaire
Wegnummers: Nationale weg, secundaire weg
Straßennummerierung : Nationalstraße, Nebenstraße

Road numbering : National road, secondary road
Numeración de las carreteras: Carretera nacional, provincial
Numerazione stradale: Strada nazionale, strada secondaria

Chemin de fer (1), gare ou point d'arrêt ouvert au trafic voyageurs (2)
Spoorweg (1), station of stopplaats open voor passagiers (2)
Eisenbahn (1), Bahnhof oder Haltpunkt für Personenverkehr (2)

Railway (1), station or stopping place open to passenger traffic (2)
Ferrocarril (1), estación o parada abierta al tráfico de pasajeros (2)
Ferrovia (1), stazione o fermata aperta al traffico passeggeri (2)

Liaison par bac
Veerdienst
Fähre

Ferry route
Ruta de transbordador (ferry)
Traghetto

Aéroport
Luchthaven
Flughafen

Airport
Aeropuerto
Aeroporto

Zone bâtie (1), zone industrielle (2)
Bebouwde kom (1), industriegebied (2)
Geschlossene Bebauung (1), Industriegebiet (2)

Built-up area (1), industrial park (2)
Zona edificada (1), polígono industrial (2)
Area edificata (1), zona industriale (2)

Bois
Bos
Wald

Woods
Bosque
Boschi

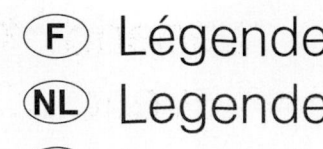

F Légende   Legend GB
NL Legende   Leyenda E
D Legende   Legenda I

Limite de département Departementsgrens Departementgrenze	━━━ ━━ ━━━	Département boundary Límite de departamento Confine di dipartimento
Limite de région Gewestgrens Regionsgrenze	━━━ ━━ ━━━	Region boundary Límite de región Confine di regione
Limite d'Etat Staatsgrens Staatsgrenze	▬ ✛ ✛ ✛ ✛ ✛ ✛ ✛	International boundary Límite de Nación Confine di stato
Hameau Gehucht Weiler	la Californie	Hamlet Aldea, caserío Paesino
Chef-lieu de commune Hoofdstad van de gemeente Gemeindehauptort	Biot	Chief town of commune Cabeza de término municipal Capoluogo di comune
Chef-lieu de canton Hoofdstad van het kanton Kantonhauptort	**Cagnes-sur-Mer**	Chief town of canton Capital de cantón Capoluogo di cantone
Chef-lieu d'arrondissement Hoofdstad van het arrondissement Arrondissementhauptort	**GRASSE**	Chief town of arrondissement Capital de arrondissement Capoluogo di arrondissement
Chef-lieu de département Hoofdstad van het departement Departementhauptort	**NICE**	Chief town of département Capital de departamento Capoluogo di dipartimento
Marais (1), Marais salants (2) Moeras (1), Zoutpan (2) Sumpf (1), Salzteiche (2)	1 2	Marsh (1), salt pans (2) Marisma, humedal (1), Salinas (2) Palude (1), Saline (2)
Région sableuse (1), Sable humide (2) Zandig gebied (1), Getijden gebied (2) Sandgebiet (1), Gezeiten (2)	1 2	Dry sand (1), wet sand (2) Zona arenosa (1), Banco de arena (2) Area sabbiosa (1), Sabbia bagnata (2)
Cathédrale (1), Abbaye (2), Église (3), Chapelle (4) Kathedraal (1), Abdij (2), Kerk (3), Kapel (4) Dom (1), Abtei (2), Kirche (3), Kapelle (4)	1 2 3 4	Cathedral (1), Abbey (2), Church (3), Chapel (4) Catedral (1), Abadía (2), Iglesia (3), Capilla (4) Cattedrale (1), Abbazia (2), Chiesa (3), Cappella (4)
Château (1), Château ouvert au public (2), Musée (3) Kasteel (1), Kasteel open voor publiek (2), Museum (3) Schloss (1), Schlossbesichtigung (2), Museum (3)	1 2 3	Castle (1), Castle open to the public (2), Museum (3) Castillo (1), Castillo abiero al público (2), Museo (3) Castello (1), Castello aperto al pubblico (2), Museo (3)
Point de vue (1), Curiosité (2) Uitzichtspunt (1), Bezienswaardigheid (2) Aussichtspunkt (1), Sehenswürdigkeit (2)	1 2	Viewpoint (1), Place of interest (2) Vista panorámica (1), Curiosidad (2) Vista panoramica (1), Curiosità (2)
Station thermale (1), Sports d'hiver (2) Kuuroord (1), Wintersportgebied (2) Kurort (1), Wintersportort (2)	1 2	Spa (1), Winter sports resort (2) Estación Termal (1), Estación de deportes de invierno (2) Stazione termale (1), Stazione di sport invernali (2)
Remparts (1), Phare (2) Borstwering (1), Vuurtoren (2) Wälle (1), Leuchtturm (2)	1 2	Rampart (1), Lighthouse (2) Muralla (1), Faro (2) Bastioni (1), Faro (2)
Vestiges antiques (1), Ruines intéressantes (2), Monument commémoratif (3) Historische overblijfselen (1), Bezienswaardige ruïne (2), Gedenkteken (3) Zeugnisse des Altertums (1), Interessante Ruinen (2), Gedänkstätte (3)	1 2 3	Ancient remains (1), Interesting ruins (2), Memorial (3) Vestigios antiguos (1), Ruinas interesantes (2), Monumento conmemorativo (3) Vestigia antiche (1), Rovine interessanti (2), Monumento commemorativo (3)
Pèlerinage Bedevaartplaats Wallfahrt	▮	Pilgrimage site Peregrinaje Luogo di pellegrinaggio
Cimetière militaire Militaire begraatplaats Soldatenfriedhof	▦	Military cemetery Cementerio militar Cimitero militare
Grotte (1), Mégalithe (2) Grot (1), Megaliet (2) Höhle (1), Megalith (2)	1 2	Cave (1), Megalith (2) Cueva (1), Megalito (2) Grotta (1), Megalite (2)
Localité ou site remarquable Interessante Stad of plaats Sehenswerter Ortschaft oder Platz	**PARIS** Baou-des-Blanc	Town or place of interest Cuidad o lugar de interés Città o luogo d'interesse

1:180,000

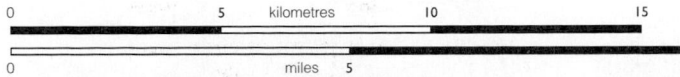

0	5	kilometres	10	15

0	miles	5	10

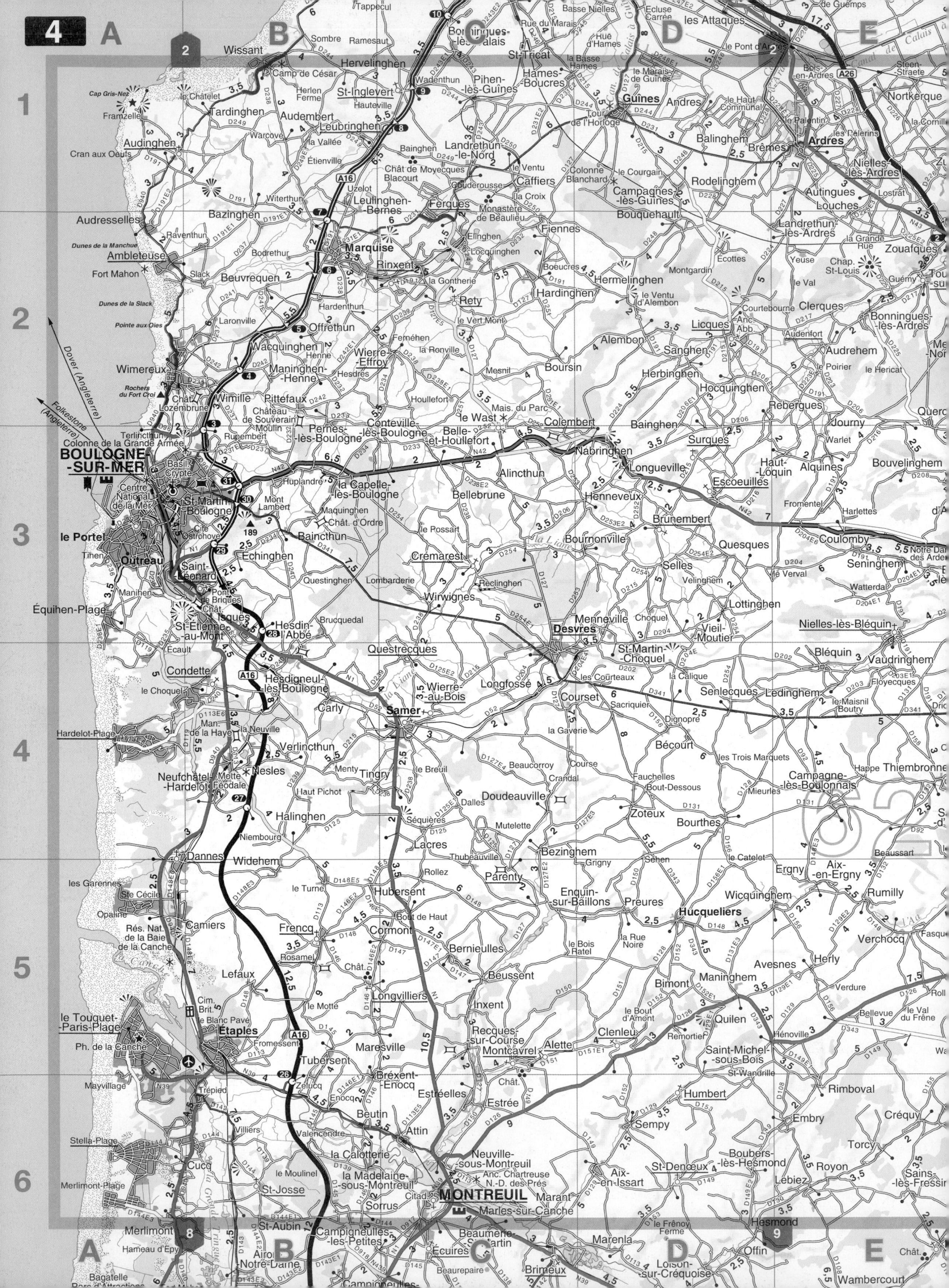

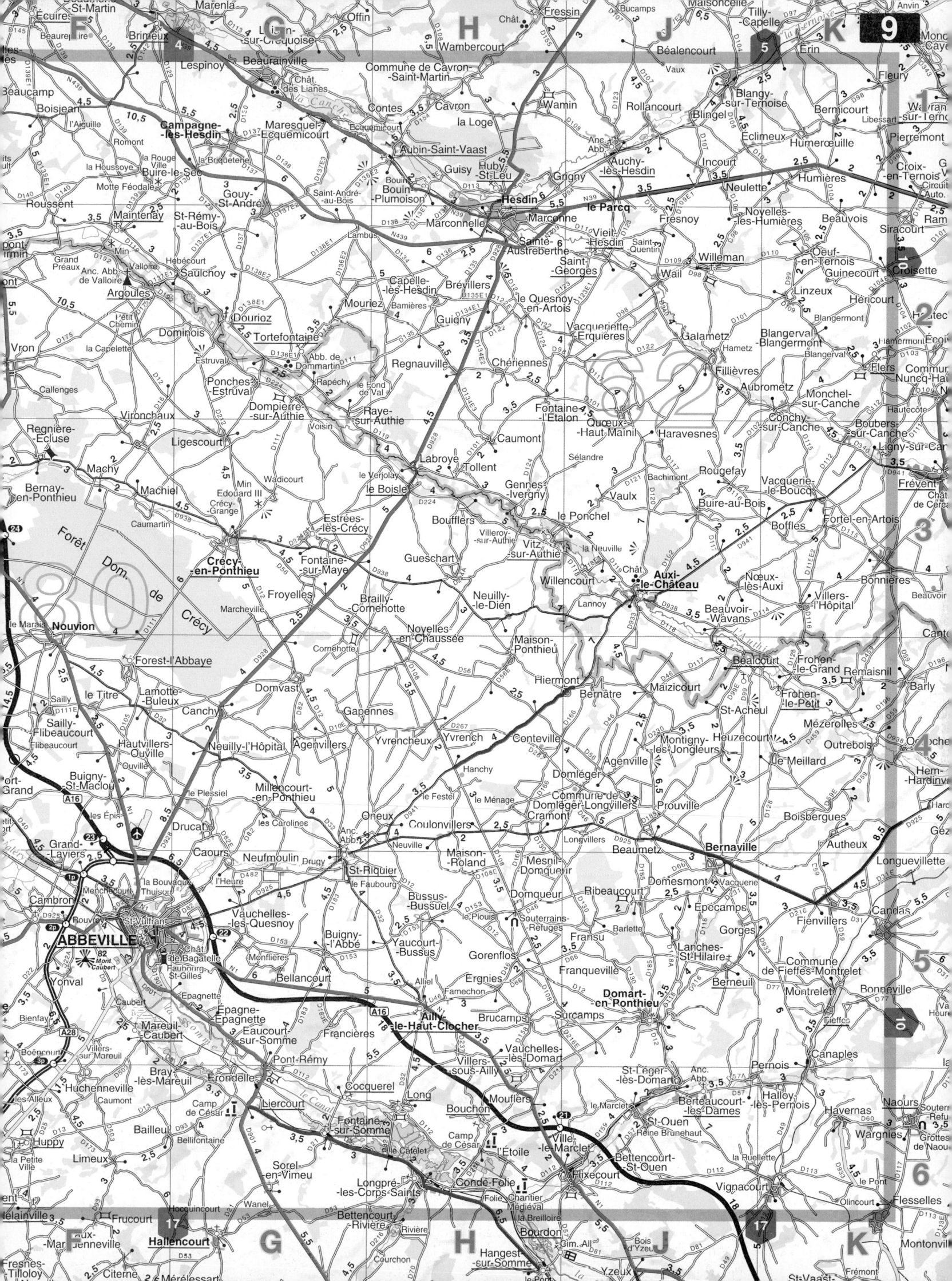

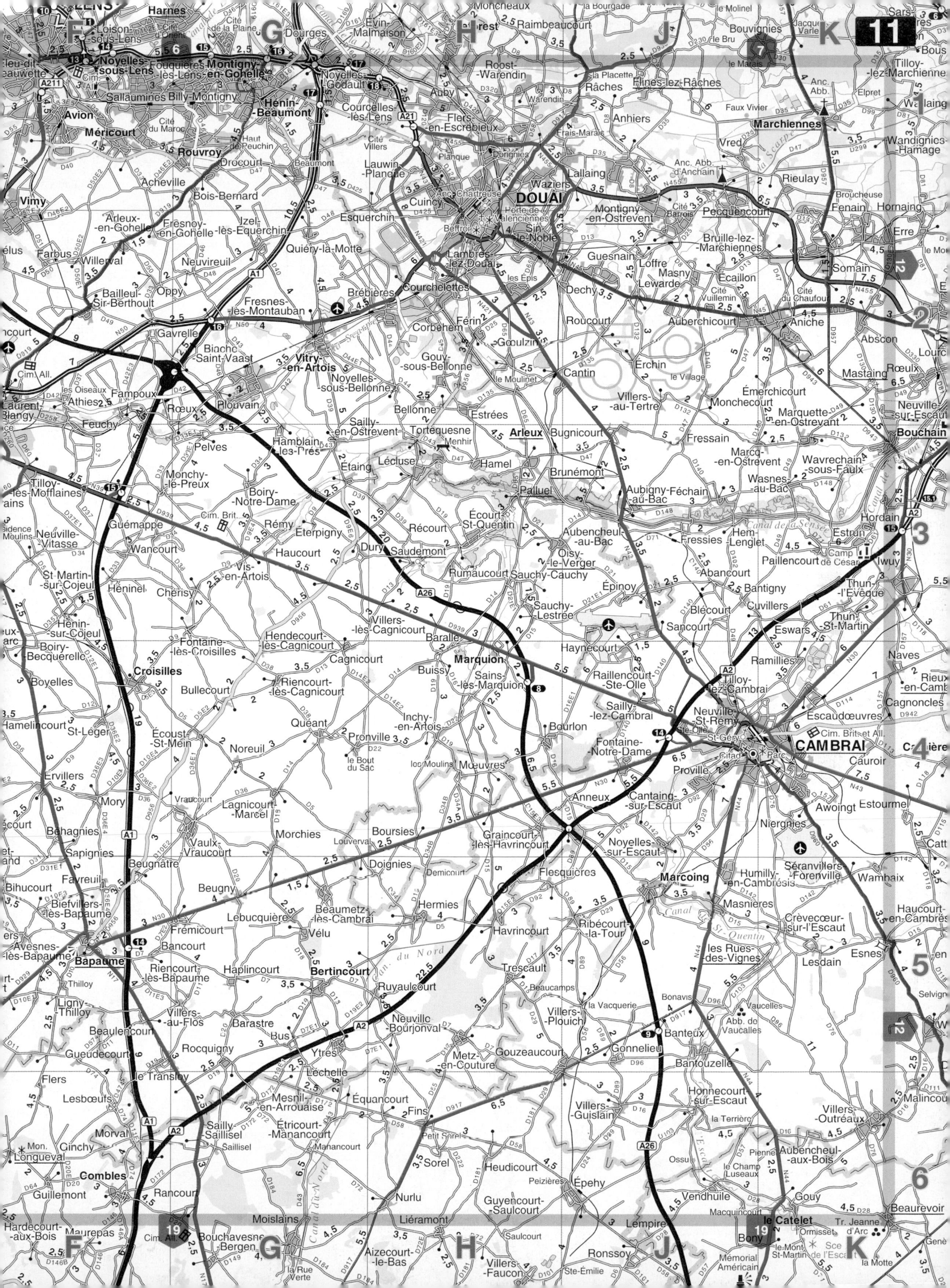

A B C D E

1

Biville-sur-Mer · Penly · Assigny · Canehan · Monchy-sur-Eu · Longroy · Gamaches · Tilloy · Floriville

Berneval-le-Grand · St-Martin-Plage · Brunville · Guilmécourt · le Coudroy · St-Martin-le-Gaillard · le Mesnil-Réaume · Millebosc · Bouillancourt-en-Séry

Belleville-sur-Mer · Bracquemont · le Petit Berneval · St-Martin-en-Campagne · Catteville · Greny · Auquemesnil · Sept-Meules · Melleville · Guerville · Bazinval · St-Milfort

2

Dieppe · Puys · Graincourt · Derchigny · Glicourt · Intraville · Tourville-la-Chapelle · St-Quentin-au-Bosc · Gratte-Panche · Avesnes-en-Val · Villy-le-Bas · Grande Vallée · Rieux · Bouttencourt

Étran · Ancourt · Sauchay · Breuilly · Bray · Bailly-en-Rivière · Brignely · Maisoncelle · Grandcourt · Folny · Dancourt · Blangy-sur-Bresle

Martin-Église · Bellengreville · St-Ouen-sous-Bailly · Auberville · Montigny · Feuilloy · le Buisson · Béthencourt · St-Rémy · Mont Rôti · Hamel

Arques-la-Bataille · Envermeu · Quartier de la Croix · Renouval · les Ifs · Fresnoy-Folny · Puisenval · Preuseville · Fallencourt

Martigny · St-Aubin-le-Cauf · St-Nicolas-d'Aliermont · Angreville · Douvrend · le Mont Landrin · Wanchy-Capval · Villeneuve · St-Pierre-des-Jonquières · Pucherin · Foucarmont

Dampierre-St-Nicolas · St-Jacques-d'Aliermont · Meulers · Notre-Dame-d'Aliermont · Bretelle · le Hamel · Béthencourt · Houppelande · Smermesnil · Crimont · Villers-sous-Foucarmont · St-Léger-aux-Bois

3

la Chapelle-du-Bourgay · St-Germain-d'Étables · Freulleville · Ste-Agathe-d'Aliermont · Épinay · Londinières · Fréauville · Bosc-Geffroy · Callengeville · Varimpré

Torcy-le-Petit · Torcy-le-Grand · Ste-Foy · St-Honoré · les Grandes Ventes · Ricarville-du-Val · Osmoy-St-Valery · Croixdalle · Bailleul-Neuville · Clais · Bailleul · Fesques · Landes-Vieilles-et-Neuves

Longueville-sur-Scie · les Hauts Champs · Muchedent · Mesnil-Follemprise · Bures-en-Bray · Isemberthéville · Mesnières-en-Bray · Lucy · Ménonval · Vatierville · Sté-Beuve-en-Rivière

4

Notre-Dame-du-Parc · Ardouval · Fresles · Haut-de-Fresles · St-Martin-l'Hortier · Mesnières-en-Bray · le Grand-Hattembuille · Neufchâtel-en-Bray · Mortemer · Flamets-Frétils · Graval · Beaussault

St-Hellier · Cressy · Orival · Pommeréval · Bully · Quièvrecourt · St-André · Neuville-Ferrières · Bouelles · Nesle-Hodeng · Conteville

Sévis · le Bosc de Sévis · Bellencombre · Forêt Domaniale · Vauchel · Martincamp · Esclavelles · Fontaine-en-Bray · Hodeng · Bethléem

5

Montreuil-en-Caux · St-Victor-l'Abbaye · Bracquetuit · Beaumont-le-Hareng · St-Saëns · Maucomble · Massy · Ste-Geneviève · Mesnil-Mauger · Beaubec-la-Rosière · le Thil-Riberpré · Serqueux

Grigneuseville · Étaimpuis · Bosc-Bérenger · St-Martin-Osmonville · Neufbosc · Bradiancourt · Bosc-Mesnil · Sommery · Compainville · Forges-les-Eaux

6

Clères · Cottévrard · Critot · Beaumont · Mathonville · Roncherolles-en-Bray · Mauquenchy · la Ferté-St-Samson

St-Germain-sous-Cailly · Cailly · Yquebeuf · Estouteville-Écalles · Buchy · Bosc-Roger-sur-Buchy · Bosc-Édeline · Rouvray-Catillon · Salmont

Mont-Cauvaire · Fontaine-le-Bourg · Vieux-Manoir · Grand Pré · Ste-Croix-sur-Buchy · Bois-Héroult · Sigy-en-Bray · Mésangueville

Bosc-Guérard-St-Adrien · St-Georges-sur-Fontaine · Pierreval · Bierville · St-Germain-des-Essourts · Ernemont-sur-Buchy · Bois-Guilbert · Argueil · Hodeng-Hodenger

Quincampoix

A B C D E

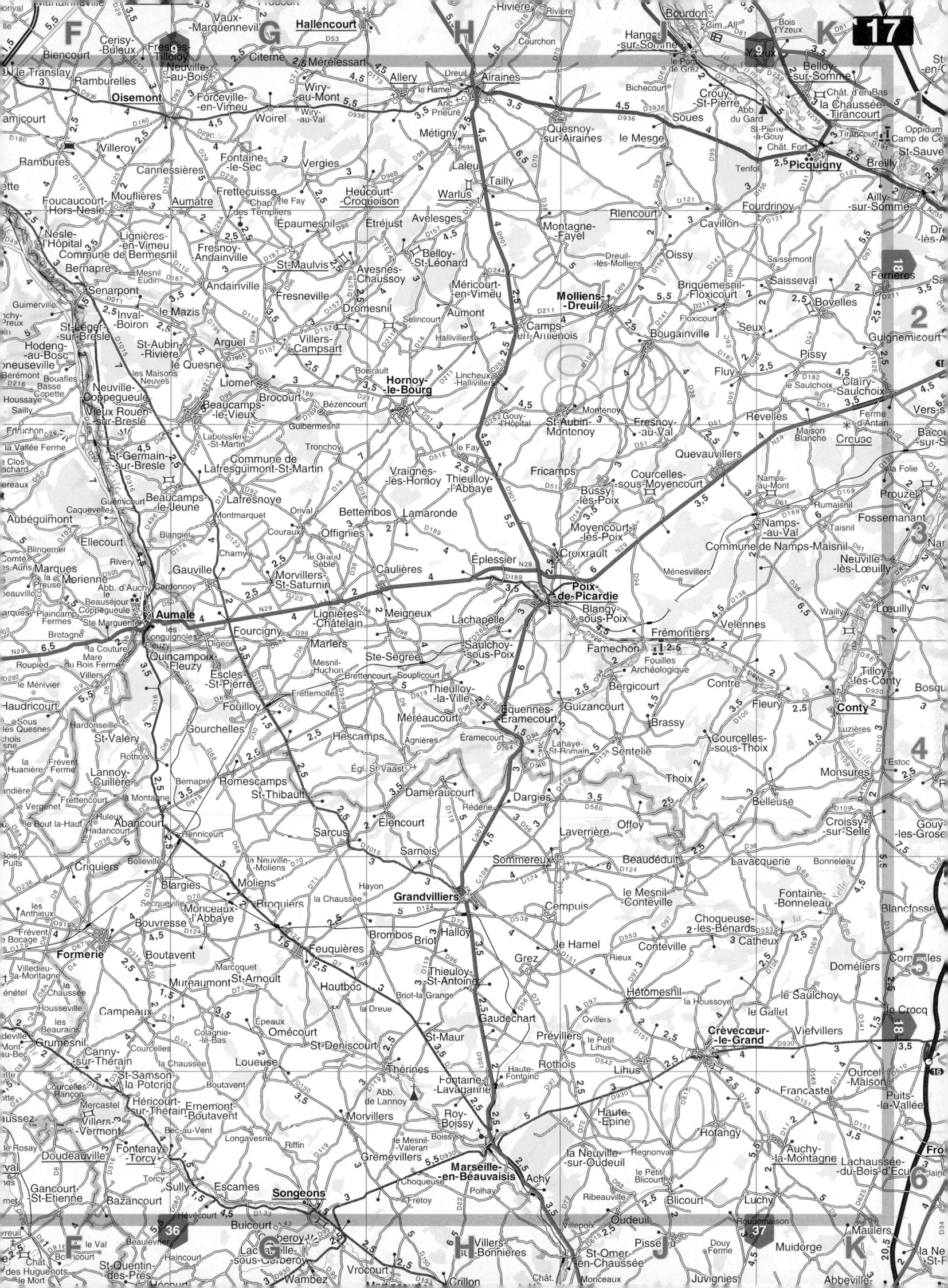

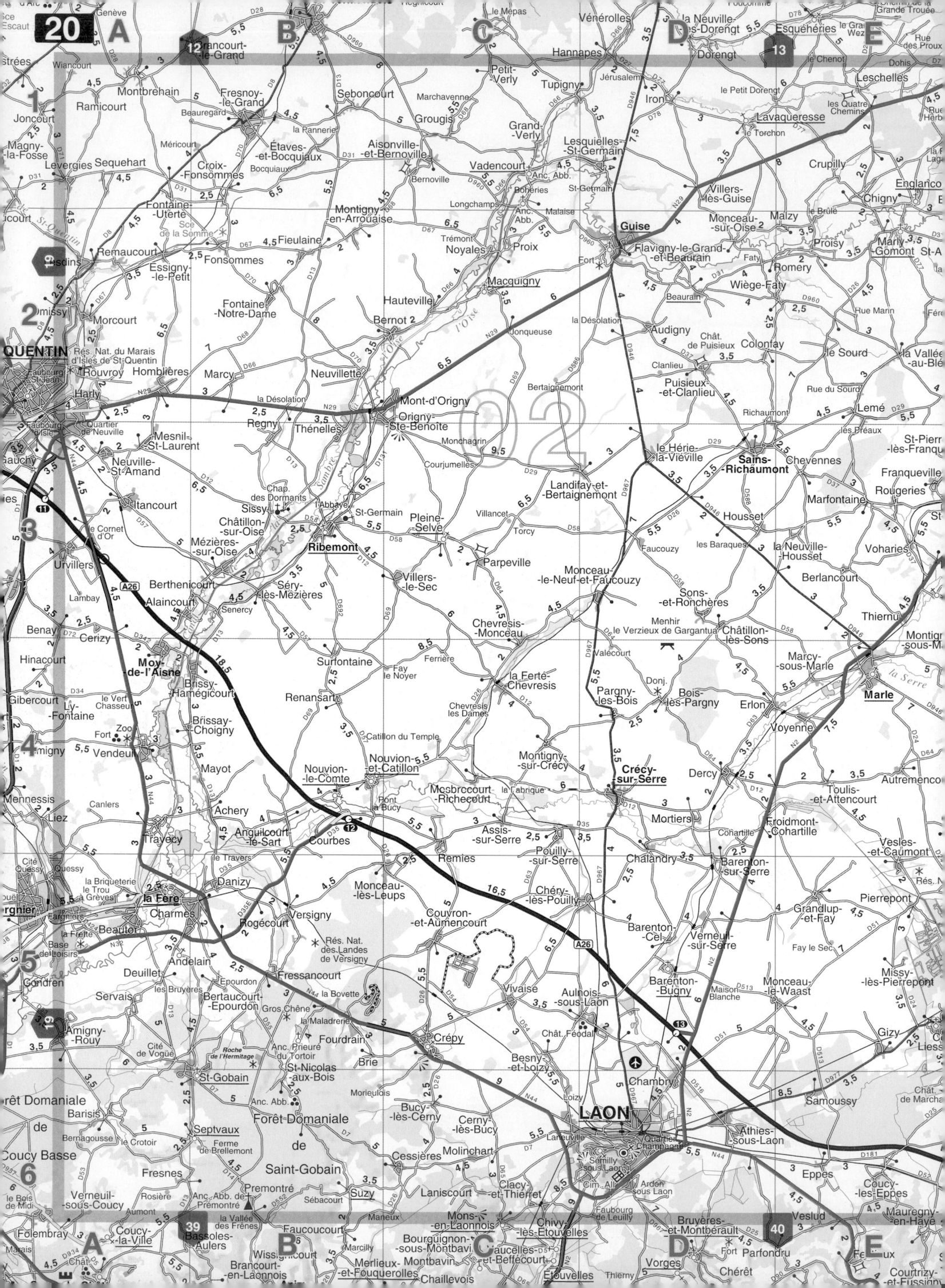

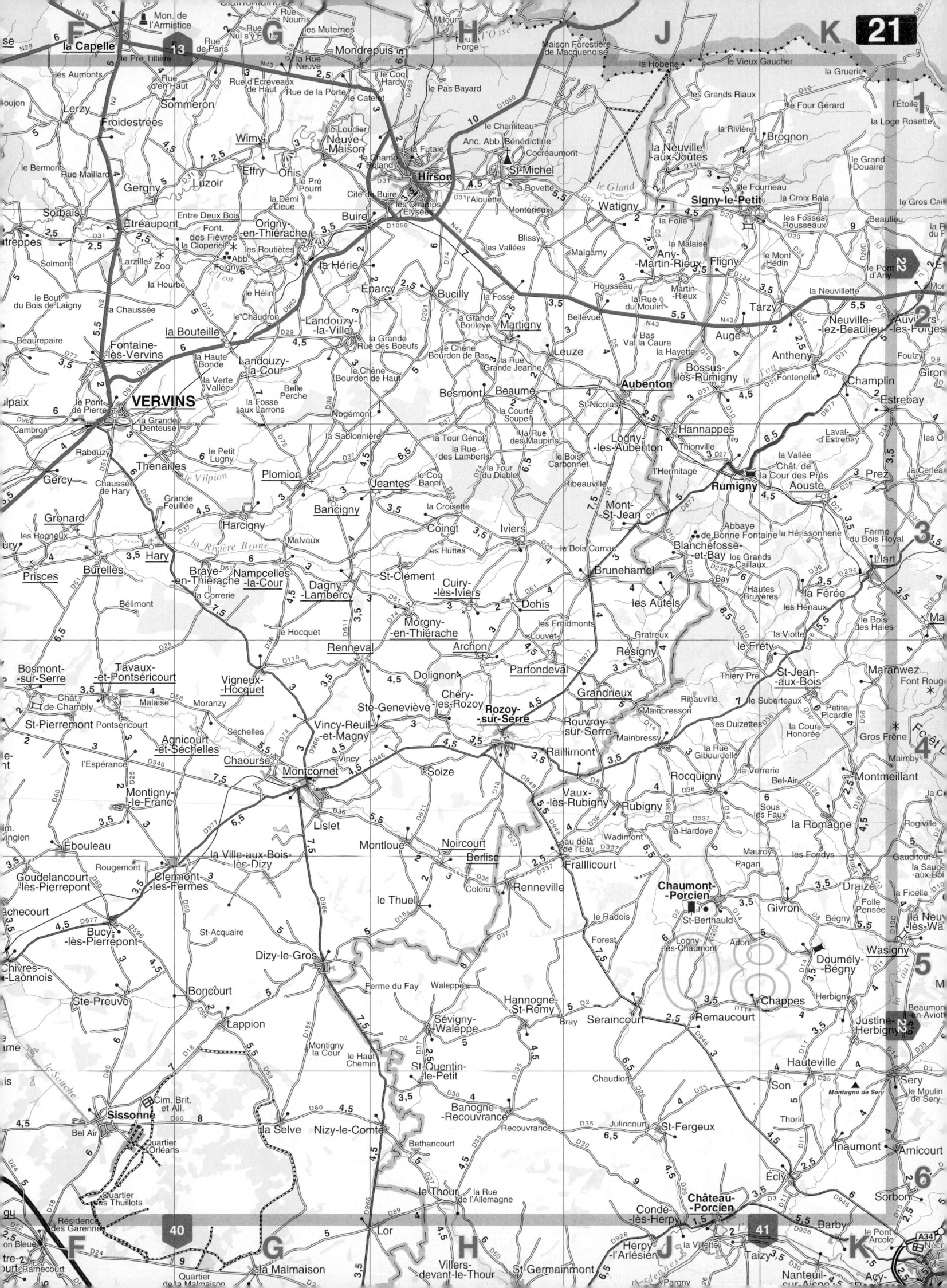

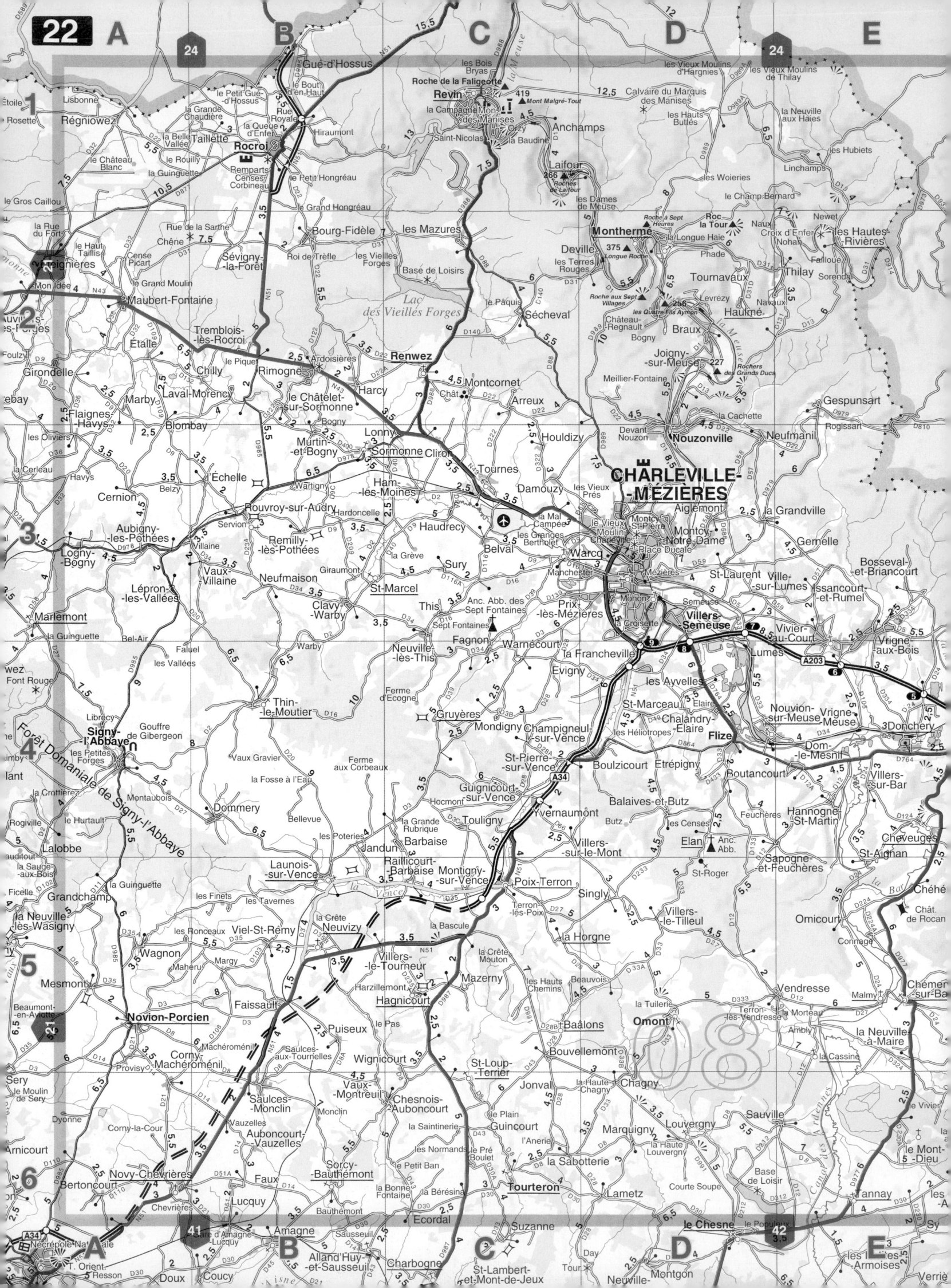

Phare
de Gatteville
Pointe de Barfleur

Réthoville Néville-
-sur-Mer
Gouberville
le Tourps
Gatteville-le-Phare
D116
Crabec
2,5
2
Tocqueville
5
D901
Barfleur
2
Ste-
-Geneviève
la Grande Ville
Clitourps
Landemer
Hameau
du Haut
Montfarville
Valcanville
D355
Anneville-
en-Saire
Canteloup
3,5
le Vicel
Crasville
Man.
de la Crasvillerie
la Froide Rue
le Vast
Table
Orient.
la Pernelle
Réville
Hameau
Néel
le Tot Ferme
Jonville
le Tronquet
Hameau
de Saint-Vaast
Pointe de Saire
Quettehou
Saint-Vaast-
-la-Hougue
Brévolle
le Venoix
les Masses
la Hougue
Fort
de la Hougue
Morsalines
cosville
Crasville
teville-
-Avenel
le Bas de Crasville
Aumeville-Lestre
Îles St-Marcouf
Lestre
audreville
Chap.
le Havre
Fort
de St-Marcouf
2
Chât
Quinéville
la Rue-
d'Ozeville
Hameau du Nord
les Gougins
Commune
d'Ozeville
Chât. de Courcy
Floxel
Fontenay-
-sur-Mer
Hameau du Sud
Rue St-Claire
udiville
Ravenoville Plage
oganville
Grand Hameau
des Dunes
St-Marcouf
les Maisons de Haut
Petit Hameau
des Dunes
Emondeville
Azeville
Ravenoville
la Selleraie
ville
Foucarville
St-Germain-
-de-Varreville
Monument
Neuville-
au-Plain
Beuzeville-
au-Plain
St-Martin-de-Varreville
la Vallée
Ste-
-Mère-Eglise
Audouville-
-la-Hubert
Utah Beach
la Grande
Dune
Turqueville
Monument
Farville
Ecoqueneauville
les Fontaines
Boutteville
le Grand
Chemin
Réserve Naturelle
de Beauguillot
Chef-
du-Pont
Pointe du Hoc
Mon.
Commune
de Sébeville
Pouppeville
Grandcamp-
-Maisy
le Bavent
le Haut
Chemin
Blosville
Hiesville
Ste-Marie-du-Mont
la Montagne
Lefevre
D514
St-Pierre-
du-Mont
Englesqueville-
-la-Percée
Vierville-
sur-Mer
les Moulins
Carquebut
l'Eglise
le Grand Vey
la Dune
Maisy
le Carrefour
Cricqueville-
-en-Bessin
Gruchy
Man.
de Veaumicel
Hamel
au Prêtre
Mon.
Omaha Beach
Liesville-
sur-Douve
Houesville
Vierville
Commune
de Brucheville
les Chapelles Cauvin
le Bas-de-Géfosse
le Wigwam
'Hermerel
Cardonville
Chât. de
Beaumont
Asnières-
en-Bessin
Louvières
Cim.
Am.
Mon.
St-Côme-
du-Mont
Angoville-
au-Plain
la Grève
la Cambe
la Vieille Place
Beauvais
Deux-
Jumeaux
St-Laurent-
-sur-Mer
le Bray
Colleville-
-sur-Mer
Appeville
la Rue
Mary
Tourlaville
St-Clément
Osmanville
St-Germain-
du-Pert
les Mares
Longueville
St-Louis
Formigny
Madeleine
Brévands
Isigny-
-sur-Mer
Canchy
Normanv
Surrain
Carentan
Commune de
St-Hilaire-Pe
Catz
l'Eglise
Cim. All.
le Bor
Commune
d'Aignerville
Ecrammeville
Russy
Auvers
Pommenauque
le Lude
Cantepie
la Fontaine
Hameau
Fontaine
la Rivière
le Quève
Montfréville
Engranville

31
32
31

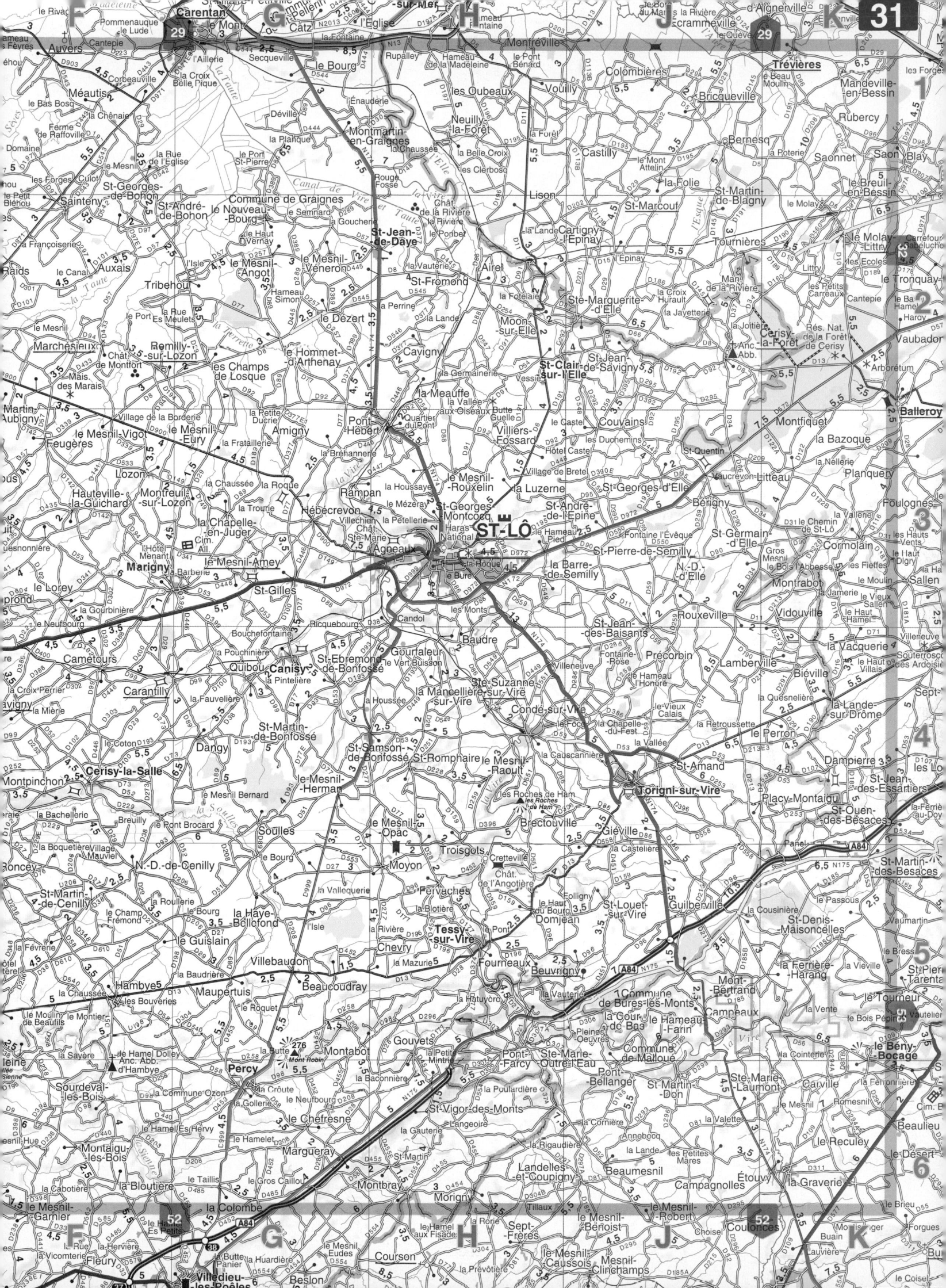

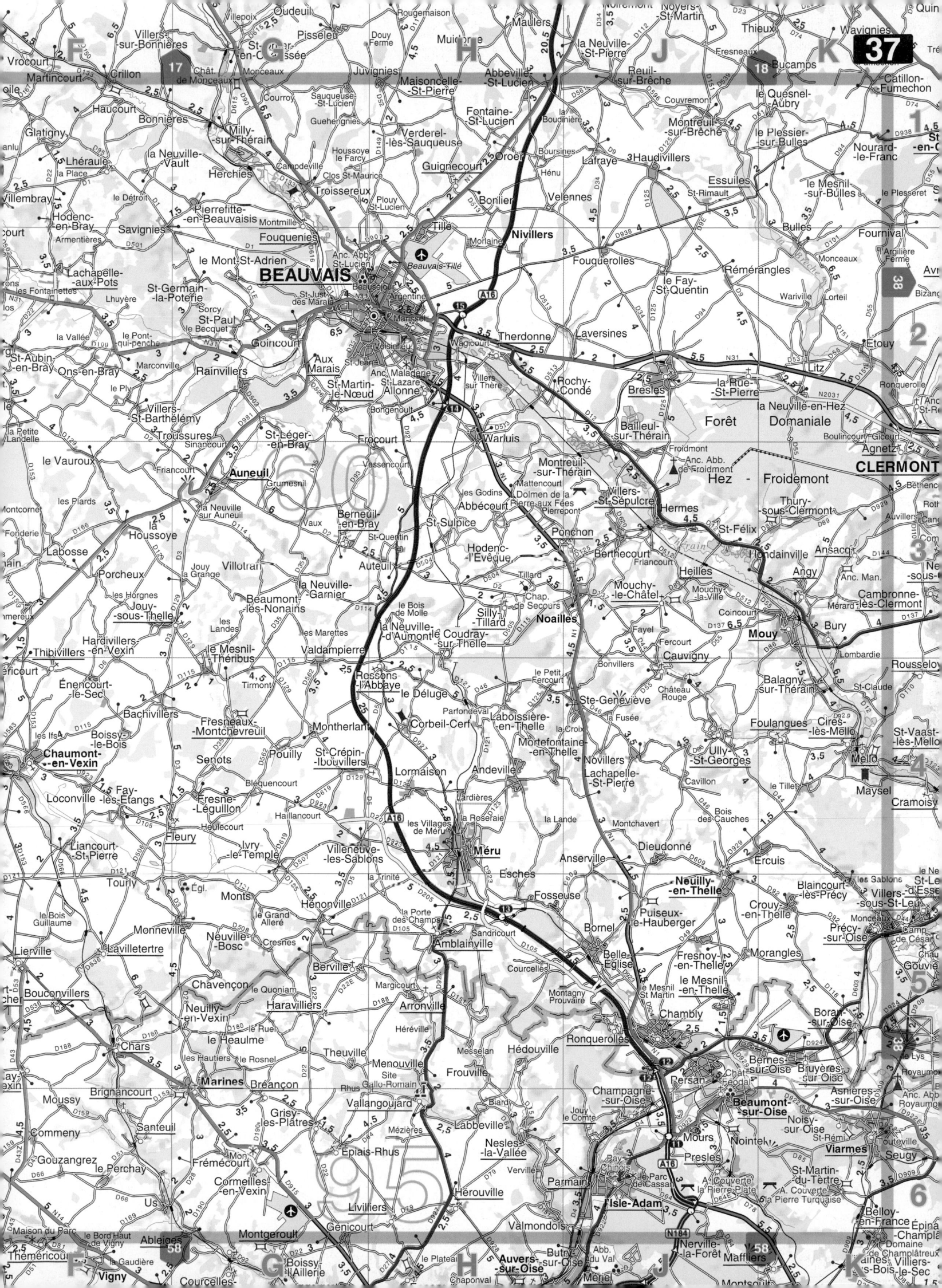

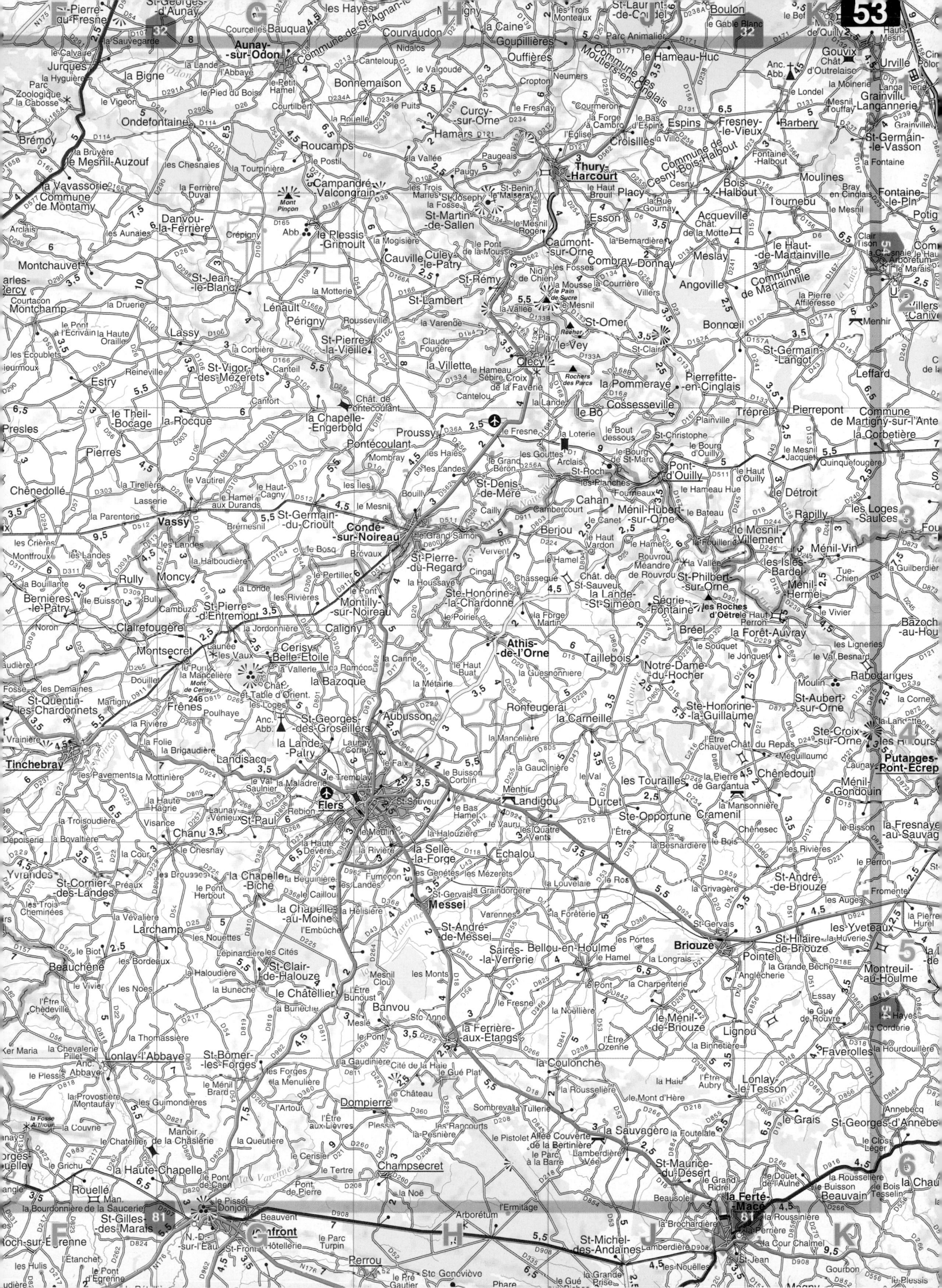

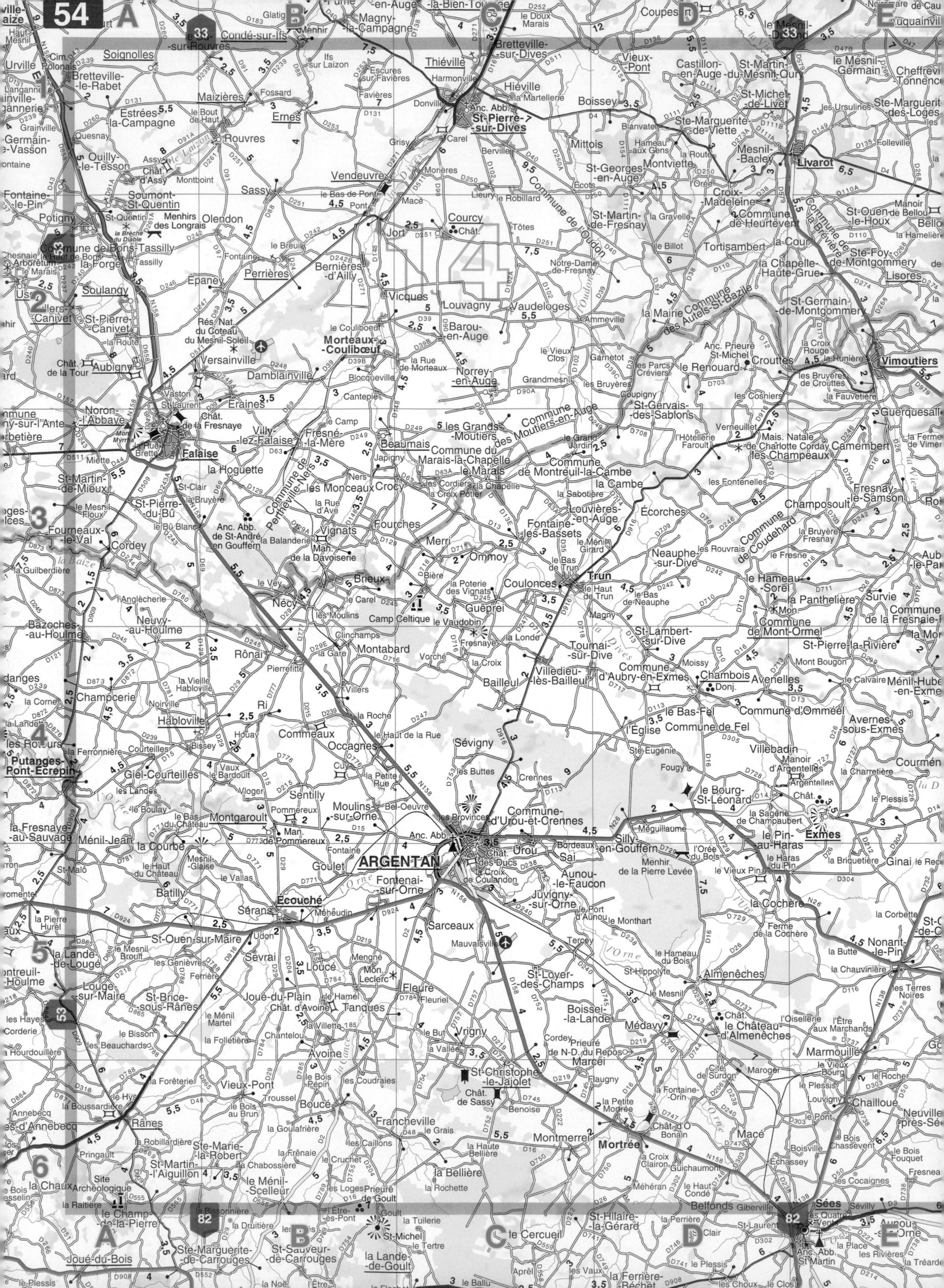

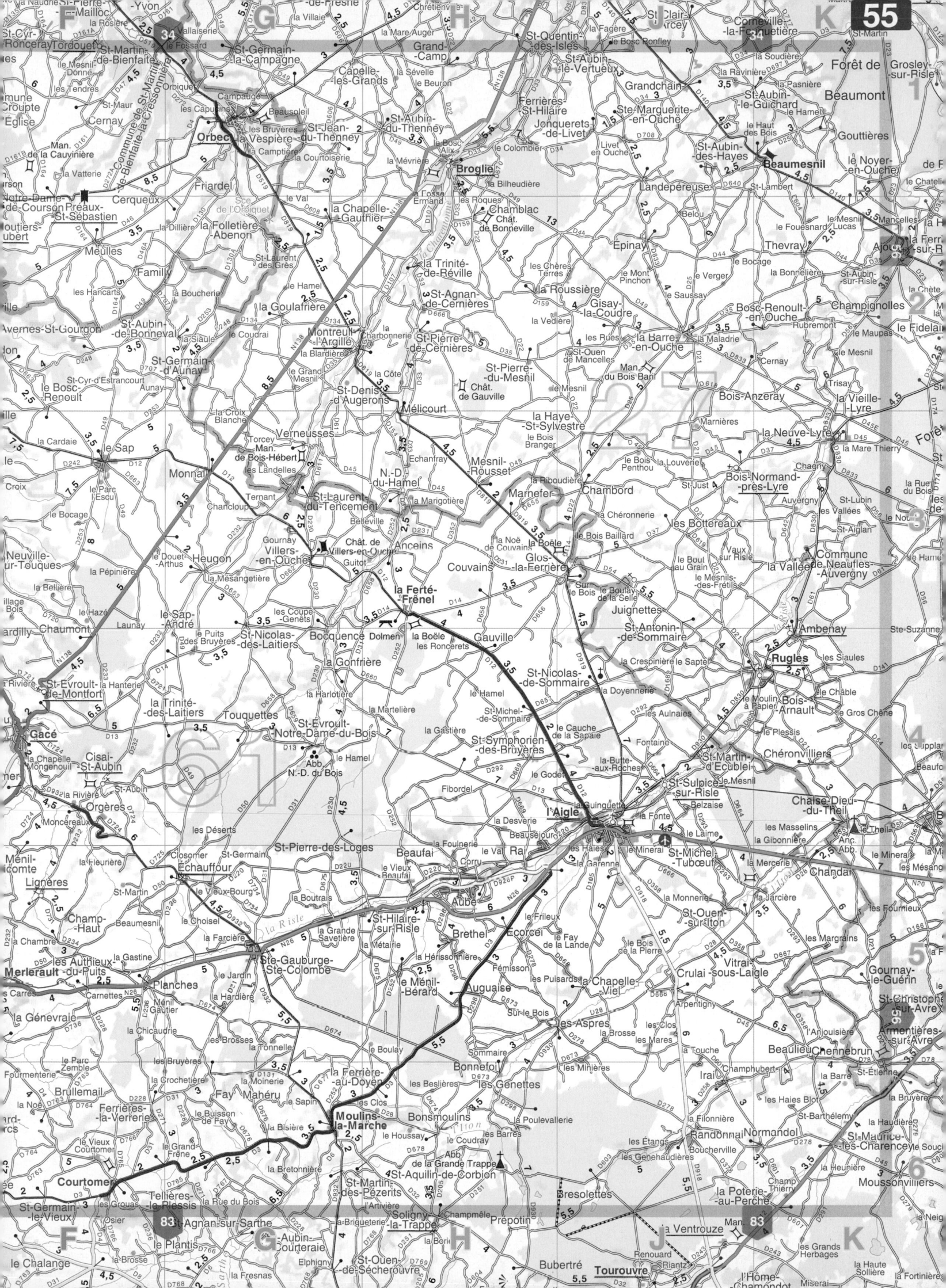

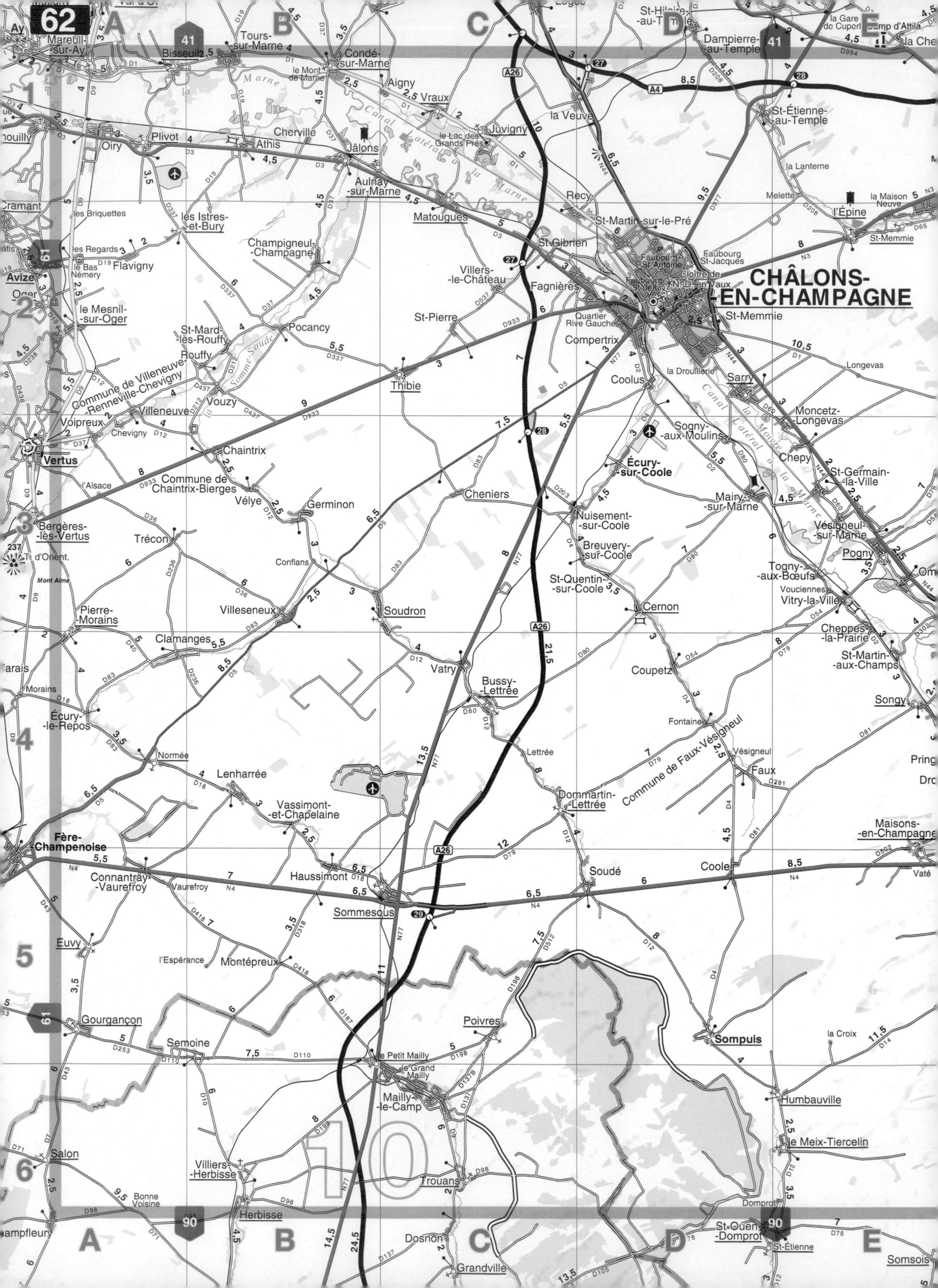

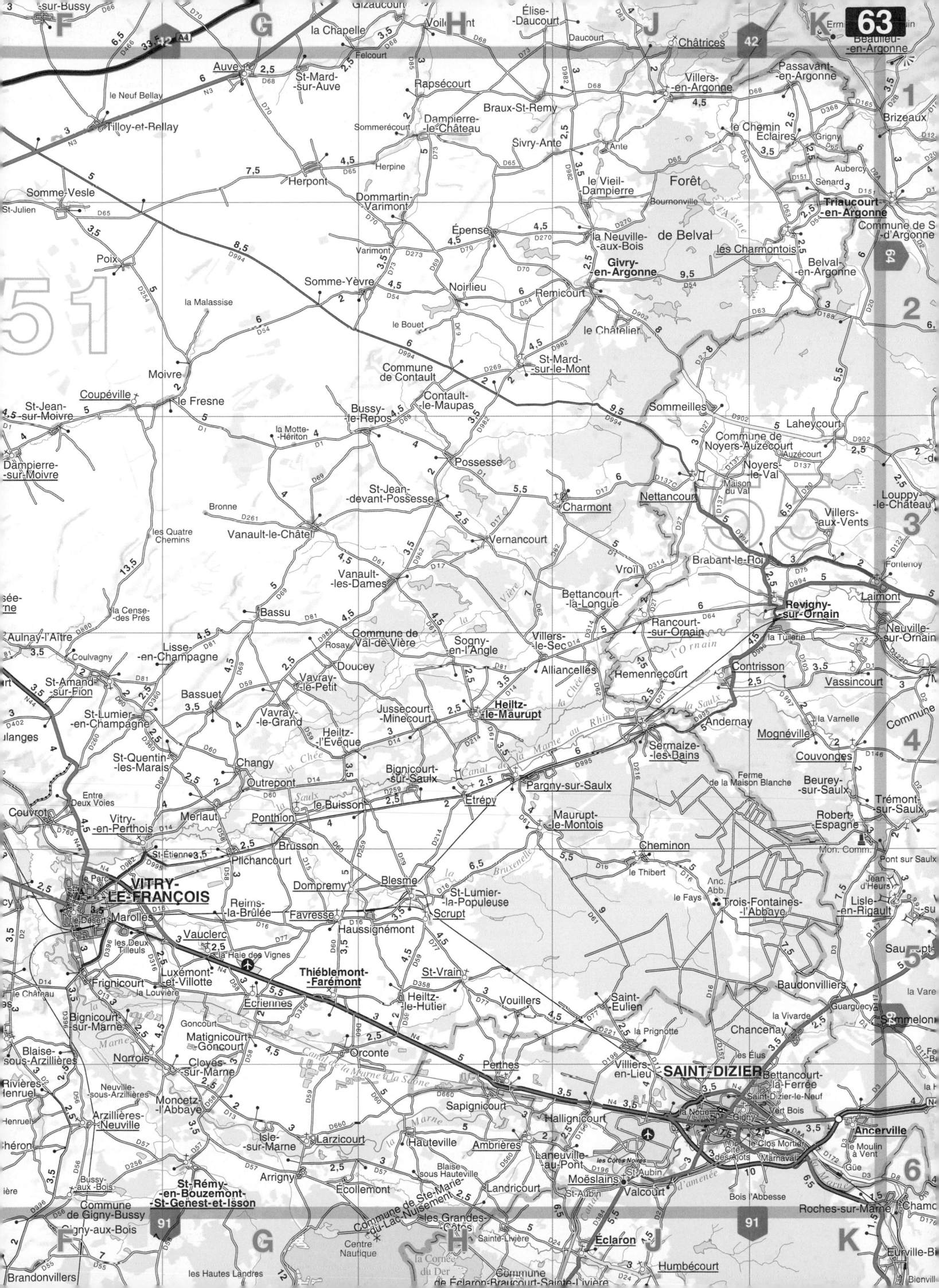

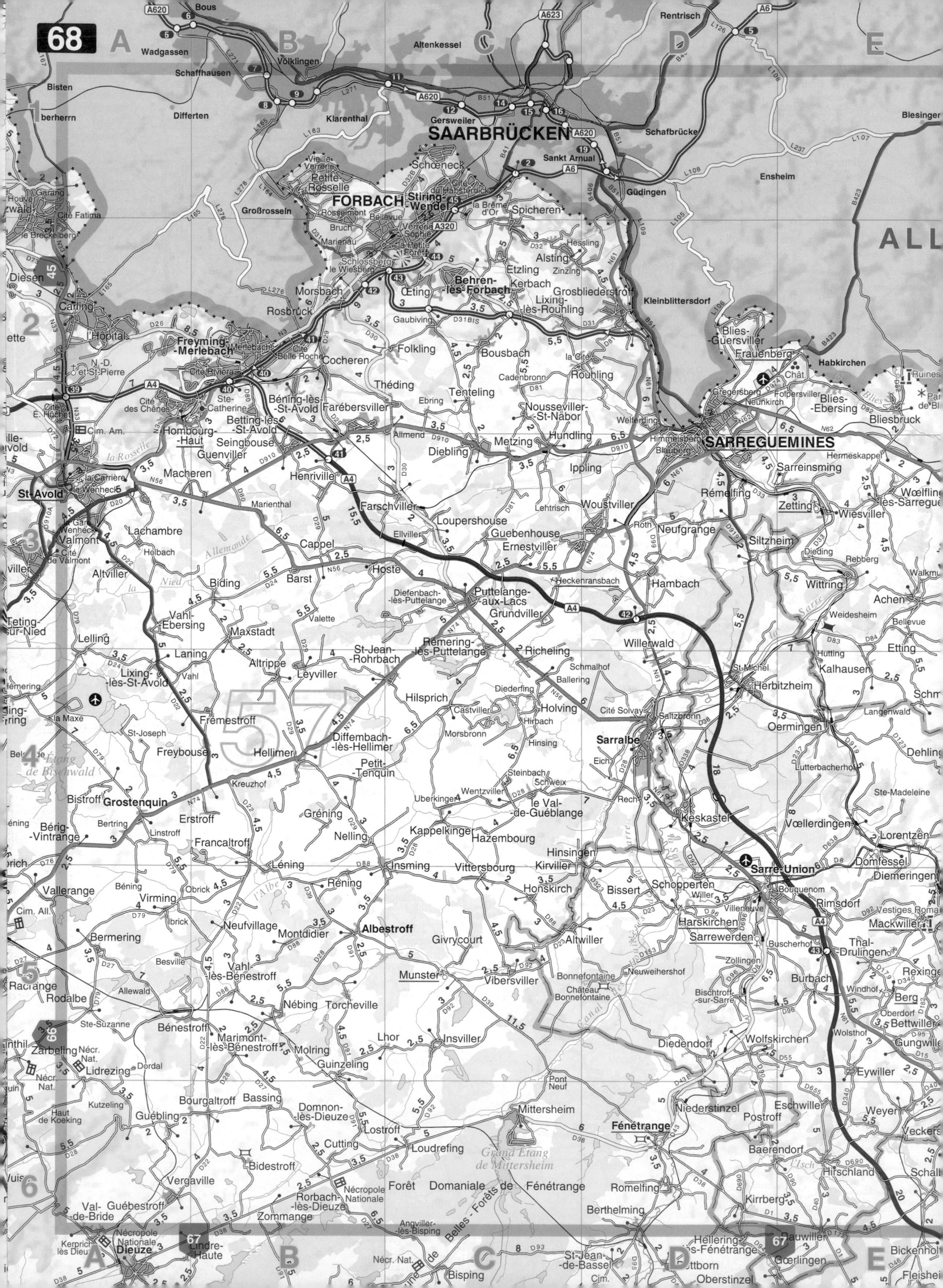

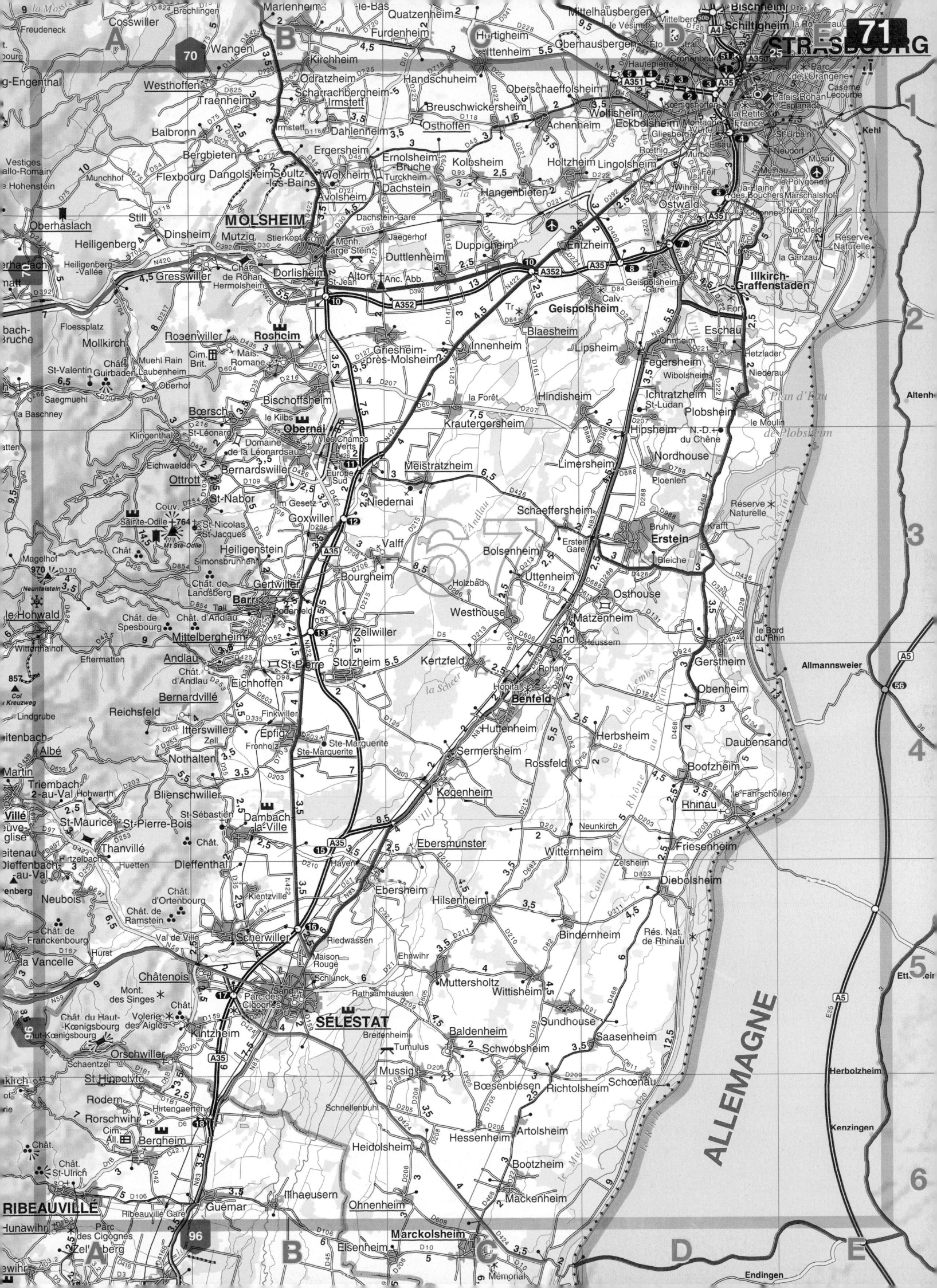

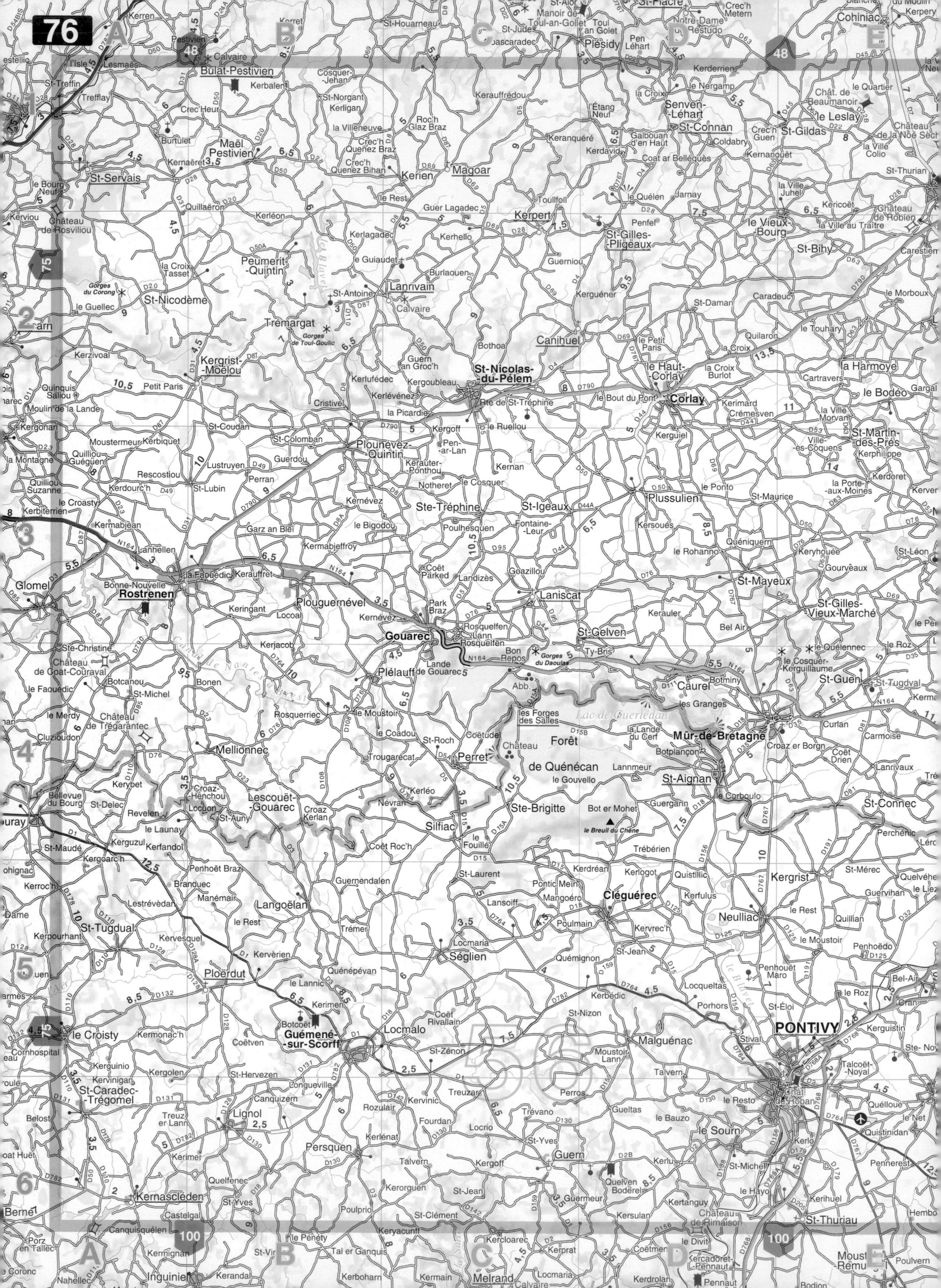

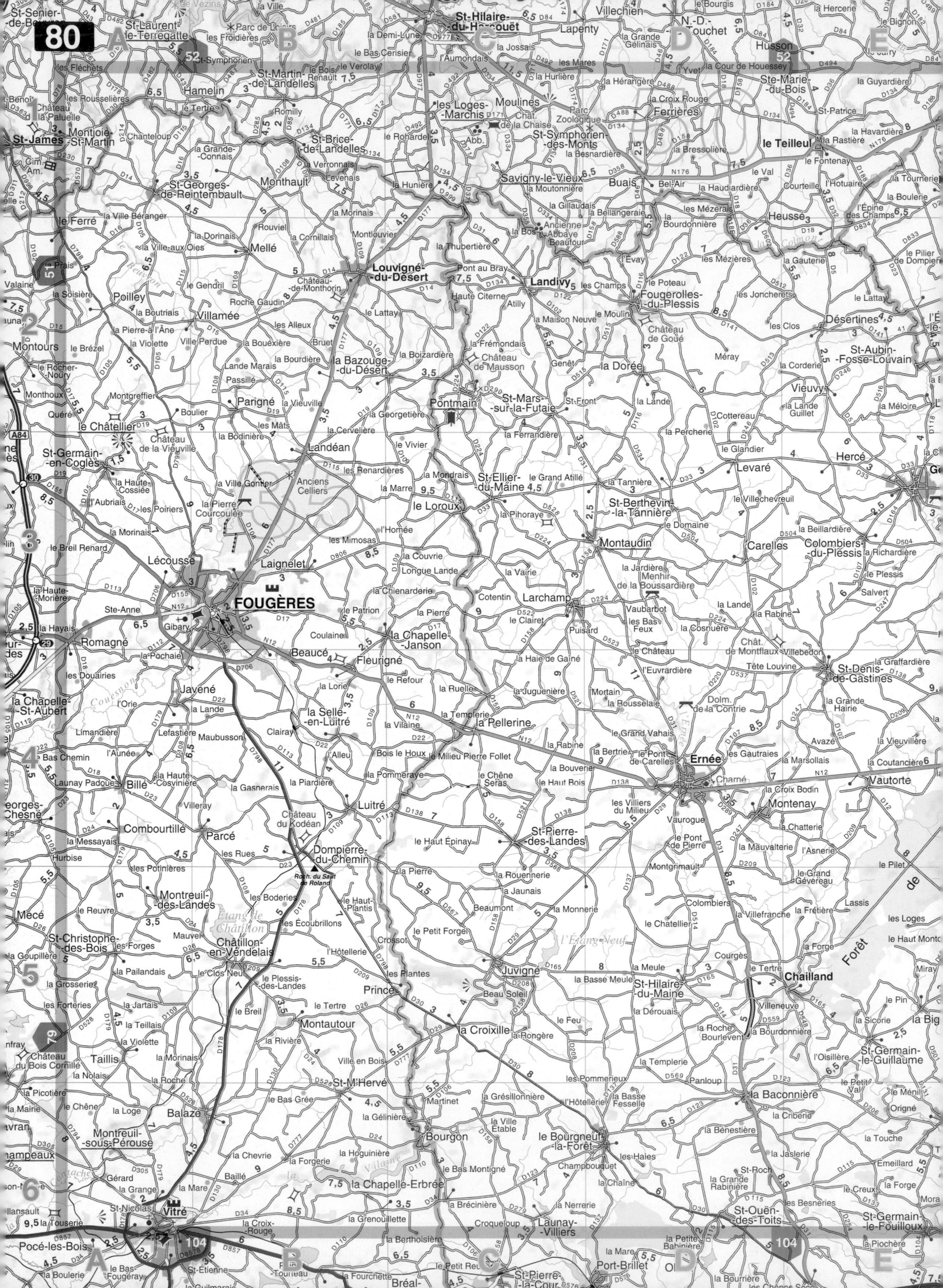

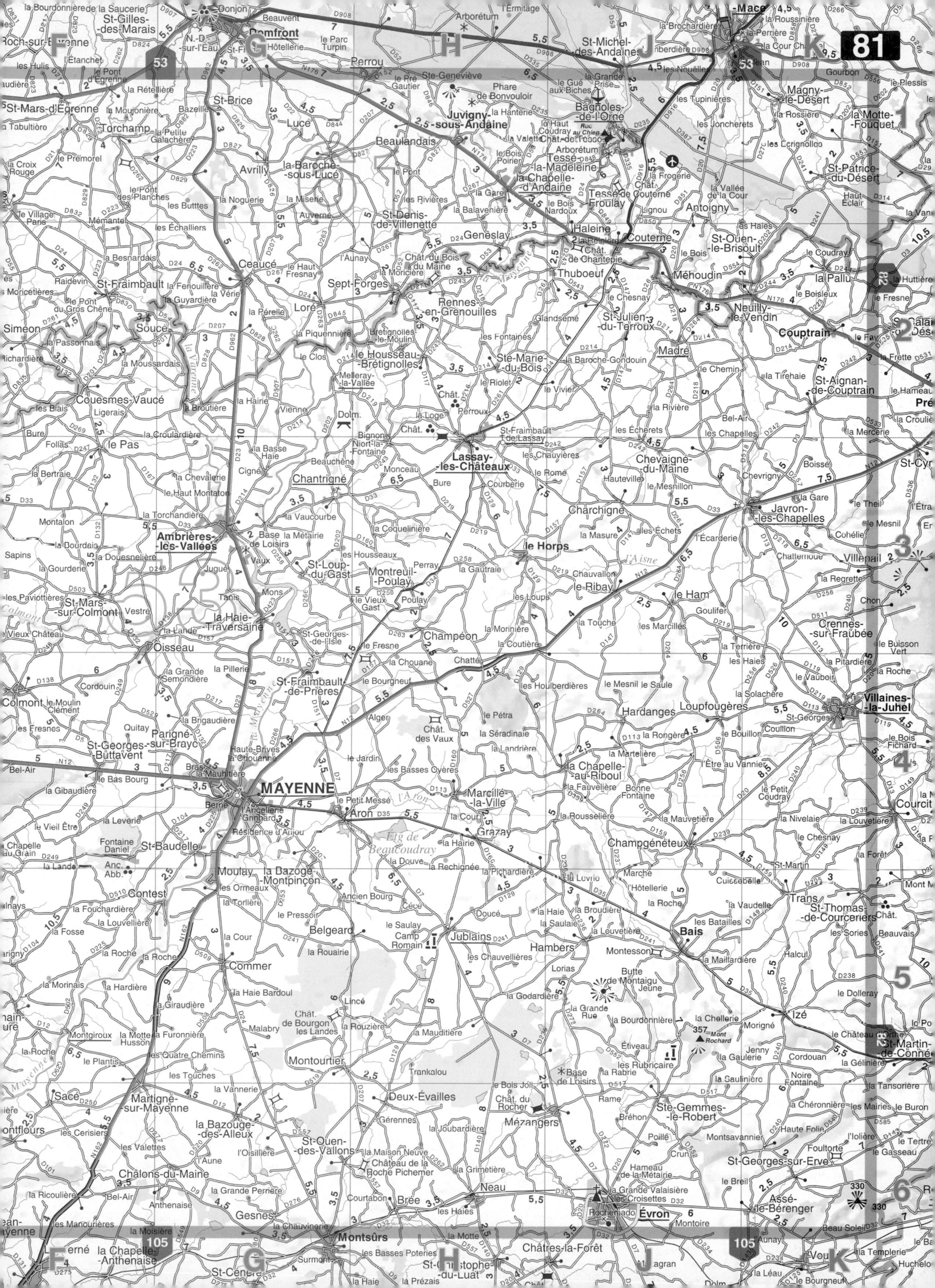

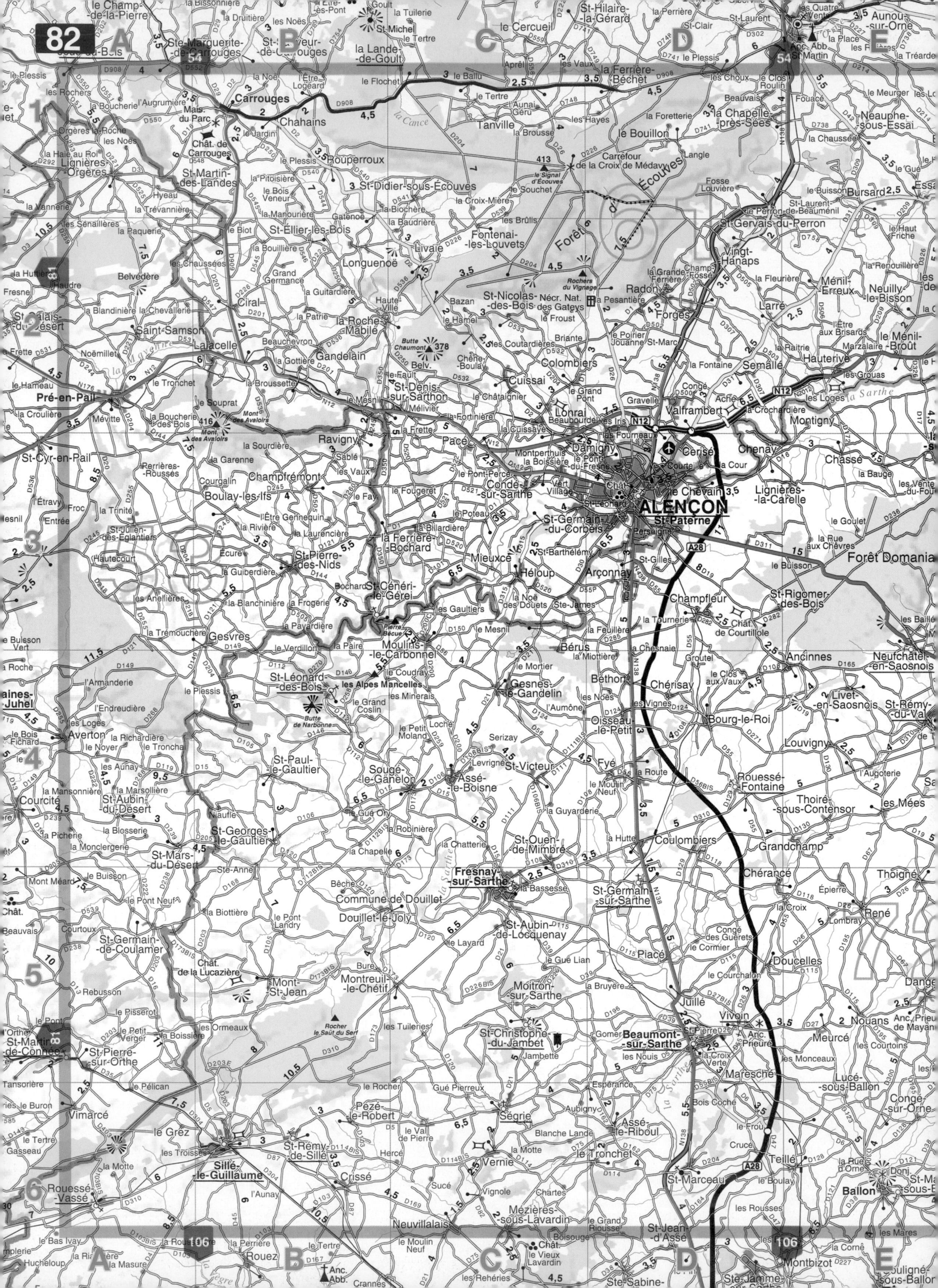

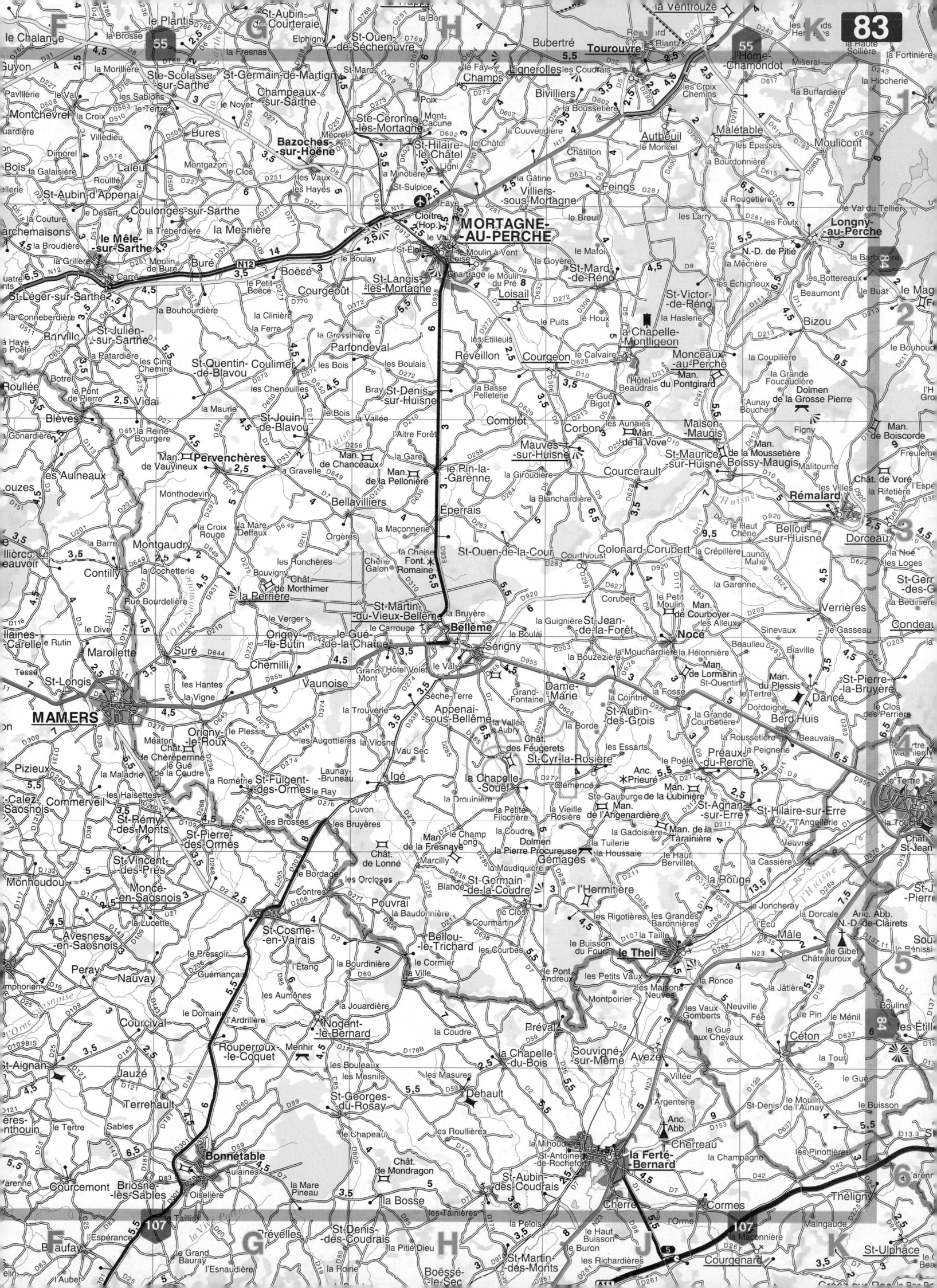

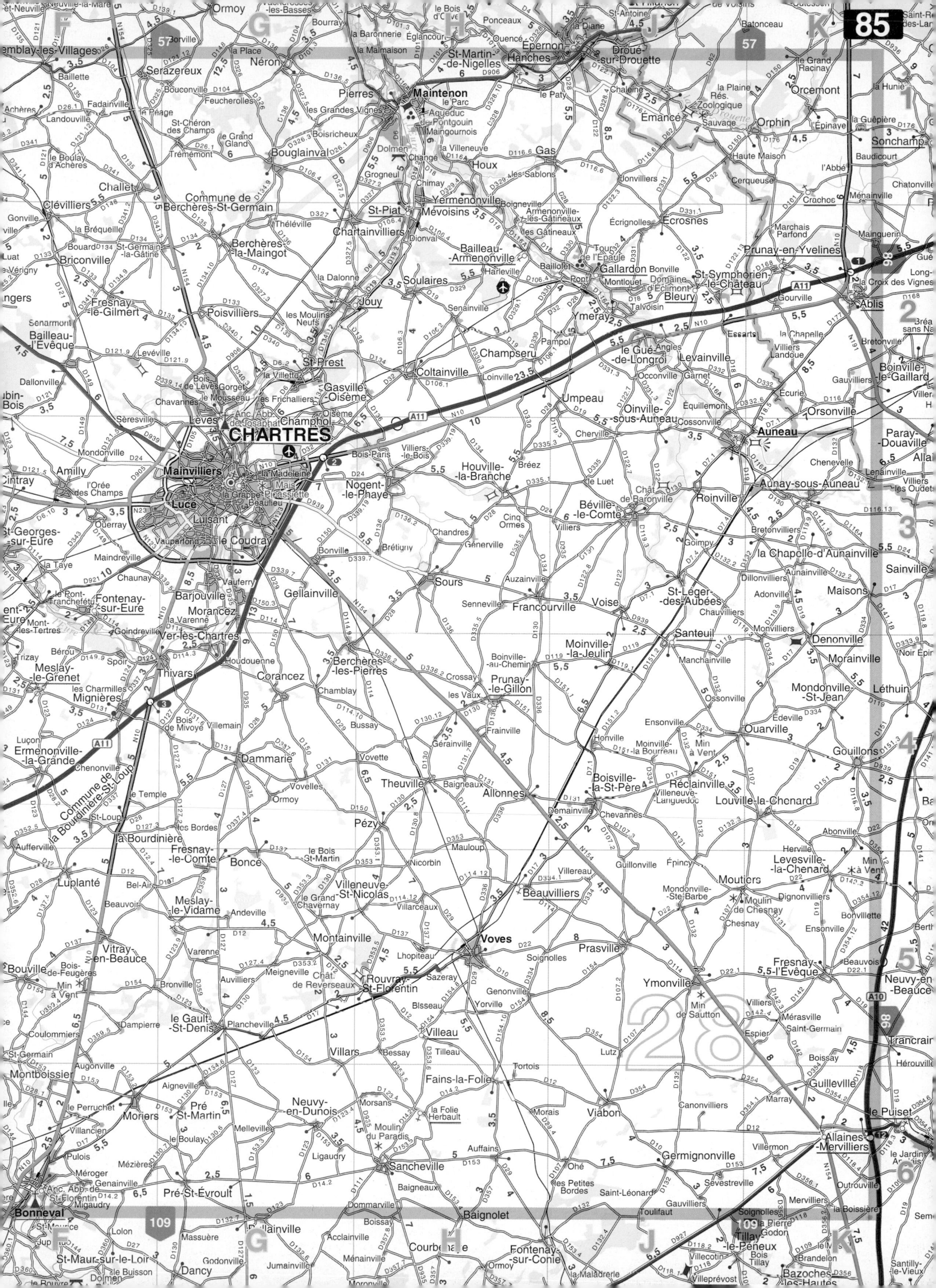

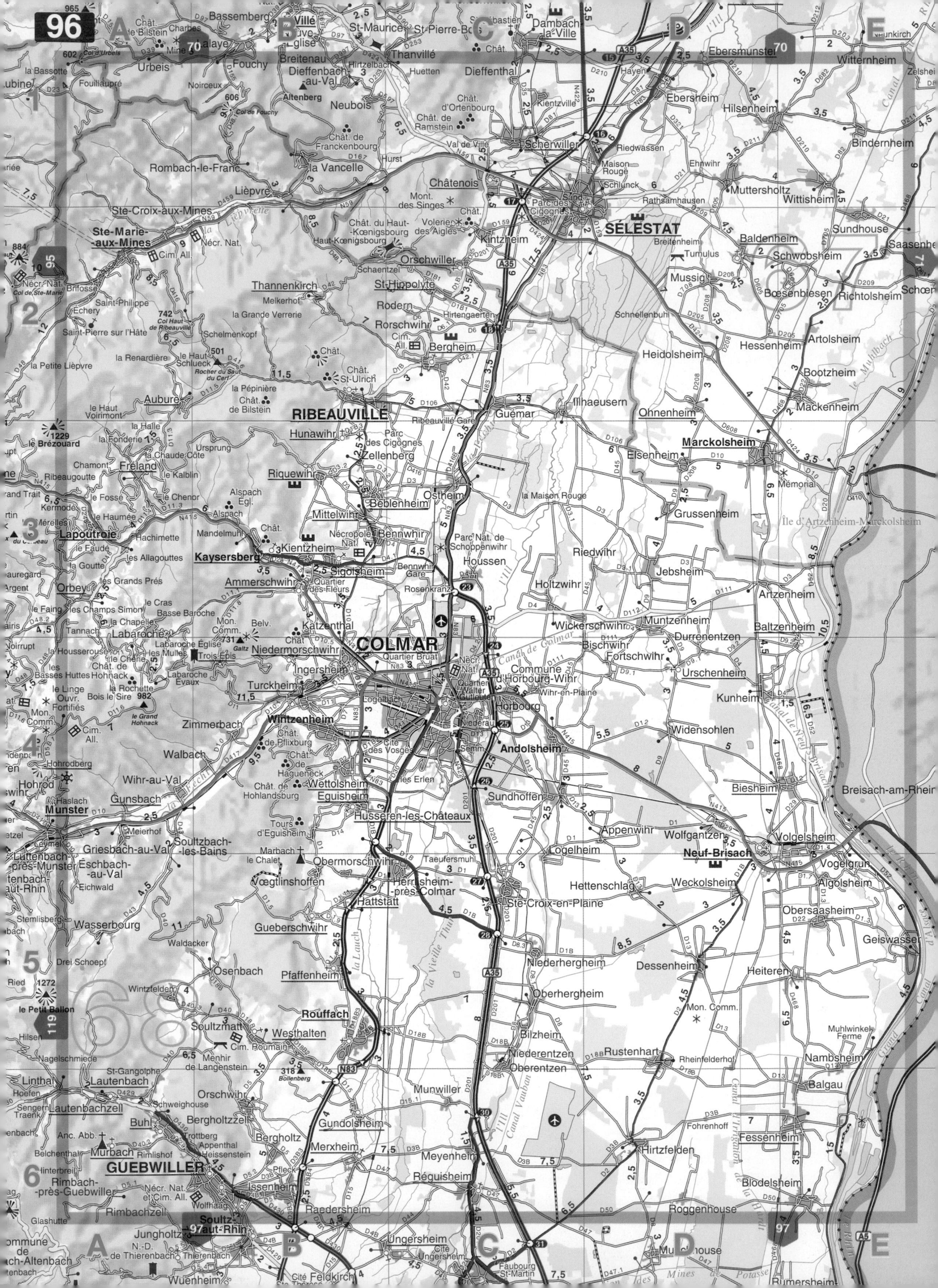

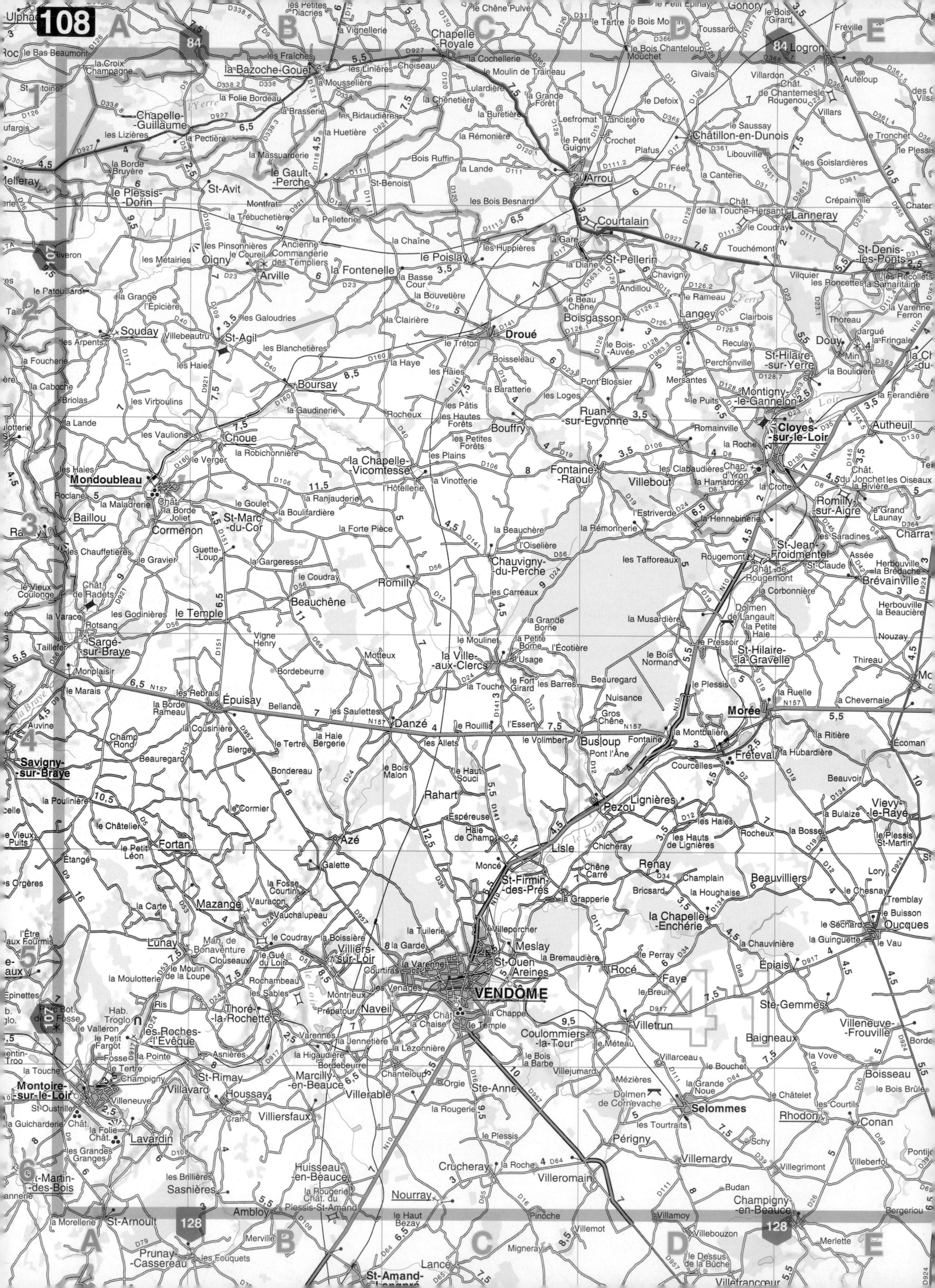

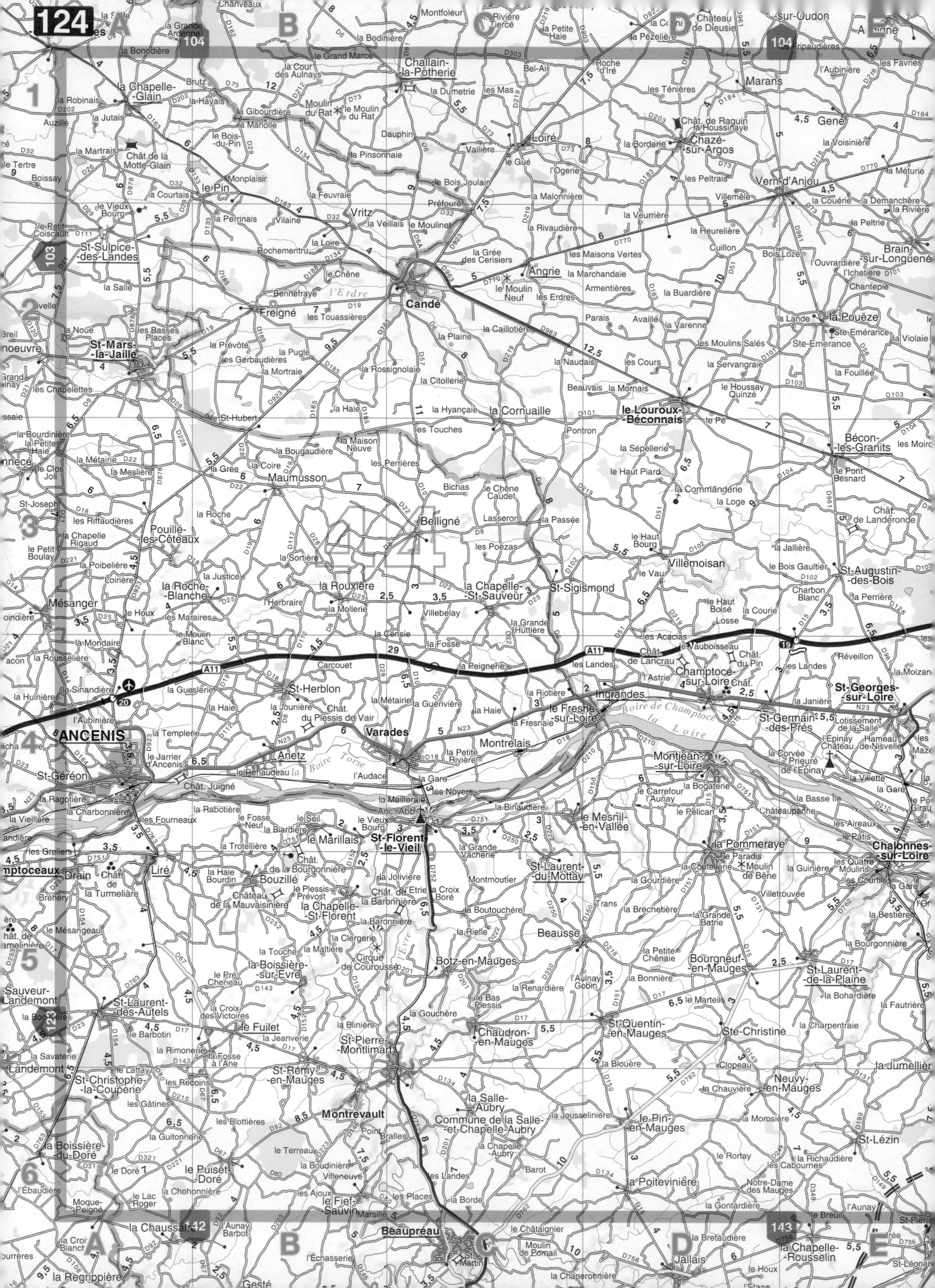

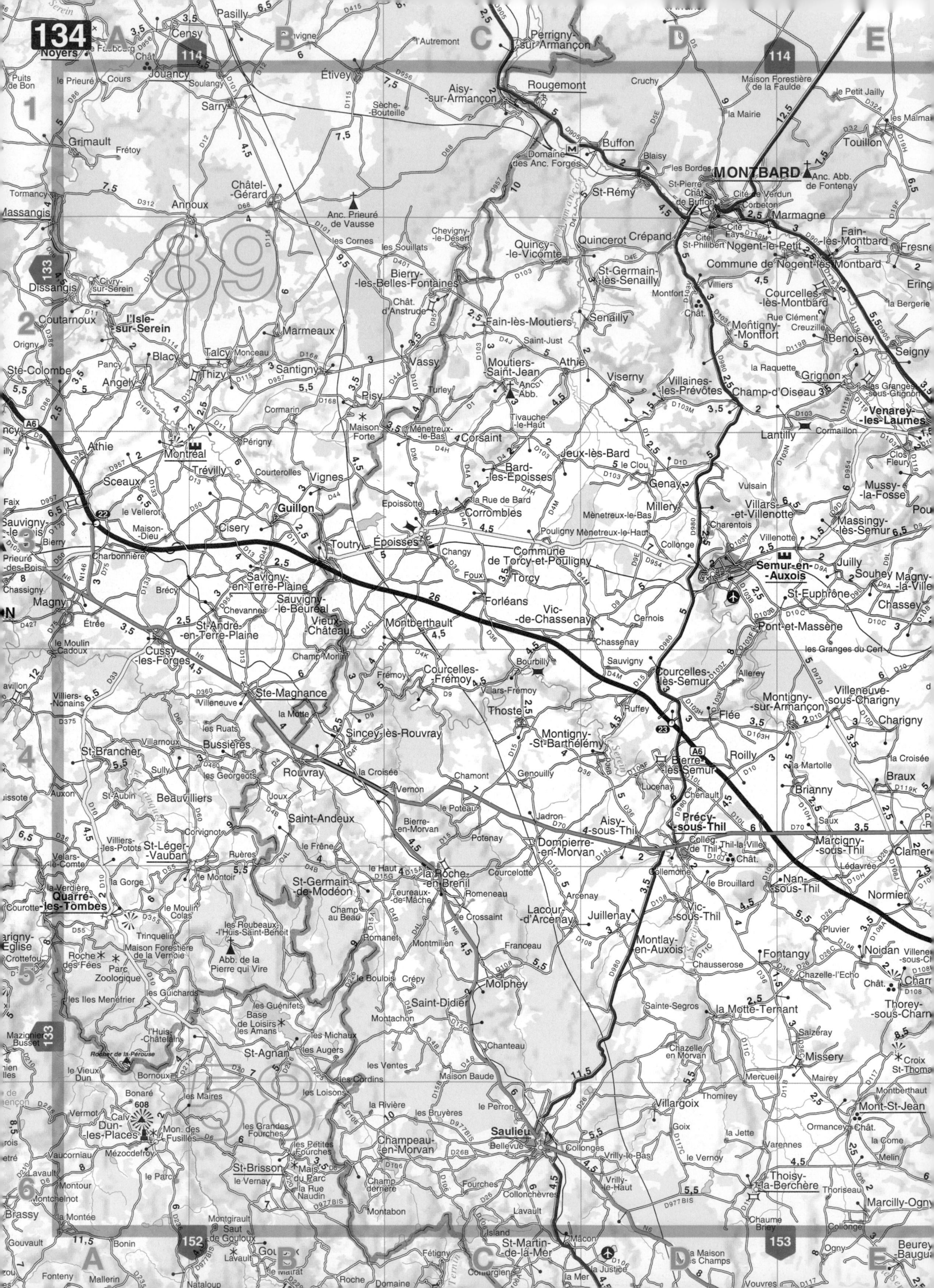

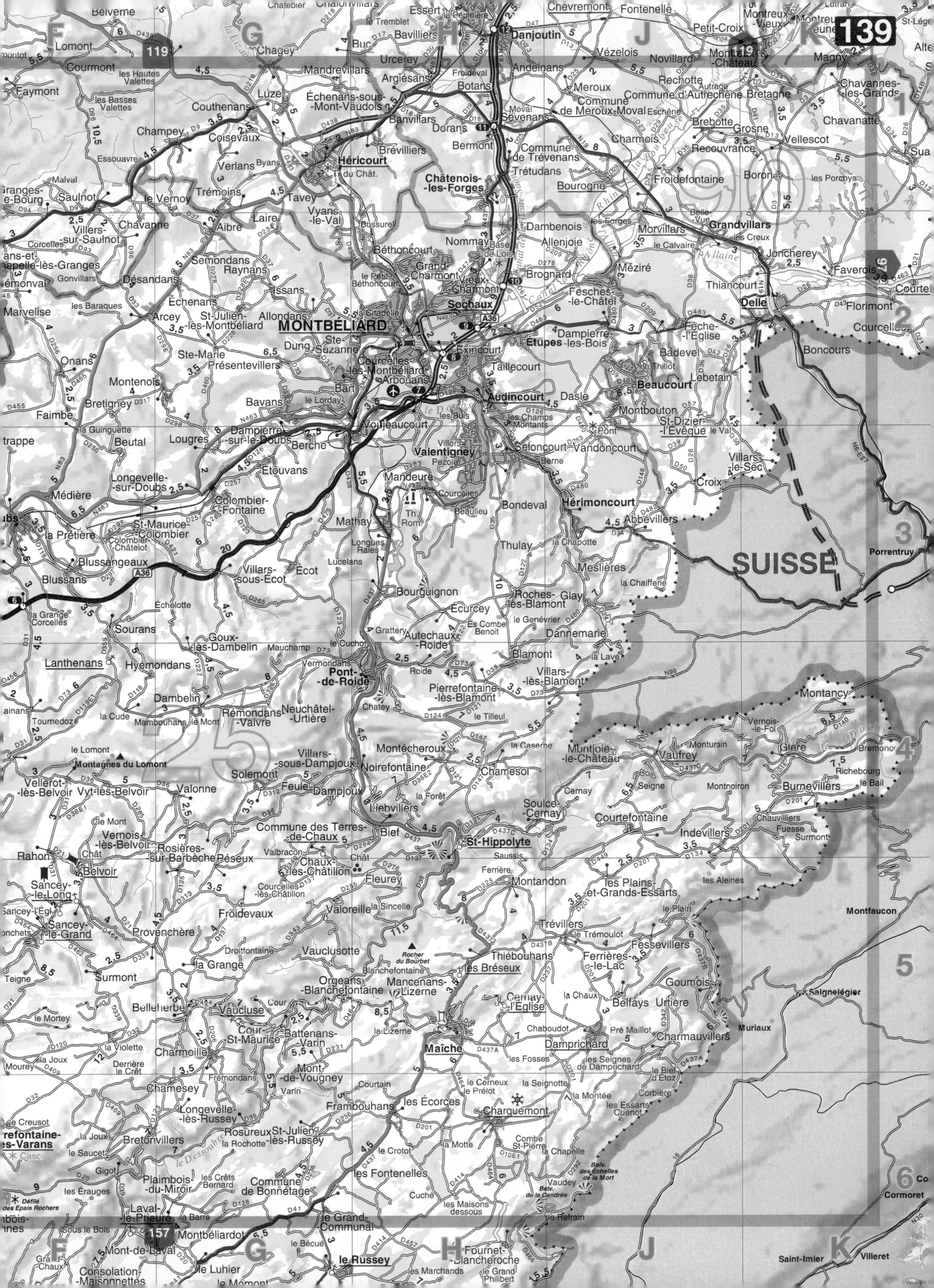

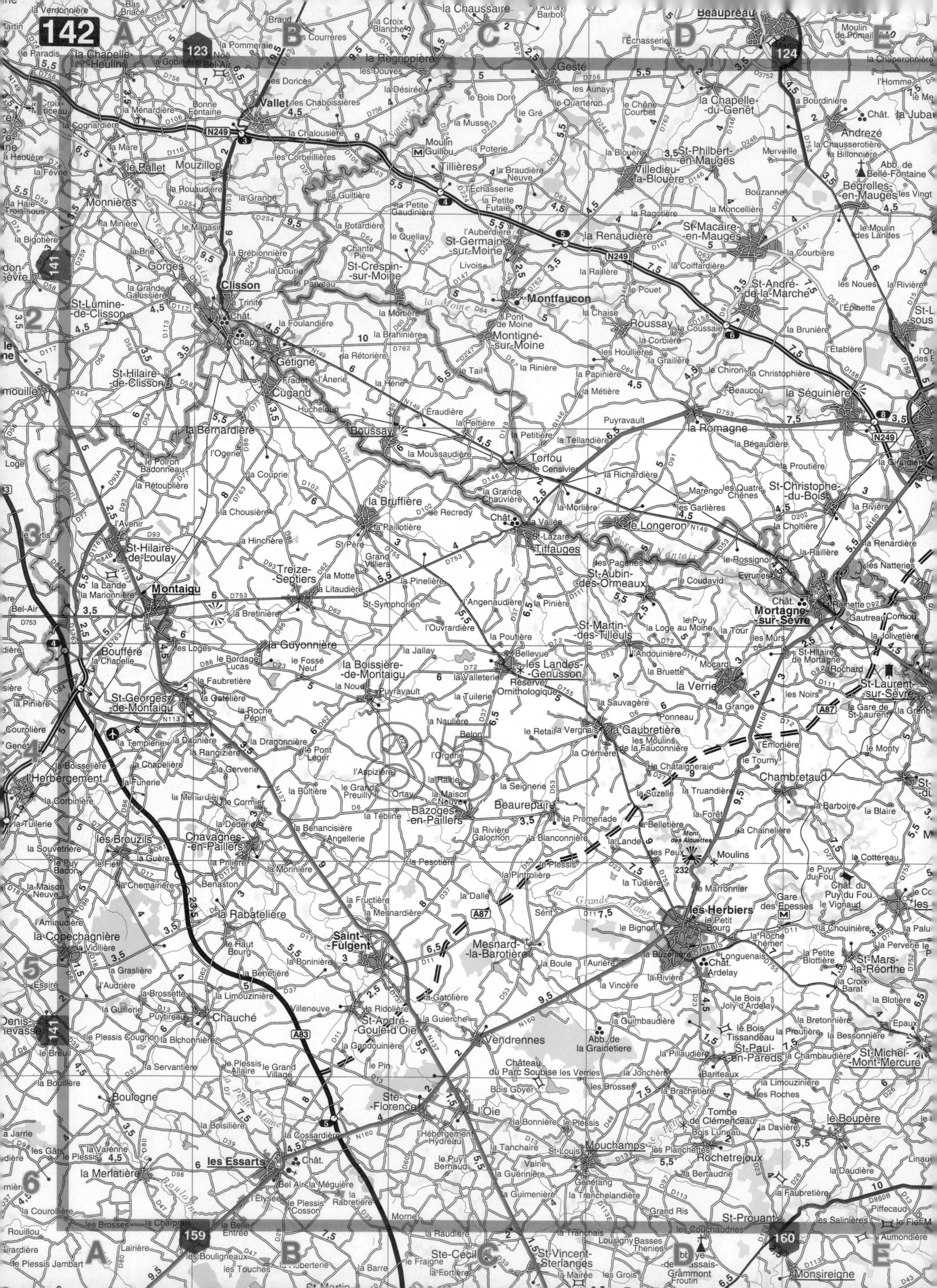

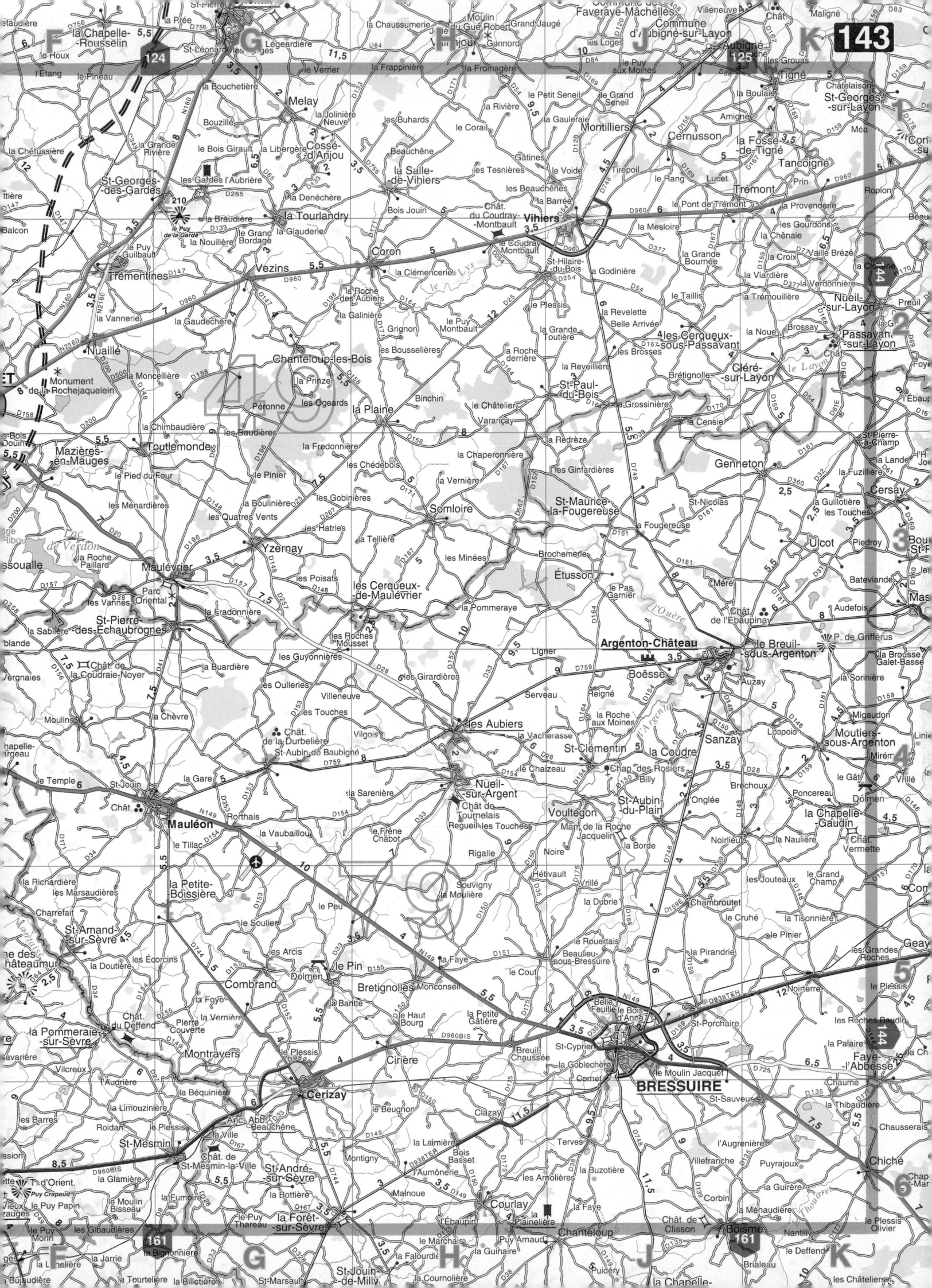

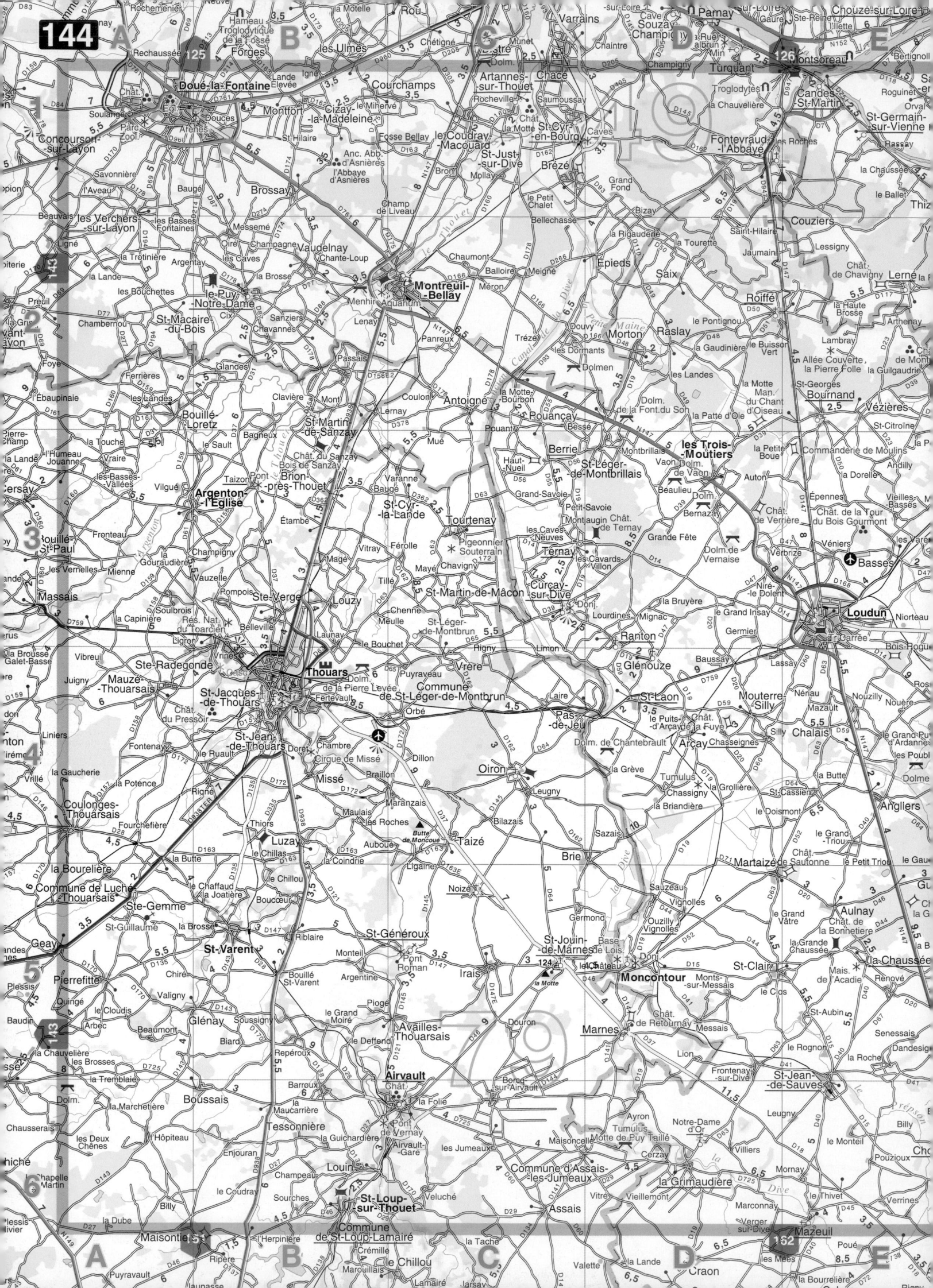

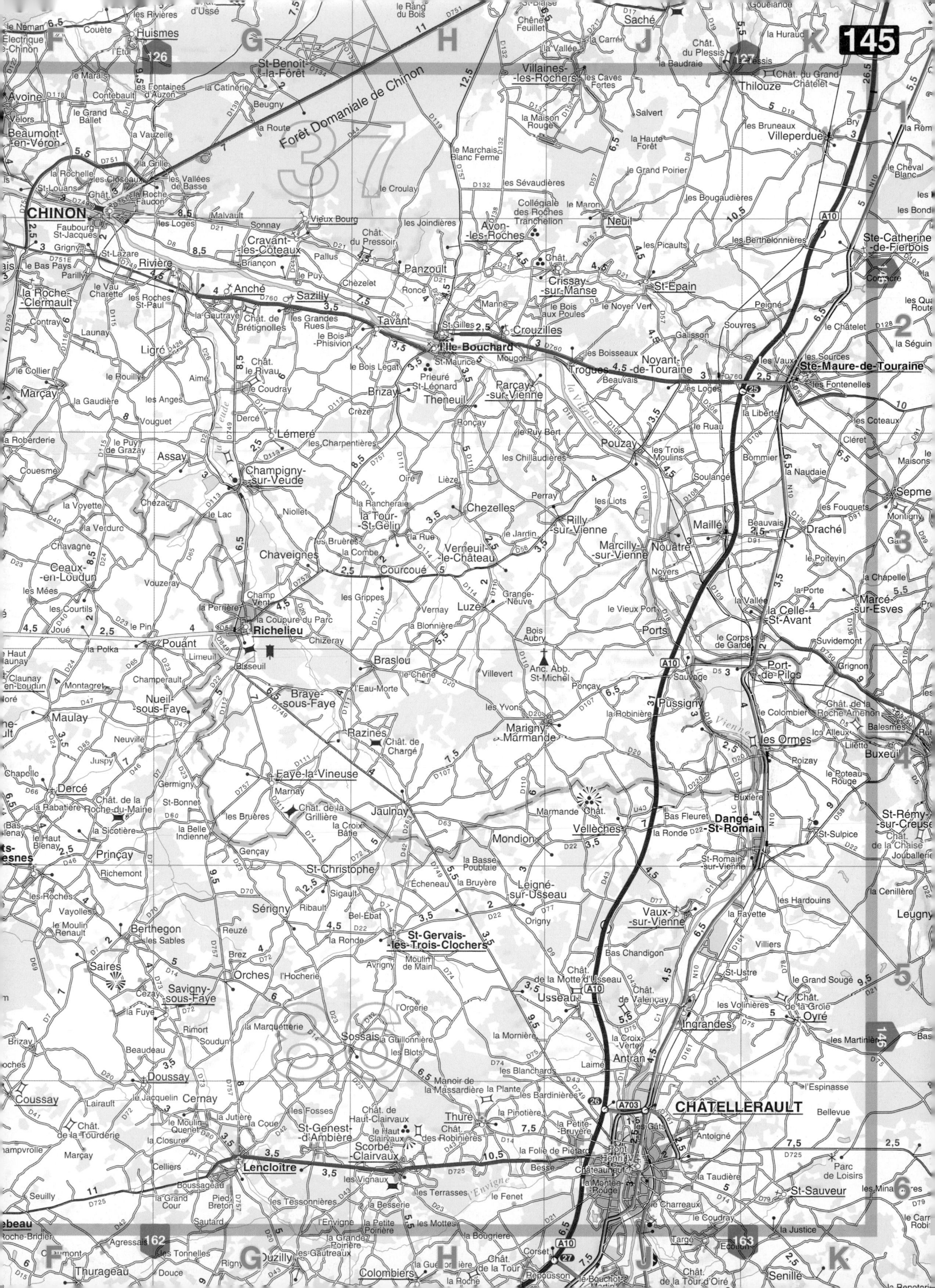

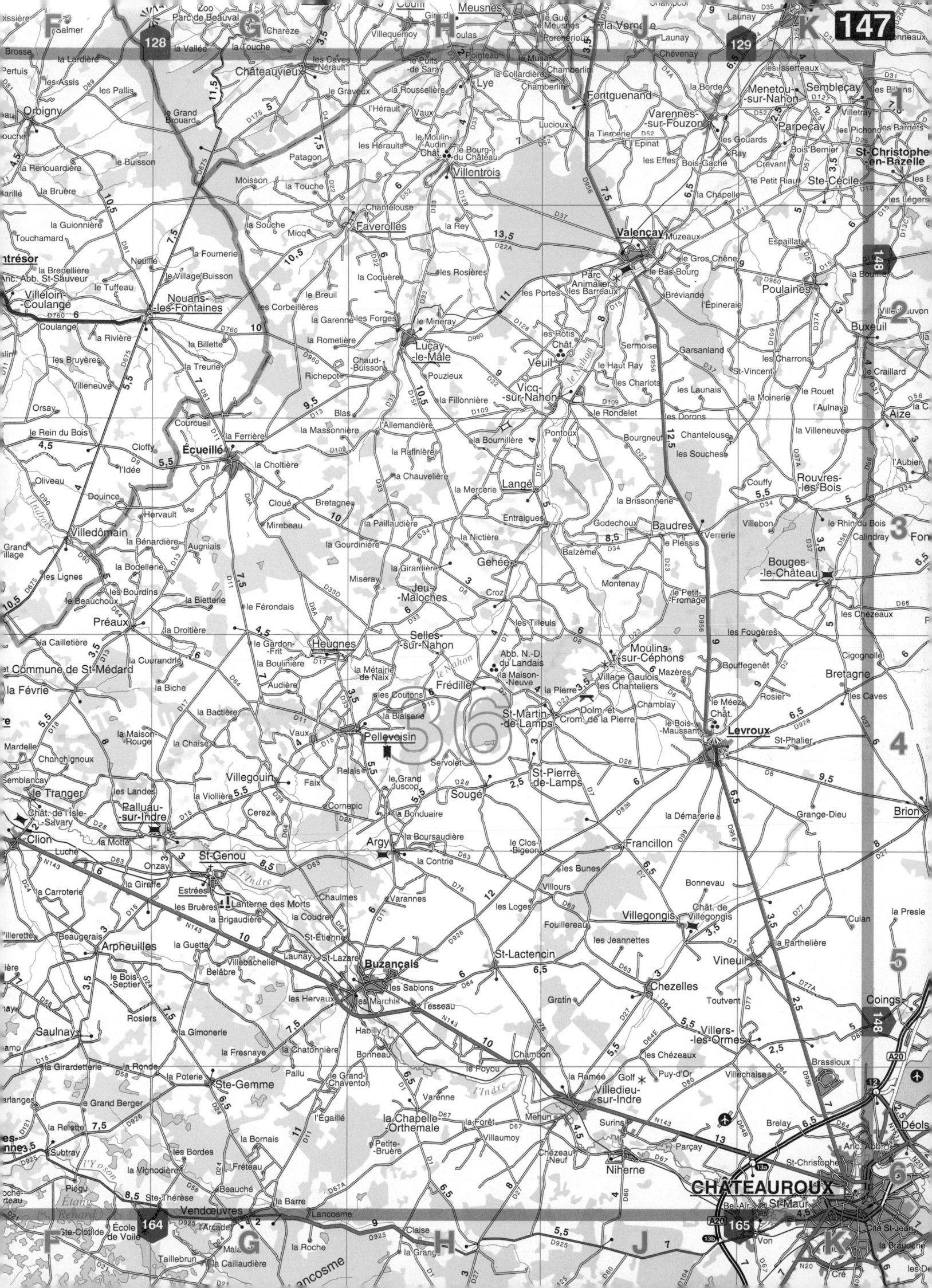

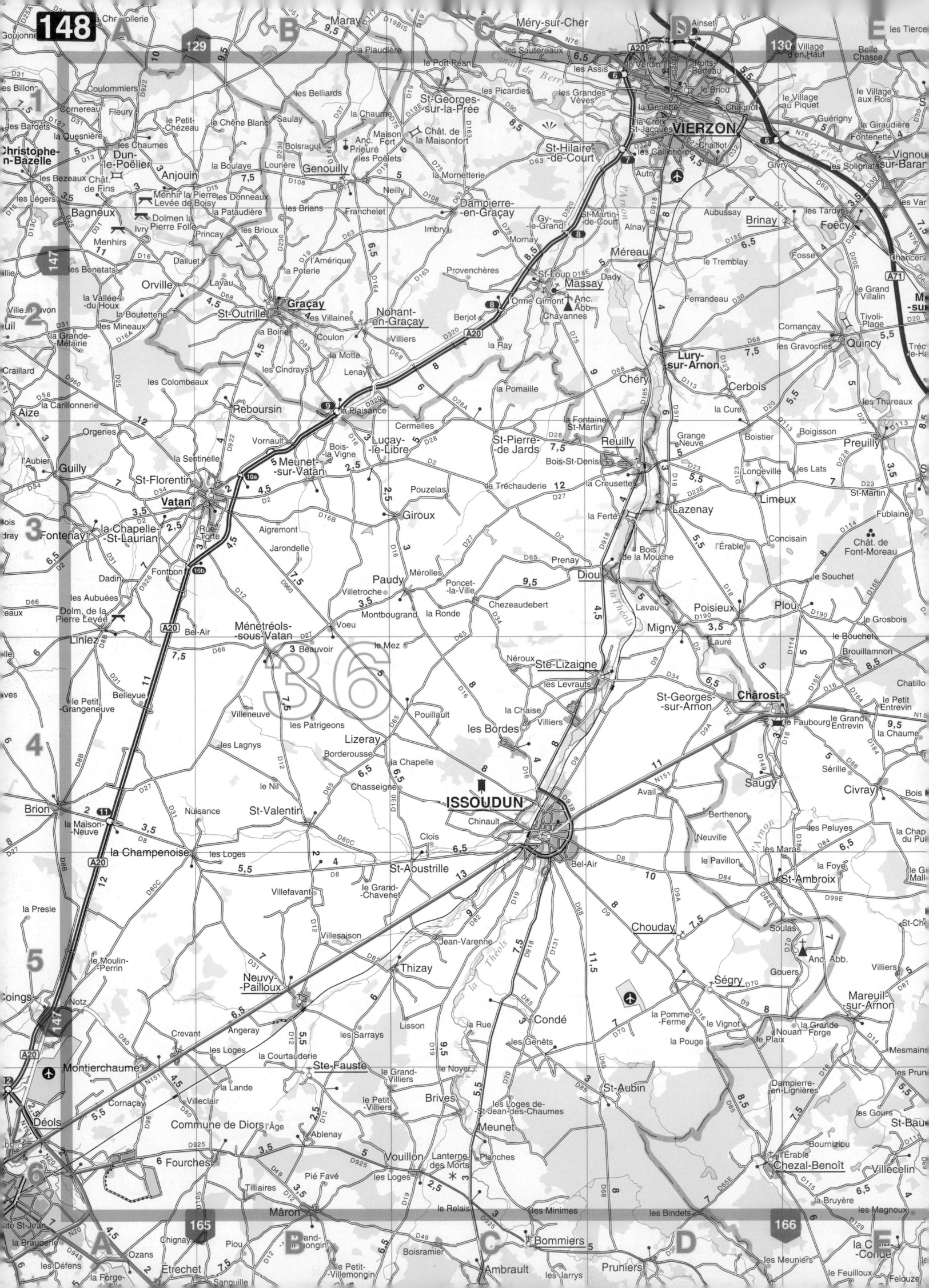

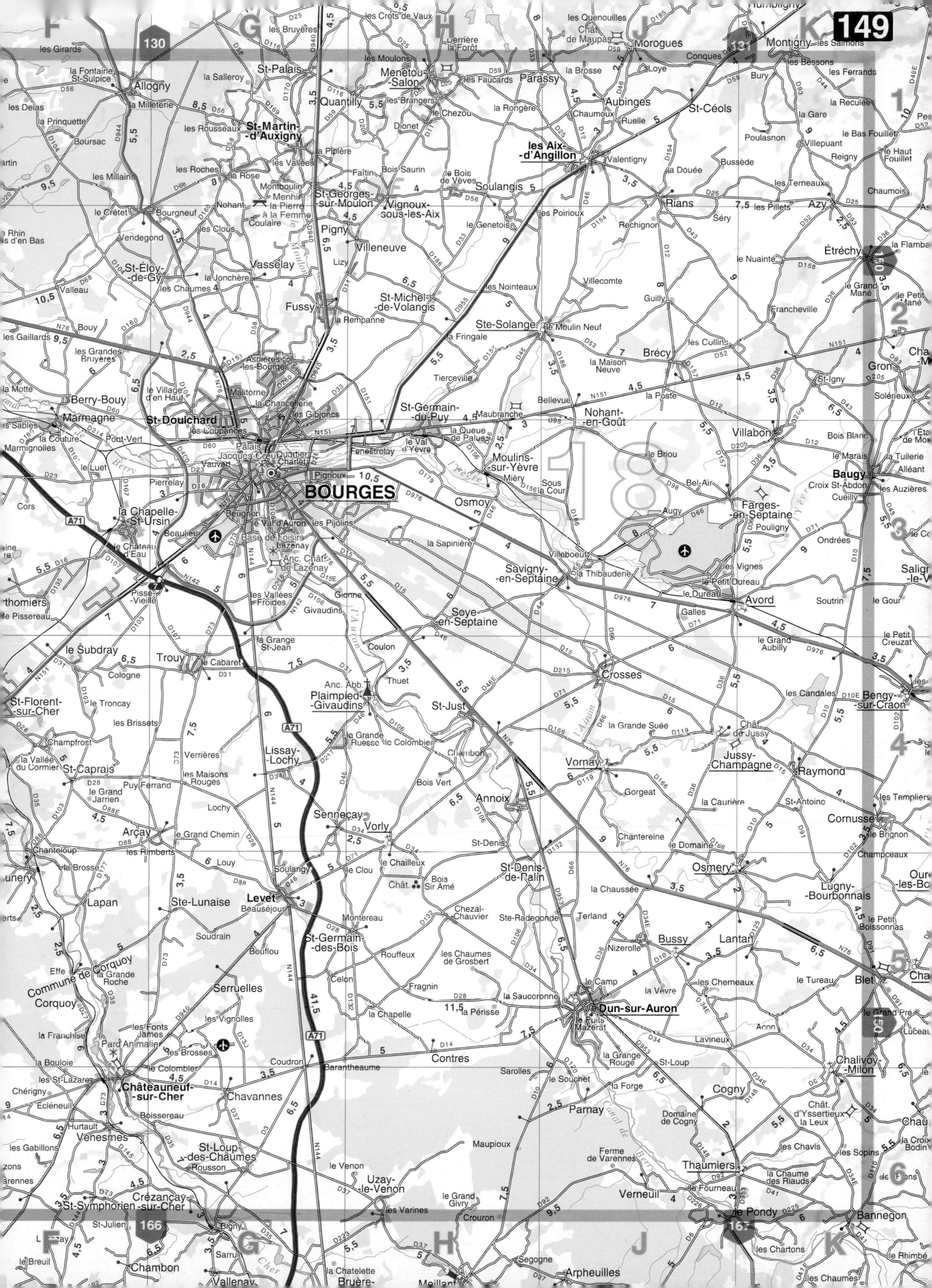

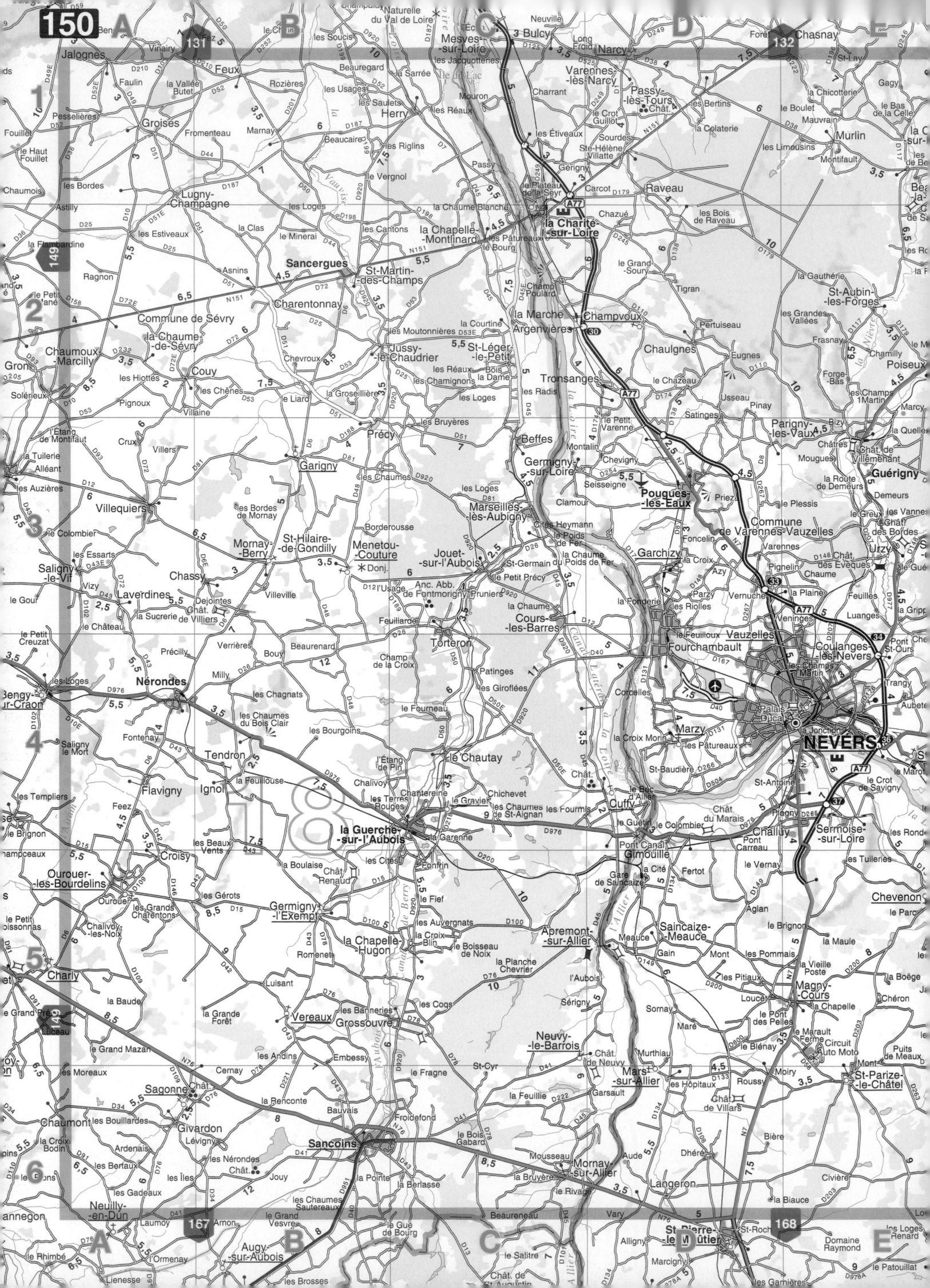

A B C D E

1

2

3

4

5

6

A B C D E

la Touche
Si... l'Océan
le Plessis
le Fenouiller
la Largerie
les Gr.
Bros...

140 Roche
Baudoin
St-Révérend
l'Essart

Croix-
de-Vie
Saint-Gilles
4,5

Commune de
St-Gilles-Croix-de-Vie
la Perpilière
la Doitière

la Chénelière
St-Grégoire
la Maigrière

le Pont
le Pont Jaunay
Givrand
l'Aiguillon
-sur-Vie
la Grève
la Fa...

la Fillonnière
Chât.
de Beaumarchais
la Boissonnière
6,5
la Savarière

la Sauzaie
4,5
la Chalonnière
la Chaize-
Giraud
Landevieille
7,5

le Prégneau
la Parée
la Trévillère
Brétignolles-
-sur-Mer
la Gaubretière

le Marais
Girard
Parc
de Loisirs
la Garenne
St-Nicolas
de Brem
St-Nicolas
de Brem
la Raffinière

la Gachère
les Granges
la Touche
Brem-sur-Mer
la Voie
Lambert
Va...

Forêt
Domaniale
d'Olonne
la Salaire
Menhir la
Conche Verte
la Brardière
la Burelière

l'Allerie
la Gobinière
Sauveterre
Observatoire
la Touche
les Barres
Champclou
Île-d'O...

la Bauduère
l'Aurière
la Girvière
la Roullère
la Salle
les Petite
Gahou...
Olonne-sur
Malag

Zoo-Marin
la Mériniè
la Gillerie
la Poitevi...
4,5

la Chaume
Fort St-Nicolas
la Marcellière

Ph. de l'Armandèche
**LES SABLES
-D'OLONNE**
Zoo...
le Pos...

Saint-Jean d'Orbe...
le Vi...
Bois d...

Ph.
des Baleines
les Portes-
-en-Ré

Villeneuve
Pertuis Breton

le Gillieux
Commune de St-Clément-
-des-Baleines
Rés. Nat.
de Lileau
des Niges

le Chabot
la Tricherie
Loix
la Déramée
le Peux
Rade de Saint-Martin

Fier d'Ars
Lavaud
Chenal des Éveillards

Grignon
Ars-en-Ré
la Passe
St-Martin-
-de-Ré
le Parc

la Couarde-
-sur-Mer
le Roulant
la Morinant
la Flotte
Abb. des Châteliers

le Bois-Plage-
-en-Ré
Fort de
la Prée

*Ensembles Littoraux et Marais
de l'Île de Ré*
les Grenettes

Rivedoux-
-Plage
la Noue
ÎLE DE RÉ
le Défens
Ste-Marie-
-de-Ré

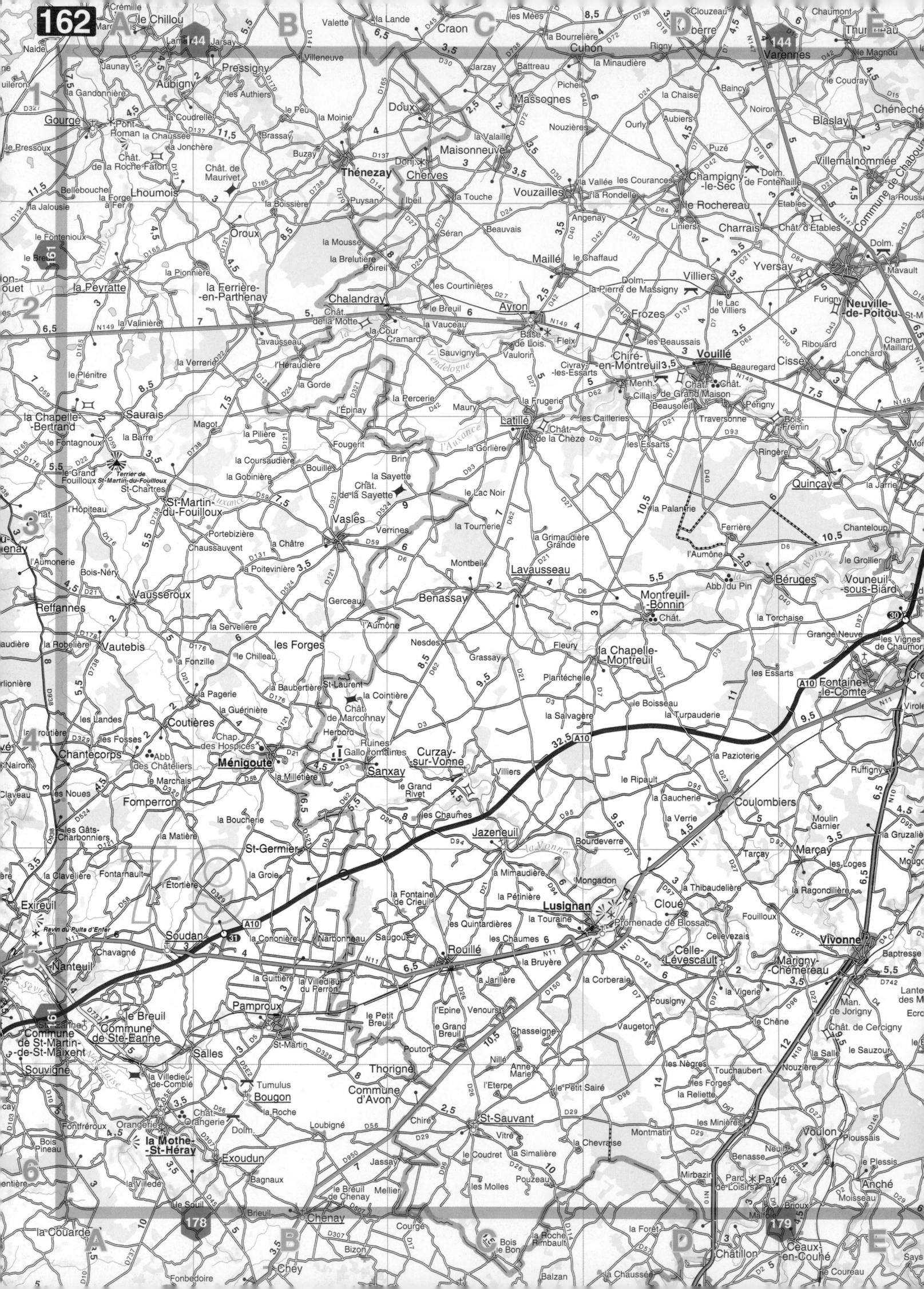

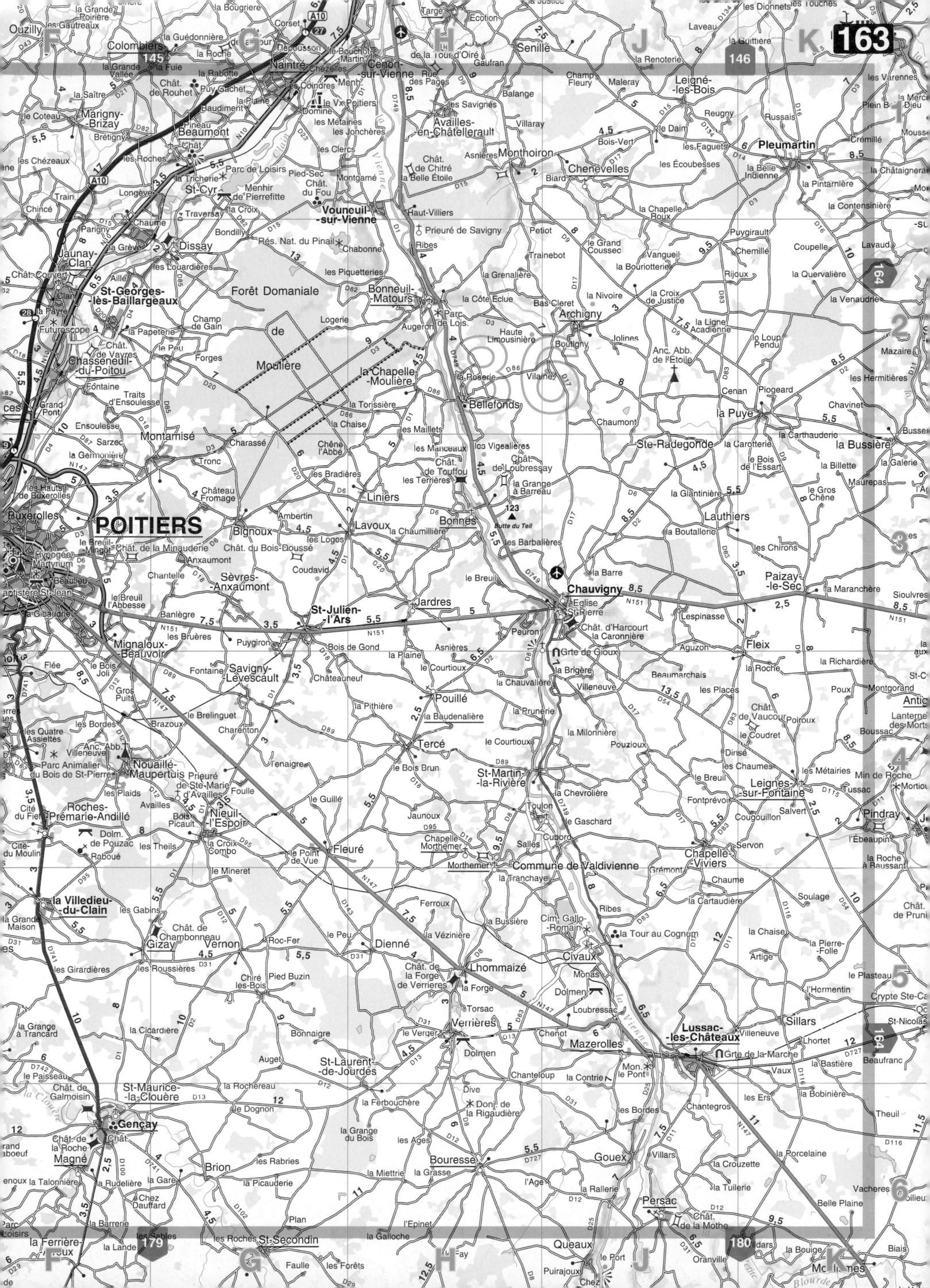

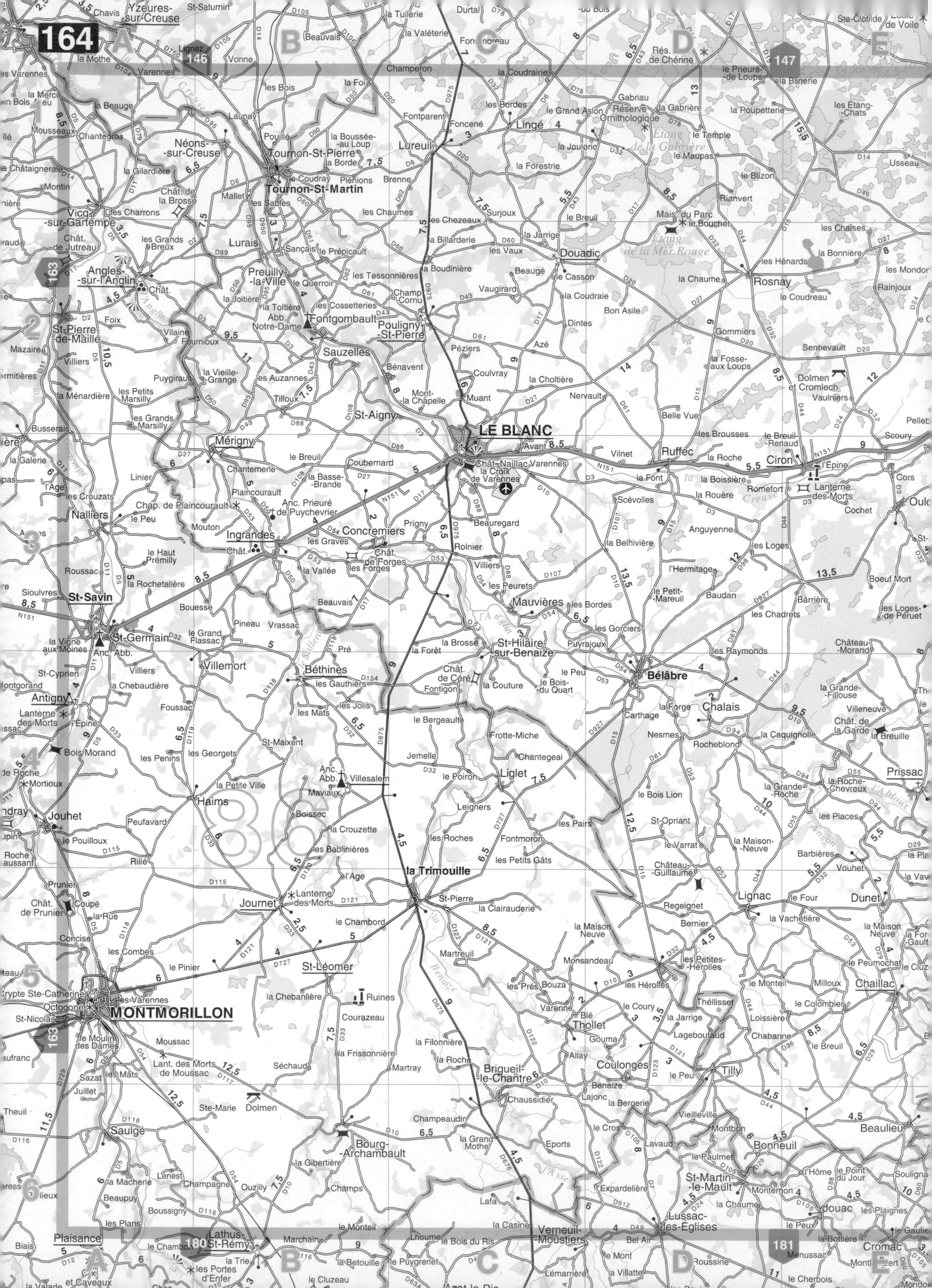

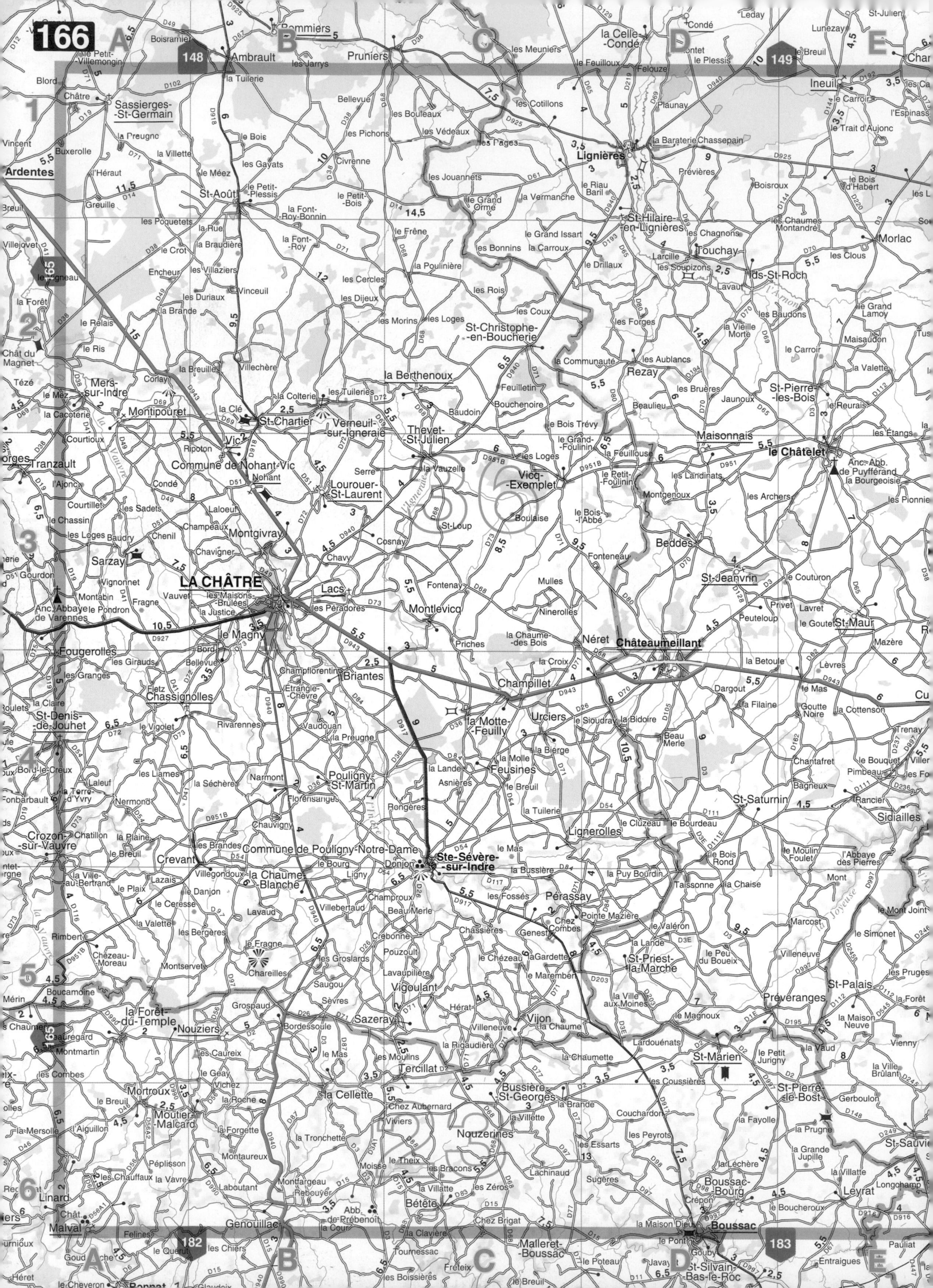

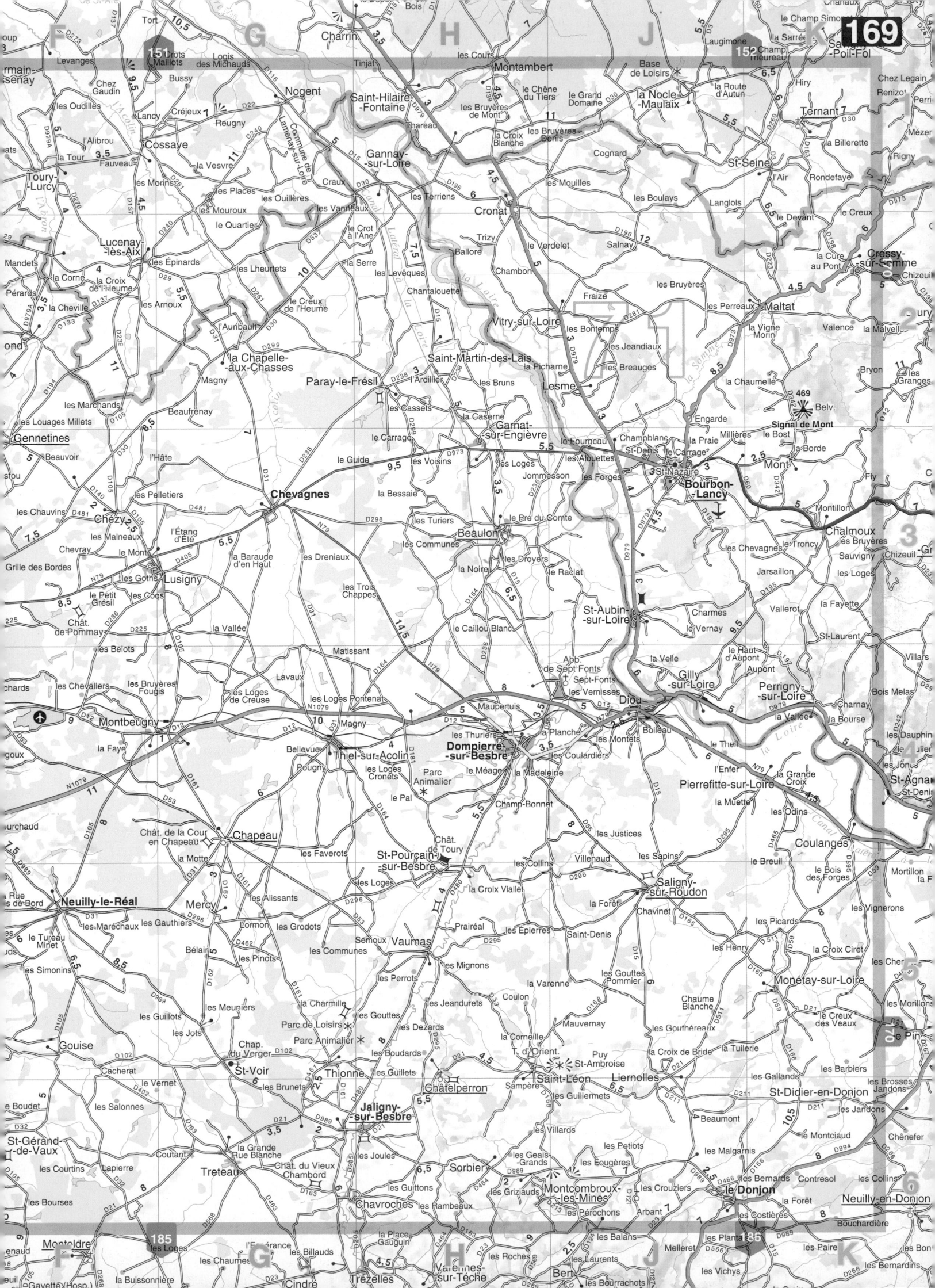

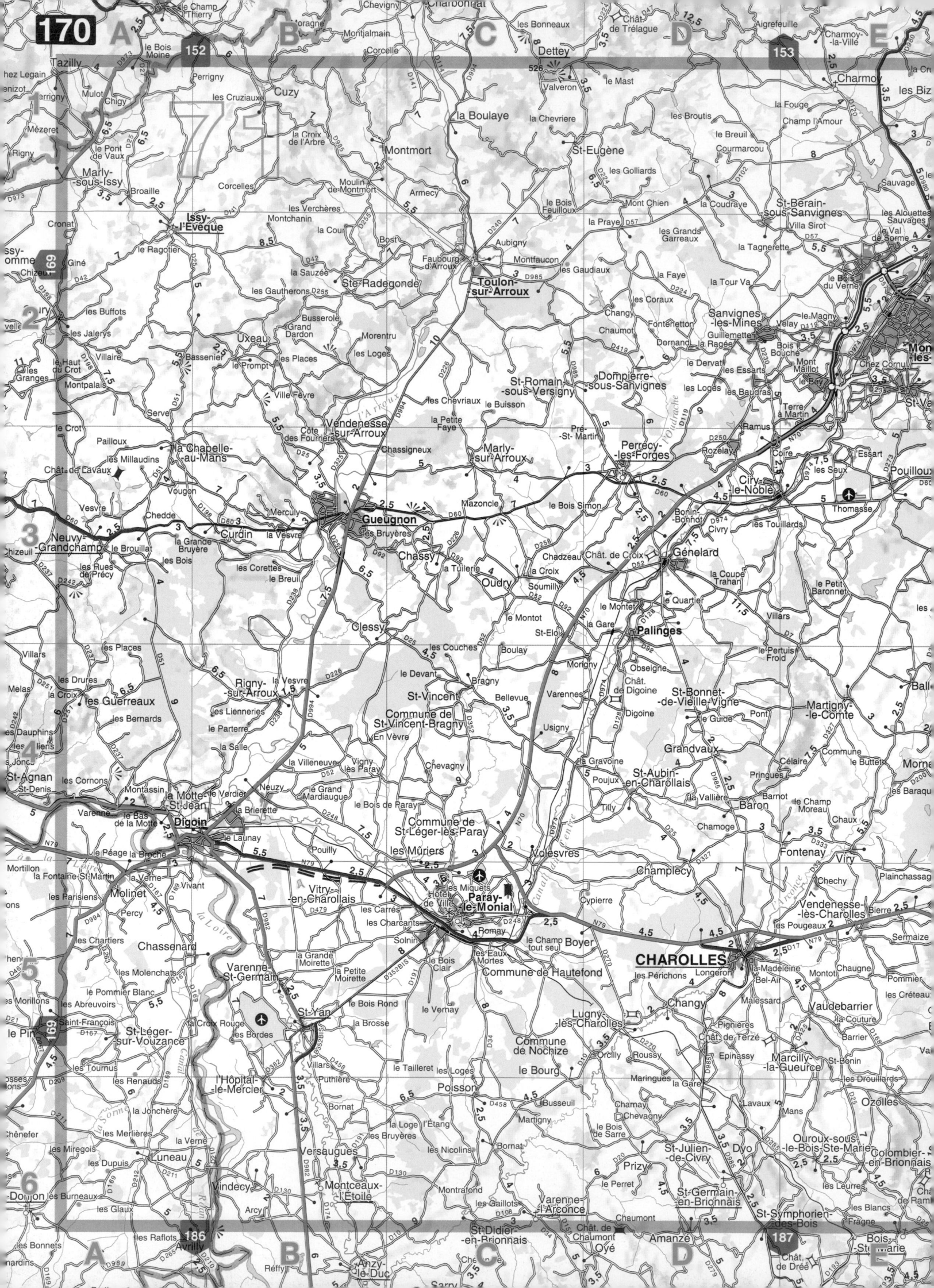

SUISSE

LAUSANNE

Orbe
la Sarraz
Cossonay
ufflens-le-Château
Morges
Préverenges
St-Sulpice

Echallens

le Mont-sur-Lausanne
Epalinges
Bussigny-près-
-Lausanne

Epesses
Chexbres

Moudon

Jules
Romont

Châtel-Saint-Denis
les Paccots

Vevey
la Tour-de-Peilz

Montreux

les Avants

Villeneuve

LAC   LÉMAN

Port Ripaille
Delta de la Dranse
le Ripaille
les Épinanches
Vongy
BAINS
oy
Tully
Sur Crête
l'Ermitage
les Bougeries
Armoy
Noyer
Chât. des Allinges
ès Château
Vieux
Orcier
Maugny
Lyaud
Reyvroz
Jouvernaisinaz
Trossy

Évian-les-Bains
Grande
Rive
Amphion
les Bains
Publier
Gros-Bissinges
Avonnex
Moruel Avulligoz
Marinel
Marin
Larringes
Champanges
Thièze
Féternes
Vérossier Haut
Vars
les Granges
Vinzier
Chevenoz

Petite
Rive
Neuvecelle Maxilly-
sur-Léman
St-Thomas
Poëse
Chez-Crosson
St-Paul-
en-Chablais
Roseires
Praubert
Bénand
Bernex Trossy
Chez Bochet
Chez Maçon

Meillerie
Troubois
le Maravant
les Plantés
Grand Roc
Lajoux
Tollon-les-Mémises
1598
Montagne des Mémises
Creusaz
2221
Dent d'Oche

Locum
Bret
St-Gingolph
les Granges
du Crêt
Novel
la Planche
Neuva
dessous
2198
Mont Gardy
2432
les Cornettes de Bise

Torgon

le Col
du Feu
Lullin
Chez
Maurice
Bellevaux
le Frêne
Col de Col
du Terrament

la Siaux
les Charges
la Baume
le Borgel
Haute-Cisère
Argence

la Vernaz
Vailly
Gorges du Pont
du Diable
le Lavouet
Chalets
de la Buchille
le Biot
Malaliutaz
Bas Thex

Nicodex
Bonnevaux
Chalets
d'Ouzon
1237
les Grands Prés
la Touvière
les Onchets

Pré Richard
Taverole
Fontany
la Forclaz
le Fion
Vacheresse
le Villard
Cercle
le Tronchet
Abondance
Frogy
Sur la Ravine
2432
Mont
de Grange
St-Guérin
les Plagnes

Darbon
Fontaine
Ubine
Richebourg
la Balme
Chalets
de Pertuis
Follebin
le Loy
Villapeyron
Très
les Pierres

Chalets
de Chevenne
la Plagne
Passengué
les Thoules
Chez
de l'Aubourry
la Chapelle
d'Abondance
le Pantiaz
la Ville du Nant
le Petit Châtel
le Moulaz
1970
le Morclan
la Vorraz
Châtel
Vonnes
Pas de Morgins
1370

Muraz

191

72

192

F   G   H   J   K

160

Pertuis Breton

Pointe d'Arçay

les Sablons

Anse à l'Aiguillon

Canal du Cur

Pointe de l'Aiguillon

Charron

1

les Portes-
-en-Ré

Ville-
neuve

ment-
Rés. Nat.
de l'ileau
des Niges

Esnandes

Chasserat

D106E2

An

les Portes

D20

4.5

le Peux

Loix

le Péramée

Lavaud

Rade de Saint-Martin

St-Martin-
-de-Ré

le Parc

Villeneuve

Villedoux

St-Ouen-
d'Aun

Marsilly

Nantilly

D105E1

D106

la Cave

D106E1

Ars-en-Ré

D735

la Passe

2.5

5

D735

le Roulant

la Flotte

Abb. des Châteliers

l'Houmeau

la Ribotelière

St-Xandre

fief des Dompierres

l'Ardillère

Ussea

2

la Couarde-
-sur-Mer

le Bois-Plage-
-en-Ré

le Morinant

**Ensembles Littoraux et Marais
de l'Île de Ré**

les Grenettes

la Noue

ÎLE DE RÉ

Ste-Marie-
-de-Ré

le Défens

Rivedoux-
-Plage

Fort de
la Prée

4.5 D735

Lauzières

les Grands
Champs

Nieul-
sur-Mer

l'Aubreçay

Lagord

le Lignon

la Rochelle-Laleu

N237

D107

Puilboreau

Dompierre-
-sur-Mer

les Brandes

N11

Chagnolet

LA ROCHELLE

Laleu

Mireuil

Vendôme

Beauty

Temple

St-Eloi

la Pallice

Vieux
Port

St-Maurice

Port Neuf

Vieux-Port

Villeneuve
des Salines

Tasdon

Périgny

St-Rogatien

3

Pertuis d'Antioche

les Minimes

la Courbe

N137

Aytré

Clave

Chât.
de Buzay

la Jarne

Salles-
sur-Mer

Chât.

la Plage
d'Aytré

Angoulins

St-Jean
des Sables

la Frénée

l'Herbaudière

Rade des Basques

Châtelaillon-
-Plage

St-Vivien

Ph. de Chassiron

la Gautrie

St-Denis-
d'Oléron

le Moulin des Combes

la Michelière

les Huttes

la Brée-
-des-Bains

les Boulassiers

Vieux
Châtelaillon

les Boucholeurs

Rés. Nat.
du Marais d'Yves

le Marouillet

4

ÎLE D'AIX

Bois Joly

Mais. de l'Empereur

Île-d'Aix

la Fumée

Baie d'Yves

Yves

**Anse du Marais Salé
ou Baie des Pilotes**

Chaucre

l'Île

le Douhet

Anse de la Maleconche

Fort Boyard

Rade de l'Île d'Aix

Pointe
de la Fumée

la Fumée

la Faye au Bois

Bassat

St-Georges-
-d'Oléron

Foulerot

la Gibertière

**Ensembles Littoraux
de l'Île d'Oléron**

Cheray

Domino

les Sables-
Vignier

l'Îleau

St-Gilles

Sauzelle

Boyardville

Embouchure
de la Charente

Fouras

Fort

St-Laurent-
de-la-Prée

Soumard

la Roche

la Menounière

Lanterne
des Morts

Arceau

Bulong

**St-Pierre-
d'Oléron**

les Allards

Île Madame

la Charente

Fort
Lupin

Fort Pe

Côte de Plédemont

Port
-des-Barques

RC

5

la Biroire

la Chefmalière

la Cotinière

Matha

Dolus-
d'Oléron

Rés. Nat.
de Moeze-d'Oléron

Piédemont

St-Nazaire-
sur-Charente

les Lauriers

St-Froult

Sc

ÎLE D'OLÉRON

la Remigeasse

les Bardières

Fort

le Château-
d'Oléron

la Gaconnière

Parcs à Huitres

Moèze

Croix Hosannière

l'Écuissière

Grésillon

St-Trojan-
les-Bains

Plage

le Grand-Village-
-Plage

Ors

Fort du Chapus

Pointe du Chapus

le Chapus

Bourcefranc-
le-Chapus

Brouage

Hiers

Commune
de Hiers-Brouage

6

Chât. de
la Gataudière

Breuil

les Bris

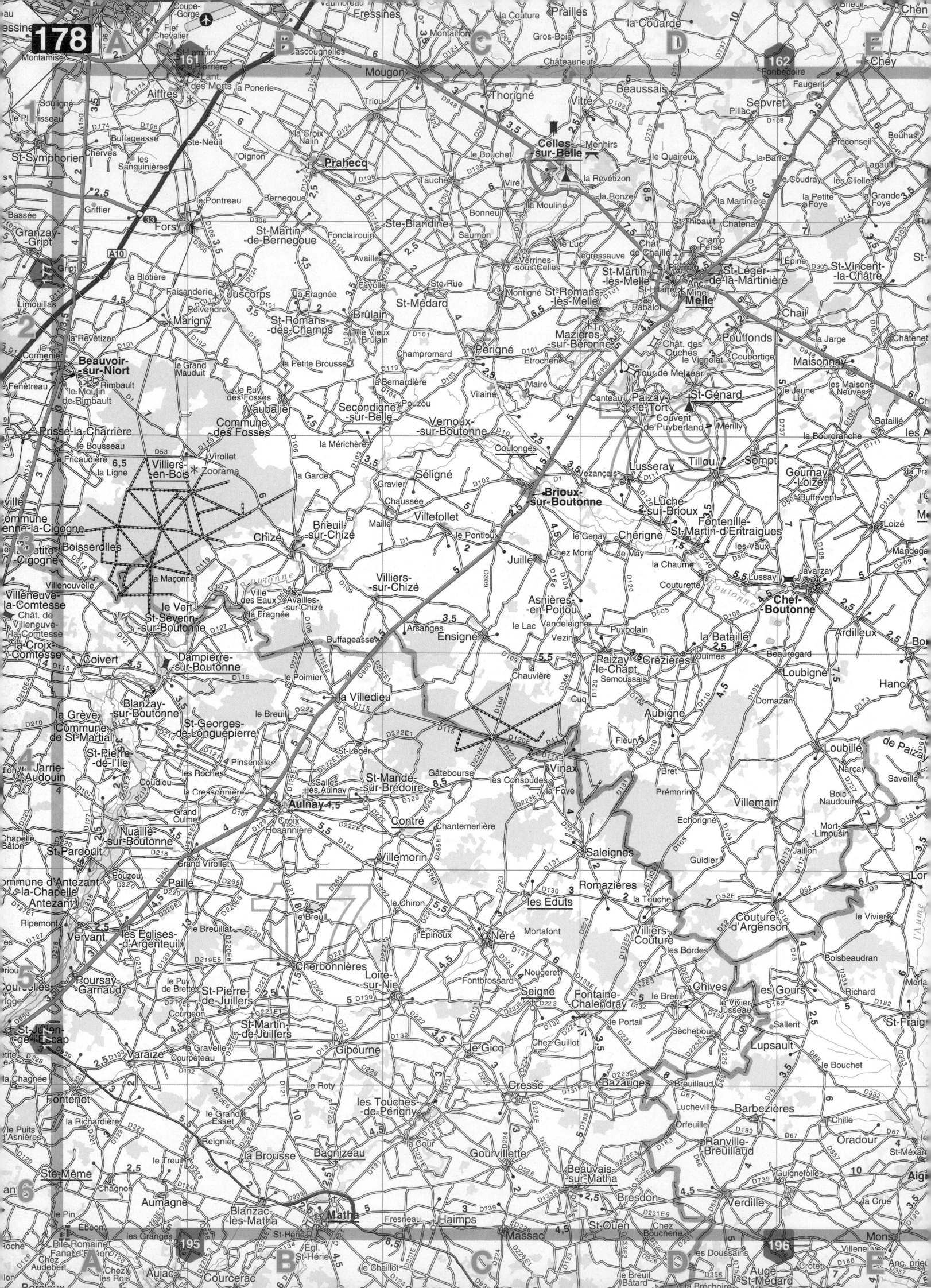

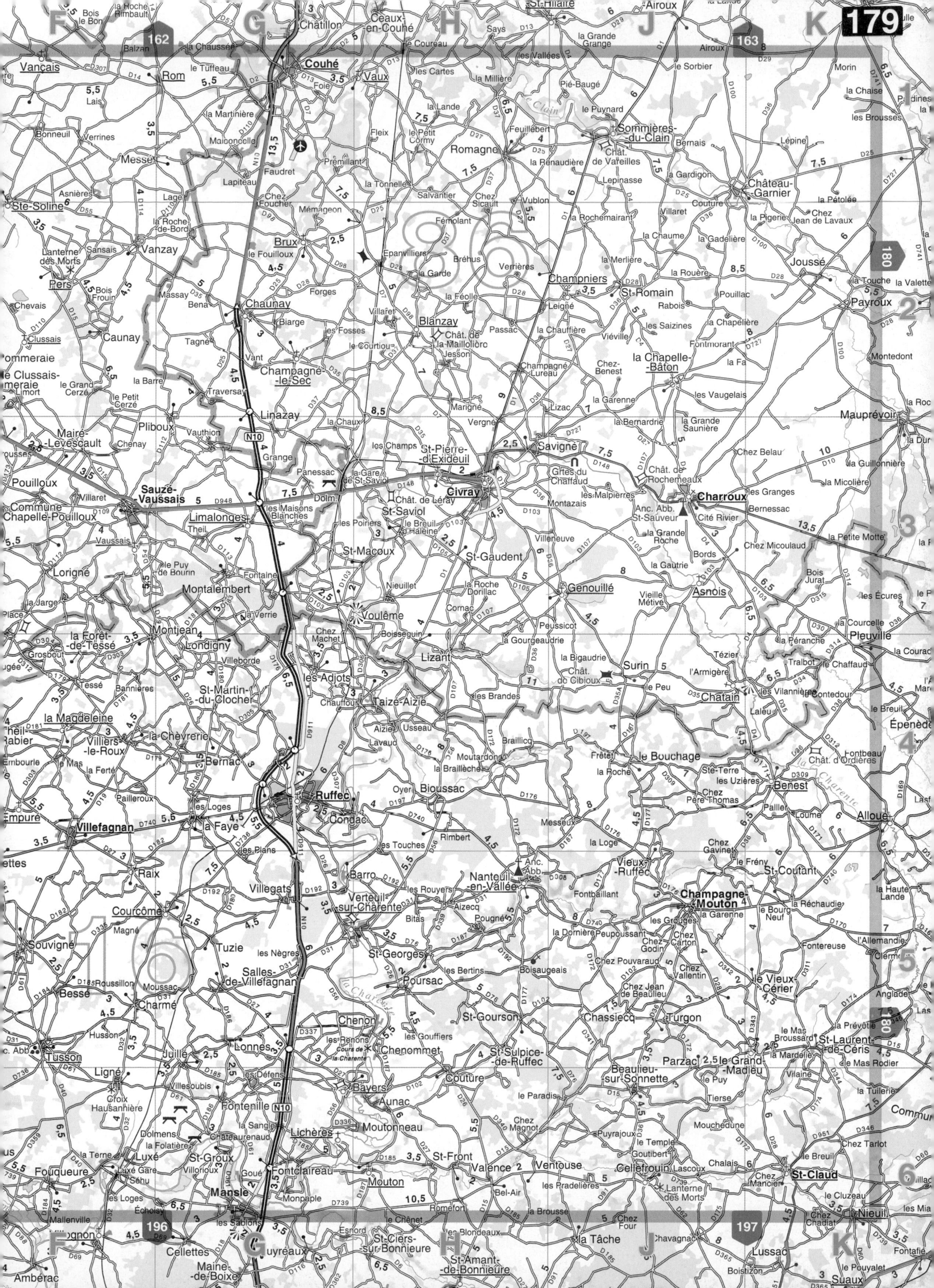

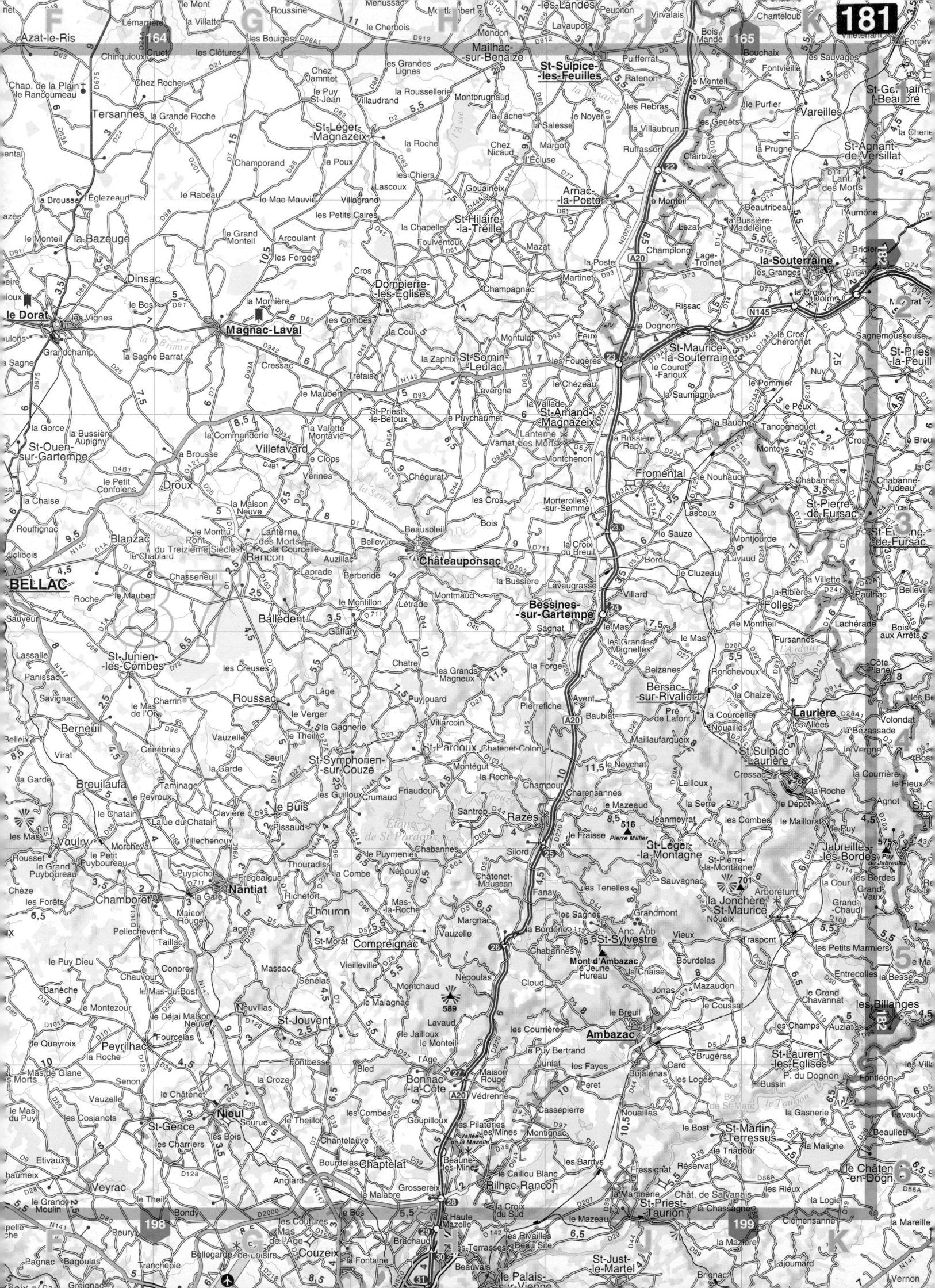

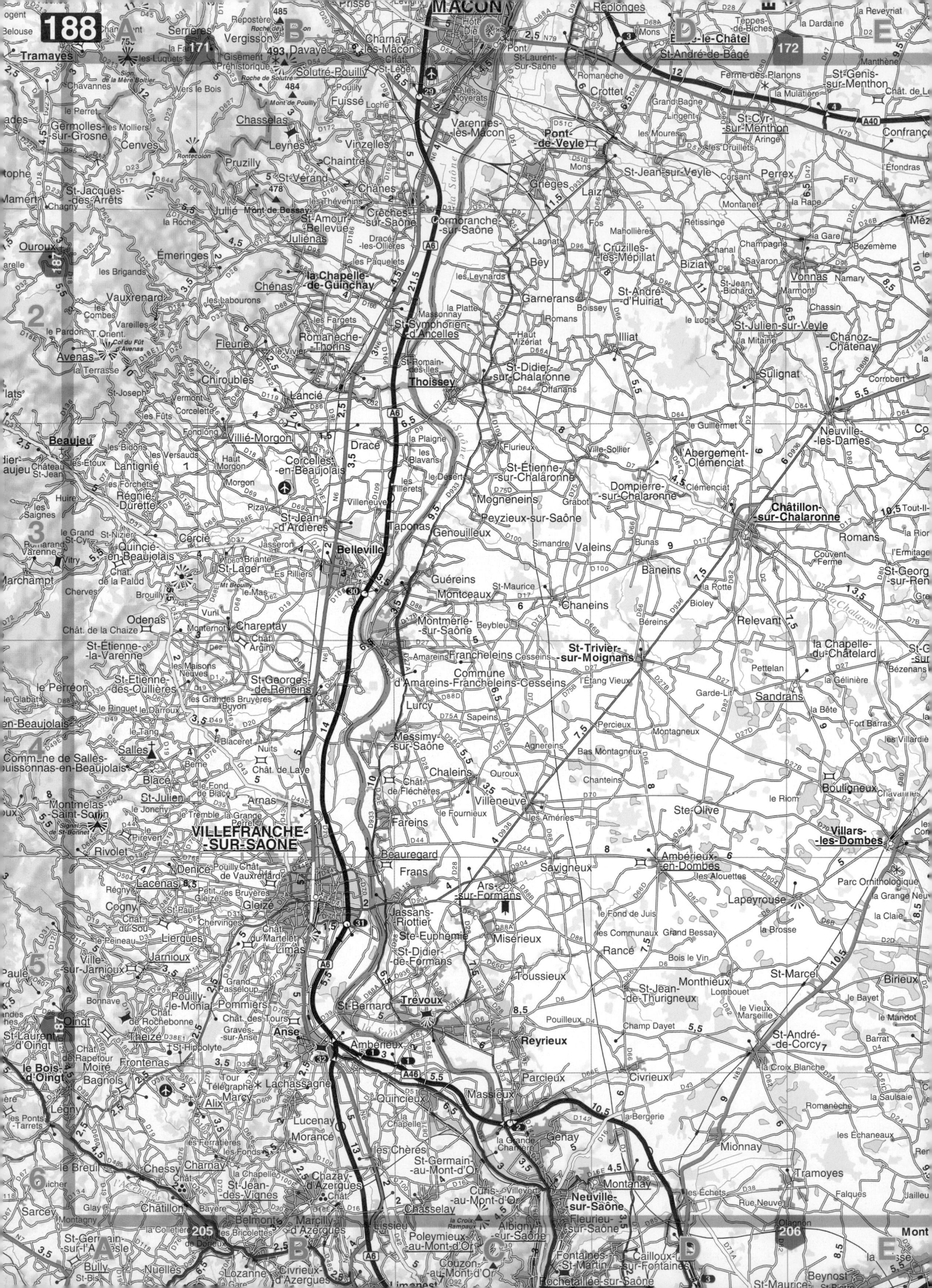

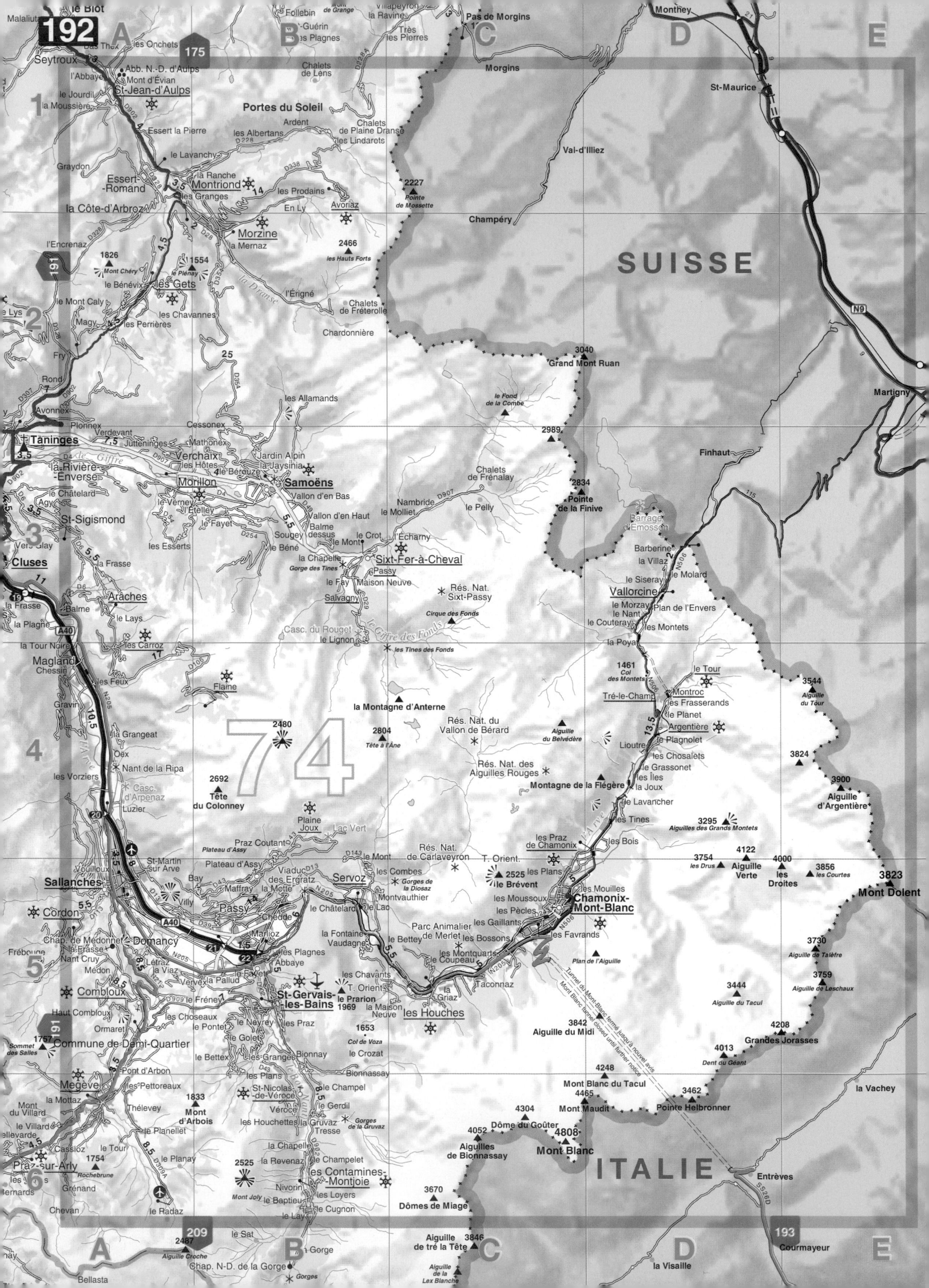

A · B · C · D · E

1
2
3
4
5
6

176

177

210

210

Pertuis de Maumusson

Pointe de Gatseau

la Plage

Marennes

la Chaînade

le Grand Breuil

St-Fort

Champagne

Pont-l'Abbé-d'Arnoult

l'Épinard 6

z Jaudon

St-Just-Luzac

la Gripperie-St-Symphorien

St-Sulpice-d'Isleau

l'Isleau

Ronce les Bains

les Brandes

St-Symphorien

les Pibles

Font Bonnet

Luzac

les Touches

60

la Tremblade

Coux

Donj.Tr. de Broue

Broue

Blénac

St-Sornin

Ste-Gemme

le Mur

Beaulieu

Forêt Domaniale

Dirée

les Fouilloux

St-Nadeau

Chez Barras

les Geais

la Moulinette

les Rivolets

Corme-Royal

de la Coubre

Avallon

Arvert

Cadeuil

Pouzaur

Nancras

les Roseaux

Étaules

Chatressac

Nieulle-sur-Seudre

St-Martin

Balanzac

20,5

la Tremblade

la Fouasse

les Mathes

Chaillevette

St-André

Anc. Abb. de Sablonceaux

le Pinier

la Fouasserie

PRESQU'ÎLE D'ARVERT

l'Île d'Étaules

Coulonges

Mornac-sur-Seudre

Sablonceaux

Chez Maulin

les Lignes

Ph. de la Coubre

Antoinette

Montsanson

l'Éguille

le Pont

Malleville

les Châtaigniers

St-Romain-de-Benet

Pointe de la Coubre

Bonne Anse

la Palmyre

Zoo

le Billeau

le Grallet

Breuillet

Plordonnier

Fontbedeau

Dercie

le Breuil

l'Ilate

le Pontet

Camp Romain de César

Toulon

les Pierrières

Tr. de Pirelongue

Villeneuve

Grande Passe de l'Ouest

Charosson

Lafond

Taupignac

St-Sulpice-de-Royan

Griffarin

la Justice

Sauvajou

le Vivier

le Romarin

Meursac

Courlay-sur-Mer

Brie

Jaffe

D14

Vertin

Saujon

Berlin

Chevret

Beaunant

le Piagnon

Corme-Écluse

la Grande Côte

la Palud

Puyravau

Vaux-sur-Mer

la Roche Châtelard

Maine Geoffroy

les Maries

Pompierrre

Chaillonnais

les Lignes

le Chay

l'Erce

les Épeaux

Ph. de Terre Nègre

Conche

St-Palais-sur-Mer

Bernon

Médis

Músson

Trignac Chât.

la Traverserie

les Courtets

Corme-Écluse

Chez Suire

Thair

Nausan

Malakoff

le Perche

Royan

Vallières

Maisonfort

Trignac

la Valade-de-Didonne

Grézac

Promenade de la Corniche

le Chay

le Parc

Plein Été

7,5

Chenaumoine

Fontenille

la Roche

Phare de Cordouan

Grande Conche

St-Georges-de-Didonne

Didonne

D730

Semussac

D730

Cozes

Embouchure de la Gironde

la Crête

Pointe de Vallières

Conche de St-Georges

Pointe de Suzac

Beloire

Bardécille

Conteneuil

Brézillas

Phare de Cordouan

Pointe de Grave

Ph. de Grave

Châtelard

Meschers-sur-Gironde

Grtes de Matata

Arces

la Grande Gorces

la Petite Gorces

Javrezac

le Pastin

Conche des Nonnes

Liboulas

Commune de Talmont-sur-Gironde

Prézelle

Soulignac

Épargnes

Plassac

le Verdon-sur-Mer

le Royannais

Site Archéologique du Fâ

le Caillaud

Talmont

Barzan

St-Seurin-d'Uzet

l'Échailler

les Huttes

les Arros

Barzan-Plage

Corm

Soulac-sur-Mer

Vieux Soulac

le Jeune Soulac

les Monards

Chenac

Commune de Chenac-St-Seurin-d'Uzet

la Gare

Neyran

Mortagne-sur-Gironde

Taffard

les Cousteaux

la Rive

Ermitage St-Martial

Saint Martial

l'Amélie

Lillan

Port de Talais

St-Seurin-d'Uzet

le Gurp

Péchaud

les Vigneaux

Talais

les Cabireaux

Port de St-Vivien

Grayan-et-l'Hôpital

la Séougue

Phare de Richard

Videau

Daugagnan

la Fosse

Commune de Jau-Dignac-et-Loirac

Euronat

la Hutte

St-Vivien-de-Médoc

la Hourcade

Port de Richard

l'Hôpital

les Piots

Jau Semensan

Dignac

le Centre

Boussan

Port de Goulée

les Colonies

Min. de Vensac

Gaudin

Sestignan

Loirac

Montalivet-les-Bains

les Cercins

Vensac

le Gua

Mayan

Larnac

la Rivière

Courbian

la Lagune

Port de By

Centre Hélio-Marin

les Abredons

Gueyt

Périgueys

le Sable

la Hontane

Condissas

By

le Blanc

Queyrac

Laujac

Canissac

Valeyrac

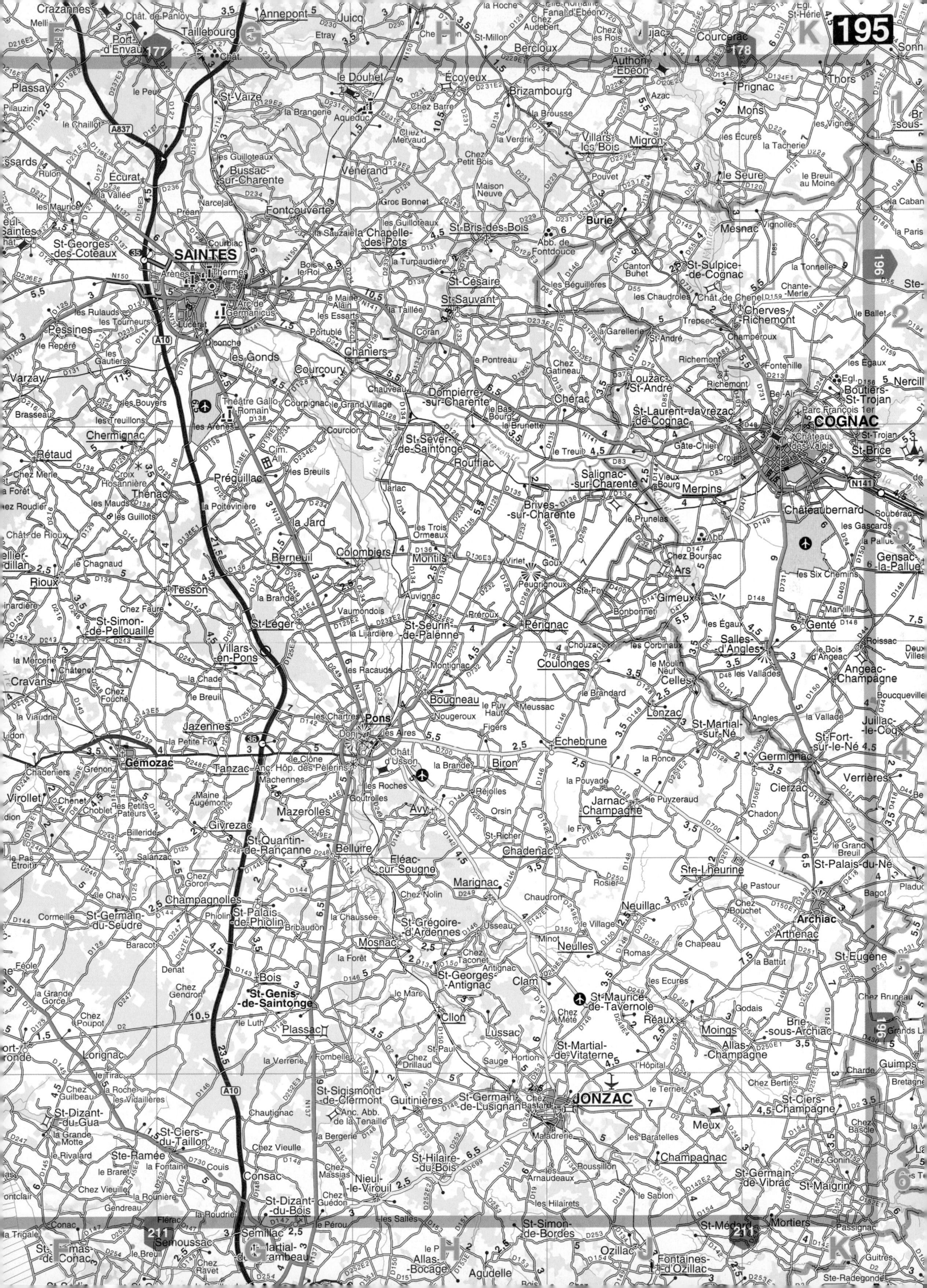

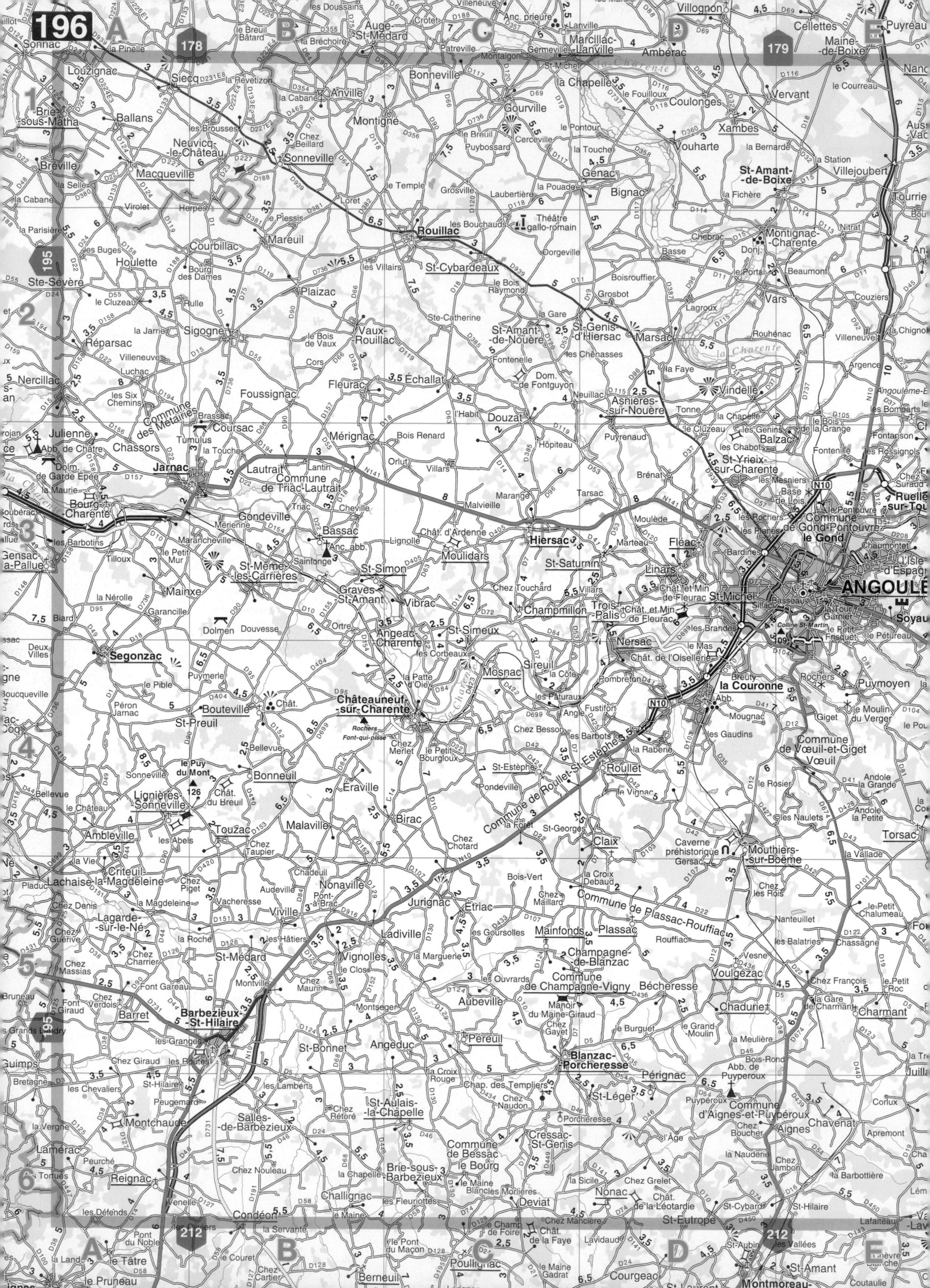

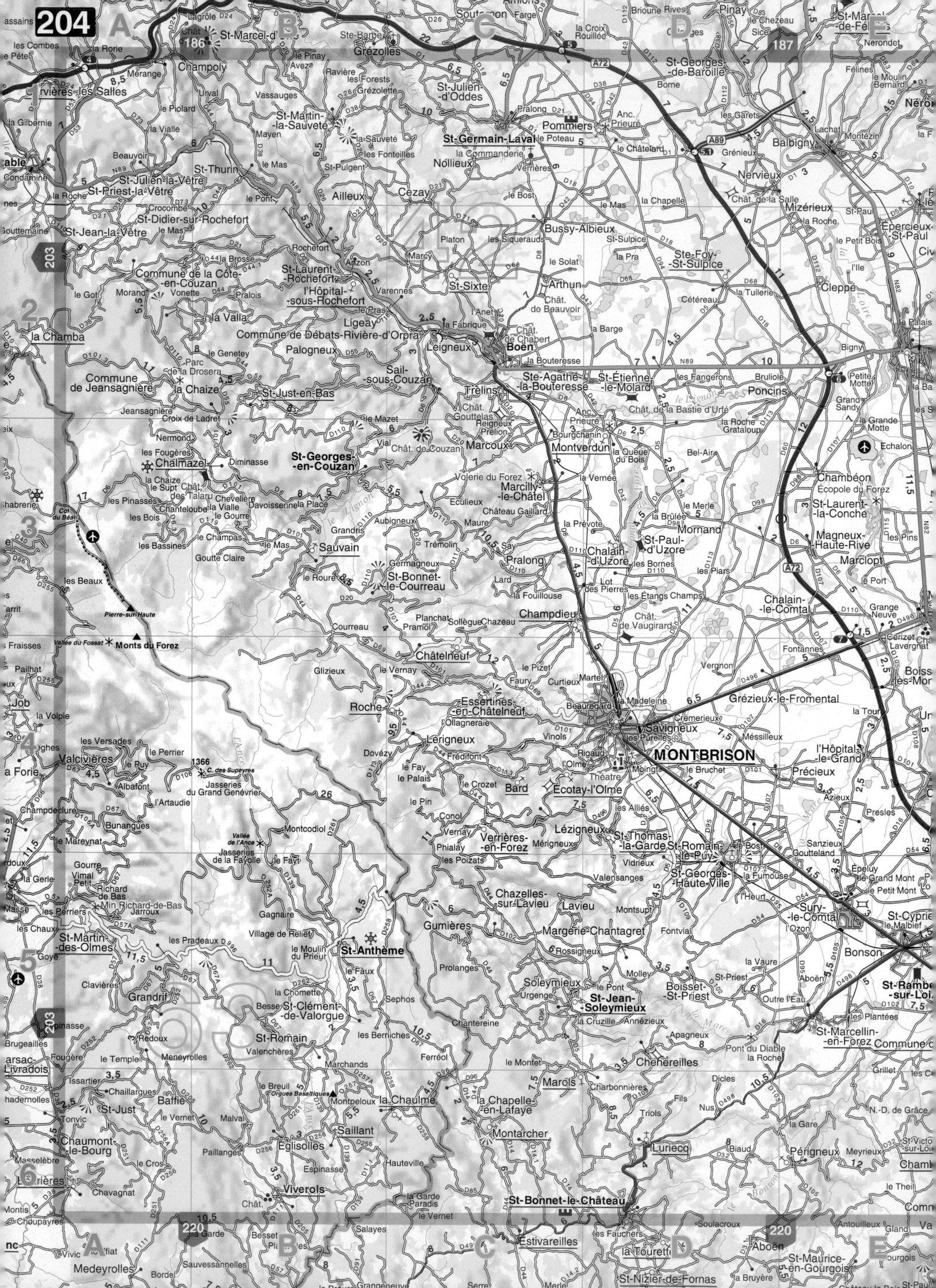

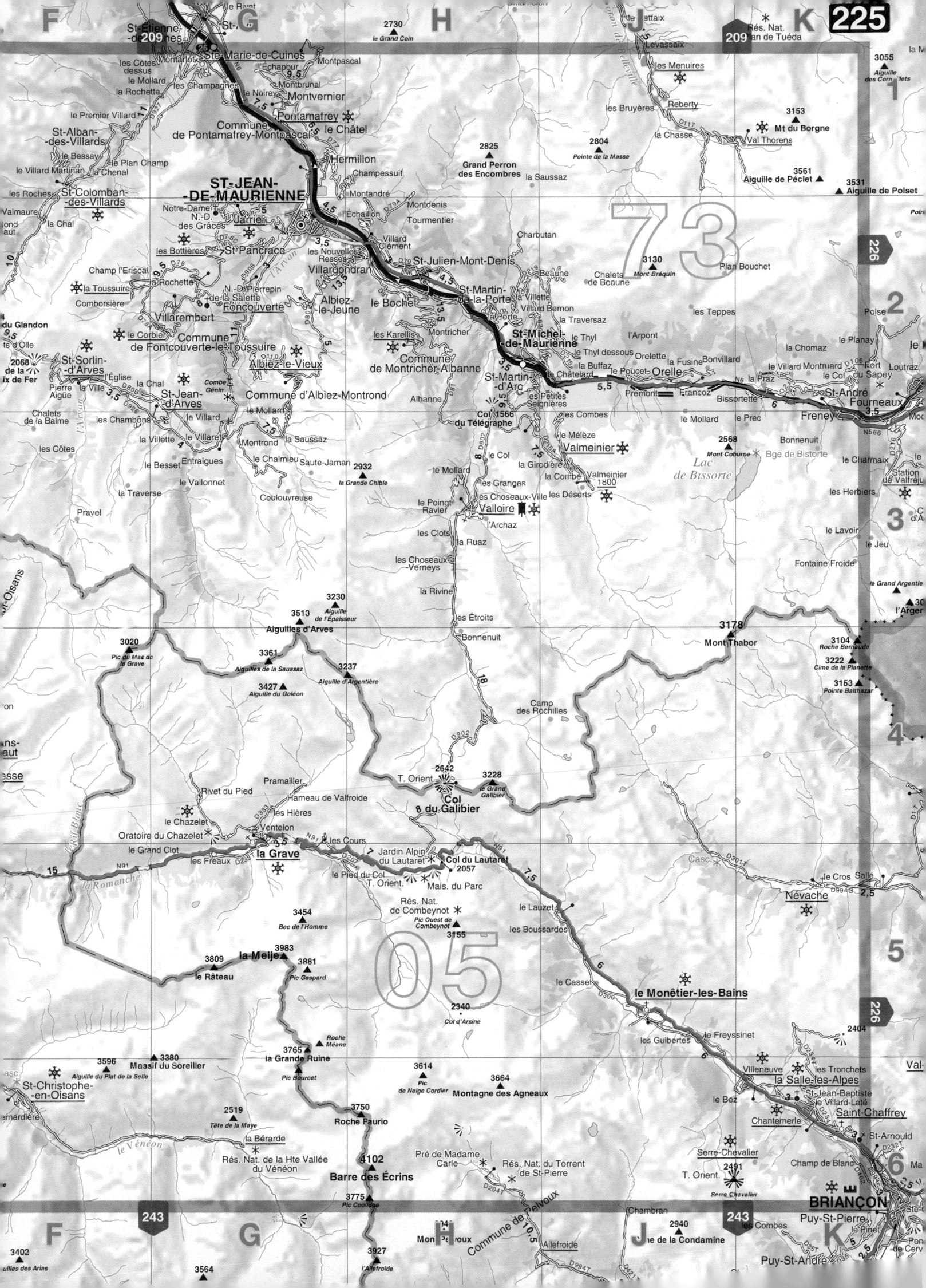

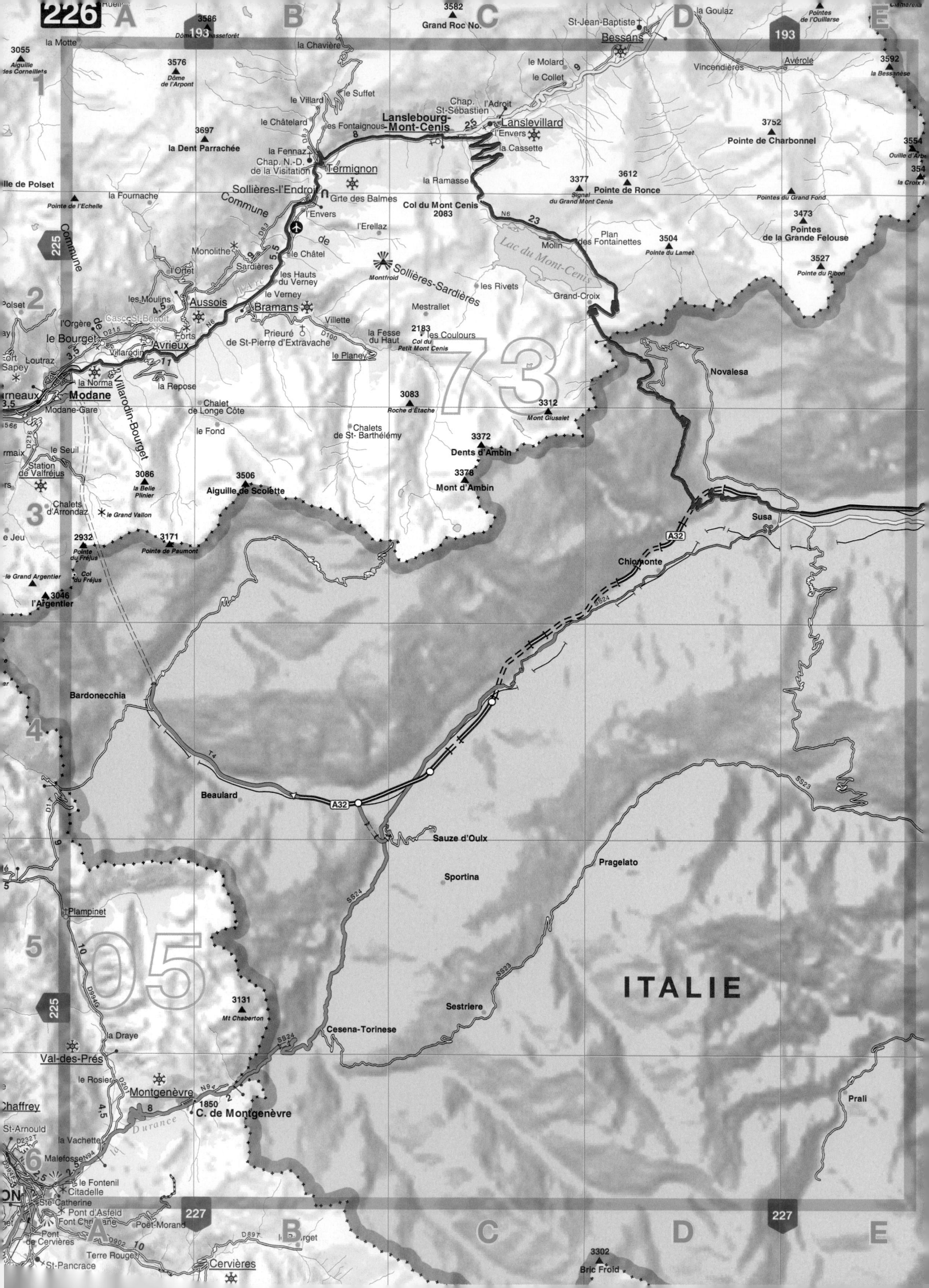

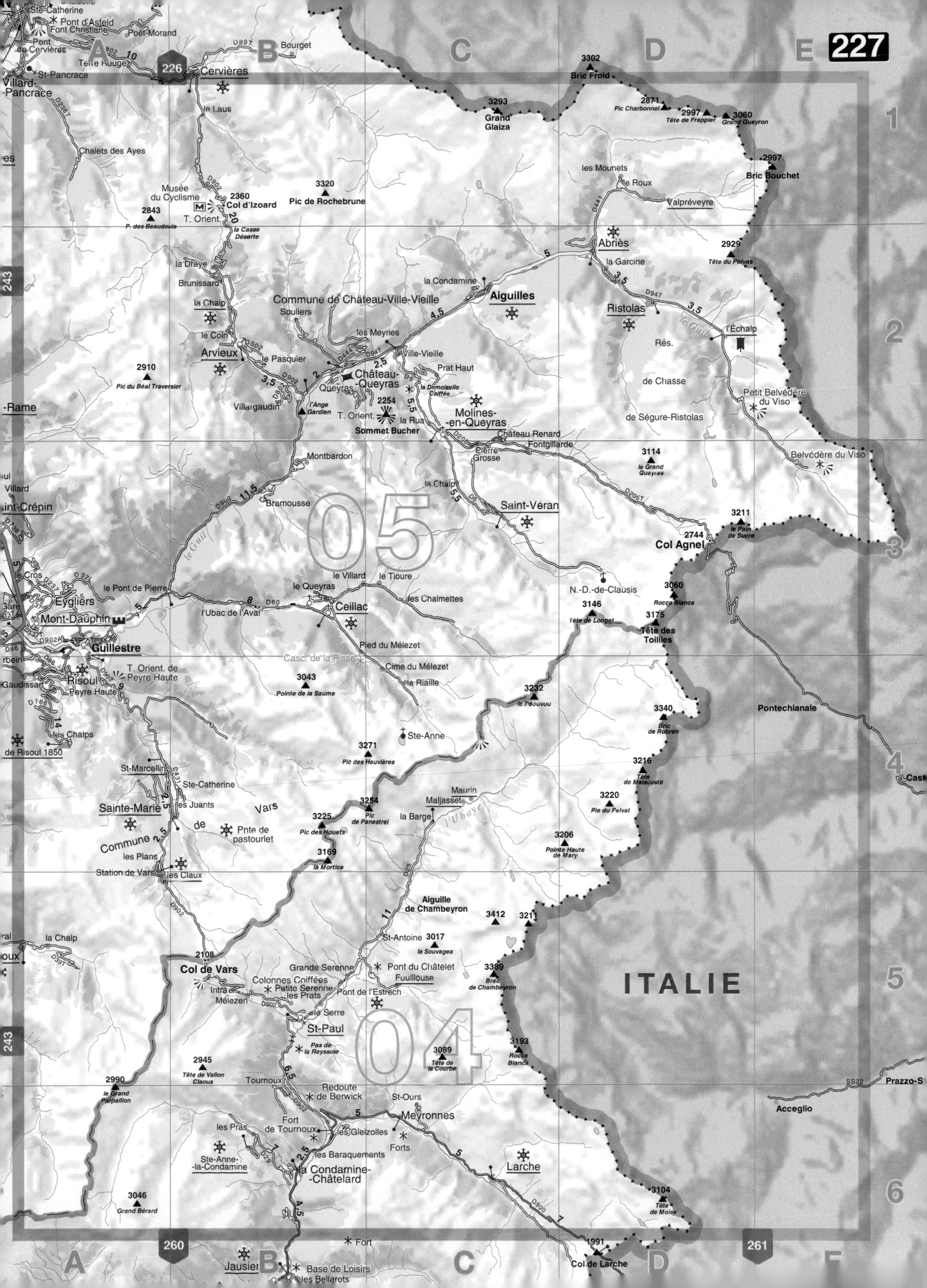

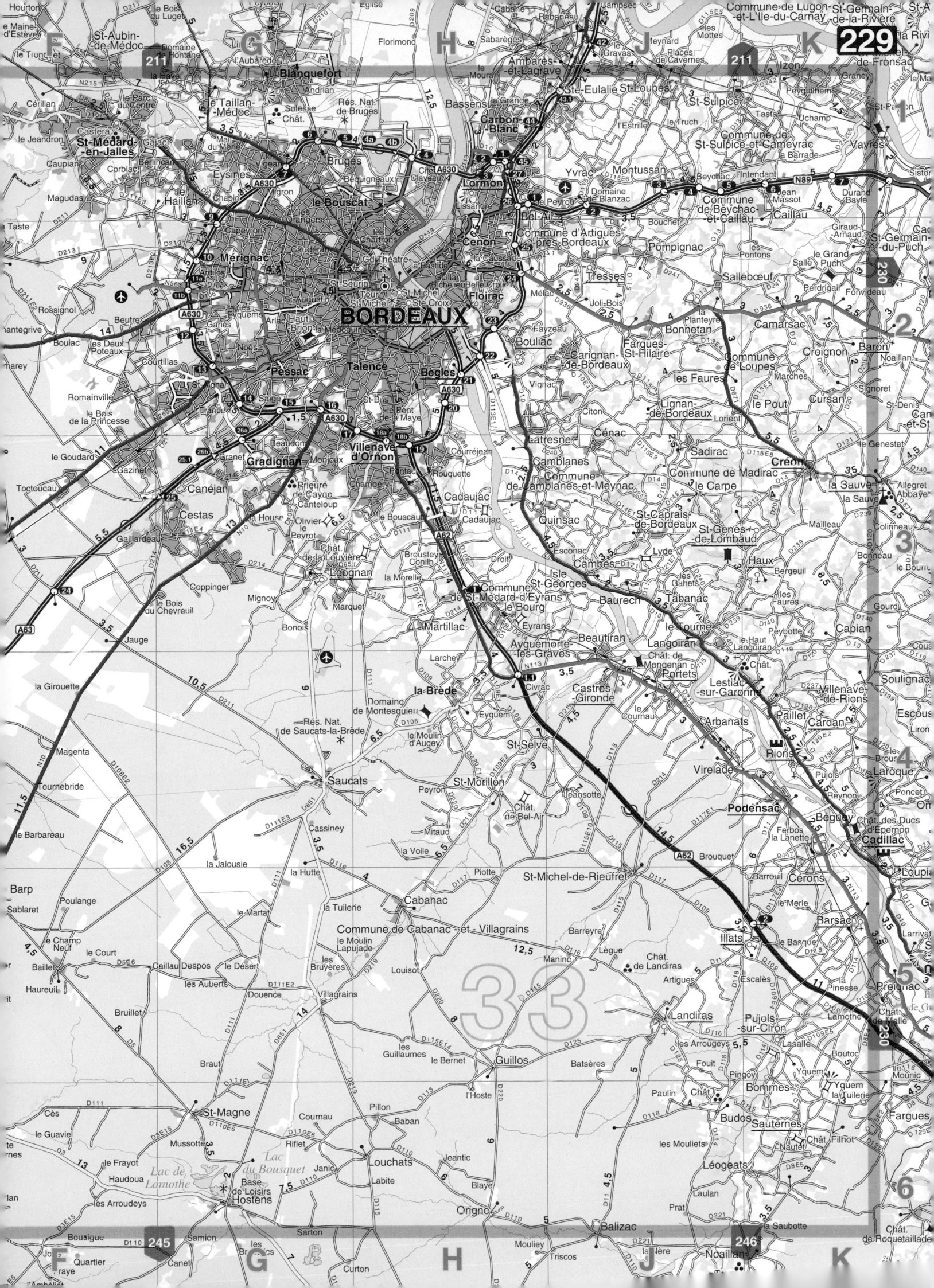

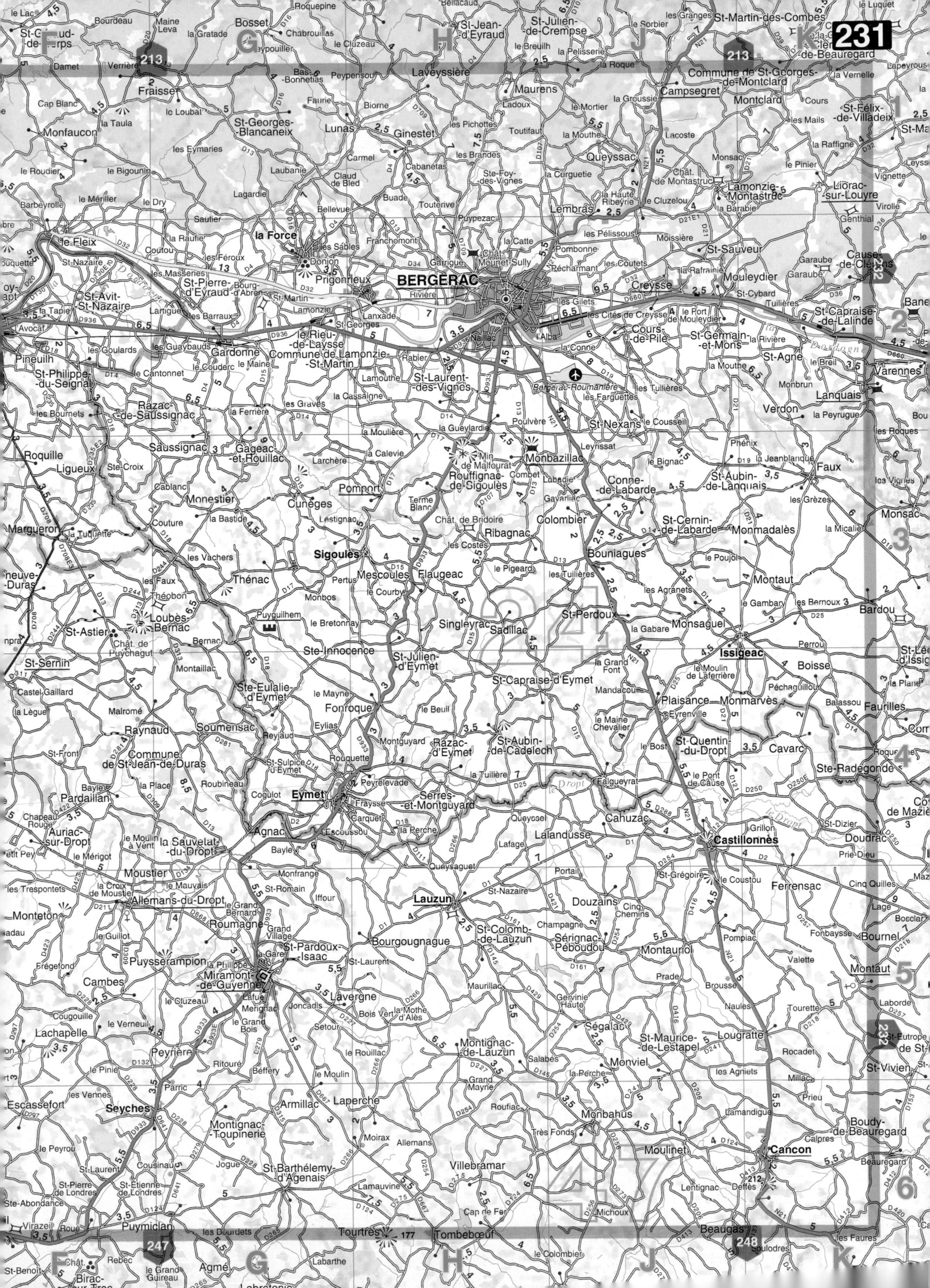

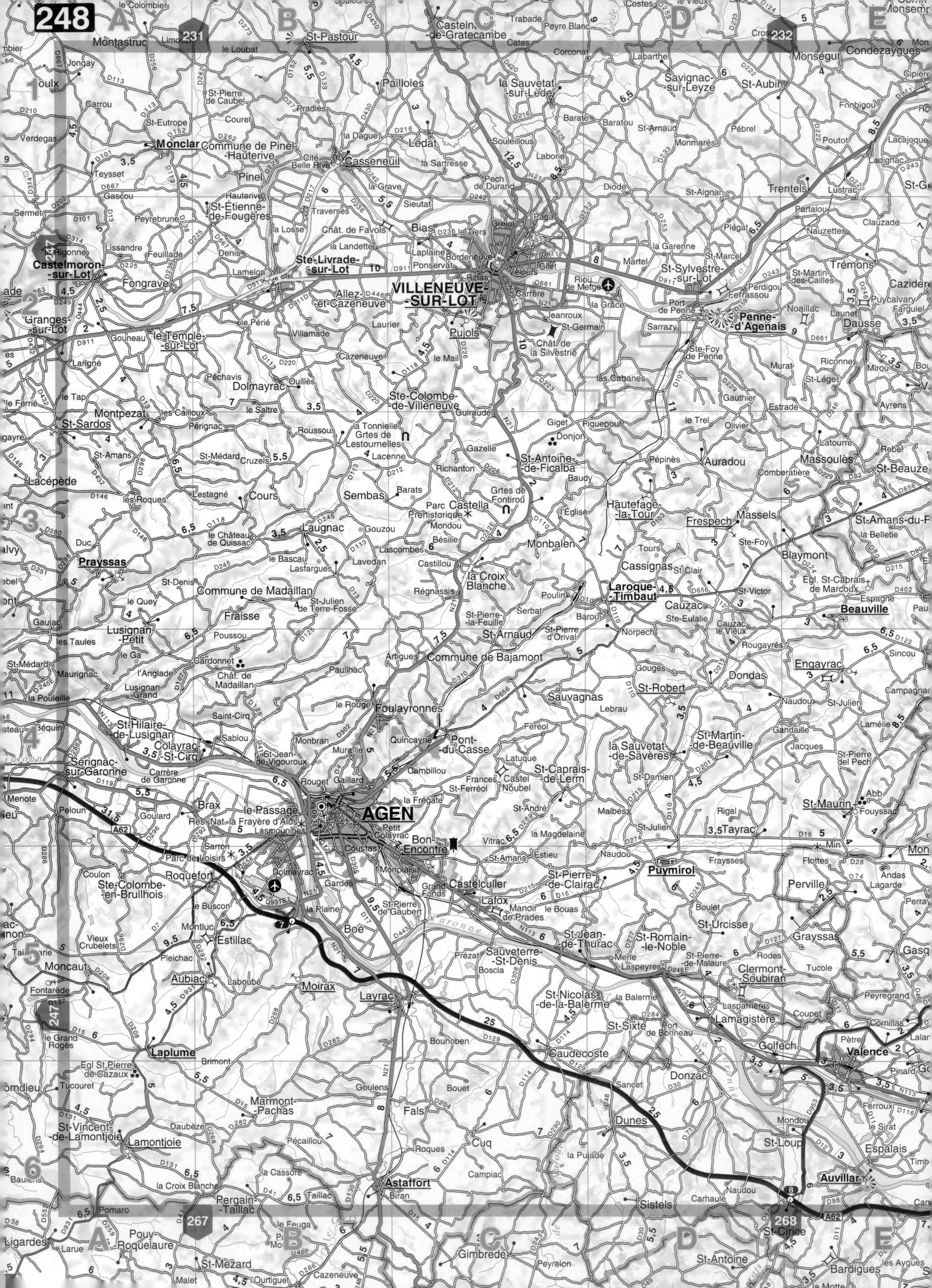

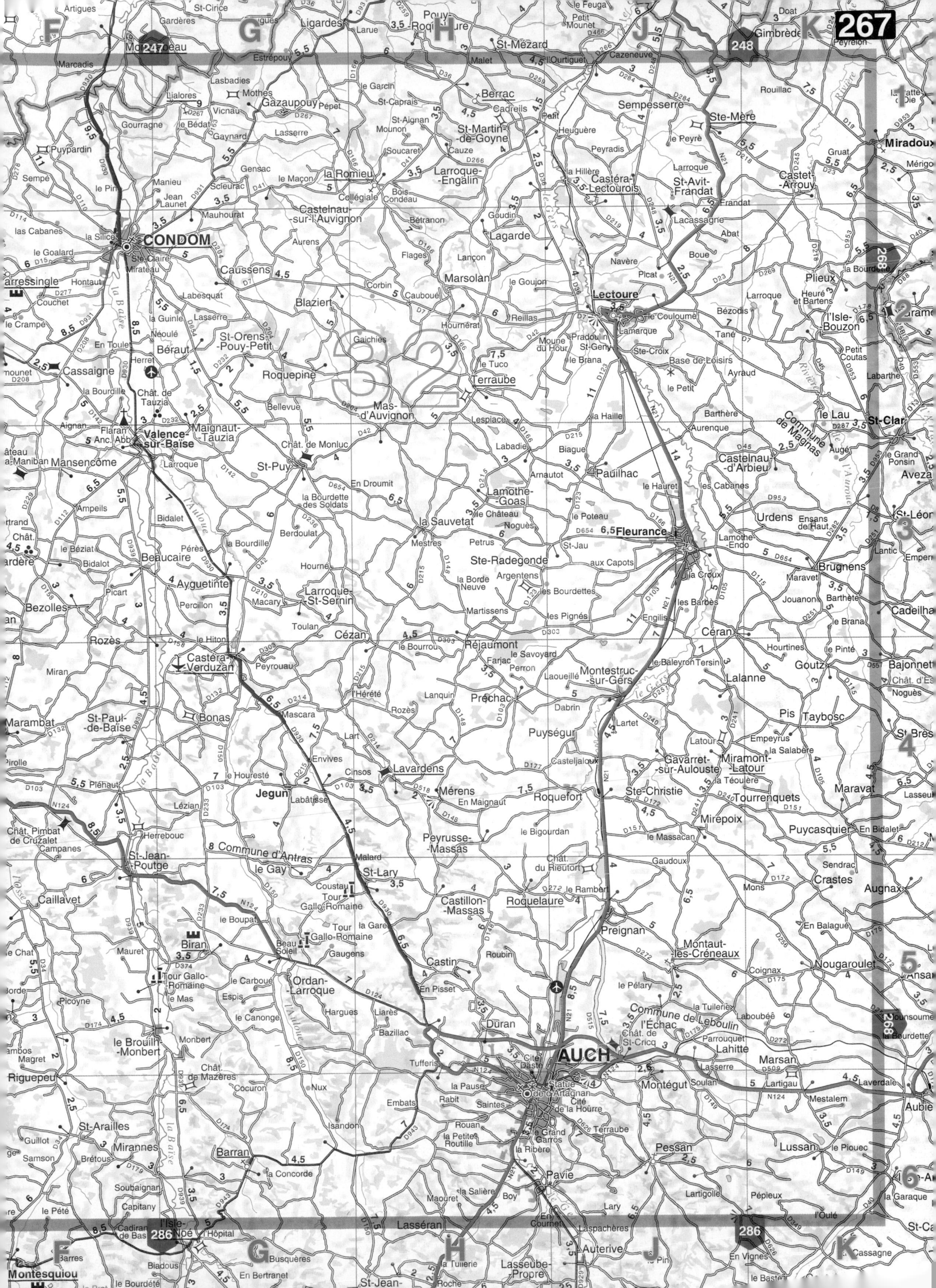

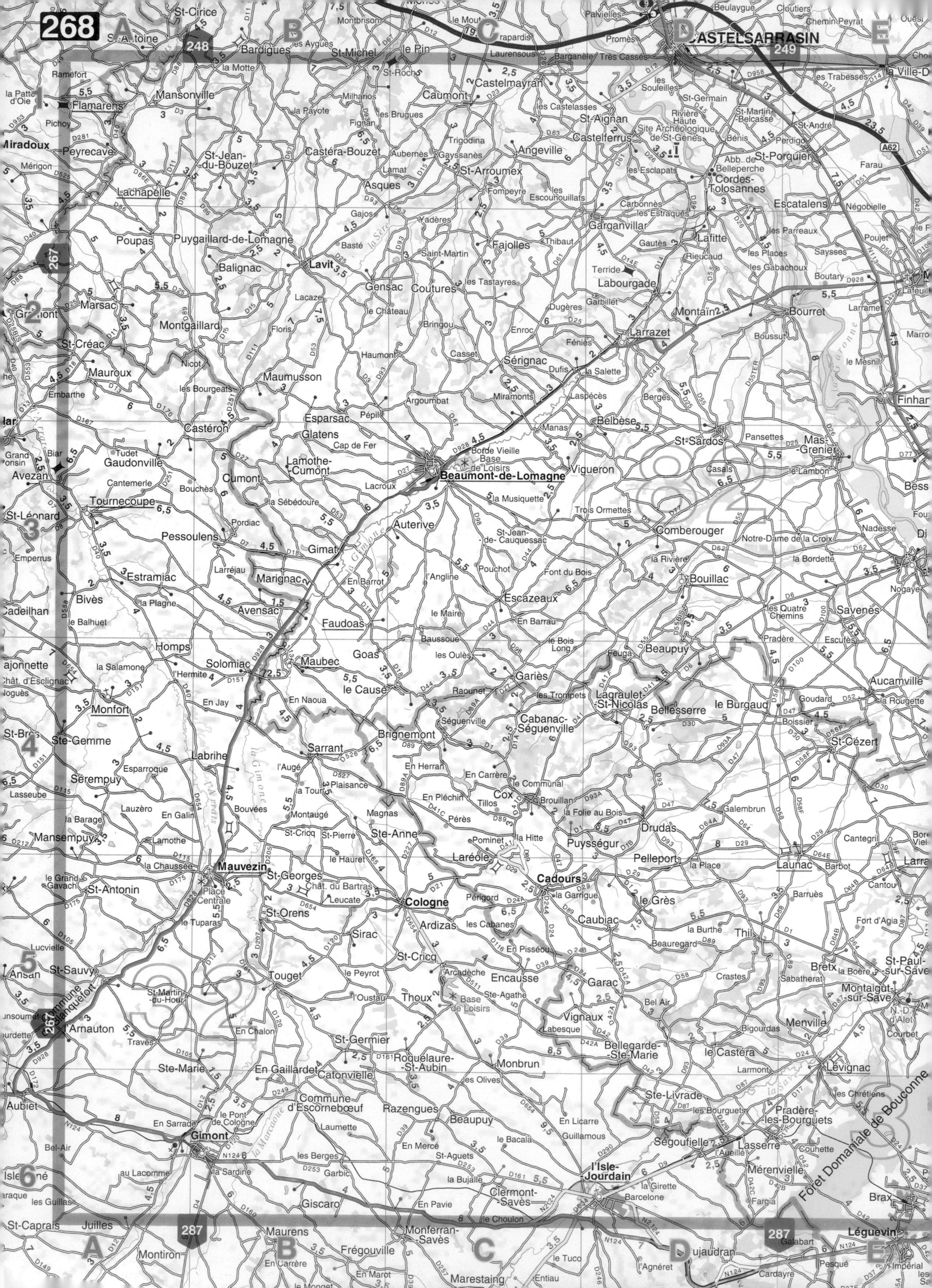

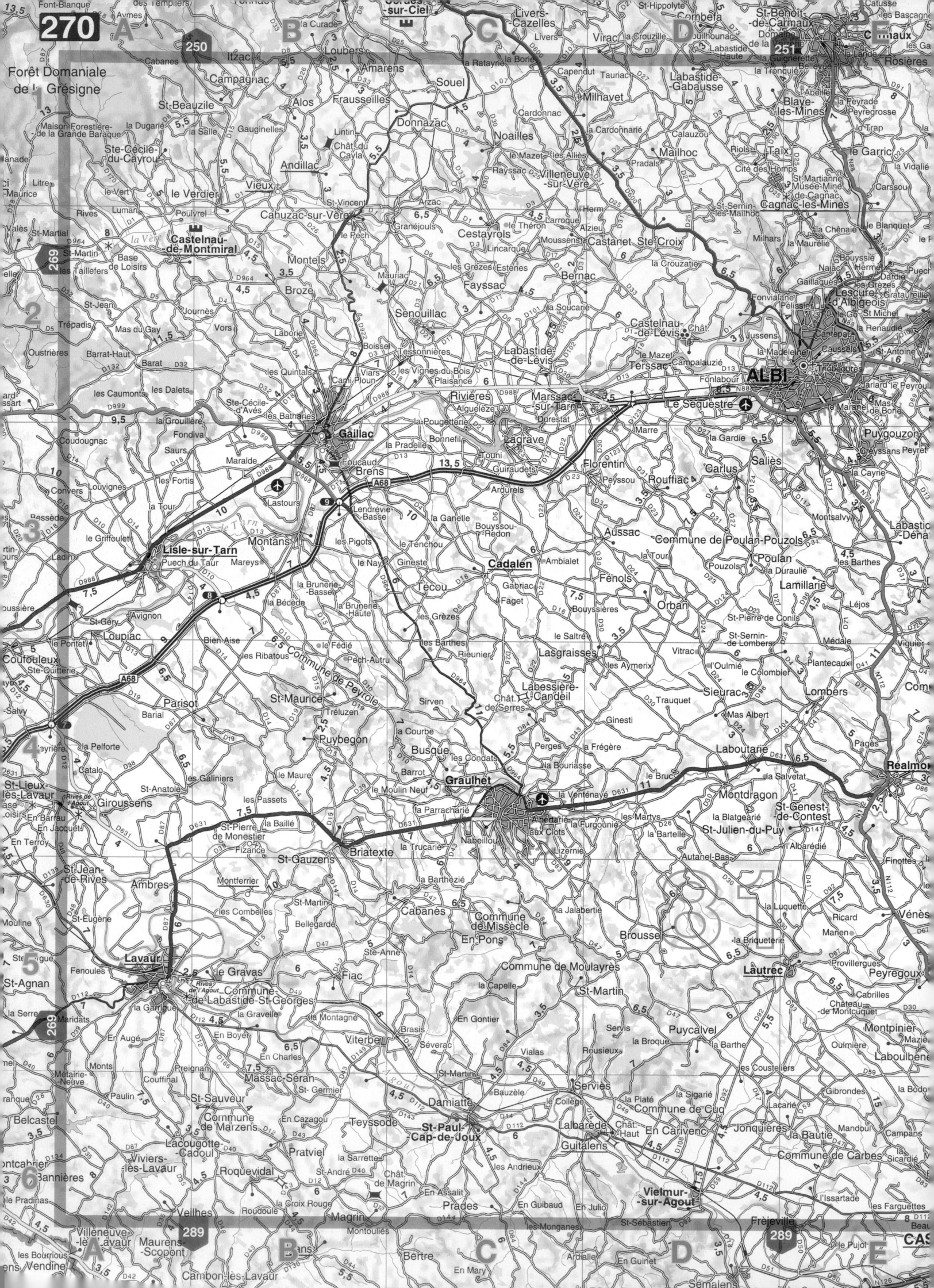

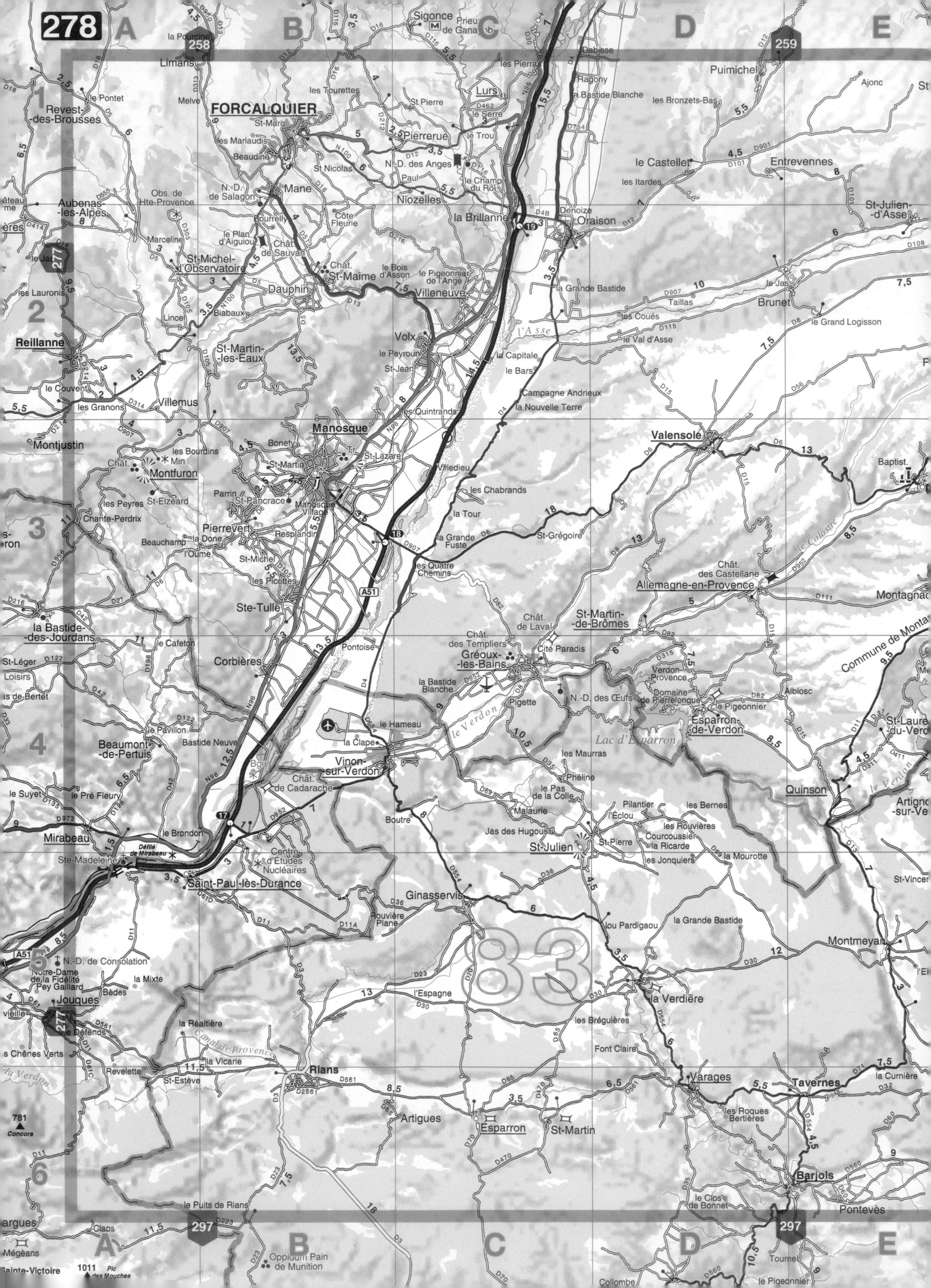

les Agres
les Pins
Parasols
les Blavets
St-Barthélémy
N7
11.5
Roquebrune-
-sur-Argens
brune
N.-D. de Pitié
le Gabre
Gaudrade
Palayson
Puget
-sur-Argens
les Belles
Terres
37
Mosquée
la Palmeraie
D4
le Capitou
de l'Esterel
280
18
la Lieutenante
D47
Parc
Zool
38
Ste-Brigitte
16.5
D637
N.-D.
de Jérusalem
D37
Cais
6.5
Mont Vinaigre
614
St-Jean de l'Estérel
Vieille
Théoule-sur-Mer
Théoule Supérieure
Miramar
Forêt
Domaniale
de l'Esterel
C. de
la Cadière
Espéro-Pax
Pic
de l'Ours
Pic d'Aurelle
la Galère
Pointe de l'Esquillon
T. Orient
le Trayas
Supérieur
le Trayas
T. Orient
16
Pic
du C. Roux
Pointe du Cap Roux
le Rastel
d'Agay
la Bastide
d'Agay
Anthéor Plage
Anthéor
la Tour de Mare
Nécr.
Nat.
Valescure
Pagode Bouddhique
Chât. Aurélien
Ste-Croix
Clair Bois
les Bastides
de Valescure
Vigne Neuve
Ste-Guitte
6
N7
Fréjus
D7
Parc
Aquatique
la Rouvière
11
Domaine
des Baux
Domaine
des Deux Collines
la Bergerie
les Petits Maures
D8
les Terrasses
les Hauts
des Issambres
les Ricards
Bouchard
la Gaillarde
les Plaines
le Petit Défens
Boulouris
Nécr.
Nat.
N98
le Dramont
Camp Long
Sém.
Cap du Dramont
St-Raphaël
Golfe de Fréjus
Fréjus-Plage
Santa-Lucia
4.5
St-Aygulf
les Rives d'Or
Val
d'Esquières
la Vigie
15
la Garonnette
les Issambres
San-Peïre-sur-Mor
les Messugues
la Baumette
la Nartelle
la Petite Corse
Pointe
des Sardinaux
Sémaphore
Guerre
Vieille
D25
Meinier
Ste-Maxime
la Croisette
Souleyas
Rayol
Golfe de St-Tropez
Rabiou
St-Tropez
Grimaud
rines de Cogolin
Plage
la Bouillabaisse
Maderbes
Bertaud
Es Marres
Moulin
l'Estagnet
Citadelle
les Canebiers
les Vanades
Ste-Anne
le Pin
la Moutte
les Salins
la Capilla
8.5
D98A
PRESQU'ÎLE
DE ST-TROPEZ
Gassin
Ramatuelle
ulins
aillas
Oumède
Pampelonne
Mistral
Bonne Terrasse
Croix-Valmer
10
131
Col de
Collebasse
le Pébriet
Cap Camarat
Camarat
l'Escalet
Gigaro
Michel
la Bastide Blanche
aire
Cap Cartaya
Cap Lardier

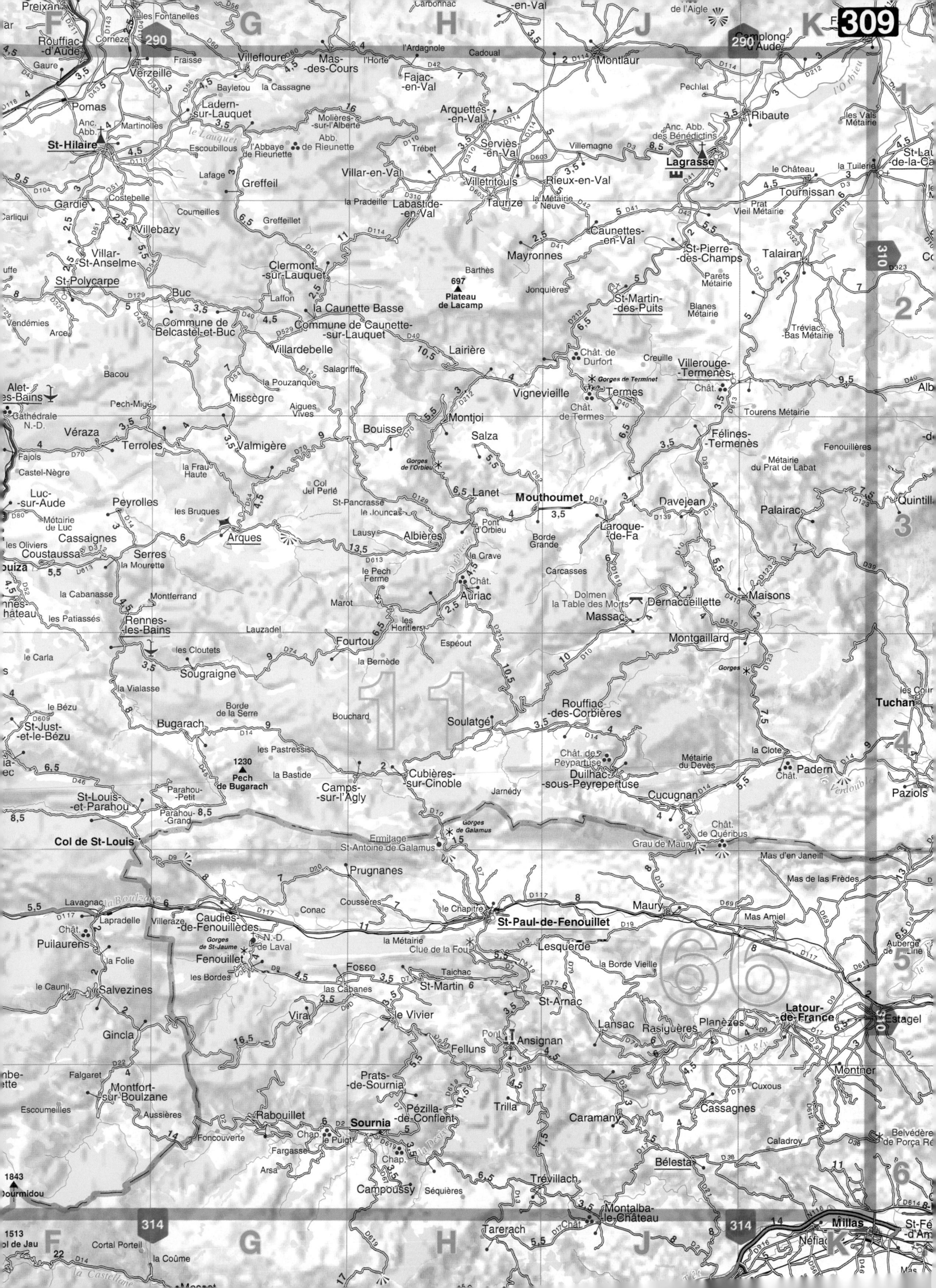

ST-OUEN
PORTE DE CLIGNANCOURT
PORTE DE ST-DENIS
PORTE DE LA CHAPELLE
PORTE D'AUBERVILLIERS
AUBERVILLIERS
PORTE DE LA VILLETTE
PANTIN

Boulevard Ney
Boulevard Ney
Boulevard Ney
Boulevard Macdonald
Bd. Macdonald

18e

Cité des Sciences et de l'Industrie
Géode
Zénith

LE PRE ST-GERVAIS

Championnet
Rue du Poteau
Boulevard Ornano
Rue Ordener
Rue de la Chapelle
Rue Marx Dormoy

Caulaincourt
Rue Custine
Barbès
Chapelle

Parc de la Villette
Cité de la Musique

Avenue Jean Lolive
Rue Gabriel Péri

LES LILAS

Sacré Coeur

Boulevard de Rochechouart
Boulevard de la Chapelle

19e

Quai de la Seine
l'Ourcq
Jean Jaurès
Avenue
Crimée

PORTE DE PANTIN

Boulevard d'Algérie
Séруrier

Avenue
Rue de Belleville

PORTE DU PRE ST GERVAIS

9e

Gare du Nord
la Fayette
Pl de Stalingrad
Avenue Secrétan
Parc des Buttes Chaumont
Rue de Crimée
Rue des Bois

PORTE DES LILAS

R ND de Lorette
La Fayette

Gare de l'Est

Quai de Valmy
Quai de Jemmapes
Pl du Col. Fabien
Rue Manin

BAGNOLET

Opéra Garnier
Bourse
Boulevard Haussman
Bd Poissonnière

Faubourg
10e
Quai de Jemmapes
Quai de Valmy

Rue de Belleville
Belleville
Gambetta

PORTE DE BAGNOLET

2e
Bd de Bonne Nouvelle
Bd Saint Martin

Rue du Faubourg du Temple
Parc de Belleville

A3

Palais Royal
Forum des Halles

Pl de la République

11e

Place Gambetta
Rue Belgrand

20e

MONTREUIL

Musée du Louvre
Pyramide

Centre Pompidou

3e
Rue du Temple
Bd du Temple
Voltaire

Cimetière du Père Lachaise

Boulevard Davout

Hôtel de Ville
Conciergerie
Ile de la Cité

Rue de Rivoli
Pl des Vosges
Rue Saint Antoine

PORTE DE MONTREUIL

St Germain des Prés
Cité Notre Dame
Ile St Louis
4e
Pl de la Bastille

Charonne
Rue d'Avron

Saint Sulpice
Opéra de Paris Bastille
Pl de la Nation
Av. de A. Netter
St Mandé

PORTE DE VINCENNES

Palais du Luxembourg Sénat
Panthéon
Jardin du Luxembourg

Diderot
Cours de Vincennes

PORTE DE SAINT-MANDÉ

Muséum National d'Histoire Naturelle
Jardin des Plantes
Gare de Lyon
12e
Reuilly

ST-MANDÉ

5e
Gare d'Austerlitz
Palais Omnisports de Paris Bercy
Av Daumesnil
Place Félix Eboué

Pl Denfert Rochereau
Bibliothèque Nationale de France
de Bercy

PORTE DORÉE

Bd Saint Jacques
Pl d'Italie
13e
Boulevard Masséna

Lac Daumesnil
Bois de Vincennes

Parc Montsouris
PORTE DE CHARENTON
PORTE DE BERCY

QUAI D'IVRY

CHARENTON-LE-PONT

Cité Universitaire
PORTE DE GENTILLY
PORTE D'ITALIE
PORTE D'IVRY
IVRY-SUR-SEINE
La Seine

Légende de plans de ville

Legende stadsplattegronden

Legende: Stadtpläne

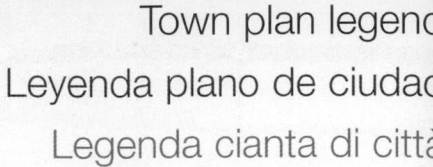

Town plan legend

Leyenda plano de ciudad

Legenda cianta di città

Autoroute, section à péage
Snelweg, tol
Autobahn, gebührenpflichtiger Abschnitt
Motorway, toll section
Autopista de peaje
Autostrada, tratto a pedaggio

Autoroute, section libre, voie à caractère autoroutier
Snelweg, vrije sectie, vierbaansweg met snelweg karakteristieken
Autobahn, gebührenfreier Abschnitt, Schnellverkehrsstraße
Motorway, free section, dual carriageway with motorway characteristics
Autovía con dos carriles en cada sentido
Autostrada, tratto senza pedaggio, doppia carreggiata di tipo autostradale

Autoroute en construction
Snelweg onder constructie
Autobahn im Bau
Motorway under construction
Autopista en construcción
Autostrada in costruzione

Échangeur : complet (1), partiel (2), numéro
Knooppunt, volledig (1), gedeeltelijk (2), nummer
Vollanschlußstelle (1), beschränkte Anschlußstelle (2), Nummer
Junction : complete (1), limited (2), number
Vía de acceso (conexión): completa (1), parcial (2), número
Svincolo: completo (1) parziale (2), numero

Barrière de péage (1), aire de service (2)
Tol slagboom (1), benzinestation (2)
Mautstelle (1), Tankstelle (2)
Toll gate (1), service area (2)
Punto de peaje (1), estación de servicio (2)
Barriera di pedaggio (1), area di servizio (2)

Autre route de liaison principale
Hoofdweg
Fernverkehrsstraße
Trunk road
Carretera nacional
Strada di grande comunicazione

Route de liaison régionale
Regionale verbindingsweg
Regionale Verbindungsstraße
Regional connecting road
Carretera regional
Strada di collegamento regionale

Autre route
Andere weg
Sonstige Straße
Other road
Carretera local
Altra strada

Tunnel
Tunnel
Straßentunnel
Road tunnel
Túnel
Galleria

Bâtiment administratif (1), église, chapelle (2), hôpital (3)
Administratief gebouw (1), kerk, kapel (2), ziekenhuis (3)
Verwaltungsgebäude (1), Kirche, Kapelle (2), Krankenhaus (3)
Administrative building (1), church, chapel (2), hospital (3)
Edificio administrative (1), iglesia, capilla (2), hospital (3)
Edificio pubblico (1), chiesa, cappella (2), ospedale (3)

Limite de commune, de canton
Gemeente-, provinciegrens
Gemeindegrenze, Kreisgrenze
Commune, canton boundary
Límite de municipio, límite de cantón
Confine di comune, confine di cantone

Limite d'arrondissement, de département
Arrondissements-, departementsgrens
Bezirksgrenze, Departementsgrenze
Arrondissement, departement boundary
Límite de arrondissement, límite de departamento
Confine di arrondissement, confine di dipartimento

Limite de région, d'État
Streek-, staatsgrens
Regiongrenze, Staatsgrenze
Region, state boundary
Límite de región, límite de estado
Confine di regione, confine di stato

Zone bâtie, superficie > 8 ha (1), < 8 ha (2), zone industrielle (3)
Bebouwde kom, groter dan 8 ha (1), kleiner dan 8 ha (2), industriegebied (3)
Geschlossene Bebauung, über 8 ha (1), unter 8 ha (2), Gewerbezone (3)
Built-up area, more than 8 ha (1), less than 8 ha (2), industrial park (3)
Zona edificada: más de 8 ha (1), menos de 8 ha (2), polígono industrial (3)
Area edificata, più di 8 ha (1), meno di 8 ha (2), zona industriale (3)

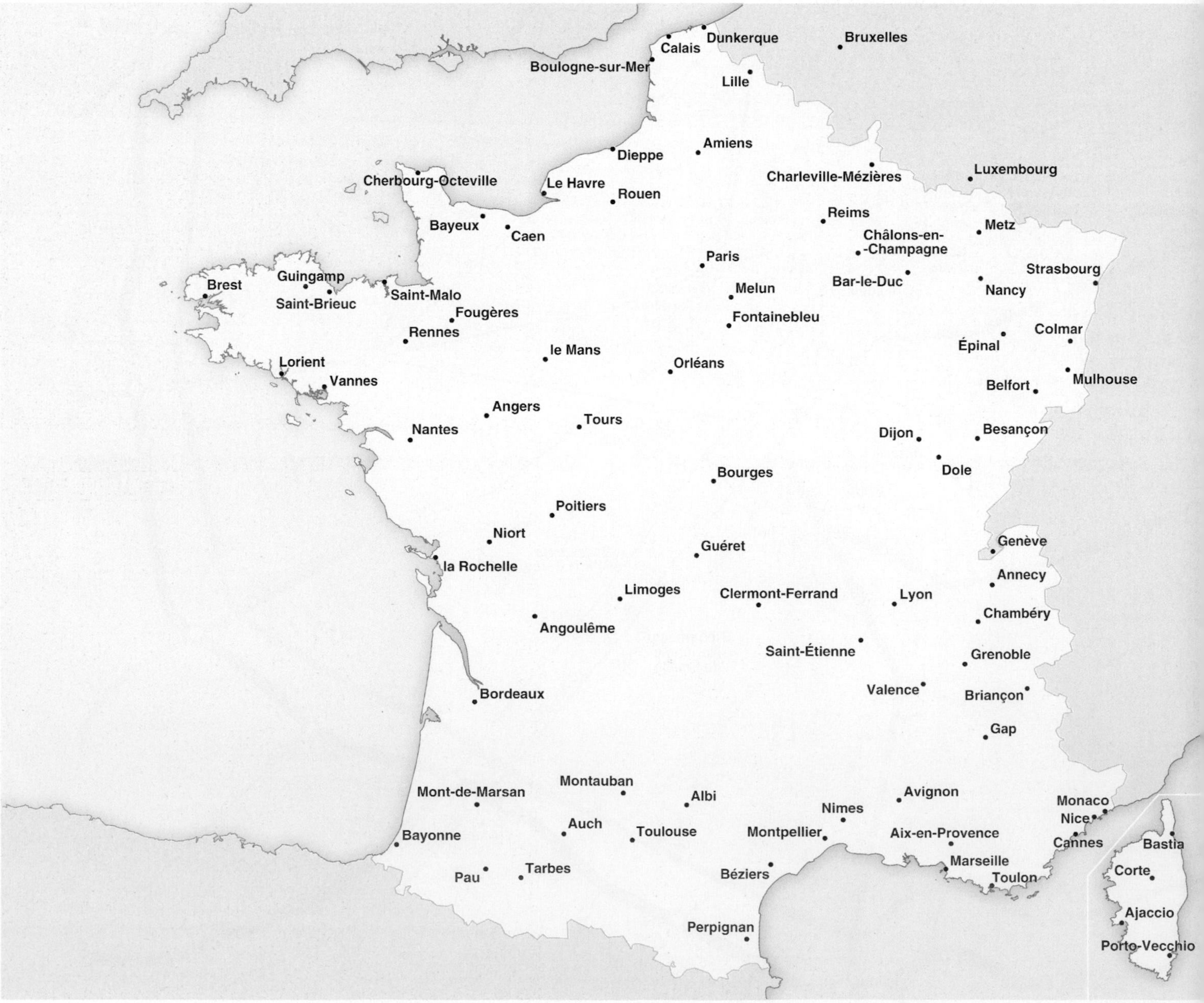

326

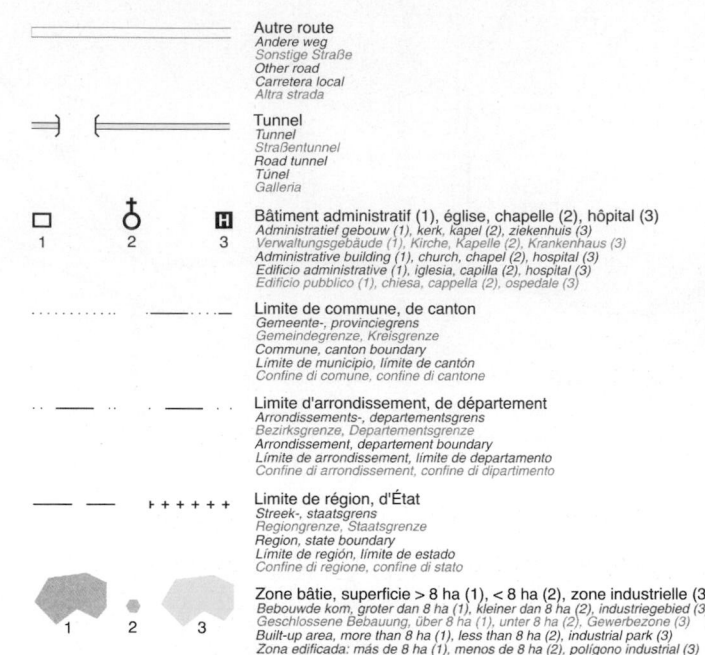

AIX-EN-PROVENCE

AJACCIO

327

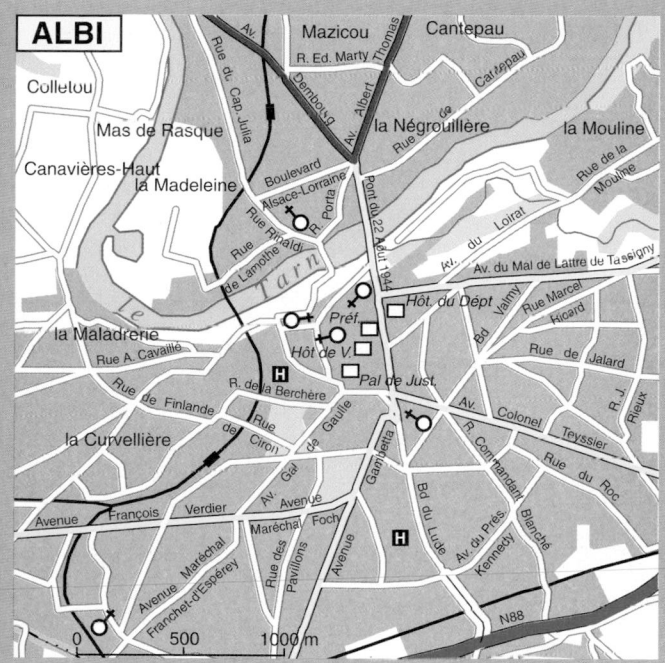

ALBI

AMIENS

ANGERS

ANGOULÊME

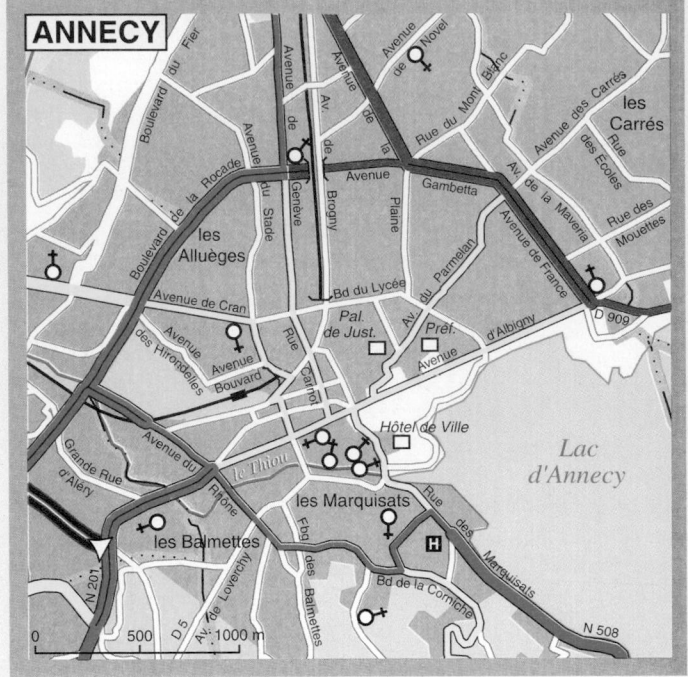

ANNECY

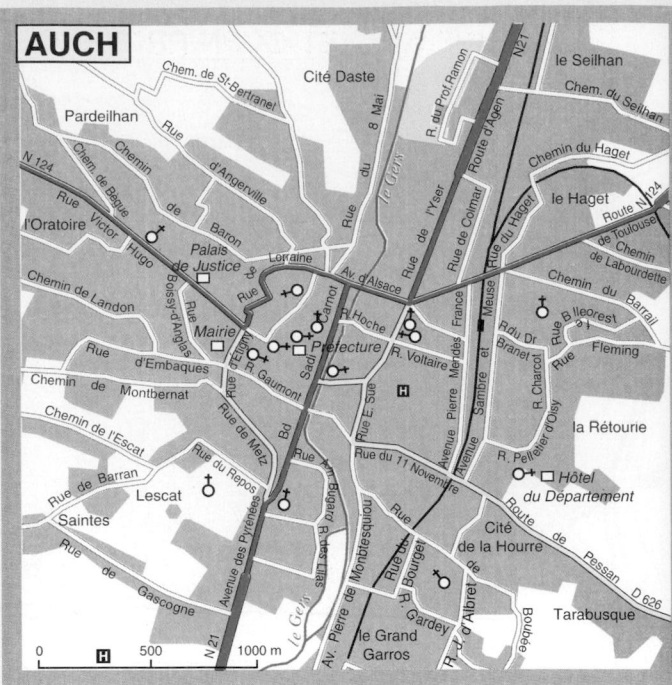

AUCH

AVIGNON

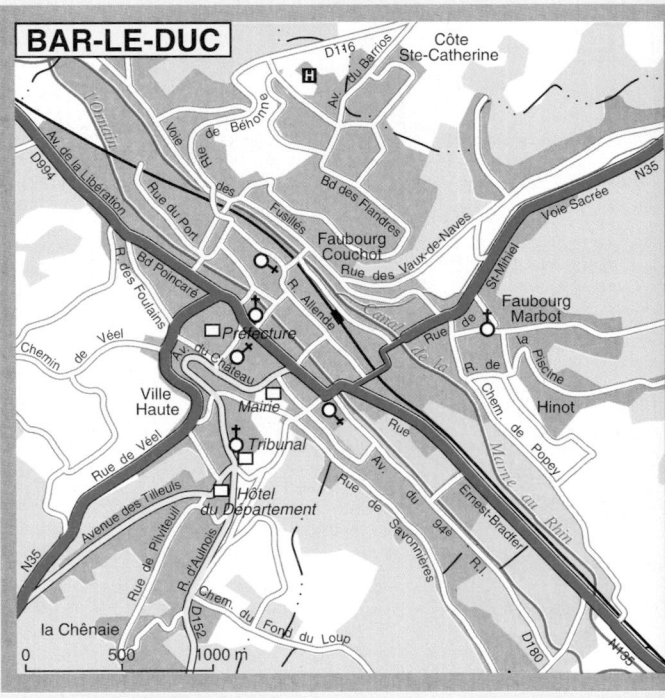

BAR-LE-DUC

BASTIA

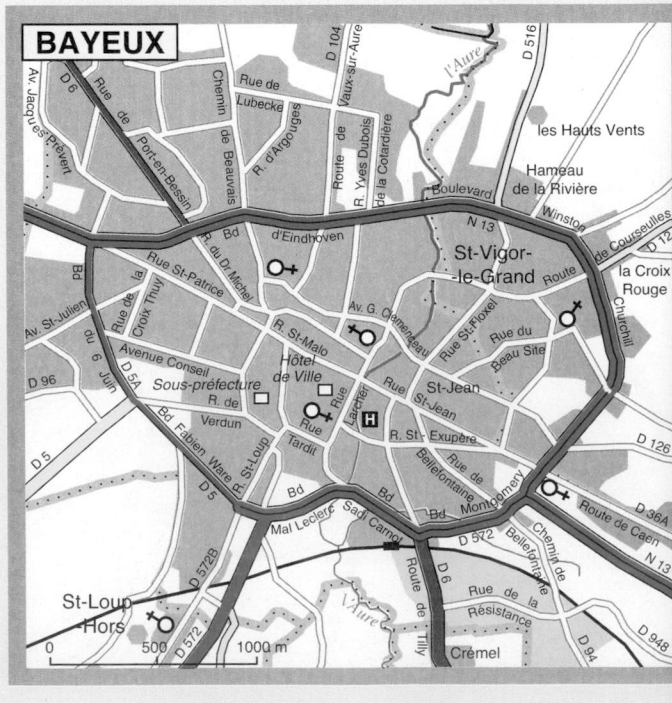

BAYEUX

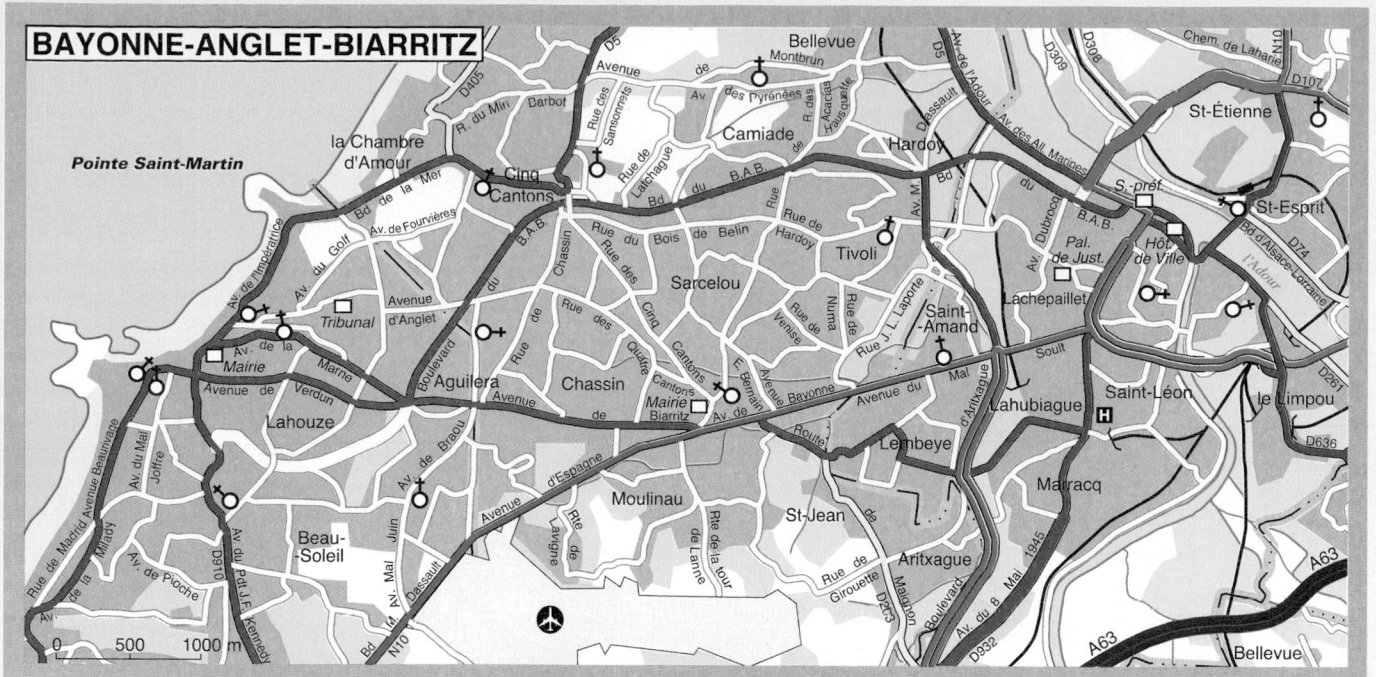

BAYONNE-ANGLET-BIARRITZ

Pointe Saint-Martin

la Chambre d'Amour

Cinq Cantons

Tribunal

Mairie

Aguilera

Chassin

Lahouze

Beau-Soleil

Mairie Biarritz

Moulinau

St-Jean

Aritxague

Sarcelou

Camiade

Bellevue

Montbrun

Hardoy

Tivoli

Saint-Amand

Lembeye

Matracq

St-Étienne

St-Esprit

Hôt. de Ville

Pal. de Just.

Lachepaillet

Lahubiague

Saint-Léon

le Limpou

Bellevue

329

BELFORT

Étang des Forges

les Forges

le Mont

les Résidences

la Miotte

Pal. de Just.

Préf.

Hôtel de Ville

Hôt. du Dépt

13

BESANÇON

la Viotte

la Vaite

les Chaprais

Battant

Hôtel de Ville

Palais de Justice

Hôtel de Région
Préfecture
Hôtel du Département

le Doubs

Brégille

BÉZIERS

la Croix de la Reille

Croix Poumeyrac

les Terries

le Rouat

Pech des Moulins

Sous-préfecture

Hôtel de Ville

Palais de Justice

Pech de la Pomme

BORDEAUX
R. Godard
Av. d'Eysines
Bd Pierre 1er
R. A. Poirson
R. de Tivoli
Cours de Luze
Rue Camille Godard
Rue Frère
Crs St-Louis
Crs Balguerie du Médoc
Quai de Bacalan
les Chartrons
Quai des Chartrons
D113
Brazza
Rue Lajaunie
Rue du Bocage
Wilson
R. de Lassseppe
Rue Johnston
Mandron
Av. C. de Gaulle
Rue E. Renan
Rue de Fondaudège
Cours de Verdun
Crs Mal Foch
Quai Louis XVIII
la Garonne
Quai des Queyries
Rue des Queyries
Rue Bouthier
Rue Mal Niel
Thiers
N10
Rue Naujac
Rue Pasteur
Rue Jules Ferry
Pdt
Rue G. Mandel
R. Thiac
R. R. Lavigne
Rue G. Carde
Avenue
Rue Laville
Crs le Rouzic
Bd Jules Simon
Poincaré
Rue R. Curie
Rue Galin
la Bastide
Rue Judaïque
Bonnac
Hôtel de la Préf.
Rue
R. B. Adour
Cardozet
Av. d'Arès
Bd
Rue de Vincennes
Brizard
Rue Georges
Mériadeck
Hôtel de Ville
Hôtel de Région
Préf. de Rég.
Crs Alsace Lorraine
Pont de Pierre
Rue de la Bénauge
Joliot
Chemin de la Sauve
Quai Deschamps
Boulevard
Gaillan Richelieu
R. du Gen. de Larminat
Bd A. Gautier
Cours Mal Juin
Pal. de Just.
Crs Ste Catherine
V. Hugo
Doumerc
R. de Canolle
d'Ornano
R. Héron
Rue Mathieu
Tondu
Pessac
Rue Pasteur
Cours de la Marne
Quai de Paludate
Pont St Jean
Quai de la Souys
D113
Bd Mal Leclerc
R. Léo Seignat
Rue du
Genès
Cours de l'Argonne
Rue de l'Yser
Malbec
Rue de la Béchade
Rue de Bethmann
R. Babin
Gallieni
Bd
Rue des Treuils
Rue de Saint
Cours de la
Rue Cazemajor
R. Furtado
Pelleport
Rue Roullet
Rue Carle Vernet
R. du Tauzin
Cours du Mal
Rue Emile Zola
Geoges V
R. A. Huc
Rue P. Kergomard
Rue B. de Goth
Cours
Rue Amédée St-Germain
Av. Paul Bert
Rue du 14 Juillet
Boulevard du Pdt Roosevelt
Sommé
Rue Jean Jacques Bosc
A 630
Semblat
St-Maurice
Rue Roustaing
Rue Lavoisier
Médoquine
Gambetta
Rue Lamartine
R.Goblet
Rue d'Aupérie
Bègles
Boulevard Jean
Av. A. Capelle
Rue M.
la Médoquine
Rue Camille Pellet
Cours
Chemin de Suzon
Boulevard Albert 1er
0
500
1000 m

BOULOGNE-SUR-MER
Avenue Percier et Fontaine
Chemin Vert
D 940
Boulevard Sainte-Beuve
Rue d'Ambleteuse
Rue du
Rue P. et M. Curie
R. A. Briand
Rue de Beaurepaire
Beaurepaire
Rue du Camp de Droite
Saint-Pierre
Rue de la Paix
Quai Amiral Huguet
Bassin Loubet
Bd Gambetta
S.-Préf.
Hôtel de Ville
Palais de Justice
Quai de l'Europe
Darse Sarraz-Bournet
Rue du Petit port
Capecure
Rue Faidherbe
Grande Rue
Rue Nationale
Bd Daunou
Bd Eurvin
Rue E. Branly
Boulevard Sarraz-Bournet
Bd A. Huguet
J. Jaurès
Viaduc
Boulevard Chanzy
Boulevard Diderot
R. d'Isly
Henriville
Bd A. Huguet
Boulevard
Av. d'Arras
Rue Carnot
Bd de la Liberté
Montesquieu
J. J. Rousseau
N 1
D 940
Av. John Kennedy
la Madeleine
D 236
D 236E
Cité Ostrohove
0
500
1000 m

BRIANÇON
Avenue professeur Forgue
N 91
Route de Grenoble
N 94
Av. du Dauphiné
le Chabas
Avenue du Lautaret
Av. de la Libération
Avenue Baldenberger
Chem. de la Tour
R. du Gen Bardot
la Guisane
Avenue
Palais de Justice
Mairie
Sainte-Catherine
Rue Roger Froger
Av. Du 159e RIA
Avenue de la République
S.-Pref.
la Durance
Pelsche
Rue Chemin Vieux
Route de Provence
Av. M.
R. Alphand
les Queyrelles
Av. du Gen. de Gaulle
Rue Pasteur
Avenue du Col de l'Izoard
Route de Puy Saint-Pierre
Route de Gap
Av. Jean Moulin
Av. Gen. Bermond Gonnet
Chemin de Font Christiane
Font Christiane
Rochas Garnier
N 94
les Toulouzanes
D 902
0
500
1000 m

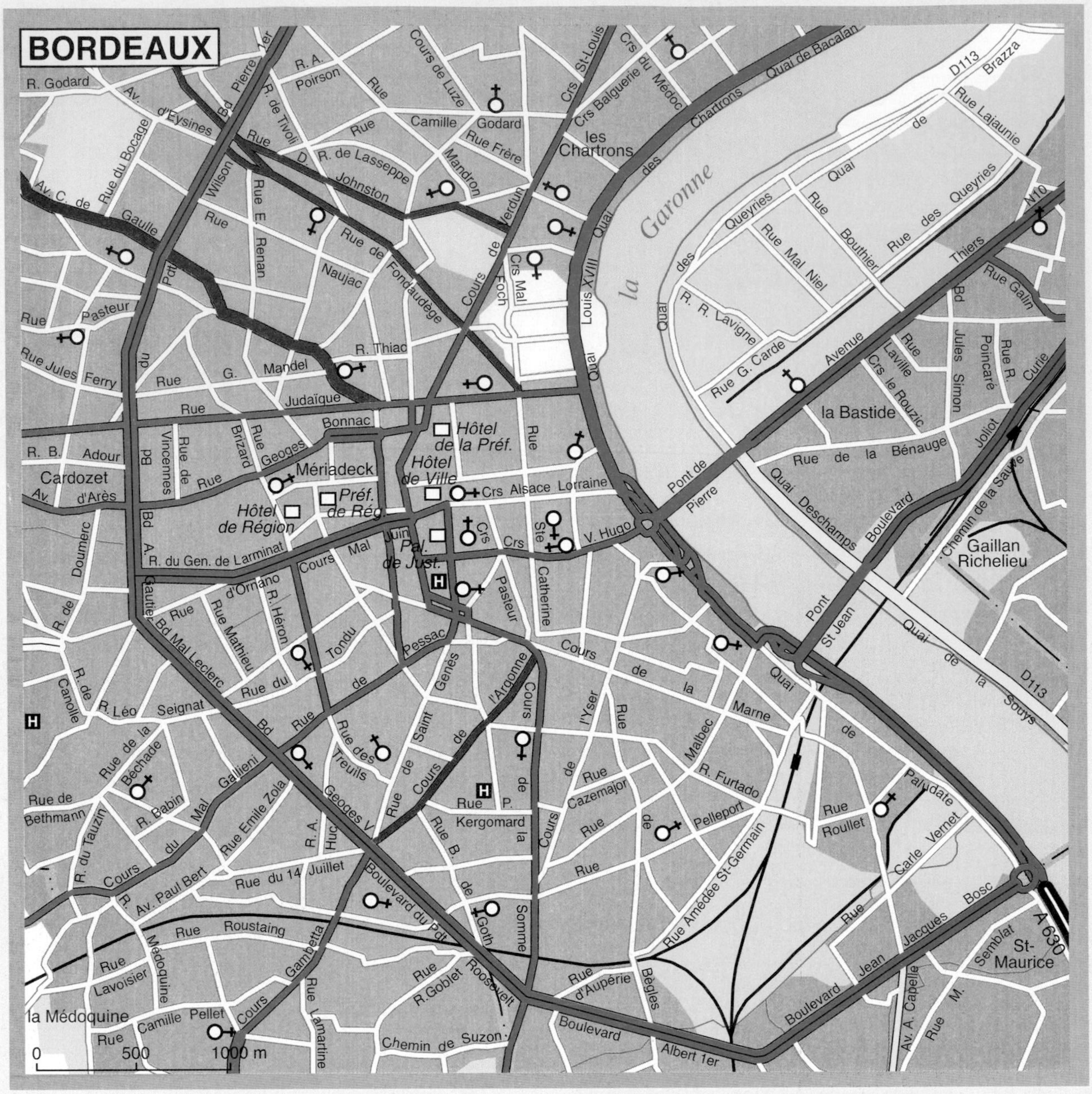

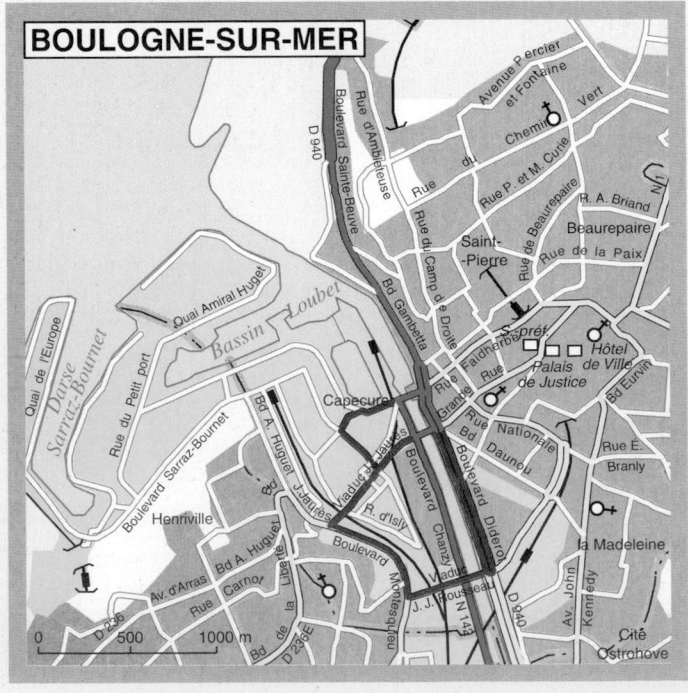

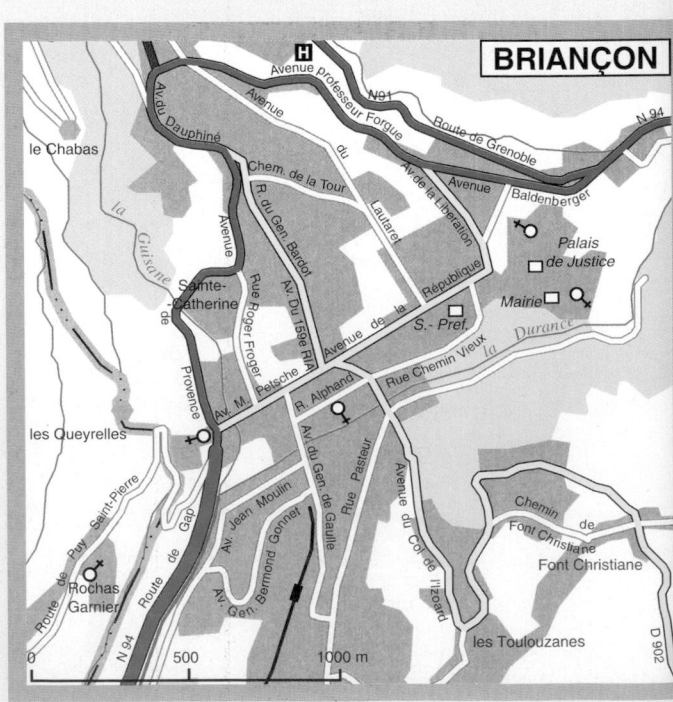

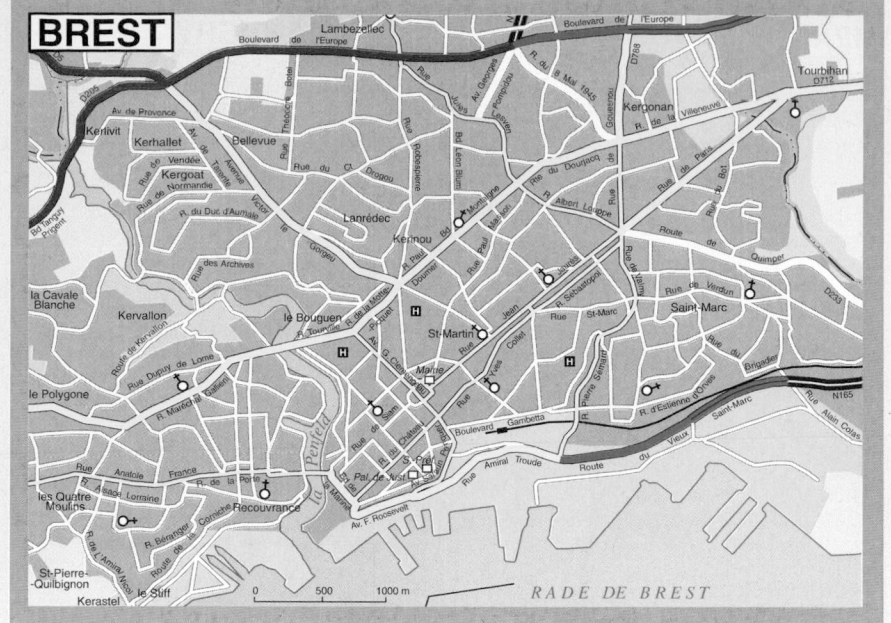

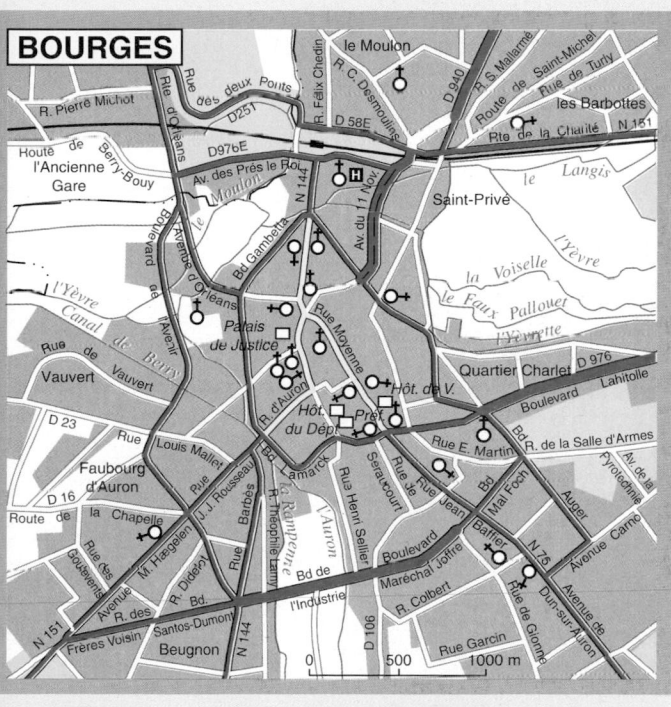

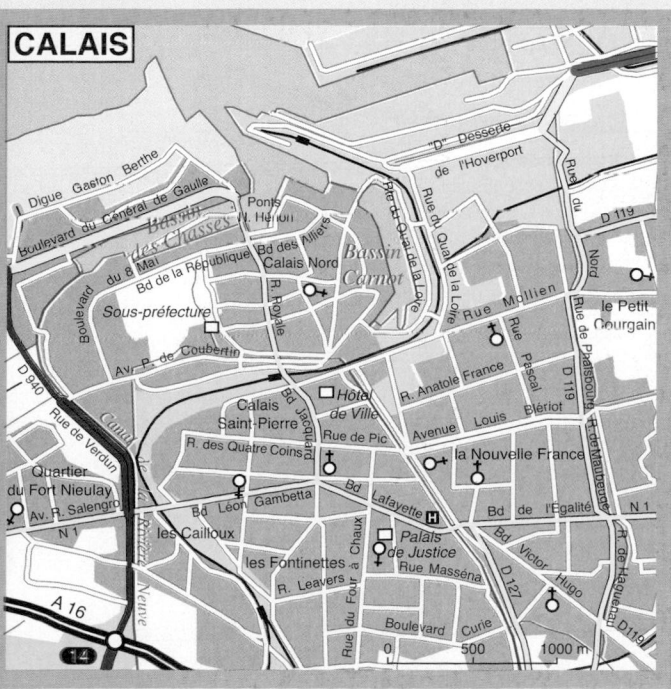

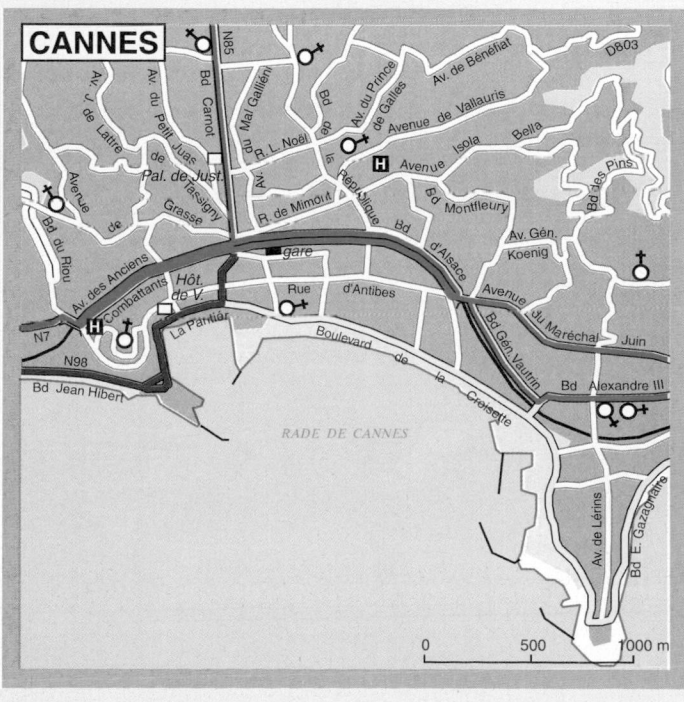

CHÂLONS-EN-CHAMPAGNE

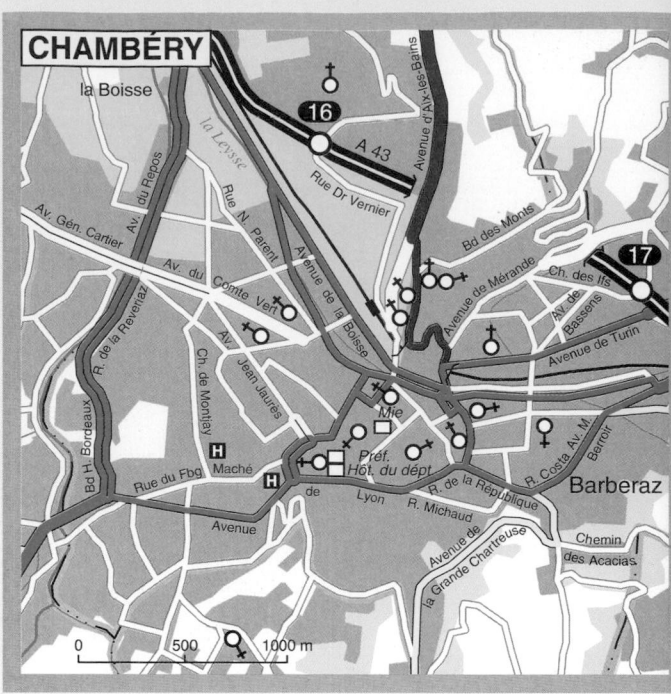

CHAMBÉRY

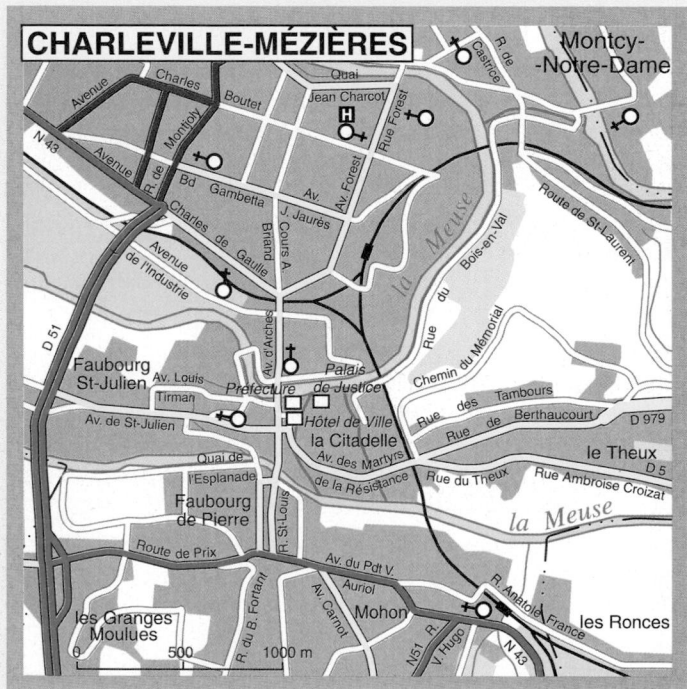

CHARLEVILLE-MÉZIÈRES

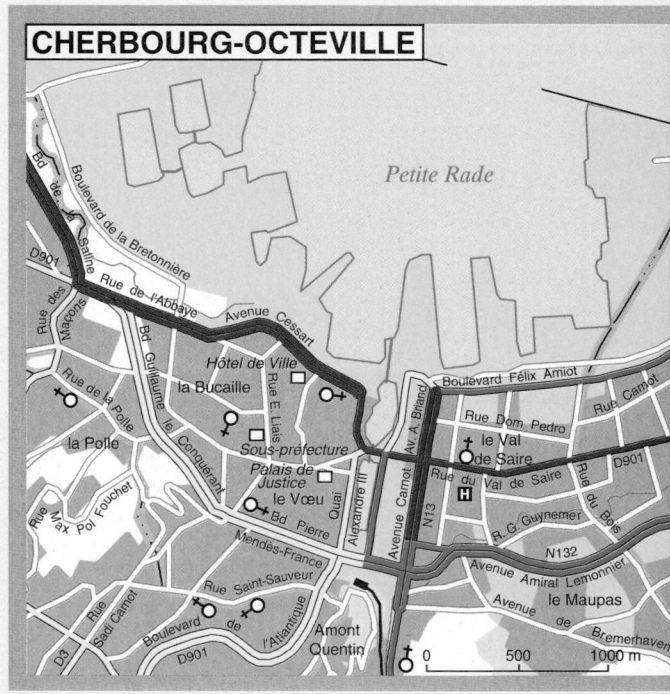

CHERBOURG-OCTEVILLE

CLERMONT-FERRAND

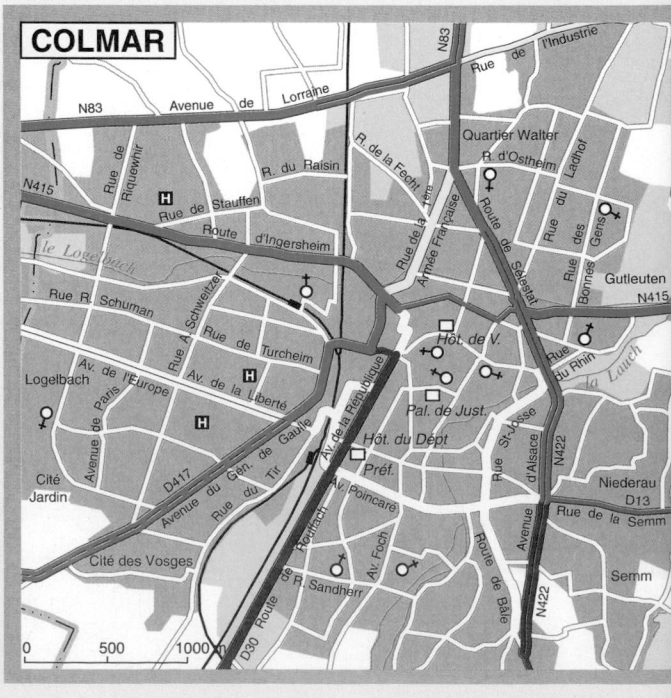

COLMAR

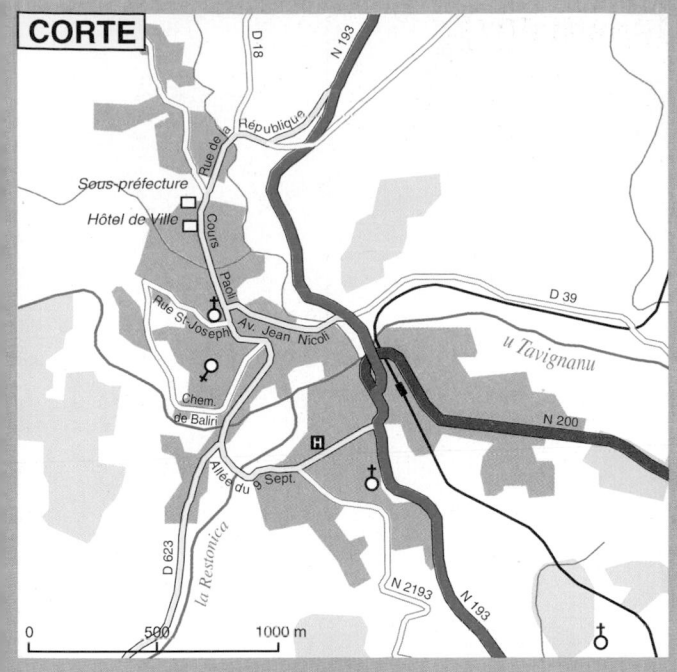

CORTE

Sous-préfecture
Hôtel de Ville
Rue de la République
D 18
N 193
Cours Paoli
Rue St-Joseph
Av. Jean Nicoli
Chem. de Baliri
D 39
D 623
Allée du 9 Sept.
la Restonica
D 2193
N 193
N 200
u Tavignanu

0   500   1000 m

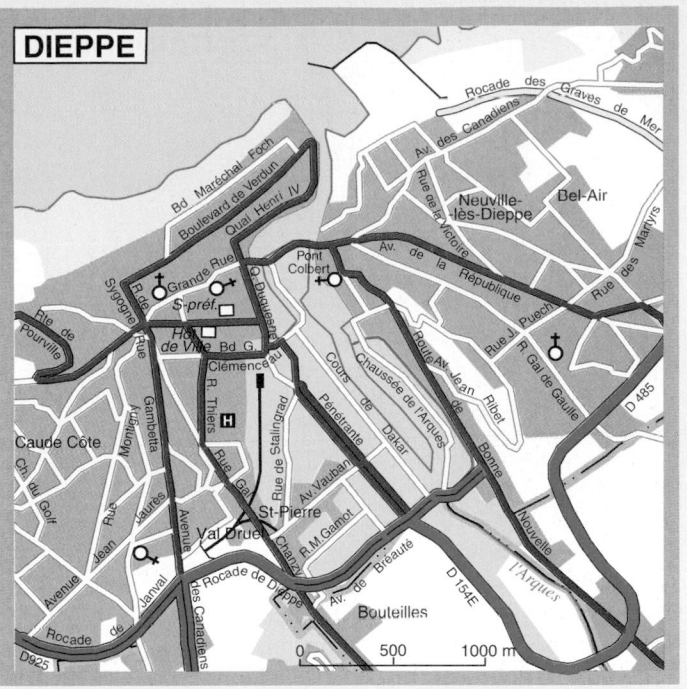

DIEPPE

Rocade des
Graves de Mer
Bd Maréchal Foch
Boulevard de Verdun
Quai Henri IV
Av. des Canadiens
Neuville-lès-Dieppe
Bel-Air
Syagone Rue
Grande Rue
Pont Colbert
Av. de la Victoire
Av. de la République
Rue J. Puech
St-préf
Rte de Fourville
Hôtel de Ville
Clémenceau
Rue J. Ribet
R. Thiers
Caude Côte
Gambetta
Rue de Stalingrad
Pénétrante
Chaussée de Dakar
Ch. du Golf
Rue Jean Jaurès
Av. Vauban
St-Pierre
R.M. Gainot
Val Druel
Av. de Bréauté
Avenue Jean
Rue de Janval
les Canadiens
Rocade de Dieppe
Bouteilles
D 925
Rocade de
D 485
Nouvelle
l'Arques
D 154E

0   500   1000 m

333

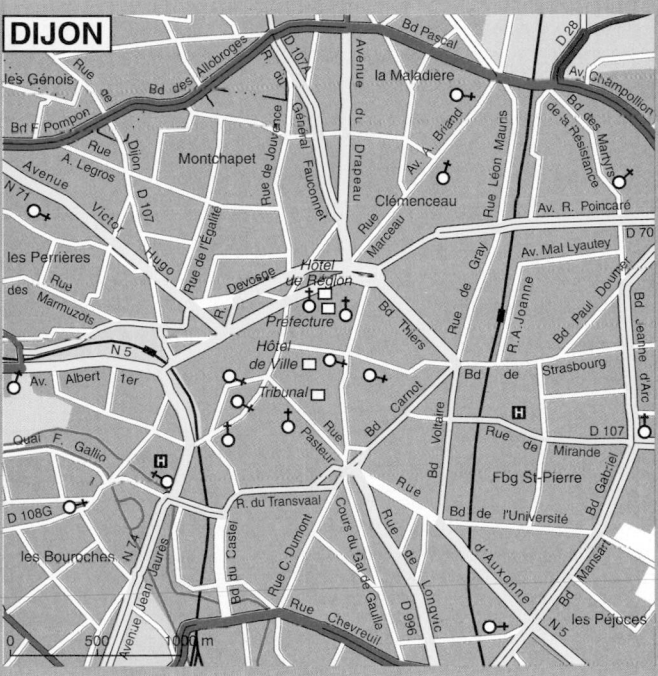

DIJON

les Génois
Bd Pascal
D 28
Bd des Allobroges
Avenue du Drapeau
Av. Champollion
Brt F. Pompon
la Maladière
Rue de la Résistance
Rue A. Briand
Bd des Martyrs
A. Legros
Montchapet
Rue de Jouvence
Rue Léon Mauris
Av. R. Poincaré
N 71
Victor
Clémenceau
Av. Mal Lyautey
les Perrières
Hugo
Rue Marceau
D 70
des Marmuzots
Rue de l'Égalité
Hôtel de Région
Av. de Gray
R.A. Joanne
Bd Paul Doumer
Devosge
Préfecture
Bd Thiers
Bd Jeanne d'Arc
N 5
Hôtel de Ville
Bd de Strasbourg
Av. Albert 1er
Tribunal
Rue Pasteur
Bd Carnot
Rue de Mirande
D 107
Quai F. Gallio
Rue
Voltaire
Fbg St-Pierre
Bd Gabriel
D 108G
R. du Transvaal
Rue
Bd de l'Université
les Bouroches
Rue C. Dumont
Cours du Gal de Gaulle
D 996
N 5
les Péjoces
Avenue Jean Jaurès
D 74
Rue du Castel
Rue Chevreuil

0   500   1000 m

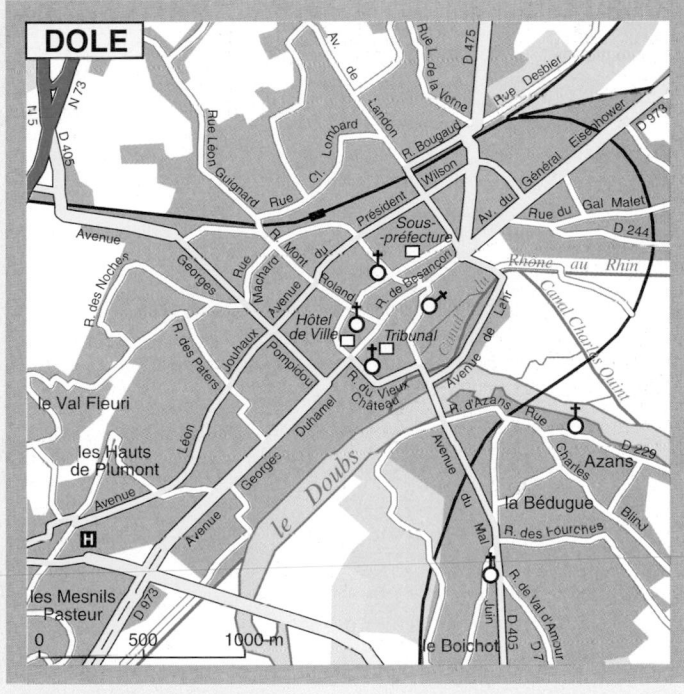

DOLE

D 475
Av. de la Verne
Rue L. Desbief
N 73
N 5
Rue Léon Guignard
R. Lombard
R. Bougaud
D 973
D 405
Rue
Ch.
Président Wilson
Av. du Général Eisenhower
Rue du Gal Malet
Avenue
Georges
Rue Mont. du
Roland
Sous-préfecture
D 244
R. des Nochier
Avenue
R. de Besançon
Rhône au Rhin
Machar.
Hôtel de Ville
Tribunal
Canal du Rhône
R. des Pâtures
Jouhaux
Pompidou
R. du Vieux Château
Avenue de Lahr
Canal Charles Quint
le Val Fleuri
Léon
Duhamel
R. d'Azans
Charles
D 229
les Hauts de Plumont
Georges
le Doubs
Azans
Avenue
Avenue
Av. du
la Bédugue
Blini
R. des Fourches
R. de Val d'Amour
les Mesnils Pasteur
D 973
Av. Juin
D 405
le Boichot

0   500   1000 m

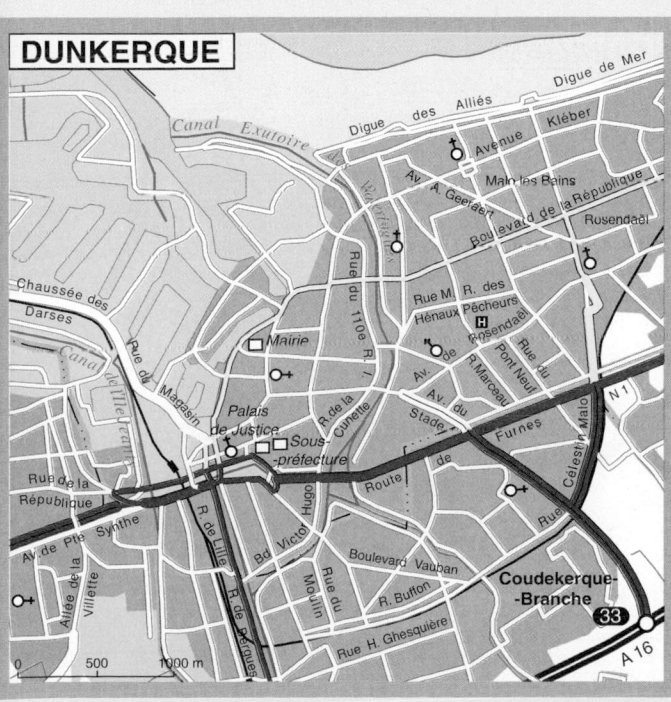

DUNKERQUE

Digue de Mer
Canal Exutoire
Digue des Alliés
Avenue Kléber
Chaussée des Darses
Av. A. Geeraert
Main les Bains
Boulevard de la République
Rosendaël
Rue du 110e R.I.
Rue M. R. des
Hénaux Pêcheurs
Rue de Rosendaël
Canal de la Villette
Rue du Magasin
Mairie
Rue Marceau
Pont Neuf
Av. du Stade
Palais de Justice
Rue de la Cunette
N 1
Sous-préfecture
Céleste Malo
Route
de
Furnes
Rue de la République
Av. de Pte Synthe
R. de Lille
Boulevard Vauban
Rue du Moulin
Rue Buffon
Coudekerque-Branche
33
Allée de la Villette
Bd Victor
R. d'Alsace
R. H. Ghesquière
A 16

0   500   1000 m

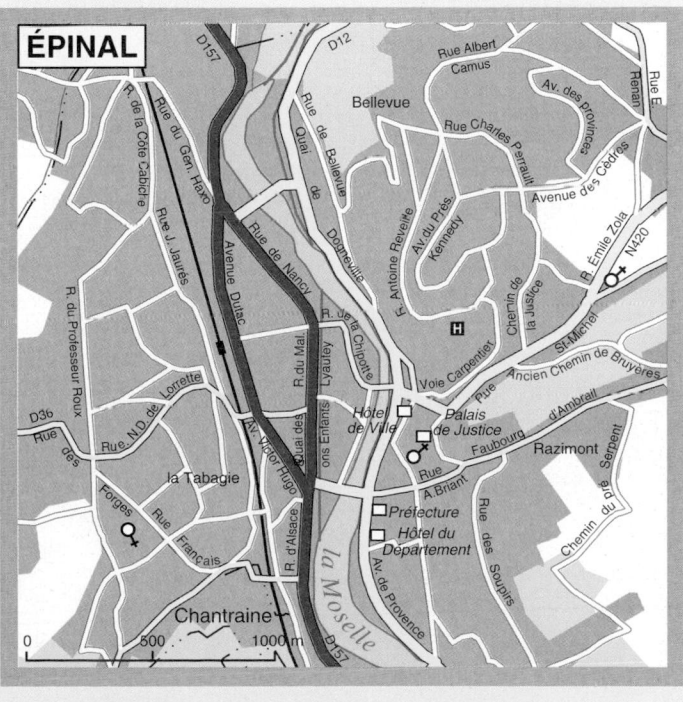

ÉPINAL

D 157
D 12
Rue Albert Camus
Bellevue
Av. des Provinces
R. de la Côte Calbère
Rue du Gén Haxo
Rue Charles Perrault
Rénan
Quai de Bellevue
Avenue des Cèdres
R. du Professeur Roux
Avenue de Nancy
R. Émile Zola
N420
Rue J. Jaurès
Av. du Prés. Kennedy
Antoine Reveille
Chemin de la Justice
Voie Carpentier
H
St-Michel
Ancien Chemin de Bruyères
D36
R. du Mal.
Rue de la Chipotte
Rue A. Briant
d'Ambrail
la Tabagie
Hôtel de Ville
Palais de Justice
Razimont
R. N.D. de Lorrette
Avenue Dutac
ons Enfants Lyautey
Faubourg
Rue des
Rue Victor Hugo
Préfecture
Chemin du
Forges
Rue Français
Hôtel du Département
la Moselle
Chantraine
D157

0   500   1000 m

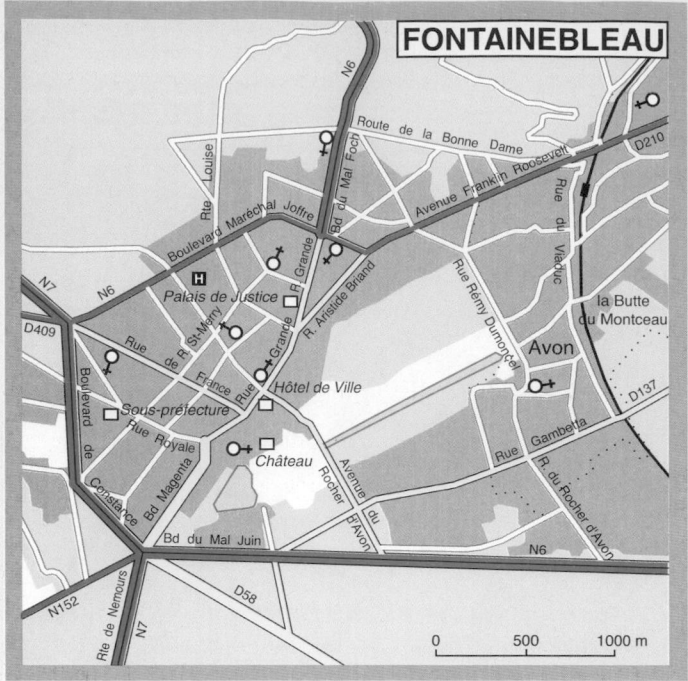

FONTAINEBLEAU

N6
Route de la Bonne Dame
D210
Route Franklin Roosevelt
Rue Rémy Dumoncel
la Butte du Montceau
Avon
Route Louise
Bd du Mal Foch
R. Grande
R. Aristide Briand
Rue du Viaduc
Boulevard Maréchal Joffre
N7
N6
H
Palais de Justice
D409
Rue St-Merry
Rue de France
Hôtel de Ville
Rue Royale
Sous-préfecture
Bd Magenta
Château
Boulevard de Constance
Rue du Rocher d'Avon
Avenue du Château
D137
Rue Gambetta
Bd du Mal Juin
N6
N152
D58
N7
Rte de Nemours

0   500   1000 m

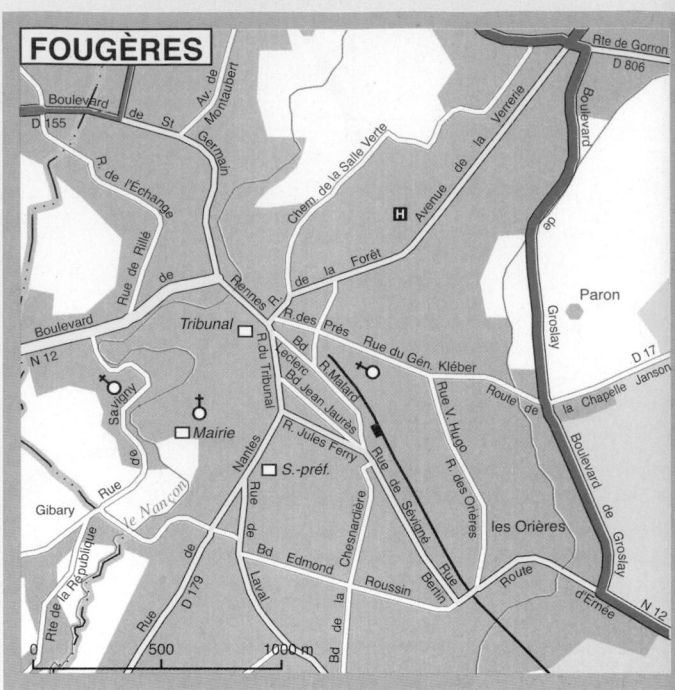

FOUGÈRES

Rte de Gorron
D 806
Boulevard de St Germain
Av. de Montaudert
Chem. de la Salle Vente
Avenue de la Verrerie
Boulevard de
D 155
Rue de Rillé
Rue de la Forêt
Rennes R.
Rue du Gén. Kléber
Paron
D 17
H
Tribunal
R. des Prés
Bd
Bd Jean Malard
la Chapelle Janson
Rue V. Hugo
Groslay
Savigny
R. du Tribunal
N 12
Nantes
Mairie
Bd Jean Jaurès
R. des Orières
Boulevard de Groslay
S.-préf.
R. Jules Ferry
R. de Séyigné
les Orières
Gibary
Rue
le Nançon
Bd Edmond
Chesnardière
Rte de la République
D 179
Rue de la
Laval
Roussin
Bernin
Route d'Emée
N 12

0   500   1000 m

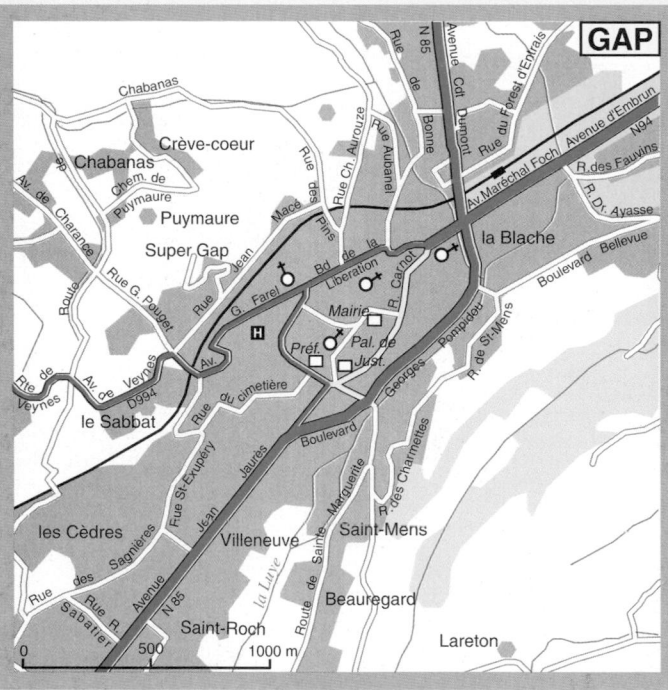

GAP

Chabanas
N 85
Avenue du Forest d'Entrais
Cdt. Dumont
Crève-coeur
Rue de Bonne
Chabanas
Chem. de Puymaure
Rue Ch. Aurouze
Rue Aubanel
R. des Fauvins
Av. de Charance
Puymaure
Macé
Super Gap
Rue G. Pouget
Bd de la Libération
R. Carnot
la Blache
R. Dr Ayasse
Boulevard Bellevue
G. Farel
Mairie
H
Pal. de Just.
Préf.
Rue de St-Mens
Rte de Veynes
Av. de Veynes
D994
Rue du cimetière
Georges-Pompidou
le Sabbat
R. des Charmettes
les Cèdres
Fue St-Exupéry
Boulevard Jaurès
R.
Saint-Mens
Villeneuve
Rue des Sagnières
Jean
Route de Sainte-Marguerite
Beauregard
N 85
Saint-Roch
la Luye
Lareton

0   500   1000 m

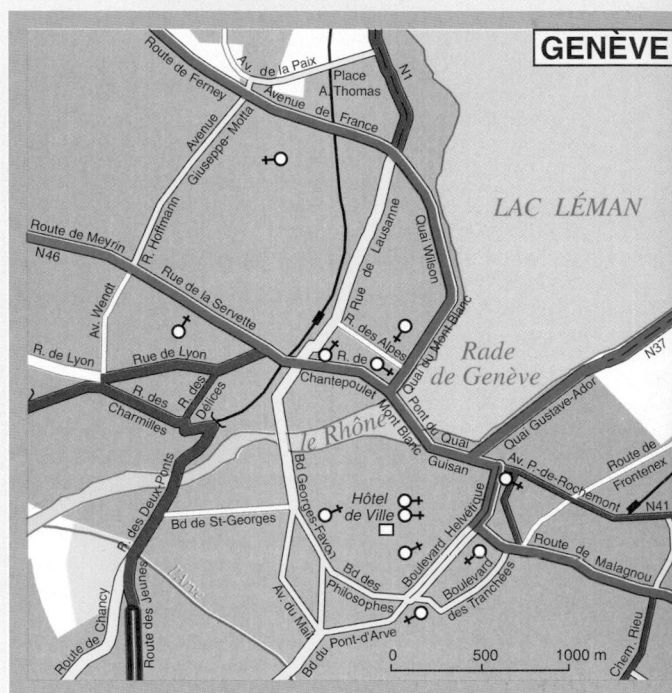

GENÈVE

Route de Ferney
Av. de la Paix
N1
Place A. Thomas
Route de Meyrin
Avenue de France
Avenue Giuseppe-Motta
LAC LÉMAN
N46
Av. Wendt
Rue de la Servette
Quai Wilson
Route de Lausanne
R. de Lyon
Rue de Lyon
R. des Alpes
Rade de Genève
R. de Lyon
Chantepoulet
Quai du Mont Blanc
N37
Charmilles
R. des Délices
Quai Gustave-Ador
Route de Frontenex
Bd James-Fazy
Quai du Pont du Quai
Guisan
Av. P.-de-Rochemont
N41
R. des Deux-Ponts
Bd Georges-Favon
Hôtel de Ville
le Rhône
Route de
Route de Chancy
Bd de St-Georges
Bd des Philosophes
Boulevard Helvétique
Route de Malagnou
Av. du Mail
Bd du Pont-d'Arve
Boulevard des Tranchées
Chem. Rieu

0   500   1000 m

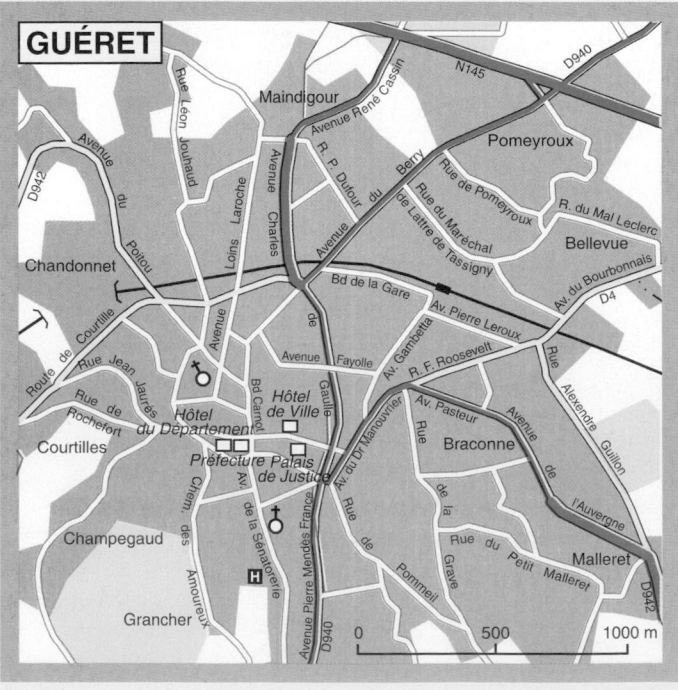

GUÉRET

N145
D940
Rue Léon Jouhaud
Maindigour
Avenue René Cassin
D942
Avenue du Pottou
R. P. Dufour
Rue de Pomeyroux
Pomeyroux
Avenue Charles
Berry
R. du Mal Leclerc
Loins
Laroche
Rue du Maréchal
R. du Mal de Lattre de Tassigny
Bellevue
Chandonnet
Bd de la Gare
Av. du Bourbonnais
Avenue
Av. Pierre Leroux
D4
Avenue Fayolle
R. F. Roosevelt
Rue de Courtille
Av. Gambetta
Rue Jean Jaurès
Hôtel du Département
Bd Carnot
Hôtel de Ville
Av. Pasteur
Avenue Guillon
Rue de Rochefort
Préfecture
Palais de Justice
Braconne
Rue du Petit Malleret
Courtilles
Av. de la Sénatorerie
Champegaud
Avenue Pierre Mendès France
Rue du Petit Malleret
Malleret
H
Grancher
Pommeil
D942

0   500   1000 m

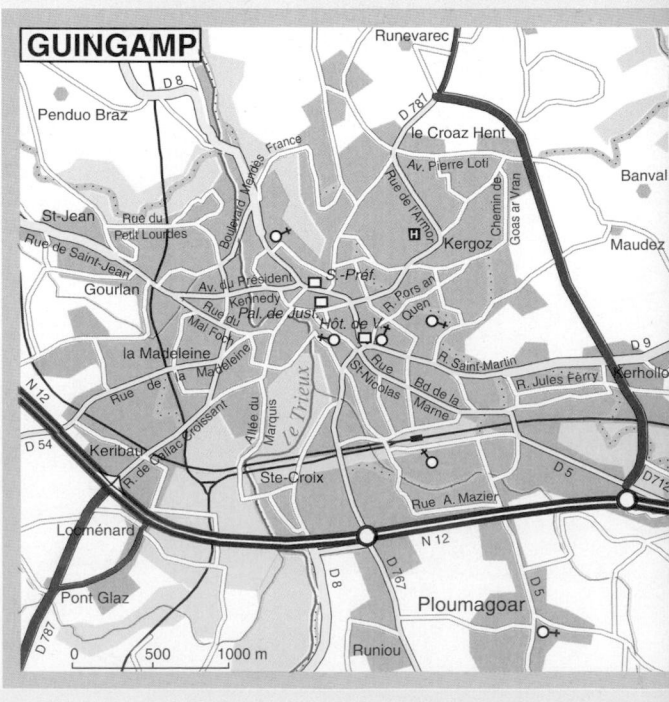

GUINGAMP

Runevarec
D 8
Penduo Braz
D 781
le Croaz Hent
Boulevard Mendès France
Av. Pierre Loti
Banval
St-Jean
Rue du Petit Lourdes
Chemin de Goas ar Vran
Kergoz
H
Rue de l'Armor
Maudez
Rue de Saint-Jean
Av. du Président Kennedy
S.-Préf.
Gourlan
Rue du Mal Foch
Pal. de Just.
R. Pors an Quen
D 9
Hôt. de V.
la Madeleine
R. Saint-Martin
R. Jules Ferry
Kerhollo
N 12
St-Nicolas
Bd de la Marne
le Trieux
D 54
Keribat
R. de Pallac
Rue de la Madeleine
Ste-Croix
Rue A. Mazier
D 5
Locménard
N 12
D 767
Pont Glaz
D 8
Ploumagoar
D 787
Runiou
D5
D712

0   500   1000 m

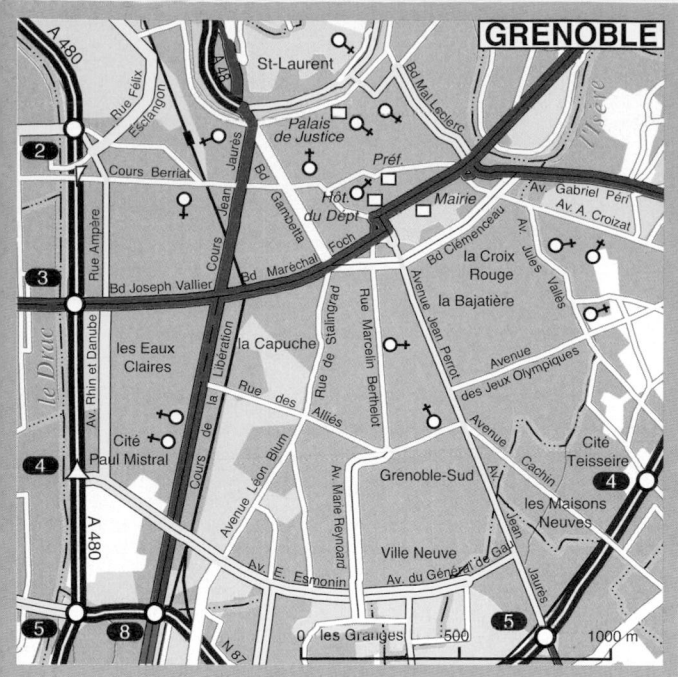

GRENOBLE

St-Laurent
Rue Félix
Esclangon
Rue Ampère
Cours Berriat
Palais de Justice
Préf.
Hôtel du Dépt
Mairie
Av. Gabriel Péri
Av. A. Croizat
Bd Clémenceau
la Croix Rouge
la Bajatière
Bd Joseph Vallier
Bd Maréchal Foch
Rue de la Libération
Rue de Stalingrad
Avenue Jean Perrot
Rue Jules Vallès
les Eaux Claires
la Capuche
Rue des Alliés
Avenue des Jeux Olympiques
Cité Paul Mistral
Avenue Léon Blum
Av. Marie Reynoard
Grenoble-Sud
Avenue Léon Cachin
Cité Teisseire
les Maisons Neuves
Ville Neuve
Av. E. Esmonin
Av. du Général de Gaulle
N 87
les Granges
0 500 1000 m
A 480
le Drac
Av. Rhin et Danube
l'Isère
Bd Mal Leclerc
Rue Jean Jaurès
Gambetta
Rue Marcelin Berthelot

2 3 4 5 8

LE HAVRE

Forêt
de Montgeon
Blèville
la Mare Rouge
R. Maurice Genevois
Samain
R. h. Gautier
la Mare au Clerc
Sanvic
R. de la Sous Bretonne
R. Barbusse
R. Weber
R. Roger
Verte
Rue L. Blanc
Rue P. Mendès France
R. Gal de Gaulle
Rue de la Cavée
Rue du 329 ème
Rue Félix Faure
R.d'Étretat
R. des Gobelins
R. G. Lafaure
Rue Mal Joffre
Rue A. Briand
Hôtel de Ville
R. A. France
S.-préf.
Pal. de just.
Bd W. Churchill
N 15
Bd Albert 1er
Bd de Strasbourg
Bd Clémenceau
Quai George V
Quai Colbert
l'Eure
Bd Amiral Mouchez
Graville
Avenue Lucien Corbeaux
Avenue C. Colomb
R. Cuvier
0 500 1000 m

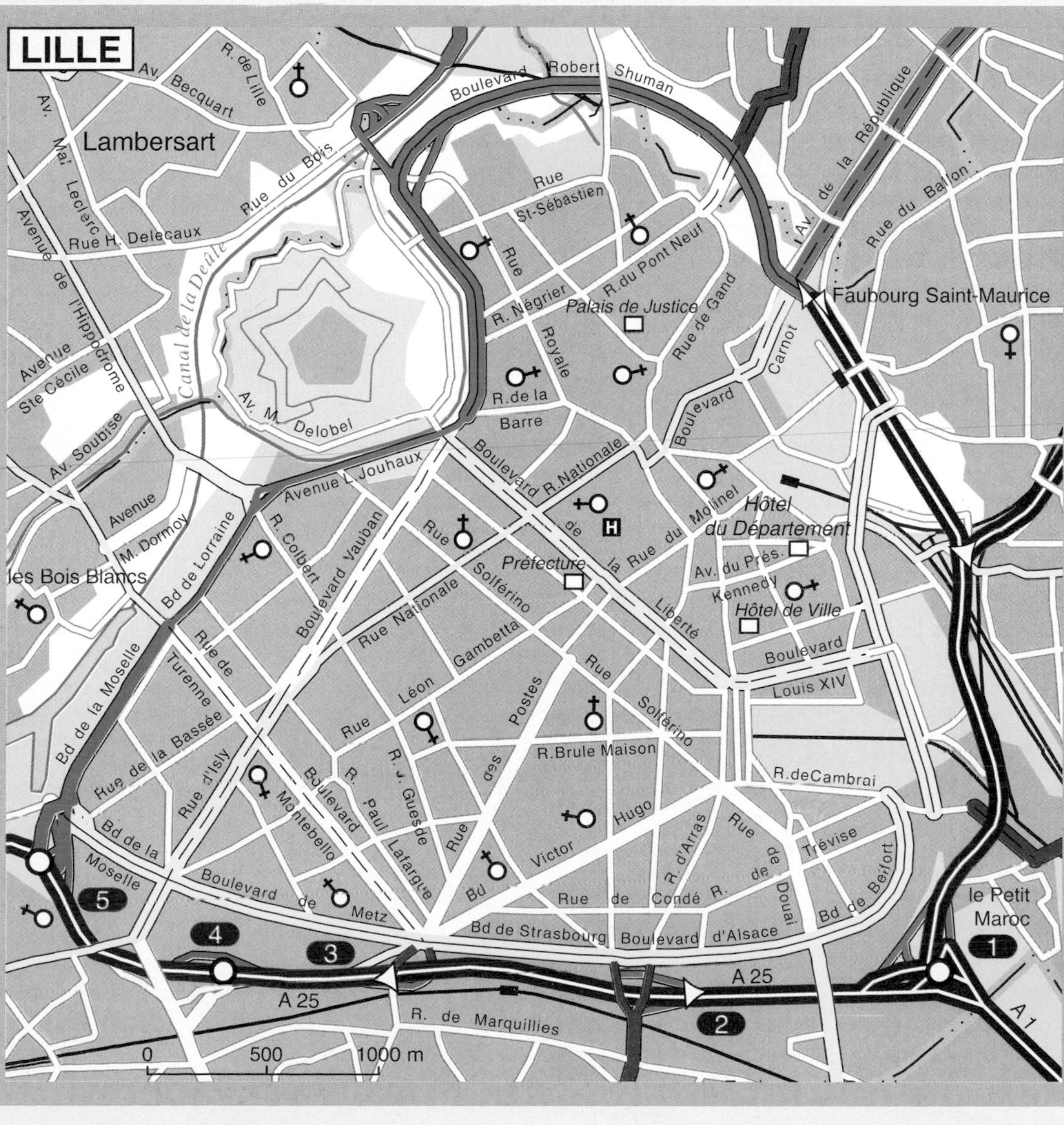

335

LILLE

Av. Becquart
R. de Lille
Lambersart
Av. Mal. Leclerc
Rue H. Delecaux
Rue du Bois
Boulevard Robert Shuman
Rue St-Sébastien
Av. de la République
Rue du Ballon
Canal de la Deûle
Avenue de l'Hippodrome
Ste Cécile
Av. Soubise
R. Négrier
Palais de Justice
Rue du Pont Neuf
Rue de Gand
Faubourg Saint-Maurice
Royale
R. de la Barre
Carnot
Av. M. Delobel
Avenue L. Jouhaux
Boulevard R. Nationale
M. Dormoy
Avenue
R. Colbert
Boulevard Vauban
Rue Solférino
Boulevard de la Rue du Molinel
Hôtel du Département
les Bois Blancs
Bd de Lorraine
Rue Nationale
Préfecture
Av. du Prés. Kennedy
Hôtel de Ville
Bd de la Moselle
Rue de Turenne
Rue de la Bassée
Rue d'Isly
Boulevard Montebello
Gambetta
Rue Léon
Rue aes Postes
R. Brule Maison
Rue Solférino
Boulevard Louis XIV
Liberté
Boulevard
R. de Cambrai
R. V. Gues de
R. Paul Lafargue
Victor Hugo
Rue d'Arras
Rue de Douai
Trévise
Bd de Belfort
le Petit Maroc
Moselle
Bd de la Moselle
Boulevard de Metz
Bd de Strasbourg
Boulevard d'Alsace
R. de Condé
R. de Marquillies
A 25
A 1
0 500 1000 m

1 2 3 4 5

LIMOGES

LE MANS

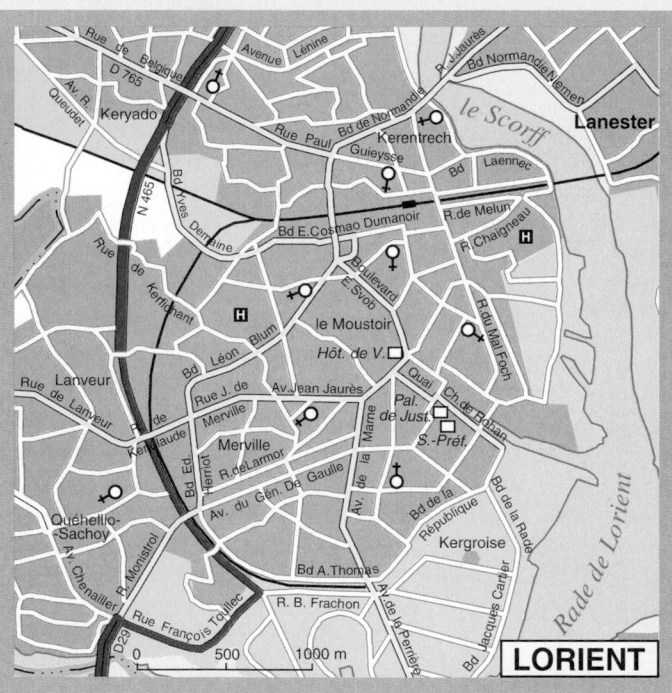

LORIENT

LA ROCHELLE

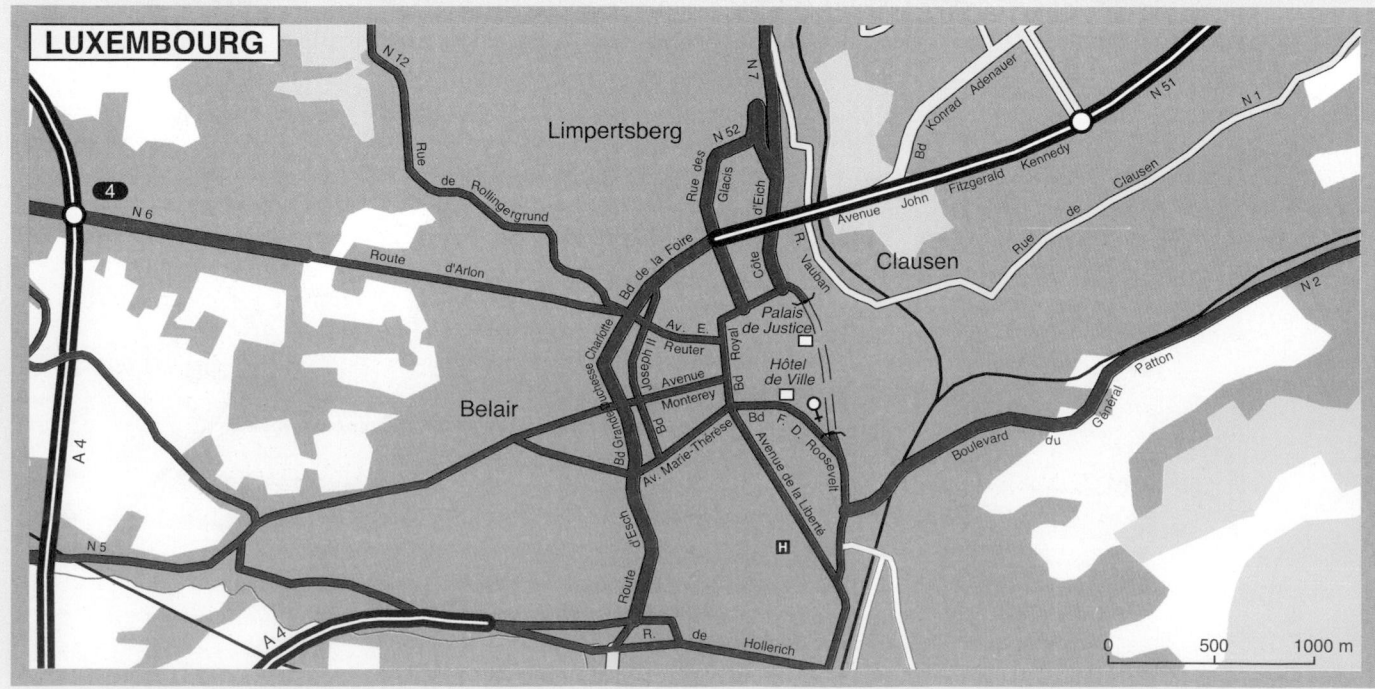

LUXEMBOURG

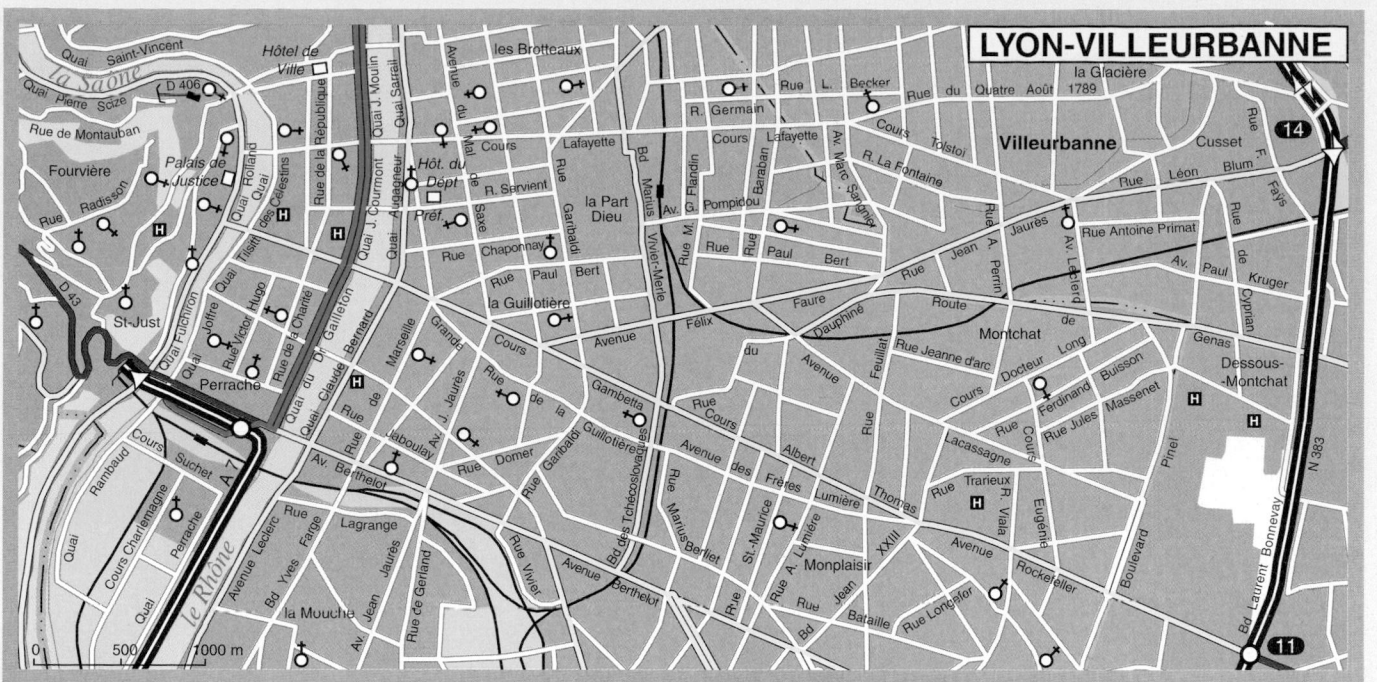

LYON-VILLEURBANNE

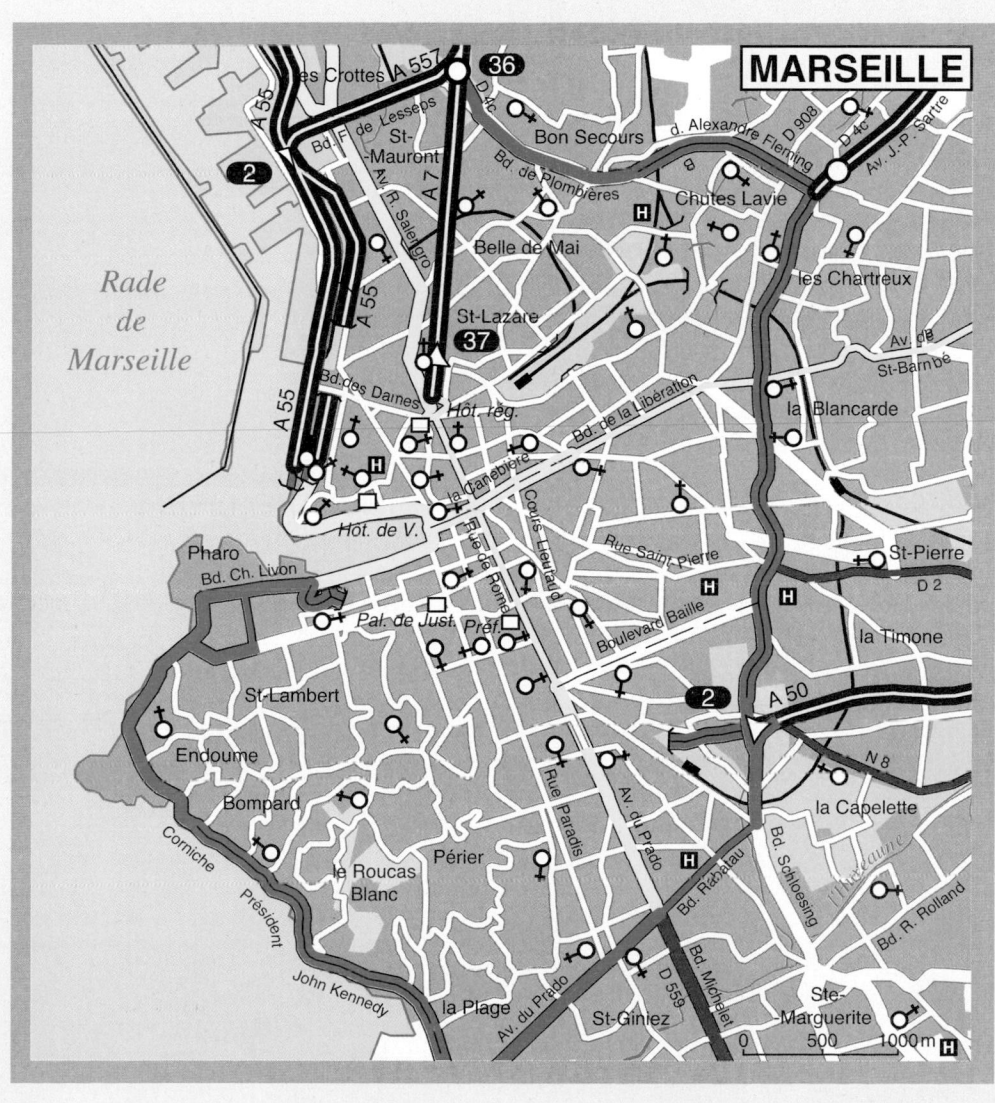

MARSEILLE

MELUN

METZ

MONACO

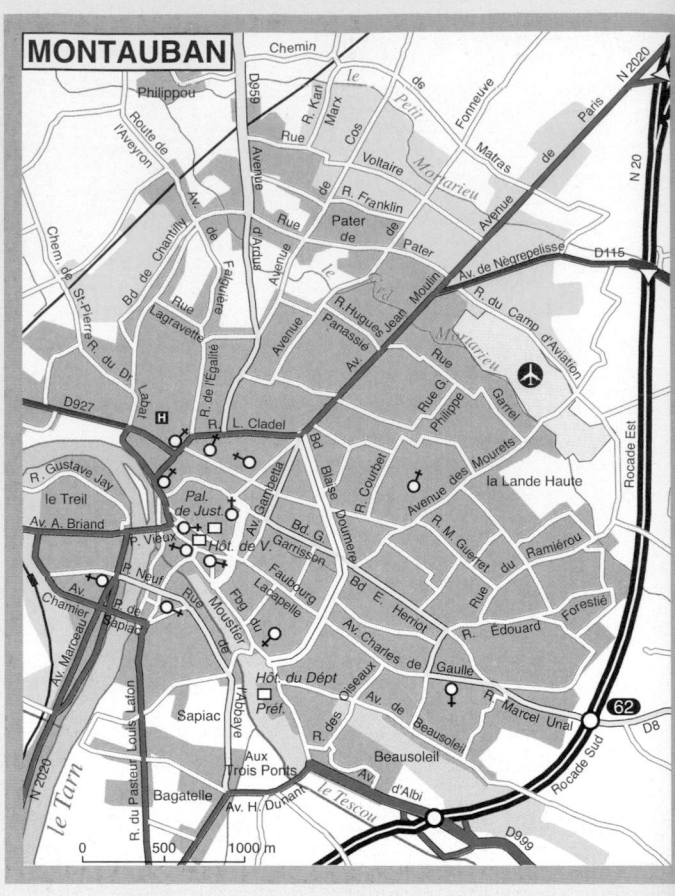

MONTAUBAN

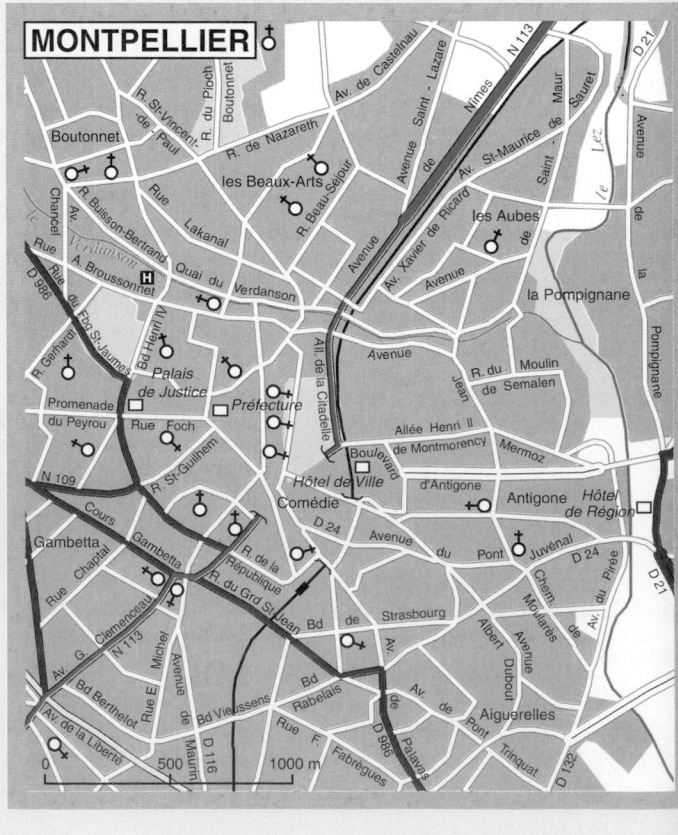

MONTPELLIER

MONT-DE-MARSAN

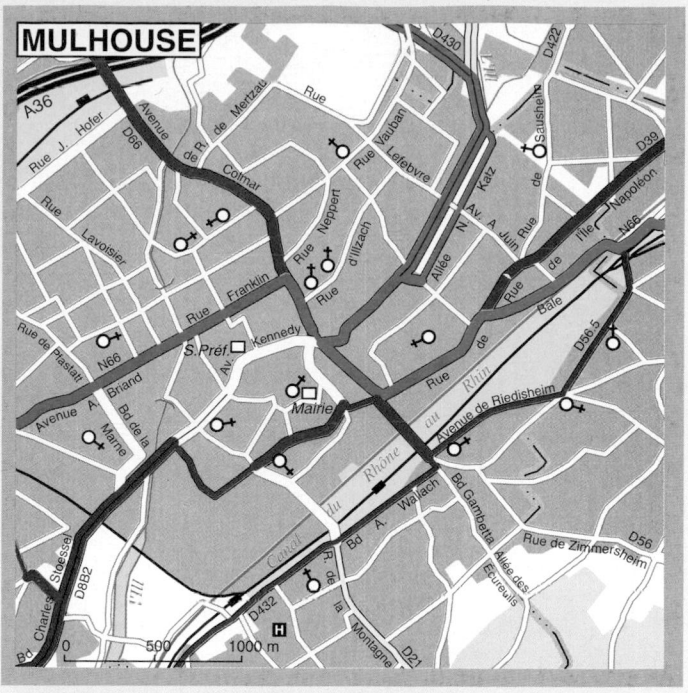

MULHOUSE

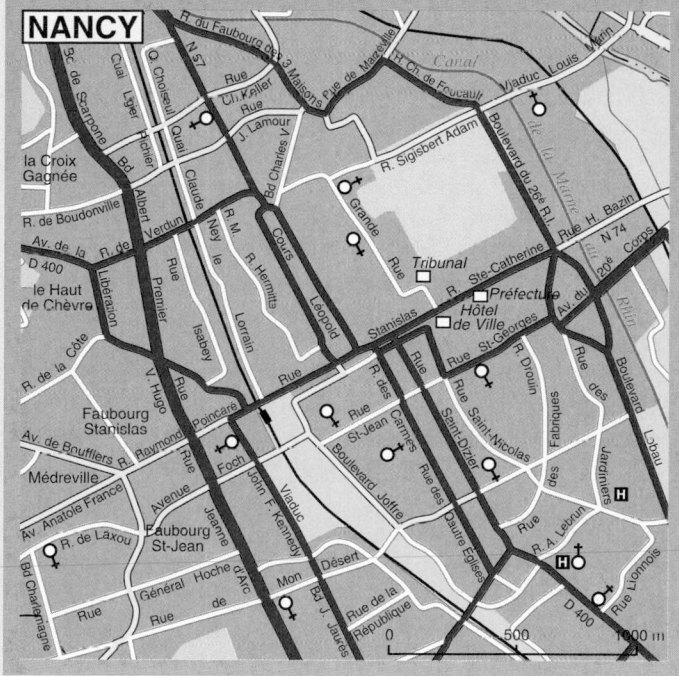

NANCY

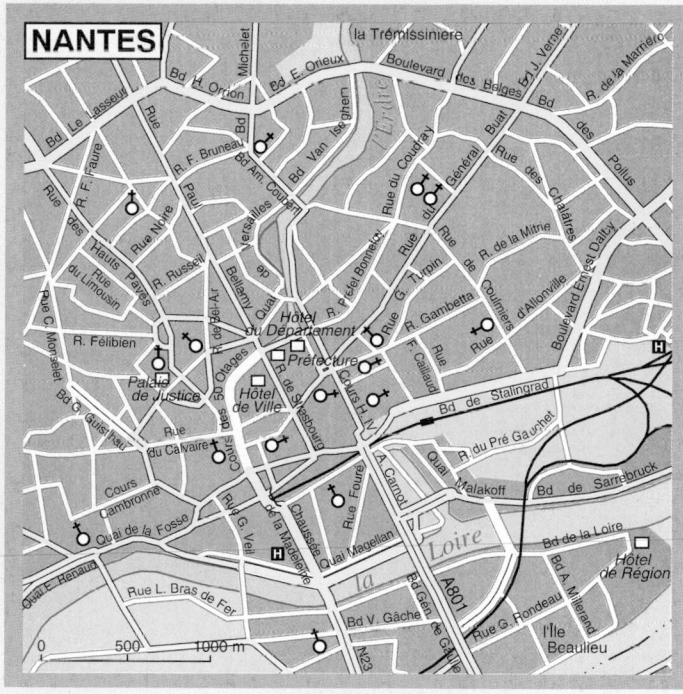

NANTES

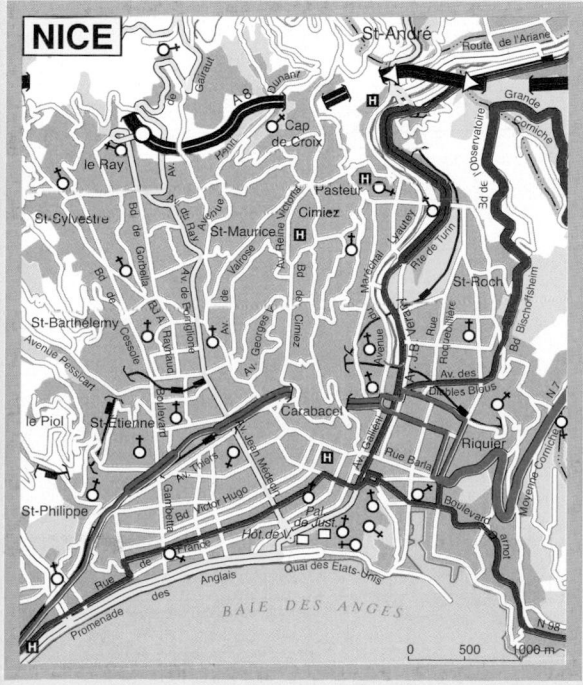

NICE

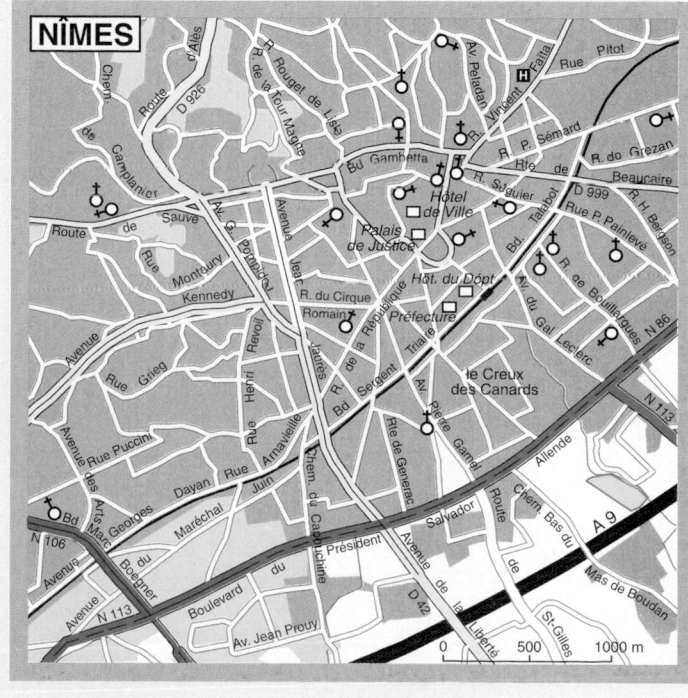

NÎMES

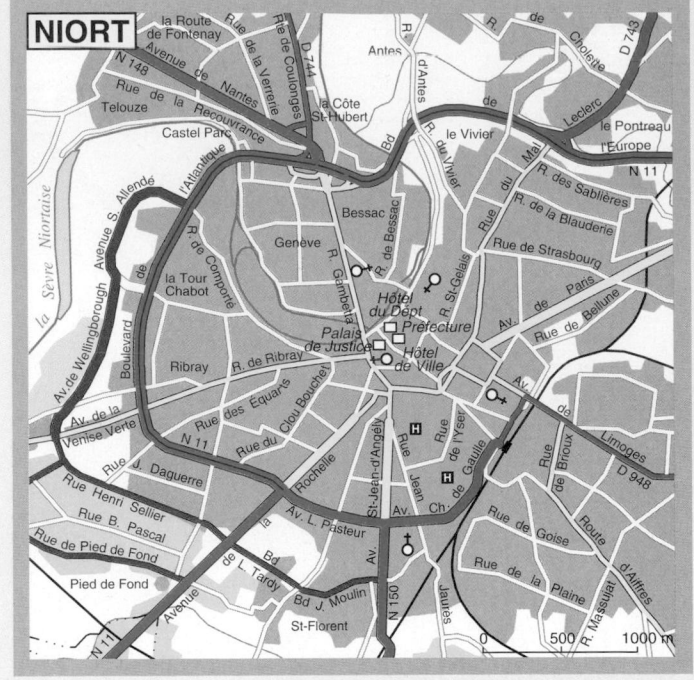

NIORT

ORLÉANS

PAU

PERPIGNAN

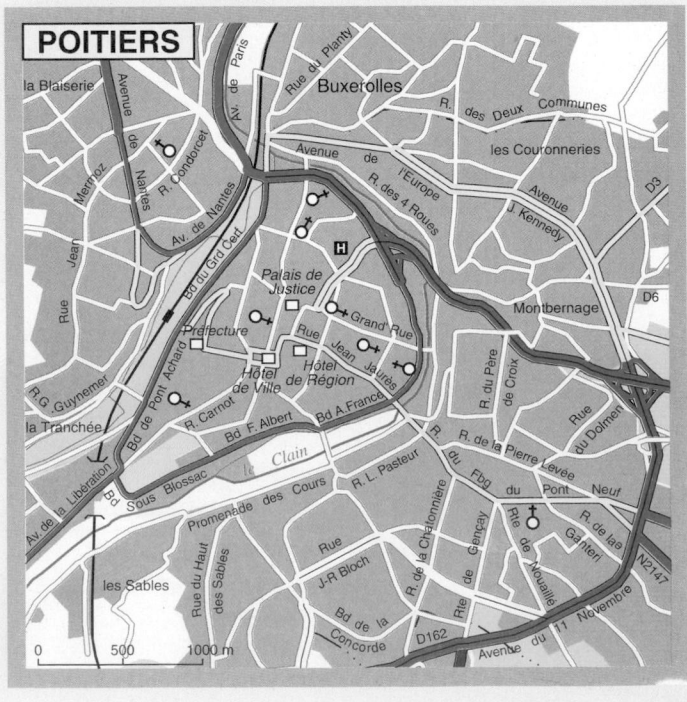

POITIERS

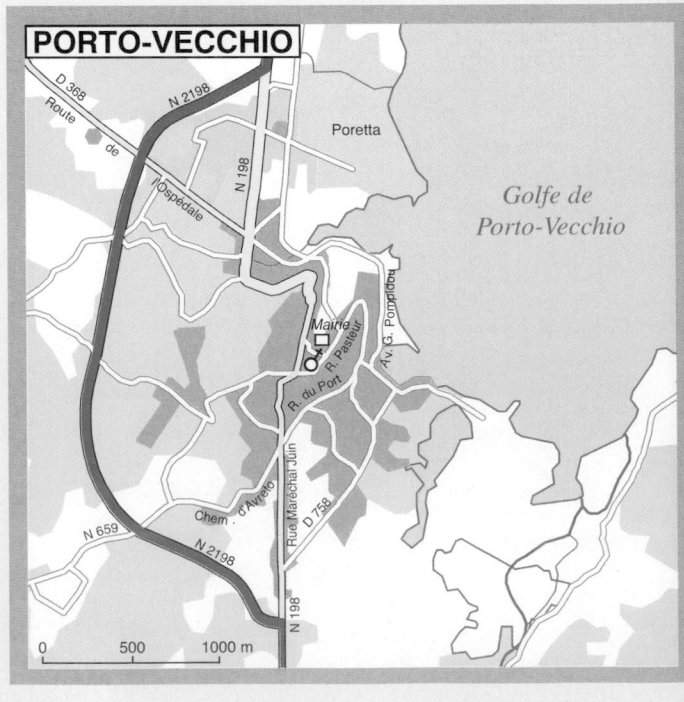

PORTO-VECCHIO

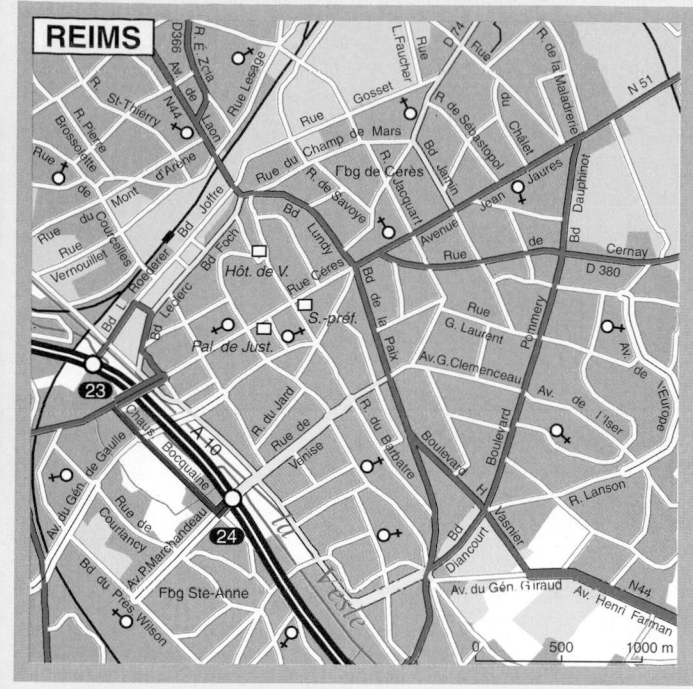

REIMS

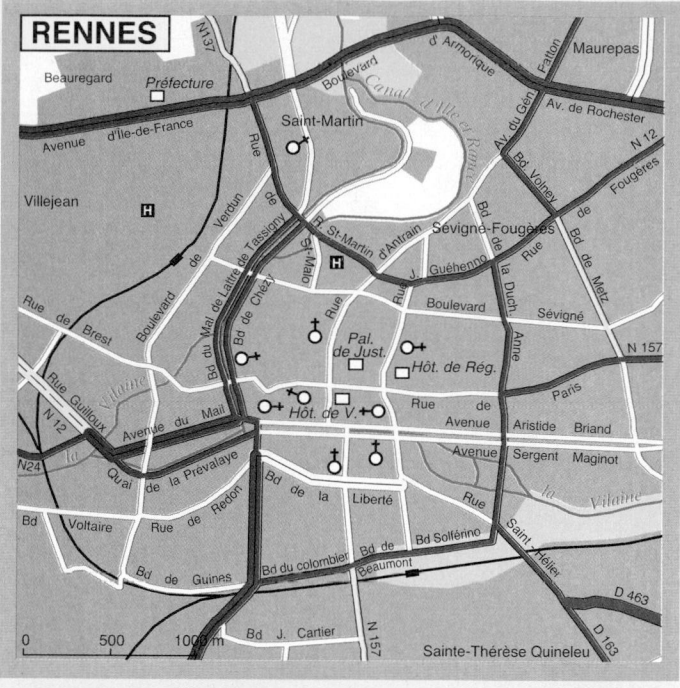

RENNES

ROUEN

SAINT-ÉTIENNE

SAINT-BRIEUC

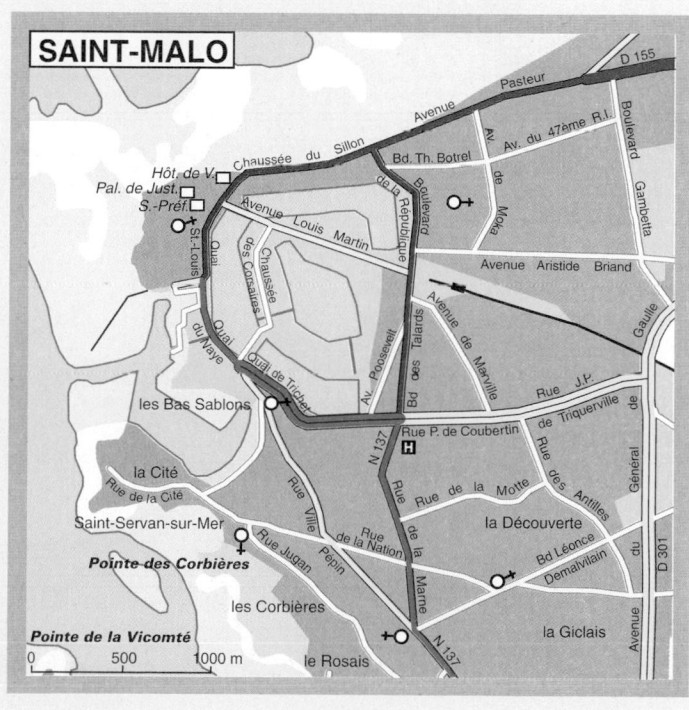

SAINT-MALO

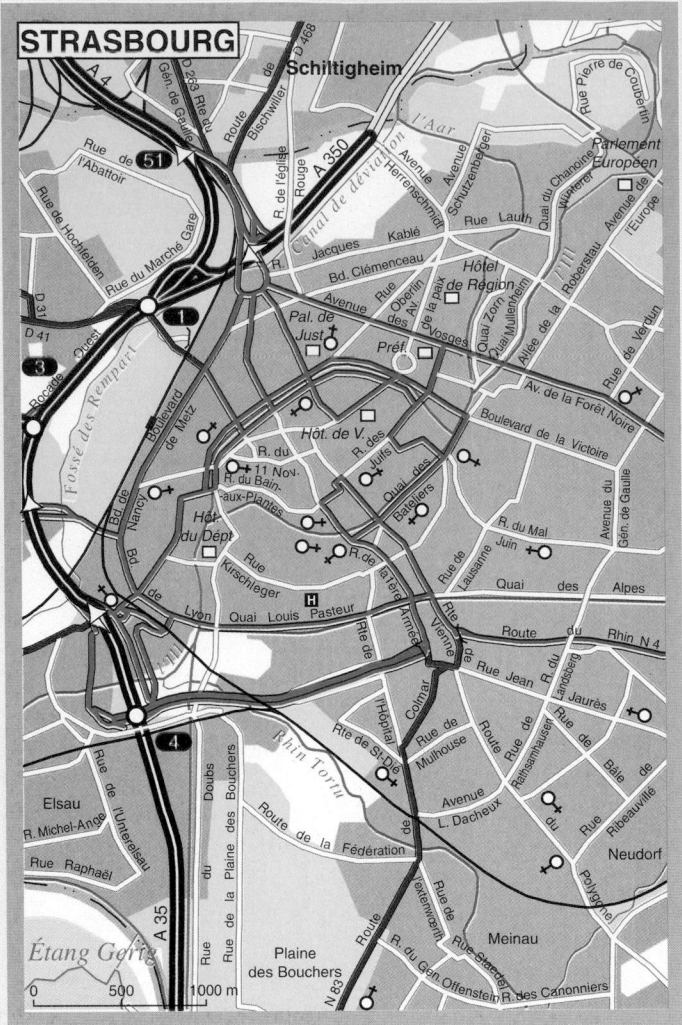

STRASBOURG

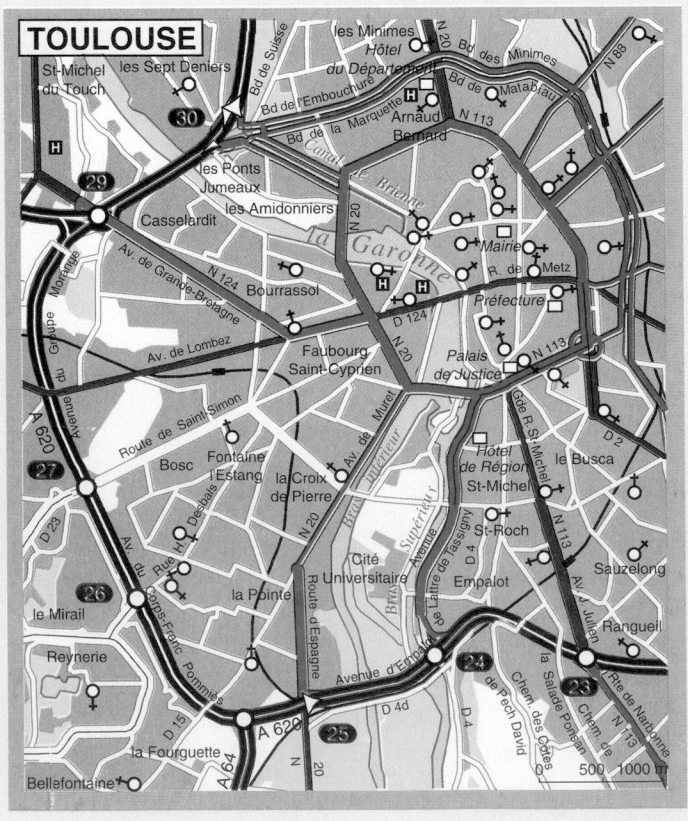

TOULOUSE

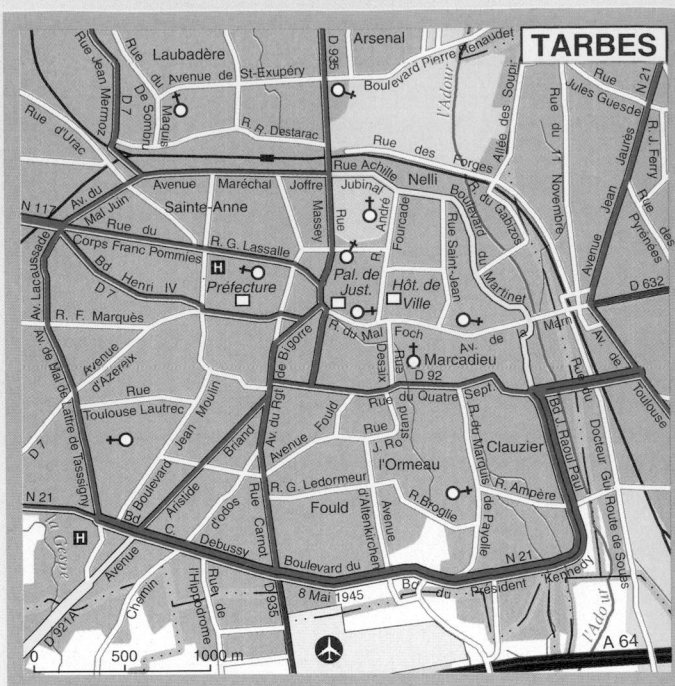

TARBES

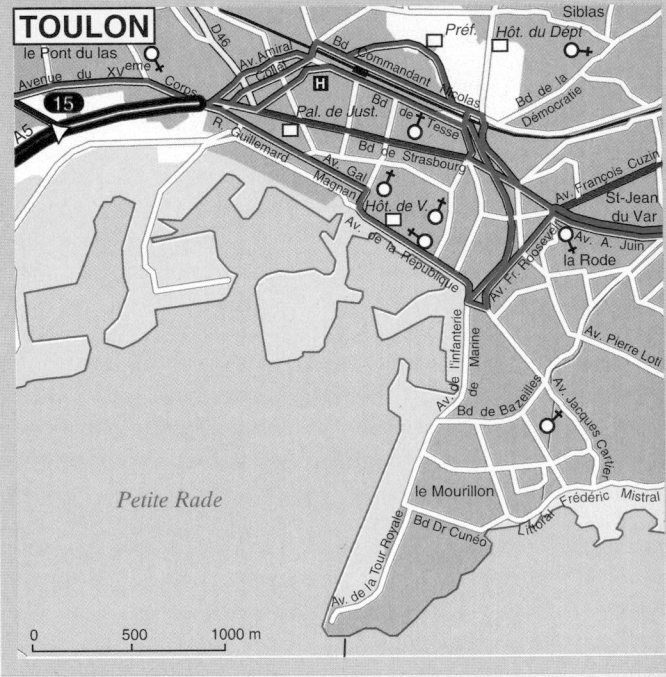

TOULON

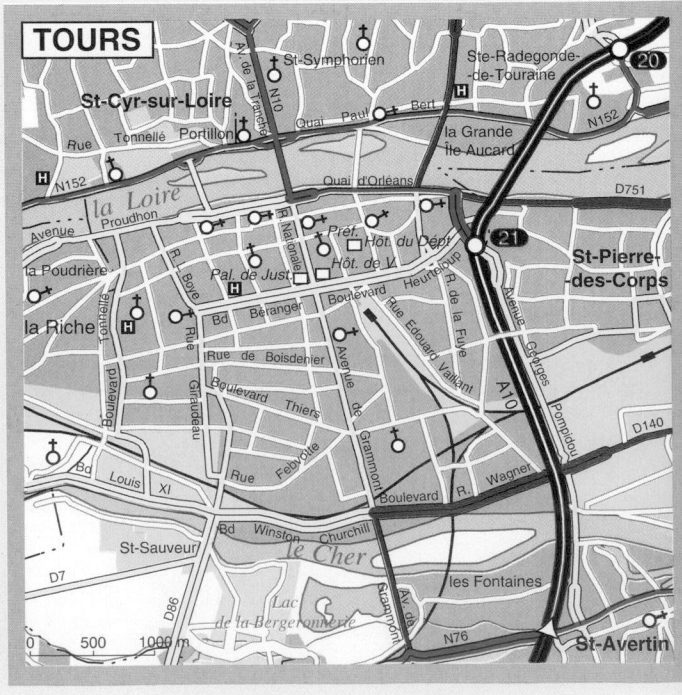

TOURS

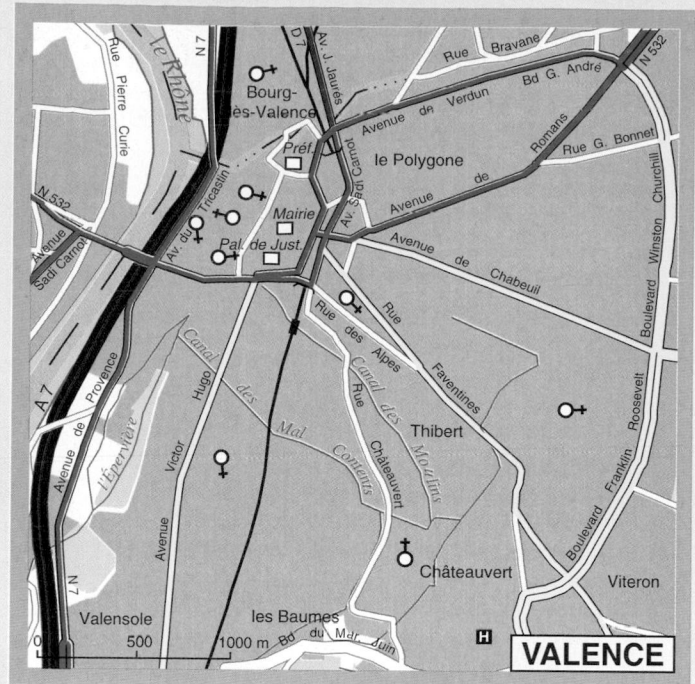

VALENCE

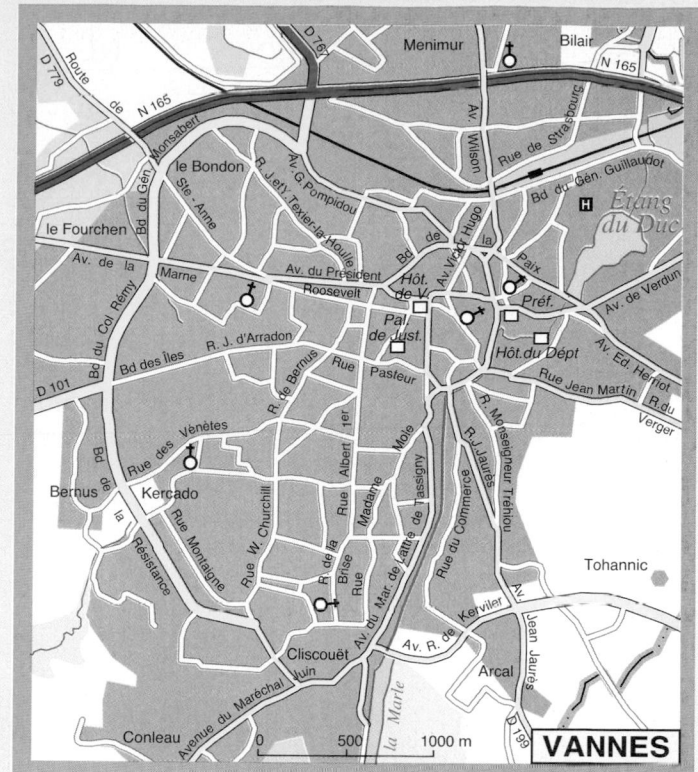

VANNES

France administrative

Overzicht Departementen

Departementskarte

 F   GB   Department map

NL   E   Mapa departamental

D   I   Carta dipartimentale

344

ILE DE FRANCE (inset)
95 VAL D'OISE
78 YVELINES
92 75 93
94
91 ESSONNE
77 SEINE-ET-MARNE

NORD PAS-DE-CALAIS
62 PAS-DE-CALAIS
59 NORD
80 SOMME

HAUTE NORMANDIE
76 SEINE-MARITIME

PICARDIE
02 AISNE
08 ARDENNES
60 OISE

95 VAL D'OISE

CHAMPAGNE-ARDENNE
55 MEUSE
51 MARNE
10 AUBE
52 HAUTE-MARNE

LORRAINE
57 MOSELLE
54 MEURTHE-ET-MOSELLE
88 VOSGES

ALSACE
67 BAS-RHIN
68 HAUT-RHIN

BASSE NORMANDIE
50 MANCHE
14 CALVADOS
27 EURE
61 ORNE

ILE DE FRANCE
78 YVELINES
77 SEINE-ET-MARNE
91 ESSONNE

BRETAGNE
22 CÔTES-D'ARMOR
29 FINISTÈRE
35 ILLE-ET-VILAINE
56 MORBIHAN

PAYS DE LA LOIRE
53 MAYENNE
72 SARTHE
44 LOIRE-ATLANTIQUE
49 MAINE-ET-LOIRE
85 VENDÉE

CENTRE
28 EURE-ET-LOIR
45 LOIRET
41 LOIR-ET-CHER
37 INDRE-ET-LOIRE
18 CHER
36 INDRE

BOURGOGNE
89 YONNE
21 CÔTE-D'OR
58 NIÈVRE
71 SAÔNE-ET-LOIRE

FRANCHE-COMTÉ
70 HAUTE-SAÔNE
90 TERRITOIRE DE BELFORT
25 DOUBS
39 JURA

POITOU-CHARENTES
17 CHARENTE-MARITIME
79 DEUX-SÈVRES
86 VIENNE
16 CHARENTE

LIMOUSIN
87 HAUTE-VIENNE
23 CREUSE
19 CORRÈZE

AUVERGNE
03 ALLIER
63 PUY-DE-DÔME
15 CANTAL
43 HAUTE-LOIRE

RHÔNE-ALPES
01 AIN
74 HAUTE-SAVOIE
69 RHÔNE
42 LOIRE
73 SAVOIE
38 ISÈRE
07 ARDÈCHE
26 DRÔME

PROVENCE-ALPES-CÔTE D'AZUR
05 HAUTES-ALPES
04 ALPES-DE-HAUTE-PROVENCE
06 ALPES-MARITIMES
84 VAUCLUSE
13 BOUCHES-DU-RHÔNE
83 VAR

AQUITAINE
33 GIRONDE
47 LOT-ET-GARONNE
40 LANDES
24 DORDOGNE
64 PYRÉNÉES-ATLANTIQUES

MIDI-PYRÉNÉES
46 LOT
12 AVEYRON
82 TARN-ET-GARONNE
81 TARN
32 GERS
31 HAUTE-GARONNE
65 HAUTES-PYRÉNÉES
09 ARIÈGE

LANGUEDOC-ROUSSILLON
48 LOZÈRE
30 GARD
34 HÉRAULT
11 AUDE
66 PYRÉNÉES-ORIENTALES

CORSE
2B HAUTE-CORSE
2A CORSE-DU-SUD

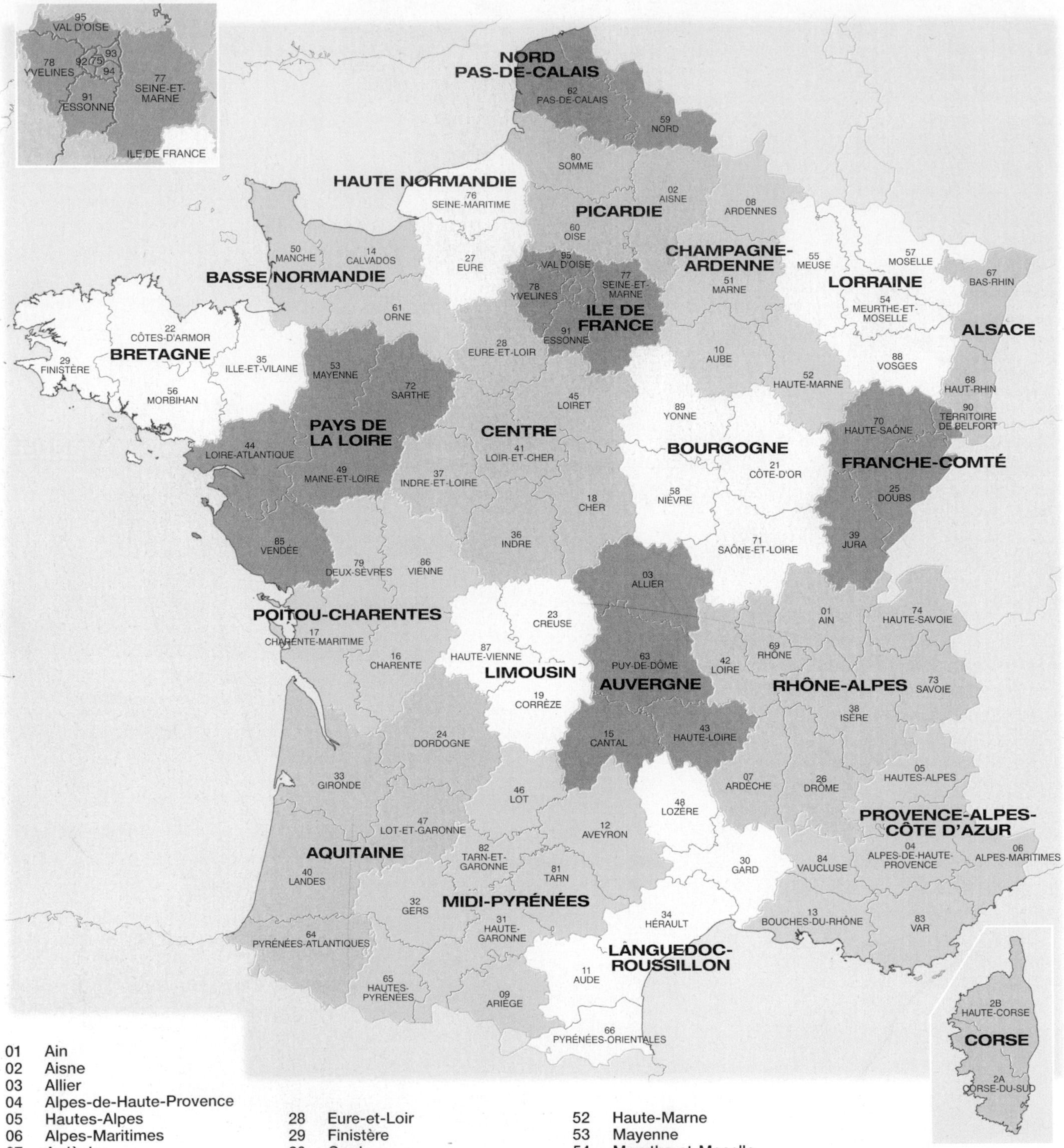

01 Ain
02 Aisne
03 Allier
04 Alpes-de-Haute-Provence
05 Hautes-Alpes
06 Alpes-Maritimes
07 Ardèche
08 Ardennes
09 Ariège
10 Aube
11 Aude
12 Aveyron
13 Bouches-du-Rhône
14 Calvados
15 Cantal
16 Charente
17 Charente-Maritime
18 Cher
19 Corrèze
2A Corse-du-Sud
2B Haute-Corse
21 Côte-d'Or
22 Côtes d'Armor
23 Creuse
24 Dordogne
25 Doubs
26 Drôme
27 Eure

28 Eure-et-Loir
29 Finistère
30 Gard
31 Haute-Garonne
32 Gers
33 Gironde
34 Hérault
35 Ille-et-Vilaine
36 Indre
37 Indre-et-Loire
38 Isère
39 Jura
40 Landes
41 Loir-et-Cher
42 Loire
43 Haute-Loire
44 Loire-Atlantique
45 Loiret
46 Lot
47 Lot-et-Garonne
48 Lozère
49 Maine-et-Loire
50 Manche
51 Marne

52 Haute-Marne
53 Mayenne
54 Meurthe-et-Moselle
55 Meuse
56 Morbihan
57 Moselle
58 Nièvre
59 Nord
60 Oise
61 Orne
62 Pas-de-Calais
63 Puy-de-Dôme
64 Pyrénées-Atlantiques
65 Hautes-Pyrénées
66 Pyrénées-Orientales
67 Bas-Rhin
68 Haut-Rhin
69 Rhône
70 Haute-Saône
71 Saône-et-Loire
72 Sarthe
73 Savoie
74 Haute-Savoie
75 Paris

76 Seine-Maritime
77 Seine-et-Marne
78 Yvelines
79 Deux-Sèvres
80 Somme
81 Tarn
82 Tarn-et-Garonne
83 Var
84 Vaucluse
85 Vendée
86 Vienne
87 Haute-Vienne
88 Vosges
89 Yonne
90 Territoire de Belfort
91 Essonne
92 Hauts-de-Seine
93 Seine-Saint-Denis
94 Val-de-Marne
95 Val-d'Oise

A

Aast (64) 285 F4
Abainville (55) 92 E1
Abancourt (59) 11 J3
Abancourt (60) 17 F4
Abaucourt (54) 66 B2
Abaucourt-Hautecourt (55) . . . 26 B6
Abbans-Dessous (25) 156 A1
Abbans-Dessus (25) 156 A2
Abbaretz (44) 103 H5
Abbécourt (02) 19 J6
Abbecourt (60) 37 H3
Abbenans (25) 138 E2
Abbeville (80) 9 G5
Abbéville-la-Rivière (91) 86 C4
Abbéville-lès-Conflans (54) . . . 26 D6
Abbeville-Saint-Lucien (60) . . . 37 H1
Abbévillers (25) 139 J3
Abeilhan (34) 292 B2
Abelcourt (70) 118 C5
Abère (64) 285 F3
l'Abergement-Clémenciat (01) . 188 D3
l'Abergement-de-Cuisery (71) . 172 A3
l'Abergement-de-Varey (01) . . 189 J4
Abergement-la-Ronce (39) . . . 155 F2
Abergement-le-Grand (39) . . . 155 J4
Abergement-le-Petit (39) 155 J4
Abergement-lès-Thésy (39) . . 156 B4
l'Abergement-Sainte-Colombe (71) . 172 A1
Abidos (64) 284 A3
Abilly (37) 146 A4
Abitain (64) 283 G2
Abjat-sur-Bandiat (24) 198 A4
Ablain-Saint-Nazaire (62) 10 E1
Ablaincourt-Pressoir (80) 19 F2
Ablainzevelle (62) 10 E4
Ablancourt (51) 62 E4
Ableiges (95) 37 G6
les Ableuvenettes (88) 94 B5
Ablis (78) 85 K2
Ablon (14) 34 A2
Ablon-sur-Seine (94) 59 F5
Aboën (42) 204 D6
Aboncourt (54) 93 J3
Aboncourt (57) 27 J5
Aboncourt-Gesincourt (70) . . . 117 K5
Aboncourt-sur-Seille (57) 66 C3
Abondance (74) 175 H6
Abondant (28) 57 F4
Abos (64) 284 B3
Abreschviller (57) 67 K5
Abrest (03) 185 J4
les Abrets (38) 207 J4
Abriès (05) 227 D2
Abscon (59) 11 K2
l'Absie (79) 161 G2
Abzac (16) 180 B3
Abzac (33) 212 B5
Accolans (25) 138 E2
Accolay (89) 133 H1
Accons (07) 239 H1
Accous (64) 303 F2
Achain (57) 66 E2
Achen (57) 68 E3
Achenheim (67) 70 E3
Achères (18) 131 F6
Achères (78) 58 C2
Achères-la-Forêt (77) 87 G4
Achery (02) 20 B4
Acheux-en-Amiénois (80) 10 C5
Acheux-en-Vimeu (80) 8 E5
Acheville (62) 11 F1
Achey (70) 137 F2
Achicourt (62) 10 E3
Achiet-le-Grand (62) 10 F5
Achiet-le-Petit (62) 10 E5
Achun (58) 151 J2
Achy (60) 17 H6
Acigné (35) 79 H4
Aclou (27) 34 E5
Acon (27) 56 C4
Acq (62) 10 D2
Acqueville (14) 53 J2
Acqueville (50) 28 B2
Acquigny (27) 35 J5
Acquin-Westbécourt (62) 2 E5
Acy (02) 39 K3
Acy-en-Multien (60) 39 F6
Acy-Romance (08) 41 H1
Adaincourt (57) 66 C1
Adainville (78) 57 H5
Adam-lès-Passavant (25) . . . 138 D5
Adam-lès-Vercel (25) 157 F1
Adamswiller (67) 67 K2
Adast (65) 304 A2
Adé (65) 285 G6
Adelange (57) 45 K6
Adelans-et-le-Val-de-Bithaine (70) . 118 D5
Adervielle-Pouchergues (65) . . 305 F4
Adilly (79) 161 J2
Adinfer (62) 10 E4
Adissan (34) 292 C1
les Adjots (16) 179 G4
Adon (45) 111 J4
les Adrets (38) 224 D2
Adriers (86) 180 C2
Afa (2A) 320 C4
Affieux (19) 200 A5
Afféville (54) 26 D5

Affoux (69) 205 G1
Affracourt (54) 94 A2
Affringues (62) 2 E6
Agassac (31) 287 F3
Agde (34) 292 C4
Agel (34) 291 G4
Agen (47) 248 B4
Agen-d'Aveyron (12) 252 C3
Agencourt (21) 154 B2
Agenville (80) 9 J4
Agenvillers (80) 9 H4
les Ageux (60) 38 B3
Ageville (52) 116 D1
Agey (21) 135 H6
Aghione (2B) 321 G4
Agincourt (54) 66 B4
Agmé (47) 247 J1
Agnac (47) 231 G4
Agnat (43) 219 H2
Agneaux (50) 31 H3
Agnetz (60) 37 K3
Agnez-lès-Duisans (62) 10 D2
Agnières (62) 10 D2
Agnières-en-Dévoluy (05) . . . 242 C3
Agnin (38) 222 B1
Agnos (64) 284 A6
Agny (62) 10 E3
Agon-Coutainville (50) 30 C4
Agonac (24) 214 A2
Agonès (34) 274 A2
Agonges (03) 168 C3
Agos-Vidalos (65) 304 B2
Agris (16) 197 F2
Agudelle (17) 211 J1
Aguessac (12) 253 G5
Aguilcourt (02) 40 E2
Aguts (81) 289 G1
Agy (14) 32 A4
Ahaxe-Alciette-Bascassan (64) . 282 E6
Ahetze (64) 263 C1
Ahéville (88) 94 B4
Ahuillé (53) 104 D2
Ahun (23) 183 F4
Ahuy (21) 136 A4
Aibes (59) 13 J3
Aibre (25) 139 G2
Aïcirits-Camou-Suhast (64) . . 283 G3
Aiffres (79) 178 A1
Aigaliers (30) 255 K6
l'Aigle (61) 55 J4
Aiglemont (08) 22 D3
Aiglepierre (39) 155 K4
Aigleville (27) 57 F1
Aiglun (04) 259 H6
Aiglun (06) 280 D2
Aignan (32) 266 C5
Aignay-le-Duc (21) 135 H1
Aigne (34) 291 F4
Aigné (72) 106 D2
Aignerville (14) 29 K6
Aignes (31) 288 D4
Aignes-et-Puypéroux (16) . . . 196 D6
Aigneville (80) 8 E6
Aigny (51) 62 C1
Aigonnay (79) 161 K6
Aigre (16) 178 E6
Aigrefeuille (31) 288 D1
Aigrefeuille-d'Aunis (17) 177 F3
Aigrefeuille-sur-Maine (44) . . 123 J6
Aigremont (30) 274 E2
Aigremont (52) 117 G2
Aigremont (78) 58 B3
Aigremont (89) 113 K6
Aiguebelette-le-Lac (73) 208 A4
Aiguebelle (73) 209 F4
Aigueblanche (73) 209 H4
Aiguefonde (81) 290 A2
Aigueperse (03) 185 G5
Aigueperse (69) 187 J1
Aigues-Juntes (09) 307 G2
Aigues-Mortes (30) 294 A3
Aigues-Vives (09) 308 B2
Aigues-Vives (11) 290 D5
Aigues-Vives (30) 275 F4
Aigues-Vives (34) 291 G4
Aiguèze (30) 256 B3
Aiguilhe (43) 220 C5
Aiguilles (05) 227 C2
l'Aiguillon (09) 308 B3
Aiguillon (47) 247 J3
l'Aiguillon-sur-Mer (85) 159 J6
l'Aiguillon-sur-Vie (85) 158 E1
Aiguines (83) 279 G3
Aigurande (36) 165 K5
Ailhon (07) 239 G5
Aillant-sur-Milleron (45) 112 A5
Aillant-sur-Tholon (89) 112 E4
Aillas (33) 230 E1
Ailleux (42) 204 B1
Aillevans (70) 138 D1
Ailleville (10) 91 G5
Aillevillers-et-Lyaumont (70) . . 118 C3
Aillianville (52) 92 E4
Aillières-Beauvoir (72) 83 F3
Aillon-le-Jeune (73) 208 D3
Aillon-le-Vieux (73) 208 D3
Ailloncourt (70) 118 D5
Ailly (27) 35 K5
Ailly-le-Haut-Clocher (80) 9 H5
Ailly-sur-Noye (80) 18 B4
Ailly-sur-Somme (80) 17 K1

Aimargues (30) 275 F5
Aime (73) 209 J4
Ainay-le-Château (03) 167 J2
Ainay-le-Vieil (18) 167 G6
Aincille (64) 282 E6
Aincourt (95) 57 K1
Aincreville (55) 43 F2
Aingeray (54) 65 J4
Aingeville (88) 93 G5
Aingoulaincourt (52) 92 C2
Ainharp (64) 283 H4
Ainhice-Mongelos (64) 282 E5
Ainhoa (64) 263 D2
Ainvelle (70) 118 B4
Ainvelle (88) 117 H2
Airaines (80) 17 H1
Airan (14) 33 G6
Aire (08) 41 G1
Aire-sur-la-Lys (62) 3 H6
Aire-sur-l'Adour (40) 265 K5
Airel (50) 31 H2
les Aires (34) 291 J1
Airion (60) 38 A2
Airon-Notre-Dame (62) 8 E1
Airon-Saint-Vaast (62) 8 E1
Airoux (11) 289 G4
Airvault (79) 144 C6
Aiserey (21) 154 D1
Aisey-et-Richecourt (70) 117 J3
Aisey-sur-Seine (21) 115 F6
Aisonville-et-Bernoville (02) . . 20 C1
Aïssey (25) 138 D5
Aisy-sous-Thil (21) 134 D4
Aisy-sur-Armançon (89) 134 C1
Aiti (2B) 319 G4
Aiton (73) 208 E4
Aix (19) 201 G4
Aix (59) 7 F6
les Aix-d'Angillon (18) 149 J1
Aix-en-Diois (26) 241 H3
Aix-en-Ergny (62) 4 E5
Aix-en-Issart (62) 4 D6
Aix-en-Othe (10) 89 H5
Aix-en-Provence (13) 296 D1
Aix-la-Fayette (63) 203 H5
Aix-les-Bains (73) 208 B2
Aix-Noulette (62) 10 E1
Aixe-sur-Vienne (87) 198 D2
Aizac (07) 239 G4
Aizanville (52) 115 J1
Aize (36) 147 K2
Aizecourt-le-Bas (80) 19 H1
Aizecourt-le-Haut (80) 19 H1
Aizelles (02) 40 D1
Aizenay (85) 141 H6
Aizier (27) 34 C2
Aizy-Jouy (02) 40 A2
Ajac (11) 308 E2
Ajaccio (2A) 320 B5
Ajain (23) 182 E2
Ajat (24) 214 D4
Ajoncourt (57) 66 B3
Ajou (27) 55 K2
Ajoux (07) 239 J3
Alaigne (11) 308 D1
Alaincourt (02) 20 A3
Alaincourt (70) 118 A3
Alaincourt-la-Côte (57) 66 C2
Alairac (11) 290 A6
Alan (31) 287 G5
Alando (2B) 319 G6
Alata (2A) 320 B4
Alba-la-Romaine (07) 239 K6
Alban (81) 271 H3
Albaret-le-Comtal (48) 236 E2
Albaret-Sainte-Marie (48) . . . 237 F2
Albas (11) 310 A2
Albas (46) 249 H1
Albé (67) 70 B6
Albefeuille-Lagarde (82) 249 J6
l'Albenc (38) 223 H3
Albens (73) 208 B1
Albepierre-Bredons (15) 218 B5
l'Albère (66) 315 G5
Albert (80) 10 D6
Albertacce (2B) 318 D6
Albertville (73) 209 G2
Albestroff (57) 67 G1
Albi (81) 270 E2
Albiac (31) 289 F1
Albiac (46) 234 B3
Albias (82) 250 A6
Albières (11) 309 H3
Albiès (09) 307 K5
Albiez-le-Jeune (73) 225 G2
Albiez-Montrond (73) 225 G2
Albignac (19) 216 A4
Albigny-sur-Saône (69) 188 C6
Albine (81) 290 D2
Albitreccia (2A) 320 D6
Albon (07) 239 H2
Albon (26) 222 B3
Alboussière (07) 222 A6
les Albres (12) 234 E6
Albussac (19) 216 B4
Alby-sur-Chéran (74) 208 C1
Alçay-Alçabéhéty-Sunharette (64) . 283 H6
Aldudes (64) 263 D5
Alembon (62) 2 D4
Alençon (61) 82 D3
Alénya (66) 315 H3
Aléria (2B) 321 K2

Alès (30) 255 G5
Alet-les-Bains (11) 309 F2
Alette (62) 4 C5
Aleu (09) 306 E4
Alex (74) 191 G5
Alexain (53) 80 E5
Aleyrac (26) 240 D6
Alfortville (94) 59 F4
Algajola (2B) 318 C2
Algans (31) 270 B6
Algolsheim (68) 96 E5
Algrange (57) 27 F4
Alièze (39) 173 G3
Alignan-du-Vent (34) 292 B2
Alincourt (08) 41 H2
Alincthun (62) 2 C5
Alise-Sainte-Reine (21) 135 F3
Alissas (07) 239 K4
Alix (69) 188 A6
Alixan (26) 222 D6
Alizay (27) 35 J3
Allain (54) 93 J1
Allaines (80) 19 G1
Allaines-Mervilliers (28) 85 K6
Allainville (28) 56 E5
Allainville (78) 86 A3
Allaire (56) 102 B4
Allamont (54) 44 B5
Allamps (54) 93 H1
Allan (26) 240 B6
Allanche (15) 218 C3
Alland'Huy-et-Sausseuil (08) . . 22 B6
Allandré (88) 95 J1
Allas-Bocage (17) 211 J1
Allas-Champagne (17) 195 K5
Allas-les-Mines (24) 232 D2
Allassac (19) 215 H3
Allauch (13) 296 D3
Allègre (43) 220 A3
Allègre-les-Fumades (30) . . . 255 J4
Alleins (13) 277 F5
Allemagne-en-Provence (04) . . 278 D3
Allemanche-Launay-et-Soyer (51) . 61 H1
Allemans (24) 213 G2
Allemans-du-Dropt (47) 231 F5
Allemant (02) 39 K1
Allemant (51) 61 J4
Allemond (38) 224 D4
Allenay (80) 8 D5
Allenc (48) 238 A6
Allenjoie (25) 139 J2
Allennes-les-Marais (59) 6 C5
Allenwiller (67) 70 B2
Allerey (21) 153 G1
Allerey-sur-Saône (71) 154 B5
Allériot (71) 154 B6
Allery (80) 17 H1
Alles-sur-Dordogne (24) 232 B2
les Alleuds (49) 125 H5
les Alleuds (79) 178 E3
les Alleux (08) 42 B1
Alleuze (15) 236 E1
Allevard (38) 208 D6
Allèves (74) 208 D1
Allex (26) 240 C3
Alleyrac (43) 238 D1
Alleyras (43) 238 A1
Alleyrat (19) 200 E4
Alleyrat (23) 183 G5
Allez-et-Cazeneuve (47) 248 B2
Alliancelles (51) 63 J4
Alliat (09) 307 J5
Allibaudières (10) 90 B1
Allichamps (52) 91 J1
Allier (65) 285 H6
Allières (09) 307 F2
les Alliés (25) 157 F4
Alligny-Cosne (58) 132 B4
Alligny-en-Morvan (58) 152 D1
Allineuc (22) 77 F3
Allinges (74) 175 F5
Allogny (18) 149 F1
Allondans (25) 139 G2
Allondaz (73) 209 F2
Allondrelle-la-Malmaison (54) . . 26 B2
Allonne (60) 37 H2
Allonne (79) 161 J3
Allonnes (28) 85 H4
Allonnes (49) 126 C6
Allonnes (72) 106 D3
Allons (04) 260 C6
Allons (47) 246 E4
Allonville (80) 18 B1
Allonzier-la-Caille (74) 191 F4
Allos (04) 260 C3
Allouagne (62) 5 J5
Alloue (16) 179 K4
Allouis (18) 148 E2
Allouville-Bellefosse (76) 15 F5
les Allues (73) 209 H5
les Alluets-le-Roi (78) 58 A3
Alluy (58) 151 J3
Alluyes (28) 85 F5
Ally (15) 217 G4
Ally (43) 219 G4
Almayrac (81) 251 H6
Almenêches (61) 54 D5
Almont-les-Junies (12) 235 G5
Alos (09) 306 D3
Alos (81) 270 B1
Alos-Sibas-Abense (64) 283 H6
Aloxe-Corton (21) 154 A3

Alpuech (12) 236 B3
Alquines (62) 2 E5
Alrance (12) 252 C5
Alsting (57) 68 C2
Altagène (2A) 323 F2
Alteckendorf (67) 69 J6
Altenach (68) 97 A4
Altenheim (67) 70 C1
Althen-des-Paluds (84) 276 C1
Altiani (2B) 321 G1
Altier (48) 254 E1
Altillac (19) 216 B6
Altkirch (68) 97 B4
Altorf (67) 70 D4
Altrippe (57) 68 B4
Altviller (57) 68 A3
Altwiller (67) 67 H1
Aluze (71) 153 J5
Alvignac (46) 234 A2
Alvimare (76) 15 F5
Alzen (09) 307 G3
Alzi (2B) 319 G6
Alzing (57) 45 J3
Alzon (30) 273 H2
Alzonne (11) 289 K5
Amage (70) 118 E4
Amagne (08) 22 B6
Amagney (25) 138 B5
Amailloux (79) 161 J1
Amance (10) 91 F4
Amance (54) 66 B4
Amance (70) 118 A4
Amancey (25) 156 C3
Amancy (74) 191 H3
Amange (39) 155 H1
Amanlis (35) 79 H5
Amanty (55) 93 F1
Amanvillers (57) 44 D4
Amanzé (71) 170 D6
Amarens (81) 270 B1
Amathay-Vésigneux (25) 156 D3
Amayé-sur-Orne (14) 32 D6
Amayé-sur-Seulles (14) 32 B6
Amazy (58) 133 G5
Ambacourt (88) 94 A3
Ambarès-et-Lagrave (33) . . . 229 J1
Ambax (31) 287 G3
Ambazac (87) 181 J5
Ambel (38) 242 D2
Ambenay (27) 55 K4
Ambérac (16) 196 D1
Ambérieu-en-Bugey (01) 189 H5
Ambérieux (69) 188 B5
Ambérieux-en-Dombes (01) . . 188 D5
Ambernac (16) 180 A5
Amberre (86) 162 D1
Ambert (63) 203 K5
Ambès (33) 211 H5
Ambeyrac (12) 251 F1
Ambialet (81) 271 G2
Ambiegna (2A) 320 C3
Ambierle (42) 186 B3
Ambiévillers (70) 118 B2
Ambillou (37) 127 G4
Ambillou-Château (49) 125 J6
Ambilly (74) 191 G2
Amblainville (60) 37 H5
Amblans-et-Velotte (70) 118 D6
Ambleny (02) 39 H3
Ambléon (01) 207 J2
Ambleteuse (62) 2 A4
Ambleville (16) 196 A4
Ambleville (95) 36 D5
Amblie (14) 32 D3
Amblimont (08) 23 G5
Ambloy (41) 108 B6
Ambly-Fleury (08) 41 K1
Ambly-sur-Meuse (55) 64 D1
Amboise (37) 128 B4
Ambon (56) 121 H1
Ambonil (26) 240 C2
Ambonnay (51) 41 G6
Ambonville (52) 91 K4
Ambrault (36) 166 B1
Ambres (81) 270 A5
Ambricourt (62) 5 F6
Ambrief (02) 39 K3
Ambrières (51) 63 H6
Ambrières-les-Vallées (53) . . . 81 G3
Ambrines (62) 10 C2
Ambronay (01) 189 H4
Ambrugeat (19) 200 D5
Ambrumesnil (76) 15 J2
Ambrus (47) 247 H4
Ambutrix (01) 189 H5
Amécourt (27) 36 D3
Amel-sur-l'Étang (55) 26 C5
Amelécourt (57) 66 D3
Amélie-les-Bains-Palalda (66) . 314 E5
Amendeuix-Oneix (64) 283 F3
Amenoncourt (54) 67 G5
Amenucourt (95) 36 D6
Ames (62) 5 H5
Amettes (62) 5 H5
Ameugny (71) 171 H4
Ameuvelle (88) 117 J3
Amfreville (14) 33 F4
Amfreville (50) 28 E5
Amfreville-la-Campagne (27) . . 35 G5
Amfreville-la-Mi-Voie (76) . . . 35 J2
Amfreville-les-Champs (27) . . . 35 K3
Amfreville-les-Champs (76) . . . 15 H4

Amfreville-sous-les-Monts (27) 35 K3
Amfreville-sur-Iton (27) 35 J5
Amfroipret (59) 13 F3
Amiens (80) 18 B2
Amifontaine (02) 40 E1
Amigny (50) 31 G3
Amigny-Rouy (02) 20 A5
Amillis (77) 60 B5
Amilly (28) 85 F3
Amilly (45) 111 J3
Amions (42) 186 E6
Amirat (06) 280 C2
Ammerschwihr (68) 96 B3
Ammerzwiller (68) 97 A3
Amné (72) 106 B2
Amnéville (57) 27 G5
Amoncourt (70) 118 A5
Amondans (25) 156 C2
Amont-et-Effreney (70) 118 E3
Amorots-Succos (64) 283 F3
Amou (40) 264 E6
Ampilly-le-Sec (21) 115 F5
Ampilly-les-Bordes (21) 135 G1
Amplepuis (69) 187 H5
Amplier (62) 10 B4
Ampoigné (53) 104 E5
Amponville (77) 87 G5
Ampriani (2B) 319 H6
Ampuis (69) 206 A5
Ampus (83) 279 H5
Amuré (79) 177 J1
Amy (60) 19 F5
Anais (16) 196 E2
Anais (17) 177 F2
Anan (31) 287 F4
Ance (64) 283 K6
Anceaumeville (76) 15 K6
Anceins (61) 55 H3
Ancelle (05) 243 F4
Ancemont (55) 43 H6
Ancenis (44) 124 A4
Ancerville (55) 63 K6
Ancerville (57) 45 H6
Ancerviller (54) 95 G1
Ancey (21) 135 J5
Anchamps (08) 22 C1
Anché (37) 145 G2
Anché (86) 162 E6
Anchenoncourt-et-Chazel (70) 118 A4
Ancienville (02) 39 H5
Ancier (70) 137 G3
Ancinnes (72) 82 E4
Ancizan (65) 305 F4
les Ancizes-Comps (63) 184 C6
Ancône (26) 240 B5
Ancourt (76) 16 A2
Ancourteville-sur-Héricourt (76) .. 15 F4
Ancretiéville-Saint-Victor (76) 15 J5
Ancretteville-sur-Mer (76) 14 E3
Ancteville (50) 30 D3
Anctoville (14) 32 B6
Anctoville-sur-Boscq (50) 51 J1
Ancy (69) 205 H1
Ancy-le-Franc (89) 114 C5
Ancy-le-Libre (89) 114 B5
Ancy-sur-Moselle (57) 44 E6
Andainville (80) 17 G2
Andance (07) 222 B3
Andancette (26) 222 B3
Andard (49) 125 J3
Andé (27) 35 K4
Andechy (80) 18 E4
Andel (22) 49 J6
Andelain (02) 20 A5
Andelaroche (03) 186 B2
Andelarre (70) 138 A1
Andelarrot (70) 138 A1
Andelat (15) 218 D5
Andelnans (90) 139 H1
Andelot-Blancheville (52) 92 C5
Andelot-en-Montagne (39) 156 B5
Andelot-Morval (39) 172 E5
Andelu (78) 57 K3
les Andelys (27) 36 A4
Andernay (55) 63 J4
Andernos-les-Bains (33) 228 C3
Anderny (54) 26 E4
Andert-et-Condon (01) 207 J1
Andeville (60) 37 H4
Andigné (49) 104 E6
Andillac (81) 270 B1
Andilly (17) 176 E1
Andilly (54) 65 H4
Andilly (74) 190 E3
Andilly (95) 58 E2
Andilly-en-Bassigny (52) 116 E3
Andiran (47) 247 H6
Andlau (67) 70 C6
Andoins (64) 284 E4
Andolsheim (68) 96 C4
Andon (06) 280 B3
Andonville (45) 86 B5
Andornay (70) 119 F6
Andouillé (53) 80 E6
Andouillé-Neuville (35) 79 H2
Andouque (81) 271 F1
Andrein (64) 283 H3
Andres (62) 2 D3
Andrest (65) 285 H4
Andrésy (78) 58 B2
Andrezé (49) 142 E1
Andrezel (77) 87 J1

Andrézieux-Bouthéon (42) 205 F5
Andryes (89) 133 F3
Anduze (30) 255 F6
Anères (65) 305 G1
Anet (28) 57 F3
Anetz (44) 124 B4
Angaïs (64) 284 E5
Angé (41) 128 D5
Angeac-Champagne (16) 195 K4
Angeac-Charente (16) 196 B3
Angecourt (08) 23 F5
Angeduc (16) 196 C5
Angely (89) 134 A2
Angeot (90) 119 K5
Angers (49) 125 G3
Angerville (14) 33 H4
Angerville (91) 86 B5
Angerville-Bailleul (76) 14 D4
Angerville-la-Campagne (27) 56 D2
Angerville-la-Martel (76) 14 E3
Angerville-l'Orcher (76) 14 C5
Angervilliers (91) 86 B1
Angeville (82) 268 C1
Angevillers (57) 27 F4
Angey (50) 51 J2
Angicourt (60) 38 B3
Angiens (76) 15 G3
Angirey (70) 137 H3
Angivillers (60) 38 B1
Anglade (33) 211 G3
Anglards-de-Saint-Flour (15) 218 E6
Anglards-de-Salers (15) 217 H3
Anglars (46) 234 C3
Anglars-Juillac (46) 249 H1
Anglars-Nozac (46) 233 H3
Anglars-Saint-Félix (12) 251 H2
Anglefort (01) 190 C5
Anglemont (88) 95 F3
les Angles (30) 276 B2
les Angles (65) 304 B1
les Angles (66) 313 J3
Anglès (81) 290 D1
Angles (85) 159 H5
les Angles-sur-Corrèze (19) 216 B2
Angles-sur-l'Anglin (86) 164 A2
Anglesqueville-la-Bras-Long (76) .. 15 G3
Anglesqueville-l'Esneval (76) 14 B5
Anglet (64) 282 B1
Angliers (17) 177 F2
Angliers (86) 144 E4
Anglure (51) 89 J1
Anglure-sous-Dun (71) 187 H2
Angluzelles-et-Courcelles (51) .. 61 J6
Angoisse (24) 198 D6
Angomont (54) 95 H1
Angos (65) 285 J5
Angoulême (16) 196 E3
Angoulins (17) 176 D3
Angoumé (40) 262 E6
Angous (64) 283 J4
Angoustrine-Villeneuve-
des-Escaldes (66) 313 G5
Angoville (14) 53 J2
Angoville-au-Plain (50) 29 G6
Angoville-sur-Ay (50) 30 D1
Angres (62) 10 E1
Angresse (40) 262 C5
Angrie (49) 124 C2
Anguerny (14) 32 E4
Anguilcourt-le-Sart (02) 20 B4
Angy (60) 37 K3
Anhaux (64) 282 D5
Anhiers (59) 11 J1
Aniane (34) 273 J5
Aniche (59) 11 K2
Anisy (14) 32 E4
Anizy-le-Château (02) 39 K1
Anjeux (70) 118 B3
Anjou (38) 222 C1
Anjouin (36) 148 B1
Anjoutey (90) 119 J5
Anla (65) 305 H2
Anlezy (58) 151 H4
Anlhiac (24) 214 E2
Annay (58) 132 A3
Annay (62) 6 C6
Annay-la-Côte (89) 133 K3
Annay-sur-Serein (89) 113 K6
Annebault (14) 33 J4
Annecy (74) 191 F5
Annecy-le-Vieux (74) 191 F5
Annelles (08) 41 J2
Annemasse (74) 191 G2
Annéot (89) 133 K3
Annepont (17) 177 J6
Annequin (62) 6 B6
Annesse-et-Beaulieu (24) 213 J4
Annet-sur-Marne (77) 59 H3
Anneux (59) 11 J4
Anneville-Ambourville (76) 35 F1
Anneville-en-Saire (50) 29 F2
Annéville-la-Prairie (52) 92 A6
Anneville-sur-Mer (50) 30 C3
Anneville-sur-Scie (76) 15 K3
Anneyron (26) 222 C2
Annezay (17) 177 H4
Annezin (62) 5 K5
Annoire (39) 154 E2
Annois (02) 19 J4
Annoisin-Chatelans (38) 207 F2
Annoix (18) 149 H4

Annonay (07) 222 A3
Annonville (52) 92 C3
Annot (04) 280 A1
Annouville-Vilmesnil (76) 14 D4
Annoux (89) 134 B2
Annoville (50) 30 D5
Annœullin (59) 6 C1
Anor (59) 13 J6
Anos (64) 284 D3
Anost (71) 152 D3
Anoux (54) 26 E5
Anoye (64) 285 F3
Anquetierville (76) 15 F6
Anrosey (52) 117 G4
Ansac-sur-Vienne (16) 180 B5
Ansacq (60) 37 K3
Ansan (32) 267 K5
Ansauville (54) 65 H3
Ansauvillers (60) 18 B6
Anse (69) 188 B5
Anserville (60) 37 J4
Ansignan (66) 309 H5
Ansost (65) 285 H2
Ansouis (84) 277 J4
Anstaing (59) 7 F4
Antagnac (47) 247 F2
Anterrieux (15) 236 D2
Anteuil (25) 139 F4
Antezant-la-Chapelle (17) 178 A5
Anthé (47) 249 F2
Anthelupt (54) 66 C6
Anthenay (51) 40 C5
Antheny (08) 21 K2
Antheuil (21) 153 K1
Antheuil-Portes (60) 38 D1
Anthien (58) 133 H5
Anthon (38) 206 E1
Anthy-sur-Léman (74) 174 E5
Antibes (06) 281 F5
Antichan (65) 305 H2
Antichan-de-Frontignes (31) 305 J3
Antignac (15) 217 J2
Antignac (31) 305 H4
Antigny (85) 160 E2
Antigny (86) 164 A4
Antigny-la-Ville (21) 153 H2
Antilly (57) 27 H6
Antilly (60) 39 F5
Antin (65) 285 K4
Antisanti (2B) 321 H2
Antist (65) 304 D1
Antogny le Tillac (37) 145 J4
Antoigné (49) 144 C2
Antoigny (61) 81 J1
Antoingt (63) 202 E5
Antonaves (05) 258 E3
Antonne-et-Trigonant (24) 214 B3
Antony (92) 58 E5
Antraigues-sur-Volane (07) 239 H4
Antrain (35) 51 J5
Antran (86) 145 J5
Antras (09) 306 B4
Antras (32) 267 G5
Antrenas (48) 237 G5
Antugnac (11) 308 E3
Antully (71) 153 G5
Anvéville (76) 15 G4
Anville (16) 196 B1
Anvin (62) 5 G6
Any-Martin-Rieux (02) 21 J2
Anzat-le-Luguet (63) 218 D2
Anzeling (57) 27 K5
Anzême (23) 182 D2
Anzex (47) 247 G3
Anzin (59) 12 D1
Anzin-Saint-Aubin (62) 10 E2
Anzy-le-Duc (71) 186 E1
Aoste (38) 207 J4
Aougny (51) 40 C5
Aouste (08) 21 K3
Aouste-sur-Sye (26) 240 E3
Aouze (88) 93 H3
Apach (57) 27 J3
Apchat (63) 218 E1
Apchon (15) 218 A3
Apinac (42) 220 D1
Appelle (81) 289 H1
Appenai-sous-Bellême (61) 83 H4
Appenans (25) 139 F3
Appenwihr (68) 96 D4
Appeville (50) 29 F6
Appeville-Annebault (27) 34 D3
Appietto (2A) 320 B4
Appilly (60) 19 J6
Appoigny (89) 113 F4
Appy (09) 307 K5
Apremont (01) 190 A2
Apremont (08) 42 E4
Apremont (60) 38 B5
Apremont (70) 137 F4
Apremont (73) 208 D2
Apremont (85) 141 G6
Apremont-la-Forêt (55) 65 F3
Apremont-sur-Allier (18) 150 D5
Aprey (52) 116 C5
Apt (84) 277 H2
Arabaux (09) 307 J3
Arâches (74) 192 A3
Aragnouet (65) 304 C5
Aragon (11) 290 A4

Aramits (64) 283 K6
Aramon (30) 276 A2
Aranc (01) 189 K4
Arancou (64) 283 F2
Arandas (01) 189 J6
Arandon (38) 207 G2
Araujuzon (64) 283 J3
Araules (43) 221 F5
Araux (64) 283 J3
Arbanats (33) 230 A4
Arbas (31) 306 B2
Arbecey (70) 117 J5
Arbellara (2A) 322 E2
Arbent (01) 173 H6
Arbéost (65) 303 J2
Arbérats-Sillègue (64) 283 G3
Arbignieu (01) 207 J2
Arbigny (01) 172 A4
Arbigny-sous-Varennes (52) 117 F4
Arbin (73) 208 D5
Arbis (33) 230 A4
Arblade-le-Bas (32) 266 A5
Arblade-le-Haut (32) 266 B4
Arbois (39) 155 K4
Arbon (31) 305 K2
Arbonne (64) 263 C1
Arbonne-la-Forêt (77) 87 G3
Arboras (34) 273 H5
Arbori (2A) 316 E6
Arbot (52) 115 K4
Arbouans (25) 139 H2
Arboucave (40) 265 H6
Arbouet-Sussaute (64) 283 G3
Arbourse (58) 132 D6
Arboussols (66) 314 C2
Arbus (64) 284 B3
Arbusigny (74) 191 G3
Arc-en-Barrois (52) 115 K3
Arc-et-Senans (25) 155 K3
Arc-lès-Gray (70) 137 F3
Arc-sous-Cicon (25) 157 F2
Arc-sous-Montenot (25) 156 B4
Arc-sur-Tille (21) 136 C5
Arcachon (33) 228 B4
Arcambal (46) 250 A1
Arcangues (64) 263 C1
Arçay (18) 149 G4
Arçay (86) 144 D4
Arceau (21) 136 C4
Arcenant (21) 154 A2
Arcens (07) 239 G1
Arces (17) 194 E4
Arces-Dilo (89) 113 G1
Arcey (21) 135 J6
Arcey (25) 139 F2
Archail (04) 259 K5
Archamps (74) 191 F3
Archelange (39) 155 G1
Arches (15) 217 G2
Arches (88) 94 E6
Archettes (88) 94 E6
Archiac (17) 195 K5
Archignac (24) 215 G6
Archignat (03) 167 F6
Archigny (86) 163 J2
Archingeay (17) 177 H5
Archon (02) 21 H4
Arcinges (42) 187 H3
Arcins (33) 211 F5
Arcis-le-Ponsart (51) 40 C4
Arcis-sur-Aube (10) 90 B2
Arcizac-Adour (65) 285 H6
Arcizac-ez-Angles (65) 304 B1
Arcizans-Avant (65) 304 A2
Arcizans-Dessus (65) 303 K2
Arcomps (18) 167 F2
Arçon (25) 157 F4
Arcon (42) 186 D5
Arconcey (21) 153 G1
Arçonnay (72) 82 D3
Arconsat (63) 186 B6
Arconville (10) 91 H6
les Arcs (83) 298 D1
Arcueil (94) 58 E4
Arcy-Sainte-Restitue (02) 39 K4
Arcy-sur-Cure (89) 133 H2
Ardelles (28) 84 D2
Ardelu (28) 86 A4
Ardenais (18) 166 E2
Ardenay-sur-Mérize (72) 107 G3
Ardengost (65) 305 F3
Ardentes (36) 165 K1
Ardes (63) 218 E1
Ardeuil-et-Montfauxelles (08) .. 42 B4
Ardiège (31) 305 J1
les Ardillats (69) 187 K2
Ardilleux (79) 178 E3
Ardillières (17) 177 F4
Ardin (79) 161 G4
Ardizas (32) 268 C5
Ardoix (07) 222 A3
Ardon (39) 156 A6
Ardon (45) 109 K5
Ardouval (76) 16 B4
Ardres (62) 2 D4
Aregno (2B) 318 C2
Areines (41) 108 C5
Aren (64) 283 K4
Arengosse (40) 264 E1

Arenthon (74) 191 H3
Arès (33) 228 B2
Aresches (39) 156 A4
Aressy (64) 284 D3
Arette (64) 302 E1
Arfeuille-Châtain (23) 183 J4
Arfeuilles (03) 186 B3
Arfons (81) 289 K3
Argagnon (64) 283 K2
Arganchy (14) 32 A4
Argançon (10) 91 F5
Argancy (57) 27 H6
Argein (09) 306 C3
Argelès (65) 304 D1
Argelès-Gazost (65) 304 A2
Argelès-sur-Mer (66) 315 J4
Argeliers (11) 291 G4
Argelliers (34) 273 K5
Argelos (40) 265 F6
Argelos (64) 284 D2
Argelouse (40) 245 J2
Argences (14) 33 G5
Argens-Minervois (11) 291 F5
Argent-sur-Sauldre (18) 131 F3
Argentan (61) 54 C5
Argentat (19) 216 C5
Argentenay (89) 114 B5
Argenteuil (95) 58 D2
Argenteuil-sur-Armançon (89) .. 114 B6
l'Argentière-la-Bessée (05) 243 K2
Argentières (77) 59 K6
Argentine (73) 209 F3
Argenton (47) 247 G2
Argenton-Château (79) 143 J4
Argenton-l'Église (79) 144 A3
Argenton-Notre-Dame (53) 105 G3
Argenton-sur-Creuse (36) 165 G3
Argentré (53) 105 G1
Argentré-du-Plessis (35) 104 B1
Argenvières (18) 150 C2
Argenvilliers (28) 84 B5
Argers (51) 42 D6
Arget (64) 284 B1
Argiésans (90) 139 H1
Argillières (70) 117 G6
Argilliers (30) 275 J1
Argilly (21) 154 C3
Argis (01) 189 J5
Argiusta-Moriccio (2A) 320 E6
Argoeuves (80) 18 A1
Argol (29) 74 B2
Argonay (74) 191 F5
Argouges (50) 51 K5
Argoules (80) 9 G2
Arguel (76) 16 D6
Arguel (25) 137 K6
Arguenos (31) 305 K3
Argut-Dessous (31) 305 J4
Argy (36) 147 H4
Arhansus (64) 283 F4
Aries-Espénan (65) 286 C4
Arifat (81) 271 G4
Arignac (09) 307 J4
Arinthod (39) 173 G5
Arith (73) 208 D2
Arjuzanx (40) 245 G6
Arlanc (63) 220 A1
Arlay (39) 155 H6
Arlebosc (07) 221 K5
Arlempdes (43) 238 C2
Arles (13) 275 K5
Arles-sur-Tech (66) 314 E6
Arlet (43) 219 H4
Arleuf (58) 152 C3
Arleux (59) 11 H3
Arleux-en-Gohelle (62) 11 F2
Arlos (31) 305 J4
Armaillé (49) 104 B6
Armancourt (60) 38 D3
Armancourt (80) 18 E5
Armaucourt (54) 66 B3
Armbouts-Cappel (59) 3 H2
Armeau (89) 112 D2
Armendarits (64) 282 E4
Armenteule (65) 305 F5
Armentières (59) 6 C3
Armentières-en-Brie (77) 60 A2
Armentières-sur-Avre (27) 56 A5
Armentières-sur-Ourcq (02) .. 39 K5
Armentieux (32) 285 H1
Armes (58) 133 G4
Armillac (47) 231 G6
Armissan (11) 291 G6
Armix (01) 190 A6
Armous-et-Cau (32) 285 J1
Armoy (74) 175 F5
Arnac (15) 217 F5
Arnac-la-Poste (87) 181 J1
Arnac-Pompadour (19) 215 G1
Arnage (72) 106 D3
Arnancourt (52) 91 J4
Arnas (69) 188 B4
Arnaud-Guilhem (31) 287 G6
Arnave (09) 307 J4
Arnaville (54) 65 J1
Arnay-le-Duc (21) 153 G2
Arnay-sous-Vitteaux (21) 135 F4
Arnayon (26) 241 G6
Arné (65) 286 C6
Arnéguy (64) 282 D6

Arnèke (59) . . . 3 H4
Arnicourt (08) . . . 21 K6
Arnières-sur-Iton (27) . . . 56 C2
Arnos (64) . . . 284 B2
Arnouville-lès-Gonesse (95) . . . 59 F2
Arnouville-lès-Mantes (78) . . . 57 J3
Aroffe (88) . . . 93 J3
Aromas (39) . . . 189 J1
Aron (53) . . . 81 G4
Aroue-Ithorots Olhaïby (64) . . . 283 H4
Aroz (70) . . . 137 K1
Arpaillargues-et-Aureillac (30) . . . 275 G1
Arpajon (91) . . . 86 D1
Arpajon-sur-Cère (15) . . . 235 H1
Arpavon (26) . . . 257 J2
Arpenans (70) . . . 138 D1
Arpheuilles (18) . . . 167 G1
Arpheuilles (36) . . . 147 F5
Arpheuilles-Saint-Priest (03) . . . 184 B2
Arphy (30) . . . 273 J1
Arquenay (53) . . . 105 G2
Arques (11) . . . 309 G3
Arques (12) . . . 252 D3
les Arques (46) . . . 233 F5
Arques (62) . . . 3 G5
Arques-la-Bataille (76) . . . 16 A2
Arquettes-en-Val (11) . . . 309 H1
Arquèves (80) . . . 10 C5
Arquian (58) . . . 132 A3
Arracourt (54) . . . 66 D4
Arradon (56) . . . 100 E5
Arraincourt (57) . . . 66 D1
Arrancourt (91) . . . 86 C4
Arrancy (02) . . . 40 C1
Arrancy-sur-Crusne (55) . . . 26 C4
Arrans (21) . . . 114 D6
Arras (62) . . . 10 E3
Arras-en-Lavedan (65) . . . 304 A2
Arras-sur-Rhône (07) . . . 222 B4
Arrast-Larrebieu (64) . . . 283 H4
Arraute-Charritte (64) . . . 283 F2
Arraye-et-Han (54) . . . 66 B3
Arrayou-Lahitte (65) . . . 304 C1
Arre (30) . . . 273 J2
Arreau (65) . . . 305 F3
Arrelles (10) . . . 114 C2
Arrembécourt (10) . . . 91 F1
Arrènes (23) . . . 182 A4
Arrens-Marsous (65) . . . 303 K3
Arrentès-de-Corcieux (88) . . . 95 H5
Arrentières (10) . . . 91 H5
Arrest (80) . . . 8 E5
Arreux (08) . . . 22 C2
Arriance (57) . . . 45 J6
Arricau-Bordes (64) . . . 285 F2
Arrien (64) . . . 285 F4
Arrien-en-Bethmale (09) . . . 306 C4
Arrigas (30) . . . 273 H1
Arrigny (51) . . . 63 G6
Arro (2A) . . . 320 C3
Arrodets (65) . . . 304 E2
Arrodets-ez-Angles (65) . . . 304 C1
Arromanches-les-Bains (14) . . . 32 C3
Arronnes (03) . . . 186 A4
Arronville (95) . . . 37 H5
Arros-de-Nay (64) . . . 284 D5
Arrosès (64) . . . 285 F1
Arrou (28) . . . 108 C1
Arrouède (32) . . . 286 C3
Arrout (09) . . . 306 C3
Arry (57) . . . 65 K1
Arry (80) . . . 9 F3
Ars (16) . . . 195 J3
Ars (23) . . . 183 F5
Ars-en-Ré (17) . . . 158 B5
Ars-Laquenexy (57) . . . 45 G5
Ars-les-Favets (63) . . . 184 C2
Ars-sur-Formans (01) . . . 188 C5
Ars-sur-Moselle (57) . . . 44 E6
Arsac (33) . . . 211 G5
Arsac-en-Velay (43) . . . 220 C6
Arsague (40) . . . 264 D6
Arsans (70) . . . 137 G4
Arsonval (10) . . . 91 G5
Arsure-Arsurette (39) . . . 174 B1
les Arsures (39) . . . 155 K4
Arsy (60) . . . 38 C2
Art-sur-Meurthe (54) . . . 66 B5
Artagnan (65) . . . 285 H3
Artaise-le-Vivier (08) . . . 22 E6
Artaix (71) . . . 186 E2
Artalens-Souin (65) . . . 304 B2
Artannes-sur-Indre (37) . . . 127 H6
Artannes-sur-Thouet (49) . . . 144 C1
Artas (38) . . . 206 E5
Artassenx (40) . . . 265 H3
Artemare (01) . . . 190 B6
Artemps (02) . . . 19 J3
Artenay (45) . . . 110 A2
Arthaz-Pont-Notre-Dame (74) . . . 191 G2
Arthel (58) . . . 151 G1
Arthémonay (26) . . . 222 D4
Arthenac (17) . . . 195 K5
Arthenas (39) . . . 173 F3
Arthès (81) . . . 270 E2
Arthez-d'Armagnac (40) . . . 265 K2
Arthez-d'Asson (64) . . . 303 J1
Arthez-de-Béarn (64) . . . 284 A2
Arthezé (72) . . . 106 B5
Arthies (95) . . . 36 E6
Arthon (36) . . . 165 J2
Arthon-en-Retz (44) . . . 122 D5
Arthonnay (89) . . . 114 C3
Arthun (42) . . . 204 C2
Artigat (09) . . . 307 G1
Artignosc-sur-Verdon (83) . . . 278 E4
Artigue (31) . . . 305 H4
Artigueloutan (64) . . . 284 E4
Artiguelouve (64) . . . 284 B4
Artiguemy (65) . . . 285 K6
Artigues (09) . . . 308 D6
Artigues (11) . . . 308 E5
Artigues (65) . . . 304 B1
Artigues (83) . . . 278 C6
les Artigues-de-Lussac (33) . . . 212 B6
Artigues-près-Bordeaux (33) . . . 229 J2
Artins (41) . . . 107 J6
Artix (09) . . . 307 H2
Artix (64) . . . 284 B3
Artolsheim (67) . . . 71 C6
Artonges (02) . . . 61 F2
Artonne (63) . . . 185 F5
Artres (59) . . . 12 D2
Artzenheim (68) . . . 96 D3
Arudy (64) . . . 284 C6
Arue (40) . . . 246 B6
Arvert (17) . . . 194 B2
Arveyres (33) . . . 230 A1
Arvieu (12) . . . 252 C5
Arvieux (05) . . . 227 B2
Arvigna (09) . . . 307 K2
Arvillard (73) . . . 208 D5
Arville (41) . . . 108 B2
Arville (77) . . . 87 G6
Arvillers (80) . . . 18 E4
Arx (40) . . . 247 F5
Arzacq-Arraziguet (64) . . . 284 C1
Arzal (56) . . . 121 J2
Arzano (29) . . . 99 K3
Arzay (38) . . . 206 E6
Arzembouy (58) . . . 151 F1
Arzenc-d'Apcher (48) . . . 236 E2
Arzenc-de-Randon (48) . . . 237 K4
Arzens (11) . . . 289 K6
Arzillières-Neuville (51) . . . 63 F6
Arzon (56) . . . 100 E6
Arzviller (57) . . . 67 K4
Asasp-Arros (64) . . . 284 A6
Ascain (64) . . . 263 B2
Ascarat (64) . . . 282 D5
Aschbach (67) . . . 25 C2
Aschères-le-Marché (45) . . . 110 B1
Asco (2B) . . . 318 E4
Ascou (09) . . . 308 B6
Ascoux (45) . . . 110 D1
Ascros (06) . . . 280 E1
Asfeld (08) . . . 41 F1
Aslonnes (86) . . . 163 F5
Asnan (58) . . . 133 G6
Asnans-Beauvoisin (39) . . . 155 F4
Asnelles (14) . . . 32 C3
Asnières (27) . . . 34 B5
Asnières-en-Bessin (14) . . . 29 J6
Asnières-en-Montagne (21) . . . 114 D6
Asnières-en-Poitou (79) . . . 178 C3
Asnières-la-Giraud (17) . . . 177 K6
Asnières-lès-Dijon (21) . . . 136 A4
Asnières-sous-Bois (89) . . . 133 G3
Asnières-sur-Blour (86) . . . 180 C3
Asnières-sur-Nouère (16) . . . 196 D2
Asnières-sur-Oise (95) . . . 37 K6
Asnières-sur-Saône (01) . . . 171 K5
Asnières-sur-Seine (92) . . . 58 D3
Asnières-sur-Vègre (72) . . . 105 K4
Asnois (58) . . . 133 G4
Asnois (86) . . . 179 J3
Aspach (57) . . . 67 H5
Aspach (68) . . . 97 B4
Aspach-le-Bas (68) . . . 97 A2
Aspach-le-Haut (68) . . . 97 A2
Aspères (30) . . . 274 D4
Asperjoc (07) . . . 239 H4
Aspet (31) . . . 306 A2
Aspin-Aure (65) . . . 305 F3
Aspin-en-Lavedan (65) . . . 304 B1
Aspiran (34) . . . 292 C1
Aspremont (05) . . . 242 B6
Aspremont (06) . . . 281 G3
les Aspres (61) . . . 55 H5
Aspres-lès-Corps (05) . . . 242 D2
Aspres-sur-Buëch (05) . . . 242 B6
Aspret-Sarrat (31) . . . 305 K1
Asprières (12) . . . 234 E6
Asque (65) . . . 304 E2
Asques (33) . . . 211 J6
Asques (82) . . . 268 B1
Asquins (89) . . . 133 H3
Assac (81) . . . 271 H2
Assainvillers (80) . . . 18 D5
Assais-les-Jumeaux (79) . . . 144 C6
Assas (34) . . . 274 C5
Assat (64) . . . 284 D5
Assay (37) . . . 145 G3
Assé-le-Bérenger (53) . . . 81 K6
Assé-le-Boisne (72) . . . 82 C4
Assé-le-Riboul (72) . . . 82 D6
Assenay (10) . . . 90 A6
Assencières (10) . . . 90 C4
Assenoncourt (57) . . . 67 G3
Assérac (44) . . . 121 J3
Assevent (59) . . . 13 H2
Assevillers (80) . . . 19 F2
Assier (46) . . . 234 C4
Assieu (38) . . . 206 B6
Assignan (34) . . . 291 G3
Assigny (18) . . . 131 J4
Assigny (76) . . . 8 B6
les Assions (07) . . . 255 H2
Assis-sur-Serre (02) . . . 20 C4
Asson (64) . . . 284 E6
Asswiller (67) . . . 69 F5
Astaffort (47) . . . 248 B6
Astaillac (19) . . . 234 B1
Asté (65) . . . 304 D2
Aste-Béon (64) . . . 303 H2
Astet (07) . . . 238 D4
Astillé (53) . . . 104 E3
Astis (64) . . . 284 D2
Aston (09) . . . 307 J5
Astugue (65) . . . 304 C1
Athée (21) . . . 136 D6
Athée (53) . . . 104 D4
Athée-sur-Cher (37) . . . 128 A5
Athesans-Étroitefontaine (70) . . . 138 E1
Athie (21) . . . 134 C2
Athie (89) . . . 134 A3
Athienville (54) . . . 66 D4
Athies (62) . . . 11 F2
Athies (80) . . . 19 H2
Athies-sous-Laon (02) . . . 20 D6
Athis (51) . . . 62 B1
Athis-de-l'Orne (61) . . . 53 H4
Athis-Mons (91) . . . 58 E5
Athos-Aspis (64) . . . 283 G2
Athose (25) . . . 156 E2
Attainville (95) . . . 58 E1
Attancourt (52) . . . 91 J1
les Attaques (62) . . . 2 D3
Attenschwiller (68) . . . 97 D4
Attiches (59) . . . 6 D5
Attichy (60) . . . 39 F2
Attignat (01) . . . 189 F1
Attignat-Oncin (73) . . . 208 A5
Attignéville (88) . . . 93 H3
Attigny (08) . . . 42 A1
Attigny (88) . . . 117 K1
Attilloncourt (57) . . . 66 C3
Attilly (02) . . . 19 J2
Attin (62) . . . 4 C6
Atton (54) . . . 65 K2
Attray (45) . . . 110 C1
Attricourt (70) . . . 136 D3
Atur (24) . . . 214 A4
Aubagnan (40) . . . 265 G5
Aubagne (13) . . . 296 E4
Aubaine (21) . . . 153 J2
Aubais (30) . . . 274 E4
Aubarède (65) . . . 285 K4
Aubas (24) . . . 215 F5
Aubazat (43) . . . 219 H4
Aubazines (19) . . . 215 K4
Aube (57) . . . 45 G6
Aube (61) . . . 55 H5
Aubéguimont (76) . . . 17 F3
Aubenas (07) . . . 239 H5
Aubenas-les-Alpes (04) . . . 278 A2
Aubenasson (26) . . . 241 F4
Aubencheul-au-Bac (59) . . . 11 J3
Aubencheul-aux-Bois (02) . . . 11 K6
Aubenton (02) . . . 21 J2
Aubepierre-Ozouer-le-Repos (77) . . . 59 K6
Aubepierre-sur-Aube (52) . . . 115 K3
l'Aubépin (39) . . . 172 E5
Auberchicourt (59) . . . 11 J2
Aubercourt (80) . . . 18 D3
Aubergenville (78) . . . 57 K2
Aubérive (51) . . . 41 J5
Auberive (52) . . . 116 A5
Auberives-en-Royans (38) . . . 223 G5
Auberives-sur-Varèze (38) . . . 206 A6
Aubermesnil-aux-Érables (76) . . . 16 E3
Aubermesnil-Beaumais (76) . . . 16 A2
Aubers (59) . . . 6 B4
Aubertin (64) . . . 284 B4
Auberville (14) . . . 33 H3
Auberville-la-Campagne (76) . . . 15 F6
Auberville-la-Manuel (76) . . . 15 F2
Auberville-la-Renault (76) . . . 14 D4
Aubervilliers (93) . . . 58 E3
Aubeterre (10) . . . 90 B3
Aubeterre-sur-Dronne (16) . . . 212 E2
Aubeville (16) . . . 196 C5
Aubevoye (27) . . . 36 A5
Aubiac (33) . . . 246 C1
Aubiac (47) . . . 248 B5
Aubiat (63) . . . 185 G5
Aubie-et-Espessas (33) . . . 211 J5
Aubière (63) . . . 202 D2
les Aubiers (79) . . . 143 H4
Aubiet (32) . . . 268 A6
Aubignan (84) . . . 257 G5
Aubignas (07) . . . 239 K5
Aubigné (35) . . . 79 G2
Aubigné (79) . . . 178 D4
Aubigné-Racan (72) . . . 106 E6
Aubigné-sur-Layon (49) . . . 143 J1
Aubignosc (04) . . . 259 G5
Aubigny (03) . . . 168 C2
Aubigny (14) . . . 54 A2
Aubigny (79) . . . 162 A1
Aubigny (80) . . . 18 C2
Aubigny (85) . . . 159 H2
Aubigny-au-Bac (59) . . . 11 J3
Aubigny-aux-Kaisnes (02) . . . 19 J3
Aubigny-en-Artois (62) . . . 10 D2
Aubigny-en-Laonnois (02) . . . 40 C1
Aubigny-en-Plaine (21) . . . 154 D2
Aubigny-la-Ronce (21) . . . 153 J4
Aubigny-les-Pothées (08) . . . 22 A3
Aubigny-lès-Sombernon (21) . . . 135 G5
Aubigny-sur-Nère (18) . . . 131 F3
Aubilly (51) . . . 40 D5
Aubin (12) . . . 235 F6
Aubin (64) . . . 284 C2
Aubin-Saint-Vaast (62) . . . 9 H1
Aubinges (18) . . . 149 J1
Auboncourt-Vauzelles (08) . . . 22 B6
Aubonne (25) . . . 156 E2
Aubord (30) . . . 275 G4
Auboué (54) . . . 27 F6
Aubous (64) . . . 266 A6
Aubres (26) . . . 257 H2
Aubréville (55) . . . 43 F5
Aubrives (08) . . . 24 C2
Aubrometz (62) . . . 9 K2
Aubry-du-Hainaut (59) . . . 12 C2
Aubry-en-Exmes (61) . . . 54 D4
Aubry-le-Panthou (61) . . . 54 E3
Aubure (68) . . . 96 A2
Aubussargues (30) . . . 275 G1
Aubusson (23) . . . 183 G5
Aubusson (61) . . . 53 H4
Aubusson-d'Auvergne (63) . . . 203 J2
Aubvillers (80) . . . 18 C4
Auby (59) . . . 11 H1
Aucaleuc (22) . . . 50 C5
Aucamville (31) . . . 269 G5
Aucamville (82) . . . 268 E4
Aucazein (09) . . . 306 B3
Aucelon (26) . . . 241 H4
Aucey-la-Plaine (50) . . . 51 J5
Auch (32) . . . 267 H6
Auchel (62) . . . 5 J6
Auchonvillers (80) . . . 10 D5
Auchy-au-Bois (62) . . . 5 H5
Auchy-la-Montagne (60) . . . 17 K6
Auchy-lès-Hesdin (62) . . . 9 J1
Auchy-les-Mines (62) . . . 6 B5
Auchy-lez-Orchies (59) . . . 7 F6
Aucun (65) . . . 303 K2
Audaux (64) . . . 283 J3
Audelange (39) . . . 155 H2
Audeloncourt (52) . . . 116 E1
Audembert (62) . . . 2 B3
Audenge (33) . . . 228 C4
Auderville (50) . . . 28 A1
Audes (03) . . . 167 G5
Audeux (25) . . . 137 J6
Audeville (45) . . . 86 D5
Audierne (29) . . . 73 C3
Audignicourt (02) . . . 39 G1
Audignies (59) . . . 13 F2
Audignon (40) . . . 265 F4
Audigny (02) . . . 20 D2
Audincourt (25) . . . 139 H2
Audincthun (62) . . . 5 F5
Audinghen (62) . . . 2 A4
Audon (40) . . . 264 D3
Audouville-la-Hubert (50) . . . 29 G5
Audrehem (62) . . . 2 E4
Audressein (09) . . . 306 C3
Audresselles (62) . . . 2 A4
Audrieu (14) . . . 32 C4
Audrix (24) . . . 232 C2
Audruicq (62) . . . 2 E3
Audun-le-Roman (54) . . . 26 E4
Audun-le-Tiche (57) . . . 26 E3
Auenheim (67) . . . 25 C4
Auffargis (78) . . . 58 A5
Auffay (76) . . . 15 K4
Aufferville (77) . . . 87 G6
Auffreville-Brasseuil (78) . . . 57 J2
Auflance (08) . . . 23 J5
Auga (64) . . . 284 C2
Augan (56) . . . 78 A6
Auge (08) . . . 21 J2
Auge (23) . . . 183 H2
Augé (79) . . . 161 J5
Auge-Saint-Médard (16) . . . 196 B1
Augea (39) . . . 172 E3
Auger-Saint-Vincent (60) . . . 38 D5
Augerans (39) . . . 155 H3
Augères (23) . . . 182 C4
Augerolles (63) . . . 203 J3
Augers-en-Brie (77) . . . 60 E6
Augerville-la-Rivière (45) . . . 87 F5
Augicourt (70) . . . 117 J5
Augignac (24) . . . 197 K4
Augirein (09) . . . 306 B3
Augisey (39) . . . 173 F3
Augnat (63) . . . 219 F1
Augnax (32) . . . 267 K5
Augne (87) . . . 199 K2
Augny (57) . . . 44 E6
Auguaise (61) . . . 55 H5
Augy (02) . . . 40 A3
Augy (89) . . . 113 G6
Augy-sur-Aubois (18) . . . 167 K1
Aujac (17) . . . 195 J1
Aujac (30) . . . 255 G3
Aujan-Mournède (32) . . . 286 C3
Aujargues (30) . . . 274 E4
Aujeurres (52) . . . 116 B5
Aujols (46) . . . 250 B2
Aulan (26) . . . 258 A4
Aulas (30) . . . 273 J1
Aulhat-Saint-Privat (63) . . . 203 F4
Aullène (2A) . . . 323 F1
Aulnat (63) . . . 202 E2
Aulnay (10) . . . 90 E2
Aulnay (17) . . . 178 B4
Aulnay (86) . . . 144 E5
Aulnay-la-Rivière (45) . . . 86 E6
Aulnay-l'Aître (51) . . . 63 F4
Aulnay-sous-Bois (93) . . . 59 F2
Aulnay-sur-Iton (27) . . . 56 C2
Aulnay-sur-Marne (51) . . . 62 B1
Aulnay-sur-Mauldre (78) . . . 57 K2
les Aulneaux (72) . . . 83 F3
Aulnois (88) . . . 93 H5
Aulnois-en-Perthois (55) . . . 64 A6
Aulnois-sous-Laon (02) . . . 20 D5
Aulnois-sur-Seille (57) . . . 66 B2
Aulnoy (77) . . . 60 B4
Aulnoy-lez-Valenciennes (59) . . . 12 D2
Aulnoy-sur-Aube (52) . . . 116 A4
Aulnoye-Aymeries (59) . . . 13 G4
Aulon (23) . . . 182 B4
Aulon (31) . . . 287 F6
Aulon (65) . . . 304 E4
Aulos (09) . . . 307 J5
Ault (80) . . . 8 C5
Aulus-les-Bains (09) . . . 307 F5
Aulx-lès-Cromary (70) . . . 138 A4
Aumagne (17) . . . 178 A6
Aumale (76) . . . 17 F3
Aumâtre (80) . . . 17 G1
Aumelas (34) . . . 273 J6
Auménancourt (51) . . . 41 F2
Aumerval (62) . . . 5 H6
Aumes (34) . . . 292 C2
Aumessas (30) . . . 273 H1
Aumetz (57) . . . 26 E3
Aumeville-Lestre (50) . . . 29 F3
Aumont (39) . . . 155 J4
Aumont (80) . . . 17 H2
Aumont-Aubrac (48) . . . 237 G4
Aumont-en-Halatte (60) . . . 38 B4
Aumontzey (88) . . . 95 G5
Aumur (39) . . . 155 F3
Aunac (16) . . . 179 H6
Aunat (11) . . . 308 D5
Aunay-en-Bazois (58) . . . 151 K2
Aunay-les-Bois (61) . . . 83 F1
Aunay-sous-Auneau (28) . . . 85 K3
Aunay-sous-Crécy (28) . . . 56 E6
Aunay-sur-Odon (14) . . . 53 G1
Auneau (28) . . . 85 J3
Auneuil (60) . . . 37 G3
Aunou-le-Faucon (61) . . . 54 C5
Aunou-sur-Orne (61) . . . 54 E6
Auppegard (76) . . . 15 K3
Aups (83) . . . 279 G5
Auquainville (14) . . . 54 E1
Auquemesnil (76) . . . 16 C1
Auradé (32) . . . 287 H1
Auradou (47) . . . 248 D3
Auragne (31) . . . 288 C3
Auray (56) . . . 100 D5
Aure (08) . . . 42 A4
Aurec-sur-Loire (43) . . . 221 F1
Aureil (87) . . . 199 G2
Aureilhan (40) . . . 244 C4
Aureilhan (65) . . . 285 H5
Aureille (13) . . . 276 D5
Aurel (26) . . . 241 G4
Aurel (84) . . . 258 A5
Aurelle-Verlac (12) . . . 253 F1
Aurensan (32) . . . 265 K6
Aurensan (65) . . . 285 H4
Aureville (31) . . . 288 C2
Auriac (11) . . . 309 H3
Auriac (19) . . . 216 E3
Auriac (64) . . . 284 D2
Auriac-du-Périgord (24) . . . 214 E5
Auriac-Lagast (12) . . . 252 B5
Auriac-l'Église (15) . . . 218 E3
Auriac-sur-Dropt (47) . . . 231 F4
Auriac-sur-Vendinelle (31) . . . 289 F2
Auriat (23) . . . 199 J1
Auribail (31) . . . 288 B4
Auribeau (84) . . . 277 J3
Auribeau-sur-Siagne (06) . . . 280 D5
Aurice (40) . . . 265 F3
Auriébat (65) . . . 285 H2
Aurières (63) . . . 202 B3
Aurignac (31) . . . 287 F5
Aurillac (15) . . . 235 H1
Aurimont (32) . . . 287 F1
Aurin (31) . . . 288 E1
Auriol (13) . . . 297 F3
Auriolles (33) . . . 230 D0
Aurions-Idernes (64) . . . 285 F1
Auris (38) . . . 224 E5
Aurons (13) . . . 277 F5
Auros (33) . . . 230 B6
Aurouër (03) . . . 168 E2
Auroux (48) . . . 238 A3
Aussac (81) . . . 270 D3
Aussac-Vadalle (16) . . . 196 E1
Ausseing (31) . . . 287 H6
Aussevielle (64) . . . 284 B3
Aussillon (81) . . . 290 B2
Aussois (73) . . . 226 A2
Ausson (31) . . . 305 H1
Aussonce (08) . . . 41 H3
Aussonne (31) . . . 269 F5
Aussos (32) . . . 286 D3
Aussurucq (64) . . . 283 G6
Autainville (41) . . . 109 F4

Autechaux (25) 138 D4
Autechaux-Roide (25) 139 H4
les Autels (02) 21 J3
les Autels-Saint-Bazile (14) 54 D2
les Autels-Villevillon (28) 84 B6
Auterive (31) 288 C4
Auterive (32) 286 D1
Auterive (82) 268 C3
Auterrive (64) 283 G2
Autet (70) 137 G2
Auteuil (60) 37 H3
Auteuil (78) 57 K4
Autevielle-Saint-Martin-Bideren (64) 283 G3
Authe (08) 42 D1
Autheuil (28) 108 E3
Autheuil (61) 83 J1
Autheuil-Authouillet (27) 35 K6
Autheuil-en-Valois (60) 39 G5
Autheux (80) 9 K4
Authevernes (27) 36 D5
Authezat (63) 202 E4
Authie (14) 32 D4
Authie (80) 10 C5
Authieule (80) 10 B4
les Authieux (27) 56 E3
les Authieux-du-Puits (61) 55 F5
les Authieux-Papion (14) 33 J6
les Authieux-Ratiéville (76) 16 A5
les Authieux-sur-Calonne (14) 34 A3
les Authieux-sur-le-Port-Saint-Ouen (76) 35 J3
Authiou (58) 132 E6
Authoison (70) 138 B3
Authon (04) 259 H3
Authon (41) 128 A1
Authon-du-Perche (28) 84 A6
Authon-Ébéon (17) 195 J1
Authon-la-Plaine (91) 86 A3
Authou (27) 34 E4
Authuille (80) 10 D6
Authume (39) 155 G2
Authumes (71) 154 E5
Autichamp (26) 240 D4
Autignac (34) 291 K2
Autigny (76) 15 H3
Autigny-la-Tour (88) 93 G3
Autigny-le-Grand (52) 92 A2
Autigny-le-Petit (52) 92 A2
Autingues (62) 2 D4
Autoire (46) 234 B2
Autoreille (70) 137 H4
Autouillet (78) 57 K3
Autrac (43) 218 E2
Autrans (38) 223 J3
Autrèche (37) 128 B3
Autrechêne (90) 139 J1
Autrêches (60) 39 G2
Autrecourt-et-Pourron (08) 23 G5
Autrécourt-sur-Aire (55) 64 A1
Autremencourt (02) 20 E4
Autrepierre (54) 67 G5
Autreppes (02) 21 F2
Autretot (76) 15 G5
Autreville (02) 19 K6
Autreville (88) 93 H2
Autréville-Saint-Lambert (55) 23 G6
Autreville-sur-la-Renne (52) 115 K1
Autreville-sur-Moselle (54) 65 K3
Autrey (54) 94 A1
Autrey (88) 95 F4
Autrey-le-Vay (70) 138 D2
Autrey-lès-Cerre (70) 138 C1
Autrey-lès-Gray (70) 136 E3
Autricourt (21) 115 G2
Autruche (08) 42 D1
Autruy-sur-Juine (45) 86 C5
Autry (08) 42 C4
Autry-Issards (03) 168 C4
Autry-le-Châtel (45) 131 G2
Autun (71) 153 F4
Auty (82) 250 A3
Auvare (06) 261 F6
Auve (51) 63 G1
Auvernaux (91) 87 F2
Auvers (43) 219 H6
Auvers (50) 31 F1
Auvers-le-Hamon (72) 105 J4
Auvers-Saint-Georges (91) 86 D2
Auvers-sous-Montfaucon (72) 106 B2
Auvers-sur-Oise (95) 58 C1
Auverse (49) 126 C3
Auvet-et-la-Chapelotte (70) 137 F3
Auvillar (82) 248 E6
Auvillars (14) 33 J5
Auvillars-sur-Saône (21) 154 C3
Auvilliers-les-Forges (08) 21 K2
Auvilliers (76) 16 E3
Auvilliers-en-Gâtinais (45) 111 F3
Aux-Aussat (32) 285 K2
Auxais (50) 31 F2
Auxange (39) 155 J1
Auxant (21) 153 J2
Auxelles-Bas (90) 119 G5
Auxelles-Haut (90) 119 G5
Auxerre (89) 113 G5
Auxi-le-Château (62) 9 J3
Aux Marais (60) 37 G2
Auxon (10) 113 K1
Auxon (70) 118 B6
Auxon-Dessous (25) 137 K5

Auxon-Dessus (25) 137 K5
Auxonne (21) 155 F1
Auxy (45) 111 F1
Auxy (71) 153 G4
Auzainvilliers (88) 93 H5
Auzances (23) 183 K5
Auzas (31) 287 F6
Auzat (09) 307 H5
Auzat-la-Combelle (63) 203 F6
Auzay (85) 160 D4
Auzebosc (76) 15 G5
Auzelles (63) 203 H4
Auzers (15) 217 H3
Auzet (04) 259 K2
Auzeville-Tolosane (31) 288 C1
Auzielle (31) 288 D1
Auzits (12) 251 J1
Auzon (43) 219 G1
Auzouer-en-Touraine (37) 128 A3
Auzouville-Auberbosc (76) 14 E5
Auzouville-l'Esneval (76) 15 H5
Auzouville-sur Ry (76) 35 K2
Auzouville-sur-Saâne (76) 15 J4
Availles-en-Châtellerault (86) 163 H1
Availles-Limouzine (86) 180 B3
Availles-sur-Seiche (35) 104 A3
Availles-Thouarsais (79) 144 C5
Avajan (65) 305 F4
Avallon (89) 133 K3
les Avanchers-Valmorel (73) 209 G5
Avançon (05) 243 F5
Avançon (08) 41 H1
Avanne-Aveney (25) 137 K6
Avant-lès-Marcilly (10) 89 G3
Avant-lès-Ramerupt (10) 90 C3
Avanton (86) 162 E2
Avapessa (2B) 318 C3
Avaray (41) 109 G6
Avaux (08) 41 F1
Aveize (69) 205 H3
Aveizieux (42) 205 G4
Avelanges (21) 136 A2
Avelesges (80) 17 H2
Avelin (59) 6 E5
Aveluy (80) 10 D6
Avenas (69) 188 A2
Avenay (14) 32 D6
Avenay-Val-d'Or (51) 41 F6
Avène (34) 272 D4
les Avenières (38) 207 H3
Avensac (32) 268 B3
Avensan (33) 211 F5
Aventignan (65) 305 H1
Averan (65) 285 G6
Averdoingt (62) 10 B2
Averdon (41) 128 E1
Avermes (03) 168 E3
Avernes (95) 37 F6
Avernes-Saint-Gourgon (61) 55 F2
Avernes-sous-Exmes (61) 54 E4
Avéron-Bergelle (32) 266 C4
Averton (53) 82 A4
Avesnelles (59) 13 H5
Avesnes (62) 4 E5
Avesnes-Chaussoy (80) 17 G2
Avesnes-en-Bray (76) 36 D1
Avesnes-en-Saosnois (72) 83 F5
Avesnes-en-Val (76) 16 C1
Avesnes-le-Comte (62) 10 C3
Avesnes-le-Sec (59) 12 B3
Avesnes-les-Aubert (59) 12 C4
Avesnes-lès-Bapaume (62) 11 F5
Avesnes-sur-Helpe (59) 13 G5
Avessac (44) 102 D4
Avessé (72) 105 K3
Aveux (65) 305 H2
Avezac-Prat-Lahitte (65) 305 F1
Avezan (32) 268 A3
Avèze (30) 273 J2
Avèze (63) 201 J4
Avezé (72) 83 J5
Aviernoz (74) 191 G4
Avignon (84) 276 B2
Avignon-lès-Saint-Claude (39) 173 K5
Avignonet (38) 224 A6
Avignonet-Lauragais (31) 289 F4
Avillers (54) 26 C5
Avillers (88) 94 B4
Avillers-Sainte-Croix (55) 44 A6
Avilley (25) 138 C3
Avilly-Saint-Léonard (60) 38 B5
Avion (62) 11 F1
Avioth (55) 23 K5
Aviré (49) 104 E6
Avirey-Lingey (10) 114 D2
Aviron (27) 56 D1
Avize (51) 62 A2
Avocourt (55) 43 F4
Avoine (37) 145 F1
Avoine (61) 54 B5
Avoise (72) 106 A4
Avolsheim (67) 70 D3
Avon (77) 87 H3
Avon (79) 162 C6
Avon-la-Pèze (10) 89 G3
Avon-les-Roches (37) 145 H2
Avondance (62) 5 F6
Avord (18) 149 J3
Avosnes (21) 135 G5
Avot (21) 136 A1
Avoudrey (25) 157 F1
Avrainville (54) 65 J4

Avrainville (88) 94 B3
Avrainville (91) 86 D1
Avranches (50) 51 K3
Avranville (88) 92 E3
Avrechy (60) 38 A2
Avremesnil (76) 15 J3
Avressieux (73) 207 K4
Avreuil (10) 114 A2
Avricourt (54) 67 G5
Avricourt (57) 67 G5
Avricourt (60) 19 G5
Avrieux (73) 226 A2
Avrigney-Virey (70) 137 H5
Avrigny (60) 38 B3
Avril (54) 26 C5
Avril-sur-Loire (58) 151 F6
Avrillé (49) 125 G3
Avrillé (85) 159 H4
Avrillé-les-Ponceaux (37) 126 E4
Avrilly (03) 170 B6
Avrilly (27) 56 D2
Avrilly (61) 81 G1
Avroult (62) 3 F6
Avy (17) 195 H4
Awoingt (59) 11 K4
Ax-les-Thermes (09) 308 A6
Axat (11) 308 E5
Axiat (09) 307 K5
Ay (51) 61 K1
Ay-sur-Moselle (57) 27 H5
Ayat-sur-Sioule (63) 184 D4
Aydat (63) 202 C3
Aydie (64) 285 F1
Aydius (64) 303 F2
Aydoilles (88) 94 E5
Ayen (19) 215 G3
Ayencourt (80) 18 D5
Ayette (62) 10 E4
Ayguatébia-Talau (66) 313 K3
Ayguemorte-les-Graves (33) 229 H3
Ayguesvives (31) 288 D3
Ayguetinte (32) 267 G3
Ayherre (64) 282 D2
Ayn (73) 207 K4
Aynac (46) 234 B3
les Aynans (70) 138 D1
Ayrens (15) 217 G6
Ayron (86) 162 C2
Ayros-Arbouix (65) 304 B2
Ayse (74) 191 J3
Ayssènes (12) 252 D6
Aytré (17) 176 D3
les Ayvelles (08) 22 D4
Ayzac-Ost (65) 304 A2
Ayzieu (32) 266 B3
Azannes-et-Soumazannes (55) 26 A5
Azas (31) 269 K5
Azat-Châtenet (23) 182 C4
Azat-le-Ris (87) 181 F1
Azay-le-Brûlé (79) 161 J5
Azay-le-Ferron (36) 146 D6
Azay-le-Rideau (37) 127 G6
Azay-sur-Cher (37) 128 A5
Azay-sur-Indre (37) 146 C1
Azay-sur-Thouet (79) 161 J2
Azé (41) 108 B4
Azé (53) 105 F4
Azé (71) 171 J5
Azelot (54) 66 B6
Azerables (23) 165 G6
Azerailles (54) 95 F1
Azerat (24) 214 E4
Azérat (43) 219 H1
Azereix (65) 285 G5
Azet (65) 305 F5
Azeville (50) 29 F4
Azillanet (34) 291 F4
Azille (11) 290 E5
Azilone-Ampaza (2A) 320 E6
Azincourt (62) 5 F6
Azolette (69) 187 J2
Azoudange (57) 67 G4
Azur (40) 262 C3
Azy (18) 149 K1
Azy-le-Vif (58) 168 D1
Azy-sur-Marne (02) 60 E2
Azzana (2A) 320 D3

B

Baâlon (55) 43 G1
Baâlons (08) 22 C5
Babeau-Bouldoux (34) 291 G3
Baboeuf (60) 19 J6
Baby (77) 88 D3
Baccarat (54) 95 F2
Baccon (45) 109 H4
Bach (46) 250 C3
Bachant (59) 13 G3
Bachas (31) 287 G5
la Bachellerie (24) 214 E4
Bachivillers (60) 37 F4
Bachos (31) 305 H4
Bachy (59) 7 F5
Bacilly (50) 51 J3
Baconnes (51) 41 H5
la Baconnière (53) 80 D6
Bacouël (60) 18 B5
Bacouel-sur-Selle (80) 18 A3

Bacourt (57) 66 C2
Bacquepuis (27) 35 H6
Bacqueville (27) 36 A3
Bacqueville-en-Caux (76) 15 J3
Badailhac (15) 235 K1
Badaroux (48) 237 J6
Badecon-le-Pin (36) 165 H4
Badefols-d'Ans (24) 215 F3
Badefols-sur-Dordogne (24) 232 B2
Baden (56) 100 E5
Badens (11) 290 C5
Badevel (25) 139 J2
Badinières (38) 207 F5
Badménil-aux-Bois (88) 94 E4
Badonviller (54) 95 H1
Badonvilliers-Gérauvilliers (55) 93 F1
Baerendorf (67) 67 J2
Baerenthal (57) 69 H4
la Baffe (88) 94 E5
Baffie (63) 204 A6
Bagard (30) 255 G6
Bagas (33) 230 C5
Bagat-en-Quercy (46) 249 H2
Bâgé-la-Ville (01) 172 A6
Bâgé-le-Châtel (01) 172 A6
Bagert (09) 306 D1
Bages (11) 310 C1
Bages (66) 315 G3
Bagiry (31) 305 J3
Bagnac-sur-Célé (46) 234 E4
Bagneaux (89) 89 G5
Bagneaux-sur-Loing (77) 87 H5
Bagnères-de-Bigorre (65) 304 D1
Bagnères-de-Luchon (31) 305 H5
Bagneux (02) 39 J2
Bagneux (03) 168 D2
Bagneux (36) 148 A1
Bagneux (51) 89 J1
Bagneux (54) 93 H1
Bagneux (92) 58 E4
Bagneux-la-Fosse (10) 114 D3
Bagnizeau (17) 178 B6
Bagnoles (11) 290 C5
Bagnoles-de-l'Orne (61) 81 J1
Bagnolet (93) 59 F3
Bagnols (63) 201 J5
Bagnols (69) 188 A6
Bagnols-en-Forêt (83) 280 B6
Bagnols-les-Bains (48) 238 A6
Bagnols-sur-Cèze (30) 256 C5
Bagnot (21) 154 C3
Baguer-Morvan (35) 51 F5
Baguer-Pican (35) 51 G4
Baho (66) 310 B6
Bahus-Soubiran (40) 265 J5
Baigneaux (28) 109 K1
Baigneaux (33) 230 B3
Baigneaux (41) 108 E5
Baignes (70) 138 A1
Baignes-Sainte-Radegonde (16) 212 B1
Baigneux-les-Juifs (21) 135 G2
Baignolet (28) 85 H6
Baigts (40) 264 D5
Baigts-de-Béarn (64) 283 J1
Baillargues (34) 274 D5
Baillé (35) 79 K1
Bailleau-Armenonville (28) 85 H2
Bailleau-le-Pin (28) 84 E4
Bailleau-l'Évêque (28) 85 F2
Baillestavy (66) 314 D4
Baillet-en-France (95) 58 E1
Bailleul (59) 6 D3
Bailleul (61) 54 C4
le Bailleul (72) 106 A5
Bailleul (80) 9 G6
Bailleul-aux-Cornailles (62) 10 B2
Bailleul-la-Vallée (27) 34 B5
Bailleul-le-Soc (60) 38 B2
Bailleul-lès-Pernes (62) 5 H6
Bailleul-Neuville (76) 16 C3
Bailleul-Sir-Berthoult (62) 11 F2
Bailleul-sur-Thérain (60) 37 J2
Bailleulmont (62) 10 D4
Bailleulval (62) 10 D4
Bailleval (60) 38 A3
Baillolet (76) 16 D3
Baillou (41) 108 A3
Bailly (60) 39 F1
Bailly (78) 58 C4
Bailly-aux-Forges (52) 91 J2
Bailly-en-Rivière (76) 16 C2
Bailly-le-Franc (10) 91 G2
Bailly-Romainvilliers (77) 59 J4
Bain-de-Bretagne (35) 103 F2
Baincthun (62) 2 B5
Bainghen (62) 2 D5
Bains (43) 220 B6
Bains-les-Bains (88) 118 B2
Bains-sur-Oust (35) 102 C3
Bainville-aux-Miroirs (54) 94 B2
Bainville-aux-Saules (88) 94 A5
Bainville-sur-Madon (54) 65 K6
Bairols (06) 261 H6
Bais (35) 79 K5
Bais (53) 81 J5
Baisieux (59) 7 F4
Baissey (52) 116 C5
Baives (59) 13 K5
Baix (07) 240 B3
Baixas (66) 310 B6
Baizieux (80) 10 C6
le Baizil (51) 61 H2

Bajamont (47) 248 C4
Bajonnette (32) 267 K4
Bajus (62) 10 C1
Balacet (09) 306 B4
Baladou (46) 233 J1
Balagny-sur-Thérain (60) 37 K4
Balaguères (09) 306 C3
Balaguier-d'Olt (12) 234 C6
Balaguier-sur-Rance (12) 271 J3
Balaiseaux (39) 155 G4
Balaives-et-Butz (08) 22 D4
Balan (01) 206 D3
Balan (08) 23 F4
Balanod (39) 172 A4
Balansun (64) 283 K1
Balanzac (17) 194 E2
Balaruc-le-Vieux (34) 293 F2
Balaruc-les-Bains (34) 292 E3
Balâtre (80) 19 G4
Balazé (35) 80 B6
Balazuc (07) 239 H6
Balbigny (42) 204 E1
Balbins (38) 206 E6
Balbronn (67) 70 C3
Baldenheim (67) 71 C5
Baldersheim (68) 97 C2
la Baleine (50) 31 F5
Baleix (64) 285 F3
Balesmes-sur-Marne (52) 116 D4
Balesta (31) 286 C5
Baleyssagues (47) 230 E4
Balgau (68) 96 E6
Balham (09) 41 G1
Balignac (82) 268 B2
Balignicourt (10) 90 E2
Bâlines (27) 56 B5
Balinghem (62) 2 D3
Baliracq-Maumusson (64) 284 E1
Baliros (64) 284 D5
Balizac (33) 229 J6
Ballainvilliers (91) 58 E6
Ballaison (74) 174 E6
Ballan-Miré (37) 127 H5
Ballancourt-sur-Essonne (91) 86 E2
Ballans (17) 196 A1
Ballay (08) 42 B2
Balledent (87) 181 G3
Ballée (53) 105 J3
Balleray (58) 151 F3
Balleroy (14) 31 K2
Ballersdorf (68) 97 A4
Balléville (88) 93 H4
Ballon (17) 177 F4
Ballon (72) 82 E6
Ballons (26) 258 C3
Ballore (71) 170 E4
Ballots (53) 104 C3
Balloy (77) 88 C3
Balma (31) 269 H6
la Balme (73) 207 K2
la Balme-de-Sillingy (74) 190 E5
la Balme-de-Thuy (74) 191 G5
la Balme-d'Épy (39) 172 A4
la Balme-les-Grottes (38) 189 H6
Balnot-la-Grange (10) 114 C3
Balnot-sur-Laignes (10) 114 D2
Balogna (2A) 316 E5
Balot (21) 114 E5
Balsac (12) 252 A2
Balschwiller (68) 97 A3
Balsièges (48) 254 A1
Baltzenheim (68) 96 E3
Balzac (16) 196 E3
Bambecque (59) 3 J3
Bambiderstroff (57) 45 J5
Ban-de-Laveline (88) 95 K4
Ban-de-Sapt (88) 95 J3
le Ban-Saint-Martin (57) 44 E5
Ban-sur-Meurthe-Clefcy (88) 95 J5
Banassac (48) 253 H2
Banca (64) 263 E5
Bancigny (02) 21 G3
Bancourt (62) 11 F5
Bandol (83) 297 G6
Baneins (01) 188 D3
Baneuil (24) 231 K2
Bangor (56) 120 B4
Banios (65) 304 E2
Banize (23) 182 E6
Bannalec (29) 99 G2
Bannans (25) 156 E4
Bannay (18) 131 K5
Bannay (51) 61 H3
Bannay (57) 45 H5
Banne (07) 255 H2
Bannegon (18) 149 K6
Bannes (46) 234 C3
Bannes (51) 61 K4
Bannes (52) 116 D3
Bannes (53) 105 J3
Banneville-la-Campagne (14) 33 F5
Banneville-sur-Ajon (14) 32 C6
Bannières (81) 270 A6
Bannoncourt (55) 64 E2
Bannost-Villegagnon (77) 60 C6
Banogne-Recouvrance (08) 21 H6
Banon (04) 258 C6
Banos (40) 265 F4
Bans (39) 155 H3
Bansat (63) 203 F6
Bantanges (71) 172 B3
Banteux (59) 11 J5

Banthelu (95) 36 E6
Bantheville (55) 42 E2
Bantigny (59) 11 J3
Bantouzelle (59) 11 J5
Bantzenheim (68) 97 D1
Banvillars (90) 139 H1
Banville (14) 32 H3
Banvou (61) 53 H5
Banyuls-dels-Aspres (66) 315 G4
Banyuls-sur-Mer (66) 315 K5
Baon (89) 114 B4
Baons-le-Comte (76) 15 G5
Bapaume (62) 11 F5
Bar (19) 216 B2
Bar-le-Duc (55) 64 B4
Bar-lès-Buzancy (08) 42 D2
Bar-sur-Aube (10) 91 G5
le Bar-sur-Loup (06) 280 E4
Bar-sur-Seine (10) 114 D1
Baracé (49) 125 J1
Baraigne (11) 289 F4
Baraize (36) 165 H4
Baralle (62) 11 H4
Baraqueville (12) 252 A4
Barastre (62) 11 G5
Baratier (05) 243 J5
Barbachen (65) 285 J2
Barbaggio (2B) 317 D5
Barbaira (11) 290 C6
Barbaise (08) 22 C4
Barbas (54) 67 G6
Barbaste (47) 247 J5
Barbâtre (85) 140 C3
Barbazan (31) 305 J4
Barbazan-Debat (65) 285 H5
Barbazan-Dessus (65) 285 J6
Barbechat (44) 123 K3
la Barben (13) 277 F5
Barbentane (13) 276 A2
Barberaz (73) 208 B4
Barberey-Saint-Sulpice (10) 90 A4
Barberier (03) 185 G2
Barbery (14) 53 K1
Barbery (60) 38 C5
Barbeville (14) 32 A3
Barbey (77) 88 B4
Barbey-Seroux (88) 95 H6
Barbezières (16) 178 E6
Barbezieux-Saint-Hilaire (16) 196 B5
Barbières (26) 222 E6
Barbirey-sur-Ouche (21) 135 H6
Barbizon (77) 87 G3
Barbonne-Fayel (51) 61 H6
Barbonville (54) 94 C1
le Barboux (25) 157 J1
Barbuise (10) 89 G1
Barby (08) 21 K6
Barby (73) 208 C4
Barc (27) 35 F6
le Barcarès (66) 310 D5
Barcelonne (26) 240 E1
Barcelonne-du-Gers (32) 265 K5
Barcelonnette (04) 260 D1
Barchain (57) 67 H4
Barcillonnette (05) 259 F1
Barcugnan (32) 286 B3
Barcus (64) 283 J5
Barcy (77) 59 K1
Bard (42) 204 C4
Bard-le-Régulier (21) 153 F2
Bard-lès-Époisses (21) 134 C3
Bard-lès-Pesmes (70) 137 G5
la Barde (17) 212 C4
Bardenac (16) 212 D2
Bardigues (82) 268 B1
le Bardon (45) 109 H5
Bardos (64) 282 E1
Bardou (24) 231 K3
Bardouville (76) 35 G2
Barèges (65) 304 C4
Bareilles (65) 305 G4
Barembach (67) 70 A5
Baren (31) 305 H4
Barentin (76) 15 J6
Barenton (50) 52 E6
Barenton-Bugny (02) 20 D5
Barenton-Cel (02) 20 D5
Barenton-sur-Serre (02) 20 D5
Barésia-sur-l'Ain (39) 173 H3
Barfleur (50) 29 G2
Bargème (83) 279 K4
Bargemon (83) 279 K5
Barges (21) 154 C1
Barges (43) 238 C2
Barges (70) 117 H4
Bargny (60) 39 F5
Barie (33) 230 B5
les Barils (27) 56 A5
Barinque (64) 284 B3
Barisey-au-Plain (54) 93 H1
Barisey-la-Côte (54) 93 H1
Barisis (02) 20 A6
Barizey (71) 153 J6
Barjac (09) 306 D2
Barjac (30) 255 K3
Barjac (48) 253 K1
Barjols (83) 278 E6
Barjon (21) 135 K1
Barjouville (28) 85 G3
Barles (04) 259 K3
Barlest (65) 285 F6
Barleux (80) 19 G2

Barlieu (18) 131 H3
Barlin (62) 5 K6
Barly (62) 10 C3
Barly (80) 10 A4
Barmainville (28) 86 A5
Barnas (07) 239 F4
Barnave (26) 241 H4
Barnay (71) 153 F2
Barneville-Carteret (50) 28 B5
Barneville-la-Bertran (14) 33 K2
Barneville-sur-Seine (27) 35 F2
la Baroche-sous-Lucé (61) 81 G1
les Baroches (54) 26 E6
Baromesnil (76) 8 C6
Baron (30) 255 J6
Baron (33) 229 K2
Baron (60) 38 D5
Baron (71) 170 D4
Baron-sur-Odon (14) 32 E5
Baronville (57) 66 E1
Barou-en-Auge (14) 54 C2
Baroville (10) 91 G6
le Barp (33) 229 F5
Barquet (27) 56 A1
Barr (67) 70 C5
Barrais-Bussolles (03) 186 B1
Barran (32) 267 G6
Barrancoueu (65) 305 F3
Barras (04) 259 H5
Barraute-Camu (64) 283 H3
Barraux (38) 208 C5
la Barre (39) 155 J1
la Barre (70) 138 B4
Barre (81) 272 B4
la Barre-de-Monts (85) 140 C4
la Barre-de-Semilly (50) 31 H3
Barre-des-Cévennes (48) 254 C4
la Barre-en-Ouche (27) 55 J2
Barrême (04) 279 H1
Barret (16) 196 A5
Barret-de-Lioure (26) 258 B4
Barret-le-Bas (05) 258 D3
Barretaine (39) 155 J5
Barrettali (2B) 317 C3
Barriac-les-Bosquets (15) 217 F4
Barro (16) 179 G5
Barrou (37) 146 A5
le Barroux (84) 257 H5
Barry (65) 285 G6
Barry-d'Islemade (82) 249 H6
Bars (24) 214 D5
Bars (32) 285 K1
Barsac (26) 241 G3
Barsac (33) 229 K5
Barst (57) 68 B3
Bart (25) 139 H2
Bartenheim (68) 97 D4
Barthe (65) 286 B4
la Barthe-de-Neste (65) 305 H1
Bartherans (25) 156 B3
les Barthes (82) 249 H6
Bartrès (65) 285 G6
Barville (27) 34 C5
Barville (61) 83 F2
Barville (88) 93 G3
Barville-en-Gâtinais (45) 111 F1
Barzan (17) 194 E5
Barzun (64) 285 F5
Barzy-en-Thiérache (02) 13 F6
Barzy-sur-Marne (02) 40 A6
Bas-en-Basset (43) 220 E2
Bas-et-Lezat (63) 185 H4
Bas-Lieu (59) 13 G4
Bas-Mauco (40) 265 G3
Bascons (40) 265 H3
Bascous (32) 266 D4
Baslieux (54) 26 D3
Baslieux-lès-Fismes (51) 40 C3
Baslieux-sous-Châtillon (51) 40 D6
Basly (14) 32 D3
Bassac (16) 196 B3
Bassan (34) 292 A3
Bassanne (33) 230 C5
Basse-Goulaine (44) 123 H4
Basse-Ham (57) 27 H4
Basse-Rentgen (57) 27 G3
la Basse-Vaivre (70) 117 K3
la Bassée (59) 6 B5
Bassemberg (67) 70 B6
Basseneville (14) 33 G4
Bassens (33) 229 H1
Bassens (73) 208 B4
Bassercles (40) 284 A1
Basses (86) 144 E3
Basseux (62) 10 D3
Bassevelle (77) 60 D2
Bassignac (15) 217 H2
Bassignac-le-Bas (19) 216 B6
Bassignac-le-Haut (19) 216 E3
Bassigney (70) 118 B4
Bassilac (24) 214 B3
Bassillon-Vauzé (64) 285 G2
Bassing (57) 67 G2
Bassoles-Aulers (02) 39 J1
Bassoncourt (52) 117 F1
Bassou (89) 113 F4
Bassoues (32) 266 E6
Bassu (51) 63 G3
Bassuet (51) 63 G4
Bassurels (48) 254 C5
Bassussarry (64) 263 D1

Bassy (74) 190 C4
Bastanès (64) 283 J3
Bastelica (2A) 320 E4
Bastelicaccia (2A) 320 C5
Bastennes (40) 264 D5
Bastia (2B) 317 E5
la Bastide (66) 314 D4
la Bastide (83) 280 A4
la Bastide-Clairence (64) 282 D2
la Bastide-de-Besplas (09) 288 A6
la Bastide-de-Bousignac (09) 308 B2
la Bastide-de-Lordat (09) 288 E6
la Bastide-de-Sérou (09) 307 G2
la Bastide-d'Engras (30) 256 B6
la Bastide-des-Jourdans (84) 277 K3
la Bastide-du-Salat (09) 306 C2
la Bastide-l'Évêque (12) 251 G3
la Bastide-Pradines (12) 272 D1
la Bastide-Puylaurent (48) 238 C5
la Bastide-Solages (12) 271 H2
la Bastide-sur-l'Hers (09) 308 B3
la Bastidonne (84) 277 K4
le Bastit (46) 233 K4
Basville (23) 201 G1
la Bataille (79) 178 D3
Bathelémont-lès-Bauzemont (54) 66 D5
Bathernay (26) 222 D3
la Bâthie (73) 209 G3
la Bâtie-des-Fonds (26) 242 A6
la Bâtie-Divisin (38) 207 J5
la Bâtie-Montgascon (38) 207 H4
la Bâtie-Montsaléon (05) 258 D1
la Bâtie-Neuve (05) 243 F5
la Bâtie-Rolland (26) 240 C5
la Bâtie-Vieille (05) 243 F5
les Bâties (70) 137 J2
Batilly (54) 44 D4
Batilly (61) 54 A5
Batilly-en-Gâtinais (45) 110 E2
Batilly-en-Puisaye (45) 131 K2
Bats (40) 265 H5
Batsère (65) 304 E1
Battenans-les-Mines (25) 138 C4
Battenans-Varin (25) 139 G5
Battenheim (68) 97 C1
Battexey (88) 94 A3
Battigny (54) 93 J2
Battrans (70) 137 G4
Batz-sur-Mer (44) 121 H5
Batzendorf (67) 69 K6
Baubigny (21) 153 J4
Baubigny (50) 28 B5
la Bauche (73) 208 A5
Baud (56) 100 D2
Baudement (51) 89 H1
Baudemont (71) 187 H1
Baudignan (40) 247 F6
Baudignécourt (55) 92 D1
Baudinard-sur-Verdon (83) 279 F4
Baudoncourt (70) 118 C5
Baudonvilliers (55) 63 K5
Baudre (50) 31 H3
Baudrecourt (52) 91 K3
Baudrecourt (57) 66 C1
Baudreix (64) 284 E5
Baudrémont (55) 64 D3
Baudres (36) 147 J3
Baudreville (28) 86 A4
Baudreville (50) 28 C6
Baudricourt (88) 93 K4
Baudrières (71) 172 B2
Bauduen (83) 279 F4
Baugé (49) 126 B2
Baugy (18) 149 K3
Baugy (60) 38 D2
Baugy (71) 186 E1
Baulay (70) 117 K5
Baule (45) 109 H5
la Baule-Escoublac (44) 121 J5
Baulme-la-Roche (21) 135 J5
Baulne (91) 86 E2
Baulne-en-Brie (02) 61 G2
Baulny (55) 42 E4
Baulon (35) 78 D6
Baulou (09) 307 H2
la Baume (74) 191 F3
la Baume-Cornillane (26) 240 C4
la Baume-de-Transit (26) 256 E2
la Baume-d'Hostun (26) 223 F5
Baume-les-Dames (25) 138 C4
Baume-les-Messieurs (39) 173 H1
Bauné (49) 125 J3
Baupte (50) 31 F1
Bauquay (14) 53 G1
Baurech (33) 229 J3
la Baussaine (35) 78 E1
Bauvin (59) 6 C5
les Baux-de-Breteuil (27) 56 A3
les Baux-de-Provence (13) 276 B4
les Baux-Sainte-Croix (27) 56 C2
Bauzemont (54) 66 D5
Bauzy (41) 129 H3
Bavans (25) 139 G2
Bavay (59) 13 F2
Bavelincourt (80) 18 C1
Bavent (14) 33 F4
Baverans (39) 155 H2
Bavilliers (90) 139 H1
Bavincourt (62) 10 D3
Bax (31) 288 A5
Bay (70) 137 H5

Bay-sur-Aube (52) 116 A5
Bayac (24) 232 A3
Bayard-sur-Marne (52) 92 A1
Bayas (33) 212 B5
Baye (29) 99 H3
Baye (51) 61 H3
Bayecourt (88) 94 D4
Bayel (88) 91 H6
Bayencourt (80) 10 D5
Bayenghem-lès-Éperlecques (62) 3 F4
Bayenghem-lès-Seninghem (62) 2 E6
Bayers (16) 179 G6
Bayet (03) 185 H2
Bayeux (14) 32 B3
Bayon (54) 94 C2
Bayon-sur-Gironde (33) 211 H5
Bayonne (64) 282 B1
Bayons (04) 259 H2
Bayonville (08) 42 C2
Bayonville-sur-Mad (54) 65 J1
Bayonvillers (80) 18 D2
Bazac (16) 212 D3
Bazaiges (36) 165 G4
Bazailles (54) 26 D4
Bazainville (78) 57 J4
Bazancourt (51) 41 G3
Bazancourt (60) 17 F6
Bazarnes (89) 133 H1
Bazas (33) 246 D1
Bazauges (17) 178 D6
Bazegney (88) 94 B4
Bazeilles (08) 23 F4
Bazeilles-sur-Othain (55) 23 K6
Bazelat (23) 165 G6
Bazemont (78) 58 A2
Bazens (47) 247 K4
Bazentin (80) 10 E6
Bazenville (14) 32 C3
Bazet (65) 285 H4
la Bazeuge (87) 181 F2
Bazian (32) 267 F5
Bazicourt (60) 38 C3
Baziège (31) 288 D2
Bazien (88) 95 F2
Bazillac (65) 285 H3
Bazincourt-sur-Epte (27) 36 E3
Bazincourt-sur-Saulx (55) 64 A5
Bazinghen (62) 2 B4
Bazinval (76) 16 E1
la Bazoche-Gouet (28) 108 B1
Bazoches (58) 133 J5
Bazoches-au-Houlme (61) 54 A4
Bazoches-en-Dunois (28) 109 H1
Bazoches-les-Gallerandes (45) 110 B1
Bazoches-les-Hautes (28) 109 K1
Bazoches-lès-Bray (77) 88 C3
Bazoches-sur-Guyonne (78) 57 K4
Bazoches-sur-Hoëne (61) 83 G1
Bazoches-sur-le-Betz (45) 112 A1
Bazoches-sur-Vesles (02) 40 B3
la Bazoge (50) 52 C5
la Bazoge (72) 106 D1
la Bazoge-Montpinçon (53) 81 G4
Bazoges-en-Paillers (85) 142 C4
Bazoges-en-Pareds (85) 160 D2
Bazoilles-et-Ménil (88) 94 A4
Bazoilles-sur-Meuse (88) 93 F4
Bazolles (58) 151 J2
Bazoncourt (57) 45 G6
la Bazoque (14) 31 K3
la Bazoque (61) 53 G4
Bazoques (27) 34 C5
Bazordan (65) 286 C5
la Bazouge-de-Chemeré (53) 105 H2
la Bazouge-des-Alleux (53) 81 G6
la Bazouge-du-Désert (35) 80 C2
Bazouges-la-Pérouse (35) 51 H6
Bazouges-sur-le-Loir (72) 106 A6
Bazugues (32) 286 A2
Bazus (31) 269 H5
Bazus-Aure (65) 305 F4
Bazus-Neste (65) 305 F2
le Béage (07) 238 E2
Béalcourt (80) 9 K4
Béalencourt (62) 9 J1
Béard (58) 151 F5
Beaubec-la-Rosière (76) 16 D5
Beaubery (71) 170 E5
Beaubray (27) 56 B3
Beaucaire (30) 275 K3
Beaucaire (32) 267 F3
Beaucamps-le-Jeune (80) 17 G3
Beaucamps-le-Vieux (80) 17 G2
Beaucamps-Ligny (59) 6 C4
Beaucé (35) 80 B4
Beaucens (65) 304 B2
le Beaucet (84) 276 E1
Beauchalot (31) 306 A1
Beauchamp (95) 58 D1
Beauchamps (50) 51 K1
Beauchamps (80) 8 D5
Beauchamps-sur-Huillard (45) 111 F3
Beauchastel (07) 240 B2
Beauchemin (52) 116 C3
Beauchêne (41) 108 B3
Beauchêne (61) 53 F5
Beauchery-Saint-Martin (77) 60 E6
Beauclair (55) 43 F1
Beaucoudray (50) 31 G5

Beaucourt (90) 139 J2
Beaucourt-en-Santerre (80) 18 D3
Beaucourt-sur-l'Ancre (80) 10 E5
Beaucourt-sur-l'Hallue (80) 18 C1
Beaucouzé (49) 125 F3
Beaucroissant (38) 223 H1
Beaudéan (65) 304 D2
Beaudignies (59) 12 D3
Beaudricourt (62) 10 B3
Beaufai (61) 55 H5
Beaufay (72) 83 F6
Beauficel (50) 52 D4
Beauficel-en-Lyons (27) 36 B2
Beaufin (38) 242 D2
Beaufort (31) 287 J2
Beaufort (34) 291 F4
Beaufort (38) 222 E1
Beaufort (39) 173 H3
Beaufort (59) 13 H3
Beaufort (73) 209 H2
Beaufort-Blavincourt (62) 10 C3
Beaufort-en-Argonne (55) 43 F1
Beaufort-en-Santerre (80) 18 E3
Beaufort-en-Vallée (49) 125 K4
Beaufort-sur-Gervanne (26) 240 E3
Beaufou (85) 141 J5
Beaufour-Druval (14) 33 H4
Beaufremont (88) 93 G5
Beaugas (47) 231 K6
Beaugeay (17) 176 E6
Beaugency (45) 109 H5
Beaugies-sous-Bois (60) 19 G5
Beaujeu (04) 260 A4
Beaujeu (69) 188 A3
Beaujeu-Saint-Vallier-
Pierrejux-et-Quitteur (70) 137 G3
Beaulandais (61) 81 H1
Beaulencourt (62) 11 F5
Beaulieu (07) 255 J2
Beaulieu (14) 31 K6
Beaulieu (15) 201 H6
Beaulieu (21) 115 H6
Beaulieu (34) 274 D5
Beaulieu (36) 164 E6
Beaulieu (38) 223 H3
Beaulieu (43) 220 C4
Beaulieu (58) 133 F6
Beaulieu (61) 55 K5
Beaulieu (63) 203 F6
Beaulieu-en-Argonne (55) 63 K1
Beaulieu-les-Fontaines (60) 19 G5
Beaulieu-lès-Loches (37) 146 D2
Beaulieu-sous-la-Roche (85) 159 G1
Beaulieu-sous-Parthenay (79) 161 K3
Beaulieu-sur-Dordogne (19) 216 B6
Beaulieu-sur-Layon (49) 125 G5
Beaulieu-sur-Loire (45) 131 J3
Beaulieu-sur-Mer (06) 281 H4
Beaulieu-sur-Oudon (53) 104 C2
Beaulieu-sur-Sonnette (16) 179 J6
Beaulon (03) 169 H3
Beaumais (14) 54 B3
Beaumarchés (32) 266 C6
Beaumat (46) 233 J4
Beaumé (02) 21 H2
la Beaume (05) 242 A5
Beauménil (88) 95 G5
Beaumerie-Saint-Martin (62) 4 C6
Beaumes-de-Venise (84) 257 G5
Beaumesnil (14) 31 J6
Beaumesnil (27) 55 K1
Beaumettes (84) 277 F3
Beaumetz (80) 9 J4
Beaumetz-lès-Aire (62) 5 G5
Beaumetz-lès-Cambrai (62) 11 G5
Beaumetz-lès-Loges (62) 10 D3
Beaumont (07) 239 F6
Beaumont (19) 216 B1
Beaumont (24) 232 A4
Beaumont (32) 266 E2
Beaumont (43) 219 G2
Beaumont (54) 65 G3
Beaumont (63) 202 D2
Beaumont (74) 191 F3
Beaumont (86) 163 G1
Beaumont (89) 113 G4
Beaumont-de-Lomagne (82) 268 C3
Beaumont-de-Pertuis (84) 278 A4
Beaumont-du-Gâtinais (77) 111 F1
Beaumont-du-Lac (87) 200 B2
Beaumont-du-Ventoux (84) 257 H4
Beaumont-en-Argonne (08) 23 G6
Beaumont-en-Auge (14) 33 J4
Beaumont-en-Beine (02) 19 J4
Beaumont-en-Cambrésis (59) 12 C5
Beaumont-en-Diois (26) 241 J5
Beaumont-en-Verdunois (55) 43 H4
Beaumont-en-Véron (37) 145 F1
Beaumont-Hague (50) 28 B2
Beaumont-Hamel (80) 10 D5
Beaumont-la-Ferrière (58) 150 E1
Beaumont-la-Ronce (37) 127 J2
Beaumont-le-Hareng (76) 16 B5
Beaumont-le-Roger (27) 34 E6
Beaumont-les-Autels (28) 84 B5
Beaumont-les-Nonains (60) 37 G3
Beaumont-lès-Randan (63) 185 J3
Beaumont-lès-Valence (26) 240 D2
Beaumont-Monteux (26) 222 C5
Beaumont-Pied-de-Boeuf (53) 105 H3
Beaumont-Pied-de-Boeuf (72) 107 F5

350

Beaumont-Sardolles (58) 151 G5
Beaumont-sur-Dême (72) 107 H6
Beaumont-sur-Grosne (71) 171 K2
Beaumont-sur-Lèze (31) 288 B3
Beaumont-sur-Oise (95) 37 J6
Beaumont-sur-Sarthe (72) 82 D5
Beaumont-sur-Vesle (51) 41 G5
Beaumont-sur-Vingeanne (21) . . 136 D3
Beaumontel (27) 34 E6
Beaumotte-Aubertans (70) 138 B3
Beaumotte-lès-Pin (70) 137 J5
Beaunay (51) 61 J3
Beaune (21) 154 A3
Beaune-d'Allier (03) 184 D1
Beaune-la-Rolande (45) 111 F2
Beaune-sur-Arzon (43) 220 B2
Beaunotte (21) 135 H1
Beaupont (01) 172 D5
Beaupouyet (24) 213 F6
Beaupréau (49) 142 D1
Beaupuy (31) 269 H6
Beaupuy (32) 268 C6
Beaupuy (47) 230 E6
Beaupuy (82) 268 D3
Beauquesne (80) 10 B5
Beaurain (59) 12 D4
Beaurains (62) 11 F3
Beaurains-lès-Noyon (60) 19 H5
Beaurainville (62) 9 G1
Beaurecueil (13) 296 E1
Beauregard (01) 188 B5
Beauregard (46) 250 D3
Beauregard-Baret (26) 222 E5
Beauregard-de-Terrasson (24) . . . 215 F4
Beauregard-et-Bassac (24) 213 K6
Beauregard-l'Évêque (63) 203 F1
Beauregard-Vendon (63) 185 F5
Beaurepaire (38) 222 D1
Beaurepaire (60) 38 B4
Beaurepaire (76) 14 B4
Beaurepaire (85) 142 C4
Beaurepaire-en-Bresse (71) 172 E2
Beaurepaire-sur-Sambre (59) . . . 13 F5
Beaurevoir (02) 11 K6
Beaurières (26) 241 K5
Beaurieux (02) 40 C2
Beaurieux (59) 13 J4
Beauronne (24) 213 G5
Beausemblant (26) 222 B3
Beausite (55) 64 B2
Beausoleil (06) 281 J3
Beaussac (24) 197 H5
Beaussais (79) 178 D1
Beaussault (76) 16 E4
Beausse (49) 124 C5
le Beausset (83) 297 H5
Beauteville (31) 288 E4
Beautheil (77) 60 B5
Beautiran (33) 229 J3
Beautor (02) 20 A5
Beautot (76) 15 K5
Beauvain (61) 53 K6
Beauvais (60) 37 H2
Beauvais-sur-Matha (17) 178 C6
Beauvais-sur-Tescou (81) 269 J2
Beauval (80) 10 A5
Beauval-en-Caux (76) 15 J4
Beauvallon (26) 240 C2
Beauvau (49) 125 K2
Beauvène (07) 239 J2
Beauvernois (71) 155 G5
Beauvezer (04) 260 C4
Beauville (31) 289 F2
Beauville (47) 248 E3
Beauvilliers (28) 85 H5
Beauvilliers (41) 108 B5
Beauvilliers (89) 134 A4
Beauvoir (50) 51 J4
Beauvoir (60) 18 B5
Beauvoir (77) 59 K6
Beauvoir (89) 112 E5
Beauvoir-de-Marc (38) 206 D5
Beauvoir-en-Lyons (76) 36 C1
Beauvoir-en-Royans (38) 223 G4
Beauvoir-sur-Mer (85) 140 D4
Beauvoir-sur-Niort (79) 178 A2
Beauvoir-Wavans (62) 9 K3
Beauvois (62) 9 K2
Beauvois-en-Cambrésis (59) 12 C4
Beauvois-en-Vermandois (02) . . . 19 J2
Beauvoisin (26) 257 J3
Beauvoisin (30) 275 G5
Beaux (43) 220 E3
Beauzac (43) 220 E3
Beauzelle (31) 269 G5
Beauziac (47) 247 F3
Bébing (57) 67 J4
Beblenheim (68) 96 B3
Bec-de-Mortagne (76) 14 D4
le Bec-Hellouin (27) 34 E4
le Bec-Thomas (27) 35 G4
Beccas (32) 285 J2
Béceleuf (79) 161 G4
Béchamps (54) 26 C6
Bécherel (35) 78 D2
Bécheresse (16) 196 D5
Béchy (57) 66 C1
Bécon-les-Granits (49) 124 E3
Bécordel-Bécourt (80) 10 E6
Bécourt (62) 2 D6
Becquigny (02) 12 C6

Becquigny (80) 18 D4
Bédarieux (34) 272 E6
Bédarrides (84) 257 F6
Beddes (18) 166 D3
Bédéchan (32) 287 F1
Bédée (35) 78 D3
Bédeille (09) 306 D1
Bédeille (64) 285 F3
Bedenac (17) 212 A4
Bédoin (84) 257 J5
Bédouès (48) 254 C3
Bedous (64) 303 F2
Béduer (46) 234 C5
Beffes (18) 150 C3
Beffia (39) 173 G3
Beffu-et-le-Morthomme (08) . . . 42 D2
Bégaar (40) 264 D3
Bégadan (33) 210 E1
Béganne (56) 102 A5
Bégard (22) 48 B4
Bègles (33) 229 H2
Begnécourt (88) 94 A5
Bégole (65) 286 A6
Bégrolles-en-Mauges (49) 142 E1
la Bégude-de-Mazenc (26) 240 D6
Bègues (03) 185 F3
Béguey (33) 229 K4
Béguios (64) 283 F5
Béhagnies (62) 11 F4
Béhasque-Lapiste (64) 283 G3
Béhen (80) 9 F5
Béhencourt (80) 18 C1
Béhéricourt (60) 19 H6
Behonne (55) 64 B4
Béhorléguy (64) 283 F6
Béhoust (78) 57 J4
Behren-lès-Forbach (57) 68 C2
Béhuard (49) 125 F4
Beignon (56) 78 B6
Beillé (72) 107 G1
Beine (89) 113 H5
Beine-Nauroy (51) 41 G4
Beinheim (67) 25 D3
Beire-le-Châtel (21) 136 C4
Beire-le-Fort (21) 136 C6
Beissat (23) 201 F2
Bélâbre (36) 164 D4
Belan-sur-Ource (21) 115 G3
Bélarga (34) 292 D1
Bélaye (46) 249 H1
Belberaud (31) 288 D2
Belbèse (82) 268 C4
Belbeuf (76) 35 J2
Belbèze-de-Lauragais (31) 288 D3
Belbèze-en-Comminges (31) 306 C1
Belcaire (11) 308 C5
Belcastel (12) 251 J2
Belcastel (81) 270 A6
Belcastel-et-Buc (11) 309 G2
Belcodène (13) 296 E2
Bélesta (09) 308 B4
Bélesta (66) 309 J6
Bélesta-en-Lauragais (31) 289 F3
Beleymas (24) 213 J6
Belfahy (70) 119 G4
Belfays (25) 139 J5
Belflou (11) 289 F4
Belfonds (61) 54 D6
Belfort (90) 119 H6
Belfort-du-Quercy (46) 250 B4
Belfort-sur-Rebenty (11) 308 D5
Belgeard (53) 81 G5
Belgentier (83) 297 J4
Belgodère (2B) 318 D2
Belhade (40) 245 J2
Belhomert-Guéhouville (28) 84 C2
le Bélieu (25) 157 H1
Béligneux (01) 189 F6
Belin-Béliet (33) 228 E6
Bélis (40) 246 A6
Bellac (87) 181 F3
Bellaffaire (04) 259 J1
Bellaing (59) 12 C2
Bellancourt (80) 9 G5
Bellange (57) 66 E2
Bellavilliers (61) 83 G3
le Bellay-en-Vexin (95) 37 F5
Belle-Église (60) 37 J5
Belle-et-Houllefort (62) 2 C5
Belle-Isle-en-Terre (22) 48 A5
Belleau (02) 39 J6
Belleau (54) 66 A3
Bellebat (33) 230 A3
Bellebrune (62) 2 C5
Bellechassagne (19) 200 E4
Bellechaume (89) 113 G2
Bellecombe (39) 173 K6
Bellecombe-en-Bauges (73) 208 D2
Bellecombe-Tarendol (26) 257 K2
Bellefond (21) 136 A4
Bellefonds (86) 163 H6
Bellefontaine (39) 174 B3
Bellefontaine (50) 52 D5
Bellefontaine (88) 118 D2
Bellefontaine (95) 38 A6
Bellefosse (67) 70 A6
Bellegarde (30) 275 J4
Bellegarde (32) 286 D3
Bellegarde (45) 111 F3
Bellegarde (81) 271 F2

Bellegarde-du-Razès (11) 308 D1
Bellegarde-en-Diois (26) 241 H5
Bellegarde-en-Forez (42) 205 F3
Bellegarde-en-Marche (23) 183 H5
Bellegarde-Poussieu (38) 222 C1
Bellegarde-Sainte-Marie (31) . . . 268 D5
Bellegarde-sur-Valserine (01) . . . 190 C3
Belleherbe (25) 139 G5
Bellemagny (68) 119 K5
Bellême (61) 83 H4
Bellenaves (03) 185 F2
Bellencombre (76) 16 B4
Belleneuve (21) 136 C5
Bellenglise (02) 19 K1
Bellengreville (14) 33 F5
Bellengreville (76) 16 B2
Bellenod-sur-Seine (21) 115 G6
Bellenot-sous-Pouilly (21) 135 F6
Bellentre (73) 193 A3
Belleray (55) 43 H5
Bellerive-sur-Allier (03) 185 J3
Belleroche (42) 187 J3
Belles-Forêts (57) 67 H3
Belleserre (81) 289 J2
Bellesserre (31) 268 D4
Belleu (02) 39 J3
Belleuse (80) 17 K4
Bellevaux (74) 191 K1
Bellevesvre (71) 155 F5
Belleville (54) 65 K3
Belleville (69) 188 B3
Belleville (79) 177 K3
Belleville-en-Caux (76) 15 J4
Belleville-et-Châtillon-sur-Bar (08) . . . 42 C1
Belleville-sur-Loire (18) 131 K3
Belleville-sur-Mer (76) 16 A1
Belleville-sur-Meuse (55) 43 H5
Belleville-sur-Vie (85) 141 K6
Bellevue-la-Montagne (43) 220 B3
Belley (01) 207 K2
Belleydoux (01) 190 B1
Bellicourt (02) 19 K1
la Bellière (61) 54 C6
la Bellière (76) 16 E5
Bellignat (01) 190 A1
Belligné (44) 124 C3
Bellignies (59) 13 F2
la Belliole (89) 112 B1
Belloc (09) 308 B2
Belloc-Saint-Clamens (32) 286 B2
Bellocq (64) 283 H1
Bellon (16) 212 E2
Bellonne (62) 11 H2
Bellot (77) 60 D3
Bellou (14) 54 C4
Bellou-en-Houlme (61) 53 J5
Bellou-le-Trichard (61) 83 H5
Bellou-sur-Huisne (61) 83 H3
Belloy (60) 18 E6
Belloy-en-France (95) 37 K6
Belloy-en-Santerre (80) 19 F2
Belloy-Saint-Léonard (80) 17 H2
Belloy-sur-Somme (80) 17 K1
Belluire (17) 195 G4
Belmesnil (76) 15 K3
Belmont (25) 138 D6
Belmont (32) 266 E5
Belmont (38) 207 G5
Belmont (39) 155 H3
Belmont (52) 117 F6
Belmont (67) 70 A5
Belmont (70) 118 E4
Belmont-Bretenoux (46) 234 C2
Belmont-d'Azergues (69) 188 B6
Belmont-de-la-Loire (42) 187 H3
Belmont-lès-Darney (88) 117 K1
Belmont-Luthézieu (01) 190 A6
Belmont-Sainte-Foi (46) 250 C3
Belmont-sur-Buttant (88) 95 G5
Belmont-sur-Rance (12) 272 A4
Belmont-sur-Vair (88) 93 J5
Belmont-Tramonet (73) 207 K4
Belmontet (46) 249 G2
Belonchamp (70) 119 F5
Belpech (11) 288 E6
Belrain (55) 64 C3
Belrupt (88) 118 A1
Belrupt-en-Verdunois (55) 43 J5
Bélus (40) 264 A6
Belval (08) 22 C3
Belval (50) 30 E4
Belval (88) 95 J2
Belval-Bois-des-Dames (08) 42 E1
Belval-en-Argonne (51) 63 K2
Belval-sous-Châtillon (51) 40 D3
Belvédère (06) 311 A3
Belvédère-Campomoro (2A) 322 C3
Belverne (70) 119 F6
Belvès (24) 232 D3
Belvès-de-Castillon (33) 230 C1
Belvèze (82) 249 G3
Belvèze-du-Razès (11) 308 D1
Belvézet (30) 255 K6
Belvézet (48) 238 B6
Belvianes-et-Cavirac (11) 308 E4
Belvis (11) 308 D1
Belvoir (25) 139 F5
Belz (56) 100 B5
Bémécourt (27) 56 A3
Bénac (09) 307 H3
Bénac (65) 285 G6
Benagues (09) 307 J1

Benais (37) 126 D6
Bénaix (09) 308 B4
Bénaménil (54) 67 F6
Bénarville (76) 14 E4
Benassay (86) 162 C3
Benay (02) 20 A3
Benayes (19) 199 H5
Bendejun (06) 281 G2
Bendorf (68) 97 C5
Bénéjacq (64) 284 E5
Benerville-sur-Mer (14) 33 H3
Bénesse-lès-Dax (40) 264 B5
Bénesse-Maremne (40) 262 C5
Benest (16) 179 K4
Bénestroff (57) 67 F2
Bénesville (76) 15 H3
Benet (85) 161 F5
Béneuvre (21) 115 K6
Bénévent-et-Charbillac (05) 242 C1
Bénévent-l'Abbaye (23) 182 B3
Beney-en-Woëvre (55) 65 G1
Benfeld (67) 70 E6
Bengy-sur-Craon (18) 150 A4
Bénifontaine (62) 6 D6
Béning-lès-Saint-Avold (57) 68 B2
la Bénisson-Dieu (42) 186 E3
Bénivay-Ollon (26) 257 J3
Bennecourt (78) 57 H1
Bennetot (76) 14 E4
Benney (54) 94 B1
Bennwihr (68) 96 B3
Bénodet (29) 98 C3
Benoisey (21) 134 E2
Benoîtville (50) 28 B3
Benon (17) 177 G2
Bénonces (01) 207 G1
Bénouville (14) 33 F4
Bénouville (76) 14 C4
Benque (31) 287 G6
Benqué (65) 304 E1
Benquet (40) 265 G3
Bentayou-Sérée (64) 285 G3
Benque-Dessous-et-Dessus (31) . . . 305 H5
Béon (01) 190 B6
Béon (89) 112 D3
Béost (64) 303 H2
Bérat (31) 287 J3
Béraut (32) 267 G2
Berbérust-Lias (65) 304 B2
Berbezit (43) 219 K2
Berbiguières (24) 232 D2
Bercenay-en-Othe (10) 89 K6
Berche (25) 139 G3
Berchères-les-Pierres (28) 85 G4
Berchères-Saint-Germain (28) . . . 85 G2
Berchères-sur-Vesgre (28) 57 G4
Berck (62) 8 E1
Bercloux (17) 195 H1
Berd'huis (61) 83 K4
Berdoues (32) 286 B2
Berentzwiller (68) 97 C4
Bérengeville-la-Campagne (27) . . . 35 H6
Bérénx (64) 283 H1
Béréziat (01) 172 B6
Berfay (72) 107 K3
Berg (67) 67 K2
Berg-sur-Moselle (57) 27 H1
Berganty (46) 250 C1
Bergbieten (67) 70 C3
Bergerac (24) 231 H2
Bergères (10) 91 G6
Bergères-lès-Vertus (51) 62 A3
Bergères-sous-Montmirail (51) . . . 61 G3
Bergesserin (71) 171 G5
Bergheim (68) 71 A4
Bergholtz (68) 96 B6
Bergholtzzell (68) 96 B6
Bergicourt (80) 17 J4
Bergnicourt (08) 41 H2
Bergonne (63) 202 E5
Bergouey (40) 264 E5
Bergouey-Viellenave (64) 283 F2
Bergueneuse (62) 5 G6
Bergues (59) 3 H2
Bergues-sur-Sambre (02) 12 E6
Berhet (22) 48 B3
Bérig-Vintrange (57) 67 F1
Bérigny (50) 31 J3
Berjou (61) 53 H3
Berlaimont (59) 13 F4
Berlancourt (02) 20 E3
Berlancourt (60) 19 H5
Berlats (81) 271 J5
Berlencourt-le-Cauroy (62) 10 B3
Berles-au-Bois (62) 10 E2
Berles-Monchel (62) 10 C2
la Berlière (08) 23 F6
Berling (57) 69 F4
Berlise (02) 21 H5
Berlou (34) 291 H2
Bermerain (59) 12 C3
Berméricourt (51) 40 E3
Bermeries (59) 13 F3
Bermering (57) 67 F1
Bermesnil (80) 17 F2
Bermicourt (62) 9 K1
Bermont (90) 139 H1

Bermonville (76) 15 F5
Bernac (16) 179 G4
Bernac (81) 270 C2
Bernac-Debat (65) 285 H6
Bernac-Dessus (65) 285 H6
la Benâte (17) 177 J4
Bernadets (64) 284 D3
Bernadets-Debat (65) 286 A3
Bernadets-Dessus (65) 285 K5
le Bernard (85) 159 H4
la Bernardière (85) 123 K6
Bernardswiller (67) 70 C5
Bernâtre (80) 9 J4
Bernaville (80) 9 K5
Bernay (27) 34 D6
Bernay (72) 106 D1
Bernay-en-Ponthieu (80) 9 F3
Bernay-Saint-Martin (17) 177 J4
Bernay-Vilbert (77) 60 A6
Berné (56) 75 K6
Bernécourt (54) 65 H3
Bernède (32) 265 K5
la Bernerie-en-Retz (44) 122 C5
Bernes (80) 19 J2
Bernes-sur-Oise (95) 37 J5
Bernesq (14) 31 J1
Berneuil (16) 212 C1
Berneuil (17) 195 G3
Berneuil (80) 9 K5
Berneuil (87) 181 F4
Berneuil-en-Bray (60) 37 G3
Berneuil-sur-Aisne (60) 39 F2
Berneval-le-Grand (76) 16 A1
Berneville (62) 10 E3
Bernex (74) 175 H5
Bernienville (27) 35 H6
Bernières (76) 14 E5
Bernières-d'Ailly (14) 54 B2
Bernières-le-Patry (14) 53 F3
Bernières-sur-Mer (14) 32 D3
Bernières-sur-Seine (27) 36 A4
Bernieulles (62) 4 C5
Bernin (38) 224 C2
Bernis (30) 275 G4
Bernolsheim (67) 70 E1
Bernon (10) 114 A3
Bernos-Beaulac (33) 246 C2
Bernot (02) 20 C2
Bernouil (89) 113 K4
Bernouville (27) 36 D4
Bernwiller (68) 97 B3
Berny-en-Santerre (80) 19 F2
Berny-Rivière (02) 39 G2
Bérou-la-Mulotière (28) 56 C5
Berrac (32) 267 H1
Berre-les-Alpes (06) 281 H2
Berre-l'Étang (13) 296 A2
Berriac (11) 290 B5
Berrias-et-Casteljau (07) 255 H2
Berric (56) 101 K5
Berrie (86) 144 C3
Berrien (29) 75 G1
Berrieux (02) 40 D1
Berrogain-Laruns (64) 283 H4
Berru (51) 41 G4
Berruyer (68) 97 B1
Berry-au-Bac (02) 40 D2
Berry-Bouy (18) 149 F2
le Bersac (05) 258 D1
Bersac-sur-Rivalier (87) 181 J4
Bersaillin (39) 155 H5
Bersée (59) 6 E6
Bersillies (59) 13 H2
Berson (33) 211 H4
Berstett (67) 70 E2
Bersteim (67) 69 K6
Bert (03) 186 B1
Bertangles (80) 18 B1
Bertaucourt-Epourdon (02) 20 B5
Berteaucourt-les-Dames (80) . . . 9 K6
Berteaucourt-lès-Thennes (80) . . . 18 C3
Bertheauville (76) 15 F3
Berthecourt (60) 37 J3
Berthegon (86) 145 F5
Berthelange (25) 155 K1
Berthelming (57) 67 J3
Berthen (59) 6 A2
Berthenay (37) 127 G5
Berthenicourt (02) 20 B3
Berthenonville (27) 36 D5
la Berthenoux (36) 166 C2
Berthez (33) 230 B6
Bertholène (12) 252 D2
Berthouville (27) 34 D5
Bertignat (63) 203 K4
Bertignolles (10) 115 F1
Bertincourt (62) 11 G5
Bertoncourt (08) 22 A6
Bertrambois (54) 67 J5
Bertrancourt (80) 10 C5
Bertrange (57) 27 G5
Bertre (81) 270 C6
Bertren (65) 305 J2
Bertreville (76) 15 F3
Bertreville-Saint-Ouen (76) 15 K3
Bertric-Burée (24) 213 G2
Bertrichamps (54) 95 G2
Bertricourt (02) 40 E2
Bertrimont (76) 15 J5
Bertrimoutier (88) 95 J4
Bertry (59) 12 C5
Béru (89) 113 K5

Béruges (86) 162 D3
Bérulle (10) 89 G6
Bérus (72) 82 C3
Berville (76) 15 H4
Berville (95) 37 G5
Berville-en-Roumois (27) 35 F3
Berville-la-Campagne (27) . . . 56 B1
Berville-sur-Mer (27) 34 B2
Berville-sur-Seine (76) 35 G1
Bervilier-en-Moselle (57) 45 K3
Berzé-la-Ville (71) 171 H6
Berzé-le-Châtel (71) 171 H5
Berzème (07) 239 K4
Berzieux (51) 42 C5
Berzy-le-Sec (02) 39 J3
la Besace (08) 23 F6
Besain (39) 155 K6
Besançon (25) 138 A6
Bésayes (26) 222 E6
Bescat (64) 284 C6
Bésignan (26) 257 K3
Bésingrand (64) 284 B3
Beslon (50) 52 B3
Besmé (02) 19 J6
Besmont (02) 21 H2
Besnans (70) 138 C3
Besné (44) 122 B1
Besneville (50) 28 C6
Besny-et-Loizy (02) 20 C5
Bessac (16) 196 C6
Bessais-le-Fromental (18) . . 167 J1
Bessamorel (43) 220 E4
Bessan (34) 292 C4
Bessancourt (95) 58 D1
Bessans (73) 226 D1
Bessas (07) 255 J3
le Bessat (42) 221 J1
Bessay (85) 160 A3
Bessay-sur-Allier (03) 168 E5
Besse (15) 217 G5
Bessé (16) 179 F5
Besse (24) 232 E4
Besse (38) 225 F4
Besse-et-Saint-Anastaise (63) . . 202 B5
Bessé-sur-Braye (72) 107 K5
Besse-sur-Issole (83) 298 A3
Bessède-de-Sault (11) 308 D1
Bessèges (30) 255 H3
Bessenay (69) 205 H2
Bessens (82) 260 C3
Besset (09) 308 A1
Bessey (42) 222 A1
Bessey-en-Chaume (21) . . . 153 K2
Bessey-la-Cour (21) 153 J2
Bessey-lès-Cîteaux (21) . . . 154 D1
la Besseyre-Saint-Mary (43) . . 219 H6
Bessières (31) 269 J4
Bessines (79) 161 G6
Bessines-sur-Gartempe (87) . . 181 J3
Bessins (38) 223 F3
Besson (03) 168 D5
Bessoncourt (90) 119 J6
Bessonies (46) 234 E3
les Bessons (48) 237 F3
Bessuéjouls (12) 236 A6
Bessy (10) 90 A1
Bessy-sur-Cure (89) 133 H2
Bestiac (09) 308 A5
Bétaille (46) 234 A1
Betaucourt (70) 117 J4
Betbèze (65) 286 C4
Betbezer-d'Armagnac (40) . . 266 A1
Betcave-Aguin (32) 286 E2
Betchat (09) 306 C1
Bétête (23) 166 C6
Béthancourt-en-Valois (60) . . 38 E4
Béthancourt-en-Vaux (02) . . . 19 J5
Béthelainville (55) 43 G5
Béthemont-la-Forêt (95) 58 D1
Béthencourt (59) 12 C4
Béthencourt-sur-Mer (80) . . . 8 D5
Béthencourt-sur-Somme (80) . . 19 G3
Bétheniville (51) 41 J3
Bétheny (51) 41 F4
Béthincourt (55) 43 G4
Béthines (86) 164 B4
Béthisy-Saint-Martin (60) . . . 38 D4
Béthisy-Saint-Pierre (60) . . . 38 D4
Bethmale (09) 306 C4
Bethon (51) 89 G1
Béthon (72) 82 D4
Béthoncourt (25) 139 H2
Béthonsart (62) 10 C1
Béthonvilliers (28) 84 B6
Béthonvilliers (90) 119 J6
Béthune (62) 6 A5
Bétignicourt (10) 90 E3
Beton-Bazoches (77) 60 D5
Betoncourt-lès-Brotte (70) . . 118 C5
Betoncourt-Saint-Pancras (70) . . 118 B3
Betoncourt-sur-Mance (70) . . 117 H4
Bétous (32) 266 C3
Betplan (65) 285 J3
Betpouey (65) 304 C4
Betpouy (65) 286 B4
Bétracq (64) 285 G1
Betschdorf (67) 25 B3
Bettainvillers (54) 26 E5
Bettancourt-la-Ferrée (52) . . . 63 K6
Bettancourt-la-Longue (51) . . 63 J3
Bettange (57) 27 K5
Bettant (01) 189 H5

Bettborn (57) 67 J3
Bettegney-Saint-Brice (88) . . 94 C4
Bettelainville (57) 27 J6
Bettembos (80) 17 G3
Bettencourt-Rivière (80) 9 H6
Bettencourt-Saint-Ouen (80) . . 9 J6
Bettendorf (68) 97 B4
Bettes (65) 304 D1
Betteville (76) 15 G6
Bettignies (59) 13 H2
Betting-lès-Saint-Avold (57) . . 68 B2
Bettlach (68) 97 D5
Betton (35) 79 G3
Betton-Bettonet (73) 208 E4
Bettoncourt (88) 94 A3
Bettrechies (59) 13 F2
Bettviller (57) 69 H3
Bettwiller (67) 67 K2
Betz (60) 39 F5
Betz-le-Château (37) 146 C4
Beugin (62) 10 C1
Beugnâtre (62) 11 F5
Beugneux (02) 39 K4
Beugnies (59) 13 H4
le Beugnon (79) 161 G3
Beugnon (89) 113 J2
Beugny (62) 11 G5
Beuil (06) 261 G5
le Beulay (88) 95 K3
Beulotte-Saint-Laurent (70) . . 119 F3
Beure (25) 137 K6
Beurey (10) 90 E6
Beurey-Bauguay (21) 134 E6
Beurey-sur-Saulx (55) 63 K4
Beurières (63) 204 A6
Beurizot (21) 135 F5
Beurlay (17) 177 G6
Beurville (52) 91 H4
Beussent (62) 4 C5
Beuste (64) 284 E5
Beutal (25) 139 F3
Beutin (62) 4 B6
Beuvardes (02) 40 A5
Beuveille (54) 26 C3
Beuvezin (54) 93 J3
Beuvillers (14) 33 K5
Beuvillers (54) 26 E4
Beuvrages (59) 12 D1
Beuvraignes (80) 19 F5
Beuvrequen (62) 2 B4
Beuvrigny (50) 31 J5
Beuvron (58) 133 F5
Beuvron-en-Auge (14) 33 H5
Beuvry (62) 6 A5
Beuvry-la-Forêt (59) 7 F6
Beux (57) 66 B1
Beuxes (86) 145 F2
Beuzec-Cap-Sizun (29) 73 C2
Beuzeville (27) 34 B3
Beuzeville-au-Plain (50) 29 F5
Beuzeville-la-Bastille (50) . . . 29 F6
Beuzeville-la-Grenier (76) . . . 14 D5
Beuzeville-la-Guérard (76) . . 15 F4
Beuzevillette (76) 14 E6
Bévenais (38) 207 G6
Beveuge (70) 138 E2
Béville-le-Comte (28) 85 J3
Bévillers (59) 12 C4
Bévons (04) 259 F4
Bévy (21) 154 A1
Bey (01) 188 C2
Bey (71) 154 B6
Bey-sur-Seille (54) 66 C3
Beychac-et-Caillau (33) 229 K1
Beylongue (40) 264 D2
Beynac (87) 198 E2
Beynac-et-Cazenac (24) . . . 232 E2
Beynat (19) 216 A4
Beynes (04) 259 J6
Beynes (78) 58 A3
Beynost (01) 206 C1
Beyrède-Jumet (65) 305 F3
Beyren-lès-Sierck (57) 27 H3
Beyrie-en-Béarn (64) 284 C3
Beyrie-sur-Joyeuse (64) . . . 283 F4
Beyries (40) 265 F6
Beyssac (19) 215 H1
Beyssenac (19) 215 G1
le Bez (81) 271 H6
Bez-et-Esparon (30) 273 J2
Bézac (09) 288 D6
Bezalles (77) 60 D6
Bézancourt (76) 36 C2
Bezange-la-Grande (54) . . . 66 D4
Bezange-la-Petite (57) 66 E4
Bezannes (51) 40 E4
Bézaudun-les-Alpes (06) . . . 280 E2
Bézaudun-sur-Bîne (26) . . . 241 F5
Bezaumont (54) 65 H4
Bèze (21) 136 C3
Bézenac (24) 232 E2
Bézenet (03) 184 C1
Bézéril (32) 287 F1
Béziers (34) 292 A4
Bezinghem (62) 4 C4
Bezins-Garraux (31) 305 J3
la Bezole (11) 308 D2
Bezolles (32) 267 F3
Bezons (95) 58 D3
Bezonvaux (55) 26 A6
Bezouce (30) 275 J3
Bézouotte (21) 136 D4

Bézu-la-Forêt (27) 36 C2
Bézu-le-Guéry (02) 60 C1
Bézu-Saint-Éloi (27) 36 D4
Bézu-Saint-Germain (02) . . . 39 K6
Bézues-Bajon (32) 286 D3
Biache-Saint-Vaast (62) 11 G2
Biaches (80) 19 G1
Bians-les-Usiers (25) 156 E3
Biard (86) 162 E3
Biarne (39) 155 G1
Biarre (80) 19 G4
Biarritz (64) 282 A1
Biarrotte (40) 262 D6
Biars-sur-Cère (46) 234 B1
Bias (40) 244 C4
Bias (47) 248 C2
Biaudos (40) 262 C6
Bibiche (57) 27 K4
Biblisheim (67) 25 A3
Bibost (69) 205 H1
Bichancourt (02) 19 K6
Biches (58) 151 J4
Bickenholtz (57) 67 K3
Bicqueley (54) 65 H6
Bidache (64) 283 F1
Bidarray (64) 263 E3
Bidart (64) 263 C1
Bidestroff (57) 67 G2
Biding (57) 68 B3
Bidon (07) 256 B2
Bidos (64) 284 A5
Biécourt (88) 93 J4
Biederthal (68) 97 D6
Bief (25) 139 H4
Bief-des-Maisons (39) 174 B1
Bief-du-Fourg (39) 156 C5
Biefmorin (39) 155 H4
Biefvillers-lès-Bapaume (62) . . 11 F5
Bielle (64) 284 A5
Biencourt (80) 17 F1
Biencourt-sur-Orge (55) 92 C1
Bienville (60) 38 E2
Bienville-la-Petite (54) 66 D5
Bienvillers-au-Bois (62) 10 D4
Biermes (08) 41 J1
Biermont (60) 18 E6
Bierné (53) 105 C5
Bierne (59) 3 H2
Bierre-lès-Semur (21) 134 D4
Bierry-les-Belles-Fontaines (89) . . 134 C2
Biert (09) 307 F4
Bierville (76) 16 B6
Biesheim (68) 96 E4
Biesles (52) 116 C1
Bietlenheim (67) 25 A5
Bieujac (33) 230 B6
Bieuxy (02) 39 H2
Bieuzy (56) 100 D1
Biéville (50) 31 K4
Biéville-Beuville (14) 32 E4
Biéville-Quétiéville (14) 33 H6
Bièvres (02) 40 C1
Bièvres (08) 23 J6
Bièvres (91) 58 D5
Biffontaine (88) 95 G5
Biganos (33) 228 D4
Bignac (16) 196 D2
Bignan (56) 101 F2
Bignay (17) 177 J5
la Bigne (14) 53 F1
Bignicourt (08) 41 J2
Bignicourt-sur-Marne (51) . . . 63 F5
Bignicourt-sur-Saulx (51) . . . 63 H4
le Bignon (44) 123 H5
le Bignon-du-Maine (53) . . . 105 G3
le Bignon-Mirabeau (45) . . . 111 K1
Bignoux (86) 163 G3
Bigorno (2B) 319 G3
la Bigottière (53) 80 E5
le Bizot (25) 157 H1
les Bizots (71) 170 E1
Bizou (61) 83 K2
Bizous (65) 305 G1
Blacé (69) 188 A4
Blacourt (60) 36 E2
Blacqueville (76) 15 H6
Blacy (51) 63 F5
Blacy (89) 134 A2
Blaesheim (67) 70 E4
Blagnac (31) 269 G6
Blagny (08) 23 H5
Blagny-sur-Vingeanne (21) . . 136 D4
Blaignac (33) 230 C6
Blaignan (33) 210 E1
Blain (44) 102 E6
Blaincourt-lès-Précy (60) . . . 37 K5
Blaincourt-sur-Aube (10) . . . 90 E3
Blainville-Crevon (76) 35 K1
Blainville-sur-l'Eau (54) 66 C6
Blainville-sur-Mer (50) 30 C4
Blainville-sur-Orne (14) 32 E4
Blairville (62) 10 E3
Blaise-sous-Arzillières (51) . . 63 H5
Blaison-Gohier (49) 125 J4
Blaisy (52) 91 K6
Blaisy-Bas (21) 135 H5
Blaisy-Haut (21) 135 H5
Blajan (31) 286 D5
Blamont (25) 139 H4
Blâmont (54) 67 G6
Blan (81) 289 H2
le Blanc (36) 164 C3
le Blanc-Mesnil (93) 59 F4

Billy-sur-Ourcq (02) 39 J5
Biltzheim (68) 96 C5
Bilwisheim (67) 70 E1
Bimont (62) 4 D5
Binarville (51) 42 D4
Binas (41) 100 G4
Bindernheim (67) 71 C5
Binges (21) 136 C5
Binic (22) 49 F5
Bining (57) 69 F3
Biniville (50) 28 E5
Binos (31) 305 H3
Binson-et-Orquigny (51) . . . 40 D6
Bio (46) 234 B3
Biol (38) 207 G5
la Biolle (73) 208 B1
Biollet (63) 184 B5
Bion (50) 52 D6
Bioncourt (57) 66 C3
Bionville (54) 95 J1
Bionville-sur-Nied (57) 45 H5
Biot (06) 281 F5
le Biot (74) 175 G6
Bioule (82) 250 B6
Bioussac (16) 179 H4
Biozat (03) 185 H4
Birac (16) 196 C4
Birac (33) 246 D1
Birac-sur-Trec (47) 247 H1
Biran (32) 267 G5
Biras (24) 213 K2
Biriatou (64) 263 A2
Birieux (01) 188 E5
Birkenwald (67) 70 B2
Biron (17) 195 H4
Biron (24) 232 B5
Biron (64) 283 K2
Biscarrosse (40) 244 D1
Bischheim (67) 25 A6
Bischholtz (67) 69 J5
Bischoffsheim (67) 70 D4
Bischwihr (68) 96 C4
Bischwiller (67) 25 B4
Bisel (68) 97 B5
Bisinchi (2B) 319 H3
Bislée (55) 64 E3
Bissert (67) 67 J1
Bisseuil (51) 62 A1
Bissey-la-Côte (21) 115 H3
Bissey-la-Pierre (21) 114 E4
Bissey-sous-Cruchaud (71) . . 171 H1
Bissezeele (59) 3 H3
Bissières (14) 33 G6
Bissy-la-Mâconnaise (71) . . . 171 J4
Bissy-sous-Uxelles (71) 171 H3
Bissy-sur-Fley (71) 171 G2
Bisten-en-Lorraine (57) 45 J4
Bistroff (57) 67 F1
Bitche (57) 69 G3
Bitry (58) 132 B3
Bitry (60) 39 G2
Bitschhoffen (67) 69 J5
Bitschwiller-lès-Thann (68) . . 119 K4
Bivès (32) 268 A3
Biviers (38) 224 B2
Biville (50) 28 B2
Biville-la-Baignarde (76) 15 K4
Biville-la-Rivière (76) 15 J3
Biville-sur-Mer (76) 16 B1
Bivilliers (61) 83 J1
Bizanet (11) 291 G6
Bizanos (64) 284 D4
Bize (52) 117 F4
Bize (65) 305 G2
Bize-Minervois (11) 291 G4
Bizeneuille (03) 167 J3
Biziat (01) 188 D2
Bizonnes (38) 207 G5

Blancafort (18) 131 G3
Blancey (21) 134 E5
Blancfossé (60) 17 K5
Blanche-Église (57) 67 F3
Blanchefosse-et-Bay (08) . . . 21 J3
Blancherupt (67) 70 A5
Blandainville (28) 84 E4
Blandas (30) 273 J2
Blandin (38) 207 G5
Blandouet (53) 105 J2
Blandy (77) 87 J1
Blandy (91) 86 D4
Blangerval-Blangermont (62) . . 9 K2
Blangy-le-Château (14) 34 A4
Blangy-sous-Poix (80) 17 J3
Blangy-sur-Bresle (76) 16 E1
Blangy-sur-Ternoise (62) . . . 9 K1
Blangy-Tronville (80) 18 C2
Blannay (89) 133 J3
Blanot (21) 152 E1
Blanot (71) 171 J4
Blanquefort (32) 268 A5
Blanquefort (33) 229 G1
Blanquefort-sur-Briolance (47) . . 232 C5
Blanzac (43) 220 B4
Blanzac (87) 181 F3
Blanzac-lès-Matha (17) 178 B6
Blanzac-Porcheresse (16) . . 196 C5
Blanzaguet-Saint-Cybard (16) . . 197 F6
Blanzat (63) 202 D1
Blanzay (86) 179 H2
Blanzay-sur-Boutonne (17) . . 178 A4
Blanzée (55) 43 K5
Blanzy (71) 170 E2
Blanzy-la-Salonnaise (08) . . 41 H4
Blanzy-lès-Fismes (02) 40 B3
Blargies (60) 17 F5
Blarians (25) 138 B4
Blaringhem (59) 3 H6
Blars (46) 234 A6
Blaru (78) 57 G1
Blasimon (33) 230 C3
Blaslay (86) 162 E1
Blassac (43) 219 H4
Blaudeix (23) 183 F2
Blausasc (06) 281 H2
Blauvac (84) 257 J6
Blauzac (30) 275 G2
Blavignac (48) 237 G2
Blavozy (43) 220 D5
Blay (14) 31 K1
Blaye (33) 211 G4
Blaye-les-Mines (81) 270 D1
Blaymont (47) 248 E3
Blaziert (32) 267 G2
Blécourt (52) 92 A3
Blécourt (59) 11 J3
Bleigny-le-Carreau (89) 113 H5
Blémerey (54) 67 F6
Blémerey (88) 93 K3
Blendecques (62) 3 G5
Bléneau (89) 132 A1
Blennes (77) 88 B5
Blénod-lès-Pont-à-Mousson (54) . . 65 K2
Blénod-lès-Toul (54) 65 H6
Bléquin (62) 2 E6
Blérancourt (02) 39 G1
Bléré (37) 128 B5
Bléruais (35) 78 C4
Blésignac (33) 230 A3
Blesle (43) 218 E2
Blesme (51) 63 H5
Blesmes (02) 60 C1
Blessac (23) 183 F5
Blessonville (52) 115 K2
Blessy (62) 5 H4
Blet (18) 149 K5
Bletterans (39) 173 F1
Bleurville (88) 117 J1
Bleury (28) 85 J2
Blevaincourt (88) 93 G6
Blèves (72) 83 F2
le Bleymard (48) 254 D1
Blicourt (60) 17 J6
Blienschwiller (67) 70 C6
Blies-Ebersing (57) 68 E2
Blies-Guersviller (57) 68 D2
Bliesbruck (57) 68 E2
Blieux (04) 279 H2
Blignicourt (10) 91 F2
Bligny (10) 91 G6
Bligny (51) 40 D5
Bligny-le-Sec (21) 135 H4
Bligny-lès-Beaune (21) 154 A4
Bligny-sur-Ouche (21) 153 J2
Blincourt (60) 38 C3
Blingel (62) 9 K1
Blis-et-Born (24) 214 C4
Blismes (58) 152 A2
Blodelsheim (68) 96 E6
Blois (41) 128 E2
Blois-sur-Seille (39) 155 J6
Blomac (11) 290 D6
Blomard (03) 184 E1
Blombay (08) 22 A2
Blond (87) 180 E4
Blondefontaine (70) 117 J4
Blonville-sur-Mer (14) 33 H3
Blosseville (76) 15 H2
Blosville (50) 29 F6
Blot-l'Église (63) 184 E4

Blotzheim (68) . . . 97 D4
Blou (49) . . . 126 B5
Blousson-Sérian (32) . . . 285 J2
la Bloutière (50) . . . 31 F6
Bloye (74) . . . 190 D6
Bluffy (74) . . . 191 G6
Blumeray (52) . . . 91 J3
Blussangeaux (25) . . . 139 F3
Blussans (25) . . . 139 F3
Blye (39) . . . 173 H2
Blyes (01) . . . 189 G6
le Bô (14) . . . 53 J2
Bobigny (93) . . . 59 F3
Bobital (22) . . . 50 C6
le Bocasse (76) . . . 15 K5
Bocé (49) . . . 126 B3
Bocognano (2A) . . . 320 E3
Bocquegney (88) . . . 94 C5
Bocquencé (61) . . . 55 G3
le Bodéo (22) . . . 76 E2
Bodilis (29) . . . 46 D5
Boé (47) . . . 248 B5
Boëcé (61) . . . 83 G2
Boëge (74) . . . 191 H1
Boeil-Bezing (64) . . . 284 E5
Boën (42) . . . 204 C2
Boersch (67) . . . 70 C4
Boeschepe (59) . . . 6 A2
Boëseghem (59) . . . 3 H6
Boesenbiesen (67) . . . 71 C5
Boësse (45) . . . 111 F1
Boësse (79) . . . 143 J4
Boëssé-le-Sec (72) . . . 107 H1
Boeurs-en-Othe (89) . . . 113 H1
Boffles (62) . . . 9 K3
Boffres (07) . . . 240 A1
Bogève (74) . . . 191 J2
Bogny-sur-Meuse (08) . . . 22 D2
Bogy (07) . . . 222 B2
Bohain-en-Vermandois (02) . . . 12 C6
Bohal (56) . . . 101 J4
la Bohalle (49) . . . 125 J4
Bohars (29) . . . 72 D4
Bohas-Meyriat-Rignat (01) . . . 189 H3
Boigneville (91) . . . 86 E4
Boigny-sur-Bionne (45) . . . 110 B4
Boinville-en-Mantois (78) . . . 57 J2
Boinville-en-Woëvre (55) . . . 44 A4
Boinville-le-Gaillard (78) . . . 86 A2
Boinvilliers (78) . . . 57 H3
Boiry-Becquerelle (62) . . . 11 F4
Boiry-Notre-Dame (62) . . . 11 G3
Boiry-Saint-Martin (62) . . . 10 E4
Boiry-Sainte-Rictrude (62) . . . 10 E4
Bois (17) . . . 195 G5
le Bois (73) . . . 209 H5
Bois-Anzeray (27) . . . 55 J2
Bois-Arnault (27) . . . 55 K4
Bois-Bernard (62) . . . 11 G1
Bois-Colombes (92) . . . 58 D3
Bois-d'Amont (39) . . . 174 C3
Bois-d'Arcy (78) . . . 58 B4
Bois-d'Arcy (89) . . . 133 H3
Bois-de-Céné (85) . . . 141 F4
Bois-de-Champ (88) . . . 95 G4
Bois-de-Gand (39) . . . 155 G5
Bois-de-la-Pierre (31) . . . 287 J4
Bois-d'Ennebourg (76) . . . 35 K2
le Bois-d'Oingt (69) . . . 188 A6
Bois-Grenier (59) . . . 6 C4
Bois-Guilbert (76) . . . 16 C6
Bois-Guillaume (76) . . . 35 H1
le Bois-Hellain (27) . . . 34 B4
Bois-Héroult (76) . . . 16 C6
Bois-Herpin (91) . . . 86 D4
Bois-Himont (76) . . . 15 G6
Bois-Jérôme-Saint-Ouen (27) . . . 36 C6
Bois-le-Roi (27) . . . 57 F3
Bois-le-Roi (77) . . . 87 H2
Bois-lès-Pargny (02) . . . 20 D4
Bois-l'Évêque (76) . . . 35 K2
Bois-Normand-près-Lyre (27) . . . 55 J3
le Bois-Plage-en-Ré (17) . . . 176 B2
le Bois-Robert (76) . . . 16 A2
Bois-Sainte-Marie (71) . . . 170 E6
Boisbergues (80) . . . 9 K4
Boisbreteau (16) . . . 212 B2
Boiscommun (45) . . . 110 E2
Boisdinghem (62) . . . 2 E5
Boisdon (77) . . . 60 C5
Boisemont (27) . . . 36 B4
Boisemont (95) . . . 58 B1
Boisgasson (28) . . . 108 D2
Boisgervilly (35) . . . 78 C3
Boisjean (62) . . . 9 F1
le Boisle (80) . . . 9 H3
Boisleux-au-Mont (62) . . . 10 E4
Boisleux-Saint-Marc (62) . . . 11 F4
Boismé (79) . . . 143 J6
Boismont (54) . . . 26 C4
Boismont (80) . . . 8 E4
Boismorand (45) . . . 111 H5
Boisney (27) . . . 34 D5
Boisredon (17) . . . 211 H2
Boisroger (50) . . . 30 D3
Boissay (76) . . . 36 A1
la Boisse (01) . . . 206 C1
Boisse (24) . . . 231 K4
Boisse-Penchot (12) . . . 235 F5
Boisseau (41) . . . 108 E5
Boisseaux (45) . . . 86 B5
Boissède (31) . . . 287 F3

Boissei-la-Lande (61) . . . 54 D5
Boisserolles (79) . . . 178 A3
Boisseron (34) . . . 274 E4
Boisset (15) . . . 235 F3
Boisset (34) . . . 290 E3
Boisset (43) . . . 220 D2
Boisset-et-Gaujac (30) . . . 255 G6
Boisset-lès-Montrond (42) . . . 204 E4
Boisset-les-Prévanches (27) . . . 56 E2
Boisset-Saint-Priest (42) . . . 204 D5
Boissets (78) . . . 57 H3
Boissettes (77) . . . 87 G2
Boisseuil (87) . . . 199 F2
Boisseuilh (24) . . . 215 F2
Boissey (01) . . . 172 A5
Boissey (14) . . . 54 D1
Boissey-le-Châtel (27) . . . 34 E4
Boissezon (81) . . . 290 B1
Boissia (39) . . . 173 H3
la Boissière (14) . . . 33 J5
la Boissière (27) . . . 57 F2
la Boissière (34) . . . 273 K5
la Boissière (39) . . . 173 G5
la Boissière (53) . . . 104 C5
la Boissière-d'Ans (24) . . . 214 D3
la Boissière-de-Montaigu (85) . . . 142 B4
la Boissière-des-Landes (85) . . . 159 H3
la Boissière-du-Doré (44) . . . 124 A6
la Boissière-École (78) . . . 57 H6
la Boissière-en-Gâtine (79) . . . 161 J3
la Boissière-sur-Èvre (49) . . . 124 B5
Boissières (30) . . . 275 F4
Boissières (46) . . . 233 H6
Boissise-la-Bertrand (77) . . . 87 G2
Boissise-le-Roi (77) . . . 87 G2
Boissy-aux-Cailles (77) . . . 87 F4
Boissy-en-Drouais (28) . . . 56 E5
Boissy-Fresnoy (60) . . . 38 E5
Boissy-la-Rivière (91) . . . 86 C4
Boissy-l'Aillerie (95) . . . 37 G6
Boissy-Lamberville (27) . . . 34 D5
Boissy-le-Bois (60) . . . 37 F4
Boissy-le-Châtel (77) . . . 60 C4
Boissy-le-Cutté (91) . . . 86 D3
Boissy-le-Repos (51) . . . 61 G3
Boissy-le-Sec (91) . . . 86 C2
Boissy-lès-Perche (28) . . . 56 A5
Boissy-Maugis (61) . . . 83 J3
Boissy-Mauvoisin (78) . . . 57 H2
Boissy-Saint-Léger (94) . . . 59 G5
Boissy-sans-Avoir (78) . . . 57 K4
Boissy-sous-Saint-Yon (91) . . . 86 D1
Boistrudan (35) . . . 79 J6
Boisville-la-Saint-Père (28) . . . 85 J4
Boisyvon (50) . . . 52 C3
Boitron (61) . . . 82 E1
Boitron (77) . . . 60 D3
Bolandoz (25) . . . 156 C3
Bolazec (29) . . . 47 J6
Bolbec (76) . . . 14 E6
Bollène (84) . . . 256 D3
la Bollène-Vésubie (06) . . . 311 A3
Bolleville (50) . . . 30 D1
Bolleville (76) . . . 14 E6
Bollezeele (59) . . . 3 H3
Bollwiller (68) . . . 97 B1
Bologne (52) . . . 92 B5
Bolozon (01) . . . 189 J2
Bolquère (66) . . . 313 J4
Bolsenheim (67) . . . 70 E5
Bombon (77) . . . 87 K1
Bommes (33) . . . 229 K5
Bommiers (36) . . . 148 C6
Bompas (09) . . . 307 J4
Bompas (66) . . . 310 C6
Bomy (62) . . . 5 G5
Bon-Encontre (47) . . . 248 C5
Bona (58) . . . 151 G3
Bonac-Irazein (09) . . . 306 B4
Bonas (32) . . . 267 G4
Bonboillon (70) . . . 137 G5
Boncé (28) . . . 85 G5
Bonchamp-lès-Laval (53) . . . 105 F1
Boncourt (02) . . . 21 G5
Boncourt (27) . . . 56 E1
Boncourt (28) . . . 57 G3
Boncourt (54) . . . 44 C5
Boncourt-le-Bois (21) . . . 154 B2
Boncourt-sur-Meuse (55) . . . 64 E4
Bondaroy (45) . . . 86 D6
Bondeval (25) . . . 139 H3
Bondigoux (31) . . . 269 H3
les Bondons (48) . . . 254 C2
Bondoufle (91) . . . 86 E1
Bondues (59) . . . 6 E3
Bondy (93) . . . 59 F3
Bongheat (63) . . . 203 G3
le Bonhomme (68) . . . 95 K5
Bonifacio (2A) . . . 323 G6
Bonlier (60) . . . 37 H1
Bonlieu (39) . . . 173 K2
Bonlieu-sur-Roubion (26) . . . 240 C5
Bonloc (64) . . . 282 D3
Bonnac (09) . . . 288 D6
Bonnac (15) . . . 218 E3
Bonnac-la-Côte (87) . . . 181 H6
Bonnal (25) . . . 138 D2
Bonnard (89) . . . 113 F4
Bonnat (23) . . . 182 D1
Bonnaud (39) . . . 172 E2
Bonnay (25) . . . 138 A5
Bonnay (71) . . . 171 H3

Bonnay (80) . . . 18 C1
Bonne (74) . . . 191 H2
Bonnebosq (14) . . . 33 J4
Bonnecourt (52) . . . 116 E3
Bonnée (45) . . . 110 D5
Bonnefamille (38) . . . 206 D4
Bonnefoi (61) . . . 55 H6
Bonnefond (19) . . . 200 C5
Bonnefont (65) . . . 286 A5
Bonnefontaine (39) . . . 173 H1
Bonnegarde (40) . . . 264 E6
Bonneil (02) . . . 60 D1
Bonnelles (78) . . . 86 B1
Bonnemain (35) . . . 51 F5
Bonnemaison (14) . . . 53 H1
Bonnemazon (65) . . . 304 E1
Bonnencontre (21) . . . 154 D2
Bonnes (16) . . . 212 A5
Bonnes (86) . . . 163 H3
Bonnesvalyn (02) . . . 39 J6
Bonnet (55) . . . 92 D1
Bonnétable (72) . . . 83 H6
Bonnétage (25) . . . 139 G6
Bonnetan (33) . . . 229 J2
Bonneuil (16) . . . 196 B4
Bonneuil (36) . . . 164 D6
Bonneuil-en-France (95) . . . 59 F2
Bonneuil-en-Valois (60) . . . 39 F4
Bonneuil-les-Eaux (60) . . . 18 A5
Bonneuil-Matours (86) . . . 163 H2
Bonneuil-sur-Marne (94) . . . 59 F4
Bonneval (28) . . . 85 F6
Bonneval (43) . . . 220 A2
Bonneval (73) . . . 209 G4
Bonneval-sur-Arc (73) . . . 193 D6
Bonnevaux (25) . . . 156 D5
Bonnevaux (30) . . . 255 G2
Bonnevaux (74) . . . 175 H6
Bonnevaux-le-Prieuré (25) . . . 156 D1
Bonneveau (41) . . . 107 K5
Bonnevent-Velloreille (70) . . . 137 J4
Bonneville (16) . . . 196 C1
la Bonneville (50) . . . 28 E5
Bonneville (74) . . . 191 H3
Bonneville (80) . . . 10 A5
Bonneville-Aptot (27) . . . 34 E4
Bonneville-et-Saint-Avit-de-Fumadières (24) . . . 230 D1
Bonneville-la-Louvet (14) . . . 34 A4
la Bonneville-sur-Iton (27) . . . 56 C2
Bonneville-sur-Touques (14) . . . 33 J3
Bonnières (60) . . . 37 F1
Bonnières (62) . . . 10 A3
Bonnières-sur-Seine (78) . . . 57 H1
Bonnieux (84) . . . 277 G3
Bonningues-lès-Ardres (62) . . . 2 E4
Bonningues-lès-Calais (62) . . . 2 C3
Bonnoeil (14) . . . 53 J2
Bonnoeuvre (44) . . . 124 A2
Bonnut (64) . . . 283 J1
Bonny-sur-Loire (45) . . . 131 K2
Bono (56) . . . 100 D5
Bonrepos (65) . . . 286 A5
Bonrepos-Riquet (31) . . . 269 J5
Bonrepos-sur-Aussonnelle (31) . . . 287 J1
Bons-en-Chablais (74) . . . 191 H1
Bons-Tassilly (14) . . . 54 A2
Bonsecours (76) . . . 35 J2
Bonsmoulins (61) . . . 55 H6
Bonson (06) . . . 281 F2
Bonson (42) . . . 204 E5
Bonvillard (73) . . . 209 F3
Bonvillaret (73) . . . 209 F4
Bonviller (54) . . . 66 D5
Bonvillers (60) . . . 18 B6
Bonvillet (88) . . . 117 K1
Bony (02) . . . 11 J6
Bonzac (33) . . . 212 A5
Bonzée (51) . . . 43 K6
Boô-Silhen (65) . . . 304 B2
Boofzheim (67) . . . 71 D4
Boos (40) . . . 264 B2
Boos (76) . . . 35 J2
Bootzheim (67) . . . 71 C6
Boqueho (22) . . . 48 E6
Bor-et-Bar (12) . . . 251 G5
Boran-sur-Oise (60) . . . 37 K5
Borce (64) . . . 303 F3
Bord-Saint-Georges (23) . . . 183 H2
Bordeaux (33) . . . 229 H2
Bordeaux-en-Gâtinais (45) . . . 111 G1
Bordeaux-Saint-Clair (76) . . . 14 C4
Bordères (64) . . . 284 E5
Bordères-et-Lamensans (40) . . . 265 J4
Bordères-Louron (65) . . . 305 F4
Bordères-sur-l'Échez (65) . . . 285 H5
les Bordes (36) . . . 148 C4
les Bordes (45) . . . 111 F5
Bordes (64) . . . 284 D5
Bordes (65) . . . 285 J5
les Bordes (71) . . . 154 C5
les Bordes (89) . . . 112 E1
les Bordes-Aumont (10) . . . 90 B6
Bordes-de-Rivière (31) . . . 305 J1
les Bordes-sur-Arize (09) . . . 307 F1
les Bordes-sur-Lez (09) . . . 306 C1
Bordezac (30) . . . 255 G3
Bords (17) . . . 177 G6
Borée (07) . . . 239 F1
Boresse-et-Martron (17) . . . 212 C2
Borest (60) . . . 38 C5
Borey (70) . . . 138 D1

Borgo (2B) . . . 319 H2
Bormes-les-Mimosas (83) . . . 298 C5
le Born (31) . . . 269 H3
le Born (48) . . . 237 J6
Bornambusc (76) . . . 14 C5
Bornay (39) . . . 173 G2
Borne (07) . . . 238 D5
Borne (43) . . . 220 B5
Bornel (60) . . . 37 J5
Boron (90) . . . 139 K1
Borre (59) . . . 3 K5
Borrèze (24) . . . 233 G1
Bors(Canton de Baignes-SainteRadegonde) (16) . . . 212 B1
Bors(Canton de Montmoreau-Saint-Cybard) (16) . . . 212 E1
Bort-les-Orgues (19) . . . 217 J1
Bort-l'Étang (63) . . . 203 G3
Borville (54) . . . 94 C2
le Bosc (09) . . . 307 G3
le Bosc (34) . . . 273 G5
Bosc-Bénard-Commin (27) . . . 35 F3
Bosc-Bénard-Crescy (27) . . . 35 F3
Bosc-Bérenger (76) . . . 16 B5
Bosc-Bordel (76) . . . 16 C6
Bosc-Edeline (76) . . . 16 C6
Bosc-Guérard-Saint-Adrien (76) . . . 15 K6
Bosc-Hyons (76) . . . 36 D2
le Bosc-le-Hard (76) . . . 16 A5
Bosc-Mesnil (76) . . . 16 C5
le Bosc-Renoult (61) . . . 55 F2
Bosc-Renoult-en-Ouche (27) . . . 55 K2
Bosc-Renoult-en-Roumois (27) . . . 34 E3
le Bosc-Roger-en-Roumois (27) . . . 35 G4
Bosc-Roger-sur-Buchy (76) . . . 16 C6
Boscamnant (17) . . . 212 C3
Bosdarros (64) . . . 284 D5
Bosgouet (27) . . . 35 F3
Bosguérard-de-Marcouville (27) . . . 35 F4
Bosjean (71) . . . 155 F6
Bosmie-l'Aiguille (87) . . . 198 E2
Bosmont-sur-Serre (02) . . . 21 F4
Bosmoreau-les-Mines (23) . . . 182 C5
Bosnormand (27) . . . 35 G4
Bosquel (80) . . . 18 A4
Bosquentin (27) . . . 36 C2
Bosrobert (27) . . . 34 E4
Bosroger (23) . . . 183 G5
la Bosse (25) . . . 157 H1
la Bosse (72) . . . 83 H6
la Bosse-de-Bretagne (35) . . . 103 G1
Bossée (37) . . . 146 A2
Bossendorf (67) . . . 69 J6
Bosset (24) . . . 213 G6
Bosseval-et-Briancourt (08) . . . 22 E3
Bossey (74) . . . 191 F2
Bossieu (38) . . . 206 D6
Bossugan (33) . . . 230 C3
Bossus-lès-Rumigny (08) . . . 21 J2
Bost (03) . . . 185 K3
Bostens (40) . . . 265 J1
Bosville (76) . . . 15 G3
Botans (90) . . . 139 H1
Botmeur (29) . . . 75 F1
Botsorhel (29) . . . 47 H5
les Bottereaux (27) . . . 55 J3
Botz-en-Mauges (49) . . . 124 C5
Bou (45) . . . 110 B4
Bouafle (78) . . . 58 A2
Bouafles (27) . . . 36 A5
Bouan (09) . . . 307 J5
Bouaye (44) . . . 123 F5
Boubers-lès-Hesmond (62) . . . 4 D6
Boubers-sur-Canche (62) . . . 9 K1
Boubiers (60) . . . 37 F5
Bouc-Bel-Air (13) . . . 296 C2
Boucagnères (32) . . . 286 D1
Boucau (64) . . . 282 B1
Boucé (03) . . . 185 K1
Boucé (61) . . . 54 B6
le Bouchage (16) . . . 179 J4
le Bouchage (38) . . . 207 H3
Bouchain (59) . . . 11 K3
Bouchamps-lès-Craon (53) . . . 104 C4
le Bouchaud (03) . . . 186 D1
Bouchavesnes-Bergen (80) . . . 19 G1
Bouchemaine (49) . . . 125 G4
Boucheporn (57) . . . 45 K5
Bouchet (26) . . . 256 E3
le Bouchet (74) . . . 209 F1
le Bouchet-Saint-Nicolas (43) . . . 238 B1
Bouchevilliers (27) . . . 36 D2
Bouchoir (80) . . . 18 E4
Bouchon (80) . . . 9 H6
le Bouchon-sur-Saulx (55) . . . 64 B6
les Bouchoux (39) . . . 173 J6
Bouchy-Saint-Genest (51) . . . 61 F6
Boucieu-le-Roi (07) . . . 222 A5
Bouclans (25) . . . 138 C6
Boucoiran-et-Nozières (30) . . . 275 F1
Bouconville (08) . . . 42 C4
Bouconville-sur-Madt (55) . . . 65 G3
Bouconville-Vauclair (02) . . . 40 C1
Bouconvillers (60) . . . 37 F5
Boucq (54) . . . 65 G4
Boudes (63) . . . 202 E6
Boudeville (76) . . . 15 H4
Boudou (82) . . . 249 F6
Boudrac (31) . . . 286 C5
Boudreville (21) . . . 115 J3

Boudy-de-Beauregard (47) . . . 231 K6
Boué (02) . . . 12 E6
Bouée (44) . . . 122 D2
Boueilh-Boueilho-Lasque (64) . . . 284 D1
Bouelles (76) . . . 16 D1
Bouër (72) . . . 107 J2
Bouère (53) . . . 105 H4
Bouessay (53) . . . 105 J4
Bouesse (36) . . . 165 J3
Bouëx (16) . . . 197 F4
la Bouëxière (35) . . . 79 J3
Bouffémont (95) . . . 58 E1
Boufféré (85) . . . 142 A4
Bouffignereux (02) . . . 40 D3
Boufflers (80) . . . 9 H3
Bouffry (41) . . . 108 C3
Bougainville (80) . . . 17 J2
Bougarber (64) . . . 284 C3
Bougé-Chambalud (38) . . . 222 C1
Bouges-le-Château (36) . . . 147 K3
Bougey (70) . . . 117 J5
Bougival (78) . . . 58 C3
Bouglainval (28) . . . 85 G1
Bougligny (77) . . . 87 H6
Bouglon (47) . . . 247 G2
Bougneau (17) . . . 195 H4
Bougnon (70) . . . 118 A6
Bougon (79) . . . 162 B6
Bougue (40) . . . 265 H2
Bouguenais (44) . . . 123 G4
Bougy (14) . . . 32 C5
Bougy-lez-Neuville (45) . . . 110 C3
Bouhans (71) . . . 154 E6
Bouhans-et-Feurg (70) . . . 136 E3
Bouhans-lès-Lure (70) . . . 118 D6
Bouhans-lès-Montbozon (70) . . . 138 C3
Bouhet (17) . . . 177 G2
Bouhey (21) . . . 153 J1
Bouhy (58) . . . 132 C3
Bouilh-Devant (65) . . . 285 K4
Bouilh-Péreuilh (65) . . . 285 J4
Bouilhonnac (11) . . . 290 C5
Bouillac (12) . . . 234 E6
Bouillac (24) . . . 232 C3
Bouillac (82) . . . 268 D3
la Bouilladisse (13) . . . 296 E3
Bouillancourt-en-Séry (80) . . . 16 E1
Bouillancourt-la-Bataille (80) . . . 18 D4
Bouillancy (60) . . . 38 E6
Bouilland (21) . . . 153 K2
Bouillargues (30) . . . 275 H4
la Bouille (76) . . . 35 G3
Bouillé-Courdault (85) . . . 161 F5
Bouillé-Loretz (79) . . . 144 A2
Bouillé-Ménard (49) . . . 104 C5
Bouillé-Saint-Paul (79) . . . 144 A3
la Bouillie (22) . . . 49 K5
le Bouillon (61) . . . 82 D1
Bouillon (64) . . . 284 B1
Bouillonville (54) . . . 65 H2
Bouilly (10) . . . 90 A6
Bouilly (51) . . . 40 D5
Bouilly-en-Gâtinais (45) . . . 110 D2
Bouin (79) . . . 178 E3
Bouin (85) . . . 140 D3
Bouin-Plumoison (62) . . . 9 H1
Bouisse (11) . . . 309 H3
Bouix (21) . . . 114 E4
Boujailles (25) . . . 156 C4
Boujan-sur-Libron (34) . . . 292 A3
Boulages (10) . . . 89 K1
Boulaincourt (88) . . . 93 K3
Boulancourt (77) . . . 87 F5
Boulange (57) . . . 26 E4
Boulaur (32) . . . 286 E1
le Boulay (37) . . . 128 A2
Boulay-les-Barres (45) . . . 109 K3
Boulay-les-Ifs (53) . . . 82 B3
le Boulay-Morin (27) . . . 35 J6
Boulay-Moselle (57) . . . 27 K6
la Boulaye (71) . . . 170 C1
Boulazac (24) . . . 214 B4
Boulbon (13) . . . 276 A3
Boulc (26) . . . 241 K4
Boule-d'Amont (66) . . . 314 D3
Bouleternère (66) . . . 314 D2
Bouleurs (77) . . . 59 K3
Bouleuse (51) . . . 40 D4
Bouliac (33) . . . 229 H2
Boulieu-lès-Annonay (07) . . . 221 K2
Bouligneux (01) . . . 188 E4
Bouligney (70) . . . 118 B3
Bouligny (55) . . . 26 C5
Boulin (65) . . . 285 J5
Boullarre (60) . . . 39 F6
le Boullay-les-Deux-Églises (28) . . . 56 E6
Boullay-les-Troux (91) . . . 58 F6
le Boullay-Mivoye (28) . . . 57 F6
le Boullay-Thierry (28) . . . 57 F6
Boulleret (18) . . . 131 K4
Boulleville (27) . . . 34 B3
Bouloc (31) . . . 269 G4
Bouloc (82) . . . 249 G3
Boulogne (85) . . . 142 A6
Boulogne-Billancourt (92) . . . 58 D4
Boulogne-la-Grasse (60) . . . 18 E5
Boulogne-sur-Gesse (31) . . . 286 D4
Boulogne-sur-Helpe (59) . . . 13 G5
Boulogne-sur-Mer (62) . . . 2 A5
Bouloire (72) . . . 107 H3
Boulon (14) . . . 32 D6
Boulot (70) . . . 137 K4

le Boulou (66) 315 G4
Boult (70) 137 K4
Boult-aux-Bois (08) 42 C2
Boult-sur-Suippe (51) 41 G2
le Boulvé (46) 249 G2
Boulzicourt (08) 22 D4
Boumourt (64) 284 B2
Bouniagues (24) 231 J3
le Boupère (85) 142 E6
Bouquehault (62) 2 D4
Bouquelon (27) 34 C2
Bouquemaison (80) 10 B4
Bouquemont (55) 64 D1
Bouquet (30) 255 J5
Bouquetot (27) 34 E3
Bouqueval (95) 59 F1
Bouranton (10) 90 B4
Bouray-sur-Juine (91) 86 E2
Bourbach-le-Bas (68) 119 K4
Bourbach-le-Haut (68) 119 K4
Bourberain (21) 136 C3
Bourbévelle (70) 117 J3
Bourbon-Lancy (71) 169 J3
Bourbon-l'Archambault (03) . . 168 B3
Bourbonne-les-Bains (52) . . . 117 G3
la Bourboule (63) 201 K4
Bourbourg (59) 3 F2
Bourbriac (22) 48 C6
Bourcefranc-le-Chapus (17) . . 176 D6
Bourcia (39) 172 E6
Bourcq (08) 42 A2
Bourdainville (76) 15 J4
Bourdalat (40) 265 K3
Bourdeau (73) 208 A2
Bourdeaux (26) 241 F5
Bourdeilles (24) 213 J2
le Bourdeix (24) 197 J4
Bourdelles (33) 230 C6
le Bourdet (79) 177 J1
Bourdettes (64) 284 D5
Bourdic (30) 275 G1
la Bourdinière-Saint-Loup (28) . . 85 F4
Bourdon (80) 17 J1
Bourdonnay (57) 67 F4
Bourdonné (78) 57 H5
Bourdons-sur-Rognon (52) . . . 92 D6
Bourecq (62) 5 J5
Bouresches (02) 60 D1
Bouresse (86) 163 H6
Bouret-sur-Canche (62) 10 A3
Boureuilles (55) 42 E4
Bourg (33) 211 H5
le Bourg (46) 234 C4
le Bourg (52) 116 C5
Bourg-Achard (27) 35 F3
Bourg-Archambault (86) 164 B6
Bourg-Argental (42) 221 J2
Bourg-Beaudouin (27) 35 K2
Bourg-Blanc (29) 72 D3
Bourg-Bruche (67) 95 K3
Bourg-Charente (16) 196 A3
Bourg-de-Bigorre (65) 304 E1
Bourg-de-Péage (26) 222 D5
Bourg-de-Sirod (39) 174 A1
Bourg-de-Thizy (69) 187 H4
Bourg-de-Visa (82) 249 F4
Bourg-des-Comptes (35) 79 F6
Bourg-des-Maisons (24) 213 H2
le Bourg-d'Hem (23) 182 C1
le Bourg-d'Iré (49) 104 C6
le Bourg-d'Oisans (38) 224 D4
Bourg-d'Oueil (31) 305 G4
le Bourg-Dun (76) 15 H2
Bourg-en-Bresse (01) 189 G2
Bourg-et-Comin (02) 40 B2
Bourg-Fidèle (08) 22 B2
Bourg-la-Reine (92) 58 E4
Bourg-Lastic (63) 201 H4
le Bourg-Saint-Léonard (61) . . 54 D4
Bourg-Saint-Maurice (73) . . . 193 A3
Bourg-Sainte-Marie (52) 93 F6
Bourg-sous-Châtelet (90) . . . 119 J6
Bourgaltroff (57) 67 F2
Bourganeuf (23) 182 C5
Bourgbarré (35) 79 G6
Bourgeauville (14) 33 J4
Bourges (18) 149 G3
le Bourget (93) 59 F2
le Bourget-du-Lac (73) 208 B3
Bourget-en-Huile (73) 208 E5
Bourgheim (67) 70 D5
Bourghelles (59) 7 F5
Bourgnac (24) 213 H6
Bourgneuf (17) 176 E2
Bourgneuf (73) 208 E4
Bourgneuf-en-Mauges (49) . . 124 D5
Bourgneuf-en-Retz (44) 122 C6
le Bourgneuf-la-Forêt (53) . . . 80 D6
Bourgogne (51) 41 F3
Bourgoin-Jallieu (38) 207 F4
Bourgon (53) 80 C6
la Bourgonce (88) 95 G3
Bourgougnague (47) 231 H5

Bourgtheroulde-Infreville (27) 35 F3
Bourguébus (14) 32 E5
Bourgueil (37) 126 D6
Bourguenolles (50) 52 A3
le Bourguet (83) 279 J3
Bourguignon (25) 139 H3
Bourguignon-lès-Conflans (70) . . 118 B4
Bourguignon-lès-la-Charité (70) . . 137 G3
Bourguignon-lès-Morey (70) 117 G6
Bourguignon-sous-Coucy (02) . . . 19 J6
Bourguignon-sous-Montbavin (02) . . 20 C6
Bourguignons (10) 114 D1
Bourgvilain (71) 171 H6
Bourideys (33) 246 A3
Bourlège (11) 308 E3
Bourigeole (11) 308 D3
Bourisp (65) 305 F4
Bourlens (47) 249 F2
Bourlon (62) 11 H4
Bourmont (52) 93 F5
Bournainville-Faverolles (27) 34 C6
Bournan (37) 146 A3
Bournand (86) 144 E2
Bournazel (12) 251 J1
Bournazel (81) 251 F6
Bourneau (85) 160 D3
Bournel (47) 231 K5
Bourneville (27) 34 D2
Bournezeau (85) 160 A2
Bourniquel (24) 232 A2
Bournois (25) 138 E2
Bournoncle-Saint-Pierre (43) 219 G2
Bournonville (62) 2 C5
Bournos (64) 284 C2
Bourogne (90) 139 J1
Bourran (47) 247 K3
Bourré (41) 128 D5
Bourréac (65) 304 B1
Bourret (82) 268 E2
Bourriot-Bergonce (40) 246 C5
Bourron-Marlotte (77) 87 H4
Bourrou (24) 213 J5
Bourrouillan (32) 266 B3
Bours (62) 5 H6
Bours (65) 285 H4
Boursault (51) 61 J1
Boursay (41) 108 B2
Bourscheid (57) 67 K3
Bourseul (22) 50 B5
Bourseville (80) 8 D5
Boursières (70) 137 K1
Boursies (59) 11 H4
Boursin (62) 2 C5
Boursonne (60) 39 F4
Bourth (27) 56 A4
Bourthes (62) 4 D4
Boury-en-Vexin (60) 36 D4
Bousbach (57) 68 C2
Bousbecque (59) 6 E1
le Bouscat (33) 229 G1
Bousies (59) 12 E4
Bousignies (59) 12 B1
Bousignies-sur-Roc (59) 13 K3
le Bousquet (11) 308 E6
le Bousquet-d'Orb (34) 272 E5
Boussac (12) 251 K4
Boussac (23) 166 D6
la Boussac (35) 51 G5
Boussac (46) 234 C5
Boussac-Bourg (23) 166 D6
Boussais (79) 144 B6
Boussan (31) 287 F5
Boussay (37) 146 C6
Boussay (44) 142 B3
Bousse (57) 27 H5
Bousse (72) 106 B5
Bousselange (21) 154 E3
Boussenac (09) 307 F4
Boussenois (21) 136 C1
Boussens (31) 287 G6
Bousseraucourt (70) 117 J2
Boussès (47) 247 G5
Bousseviller (57) 69 H2
Boussey (21) 135 F5
Boussicourt (80) 18 D4
Boussières (25) 156 A1
Boussières-en-Cambrésis (59) . . 12 B4
Boussières-sur-Sambre (59) . . 13 H2
Boussois (59) 13 H2
Boussy (59) 190 E6
Boussy-Saint-Antoine (91) . . . 59 G5
Boust (57) 27 G3
Boustroff (57) 45 K6
Bout-du-Pont-de-Larn (81) 290 B2
Boutancourt (08) 22 D4
Boutavent (60) 17 F5
la Bouteille (02) 21 G2
Bouteilles-Saint-Sébastien (24) . . 213 G1
Boutenac (11) 291 F6
Boutenac-Touvent (17) 194 E5
Boutencourt (60) 36 E3
Boutervilliers (91) 86 B3
Bouteville (16) 196 B4
Boutiers-Saint-Trojan (16) . . . 195 K2
Boutigny (77) 59 K3
Boutigny-Prouais (28) 57 H5
Boutigny-sur-Essonne (91) . . . 86 E3
Bouttencourt (80) 16 E1
Boutteville (50) 29 G5
Boutx (31) 305 J3
Bouvaincourt-sur-Bresle (80) 8 D6

Bouvancourt (51) 40 D3
Bouvante (26) 223 G6
Bouvelinghem (62) 2 E5
Bouvellemont (08) 22 C5
Bouverans (25) 156 D5
Bouvesse-Quirieu (38) 207 G1
Bouvières (26) 241 F6
Bouvignies (59) 11 K1
Bouvigny-Boyeffles (62) 10 D1
Bouville (28) 85 F5
Bouville (76) 15 H6
Bouville (91) 86 D3
Bouvincourt-en-Vermandois (80) . . 19 H2
Bouvines (59) 7 F5
Bouvresse (60) 17 F5
Bouvron (44) 122 E1
Bouvron (54) 65 H4
Boux-sous-Salmaise (21) 135 G3
Bouxières-aux-Bois (88) 94 C4
Bouxières-aux-Chênes (54) . . 66 B4
Bouxières-aux-Dames (54) . . . 66 A4
Bouxières-sous-Froidmont (54) . . 65 K1
Bouxurulles (88) 94 B3
Bouxwiller (67) 69 H6
Bouxwiller (68) 97 C5
Bouy (51) 41 J6
Bouy-Luxembourg (10) 90 C3
Bouy-sur-Orvin (10) 89 F3
Bouyon (06) 281 F2
le Bouyssou (46) 234 C4
Bouzais (18) 167 G2
Bouzancourt (52) 91 K4
Bouzanville (54) 94 A3
Bouze-lès-Beaune (21) 153 K3
Bouzel (63) 203 F2
Bouzemont (88) 94 B4
Bouzeron (71) 153 K5
Bouzic (24) 233 F4
Bouziès (46) 250 C1
Bouzigues (34) 292 E2
Bouzillé (49) 124 B5
Bouzin (31) 287 F6
Bouzincourt (80) 10 D6
Bouzon-Gellenave (32) 266 C5
Bouzonville (57) 45 J3
Bouzonville-aux-Bois (45) . . . 110 D1
Bouzy (51) 41 G6
Bouzy-la-Forêt (45) 110 E5
Bovée-sur-Barboure (55) 64 E6
Bovel (35) 78 D6
Bovelles (80) 17 K2
Boves (80) 18 B2
Boviolles (55) 64 D6
Boyaval (62) 5 G6
Boyelles (62) 11 F4
Boyer (42) 187 G3
Boyer (71) 171 K3
Boyeux-Saint-Jérôme (01) . . . 189 J4
Boynes (45) 110 E1
Boz (01) 171 K5
Bozas (07) 221 K5
Bozel (73) 209 J5
Bozouls (12) 252 D1
Brabant-le-Roi (55) 63 K3
Brabant-sur-Meuse (55) 43 H3
Brach (33) 210 D5
Brachay (52) 91 K3
Braches (80) 18 C4
Brachy (76) 15 J3
Bracieux (41) 129 G3
Bracon (39) 156 A4
Bracquemont (76) 16 A1
Bracquetuit (76) 16 A5
Bradiancourt (76) 16 C5
Braffais (50) 52 A4
Bragassargues (30) 274 D2
Bragayrac (31) 287 H2
Brageac (15) 217 G3
Bragelogne-Beauvoir (10) . . . 114 C3
Bragny-sur-Saône (71) 154 C4
Braillans (25) 138 A5
Brailly-Cornehotte (80) 9 H3
Brain (21) 135 F3
Brain-sur-Allonnes (49) 126 C5
Brain-sur-l'Authion (49) 125 H4
Brain-sur-Longuenée (49) . . . 124 E2
Brainans (39) 155 H5
Braine (02) 40 A3
Brains (44) 123 F4
Brains-sur-Gée (72) 106 C2
Brains-sur-les-Marches (53) . . 104 A3
Brainville (50) 30 D3
Brainville (54) 44 B5
Brainville-sur-Meuse (52) 93 F6
Braisnes (60) 38 D1
Braize (03) 167 H2
Bralleville (54) 94 B3
Bram (11) 289 J5
Bramans (73) 226 B2
Bramevaque (65) 305 H3
Bran (17) 212 A1
Branceilles (19) 216 A6
Branches (89) 113 F4
Brancourt-en-Laonnois (02) 39 K1
Brancourt-le-Grand (02) 20 A1
Brandérion (56) 100 B3
Brandeville (55) 43 G2
Brandivy (56) 100 D3
Brando (2B) 317 E4
Brandon (71) 171 G6
Brandonnet (12) 251 G2

Brandonvillers (51) 91 F1
Branges (71) 172 C2
Brangues (38) 207 H2
Brannay (89) 88 B5
Branne (25) 138 E4
Branne (33) 230 B3
Brannens (33) 230 B6
Branoux-les-Taillades (30) . . . 255 F4
Brans (39) 137 F6
Bransat (03) 185 G1
Branscourt (51) 40 D4
Bransles (77) 111 K1
Brantes (84) 257 K4
Brantigny (88) 94 B3
Brantôme (24) 213 K1
Branville (14) 33 H4
Branville-Hague (50) 28 B2
Braquis (55) 44 A5
Bras (83) 297 J1
Bras-d'Asse (04) 278 E1
Bras-sur-Meuse (55) 43 H4
Brasc (12) 271 J2
Brasles (02) 60 E1
Braslou (37) 145 H4
Brasparts (29) 74 D2
Brassac (09) 307 H3
Brassac (81) 271 H6
Brassac (82) 249 F4
Brassac-les-Mines (63) 219 G1
Brassempouy (40) 264 E5
Brasseuse (60) 38 C4
Brassy (58) 133 K6
Brassy (80) 17 J4
Bratte (54) 66 A3
Braud-et-Saint-Louis (33) . . . 211 G2
Brauvilliers (55) 92 B1
Braux (04) 260 D6
Braux (10) 90 E2
Braux (21) 134 E4
Braux-le-Châtel (52) 115 K1
Braux-Saint-Remy (51) 63 H1
Braux-Sainte-Cohière (51) . . . 42 C6
Brax (31) 268 E6
Brax (47) 248 A4
Bray (27) 35 F6
Bray (71) 171 J4
Bray-Dunes (59) 3 J1
Bray-en-Val (45) 110 E5
Bray-et-Lû (95) 36 D6
Bray-lès-Mareuil (80) 9 G4
Bray-Saint-Christophe (02) 19 J3
Bray-sur-Seine (77) 88 D3
Bray-sur-Somme (80) 18 E1
Braye (02) 39 J2
Braye-en-Laonnois (02) 40 B2
Braye-en-Thiérache (02) 21 G3
Braye-sous-Faye (37) 145 G4
Braye-sur-Maulne (37) 126 E2
Brazey-en-Morvan (21) 152 E1
Brazey-en-Plaine (21) 154 D2
Bréal-sous-Montfort (35) 78 E5
Bréal-sous-Vitré (35) 104 C1
Bréançon (95) 37 G6
Bréau (77) 87 K1
Bréau-et-Salagosse (30) 273 J1
Bréauté (76) 14 D5
Bréban (51) 90 D1
Brebières (62) 11 H2
Brebotte (90) 139 J1
Brécé (35) 79 J4
Brécé (53) 80 E3
Brécey (50) 52 B4
Brech (56) 100 D4
Brechainville (88) 92 E3
Bréchamps (28) 57 G6
Bréchaumont (68) 119 K6
Brèches (37) 127 F2
Breconchaux (25) 138 C4
Brectouville (50) 31 H4
Brécy (02) 39 K5
Brécy (18) 149 J2
Brécy-Brières (08) 42 C3
la Brède (33) 229 H4
Brée (53) 81 H6
la Brée-les-Bains (17) 176 B4
Bréel (61) 53 J4
Brégnier-Cordon (01) 207 J3
Brégy (60) 38 E6
Bréhain (57) 66 D2
Bréhain-la-Ville (54) 26 E3
Bréhal (50) 30 D6
Bréhan (56) 77 G6
Bréhand (22) 77 H2
Bréhémont (37) 127 F6
Bréhéville (55) 43 H2
Breidenbach (57) 69 G2
Breil (49) 126 D3
le Breil-sur-Mérize (72) 107 G2
Breil-sur-Roya (06) 311 C4
la Breille-les-Pins (49) 126 C5
Breilly (80) 17 K1
Breistroff-la-Grande (57) 27 H3
Breitenau (67) 96 B1
Breitenbach (67) 70 B6
Breitenbach-Haut-Rhin (68) . . 119 K1
Brélès (29) 72 B3
Brélidy (22) 48 C4
Brem-sur-Mer (85) 158 E2
Bréménil (54) 95 H1
Brêmes (62) 2 D4
Brémoncourt (54) 94 C1
Bremondans (25) 138 D6

Brémontier-Merval (76) 36 C1
Brémoy (14) 53 F1
Brémur-et-Vaurois (21) 115 G6
Bren (26) 222 C4
Brenac (11) 308 E4
Brenas (34) 273 F6
Brenat (63) 203 F5
Brénaz (01) 190 B5
Brenelle (02) 40 A3
Brengues (46) 234 B5
Brennes (52) 116 C5
Brennilis (29) 75 F1
Brénod (01) 190 A4
Brenon (83) 279 K3
Brenouille (60) 38 B4
Brenoux (48) 254 B1
Brens (01) 207 K2
Brens (81) 270 B3
Brenthonne (74) 174 E6
Breny (02) 39 J5
la Bréole (04) 243 G6
Brères (25) 156 A2
Bréry (39) 155 H6
Bresdon (17) 178 D6
les Bréseux (25) 139 H5
Bresilley (70) 137 G6
Bresle (80) 18 D1
Bresles (60) 37 J2
Bresnay (03) 168 D5
Bresolettes (61) 55 J6
la Bresse (88) 119 H2
Bresse-sur-Grosne (71) 171 J3
Bressey-sur-Tille (21) 136 C5
Bressieux (38) 223 G1
Bressolles (01) 189 F6
Bressolles (03) 168 E4
Bressols (82) 269 F2
Bresson (38) 224 B4
Bressuire (79) 143 J5
Brest (29) 72 D4
Brestot (27) 34 E3
Bretagne (36) 147 K1
Bretagne (90) 139 K1
Bretagne-d'Armagnac (32) . . . 266 D2
Bretagne-de-Marsan (40) . . . 265 H3
Bretagnolles (27) 57 F2
Breteau (45) 131 K1
Breteil (35) 78 E4
Bretenière (21) 136 B6
la Bretenière (25) 138 C4
la Bretenière (39) 155 J2
Bretenières (39) 155 H4
Bretenoux (46) 234 B1
Breteuil (27) 56 B4
Breteuil (60) 18 A5
Brethel (61) 55 H5
Brethenay (52) 92 B6
le Brethon (03) 167 J3
Bretigney (25) 139 F2
Bretigney-Notre-Dame (25) . . . 138 C5
Bretignolles (79) 143 H5
Bretignolles-sur-Mer (85) . . . 158 D2
Bretigny (21) 136 B4
Brétigny (27) 34 E4
Brétigny (60) 19 J6
Brétigny-sur-Orge (91) 86 E1
Bretoncelles (61) 84 A3
la Bretonnière (85) 159 K4
Bretonvillers (25) 139 F6
Brette (26) 241 G5
Brette-les-Pins (72) 107 F4
Bretten (68) 119 K5
Brettes (16) 179 F5
Bretteville (50) 28 D2
Bretteville-du-Grand-Caux (76) . . 14 D4
Bretteville-le-Rabet (14) 54 A1
Bretteville-l'Orgueilleuse (14) . . 32 C4
Bretteville-Saint-Laurent (76) . . 15 H3
Bretteville-sur-Ay (50) 30 C1
Bretteville-sur-Dives (14) 54 C1
Bretteville-sur-Laize (14) 53 K1
Bretteville-sur-Odon (14) 32 D5
Brettnach (57) 45 J3
Bretx (31) 268 E5
Breuches (70) 118 C4
Breuchotte (70) 118 D4
Breugnon (58) 133 F4
le Breuil (03) 186 B2
le Breuil (51) 40 C3
le Breuil (51) 61 G2
le Breuil (69) 188 A6
le Breuil (71) 153 G6
le Breuil (80) 19 G4
Breuil-Barret (85) 161 F2
le Breuil-Bernard (79) 161 G1
Breuil-Bois-Robert (78) 57 J2
le Breuil-en-Auge (14) 33 K4
le Breuil-en-Bessin (14) 31 K2
Breuil-la-Réorte (17) 177 H4
Breuil-le-Sec (60) 38 A3
Breuil-le-Vert (60) 38 A3
Breuil-Magné (17) 177 F4
le Breuil-sous-Argenton (79) . . 143 K3
le Breuil-sur-Couze (63) 203 F6
Breuilaufa (87) 181 F4
Breuilh (24) 214 A5
Breuillet (17) 194 C2
Breuillet (91) 86 C1
Breuilpont (27) 57 F2
Breurey-lès-Faverney (70) . . . 118 A5
Breuschwickersheim (67) 70 E3
Breuvannes-en-Bassigny (52) . . 117 F1

Breuvery-sur-Coole (51) 62 D3
Breuville (50) 28 C3
Breux (55) 23 K5
Breux-Jouy (91) 86 C1
Breux-sur-Avre (27) 56 C4
Brévainville (41) 108 E3
Bréval (78) 57 G2
Brévands (50) 29 G6
Brevans (39) 155 G2
le Brévedent (14) 34 A4
Brèves (58) 133 G4
les Bréviaires (78) 57 K5
Bréviandes (10) 90 B5
la Brévière (14) 54 E2
Bréville (14) 33 F4
Bréville (16) 196 A1
Bréville-sur-Mer (50) 30 D6
Brévillers (62) 9 H5
Brévillers (80) 10 B4
Brevilliers (70) 139 H1
Brévilly (08) 23 G4
Brévonnes (10) 90 D4
Bréxent-Enocq (62) 4 B5
Brey-et-Maison-du-Bois (25) . . . 156 E6
Brézé (49) 144 C1
Bréziers (05) 259 J1
Brézilhac (11) 289 J6
Brézins (38) 223 G1
Brezolles (28) 56 C5
Brezons (15) 218 B6
Briançon (05) 225 K6
Brianny (21) 134 E4
Briant (71) 187 F1
Briantes (36) 166 B4
Briare (45) 131 J2
Briarres-sur-Essonne (45) 87 F6
Brias (62) 10 B1
Briastre (59) 12 C4
Briatexte (81) 270 B4
Briaucourt (52) 92 B5
Briaucourt (70) 118 B4
Bricon (52) 115 K1
Briconville (28) 85 F2
Bricquebec (50) 28 C4
Bricquebosq (50) 28 C3
Bricqueville (50) 31 J1
Bricqueville-la-Blouette (50) . . . 30 D4
Bricqueville-sur-Mer (50) 30 D6
Bricy (45) 109 J3
Brides-les-Bains (73) 209 H5
la Bridoire (73) 207 K4
Bridoré (37) 146 D3
Brie (02) 20 B5
Brie (09) 288 C6
Brie (16) 197 F2
Brie (35) 79 H6
Brie (79) 144 D4
Brie (80) 19 G2
Brie-Comte-Robert (77) 59 G5
Brié-et-Angonnes (38) 224 B4
Brie-sous-Archiac (17) 195 K5
Brie-sous-Barbezieux (16) 196 C6
Brie-sous-Chalais (16) 212 D2
Brie-sous-Matha (17) 196 A1
Brie-sous-Mortagne (17) 195 F5
Briec (29) 74 E4
Briel-sur-Barse (10) 90 D6
Brielles (35) 104 B2
Brienne (71) 172 B3
Brienne-la-Vieille (10) 91 F3
Brienne-le-Château (10) 91 F3
Brienne-sur-Aisne (08) 41 F2
Briennon (42) 187 F3
Brienon-sur-Armançon (89) . . . 113 G3
Brières-les-Scellés (91) 86 C3
Brieuil-sur-Chizé (79) 178 B3
Brieulles-sur-Bar (08) 42 C1
Brieulles-sur-Meuse (55) 43 F3
Brieux (61) 54 B3
Briey (54) 26 E6
Briffons (63) 201 J3
Brignac (34) 273 H6
Brignac (56) 77 K5
Brignac-la-Plaine (19) 215 G4
Brignais (69) 205 K3
Brignancourt (95) 37 F6
Brigné (49) 125 J6
Brignemont (31) 268 C4
Brignogan-Plage (29) 46 B3
Brignoles (83) 297 K2
Brignon (30) 275 F1
le Brignon (43) 238 C1
la Brigue (06) 311 D2
Brigueil-le-Chantre (86) 164 C6
Brigueuil (16) 180 D5
Briis-sous-Forges (91) 58 C6
Brillac (16) 180 C4
la Brillanne (04) 278 C2
Brillecourt (10) 90 D2
Brillevast (50) 28 E2
Brillon (59) 11 K1
Brillon-en-Barrois (55) 64 A5
Brimeux (62) 4 C6
Brimont (51) 41 F3
Brin-sur-Seille (54) 66 C4
Brinay (18) 148 E2
Brinay (58) 151 K4
Brinckheim (68) 97 D4
Brindas (69) 205 K2
Bringolo (22) 48 E5
Brinon-sur-Beuvron (58) 133 F6

Brinon-sur-Sauldre (18) 130 D2
Briod (39) 173 G2
Briollay (49) 125 H2
Brion (01) 189 K2
Brion (36) 148 A4
Brion (38) 223 G2
Brion (48) 236 E3
Brion (49) 126 A4
Brion (71) 152 E5
Brion (86) 163 G6
Brion (89) 113 F3
Brion-près-Thouet (79) 144 B3
Brion-sur-Ource (21) 115 G3
la Brionne (23) 182 C3
Brionne (27) 34 E5
Briord (01) 207 G1
Briosne-lès-Sables (72) 83 F6
Briot (60) 17 H5
Briou (41) 109 G5
Brioude (43) 219 H2
Brioux-sur-Boutonne (79) . . . 178 C3
Briouze (61) 53 J5
Briquemesnil-Floxicourt (80) . . . 17 J2
Briquenay (08) 42 D1
Briscous (64) 282 D2
Brison-Saint-Innocent (73) . . . 208 B2
Brissac (34) 274 A3
Brissac-Quincé (49) 125 H5
Brissarthe (49) 105 H6
Brissay-Choigny (02) 20 A4
Brissy-Hamégicourt (02) 20 B4
Brive-la-Gaillarde (19) 215 J4
Brives (36) 148 C6
Brives-Charensac (43) 220 C5
Brives-sur-Charente (17) 195 H3
Brivezac (19) 216 B6
Brix (50) 28 D3
Brixey-aux-Chanoines (55) . . . 93 G2
Brizambourg (17) 195 H1
Brizay (37) 145 H2
Brizeaux (55) 63 K1
Brizon (74) 191 J3
le Broc (06) 281 F2
Broc (49) 126 D2
le Broc (63) 202 E5
Brocas (40) 245 K6
Brochon (21) 135 K6
Brocourt (80) 17 G2
Broglie (27) 55 H1
Brognard (25) 139 H2
Brognon (08) 21 K1
Brognon (21) 136 B4
Broin (21) 154 D2
Broindon (21) 154 C1
Broissia (39) 173 F6
Brombos (60) 17 H5
Bromeilles (45) 87 F6
Brommat (12) 236 A2
Bromont-Lamothe (63) 202 A1
Bron (69) 206 B2
Bronvaux (57) 27 G6
Broons (22) 78 B1
la Broque (67) 70 A5
Broquiers (60) 17 G5
Broquiès (12) 271 K1
Brossac (16) 212 C1
Brossainc (07) 222 A2
Drocsay (49) 144 B1
la Brosse-Montceaux (77) . . . 88 B4
Brosses (89) 133 H3
Brosville (27) 35 H6
Brotte-lès-Luxeuil (70) 118 C4
Brotte-lès-Ray (70) 137 G1
Brou (28) 84 D6
Brou-sur-Chantereine (77) . . . 59 H3
Brouains (50) 52 D5
Broualan (35) 51 G5
Brouay (14) 32 C4
Brouchaud (24) 214 D3
Brouchy (80) 19 J4
Brouck (57) 45 J5
Brouckerque (59) 3 G2
Brouderdorff (57) 67 K4
Broué (28) 57 G5
Brouennes (55) 23 J6
le Brouilh-Monbert (32) 267 F5
Brouilla (66) 315 G3
Brouillet (51) 40 C4
Brouqueyran (33) 230 B6
la Brousse (17) 178 B6
Brousse (23) 183 J5
Brousse (63) 203 G4
Brousse (81) 270 D5
Brousse-le-Château (12) 271 J1
Brousses-et-Villaret (11) 290 A4
Brousseval (52) 91 K2
Broussey-en-Blois (55) 64 E6
Broussey-Raulecourt (55) . . . 65 F3
Broussy-le-Grand (51) 61 J4
Broussy-le-Petit (51) 61 J4
Brouvelieures (88) 95 G4
Brouville (54) 95 G1
Brouviller (57) 67 K3
Brouy (91) 86 D4
Brouzet-lès-Alès (30) 255 J5
Brouzet-lès-Quissac (30) 274 D3
les Brouzils (85) 142 A4
Broxeele (59) 3 G4
Broye (71) 153 F5
Broye-Aubigney-Montseugny (70) . 137 F5
Broye-les-Loups-et-Verfontaine (70) . 136 E3

Broyes (51) 61 H5
Broyes (60) 18 C5
Broze (81) 270 B2
Brû (88) 95 F3
Bruailles (71) 172 D3
Bruay-la-Buissière (62) 5 K6
Bruay-sur-l'Escaut (59) 12 D1
Bruc-sur-Aff (35) 102 C2
Brucamps (80) 9 J5
Bruch (47) 247 K4
Brucheville (50) 29 G6
Brucourt (14) 33 G4
Brue-Auriac (83) 297 J1
Bruebach (68) 97 C3
Brueil-en-Vexin (78) 57 K1
la Bruère-sur-Loir (72) 127 F1
la Bruffière (85) 142 B3
Brugairolles (11) 308 E1
le Brugeron (63) 203 K3
Bruges (33) 229 G1
Bruges-Capbis-Mifaget (64) . . . 284 D6
Brugheas (03) 185 H4
Brugnac (47) 247 K1
Brugnens (32) 267 K3
Bruguières (31) 269 G5
Bruille-lez-Marchiennes (59) . . . 11 K2
Bruille-Saint-Amand (59) 7 J6
Bruis (05) 241 J6
Brûlain (79) 178 B2
les Brulais (35) 102 C1
Brulange (57) 66 D1
la Brûlatte (53) 104 D1
Bruley (54) 65 H5
Brullemail (61) 55 F6
Brullioles (69) 205 H2
Brûlon (72) 105 K3
Brumath (67) 25 A3
Brumetz (02) 39 H6
Brunehamel (02) 21 J3
Brunelles (28) 84 A4
les Brunels (11) 289 H3
Brunembert (62) 2 D5
Brunémont (59) 11 J3
Brunet (04) 278 E2
Bruniquel (82) 250 C6
Brunoy (91) 59 F5
Brunstatt (68) 97 C3
Brunville (76) 16 B1
Brunvillers-la-Motte (60) 18 C6
Brusque (12) 272 C4
le Brusquet (04) 259 K4
Brussey (70) 137 H5
Brussieu (69) 205 H2
Brusson (51) 63 G4
Brusvily (22) 50 C6
Brutelles (80) 8 D4
Bruville (54) 44 C5
Brux (86) 179 G2
la Bruyère (70) 118 E4
Bruyères (88) 95 F5
Bruyères-et-Montbérault (02) . . . 40 B1
Bruyères-le-Châtel (91) 86 D1
Bruyères-sur-Fère (02) 39 K5
Bruyères-sur-Oise (95) 37 K5
Bruys (02) 40 A4
Bruz (35) 79 H4
Bry (59) 12 E2
Bry-sur-Marne (94) 59 G4
Bû (28) 57 G4
le Bû-sur-Rouvres (14) 54 B1
Buais (50) 80 D1
Buanes (40) 265 H4
Bubertré (61) 83 H1
Bubry (56) 100 C1
Buc (78) 58 C4
Buc (90) 139 H1
Bucamps (60) 37 K1
Bucéels (14) 32 B4
Bucey-en-Othe (10) 89 J5
Bucey-lès-Gy (70) 137 J4
Bucey-lès-Traves (70) 137 K1
Buchelay (78) 57 J2
Buchères (10) 90 B5
Buchy (57) 66 B1
Buchy (76) 16 E5
Bucilly (02) 21 H2
Bucquoy (62) 10 E4
Bucy-le-Long (02) 39 K2
Bucy-le-Roi (45) 110 A2
Bucy-lès-Cerny (02) 20 C6
Bucy-lès-Pierrepont (02) 21 F5
Bucy-Saint-Liphard (45) 109 J3
Budelière (23) 183 K2
Buding (57) 27 J4
Budling (57) 27 J4
Budos (33) 229 J6
Bué (18) 131 J6
Bueil (27) 57 G2
Bueil-en-Touraine (37) 127 H1
Buellas (01) 189 F2
Buethwiller (68) 97 A3
Buffard (25) 155 K3
Buffières (71) 171 G5
Buffignécourt (70) 117 K4
Buffon (21) 134 D1
Bugarach (11) 309 G4
Bugard (65) 286 A5
Bugeat (19) 200 B4
Bugnein (64) 283 J1

Bugnicourt (59) 11 J3
Bugnières (52) 116 A3
Bugny (25) 157 F3
le Bugue (24) 232 C1
Buhl (67) 25 C2
Buhl (68) 96 A6
Buhl-Lorraine (57) 67 J4
Buhy (95) 36 D5
Buicourt (60) 17 G6
Buigny-l'Abbé (80) 9 H5
Buigny-lès-Gamaches (80) 8 D6
Buigny-Saint-Maclou (80) 9 G4
Buire (02) 21 G2
Buire-au-Bois (62) 9 K3
Buire-Courcelles (80) 19 H1
Buire-le-Sec (62) 9 G1
Buire-sur-l'Ancre (80) 18 D1
Buironfosse (02) 20 E1
le Buis (87) 181 G4
Buis-les-Baronnies (26) 257 J3
Buis-sur-Damville (27) 56 D4
Buissard (05) 243 F4
la Buisse (38) 223 K1
la Buissière (38) 208 C6
le Buisson (48) 237 F5
le Buisson (51) 63 H4
le Buisson (84) 257 G3
le Buisson-de-Cadouin (24) . . . 232 C2
Buissoncourt (54) 66 C5
Buisson (84) 257 G3
Bujaleuf (87) 199 J2
Bulan (65) 304 E2
Bulat-Pestivien (22) 76 B1
Bulcy (58) 150 C1
Buléon (56) 101 G2
Bulgnéville (88) 93 H5
Bulhon (63) 185 J6
Bullainville (28) 85 G6
Bulle (25) 156 D4
Bullecourt (62) 11 G4
Bulles (60) 37 K2
Bulligny (54) 65 H6
Bullion (78) 58 B6
Bullou (28) 84 E5
Bully (42) 186 E6
Bully (69) 205 J1
Bully (76) 16 C4
Bully-les-Mines (62) 10 E1
Bulson (08) 23 F5
Bult (88) 94 E4
Bun (65) 304 A2
Buncey (21) 115 F5
Buneville (62) 10 B2
Buno-Bonnevaux (91) 86 E4
Bunus (64) 283 F5
Bunzac (16) 197 G3
Buoux (84) 277 H3
Burbach (67) 67 J2
la Burbanche (01) 189 K6
Burburre (62) 5 J5
Burcin (38) 207 G6
Burcy (14) 53 F3
Burcy (77) 87 G5
Burdignes (42) 221 J2
Burdignin (74) 191 J1
Bure (55) 92 C2
Buré (61) 83 G2
Bure-les-Templiers (21) 115 J6
Burelles (02) 21 F3
Bures (54) 66 E4
Bures (61) 83 G1
Bures-en-Bray (76) 16 C3
Bures-les-Monts (14) 31 J5
Bures-sur-Yvette (91) 58 C5
le Buret (53) 105 H3
Burey (27) 56 B2
Burey-en-Vaux (55) 93 F1
Burey-la-Côte (55) 93 G2
Burg (65) 286 A6
Burgalays (31) 305 J4
le Burgaud (31) 268 D4
Burgille (25) 137 H5
Burgnac (87) 198 E2
Burgy (71) 171 K4
Burie (17) 195 J2
Buriville (54) 95 F1
Burlats (81) 271 F6
Burlioncourt (57) 66 E2
Burnand (71) 171 H3
Burnevillers (25) 139 K4
Buros (64) 284 D3
Burosse-Mendousse (64) 284 E1
Burret (09) 307 H3
Bursard (61) 82 E1
Burthecourt-aux-Chênes (54) . . . 66 B6
Burtoncourt (57) 27 K6
Bury (60) 37 K3
Burzet (07) 239 F3
Burzy (71) 171 G3
Bus (62) 11 G5
Bus-la-Mésière (80) 18 E5
Bus-lès-Artois (80) 10 C5
Bus-Saint-Rémy (27) 36 C5
Busigny (59) 12 C6
Busloup (41) 108 C2
Busnes (62) 5 J5
Busque (81) 270 C4
Bussac (24) 213 K2

Bussac-Forêt (17) 211 K3
Bussac-sur-Charente (17) . . . 195 G1
Bussang (88) 119 H3
le Busseau (79) 161 G3
Busseaut (21) 115 G6
Busséol (63) 202 E3
Busserolles (24) 197 J3
Busserotte-et-Montenaille (21) . . 135 K1
Busset (03) 185 K4
Bussiares (02) 39 H6
la Bussière (45) 111 J6
la Bussière (86) 163 K3
Bussière-Badil (24) 197 J3
Bussière-Boffy (87) 180 D4
Bussière-Dunoise (23) 182 C2
Bussière-Galant (87) 198 C5
Bussière-Nouvelle (23) 183 J5
Bussière-Poitevine (87) 180 D2
Bussière-Saint-Georges (23) . . . 166 C6
la Bussière-sur-Ouche (21) . . . 153 J1
Bussières (21) 135 K1
Bussières (42) 205 F1
Bussières (63) 184 A4
Bussières (70) 137 K5
Bussières (71) 171 H6
Bussières (77) 60 C3
Bussières (89) 134 B4
Bussières-et-Pruns (63) 185 G5
Busson (52) 92 D4
Bussu (80) 19 H1
Bussunarits-Sarrasquette (64) . . 282 E5
Bussus-Bussuel (80) 9 H5
Bussy (18) 149 J5
Bussy (60) 19 H5
Bussy-Albieux (42) 204 C2
Bussy-en-Othe (89) 113 F2
Bussy-la-Pesle (21) 135 H5
Bussy-la-Pesle (58) 133 F6
Bussy-le-Château (51) 42 A6
Bussy-le-Grand (21) 135 F2
Bussy-le-Repos (51) 63 H3
Bussy-le-Repos (89) 112 D2
Bussy-lès-Daours (80) 18 C2
Bussy-lès-Poix (80) 17 J3
Bussy-Lettrée (51) 62 C4
Bussy-Saint-Georges (77) . . . 59 H4
Bussy-Saint-Martin (77) 59 H3
Bust (67) 69 F6
Bustanico (2B) 319 G5
Bustince-Iriberry (64) 282 E5
Buswiller (67) 69 J6
Busy (25) 156 B1
Buthiers (70) 138 A4
Buthiers (77) 87 F5
Butot (76) 15 K5
Butot-Vénesville (76) 15 F3
Butry-sur-Oise (95) 37 J6
Butteaux (89) 113 J3
Butten (67) 69 F4
Buverchy (80) 19 H4
Buvilly (39) 155 J5
la Buxerette (36) 165 K4
Buxerolles (21) 115 K5
Buxerolles (86) 163 F3
Buxeuil (10) 114 E2
Buxeuil (36) 147 K2
Buxeuil (86) 146 A4
Buxières-d'Aillac (36) 165 J3
Buxières-lès-Clefmont (52) . . . 116 E1
Buxières-les-Mines (03) 168 A5
Buxières-lès-Villiers (52) 116 A1
Buxières-sous-les-Côtes (55) . . . 65 F2
Buxières-sous-Montaigut (63) . . . 184 D2
Buxières-sur-Arce (10) 114 E1
Buxy (71) 171 H1
Buysscheure (59) 3 H4
Buzan (09) 306 B3
Buzançais (36) 147 H5
Buzancy (02) 39 J3
Buzancy (08) 42 D2
Buzeins (12) 253 F2
Buzet-sur-Baïse (47) 247 J4
Buzet-sur-Tarn (31) 269 J4
Buziet (64) 284 B6
Buzignargues (34) 274 D4
Buzon (65) 285 J2
Buzy (64) 284 C6
Buzy-Darmont (55) 44 A5
By (25) 156 A3
Byans-sur-Doubs (25) 156 A2

C

Cabanac (65) 285 K4
Cabanac-Cazaux (31) 305 K2
Cabanac-et-Villagrains (33) . . . 229 H5
Cabanac-Séguenville (31) 268 C4
la Cabanasse (66) 313 J4
Cabanès (12) 251 J5
Cabanès (81) 270 C5
le Cabanial (31) 289 G2
les Cabannes (09) 307 K5
Cabannes (13) 276 C3
les Cabannes (81) 251 F6
Cabara (33) 230 B2
Cabariot (17) 177 G5
Cabas-Loumassès (32) 286 D3
Cabasse (83) 298 B2
Cabestany (66) 315 H2
Cabidos (64) 284 C1

Cabourg (14) . . . 33 G3
Cabrerets (46) . . . 250 C1
Cabrerolles (34) . . . 291 K1
Cabrespine (11) . . . 290 C4
Cabrières (30) . . . 275 H2
Cabrières (34) . . . 292 B1
Cabrières-d'Aigues (84) . . . 277 J3
Cabrières-d'Avignon (84) . . . 276 E2
Cabriès (13) . . . 296 C2
Cabris (06) . . . 280 C4
Cachan (94) . . . 58 E4
Cachen (40) . . . 246 A6
Cachy (80) . . . 18 C2
Cadalen (81) . . . 270 C3
Cadarcet (09) . . . 307 H2
Cadarsac (33) . . . 230 A2
Cadaujac (33) . . . 229 H3
Cadéac (65) . . . 305 F4
Cadeilhan (32) . . . 267 K3
Cadeilhan-Trachère (65) . . . 304 E4
Cadeillan (32) . . . 287 F3
Cademène (25) . . . 156 B2
Caden (56) . . . 102 A4
Cadenet (84) . . . 277 H4
Caderousse (84) . . . 256 D5
la Cadière-d'Azur (83) . . . 297 G5
la Cadière-et-Cambo (30) . . . 274 B2
Cadillac (33) . . . 229 K4
Cadillac-en-Fronsadais (33) . . . 211 K6
Cadillon (64) . . . 285 F1
Cadix (81) . . . 271 H2
Cadolive (13) . . . 296 E3
Cadours (31) . . . 268 C5
Cadrieu (46) . . . 250 E1
Caen (14) . . . 32 E5
Caëstre (59) . . . 3 K5
Caffiers (62) . . . 2 C4
Cagnac-les-Mines (81) . . . 270 E2
Cagnano (2B) . . . 317 D3
Cagnes-sur-Mer (06) . . . 281 F4
Cagnicourt (62) . . . 11 G4
Cagnoncles (59) . . . 11 K4
Cagnotte (40) . . . 264 B6
Cagny (14) . . . 33 F6
Cagny (80) . . . 18 B2
Cahagnes (14) . . . 32 A6
Cahagnolles (14) . . . 32 A5
Cahaignes (27) . . . 36 C5
Cahan (61) . . . 53 J3
Caharet (65) . . . 286 A6
Cahon (80) . . . 9 F5
Cahors (46) . . . 249 K1
Cahus (46) . . . 234 C1
Cahuzac (11) . . . 289 F6
Cahuzac (47) . . . 231 J4
Cahuzac (81) . . . 289 J2
Cahuzac-sur-Adour (32) . . . 266 B6
Cahuzac-sur-Vère (81) . . . 270 D2
Caignac (31) . . . 288 E4
le Cailar (30) . . . 275 F5
Cailhau (11) . . . 289 J6
Cailhavel (11) . . . 289 H6
Cailla (11) . . . 308 E5
Caillac (46) . . . 249 J1
Caillavet (32) . . . 267 F5
Caille (06) . . . 280 B3
la Caillère-Saint-Hilaire (85) . . . 160 D2
Cailleville (76) . . . 15 G2
Caillouël-Crépigny (02) . . . 19 J5
Caillouet-Orgeville (27) . . . 56 E1
Cailloux-sur-Fontaines (69) . . . 188 D6
Cailly (76) . . . 16 B6
Cailly-sur-Eure (27) . . . 35 J6
la Caine (14) . . . 53 H1
Cairanne (84) . . . 257 F4
le Caire (04) . . . 259 G2
Cairon (14) . . . 32 D4
Caisnes (60) . . . 39 G1
Caissargues (30) . . . 275 G4
Caix (80) . . . 18 E3
Caixas (66) . . . 314 E3
Caixon (65) . . . 285 H3
Cajarc (46) . . . 250 E1
Calacuccia (2B) . . . 318 E5
Calais (62) . . . 2 C1
Calamane (46) . . . 233 G6
Calan (56) . . . 100 A2
Calanhel (22) . . . 47 K6
Calavanté (65) . . . 285 J5
Calcatoggio (2A) . . . 320 B4
Calce (66) . . . 310 A5
Calenzana (2B) . . . 318 C3
Calès (24) . . . 232 B2
Calès (46) . . . 233 J3
Calignac (47) . . . 247 K5
Caligny (61) . . . 53 G4
Callac (22) . . . 75 K1
Callas (83) . . . 279 K6
Callen (40) . . . 246 A3
Callengeville (76) . . . 10 D3
Calleville (27) . . . 34 E5
Calleville-les-Deux-Églises (76) . . . 15 H4
Callian (32) . . . 266 E6
Callian (83) . . . 280 B5
Calmeilles (66) . . . 314 E4
Calmels-et-le-Viala (12) . . . 272 A2
la Calmette (30) . . . 275 F2
Calmont (12) . . . 252 B4
Calmont (31) . . . 288 D5
Calmoutier (70) . . . 118 C6
Caloire (42) . . . 204 E6
Calonges (47) . . . 247 H2

Calonne-Ricouart (62) . . . 5 J6
Calonne-sur-la-Lys (62) . . . 5 K4
Calorguen (22) . . . 50 D6
la Calotterie (62) . . . 4 B6
Caluire-et-Cuire (69) . . . 206 A1
Calvi (2B) . . . 318 B3
Calviac (46) . . . 234 D1
Calviac-en-Périgord (24) . . . 233 G2
Calvignac (46) . . . 250 D1
Calvinet (15) . . . 235 G4
Calvisson (30) . . . 275 F4
Calzan (09) . . . 307 K2
Camalès (65) . . . 285 H3
Camarade (09) . . . 307 F1
Camarès (12) . . . 272 B4
Camaret-sur-Aigues (84) . . . 257 F5
Camaret-sur-Mer (29) . . . 72 C6
Camarsac (33) . . . 229 K2
Cambayrac (46) . . . 249 J2
la Cambe (14) . . . 29 J6
Cambernard (31) . . . 287 J2
Cambernon (50) . . . 30 E3
Cambes (33) . . . 229 J3
Cambes (46) . . . 234 C5
Cambes (47) . . . 231 F5
Cambes-en-Plaine (14) . . . 32 E4
Cambia (2B) . . . 319 G5
Cambiac (31) . . . 289 F2
Cambieure (11) . . . 308 D1
Camblain-Châtelain (62) . . . 5 J6
Camblain-l'Abbé (62) . . . 10 D2
Camblanes-et-Meynac (33) . . . 229 H3
Cambligneul (62) . . . 10 D1
Cambo-les-Bains (64) . . . 263 E2
Cambon (81) . . . 270 E2
Cambon-et-Salvergues (34) . . . 272 B6
Cambon-lès-Lavaur (81) . . . 289 G1
Camboulazet (12) . . . 252 A4
Camboulit (46) . . . 234 C5
Cambounès (81) . . . 290 C1
Cambounet-sur-le-Sor (81) . . . 289 J1
le Cambout (22) . . . 77 H6
Cambrai (59) . . . 11 J4
Cambremer (14) . . . 33 H5
Cambrin (62) . . . 6 B5
Cambron (80) . . . 9 F5
Cambronne-lès-Clermont (60) . . . 38 A3
Cambronne-lès-Ribécourt (60) . . . 38 E1
Camburat (46) . . . 234 D5
Came (64) . . . 283 F2
Camélas (66) . . . 314 E2
Camelin (02) . . . 39 G1
Camembert (61) . . . 54 E3
Cametours (50) . . . 31 F4
Camiac-et-Saint-Denis (33) . . . 230 A2
Camiers (62) . . . 4 A5
Camiran (33) . . . 230 C5
Camjac (12) . . . 251 K5
Camlez (22) . . . 48 B2
les Cammazes (81) . . . 289 J3
Camoël (56) . . . 121 J2
Camon (09) . . . 308 C2
Camon (80) . . . 18 B2
Camors (56) . . . 100 D3
Camou-Cihigue (64) . . . 283 H6
Camous (65) . . . 305 F3
Campagna-de-Sault (11) . . . 308 D5
Campagnac (12) . . . 253 G2
Campagnac (81) . . . 270 B1
Campagnac-lès-Quercy (24) . . . 232 E4
Campagnan (34) . . . 292 D1
Campagne (24) . . . 232 C1
Campagne (34) . . . 274 D4
Campagne (40) . . . 265 F3
Campagne (60) . . . 19 G5
Campagne-d'Armagnac (32) . . . 266 C3
Campagne-lès-Boulonnais (62) . . . 4 E4
Campagne-lès-Guines (62) . . . 2 D4
Campagne-lès-Hesdin (62) . . . 9 G1
Campagne-lès-Wardrecques (62) . . . 3 H5
Campagne-sur-Arize (09) . . . 307 F1
Campagne-sur-Aude (11) . . . 308 D3
Campagnolles (14) . . . 31 J6
Campan (65) . . . 304 D2
Campana (2B) . . . 319 H5
Campandré-Valcongrain (14) . . . 53 H1
Camparan (65) . . . 305 F4
Campbon (44) . . . 122 D1
Campeaux (14) . . . 31 J5
Campeaux (60) . . . 17 F5
Campel (35) . . . 78 D6
Campénéac (56) . . . 70 A6
Campestre-et-Luc (30) . . . 273 H2
Campet-et-Lamolère (40) . . . 265 F2
Camphin-en-Carembault (59) . . . 6 D5
Camphin-en-Pévèle (59) . . . 7 F4
Campi (2B) . . . 319 J6
Campigneulles-les-Grandes (62) . . . 9 F1
Campigneulles-les-Petites (62) . . . 4 B6
Campigny (14) . . . 32 A4
Campigny (27) . . . 34 C3
Campile (2B) . . . 319 H3
Campistrous (65) . . . 286 A6
Camplong (34) . . . 272 E6
Camplong-d'Aude (11) . . . 309 K1
Campneuseville (76) . . . 17 F2
Campo (2A) . . . 320 D5
Campôme (66) . . . 314 B2
Campouriez (12) . . . 235 K4
Campoussy (66) . . . 309 H6
Campremy (60) . . . 18 B6

Camprond (50) . . . 31 F3
Camps-en-Amiénois (80) . . . 17 H2
Camps-la-Source (83) . . . 297 K2
Camps-Saint-Mathurin-Léobazel (19) . . . 216 D6
Camps-sur-l'Agly (11) . . . 309 G4
Camps-sur-l'Isle (33) . . . 212 C5
Campsas (82) . . . 269 F3
Campsegret (24) . . . 231 J1
Campuac (12) . . . 235 K6
Campugnan (33) . . . 211 H3
Campuzan (65) . . . 286 B5
Camurac (11) . . . 308 B5
Canale-di-Verde (2B) . . . 319 J6
Canals (82) . . . 269 F3
Canaples (80) . . . 9 K5
Canappeville (27) . . . 35 H5
Canapville (14) . . . 33 J3
Canapville (61) . . . 55 F2
Canari (2B) . . . 317 C3
Canaules-et-Argentières (30) . . . 274 D1
Canavaggia (2B) . . . 319 G3
Cancale (35) . . . 51 F3
Canchy (14) . . . 29 J6
Canchy (80) . . . 9 G4
Cancon (47) . . . 231 K6
Candas (80) . . . 10 A5
Candé (49) . . . 124 C2
Candé-sur-Beuvron (41) . . . 128 E3
Candes-Saint-Martin (37) . . . 144 E1
Candillargues (34) . . . 274 D6
Candor (60) . . . 19 G5
Candresse (40) . . . 264 B6
Canehan (76) . . . 16 C1
Canéjan (33) . . . 229 G3
Canens (31) . . . 288 A5
Canenx-et-Réaut (40) . . . 265 H1
Canet (11) . . . 291 G5
Canet (34) . . . 273 H6
Canet-de-Salars (12) . . . 252 B5
Canet-en-Roussillon (66) . . . 310 D6
Canettemont (62) . . . 10 B3
Cangey (37) . . . 128 C4
Caniac-du-Causse (46) . . . 233 K5
Canihuel (22) . . . 76 C2
Canilhac (48) . . . 253 H1
Canisy (50) . . . 31 G4
Canlers (62) . . . 5 F6
Canly (60) . . . 38 C2
Cannectancourt (60) . . . 19 G6
Cannelle (2A) . . . 320 C3
Cannes (06) . . . 280 E6
Cannes-Écluse (77) . . . 88 A4
Cannes-et-Clairan (30) . . . 274 E2
le Cannet (06) . . . 280 E6
Cannet (32) . . . 266 B6
le Cannet-des-Maures (83) . . . 298 C2
Canny-sur-Matz (60) . . . 19 F5
Canny-sur-Thérain (60) . . . 17 F5
Canohès (66) . . . 315 G2
la Canourgue (48) . . . 253 H2
Canouville (76) . . . 15 F3
Cantaing-sur-Escaut (59) . . . 11 J4
Cantaous (65) . . . 305 G1
Cantaron (06) . . . 281 H3
Canté (09) . . . 288 C5
Cantel (76) . . . 35 H4
Canteleu (62) . . . 10 A4
Canteloup (14) . . . 33 G5
Canteloup (50) . . . 29 F2
Cantenac (33) . . . 211 G5
Cantenay-Épinard (49) . . . 125 G2
Cantiers (27) . . . 36 C4
Cantigny (80) . . . 18 C5
Cantillac (24) . . . 213 K1
Cantin (59) . . . 11 H2
Cantois (33) . . . 230 A4
Canville-la-Rocque (50) . . . 28 C6
Canville-les-Deux-Églises (76) . . . 15 H3
Cany-Barville (76) . . . 15 F3
Caorches-Saint-Nicolas (27) . . . 34 C6
Caouënnec-Lanvézéac (22) . . . 48 A3
Caours (80) . . . 9 G5
Cap-d'Ail (06) . . . 281 J3
Capbreton (40) . . . 262 B5
Capdenac (46) . . . 234 D6
Capdenac-Gare (12) . . . 234 E6
Capdrot (24) . . . 232 C4
la Capelle (02) . . . 21 F1
Capelle (59) . . . 12 D3
la Capelle-Balaguier (12) . . . 251 F2
la Capelle-Bleys (12) . . . 251 H3
la Capelle-Bonance (12) . . . 253 F1
la Capelle-et-Masmolène (30) . . . 256 R6
Capelle-Fermont (62) . . . 10 D2
la Capelle-lès-Boulogne (62) . . . 2 A3
Capelle-les-Grands (27) . . . 55 G1
Capelle-lès-Hesdin (62) . . . 9 H2
Capendu (11) . . . 290 D6
Capens (31) . . . 287 K4
Capestang (34) . . . 291 J4
Capian (33) . . . 229 K3
Caplong (33) . . . 230 E3
Capoulet-et-Junac (09) . . . 307 J5
Cappel (57) . . . 68 C2
Cappelle-Brouck (59) . . . 3 G3
Cappelle-en-Pévèle (59) . . . 6 E5
Cappelle-la-Grande (59) . . . 3 H2

Cappy (80) . . . 19 F1
Captieux (33) . . . 246 C3
Capvern (65) . . . 305 F1
Caragoudes (31) . . . 288 E2
Caraman (31) . . . 289 F1
Caramany (66) . . . 309 J6
Carantec (29) . . . 47 F3
Carantilly (50) . . . 31 F4
Carayac (46) . . . 234 C6
Carbay (49) . . . 104 A5
Carbes (81) . . . 270 E6
Carbini (2A) . . . 323 G2
Carbon-Blanc (33) . . . 229 H1
Carbonne (31) . . . 287 K4
Carbuccia (2A) . . . 320 D3
Carcagny (14) . . . 32 C4
Carcanières (09) . . . 308 D6
Carcans (33) . . . 210 C4
Carcarès-Sainte-Croix (40) . . . 264 D3
Carcassonne (11) . . . 290 B5
Carcen-Ponson (40) . . . 264 D2
Carcès (83) . . . 298 A1
Carcheto-Brustico (2B) . . . 319 H5
Cardaillac (46) . . . 234 D4
Cardan (33) . . . 229 K4
Cardeilhac (31) . . . 286 D5
Cardesse (64) . . . 284 A4
Cardet (30) . . . 274 D1
Cardo-Torgia (2A) . . . 320 E6
Cardonette (80) . . . 18 B1
le Cardonnois (80) . . . 18 C5
Cardonville (14) . . . 29 H6
Cardroc (35) . . . 78 E2
Carelles (53) . . . 80 D3
Carency (62) . . . 10 E1
Carennac (46) . . . 234 A1
Carentan (50) . . . 31 G1
Carentoir (56) . . . 102 B2
Cargèse (2A) . . . 316 C6
Cargiaca (2A) . . . 323 F2
Carhaix-Plouguer (29) . . . 75 J3
Carignan (08) . . . 23 H5
Carignan-de-Bordeaux (33) . . . 229 J2
Carisey (89) . . . 113 J4
Carla-Bayle (09) . . . 288 B6
Carla-de-Roquefort (09) . . . 308 A3
le Carlaret (09) . . . 288 E6
Carlat (15) . . . 235 J2
Carlencas-et-Levas (34) . . . 273 F6
Carlepont (60) . . . 39 F1
Carling (57) . . . 68 A2
Carlipa (11) . . . 289 J4
Carlucet (46) . . . 233 K4
Carlus (81) . . . 270 D3
Carlux (24) . . . 233 G2
Carly (62) . . . 2 B6
Carmaux (81) . . . 270 E1
Carnac (56) . . . 100 C6
Carnac-Rouffiac (46) . . . 249 H2
Carnas (30) . . . 274 D3
la Carneille (61) . . . 53 J4
Carnet (50) . . . 51 K5
Carnetin (77) . . . 59 H3
Carneville (50) . . . 28 E2
Carnières (59) . . . 12 B4
Carnin (59) . . . 6 D5
Carnoët (22) . . . 75 J1
Carnoules (83) . . . 298 B3
Carnoux-en-Provence (13) . . . 296 E4
Carnoy (80) . . . 19 F1
Caro (56) . . . 101 K3
Caro (64) . . . 282 E6
Caromb (84) . . . 257 H5
Carpentras (84) . . . 257 G6
Carpineto (2B) . . . 319 H5
Carpiquet (14) . . . 32 D5
Carquebut (50) . . . 29 F6
Carquefou (44) . . . 123 H3
Carqueiranne (83) . . . 297 K6
Carrépuis (80) . . . 19 F4
Carrère (64) . . . 284 E2
Carresse-Cassaber (64) . . . 283 G2
Carrières-sous-Poissy (78) . . . 58 B2
Carrières-sur-Seine (78) . . . 58 D3
Carros (06) . . . 281 F3
Carrouges (61) . . . 82 B1
Carry-le-Rouet (13) . . . 296 A4
Cars (33) . . . 211 G4
les Cars (87) . . . 198 D3
Carsac-Aillac (24) . . . 233 F2
Carsac-de-Gurson (24) . . . 212 E6
Carsan (30) . . . 256 C4
Carsix (27) . . . 34 D5
Carspach (68) . . . 97 B4
Cartelègue (33) . . . 211 H3
Carticasi (2B) . . . 319 G5
Cartignies (59) . . . 13 G5
Cartigny (80) . . . 19 H2
Cartigny-l'Épinay (14) . . . 31 J2
Carves (24) . . . 232 D3
Carville (14) . . . 31 K6
Carville-la-Folletière (76) . . . 15 H4
Carville-Pot-de-Fer (76) . . . 15 G4
Carvin (62) . . . 6 D6
Casabianca (2B) . . . 319 H4
Casaglione (2A) . . . 320 C3
Casalabriva (2A) . . . 322 D1
Casalta (2B) . . . 319 H4
Casamaccioli (2B) . . . 318 D6
Casanova (2B) . . . 319 F6
Cascastel-des-Corbières (11) . . . 310 A3
Casefabre (66) . . . 314 E3

Caseneuve (84) . . . 277 J2
Cases-de-Pène (66) . . . 310 A5
Casevecchie (2B) . . . 321 H2
Cassagnabère-Tournas (31) . . . 286 E5
Cassagnas (48) . . . 254 D4
la Cassagne (24) . . . 215 G5
Cassagne (31) . . . 306 C1
Cassagnes (46) . . . 232 E6
Cassagnes (66) . . . 309 J6
Cassagnes-Bégonhès (12) . . . 252 B5
Cassagnoles (30) . . . 274 E1
Cassagnoles (34) . . . 290 E3
la Cassaigne (11) . . . 289 H6
Cassaigne (32) . . . 267 F2
Cassaignes (11) . . . 309 F3
Cassaniouze (15) . . . 235 H4
Cassel (59) . . . 3 J4
Cassen (40) . . . 264 D4
Casseneuil (47) . . . 248 B1
les Cassés (11) . . . 289 G3
Casseuil (33) . . . 230 B5
Cassignas (47) . . . 248 D3
Cassis (13) . . . 296 E5
Casson (44) . . . 123 G2
Cassuéjouls (12) . . . 236 B4
Cast (29) . . . 74 D4
Castagnac (31) . . . 288 A5
Castagnède (31) . . . 306 B2
Castagnède (64) . . . 283 G2
Castagniers (06) . . . 281 G3
Castaignos-Souslens (40) . . . 265 F6
Castandet (40) . . . 265 J3
Castanet (12) . . . 251 J4
Castanet (81) . . . 270 C2
Castanet (82) . . . 251 F4
Castanet-le-Haut (34) . . . 272 C5
Castanet-Tolosan (31) . . . 288 C2
Castans (11) . . . 290 C3
Casteide-Cami (64) . . . 284 B2
Casteide-Candau (64) . . . 284 B1
Casteide-Doat (64) . . . 285 G3
Casteil (66) . . . 314 B4
Castel-Sarrazin (40) . . . 264 D6
Castelbajac (65) . . . 286 A6
Castelbiague (31) . . . 306 B2
Castelculier (47) . . . 248 C5
Castelferrus (82) . . . 268 D1
Castelfranc (46) . . . 249 H1
Castelgaillard (31) . . . 287 G4
Castelginest (31) . . . 269 G5
Casteljaloux (47) . . . 247 G3
Castella (47) . . . 248 C3
Castellane (04) . . . 279 J2
Castellar (06) . . . 281 J2
le Castellard-Melan (04) . . . 259 H4
Castellare-di-Casinca (2B) . . . 319 J3
Castellare-di-Mercurio (2B) . . . 319 G6
le Castellet (04) . . . 278 D1
le Castellet (83) . . . 297 G5
Castellet (84) . . . 277 J3
Castellet-lès-Sausses (04) . . . 260 E6
Castello-di-Rostino (2B) . . . 319 G4
Castelmary (12) . . . 251 J5
Castelmaurou (31) . . . 269 H5
Castelmayran (82) . . . 268 C1
Castelmoron-d'Albret (33) . . . 230 C4
Castelmoron-sur-Lot (47) . . . 248 A2
Castelnau-Barbarens (32) . . . 286 E1
Castelnau-Chalosse (40) . . . 264 D5
Castelnau-d'Anglès (32) . . . 266 E6
Castelnau-d'Arbieu (32) . . . 267 K3
Castelnau-d'Aude (11) . . . 290 E5
Castelnau-d'Auzan (32) . . . 266 D2
Castelnau-de-Brassac (81) . . . 271 H6
Castelnau-de-Guers (34) . . . 292 C3
Castelnau-de-Lévis (81) . . . 270 D2
Castelnau-de-Mandailles (12) . . . 236 C6
Castelnau-de-Médoc (33) . . . 211 F5
Castelnau-de-Montmiral (81) . . . 270 A2
Castelnau-d'Estrétefonds (31) . . . 269 F4
Castelnau-Durban (09) . . . 307 F2
Castelnau-le-Lez (34) . . . 274 C5
Castelnau-Magnoac (65) . . . 286 C4
Castelnau-Montratier (46) . . . 249 J4
Castelnau-Pégayrols (12) . . . 253 F5
Castelnau-Picampeau (31) . . . 287 H4
Castelnau-Rivière-Basse (65) . . . 266 B6
Castelnau-sur-Gupie (47) . . . 230 E5
Castelnau-sur-l'Auvignon (32) . . . 267 G1
Castelnau-Tursan (40) . . . 265 H5
Castelnau-Valence (30) . . . 275 F1
Castelnaud-de-Gratecambe (47) . . . 248 C1
Castelnaud-la-Chapelle (24) . . . 232 E2
Castelnaudary (11) . . . 289 H4
Castelnavet (32) . . . 266 D5
Castelner (40) . . . 284 B1
Castelnou (66) . . . 314 E3
Castelreng (11) . . . 308 E2
Castels (24) . . . 232 D2
Castelsagrat (82) . . . 248 E5
Castelsarrasin (82) . . . 268 D1
Castelvieilh (65) . . . 285 J4
Castelviel (33) . . . 230 B4
le Castéra (31) . . . 268 D5
Castéra-Bouzet (82) . . . 268 B1
Castéra-Lanusse (65) . . . 285 K6
Castéra-Lectourois (32) . . . 267 J1
Castéra-Lou (65) . . . 285 J4
Castéra-Loubix (64) . . . 285 G3
Castéra-Verduzan (32) . . . 267 G4
Castéra-Vignoles (31) . . . 286 E5
Castéras (09) . . . 307 G1

Casterets (65) 286 C4
Castéron (32) 268 B3
Castet (64) 303 H1
Castet-Arrouy (32) 267 K1
Castetbon (64) 283 J3
Castétis (64) 283 K2
Castetnau-Camblong (64) 283 J3
Castetner (64) 283 J2
Castetpugon (64) 284 E1
Castets (40) 262 E2
Castets-en-Dorthe (33) 230 B5
Castex (09) 288 A6
Castex (32) 286 A3
Castex-d'Armagnac (32) 266 A3
Casties-Labrande (31) 287 H1
Castifao (2B) 318 E3
Castiglione (2B) 319 F4
Castillon (06) 281 K5
Castillon (14) 32 A4
Castillon (65) 304 D1
Castillon(Canton d'Arthez-
  de-Béarn) (64) 284 B2
Castillon(Canton de
  Lembeye) (64) 285 F2
Castillon-de-Castets (33) 230 B6
Castillon-de-Larboust (31) 305 H5
Castillon-de-Saint-Martory (31) . . 287 F6
Castillon-Debats (32) 266 E4
Castillon-du-Gard (30) 275 J1
Castillon-en-Auge (14) 54 D1
Castillon-en-Couserans (09) . . . 306 C3
Castillon-la-Bataille (33) 230 C2
Castillon-Massas (32) 267 H5
Castillon-Savès (32) 287 H1
Castillonnès (47) 231 J4
Castilly (14) 31 J1
Castin (32) 267 H5
Castineta (2B) 319 G4
Castirla (2B) 319 F5
Castrès (02) 19 K3
Castres (81) 271 F6
Castres-Gironde (33) 229 J4
Castries (34) 274 D5
le Cateau-Cambrésis (59) 12 D5
le Catelet (02) 11 K6
le Catelier (76) 16 A3
Catenay (76) 36 A1
Catenoy (60) 38 B3
Cateri (2B) 318 C3
Cathervielle (31) 305 G5
Catheux (60) 17 K5
Catigny (60) 19 G5
Catillon-Fumechon (60) 37 K1
Catillon-sur-Sambre (59) 12 E5
Catllar (66) 314 C3
Catonvielle (32) 268 B5
Cattenières (59) 12 B4
Cattenom (57) 27 H3
Catteville (50) 28 D6
Catus (46) 233 G6
Catz (50) 31 G1
Caubeyres (47) 247 H4
Caubiac (31) 268 D5
Caubios-Loos (64) 284 C2
Caubon-Saint-Sauveur (47) . . . 230 E5
Caubous (31) 305 H4
Caubous (65) 286 B5
Caucalières (81) 290 A2
la Cauchie (62) 10 D4
Cauchy-à-la-Tour (62) 5 J6
Caucourt (62) 10 D1
Caudan (56) 100 A3
Caudebec-en-Caux (76) 15 G6
Caudebec-lès-Elbeuf (76) 35 H4
Caudebronde (11) 290 A3
Caudecoste (47) 248 C5
Caudeval (11) 308 C1
Caudiès-de-Conflent (66) 313 K3
Caudiès-de-Fenouillèdes (66) . . 309 G5
Caudrot (33) 230 B5
Caudry (59) 12 C5
Cauffry (60) 38 A3
Caugé (27) 56 C1
Caujac (31) 288 C4
Caulaincourt (02) 19 J2
le Caule-Sainte-Beuve (76) . . . 16 E3
Caulières (80) 17 H3
Caullery (59) 12 B5
Caulnes (22) 78 B2
Caumont (02) 19 J5
Caumont (09) 306 D2
Caumont (27) 35 G3
Caumont (32) 266 B5
Caumont (33) 230 C4
Caumont (62) 9 H3
Caumont (82) 268 C1
Caumont-l'Éventé (14) 32 A6
Caumont-sur-Durance (84) . . . 276 C2
Caumont-sur-Garonne (47) . . . 247 H1
Caumont-sur-Orne (14) 53 H2
Cauna (40) 265 F4
Caunay (79) 179 F2
Cauneille (40) 264 B6
Caunes-Minervois (11) 290 D4
la Caunette (34) 291 F4
Caunette-sur-Lauquet (11) . . . 309 G2
Caunettes-en-Val (11) 309 J2
Caupenne (40) 264 E5
Caupenne-d'Armagnac (32) . . . 266 B4
la Caure (51) 61 H3
Caurel (22) 76 D4
Caurel (51) 41 G3

Cauro (2A) 320 D5
Cauroir (59) 11 K4
Cauroy (08) 41 K3
Cauroy-lès-Hermonville (51) . . . 40 E3
le Causé (82) 268 C4
Cause-de-Clérans (24) 231 K2
Caussade (82) 250 B5
Caussade-Rivière (65) 285 H1
Causse-Bégon (30) 253 K6
Causse-de-la-Selle (34) 273 K4
Causse-et-Diège (12) 234 D6
Caussens (32) 267 G2
Causses-et-Veyran (34) 291 J2
Caussiniojouls (34) 291 K1
Caussols (06) 280 D3
Caussou (09) 308 A5
Cauterets (65) 304 A3
Cauverville-en-Roumois (27) . . . 34 D3
Cauvicourt (14) 54 A1
Cauvignac (33) 246 E1
Cauvigny (60) 37 J4
Cauville (14) 53 H2
Cauville (76) 14 A5
Caux (34) 292 B2
Caux-et-Sauzens (11) 290 A5
Cauzac (47) 248 D3
Cavagnac (46) 215 K6
Cavaillon (84) 276 D3
Cavalaire-sur-Mer (83) 298 E5
la Cavalerie (12) 272 E1
Cavan (22) 48 B3
Cavanac (11) 290 B6
Cavarc (47) 231 K4
Caveirac (30) 275 F3
Caves (11) 310 C3
Cavignac (33) 211 K4
Cavigny (50) 31 H2
Cavillargues (30) 256 B5
Cavillon (80) 17 J1
Cavron-Saint-Martin (62) 9 H1
Caychax (09) 307 K5
Cayeux-en-Santerre (80) 18 D3
Cayeux-sur-Mer (80) 8 D4
le Caylar (34) 273 G3
Caylus (82) 250 D4
Cayrac (82) 250 A6
Cayres (43) 238 B1
Cayriech (82) 250 B4
le Cayrol (12) 236 B5
Cayrols (15) 235 F2
Cazac (31) 287 G2
Cazalis (33) 246 B2
Cazalis (40) 265 F5
Cazalrenoux (11) 289 G6
Cazals (46) 233 F5
Cazals (82) 250 C5
Cazals-des-Baylès (09) 308 C1
Cazaril-Laspènes (31) 305 H5
Cazaril-Tambourès (31) 286 C6
Cazarilh (65) 305 H3
Cazats (33) 246 D1
Cazaubon (32) 266 B2
Cazaugitat (33) 230 D3
Cazaunous (31) 305 K2
Cazaux (09) 307 H2
Cazaux-d'Anglès (32) 266 E5
Cazaux-Debat (65) 305 F4
Cazaux-Fréchet-
  Anéran-Camors (65) 305 F4
Cazaux-Layrisse (31) 305 H4
Cazaux-Savès (32) 287 G1
Cazaux-Villecomtal (32) 285 J2
Cazavet (09) 306 C2
Cazeaux-de-Larboust (31) . . . 305 H5
Cazedarnes (34) 291 J3
Cazenave-Serres-et-Allens (09) . 307 J4
Cazeneuve (32) 266 D2
Cazeneuve-Montaut (31) 287 F6
Cazères (31) 287 H5
Cazères-sur-l'Adour (40) 265 J4
Cazes-Mondenard (82) 249 H4
Cazevieille (34) 274 B4
Cazideroque (47) 248 E2
Cazilhac (11) 290 B6
Cazilhac (34) 274 A2
Cazillac (46) 215 K6
Cazoulès (24) 233 H2
Cazouls-d'Hérault (34) 292 C2
Cazouls-lès-Béziers (34) 291 J3
Ceaucé (61) 81 G2
Ceaulmont (36) 165 G4
Céaux (50) 51 K3
Céaux-d'Allègre (43) 220 A4
Ceaux-en-Couhé (86) 162 E6
Ceaux-en-Loudun (86) 145 F3
Cébazan (34) 291 H3
Cébazat (63) 202 D1
Ceffonds (52) 91 H2
Ceignes (01) 189 J3
Ceilhes-et-Rocozels (34) 272 E4
Ceillac (05) 227 B3
Ceilloux (63) 203 H3
Ceintrey (54) 94 A1
la Celette (18) 167 G2
la Celle (03) 184 C2
la Celle (18) 167 F1
Cellé (41) 107 K5
la Celle (63) 201 H1
la Celle (83) 297 K2
la Celle-Condé (18) 148 E6
la Celle-Dunoise (23) 182 C1
la Celle-en-Morvan (71) 152 E3

la Celle-Guenand (37) 146 C4
la Celle-les-Bordes (78) 58 A6
la Celle-Lévescault (86) 162 D5
la Celle-Saint-Avant (37) 145 K3
la Celle-Saint-Cloud (78) 58 C3
la Celle-Saint-Cyr (89) 112 D3
la Celle-sous-Chantemerle (51) . 61 G6
la Celle-sous-Gouzon (23) . . . 183 G2
la Celle-sous-Montmirail (02) . . 61 F3
la Celle-sur-Loire (58) 132 A4
la Celle-sur-Morin (77) 60 A4
la Celle-sur-Nièvre (58) 150 E1
Cellefrouin (16) 179 J6
Celles (09) 307 K3
Celles (15) 218 C4
Celles (17) 195 J4
Celles (24) 213 H2
Celles (34) 273 G6
Celles-en-Bassigny (52) 117 F3
Celles-lès-Condé (02) 61 F1
Celles-sur-Aisne (02) 40 A2
Celles-sur-Belle (79) 178 C1
Celles-sur-Durolle (63) 203 J1
Celles-sur-Ource (10) 114 C2
Celles-sur-Plaine (88) 95 H2
la Cellette (23) 166 B6
la Cellette (63) 184 B4
Cellettes (16) 179 G6
Cellettes (41) 129 F3
le Cellier (44) 123 J3
Cellier-du-Luc (07) 238 C4
Cellieu (42) 205 H5
Cellule (63) 185 H5
Celon (36) 165 G4
Celoux (15) 219 H4
Celsoy (52) 116 E4
Cély (77) 87 G3
Cemboing (70) 117 H4
Cempuis (60) 17 H5
Cénac (33) 229 J3
Cénac-et-Saint-Julien (24) . . . 233 F3
Cenans (70) 138 B3
Cendras (30) 255 G5
le Cendre (63) 202 E3
Cendrecourt (70) 117 J4
Cendrey (25) 138 C4
Cendrieux (24) 214 B6
Cénevières (46) 250 D1
Cenne-Monestiés (11) 289 J4
Cenon (33) 229 H2
Cenon-sur-Vienne (86) 163 H1
Censeau (39) 156 C5
Censerey (21) 153 F1
Censy (89) 114 A6
les Cent-Acres (76) 16 A3
Centrès (12) 251 K5
Centuri (2B) 317 D2
Cenves (69) 188 A1
Cépet (31) 269 G4
Cépie (11) 309 F1
Cepoy (45) 111 J2
Céran (32) 267 J3
Cérans-Foulletourte (72) 106 C5
Cerbère (66) 315 K5
Cerbois (18) 148 D2
Cercié (69) 188 B3
Cercier (74) 190 E4
Cercles (24) 213 H1
Cercottes (45) 110 A3
Cercoux (17) 212 B4
le Cercueil (61) 82 C1
Cercy-la-Tour (58) 151 J5
Cerdon (01) 189 J3
Cerdon (45) 130 E2
Cère (40) 265 G1
Céré-la-Ronde (37) 128 C6
Cerelles (37) 127 J3
Cérences (50) 30 E6
Céreste (04) 277 K3
Céret (66) 315 F4
Cerfontaine (59) 13 H3
le Cergne (42) 187 H3
Cergy (95) 58 B1
Cérilly (03) 167 K3
Cérilly (21) 115 F4
Cérilly (89) 89 G6
Cerisé (61) 82 D3
Cerisières (52) 92 A4
Cerisiers (89) 113 F1
Cerisy (80) 18 E2
Cerisy-Belle-Étoile (61) 53 G4
Cerisy-Buleux (80) 17 F1
Cerisy-la-Forêt (50) 31 J2
Cerisy-la-Salle (50) 31 F4
Cerizay (79) 143 G6
Cérizols (09) 306 C1
Cerizy (02) 20 A3
la Cerlangue (76) 34 B1
Cernans (39) 156 B4
Cernay (14) 55 F1
Cernay (28) 84 E4
Cernay (68) 97 A2
Cernay (86) 145 G6
Cernay-en-Dormois (51) 42 C4
Cernay-la-Ville (78) 58 B6
Cernay-l'Église (25) 139 H5
Cernay-lès-Reims (51) 41 F4
Cerneux (77) 60 D5
Cernex (74) 190 E3
Cerniébaud (39) 156 C6
Cernion (08) 22 A3
Cernon (39) 173 H5

Cernon (51) 62 D3
Cernoy (60) 38 B2
Cernoy-en-Berry (45) 131 H3
Cernusson (49) 143 J1
Cerny (91) 86 E2
Cerny-en-Laonnois (02) 40 B2
Cerny-lès-Bucy (02) 20 C5
Céron (71) 186 D1
Cérons (33) 229 K4
Cerqueux (14) 55 F1
les Cerqueux (49) 143 H3
les Cerqueux-sous-Passavant (49) . 143 J2
Cerre-lès-Noroy (70) 138 C1
Cers (34) 292 B4
Cersay (79) 143 K3
Cerseuil (02) 40 A3
Cersot (71) 171 H1
Certilleux (88) 93 G4
Certines (01) 189 G3
Cervens (74) 175 F6
Cervières (05) 227 B1
Cervières (42) 204 A1
Cerville (54) 66 B5
Cervione (2B) 319 J5
Cervon (58) 151 K1
Cerzat (43) 219 H4
Cesancey (39) 173 F2
Césarches (73) 209 G2
Césarville-Dossainville (45) . . . 86 D5
Cescau (09) 306 C3
Cescau (64) 284 B3
Cesny-aux-Vignes-Ouézy (14) . . 33 G6
Cesny-Bois-Halbout (14) 53 J1
Cessac (33) 230 B3
Cessales (31) 288 E2
Cesse (55) 23 H6
Cessenon-sur-Orb (34) 291 J2
Cessens (73) 208 B1
Cesseras (34) 290 E4
Cesset (03) 185 G1
Cesseville (27) 35 G5
Cessey (25) 156 A2
Cessey-sur-Tille (21) 136 C6
Cessières (02) 20 C6
Cessieu (38) 207 G4
Cesson (77) 87 G1
Cesson-Sévigné (35) 79 G4
Cessoy-en-Montois (77) 88 C2
Cessy (01) 174 B6
Cessy-les-Bois (58) 132 C5
Cestas (33) 229 G3
Cestayrols (81) 270 C2
Ceton (61) 83 K5
Cette-Eygun (64) 303 F3
Cevins (73) 209 G3
Ceyras (34) 273 H6
Ceyrat (63) 202 D2
Ceyreste (13) 297 F5
Ceyroux (23) 182 B4
Ceyssac (43) 220 B5
Ceyssat (63) 202 B2
Ceyzériat (01) 189 H2
Ceyzérieu (01) 190 B6
Cézac (33) 211 J4
Cézac (46) 249 J3
Cezais (85) 160 D3
Cézan (32) 267 H3
Cezay (42) 204 C1
Cézens (15) 218 B6
Cézia (39) 173 G5
Cézy (89) 112 E3
Chabanais (16) 180 B6
la Chabanne (03) 186 C4
Chabestan (05) 242 B6
Chabeuil (26) 240 D1
Chablis (89) 113 J5
Châbons (38) 207 G6
Chabottes (05) 243 F4
Chabournay (86) 162 E1
Chabrac (16) 180 C6
Chabreloche (63) 186 B6
Chabrignac (19) 215 G2
Chabrillan (26) 240 D3
Chabris (36) 129 H6
Chacé (49) 144 C1
Chacenay (10) 115 F1
Chacrise (02) 39 K3
Chadeleuf (63) 202 E4
Chadenac (17) 195 J4
Chadenet (48) 237 K6
Chadrac (43) 220 C5
Chadron (43) 220 D6
Chadurie (16) 196 D5
le Chaffal (26) 241 F1
le Chaffaut-Saint-Jurson (04) . . 259 J6
Chaffois (25) 156 E4
Chagey (70) 139 G1
Chagnon (42) 205 H5
Chagny (08) 22 D6
Chagny (71) 153 K5
Chahaignes (72) 107 G6
Chahains (61) 82 B1
Chaignay (21) 136 A3
Chaignes (27) 57 G1
Chail (79) 178 J2
Chaillac (36) 164 E5
Chaillac-sur-Vienne (87) 180 D6
Chailland (53) 80 E5
Chaillé-les-Marais (85) 160 B5
Chaillé-sous-les-Ormeaux (85) . 159 J3
Chailles (41) 128 E3
Chaillevette (17) 194 C2

Chaillevois (02) 40 A1
Chailley (89) 113 H2
Chaillon (55) 65 F2
Chailloué (61) 54 E6
Chailly-en-Bière (77) 87 G3
Chailly-en-Brie (77) 60 B4
Chailly-en-Gâtinais (45) 111 G3
Chailly-lès-Ennery (57) 27 H6
Chailly-sur-Armançon (21) . . . 135 F6
Chainaz-les-Frasses (74) 208 C1
Chaînée-des-Coupis (39) 155 G4
Chaingy (45) 109 J4
Chaintré (71) 188 B1
Chaintreaux (77) 87 J6
Chaintrix-Bierges (51) 62 B3
la Chaise (10) 91 G4
la Chaise-Baudouin (50) 52 B4
la Chaise-Dieu (43) 220 A2
Chaise-Dieu-du-Theil (27) . . . 55 K4
Chaix (85) 160 D5
la Chaize-Giraud (85) 158 E2
la Chaize-le-Vicomte (85) . . . 159 K1
Chalabre (11) 308 C3
Chalagnac (24) 213 K5
Chalain-d'Uzore (42) 204 D3
Chalain-le-Comtal (42) 204 E3
Chalaines (55) 65 F6
Chalais (16) 212 E2
Chalais (36) 164 D4
Chalais (86) 144 E4
Chalamont (01) 189 F4
Chalampé (68) 97 E1
Chalancey (52) 116 B2
Chalancon (26) 241 H6
Chalandray (86) 162 B1
Chalandry (02) 20 D4
Chalandry-Elaire (08) 22 D4
le Chalange (61) 83 F1
le Chalard (87) 198 D5
Chalaux (58) 133 K5
Chaleins (01) 188 C4
Chaleix (24) 198 B5
Chalencon (07) 239 K1
les Chalesmes (39) 174 B1
Châlette-sur-Loing (45) 111 J3
Chalette-sur-Voire (10) 90 E3
Chaley (01) 189 K5
Chalèze (25) 138 A5
Chalezeule (25) 138 A5
Chaliers (15) 237 F1
Chalifert (77) 59 J3
Chaligny (54) 65 K6
Chalinargues (15) 218 C4
Chalindrey (52) 116 E5
Chalivoy-Milon (18) 149 K6
Challain-la-Potherie (49) 124 C1
Challans (85) 141 F5
Challement (58) 133 G5
Challerange (08) 42 B3
Challes (01) 189 J3
Challes (72) 107 G3
Challes-les-Eaux (73) 208 C4
Challet (28) 85 F1
Challex (01) 190 D2
Challignac (16) 196 B6
Challonges (74) 190 C4
Challuy (58) 150 D4
Chalmaison (77) 88 D2
Chalmazel (42) 204 B3
Chalmoux (71) 169 K3
Chalo-Saint-Mars (91) 86 B3
le Chalon (26) 222 E4
Chalon-sur-Saône (71) 154 A6
Chalonnes-sous-le-Lude (49) . . 126 D2
Chalonnes-sur-Loire (49) 124 E5
Châlons (38) 206 B6
Châlons-du-Maine (53) 81 G6
Châlons-en-Champagne (51) . . 62 D2
Châlons-sur-Vesle (51) 40 E4
Châlonvillars (70) 119 H6
Chalou-Moulineux (91) 86 B4
Chaltrait (51) 61 J2
Chalus (63) 202 E6
Châlus (87) 198 C5
Chalvignac (15) 217 F3
Chalvraines (52) 92 C5
Chamadelle (33) 212 C4
Chamagne (88) 94 B2
Chamagnieu (38) 206 E3
Chamalières (63) 202 D2
Chamalières-sur-Loire (43) . . . 220 D3
Chamaloc (26) 241 F2
Chamant (60) 38 D4
Chamarande (91) 86 D2
Chamarandes-Choignes (52) . . 116 B3
Chamaret (26) 257 F2
la Chamba (42) 203 K2
Chambain (21) 115 K5
Chambeire (21) 136 C5
Chambellay (49) 105 F6
Chambéon (42) 204 E3
Chambérat (03) 167 F5
Chamberaud (23) 183 F4
Chamberet (19) 199 K4
Chambéria (39) 173 G4
Chambéry (73) 208 B4
Chambeugle (89) 112 B4
Chambezon (43) 219 F6
Chambilly (71) 186 E1
Chamblac (27) 55 H2

Chamblanc (21) . . . 154 D3
Chamblay (39) . . . 155 J3
Chambles (42) . . . 204 E6
Chamblet (03) . . . 104 B1
Chambley-Bussières (54) . . . 44 C6
Chambly (60) . . . 37 J5
Chamboeuf (21) . . . 135 K6
Chamboeuf (42) . . . 205 F4
Chambois (61) . . . 54 D4
Chambolle-Musigny (21) . . . 154 B1
le Chambon (07) . . . 239 G2
Chambon (17) . . . 177 G3
Chambon (18) . . . 166 E1
Chambon (30) . . . 255 G3
Chambon (37) . . . 146 B6
le Chambon-Feugerolles (42) . . . 221 G1
Chambon-la-Forêt (45) . . . 110 E2
Chambon-le-Château (48) . . . 237 K2
Chambon-Sainte-Croix (23) . . . 165 K6
Chambon-sur-Cisse (41) . . . 128 D2
Chambon-sur-Dolore (63) . . . 203 J3
Chambon-sur-Lac (63) . . . 202 B4
le Chambon-sur-Lignon (43) . . . 221 G5
Chambon-sur-Voueize (23) . . . 183 J2
Chambonas (07) . . . 255 H2
Chambonchard (23) . . . 183 K3
la Chambonie (42) . . . 203 K2
Chamborand (23) . . . 182 A3
Chambord (27) . . . 55 J3
Chambord (41) . . . 129 G2
Chamboret (87) . . . 181 F5
Chamborigaud (30) . . . 255 F3
Chambornay-lès-Bellevaux (70) . . . 138 A4
Chambornay-lès-Pin (70) . . . 137 J5
Chambors (60) . . . 36 E4
Chambost-Allières (69) . . . 187 K4
Chambost-Longessaigne (69) . . . 205 G2
Chamboulive (19) . . . 199 K6
Chambourcy (78) . . . 58 B3
Chambourg-sur-Indre (37) . . . 146 C1
Chambray (27) . . . 35 K6
Chambray-lès-Tours (37) . . . 127 J5
la Chambre (73) . . . 209 F6
Chambrecy (51) . . . 40 D5
les Chambres (50) . . . 51 K2
Chambretaud (85) . . . 142 D4
Chambrey (57) . . . 66 D3
Chambroncourt (52) . . . 92 D3
Chambry (02) . . . 20 D6
Chambry (77) . . . 59 K2
Chaméane (63) . . . 203 G5
Chamelet (69) . . . 187 K5
Chamery (51) . . . 40 E5
Chamesey (25) . . . 139 G6
Chamesol (25) . . . 139 H4
Chamesson (21) . . . 115 K5
Chameyrat (19) . . . 216 A3
Chamigny (77) . . . 60 C2
Chamilly (71) . . . 153 J5
Chammes (53) . . . 105 J1
Chamole (39) . . . 155 J5
Chamonix-Mont Blanc (74) . . . 192 C5
Chamouillac (17) . . . 211 J2
Chamouille (02) . . . 40 B1
Chamouilley (52) . . . 63 K6
Chamousset (73) . . . 208 E4
Chamoux (89) . . . 133 H4
Chamoux-sur-Gelon (73) . . . 208 E4
Chamoy (10) . . . 113 K1
le Champ-de-la-Pierre (61) . . . 54 A4
Champ-d'Oiseau (21) . . . 134 D2
Champ-Dolent (27) . . . 56 C2
Champ-du-Boult (14) . . . 52 D4
Champ-Haut (61) . . . 55 F5
Champ-Laurent (73) . . . 208 E4
Champ-le-Duc (88) . . . 95 F5
le Champ-près-Froges (38) . . . 224 C2
le Champ-Saint-Père (85) . . . 159 J3
Champ-sur-Barse (10) . . . 90 A5
Champ-sur-Drac (38) . . . 224 A4
Champ-sur-Layon (49) . . . 125 G6
Champagnac (15) . . . 217 H1
Champagnac (17) . . . 195 J6
Champagnac-de-Belair (24) . . . 214 A1
Champagnac-la-Noaille (19) . . . 216 D2
Champagnac-la-Prune (19) . . . 216 C4
Champagnac-la-Rivière (87) . . . 198 B3
Champagnac-le-Vieux (43) . . . 219 J1
Champagnat (23) . . . 183 H5
Champagnat (71) . . . 172 E4
Champagnat-le-Jeune (63) . . . 203 G6
Champagne (07) . . . 222 B2
Champagne (17) . . . 194 D1
Champagne (28) . . . 57 H5
Champagné (72) . . . 107 F2
Champagne-au-Mont-d'Or (69) . . . 206 A1
Champagne-en-Valromey (01) . . . 190 B5
Champagne-et-Fontaine (24) . . . 197 F6
Champagne-le-Sec (86) . . . 179 G2
Champagne-les-Marais (85) . . . 160 A5
Champagné-Mouton (16) . . . 179 J5
Champagné-Saint-Hilaire (86) . . . 162 E6
Champagne-sur-Loue (39) . . . 155 K3
Champagne-sur-Oise (95) . . . 37 J6
Champagne-sur-Seine (77) . . . 87 J3
Champagne-sur-Vingeanne (21) . . . 136 D3
Champagne-Vigny (16) . . . 196 C5
Champagneux (73) . . . 207 J3
Champagney (25) . . . 137 J6
Champagney (39) . . . 137 F6
Champagney (70) . . . 119 G5
Champagnier (38) . . . 224 A4

Champagnole (39) . . . 156 B6
Champagnolles (17) . . . 195 G5
Champagny (21) . . . 135 H3
Champagny-en-Vanoise (73) . . . 209 K6
Champagny-sous-Uxelles (71) . . . 171 J3
Champallement (58) . . . 151 H1
Champanges (74) . . . 175 G5
Champaubert (51) . . . 61 H3
Champcella (05) . . . 243 K3
Champcenest (77) . . . 60 D6
Champcerie (61) . . . 54 A4
Champcervon (50) . . . 51 K2
Champcevinel (24) . . . 214 A3
Champcevrais (89) . . . 112 A6
Champcey (50) . . . 51 J2
Champclause (43) . . . 221 F5
Champcueil (91) . . . 87 F2
Champdeniers-Saint-Denis (79) . . . 161 H4
Champdeuil (77) . . . 59 J6
Champdieu (42) . . . 204 C3
Champdivers (39) . . . 155 F3
Champdolent (17) . . . 177 G5
Champdor (01) . . . 190 A4
Champdôtre (21) . . . 154 E1
Champdray (88) . . . 95 G6
Champeau-en-Morvan (21) . . . 134 B6
Champeaux (35) . . . 79 K4
Champeaux (50) . . . 51 J2
les Champeaux (61) . . . 54 D3
Champeaux (77) . . . 87 J1
Champeaux-et-la-Chapelle-Pommier (24) . . . 197 J6
Champeaux-sur-Sarthe (61) . . . 83 G1
Champeix (63) . . . 202 D4
Champenard (27) . . . 36 A6
la Champenoise (36) . . . 148 A5
Champenoux (54) . . . 66 C4
Champéon (53) . . . 81 H3
Champétières (63) . . . 203 K5
Champey (70) . . . 139 G1
Champey-sur-Moselle (54) . . . 65 K1
Champfleur (72) . . . 82 D3
Champfleury (10) . . . 62 A6
Champfleury (51) . . . 41 F5
Champforgeuil (71) . . . 154 A6
Champfrémont (53) . . . 82 B3
Champfromier (01) . . . 190 C2
Champgenéteux (53) . . . 81 J4
Champguyon (51) . . . 61 F4
Champhol (28) . . . 85 G3
Champien (80) . . . 19 G4
Champier (38) . . . 207 F5
Champigné (49) . . . 125 G1
Champigneulle (08) . . . 42 D3
Champigneul-Champagne (51) . . . 62 B2
Champigneul-sur-Vence (08) . . . 22 C4
Champigneulles (54) . . . 66 A4
Champigneulles-en-Bassigny (52) . . . 93 F6
Champignol-lez-Mondeville (10) . . . 115 G1
Champignolles (21) . . . 153 H3
Champignolles (27) . . . 55 K2
Champigny (51) . . . 40 E4
Champigny (89) . . . 88 C4
Champigny-en-Beauce (41) . . . 108 E6
Champigny-la-Futelaye (27) . . . 56 E3
Champigny-le-Sec (86) . . . 162 D1
Champigny-lès-Langres (52) . . . 116 D4
Champigny-sous-Varennes (52) . . . 117 F4
Champigny-sur-Aube (10) . . . 90 A1
Champigny-sur-Marne (94) . . . 59 G4
Champigny-sur-Veude (37) . . . 145 G3
Champillet (36) . . . 165 G6
Champillon (51) . . . 40 E4
Champis (07) . . . 222 A6
Champlan (91) . . . 58 D5
Champlat-et-Boujacourt (51) . . . 40 D5
Champlay (89) . . . 112 E3
Champlecy (71) . . . 170 D4
Champlemy (58) . . . 132 E6
Champlin (08) . . . 21 K2
Champlin (58) . . . 151 G1
Champlitte (70) . . . 136 E1
Champlive (25) . . . 138 C5
Champlost (89) . . . 113 H2
Champmillon (16) . . . 196 C3
Champmotteux (91) . . . 86 E4
Champnétery (87) . . . 199 J1
Champneuville (55) . . . 43 H4
Champniers (16) . . . 196 E2
Champniers (86) . . . 179 J2
Champniers-et-Reilhac (24) . . . 197 K3
Champoléon (05) . . . 243 G3
Champoly (42) . . . 204 A1
Champosoult (61) . . . 54 E3
Champougny (55) . . . 93 G1
Champoulet (45) . . . 132 A1
Champoux (25) . . . 138 B5
Champrenault (21) . . . 135 G4
Champrepus (50) . . . 52 A3
Champrond (72) . . . 107 K2
Champrond-en-Gâtine (28) . . . 84 C3
Champrond-en-Perchet (28) . . . 84 A4
Champrougier (39) . . . 155 G5
Champs (02) . . . 193 K6
Champs (61) . . . 83 H1
Champs (63) . . . 185 F4
les Champs-de-Losque (50) . . . 31 G2
les Champs-Géraux (22) . . . 50 D6
Champs-Romain (24) . . . 198 A5
Champs-sur-Marne (77) . . . 59 G4
Champs-sur-Tarentaine-Marchal (15) . . . 217 J1

Champs-sur-Yonne (89) . . . 113 G6
Champsac (87) . . . 198 C3
Champsanglard (23) . . . 182 D1
Champsecret (61) . . . 53 H6
Champseru (28) . . . 85 H2
Champsevraine (52) . . . 117 F5
Champtercier (04) . . . 259 J5
Champteussé-sur-Baconne (49) . . . 125 F1
Champtocé-sur-Loire (49) . . . 124 D4
Champtoceaux (49) . . . 123 K2
Champtonnay (70) . . . 137 G4
Champvallon (89) . . . 112 E3
Champvans (39) . . . 155 G2
Champvans (70) . . . 137 F4
Champvans-les-Moulins (25) . . . 137 J6
Champvert (58) . . . 151 H6
Champvoisy (51) . . . 40 B6
Champvoux (58) . . . 150 D2
Chamrousse (38) . . . 224 C4
Chamvres (89) . . . 112 E3
Chanac (48) . . . 253 K1
Chanac-les-Mines (19) . . . 216 B3
Chanaleilles (43) . . . 237 J2
Chanas (38) . . . 222 B2
Chanat-la-Mouteyre (63) . . . 202 C1
Chanay (01) . . . 190 C4
Chanaz (73) . . . 208 A1
Chançay (37) . . . 128 A4
Chancé (35) . . . 79 J5
Chanceaux (21) . . . 135 H3
Chanceaux-près-Loches (37) . . . 146 C2
Chanceaux-sur-Choisille (37) . . . 127 J3
Chancelade (24) . . . 213 K3
Chancenay (52) . . . 63 K5
Chancey (70) . . . 137 G5
Chancia (39) . . . 173 H6
Chandai (61) . . . 55 K5
Chandolas (07) . . . 255 J2
Chandon (42) . . . 187 G3
Chanéac (07) . . . 239 G1
Chaneins (01) . . . 188 C3
Chânes (71) . . . 188 B1
le Change (24) . . . 214 C3
Changé (53) . . . 104 E1
Change (71) . . . 163 J4
Changé (72) . . . 106 E3
Changey (52) . . . 116 D3
Changis-sur-Marne (77) . . . 60 A2
Changy (42) . . . 186 D3
Changy (51) . . . 63 G4
Changy (71) . . . 170 D5
Chaniat (43) . . . 219 J2
Chaniers (17) . . . 195 H2
Channay (21) . . . 114 D4
Channay-sur-Lathan (37) . . . 126 E3
Channes (10) . . . 114 C3
Chanonat (63) . . . 202 D3
Chanos-Curson (26) . . . 222 C5
Chanousse (05) . . . 258 C2
Chanoy (52) . . . 116 C3
Chanoz-Châtenay (01) . . . 188 E2
Chanteau (41) . . . 110 B3
Chantecoq (45) . . . 112 A2
Chantecorps (79) . . . 162 A4
Chanteheux (54) . . . 66 D6
Chanteix (19) . . . 215 K2
Chantelle (03) . . . 185 F2
Chanteloup (27) . . . 56 C3
Chanteloup (35) . . . 79 G6
Chanteloup (50) . . . 30 D6
Chanteloup (79) . . . 143 J6
Chanteloup-en-Brie (77) . . . 59 J3
Chanteloup-les-Bois (49) . . . 143 G2
Chanteloup-les-Vignes (78) . . . 58 B2
Chantelouve (38) . . . 224 D5
Chantemerle (51) . . . 89 G1
Chantemerle-les-Blés (26) . . . 222 C4
Chantemerle-les-Grignan (26) . . . 256 F2
Chantemerle-sur-la-Soie (17) . . . 177 J5
Chantenay-Saint-Imbert (58) . . . 168 D1
Chantenay-Villedieu (72) . . . 106 A3
Chantepie (35) . . . 79 G4
Chantérac (24) . . . 213 H4
Chanteraine (55) . . . 64 D5
Chanterelle (15) . . . 218 B1
Chantes (70) . . . 137 J1
Chantesse (38) . . . 223 H2
Chanteuges (43) . . . 219 J5
Chantillac (16) . . . 212 A2
Chantilly (60) . . . 38 A5
Chantonnay (85) . . . 160 B1
Chantraine (88) . . . 94 D5
Chantraines (52) . . . 92 C5
Chantrans (25) . . . 156 D2
Chantrigné (53) . . . 81 G3
Chanu (61) . . . 53 G5
Chanville (57) . . . 45 H6
Chanzeaux (49) . . . 125 F6
Chaon (41) . . . 130 C2
Chaouilley (54) . . . 93 K2
Chaource (10) . . . 114 B2
Chaourse (02) . . . 21 G4
Chapaize (71) . . . 171 J3
Chapareillan (38) . . . 208 C5
Chapdes-Beaufort (63) . . . 184 D6
Chapdeuil (24) . . . 213 H1
Chapeau (03) . . . 169 G4
Chapeiry (74) . . . 190 E6
Chapelaine (51) . . . 90 E1
la Chapelaude (03) . . . 167 G5
la Chapelle (03) . . . 186 A3
la Chapelle (08) . . . 23 F3

la Chapelle (16) . . . 196 D1
la Chapelle (73) . . . 209 F6
la Chapelle-Achard (85) . . . 159 F2
la Chapelle-Agnon (63) . . . 203 J4
la Chapelle-Anthenaise (53) . . . 105 F1
la Chapelle-au-Mans (71) . . . 170 A3
la Chapelle-au-Moine (61) . . . 53 G5
la Chapelle-au-Riboul (53) . . . 81 J4
la Chapelle-Aubareil (24) . . . 215 F6
la Chapelle-aux-Bois (88) . . . 118 C1
la Chapelle-aux-Brocs (19) . . . 215 K4
la Chapelle-aux-Chasses (03) . . . 169 G2
la Chapelle-aux-Choux (72) . . . 126 E1
la Chapelle-aux-Filtzméens (35) . . . 51 F6
la Chapelle-aux-Lys (85) . . . 161 F2
la Chapelle-aux-Naux (37) . . . 127 F5
la Chapelle-aux-Saints (19) . . . 216 A6
la Chapelle-Baloue (23) . . . 165 H6
la Chapelle-Basse-Mer (44) . . . 123 J3
la Chapelle-Bâton (79) . . . 161 J4
la Chapelle-Bâton (86) . . . 179 J2
la Chapelle-Bayvel (27) . . . 34 B4
la Chapelle-Bertin (43) . . . 219 K3
la Chapelle-Bertrand (79) . . . 162 A4
la Chapelle-Biche (61) . . . 53 G5
la Chapelle-Blanche (22) . . . 78 C2
la Chapelle-Blanche (73) . . . 208 D5
la Chapelle-Blanche-Saint-Martin (37) . . . 146 B3
la Chapelle-Bouëxic (35) . . . 78 D6
la Chapelle-Caro (56) . . . 101 J3
la Chapelle-Cécelin (50) . . . 52 B3
la Chapelle-Chaussée (35) . . . 78 E2
la Chapelle-Craonnaise (53) . . . 104 D3
la Chapelle-d'Abondance (74) . . . 175 J3
la Chapelle-d'Alagnon (15) . . . 218 C5
la Chapelle-d'Aligné (72) . . . 105 K6
la Chapelle-d'Andaine (61) . . . 81 H1
la Chapelle-d'Angillon (18) . . . 131 F5
la Chapelle-d'Armentières (59) . . . 6 C3
la Chapelle-d'Aunainville (28) . . . 85 K3
la Chapelle-d'Aurec (43) . . . 221 F2
la Chapelle-de-Bragny (71) . . . 171 J2
la Chapelle-de-Brain (35) . . . 102 D3
la Chapelle-de-Guinchay (71) . . . 188 B2
la Chapelle-de-la-Tour (38) . . . 207 G4
la Chapelle-de-Mardore (69) . . . 187 H4
la Chapelle-de-Surieu (38) . . . 222 C1
la Chapelle-des-Bois (25) . . . 174 B2
la Chapelle-des-Fougeretz (35) . . . 79 F3
la Chapelle-des-Marais (44) . . . 122 A1
la Chapelle-des-Pots (17) . . . 195 H2
la Chapelle-devant-Bruyères (88) . . . 95 G5
Chapelle-d'Huin (25) . . . 156 D4
la Chapelle-du-Bard (38) . . . 208 D6
la Chapelle-du-Bois (72) . . . 107 H2
la Chapelle-du-Bois-des-Faulx (27) . . . 35 J8
la Chapelle-du-Bourgay (76) . . . 16 A3
la Chapelle-du-Châtelard (01) . . . 188 E4
la Chapelle-du-Genêt (49) . . . 142 D1
la Chapelle-du-Lou (35) . . . 78 D3
la Chapelle-du-Mont-de-France (71) . . . 171 G6
la Chapelle-du-Mont-du-Chat (73) . . . 208 A2
la Chapelle-du-Noyer (28) . . . 108 E2
la Chapelle-en-Juger (50) . . . 31 G3
la Chapelle-en-Lafaye (42) . . . 204 C6
la Chapelle-en-Serval (60) . . . 38 B6
la Chapelle-en-Valgaudémar (05) . . . 243 F2
la Chapelle-en-Vercors (26) . . . 223 H6
la Chapelle-en-Vexin (95) . . . 36 D5
la Chapelle-Enchérie (41) . . . 108 D5
la Chapelle-Engerbold (14) . . . 53 G3
la Chapelle-Erbrée (35) . . . 80 B6
la Chapelle-Faucher (24) . . . 214 A1
la Chapelle-Felcourt (51) . . . 63 G1
la Chapelle-Forainvilliers (28) . . . 57 G5
la Chapelle-Fortin (28) . . . 56 A6
la Chapelle-Gaceline (56) . . . 102 C2
la Chapelle-Gaudin (79) . . . 143 K4
la Chapelle-Gaugain (72) . . . 107 J5
la Chapelle-Gauthier (37) . . . 55 G2
la Chapelle-Gauthier (77) . . . 87 K2
la Chapelle-Geneste (43) . . . 219 K1
la Chapelle-Glain (44) . . . 124 A1
la Chapelle-Gonaguet (24) . . . 213 K3
la Chapelle-Grésignac (24) . . . 213 G1
Chapelle-Guillaume (28) . . . 108 A1
la Chapelle-Hareng (27) . . . 34 B6
la Chapelle-Haute-Grue (14) . . . 54 D2
la Chapelle-Hermier (85) . . . 159 F1
la Chapelle-Heulin (44) . . . 123 J4
la Chapelle-Hugon (18) . . . 150 C5
la Chapelle-Hullin (49) . . . 104 B5
la Chapelle-Huon (72) . . . 107 K4
la Chapelle-Iger (77) . . . 60 A4
la Chapelle-Janson (35) . . . 80 B3
la Chapelle-la-Reine (77) . . . 87 G4
la Chapelle-Lasson (51) . . . 61 J6
la Chapelle-Launay (44) . . . 122 C2
la Chapelle-Laurent (15) . . . 219 F4
la Chapelle-lès-Luxeuil (70) . . . 118 D5
la Chapelle-Marcousse (63) . . . 202 D6
la Chapelle-Montabourlet (24) . . . 213 H1
la Chapelle-Montbrandeix (87) . . . 198 B3
la Chapelle-Monthodon (02) . . . 61 G1
la Chapelle-Montligeon (61) . . . 83 J2
la Chapelle-Montlinard (18) . . . 150 C2
la Chapelle-Montmartin (41) . . . 129 J6
la Chapelle-Montmoreau (24) . . . 197 J6
la Chapelle-Montreuil (86) . . . 162 D4
la Chapelle-Moulière (86) . . . 163 H2

la Chapelle-Moutils (77) . . . 60 E4
la Chapelle-Naude (71) . . . 172 C3
la Chapelle-Neuve (22) . . . 48 A6
la Chapelle-Neuve (56) . . . 100 E2
la Chapelle-Onzerain (45) . . . 109 H2
la Chapelle-Orthemale (36) . . . 147 H6
la Chapelle-Palluau (85) . . . 141 H6
la Chapelle-Pouilloux (79) . . . 179 F3
la Chapelle-près-Sées (61) . . . 82 D1
la Chapelle-Rablais (77) . . . 88 C2
la Chapelle-Rainsouin (53) . . . 105 H1
la Chapelle-Rambaud (74) . . . 191 G3
la Chapelle-Réanville (27) . . . 36 A6
la Chapelle-Rousselin (49) . . . 124 E6
Chapelle-Royale (28) . . . 108 C1
la Chapelle-Saint-André (58) . . . 132 E5
la Chapelle-Saint-Aubert (35) . . . 79 K2
la Chapelle-Saint-Aubin (72) . . . 106 D2
la Chapelle-Saint-Étienne (79) . . . 161 G2
la Chapelle-Saint-Florent (49) . . . 124 B5
la Chapelle-Saint-Fray (72) . . . 106 D1
la Chapelle-Saint-Géraud (19) . . . 216 C5
la Chapelle-Saint-Jean (24) . . . 214 E3
la Chapelle-Saint-Laud (49) . . . 125 J1
la Chapelle-Saint-Laurent (79) . . . 161 H1
la Chapelle-Saint-Laurian (36) . . . 148 A3
la Chapelle-Saint-Luc (10) . . . 90 A1
la Chapelle-Saint-Martial (23) . . . 182 D5
la Chapelle-Saint-Martin (73) . . . 207 K3
la Chapelle-Saint-Martin-en-Plaine (41) . . . 109 F6
la Chapelle-Saint-Maurice (74) . . . 208 D1
la Chapelle-Saint-Mesmin (45) . . . 109 K4
la Chapelle-Saint-Ouen (76) . . . 16 C6
la Chapelle-Saint-Quillain (70) . . . 137 H3
la Chapelle-Saint-Rémy (72) . . . 107 G1
la Chapelle-Saint-Sauveur (44) . . . 124 C3
la Chapelle-Saint-Sauveur (71) . . . 154 E5
la Chapelle-Saint-Sépulcre (45) . . . 111 K2
la Chapelle-Saint-Sulpice (77) . . . 88 C1
la Chapelle-Saint-Ursin (18) . . . 149 F3
la Chapelle-Souëf (61) . . . 83 H4
la Chapelle-sous-Brancion (71) . . . 171 J3
la Chapelle-sous-Dun (71) . . . 187 H1
la Chapelle-sous-Orbais (51) . . . 61 H3
la Chapelle-sous-Uchon (71) . . . 152 E6
Chapelle-Spinasse (19) . . . 216 D1
la Chapelle-sur-Chézy (02) . . . 60 E2
la Chapelle-sur-Coise (69) . . . 205 H3
la Chapelle-sur-Dun (76) . . . 15 H2
la Chapelle-sur-Erdre (44) . . . 123 G3
la Chapelle-sur-Furieuse (39) . . . 156 A3
la Chapelle-sur-Loire (37) . . . 126 E6
la Chapelle-sur-Oreuse (89) . . . 88 D5
la Chapelle-sur-Oudon (49) . . . 104 E6
la Chapelle-sur-Usson (63) . . . 203 G6
la Chapelle-Taillefert (23) . . . 182 D4
la Chapelle-Thècle (71) . . . 172 C3
la Chapelle-Thémer (85) . . . 160 C3
la Chapelle-Thireuil (79) . . . 161 G3
la Chapelle-Thouarault (35) . . . 78 E4
la Chapelle-Urée (50) . . . 52 B5
Chapelle-Vallon (10) . . . 90 A3
la Chapelle-Vaupelteigne (89) . . . 113 H5
la Chapelle-Vendômoise (41) . . . 128 D1
la Chapelle-Vicomtesse (41) . . . 108 C3
la Chapelle-Viel (61) . . . 55 J5
la Chapelle-Villars (42) . . . 205 K5
la Chapelle-Viviers (86) . . . 163 J4
Chapelle-Voland (39) . . . 155 F6
la Chapelle-Yvon (14) . . . 34 A6
les Chapelles (73) . . . 193 A3
les Chapelles-Bourbon (77) . . . 59 K5
Chapelon (45) . . . 111 G2
Chapelotte (18) . . . 131 G5
Chapet (78) . . . 58 A2
Chapois (39) . . . 156 B5
Chaponnay (69) . . . 206 B3
Chaponost (69) . . . 205 K2
Chappes (03) . . . 168 A6
Chappes (08) . . . 21 J3
Chappes (10) . . . 90 C6
Chappes (63) . . . 202 E1
Chaptelat (87) . . . 181 H6
Chaptuzat (63) . . . 185 G4
Charancieu (38) . . . 207 J5
Charantonnay (38) . . . 206 D5
Charavines (38) . . . 207 H6
Charbogne (08) . . . 42 A1
Charbonnat (71) . . . 152 D6
Charbonnier-les-Mines (63) . . . 219 G1
Charbonnières (28) . . . 84 B6
Charbonnières (71) . . . 171 K5
Charbonnières-les-Bains (69) . . . 205 K2
Charbonnières-les-Sapins (25) . . . 156 D1
Charbonnières-les-Varennes (63) . . . 184 E6
Charbonnières-les-Vieilles (63) . . . 184 E5
Charbuy (89) . . . 113 F5
la Charce (26) . . . 241 J6
Charcé-Saint-Ellier-sur-Aubance (49) . . . 125 H5
Charcenne (70) . . . 137 H4
Charchigné (53) . . . 81 J3
Charchilla (39) . . . 173 H4
Charcier (39) . . . 173 J2
Chard (23) . . . 183 K6
Chardeny (08) . . . 42 A2
Chardogne (55) . . . 64 A3
Chardonnay (71) . . . 171 K4
Chareil-Cintrat (03) . . . 185 G1
Charencey (21) . . . 135 G4

Commune	Page	Grid
Charency (39)	156	B6
Charency-Vezin (54)	26	A3
Charens (26)	241	J5
Charensat (63)	184	A5
Charentay (69)	188	B3
Charentenay (89)	133	F1
Charentilly (37)	127	H3
Charenton-du-Cher (18)	167	H1
Charenton-le-Pont (94)	59	F4
Charentonnay (18)	150	B2
Charette (38)	207	F1
Charette-Varennes (71)	154	D4
Charey (54)	65	H1
Charézier (39)	173	H2
Chargé (37)	128	B4
Chargey-lès-Gray (70)	137	F3
Chargey-lès-Port (70)	117	K5
Chariez (70)	138	A1
Charigny (21)	134	E4
la Charité-sur-Loire (58)	150	C2
Charix (01)	190	B2
Charlas (31)	286	E5
Charleval (13)	277	F4
Charleval (27)	36	A3
Charleville (51)	61	G4
Charleville-Mézières (08)	22	D3
Charleville-sous-Bois (57)	27	K6
Charlieu (42)	187	F3
Charly (02)	60	D2
Charly (18)	150	A5
Charly (69)	206	A3
Charly-Oradour (57)	27	H6
Charmant (16)	196	E5
Charmauvillers (25)	139	J5
Charmé (16)	179	F5
la Charme (39)	155	H5
le Charme (45)	112	A5
la Charmée (71)	171	J1
Charmeil (03)	185	J3
le Charmel (02)	40	A6
Charmensac (15)	218	E3
Charmentray (77)	59	J2
Charmes (02)	20	B5
Charmes (03)	185	G4
Charmes (21)	136	D4
Charmes (52)	116	D3
Charmes (88)	94	B3
Charmes-en-l'Angle (52)	91	K3
Charmes-la-Côte (54)	65	H6
Charmes-la-Grande (52)	91	K3
Charmes-Saint-Valbert (70)	117	G5
Charmes-sur-l'Herbasse (26)	222	D4
Charmes-sur-Rhône (07)	240	B2
Charmoille (25)	139	G5
Charmoille (70)	118	A6
Charmois (54)	94	C1
Charmois (90)	139	J1
Charmois-devant-Bruyères (88)	94	E5
Charmois-l'Orgueilleux (88)	94	B6
Charmont (51)	63	J3
Charmont (95)	36	E6
Charmont-en-Beauce (45)	86	C5
Charmont-sous-Barbuise (10)	90	B3
les Charmontois (51)	63	K2
Charmoy (10)	89	G3
Charmoy (71)	170	E1
Charmoy (89)	113	F3
Charnas (07)	222	A1
Charnat (63)	185	J5
Charnay (25)	156	B1
Charnay (69)	188	B6
Charnay-lès-Chalon (71)	154	C4
Charnay-lès-Mâcon (71)	188	C1
Charnècles (38)	223	J1
Charnizay (37)	146	C5
Charnod (39)	173	F6
Charnois (08)	24	C2
Charnoz-sur-Ain (01)	189	G6
Charny (21)	134	E5
Charny (77)	59	J2
Charny (89)	112	B4
Charny-le-Bachot (10)	89	K1
Charny-sur-Meuse (55)	43	H4
Charolles (71)	170	D5
Charols (26)	240	D5
Charonville (28)	84	E5
Chârost (18)	148	D4
Charpentry (55)	42	E4
Charpey (26)	222	E6
Charpont (28)	57	F5
Charquemont (25)	139	H6
Charrais (86)	162	E2
Charraix (43)	219	J6
Charras (16)	197	G5
Charray (28)	108	E3
Charre (64)	283	H4
Charrecey (71)	153	J5
Charrey-sur-Saône (21)	154	D2
Charrey-sur-Seine (21)	115	F3
Charrin (58)	151	J6
Charritte-de-Bas (64)	283	H4
Charron (17)	160	B6
Charron (23)	184	A4
Charroux (03)	185	F3
Charroux (86)	179	J3
Chars (95)	37	F5
Charsonville (45)	109	H4
Chartainvilliers (28)	85	G2
Chartèves (02)	40	A6
la Chartre-sur-le-Loir (72)	107	H6
Chartrené (49)	126	A3
Chartres (28)	85	G3
Chartres-de-Bretagne (35)	79	F5
Chartrettes (77)	87	H2
Chartrier-Ferrière (19)	215	H5
Chartronges (77)	60	D5
Chartuzac (17)	211	J1
Charvieu-Chavagneux (38)	206	D2
Charvonnex (74)	191	H5
Chas (63)	203	F2
Chaserey (10)	114	B3
Chasnais (85)	159	K4
Chasnans (25)	156	E2
Chasnay (58)	150	E1
Chasné-sur-Illet (35)	79	H2
Chaspinhac (43)	220	C5
Chaspuzac (43)	220	A5
la Chassagne (39)	155	G5
Chassagne (63)	202	D5
Chassagne-Montrachet (21)	153	K4
Chassagne-Saint-Denis (25)	156	C2
Chassagnes (43)	219	J3
Chassagny (69)	205	K4
Chassaignes (24)	213	F3
Chassal (39)	173	J5
Chassant (28)	84	C5
Chassé (72)	82	E3
Chasse-sur-Rhône (38)	206	A4
Chasseguey (50)	52	C5
Chasselas (71)	188	B1
Chasselay (38)	223	G2
Chasselay (69)	188	C6
Chassemy (02)	40	A2
Chassenard (03)	170	B5
Chasseneuil (36)	165	G2
Chasseneuil-du-Poitou (86)	163	F2
Chasseneuil-sur-Bonnieure (16)	197	H1
Chassenon (16)	198	A1
Chasseradès (48)	238	B6
Chassey (21)	134	E3
Chassey-Beaupré (55)	92	D2
Chassey-le-Camp (71)	153	J5
Chassey-lès-Montbozon (70)	138	C2
Chassey-lès-Scey (70)	137	K1
Chassiecq (16)	179	J5
Chassiers (07)	239	G6
Chassieu (69)	206	C2
Chassignelles (89)	114	C6
Chassignieu (38)	207	H5
Chassignolles (36)	166	A4
Chassignolles (43)	219	J1
Chassigny (52)	116	D6
Chassigny-sous-Dun (71)	187	H2
Chassillé (72)	106	B2
Chassors (16)	196	A2
Chassy (18)	150	B3
Chassy (71)	170	C3
Chassy (89)	112	E4
le Chastang (19)	216	A4
Chastanier (48)	238	B4
Chasteaux (19)	215	H5
Chastel (43)	219	G5
Chastel-Arnaud (26)	241	F4
Chastel-Nouvel (48)	237	J6
Chastel-sur-Murat (15)	218	B4
Chastellux-sur-Cure (89)	133	K5
Chastreix (63)	201	K5
la Châtaigneraie (85)	160	E2
Chatain (86)	179	J4
Châtaincourt (28)	56	E5
Châtas (88)	95	J3
Château (71)	171	G5
Château-Arnoux-Saint-Auban (04)	259	G5
Château-Bernard (38)	223	K6
Château-Bréhain (57)	66	D2
Château-Chalon (39)	155	J6
Château-Chervix (87)	199	G4
Château-Chinon(Campagne) (58)	152	B3
Château-Chinon(Ville) (58)	152	B3
le Château-d'Almenêches (61)	54	D5
Château-des-Prés (39)	173	K4
le Château-d'Oléron (17)	176	C6
Château-d'Olonne (85)	158	E3
Château-du-Loir (72)	107	G6
Château-Garnier (86)	179	J1
Château-Gontier (53)	105	F4
Château-Guibert (85)	159	K3
Château-la-Vallière (37)	127	F2
Château-Landon (77)	111	H1
Château-Larcher (86)	162	E5
Château-l'Évêque (24)	214	A3
Château-l'Hermitage (72)	106	D5
Château-Porcien (08)	21	J6
Château-Renard (45)	112	A4
Château-Renault (37)	128	A2
Château-Rouge (57)	45	J3
Château-Salins (57)	66	D3
Château-sur-Allier (03)	168	B1
Château-sur-Cher (63)	184	A3
Château-sur-Epte (27)	36	D5
Château-Thébaud (44)	123	H5
Château-Thierry (02)	60	E1
Château-Verdun (09)	307	K5
Château-Ville-Vieille (05)	227	B2
Château-Voué (57)	66	D3
Châteaubernard (16)	195	K3
Châteaubleau (77)	88	B1
Châteaubourg (07)	222	B6
Châteaubourg (35)	79	J4
Châteaubriant (44)	103	J3
Châteaudouble (26)	240	E1
Châteaudouble (83)	279	J5
Châteaudun (28)	108	E2
Châteaufort (04)	259	G3
Châteaufort (78)	58	C5
Châteaugay (63)	202	D1
Châteaugiron (35)	79	H5
Châteaulin (29)	74	D3
Châteaumeillant (18)	166	D4
Châteauneuf (21)	153	J1
Châteauneuf (42)	205	J5
Châteauneuf (71)	187	G2
Châteauneuf (73)	208	E4
Châteauneuf (85)	140	E4
Châteauneuf-de-Bordette (26)	257	H2
Châteauneuf-de-Chabre (05)	258	E3
Châteauneuf-de-Gadagne (84)	276	C2
Châteauneuf-de-Galaure (26)	222	C3
Châteauneuf-de-Randon (48)	238	A5
Châteauneuf-de-Vernoux (07)	239	K1
Châteauneuf-d'Entraunes (06)	261	F4
Châteauneuf-d'Ille-et-Vilaine (35)	50	E4
Châteauneuf-d'Oze (05)	242	C6
Châteauneuf-du-Faou (29)	75	G4
Châteauneuf-du-Pape (84)	256	E6
Châteauneuf-du-Rhône (26)	240	A6
Châteauneuf-en-Thymerais (28)	84	E1
Châteauneuf-Grasse (06)	280	D4
Châteauneuf-la-Forêt (87)	199	J3
Châteauneuf-le-Rouge (13)	296	E1
Châteauneuf-les-Bains (63)	184	D4
Châteauneuf-les-Martigues (13)	296	A3
Châteauneuf-Miravail (04)	258	D4
Châteauneuf-sur-Charente (16)	196	C4
Châteauneuf-sur-Cher (18)	149	F6
Châteauneuf-sur-Isère (26)	222	C5
Châteauneuf-sur-Loire (45)	110	D4
Châteauneuf-sur-Sarthe (49)	105	H6
Châteauneuf-Val-de-Bargis (58)	132	D6
Châteauneuf-Val-Saint-Donat (04)	259	G5
Châteauneuf-Villevieille (06)	281	G2
Châteauponsac (87)	181	H3
Châteauredon (04)	259	J4
Châteaurenard (13)	276	C2
Châteauroux (36)	147	K6
Châteauroux-les-Alpes (05)	243	J4
Châteauvert (83)	297	K1
Châteauvieux (05)	242	E6
Châteauvieux (41)	147	G1
Châteauvieux (83)	279	K3
Châteauvieux-les-Fossés (25)	156	D2
Châteauvilain (38)	207	F5
Châteauvillain (52)	115	J2
le Châtel (73)	225	G1
Châtel (74)	175	J6
Châtel-Censoir (89)	133	G3
Châtel-Chéhéry (08)	42	D3
Châtel-de-Joux (39)	173	J3
Châtel-de-Neuvre (03)	168	E5
Châtel-Gérard (89)	134	B1
Châtel-Montagne (03)	186	B3
Châtel-Moron (71)	153	J6
Châtel-Saint-Germain (57)	44	E5
Châtel-sur-Moselle (88)	94	C4
Châtelaillon-Plage (17)	176	E3
Châtelain (53)	105	G5
la Châtelaine (39)	155	K5
Châtelais (49)	104	D5
Châtelard (23)	183	K5
le Châtelard (73)	208	D2
Châtelaudren (22)	48	E5
Chatelay (39)	155	J3
Châtelblanc (25)	174	B1
Châteldon (63)	185	K5
le Châtelet (18)	166	E3
le Châtelet-en-Brie (77)	87	J2
le Châtelet-sur-Meuse (52)	117	F2
le Châtelet-sur-Retourne (08)	41	H2
le Châtelet-sur-Sormonne (08)	22	B2
les Châtelets (28)	56	C6
le Chateley (39)	155	H5
Châtelguyon (63)	185	F6
Châtellenot (21)	135	F6
Châtellerault (86)	145	J6
le Châtellier (35)	80	A3
le Châtellier (61)	53	G5
les Châtelliers-Châteaumur (85)	143	F5
les Châtelliers-Notre-Dame (28)	84	D4
Châtelneuf (39)	173	K1
Châtelneuf (42)	204	C4
Châtelperron (03)	169	H5
Châtelraould-Saint-Louvent (51)	63	F5
Châtelus (03)	186	B2
Châtelus (38)	223	H5
Châtelus (42)	205	G4
Châtelus-le-Marcheix (23)	182	A5
Châtelus-Malvaleix (23)	182	E1
Châtenay (01)	189	G4
Châtenay (28)	86	A4
Châtenay (38)	223	F1
Châtenay (71)	187	H1
Châtenay-en-France (95)	59	F1
Châtenay-Mâcheron (52)	116	D4
Châtenay-Malabry (92)	58	D5
Châtenay-sur-Seine (77)	88	B3
Châtenay-Vaudin (52)	116	E4
Chatenet (17)	212	A2
le Châtenet-en-Dognon (87)	181	K6
Châtenay (70)	118	C6
Châtenois (39)	155	H1
Châtenois (67)	71	B5
Châtenois (70)	118	C6
Châtenois (88)	93	H4
Châtenois-les-Forges (90)	139	H1
Châtenoy (45)	110	E4
Châtenoy (77)	87	H5
Châtenoy-en-Bresse (71)	154	B6
Châtenoy-le-Royal (71)	154	A6
Châtignac (16)	212	D1
Chatignonville (91)	86	A3
Châtillon (03)	168	C5
Châtillon (39)	173	H2
Châtillon (69)	188	A6
Châtillon (86)	162	D6
Châtillon (92)	58	E4
Châtillon-Coligny (45)	111	K5
Châtillon-en-Bazois (58)	151	J3
Châtillon-en-Diois (26)	241	J3
Châtillon-en-Dunois (28)	108	D1
Châtillon-en-Michaille (01)	190	C2
Châtillon-en-Vendelais (35)	80	B5
Châtillon-Guyotte (25)	138	B5
Châtillon-la-Borde (77)	87	J2
Châtillon-la-Palud (01)	189	G1
Châtillon-le-Duc (25)	137	K5
Châtillon-le-Roi (45)	86	C6
Châtillon-lès-Sons (02)	20	D3
Châtillon-Saint-Jean (26)	222	D4
Châtillon-sous-les-Côtes (55)	43	K5
Châtillon-sur-Broué (51)	91	G1
Châtillon-sur-Chalaronne (01)	188	D3
Châtillon-sur-Cher (41)	129	G6
Châtillon-sur-Cluses (74)	191	K3
Châtillon-sur-Colmont (53)	81	F4
Châtillon-sur-Indre (36)	146	E4
Châtillon-sur-Lison (25)	156	B2
Châtillon-sur-Loire (45)	131	J2
Châtillon-sur-Marne (51)	40	C6
Châtillon-sur-Morin (51)	61	G5
Châtillon-sur-Oise (02)	20	B3
Châtillon-sur-Saône (88)	117	J3
Châtillon-sur-Seine (21)	115	F4
Châtillon-sur-Thouet (79)	161	K2
Châtin (58)	152	B2
Châtonnay (38)	206	E5
Chatonnay (39)	173	G5
Chatonrupt-Sommermont (52)	92	A2
Chatou (78)	58	C3
la Châtre (36)	166	B3
la Châtre-Langlin (36)	165	F5
Châtres (10)	89	J2
Châtres (24)	215	F4
Châtres (77)	59	J5
Châtres-la-Forêt (53)	81	J6
Châtres-sur-Cher (41)	130	A6
Châtrices (51)	63	J1
Chattancourt (55)	43	G4
Chatte (38)	223	G4
Chatuzange-le-Goubet (26)	222	E5
Chaucenne (25)	137	J5
Chauchailles (48)	236	E3
Chauché (85)	142	B5
le Chauchet (23)	183	H4
Chauchigny (10)	89	K3
Chauconin-Neufmontiers (77)	59	J2
Chaudardes (02)	40	C2
Chaudebonne (26)	241	F6
Chaudefonds-sur-Layon (49)	125	F5
Chaudefontaine (25)	138	B4
Chaudefontaine (51)	42	D6
Chaudenay (52)	116	E4
Chaudenay (71)	153	K5
Chaudenay-la-Ville (21)	153	J1
Chaudenay-le-Château (21)	153	J1
Chaudeney-sur-Moselle (54)	65	H5
Chaudes-Aigues (15)	236	D2
Chaudeyrac (48)	238	B4
Chaudeyrolles (43)	239	F1
la Chaudière (26)	241	F4
Chaudon (28)	57	G6
Chaudon-Norante (04)	279	G1
Chaudrey (10)	90	C2
Chaudron-en-Mauges (49)	124	C5
Chaudun (02)	39	H3
Chauffailles (71)	187	H2
Chauffayer (05)	242	D3
Chauffecourt (88)	94	A3
Chauffour-lès-Bailly (10)	90	D6
Chauffour-lès-Étréchy (91)	86	C2
Chauffour-sur-Vell (19)	215	K6
Chauffours (28)	85	F3
Chauffourt (52)	116	D2
Chauffry (77)	60	C4
Chaufour-lès-Bonnières (78)	57	G1
Chaufour-Notre-Dame (72)	106	C2
Chaugey (21)	115	K5
Chaulgnes (58)	150	D2
Chaulhac (48)	237	F1
Chaulieu (50)	52	E4
la Chaulme (63)	204	C6
Chaulnes (80)	19	F3
Chaum (31)	305	J3
Chaumard (58)	152	B2
la Chaume (21)	115	J4
Chaume-et-Courchamp (21)	136	D2
Chaume-lès-Baigneux (21)	135	F1
Chaumeil (19)	200	B6
Chaumercenne (70)	137	G5
Chaumes-en-Brie (77)	59	K6
Chaumesnil (10)	91	H4
Chaumont (18)	150	A6
Chaumont (52)	116	B1
Chaumont (61)	55	F3
Chaumont (74)	190	D4
Chaumont (89)	88	B4
Chaumont-d'Anjou (49)	125	K2
Chaumont-devant-Damvillers (55)	43	J3
Chaumont-en-Vexin (60)	37	F4
Chaumont-la-Ville (52)	93	F6
Chaumont-le-Bois (21)	115	F3
Chaumont-le-Bourg (63)	204	A6
Chaumont-Porcien (08)	21	J5
Chaumont-sur-Aire (55)	64	B2
Chaumont-sur-Loire (41)	128	D3
Chaumont-sur-Tharonne (41)	130	A2
Chaumontel (95)	38	A6
Chaumot (58)	133	H6
Chaumot (89)	112	C2
Chaumousey (88)	94	C5
Chaumoux-Marcilly (18)	150	A2
Chaumussay (37)	146	B5
la Chaumusse (39)	173	K3
Chaumuzy (51)	40	D5
Chaunac (17)	211	K1
Chaunay (86)	179	G2
Chauny (02)	19	K5
Chauray (79)	161	H6
Chauriat (63)	203	F2
la Chaussade (23)	183	G5
la Chaussaire (49)	124	A6
Chaussan (69)	205	J3
la Chaussée (76)	16	A3
la Chaussée (86)	144	E5
la Chaussée-d'Ivry (28)	57	G3
la Chaussée-Saint-Victor (41)	129	F2
la Chaussée-sur-Marne (51)	62	E3
la Chaussée-Tirancourt (80)	17	K1
Chaussenac (15)	217	G4
Chaussenans (39)	155	J5
Chausseterre (42)	186	C6
Chaussin (39)	155	F4
Chaussoy-Epagny (80)	18	B4
Chaussy (45)	86	B6
Chaussy (95)	36	D6
le Chautay (18)	150	C4
Chauvac (26)	258	B2
Chauvé (44)	122	C4
Chauvency-le-Château (55)	23	J6
Chauvency-Saint-Hubert (55)	23	J6
Chauvigné (35)	79	J1
Chauvigny (86)	163	J3
Chauvigny-du-Perche (41)	108	C3
Chauvincourt-Provemont (27)	36	D4
Chauvirey-le-Châtel (70)	117	H5
Chauvirey-le-Vieil (70)	117	H5
Chauvoncourt (55)	64	E2
Chauvry (95)	58	D1
Chaux (21)	154	B2
la Chaux (25)	157	F3
la Chaux (61)	53	K6
la Chaux (71)	154	E5
Chaux (90)	119	H5
Chaux-Champagny (39)	156	A4
Chaux-des-Crotenay (39)	174	A2
Chaux-des-Prés (39)	173	K4
la Chaux-du-Dombief (39)	173	K2
la Chaux-en-Bresse (39)	155	G5
Chaux-la-Lotière (70)	137	K4
Chaux-lès-Clerval (25)	138	E4
Chaux-lès-Passavant (25)	138	D6
Chaux-lès-Port (70)	117	K6
Chaux-Neuve (25)	174	B1
Chauzon (07)	255	K1
Chavagnac (15)	218	C4
Chavagnac (24)	215	G5
Chavagne (35)	79	F5
Chavagnes (49)	125	H6
Chavagnes-en-Paillers (85)	142	B4
Chavagnes-les-Redoux (85)	160	D1
Chavaignes (49)	126	C2
Chavanac (19)	200	D4
Chavanat (23)	182	E5
Chavanatte (90)	139	K1
Chavanay (42)	205	K6
Chavanges (10)	91	F2
Chavaniac-Lafayette (43)	219	J4
Chavannaz (74)	190	E3
Chavanne (70)	139	F2
la Chavanne (73)	208	D5
Chavannes (18)	149	G6
Chavannes (26)	222	C4
les Chavannes-en-Maurienne (73)	209	F6
Chavannes-les-Grands (90)	139	K1
Chavannes-sur-l'Étang (68)	119	K6
Chavannes-sur-Reyssouze (01)	172	A5
Chavannes-sur-Suran (01)	189	J1
Chavanod (74)	190	E5
Chavanoz (38)	206	E1
Chavaroux (63)	203	F1
la Chavatte (80)	19	F4
Chaveignes (37)	145	G3
Chavelot (88)	94	D5
Chavenat (16)	196	E6
Chavençon (60)	37	G5
Chavenon (03)	168	A5
Chavéria (39)	173	G4
Chaveroche (19)	201	F4
Chaveyriat (01)	188	E2
Chavignon (02)	40	A1
Chavigny (02)	39	J2
Chavigny (54)	66	A5
Chavigny-Bailleul (27)	56	D3
Chaville (92)	58	D4
Chavin (36)	165	H4
Chavonne (02)	40	B2

Chavornay (01) 190 B6
Chavot-Courcourt (51) 61 K1
Chavoy (50) 51 K2
Chavroches (03) 169 G6
le Chay (17) 194 D3
Chay (25) 156 A3
Chazay-d'Azergues (69) 188 B6
la Chaze-de-Peyre (48) 237 F6
Chazé-Henry (49) 104 B5
Chazé-sur-Argos (49) 124 D1
Chazeaux (07) 239 G5
Chazelet (36) 165 F4
Chazelles (15) 219 G5
Chazelles (16) 197 G3
Chazelles (39) 172 E5
Chazelles (43) 219 J6
Chazelles-sur-Albe (54) 67 G6
Chazelles-sur-Lavieu (42) 204 C5
Chazelles-sur-Lyon (42) 205 G3
Chazemais (03) 167 G2
Chazeuil (21) 136 C2
Chazeuil (58) 132 E6
Chazey-Bons (01) 207 J1
Chazey-sur-Ain (01) 189 G6
Chazilly (21) 153 H1
Chazot (25) 139 F4
Chécy (45) 110 B4
Chédigny (37) 146 D1
Chef-Boutonne (79) 178 E3
Chef-du-Pont (50) 29 F5
Chef-Haut (88) 93 K3
Cheffes (49) 125 H1
Cheffois (85) 160 E2
Cheffreville-Tonnencourt (14) . . 54 E1
le Chefresne (50) 31 G6
Chéhéry (08) 22 E5
Cheignieu-la-Balme (01) 207 J1
Cheillé (37) 127 G6
Cheilly-lès-Maranges (71) 153 J5
Chein-Dessus (31) 306 B2
Cheissoux (87) 199 J1
le Cheix (63) 185 G5
Cheix-en-Retz (44) 122 E4
Chélan (32) 286 C4
Chelers (62) 10 C1
Chélieu (38) 207 H5
Chelle-Debat (65) 285 K4
Chelle-Spou (65) 285 K6
Chelles (60) 39 F3
Chelles (77) 59 G3
Chelun (35) 104 A4
Chemaudin (25) 137 J6
Chemazé (53) 104 E5
Chemellier (49) 125 J5
Chemenot (39) 155 H5
Chéméré (44) 122 D5
Chéméré-le-Roi (53) 105 H3
Chémery (41) 129 G5
Chémery-les-Deux (57) 27 K5
Chémery-sur-Bar (08) 22 E6
Chemilla (39) 173 G6
Chemillé (49) 124 E6
Chemillé-sur-Dême (37) 127 J1
Chemillé-sur-Indrois (37) 146 E2
Chemilli (61) 83 G4
Chemilly (03) 168 E4
Chemilly (70) 137 K1
Chemilly-sur-Serein (89) 113 J5
Chemilly-sur-Yonne (89) 113 G4
Chemin (39) 154 E4
le Chemin (51) 63 J1
Chemin-d'Aisey (21) 115 F6
Cheminas (07) 222 B4
Cheminon (51) 63 J5
Cheminot (57) 66 B2
Chemiré-en-Charnie (72) 106 A2
Chemiré-le-Gaudin (72) 106 C3
Chemiré-sur-Sarthe (49) 105 H5
Chemy (59) 6 D5
Chenac-Saint-Seurin-d'Uzet (17) 194 E4
Chenailler-Mascheix (19) 216 B5
la Chenalotte (25) 157 J1
Chénas (69) 188 B2
Chenaud (24) 212 E3
Chenay (51) 40 E3
Chenay (72) 82 D3
Chenay (79) 162 B6
Chenay-le-Châtel (71) 186 D2
le Chêne (10) 90 B1
Chêne-Arnoult (89) 112 B4
Chêne-Bernard (39) 155 G4
Chêne-en-Semine (74) 190 C4
Chêne-Sec (39) 155 G5
Chenebier (70) 119 G6
Chenecey-Buillon (25) 156 B1
Chenché (86) 162 E1
Chênedollé (53) 53 F3
Chênedouit (61) 53 K4
Chênehutte-Trèves-Cunault (49) . 126 A5
Chénelette (69) 187 K2
Chénérailles (23) 183 G3
Chenereilles (42) 204 D5
Chenereilles (43) 221 F1
Chenevelles (86) 163 J1
Chenevières (54) 94 E1
Chenevrey-et-Morogne (70) . . 137 H5
Chênex (74) 190 E3
Cheney (89) 113 K4
Chenicourt (54) 66 B3
Chenières (54) 26 D3
Chéniers (23) 165 K6
Cheniers (51) 62 C3

Chenillé-Changé (49) 105 F6
Cheniménil (88) 94 E6
Chennebrun (27) 55 K5
Chennegy (10) 89 J5
Chennevières-lès-Louvres (95) . 59 G1
Chennevières-sur-Marne (94) . . 59 G4
Chenois (57) 66 D1
Chenoise (77) 88 C1
Chenommet (16) 179 H5
Chenon (16) 179 H5
Chenonceaux (37) 128 C5
Chenou (77) 87 H6
Chenôve (21) 136 A5
Chenôves (71) 171 H2
Chens-sur-Léman (74) 174 D6
Chenu (72) 127 F2
Chepniers (17) 212 A2
Chepoix (60) 18 B5
la Cheppe (51) 62 E1
Cheppes-la-Prairie (51) 62 E3
Cheppy (55) 42 E4
Cheptainville (91) 86 D2
Chepy (51) 62 E3
Chépy (80) 8 E5
Chérac (17) 195 J2
Chérancé (53) 104 D5
Chérancé (72) 82 D5
Chéraute (64) 283 H5
Cherbonnières (17) 178 B5
Cherbourg Octeville (50) 28 D2
Chérence (95) 36 D6
Chérencé-le-Héron (50) 52 B3
Chérencé-le-Roussel (50) 52 C5
Chéreng (59) 7 F4
les Chères (69) 188 B6
Chérêt (02) 40 C1
Chériennes (62) 9 J2
Cherier (42) 186 D5
Chérigné (79) 178 D3
Chérisay (72) 82 D4
Chérisey (57) 45 F6
Chérisy (28) 57 F5
Chérisy (62) 11 G3
Chérizet (71) 171 G4
Chermignac (17) 195 F3
Chermisey (88) 93 G3
Chermizy-Ailles (02) 40 C1
Chéronnac (87) 198 A2
Chéronvilliers (27) 55 K4
Chéroy (89) 88 A6
Cherré (49) 105 G6
Cherré (72) 83 J6
Cherreau (72) 83 J6
Cherrueix (35) 51 G4
Cherval (24) 213 G1
Cherveix-Cubas (24) 214 E2
Cherves (86) 162 C1
Cherves-Châtelars (16) 197 H1
Cherves-Richemont (16) 195 J2
Chervettes (17) 177 H4
Cherveux (79) 161 J5
Chervey (10) 114 E1
Cherville (51) 62 B1
Chéry (18) 148 D2
Chéry-Chartreuve (02) 40 B4
Chéry-lès-Pouilly (02) 20 D5
Chéry-lès-Rozoy (02) 21 H4
Chesley (10) 114 B3
le Chesnay (78) 58 C4
le Chesne (08) 22 D6
le Chesne (27) 56 B3
Chesnois-Aubencourt (08) . . . 22 B6
Chesny (57) 45 F6
Chessenaz (74) 190 D4
Chessy (69) 188 A6
Chessy (77) 59 J3
Chessy-les-Prés (10) 113 K2
Chéu (89) 113 H3
Cheuge (21) 136 D4
Cheust (65) 304 B1
Cheux (14) 32 C5
Chevagnes (03) 169 G3
Chevagny-les-Chevrières (71) . . 171 J6
Chevagny-sur-Guye (71) 171 F4
Chevaigné (35) 79 G3
Chevaigné-du-Maine (53) 81 J3
le Chevain (72) 82 D3
Cheval-Blanc (84) 276 E3
Chevaline (74) 208 E1
la Chevallerais (44) 123 F1
Chevanceaux (17) 212 B2
Chevannay (21) 135 G4
Chevannes (21) 154 A1
Chevannes (45) 111 K1
Chevannes (89) 113 F6
Chevannes (91) 87 F2
Chevannes-Changy (58) 133 F6
Chevennes (02) 20 E3
Chevenon (58) 150 E3
Chevenoz (74) 175 G5
Cheverny (41) 129 F3
Cheveuges (08) 22 E4
Chevières (08) 42 D3
Chevigney (70) 137 F5
Chevigney-lès-Vercel (25) . . . 157 F1
Chevigney-sur-l'Ognon (25) . . 137 J5
Chevigny (39) 155 G1
Chevigny-en-Valière (21) 154 B4
Chevigny-Saint-Sauveur (21) . . 136 B5

Chevillé (72) 106 A3
Chevillon (52) 92 A1
Chevillon (89) 112 C4
Chevillon-sur-Huillard (45) . . . 111 H3
la Chevillotte (25) 138 B3
Chevilly (45) 110 A2
Chevilly-Larue (94) 58 E5
Chevinay (69) 205 J2
Chevincourt (60) 38 E1
Cheviré-le-Rouge (49) 126 A2
Chevrainvilliers (77) 87 G5
Chevreaux (39) 172 E4
Chevregny (02) 40 B1
Chèvremont (90) 119 J6
la Chèvrerie (16) 179 G4
Chevresis-Monceau (02) 20 C3
Chevreuse (78) 58 B5
Chèvreville (50) 52 C6
Chèvreville (60) 38 A6
Chevrier (74) 190 D3
Chevrières (38) 223 G3
Chevrières (42) 205 G4
Chevrières (60) 38 C3
Chevroches (58) 133 G4
la Chevrolière (44) 123 G5
Chevrotaine (39) 173 J2
Chevroux (01) 172 A5
Chevroz (25) 137 K5
Chevru (77) 60 C5
Chevry (01) 174 B6
Chevry (50) 31 H5
Chevry-Cossigny (77) 59 H5
Chevry-en-Sereine (77) 88 A5
Chevry-sous-le-Bignon (45) . . 111 K1
Chey (79) 178 E1
Cheylade (15) 218 A3
les Choux (45) 111 H5
le Choylard (07) 239 H1
Cheylard-l'Évêque (48) 238 B5
le Cheylas (38) 208 C6
Cheyssieu (38) 206 B6
Chezal-Benoît (18) 148 D6
la Chèze (22) 77 G5
Chèze (65) 304 B3
Chezelle (03) 185 F2
Chezelles (36) 147 J5
Chezelles (37) 145 H3
Chèzeneuve (38) 206 E4
Chézery-Forens (01) 190 C1
Chézy (03) 169 F3
Chézy-en-Orxois (02) 39 H6
Chézy-sur-Marne (02) 60 E2
Chiatra (2B) 319 J6
Chiché (79) 143 K6
Chichée (89) 113 J5
Chichery (89) 113 F4
Chichey (51) 61 H5
Chichilianne (38) 241 K2
Chicourt (57) 66 D2
Chiddes (58) 152 B5
Chiddes (71) 171 G5
Chidrac (63) 202 D5
Chierry (02) 60 E1
Chieulles (57) 45 F5
Chigné (49) 126 C2
Chignin (73) 208 C1
Chigny (02) 20 E1
Chigny-les-Roses (51) 41 F5
Chigy (89) 89 F6
Chilhac (43) 219 H4
Chillac (16) 212 C1
Chille (39) 173 G1
Chilleurs-aux-Bois (45) 110 C2
le Chillou (79) 162 A1
Chilly (08) 22 B2
Chilly (74) 190 D4
Chilly (80) 19 F3
Chilly-le-Vignoble (39) 173 F2
Chilly-Mazarin (91) 58 E5
Chilly-sur-Salins (39) 156 A4
Chimilin (38) 207 J4
Chindrieux (73) 208 A1
Chinon (37) 145 F1
Chipilly (80) 18 E2
Chirac (16) 180 B6
Chirac (48) 237 G6
Chirac-Bellevue (19) 201 F6
Chirassimont (42) 187 H6
Chirat-l'Église (03) 184 E2
Chiré-en-Montreuil (86) 162 D2
Chirens (38) 207 H6
Chiroubles (69) 188 A2
Chirols (07) 239 G4
Chiry-Ourscamps (60) 19 G6
Chis (65) 285 H4
Chisa (2B) 321 H6
Chissay-en-Touraine (41) 128 C5
Chisseaux (37) 128 C5
Chisséria (39) 173 G5
Chissey-en-Morvan (71) 152 E2
Chissey-lès-Mâcon (71) 171 J4
Chissey-sur-Loue (39) 155 J3
Chitenay (41) 129 F3
Chitray (36) 165 F3
Chitry (89) 113 H6
Chitry-les-Mines (58) 133 H6
Chives (17) 178 D5
Chivres (21) 154 C4
Chivres-en-Laonnois (02) 21 F5
Chivres-Val (02) 39 K2
Chivy-lès-Étouvelles (02) 20 C6

Chizé (79) 178 B3
Chocques (62) 5 K5
Choilley-Dardenay (52) 136 D1
Choisel (78) 58 B6
Choiseul (52) 117 F1
Choisey (39) 155 G2
Choisies (59) 13 H3
Choisy (74) 190 E4
Choisy-au-Bac (60) 38 E2
Choisy-en-Brie (77) 60 C5
Choisy-la-Victoire (60) 38 B3
Choisy-le-Roi (94) 59 F5
Cholet (49) 142 E2
Cholonge (38) 224 B5
Choloy-Ménillot (54) 65 H5
la Chomette (43) 219 H3
Chonas-l'Amballan (38) 206 A6
Chonville-Malaumont (55) . . . 64 E4
Chooz (08) 24 C2
Choqueuse-les-Bénards (60) . . 17 J5
Choranche (38) 223 H5
Chorey-les-Beaune (21) 154 A3
Chorges (05) 243 G5
Chouain (14) 32 B4
Chouday (36) 148 D5
Choue (41) 108 B3
Chougny (58) 151 K3
Chouilly (51) 62 A1
Chouppes (86) 144 E6
Chourgnac (24) 214 D3
Choussy (41) 128 E5
Chouvigny (03) 184 E3
Choux (39) 173 J6
les Choux (45) 111 H5
Chouy (02) 39 H5
Chouzé-sur-Loire (37) 126 D6
Chouzelot (25) 156 A2
Chouzy-sur-Cisse (41) 128 D3
Choye (70) 137 H4
Chozeau (38) 206 E2
Chuelles (45) 112 A3
Chuffilly-Roche (08) 42 A1
Chuignes (80) 19 F2
Chuignolles (80) 18 E2
Chuisnes (28) 84 D3
Chusclan (30) 256 D5
Chuyer (42) 205 K6
Chuzelles (38) 206 B4
Ciadoux (31) 286 E5
Ciamannacce (2A) 321 F4
Ciboure (64) 263 B1
Cideville (76) 15 H5
Ciel (71) 154 C5
Cier-de-Luchon (31) 305 H4
Cier-de-Rivière (31) 305 J1
Cierges (02) 40 B5
Cierges-sous-Montfaucon (55) . 43 F3
Cierp-Gaud (31) 305 J3
Cierrey (27) 56 E1
Cierzac (17) 195 K4
Cieurac (46) 250 A2
Cieutat (65) 285 J6
Cieux (87) 181 F5
Ciez (58) 132 C4
Cigogné (37) 128 A6
Cilly (02) 21 F4
Cinais (37) 145 F2
Cindré (03) 185 K1
Cinq-Mars-la-Pile (37) 127 G5
Cinqueux (60) 38 B3
Cintegabelle (31) 288 C4
Cintheaux (14) 32 K6
Cintray (27) 56 A4
Cintray (28) 85 F3
Cintré (35) 78 E4
Cintrey (70) 117 H5
la Ciotat (13) 297 F5
Cipières (06) 280 D3
Ciral (61) 82 B2
Ciran (37) 146 B3
Circourt (88) 94 B4
Circourt-sur-Mouzon (88) . . . 93 G4
Ciré-d'Aunis (17) 177 F4
Cirès (31) 305 G4
Cires-lès-Mello (60) 37 K4
Cirey (70) 138 B4
Cirey-lès-Mareilles (52) 92 C3
Cirey-lès-Pontailler (21) 136 D5
Cirey-sur-Blaise (52) 91 J4
Cirey-sur-Vezouze (54) 67 H6
Cirfontaines-en-Azois (52) . . . 115 J1
Cirfontaines-en-Ornois (52) . . 92 D2
Cirière (79) 143 H5
Ciron (36) 164 E3
Ciry-le-Noble (71) 170 D3
Ciry-Salsogne (02) 39 K3
Cisai-Saint-Aubin (61) 55 F4
Cisery (89) 134 B3
Cissac-Médoc (33) 210 E3
Cissé (86) 162 E2
Cisternes-la-Forêt (63) 201 K2
Cistrières (43) 219 K2
Citerne (80) 17 G1
Citers (70) 118 D5
Citey (70) 137 H3
Citou (11) 290 D3
Citry (77) 60 C2
Civaux (86) 163 J5
Civens (42) 204 E2
Civières (27) 36 C5

Civrac-de-Blaye (33) 211 J4
Civrac-en-Médoc (33) 210 E1
Civrac-sur-Dordogne (33) . . . 230 C2
Civray (18) 148 E4
Civray (86) 179 H3
Civray-de-Touraine (37) 128 C5
Civray-sur-Esves (37) 146 A3
Civrieux (01) 188 D5
Civrieux-d'Azergues (69) 188 B6
Civry (28) 109 G2
Civry-en-Montagne (21) 135 G6
Civry-la-Forêt (78) 57 H3
Cizancourt (80) 19 G2
Cizay-la-Madeleine (49) 144 B1
Cize (01) 189 J2
Cize (39) 173 K1
Cizely (58) 151 H4
Cizos (65) 286 B5
Clacy-et-Thierret (02) 20 C5
Cladech (24) 232 D2
Claira (66) 310 C5
Clairac (47) 247 J2
Clairavaux (23) 200 E2
Clairefontaine-en-Yvelines (78) . 86 A1
Clairefougère (61) 53 F1
Clairegoutte (70) 119 F6
Clairfayts (59) 13 J4
Clairfontaine (02) 13 H6
Clairmarais (62) 3 G5
Clairoix (60) 38 E2
Clairvaux-d'Aveyron (12) 251 K2
Clairvaux-les-Lacs (39) 173 J3
Clairy-Saulchoix (80) 17 K2
Clais (76) 16 D3
Claix (16) 196 D4
Claix (38) 224 A4
Clam (17) 195 H5
Clamanges (51) 62 A4
Clamart (92) 58 D4
Clamecy (02) 39 J2
Clamecy (58) 133 F4
Clamensane (04) 259 H2
Clamerey (21) 134 E2
Clans (06) 261 J6
Clans (70) 137 K1
Clansayes (26) 256 E2
le Claon (55) 42 E5
le Clapier (12) 272 E3
Clapiers (34) 274 C5
Clara (66) 314 C3
Clarac (31) 305 J1
Clarac (65) 285 K5
Claracq (64) 284 D1
Clarafond (74) 190 D3
Clarbec (14) 33 J4
Clarens (65) 286 B6
Clarensac (30) 275 F3
Claret (04) 259 F2
Claret (34) 274 C3
Clarques (62) 3 G6
Clary (59) 12 C5
Classun (40) 265 H5
Clastres (02) 19 K4
Clasville (76) 15 F3
le Clat (11) 308 E5
Claudon (88) 117 K2
le Claux (15) 218 A4
Clavans-en-Haut-Oisans (38) . . 225 F4
Clavé (79) 161 K4
Claveisolles (69) 187 K3
Clavette (17) 176 E2
Claveyson (26) 222 C3
Clavières (15) 219 G6
Claviers (83) 279 K5
Claville (27) 56 C1
Claville-Motteville (76) 16 A5
Clavy-Warby (08) 22 B3
la Claye (85) 159 K4
Claye-Souilly (77) 59 H2
Clayes (35) 78 E3
les Clayes-sous-Bois (78) . . . 58 B4
la Clayette (71) 187 H1
Clayeures (54) 94 C2
Clécy (14) 53 H2
Cléden-Cap-Sizun (29) 73 B3
Cléden-Poher (29) 75 H3
Cléder (29) 46 D3
Clèdes (40) 265 H6
Cleebourg (67) 25 D1
Clefmont (52) 116 E1
Clefs (49) 126 B1
les Clefs (74) 191 H6
Cléguer (56) 99 K3
Cléguérec (56) 76 D2
Clelles (38) 241 K2
Clémencey (21) 135 J6
Clémensat (63) 202 D5
Clémery (54) 66 A2
Clémont (18) 130 E2
Clénay (21) 136 B4
Clenleu (62) 4 D5
Cléon (76) 35 H3
Cléon-d'Andran (26) 240 D5
Cleppé (42) 204 E2
Clérac (17) 212 B3
Cléré-du-Bois (36) 146 E3
Cléré-les-Pins (37) 127 F4
Cléré-sur-Layon (49) 143 K2
Clères (76) 15 K5
Clérey (10) 90 C6
Clérey-la-Côte (88) 93 G2
Clérey-sur-Brenon (54) 94 A1

359

Clergoux (19)	216	D2
Clérieux (26)	222	D5
les Clérimois (89)	88	E5
le Clerjus (88)	118	C2
Clerlande (63)	185	G6
Clermain (71)	171	G6
Clermont (09)	307	F2
Clermont (40)	264	C5
Clermont (60)	38	A3
Clermont (74)	190	D5
Clermont-Créans (72)	106	B6
Clermont-de-Beauregard (24)	231	K1
Clermont-Dessous (47)	247	K4
Clermont-d'Excideuil (24)	214	D1
Clermont-en-Argonne (55)	42	E6
Clermont-Ferrand (63)	202	D2
Clermont-le-Fort (31)	288	B2
Clermont-les-Fermes (02)	21	G5
Clermont-l'Hérault (34)	273	H6
Clermont-Pouyguillès (32)	286	C6
Clermont-Savès (32)	268	C6
Clermont-Soubiran (47)	248	D5
Clermont-sur-Lauquet (11)	309	G2
Cléron (25)	156	C2
Clerques (62)	2	E4
Clerval (25)	138	E4
Cléry (21)	136	E5
Cléry (73)	209	F3
Cléry-en-Vexin (95)	36	E6
Cléry-Grand (55)	43	F2
Cléry-Petit (55)	43	F2
Cléry-Saint-André (45)	109	J5
Cléry-sur-Somme (80)	19	G1
Clesles (51)	89	J2
Clessé (71)	171	J5
Clessé (79)	161	H1
Clessy (71)	170	B3
Cléty (62)	3	F6
Cleurie (88)	119	F1
Cleuville (76)	15	F4
Cléville (14)	33	G5
Cléville (76)	15	F5
Clévilliers (28)	85	F2
Cleyrac (33)	230	C3
Cleyzieu (01)	189	K5
Clézentaine (88)	94	E2
Clichy (92)	58	E3
Clichy-sous-Bois (93)	59	G3
Climbach (67)	25	B1
Clinchamp (52)	92	E5
Clinchamps-sur-Orne (14)	32	D6
Clion (17)	195	H5
Clion (36)	147	F4
Cliousclat (26)	240	C3
Cliponville (76)	15	F4
Cliron (08)	22	C3
la Clisse (17)	195	F2
Clisson (44)	123	K6
Clitourps (50)	29	F2
Clohars-Carnoët (29)	99	H4
Clohars-Fouesnant (29)	98	D2
le Cloître-Pleyben (29)	75	F3
le Cloître-Saint-Thégonnec (29)	47	G6
Clomot (21)	153	G1
Clonas-sur-Varèze (38)	206	A6
Clos-Fontaine (77)	88	A1
la Clotte (17)	212	B4
Clouange (57)	27	G5
Cloué (86)	162	D5
les Clouzeaux (85)	159	H2
Cloyes-sur-le-Loir (28)	108	D3
Cloyes-sur-Marne (51)	63	G6
Clucy (39)	156	A4
Clugnat (23)	183	F1
Cluis (36)	165	J4
Clumanc (04)	260	A6
Cluny (71)	171	H5
la Clusaz (74)	191	J5
la Cluse (05)	242	C4
la Cluse-et-Mijoux (25)	157	F4
les Cluses (66)	315	G4
Cluses (74)	191	K3
Clussais-la-Pommeraie (79)	179	F2
Clux (71)	154	D4
Coadout (22)	48	C5
Coaraze (06)	281	G2
Coarraze (64)	284	E6
Coat-Méal (29)	72	D3
Coatascorn (22)	48	C3
Coatréven (22)	48	B2
Cobonne (26)	240	E3
Cobrieux (59)	7	H5
la Cochère (61)	54	D5
Cocherel (77)	60	B1
Cocheren (57)	68	B2
Coclois (10)	90	D2
Cocquerel (80)	9	H6
Cocumont (47)	247	F1
Cocurès (48)	254	C3
Codalet (66)	314	B3
Codognan (30)	275	F4
Codolet (30)	256	D5
Coësmes (35)	103	J1
Coëtlogon (22)	77	H5
Coëtmieux (22)	49	H6
Coeuvres-et-Valsery (02)	39	G3
Coëx (85)	158	E1
Coggia (2A)	316	B4
Coglès (35)	51	K6
Cogna (39)	173	J3
Cognac (16)	195	K3
Cognac-la-Forêt (87)	198	C1
Cognat-Lyonne (03)	185	H3
Cogners (72)	107	J4
Cognet (38)	242	B1
Cognières (70)	138	C3
Cognin (73)	208	B4
Cognin-les-Gorges (38)	223	H3
Cogny (18)	149	K6
Cogny (69)	188	A5
Cogolin (83)	298	E4
Cohade (43)	219	G2
Cohennoz (73)	209	G1
Cohiniac (22)	48	E6
Cohons (52)	116	D5
Coiffy-le-Bas (52)	117	G3
Coiffy-le-Haut (52)	117	G3
Coigneux (80)	10	C5
Coignières (78)	58	A5
Coigny (50)	28	E6
Coimères (33)	230	A6
Coin-lès-Cuvry (57)	45	F6
Coin-sur-Seille (57)	66	A1
Coinces (45)	109	J3
Coinches (88)	95	J4
Coincourt (54)	66	E4
Coincy (02)	39	K5
Coincy (57)	45	G5
Coings (36)	148	A5
Coingt (02)	21	H3
Coirac (33)	230	B4
Coise (69)	205	H4
Coise-Saint-Jean-Pied-Gauthier (73)	208	D4
Coiserette (39)	173	J6
Coisevaux (70)	139	G1
Coisia (39)	173	G6
Coisy (80)	18	B1
Coivert (17)	178	A4
Coivrel (60)	18	D6
Coizard-Joches (51)	61	J4
Colayrac-Saint-Cirq (47)	248	B4
Colembert (62)	2	C5
Coligny (01)	172	E5
Colincamps (80)	10	D5
Collan (89)	113	J5
la Collancelle (58)	151	J2
Collandres (15)	217	K3
Collandres-Quincarnon (27)	56	A2
Collanges (63)	202	E6
Collat (43)	219	K3
la Colle-sur-Loup (06)	281	F4
Collégien (77)	59	H4
Collemiers (89)	112	D1
Colleret (59)	13	J3
le Collet-de-Dèze (48)	255	F4
Colletot (27)	34	D3
Colleville (76)	14	D3
Colleville-Montgomery (14)	32	E4
Colleville-sur-Mer (14)	29	K6
Collias (30)	275	H2
Colligis-Crandelain (02)	40	B1
Colligny (57)	45	G5
Colline-Beaumont (62)	8	E2
Collinée (22)	77	J3
Collioure (66)	315	J4
Collobrières (83)	298	C4
Collonge-en-Charollais (71)	171	G2
Collonge-la-Madeleine (71)	153	H4
Collonges (01)	190	D2
Collonges-au-Mont-d'Or (69)	206	A1
Collonges-la-Rouge (19)	215	K5
Collonges-lès-Bévy (21)	154	A1
Collonges-lès-Premières (21)	136	C6
Collonges-sous-Salève (74)	191	F2
Collongues (06)	280	C2
Collongues (65)	285	J4
Collorec (29)	75	G2
Collorgues (30)	275	G1
Colmar (68)	96	C4
Colmars (04)	260	C4
Colmen (57)	45	J2
Colméry (58)	132	D5
Colmesnil-Manneville (76)	15	K2
Colmey (54)	26	B3
Colmier-le-Bas (52)	115	K5
Colmier-le-Haut (52)	115	K5
Colognac (30)	274	B1
Cologne (32)	268	C6
Colomars (06)	281	G3
Colombe (38)	207	G6
la Colombe (41)	109	F4
la Colombe (50)	31	G6
Colombé-la-Fosse (10)	91	H5
Colombé-le-Sec (10)	91	H5
Colombelles (14)	32	E4
Colombes (92)	58	D3
Colombey-les-Belles (54)	93	H1
Colombey-les-Deux-Églises (52)	91	J5
Colombier (03)	184	C1
Colombier (21)	153	J1
Colombier (24)	231	J3
Colombier (42)	221	K1
Colombier (70)	118	B6
Colombier-en-Brionnais (71)	170	E6
Colombier-Fontaine (25)	139	G3
Colombier-le-Cardinal (07)	222	A2
Colombier-le-Jeune (07)	222	A5
Colombier-le-Vieux (07)	222	A5
Colombier-Saugnieu (69)	206	D2
Colombières (14)	31	J1
Colombières-sur-Orb (34)	291	H1
Colombiers (17)	195	H3
Colombiers (18)	167	G2
Colombiers (34)	291	K4
Colombiers (61)	82	C2
Colombiers (86)	163	G1
Colombiers-du-Plessis (53)	80	E3
Colombiers-sur-Seulles (14)	32	D3
Colombiès (12)	251	J3
Colombotte (70)	118	C6
Colomby (50)	28	D4
Colomby-sur-Thaon (14)	32	D4
Colomiers (31)	269	F6
Colomieu (01)	207	J2
Colonard-Corubert (61)	83	J3
Colondannes (23)	182	A1
Colonfay (02)	20	D2
Colonne (39)	155	H5
Colonzelle (26)	257	F2
Colpo (56)	101	F3
Colroy-la-Grande (88)	95	K3
Colroy-la-Roche (67)	70	A6
Coltainville (28)	85	H2
Coltines (15)	218	D5
Coly (24)	215	F5
Combaillaux (34)	274	A5
Combas (30)	274	E3
la Combe-de-Lancey (38)	224	C2
Combeaufontaine (70)	117	J6
Combefa (81)	251	G6
Comberanche-et-Épeluche (24)	213	F2
Comberjon (70)	118	B6
Comberouger (82)	268	D3
Combertault (21)	154	B4
les Combes (25)	157	G2
Combes (34)	272	D6
Combiers (16)	197	G5
Comblanchien (21)	154	B2
Combles (80)	11	F6
Combles-en-Barrois (55)	64	A4
Combleux (45)	110	B4
Comblessac (35)	102	C1
Comblot (61)	83	H2
Combloux (74)	192	A5
Combon (27)	35	F6
Combourg (35)	51	F6
Combourtillé (35)	80	A4
Combovin (26)	240	E1
Combrailles (63)	201	J1
Combrand (79)	143	G5
Combray (14)	53	J2
Combre (42)	187	G4
Combrée (49)	104	C6
Combres (28)	84	C4
Combres-sous-les-Côtes (55)	44	A6
Combressol (19)	200	E6
Combret (12)	271	K3
Combreux (45)	110	E3
Combrimont (88)	95	K4
Combrit (29)	98	C2
Combronde (63)	185	F5
Combs-la-Ville (77)	59	G6
la Comelle (71)	152	D5
Comiac (46)	234	D1
Comigne (11)	290	D6
Comines (59)	6	D2
Commana (29)	46	E6
Commarin (21)	135	G6
Commeaux (61)	54	B4
Commelle (38)	206	E6
Commelle-Vernay (42)	187	F5
Commenailles (39)	155	G6
Commenchon (02)	19	J5
Commensacq (40)	245	G4
Commentry (03)	184	B1
Commeny (95)	37	H6
Commequiers (85)	141	F6
Commer (53)	81	G5
Commercy (55)	64	E4
Commerveil (72)	83	F4
Commes (14)	32	B3
Communailles-en-Montagne (39)	156	C6
Communay (69)	206	A4
Compains (63)	202	B6
Compainville (76)	16	E5
Compans (77)	59	H2
le Compas (23)	183	J5
Compertrix (51)	62	D2
Compeyre (12)	253	G5
Compiègne (60)	38	D2
Compigny (89)	88	D4
Compolibat (12)	251	H2
la Compôte (73)	208	D2
Comprégnac (12)	253	F6
Compreignac (87)	181	H5
Comps (26)	240	E5
Comps (30)	275	K3
Comps (33)	211	H5
Comps-la-Grand-Ville (12)	252	B4
Comps-sur-Artuby (83)	279	J4
la Comté (62)	10	C1
Comus (11)	308	B5
Conan (41)	108	E6
Conand (01)	189	J6
Conat (66)	314	B3
Conca (2A)	323	J1
Concarneau (29)	98	E3
Conceveux (02)	40	C2
Concèze (19)	215	G1
Conches-en-Ouche (27)	56	B2
Conches-sur-Gondoire (77)	59	H3
Conchez-de-Béarn (64)	285	F1
Conchil-le-Temple (62)	8	E2
Conchy-les-Pots (60)	18	E5
Conchy-sur-Canche (62)	9	K2
Concorès (46)	233	H4
Concoret (56)	78	B4
Concots (46)	250	C2
Concoules (30)	255	F2
Concourson-sur-Layon (49)	144	A1
Concremiers (36)	164	B3
Concressault (18)	131	G3
Concriers (41)	109	G6
Condac (16)	179	G4
Condal (71)	172	D4
Condamine (01)	189	K3
Condamine (39)	173	F2
la Condamine-Châtelard (04)	227	B6
Condat (15)	218	A2
Condat (46)	215	K6
Condat-en-Combraille (63)	201	J1
Condat-lès-Montboissier (63)	203	H5
Condat-sur-Ganaveix (19)	199	D3
Condat-sur-Trincou (24)	214	A1
Condat-sur-Vézère (24)	215	F4
Condat-sur-Vienne (87)	198	E2
Condé (36)	148	C5
Condé-en-Brie (02)	61	F1
Condé-Folie (80)	9	H6
Condé-lès-Autry (08)	42	C4
Condé-lès-Herpy (08)	21	J6
Condé-Northen (57)	45	H4
Condé-Sainte-Libiaire (77)	59	J3
Condé-sur-Aisne (02)	39	K2
Condé-sur-Huisne (61)	84	A4
Condé-sur-Ifs (14)	54	B1
Condé-sur-Iton (27)	56	B4
Condé-sur-l'Escaut (59)	7	J6
Condé-sur-Marne (51)	62	B1
Condé-sur-Noireau (14)	53	H3
Condé-sur-Risle (27)	34	D3
Condé-sur-Sarthe (61)	82	C3
Condé-sur-Seulles (14)	32	B4
Condé-sur-Suippe (02)	40	E2
Condé-sur-Vesgre (78)	57	H5
Condé-sur-Vire (50)	31	H4
Condeau (61)	84	A3
Condécourt (95)	58	A1
Condeissiat (01)	188	E2
Condéon (16)	196	B6
Condes (39)	173	G6
Condes (52)	92	B6
Condette (62)	2	A6
Condezaygues (47)	248	E1
Condillac (26)	240	B4
Condom (32)	267	F2
Condom-d'Aubrac (12)	236	C5
Condorcet (26)	257	J1
Condren (02)	19	K5
Condrieu (69)	206	A6
Conflandey (70)	117	K5
Conflans-en-Jarnisy (54)	44	C5
Conflans-Sainte-Honorine (78)	58	C2
Conflans-sur-Anille (72)	107	K3
Conflans-sur-Lanterne (70)	118	B4
Conflans-sur-Loing (45)	111	J3
Conflans-sur-Seine (51)	89	H1
Confolens (16)	180	B5
Confolent-Port-Dieu (19)	201	H5
Confort (01)	190	C2
Confracourt (70)	117	J6
Confrançon (01)	188	E1
Congé-sur-Orne (72)	82	E6
Congénies (30)	274	E4
Congerville-Thionville (91)	86	B4
Congis-sur-Thérouanne (77)	60	A1
Congrier (53)	104	B4
Congy (51)	61	J3
Conie-Molitard (28)	109	F1
Conilhac-Corbières (11)	290	E6
Conilhac-de-la-Montagne (11)	308	D5
Conjux (73)	208	A1
Conlie (72)	106	C1
Conliège (39)	173	G2
Connac (12)	271	J1
Connangles (43)	219	K2
Connantray-Vaurefroy (51)	62	A5
Connantre (51)	61	K5
Connaux (30)	256	C6
Conne-de-Labarde (24)	231	J3
Connelles (27)	35	K4
Connerré (72)	107	G2
Connezac (24)	197	H5
Connigis (02)	61	F1
Conquereuil (44)	103	F4
Conques (12)	235	H5
Conques-sur-Orbiel (11)	290	B5
le Conquet (29)	72	A4
Conqueyrac (30)	274	C2
Cons-la-Grandville (54)	26	C3
Cons-Sainte-Colombe (74)	209	F1
Consac (17)	195	G6
Conségudes (06)	280	E2
Consenvoye (55)	43	G3
Consigny (52)	92	D6
Consolation-Maisonnettes (25)	157	H1
Contalmaison (80)	10	E6
Contamine-Sarzin (74)	190	D4
Contamine-sur-Arve (74)	191	H2
les Contamines-Montjoie (74)	192	B6
Contault (51)	63	H2
Contay (80)	10	C6
Conte (39)	156	B6
Contes (06)	281	H2
Contes (62)	9	H1
Contescourt (02)	19	K3
Contest (53)	81	G5
Conteville (14)	33	F6
Conteville (27)	34	B2
Conteville (60)	17	J5
Conteville (76)	16	E4
Conteville (80)	9	J4
Conteville-en-Ternois (62)	10	A1
Conteville-lès-Boulogne (62)	2	B5
Conthil (57)	66	E2
Contigné (49)	105	H6
Contigny (03)	168	E6
Contilly (72)	83	F3
Continvoir (37)	126	E4
Contoire (80)	18	D4
Contrazy (09)	306	E2
Contré (17)	178	C4
Contréglise (70)	117	K4
Contremoulins (76)	14	D4
Contres (18)	149	H5
Contres (41)	129	F4
Contreuve (08)	42	A3
Contrevoz (01)	207	J1
Contrexéville (88)	93	J5
Contrières (50)	30	E5
Contrisson (55)	63	J4
Conty (80)	17	K4
Contz-les-Bains (57)	27	J3
Conzieu (01)	207	J2
Coole (51)	62	D5
Coolus (51)	62	D2
la Copechagnière (85)	142	A5
Copponex (74)	190	E3
Coquainvilliers (14)	33	K5
Coquelles (62)	2	C3
la Coquille (24)	198	C5
Corancez (28)	85	G4
Corancy (58)	152	B2
Coray (29)	75	F5
Corbara (2B)	318	C2
Corbarieu (82)	269	G2
Corbas (69)	206	B3
Corbehem (62)	11	H2
Corbeil (51)	90	E1
Corbeil-Cerf (60)	37	H4
Corbeil-Essonnes (91)	87	F1
Corbeilles (45)	111	G2
Corbel (73)	208	A6
Corbelin (38)	207	H3
Corbenay (70)	118	C3
Corbeny (02)	40	D1
Corbère (66)	314	E2
Corbère-Abères (64)	285	F2
Corbère-les-Cabanes (66)	314	E2
Corberon (21)	154	B3
Corbès (30)	255	F6
Corbie (80)	18	C2
la Corbière (70)	118	E4
Corbières (04)	278	B4
Corbières (11)	308	C2
Corbigny (58)	133	H6
Corbon (14)	33	H5
Corbon (61)	83	J3
Corbonod (01)	190	C5
Corbreuse (91)	86	B2
Corcelle-Mieslot (25)	138	B4
Corcelles (01)	189	K4
Corcelles-en-Beaujolais (69)	188	B3
Corcelles-Ferrières (25)	137	H6
Corcelles-les-Arts (21)	153	K4
Corcelles-lès-Cîteaux (21)	154	C1
Corcelles-les-Monts (21)	135	K5
Corcieux (88)	95	H5
Corcondray (25)	137	J6
Corconne (30)	274	C3
Corcoué-sur-Logne (44)	141	H3
Corcy (02)	39	H4
Cordéac (38)	242	C2
Cordebugle (14)	34	B4
Cordelle (42)	186	E5
Cordemais (44)	122	D3
Cordes-sur-Ciel (81)	251	F6
Cordes-Tolosannes (82)	268	D1
Cordesse (71)	153	F3
Cordey (14)	54	A3
Cordon (74)	192	A5
Cordonnet (70)	137	K4
Coren (15)	218	E5
Corenc (38)	224	B3
Corent (63)	202	E3
Corfélix (51)	61	H4
Corgengoux (21)	154	B4
Corgnac-sur-l'Isle (24)	214	C1
Corgoloin (21)	154	B2
Corignac (17)	211	K2
Corlay (22)	76	D2
Corlier (01)	189	K4
Cormainville (28)	109	H1
Cormaranche-en-Bugey (01)	190	A5
Cormatin (71)	171	H3
Corme-Écluse (17)	194	E3
Corme-Royal (17)	194	E2
Cormeilles (27)	34	B4
Cormeilles (60)	17	K5
Cormeilles-en-Parisis (95)	58	D2
Cormeilles-en-Vexin (95)	37	G6
Cormelles-le-Royal (14)	32	E5
Cormenon (41)	108	A3
Cormeray (41)	129	F3
Cormery (37)	127	K6
Cormes (72)	83	J6

Cormicy (51) . . . 40 D3
le Cormier (27) . . . 56 E2
Cormolain (14) . . . 31 K3
Cormont (62) . . . 4 C5
Cormontreuil (51) . . . 41 F4
Cormoranche-sur-Saône (01) . . . 188 C2
Cormost (10) . . . 90 B6
Cormot-le-Grand (21) . . . 153 J4
Cormoyeux (51) . . . 40 E6
Cormoz (01) . . . 172 D4
Corn (46) . . . 234 C5
Cornac (46) . . . 234 C1
Cornant (89) . . . 112 C1
Cornas (07) . . . 222 C6
Cornay (08) . . . 42 D3
Corné (49) . . . 125 J3
Cornebarrieu (31) . . . 269 F6
Corneilhan (34) . . . 291 K3
Corneilla-de-Conflent (66) . . . 314 B4
Corneilla-del-Vercol (66) . . . 315 H3
Corneilla-la-Rivière (66) . . . 310 A6
Corneillan (32) . . . 266 A5
Corneuil (27) . . . 56 D3
Corneville-la-Fouquetière (27) . . . 34 E6
Corneville-sur-Risle (27) . . . 34 D3
Cornier (74) . . . 191 G3
Cornil (19) . . . 216 A3
Cornillac (26) . . . 258 A1
Cornille (24) . . . 214 B3
Cornillé (35) . . . 79 K5
Cornillé-les-Caves (49) . . . 125 J3
Cornillon (30) . . . 256 B4
Cornillon-Confoux (13) . . . 295 K3
Cornillon-en-Trièves (38) . . . 242 A2
Cornillon-sur-l'Oule (26) . . . 257 K1
Cornimont (88) . . . 119 H2
Cornod (39) . . . 173 G6
Cornot (70) . . . 117 H6
la Cornuaille (49) . . . 124 C3
Cornus (12) . . . 272 E3
Cornusse (18) . . . 149 K4
Corny (27) . . . 36 B4
Corny-Machéroménil (08) . . . 22 A6
Corny-sur-Moselle (57) . . . 44 E6
Coron (49) . . . 143 H4
Corpe (85) . . . 160 A4
Corpeau (21) . . . 153 K4
Corpoyer-la-Chapelle (21) . . . 135 G2
Corps (38) . . . 242 D2
Corps-Nuds (35) . . . 79 G6
Corquilleroy (45) . . . 111 K4
Corquoy (18) . . . 149 F5
Corrano (2A) . . . 321 F5
Corravillers (70) . . . 119 F3
Corre (70) . . . 117 K3
Corrençon-en-Vercors (38) . . . 223 J5
Correns (83) . . . 297 K1
Corrèze (19) . . . 216 C1
Corribert (51) . . . 61 H2
Corrobert (51) . . . 61 G3
Corrombles (21) . . . 134 C3
Corronsac (31) . . . 288 C2
Corroy (51) . . . 61 K5
Corsaint (21) . . . 134 C3
Corsavy (66) . . . 314 D5
Corscia (2B) . . . 318 E5
Corsept (44) . . . 122 C3
Corseul (22) . . . 50 B5
Cortambert (71) . . . 171 H4
Corte (2B) . . . 319 F6
Cortevaix (71) . . . 171 H4
Cortrat (45) . . . 111 J4
les Corvées-les-Yys (28) . . . 84 D4
Corveissiat (01) . . . 189 J1
Corvol-d'Embernard (58) . . . 132 E6
Corvol-l'Orgueilleux (58) . . . 132 E4
Corzé (49) . . . 125 J2
Cos (09) . . . 307 H3
Cosges (39) . . . 172 E1
Coslédaà-Lube-Boast (64) . . . 284 C1
Cosmes (53) . . . 104 D3
Cosnac (19) . . . 215 J4
Cosne-Cours-sur-Loire (58) . . . 132 A4
Cosne-d'Allier (03) . . . 167 K5
Cosnes-et-Romain (54) . . . 26 C2
Cosqueville (50) . . . 28 E2
Cossaye (58) . . . 169 F1
Cossé-d'Anjou (49) . . . 143 G1
Cossé-en-Champagne (53) . . . 105 J3
Cossé-le-Vivien (53) . . . 104 D3
Cossesseville (14) . . . 53 J3
Cosswiller (67) . . . 70 C2
Costa (2B) . . . 318 D2
Costaros (43) . . . 238 C1
les Costes (05) . . . 242 E3
les Costes-Gozon (12) . . . 272 A1
la Côte (70) . . . 119 F6
la Côte-d'Aime (73) . . . 209 J4
la Côte-d'Arbroz (74) . . . 192 A1
la Côte-en-Couzan (42) . . . 204 A2
la Côte-Saint-André (38) . . . 207 F6
le Coteau (42) . . . 187 F4
Côtebrune (25) . . . 138 C5
les Côtes-d'Arey (38) . . . 206 B6
les Côtes-de-Corps (38) . . . 242 C2
Coti-Chiavari (2A) . . . 322 C1
Cotignac (83) . . . 298 A1
Cottance (42) . . . 205 F2
Cottenchy (80) . . . 18 B3
Cottévrard (76) . . . 16 B5
Cottun (14) . . . 32 A3
la Couarde (79) . . . 162 A6

la Couarde-sur-Mer (17) . . . 176 A2
Couargues (18) . . . 132 A6
Coubert (77) . . . 59 H6
Coubeyrac (33) . . . 230 D3
Coubisou (12) . . . 236 A6
Coubjours (24) . . . 215 F3
Coublanc (52) . . . 116 E6
Coublanc (71) . . . 187 G2
Coublevie (38) . . . 223 K1
Coublucq (64) . . . 284 D1
Coubon (43) . . . 220 C6
Coubron (93) . . . 59 G3
Couches (71) . . . 153 H5
Couchey (21) . . . 135 K6
la Coucourde (26) . . . 240 B4
Coucouron (07) . . . 238 D3
Coucy (08) . . . 41 J1
Coucy-la-Ville (02) . . . 20 A6
Coucy-le-Château-Auffrique (02) . . . 39 J1
Coucy-lès-Eppes (02) . . . 20 E6
Couddes (41) . . . 129 F5
Coudehard (61) . . . 54 D3
Coudekerque (59) . . . 3 H2
Coudekerque-Branche (59) . . . 3 H1
Coudes (63) . . . 202 E4
Coudeville-sur-Mer (50) . . . 30 D6
Coudoux (13) . . . 296 B1
Coudray (27) . . . 36 B3
le Coudray (28) . . . 85 G3
Coudray (45) . . . 86 E5
Coudray (53) . . . 105 F5
Coudray-au-Perche (28) . . . 84 A5
le Coudray-Macouard (49) . . . 144 C1
le Coudray-Montceaux (91) . . . 87 F1
Coudray-Rabut (14) . . . 33 K3
le Coudray-Saint-Germer (60) . . . 36 E2
le Coudray-sur-Thelle (60) . . . 37 H3
la Coudre (79) . . . 143 J4
Coudreceau (28) . . . 84 B4
Coudrecieux (72) . . . 107 J3
Coudres (28) . . . 56 E3
Coudroy (45) . . . 111 F4
Coudun (60) . . . 38 D2
Coudures (40) . . . 265 G5
Coueilles (31) . . . 287 F4
Couëron (44) . . . 123 F4
Couesmes (37) . . . 127 F2
Couesmes-Vaucé (53) . . . 81 F2
Couffé (44) . . . 123 K2
Couffoulens (11) . . . 290 A6
Couffy (41) . . . 129 F6
Couffy-sur-Sarsonne (19) . . . 201 F3
Couflens (09) . . . 306 E5
Coufouleux (81) . . . 269 K4
Couhé (86) . . . 179 G1
Couilly-Pont-aux-Dames (77) . . . 59 K3
Couin (62) . . . 10 C5
Couiza (11) . . . 309 F3
Couladère (31) . . . 287 H6
Coulaines (72) . . . 106 E2
Coulandon (03) . . . 168 D4
Coulangeron (89) . . . 133 F1
Coulanges (03) . . . 169 K4
Coulanges (41) . . . 128 D3
Coulanges-la-Vineuse (89) . . . 113 G6
Coulanges-lès-Nevers (58) . . . 150 E4
Coulanges-sur-Yonne (89) . . . 133 F3
Coulans-sur-Gée (72) . . . 106 C2
Coulaures (24) . . . 214 D2
Couleuvre (03) . . . 168 A2
Coulevon (70) . . . 118 B6
Coulgens (16) . . . 197 F1
Coulimer (61) . . . 83 G2
Coullemelle (80) . . . 18 C5
Coullemont (62) . . . 10 C4
Coullons (45) . . . 131 F2
Coulmer (61) . . . 55 F4
Coulmier-le-Sec (21) . . . 115 F6
Coulmiers (45) . . . 109 H4
Coulobres (34) . . . 292 A2
Coulogne (62) . . . 2 D3
Couloisy (60) . . . 39 F2
Coulombiers (72) . . . 82 D4
Coulombiers (86) . . . 162 D4
Coulombs (14) . . . 32 C4
Coulombs (28) . . . 57 G6
Coulombs-en-Valois (77) . . . 60 B1
Coulomby (62) . . . 2 E5
Coulommes (77) . . . 59 K3
Coulommes-et-Marqueny (08) . . . 42 A2
Coulommes-la-Montagne (51) . . . 40 E4
Coulommiers (77) . . . 60 B4
Coulommiers-la-Tour (41) . . . 108 D5
Coulon (79) . . . 161 F6
Coulonces (14) . . . 31 J6
Coulonces (61) . . . 54 C3
la Coulonche (61) . . . 53 J6
Coulongé (72) . . . 106 D6
Coulonges (16) . . . 196 D1
Coulonges (17) . . . 195 J4
Coulonges (86) . . . 164 D5
Coulonges-Cohan (02) . . . 40 B5
Coulonges-les-Sablons (61) . . . 84 A3
Coulonges-sur-l'Autize (79) . . . 161 F4
Coulonges-sur-Sarthe (61) . . . 83 G2
Coulonges-Thouarsais (79) . . . 144 A4
Coulonvillers (80) . . . 9 H4
Couloumé-Mondebat (32) . . . 266 C6
Coulounieix-Chamiers (24) . . . 214 A3
Coulours (89) . . . 89 G6
Couloutre (58) . . . 132 D4

Coulouvray-Boisbenâtre (50) . . . 52 C4
Coulvain (14) . . . 32 A6
Coulx (47) . . . 248 A1
Coume (57) . . . 45 J4
Counozouls (11) . . . 308 E6
Coupelle-Neuve (62) . . . 5 F6
Coupelle-Vieille (62) . . . 5 F5
Coupesarte (14) . . . 33 J4
Coupéville (51) . . . 63 F2
Coupiac (12) . . . 271 J2
Coupray (52) . . . 115 K3
Coupru (02) . . . 60 D1
Couptrain (53) . . . 81 K2
Coupvray (77) . . . 59 J3
Courances (91) . . . 87 F3
Courant (17) . . . 177 J4
Courban (21) . . . 115 J3
la Courbe (61) . . . 54 A4
Courbehaye (28) . . . 109 H1
Courbépine (27) . . . 34 C6
Courbes (02) . . . 20 B4
Courbesseaux (54) . . . 66 C5
Courbette (39) . . . 173 G3
Courbeveille (53) . . . 104 D2
Courbevoie (92) . . . 58 D3
Courbiac (47) . . . 249 F2
Courbillac (16) . . . 196 A2
Courbon (02) . . . 01 F2
Courbouzon (39) . . . 173 F2
Courbouzon (41) . . . 109 G6
Courçais (03) . . . 167 F5
Courçay (37) . . . 128 A6
Courceboeufs (72) . . . 106 E1
Courcelette (80) . . . 10 E5
Courcelles (17) . . . 178 A5
Courcelles (25) . . . 156 B2
Courcelles (54) . . . 93 K3
Courcelles (58) . . . 132 E4
Courcelles (90) . . . 97 A5
Courcelles-au-Bois (80) . . . 10 D5
Courcelles-Chaussy (57) . . . 45 H5
Courcelles-de-Touraine (37) . . . 126 E3
Courcelles-en-Barrois (55) . . . 64 D3
Courcelles-en-Bassée (77) . . . 88 B3
Courcelles-en-Montagne (52) . . . 116 C4
Courcelles-Epayelles (60) . . . 18 D6
Courcelles-Frémoy (21) . . . 134 C4
Courcelles-la-Forêt (72) . . . 106 C5
Courcelles-le-Comte (62) . . . 10 E4
Courcelles-lès-Gisors (60) . . . 36 D4
Courcelles-lès-Lens (62) . . . 11 H1
Courcelles-lès-Montbard (21) . . . 134 C3
Courcelles-lès-Montbéliard (25) . . . 139 H2
Courcelles-lès-Semur (21) . . . 134 D4
Courcelles-Sapicourt (51) . . . 40 D4
Courcelles-sous-Châtenois (88) . . . 93 H4
Courcelles-sous-Moyencourt (80) . . . 17 J3
Courcelles-sous-Thoix (80) . . . 17 J4
Courcelles-sur-Aire (55) . . . 64 B2
Courcelles-sur-Blaise (52) . . . 91 J3
Courcelles-sur-Nied (57) . . . 45 G6
Courcelles-sur-Seine (27) . . . 36 A5
Courcelles-sur-Vesles (02) . . . 40 B3
Courcelles-sur-Viosne (95) . . . 37 G6
Courcelles-sur-Voire (10) . . . 91 F2
Courcemain (51) . . . 61 K6
Courcemont (72) . . . 83 F6
Courcerac (17) . . . 195 J1
Courcerault (61) . . . 83 J3
Courceroy (10) . . . 88 E3
Courchamp (77) . . . 60 D6
Courchamps (02) . . . 39 H6
Courchamps (49) . . . 144 C1
Courchapon (25) . . . 137 H6
Courchaton (70) . . . 138 E2
Courchelettes (59) . . . 11 H2
Courcité (53) . . . 81 K4
Courcival (72) . . . 83 F5
Courçôme (16) . . . 179 G5
Courçon (17) . . . 177 G1
Courcoué (37) . . . 145 H3
Courcouronnes (91) . . . 87 F1
Courcoury (17) . . . 195 G2
Courcuire (70) . . . 137 H5
Courcy (14) . . . 54 C2
Courcy (50) . . . 30 E4
Courcy (51) . . . 40 E3
Courcy-aux-Loges (45) . . . 110 D2
Courdemanche (27) . . . 56 E4
Courdemanche (72) . . . 107 H5
Courdemanges (51) . . . 63 H5
Courdimanche (95) . . . 58 B1
Courdimanche-sur-Essonne (91) . . . 86 E3
Courgeac (16) . . . 212 E1
Courgenard (72) . . . 107 K1
Courgenay (89) . . . 89 F3
Courgent (78) . . . 57 H3
Courgeon (61) . . . 83 J1
Courgeoût (61) . . . 83 G2
Courgis (89) . . . 113 H5
Courgivaux (51) . . . 61 F5

Courgoul (63) . . . 202 C5
Courjeonnet (51) . . . 61 J4
Courlac (16) . . . 212 E2
Courlandon (51) . . . 40 C3
Courlans (39) . . . 173 F2
Courlaoux (39) . . . 173 F2
Courlay (79) . . . 143 H6
Courléon (49) . . . 126 A4
Courlon (21) . . . 136 A1
Courlon-sur-Yonne (89) . . . 88 C4
Courmangoux (01) . . . 172 E6
Courmas (51) . . . 40 E5
Courmelles (02) . . . 39 J3
Courmemin (41) . . . 129 H4
Courménil (61) . . . 54 E4
Courmes (06) . . . 280 E3
Courmont (02) . . . 40 B5
Courmont (70) . . . 139 F1
Cournanel (11) . . . 308 E2
Courniou (34) . . . 290 E2
Cournols (63) . . . 202 C4
Cournon (56) . . . 102 C3
Cournon-d'Auvergne (63) . . . 202 E2
Cournonsec (34) . . . 293 F1
Cournonterral (34) . . . 293 F1
la Couronne (16) . . . 196 D4
Courouvre (55) . . . 64 C2
Courpalay (77) . . . 60 A6
Courpiac (33) . . . 230 B3
Courpière (63) . . . 203 H2
Courpignac (17) . . . 211 J1
Courquetaine (77) . . . 59 J6
Courrensan (32) . . . 266 E4
Courrières (62) . . . 6 C6
Courris (81) . . . 271 G2
Courry (30) . . . 255 H3
Cours (46) . . . 233 J6
Cours (47) . . . 248 B3
le Cours (56) . . . 101 J4
Cours (79) . . . 161 H4
Cours-de-Monségur (33) . . . 230 E4
Cours-de-Pile (24) . . . 231 J2
Cours-la-Ville (69) . . . 187 H3
Cours-les-Bains (33) . . . 247 F2
Cours-les-Barres (18) . . . 150 C3
Coursac (24) . . . 213 K4
Coursan (11) . . . 291 J5
Coursan-en-Othe (10) . . . 113 J2
Coursegoules (06) . . . 280 E3
Courset (62) . . . 2 C6
Courseulles-sur-Mer (14) . . . 32 D3
Courson (14) . . . 52 C3
Courson-les-Carrières (89) . . . 133 F2
Courson-Monteloup (91) . . . 86 C1
Courtacon (77) . . . 60 D5
Courtagnon (51) . . . 40 E5
Courtalain (28) . . . 108 D2
Courtaoult (10) . . . 113 J2
Courtauly (11) . . . 308 D2
Courtavon (68) . . . 97 B6
Courtefontaine (25) . . . 139 J4
Courtefontaine (39) . . . 155 K2
Courteilles (27) . . . 56 B5
Courteix (19) . . . 201 F4
Courtelevant (90) . . . 97 A5
Courtemanche (80) . . . 18 D5
Courtemaux (45) . . . 112 A2
Courtémont (51) . . . 42 C5
Courtemont-Varennes (02) . . . 40 A6
Courtempierre (45) . . . 111 G1
Courtenay (38) . . . 207 G2
Courtenay (45) . . . 112 B2
Courtenot (10) . . . 90 D6
Courteranges (10) . . . 90 C5
Courteron (10) . . . 114 E2
Courtes (01) . . . 172 B4
Courtesoult-et-Gatey (70) . . . 137 F1
Courtetain-et-Salans (25) . . . 138 D5
la Courtète (11) . . . 289 H6
Courteuil (60) . . . 38 B5
Courthézon (84) . . . 257 F6
Courthiézy (51) . . . 61 G1
Courties (32) . . . 285 J1
Courtieux (60) . . . 39 G2
Courtillers (72) . . . 105 K5
Courtils (50) . . . 51 K3
la Courtine (23) . . . 201 F3
Courtisols (51) . . . 62 E2
Courtivron (21) . . . 135 K2
Courtoin (89) . . . 112 B1
Courtois-sur-Yonne (89) . . . 88 D6
Courtomer (61) . . . 55 F6
Courtomer (77) . . . 59 K6
Courtonne-la-Meurdrac (14) . . . 34 A6
Courtonne-les-Deux-Églises (14) . . . 34 B6
Courtrizy-et-Fussigny (02) . . . 40 C1
Courtry (77) . . . 59 G3
Courvaudon (14) . . . 53 H1
Courville (51) . . . 40 C4
Courville-sur-Eure (28) . . . 84 E3
Courzieu (69) . . . 205 H2
Cousance (39) . . . 172 E3
Cousances-les-Forges (55) . . . 64 C6
Cousances-lès-Triconville (55) . . . 64 D4
Cousolre (59) . . . 13 J3
Coussa (09) . . . 307 K2
Coussac-Bonneval (87) . . . 199 F5
Coussan (65) . . . 285 J5
Coussay (86) . . . 145 F6
Coussay-les-Bois (86) . . . 146 A6

Coussegrey (10) . . . 114 A3
Coussergues (12) . . . 252 E2
Coussey (88) . . . 93 G3
Coust (18) . . . 167 H2
Coustaussa (11) . . . 309 F3
Coustouge (11) . . . 310 A2
Coustouges (66) . . . 314 E6
Coutances (50) . . . 30 E4
Coutansouze (03) . . . 184 E2
Coutarnoux (89) . . . 134 A2
Coutençon (77) . . . 88 A2
Coutens (09) . . . 308 A1
Couterne (61) . . . 81 J2
Couternon (21) . . . 136 B5
Couteuges (43) . . . 219 J4
Coutevroult (77) . . . 59 K3
Couthenans (70) . . . 139 G1
Couthures-sur-Garonne (47) . . . 230 D6
Coutiches (59) . . . 7 F6
Coutières (79) . . . 162 A4
Coutouvre (42) . . . 187 G4
Coutras (33) . . . 212 B5
Couture (16) . . . 179 H6
la Couture (62) . . . 6 A5
la Couture (85) . . . 159 K3
la Couture-Boussey (27) . . . 57 F3
Couture-d'Argenson (79) . . . 178 D5
Couture-sur-Loir (41) . . . 107 J6
Couturelle (62) . . . 10 C4
Coutures (24) . . . 213 H2
Coutures (33) . . . 230 D4
Coutures (49) . . . 125 J5
Coutures (82) . . . 268 C2
Couvains (50) . . . 31 J3
Couvains (61) . . . 55 H3
la Couvertoirade (12) . . . 273 G2
Couvertpuis (55) . . . 92 C1
Couvignon (10) . . . 91 G6
Couville (50) . . . 28 C3
Couvonges (55) . . . 63 K4
Couvrelles (02) . . . 40 A3
Couvron-et-Aumencourt (02) . . . 20 C5
Couvrot (51) . . . 63 F4
Coux (07) . . . 239 K3
Coux (17) . . . 211 K2
Coux-et-Bigaroque (24) . . . 232 C2
Couy (18) . . . 150 A2
la Couyère (35) . . . 103 H1
Couze-et-Saint-Front (24) . . . 232 A2
Couzeix (87) . . . 181 G6
Couziers (37) . . . 144 E2
Couzon (03) . . . 168 C2
Couzon-au-Mont-d'Or (69) . . . 206 A1
Couzou (46) . . . 233 K3
Cox (31) . . . 268 C4
Coye-la-Forêt (60) . . . 38 A6
Coyecques (62) . . . 5 F4
Coyolles (02) . . . 39 F4
Coyrière (39) . . . 173 K6
Coyron (39) . . . 173 H4
Coyviller (54) . . . 66 B6
Cozes (17) . . . 194 E4
Cozzano (2A) . . . 321 F5
Crach (56) . . . 100 D5
Crachier (38) . . . 206 E4
Crain (89) . . . 133 G3
Craincourt (57) . . . 66 B2
Craintilleux (42) . . . 204 E4
Crainvilliers (88) . . . 93 H6
Cramaille (02) . . . 39 K4
Cramans (39) . . . 155 K3
Cramant (51) . . . 61 K2
Cramchaban (17) . . . 177 H2
Craménil (61) . . . 53 J4
Cramoisy (60) . . . 38 A4
Cramont (80) . . . 9 J4
Crampagna (09) . . . 307 J2
Cran-Gevrier (74) . . . 191 F5
Crancey (10) . . . 89 G2
Crançot (39) . . . 173 H1
Crandelles (15) . . . 235 G1
Crannes-en-Champagne (72) . . . 106 B3
Crans (01) . . . 189 G3
Crans (39) . . . 174 A1
Cransac (12) . . . 235 G6
Crantenoy (54) . . . 94 B2
Cranves-Sales (74) . . . 191 G2
Craon (53) . . . 104 D4
Craon (86) . . . 144 D6
Craonne (02) . . . 40 C2
Craonnelle (02) . . . 40 C2
Crapeaumesnil (60) . . . 19 F5
Craponne (69) . . . 205 K2
Craponne-sur-Arzon (43) . . . 220 B2
Cras (00) . . . 223 H2
Cras (46) . . . 233 J6
Cras-sur-Reyssouze (01) . . . 172 C6
Crastatt (67) . . . 70 C2
Crastes (32) . . . 267 K5
Craville (27) . . . 35 H5
Crasville (50) . . . 29 F3
Crasville-la-Mallet (76) . . . 15 G3
Crasville-la-Rocquefort (76) . . . 15 H3
la Crau (83) . . . 297 K5
Cravanche (90) . . . 119 H6
Cravans (17) . . . 195 F4
Cravant (45) . . . 109 H5
Cravant (89) . . . 133 H1
Cravant-les-Côteaux (37) . . . 145 G4
Cravencères (32) . . . 266 C4
Cravent (78) . . . 57 G2
Crayssac (46) . . . 233 G6

Craywick (59)	3	G2	
Crazannes (17)	177	H6	
Cré (72)	126	A1	
Créances (50)	30	D2	
Créancey (21)	135	G6	
Crécey-sur-Tille (21)	136	B2	
la Crèche (79)	161	J6	
Crêches-sur-Saône (71)	188	C1	
Créchets (65)	305	H2	
Créchy (03)	185	J2	
Crécy-au-Mont (02)	39	J1	
Crécy-Couvé (28)	56	E6	
Crécy-en-Ponthieu (80)	9	G3	
Crécy-la-Chapelle (77)	59	K3	
Crécy-sur-Serre (02)	20	D4	
Crédin (56)	77	F6	
Crégols (46)	250	C1	
Crégy-lès-Meaux (77)	59	K2	
Créhange (57)	45	J6	
Créhen (22)	50	B4	
Creil (60)	38	A4	
Creissan (34)	291	H3	
Creissels (12)	253	G6	
Crémarest (62)	2	C4	
Cremeaux (42)	186	D6	
Crémery (80)	19	F4	
Crémieu (38)	206	E2	
Crempigny-Bonneguête (74)	190	D5	
Cremps (46)	250	B2	
Crenans (39)	173	H4	
Creney-près-Troyes (10)	90	B4	
Crennes-sur-Fraubée (53)	81	K3	
Créon (33)	229	K3	
Créon-d'Armagnac (40)	266	B1	
Créot (71)	153	J5	
Crépand (21)	134	D2	
Crépey (54)	93	J1	
Crépol (26)	222	E3	
Crépon (14)	32	C4	
Crépy (02)	20	C5	
Crépy (62)	5	G6	
Crépy-en-Valois (60)	38	E4	
Créquy (62)	4	E6	
le Crès (34)	274	C6	
Cresancey (70)	137	G4	
Crésantignes (10)	114	A1	
les Cresnays (50)	52	C4	
Crespian (30)	274	E3	
Crespières (78)	58	A3	
Crespin (12)	251	J5	
Crespin (59)	12	E1	
Crespin (81)	271	F1	
Crespinet (81)	271	F2	
Crespy-le-Neuf (10)	91	F3	
Cressac-Saint-Genis (16)	196	C6	
Cressanges (03)	168	C5	
Cressat (23)	183	F3	
la Cresse (12)	253	H5	
Cressé (17)	178	C6	
Cressensac (46)	215	J6	
Cresserons (14)	32	E3	
Cresseveuille (14)	33	H4	
Cressia (39)	173	F3	
Cressin-Rochefort (01)	207	K1	
Cressonsacq (60)	38	B2	
Cressy (76)	16	A4	
Cressy-Omencourt (80)	19	G4	
Cressy-sur-Somme (71)	169	K2	
Crest (26)	240	D3	
le Crest (63)	202	D3	
Crest-Voland (73)	209	H1	
Creste (63)	202	C5	
le Crestet (07)	221	K5	
Crestet (84)	257	H4	
Crestot (27)	35	G5	
Créteil (94)	59	F4	
Cretteville (50)	28	E6	
Creully (14)	32	C3	
la Creuse (70)	118	C6	
Creuse (80)	17	K3	
le Creusot (71)	153	G6	
Creutzwald (57)	68	A1	
Creuzier-le-Neuf (03)	185	J3	
Creuzier-le-Vieux (03)	185	J3	
Crevans-et-la-Chapelle-lès-Granges (70)	139	F2	
Crevant (36)	166	B4	
Crevant-Laveine (63)	185	J6	
Crévéchamps (54)	94	B1	
Crèvecoeur-en-Auge (14)	33	H6	
Crèvecoeur-en-Brie (77)	59	K5	
Crèvecoeur-le-Grand (60)	17	J5	
Crèvecoeur-le-Petit (60)	18	C6	
Crèvecoeur-sur-l'Escaut (59)	11	K5	
Creveney (70)	118	C6	
Crévic (54)	66	C5	
Crévin (35)	79	G6	
Crévoux (05)	227	A5	
Creys-Mépieu (38)	207	H2	
Creyssac (24)	213	J2	
Creysse (24)	231	J2	
Creysse (46)	233	K2	
Creysseilles (07)	239	J3	
Creyssensac-et-Pissot (24)	213	K5	
Crézançay-sur-Cher (18)	149	G6	
Crézancy (02)	61	F1	
Crézancy-en-Sancerre (18)	131	J6	
Crézières (79)	178	D3	
Crézilles (54)	65	H6	
Cricqueboeuf (14)	33	J2	
Cricqueville-en-Auge (14)	33	H4	
Cricqueville-en-Bessin (14)	29	J6	
Criel-sur-Mer (76)	8	B6	
Crillon (60)	37	F1	
Crillon-le-Brave (84)	257	H5	
Crimolois (21)	136	B6	
Crion (54)	66	D5	
la Crique (76)	16	A4	
Criquebeuf-en-Caux (76)	14	C4	
Criquebeuf-la-Campagne (27)	35	G5	
Criquebeuf-sur-Seine (27)	35	H3	
Criquetot-le-Mauconduit (76)	14	C3	
Criquetot-l'Esneval (76)	14	C5	
Criquetot-sur-Longueville (76)	15	K3	
Criquetot-sur-Ouville (76)	15	H4	
Criquiers (76)	17	F5	
Crisenoy (77)	87	J1	
Crisolles (60)	19	H5	
Crissay-sur-Manse (37)	145	J2	
Crissé (72)	82	B6	
Crissey (39)	155	G2	
Crissey (71)	154	A6	
Cristinacce (2A)	320	C1	
Cristot (14)	32	C4	
Criteuil-la-Magdeleine (16)	196	A5	
Critot (76)	16	B5	
Croce (2B)	319	H4	
Crochte (59)	3	H3	
Crocicchia (2B)	319	H4	
Crocq (23)	201	G1	
le Crocq (60)	17	K5	
Crocy (14)	54	C3	
Croettwiller (67)	25	C2	
Croignon (33)	229	K2	
Croisances (43)	237	K1	
Croisette (62)	10	A2	
le Croisic (44)	121	H5	
la Croisille (27)	56	B2	
la Croisille-sur-Briance (87)	199	J4	
Croisilles (14)	53	J1	
Croisilles (28)	57	G5	
Croisilles (61)	54	E4	
Croisilles (62)	11	F4	
Croismare (54)	66	E6	
Croissanville (14)	33	G5	
Croissy-Beaubourg (77)	59	H4	
Croissy-sur-Celle (60)	17	K4	
Croissy-sur-Seine (78)	58	C3	
le Croisty (56)	76	A5	
Croisy (18)	150	A5	
Croisy-sur-Andelle (76)	36	A2	
Croisy-sur-Eure (27)	57	F1	
Croix (59)	6	E3	
Croix (90)	139	J3	
la Croix-aux-Bois (08)	42	C2	
la Croix-aux-Mines (88)	95	J4	
la Croix-Avranchin (50)	51	K4	
la Croix-Blanche (47)	248	C3	
Croix-Caluyau (59)	12	D4	
Croix-Chapeau (17)	176	E3	
la Croix-Comtesse (17)	177	K3	
la Croix-de-la-Rochette (73)	208	D5	
la Croix-du-Perche (28)	84	C5	
la Croix-en-Brie (77)	88	B1	
la Croix-en-Champagne (51)	42	B6	
Croix-en-Ternois (62)	10	A1	
la Croix-en-Touraine (37)	128	B5	
Croix-Fonsommes (02)	20	B1	
la Croix-Helléan (56)	101	J1	
Croix-Mare (76)	15	H5	
Croix-Moligneaux (80)	19	H3	
la Croix-Saint-Leufroy (27)	35	K6	
la Croix-sur-Gartempe (87)	180	E3	
la Croix-sur-Ourcq (02)	39	J5	
la Croix-sur-Roudoule (06)	261	F6	
la Croix-Valmer (83)	299	F4	
Croixanvec (56)	76	E5	
Croixdalle (76)	16	C4	
la Croixille (53)	80	C5	
Croixrault (80)	17	H3	
Croizet-sur-Gand (42)	187	G6	
Crolles (38)	224	C2	
Crollon (50)	51	K4	
Cromac (87)	164	E6	
Cromary (70)	138	A4	
Cronat (71)	169	H1	
Cronce (43)	219	G5	
la Cropte (53)	105	H3	
Cropus (76)	16	A4	
Cros (30)	274	B1	
le Cros (34)	273	G3	
Cros (63)	201	J6	
Cros-de-Géorand (07)	238	E3	
Cros-de-Montvert (15)	216	E5	
Cros-de-Ronesque (15)	235	K2	
Crosey-le-Grand (25)	138	E4	
Crosey-le-Petit (25)	138	E4	
Crosmières (72)	106	A6	
Crosne (91)	59	F5	
Crossac (44)	122	B1	
Crosses (18)	149	J4	
Crosville-la-Vieille (27)	35	G5	
Crosville-sur-Douve (50)	28	E5	
Crosville-sur-Scie (76)	15	K3	
Crotelles (37)	128	A3	
Crotenay (39)	155	K6	
Croth (27)	57	F3	
le Crotoy (80)	8	E2	
Crots (05)	243	J6	
Crottes-en-Pithiverais (45)	110	B1	
Crottet (01)	188	D1	
le Crouais (35)	78	C3	
Crouay (14)	32	A3	
la Croupte (14)	55	F1	
Crouseilles (64)	285	F1	
Croutelle (86)	162	E4	
les Croûtes (10)	113	J3	
Croutoy (60)	39	F2	
Crouttes (61)	54	D2	
Crouttes-sur-Marne (02)	60	C2	
Crouy (02)	39	J2	
Crouy-en-Thelle (60)	37	K5	
Crouy-Saint-Pierre (80)	17	J1	
Crouy-sur-Cosson (41)	129	H1	
Crouy-sur-Ourcq (77)	39	G6	
le Crouzet (25)	174	B1	
Crouzet-Migette (25)	156	B4	
la Crouzille (63)	184	C3	
Crouzilles (37)	145	H2	
Crozant (23)	165	H6	
Croze (23)	200	E1	
Crozes-Hermitage (26)	222	B4	
Crozet (01)	174	B6	
le Crozet (42)	186	C3	
les Crozets (39)	173	J4	
Crozon (29)	72	D6	
Crozon-sur-Vauvre (36)	166	A4	
Cruas (07)	240	B4	
Crucey-Villages (28)	56	C6	
Crucheray (41)	108	C6	
Cruéjouls (12)	252	E1	
Cruet (73)	208	D4	
Crugey (21)	153	J1	
Crugny (51)	40	D6	
Cruguel (56)	101	H2	
Cruis (04)	258	E6	
Crulai (61)	55	J5	
Crupies (26)	241	F5	
Crupilly (02)	20	E1	
Cruscades (11)	291	G6	
Cruseilles (74)	191	F4	
Crusnes (54)	26	E3	
Cruviers-Lascours (30)	275	F1	
Crux-la-Ville (58)	151	H2	
Cruzille (71)	171	J4	
Cruzilles-lès-Mépillat (01)	188	D2	
Cruzy (34)	291	H4	
Cruzy-le-Châtel (89)	114	C4	
Cry (89)	114	C6	
Cubelles (43)	219	J6	
Cubières (48)	254	D1	
Cubières-sur-Cinoble (11)	309	H4	
Cubiérettes (48)	254	D1	
Cubjac (24)	214	C3	
Cublac (19)	215	G4	
Cublize (69)	187	H4	
Cubnezais (33)	211	J5	
Cubrial (25)	138	D2	
Cubry (25)	138	D2	
Cubry-lès-Faverney (70)	118	A4	
Cubzac-les-Ponts (33)	211	J6	
Cucharmoy (77)	88	C1	
Cuchery (51)	40	D6	
Cucq (62)	4	A6	
Cucugnan (11)	309	J4	
Cucuron (84)	277	H4	
Cudos (33)	246	D2	
Cudot (89)	112	C3	
Cuébris (06)	280	E1	
Cuélas (32)	286	B4	
Cuers (83)	297	K4	
Cuffies (02)	39	J2	
Cuffy (18)	150	D4	
Cugand (85)	123	K6	
Cuges-les-Pins (13)	297	F4	
Cugnaux (31)	288	A1	
Cugney (70)	137	G4	
Cugny (02)	19	J4	
Cuguen (35)	51	G6	
Cuguron (31)	305	H1	
Cuhon (86)	162	C1	
Cuignières (60)	38	A2	
Cuigy-en-Bray (60)	36	E2	
Cuillé (53)	104	B2	
Cuinchy (62)	6	B5	
Cuincy (59)	11	H1	
le Cuing (31)	286	D6	
Cuinzier (42)	187	G3	
Cuirieux (02)	20	E4	
Cuiry-Housse (02)	40	A4	
Cuiry-lès-Chaudardes (02)	40	C2	
Cuiry-lès-Iviers (02)	21	H3	
Cuis (51)	61	K2	
Cuise-la-Motte (60)	39	F2	
Cuiseaux (71)	172	E4	
Cuiserey (21)	136	D4	
Cuisery (71)	172	A3	
Cuisia (39)	172	E3	
Cuissai (61)	82	C2	
Cuissy-et-Geny (02)	40	C2	
Cuisy (55)	43	F4	
Cuisy (77)	59	J1	
Cuisy-en-Almont (02)	39	H2	
Culan (18)	166	E4	
Culètre (21)	153	H2	
Culey-le-Patry (14)	53	H2	
Culhat (63)	203	F1	
Culin (38)	206	E5	
Culles-les-Roches (71)	171	H2	
Cully (14)	32	C4	
Culmont (52)	116	E4	
Culoz (01)	190	D6	
Cult (70)	137	H5	
Cultures (48)	253	K1	
Cumières (51)	40	E6	
Cumières-le-Mort-Homme (55)	43	G4	
Cumiès (11)	289	F4	
Cumont (82)	268	B3	
Cunac (81)	270	E2	
Cuncy-lès-Varzy (58)	133	F5	
Cunèges (24)	231	G3	
Cunel (55)	43	F3	
Cunelières (90)	119	J6	
Cunfin (10)	115	G2	
Cunlhat (63)	203	H4	
Cuon (49)	126	B3	
Cuperly (51)	41	J6	
Cuq (47)	248	C5	
Cuq (81)	270	D6	
Cuq-Toulza (81)	289	G1	
Cuqueron (64)	284	B4	
Curac (16)	212	D2	
Curan (12)	252	E5	
Curbans (04)	259	G1	
Curbigny (71)	187	H1	
Curçay-sur-Dive (86)	144	C3	
Curchy (80)	19	G3	
Curciat-Dongalon (01)	172	C4	
Curcy-sur-Orne (14)	53	H1	
Curdin (71)	170	B3	
Curel (04)	258	D4	
Curel (52)	92	A2	
Curemonte (19)	216	A6	
Cures (72)	106	C1	
Curgies (59)	12	D2	
Curgy (71)	153	F4	
Curienne (73)	208	C4	
Curières (12)	236	C5	
Curis-au-Mont-d'Or (69)	188	C6	
Curley (21)	154	B1	
Curlu (80)	19	F1	
Curmont (52)	91	K5	
Curnier (26)	257	J2	
Cursan (33)	229	K2	
Curtafond (01)	188	E1	
Curtil-Saint-Seine (21)	135	K3	
Curtil-sous-Buffières (71)	171	G5	
Curtil-sous-Burnand (71)	171	H3	
Curtil-Vergy (21)	154	A1	
Curvalle (81)	271	H2	
Curzay-sur-Vonne (86)	162	C4	
Curzon (85)	159	J4	
Cusance (25)	138	E5	
Cuse-et-Adrisans (25)	138	D3	
Cusey (52)	136	D1	
Cussac (15)	218	C6	
Cussac (87)	198	B3	
Cussac-Fort-Médoc (33)	211	F4	
Cussac-sur-Loire (43)	220	C6	
Cussangy (10)	114	B2	
Cussay (37)	146	B3	
Cusset (03)	185	J3	
Cussey-les-Forges (21)	136	A1	
Cussey-sur-Lison (25)	156	B2	
Cussey-sur-l'Ognon (25)	137	K5	
Cussy (14)	32	A3	
Cussy-en-Morvan (71)	152	D2	
Cussy-la-Colonne (21)	153	J3	
Cussy-le-Châtel (21)	153	H1	
Cussy-les-Forges (89)	134	A3	
Custines (54)	66	A3	
Cusy (74)	208	C1	
Cutry (02)	39	H3	
Cutry (54)	26	C3	
Cuts (60)	19	J6	
Cutting (57)	67	G2	
Cuttoli-Corticchiato (2A)	320	D4	
Cuttura (39)	173	J5	
Cuvat (74)	191	F4	
Cuve (70)	118	B3	
Cuvergnon (60)	39	F5	
Cuverville (14)	33	F5	
Cuverville (27)	36	A4	
Cuverville (76)	14	C4	
Cuverville-sur-Yères (76)	16	C1	
Cuves (50)	52	C4	
Cuves (52)	116	D1	
Cuvier (39)	156	C5	
Cuvillers (59)	11	J3	
Cuvilly (60)	18	E6	
Cuvry (57)	45	F6	
Cuxac-Cabardès (11)	290	A3	
Cuxac-d'Aude (11)	291	H5	
Cuy (60)	19	G6	
Cuy (89)	88	D5	
Cuy-Saint-Fiacre (76)	36	D1	
Cuzac (46)	234	E5	
Cuzance (46)	233	J1	
Cuzieu (01)	207	J1	
Cuzieu (42)	205	F4	
Cuzion (36)	165	H5	
Cuzorn (47)	232	C6	
Cuzy (71)	170	B1	
Cys-la-Commune (02)	40	B2	
Cysoing (59)	7	F5	

D

Dabo (57)	70	A2	
Dachstein (67)	70	D3	
Dadonville (45)	110	D1	
Daglan (24)	233	F3	
Dagneux (01)	188	E6	
Dagny (77)	60	C5	
Dagny-Lambercy (02)	21	G3	
Dagonville (55)	64	D4	
la Daguenière (49)	125	H4	
Dahlenheim (67)	70	D3	
Daignac (33)	230	A2	
Daigny (08)	23	F4	
Daillancourt (52)	91	K4	
Daillecourt (52)	116	E1	
Dainville (62)	10	E3	
Dainville-Bertheléville (55)	92	E2	
Daix (21)	136	A5	
Dalem (57)	45	K3	
Dalhain (57)	66	E2	
Dallet (63)	202	E2	
Dallon (02)	19	K3	
Dalou (09)	307	J2	
Dalstein (57)	27	J5	
Daluis (06)	260	E6	
Damas-aux-Bois (88)	94	D3	
Damas-et-Bettegney (88)	94	B5	
Damazan (47)	247	H3	
Dambach (67)	69	J4	
Dambach-la-Ville (67)	71	B4	
Dambelin (25)	139	G4	
Dambenois (25)	139	H2	
Dambenoît-lès-Colombe (70)	118	D5	
Damblain (88)	117	F1	
Damblainville (14)	54	B2	
Dambron (28)	109	K1	
Dame-Marie (27)	56	B4	
Dame-Marie (61)	83	J4	
Dame-Marie-les-Bois (37)	128	B3	
Dameleviéres (54)	66	C6	
Daméraucourt (60)	17	H4	
Damerey (71)	154	C5	
Damery (51)	40	D6	
Damery (80)	18	E4	
Damgan (56)	121	H2	
Damiatte (81)	270	C6	
Damigny (61)	82	D3	
Damloup (55)	26	A6	
Dammard (02)	39	H5	
Dammarie (28)	85	G4	
Dammarie-en-Puisaye (45)	131	K2	
Dammarie-les-Lys (77)	87	H2	
Dammarie-sur-Loing (45)	111	K5	
Dammarie-sur-Saulx (55)	64	B6	
Dammartin-en-Goële (77)	59	H1	
Dammartin-en-Serve (78)	57	H3	
Dammartin-les-Templiers (25)	138	C5	
Dammartin-Marpain (39)	137	F6	
Dammartin-sur-Meuse (52)	117	F2	
Dammartin-sur-Tigeaux (77)	59	K4	
Damousies (59)	13	H3	
Damouzy (08)	22	C3	
Damparis (39)	155	F2	
Dampierre (10)	90	D1	
Dampierre (14)	31	K4	
Dampierre (39)	155	J1	
Dampierre (52)	116	D3	
Dampierre-au-Temple (51)	62	D1	
Dampierre-en-Bray (76)	16	E6	
Dampierre-en-Bresse (71)	154	D5	
Dampierre-en-Burly (45)	111	G6	
Dampierre-en-Crot (18)	131	G4	
Dampierre-en-Graçay (18)	148	C2	
Dampierre-en-Montagne (21)	135	F4	
Dampierre-en-Yvelines (78)	58	B5	
Dampierre-et-Flée (21)	136	D3	
Dampierre-le-Château (51)	63	H1	
Dampierre-les-Bois (25)	139	J2	
Dampierre-lès-Conflans (70)	118	B4	
Dampierre-Saint-Nicolas (76)	16	A2	
Dampierre-sous-Bouhy (58)	132	C3	
Dampierre-sous-Brou (28)	84	C6	
Dampierre-sur-Avre (28)	56	D4	
Dampierre-sur-Boutonne (17)	178	A4	
Dampierre-sur-Doubs (25)	139	G3	
Dampierre-sur-Linotte (70)	138	B2	
Dampierre-sur-Moivre (51)	63	F3	
Dampierre-sur-Salon (70)	137	G2	
Dampjoux (25)	139	G4	
Dampleux (02)	39	G4	
Dampmart (77)	59	J3	
Dampniat (19)	215	K4	
Damprichard (25)	139	J5	
les Damps (27)	35	J3	
Dampsmesnil (27)	36	C5	
Dampvalley-lès-Colombe (70)	138	C1	
Dampvalley-Saint-Pancras (70)	118	B3	
Dampvitoux (54)	65	H1	
Damrémont (52)	117	F3	
Damville (27)	56	C3	
Damvillers (55)	43	H3	
Damvix (85)	160	E6	
Dancé (42)	186	E6	
Dancé (61)	83	K4	
Dancevoir (52)	115	J3	
Dancourt (76)	16	E2	
Dancourt-Popincourt (80)	18	E5	
Dancy (28)	109	J3	
Danestal (14)	33	H4	
Dangé-Saint-Romain (86)	145	K4	
Dangeau (28)	84	E6	
Dangers (28)	85	F2	
Dangeul (72)	82	E5	
Dangolsheim (67)	70	C3	
Dangu (27)	36	D4	
Dangy (50)	31	G4	
Danizy (02)	20	B5	
Danjoutin (90)	139	H1	
Danne-et-Quatre-Vents (57)	70	B1	
Dannelbourg (57)	70	A1	

Dannemarie (25) 139 J3
Dannemarie (68) 97 A4
Dannemarie (78) 57 H5
Dannemarie-sur-Crète (25) 137 J6
Dannemoine (89) 113 K4
Dannemois (91) 87 F3
Dannes (62) 4 A4
Dannevoux (55) 43 G3
Danvou-la-Ferrière (14) 53 G2
Danzé (41) 108 C4
Daon (53) 105 F5
Daoulas (29) 74 C1
Daours (80) 18 C2
Darazac (19) 216 E4
Darbonnay (39) 155 H5
Darbres (07) 239 J4
Darcey (21) 135 F2
Dardenac (33) 230 A3
Dardez (27) 35 J6
Dardilly (69) 205 K1
Dareizé (69) 187 K6
Dargies (60) 17 H4
Dargnies (80) 8 D6
Dargoire (42) 205 J4
Darmannes (52) 92 B6
Darnac (87) 180 E2
Darnétal (76) 35 J2
Darnets (19) 200 D6
Darney (88) 117 K1
Darney-aux-Chênes (88) 93 H4
Darnieulles (88) 94 C5
Darois (21) 135 K4
Darvault (77) 87 J5
Darvoy (45) 110 C4
Dasle (25) 139 J2
Daubensand (67) 71 D4
Daubeuf-la-Campagne (27) 35 H5
Daubeuf-près-Vatteville (27) 35 K4
Daubeuf-Serville (76) 14 E4
Daubèze (33) 230 B3
Dauendorf (67) 69 K6
Daumazan-sur-Arize (09) 288 A6
Daumeray (49) 105 J6
Dauphin (04) 278 B2
Dausse (47) 248 E2
Daux (31) 269 F5
Dauzat-sur-Vodable (63) 202 D6
Davayat (63) 185 F5
Davayé (71) 188 B1
Davejean (11) 309 J3
Davenescourt (80) 18 D4
Davézieux (07) 222 A2
Davignac (19) 200 D6
Davrey (10) 113 K2
Davron (78) 58 A3
Dax (40) 264 B4
Deauville (14) 33 J3
Deaux (30) 255 H6
Débats-Rivière-d'Orpra (42) 204 B2
Decazeville (12) 235 F6
Dechy (59) 11 J2
Décines-Charpieu (69) 206 C2
Decize (58) 151 G6
Dégagnac (46) 233 G4
Degré (72) 106 C2
Dehault (72) 83 H6
Dehéries (59) 12 B5
Dehlingen (67) 68 E4
Deinvillers (88) 94 E2
Delain (70) 137 G2
Delettes (62) 5 G4
Delincourt (60) 36 E4
Delle (90) 139 K2
Delme (57) 66 C2
Delouze-Rosières (55) 92 E1
le Déluge (60) 37 H4
Delut (55) 43 J2
Deluz (25) 138 B5
Demandolx (04) 279 K2
Demange-aux-Eaux (55) 64 D6
Demangevelle (70) 117 K3
Demi-Quartier (74) 192 A6
la Demie (70) 138 B1
Demigny (71) 154 A4
Démouville (14) 33 F5
Dému (32) 266 D4
Démuin (80) 18 D3
Denain (59) 12 C2
Dénat (81) 270 E3
Denazé (53) 104 D4
Denée (49) 125 G4
Dénestanville (76) 15 K3
Deneuille-lès-Chantelle (03) 185 F2
Deneuille-les-Mines (03) 167 J6
Deneuvre (54) 95 F2
Denèvre (70) 137 G2
Dénezé-sous-Doué (49) 125 K6
Dénezé-sous-le-Lude (49) 126 D3
Denezières (39) 173 J2
Denguin (64) 284 B3
Denicé (69) 188 A5
Denier (62) 10 B3
Denipaire (88) 95 J3
Dennebroeucq (62) 5 F5
Denneville (50) 28 C6
Dennevy (71) 153 J5
Denney (90) 119 J6
Denonville (28) 85 K3
Denting (57) 45 J4
Déols (36) 147 K6
Derbamont (88) 94 B4
Dercé (86) 145 F4
Derchigny (76) 16 A1
Dercy (02) 20 D4
Dernacueillette (11) 309 J3
Dernancourt (80) 18 D1
Derval (44) 103 F4
Désaignes (07) 221 J6
Désandans (25) 139 G2
Descartes (37) 146 A4
le Deschaux (39) 155 G4
le Désert (14) 31 K6
Désertines (03) 167 H6
Désertines (53) 80 E2
les Déserts (73) 208 C3
Déservillers (25) 156 C3
Desges (43) 219 H6
Desingy (74) 190 D4
Desmonts (45) 87 F6
Desnes (39) 155 G6
Desseling (57) 67 G3
Dessenheim (68) 96 D5
Dessia (39) 173 F5
Destord (88) 95 F4
la Destrousse (13) 296 E3
Destry (57) 66 E1
Desvres (62) 2 C6
Détain-et-Bruant (21) 153 K1
Détrier (73) 208 D5
le Détroit (14) 53 K3
Dettey (71) 170 C1
Dettwiller (67) 70 C1
Deuil-la-Barre (95) 58 E2
Deuillet (02) 20 A5
Deûlémont (59) 6 C3
Deux-Chaises (03) 168 B6
Deux-Évailles (53) 81 H6
les Deux-Fays (39) 155 G5
Deux-Jumeaux (14) 29 J6
Deux-Verges (15) 236 D3
les Deux-Villes (08) 23 H4
Deuxville (54) 66 D5
Devay (58) 151 H6
Devecey (25) 137 K5
Devesset (07) 221 H5
Devèze (65) 286 C5
Deviat (16) 196 C6
Dévillac (47) 232 B5
Deville (08) 22 D2
Déville-lès-Rouen (76) 35 H1
Devise (80) 19 H2
Devrouze (71) 154 D6
Deycimont (88) 95 F5
Deyme (31) 288 C2
Deyvillers (88) 94 E5
le Dézert (50) 31 G2
Dezize-lès-Maranges (71) 153 J5
D'Huison-Longueville (91) 86 E3
Dhuisy (77) 60 C1
Dhuizel (02) 40 B3
Dhuizon (41) 129 H2
Diancey (21) 153 H1
Diane-Capelle (57) 67 H4
Diant (77) 88 A5
Diarville (54) 94 A3
Diconne (71) 154 D6
Dicy (89) 112 B3
Didenheim (68) 97 C3
Die (26) 241 H3
Diebling (57) 68 C3
Diebolsheim (67) 71 D5
Diedendorf (67) 67 J2
Dieffenbach-au-Val (67) 71 A5
Dieffenbach-lès-Woerth (67) 25 A2
Dieffenthal (67) 71 B5
Diefmatten (68) 97 A3
Dième (69) 187 J5
Diemeringen (67) 67 K1
Diémoz (38) 206 D4
Diénay (21) 136 A3
Dienne (15) 218 B4
Dienné (86) 163 H5
Diennes-Aubigny (58) 151 J5
Dienville (10) 91 F4
Dieppe (76) 15 K1
Dieppe-sous-Douaumont (55) 26 A6
Dierre (37) 128 B5
Dierrey-Saint-Julien (10) 89 J4
Dierrey-Saint-Pierre (10) 89 J4
Diesen (57) 45 K4
Dietwiller (68) 97 C3
Dieudonné (60) 37 J4
Dieue-sur-Meuse (55) 43 J6
Dieulefit (26) 240 E6
Dieulivol (33) 230 E4
Dieulouard (54) 65 K3
Dieupentale (82) 269 F3
Dieuze (57) 67 F3
Diéval (62) 10 C1
Diffembach-lès-Hellimer (57) 68 B4
Diges (89) 112 E6
Digna (39) 172 E4
Dignac (16) 197 F4
la Digne-d'Amont (11) 308 E2
la Digne-d'Aval (11) 308 E2
Digne-les-Bains (04) 259 J5
Dignonville (88) 94 D4
Digny (28) 84 D2
Digoin (71) 170 A4
Digosville (50) 28 D2
Digulleville (50) 28 A1
Dijon (21) 136 A5
Dimancheville (45) 87 F5
Dimbsthal (67) 70 B2
Dimechaux (59) 13 H4
Dimont (59) 13 H4
Dinan (22) 50 D5
Dinard (35) 50 D3
Dinéault (29) 74 C3
Dingé (35) 79 G1
Dingsheim (67) 70 E2
Dingy-en-Vuache (74) 190 D3
Dingy-Saint-Clair (74) 191 G5
Dinozé (88) 94 D6
Dinsac (87) 181 F2
Dinsheim (67) 70 C4
Dinteville (52) 115 H2
Dio-et-Valquières (34) 273 F5
Dionay (38) 223 F3
Dions (30) 275 G2
Diors (36) 148 B6
Diou (03) 169 J4
Diou (36) 148 D3
Dirac (16) 197 F4
Dirinon (29) 46 C6
Dirol (58) 133 H5
Dissangis (89) 134 A2
Dissay (86) 163 G2
Dissay-sous-Courcillon (72) 127 G1
Dissé-sous-Ballon (72) 83 F5
Dissé-sous-le-Lude (72) 126 D2
Distré (49) 144 C1
Distroff (57) 27 H4
Diusse (64) 285 F1
Divajeu (26) 240 D4
Dives (60) 19 G6
Dives-sur-Mer (14) 33 G3
Divion (62) 5 J6
Divonne-les-Bains (01) 174 C5
Dixmont (89) 112 E2
Dizimieu (38) 207 F2
Dizy (51) 40 E6
Dizy-le-Gros (02) 21 G5
Doazit (40) 265 F5
Doazon (64) 284 B2
Docelles (88) 95 F6
Doeuil-sur-le-Mignon (17) 177 K3
Dognen (64) 283 J4
Dogneville (88) 94 D5
Dohem (62) 3 F6
Dohis (02) 21 H3
Doignies (59) 11 H5
Doingt (80) 19 G1
Doissat (24) 232 D4
Doissin (38) 207 G5
Doix (85) 160 D5
Doizieux (42) 205 J6
Dol-de-Bretagne (35) 51 F4
Dolaincourt (88) 93 H4
Dolancourt (10) 91 G5
Dolcourt (54) 93 J2
Dole (39) 155 G2
Dolignon (02) 21 H4
Dolleren (68) 119 J4
Dollon (72) 107 H2
Dollot (89) 88 B6
Dolmayrac (47) 248 B2
Dolo (22) 50 A6
Dolomieu (38) 207 H3
Dolus-d'Oléron (17) 176 C5
Dolus-le-Sec (37) 146 C2
Dolving (57) 67 J3
Dom-le-Mesnil (08) 22 E4
Domagné (35) 79 J5
Domaize (63) 203 H3
Domalain (35) 104 A2
Domancy (74) 192 A5
Domarin (38) 206 E4
Domart-en-Ponthieu (80) 9 J5
Domart-sur-la-Luce (80) 18 C3
Domats (89) 112 B1
Domazan (30) 275 K2
Dombasle-devant-Darney (88) 93 K6
Dombasle-en-Argonne (55) 43 G5
Dombasle-en-Xaintois (88) 93 J4
Dombasle-sur-Meurthe (54) 66 C5
Domblain (52) 91 K2
Domblans (39) 155 H6
Dombras (55) 26 A4
Dombrot-le-Sec (88) 93 J6
Dombrot-sur-Vair (88) 93 H4
Domecy-sur-Cure (89) 133 J4
Domecy-sur-le-Vault (89) 133 J3
Doméliers (60) 17 K5
Domène (38) 224 B3
Domérat (03) 167 G6
Domesmont (80) 9 K5
Domessargues (30) 274 E1
Domessin (73) 207 K4
Domèvre-en-Haye (54) 65 J3
Domèvre-sous-Montfort (88) 93 K5
Domèvre-sur-Avière (88) 94 C5
Domèvre-sur-Durbion (88) 94 D4
Domèvre-sur-Vezouze (54) 67 G6
Domeyrat (43) 219 J3
Domeyrot (23) 183 G2
Domezain-Berraute (64) 283 G3
Domfaing (88) 95 G4
Domfessel (67) 67 K1
Domfront (60) 18 D5
Domfront (61) 53 G6
Domfront-en-Champagne (72) 106 C1
Domgermain (54) 65 H5
la Dominelais (35) 103 F3
Dominois (80) 9 G2
Domjean (50) 31 H5
Domjevin (54) 67 F6
Domjulien (88) 93 J5
Domléger-Longvillers (80) 9 J4
Domloup (35) 79 H5
Dommarie-Eulmont (54) 93 K2
Dommarien (52) 116 D6
Dommartemont (54) 66 B4
Dommartin (01) 172 A6
Dommartin (25) 156 E4
Dommartin (58) 152 A3
Dommartin (69) 205 K1
Dommartin (80) 18 B3
Dommartin-aux-Bois (88) 94 B6
Dommartin-Dampierre (51) 42 C6
Dommartin-la-Chaussée (54) 65 H1
Dommartin-la-Montagne (55) 43 K6
Dommartin-le-Coq (10) 90 D2
Dommartin-le-Franc (52) 91 K3
Dommartin-le-Saint-Père (52) 91 J3
Dommartin-lès-Cuiseaux (71) 172 D4
Dommartin-lès-Remiremont (88) 119 F2
Dommartin-lès-Toul (54) 65 H5
Dommartin-lès-Vallois (88) 94 A6
Dommartin-Lettrée (51) 62 C4
Dommartin-sous-Amance (54) 66 B4
Dommartin-sous-Hans (51) 42 C5
Dommartin-sur-Vraine (88) 93 J4
Dommartin-Varimont (51) 63 H2
Dommary-Baroncourt (55) 26 C5
Domme (24) 233 F3
Dommery (08) 22 B4
Dommiers (02) 39 H3
Domnon-lès-Dieuze (57) 67 G2
Domont (95) 58 E1
Dompaire (88) 94 B5
Dompcevrin (55) 64 D2
Dompierre (60) 18 D6
Dompierre (61) 53 H6
Dompierre (88) 94 E4
Dompierre-aux-Bois (55) 64 E1
Dompierre-Becquincourt (80) 19 F2
Dompierre-du-Chemin (35) 80 B4
Dompierre-en-Morvan (21) 134 C4
Dompierre-les-Églises (87) 181 H2
Dompierre-les-Ormes (71) 171 F6
Dompierre-les-Tilleuls (25) 156 D5
Dompierre-sous-Sanvignes (71) 170 D2
Dompierre-sur-Authie (80) 9 H2
Dompierre-sur-Besbre (03) 169 H4
Dompierre-sur-Chalaronne (01) 188 D3
Dompierre-sur-Charente (17) 195 H2
Dompierre-sur-Helpe (59) 13 G4
Dompierre-sur-Héry (58) 133 G6
Dompierre-sur-Mer (17) 176 E2
Dompierre-sur-Mont (39) 173 G3
Dompierre-sur-Nièvre (58) 150 E1
Dompierre-sur-Veyle (01) 189 G4
Dompierre-sur-Yon (85) 141 K6
Dompnac (07) 238 E6
Domprel (25) 138 E6
Dompremy (51) 63 G5
Domprix (54) 26 D5
Domps (87) 199 K3
Domptail (88) 94 E2
Domptail-en-l'Air (54) 94 C1
Domptin (02) 60 D1
Domqueur (80) 9 J5
Domremy-la-Canne (55) 26 C5
Domrémy-la-Pucelle (88) 93 F2
Domremy-Landéville (52) 92 C3
Domsure (01) 172 D5
Domvallier (88) 93 K4
Domvast (80) 9 H4
Don (59) 6 C5
Donazac (11) 308 D1
Donchery (08) 22 E4
Doncières (88) 95 F2
Doncourt-aux-Templiers (55) 44 B6
Doncourt-lès-Conflans (54) 44 D5
Doncourt-lès-Longuyon (54) 26 C3
Doncourt-sur-Meuse (52) 93 F6
Dondas (47) 248 D4
Donges (44) 122 B2
Donjeux (52) 92 B3
Donjeux (57) 66 C2
le Donjon (03) 169 J6
Donnay (14) 53 J2
Donnazac (81) 270 C1
Donnelay (57) 67 F4
Donnemain-Saint-Mamès (28) 109 F1
Donnemarie-Dontilly (77) 88 C2
Donnement (10) 90 E2
Donnenheim (67) 70 E1
Donnery (45) 110 C4
Donneville (31) 288 C2
Donnezac (33) 211 J2
Dontreix (23) 184 A5
Dontrien (51) 41 J4
Donville-les-Bains (50) 30 C6
Donzac (33) 230 A4
Donzac (82) 248 D6
Donzacq (40) 264 D5
le Donzeil (23) 182 E5
Donzenac (19) 215 J3
Donzère (26) 256 D1
Donzy (58) 132 C5
Donzy-le-National (71) 171 G5
Donzy-le-Pertuis (71) 171 J5
Doranges (63) 219 K1
Dorans (90) 139 H1
Dorat (63) 185 K6
le Dorat (87) 181 F2
Dorceau (61) 83 K3
Dordives (45) 111 J1
Dore-l'Église (63) 220 A1
la Dorée (53) 80 D2
Dorengt (02) 20 D1
Dorlisheim (67) 70 D4
Dormans (51) 40 B6
Dormelles (77) 87 K4
la Dornac (24) 215 G5
Dornas (07) 239 G2
Dornecy (58) 133 G4
Dornes (58) 168 E2
Dornot (57) 44 E6
Dorres (66) 313 G5
Dortan (01) 173 H6
Dosches (10) 90 C4
Dosnon (10) 62 C6
Dossenheim-Kochersberg (67) 70 D2
Dossenheim-sur-Zinsel (67) 69 G6
Douadic (36) 164 C2
Douai (59) 11 H2
Douains (27) 57 F1
Douarnenez (29) 73 E2
Douaumont (55) 26 A6
Doubs (25) 157 F4
Doucelles (72) 82 D5
Douchapt (24) 213 H3
Douchy (02) 19 J3
Douchy (45) 112 B3
Douchy-lès-Ayette (62) 10 E4
Douchy-les-Mines (59) 12 C2
Doucier (39) 173 J2
Doucy-en-Bauges (73) 208 D2
Doudeauville (62) 4 C4
Doudeauville (76) 17 F6
Doudeauville-en-Vexin (27) 36 C3
Doudelainville (80) 9 F6
Doudeville (76) 15 G4
Doudrac (47) 231 K4
Doue (77) 60 C3
Doué-la-Fontaine (49) 144 A1
Douelle (46) 249 K1
le Douhet (17) 195 G1
Douillet (72) 82 D5
Douilly (80) 19 H3
Doulaincourt-Saucourt (52) 92 B4
Doulcon (55) 43 F2
Doulevant-le-Château (52) 91 J3
Doulevant-le-Petit (52) 91 K2
Doulezon (33) 230 D3
le Doulieu (59) 6 A3
Doullens (80) 10 B4
Doumely-Bégny (08) 21 K5
Doumy (64) 284 D2
Dounoux (88) 94 D6
Dourbies (30) 254 A6
Dourdain (35) 79 K3
Dourdan (91) 86 B2
Dourges (62) 11 G1
Dourgne (81) 289 J2
Douriez (62) 9 G2
Dourlers (59) 13 G4
le Dourn (81) 271 H1
Dournazac (87) 198 B4
Dournon (39) 156 B4
Dours (65) 285 J4
Doussard (74) 208 E1
Doussay (86) 145 F5
Douvaine (74) 174 D6
Douville (24) 213 J6
Douville-en-Auge (14) 33 H4
Douville-sur-Andelle (27) 35 K3
Douvrend (76) 16 C2
Douvres (01) 189 H4
Douvres-la-Délivrande (14) 32 E3
Douvrin (62) 6 B6
Doux (08) 41 J1
Doux (79) 162 C1
Douy (28) 108 E2
Douy-la-Ramée (77) 59 K1
Douzains (47) 231 J5
Douzat (16) 196 C2
la Douze (24) 214 B5
Douzens (11) 290 D6
Douzillac (24) 213 H5
Douzy (08) 23 G4
Doville (50) 28 D6
Doye (39) 156 C6
Doyet (03) 184 C1
Dozulé (14) 33 H4
Dracé (69) 188 B3
Draché (37) 145 K3
Drachenbronn-Birlenbach (67) 25 B2
Dracy (89) 112 D6
Dracy-le-Fort (71) 153 K6
Dracy-lès-Couches (71) 153 H5
Dracy-Saint-Loup (71) 153 F3
Dragey-Ronthon (50) 51 J2
Draguignan (83) 279 J6
Drain (49) 124 A5
Draix (04) 260 A4
Draize (08) 21 K5
Drambon (21) 136 D5
Dramelay (39) 173 G5
Drancy (93) 59 F3
Drap (06) 281 H3
Dravegny (02) 40 B5
Draveil (91) 59 F6
Drée (21) 135 H5
Drefféac (44) 102 C6
Drémil-Lafage (31) 269 J6
le Drennec (29) 46 B4

364

Dreuil-lès-Amiens (80)	18	A2
Dreuilhe (09)	308	B3
Dreux (28)	57	F5
Drevant (18)	167	G2
Dricourt (08)	41	K2
Driencourt (80)	19	H1
Drincham (59)	3	G3
Drocourt (62)	11	G1
Drocourt (78)	57	J1
Droisy (27)	56	D4
Droisy (74)	190	D5
Droiturier (03)	186	B2
Droizy (02)	39	K4
Drom (01)	189	H2
Dromesnil (80)	17	G2
Drosay (76)	15	G3
Drosnay (51)	91	F1
Droué (41)	108	C2
Droue-sur-Drouette (28)	85	J1
Drouges (35)	104	A3
Drouilly (51)	62	E4
Droupt-Saint-Basle (10)	89	K2
Droupt-Sainte-Marie (10)	89	K2
Drouville (54)	66	C5
Drouvin-le-Marais (62)	6	A6
Droux (87)	181	G3
Droyes (52)	91	G2
Drubec (14)	33	J4
Drucat (80)	9	G4
Drucourt (27)	34	C6
Drudas (31)	268	D4
Druelle (12)	252	A3
Drugeac (15)	217	H4
Druillat (01)	189	H4
Drulhe (12)	251	G1
Drulingen (67)	67	K2
Drumettaz-Clarafond (73)	208	B3
Drusenheim (67)	25	C4
Druy-Parigny (58)	151	G5
Druye (37)	127	G5
Druyes-les-Belles-Fontaines (89)	132	E3
Dry (45)	109	J5
Duault (22)	75	K2
Ducey (50)	52	A6
Duclair (76)	35	F1
Ducy-Sainte-Marguerite (14)	32	C4
Duerne (69)	205	H3
Duesme (21)	135	G1
Duffort (32)	286	B4
Dugny (93)	59	F2
Dugny-sur-Meuse (55)	43	H6
Duhort-Bachen (40)	265	J4
Duilhac-sous-Peyrepertuse (11)	309	J4
Duingt (74)	191	G6
Duisans (62)	10	E2
Dullin (73)	207	K4
Dumes (40)	265	F5
Dun (09)	308	A2
Dun-le-Palestel (23)	182	B1
Dun-le-Poëlier (36)	148	A1
Dun-les-Places (58)	134	A6
Dun-sur-Auron (18)	149	J5
Dun-sur-Grandry (58)	152	A3
Dun-sur-Meuse (55)	43	F2
Duneau (72)	107	H2
Dunes (82)	248	D6
Dunet (36)	164	E5
Dung (25)	139	G2
Dunières (43)	221	G3
Dunières-sur-Eyrieux (07)	240	A2
Dunkerque (59)	3	H1
Duntzenheim (67)	70	D2
Duppigheim (67)	70	E4
Duran (32)	267	H5
Durance (47)	247	G5
Duranus (06)	281	G1
Duranville (27)	34	C5
Duras (47)	230	E4
Duravel (46)	232	D6
Durban (32)	286	C1
Durban-Corbières (11)	310	B2
Durban-sur-Arize (09)	307	F2
Durbans (46)	234	B4
Durcet (61)	53	J4
Durdat-Larequille (03)	184	B2
Dureil (72)	106	A4
Durenque (12)	252	C6
Durfort (09)	288	C5
Durfort (81)	289	J3
Durfort-et-Saint-Martin-de-Sossenac (30)	274	C1
Durfort-Lacapelette (82)	249	G5
Durlinsdorf (68)	97	B6
Durmenach (68)	97	C5
Durmignat (63)	184	D3
Durnes (25)	156	D2
Durningen (67)	70	D2
Durrenbach (67)	25	A3
Durrenentzen (68)	96	D4
Durstel (67)	67	K2
Durtal (49)	125	K1
Durtol (63)	202	D2
Dury (02)	19	J4
Dury (62)	11	G5
Dury (80)	18	A2
Dussac (24)	214	E1
Duttlenheim (67)	70	D4
Duvy (60)	38	E4
Duzey (55)	26	B4
Dyé (89)	113	J4
Dyo (71)	170	D6

E

Eancé (35)	104	A4
Eaubonne (95)	58	D2
Eaucourt-sur-Somme (80)	9	G5
Eaunes (31)	288	B3
Eaux-Bonnes (64)	303	H2
Eaux-Puiseaux (10)	113	K1
Eauze (32)	266	D3
Ebaty (21)	153	K4
Ebblinghem (59)	3	H5
Eberbach-Seltz (67)	25	D1
Ebersheim (67)	71	B5
Ebersmunster (67)	71	C4
Ebersviller (57)	27	J5
Éblange (57)	27	K6
Ébouleau (02)	21	F4
Ébréon (16)	179	F5
Ébreuil (03)	185	F3
l'Écaille (08)	41	G2
Écaillon (59)	11	J2
Écalles-Alix (76)	15	H5
Écaquelon (27)	34	E4
Écardenville-la-Campagne (27)	35	F6
Écardenville-sur-Eure (27)	35	K6
Écausseville (50)	29	F4
Écauville (27)	35	G6
Eccica-Suarella (2A)	320	D5
Eccles (59)	13	J3
Échalas (69)	205	K4
Échallat (16)	196	C2
Échallon (01)	190	B2
Échalot (21)	135	J2
Échalou (61)	53	H5
Échandelys (63)	203	H5
Échannay (21)	135	G6
Écharcon (91)	87	F1
Échassières (03)	184	D3
Échauffour (61)	55	G5
Échavanne (70)	119	G6
Échay (25)	156	B3
Echebrune (17)	195	H4
l'Échelle (08)	22	B3
l'Échelle-Saint-Aurin (80)	18	E4
les Échelles (73)	207	K6
Échemines (10)	89	J3
Échemiré (49)	126	A2
Échenans (25)	139	G2
Échenans-sous-Mont-Vaudois (70)	139	G1
Échenay (52)	92	C2
Échenevex (01)	174	B6
Échenon (21)	154	E2
Échenoz-la-Méline (70)	138	B1
Échenoz-le-Sec (70)	138	A2
Echevannes (21)	136	B2
Échevannes (25)	156	D2
Échevis (26)	223	H5
Échevronne (21)	154	A2
Échigey (21)	154	D1
Échillais (17)	177	F6
Échilleuses (45)	87	F6
Echinghen (62)	2	B5
Échiré (79)	161	H5
Échirolles (38)	224	A4
Échouboulains (77)	88	A3
Échourgnac (24)	213	F4
Eckartswiller (67)	70	B1
Eckbolsheim (67)	71	D1
Eckwersheim (67)	25	A5
Éclaibes (59)	13	G4
Éclaires (51)	63	K1
Éclance (10)	91	G4
Éclans-Nenon (39)	155	H2
Éclaron-Braucourt-Sainte-Livière (52)	91	J1
Eclassan (07)	222	B4
Écleux (39)	155	J3
Éclimeux (62)	9	K1
Eclose (38)	207	F5
Éclusier-Vaux (80)	19	F1
Écluzelles (28)	57	F5
Écly (08)	21	K6
Écoche (42)	187	H3
Écoivres (62)	10	A2
École (73)	208	E3
École-Valentin (25)	137	K5
Écollemont (51)	63	G6
Écommoy (72)	106	E5
Écoquenéauville (50)	29	F5
Ecorcei (61)	55	H5
les Écorces (25)	139	H6
Écorches (61)	54	D3
Écordal (08)	22	C6
Écorpain (72)	107	J3
Écos (27)	36	C5
Écot (25)	139	G3
Ecot-la-Combe (52)	92	D5
Écotay-l'Olme (42)	204	C4
Écouché (61)	54	B5
Écouen (95)	58	E1
Écouflant (49)	125	G2
Écouis (27)	36	B3
Écourt-Saint-Quentin (62)	11	H3
Écoust-Saint-Mein (62)	11	G4
Écouviez (55)	26	A2
l'Écouvotte (25)	138	C4
Écoyeux (17)	195	H1
Ecquedecques (62)	5	J5
Ecques (62)	3	G6
Ecquetot (27)	35	H5
Ecquevilly (78)	58	A2

Écrainville (76)	14	C5
Écrammeville (14)	29	J6
les Écrennes (77)	87	K2
Écretteville-lès-Baons (76)	15	F5
Écretteville-sur-Mer (76)	14	E3
Écriennes (51)	63	G5
Écrille (39)	173	G4
Écromagny (70)	118	E4
Écrosnes (28)	85	J2
Écrouves (54)	65	H5
Ectot-l'Auber (76)	15	J3
Ectot-lès-Baons (76)	15	H5
Écueil (51)	40	E5
Écueillé (36)	147	G3
Écuélin (59)	13	G4
Écuelle (70)	137	F2
Écuelles (71)	154	C4
Écuelles (77)	87	J4
Écuillé (49)	125	G1
Écuires (62)	4	C6
Écuisses (71)	171	G1
Éculleville (50)	28	B1
Écully (69)	206	A2
Écuras (16)	197	J3
Écurat (17)	195	F1
Écurcey (25)	139	H3
Écurey-en-Verdunois (55)	43	H2
Écurie (62)	10	E2
Écury-le-Repos (51)	62	A4
Écury-sur-Coole (51)	62	D3
Écutigny (21)	153	J2
Écuvilly (60)	19	G5
Edern (29)	74	E4
Edon (16)	197	G5
les Eduts (17)	178	C5
Eecke (59)	3	K5
Effiat (63)	185	G4
Effincourt (52)	92	C2
Effry (02)	21	G1
Égat (66)	313	H4
Égleny (89)	112	E5
Égletons (19)	216	D1
Égligny (77)	88	B3
Eglingen (68)	97	A3
l'Église-aux-Bois (19)	200	A4
Église-Neuve-de-Vergt (24)	214	A5
Église-Neuve-d'Issac (24)	213	H6
Égliseneuve-d'Entraigues (63)	218	B1
Égliseneuve-des-Liards (63)	203	G4
Égliseneuve-près-Billom (63)	203	G3
les Églises-d'Argenteuil (17)	178	A5
Églisolles (63)	204	B6
les Églisottes-et-Chalaures (33)	212	C4
Égly (91)	86	D1
Egreville (77)	87	K6
Égriselles-le-Bocage (89)	112	C1
Egry (45)	111	F1
Éguelshardt (57)	69	H3
Eguenigue (90)	119	G4
l'Éguille (17)	194	C2
Éguilles (13)	277	H6
Éguilly (21)	135	F5
Éguilly-sous-Bois (10)	115	F1
Éguisheim (68)	96	B4
Éguzon-Chantôme (36)	165	H5
Éhuns (70)	118	C5
Eichhoffen (67)	70	C6
Eincheville (57)	66	E1
Einvaux (54)	94	C1
Einville-au-Jard (54)	66	D5
Eix (55)	43	J5
Elan (08)	22	D4
Élancourt (78)	58	B4
Elbach (68)	119	K6
Elbeuf (76)	35	H4
Elbeuf-en-Bray (76)	36	D1
Elbeuf-sur-Andelle (76)	36	A1
Élencourt (60)	17	H4
Élesmes (59)	13	H2
Éleu-dit-Leauwette (62)	11	F1
Élincourt (59)	12	B6
Élincourt-Sainte-Marguerite (60)	38	D1
Élise-Daucourt (51)	63	H1
Ellecourt (76)	17	F3
Elliant (29)	75	F6
Ellon (14)	32	B4
Elne (66)	315	H3
Elnes (62)	3	F6
Éloie (90)	119	H5
Éloise (74)	190	C3
Éloyes (88)	95	F6
Elsenheim (67)	71	C6
Elvange (57)	45	J6
Elven (56)	101	H4
Elzange (57)	27	H4
Émagny (25)	137	J5
Émalleville (27)	35	J6
Émancé (78)	85	J1
Émanville (27)	56	B1
Émanville (76)	15	J5
Emberménil (54)	67	F5
Embres-et-Castelmaure (11)	310	B3
Embreville (80)	8	D6
Embrun (05)	243	J5
Embry (62)	4	E6
Émerainville (77)	59	H4
Émerchicourt (59)	11	K2
Émeringes (69)	188	B2
Éméville (60)	39	F4
Émiéville (14)	33	F5
Emlingen (68)	97	B4

Emmerin (59)	6	D4
Émondeville (50)	29	F4
Empeaux (31)	287	J1
Empurany (07)	221	K5
Empuré (16)	179	F4
Empury (58)	133	J5
Encausse (32)	268	C5
Encausse-les-Thermes (31)	305	K2
Enchastrayes (04)	260	D1
Enchenberg (57)	69	G4
Encourtiech (09)	306	E3
Endoufielle (32)	287	H1
Énencourt-le-Sec (60)	37	F4
Énencourt-Léage (60)	36	E3
Enfonvelle (52)	117	H3
Engayrac (47)	248	E4
Engente (10)	91	H5
Engenville (45)	86	D5
Engins (38)	223	K3
Englancourt (02)	20	E1
Englebelmer (80)	10	D5
Englefontaine (59)	12	E4
Englesqueville-en-Auge (14)	33	J3
Englesqueville-la-Percée (14)	29	J6
Englos (59)	6	D4
Engomer (09)	306	C3
Enguinegatte (62)	5	G4
Engwiller (67)	69	J5
Ennemain (80)	19	G2
Ennery (57)	27	H6
Ennery (95)	58	C1
Ennetières-en-Weppes (59)	6	C4
Ennevelin (59)	6	E5
Ennezat (63)	185	G6
Ennordres (18)	130	E4
Enquin-les-Mines (62)	5	G5
Enquin-sur-Baillons (62)	4	C5
Ens (65)	305	F5
Ensigné (79)	178	C3
Ensisheim (68)	97	C1
Ensués-la-Redonne (13)	296	A3
Entrages (04)	259	K6
Entraigues (38)	242	D1
Entraigues (63)	185	G6
Entraigues-sur-la-Sorgue (84)	276	C1
Entrains-sur-Nohain (58)	132	D4
Entrammes (53)	105	F2
Entrange (57)	27	G3
Entraunes (06)	260	E4
Entraygues-sur-Truyère (12)	235	J3
Entre-deux-Eaux (88)	95	J4
Entre-deux-Guiers (38)	207	K6
Entre-deux-Monts (39)	174	A2
Entrecasteaux (83)	298	B1
Entrechaux (84)	257	H4
Entremont (74)	191	H4
Entremont-le-Vieux (73)	208	B5
Entrepierres (04)	259	G4
Entrevaux (04)	280	C1
Entrevennes (04)	278	D1
Entrevernes (74)	208	E1
Entzheim (67)	70	E4
Enval (63)	184	E6
Enveitg (66)	313	G5
Envermeu (76)	16	B2
Environville (76)	15	F5
Éourres (05)	258	D4
Eoux (31)	287	F5
Épagne (10)	90	E3
Épagne-Épagnette (80)	9	G5
Épagny (02)	39	H1
Épagny (21)	136	A3
Épagny (74)	191	F5
Épaignes (27)	34	B4
Épaney (14)	54	B2
Épannes (79)	177	J2
Éparcy (02)	21	H2
les Éparges (55)	43	K6
Épargnes (17)	194	E4
les Éparres (38)	207	F4
Épaumesnil (80)	17	G2
Épaux-Bézu (02)	39	J6
Épeautrolles (28)	84	E4
Épécamps (80)	9	K5
Épégard (27)	35	F5
Épehy (80)	11	J6
Épeigné-les-Bois (37)	128	C6
Épeigné-sur-Dême (37)	127	H1
Épénancourt (80)	19	G3
Épenède (16)	180	A4
Épenouse (25)	138	D6
Épenoy (25)	157	F1
Épense (51)	63	H2
Épercieux-Saint-Paul (42)	204	E2
Éperlecques (62)	3	F4
Épernay (51)	61	K1
Épernay-sous-Gevrey (21)	154	C1
Épernon (28)	85	J1
Éperrais (61)	83	H3
Épersy (73)	208	B2
Épertully (71)	153	J4
Épervans (71)	171	K1
les Epesses (85)	142	E5
Épeugney (25)	156	B2
Epfig (67)	70	C6
Épiais (41)	108	E5
Épiais-lès-Louvres (95)	59	G1
Épiais-Rhus (95)	37	G6
Épieds (02)	39	K6
Épieds (27)	57	F2
Épieds (49)	144	D2

Épieds-en-Beauce (45)	109	H3
Épierre (73)	209	F5
Épiez-sur-Chiers (54)	26	A3
Épiez-sur-Meuse (55)	93	F1
Épinac (71)	153	H4
Épinal (88)	94	D5
Épinay (27)	55	J2
Épinay-Champlâtreux (95)	38	A6
l'Épinay-le-Comte (61)	80	E2
Épinay-sous-Sénart (91)	59	G5
Épinay-sur-Duclair (76)	15	H6
Épinay-sur-Odon (14)	32	B6
Épinay-sur-Orge (91)	58	E6
Épinay-sur-Seine (93)	58	E2
l'Épine (05)	258	C1
l'Épine (51)	62	C2
l'Épine (85)	140	B3
l'Épine-aux-Bois (02)	60	E3
Épineau-les-Voves (89)	113	F3
Épineu-le-Chevreuil (72)	106	B2
Épineuil (89)	114	A4
Épineuil-le-Fleuriel (18)	167	H4
Épineuse (60)	38	B2
Épineux-le-Seguin (53)	105	J3
Épiniac (35)	51	G5
Épinonville (55)	42	E3
Épinouze (26)	222	C2
Épinoy (62)	11	J3
Epiry (58)	151	K1
Épisy (77)	87	J4
Épizon (52)	92	C3
Éplessier (80)	17	H3
Éply (54)	66	A2
Époisses (21)	134	C3
Épône (78)	57	K2
Épothémont (10)	91	G3
Épouville (76)	14	B6
Époye (51)	41	H3
Eppe-Sauvage (59)	13	K5
Eppes (02)	20	E6
Eppeville (80)	19	H4
Epping (57)	69	F2
Épretot (76)	14	C6
Épreville (76)	14	D4
Épreville-en-Lieuvin (27)	34	C5
Épreville-en-Roumois (27)	34	E3
Épreville-près-le-Neubourg (27)	35	F5
Épron (14)	32	E4
Eps (62)	5	G6
Épuisay (41)	108	B4
Équancourt (80)	11	H6
Équemauville (14)	33	K2
Équennes-Eramecourt (80)	17	H4
Équeurdreville-Hainneville (50)	28	C2
Équevilley (70)	118	B5
Équevillon (39)	156	B6
Équihen-Plage (62)	2	A6
Équilly (50)	51	K1
Équirre (62)	5	G6
Éragny (95)	58	C1
Éragny-sur-Epte (60)	36	E3
Eraines (14)	54	B2
Éraville (16)	196	B4
Erbajolo (2B)	319	G6
Erbéviller-sur-Amezule (54)	66	C4
Erbray (44)	103	K4
Erbrée (35)	104	B1
Ercé (09)	307	F4
Ercé-en-Lamée (35)	103	H2
Ercé-près-Liffré (35)	79	H2
Erceville (45)	86	B5
Erches (80)	18	E4
Ercheu (80)	19	G4
Erchin (59)	11	J2
Erching (57)	69	F2
Erckartswiller (67)	69	G5
Ercourt (80)	9	F6
Ercuis (60)	37	K4
Erdeven (56)	100	B5
Éréac (22)	78	A2
Ergersheim (67)	70	D3
Ergnies (80)	9	J5
Ergny (62)	4	E5
Ergué-Gabéric (29)	74	D6
Érin (62)	9	K1
Eringes (21)	134	E2
Eringhem (59)	3	H3
Érize-la-Brûlée (55)	64	C3
Érize-la-Petite (55)	64	B2
Érize-Saint-Dizier (55)	64	C3
Erlon (02)	20	D4
Erloy (02)	20	E1
Ermenonville (60)	38	C6
Ermenonville-la-Grande (28)	85	F4
Ermenonville-la-Petite (28)	85	F5
Ermenouville (76)	15	G3
Ermont (95)	58	D2
Ernée (53)	80	D4
Ernemont-Boutavent (60)	17	G6
Ernemont-la-Villette (76)	36	D2
Ernemont-sur-Buchy (76)	16	C6
Ernes (14)	54	B1
Ernestviller (57)	68	C3
Erneville-aux-Bois (55)	64	D4
Ernolsheim-Bruche (67)	70	D3
Ernolsheim-lès-Saverne (67)	69	G6
Erny-Saint-Julien (62)	5	G5
Érôme (26)	222	B4
Érondelle (80)	9	G6
Erone (2B)	319	G5
Éroudeville (50)	28	E4
Erp (09)	306	E3

Erquery (60)............38 A2
Erquinghem-le-Sec (59).....6 C4
Erquinghem-Lys (59).....6 C3
Erquinvillers (60)........38 A2
Erquy (22).....49 K4
Err (66).......313 H5
Erre (59).....11 K2
Errevet (70)......119 G6
Errouville (54)....26 E3
Ersa (2B).....317 D2
Erstein (67).....71 D3
Erstroff (57).....67 F1
Ervauville (45)....112 A2
Ervillers (62).....11 F4
Ervy-le-Châtel (10)....113 K2
Esbareich (65)....305 H3
Esbarres (21)....154 D2
Esboz-Brest (70)....118 D4
Escala (65)....305 F1
Escalans (40)....266 C1
l'Escale (04)....259 G5
Escales (11)....290 E5
Escalles (62)....2 B3
Escalquens (31)....288 D2
Escames (60)....17 G6
Escamps (46)....250 C2
Escamps (89)....113 F6
Escandolières (12)....251 J1
Escanecrabe (31)....286 E5
Escardes (51)....61 F5
l'Escarène (06)....281 H2
Escarmain (59)....12 D3
Escaro (66)....314 A4
Escassefort (47)....231 F6
Escatalens (82)....268 E1
Escaudain (59)....12 B2
Escaudes (33)....246 D3
Escaudoeuvres (59)....11 H4
Escaunets (65)....285 F3
Escautpont (59)....12 D1
Escazeaux (82)....268 C4
Eschau (67)....71 D2
Eschbach (67)....25 A3
Eschbach-au-Val (68)....96 A4
Eschbourg (67)....69 F6
Eschentzwiller (68)....97 C3
Escherange (57)....27 F3
Esches (60)....37 H5
Eschwiller (67)....67 K2
Esclagne (09)....308 B3
Esclainvillers (80)....18 B4
Esclanèdes (48)....253 K1
Esclassan-Labastide (32)....286 C3
Esclauzels (46)....250 B2
Esclavelles (76)....16 C4
Esclavolles-Lurey (51)....89 G1
Escles (88)....94 D6
Escles-Saint-Pierre (60)....17 G4
Esclottes (33)....230 E4
Escobecques (59)....6 C4
Escoeuilles (62)....2 D5
Escoire (24)....214 B3
Escolives-Sainte-Camille (89)....113 G6
Escombres-et-le-Chesnois (08)....23 G4
Escondeaux (65)....285 J4
Esconnets (65)....304 E1
Escorailles (15)....217 G4
Escorneboeuf (32)....260 B6
Escorpain (28)....56 D5
Escos (64)....283 G2
Escosse (09)....307 H1
Escot (64)....303 F1
Escots (65)....304 E1
Escou (64)....284 B5
Escoubès (64)....284 E3
Escoubès-Pouts (65)....304 C1
Escoulis (31)....306 C1
Escouloubre (11)....308 D6
Escource (40)....244 E4
Escoussans (33)....230 A4
Escoussens (81)....289 K2
Escout (64)....284 B5
Escoutoux (63)....203 H1
Escoville (14)....33 F4
Escragnolles (06)....280 B4
Escrennes (45)....110 D1
Escrignelles (45)....111 J6
Escroux (81)....271 J2
Escueillens-et-Saint-Just-de-Bélengard (11)....308 C1
Escurès (64)....285 F2
Escurolles (03)....185 G3
Eslettes (76)....15 K6
Esley (88)....93 K6
Eslourenties-Daban (64)....285 K4
Esmans (77)....88 A4
Esmery-Hallon (80)....19 H4
Esmoulières (70)....119 F4
Esmoulins (70)....137 F6
Esnandes (17)....176 D1
Esnans (25)....138 C4
Esnes (59)....11 K5
Esnes-en-Argonne (55)....43 G4
Esnon (89)....113 G3
Esnouveaux (52)....92 D6
Espagnac (19)....216 C3
Espagnac-Sainte-Eulalie (46)....234 B5
Espalais (82)....248 E6
Espalem (43)....219 F2
Espalion (12)....236 B6
Espaly-Saint-Marcel (43)....220 C5

Espanès (31)....288 C2
Espaon (32)....287 F3
Esparron (05)....242 C6
Esparron (31)....287 F5
Esparron (83)....278 C6
Esparron-de-Verdon (04)....278 D4
Esparros (65)....305 F2
Esparsac (82)....268 B2
Espartignac (19)....215 K1
Espas (32)....266 C4
Espaubourg (60)....37 F2
Espèche (65)....304 E1
Espéchède (64)....284 E4
Espédaillac (46)....234 B5
Espelette (64)....263 D2
Espeluche (26)....240 B6
Espenel (26)....241 F4
Espérausses (81)....271 H5
Espéraza (11)....308 E3
Esperce (31)....288 B4
Espère (46)....233 G6
Espès-Undurein (64)....283 H4
Espeyrac (12)....235 J5
Espeyroux (46)....234 C3
Espezel (11)....308 C5
Espieilh (65)....304 E1
Espiens (47)....247 J5
Espiet (33)....230 A2
Espinas (82)....250 D5
Espinasse (15)....236 C2
Espinasse (63)....184 B4
Espinasse-Vozelle (03)....185 H3
Espinasses (05)....243 G6
Espinchal (63)....218 C1
Espins (14)....53 J1
Espira-de-Conflent (66)....314 C3
Espira-de-l'Agly (66)....310 B5
Espirat (63)....203 F2
Espiute (64)....283 H3
Esplantas (43)....237 J1
Esplas (09)....288 C6
Esplas-de-Sérou (09)....307 F3
Espoey (64)....285 F5
Espondeilhan (34)....292 A3
Esprels (70)....138 D2
Esquay-Notre-Dame (14)....32 D6
Esquay-sur-Seulles (14)....32 C3
Esquéhéries (02)....13 F6
Esquelbecq (59)....3 H3
Esquennoy (60)....18 A5
Esquerchin (59)....11 G1
Esquerdes (62)....3 F5
Esquibien (29)....73 C3
Esquièze-Sère (65)....304 B4
Esquiule (64)....283 K5
les Essards (16)....212 E3
les Essards (17)....195 F1
les Essards (37)....126 E5
les Essards-Taignevaux (39)....155 F4
Essarois (21)....115 H5
Essars (62)....6 A5
les Essarts (27)....56 B3
les Essarts (41)....107 J6
les Essarts (85)....142 B6
les Essarts-le-Roi (78)....58 A5
les Essarts-le-Vicomte (51)....61 F6
les Essarts-lès-Sézanne (51)....61 G5
Essay (61)....82 E1
Esse (16)....180 C4
Essé (35)....79 J6
Essegney (88)....94 C3
les Esseintes (33)....230 C5
Essert (90)....119 H6
Essert-Romand (74)....192 A1
Essertaux (80)....18 A4
Essertenne (71)....153 H6
Essertenne-et-Cecey (70)....136 E4
Essertines-en-Châtelneuf (42)....204 C4
Essertines-en-Donzy (42)....205 F2
Esserts-Blay (73)....209 G3
Esserval-Combe (39)....156 C4
Esserval-Tartre (39)....156 C5
Essey (21)....153 H1
Essey-et-Maizerais (54)....65 G2
Essey-la-Côte (54)....94 D2
Essey-lès-Nancy (54)....66 B4
Essia (39)....173 G2
Essigny-le-Grand (02)....19 K3
Essigny-le-Petit (02)....20 A2
Essises (02)....60 E2
Essômes-sur-Marne (02)....60 E1
Esson (14)....53 J2
Essuyès (10)....115 F2
Essuiles (60)....37 J1
les Estables (43)....238 E1
Estables (48)....237 J4
Establet (26)....241 J6
Estadens (31)....306 A2
Estagel (66)....309 K5
Estaing (12)....235 J4
Estaing (65)....303 K3
Estaires (59)....6 A4
Estal (46)....234 C1
Estampes (32)....285 K3
Estampures (65)....285 K3
Estancarbon (31)....305 K1
Estandeuil (63)....203 G3
Estang (32)....266 B3
Estarvielle (65)....305 F4
Esteil (63)....203 G6
Esténos (31)....305 J3

Estensan (65)....305 F4
Estérençuby (64)....282 E6
Esternay (51)....61 F5
Esterre (65)....304 B4
Estevelles (62)....6 C1
Esteville (76)....16 B5
Estézargues (30)....275 K2
Estialescq (64)....284 B5
Estibeaux (40)....264 C6
Estigarde (40)....246 E6
Estillac (47)....248 B5
Estipouy (32)....286 A1
Estirac (65)....285 H2
Estissac (10)....89 J5
Estivals (19)....215 H6
Estivareilles (03)....167 H5
Estivareilles (42)....204 C6
Estivaux (19)....215 H2
Estoher (66)....314 C3
Estos (64)....284 A5
Estoublon (04)....279 F1
Estouches (91)....86 C5
Estourmel (59)....11 K4
Estouteville-Écalles (76)....16 B6
Estouy (45)....86 K6
Estrablin (38)....206 C5
Estramiac (32)....268 A3
Estrebay (08)....21 K2
Estrébœuf (80)....8 E4
l'Estréchure (30)....254 D6
Estrée (62)....4 C6
Estrée-Blanche (62)....5 H4
Estrée-Cauchy (62)....10 D1
Estrée-Wamin (62)....10 B3
Estréelles (62)....4 C6
Estrées (02)....19 K1
Estrées (59)....11 H2
Estrées-Deniécourt (80)....19 F2
Estrées-la-Campagne (14)....54 A1
Estrées-lès-Crécy (80)....9 H3
Estrées-Mons (80)....19 H2
Estrées-Saint-Denis (60)....38 C2
Estrées-sur-Noye (80)....18 B3
Estrennes (88)....93 K4
Estreux (59)....12 D2
Estrun (59)....11 K3
Estry (14)....53 F2
Esvès-le-Moutier (37)....146 C3
Esvres (37)....127 K6
Eswars (59)....11 K3
Étable (73)....208 D3
Étables (07)....222 A4
Étables-sur-Mer (22)....49 F4
Étagnac (16)....180 C6
Étaimpuis (76)....16 A6
Étain (55)....26 C6
Étaing (62)....11 G3
Étainhus (76)....14 C6
Étais (21)....114 E6
Étais-la-Sauvin (89)....132 E3
Étalans (25)....156 E1
Étalante (21)....135 H1
Étalle (08)....22 A2
Étalleville (76)....15 H4
Étalon (80)....19 G3
Étalondes (76)....8 C6
Étampes (91)....86 C3
Étampes-sur-Marne (02)....60 E1
l'Étang-Bertrand (50)....28 D4
l'Étang-la-Ville (78)....58 C3
l'Étang-Vergy (21)....154 A1
les Étangs (57)....45 H5
Étaples (62)....4 B5
Étaule (89)....133 K3
Étaules (17)....194 B2
Étaules (21)....135 K4
Étauliers (33)....211 H3
Étaux (74)....191 G3
Étaves-et-Bocquiaux (02)....20 B1
Étavigny (60)....39 F6
Etcharry (64)....283 H3
Etchebar (64)....302 C1
Éteignières (08)....22 A2
Éteimbes (68)....119 K5
Étel (56)....100 B5
Ételfay (80)....18 D5
Étercy (74)....190 E6
Éternoz (25)....156 C3
Éterpigny (62)....11 G3
Éterpigny (80)....19 G2
Éterville (14)....32 D5
Étevaux (21)....136 D5
Eth (59)....12 C2
Étienville (50)....28 E5
Étigny (89)....112 D1
les Étilleux (28)....84 A5
Étinehem (80)....18 E1
Étiolles (91)....59 F6
Étival (39)....173 J4
Étival-Clairefontaine (88)....95 H3
Étival-lès-le-Mans (72)....106 D3
Étivey (89)....134 B1
Étobon (70)....119 G6
Étoges (51)....61 J3
l'Étoile (39)....173 F1
l'Étoile (80)....9 J6
Étoile-Saint-Cyrice (05)....258 C2
Étoile-sur-Rhône (26)....240 C2
Éton (55)....26 C5
Étormay (21)....135 F2
Étouars (24)....197 J4

Étourvy (10)....114 B3
Étoutteville (76)....15 G4
Étouvans (25)....139 G3
Étouvelles (02)....40 B1
Étouvy (14)....31 K6
Étouy (60)....37 K2
Étrabonne (25)....137 H6
Étrappe (25)....139 F3
l'Étrat (42)....205 G5
Étray (25)....156 E1
Étraye (55)....43 H3
Étréaupont (02)....21 F2
Étrechet (36)....165 K1
Étréchy (18)....149 K2
Étréchy (51)....61 K3
Étréchy (91)....86 D2
Étréham (14)....32 A3
Étréjust (80)....17 H2
Étrelles (35)....104 A1
Étrelles-et-la-Montbleuse (70)....137 J3
Étrelles-sur-Aube (10)....89 J1
Étrembières (74)....191 G2
Étrépagny (27)....36 C3
Étrepigney (39)....155 J2
Étrépigny (08)....22 D4
Étrépilly (02)....39 J6
Étrépilly (77)....59 K1
Étrepy (51)....63 H4
Étretat (76)....14 B4
Étreux (02)....12 E6
Étreval (54)....93 K2
Étréville (27)....34 D3
Étrez (01)....172 C6
Étriac (16)....196 C5
Étriché (49)....125 H1
Étricourt-Manancourt (80)....11 G6
Étrigny (71)....171 J3
Étrochey (21)....115 F4
Étrœungt (59)....13 G5
Étroussat (03)....185 G2
Étrun (62)....10 E2
Ettendorf (67)....69 J6
Etting (57)....68 E3
Étueffont (90)....119 J5
Étupes (25)....139 H2
Éturqueraye (27)....34 D3
Étusson (79)....143 J3
Étuz (70)....137 K4
Etzling (57)....68 C2
Eu (76)....8 C6
Euffigneix (52)....116 A1
Eugénie-les-Bains (40)....265 H5
Euilly-et-Lombut (08)....23 G5
Eulmont (54)....66 B4
Eup (31)....305 J3
Eurre (26)....240 D3
Eurville-Bienville (52)....91 K1
Eus (66)....314 C3
Euvezin (54)....65 H2
Euville (55)....65 F4
Euvy (51)....62 A5
Euzet (30)....255 J6
Évaillé (72)....107 J4
Évans (39)....155 K1
Évaux-et-Ménil (88)....94 C4
Évaux-les-Bains (23)....183 K3
Ève (60)....38 C6
Évecquemont (78)....58 A1
Évenos (83)....297 H5
Évergnicourt (02)....41 F2
Éverly (77)....88 D3
Évette-Salbert (90)....119 H6
Eveux (69)....205 J1
Évian-les-Bains (74)....175 G5
Évigny (08)....22 C4
Évillers (25)....156 D3
Évin-Malmaison (62)....11 H1
Évires (74)....191 G4
Évisa (2A)....316 E4
Évosges (01)....189 K5
Évran (22)....50 D6
Évrange (57)....27 G2
Évrecy (14)....32 C6
Évres (55)....64 A1
Évreux (27)....56 D1
Évricourt (60)....19 G6
Évriguet (56)....77 K8
Évron (53)....81 J6
Évry (89)....88 D3
Évry (91)....59 F6
Evry-Grégy-sur-Yerre (77)....59 H6
Excenevex (74)....174 E5
Excideuil (24)....214 D2
Exermont (08)....42 E3
Exideuil (16)....180 B6
Exincourt (25)....139 H2
Exireuil (79)....161 K5
Exmes (61)....54 E4
Exoudun (79)....162 B6
Expiremont (17)....211 K1
Eybens (38)....224 B3
Eybouleuf (87)....199 H2
Eyburie (19)....199 J6
Eycheil (09)....306 D3
Eydoche (38)....207 F6
Eygalayes (26)....258 C3
Eygalières (13)....276 D4
Eygaliers (26)....257 J4
Eygliers (05)....227 A3
Eygluy-Escoulin (26)....241 F2

Eyguians (05)....258 E2
Eyguières (13)....276 D5
Eygurande (19)....201 G3
Eygurande-et-Gardedeuil (24)....212 E5
Eyjeaux (87)....199 G3
Eyliac (24)....214 B4
Eymet (24)....231 G4
Eymeux (26)....223 F5
Eymouthiers (16)....197 H3
Eymoutiers (87)....199 K2
Eyne (66)....313 J5
Eynesse (33)....230 E2
Eyragues (13)....276 B3
Eyrans (33)....211 G3
Eyrein (19)....216 C2
Eyres-Moncube (40)....265 G4
Eyroles (26)....257 J1
Eysines (33)....229 G1
Eysson (25)....138 E6
Eysus (64)....284 A6
Eyvirat (24)....214 A2
Eywiller (67)....67 K2
Eyzahut (26)....240 D5
Eyzerac (24)....214 C1
les Eyzies-de-Tayac-Sireuil (24)....232 D1
Eyzin-Pinet (38)....206 C5
Ézanville (95)....58 E1
Èze (06)....281 H3
Ézy-sur-Eure (27)....57 F3

F

Fa (11)....308 E3
Faÿ-lès-Nemours (77)....87 H5
Fabas (09)....306 D1
Fabas (31)....287 G4
Fabas (82)....269 F3
Fabras (07)....239 G4
Fabrègues (34)....293 F1
Fabrezan (11)....309 K1
Faches-Thumesnil (59)....6 E4
Fâchin (58)....152 C4
la Fage-Montivernoux (48)....236 E3
la Fage-Saint-Julien (48)....237 F3
le Faget (31)....289 F1
Faget-Abbatial (32)....286 E2
Fagnières (51)....62 D2
Fagnon (08)....22 C4
Fahy-lès-Autrey (70)....136 E3
Failly (57)....45 F5
Faimbe (25)....139 F2
Fain-lès-Montbard (21)....134 E2
Fain-lès-Moutiers (21)....134 C2
Fains (27)....57 F2
Fains-la-Folie (28)....85 H6
Fains-Véel (55)....64 A4
Faissault (08)....22 B5
Fajac-en-Val (11)....309 H1
Fajac-la-Relenque (11)....288 E6
Fajoles (46)....233 H3
la Fajolle (11)....308 C5
Fajolles (82)....268 C2
Falaise (08)....42 B2
Falaise (14)....54 A3
la Falaise (78)....57 K2
Falck (57)....45 K4
Faleyras (33)....230 A3
Falga (31)....289 G2
le Falgoux (15)....217 K4
Falicon (06)....281 G3
Falkwiller (68)....97 A3
Fallencourt (76)....16 E2
Fallerans (25)....156 E1
Falleron (85)....141 G4
Falletans (39)....155 H2
Fallon (70)....138 D2
la Faloise (80)....18 B4
Fals (47)....248 C6
Falvy (80)....19 G3
Famars (59)....12 D2
Famechon (62)....10 C4
Famechon (80)....17 J3
Fameck (57)....27 G5
Familly (14)....55 F2
Fampoux (62)....11 F2
Fanjeaux (11)....289 H6
Fanlac (24)....214 E5
le Faou (29)....74 C2
le Faouët (22)....48 D3
le Faouët (56)....75 J6
Faramans (01)....189 F6
Faramans (38)....206 E6
Farbus (62)....11 F2
Farceaux (27)....36 B4
la Fare-en-Champsaur (05)....242 E4
la Fare-les-Oliviers (13)....296 A1
Farébersviller (57)....68 B3
Fareins (01)....188 B4
Faremoutiers (77)....60 A4
Farges (01)....190 D2
les Farges (24)....215 F4
Farges-Allichamps (18)....167 F1
Farges-en-Septaine (18)....149 J3
Farges-lès-Chalon (71)....154 A6
Farges-lès-Mâcon (71)....171 K6
Fargues (33)....229 K6
Fargues (40)....265 H4
Fargues (46)....249 H2
Fargues-Saint-Hilaire (33)....229 J2
Fargues-sur-Ourbise (47)....247 G4

Farincourt (52) ... 117 G6
Farinole (2B) ... 317 D5
la Farlède (83) ... 297 K5
Farnay (42) ... 205 J5
Farschviller (57) ... 68 C3
Fatines (72) ... 107 F2
Fatouville-Grestain (27) ... 34 A4
le Fau (15) ... 217 J5
Fau-de-Peyre (48) ... 237 F3
Fauch (81) ... 271 F3
Faucigny (74) ... 191 H2
Faucogney-et-la-Mer (70) ... 118 E4
Faucompierre (88) ... 95 F6
Faucon (84) ... 257 H3
Faucon-de-Barcelonnette (04) ... 260 D1
Faucon-du-Caire (04) ... 259 H1
Fauconcourt (88) ... 94 E3
Faucoucourt (02) ... 20 B4
Faudoas (82) ... 268 B3
le Fauga (31) ... 288 A3
Faugères (07) ... 255 H1
Faugères (34) ... 291 K1
Fauguernon (14) ... 34 A5
Fauguerolles (47) ... 247 H1
Fauillet (47) ... 247 J1
le Faulq (14) ... 34 A4
Faulquemont (57) ... 45 K6
Faulx (54) ... 66 A3
Faumont (59) ... 6 E6
Fauquembergues (62) ... 5 F4
la Faurie (05) ... 242 B5
Faurilles (24) ... 231 K4
Fauroux (82) ... 249 F4
Faussergues (81) ... 271 H1
la Faute-sur-Mer (85) ... 159 J6
Fauverney (21) ... 136 B6
Fauville (27) ... 56 D1
Fauville-en-Caux (76) ... 15 F5
Faux (08) ... 22 B6
Faux (24) ... 231 K3
Faux-Fresnay (51) ... 61 K6
Faux-la-Montagne (23) ... 200 B2
Faux-Mazuras (23) ... 182 C6
Faux-Vésigneul (51) ... 62 D4
Faux-Villecerf (10) ... 89 H4
Favalello (2B) ... 319 G6
Favars (19) ... 216 A3
Faveraye-Mâchelles (49) ... 125 G6
Faverdines (18) ... 167 G3
Faverelles (45) ... 132 A2
Faverges (74) ... 209 F1
Faverges-de-la-Tour (38) ... 207 H4
Faverney (70) ... 118 A5
Faverois (90) ... 139 K2
Faverolles (02) ... 39 H4
Faverolles (15) ... 236 E1
Faverolles (28) ... 57 H5
Faverolles (36) ... 147 H2
Faverolles (52) ... 116 B3
Faverolles (61) ... 53 K5
Faverolles (80) ... 18 D5
Faverolles-et-Coëmy (51) ... 40 D4
Faverolles-la-Campagne (27) ... 56 B1
Faverolles-lès-Lucey (21) ... 115 J4
Faverolles-sur-Cher (41) ... 128 D5
la Favière (39) ... 156 C6
Favières (28) ... 84 D2
Favières (54) ... 93 J2
Favières (77) ... 59 J5
Favières (80) ... 8 E3
Favresse (51) ... 63 G5
Favreuil (62) ... 11 F5
Favrieux (78) ... 57 H2
le Favril (27) ... 34 C5
le Favril (28) ... 84 D3
le Favril (59) ... 13 F5
Fay (61) ... 55 G6
le Fay (71) ... 172 E2
Fay (72) ... 106 C2
Fay (80) ... 19 F2
Fay-aux-Loges (45) ... 110 C4
Fay-de-Bretagne (44) ... 122 E1
Fay-en-Montagne (39) ... 155 J6
Fay-le-Clos (26) ... 222 C3
Fay-les-Étangs (60) ... 37 F4
Fay-lès-Marcilly (10) ... 89 G3
le Fay-Saint-Quentin (60) ... 37 J2
Fay-sur-Lignon (43) ... 221 F6
Faycelles (46) ... 234 D6
la Faye (16) ... 179 G4
Faye (41) ... 108 D5
Faye-d'Anjou (49) ... 125 G5
Faye-la-Vineuse (37) ... 145 G4
Faye-l'Abbesse (79) ... 143 K6
Faye-sur-Ardin (79) ... 161 G5
le Fayel (60) ... 38 C3
Fayence (83) ... 280 B5
Fayet (02) ... 19 K2
Fayet (12) ... 272 C4
Fayet-le-Château (63) ... 203 G3
Fayet-Ronaye (63) ... 203 H6
Fayl-la-Forêt (52) ... 117 F5
Faymont (70) ... 139 F1
Faymoreau (85) ... 161 F3
Fays (52) ... 91 K2
Fays (88) ... 95 F5
Fays-la-Chapelle (10) ... 114 A1
Fayssac (81) ... 270 C2
Féas (64) ... 283 K6
Febvin-Palfart (62) ... 5 H5
Fécamp (76) ... 14 D3
Féchain (59) ... 11 J3

Fêche-l'Église (90) ... 139 J2
Fécocourt (54) ... 93 K3
Fédry (70) ... 137 J1
Fegersheim (67) ... 71 D2
Fégréac (44) ... 102 C5
Feigères (74) ... 190 E3
Feigneux (60) ... 38 E4
Feignies (59) ... 13 G2
Feillens (01) ... 171 K6
Feings (41) ... 128 E4
Feings (61) ... 83 J1
Feins (35) ... 79 G1
Feins-en-Gâtinais (45) ... 111 K6
Feissons-sur-Isère (73) ... 209 G4
Feissons-sur-Salins (73) ... 209 H5
le Fel (12) ... 235 J5
Fel (61) ... 54 D4
Felce (2B) ... 319 G6
Feldbach (68) ... 97 B5
Feldkirch (68) ... 97 B1
Feliceto (2B) ... 318 C2
Félines (07) ... 222 A2
Félines (43) ... 220 A2
Félines-Minervois (34) ... 290 D4
Félines-sur-Rimandoule (26) ... 240 E5
Félines-Termenès (11) ... 309 J3
Felleries (59) ... 13 H4
Fellering (68) ... 119 J3
Felletin (23) ... 183 G6
Felluns (66) ... 309 H5
Felon (90) ... 119 J5
Felzins (46) ... 234 E5
Fenain (59) ... 11 K2
Fénay (21) ... 136 A6
Fendeille (11) ... 289 G5
Fénery (79) ... 161 J2
Fénétrange (57) ... 67 J2
Feneu (49) ... 125 G2
Féneyrols (82) ... 250 D5
Féniers (23) ... 200 D2
Fenioux (17) ... 177 J6
Fenioux (79) ... 161 K3
Fenneviller (54) ... 95 H1
Fénols (81) ... 270 D3
le Fenouiller (85) ... 140 E6
Fenouillet (31) ... 269 G5
Fenouillet (66) ... 309 G5
Fenouillet-du-Razès (11) ... 289 H6
Fépin (08) ... 24 C3
Fercé (44) ... 103 J2
Fercé-sur-Sarthe (72) ... 106 B4
Ferdrupt (88) ... 119 G3
la Fère (02) ... 20 A5
Fère-Champenoise (51) ... 61 K5
Fère-en-Tardenois (02) ... 40 A5
Fèrebrianges (51) ... 61 J3
la Férée (08) ... 21 K3
Férel (56) ... 121 K2
Ferfay (62) ... 5 J5
Féricy (77) ... 87 J4
Férin (59) ... 11 H2
Fermanville (50) ... 28 E2
la Fermeté (58) ... 151 F4
Ferney-Voltaire (01) ... 191 F1
Fernoël (63) ... 201 G2
Férolles (45) ... 110 C5
Férolles-Attilly (77) ... 59 H5
Féron (59) ... 13 H5
Ferques (62) ... 2 C4
Ferrals-les-Corbières (11) ... 291 F6
Ferrals-les-Montagnes (34) ... 290 E3
Ferran (11) ... 289 J6
Ferrassières (26) ... 258 B5
le Ferré (35) ... 80 A2
Ferrensac (47) ... 231 K5
Ferrère (65) ... 305 H3
les Ferres (06) ... 280 E2
Ferrette (68) ... 97 C5
Ferreux-Quincey (10) ... 89 G3
la Ferrière (22) ... 77 H5
la Ferrière (37) ... 127 K1
la Ferrière (38) ... 224 E1
la Ferrière (85) ... 159 J1
la Ferrière-Airoux (86) ... 163 F6
la Ferrière-au-Doyen (61) ... 55 H6
la Ferrière-aux-Étangs (61) ... 53 H5
la Ferrière-Béchet (61) ... 82 D1
la Ferrière-Bochard (61) ... 82 C3
la Ferrière-de-Flée (49) ... 104 D6
la Ferrière-en-Parthenay (79) ... 162 B2
Ferrière-et-Lafolie (52) ... 92 A3
la Ferrière-Harang (14) ... 31 K5
la Ferrière-la-Grande (59) ... 13 H3
la Ferrière-la-Petite (59) ... 13 H3
Ferrière-Larçon (37) ... 146 C4
Ferrière-sur-Beaulieu (37) ... 146 D2
la Ferrière-sur-Risle (27) ... 55 K2
Ferrières (17) ... 177 G1
Ferrières (45) ... 111 J4
Ferrières (50) ... 80 D1
Ferrières (54) ... 66 B6
Ferrières (60) ... 18 D6
Ferrières (65) ... 303 J2
Ferrières (80) ... 17 K2
Ferrières (81) ... 271 H6
Ferrières-en-Bray (76) ... 36 D1
Ferrières-en-Brie (77) ... 59 H4
Ferrières-Haut-Clocher (27) ... 56 B1
la Ferrière-la-Verrerie (61) ... 55 F6
Ferrières-le-Lac (25) ... 139 J5
Ferrières-les-Bois (25) ... 137 H6
Ferrières-lès-Ray (70) ... 137 H2

Ferrières-lès-Scey (70) ... 117 K6
Ferrières-les-Verreries (34) ... 274 B3
Ferrières-Poussarou (34) ... 291 G2
Ferrières-Saint-Hilaire (27) ... 55 H1
Ferrières-Saint-Mary (15) ... 218 D4
Ferrières-sur-Ariège (09) ... 307 J3
Ferrières-sur-Sichon (03) ... 186 B6
Ferrussac (43) ... 219 H5
Fertans (25) ... 156 C2
la Ferté (39) ... 155 J4
la Ferté-Alais (91) ... 86 E2
la Ferté-Beauharnais (41) ... 129 K3
la Ferté-Bernard (72) ... 83 J6
la Ferté-Chevresis (02) ... 20 C4
la Ferté-Frênel (61) ... 55 H3
la Ferté-Gaucher (77) ... 60 D4
la Ferté-Hauterive (03) ... 168 E6
la Ferté-Imbault (41) ... 130 A5
la Ferté-Loupière (89) ... 112 D4
la Ferté-Macé (61) ... 53 J6
la Ferté-Milon (02) ... 39 G5
la Ferté-Saint-Aubin (45) ... 110 A6
la Ferté-Saint-Cyr (41) ... 129 H1
la Ferté-Saint-Samson (76) ... 16 D6
la Ferté-sous-Jouarre (77) ... 60 B2
la Ferté-sur-Chiers (08) ... 23 J5
la Ferté-Vidame (28) ... 56 B6
la Ferté-Villeneuil (28) ... 108 E3
Fertrève (58) ... 151 J4
Fervaches (50) ... 31 H5
Fervaques (14) ... 54 E1
Fescamps (80) ... 18 E5
Fesches-le-Châtel (25) ... 139 J2
Fesmy-le-Sart (02) ... 12 E6
Fesques (76) ... 16 D3
Fessanvilliers-Mattanvilliers (28) ... 56 C5
Fessenheim (68) ... 96 E6
Fessenheim-le-Bas (67) ... 70 D2
Fessevillers (25) ... 139 J5
les Fessey (70) ... 118 E4
Fessy (74) ... 174 E6
Festalemps (24) ... 213 F3
Festes-et-Saint-André (11) ... 308 E3
Festieux (02) ... 40 C1
Festigny (51) ... 61 H1
Festigny (89) ... 133 F2
Festubert (62) ... 6 B5
le Fête (21) ... 153 H1
Féternes (74) ... 175 G5
Fétigny (39) ... 173 G4
Feucherolles (78) ... 58 B3
Feuchy (62) ... 11 F3
Feugarolles (47) ... 247 J4
Feugères (50) ... 31 F3
Feuges (10) ... 90 B3
Feuguerolles (27) ... 35 H6
Feuguerolles-Bully (14) ... 32 D5
Feuilla (11) ... 310 C3
Feuillade (16) ... 197 H4
la Feuillade (24) ... 215 H4
la Feuillée (29) ... 75 F1
Feuillères (80) ... 19 F1
la Feuillie (50) ... 30 D2
la Feuillie (76) ... 36 B1
Feule (25) ... 139 G4
Feuquières (60) ... 17 G5
Feuquières-en-Vimeu (80) ... 8 E5
Feurs (42) ... 204 E2
Feusines (36) ... 166 C4
Feux (18) ... 150 B1
Fèves (57) ... 27 G6
Féy (57) ... 44 E6
Fey-en-Haye (54) ... 65 J2
Feyt (19) ... 201 H3
Feytiat (87) ... 199 F1
Feyzin (69) ... 206 B3
Fiac (81) ... 270 B5
Ficaja (2B) ... 319 H4
Ficheux (62) ... 10 E3
Fichous-Riumayou (64) ... 284 C2
le Fidelaire (27) ... 56 A2
le Fied (39) ... 155 J6
le Fief-Sauvin (49) ... 124 B6
Fieffes-Montrelet (80) ... 9 K5
Fiefs (62) ... 5 H6
Fiennes (62) ... 2 C4
Fienvillers (80) ... 9 K5
Fierville-Bray (14) ... 33 F6
Fierville-les-Mines (50) ... 28 C5
Fierville-les-Parcs (14) ... 33 K4
le Fieu (33) ... 212 C5
Fieulaine (02) ... 20 B2
Fieux (47) ... 247 K6
Figanières (83) ... 279 J6
Figari (2A) ... 323 G5
Figarol (31) ... 306 B1
Figeac (46) ... 234 D5
Fignévelle (88) ... 117 J2
Fignières (80) ... 18 D4
Filain (02) ... 40 A1
Filain (70) ... 138 B2
Fillé (72) ... 106 D4
Fillières (54) ... 26 D4
Fillièvres (62) ... 9 K2
Fillinges (74) ... 191 H2
Fillols (66) ... 314 B4
Filstroff (57) ... 45 J2
Fiménil (88) ... 95 F5
Finestret (66) ... 314 C3
Finhan (82) ... 268 E4
les Fins (25) ... 157 H2
Fins (80) ... 11 H6

Fiquefleur-Equainville (27) ... 34 A2
Firbeix (24) ... 198 C4
Firfol (14) ... 34 A5
Firmi (12) ... 235 G6
Firminy (42) ... 221 G1
Fislis (68) ... 97 C5
Fismes (51) ... 40 C3
Fitilieu (38) ... 207 H4
Fitou (11) ... 310 C4
Fitz-James (60) ... 38 A2
Fix-Saint-Geneys (43) ... 219 K4
Fixem (57) ... 27 H3
Fixin (21) ... 135 K6
Flacey (21) ... 136 B4
Flacey (28) ... 109 F1
Flacey-en-Bresse (71) ... 172 E3
la Flachère (38) ... 208 C6
Flachères (38) ... 207 F5
Flacourt (78) ... 57 H2
Flacy (89) ... 89 G5
Flagey (25) ... 156 C3
Flagey (52) ... 116 C5
Flagey-Echézeaux (21) ... 154 B1
Flagey-lès-Auxonne (21) ... 155 F1
Flagey-Rigney (25) ... 138 B3
Flagnac (12) ... 235 F5
Flagy (70) ... 118 B6
Flagy (71) ... 171 H4
Flagy (77) ... 87 K4
Flaignes-Havys (08) ... 22 A3
Flainval (54) ... 66 C5
Flamanville (50) ... 28 A3
Flamanville (76) ... 15 H5
Flamarens (32) ... 268 A1
la Flamengrie (02) ... 13 G6
la Flamengrie (59) ... 12 E2
Flammerans (21) ... 136 E6
Flammerécourt (52) ... 92 A3
Flancourt-Catelon (27) ... 34 E3
Flangebouche (25) ... 157 G1
Flassan (84) ... 257 J5
Flassans-sur-Issole (83) ... 298 D5
Flassigny (55) ... 26 A3
Flastroff (57) ... 45 J2
Flat (63) ... 203 F4
Flaucourt (80) ... 19 G2
Flaugeac (24) ... 231 H3
Flaujac-Gare (46) ... 234 B4
Flaujac-Poujols (46) ... 250 A2
Flaujagues (33) ... 230 D2
Flaumont-Waudrechies (59) ... 13 H4
Flaux (30) ... 275 J1
Flavacourt (60) ... 36 E3
Flaviac (07) ... 240 A3
Flavignac (87) ... 198 D3
Flavignerot (21) ... 135 K6
Flavigny (18) ... 150 A4
Flavigny (51) ... 62 A2
Flavigny-le-Grand-et-Beaurain (02) ... 20 D2
Flavigny-sur-Moselle (54) ... 66 A6
Flavigny-sur-Ozerain (21) ... 135 F3
Flavin (12) ... 252 B3
Flavy-le-Martel (02) ... 19 K4
Flavy-le-Meldeux (60) ... 19 H4
Flaxieu (01) ... 207 K1
Flaxlanden (68) ... 97 C3
Flayat (23) ... 201 G2
Flayosc (83) ... 279 H6
Fléac (16) ... 196 D3
Fléac-sur-Seugne (17) ... 195 H5
la Flèche (72) ... 106 B6
Fléchin (62) ... 5 H5
Fléchy (60) ... 18 A5
Flée (21) ... 134 D4
Flée (72) ... 107 G6
Fleigneux (08) ... 23 F3
Fleisheim (57) ... 67 K3
le Fleix (24) ... 231 F2
Fleix (86) ... 163 K3
Fléré-la-Rivière (36) ... 146 E3
Flers (61) ... 53 H4
Flers (62) ... 10 A2
Flers (80) ... 11 F6
Flers-en-Escrebieux (59) ... 11 H1
Flers-sur-Noye (80) ... 18 A4
Flesquières (59) ... 11 H5
Flesselles (80) ... 10 A6
Flétrange (57) ... 45 J6
Fléty (58) ... 152 B6
Fleurac (16) ... 196 B2
Fleurac (24) ... 214 D6
Fleurance (32) ... 267 J3
Fleurat (23) ... 182 B2
Fleurbaix (62) ... 6 B4
Fleuré (61) ... 54 C5
Fleuré (86) ... 163 G4
Fleurey (21) ... 135 H5
Fleurey-lès-Faverney (70) ... 118 A5
Fleurey-lès-Lavoncourt (70) ... 117 H6
Fleurey-lès-Saint-Loup (70) ... 118 C3
Fleurey-sur-Ouche (21) ... 135 C5
Fleurie (69) ... 188 B2
Fleuriel (03) ... 185 G1
Fleurieu-sur-Saône (69) ... 188 C6
Fleurieux-sur-l'Arbresle (69) ... 205 J3
Fleurigné (35) ... 80 B4
Fleurines (60) ... 38 B4
Fleurville (71) ... 171 K5
Fleury (02) ... 39 G4

Fleury (11) ... 291 K5
Fleury (50) ... 52 A3
Fleury (57) ... 45 F6
Fleury (60) ... 37 F4
Fleury (62) ... 10 A1
Fleury (80) ... 17 K4
Fleury-devant-Douaumont (55) ... 43 J4
Fleury-en-Bière (77) ... 87 G3
Fleury-la-Forêt (27) ... 36 C2
Fleury-la-Montagne (71) ... 187 F2
Fleury-la-Rivière (51) ... 40 D6
Fleury-la-Vallée (89) ... 113 F4
Fleury-les-Aubrais (45) ... 110 A4
Fleury-Mérogis (91) ... 58 E6
Fleury-sur-Andelle (27) ... 36 A3
Fleury-sur-Loire (58) ... 151 F6
Fleury-sur-Orne (14) ... 32 E5
Fléville (08) ... 42 D3
Fléville-devant-Nancy (54) ... 66 A5
Fléville-Lixières (54) ... 26 D6
Flévy (57) ... 27 H6
Flexanville (78) ... 57 J3
Flexbourg (67) ... 70 C3
Fley (71) ... 171 H2
Fleys (89) ... 113 J5
Flez-Cuzy (58) ... 133 G5
Fligny (08) ... 21 J2
Flin (54) ... 95 F1
Flines-lès-Mortagne (59) ... 7 H5
Flines-lez-Raches (59) ... 11 J1
Flins-Neuve-Église (78) ... 57 H3
Flins-sur-Seine (78) ... 58 A2
Flipou (27) ... 35 K3
Flirey (54) ... 65 H3
Flixecourt (80) ... 9 J6
Flize (08) ... 22 D4
la Flocellière (85) ... 142 E5
Flocourt (57) ... 66 C1
Flocques (76) ... 8 C6
Flogny-la-Chapelle (89) ... 113 J3
Floing (08) ... 23 F4
Floirac (17) ... 195 F5
Floirac (33) ... 229 H2
Floirac (46) ... 233 K1
Florac (48) ... 254 B3
Florange (57) ... 27 G5
Florémont (88) ... 94 B3
Florensac (34) ... 292 C3
Florentia (39) ... 173 F5
Florentin (81) ... 270 D3
Florentin-la-Capelle (12) ... 235 K5
Floressas (46) ... 249 G1
Florimont (90) ... 139 K2
Florimont-Gaumier (24) ... 233 F4
Floringhem (62) ... 5 J6
la Flotte (17) ... 176 B2
Flottemanville (50) ... 28 E4
Flottemanville-Hague (50) ... 28 C2
Floudès (33) ... 230 C5
Floure (11) ... 290 C6
Flourens (31) ... 269 H6
Floursies (59) ... 13 H4
Floyon (59) ... 13 G6
Flumet (73) ... 191 K6
Fluquières (02) ... 19 J3
Fluy (80) ... 17 J2
Foameix-Ornel (55) ... 26 B6
Foce (2A) ... 323 F3
Focicchia (2B) ... 319 G6
Foëcy (18) ... 148 E2
le Foeil (22) ... 76 E1
Foisches (08) ... 24 C1
Foissac (12) ... 234 D6
Foissac (30) ... 255 K6
Foissiat (01) ... 172 C5
Foissy (21) ... 153 H2
Foissy-lès-Vézelay (89) ... 133 J4
Foissy-sur-Vanne (89) ... 89 F6
Foix (09) ... 307 J3
Folcarde (31) ... 289 F3
Folembray (02) ... 20 A6
Folgensbourg (68) ... 97 C5
la Folie (14) ... 31 J1
Folies (80) ... 18 E3
Folkling (57) ... 68 C2
Follainville-Dennemont (78) ... 57 J1
Folles (87) ... 181 K3
la Folletière (76) ... 15 G6
la Folletière-Abenon (14) ... 55 G2
Folleville (27) ... 34 C5
Folleville (80) ... 18 B5
Folligny (50) ... 51 K1
Folschviller (57) ... 68 A3
Fomerey (88) ... 94 C5
Fomperron (79) ... 162 A4
Fonbeauzard (31) ... 269 G5
Foncegrive (21) ... 136 B1
Fonches-Fonchette (80) ... 19 F3
Foncine-le-Bas (39) ... 174 A2
Foncine-le-Haut (39) ... 174 B2
Foncquevillers (62) ... 10 D4
Fondamente (12) ... 272 E3
Fondettes (37) ... 127 H4
Fondremand (70) ... 137 K3
Fongrave (47) ... 248 A2
Fonguenoussemare (76) ... 14 C4
Fonroque (24) ... 231 H4
Fons (07) ... 239 G5
Fons (30) ... 275 F2
Fons (46) ... 234 C4

Fons-sur-Lussan (30) 255 K4
Fonsommes (02) 20 B2
Fonsorbes (31) 287 K1
Font-Romeu-Odeillo-Via (66) . . . 313 H4
Fontain (25) 138 A6
Fontaine (10) 91 G5
Fontaine (38) 224 A3
Fontaine (90) 119 J6
Fontaine-au-Bois (59) 12 E4
Fontaine-au-Pire (59) 12 B5
Fontaine-Bellenger (27) 35 K5
Fontaine-Bonneleau (60) 17 K5
Fontaine-Chaalis (60) 38 C5
Fontaine-Chalendray (17) 178 D5
Fontaine-Couverte (53) 104 B3
Fontaine-de-Vaucluse (84) 276 E2
Fontaine-Denis-Nuisy (51) 61 H6
Fontaine-en-Bray (76) 16 C5
Fontaine-en-Dormois (51) 42 B4
Fontaine-Étoupefour (14) 32 D5
Fontaine-Fourches (77) 88 E3
Fontaine-Française (21) 136 D2
Fontaine-Guérin (49) 126 A3
Fontaine-Henry (14) 32 D3
Fontaine-Heudebourg (27) 35 J6
Fontaine-la-Gaillarde (89) 88 E6
Fontaine-la-Guyon (28) 84 E2
Fontaine-la-Louvet (27) 34 B5
Fontaine-la-Mallet (76) 14 B6
Fontaine-la-Rivière (91) 86 C4
Fontaine-la-Soret (27) 34 E5
Fontaine-l'Abbé (27) 34 E6
Fontaine-Lavaganne (60) 17 H6
Fontaine-le-Bourg (76) 16 A6
Fontaine-le-Comte (86) 162 E4
Fontaine-le-Dun (76) 15 H3
Fontaine-le-Pin (14) 53 K2
Fontaine-le-Port (77) 87 J2
Fontaine-le-Puits (73) 209 H5
Fontaine-le-Sec (80) 17 G1
Fontaine-les-Bassets (61) 54 C3
Fontaine-lès-Boulans (62) 5 G6
Fontaine-lès-Cappy (80) 19 E4
Fontaine-lès-Clercs (02) 19 K3
Fontaine-lès-Clerval (25) 138 E3
Fontaine-lès-Coteaux (41) 107 K5
Fontaine-lès-Croisilles (62) 11 G3
Fontaine-lès-Dijon (21) 136 A5
Fontaine-lès-Grès (10) 89 H3
Fontaine-lès-Hermans (62) 5 H5
Fontaine-lès-Luxeuil (70) 118 C4
Fontaine-lès-Ribouts (28) 56 E6
Fontaine-lès-Vervins (02) 21 F2
Fontaine-l'Étalon (62) 9 J4
Fontaine-Mâcon (10) 89 F3
Fontaine-Milon (49) 125 K3
Fontaine-Notre-Dame (02) 20 B2
Fontaine-Notre-Dame (59) 11 J4
Fontaine-Raoul (41) 108 D3
Fontaine-Saint-Lucien (60) 37 H1
la Fontaine-Saint-Martin (72) 106 C5
Fontaine-Simon (28) 84 C2
Fontaine-sous-Jouy (27) 56 E1
Fontaine-sous-Montdidier (80) 18 D5
Fontaine-sous-Préaux (76) 35 J1
Fontaine-sur-Ay (51) 41 F6
Fontaine-sur-Maye (80) 9 H3
Fontaine-sur-Somme (80) 9 H6
Fontaine-Uterte (02) 20 A1
Fontainebleau (77) 87 H3
Fontainebrux (39) 172 K1
Fontaines (71) 153 K5
Fontaines (85) 160 D5
Fontaines (89) 132 D1
Fontaines-d'Ozillac (17) 211 K1
Fontaines-en-Duesmois (21) 135 F1
Fontaines-en-Sologne (41) 129 G3
Fontaines-les-Sèches (21) 114 D5
Fontaines-Saint-Clair (55) 43 G2
Fontaines-Saint-Martin (69) 206 A1
Fontaines-sur-Marne (52) 92 A1
Fontaines-sur-Saône (69) 206 A1
Fontains (77) 88 J2
Fontan (06) 311 D3
Fontanès (30) 274 E3
Fontanès (34) 274 C4
Fontanès (42) 205 G5
Fontanes (46) 250 A3
Fontanes (48) 238 B3
Fontanès-de-Sault (11) 308 D5
Fontanes-du-Causse (46) 233 K4
Fontanges (15) 217 J5
Fontangy (21) 134 D5
Fontanières (23) 183 K3
Fontanil-Cornillon (38) 223 K2
Fontannes (43) 219 H2
Fontans (48) 237 H3
Fontarèches (30) 256 A5
Fontclaireau (16) 179 G6
Fontcouverte (11) 290 F6
Fontcouverte (17) 195 G2
Fontcouverte-la-Toussuire (73) 225 G2
la Fontelaye (76) 15 H4
Fontenai-les-Louvets (61) 82 C2
Fontenai-sur-Orne (61) 54 B5
Fontenailles (77) 88 A1
Fontenailles (89) 133 F2
Fontenay (27) 36 C5
Fontenay (36) 148 A3
Fontenay (50) 52 C6
Fontenay (71) 170 E4
Fontenay (76) 14 B6

Fontenay (88) 94 E5
Fontenay-aux-Roses (92) 58 D4
Fontenay-de-Bossery (10) 89 F3
Fontenay-en-Parisis (95) 59 F1
Fontenay-le-Comte (85) 160 D4
Fontenay-le-Fleury (78) 58 B4
Fontenay-le-Marmion (14) 32 E6
Fontenay-le-Pesnel (14) 32 C5
Fontenay-le-Vicomte (91) 87 F2
Fontenay-lès-Briis (91) 58 C6
Fontenay-Mauvoisin (78) 57 H2
Fontenay-près-Chablis (89) 113 J4
Fontenay-près-Vézelay (89) 133 J4
Fontenay-Saint-Père (78) 57 J1
Fontenay-sous-Bois (94) 59 F3
Fontenay-sous-Fouronnes (89) 133 G2
Fontenay-sur-Conie (28) 85 H6
Fontenay-sur-Eure (28) 85 H3
Fontenay-sur-Loing (45) 111 J1
Fontenay-sur-Mer (50) 29 F4
Fontenay-sur-Vègre (72) 106 A4
Fontenay-Torcy (60) 17 F6
Fontenay-Trésigny (77) 59 K5
Fontenelle (02) 13 G6
Fontenelle (21) 136 D3
la Fontenelle (35) 51 J5
la Fontenelle (41) 108 C2
Fontenelle (90) 119 J6
Fontenelle-en-Brie (02) 61 F3
Fontenelle-Montby (25) 138 D3
les Fontenelles (25) 139 G6
Fontenermont (14) 52 C3
Fontenet (17) 178 A6
Fontenille (16) 179 G6
Fontenille-Saint-
   Martin-d'Entraigues (79) 178 D3
Fontenilles (31) 287 K1
Fontenois-la-Ville (70) 118 K3
Fontenois-lès-Montbozon (70) 138 C3
Fontenotte (25) 138 C4
Fontenouilles (89) 112 B4
Fontenoy (02) 39 H1
Fontenoy (89) 132 D1
Fontenoy-la-Joûte (54) 95 F2
Fontenoy-le-Château (88) 118 B2
Fontenoy-sur-Moselle (54) 65 J5
Fontenu (39) 173 J2
Fonteny (57) 66 D2
Fonters-du-Razès (11) 209 G5
Fontès (34) 292 B1
Fontet (33) 230 C5
Fontette (10) 115 G1
Fontevraud-l'Abbaye (49) 144 D1
Fontgombault (36) 164 B2
Fontguenand (36) 147 J1
Fontienne (04) 258 E6
Fontiers-Cabardès (11) 290 A4
Fontiès-d'Aude (11) 290 C6
Fontjoncouse (11) 310 A2
Fontoy (57) 27 F4
Fontpédrouse (66) 313 K4
Fontrabiouse (66) 313 J3
Fontrailles (65) 286 A4
Fontvannes (10) 89 J5
Fontvieille (13) 276 A4
Forbach (57) 68 C2
Forcalqueiret (83) 297 K3
Forcalquier (04) 278 B1
la Force (11) 289 J6
la Force (24) 231 G2
Forcé (53) 105 F2
Forcelles-Saint-Gorgon (54) 93 K2
Forcelles-sous-Gugney (54) 93 K3
Forceville (80) 10 C5
Forceville-en-Vimeu (80) 17 G1
Forcey (52) 92 D6
Forciolo (2A) 320 E6
la Forclaz (74) 175 G6
Forest-en-Cambrésis (59) 12 D4
Forest-l'Abbaye (80) 9 G4
la Forest-Landerneau (29) 46 B6
Forest-Montiers (80) 9 F3
Forest-Saint-Julien (05) 243 F4
Forest-sur-Marque (59) 7 F4
Foreste (02) 19 J3
la Forestière (51) 61 G6
la Forêt-Auvray (61) 53 K4
la Forêt-de-Tessé (16) 179 F4
la Forêt-du-Parc (27) 56 E3
la Forêt-du-Temple (23) 166 A5
la Forêt-Fouesnant (29) 98 E2
Forêt-la-Folie (27) 36 C4
la Forêt-le-Roi (91) 86 B2
la Forêt-Sainte-Croix (91) 86 D4
la Forêt-sur-Sèvre (79) 143 G6
Forfry (77) 59 K1
la Forge (88) 95 G5
Forges (17) 177 F3
Forgès (19) 216 C4
Forges (49) 144 B1
les Forges (56) 77 G6
Forges (61) 82 D2
Forges (77) 88 A3
les Forges (79) 162 B4
les Forges (88) 94 D5
Forges-la-Forêt (35) 103 K2
Forges-les-Bains (91) 86 C6
Forges-les-Eaux (76) 16 D5
Forges-sur-Meuse (55) 43 G4
Forgues (31) 287 H3
la Forie (63) 204 A4
Forléans (21) 134 C3

Formentin (14) 33 J5
Formerie (60) 17 F5
Formigny (14) 29 K6
Formiguères (66) 313 J3
Fornex (09) 287 K6
Fors (79) 178 A1
Forstfeld (67) 25 D3
Forstheim (67) 69 K5
Fort-du-Plasne (39) 174 A2
Fort-Louis (67) 25 D4
Fort-Mahon-Plage (80) 8 D2
Fort-Mardyck (59) 3 G1
Fort-Moville (27) 34 B3
Fortan (41) 108 A5
Fortel-en-Artois (62) 9 K3
la Forteresse (38) 223 H2
Fortschwihr (68) 96 D4
Fos (31) 305 K4
Fos (34) 292 A1
Fos-sur-Mer (13) 295 H5
le Fossat (09) 288 B6
Fossé (08) 42 E1
Fossé (41) 128 E2
Fosse (66) 309 G5
le Fossé (76) 16 E5
la Fosse-Corduan (10) 89 G3
la Fosse-de-Tigné (49) 143 K1
Fossemagne (24) 214 D4
Fossemanant (80) 17 K3
les Fosses (79) 178 B2
Fosses (95) 38 B6
Fossès-et-Baleyssac (33) 230 D5
Fosseuse (60) 37 H5
Fosseux (62) 10 E3
Fossieux (57) 66 B3
Fossoy (02) 61 F1
Foucarmont (76) 16 E2
Foucart (76) 15 F5
Foucarville (50) 29 G5
Foucaucourt-en-Santerre (80) 19 F2
Foucaucourt-Hors-Nesle (80) 17 F2
Foucaucourt-sur-Thabas (55) 64 A1
Fouchécourt (70) 117 K5
Fouchécourt (88) 117 H2
Foucherans (25) 156 C1
Foucherans (39) 155 G2
Fouchères (10) 90 C6
Fouchères (89) 88 C6
Fouchères-aux-Bois (55) 64 B6
Foucherolles (45) 112 A2
Fouchy (67) 96 B1
Foucrainville (27) 56 E2
Fouday (67) 70 A5
Fouencamps (80) 18 C3
Fouesnant (29) 98 D2
Foufflin-Ricametz (62) 10 B2
Foug (54) 65 G5
Fougaron (31) 306 B2
Fougax-et-Barrineuf (09) 308 B4
Fougeré (49) 126 A1
Fougeré (85) 159 K2
Fougères (35) 80 B3
Fougères-sur-Bièvre (41) 128 E4
les Fougerêts (56) 102 B3
Fougerolles (36) 166 A4
Fougerolles (70) 118 D3
Fougerolles-du-Plessis (53) 80 D2
Fougueyrolles (24) 230 E2
la Fouillade (12) 251 G4
la Fouillouse (42) 205 F5
le Fouilloux (17) 212 C3
Fouilloy (60) 17 G2
Fouilloy (80) 18 C2
Fouju (77) 87 J1
Foulain (52) 116 B2
Foulangues (60) 37 K4
Foulayronnes (47) 248 B4
Foulbec (27) 34 B2
Foulcrey (57) 67 G5
Fouleix (24) 213 K6
Foulenay (39) 155 G5
Fouligny (57) 45 J5
Foulognes (14) 32 A5
Fouquebrune (16) 196 E5
Fouquenies (60) 37 H3
Fouquereuil (62) 5 K5
Fouquerolles (60) 37 J2
Fouquescourt (80) 19 F3
Fouqueure (16) 179 F6
Fouqueville (27) 35 G4
Fouquières-lès-Béthune (62) 5 K5
Fouquières-lès-Lens (62) 11 G1
Four (38) 206 E4
Fouras (17) 176 E4
Fourbanne (25) 138 C5
Fourcatier-et-Maison-Neuve (25) 156 E6
Fourcès (32) 266 E1
Fourchambault (58) 150 D4
Fourches (14) 54 B3
Fourcigny (80) 17 G3
Fourdrain (02) 20 B5
Fourdrinoy (80) 17 J2
Fourg (25) 156 A2
Fourges (27) 36 D6
les Fourgs (25) 157 F5
Fourilles (03) 185 G2
Fourmagnac (46) 234 D4
Fourmetot (27) 34 D2
Fourmies (59) 13 H6
Fournaudin (89) 113 G1

Fourneaux (42) 187 G5
Fourneaux (50) 31 H5
Fourneaux (73) 225 K3
Fourneaux-le-Val (14) 54 A3
Fournels (48) 236 E2
Fournès (30) 275 K2
Fournes-Cabardès (11) 290 B4
Fournes-en-Weppes (59) 6 C5
le Fournet (14) 33 J5
Fournet-Blancheroche (25) 139 H4
Fournets-Luisans (25) 157 G1
Fourneville (14) 33 K3
Fournival (60) 37 K1
Fournols (63) 203 J5
Fournoulès (15) 235 F4
Fouronnes (89) 133 G2
Fourques (30) 275 K5
Fourques (66) 315 F3
Fourques-sur-Garonne (47) 247 G1
Fourqueux (78) 58 B3
Fourquevaux (31) 288 D2
Fours (33) 211 G3
Fours (58) 151 K6
Fours-en-Vexin (27) 36 C5
Fourtou (11) 309 G4
Foussais-Payré (85) 161 F3
Foussemagne (90) 119 K6
le Fousseret (31) 287 H5
Foussignac (16) 196 B2
Fouvent-Saint-Andoche (70) 137 G1
Fouzilhon (34) 292 A2
Foville (57) 66 B2
Fox-Amphoux (83) 278 E6
la Foye-Monjault (79) 177 K2
Fozières (34) 273 G4
Fozzano (2A) 322 E2
Fragnes (71) 154 A6
Frahier-et-Chatebier (70) 119 G6
Fraignot-et-Vesvrotte (21) 135 K1
Fraillicourt (08) 21 J4
Fraimbois (54) 94 E1
Frain (88) 117 J1
Frais (90) 119 J6
Fraisans (39) 155 K1
Fraisnes-en-Saintois (54) 93 K3
Fraisse (24) 231 G1
Fraisse-Cabardès (11) 290 A4
Fraissé-des-Corbières (11) 310 B3
Fraisse-sur-Agout (34) 272 A6
Fraisses (42) 221 H1
Fraissinet-de-Fourques (48) 254 B4
Fraissinet-de-Lozère (48) 254 D2
Fraize (88) 95 J5
Fralignes (10) 90 D6
la Framboisière (28) 84 C1
Frambouhans (25) 139 H6
Framecourt (62) 10 A2
Framerville-Rainecourt (80) 18 E2
Framicourt (80) 17 F1
Framont (70) 137 F2
Frampas (52) 91 H2
Francalmont (70) 118 C4
Francaltroff (57) 67 G1
Francarville (31) 288 E1
Francastel (60) 17 K6
Françay (41) 128 C2
Francazal (31) 306 C2
Francescas (47) 247 K6
Francheleins (01) 188 C4
Franchesse (03) 168 B3
Francheval (08) 23 G4
Franchevelle (70) 118 D5
la Francheville (08) 22 D4
Francheville (21) 135 J3
Francheville (27) 56 A4
Francheville (39) 155 G5
Francheville (51) 63 F3
Francheville (54) 65 J4
Francheville (61) 54 B6
Francheville (69) 205 K2
Francières (60) 38 C2
Francières (80) 9 H5
Francillon (36) 147 J2
Francillon-sur-Roubion (26) 240 D6
Francilly-Selency (02) 19 K2
Francin (73) 208 C5
Franclens (74) 190 C4
François (79) 161 J5
Françon (31) 287 G5
Franconville (54) 94 D1
Franconville (95) 58 D2
Francoulès (46) 233 H6
Francourt (70) 137 H1
Francourville (28) 85 H3
Francs (33) 212 D6
Francueil (37) 128 C5
Franey (25) 137 H6
Frangy (74) 190 D4
Frangy-en-Bresse (71) 172 E1
Franken (68) 97 C4
Franleu (80) 8 E5
Franois (25) 137 J6
Franquevielle (31) 286 C6
Franqueville (02) 20 E3
Franqueville (27) 34 E5
Franqueville (80) 9 J5
Franqueville-Saint-Pierre (76) 35 J2
Frans (01) 188 C5
Fransart (80) 19 F3
Fransèches (23) 183 F5
Fransu (80) 9 J5

Fransures (80) 18 A4
Franvillers (80) 18 C1
Franxault (21) 154 E3
Frapelle (88) 95 K4
Fraquelfing (57) 67 J5
Fraroz (39) 156 C6
Frasnay-Reugny (58) 151 H4
Frasne (25) 156 D5
Frasne (39) 155 G1
Frasne-le-Château (70) 137 J3
la Frasnée (39) 173 J3
le Frasnois (39) 173 K2
Frasnoy (59) 12 E3
Frasseto (2A) 320 E5
Frauenberg (57) 68 E2
Frausseilles (81) 270 B1
Fravaux (10) 91 G5
le Fraysse (81) 271 G3
Frayssinet (46) 233 H4
Frayssinet-le-Gélat (46) 232 E5
Frayssinhes (46) 234 C2
Frazé (28) 84 C5
Fréauville (76) 16 C3
Frebécourt (88) 93 F3
Frébuans (39) 173 F2
le Frêche (40) 265 K2
Fréchède (65) 285 K3
Fréchencourt (80) 18 C1
Fréchendets (65) 304 E1
le Fréchet (31) 287 G6
Fréchet-Aure (65) 305 F3
Fréchou (47) 247 J6
Fréchou-Fréchet (65) 285 J6
Frécourt (52) 116 E3
Frédéric-Fontaine (70) 119 F6
la Frédière (17) 177 J6
Frédille (36) 147 H4
Frégimont (47) 247 K3
Frégouville (32) 287 G1
Fréhel (22) 50 A3
Freigné (49) 124 B2
Freissinières (05) 243 J2
la Freissinouse (05) 242 D5
Freistroff (57) 27 K5
Freix-Anglards (15) 217 H6
Fréjairolles (81) 270 E3
Fréjeville (81) 270 E6
Fréjus (83) 299 C3
Fréland (68) 96 A3
Frelinghien (59) 6 C3
Frémainville (95) 58 A1
Frémécourt (95) 37 G6
Fréménil (54) 67 F6
Frémeréville-sous-les-Côtes (55) 65 F4
Frémery (57) 66 D2
Frémestroff (57) 68 B4
Frémicourt (62) 11 G5
Fremifontaine (88) 95 F4
Frémontiers (80) 17 J4
Frémonville (54) 67 H6
la Frénaye (76) 14 E6
Frencq (62) 4 B5
Frenelle-la-Grande (88) 93 K3
Frenelle-la-Petite (88) 93 K3
Frênes (61) 53 G4
Freneuse (76) 35 H3
Freneuse (78) 57 H1
Freneuse-sur-Risle (27) 34 D4
Freney (73) 225 K2
le Freney-d'Oisans (38) 224 E5
Fréniches (60) 19 H5
Frénois (21) 135 J3
Frénois (88) 94 A5
Frénouville (14) 33 H5
Frépillon (95) 58 D1
Fresles (76) 16 C4
la Fresnaie-Fayel (61) 54 E4
la Fresnais (35) 51 F4
Fresnay (10) 91 H4
Fresnay-en-Retz (44) 122 D6
Fresnay-le-Comte (28) 85 G5
Fresnay-le-Gilmert (28) 85 G3
Fresnay-le-Long (76) 15 K5
Fresnay-le-Samson (61) 54 E3
Fresnay-l'Évêque (28) 85 K5
Fresnay-sur-Sarthe (72) 82 C5
la Fresnaye-au-Sauvage (61) 54 A5
la Fresnaye-sur-Chédouet (72) 82 E3
le Fresne (27) 56 B2
le Fresne (51) 63 F2
le Fresne-Camilly (14) 32 D4
Fresné-la-Mère (14) 54 B3
Fresne-l'Archevêque (27) 36 A4
Fresne-le-Plan (76) 35 K2
Fresne-Léguillon (60) 37 G4
Fresne-lès-Reims (51) 41 F3
le Fresne-Poret (50) 52 E5
Fresne-Saint-Mamès (70) 137 J2
Fresne-sur-Loire (44) 124 D4
Fresneaux-Montchevreuil (60) 37 G4
Fresnes (02) 20 A4
Fresnes (21) 134 E2
Fresnes (41) 129 F4
Fresnes (89) 114 A6
Fresnes (94) 58 E5
Fresnes-au-Mont (55) 64 D2
Fresnes-en-Saulnois (57) 66 C3
Fresnes-en-Tardenois (02) 40 A5
Fresnes-en-Woëvre (55) 44 A6
Fresnes-lès-Montauban (62) 11 G2
Fresnes-Mazancourt (80) 19 G2

Fresnes-sur-Apance (52) . . . 117 H3
Fresnes-sur-Escaut (59) . . . 12 D1
Fresnes-sur-Marne (77) . . . 59 J2
Fresnes-Tilloloy (80) . . . 17 F1
Fresneville (80) . . . 17 G2
Fresney (27) . . . 56 E2
Fresney-le-Puceux (14) . . . 32 E6
Fresney-le-Vieux (14) . . . 53 J1
Fresnicourt-le-Dolmen (62) . . . 10 D1
Fresnières (60) . . . 19 F5
Fresnois-la-Montagne (54) . . . 26 B3
Fresnoy (62) . . . 9 J2
Fresnoy-Andainville (80) . . . 17 G2
Fresnoy-au-Val (80) . . . 17 J3
Fresnoy-en-Chaussée (80) . . . 18 D3
Fresnoy-en-Gohelle (62) . . . 11 F2
Fresnoy-en-Thelle (60) . . . 37 J5
Fresnoy-Folny (76) . . . 16 C2
Fresnoy-la-Rivière (60) . . . 38 E4
Fresnoy-le-Château (10) . . . 90 C6
Fresnoy-le-Grand (02) . . . 20 B1
Fresnoy-le-Luat (60) . . . 38 D5
Fresnoy-lès-Roye (80) . . . 19 F4
Frespech (47) . . . 248 D3
Fresquiennes (76) . . . 15 J6
Fressac (30) . . . 274 C1
Fressain (59) . . . 11 J3
Fressancourt (02) . . . 20 B5
Fresse (70) . . . 119 F5
Fresse-sur-Moselle (88) . . . 119 G3
Fresselines (23) . . . 165 J6
Fressenneville (80) . . . 8 D5
Fressies (59) . . . 11 J3
Fressin (62) . . . 4 E6
Fressines (79) . . . 161 J6
le Frestoy-Vaux (60) . . . 18 D6
Fresville (50) . . . 29 F5
Fréterive (73) . . . 208 E4
Fréteval (41) . . . 108 D4
Fréthun (62) . . . 2 C3
Fretigney-et-Velloreille (70) . . . 137 K3
Frétigny (28) . . . 84 B4
Fretin (59) . . . 6 E5
Frétoy (77) . . . 60 C5
Frétoy-le-Château (60) . . . 19 H5
la Frette (38) . . . 207 G6
la Frette (71) . . . 172 B2
la Frette-sur-Seine (95) . . . 58 D2
Frettecuisse (80) . . . 17 G1
Frettemeule (80) . . . 8 E6
Fretterans (71) . . . 154 E4
le Fréty (08) . . . 21 K4
Freulleville (76) . . . 16 B3
Frévent (62) . . . 10 A3
Fréville (76) . . . 15 H6
Fréville (88) . . . 93 F4
Fréville-du-Gâtinais (45) . . . 111 F2
Frévillers (62) . . . 10 C1
Frévin-Capelle (62) . . . 10 D2
Freybouse (57) . . . 68 B4
Freycenet-la-Cuche (43) . . . 238 E1
Freycenet-la-Tour (43) . . . 238 E1
Freychenet (09) . . . 307 K4
Freyming-Merlebach (57) . . . 68 B2
Freyssenet (07) . . . 239 J4
Friaize (28) . . . 84 D3
Friardel (14) . . . 55 G1
Friaucourt (80) . . . 8 D5
Friauville (54) . . . 44 C5
Fribourg (57) . . . 67 G3
Fricamps (80) . . . 17 J3
Frichemesnil (76) . . . 16 A5
Fricourt (80) . . . 10 E6
Fridefont (15) . . . 236 E1
Friedolsheim (67) . . . 70 C2
Frières-Faillouël (02) . . . 19 K4
Friesen (68) . . . 97 A5
Friesenheim (67) . . . 71 D4
Frignicourt (51) . . . 63 F5
Frise (80) . . . 19 F1
Friville-Escarbotin (80) . . . 8 D5
Frizon (88) . . . 94 C4
Froberville (76) . . . 14 C4
Frocourt (60) . . . 37 H3
Froeningen (68) . . . 97 B3
Froeschwiller (67) . . . 69 K4
Froges (38) . . . 224 C2
Frohen-le-Grand (80) . . . 9 K4
Frohen-le-Petit (80) . . . 9 K4
Frohmuhl (67) . . . 69 F5
Froideconche (70) . . . 118 D4
Froidefontaine (90) . . . 139 J1
Froidestrées (02) . . . 21 F1
Froideterre (70) . . . 118 E5
Froidevaux (25) . . . 139 G5
Froideville (39) . . . 155 G6
Froidfond (85) . . . 141 G4
Froidmont-Cohartille (02) . . . 20 D4
Froidos (55) . . . 43 F6
Froissy (60) . . . 18 A6
Frôlois (21) . . . 135 G3
Frolois (54) . . . 66 A6
Fromelennes (08) . . . 24 D1
Fromelles (59) . . . 6 C4
Fromental (87) . . . 181 J3
Fromentières (51) . . . 61 H3
Fromentières (53) . . . 105 F4
Fromeréville-les-Vallons (55) . . . 43 G5
Fromezey (55) . . . 26 B6
Fromont (77) . . . 87 F5
Fromy (08) . . . 23 J5
Froncles (52) . . . 92 B4

Fronsac (31) . . . 305 J3
Fronsac (33) . . . 230 A1
Frontenac (33) . . . 230 B3
Frontenac (46) . . . 234 C6
Frontenard (71) . . . 154 D4
Frontenas (69) . . . 188 A5
Frontenaud (71) . . . 172 D3
Frontenay (39) . . . 155 H6
Frontenay-Rohan-Rohan (79) . . . 177 K1
Frontenex (73) . . . 209 F3
Frontignan (34) . . . 293 F2
Frontignan-de-Comminges (31) . . . 305 J3
Frontignan-Savès (31) . . . 287 G3
Fronton (31) . . . 269 G3
Frontonas (38) . . . 206 E3
Fronville (52) . . . 92 B3
Frossay (44) . . . 122 D3
Frotey-lès-Lure (70) . . . 118 E6
Frotey-lès-Vesoul (70) . . . 138 B1
Frouard (54) . . . 66 A4
Frouville (95) . . . 37 H5
Frouzins (31) . . . 288 A2
Froville (54) . . . 94 C2
Froyelles (80) . . . 9 H3
Frozes (86) . . . 162 D2
Frucourt (80) . . . 9 G6
Frugères-les-Mines (43) . . . 219 G1
Fruges (62) . . . 5 F5
Frugières-le-Pin (43) . . . 219 J3
Fruncé (28) . . . 84 D3
Fry (76) . . . 16 D6
Fuans (25) . . . 157 G1
Fublaines (77) . . . 60 A2
le Fugeret (04) . . . 260 D6
le Fuilet (49) . . . 124 B5
Fuilla (66) . . . 314 B4
Fuissé (71) . . . 188 B1
Fuligny (10) . . . 91 G4
Fulleren (68) . . . 97 A4
Fultot (76) . . . 15 G3
Fulvy (89) . . . 114 C6
Fumay (08) . . . 24 B3
Fumel (47) . . . 249 F1
Fumichon (14) . . . 34 B5
Furchhausen (67) . . . 70 C1
Furdenheim (67) . . . 70 D3
Furiani (2B) . . . 317 D5
Furmeyer (05) . . . 242 C5
Fussey (21) . . . 154 A2
Fussy (18) . . . 149 G2
Fustérouau (32) . . . 266 C5
Fustignac (31) . . . 287 G4
Futeau (55) . . . 42 E6
Fuveau (13) . . . 296 E2
Fyé (72) . . . 82 D4

G

Gaas (40) . . . 264 B5
Gabarnac (33) . . . 230 A5
Gabarret (40) . . . 266 C1
Gabaston (64) . . . 284 E3
Gabat (64) . . . 283 G3
Gabian (34) . . . 292 A2
Gabillou (24) . . . 214 D3
Gabriac (12) . . . 252 D1
Gabriac (48) . . . 254 D5
Gabrias (48) . . . 237 H6
Gacé (61) . . . 55 F4
la Gacilly (56) . . . 102 B2
Gâcogne (58) . . . 152 B1
Gadancourt (95) . . . 36 E6
Gadencourt (27) . . . 57 F2
Gaël (35) . . . 78 B4
Gageac-et-Rouillac (24) . . . 231 G3
Gagnac-sur-Cère (46) . . . 234 C1
Gagnac-sur-Garonne (31) . . . 269 G5
Gagnières (30) . . . 255 H3
Gagny (93) . . . 59 G3
Gahard (35) . . . 79 H2
Gailhan (30) . . . 274 D3
Gaillac (81) . . . 270 B3
Gaillac-d'Aveyron (12) . . . 253 F3
Gaillac-Toulza (31) . . . 288 C5
Gaillagos (65) . . . 303 K2
Gaillan-en-Médoc (33) . . . 210 D1
Gaillard (74) . . . 191 G2
Gaillardbois-Cressenville (27) . . . 36 A3
la Gaillarde (76) . . . 15 H2
Gaillefontaine (76) . . . 16 E5
Gaillères (40) . . . 265 J2
Gaillon (27) . . . 36 A5
Gaillon-sur-Montcient (78) . . . 58 A1
Gainneville (76) . . . 14 C6
Gaja-et-Villedieu (11) . . . 308 E1
Gaja-la-Selve (11) . . . 289 G6
Gajac (33) . . . 246 E1
Gajan (09) . . . 306 D2
Gajan (30) . . . 275 F2
Gajoubert (87) . . . 180 D3
Galametz (62) . . . 9 J2
Galan (65) . . . 286 B5
Galapian (47) . . . 247 K3
Galargues (34) . . . 274 D4
Galéria (2B) . . . 316 C3
Galey (09) . . . 306 B3
Galez (65) . . . 286 B6
Galfingue (68) . . . 97 B3
Galgan (12) . . . 251 H1

Galgon (33) . . . 212 A6
Galiax (32) . . . 266 C6
Galié (31) . . . 305 J2
Galinagues (11) . . . 308 D5
Gallardon (28) . . . 85 J2
Gallargues-le-Montueux (30) . . . 274 E5
le Gallet (60) . . . 17 K5
Galluis (78) . . . 57 K4
Gamaches (80) . . . 8 D6
Gamaches-en-Vexin (27) . . . 36 C4
Gamarde-les-Bains (40) . . . 264 D4
Gamarthe (64) . . . 282 E5
Gambais (78) . . . 57 J4
Gambaiseuil (78) . . . 57 J5
Gambsheim (67) . . . 25 B5
Gan (64) . . . 284 C5
Ganac (09) . . . 307 H3
Ganagobie (04) . . . 259 F6
Gancourt-Saint-Etienne (76) . . . 17 F6
Gandelain (61) . . . 82 B2
Gandelu (02) . . . 39 H6
Gandrange (57) . . . 27 G5
Ganges (34) . . . 274 A2
Gannat (03) . . . 185 G4
Gannay-sur-Loire (03) . . . 169 H1
Gannes (60) . . . 18 C6
Gans (33) . . . 246 D1
Ganties (31) . . . 306 A1
Ganzeville (76) . . . 14 D4
Gap (05) . . . 242 E5
Gapennes (80) . . . 9 H4
Gâprée (61) . . . 55 F6
Garac (31) . . . 268 D5
Garancières (78) . . . 57 J4
Garancières-en-Beauce (28) . . . 86 A3
Garancières-en-Drouais (28) . . . 56 E5
Garanou (09) . . . 307 K5
Garat (16) . . . 197 F4
Garcelles-Secqueville (14) . . . 32 E6
Garches (92) . . . 58 D4
Garchizy (58) . . . 150 D3
Garchy (58) . . . 132 B6
Gardanne (13) . . . 296 D2
la Garde (04) . . . 279 K2
la Garde (38) . . . 224 D4
la Garde (83) . . . 297 K6
la Garde-Adhémar (26) . . . 256 D2
la Garde-Freinet (83) . . . 298 D3
Gardefort (18) . . . 131 K6
Gardegan-et-Tourtirac (33) . . . 230 C1
Gardères (65) . . . 285 F4
Gardes-le-Pontaroux (16) . . . 197 F5
Gardie (11) . . . 309 F1
Gardonne (24) . . . 231 G2
Gardouch (31) . . . 288 E3
Garein (40) . . . 245 J6
Garencières (27) . . . 56 E2
la Garenne-Colombes (92) . . . 58 D3
Garennes-sur-Eure (27) . . . 57 F3
Garentreville (77) . . . 87 G5
Garéoult (83) . . . 297 K3
Garganvillar (82) . . . 268 D2
Gargas (31) . . . 269 H4
Gargas (84) . . . 277 H2
Gargenville (78) . . . 57 K2
Garges-lès-Gonesse (95) . . . 59 F3
Gargilesse-Dampierre (36) . . . 165 H4
Garidech (31) . . . 269 H5
Gariès (82) . . . 268 C5
Garigny (18) . . . 150 B3
Garin (31) . . . 305 G5
Garindein (64) . . . 283 H5
Garlan (29) . . . 47 G4
Garlède-Mondebat (64) . . . 284 D1
Garlin (64) . . . 284 E1
le Garn (30) . . . 256 B3
la Garnache (85) . . . 141 F4
Garnat-sur-Engièvre (03) . . . 169 H3
Garnay (28) . . . 57 F5
Garnerans (01) . . . 188 C2
Garons (30) . . . 275 H4
Garos (64) . . . 284 C1
Garravet (32) . . . 287 G3
Garrebourg (57) . . . 70 A2
Garrevaques (81) . . . 289 H2
Garrey (40) . . . 264 C5
le Garric (81) . . . 270 E1
Garrigues (34) . . . 274 D4
Garrigues (81) . . . 269 K5
Garrigues-Sainte-Eulalie (30) . . . 275 G1
Garris (64) . . . 283 F3
Garrosse (40) . . . 245 F6
Gars (06) . . . 280 C2
Gartempe (23) . . . 182 C3
Gas (28) . . . 85 J1
Gasny (27) . . . 36 C6
Gasques (82) . . . 248 E5
Gassin (83) . . . 299 F4
le Gast (14) . . . 52 C4
Gastes (40) . . . 244 D2
Gastines (53) . . . 104 B3
Gastins (77) . . . 60 A6
Gasville-Oisème (28) . . . 85 G3
Gatey (39) . . . 155 G4
Gathemo (50) . . . 52 D4
Gatteville-le-Phare (50) . . . 29 G2
Gattières (06) . . . 281 F3
Gatuzières (48) . . . 254 B4
Gaubertin (45) . . . 111 F1
la Gaubretière (85) . . . 142 D4
Gauchin-Légal (62) . . . 10 D1
Gauchin-Verloingt (62) . . . 10 A1

Gauchy (02) . . . 19 K3
Gauciel (27) . . . 56 E1
la Gaudaine (28) . . . 84 B5
la Gaude (06) . . . 281 F3
Gaudechart (60) . . . 17 H5
Gaudent (65) . . . 305 H2
Gaudiempré (62) . . . 10 C4
Gaudiès (09) . . . 288 E6
Gaudonville (32) . . . 268 A3
Gaudreville-la-Rivière (27) . . . 56 C2
Gaugeac (24) . . . 232 B4
Gaujac (30) . . . 256 C6
Gaujac (32) . . . 287 F2
Gaujac (47) . . . 230 E6
Gaujacq (40) . . . 264 E5
Gaujan (32) . . . 286 E3
le Gault-Perche (41) . . . 108 B1
le Gault-Saint-Denis (28) . . . 85 G5
le Gault-Soigny (51) . . . 61 G2
Gauré (31) . . . 269 J6
Gauriac (33) . . . 211 G5
Gauriaguet (33) . . . 211 K5
Gaussan (65) . . . 286 B5
Gausson (22) . . . 77 G3
Gauville (61) . . . 55 H4
Gauville (80) . . . 17 G3
Gauville-la-Campagne (27) . . . 56 C1
Gavarnie (65) . . . 304 B5
Gavarret-sur-Aulouste (32) . . . 267 J4
Gavaudun (47) . . . 232 C6
Gavignano (2B) . . . 319 G4
Gavisse (57) . . . 27 H3
Gavray (50) . . . 30 E6
Gavrelle (62) . . . 11 F2
le Gâvre (44) . . . 103 F6
Gâvres (56) . . . 99 K5
Gavrus (14) . . . 32 C5
Gayan (65) . . . 285 H4
Gaye (51) . . . 61 J3
Gayon (64) . . . 285 F2
Gazaupouy (32) . . . 267 G1
Gazave (65) . . . 305 G2
Gazax-et-Baccarisse (32) . . . 266 D6
Gazeran (78) . . . 57 J6
Gazost (65) . . . 304 B2
Géanges (71) . . . 154 B4
Geaune (40) . . . 265 H5
Geay (17) . . . 177 H6
Geay (79) . . . 144 A5
Gèdre (65) . . . 304 B5
Gée (49) . . . 125 K3
Gée-Rivière (32) . . . 266 A5
Geffosses (50) . . . 30 D3
Géfosse-Fontenay (14) . . . 29 H6
Gehée (36) . . . 147 H3
Geishouse (68) . . . 119 K3
Geispitzen (68) . . . 97 D3
Geispolsheim (67) . . . 70 E4
Geiswasser (68) . . . 96 E5
Geiswiller (67) . . . 69 H6
Gélacourt (54) . . . 95 F1
Gélannes (10) . . . 89 G2
Gélaucourt (54) . . . 93 J2
Gellainville (28) . . . 85 G3
Gellenoncourt (54) . . . 66 C5
Gelles (63) . . . 202 A2
Gellin (25) . . . 156 E6
Gelos (64) . . . 284 D4
Geloux (40) . . . 265 F1
Gelucourt (57) . . . 67 F4
Gelvécourt-et-Adompt (88) . . . 94 A5
Gémages (61) . . . 83 J5
Gemaingoutte (88) . . . 95 K4
Gembrie (65) . . . 305 H2
Gemeaux (21) . . . 136 B3
Gémenos (13) . . . 297 F4
Gémigny (45) . . . 109 J3
Gémil (31) . . . 269 J5
Gemmelaincourt (88) . . . 93 J4
Gémonval (25) . . . 139 F2
Gémonville (54) . . . 93 H3
Gémozac (17) . . . 195 F4
Genac (16) . . . 196 C1
Genainville (95) . . . 36 E6
Genas (69) . . . 206 C2
Génat (09) . . . 307 H5
Genay (21) . . . 134 D3
Genay (69) . . . 188 C6
Gençay (86) . . . 163 F6
Gendreville (88) . . . 93 G5
Gendrey (39) . . . 137 G6
Gené (49) . . . 124 E1
Génébrières (82) . . . 269 H1
Genech (59) . . . 7 F5
Génelard (71) . . . 170 D3
Générac (30) . . . 275 G4
Générac (33) . . . 211 H3
Générargues (30) . . . 255 F6
Générest (65) . . . 305 H2
Generville (11) . . . 289 G5
Geneslay (61) . . . 81 H2
le Genest-Saint-Isle (53) . . . 104 D1
Genestelle (07) . . . 239 H4
Geneston (44) . . . 123 H6
la Genête (71) . . . 172 B3
la Genétouze (17) . . . 212 C3
la Genétouze (85) . . . 159 H1
Genêts (50) . . . 51 J3
Geneuille (25) . . . 137 K5
la Genevraie (61) . . . 55 F5
la Genevraye (77) . . . 87 J4

Genevreuille (70) . . . 118 D6
Genevrey (70) . . . 118 C5
Genevrières (52) . . . 117 F6
la Genevroye (52) . . . 92 A5
Geney (25) . . . 139 F2
la Geneytouse (87) . . . 199 H2
Génicourt (95) . . . 37 G6
Génicourt-sur-Meuse (55) . . . 64 D1
Genilac (42) . . . 205 J5
Genillé (37) . . . 146 E1
Génis (24) . . . 214 E2
Génissac (33) . . . 230 A2
Génissieux (26) . . . 222 E4
Genlis (21) . . . 136 C6
Gennes (25) . . . 138 B6
Gennes (49) . . . 125 K5
Gennes-Ivergny (62) . . . 9 J3
Gennes-sur-Glaize (53) . . . 105 G4
Gennes-sur-Seiche (35) . . . 104 B2
Genneteil (49) . . . 126 C2
Gennetines (03) . . . 169 F3
Genneton (79) . . . 143 K3
Genneville (14) . . . 34 A2
Gennevilliers (92) . . . 58 E2
Genod (39) . . . 173 G6
Génolhac (30) . . . 255 F3
Génos (31) . . . 305 J2
Génos (65) . . . 305 G5
Genouillac (16) . . . 197 J1
Genouillac (23) . . . 166 B6
Genouillé (17) . . . 177 G4
Genouillé (86) . . . 179 J3
Genouilleux (01) . . . 188 C3
Genouilly (18) . . . 148 B1
Genouilly (71) . . . 171 G2
Gensac (33) . . . 230 D2
Gensac (65) . . . 285 H2
Gensac (82) . . . 268 B2
Gensac-de-Boulogne (31) . . . 286 C5
Gensac-la-Pallue (16) . . . 196 A3
Gensac-sur-Garonne (31) . . . 287 J5
Genté (16) . . . 195 K3
Gentelles (80) . . . 18 C2
Gentilly (94) . . . 58 E4
Gentioux-Pigerolles (23) . . . 200 C2
Genvry (60) . . . 19 H5
Georfans (70) . . . 138 E2
Géovreisset (01) . . . 190 A1
Géovreissiat (01) . . . 189 K2
Ger (50) . . . 53 F5
Ger (64) . . . 285 G5
Ger (65) . . . 304 B1
Geraise (39) . . . 156 B4
Gérardmer (88) . . . 119 H1
Géraudot (10) . . . 90 D4
Gerbaix (73) . . . 207 K3
Gerbamont (88) . . . 119 G2
Gerbécourt (57) . . . 66 D3
Gerbécourt-et-Haplemont (54) . . . 94 A2
Gerbépal (88) . . . 95 H5
Gerberoy (60) . . . 17 G6
Gerbéviller (54) . . . 94 D1
Gercourt-et-Drillancourt (55) . . . 43 G3
Gercy (02) . . . 21 F3
Gerde (65) . . . 304 D1
Gerderest (64) . . . 285 F3
Gère-Bélesten (64) . . . 303 H2
Gergny (02) . . . 21 F1
Gergueil (21) . . . 135 J6
Gergy (71) . . . 154 B5
Gerland (21) . . . 154 C2
Germ (65) . . . 305 G5
Germagnat (01) . . . 173 F6
Germagny (71) . . . 171 G2
Germaine (02) . . . 19 J3
Germaine (51) . . . 41 F6
Germaines (52) . . . 116 A5
Germainville (28) . . . 57 G5
Germainvilliers (52) . . . 117 F1
Germay (52) . . . 92 D3
Germéfontaine (25) . . . 138 E6
Germenay (58) . . . 133 G6
Germignac (17) . . . 195 K4
Germigney (39) . . . 155 J3
Germigney (70) . . . 137 F4
Germignonville (28) . . . 85 J6
Germigny (51) . . . 40 D4
Germigny (89) . . . 113 J3
Germigny-des-Prés (45) . . . 110 D5
Germigny-l'Évêque (77) . . . 60 A2
Germigny-l'Exempt (18) . . . 150 B5
Germigny-sous-Coulombs (77) . . . 60 C1
Germigny-sur-Loire (58) . . . 150 C3
Germinon (51) . . . 62 B3
Germiny (54) . . . 93 J1
Germisay (52) . . . 92 D3
Germolles-sur-Grosne (71) . . . 188 A1
Germond-Rouvre (79) . . . 161 H4
Germondans (25) . . . 138 B4
Germont (08) . . . 42 D2
Germonville (54) . . . 94 B3
Germs-sur-l'Oussouet (65) . . . 304 C1
Gernelle (08) . . . 22 E3
Gernicourt (02) . . . 40 D2
Géronce (64) . . . 283 K5
Gerponville (76) . . . 14 E3
Gerrots (14) . . . 33 H5
Gerstheim (67) . . . 71 D6
Gertwiller (67) . . . 70 C5
Geruge (39) . . . 173 F2
Gervans (26) . . . 222 B4
Gerville (76) . . . 14 C4

Géry (55) . . . 64 C4
Gerzat (63) . . . 202 D1
Gesnes (53) . . . 81 G6
Gesnes-en-Argonne (55) . . . 42 E3
Gesnes-le-Gandelin (72) . . . 82 C4
Gespunsart (08) . . . 22 E2
Gestas (64) . . . 283 H3
Gesté (49) . . . 142 C1
Gestel (56) . . . 99 K4
Gestiès (09) . . . 307 H5
Gesvres (53) . . . 82 B3
Gesvres-le-Chapitre (77) . . . 59 K1
Gétigné (44) . . . 123 K6
les Gets (74) . . . 192 A2
Geu (65) . . . 304 B2
Geudertheim (67) . . . 25 A5
Géus-d'Arzacq (64) . . . 284 B2
Géus-d'Oloron (64) . . . 283 K4
Gévezé (35) . . . 79 F3
Gevigney-et-Mercey (70) . . . 117 J5
Geville (55) . . . 65 F4
Gevingey (39) . . . 173 F2
Gevresin (25) . . . 156 C3
Gevrey-Chambertin (21) . . . 135 K6
Gevrolles (21) . . . 115 H3
Gevry (39) . . . 155 G3
Gex (01) . . . 174 B6
Geyssans (26) . . . 222 E4
Gez (65) . . . 304 A2
Gez-ez-Angles (65) . . . 304 C1
Gézaincourt (80) . . . 10 A4
Gézier-et-Fontenelay (70) . . . 137 J4
Gézoncourt (54) . . . 65 J3
Ghisonaccia (2B) . . . 321 J3
Ghisoni (2B) . . . 321 G2
Ghissignies (59) . . . 12 E3
Ghyvelde (59) . . . 3 J1
Giat (63) . . . 201 H2
Gibeaumeix (54) . . . 65 G6
Gibel (31) . . . 288 E4
Gibercourt (02) . . . 19 K4
Giberville (14) . . . 33 F5
Gibles (71) . . . 170 E6
Gibourne (17) . . . 178 B5
Gibret (40) . . . 264 D5
le Gicq (17) . . . 178 C5
Gidy (45) . . . 109 K3
Giel-Courteilles (61) . . . 54 A4
Gien (45) . . . 131 H1
Gien-sur-Cure (58) . . . 152 D2
Gières (38) . . . 224 B3
la Giettaz (73) . . . 191 J6
Giéville (50) . . . 31 J4
Gièvres (41) . . . 129 H6
Giey-sur-Aujon (52) . . . 116 A3
Giez (74) . . . 208 E1
Gif-sur-Yvette (91) . . . 58 C5
Giffaumont-Champaubert (51) . . . 91 H1
Gigean (34) . . . 293 F2
Gignac (34) . . . 273 J6
Gignac (46) . . . 215 H6
Gignac (84) . . . 277 J2
Gignac-la-Nerthe (13) . . . 296 B3
Gignat (63) . . . 202 E6
Gignéville (88) . . . 117 J1
Gigney (88) . . . 94 C5
Gigny (39) . . . 173 F4
Gigny (89) . . . 114 D5
Gigny-Bussy (51) . . . 63 F6
Gigny-sur-Saône (71) . . . 172 A2
Gigondas (84) . . . 257 G5
Gigors (04) . . . 259 H1
Gigors-et-Lozeron (26) . . . 240 E2
Gigouzac (46) . . . 233 H5
Gijounet (81) . . . 271 J5
Gildwiller (68) . . . 97 A3
Gilette (06) . . . 281 F2
Gilhac-et-Bruzac (07) . . . 240 A2
Gilhoc-sur-Ormèze (07) . . . 222 A6
Gillancourt (52) . . . 91 K6
Gillaumé (52) . . . 92 C2
Gilles (28) . . . 57 G3
Gilley (25) . . . 157 G2
Gilley (52) . . . 117 G6
Gillois (39) . . . 174 A1
Gillonnay (38) . . . 207 F6
Gilly-lès-Cîteaux (21) . . . 154 B1
Gilly-sur-Isère (73) . . . 209 F3
Gilly-sur-Loire (71) . . . 169 J4
Gilocourt (60) . . . 38 E4
Gimat (82) . . . 268 B3
Gimbrède (32) . . . 267 K1
Gimeaux (63) . . . 185 F6
Gimécourt (55) . . . 64 C3
Gimel-les-Cascades (19) . . . 216 B2
Gimeux (16) . . . 195 J3
la Gimond (42) . . . 205 G4
Gimont (32) . . . 268 B6
Gimouille (58) . . . 150 D4
Ginai (61) . . . 54 E5
Ginals (82) . . . 250 E5
Ginasservis (83) . . . 278 C5
Ginchy (80) . . . 11 F6
Gincla (11) . . . 309 F5
Gincrey (55) . . . 26 B6
Gindou (46) . . . 233 F5
Ginestas (11) . . . 291 G5
Ginestet (24) . . . 231 H1
Gingsheim (67) . . . 70 D1
Ginoles (11) . . . 308 E4
Ginouillac (46) . . . 233 J4
Gintrac (46) . . . 234 A2

Giocatojo (2B) . . . 319 H4
Gionges (51) . . . 61 K2
Giou-de-Mamou (15) . . . 235 J1
Gioux (23) . . . 200 D2
Gipcy (03) . . . 168 B4
Girac (46) . . . 234 B1
Girancourt (88) . . . 94 C6
Giraumont (54) . . . 44 C4
Giraumont (60) . . . 38 D1
Girauvoisin (55) . . . 65 F3
Gircourt-lès-Viéville (88) . . . 94 B3
Girecourt-sur-Durbion (88) . . . 94 E4
Girefontaine (70) . . . 118 B3
Giremoutiers (77) . . . 60 B4
Girgols (15) . . . 217 H5
Giriviller (54) . . . 94 D2
Girmont (88) . . . 94 D4
Girmont-Val-d'Ajol (88) . . . 118 E2
Girolles (45) . . . 111 H2
Girolles (89) . . . 133 J3
Giromagny (90) . . . 119 H5
Giron (01) . . . 190 B1
Gironcourt-sur-Vraine (88) . . . 93 J4
Gironde-sur-Dropt (33) . . . 230 C5
Girondelle (08) . . . 22 A2
Gironville (77) . . . 87 G6
Gironville-sur-Essonne (91) . . . 86 E4
le Girouard (85) . . . 159 G3
Giroussens (81) . . . 270 A4
Giroux (36) . . . 148 C3
Giry (58) . . . 151 F1
Gisay-la-Coudre (27) . . . 55 J2
Giscaro (32) . . . 268 B6
Giscos (33) . . . 246 D3
Gisors (27) . . . 36 E4
Gissac (12) . . . 272 C3
Gissey-le-Vieil (21) . . . 135 F5
Gissey-sous-Flavigny (21) . . . 135 G3
Gissey-sur-Ouche (21) . . . 135 H6
Gisy-les-Nobles (89) . . . 88 D5
Giuncaggio (2B) . . . 321 H1
Giuncheto (2A) . . . 322 K6
Givardon (18) . . . 150 A6
Givarlais (03) . . . 167 H5
Givenchy-en-Gohelle (62) . . . 10 E1
Givenchy-le-Noble (62) . . . 10 C2
Givenchy-lès-la-Bassée (62) . . . 6 B5
Giverny (27) . . . 36 B6
Giverville (27) . . . 34 D5
Givet (08) . . . 24 C1
Givonne (08) . . . 23 F4
Givors (69) . . . 206 A4
Givraines (45) . . . 110 E1
Givrand (85) . . . 158 D1
Givrauval (55) . . . 64 C5
le Givre (85) . . . 159 J4
Givrezac (17) . . . 195 G4
Givron (08) . . . 21 K5
Givry (08) . . . 41 K1
Givry (71) . . . 153 K6
Givry (89) . . . 133 J3
Givry-en-Argonne (51) . . . 63 J2
Givry-lès-Loisy (51) . . . 61 K3
Givrycourt (57) . . . 67 H1
Gizaucourt (51) . . . 42 C6
Gizay (86) . . . 163 F5
Gizeux (37) . . . 126 D4
Gizia (39) . . . 172 E3
Gizy (02) . . . 20 E5
la Glacerie (50) . . . 28 D2
Glageon (59) . . . 13 J5
Glaignes (60) . . . 38 E4
Glaine-Montaigut (63) . . . 203 G2
Glaire (08) . . . 23 F4
le Glaizil (05) . . . 242 D3
Glamondans (25) . . . 138 C5
Gland (02) . . . 60 E1
Gland (89) . . . 114 C5
Glandage (26) . . . 241 K4
Glandon (87) . . . 198 E6
Glanes (46) . . . 234 C1
Glanges (87) . . . 199 G3
Glannes (51) . . . 63 F5
Glanon (21) . . . 154 D3
Glanville (14) . . . 33 J3
Glatens (82) . . . 268 B3
Glatigny (50) . . . 30 C1
Glatigny (57) . . . 45 G5
Glatigny (60) . . . 37 F1
Glay (25) . . . 139 J3
Gleizé (69) . . . 188 B5
Glénac (56) . . . 102 B3
Glénat (15) . . . 235 F1
Glénay (79) . . . 144 B5
Glénic (23) . . . 182 D2
Glennes (02) . . . 40 C3
Glénouze (86) . . . 144 D4
Glère (25) . . . 139 K4
Glicourt (76) . . . 16 B1
Glisolles (27) . . . 56 C2
Glisy (80) . . . 18 B2
Glomel (22) . . . 76 A3
Glonville (54) . . . 95 F1
Glorianes (66) . . . 314 D3
Glos (14) . . . 34 A6
Glos-la-Ferrière (61) . . . 55 J3
Glos-sur-Risle (27) . . . 34 E4
Gluiras (07) . . . 239 J2
Glun (07) . . . 222 B5
Glux-en-Glenne (58) . . . 152 C4
Goas (82) . . . 268 C4
la Godefroy (50) . . . 52 A5

Godenvillers (60) . . . 18 D6
Goderville (76) . . . 14 D5
Godewaersvelde (59) . . . 3 K4
Godisson (61) . . . 54 E5
la Godivelle (63) . . . 218 C1
Godoncourt (88) . . . 117 J2
Goerlingen (67) . . . 67 J3
Goersdorf (67) . . . 25 A2
Goès (64) . . . 284 A5
Goetzenbruck (57) . . . 69 G4
Goeulzin (59) . . . 11 H2
Gogney (54) . . . 67 G5
Gognies-Chaussée (59) . . . 13 G2
la Gohannière (50) . . . 52 A5
Gohory (28) . . . 84 D6
Goin (57) . . . 66 A1
Goincourt (60) . . . 37 G2
Golancourt (60) . . . 19 H4
Golbey (88) . . . 94 D5
Goldbach-Altenbach (68) . . . 119 K3
Golfech (82) . . . 248 D5
Golinhac (12) . . . 235 J5
Golleville (50) . . . 28 D5
Gombergean (41) . . . 128 C1
Gomelange (57) . . . 27 K5
Gomené (22) . . . 77 J4
Gomer (64) . . . 284 E5
Gometz-la-Ville (91) . . . 58 C6
Gometz-le-Châtel (91) . . . 58 C6
Gomiécourt (62) . . . 11 F4
Gommecourt (62) . . . 10 E4
Gommecourt (78) . . . 36 C6
Gommegnies (59) . . . 12 E3
Gommenec'h (22) . . . 48 C1
Gommersdorf (68) . . . 97 A4
Gommerville (28) . . . 86 A4
Gommerville (76) . . . 14 D6
Gomméville (21) . . . 115 F3
Gomont (08) . . . 41 G1
Goncelin (38) . . . 224 D1
Goncourt (52) . . . 93 F5
Gond-Pontouvre (16) . . . 196 B3
Gondecourt (59) . . . 6 D5
Gondenans-les-Moulins (25) . . . 138 D3
Gondenans-Montby (25) . . . 138 E3
Gondeville (16) . . . 196 B3
Gondrecourt-Aix (54) . . . 26 D6
Gondrecourt-le-Château (55) . . . 92 E1
Gondreville (45) . . . 111 H2
Gondreville (54) . . . 65 J5
Gondreville (60) . . . 39 F5
Gondrexange (57) . . . 67 H4
Gondrexon (54) . . . 67 G5
Gondrin (32) . . . 266 E3
les Gonds (17) . . . 195 G2
Gonesse (95) . . . 59 F2
Gonez (65) . . . 285 J5
Gonfaron (83) . . . 298 C3
Gonfreville (50) . . . 30 C2
Gonfreville-Caillot (76) . . . 14 D5
Gonfreville-l'Orcher (76) . . . 33 K1
la Gonfrière (61) . . . 55 G4
Gonnehem (62) . . . 5 K5
Gonnelieu (59) . . . 11 J5
Gonnetot (76) . . . 15 H3
Gonneville (50) . . . 28 E2
Gonneville-en-Auge (14) . . . 33 F4
Gonneville-la-Mallet (76) . . . 14 B5
Gonneville-sur-Honfleur (14) . . . 34 A2
Gonneville-sur-Mer (14) . . . 33 H3
Gonneville-sur-Scie (76) . . . 15 K3
Gonsans (25) . . . 138 C6
Gontaud-de-Nogaret (47) . . . 247 J1
la Gonterie-Boulouneix (24) . . . 213 K1
Gonzeville (76) . . . 15 H3
Goos (40) . . . 264 C4
Gorbio (06) . . . 281 J2
Gorcy (54) . . . 26 C2
Gordes (84) . . . 277 F2
Gorenflos (80) . . . 9 J5
Gorges (44) . . . 123 K5
Gorges (50) . . . 30 D4
Gorges (80) . . . 9 K5
Gorhey (88) . . . 94 B5
Gornac (33) . . . 230 B4
Gorniès (34) . . . 273 K3
Gorre (87) . . . 198 C2
Gorrevod (01) . . . 172 A5
Gorron (53) . . . 80 E3
Gorses (46) . . . 234 D3
Gorze (57) . . . 44 D6
Gosnay (62) . . . 5 K6
Gosné (35) . . . 79 K3
Gosselming (57) . . . 67 J3
Gotein-Libarrenx (64) . . . 283 H5
Gottenhouse (67) . . . 70 B1
Gottesheim (67) . . . 70 C1
Gouaix (77) . . . 88 D2
Goualade (33) . . . 246 D3
Gouarec (22) . . . 76 C3
Gouaux (65) . . . 305 F4
Gouaux-de-Larboust (31) . . . 305 G5
Gouaux-de-Luchon (31) . . . 305 H4
Gouberville (50) . . . 28 E1
Gouchaupre (76) . . . 16 B1
Goudargues (30) . . . 256 A4
Goudelancourt-lès-Berrieux (02) . . . 40 D1
Goudelancourt-lès-Pierrepont (02) . . . 21 F1
Goudelin (22) . . . 48 E5
Goudet (43) . . . 238 C1
Goudex (31) . . . 287 G3

Goudon (65) . . . 285 K5
Goudourville (82) . . . 248 E5
Gouesnach (29) . . . 98 C2
la Gouesnière (35) . . . 50 E4
Gouesnou (29) . . . 46 A5
Gouex (86) . . . 163 J6
Gouézec (29) . . . 74 E4
Gougenheim (67) . . . 70 D2
Gouhelans (25) . . . 138 D3
Gouhenans (70) . . . 138 E1
Gouillons (28) . . . 85 K4
Gouise (03) . . . 169 F5
Goujounac (46) . . . 233 F5
la Goulafrière (27) . . . 55 G2
Goulet (61) . . . 54 B5
Goulien (29) . . . 73 C3
Goulier (09) . . . 307 H5
Goulles (19) . . . 216 E5
les Goulles (21) . . . 115 J4
Gouloux (58) . . . 134 B6
Goult (84) . . . 277 F3
Goulven (29) . . . 46 C3
Goumois (25) . . . 139 J5
Goupillières (14) . . . 53 J1
Goupillières (27) . . . 34 E6
Goupillières (76) . . . 15 J6
Goupillières (78) . . . 57 J3
Gouraincourt (55) . . . 26 C5
Gourbera (40) . . . 264 B3
Gourbesville (50) . . . 28 E5
Gourbit (09) . . . 307 H4
Gourchelles (60) . . . 17 G4
Gourdan-Polignan (31) . . . 305 H1
Gourdièges (15) . . . 236 C1
Gourdon (06) . . . 280 D4
Gourdon (07) . . . 239 H3
Gourdon (46) . . . 233 G3
Gourdon (71) . . . 171 F2
Gourdon-Murat (19) . . . 200 B5
Gourfaleur (50) . . . 31 H4
Gourgançon (51) . . . 62 A5
Gourgé (79) . . . 162 A1
Gourgeon (70) . . . 117 H6
Gourgue (65) . . . 285 K6
Gourhel (56) . . . 101 K2
Gourin (56) . . . 75 H4
Gourlizon (29) . . . 74 B5
Gournay (36) . . . 165 J3
Gournay-en-Bray (76) . . . 36 D1
Gournay-le-Guérin (27) . . . 55 K5
Gournay-Loizé (79) . . . 178 E3
Gournay-sur-Aronde (60) . . . 38 C1
Gournay-sur-Marne (93) . . . 59 G3
les Gours (16) . . . 178 E5
Gours (33) . . . 212 D6
Gourvieille (11) . . . 289 F4
Gourville (16) . . . 196 C1
Gourvillette (17) . . . 178 C6
Goussaincourt (55) . . . 93 G2
Goussainville (28) . . . 57 H4
Goussainville (95) . . . 59 F1
Goussancourt (02) . . . 40 B5
Gousse (40) . . . 264 C4
Goussonville (78) . . . 57 J3
Goustranville (14) . . . 33 G4
Gout-Rossignol (24) . . . 197 G6
la Goutelle (63) . . . 202 A1
Goutevernisse (31) . . . 287 J5
Goutrens (12) . . . 251 K1
Gouts (40) . . . 264 D3
Gouttières (27) . . . 55 K1
Gouttières (63) . . . 184 C4
Goutz (32) . . . 267 K4
Gouvernes (77) . . . 59 H3
Gouves (62) . . . 10 D2
Gouvets (50) . . . 31 H5
Gouvieux (60) . . . 38 A5
Gouville (27) . . . 56 B3
Gouville-sur-Mer (50) . . . 30 C3
Gouvix (14) . . . 53 K1
Goux (32) . . . 266 B6
Goux-lès-Dambelin (25) . . . 139 G4
Goux-les-Usiers (25) . . . 156 E3
Goux-sous-Landet (25) . . . 156 B2
Gouy (02) . . . 11 K6
Gouy (76) . . . 35 J3
Gouy-en-Artois (62) . . . 10 D3
Gouy-en-Ternois (62) . . . 10 B2
Gouy-les-Groseillers (60) . . . 18 A4
Gouy-Saint-André (62) . . . 9 G2
Gouy-Servins (62) . . . 10 D1
Gouy-sous-Bellonne (62) . . . 11 H2
Gouzangrez (95) . . . 37 F6
Gouzeaucourt (59) . . . 11 J5
Gouzens (31) . . . 287 J6
Gouzon (23) . . . 183 G2
Goven (35) . . . 78 E5
Goviller (54) . . . 93 J1
Goxwiller (67) . . . 70 D5

Graincourt-lès-Havrincourt (62) . . . 11 H4
Grainville (27) . . . 36 A3
Grainville-la-Teinturière (76) . . . 15 F4
Grainville-Langannerie (14) . . . 54 A1
Grainville-sur-Odon (14) . . . 32 C5
Grainville-sur-Ry (76) . . . 35 K1
Grainville-Ymauville (76) . . . 14 D5
le Grais (61) . . . 53 K6
Graissac (12) . . . 236 B3
Graissessac (34) . . . 272 C5
Graix (42) . . . 221 J1
Gramat (46) . . . 234 A3
Gramazie (11) . . . 308 D1
Grambois (84) . . . 277 K4
Grammond (42) . . . 205 G4
Grammont (70) . . . 138 E2
Gramond (12) . . . 251 K4
Gramont (82) . . . 267 K2
Granace (2A) . . . 322 E6
Grancey-le-Château-Neuvelle (21) . . . 136 A1
Grancey-sur-Ource (21) . . . 115 F2
Grand (88) . . . 92 E3
le Grand-Abergement (01) . . . 190 B4
le Grand-Auverné (44) . . . 103 K5
le Grand-Bornand (74) . . . 191 J5
le Grand-Bourg (23) . . . 182 B3
Grand-Brassac (24) . . . 213 H2
Grand-Camp (27) . . . 55 H1
Grand-Camp (76) . . . 15 F6
le Grand-Celland (50) . . . 52 B5
Grand-Champ (56) . . . 100 E4
Grand-Charmont (25) . . . 139 H2
la Grand-Combe (30) . . . 255 G6
Grand-Corent (01) . . . 189 J2
Grand-Couronne (76) . . . 35 H3
la Grand-Croix (42) . . . 205 J5
Grand-Failly (54) . . . 26 A4
Grand-Fayt (59) . . . 13 F5
Grand-Fort-Philippe (59) . . . 3 F2
Grand-Fougeray (35) . . . 103 F3
Grand-Laviers (80) . . . 9 F5
le Grand-Lemps (38) . . . 207 G6
le Grand-Lucé (72) . . . 107 G4
le Grand-Madieu (16) . . . 179 K5
le Grand-Pressigny (37) . . . 146 B5
le Grand-Quevilly (76) . . . 35 H2
Grand-Rozoy (02) . . . 39 K4
Grand-Rullecourt (62) . . . 10 C3
le Grand-Serre (26) . . . 222 E2
Grand-Vabre (12) . . . 235 G5
Grand-Verly (02) . . . 20 C1
le Grand-Village-Plage (17) . . . 176 C6
Grandcamp-Maisy (14) . . . 29 H5
Grandchain (27) . . . 55 J1
Grandchamp (08) . . . 22 A5
Grandchamp (52) . . . 116 E6
Grandchamp (72) . . . 82 E4
Grandchamp (78) . . . 57 H5
Grandchamp (89) . . . 112 C5
Grandchamp-le-Château (14) . . . 33 J6
Grandchamps-des-Fontaines (44) . . . 123 G2
Grand'Combe-Châteleu (25) . . . 157 H2
Grand'Combe-des-Bois (25) . . . 157 K1
Grandcourt (76) . . . 16 D2
Grandcourt (80) . . . 10 E5
la Grande-Fosse (88) . . . 95 K3
la Grande-Motte (34) . . . 293 J1
la Grande-Paroisse (77) . . . 87 K4
la Grande-Résie (70) . . . 137 F5
Grande-Rivière (39) . . . 173 K3
Grande-Synthe (59) . . . 3 G2
la Grande-Verrière (71) . . . 152 D4
Grandecourt (70) . . . 137 J1
les Grandes-Armoises (08) . . . 22 C6
les Grandes-Chapelles (10) . . . 90 A2
les Grandes-Loges (51) . . . 41 H6
les Grandes-Ventes (76) . . . 16 B3
Grandeyrolles (63) . . . 202 D4
Grandfontaine (25) . . . 137 J6
Grandfontaine (67) . . . 95 K1
Grandfontaine-sur-Creuse (25) . . . 138 E6
Grandfresnoy (60) . . . 38 C3
Grandham (08) . . . 42 C3
Grandjean (17) . . . 177 J6
Grand'Landes (85) . . . 141 H5
Grandlup-et-Fay (02) . . . 20 E5
Grandpré (08) . . . 42 D3
Grandpuits-Bailly-Carrois (77) . . . 88 A1
Grandrieu (48) . . . 237 K3
Grandrieux (02) . . . 21 J4
Grandrif (63) . . . 204 A5
Grandris (69) . . . 187 J4
Grandrû (60) . . . 19 J5
Grandrupt (88) . . . 95 J3
Grandrupt-de-Bains (88) . . . 118 B1
les Grands-Chézeaux (87) . . . 165 F6
Grandsaigne (19) . . . 200 B6
Grandval (63) . . . 203 J4
Grandvals (48) . . . 236 D3
Grandvaux (71) . . . 170 D4
Grandvelle-et-le-Perrenot (70) . . . 137 K2
Grandvillars (90) . . . 139 J2
la Grandville (08) . . . 22 D3
Grandville (10) . . . 90 C1
Grandvillers (88) . . . 95 F4
Grandvillers-aux-Bois (60) . . . 38 C2
Grandvilliers (27) . . . 56 C4
Grandvilliers (60) . . . 17 H5
Grane (26) . . . 240 C3
Granès (11) . . . 309 F4
la Grange (25) . . . 139 G5
Grange-de-Vaivre (39) . . . 156 A3

Grangermont (45). 87 F6
les Granges (10). 114 A2
Granges (71). 171 J1
Granges-d'Ans (24). 214 E3
les Granges-Gontardes (26). 256 D1
Granges-la-Ville (70). 139 F1
Granges-le-Bourg (70). 139 F1
les Granges-le-Roi (91). 86 B2
Granges-les-Beaumont (26). 222 D5
Granges-Narboz (25). 156 K4
Granges-sur-Aube (51). 89 J1
Granges-sur-Baume (39). 173 G1
Granges-sur-Lot (47). 248 A2
Granges-sur-Vologne (88). 95 G6
les Grangettes (25). 156 E5
Grangues (14). 33 H4
Granier (73). 209 J3
Granieu (38). 207 J4
Grans (13). 276 E6
Granville (50). 51 H1
Granzay-Gript (79). 178 A2
Gras (07). 256 B1
les Gras (25). 157 G3
Grassac (16). 197 G4
Grasse (06). 280 D4
Grassendorf (67). 69 J6
Grateloup (47). 247 K4
Gratens (31). 287 J4
Gratentour (31). 269 G5
Gratibus (80). 18 D4
Gratot (50). 30 D4
Gratreuil (51). 42 B4
Grattepanche (80). 18 A3
le Gratteris (25). 156 C1
Grattery (70). 118 A6
le Grau-du-Roi (30). 293 K1
les Graulges (24). 197 G5
Graulhet (81). 270 C4
Grauves (51). 61 K2
Graval (76). 16 D4
la Grave (05). 225 G4
Gravelines (59). 3 F2
la Gravelle (53). 104 C1
Gravelotte (57). 44 D5
la Graverie (14). 31 K6
Graveron-Sémerville (27). 35 G6
Graves-Saint-Amant (16). 196 B3
Graveson (13). 276 B3
Gravières (07). 255 G2
Gravigny (27). 56 D1
Gravon (77). 88 B3
Gray (70). 137 F3
Gray-la-Ville (70). 137 F3
Grayan-et-l'Hôpital (33). 194 B5
Graye-et-Charnay (39). 173 F4
Graye-sur-Mer (14). 32 D3
Grayssas (47). 248 E5
Grazac (31). 288 C4
Grazac (43). 221 F3
Grazac (81). 269 J3
Grazay (53). 81 H4
Gréalou (46). 234 C6
Gréasque (13). 296 E2
Grébault-Mesnil (80). 9 F6
Grécourt (80). 19 H4
Gredisans (39). 155 G1
la Grée-Saint-Laurent (56). 101 J1
Gréez-sur-Roc (72). 107 K1
Greffeil (11). 309 G1
Grèges (76). 16 A1
Grémecey (57). 66 C3
Grémévillers (60). 17 H6
Gremilly (55). 26 A5
Grémonville (76). 15 H4
Grenade (31). 269 F4
Grenade-sur-l'Adour (40). 265 H4
Grenand-lès-Sombernon (21). . . . 135 H6
Grenant (52). 116 E6
Grenay (38). 206 D3
Grenay (62). 6 B6
Grendelbruch (67). 70 B4
Greneville-en-Beauce (45). 86 C6
Grenier-Montgon (43). 219 F2
Gréning (57). 67 G1
Grenoble (38). 224 A3
Grenois (58). 133 F5
Grentheville (14). 32 E5
Grentzingen (68). 97 C5
Greny (76). 16 B1
Gréolières (06). 280 D3
Gréoux-les-Bains (04). 278 C4
Grépiac (31). 288 B3
le Grès (31). 268 D5
Grésigny-Sainte-Reine (21). . . . 135 F2
Gresin (73). 207 K3
la Gresle (42). 187 H4
Gresse-en-Vercors (38). 241 K1
Gressey (78). 57 H4
Gresswiller (67). 70 C4
Gressy (77). 59 H2
Grésy-sur-Aix (73). 208 B2
Grésy-sur-Isère (73). 208 E3
Gretz-Armainvilliers (77). 59 J5
Greucourt (70). 137 J2
Greuville (76). 15 J3
Greux (88). 93 F2
la Grève-sur-Mignon (17). 177 H1
Gréville-Hague (50). 28 B2
Grévillers (62). 11 F5
Grevilly (71). 171 J4
Grez (60). 17 H5
le Grez (72). 82 A6

Grez-en-Bouère (53). 105 H4
Grez-Neuville (49). 125 F1
Grez-sur-Loing (77). 87 H4
Grézac (17). 194 E4
Grézels (46). 249 G1
Grèzes (24). 215 G5
Grèzes (43). 237 J1
Grèzes (46). 234 B5
Grèzes (48). 237 G6
Grézet-Cavagnan (47). 247 G2
Grézian (65). 305 F4
Grézieu-la-Varenne (69). 205 K2
Grézieu-le-Marché (69). 205 J3
Grézieux-le-Fromental (42). . . . 204 D4
Grézillac (33). 230 A2
Grézillé (49). 125 J5
Grézolles (42). 204 B1
Gricourt (02). 19 K2
Grièges (01). 188 C1
Gries (67). 25 B4
Griesbach-au-Val (68). 96 A4
Griesheim-près-Molsheim (67). . . 70 D4
Griesheim-sur-Souffel (67). . . . 70 E2
Grignan (26). 257 F1
Grigneuseville (76). 16 A5
Grignols (24). 213 J5
Grignols (33). 246 E2
Grignon (21). 134 D2
Grignon (73). 209 G3
Grignoncourt (88). 117 J3
Grigny (62). 9 J1
Grigny (69). 206 A4
Grigny (91). 58 E6
la Grigonnais (44). 103 F6
Grillon (84). 257 F2
Grilly (01). 174 B6
Grimaucourt-en-Woëvre (55). . . 43 K5
Grimaucourt-près-Sampigny (55). . 64 D4
Grimaud (83). 298 E4
la Grimaudière (86). 144 D6
Grimault (89). 134 A1
Grimbosq (14). 32 D6
Grimesnil (50). 30 E5
Grimonviller (54). 93 K3
Grincourt-lès-Pas (62). 10 C4
Grindorff (57). 45 J2
la Gripperie-Saint-
    Symphorien (17). 194 D1
Gripport (54). 94 B2
Griscourt (54). 65 J3
Griselles (21). 114 D4
Griselles (45). 111 J2
Grisolles (02). 39 J5
Grisolles (82). 269 F3
Grisy-les-Plâtres (95). 37 G6
Grisy-Suisnes (77). 59 H6
Grisy-sur-Seine (77). 88 D3
Grives (24). 232 D3
Grivesnes (80). 18 C4
Grivillers (80). 18 E5
Grivy-Loisy (08). 42 A2
Groffliers (62). 8 E1
la Groise (59). 12 E5
Groises (18). 150 A1
Groissiat (01). 190 A2
Groisy (74). 191 H4
Groix (56). 99 J6
Groléjac (24). 233 G2
Gron (18). 149 K2
Gron (89). 112 D1
Gronard (02). 21 F3
Gros-Chastang (19). 216 D3
Gros-Réderching (57). 68 E3
le Gros-Theil (27). 35 F4
Grosbliederstroff (57). 68 D2
Grosbois (25). 138 C4
Grosbois-en-Montagne (21). . . . 135 G5
Grosbois-lès-Tichey (21). 154 E3
Grosbreuil (85). 159 F3
les Groseillers (79). 161 H4
Groslay (95). 58 E2
Groslée (01). 207 H2
Grosley-sur-Risle (27). 56 A1
Grosmagny (90). 119 H5
Grosne (90). 139 K1
Grospierres (07). 255 J2
Grosrouvre (78). 57 J4
Grosrouvres (54). 65 H3
Grossa (2A). 322 D3
Grosseto-Prugna (2A). 320 E6
Grossoeuvre (27). 56 D2
Grossouvre (18). 150 C5
Grostenquin (57). 67 F1
Grosville (50). 28 B4
Grouches-Luchuel (80). 10 B4
Grougis (02). 20 C1
la Groutte (18). 167 G2
Grozon (39). 155 J5
Gruchet-le-Valasse (76). 14 E6
Gruchet-Saint-Siméon (76). . . . 15 H3
Grues (85). 159 J5
Gruey-lès-Surance (88). 118 B1
Gruffy (74). 208 C1
Grugé-l'Hôpital (49). 104 C5
Grugies (02). 19 K3
Grugny (76). 15 K5
Grumesnil (76). 17 F5
Grun-Bordas (24). 213 K5
Grundviller (57). 68 C3
Gruny (80). 19 F4
Grury (71). 170 A2

Gruson (59). 7 F4
Grusse (39). 173 F3
Grussenheim (68). 96 D3
Grust (65). 304 B3
Gruyères (08). 22 C4
le Gua (17). 194 D2
le Gua (38). 223 K5
Guagno (2A). 320 C6
Guainville (28). 57 G3
Guarbecque (62). 5 J4
Guargualé (2A). 320 D6
Guchan (65). 305 F4
Guchen (65). 305 F4
Gudas (09). 307 K2
Gudmont-Villiers (52). 92 B4
le Gué-d'Alleré (17). 177 G2
le Gué-de-la-Chaîne (61). . . . 83 H4
le Gué-de-Longroi (28). 85 J2
le Gué-de-Velluire (85). 160 C5
Gué-d'Hossus (08). 22 B1
Guebenhouse (57). 68 C3
Gueberschwihr (68). 96 B5
Guébestroff (57). 67 F3
Guéblange-lès-Dieuze (57). . . . 67 F3
Guébling (57). 67 F2
Guebwiller (68). 96 B6
Guécélard (72). 106 D4
le Guédéniac (49). 126 B3
Guégon (56). 101 H2
Guéhébert (50). 30 E5
Guéhenno (56). 101 G2
Gueltas (56). 77 F5
Guémappe (62). 11 F3
Guémené-Penfao (44). 102 E4
Guémené-sur-Scorff (56). . . . 76 B5
Guemps (62). 2 E3
Guénange (57). 27 H5
Guengat (29). 74 C5
Guénin (56). 100 D2
Guenroc (22). 78 C1
Guenrouet (44). 102 D6
Guenviller (57). 68 B3
Guêprei (61). 54 C3
Guer (56). 102 B3
Guérande (44). 121 J4
Guérard (77). 60 A4
Guerbigny (80). 18 E4
la Guerche (37). 146 A5
la Guerche-de-Bretagne (35). . . 104 A3
la Guerche-sur-l'Aubois (18). . . 150 C4
Guercheville (77). 87 G5
Guerchy (89). 112 E4
Guéreins (01). 188 C3
Guéret (23). 182 D3
Guerfand (71). 154 C6
Guérigny (58). 150 D3
Guérin (47). 247 F2
la Guérinière (85). 140 B3
Guerlesquin (29). 47 J5
Guermange (57). 67 G3
Guermantes (77). 59 H3
Guern (56). 76 C6
Guernanville (27). 56 A3
Guernes (78). 57 H1
le Guerno (56). 101 H3
Guerny (27). 36 D5
Guéron (14). 32 B4
la Guéroulde (27). 56 A4
Guerpont (55). 64 B5
Guerquesalles (61). 54 E3
les Guerreaux (71). 170 A4
Guerstling (57). 45 J2
Guerting (57). 45 K4
Guerville (76). 16 D1
Guerville (78). 57 J2
Gueschart (80). 9 H3
Guesnain (59). 11 J2
Guesnes (86). 144 E5
Guessling-Hémering (57). . . . 45 K6
Guéthary (64). 263 C1
Gueudecourt (80). 11 F5
Gueugnon (71). 170 B3
Gueures (76). 15 J2
Gueutteville (76). 15 J5
Gueutteville-les-Grès (76). . . . 15 G2
Gueux (51). 40 E4
Guevenatten (68). 119 K5
Guewenheim (68). 119 K5
Gueytes-et-Labastide (11). . . . 308 C2
Gugnécourt (88). 95 F4
Gugney (54). 93 K3
Gugney-aux-Aulx (88). 94 B4
Guibeville (91). 86 D1
Guichainville (27). 56 D2
Guiche (64). 282 E1
la Guiche (71). 171 F4
Guichen (35). 79 F6
Guiclan (29). 47 F5
Guidel (56). 99 J4
la Guierche (72). 106 E1
Guignecourt (60). 17 H1
Guignemicourt (80). 17 K2
Guignen (35). 102 E1
Guignes (77). 59 J6
Guigneville (45). 86 C6
Guigneville-sur-Essonne (91). . . 86 E2
Guignicourt (02). 40 E2
Guignicourt-sur-Vence (08). . . 22 C4
Guigny (62). 9 H2
Guilberville (50). 31 J5
Guiler-sur-Goyen (29). 73 E3

Guilers (29). 72 C4
Guilherand-Granges (07). . . . 240 C1
Guillac (33). 230 A2
Guillac (56). 101 J2
Guillaucourt (80). 18 D2
Guillaumes (06). 261 F5
Guillemont (80). 11 F6
la Guillermie (03). 186 A5
Guillerval (91). 86 C4
Guillestre (05). 227 A3
Guilleville (28). 85 K6
Guilliers (56). 77 K6
Guilligomarc'h (29). 99 K2
Guillon (89). 134 B3
Guillon-les-Bains (25). 138 D5
Guillonville (28). 109 H2
Guillos (33). 229 H5
Guilly (36). 148 A3
Guilly (45). 110 D5
Guilmécourt (76). 16 B1
Guilvinec (29). 73 E6
Guimaëc (29). 47 H3
Guimiliau (29). 46 E5
Guimps (16). 196 A5
Guinarthe-Parenties (64). . . . 283 G3
Guincourt (08). 22 C6
Guindrecourt-aux-Ormes (52). . . 91 K2
Guindrecourt-sur-Blaise (52). . . 91 K4
Guinecourt (62). 9 K2
Guînes (62). 2 D3
Guingamp (22). 48 C5
Guinglange (57). 45 J5
Guinkirchen (57). 27 K6
Guinzeling (57). 67 G2
Guipavas (29). 46 A6
Guipel (35). 79 F2
Guipronvel (29). 72 C3
Guipry (35). 102 E2
Guipy (58). 151 H1
Guiry-en-Vexin (95). 36 E6
Guiscard (60). 19 H5
Guiscriff (56). 75 H5
Guise (02). 20 D2
le Guislain (50). 31 G5
Guissény (29). 46 B3
Guisy (62). 9 J1
Guitalens (81). 270 D6
Guitera-les-Bains (2A). 321 F5
Guitinières (17). 195 H6
Guitrancourt (78). 57 K1
Guîtres (33). 212 B5
Guitry (27). 36 C5
Guitté (22). 78 C2
Guivry (02). 19 J5
Guizancourt (80). 17 H4
Guizengeard (16). 212 C2
Guizerix (65). 286 B4
Gujan-Mestras (33). 228 C4
Gumbrechtshoffen (67). 69 J5
Gumery (10). 88 E3
Gumiane (26). 241 G6
Gumières (42). 204 C5
Gumond (19). 216 D3
Gundershoffen (67). 69 K5
Gundolsheim (68). 96 B6
Gungwiller (67). 67 K2
Gunsbach (68). 96 A4
Gunstett (67). 25 A2
Guntzviller (57). 67 K4
Guny (02). 39 H1
Guran (31). 305 H4
Gurat (16). 197 F6
Gurcy-le-Châtel (77). 88 B2
Gurgy (89). 113 G4
Gurgy-la-Ville (21). 115 K4
Gurgy-le-Château (21). 115 K4
Gurmençon (64). 284 A6
Gurs (64). 283 J4
Gurunhuel (22). 48 B5
Gury (60). 19 F6
Gussainville (55). 44 A5
Gussignies (59). 13 F2
Guyancourt (78). 58 C4
Guyans-Durnes (25). 156 D1
Guyans-Vennes (25). 157 G1
Guyencourt (02). 40 D3
Guyencourt-Saulcourt (80). . . . 11 H6
Guyencourt-sur-Noye (80). . . . 18 B3
la Guyonnière (85). 142 B4
Guyonvelle (52). 117 G4
Guzargues (34). 274 C5
Gy (70). 137 H4
Gy-en-Sologne (41). 129 H5
Gy-les-Nonains (45). 111 K3
Gy-l'Évêque (89). 113 G6
Gye (54). 65 H6
Gyé-sur-Seine (10). 114 C2

H

l'Haÿ-les-Roses (94). 58 E4
Habarcq (62). 10 D2
Habas (40). 264 C6
Habère-Lullin (74). 191 J1
Habère-Poche (74). 191 J1
l'Habit (27). 57 F3
Hablainville (54). 95 F1
Habloville (61). 54 B4
Haboudange (57). 66 E2

Habsheim (68). 97 D2
Hachan (65). 286 B4
Hâcourt (52). 93 F6
Hacqueville (27). 36 C4
Hadancourt-le-Haut-Clocher (60). . 36 E5
Hadigny-les-Verrières (88). . . . 94 D3
Hadol (88). 94 D6
Haegen (67). 70 B2
Hagécourt (88). 94 A5
Hagedet (65). 285 G1
Hagen (57). 27 G2
Hagenbach (68). 97 A4
Hagenthal-le-Bas (68). 97 D5
Hagenthal-le-Haut (68). 97 D5
Haget (32). 285 J3
Hagetaubin (64). 284 A1
Hagetmau (40). 265 F5
Hagéville (54). 44 C6
Hagnéville-et-Roncourt (88). . . 93 H5
Hagnicourt (08). 22 C5
Hagondange (57). 27 G5
Haguenau (67). 25 A4
la Haie-Fouassière (44). 123 J5
la Haie-Traversaine (53). . . . 81 G3
les Haies (69). 205 K5
Haigneville (54). 94 C1
Haillainville (88). 94 D3
le Haillan (33). 229 G1
Hailles (80). 18 C3
Haillicourt (62). 5 K6
Haimps (17). 178 C6
Haims (86). 164 A4
Hainvilliers (60). 18 E6
Haironville (55). 64 A5
Haisnes (62). 6 B6
Haleine (61). 81 J2
Halinghen (62). 4 B4
Hallencourt (80). 9 G6
Hallennes-lez-Haubourdin (59). . 6 D4
Hallering (57). 45 J5
les Halles (69). 205 G2
Halles-sous-les-Côtes (55). . . . 43 F1
Hallignicourt (52). 63 J6
Hallines (62). 3 F5
Hallivillers (80). 18 A4
la Hallotière (76). 36 B1
Halloville (54). 67 H6
Halloy (60). 17 H5
Halloy (62). 10 B4
Halloy-lès-Pernois (80). 9 K6
Hallu (80). 19 F3
Halluin (59). 6 E2
Halsou (64). 263 D2
Halstroff (57). 27 K4
le Ham (50). 28 E5
le Ham (53). 81 J3
Ham (80). 19 H4
Ham-en-Artois (62). 5 J5
Ham-les-Moines (08). 22 C3
Ham-sous-Varsberg (57). . . . 45 K4
Ham-sur-Meuse (08). 24 C2
Hamars (14). 53 H1
Hambach (57). 68 D3
Hambers (53). 81 J5
Hamblain-les-Prés (62). 11 G3
Hambye (50). 31 F5
Hamel (59). 11 H3
le Hamel (60). 17 H5
le Hamel (80). 18 D2
Hamelet (80). 18 D2
Hamelin (50). 80 B1
Hamelincourt (62). 11 F4
Hames-Boucres (62). 2 C3
Hammeville (54). 93 K1
Hamonville (54). 65 G3
Hampigny (10). 91 F2
Hampont (57). 66 E3
Han-devant-Pierrepont (54). . . 26 C4
Han-lès-Juvigny (55). 43 H1
Han-sur-Meuse (55). 64 E3
Han-sur-Nied (57). 66 C1
Hanc (79). 178 E4
Hanches (28). 85 H1
Hancourt (80). 19 H2
Handschuheim (67). 70 D3
Hangard (80). 18 C3
Hangenbieten (67). 70 E3
Hangest-en-Santerre (80). . . . 18 D4
Hangest-sur-Somme (80). . . . 17 J1
Hangviller (57). 69 F6
Hannaches (60). 36 E1
Hannapes (02). 20 D1
Hannappes (08). 21 J3
Hannescamps (62). 10 D4
Hannocourt (57). 66 C2
Hannogne-Saint-Martin (08). . . 22 E4
Hannogne-Saint-Rémy (08). . . 21 H5
Hannonville-sous-les-Côtes (55). . 44 A6
Hannonville-Suzémont (54). . . 44 C5
le Hanouard (76). 15 F4
Hans (51). 42 C6
Hantay (59). 6 C5
Hanvec (29). 74 D2
Hanviller (57). 69 H2
Hanvoile (60). 37 F1
Haplincourt (62). 11 G5
Happencourt (02). 19 J3
Happonvilliers (28). 84 C4
Haramont (02). 39 G4
Haraucourt (08). 23 F5
Haraucourt (54). 66 C5
Haraucourt-sur-Seille (57). . . . 66 E3

Haravesnes (62) 9 J3
Haravilliers (95) 37 G5
Harbonnières (80) 18 E2
Harbouey (54) 67 H6
Harcanville (76) 15 G4
Harchéchamp (88) 93 G3
Harcigny (02) 21 G3
Harcourt (27) 34 E5
Harcy (08) 22 B2
Hardancourt (88) 94 E3
Hardanges (53) 81 J4
Hardecourt-aux-Bois (80) 11 F6
Hardencourt-Cocherel (27) . . . 56 E1
Hardifort (59) 3 J4
Hardinghen (62) 2 C4
Hardinvast (50) 28 C3
Hardivillers (60) 18 A5
Hardivillers-en-Vexin (60) 37 F3
Hardricourt (78) 58 A1
la Harengère (27) 35 G4
Haréville (88) 93 K5
Harfleur (76) 33 K1
Hargarten-aux-Mines (57) 45 K4
Hargeville (78) 57 J3
Hargicourt (02) 19 J1
Hargicourt (80) 18 D4
Hargnies (08) 24 C3
Hargnies (59) 13 G3
Harly (02) 20 A2
Harmonville (88) 93 H2
la Harmoye (22) 76 E2
Harnes (62) 6 C6
Harol (88) 94 B6
Haroué (54) 94 A2
Harponville (80) 10 C6
Harprich (57) 66 E1
Harquency (27) 36 B4
Harreberg (57) 67 K5
Harréville-les-Chanteurs (52) . . 93 F5
Harricourt (08) 42 D2
Harsault (88) 118 B1
Harskirchen (67) 67 J1
Hartennes-et-Taux (02) 39 J4
Hartmannswiller (68) 97 B1
Hartzviller (57) 67 K5
Harville (55) 44 B5
Hary (02) 21 F3
Haselbourg (57) 70 A2
Hasnon (59) 12 C1
Hasparren (64) 282 D3
Haspelschiedt (57) 69 H3
Haspres (59) 12 C3
Hastingues (40) 283 F1
Hatrize (54) 26 E6
Hatten (67) 25 C3
Hattencourt (80) 19 F3
Hattenville (76) 14 E5
Hattigny (57) 67 H5
Hattmatt (67) 69 H4
Hattstatt (68) 96 B5
Hauban (65) 304 D1
Haubourdin (59) 6 D4
Hauconcourt (57) 27 H6
Haucourt (60) 37 F1
Haucourt (62) 11 G3
Haucourt (76) 17 F5
Haucourt-en-Cambrésis (59) . . . 12 B5
Haucourt-Moulaine (54) 26 D3
Haudainville (55) 43 J5
Haudiomont (55) 43 K5
Haudivillers (60) 37 J1
Haudonville (54) 94 D1
Haudrecy (08) 22 C3
Haudricourt (76) 17 F4
Haulchin (59) 12 C2
Haulies (32) 286 D1
Haulmé (08) 22 D2
Haumont-près-Samogneux (55) . . 43 H3
Hauriet (40) 264 E4
Hausgauen (68) 97 C4
Haussez (76) 17 F6
Haussignémont (51) 63 H5
Haussimont (51) 62 B5
Haussonville (54) 94 C1
Haussy (59) 12 C3
Haut-Clocher (57) 67 J4
le Haut-Corlay (22) 76 D2
Haut-de-Bosdarros (64) 284 D6
Haut-du-Them-Château-
    Lambert (70) 119 G4
Haut-Lieu (59) 13 G5
Haut-Loquin (62) 2 D5
Haut-Mauco (40) 265 G3
Hautaget (65) 305 G2
Hautbos (60) 17 G5
Haute-Amance (52) 117 F4
Haute-Avesnes (62) 10 D2
la Haute-Beaume (05) 242 A5
la Haute-Chapelle (61) 53 G6
Haute-Épine (61) 17 J6
Haute-Goulaine (44) 123 H4
Haute-Isle (95) 36 D6
la Haute-Kontz (57) 27 J3
la Haute-Maison (77) 60 A3
Haute-Rivoire (69) 205 G2
Haute-Vigneulles (57) 45 J3
Hautecloque (62) 10 A2
Hautecour (39) 173 J3
Hautecour (73) 209 H4
Hautecourt-Romanèche (01) . . . 189 J2
Hautefage (19) 216 D5
Hautefage-la-Tour (47) 248 D3

Hautefaye (24) 197 H5
Hautefeuille (77) 60 A5
Hautefond (71) 170 D5
Hautefort (24) 214 E3
Hauteluce (73) 209 H1
Hautepierre-le-Châtelet (25) . . . 156 E2
Hauterive (03) 185 J4
Hauterive (61) 82 E2
Hauterive (89) 113 G4
Hauterive-la-Fresse (25) 157 F3
Hauterives (26) 222 D2
Hauteroche (21) 135 F3
Hautes-Duyes (04) 259 J4
les Hautes-Rivières (08) 22 E2
Hautesvignes (47) 247 J1
Hautevelle (70) 118 C4
Hautevesnes (02) 39 H6
Hauteville (02) 20 C2
Hauteville (08) 21 K6
Hauteville (51) 63 H6
Hauteville (62) 10 D3
Hauteville (73) 208 E4
la Hauteville (78) 57 H5
Hauteville-la-Guichard (50) . . . 31 F3
Hauteville-lès-Dijon (21) 136 A5
Hauteville-Lompnes (01) 190 A5
Hauteville-sur-Fier (74) 190 D5
Hauteville-sur-Mer (50) 30 D5
Haution (02) 21 F2
Hautmont (59) 13 G4
Hautmougey (88) 118 B2
Hautot-l'Auvray (76) 15 G3
Hautot-le-Vatois (76) 15 G5
Hautot-Saint-Sulpice (76) 15 G4
Hautot-sur-Mer (76) 15 K2
Hautot-sur-Seine (76) 35 G3
les Hauts-de-Chée (55) 64 B3
Hautteville-Bocage (50) 28 C5
Hautvillers (51) 40 E6
Hautvillers-Ouville (80) 9 G4
Hauville (27) 34 E2
Hauviné (08) 41 J3
Haux (33) 229 K3
Haux (64) 302 C1
Havange (57) 27 F4
Havelu (28) 57 G4
Haveluy (59) 12 C2
Havernas (80) 9 K6
Haverskerque (59) 3 J6
le Havre (76) 33 J1
Havrincourt (62) 11 H5
Hayange (57) 27 F4
Haybes (08) 24 B3
la Haye (76) 36 B1
la Haye (88) 118 B1
la Haye-Aubrée (27) 34 E2
la Haye-Bellefond (50) 31 G5
la Haye-de-Calleville (27) 34 E5
la Haye-de-Routot (27) 34 E2
la Haye-d'Ectot (50) 28 B5
la Haye-du-Puits (50) 30 D1
la Haye-du-Theil (27) 35 F4
la Haye-le-Comte (27) 35 J5
la Haye-Malherbe (27) 35 H4
la Haye-Pesnel (50) 51 K1
la Haye-Saint-Sylvestre (27) . . . 55 J3
les Hayes (41) 107 K6
Hayes (57) 45 G4
Haynecourt (59) 11 J4
les Hays (39) 155 F4
Hazebrouck (59) 3 J5
Hazembourg (57) 67 H1
le Heaulme (95) 37 G5
Héauville (50) 28 B3
Hébécourt (27) 36 D3
Hébécourt (80) 18 A3
Hébécrevon (50) 31 G3
Héberville (76) 15 H3
Hébuterne (62) 10 D5
Hèches (65) 305 F2
Hecken (68) 97 A3
Hecmanville (27) 34 D5
Hécourt (27) 57 F2
Hécourt (60) 36 E1
Hecq (59) 12 E4
Hectomare (27) 35 G5
Hédauville (80) 10 D6
Hédé (35) 79 F2
Hédouville (95) 37 H5
Hegeney (67) 25 A3
Hégenheim (68) 97 E4
Heidolsheim (67) 71 C6
Heidwiller (68) 97 B3
Heiligenberg (67) 70 C4
Heiligenstein (67) 70 C5
Heillecourt (54) 66 A5
Heilles (60) 37 J3
Heilly (80) 18 D1
Heiltz-le-Hutier (51) 63 H5
Heiltz-le-Maurupt (51) 63 H4
Heiltz-l'Évêque (51) 63 G4
Heimersdorf (68) 97 B4
Heimsbrunn (68) 97 B3
Heining-lès-Bouzonville (57) . . . 45 J2
Heippes (55) 64 C1
Heiteren (68) 96 E5
Heiwiller (68) 97 C4
Hélesmes (59) 12 B2
Hélette (64) 282 D4
Helfaut (62) 3 G6
Helfrantzkirch (68) 97 D4

Helléan (56) 101 J1
Hollering-lès-Fénétrange (57) . . 67 J3
Helleville (50) 28 B3
Hellimer (57) 68 B4
Héloup (61) 82 C3
Helstroff (57) 45 H4
Hem (59) 7 F4
Hem-Hardinval (80) 10 A4
Hem-Lenglet (59) 11 J3
Hem-Monacu (80) 19 F1
Hémevez (50) 28 E4
Hémévillers (60) 38 C2
Hémilly (57) 45 J6
Héming (57) 67 H4
Hémonstoir (22) 77 F4
Hénaménil (54) 66 E5
Hénanbihen (22) 50 A4
Hénansal (22) 49 K6
Hendaye (64) 280 A2
Hendecourt-lès-Cagnicourt (62) . . 11 G4
Hendecourt-lès-Ransart (62) . . . 10 E4
Hénencourt (80) 10 D6
Henflingen (68) 97 C4
Hengoat (22) 48 C3
Hengwiller (67) 70 B2
Hénin-Beaumont (62) 11 G1
Hénin-sur-Cojeul (62) 11 F3
Héninel (62) 11 F3
Hennebont (56) 100 A3
Hennecourt (88) 94 C5
Hennemont (55) 44 A5
Henneveux (62) 2 C5
Hennezel (88) 118 A1
Hennezis (27) 36 B5
Hénon (22) 77 G2
Hénonville (60) 37 G5
Hénouville (76) 35 G2
Henrichemont (18) 131 G6
Henridorff (57) 70 A1
Henriville (57) 68 B3
Hénu (62) 10 C4
Henvic (29) 47 F4
Hérange (57) 67 K3
Herbault (41) 128 C2
Herbécourt (80) 19 F1
Herbelles (62) 3 G6
l'Herbergement (85) 141 K4
Herbeuval (08) 23 J5
Herbeuville (55) 44 A6
Herbeville (78) 58 A3
Herbéviller (54) 67 G6
Herbeys (38) 224 B4
les Herbiers (85) 142 D5
Herbignac (44) 121 K3
Herbinghen (62) 2 D5
Herbisse (10) 62 B6
Herbitzheim (67) 68 D4
Herblay (95) 58 D4
Herbsheim (67) 70 E6
Hercé (53) 80 E3
Herchies (60) 37 G1
la Hérelle (60) 18 C6
Hérenguerville (50) 30 D5
Hérépian (34) 291 J1
Hères (65) 285 G1
Hergnies (59) 7 J6
Hergugney (88) 94 B3
Héric (44) 123 F1
Héricourt (62) 10 A2
Héricourt (70) 139 G1
Héricourt-en-Caux (76) 15 G4
Héricourt-sur-Thérain (60) 17 F6
Héricy (77) 87 J3
la Hérie (02) 21 G2
le Hérie-la-Viéville (02) 20 D3
Hériménil (54) 66 D6
Hérimoncourt (25) 139 J3
Hérin (59) 12 C2
Hérissart (80) 10 B6
Hérisson (03) 167 J4
Herleville (80) 19 F2
la Herlière (62) 10 C4
Herlies (59) 6 C5
Herlin-le-Sec (62) 10 A2
Herlincourt (62) 10 A2
Herly (62) 4 E5
Herly (80) 19 H4
l'Herm (09) 307 K3
Herm (40) 262 E3
Hermanville (76) 15 J3
Hermanville-sur-Mer (14) 32 E3
les Hermaux (48) 236 E6
Hermaville (62) 10 D2
Hermé (77) 88 D2
Hermelange (57) 67 J4
Hermelinghen (62) 2 C4
l'Hermenault (85) 160 D3
Herment (63) 201 J2
Hermeray (78) 57 J6
Hermes (60) 37 J3
Hermeville (76) 14 C5
Herméville-en-Woëvre (55) . . . 43 K5
Hermies (62) 11 H5
Hermillon (73) 225 G1
Hermin (62) 10 C1
l'Hermitage (35) 78 E4
l'Hermitage-Lorge (22) 77 F2
les Hermites (37) 127 K1
l'Hermitière (61) 83 J4
Hermival-les-Vaux (14) 34 A5
Hermonville (51) 40 E3
Hernicourt (62) 10 A1

Herny (57) 66 D1
le Héron (76) 36 A1
Héronchelles (76) 16 C6
Hérouville (95) 37 H6
Hérouville-Saint-Clair (14) 32 E4
Hérouvillette (14) 33 F4
Herpelmont (88) 95 G5
Herpont (51) 63 G1
Herpy-l'Arlésienne (08) 21 J6
Herqueville (27) 35 K4
Herqueville (50) 28 A2
Herran (31) 306 C1
Herré (40) 266 B1
Herrère (64) 284 B6
Herrin (59) 6 D1
Herrlisheim (67) 25 C5
Herrlisheim-près-Colmar (68) . . 96 C5
Herry (18) 150 C1
Herserange (54) 26 A1
Hersin-Coupigny (62) 6 A6
Hertzing (57) 67 H4
Hervelinghen (62) 2 B3
Hervilly (80) 19 J1
Héry (58) 133 G6
Héry (89) 113 G4
Héry-sur-Alby (74) 208 C1
Herzeele (59) 3 J3
Hesbécourt (80) 19 J1
Hescamps (80) 17 G6
Hesdigneul-lès-Béthune (62) . . . 5 K6
Hesdigneul-lès-Boulogne (62) . . 2 B5
Hesdin (62) 9 J2
Hesdin-l'Abbé (62) 2 B6
Hésingue (68) 97 E4
Hesmond (62) 4 D6
Hesse (57) 67 J4
Hessenheim (67) 71 C6
Hestroff (57) 27 K5
Hestrud (59) 13 J4
Hestrus (62) 5 H6
Hétomesnil (60) 17 J5
Hettange-Grande (57) 27 G3
Hettenschlag (68) 96 D5
Heubécourt-Haricourt (27) 36 C6
Heuchin (62) 5 G6
Heucourt-Croquoison (80) 17 H1
Heudebouville (27) 35 K5
Heudicourt (27) 36 D3
Heudicourt (80) 11 H6
Heudicourt-sous-les-Côtes (55) . . 65 F2
Heudreville-en-Lieuvin (27) . . . 34 C5
Heudreville-sur-Eure (27) 35 J3
Heugas (40) 264 A5
Heugleville-sur-Scie (76) 15 K4
Heugnes (36) 147 G3
Heugon (61) 55 G3
Heugueville-sur-Sienne (50) . . . 30 D4
Heuilley-Cotton (52) 116 D5
Heuilley-le-Grand (52) 116 D5
Heuilley-sur-Saône (21) 136 E5
Heuland (14) 33 H4
Heume-l'Église (63) 201 K3
la Heunière (27) 57 F1
Heuqueville (27) 36 A4
Heuqueville (76) 14 B5
Heuringhem (62) 3 G6
Heurteauville (76) 35 F2
Heurtevent (14) 54 D2
Heussé (50) 80 D2
Heutrégiville (51) 41 H3
Heuzecourt (80) 9 K4
Hévilliers (55) 64 C6
Heyrieux (38) 206 D3
Hézecques (62) 5 F5
le Hézo (56) 101 G6
Hibarette (65) 285 H6
Hières-sur-Amby (38) 207 F1
Hierges (08) 24 C2
Hiermont (80) 9 J4
Hiers-Brouage (17) 176 E6
Hiersac (16) 196 C3
Hiesse (16) 180 A4
Hiesville (50) 29 F6
Hiéville (14) 54 C1
Higuères-Souye (64) 284 E3
Hiis (65) 285 H6
Hilbesheim (57) 67 J3
Hillion (22) 49 H6
Hilsenheim (67) 71 C5
Hilsprich (57) 68 C4
Hinacourt (02) 20 A4
Hinckange (57) 27 K6
Hindisheim (67) 70 E4
Hindlingen (68) 97 A5
Hinges (62) 5 K5
le Hinglé (22) 50 C6
Hinsbourg (67) 69 F5
Hinsingen (67) 67 H1
Hinx (40) 264 C4
Hipsheim (67) 71 D2
Hirel (35) 51 F4
Hirschland (67) 67 K2
Hirsingue (68) 97 B4
Hirson (02) 21 H1
Hirtzbach (68) 97 B4
Hirtzfelden (68) 96 D6
His (31) 306 B1
Hitte (65) 285 J6
Hochfelden (67) 70 D1
Hochstatt (68) 97 B3
Hochstett (67) 69 K6
Hocquigny (50) 51 K1

Hocquinghen (62) 2 D5
Hodenc-en-Bray (60) 37 F1
Hodenc-l'Évêque (60) 37 H3
Hodeng-au-Bosc (76) 17 F2
Hodeng-Hodenger (76) 36 C1
Hodent (95) 36 E5
Hœdic (56) 120 E4
Hœnheim (67) 25 A6
Hœrdt (67) 25 A5
Hœville (54) 66 D4
Hoffen (67) 25 C2
les Hogues (27) 36 A2
la Hoguette (14) 54 B3
Hohatzenheim (67) 70 E1
Hohengœft (67) 70 C2
Hohfrankenheim (67) 70 D1
Hohrod (68) 119 K1
le Hohwald (67) 70 B5
Holacourt (57) 66 D1
Holling (57) 27 K5
Holnon (02) 19 K2
Holque (59) 3 F4
Holtzheim (67) 70 E3
Holtzwihr (68) 96 C3
Holving (57) 68 C4
Hombleux (80) 19 H4
Homblières (02) 20 A2
Hombourg (68) 97 D2
Hombourg-Budange (57) 27 J5
Hombourg-Haut (57) 68 A2
l'Hôme-Chamondot (61) 83 K1
Homécourt (54) 27 F6
Hommarting (57) 67 K4
Hommert (57) 67 K4
Hommes (37) 126 E4
le Hommet-d'Arthenay (50) . . . 31 G2
Homps (11) 291 F5
Homps (32) 268 A4
Hon-Hergies (59) 13 F2
Hondainville (60) 37 J3
Hondeghem (59) 3 J5
Hondevilliers (77) 60 D3
Hondouville (27) 35 H5
Hondschoote (59) 3 K2
Honfleur (14) 33 K2
Honguemare-Guenouville (27) . . 35 F3
Honnechy (59) 12 C5
Honnecourt-sur-Escaut (59) . . . 11 J6
l'Honor-de-Cos (82) 249 J5
Honskirch (57) 67 H1
Hontanx (40) 265 K3
l'Hôpital (57) 68 A2
Hôpital-Camfrout (29) 74 C1
l'Hôpital-d'Orion (64) 283 H2
l'Hôpital-du-Grosbois (25) 156 D1
l'Hôpital-le-Grand (42) 204 E4
l'Hôpital-le-Mercier (71) 170 B6
l'Hôpital-Saint-Blaise (64) 283 J4
l'Hôpital-Saint-Lieffroy (25) . . . 138 E4
l'Hôpital-sous-Rochefort (42) . . 204 B2
les Hôpitaux-Neufs (25) 157 F6
les Hôpitaux-Vieux (25) 157 F6
Horbourg-Wihr (68) 96 C4
Hordain (59) 11 K3
la Horgne (08) 22 C5
Horgues (65) 285 H6
l'Horme (42) 205 H5
Hornaing (59) 11 K2
Hornoy-le-Bourg (80) 17 H2
le Horps (53) 81 H3
Horsarrieu (40) 265 F5
Horville-en-Ornois (55) 92 E1
l'Hosmes (27) 56 C4
l'Hospitalet (04) 258 D5
l'Hospitalet-du-Larzac (12) . . . 272 E2
l'Hospitalet-près-l'Andorre (09) . . 313 F5
Hosta (64) 283 F5
Hoste (57) 68 B3
Hostens (33) 229 G6
Hostias (01) 189 K6
Hostun (26) 223 F5
l'Hôtellerie (14) 34 B5
l'Hôtellerie-de-Flée (49) 104 D5
Hotonnes (01) 190 B4
Hotot-en-Auge (14) 33 H5
Hottot-les-Bagues (14) 32 B5
Hottviller (57) 69 G3
la Houblonnière (14) 33 J6
les Houches (74) 192 C5
Houchin (62) 5 K6
Houdain (62) 5 K6
Houdain-lez-Bavay (59) 13 F2
Houdan (78) 57 H4
Houdancourt (60) 38 C3
Houdelaincourt (55) 92 E1
Houdelmont (54) 93 K1
Houdemont (54) 66 A5
Houdetot (76) 15 H3
Houdilcourt (08) 41 F2
Houdreville (54) 93 K1
Houécourt (88) 93 J4
Houeillès (47) 247 F4
Houesville (50) 29 F6
Houetteville (27) 35 H6
Houéville (88) 93 H3
Houeydets (65) 286 A6
le Houga (32) 266 A4
Houilles (78) 58 D3
Houlbec-Cocherel (27) 36 A6
Houlbec-près-le-Gros-Theil (27) . . 35 F4
Houldizy (08) 22 C3
Houlette (16) 196 A2

372

Houlgate (14)	33	G3
Houlle (62)	3	F4
le Houlme (76)	35	H1
l'Houmeau (17)	176	D2
Hounoux (11)	308	C1
Houplin-Ancoisne (59)	6	D5
Houplines (59)	6	C3
Houppeville (76)	35	H1
Houquetot (76)	14	D5
Hourc (65)	285	J5
Hourges (51)	40	C4
Hours (64)	285	F5
Hourtin (33)	210	C3
Houry (02)	21	F3
Houssay (41)	108	B6
Houssay (53)	105	F3
la Houssaye (27)	56	A2
la Houssaye-Béranger (76)	15	K5
la Houssaye-en-Brie (77)	59	K5
le Housseau-Brétignolles (53)	81	H2
Houssen (68)	96	C3
Housseras (88)	95	F3
Housset (02)	20	D3
Housséville (54)	94	A3
la Houssière (88)	95	H5
la Houssoye (60)	37	F3
Houtaud (25)	156	C4
Houtkerque (59)	3	K3
Houtteville (50)	29	F6
Houville-en-Vexin (27)	36	A4
Houville-la-Branche (28)	85	H3
Houvin-Houvigneul (62)	10	B2
Houx (28)	85	H1
Hoymille (59)	3	J2
Huanne-Montmartin (25)	138	D3
Hubersent (62)	4	B5
Hubert-Folie (14)	32	E5
Huberville (50)	28	E4
Huby-Saint-Leu (62)	9	J1
Huchenneville (80)	9	F6
Huclier (62)	10	B1
Hucqueliers (62)	4	D5
Hudimesnil (50)	30	D4
Hudiviller (54)	66	C6
Huelgoat (29)	75	G1
Huest (27)	56	D1
Huêtre (45)	109	K2
Huez (38)	224	E4
Hugier (70)	137	G5
Hugleville-en-Caux (76)	15	J5
Huillé (49)	125	J1
Huilliécourt (52)	92	E6
Huilly-sur-Seille (71)	172	B3
Huiron (51)	63	F5
Huismes (37)	126	E6
Huisnes-sur-Mer (50)	51	J4
Huisseau-en-Beauce (41)	108	B6
Huisseau-sur-Cosson (41)	129	F2
Huisseau-sur-Mauves (45)	109	J4
l'Huisserie (53)	104	E2
Hulluch (62)	6	B6
Hultehouse (57)	70	A2
Humbauville (51)	62	E6
Humbécourt (52)	91	J1
Humbercamps (62)	10	D4
Humbercourt (80)	10	C4
Humbert (62)	4	D6
Humberville (52)	92	D4
Humbligny (18)	131	H6
Humeroeuille (62)	9	K1
Humes-Jorquenay (52)	116	C3
Humières (62)	9	K1
Hunawihr (68)	71	A6
Hundling (57)	68	C3
Hundsbach (68)	97	C4
Huningue (68)	97	E4
Hunspach (67)	25	C2
Hunting (57)	27	J3
Huos (31)	305	H1
Huparlac (12)	236	B4
Huppy (80)	9	F6
Hurbache (88)	95	H3
Hure (33)	230	C6
Hurecourt (70)	118	A3
Hures-la-Parade (48)	253	K4
Huriel (03)	167	G6
Hurigny (71)	171	J6
Hurtières (38)	224	D2
Hurtigheim (67)	70	D3
Husseren-les-Châteaux (68)	96	B4
Husseren-Wesserling (68)	119	J3
Hussigny-Godbrange (54)	26	E3
Husson (50)	80	E1
Huttendorf (67)	69	K6
Huttenheim (67)	70	E6
Hyds (03)	184	C1
Hyémondans (25)	139	F4
Hyencourt-le-Grand (80)	19	F3
Hyenville (50)	30	D5
Hyères (83)	298	A6
Hyet (70)	138	A3
Hyèvre-Magny (25)	138	D4
Hyèvre-Paroisse (25)	138	D4
Hymont (88)	94	A4

I

Ibarrolle (64)	283	F5
Ibigny (57)	67	H5
Ibos (65)	285	G5
Ichtratzheim (67)	71	D2
Ichy (77)	87	G6
Idaux-Mendy (64)	283	H5
Idrac-Respaillès (32)	286	B1
Idron-Ousse-Sendets (64)	284	D4
Ids-Saint-Roch (18)	166	D2
Iffendic (35)	78	C4
les Iffs (35)	78	E2
Ifs (14)	32	E5
les Ifs (76)	16	C2
Igé (61)	83	H4
Igé (71)	171	J5
Ignaucourt (80)	18	D3
Ignaux (09)	308	A6
Igney (54)	67	G5
Igney (88)	94	C4
Ignol (18)	150	D3
Igny (70)	137	H3
Igny (91)	58	D5
Igny-Comblizy (51)	61	H1
Igon (64)	284	E6
Igornay (71)	153	F3
Igoville (27)	35	J3
Iguerande (71)	187	F2
Iholdy (64)	282	E4
Île-aux-Moines (56)	100	E6
Île-Bouchard (37)	145	H2
Île-d'Aix (17)	176	D4
Île-d'Arz (56)	101	F6
Île-de-Batz (29)	46	E2
Île-de-Bréhat (22)	48	E1
Île-de-Sein (29)	73	A6
Île-d'Elle (85)	160	C6
Île-d'Houat (56)	120	D3
Île-d'Olonne (85)	158	E3
Île-d'Yeu (85)	140	B6
Île-Molène (29)	72	A6
l'Île-Rousse (2B)	318	C2
l'Île-Saint-Denis (93)	58	E2
Île-Tudy (29)	98	C3
Ilharre (64)	283	G3
Ilhat (09)	308	A3
les Ilhes (11)	290	B4
Ilhet (65)	305	F3
Ilheu (65)	305	H2
Illange (57)	27	G4
Illartein (09)	306	B3
Illats (33)	229	K5
Ille-sur-Têt (66)	314	E2
Illeville-sur-Montfort (27)	34	E3
Illfurth (68)	97	B3
Illhaeusern (68)	71	B6
Illiat (01)	188	D2
Illier-et-Laramade (09)	307	H5
Illiers-Combray (28)	84	E5
Illiers-l'Évêque (27)	56	E4
Illies (59)	6	B5
Illifaut (22)	77	K5
Illkirch-Graffenstaden (67)	71	D2
Illois (76)	16	E4
Illoud (52)	93	F5
Illy (08)	23	F3
Illzach (68)	97	C2
Ilonse (06)	261	H5
Imbleville (76)	15	J4
Imécourt (08)	42	D2
Imling (57)	67	J4
Imphy (58)	151	F5
Inaumont (08)	21	K6
Incarville (27)	35	J4
Incheville (76)	8	D6
Inchy (59)	12	C5
Inchy-en-Artois (62)	11	H4
Incourt (62)	9	K1
Indevillers (25)	139	J4
Indre (44)	123	F4
Ineuil (18)	166	E1
les Infournas (05)	242	E3
Ingenheim (67)	70	D1
Ingersheim (68)	96	B4
Inghem (62)	3	G6
Inglange (57)	27	H4
Ingolsheim (67)	25	C2
Ingouville (76)	15	G2
Ingrandes (36)	164	B3
Ingrandes (49)	124	D4
Ingrandes (86)	145	J5
Ingrandes-de-Touraine (37)	126	E6
Ingrannes (45)	110	D3
Ingré (45)	109	K4
Inguiniel (56)	100	B1
Ingwiller (67)	69	H5
Injoux-Génissiat (01)	190	C4
Innenheim (67)	70	D4
Innimond (01)	207	H1
Inor (55)	23	H6
Insming (57)	67	G1
Insviller (57)	67	H2
Intraville (76)	16	B1
Intres (07)	221	G6
Intréville (28)	86	A5
Intville-la-Guétard (45)	86	D5
Inval-Boiron (80)	17	F2
Inxent (62)	4	C5
Inzinzac-Lochrist (56)	100	B2
Ippécourt (55)	64	B1
Ippling (57)	68	D3
Irai (61)	55	J6
Irais (79)	144	C3
Irancy (89)	113	H6
Iré-le-Sec (55)	43	H1
Irigny (69)	206	A3
Irissarry (64)	282	E4
Irles (80)	10	E5
Irodouër (35)	78	D2
Iron (02)	20	D1
Irouléguy (64)	282	D5
Irreville (27)	35	J6
Irvillac (29)	74	C1
Is-en-Bassigny (52)	116	E2
Is-sur-Tille (21)	136	B3
Isbergues (62)	5	J4
Isches (88)	117	H2
Isdes (45)	130	D1
Isenay (58)	151	K5
Isigny-le-Buat (50)	52	B6
Isigny-sur-Mer (14)	29	H6
Island (89)	133	J3
Isle (87)	198	E2
l'Isle-Adam (95)	37	J6
l'Isle-Arné (32)	267	K6
Isle-Aubigny (10)	90	C2
Isle-Aumont (10)	90	B6
l'Isle-Bouzon (32)	267	K2
l'Isle-d'Abeau (38)	206	E3
l'Isle-de-Noé (32)	267	G6
l'Isle-d'Espagnac (16)	196	E3
l'Isle-en-Dodon (31)	287	F3
Isle-et-Bardais (03)	167	K2
l'Isle-Jourdain (32)	268	D6
l'Isle-Jourdain (86)	180	B2
Isle-Saint-Georges (33)	229	J3
l'Isle-sur-la-Sorgue (84)	276	D2
l'Isle-sur-le-Doubs (25)	139	F3
Isle-sur-Marne (51)	63	G6
l'Isle-sur-Serein (89)	134	A2
les Isles-Bardel (14)	53	K3
Isles-les-Meldeuses (77)	60	A2
Isles-lès-Villenoy (77)	59	J3
Isles-sur-Suippe (51)	41	G3
les Islettes (55)	42	E6
Isneauville (76)	35	J1
Isola (06)	261	H3
Isolaccio-di-Fiumorbo (2B)	321	H4
Isômes (52)	136	C1
Ispagnac (48)	254	B2
Ispoure (64)	282	D5
Isques (62)	2	B6
Issac (24)	213	H6
Issamoulenc (07)	239	J3
Issancourt-et-Rumel (08)	22	E3
Issanlas (07)	238	D3
Issans (25)	139	G2
les Issards (09)	307	K1
Issarlès (07)	238	D2
Issé (44)	103	H5
Isse (51)	41	G6
Issel (11)	289	H4
Issendolus (46)	234	B3
Issenhausen (67)	69	J6
Issenheim (68)	96	B6
Issepts (46)	234	C4
Isserpent (03)	186	A3
Isserteaux (63)	203	G3
Issigeac (24)	231	J3
Issirac (30)	256	B3
Issoire (63)	202	E5
Issor (64)	283	K6
Issou (78)	57	K2
Issoudun (36)	148	C4
Issoudun-Létrieix (23)	183	F4
Issus (31)	288	C3
Issy-les-Moulineaux (92)	58	D4
Issy-l'Évêque (71)	170	A2
Istres (13)	295	J4
les Istres-et-Bury (51)	62	A2
Isturits (64)	282	E3
Itancourt (02)	20	A3
Iteuil (86)	162	E4
Ittenheim (67)	70	D3
Itterswiller (67)	70	C6
Itteville (91)	86	E2
Itxassou (64)	263	D2
Itzac (81)	270	B1
Ivergny (62)	10	B3
Iverny (77)	59	J2
Iviers (02)	21	H3
Iville (27)	35	G5
Ivory (39)	156	A4
Ivoy-le-Pré (18)	131	F5
Ivry-en-Montagne (21)	153	J3
Ivry-la-Bataille (27)	57	G3
Ivry-le-Temple (60)	37	G4
Ivry-sur-Seine (94)	58	E4
Iwuy (59)	11	K3
Izaourt (65)	305	H2
Izaut-de-l'Hôtel (31)	305	K2
Izaux (65)	305	F1
Izé (53)	81	K5
Izeaux (38)	223	H1
Izel-lès-Équerchin (62)	11	G2
Izel-lès-Hameaux (62)	10	C2
Izenave (01)	189	K4
Izernore (01)	189	K2
Izeste (64)	303	D1
Izeure (21)	154	D1
Izier (21)	136	C6
Izieu (01)	207	J3
Izon (33)	229	K1
Izon-la-Bruisse (26)	258	C3
Izotges (32)	266	B5

J

Jablines (77)	59	J3
Jabreilles-les-Bordes (87)	181	K5
Jabrun (15)	236	D3
Jacob-Bellecombette (73)	208	B4
Jacou (34)	274	C5
Jacque (65)	285	J4
Jagny-sous-Bois (95)	38	A6
Jaignes (77)	60	B2
Jaillans (26)	223	F5
la Jaille-Yvon (49)	105	F6
Jaillon (54)	65	J4
Jailly (58)	151	H3
Jailly-les-Moulins (21)	135	G3
Jainvillotte (88)	93	G5
Jalesches (23)	183	F1
Jaleyrac (15)	217	G3
Jaligny-sur-Besbre (03)	169	H6
Jallais (49)	143	F1
Jallanges (21)	154	D3
Jallans (28)	109	F2
Jallaucourt (57)	66	C3
Jallerange (25)	137	H6
Jalognes (18)	150	A1
Jalogny (71)	171	H5
Jâlons (51)	62	B1
Jambles (71)	153	J6
Jambville (78)	57	K1
Jaméricourt (60)	37	F3
Jametz (55)	43	H1
Janailhac (87)	198	E4
Janaillat (23)	182	C4
Jancigny (21)	136	E4
Jandun (08)	22	B4
Janneyrias (38)	206	D2
Janville (14)	33	G5
Janville (28)	86	A6
Janville (60)	38	E2
Janville-sur-Juine (91)	86	D2
Janvilliers (51)	61	G3
Janvry (51)	40	D4
Janvry (91)	58	C6
Janzé (35)	79	H6
Jarcieu (38)	222	C1
la Jard (17)	195	J4
Jard-sur-Mer (85)	159	G5
le Jardin (19)	216	D2
Jardin (38)	206	B5
Jardres (86)	163	H3
Jargeau (45)	110	C4
Jarjayes (05)	242	E6
Jarménil (88)	94	E6
Jarnac (16)	196	A3
Jarnac-Champagne (17)	195	J4
Jarnages (23)	183	F3
la Jarne (17)	176	E3
Jarnioux (69)	188	A5
Jarnosse (42)	187	G3
Jarny (54)	44	C5
Jarret (65)	304	B1
la Jarrie (17)	176	E3
Jarrie (38)	224	B4
la Jarrie-Audouin (17)	177	K4
Jarrier (73)	225	G2
Jars (18)	131	H5
Jarsy (73)	208	E3
Jarville-la-Malgrange (54)	66	A5
Jarzé (49)	125	K2
Jas (42)	205	F2
Jasney (70)	118	B4
Jassans-Riottier (01)	188	B5
Jasseines (10)	90	D2
Jasseron (01)	189	H2
Jasses (64)	283	J4
Jatxou (64)	263	D2
Jau-Dignac-et-Loirac (33)	194	C6
Jaucourt (10)	91	G5
la Jaudonnière (85)	160	C2
Jaudrais (28)	84	D1
Jaujac (07)	239	G5
Jauldes (16)	197	F2
Jaulges (89)	113	J3
Jaulgonne (02)	40	A6
Jaulnay (37)	145	H4
Jaulnes (77)	88	D3
Jaulny (54)	65	H1
Jaulzy (60)	39	G2
Jaunac (07)	239	H1
Jaunay-Clan (86)	163	F2
Jaure (24)	213	J5
Jausiers (04)	260	D1
Jaux (60)	38	D2
Jauzé (72)	83	F6
Javaugues (43)	219	H2
Javené (35)	80	A4
Javerdat (87)	180	E5
Javerlhac-et-la-Chapelle-Saint-Robert (24)	197	J4
Javernant (10)	90	A6
la Javie (04)	260	A4
Javols (48)	237	G4
Javrezac (16)	195	J2
Javron-les-Chapelles (53)	81	K3
Jax (43)	219	K4
Jaxu (64)	282	E5
Jayac (24)	215	G5
Jayat (01)	172	C6
Jazeneuil (86)	162	C4
Jazennes (17)	195	G4
Joancourt (02)	19	J1
Jeandelaincourt (54)	66	B3
Jeandelize (54)	44	B5
Jeanménil (88)	95	F3
Jeansagnière (42)	204	A2
Jeantes (02)	21	H3
Jebsheim (68)	96	D3
Jegun (32)	267	G4
la Jemaye (24)	213	F4
Jenlain (59)	12	E2
Jenzat (03)	185	G3
Jésonville (88)	94	A6
Jessains (10)	91	F4
Jetterswiller (67)	70	C2
Jettingen (68)	97	C4
Jeu-les-Bois (36)	165	K2
Jeu-Maloches (36)	147	H3
Jeufosse (78)	57	G1
Jeugny (10)	114	A1
Jeumont (59)	13	J2
Jeurre (39)	173	H5
Jeux-lès-Bard (21)	134	C3
Jeuxey (88)	94	D5
Jevoncourt (54)	94	A2
Jezainville (54)	65	K2
Jézeau (65)	305	F3
Joannas (07)	239	G5
Job (63)	203	K4
Jobourg (50)	28	A1
Joch (66)	314	D3
Joeuf (54)	27	F6
Joganville (50)	29	F4
Joigny (89)	112	E3
Joigny-sur-Meuse (08)	22	D2
Joinville (52)	92	B2
Joinville-le-Pont (94)	59	F4
Joiselle (51)	61	F4
Jolimetz (59)	12	E3
Jolivet (54)	66	D6
Jonage (69)	206	C1
Joncels (34)	272	E5
la Jonchère (85)	159	J4
la Jonchère-Saint-Maurice (87)	181	K5
Jonchères (26)	241	H5
Joncherey (90)	139	K2
Jonchery (52)	92	A6
Jonchery-sur-Suippe (51)	41	K5
Jonchery-sur-Vesle (51)	40	D4
Joncourt (02)	20	A1
Joncreuil (10)	91	F2
Joncy (71)	171	G3
Jongieux (73)	208	A2
Jonquerets-de-Livet (27)	55	J3
Jonquerettes (84)	276	C2
Jonquery (51)	40	D5
Jonquières (11)	310	A2
Jonquières (34)	273	H5
Jonquières (60)	38	D2
Jonquières (81)	270	D6
Jonquières (84)	257	F5
Jonquières-Saint-Vincent (30)	275	J3
Jons (69)	206	D1
Jonval (08)	22	C6
Jonville-en-Woëvre (55)	44	B6
Jonzac (17)	195	J6
Jonzier-Épagny (74)	190	E3
Jonzieux (42)	221	G2
Joppécourt (54)	26	D4
Jort (14)	54	B2
Jorxey (88)	94	B4
Josat (43)	219	K3
Joserand (63)	185	F5
Josnes (41)	109	G5
Josse (40)	262	D5
Josselin (56)	101	H1
Jossigny (77)	59	J4
Jou-sous-Monjou (15)	235	K1
Jouac (87)	164	E6
Jouaignes (02)	40	A3
Jouancy (89)	134	A1
Jouarre (77)	60	B2
Jouars-Pontchartrain (78)	58	A4
Jouaville (54)	44	D5
Joucas (84)	277	F2
Joucou (11)	308	D5
Joudes (71)	172	E4
Joudreville (54)	26	D5
Joué-du-Bois (61)	82	A1
Joué-du-Plain (61)	54	B5
Joué-en-Charnie (72)	106	A2
Joué-l'Abbé (72)	106	E1
Joué-lès-Tours (37)	127	J5
Joué-sur-Erdre (44)	103	J6
Jouet-sur-l'Aubois (18)	150	C3
Jouey (21)	153	G2
Jougne (25)	157	F6
Jouhe (39)	155	G1
Jouhet (86)	164	A4
Jouillat (23)	182	D2
Jouques (13)	278	A5
Jouqueviel (81)	251	G5
Jourgnac (87)	198	E3
Journans (01)	189	H3
Journet (86)	164	B5
Journiac (24)	214	C6
Journy (62)	2	E5
Jours-en-Vaux (21)	153	H3
Jours-lès-Baigneux (21)	135	G1
Joursac (15)	218	D4
Joussé (86)	179	K2
Jouvençon (71)	172	B3

Joux (69) 187 H6
Joux-la-Ville (89) 133 J2
Jouy (28) 85 G2
Jouy (89) 88 A6
Jouy-aux-Arches (57) 44 E6
Jouy-en-Argonne (55) 43 G5
Jouy-en-Josas (78) 58 C4
Jouy-en-Pithiverais (45) 110 C1
Jouy-le-Châtel (77) 60 B6
Jouy-le-Moutier (95) 58 B1
Jouy-le-Potier (45) 109 K6
Jouy-lès-Reims (51) 40 E4
Jouy-Mauvoisin (78) 57 H2
Jouy-sous-Thelle (60) 37 F3
Jouy-sur-Eure (27) 56 E1
Jouy-sur-Morin (77) 60 D4
Joyeuse (07) 255 J1
Joyeux (01) 189 F5
Joze (63) 203 F1
Jû-Belloc (32) 266 C6
Juaye-Mondaye (14) 32 B4
Jubainville (88) 93 G2
la Jubaudière (49) 142 E1
Jublains (53) 81 H5
le Juch (29) 74 B5
Jugazan (33) 230 B3
Jugeals-Nazareth (19) 215 J5
Jugon-les-Lacs (22) 50 A6
Jugy (71) 171 K3
Juicq (17) 177 K6
Juif (71) 172 C2
Juignac (16) 212 E1
Juigné-des-Moutiers (44) . . . 104 A6
Juigné-sur-Loire (49) 125 H4
Juigné-sur-Sarthe (72) 105 K4
Juignettes (27) 55 J3
Juillac (19) 215 G2
Juillac (32) 285 J1
Juillac (33) 230 D2
Juillac-le-Coq (16) 195 K4
Juillaguet (16) 196 E5
Juillan (65) 285 G5
Juillé (16) 179 G5
Juillé (72) 82 D5
Juillé (79) 178 C3
Juillenay (21) 134 D5
Juilles (32) 268 A6
Juilley (50) 51 K4
Juilly (21) 134 E3
Juilly (77) 60 H1
Jujols (66) 314 A3
Jujurieux (01) 189 J4
Julianges (48) 237 G1
Juliénas (69) 188 B2
Julienne (16) 196 A3
Jullianges (43) 220 B2
Jullié (69) 188 B2
Jullouville (50) 51 H2
Jully (89) 114 D5
Jully-lès-Buxy (71) 171 H2
Jully-sur-Sarce (10) 114 D1
Julos (65) 285 G6
Julvécourt (55) 43 G6
Jumeauville (78) 57 K3
Jumeaux (63) 203 F6
Jumel (80) 18 B4
Jumelles (27) 56 D3
la Jumellière (49) 124 E5
Jumencourt (02) 39 J1
Jumièges (76) 35 F2
Jumigny (02) 40 C2
Jumilhac-le-Grand (24) 198 D5
Junas (30) 274 E4
Junay (89) 113 K4
Juncalas (65) 304 B1
Jungholtz (68) 96 A6
Junhac (15) 235 H4
les Junies (46) 233 F6
Juniville (08) 41 J2
Jupilles (72) 107 F5
Jurançon (64) 284 C4
Juranville (45) 111 F2
Juré (42) 186 D6
Jurignac (16) 196 C5
Jurques (14) 53 F1
Jurvielle (31) 305 G5
Jury (57) 45 F6
Juscorps (79) 178 B2
Jusix (47) 230 D2
Jussac (15) 217 H6
Jussarupt (88) 95 G5
Jussas (17) 211 K2
Jussecourt-Minecourt (51) . . . 63 H4
Jussey (70) 117 J4
Jussy (02) 19 K4
Jussy (57) 44 E5
Jussy (89) 113 G6
Jussy-Champagne (18) 149 J4
Jussy-le-Chaudrier (18) 150 B2
Justian (32) 267 F3
Justine-Herbigny (08) 21 K5
Jutigny (77) 88 C2
Juvaincourt (88) 93 K4
Juvancourt (10) 115 H1
Juvanzé (10) 91 F4
Juvardeil (49) 125 H1
Juvelize (57) 66 E4
Juvignac (34) 274 B6
Juvigné (53) 80 C5
Juvignies (60) 37 H1
Juvigny (02) 39 J2

Juvigny (51) 62 C1
Juvigny (74) 191 G1
Juvigny-en-Perthois (55) 64 B6
Juvigny-le-Tertre (50) 52 C5
Juvigny-sous-Andaine (61) . . . 81 H1
Juvigny-sur-Loison (55) 43 H1
Juvigny-sur-Orne (61) 54 C5
Juvigny-sur-Seulles (14) 32 C5
Juville (57) 66 C2
Juvinas (07) 239 G4
Juvincourt-et-Damary (02) . . . 40 D2
Juvisy-sur-Orge (91) 58 E5
Juvrecourt (54) 66 E4
Juxue (64) 283 F5
Juzanvigny (10) 91 F3
Juzennecourt (52) 91 K6
Juzes (31) 289 F2
Juzet-de-Luchon (31) 305 H5
Juzet-d'Izaut (31) 305 K3
Juziers (78) 57 K2

K

Kalhausen (57) 68 E4
Kaltenhouse (67) 25 B4
Kanfen (57) 27 G3
Kappelen (68) 97 D4
Kappelkinger (57) 67 H1
Katzenthal (68) 96 B3
Kauffenheim (67) 25 C3
Kaysersberg (68) 96 B3
Kédange-sur-Canner (57) . . . 27 J5
Keffenach (67) 25 B2
Kembs (68) 97 D3
Kemplich (57) 27 J4
Kerbach (57) 68 C2
Korbors (22) 48 C2
Kerfot (22) 48 C5
Kerfourn (56) 77 F6
Kergloff (29) 75 H3
Kergrist (56) 76 E5
Kergrist-Moëlou (22) 76 B2
Kerien (22) 76 C1
Kerlaz (29) 74 B4
Kerling-lès-Sierck (57) 27 J4
Kerlouan (29) 46 B3
Kermaria-Sulard (22) 48 B2
Kermoroc'h (22) 48 C4
Kernascléden (56) 76 A6
Kernilis (29) 46 A4
Kernouës (29) 46 B4
Kerpert (22) 76 C2
Kerprich-aux-Bois (57) 67 H4
Kersaint-Plabennec (29) 46 B5
Kertzfeld (67) 70 D6
Kervignac (56) 100 B3
Keskastel (67) 67 J1
Kesseldorf (67) 25 D3
Kienheim (67) 70 D2
Kientzheim (68) 96 B3
Kiffis (68) 97 C6
Killem (59) 3 K2
Kilstett (67) 25 B5
Kindwiller (67) 69 J5
Kingersheim (68) 97 C2
Kintzheim (67) 71 A5
Kirchberg (68) 119 J4
Kirchheim (67) 70 D3
Kirrberg (67) 67 J3
Kirrwiller-Bosselshausen (67) . . . 69 J6
Kirsch-lès-Sierck (57) 27 J3
Kirschnaumen (57) 27 K3
Kirviller (57) 67 H1
Klang (57) 27 J4
Kleingoeft (67) 70 C2
Knoeringue (68) 97 D4
Knoersheim (67) 70 C2
Knutange (57) 27 F4
Koenigsmacker (57) 27 H4
Koestlach (68) 97 B5
Koetzingue (68) 97 C3
Koeur-la-Grande (55) 64 D3
Koeur-la-Petite (55) 64 E3
Kogenheim (67) 70 D6
Kolbsheim (67) 70 D3
Krautergersheim (67) 70 D4
Krautwiller (67) 70 E1
le Kremlin-Bicêtre (94) 58 E4
Kriegsheim (67) 25 A4
Kruth (68) 119 J2
Kunheim (68) 96 D4
Kuntzig (57) 27 H4
Kurtzenhouse (67) 25 B5
Kuttolsheim (67) 70 D2
Kutzenhausen (67) 25 B2

L

Laà-Mondrans (64) 283 J2
Laas (32) 286 A2
Laas (45) 110 D1
Laàs (64) 283 H3
Labalme (01) 189 J3
Labarde (33) 211 G5
Labaroche (68) 96 A3
Labarrère (32) 266 D2
Labarthe (32) 286 C2
Labarthe (82) 249 J4
Labarthe-Bleys (81) 250 E6

Labarthe-Inard (31) 306 A1
Labarthe-Rivière (31) 305 J1
Labarthe-sur-Lèze (31) 288 B2
Labarthète (32) 266 A6
Labassère (65) 304 C1
Labastide (65) 305 F2
Labastide-Beauvoir (31) 288 E2
Labastide-Castel-Amouroux (47) . . . 247 G3
Labastide-Cézéracq (64) 284 B3
Labastide-Chalosse (40) 265 F6
Labastide-Clermont (31) 287 J4
Labastide-d'Anjou (11) 289 F4
Labastide-d'Armagnac (40) . . . 266 A1
Labastide-de-Lévis (81) 270 C2
Labastide-de-Penne (82) 250 B3
Labastide-de-Virac (07) 256 A2
Labastide-Dénat (81) 270 E3
Labastide-du-Haut-Mont (46) . . . 234 E2
Labastide-du-Temple (82) . . . 249 H6
Labastide-du-Vert (46) 233 F6
Labastide-en-Val (11) 309 H1
Labastide-Esparbairenque (11) . . . 290 B3
Labastide-Gabausse (81) 270 D1
Labastide-Marnhac (46) 249 K2
Labastide-Monréjeau (64) . . . 284 B3
Labastide-Murat (46) 233 J5
Labastide-Paumès (31) 287 G4
Labastide-Rouairoux (81) . . . 290 E2
Labastide-Saint-Georges (81) . . . 270 B5
Labastide-Saint-Pierre (82) . . . 269 G2
Labastide-Saint-Sernin (31) . . . 269 H5
Labastide-Savès (32) 287 G2
Labastide-sur-Bésorgues (07) . . . 239 G3
Labastide-Villefranche (64) . . . 283 G2
Labastidette (31) 287 K2
Labathude (46) 234 D4
Labatie-d'Andaure (07) 221 J5
Labatmale (64) 285 F5
Labatut (09) 288 C5
Labatut (40) 264 B6
Labatut (64) 285 G3
Labatut-Rivière (65) 285 H1
Labbeville (95) 37 H6
Labeaume (07) 255 J1
Labécède-Lauragais (11) 289 H3
Labège (31) 288 C1
Labégude (07) 239 H4
Labéjan (32) 286 C1
Labenne (40) 262 B6
Labergement-du-Navois (25) . . . 156 C3
Labergement-Foigney (21) . . . 136 C6
Labergement-lès-Auxonne (21) . . . 155 F1
Labergement-lès-Seurre (21) . . . 154 C3
Labergement-Sainte-Marie (25) . . . 156 E6
Laberlière (60) 19 F6
Labescau (33) 246 E1
Labesserette (15) 235 H3
Labessette (63) 201 H4
Labessière-Candeil (81) 270 C4
Labets-Biscay (64) 283 F3
Labeuville (55) 44 B5
Labeuvrière (62) 5 K5
Labeyrie (64) 284 A1
Lablachère (07) 255 J1
Laboissière-en-Santerre (80) . . . 18 E5
Laboissière-en-Thelle (60) . . . 37 H4
Laborde (65) 304 E2
Laborel (26) 258 D3
Labosse (60) 37 F3
Labouheyre (40) 245 F4
Laboulbène (81) 270 E5
Laboule (07) 239 F5
Labouquerie (24) 232 B3
Labourgade (82) 268 D2
Labourse (62) 6 A6
Laboutarie (81) 270 D4
Labretonie (47) 247 J1
Labrihe (32) 268 B4
Labrit (40) 245 K5
Labroquère (31) 305 H2
Labrosse (45) 86 E5
Labrousse (15) 235 J2
Labroye (62) 9 H3
Labruguière (81) 290 B1
Labruyère (21) 154 D3
Labruyère (60) 38 B3
Labruyère-Dorsa (31) 288 C3
Labry (54) 44 C4
Laburgade (46) 250 B2
Lac-des-Rouges-Truites (39) . . . 174 A2
le Lac-d'Issarlès (07) 238 E2
Lacabarède (81) 290 D2
Lacadée (64) 284 A1
Lacajunte (40) 265 H6
Lacalm (12) 236 C3
Lacanau (33) 210 D2
Lacapelle-Barrès (15) 236 A1
Lacapelle-Biron (47) 232 C5
Lacapelle-Cabanac (46) 249 G1
Lacapelle-del-Fraisse (15) . . . 235 H3
Lacapelle-Livron (82) 250 D4
Lacapelle-Marival (46) 234 C4
Lacapelle-Pinet (81) 251 J6
Lacapelle-Ségalar (81) 251 F6
Lacapelle-Viescamp (15) 235 F1
Lacarre (64) 282 E5
Lacarry-Arhan-Charritte-
de-Haut (64) 302 C1
Lacassagne (65) 285 J3
Lacaugne (31) 287 K4

Lacaune (81) 271 K5
Lacaussade (47) 232 B6
Lacave (09) 306 C2
Lacave (46) 233 J2
Lacaze (81) 271 H5
Lacelle (19) 200 A4
Lacenas (69) 188 A5
Lacépède (47) 247 K3
Lachaise (16) 196 A5
Lachalade (55) 42 D5
Lachambre (57) 68 A3
Lachamp (48) 237 H5
Lachamp-Raphaël (07) 239 G2
Lachapelle (47) 231 F5
Lachapelle (54) 95 G2
Lachapelle (80) 17 H3
Lachapelle (82) 268 A1
Lachapelle-aux-Pots (60) 37 F2
Lachapelle-Auzac (46) 233 H1
Lachapelle-en-Blaisy (52) . . . 91 K6
Lachapelle-Graillouse (07) . . . 238 D2
Lachapelle-Saint-Pierre (60) . . . 37 J4
Lachapelle-sous-Aubenas (07) . . . 239 H5
Lachapelle-sous-Chanéac (07) . . . 239 G1
Lachapelle-sous-Chaux (90) . . . 119 H5
Lachapelle-sous-Gerberoy (60) . . . 17 G6
Lachapelle-sous-Rougemont (90) . . . 119 K5
Lachassagne (69) 188 B5
Lachau (26) 258 C4
Lachaussée (55) 44 C6
Lachaussée-du-Bois-d'Écu (60) . . . 17 K6
Lachaux (63) 186 A5
Lachelle (60) 38 D2
Lachy (51) 61 H4
Lacollonge (90) 119 J6
Lacombe (11) 289 K3
Lacommande (64) 284 B4
Lacoste (34) 273 H6
Lacoste (84) 277 G3
Lacougotte-Cadoul (81) 270 A6
Lacour (82) 248 E3
Lacour-d'Arcenay (21) 134 C5
Lacourt (09) 306 D3
Lacourt-Saint-Pierre (82) . . . 269 F1
Lacq (64) 284 A2
Lacquy (40) 265 K2
Lacrabe (40) 265 F6
Lacres (62) 4 C2
Lacroisille (81) 289 G1
Lacroix-Barrez (12) 235 K3
Lacroix-Saint-Ouen (60) 38 D3
Lacroix-sur-Meuse (55) 64 E1
Lacropte (24) 214 B5
Lacrost (71) 172 A3
Lacrouzette (81) 271 G6
Lacs (36) 166 B3
Ladapeyre (23) 183 F2
Ladaux (33) 230 A4
Ladern-sur-Lauquet (11) 309 G1
Ladevèze-Rivière (32) 285 H1
Ladevèze-Ville (32) 285 H1
Ladignac-le-Long (87) 198 D4
Ladignac-sur-Rondelles (19) . . . 216 B3
Ladinhac (15) 235 J3
Ladirat (46) 234 C3
Ladiville (16) 196 B5
Ladoix-Serrigny (21) 154 A3
Ladon (45) 111 G3
Lados (33) 246 D1
Ladoye-sur-Seille (39) 155 J6
Laduz (89) 112 E4
Lafage (11) 289 G6
Lafage-sur-Sombre (19) 216 E2
Lafare (84) 257 G5
Lafarre (07) 221 J5
Lafarre (43) 238 D2
Lafat (23) 182 A1
Lafauche (52) 92 E4
Laféline (03) 168 C6
Laferté-sur-Amance (52) 117 G4
Laferté-sur-Aube (52) 115 H1
Lafeuillade-en-Vézie (15) . . . 235 H3
Laffaux (02) 39 K2
Laffite-Toupière (31) 287 G6
Laffrey (38) 224 B5
Lafitole (65) 285 H2
Lafitte (82) 268 D2
Lafitte-sur-Lot (47) 247 K2
Lafitte-Vigordane (31) 287 J4
Lafox (47) 248 C5
Lafrançaise (82) 249 H5
Lafraye (60) 37 J1
Lafresguimont-Saint-Martin (80) . . . 17 G3
Lafrimbolle (57) 67 J6
Lagamas (34) 273 J5
Lagarde (09) 308 D2
Lagarde (31) 288 E4
Lagarde (32) 267 H2
Lagarde (57) 67 F4
Lagarde (65) 285 H4
Lagarde-d'Apt (84) 277 J1
Lagarde-Enval (19) 216 B4
Lagarde-Hachan (32) 286 C3
Lagarde-Paréol (84) 256 E4
Lagarde-sur-le-Né (16) 196 A5
Lagardelle (46) 249 H1
Lagardelle-sur-Lèze (31) 288 B3
Lagardère (32) 267 F3
Lagardiolle (81) 289 J2
Lagarrigue (47) 247 J3
Lagarrigue (81) 290 A1

Lageon (79) 161 K1
Lagery (51) 40 C3
Lagesse (10) 114 B2
Lagleygeolle (19) 216 A5
Laglorieuse (40) 265 H3
Lagnes (84) 276 E2
Lagney (54) 65 H4
Lagnicourt-Marcel (62) 11 G4
Lagnieu (01) 189 H6
Lagny (60) 19 G5
Lagny-le-Sec (60) 38 D6
Lagny-sur-Marne (77) 59 H3
Lagor (64) 284 A3
Lagorce (07) 256 A1
Lagorce (33) 212 B5
Lagord (17) 176 D2
Lagos (64) 284 E5
Lagrâce-Dieu (31) 288 B4
Lagrand (05) 258 D2
Lagrange (40) 266 B1
Lagrange (65) 286 A6
Lagrange (90) 119 J6
Lagrasse (11) 309 J1
Lagraulet-du-Gers (32) 266 E2
Lagraulet-Saint-Nicolas (31) . . . 268 D4
Lagraulière (19) 215 K2
Lagrave (81) 270 C3
Lagruère (47) 247 H2
Laguenne (19) 216 B3
Laguépie (82) 251 F5
Laguian-Mazous (32) 285 K3
Laguinge-Restoue (64) 302 C1
Laguiole (12) 236 B4
Lagupie (47) 230 E5
Lahage (31) 287 H3
Lahas (32) 287 G1
Lahaymeix (55) 64 D2
Lahayville (55) 65 G2
Laheycourt (55) 63 K3
Lahitère (31) 287 K6
Lahitte (32) 267 J5
Lahitte-Toupière (65) 285 G2
Lahonce (64) 282 C1
Lahosse (40) 264 D4
Lahourcade (64) 284 A3
Lahoussoye (80) 18 C1
Laifour (08) 22 C1
la Laigne (17) 177 H2
Laigné (53) 104 E4
Laigné-en-Belin (72) 106 E4
Laignelet (35) 80 B3
Laignes (21) 114 D4
Laigneville (60) 38 A4
Laigny (02) 21 F2
Laillé (35) 79 F6
Lailly (89) 89 F5
Lailly-en-Val (45) 109 J6
Laimont (55) 63 K3
Lain (89) 132 E2
Laines-aux-Bois (10) 90 A5
Lains (39) 173 F5
Lainsecq (89) 132 D3
Lainville-en-Vexin (78) 57 K1
Laire (25) 139 G2
Laires (62) 5 G5
Lairière (11) 309 H2
Lairoux (85) 159 K4
Laissac (12) 252 E2
Laissaud (73) 208 C5
Laissey (25) 138 C5
Laître-sous-Amance (54) 66 B4
Laives (71) 171 K2
Laix (54) 26 D3
Laiz (01) 188 D1
Laizé (71) 171 J5
Laize-la-Ville (14) 32 E6
Laizy (71) 152 E5
Lajo (48) 237 H2
Lajoux (39) 174 A5
Lalacelle (61) 82 B2
Lalande (89) 132 D1
Lalande-de-Pomerol (33) . . . 212 B6
Lalande-en-Son (60) 36 E2
Lalandelle (60) 37 F2
Lalandusse (47) 231 J4
Lalanne (32) 267 J4
Lalanne (65) 286 C5
Lalanne-Arqué (32) 286 D4
Lalanne-Trie (65) 286 A4
Lalaye (67) 96 B1
Lalbarède (81) 270 D6
Lalbenque (46) 250 B3
Laleu (61) 83 H1
Laleu (80) 17 H1
Lalevade-d'Ardèche (07) 239 G4
Lalheue (71) 171 J2
Lalinde (24) 232 A2
Lalizolle (03) 184 E3
Lallaing (59) 11 J1
Lalleu (35) 103 H2
Lalley (38) 242 A3
Lalleyriat (01) 190 B2
Lalobbe (08) 22 A4
Laloeuf (54) 93 K2
Lalongue (64) 284 E2
Lalonquette (64) 284 D2
Laloubère (65) 285 H5
Lalouret-Laffiteau (31) 286 E6
Lalouvesc (07) 221 J4
Laluque (40) 264 B3
Lama (2B) 319 F2

373

Lamadeleine-Val-des-Anges (90) . . 119 J5
Lamagdelaine (46) 250 A1
Lamagistère (82) 248 D5
Lamaguère (32) 286 D2
Lamaids (03) 183 J1
Lamalou-les-Bains (34) 272 D6
Lamancine (52) 92 A5
Lamanère (66) 314 D6
Lamanon (13) 276 E5
Lamarche (88) 117 H1
Lamarche-sur-Saône (21) 136 D6
Lamargelle (21) 135 J2
Lamaronde (80) 17 H3
Lamarque (33) 211 F4
Lamarque-Pontacq (65) 285 F6
Lamarque-Rustaing (65) 285 K4
Lamasquère (31) 287 K2
Lamastre (07) 221 K6
Lamath (54) 94 D1
Lamativie (46) 234 D1
Lamayou (64) 285 G3
Lamazère (32) 286 B1
Lamazière-Basse (19) 216 E1
Lamazière-Haute (19) 201 G3
Lambach (57) 69 G3
Lamballe (22) 77 J1
Lambersart (59) 6 D4
Lamberville (50) 31 H4
Lamberville (76) 15 J3
Lambesc (13) 277 G5
Lamblore (28) 56 B6
Lambres (62) 5 H4
Lambres-lez-Douai (59) 11 H2
Lambrey (70) 117 J5
Lambruisse (04) 260 B5
Laméac (65) 285 K4
Lamécourt (60) 38 A4
Lamelouze (30) 255 F4
Lamenay-sur-Loire (58) 169 G1
Lamérac (16) 196 A6
Lametz (08) 22 D6
Lamillarié (81) 270 E3
Lammerville (76) 15 J3
Lamnay (72) 107 J1
Lamongerie (19) 199 J5
Lamontélarié (81) 271 J6
Lamontgie (63) 203 F6
Lamontjoie (47) 248 A6
Lamonzie-Montastruc (24) 231 J1
Lamonzie-Saint-Martin (24) 231 G2
Lamorlaye (60) 38 A5
Lamorville (55) 64 E2
Lamothe (40) 265 F3
Lamothe (43) 219 H2
Lamothe-Capdeville (82) 249 K6
Lamothe-Cassel (46) 233 J5
Lamothe-Cumont (82) 268 B3
Lamothe-en-Blaisy (52) 91 K5
Lamothe-Fénelon (46) 233 H2
Lamothe-Goas (32) 267 H3
Lamothe-Landerron (33) 230 D5
Lamothe-Montravel (24) 230 D2
Lamotte-Beuvron (41) 130 D2
Lamotte-Brebière (80) 18 B2
Lamotte-Buleux (80) 9 G4
Lamotte-du-Rhône (84) 256 D6
Lamotte-Warfusée (80) 18 D2
Lamouilly (55) 23 H6
Lamoura (39) 174 A5
Lampaul-Guimiliau (29) 46 E5
Lampaul-Plouarzel (29) 72 B3
Lampaul-Ploudalmézeau (29) 72 C2
Lampertheim (67) 25 A6
Lampertsloch (67) 25 A2
Lamure-sur-Azergues (69) 187 K4
Lanans (25) 138 E5
Lanarce (07) 238 D3
Lanarvily (29) 46 B4
Lanas (07) 239 H6
Lancé (41) 128 C1
Lanchères (80) 8 D4
Lanches-Saint-Hilaire (80) 9 J5
Lanchy (02) 19 H3
Lancié (69) 188 B2
Lancieux (22) 50 C3
Lancôme (41) 128 C1
Lançon (08) 42 D4
Lançon (65) 305 F4
Lançon-Provence (13) 276 E6
Lancrans (01) 190 C3
Landange (57) 67 H5
Landas (59) 7 H5
Landaul (56) 100 C4
Landaville (88) 93 G4
Landavran (35) 79 K4
la Lande-Chasles (49) 126 B3
la Lande-d'Airou (50) 52 A3
la Lande-de-Fronsac (33) 211 K6
la Lande-de-Goult (61) 82 C1
la Lande-de-Lougé (61) 54 A5
la Lande-Patry (61) 53 J6
la Lande-Saint-Léger (27) 34 B3
la Lande-Saint-Siméon (61) 53 J6
la Lande-sur-Drôme (14) 31 K4
la Lande-sur-Eure (61) 84 A1
Landéan (35) 80 B3
Landebaëron (22) 48 C4
Landébia (22) 50 A4
le Landec (22) 50 B5
Landécourt (54) 94 C1
Landéda (29) 72 D2
Landéhen (22) 77 J1

Landeleau (29) 75 G3
Landelles (28) 84 D2
Landelles-et-Coupigny (14) 31 J6
Landemont (49) 123 K3
Landepéreuse (27) 55 J1
Landerneau (29) 46 C6
Landeronde (85) 159 G2
Landerrouat (33) 230 E3
Landerrouet-sur-Ségur (33) 230 C4
Landersheim (67) 70 C2
Landes (17) 177 J4
les Landes-Genusson (85) 142 C4
Landes-le-Gaulois (41) 128 D1
Landes-sur-Ajon (14) 32 C6
Landes-Vieilles-et-Neuves (76) . . . 16 E3
Landévant (56) 100 C3
Landévennec (29) 74 C2
Landevieille (85) 158 E2
Landeyrat (15) 218 C3
Landifay-et-Bertaignemont (02) . . 20 D3
Landigou (61) 53 H4
le Landin (27) 35 F2
Landiras (33) 229 J5
Landisacq (61) 53 G4
Landivisiau (29) 46 E5
Landivy (53) 80 C2
Landogne (63) 201 J1
Landorthe (31) 286 E6
Landos (43) 238 B2
Landouzy-la-Cour (02) 21 G2
Landouzy-la-Ville (02) 21 G2
Landrais (17) 177 G3
le Landreau (44) 123 K4
Landrecies (59) 12 E5
Landrecourt-Lempire (55) 43 H6
Landremont (54) 66 A3
Landres (54) 26 D5
Landres-et-Saint-Georges (08) . . . 42 E3
Landresse (25) 138 E5
Landrethun-le-Nord (62) 2 C4
Landrethun-lès-Ardres (62) 2 D4
Landrévarzec (29) 74 D5
Landreville (10) 114 E2
Landrichamps (08) 24 D2
Landricourt (02) 39 J1
Landricourt (51) 63 H6
Landroff (57) 66 E1
Landry (73) 193 A3
Landser (68) 97 C3
Landudal (29) 74 E5
Landudec (29) 73 E3
Landujan (35) 78 D2
Landunvez (29) 72 B2
Lanespède (65) 285 K6
Lanester (56) 100 A3
Lanet (11) 309 H3
Laneuvelle (52) 117 G3
Laneuvelotte (54) 66 B4
Laneuveville-aux-Bois (54) 67 F5
Laneuveville-derrière-Foug (54) . . 65 G5
Laneuveville-devant-Bayon (54) . . 94 B2
Laneuveville-devant-Nancy (54) . . 66 B5
Laneuveville-en-Saulnois (57) . . . 66 C2
Laneuveville-lès-Lorquin (57) 67 J5
Laneuville-au-Pont (52) 63 J6
Laneuville-au-Rupt (55) 64 E5
Laneuville-sur-Meuse (55) 43 F1
Laneuvilleroy (60) 38 B1
Lanfains (22) 76 E2
Lanfroicourt (54) 66 B3
Langan (35) 78 E1
Langast (22) 77 G3
Langatte (57) 67 H4
Langé (36) 147 H3
Langeac (43) 219 J5
Langeais (37) 127 F5
Langensoultzbach (67) 25 A2
Langeron (58) 150 D6
Langesse (45) 111 H5
Langey (28) 108 D2
Langlade (30) 275 F4
Langley (88) 94 C3
Langoat (22) 48 B3
Langoëlan (56) 76 B5
Langogne (48) 238 C4
Langoiran (33) 229 J3
Langolen (29) 74 E5
Langon (33) 230 A5
Langon (35) 102 E6
Langon (41) 129 K6
le Langon (85) 160 C5
Langonnet (56) 75 J5
Langouet (35) 78 E2
Langourla (22) 77 K3
Langres (52) 116 D4
Langrolay-sur-Rance (22) 50 D4
Langrune-sur-Mer (14) 32 E3
Languédias (22) 50 B6
Languenan (22) 50 C5
Langueux (22) 49 G6
Languevoisin-Quiquery (80) 19 G4
Languidic (56) 100 C2
Languimberg (57) 67 G4
Langy (03) 185 J1
Lanhélin (35) 51 F5
Lanhères (54) 26 C4
Lanhouarneau (29) 46 C4
Lanilduc (29) 72 B3
Laning (57) 68 B4
Laniscat (22) 76 C3
Laniscourt (02) 20 C4
Lanleff (22) 48 D3

Lanloup (22) 48 E3
Lanmérin (22) 48 B3
Lanmeur (22) 47 H4
Lanmodez (22) 48 D1
Lanne (65) 285 G6
Lanne-en-Barétous (64) 283 J6
Lanne-Soubiran (32) 266 A4
Lannéanou (29) 47 H6
Lannebert (22) 48 E4
Lannecaube (64) 284 E2
Lannédern (29) 75 F2
Lannemaignan (32) 265 K2
Lannemezan (65) 305 F1
Lannepax (32) 266 E4
Lanneplaà (64) 283 J2
Lanneray (28) 108 E2
Lannes (47) 247 J6
Lanneuffret (29) 46 C5
Lannilis (29) 72 D2
Lannion (22) 48 A3
Lannoy (59) 7 F4
Lannoy-Cuillère (60) 17 F4
Lannux (32) 265 K5
Lano (2B) 319 G5
Lanobre (15) 201 H6
Lanouaille (24) 214 E1
Lanouée (56) 101 H1
Lanoux (09) 307 G1
Lanquais (24) 231 K2
Lanques-sur-Rognon (52) 116 D1
Lanquetot (76) 14 E6
Lanrelas (22) 78 A2
Lanrigan (35) 51 G6
Lanrivain (22) 76 C2
Lanrivoaré (29) 72 C3
Lanrodec (22) 48 D6
Lans (71) 154 B6
Lans-en-Vercors (38) 223 K4
Lansac (33) 211 H5
Lansac (65) 285 J5
Lansac (66) 309 J5
Lansargues (34) 274 D6
Lanslebourg-Mont-Cenis (73) . . . 226 C1
Lanslevillard (73) 226 C1
Lanta (31) 288 E1
Lantabat (64) 283 F4
Lantages (10) 114 C2
Lantan (18) 149 K5
Lantéfontaine (54) 26 E6
Lantenay (01) 189 K4
Lantenay (21) 135 J5
Lantenne-Vertière (25) 137 H6
Lantenot (70) 118 E5
la Lanterne-et-les-Armonts (70) . . 118 E4
Lanteuil (19) 215 K4
Lanthenans (25) 139 F4
Lanthes (21) 154 D3
Lantheuil (14) 32 C4
Lantic (22) 49 F5
Lantignié (69) 188 A3
Lantillac (56) 101 G1
Lantilly (21) 134 E2
Lanton (33) 228 C3
Lantosque (06) 311 A4
Lantriac (43) 220 D6
Lanty (21) 152 A6
Lanty-sur-Aube (52) 115 H2
Lanuéjols (30) 253 K5
Lanuéjols (48) 254 B1
Lanuéjouls (12) 251 H2
Lanvallay (22) 50 D5
Lanvaudan (56) 100 B2
Lanvellec (22) 47 K4
Lanvénégen (56) 75 J6
Lanvéoc (29) 72 D6
Lanvollon (22) 48 E4
Lanzac (46) 233 H2
Laon (02) 20 D6
Laons (28) 56 D5
Lapalisse (03) 186 A2
Lapalud (84) 256 D3
Lapan (18) 149 F5
Lapanouse (12) 253 G3
Lapanouse-de-Cernon (12) 272 D1
Laparade (47) 247 K2
Laparrouquial (81) 251 F6
Lapège (09) 307 H5
Lapenche (82) 250 B4
Lapenne (09) 288 E6
Lapenty (50) 52 C6
Laperche (47) 231 H6
Laperrière-sur-Saône (21) 155 F2
Lapeyre (65) 286 A4
Lapeyrère (31) 288 A5
Lapeyrouse (01) 188 E5
Lapeyrouse (63) 184 D2
Lapeyrouse-Fossat (31) 269 H5
Lapeyrouse-Mornay (26) 222 D2
Lapeyrugue (15) 235 J4
Lapleau (19) 216 E2
Laplume (47) 248 A5
Lapoutroie (68) 96 A3
Lapouyade (33) 211 J4
Lappion (02) 21 G5
Laprade (11) 290 A3
Laprade (16) 213 F2
Laprugne (03) 186 B5
Laps (63) 203 F3
Lapte (43) 221 F3
Lapugnoy (62) 5 K5
Laquenexy (57) 45 G6
Laqueuille (63) 201 K4

Laragne-Montéglin (05) 258 E2
Larajasse (69) 205 H4
Laramière (46) 250 E3
Laran (65) 286 B5
Larbey (40) 264 E4
Larbont (09) 307 G2
Larcan (31) 286 E6
Larcat (09) 307 J5
Larçay (37) 127 K5
Larceveau-Arros-Cibits (64) 283 F5
Larchamp (53) 80 C3
Larchamp (61) 53 F5
Larchant (77) 87 G5
Larche (04) 227 C6
Larche (19) 215 H4
le Larderet (39) 156 B5
Lardier-et-Valença (05) 259 G1
Lardiers (04) 258 C5
le Lardin-Saint-Lazare (24) 215 F4
Lardy (91) 86 D2
Larée (32) 266 B2
Laréole (31) 268 C5
Largeasse (79) 161 G1
Largentière (07) 239 G6
Largillay-Marsonnay (39) 173 H3
Largitzen (68) 97 B5
Largny-sur-Automne (02) 39 F4
Larians-et-Munans (70) 138 C3
Larivière (90) 119 J6
Larivière-Arnoncourt (52) 117 G2
Larmor-Baden (56) 100 E6
Larmor-Plage (56) 99 K5
Larnage (26) 222 C4
Larnagol (46) 250 D1
Larnas (07) 256 C1
Larnat (09) 307 J5
Larnaud (39) 173 F1
Larnod (25) 156 B1
Laroche-près-Feyt (19) 201 H3
Laroche-Saint-Cydroine (89) 113 F3
Larochemillay (58) 152 C5
Larodde (63) 201 H5
Laroin (64) 284 C4
Laronxe (54) 94 E1
Laroque (33) 229 K4
Laroque (34) 274 A2
Laroque-de-Fa (11) 309 J3
Laroque-des-Albères (66) 315 H4
Laroque-des-Arcs (46) 250 A1
Laroque-d'Olmes (09) 308 D3
Laroque-Timbaut (47) 248 D3
Laroquebrou (15) 217 F6
Laroquevieille (15) 217 J6
Larouillies (59) 13 G6
Larra (31) 268 E5
Larrau (64) 302 B2
Larrazet (82) 268 D2
Larré (56) 101 H4
Larressingle (32) 267 F2
Larressore (64) 263 D2
Larret (70) 137 F1
Larreule (64) 284 C2
Larreule (65) 285 G2
Larrey (21) 114 E4
Larribar-Sorhapuru (64) 283 G4
Larringes (74) 175 G5
Larrivière (40) 265 H4
Larrivoire (39) 173 J6
Larroque (31) 286 D6
Larroque (65) 286 B4
Larroque (81) 269 K1
Larroque-Engalin (32) 267 H1
Larroque-Saint-Sernin (32) 267 G3
Larroque-sur-l'Osse (32) 266 E1
Larroque-Toirac (46) 234 C6
Lartigue (32) 286 E1
Lartigue (33) 246 E4
Laruns (64) 303 H2
Laruscade (33) 211 K4
Larzac (24) 232 D3
Larzicourt (51) 63 G6
Lasalle (30) 254 E6
Lasbordes (11) 289 H4
Lascabanes (46) 249 J3
Lascaux (19) 215 G2
Lascazères (65) 285 G1
Lascelle (15) 217 J6
Lasclaveries (64) 284 D2
Lasfaillades (81) 290 C1
Lasgraisses (81) 270 D4
Laslades (65) 285 J5
Lassales (65) 286 B5
Lassay-les-Châteaux (53) 81 H3
Lassay-sur-Croisne (41) 129 H5
Lasse (49) 126 C2
Lasse (64) 282 D5
Lasserade (32) 266 C6
Lasséran (32) 267 H6
Lasserre (09) 306 D1
Lasserre (31) 268 E6
Lasserre (47) 247 K6
Lasserre (64) 285 F1
Lasserre-de-Prouille (11) 289 J6
Lasseube (64) 284 B5
Lasseube-Propre (32) 286 C1
Lasseubetat (64) 284 C6
Lassicourt (10) 90 E3
Lassigny (60) 19 F6
Lasson (14) 32 D4
Lasson (89) 113 J2

Lassouts (12) 252 E1
Lassur (09) 307 K5
Lassy (14) 53 G2
Lassy (35) 78 E6
Lassy (95) 38 A6
Lastic (15) 219 F4
Lastic (63) 201 J3
Lastours (11) 290 B4
Lataule (60) 18 E6
le Latet (39) 156 B6
la Latette (39) 156 C6
Lathuile (74) 208 E1
Lathus-Saint-Rémy (86) 164 B6
Latillé (86) 162 C3
Latilly (02) 39 J5
Latoue (31) 286 E6
Latouille-Lentillac (46) 234 C2
Latour (31) 288 A6
Latour-Bas-Elne (66) 315 H3
Latour-de-Carol (66) 313 G5
Latour-de-France (66) 309 K5
Latour-en-Woëvre (55) 44 B6
Latrape (31) 288 A5
Latrecey-Ormoy-sur-Aube (52) . . . 115 J3
Latresne (33) 229 H2
Latrille (40) 265 J6
Latronche (19) 217 F2
Latronquière (46) 234 E3
Lattainville (60) 36 E4
Lattes (34) 293 H1
Lattre-Saint-Quentin (62) 10 D3
Lau-Balagnas (65) 304 A2
Laubach (67) 25 A3
Laubert (48) 237 K5
les Laubies (48) 237 H4
Laubressel (10) 90 C4
Laubrières (53) 104 B3
Laucourt (80) 19 F5
Laudrefang (57) 45 K4
Laudun (30) 256 C5
Laugnac (47) 248 B3
Laujuzan (32) 266 A3
Laulne (50) 30 E1
Laumesfeld (57) 27 K4
Launac (31) 268 E4
Launaguet (31) 269 G5
Launay (27) 34 E6
Launay-Villiers (53) 80 C6
Launois-sur-Vence (08) 22 B5
Launoy (02) 39 K4
Launstroff (57) 27 K3
la Laupie (26) 240 C5
Laurabuc (11) 289 H5
Laurac (11) 289 H5
Laurac-en-Vivarais (07) 239 G6
Lauraët (32) 266 E2
Lauraguel (11) 308 E1
Laure-Minervois (11) 290 D5
Laurède (40) 264 D4
Laurenan (22) 77 J4
Laurens (34) 291 K2
Lauresses (46) 234 E3
Lauret (34) 274 C3
Lauret (40) 284 D1
Laurie (15) 218 E2
Laurière (87) 181 K4
Lauris (84) 277 G4
Lauroux (34) 273 F4
Laussonne (43) 220 D6
Laussou (47) 232 B5
Lautenbach (68) 96 A6
Lautenbachzell (68) 96 A6
Lauterbourg (67) 25 E2
Lauthiers (86) 163 J3
Lautignac (31) 287 H3
Lautrec (81) 270 E5
Lauw (68) 119 K5
Lauwin-Planque (59) 11 H1
Laux-Montaux (26) 258 B2
Lauzach (56) 101 H6
Lauzerte (82) 249 G4
Lauzerville (31) 288 D1
Lauzès (46) 233 J6
le Lauzet-Ubaye (04) 260 A1
Lauzun (47) 231 H5
Lavacquerie (60) 17 J4
Laval (38) 224 C2
Laval (53) 104 E1
Laval-Atger (48) 238 A4
Laval-d'Aix (26) 241 H3
Laval-d'Aurelle (07) 238 D6
Laval-de-Cère (46) 234 C1
Laval-du-Tarn (48) 253 K3
Laval-en-Brie (77) 88 A3
Laval-en-Laonnois (02) 40 B1
Laval-le-Prieuré (25) 139 F6
Laval-Morency (08) 22 B2
Laval-Pradel (30) 255 G4
Laval-Roquecezière (12) 271 K4
Laval-Saint-Roman (30) 256 B3
Laval-sur-Doulon (43) 219 J1
Laval-sur-Luzège (19) 216 E3
Laval-sur-Tourbe (51) 42 B5
Laval-sur-Vologne (88) 95 F5
Lavalade (24) 232 B4
Lavaldens (38) 224 C5
Lavalette (11) 290 A6
Lavalette (31) 269 J6
Lavalette (34) 273 F5
Lavallée (55) 64 C3
Lavancia-Épercy (39) 173 H6
le Lavandou (83) 298 D5

Lavangeot (39)	155 H1	Lect (39)	173 H5
Lavannes (51)	41 G3	Lectoure (32)	267 J2
Lavans-lès-Dole (39)	155 H1	Lecumberry (64)	282 E6
Lavans-lès-Saint-Claude (39)	173 J5	Lécussan (31)	286 C6
Lavans-Quingey (25)	156 A2	Lédas-et-Penthiès (81)	251 K6
Lavans-sur-Valouse (39)	173 G6	Lédat (47)	248 C1
Lavans-Vuillafans (25)	156 D2	Lédenon (30)	275 J2
Lavaqueresse (02)	20 D1	Lédergues (12)	252 A6
Lavardac (47)	247 J5	Lederzeele (59)	3 G4
Lavardens (32)	267 H4	Lédignan (30)	274 E1
Lavardin (41)	108 A6	Ledinghem (62)	2 E6
Lavardin (72)	106 C1	Ledringhem (59)	3 H1
Lavaré (72)	107 J2	Lée (64)	284 D4
Lavars (38)	242 A1	Leers (59)	7 F3
Lavastrie (15)	236 D1	Lées-Athas (64)	303 F2
Lavatoggio (2B)	318 C5	Lefaux (62)	4 B5
Lavau (10)	90 B4	Leffard (14)	53 K2
Lavau (89)	132 A2	Leffincourt (08)	41 K2
Lavau-sur-Loire (44)	122 C3	Leffonds (52)	116 B3
Lavaudieu (43)	219 H3	Leffrinckoucke (59)	3 H1
Lavaufranche (23)	183 H1	Leforest (62)	11 H1
Lavault-de-Frétoy (58)	152 C2	Lège (31)	305 H4
Lavault-Sainte-Anne (03)	184 A1	Legé (44)	141 H4
Lavaur (24)	232 D5	Lège-Cap-Ferret (33)	228 B2
Lavaur (81)	270 A5	Légéville-et-Bonfays (88)	94 A5
Lavaurette (82)	250 C4	Léglantiers (60)	38 B1
Lavausseau (86)	162 C3	Légna (39)	173 G5
Lavaveix-les-Mines (23)	183 F4	Légny (69)	188 A6
Lavazan (33)	246 E2	Léguevin (31)	268 E6
Laveissenet (15)	218 C5	Léguillac-de-Cercles (24)	213 J1
Laveissière (15)	218 B4	Léguillac-de-l'Auche (24)	213 J3
Lavelanet (09)	308 B3	Lehaucourt (02)	19 K1
Lavelanet-de-Comminges (31)	287 J5	Léhon (22)	50 D5
Laveline-devant-Bruyères (88)	95 G5	Leigné-les-Bois (86)	163 J1
Laveline-du-Houx (88)	95 F6	Leigné-sur-Usseau (86)	145 H5
Lavenay (72)	107 J5	Leignes-sur-Fontaine (86)	163 K4
Laventie (62)	6 B4	Leigneux (42)	204 C2
Laveraët (32)	285 J1	Leimbach (68)	119 K4
Lavercantière (46)	233 G5	Leintrey (54)	67 F5
Laverdines (18)	150 A3	Lélex (01)	174 A6
Lavergne (46)	234 A3	Lelin-Lapujolle (32)	266 C5
Lavergne (47)	231 G5	Lelling (57)	68 A4
Lavernat (72)	107 F6	Lemainville (54)	94 B1
Lavernay (25)	137 H6	Lembach (67)	25 A1
Lavernhe (12)	253 F3	Lemberg (57)	69 G4
Lavernose-Lacasse (31)	287 K3	Lembeye (64)	285 F2
Lavernoy (52)	117 F3	Lembras (24)	231 J1
Laverrière (60)	17 J4	Lemé (02)	20 E2
Laversine (02)	39 H3	Lème (64)	284 D2
Laversines (60)	37 J2	Leménil-Mitry (54)	94 B2
Lavérune (34)	293 G1	Lémeré (37)	145 G3
Laveyron (26)	222 B3	Lemmecourt (88)	93 G5
Laveyrune (07)	238 C5	Lemmes (55)	43 G6
Laveyssière (24)	231 H1	Lemoncourt (57)	66 C2
Lavieu (42)	204 C5	Lempaut (81)	289 J2
Laviéville (80)	10 D6	Lempdes (63)	202 E2
Lavigerie (15)	218 A4	Lempdes-sur-Allagnon (43)	219 F1
Lavignac (87)	198 D3	Lempire (02)	11 J6
Lavigney (70)	117 H6	Lemps (07)	222 B4
Lavigny (39)	173 G1	Lemps (26)	258 A2
Lavillatte (07)	238 D3	Lempty (63)	203 F1
Laville-aux-Bois (52)	116 C1	Lempzours (24)	214 B1
Lavilledieu (07)	239 J5	Lemud (57)	45 G6
Lavilleneuve (52)	116 E2	Lemuy (39)	156 B4
Lavilletertre (60)	37 F5	Lénault (14)	53 G2
Lavincourt (55)	64 B5	Lenax (03)	186 C1
Laviolle (07)	239 G3	Lencloître (86)	145 G6
Laviron (25)	139 F5	Lencouacq (40)	246 B5
Lavit (82)	268 R2	Lengelsheim (57)	69 G2
Lavoine (03)	186 B5	Lengronne (50)	30 E5
Lavoncourt (70)	137 H1	Lenharrée (51)	62 B4
Lavours (01)	207 K1	Léning (57)	67 G1
Lavoûte-Chilhac (43)	219 H4	Lennon (29)	75 F3
Lavoûte-sur-Loire (43)	220 C4	Lenoncourt (54)	66 B5
Lavoux (86)	163 G3	Lens (62)	11 F1
Lavoye (55)	43 F6	Lens-Lestang (26)	222 D2
Lawarde-Mauger-l'Hortoy (80)	18 A4	Lent (01)	189 G3
Laxou (54)	66 A5	Lent (39)	156 B6
Lay (42)	187 G5	Lentigny (42)	186 E5
Lay-Lamidou (64)	303 H4	Lentillac-du-Causse (46)	233 K6
Lay-Saint-Christophe (54)	66 A4	Lentillac-Saint-Blaise (46)	234 E5
Lay-Saint-Remy (54)	65 G5	Lentillères (07)	239 G5
Laye (05)	242 E4	Lentilles (10)	91 F2
Laymont (32)	287 G3	Lentilly (69)	205 J1
Layrac (47)	248 C5	Lentiol (38)	222 E2
Layrac-sur-Tarn (31)	269 H3	Lento (2B)	319 G3
Layrisse (65)	285 H6	Léobard (46)	233 G4
Lays-sur-le-Doubs (71)	154 C4	Léogeats (33)	229 K6
Laz (29)	75 F4	Léognan (33)	229 H4
Lazenay (18)	148 D3	Léojac (82)	269 G1
Lazer (05)	258 E2	Léon (40)	262 D2
Léalvillers (80)	10 C5	Léoncel (26)	241 F1
Léaupartie (14)	33 H5	Léotoing (43)	219 F1
Léaz (01)	190 D3	Léouville (45)	86 C6
Lebetain (90)	139 J2	Léoville (17)	211 K1
Lebeuville (54)	94 B2	Lépanges-sur-Vologne (88)	95 F5
Lebiez (62)	4 E6	Lépaud (23)	183 J2
Leboulin (32)	267 J5	Lépin-le-Lac (73)	208 A4
Lebreil (46)	249 H3	Lépinas (23)	182 D4
Lebucquière (62)	11 G5	Lépine (62)	9 F1
Lécaude (14)	33 J6	Lépron-les-Vallées (08)	22 A3
Lecci (2A)	323 H2	Lepuix (90)	119 H5
Lecelles (59)	7 G6	Lepuix-Neuf (90)	97 A5
Lecey (52)	116 E4	Léran (09)	308 B3
Lechâtelet (21)	154 D3	Lercoul (09)	307 H5
Léchelle (62)	11 G5	Léré (18)	131 K4
Léchelle (77)	88 E1	Léren (64)	283 G1
la Léchère (73)	209 H4	Lérigneux (42)	204 C4
les Lèches (24)	213 G6	Lerm-et-Musset (33)	246 D3
Lécluse (59)	11 H3	Lerné (37)	144 E2
Lécousse (35)	80 A3	Lérouville (55)	64 E4
Lecques (30)	274 D3		

Lerrain (88)	94 A6	les Lèves-et-Thoumeyragues (33)	230 E3
Léry (21)	135 J2	Levesville-la-Chenard (28)	85 K5
Léry (27)	35 J4	Levet (18)	149 G5
Lerzy (02)	21 F1	Levie (2A)	323 F2
Les Adrets-de-l'Estérel (83)	280 C6	Levier (25)	156 C4
Lesbœufs (80)	11 F6	Lévignac (31)	268 E5
Lesbois (53)	80 F2	Lévignac-de-Guyenne (47)	230 E5
Lescar (64)	284 C4	Lévignacq (40)	244 B6
Leschaux (74)	208 D1	Lévignen (60)	38 D5
Leschelles (02)	20 E1	Lévigny (10)	91 G4
Lescheraines (73)	208 D2	Levis (89)	132 D1
Leschères (39)	173 G4	Lévis-Saint-Nom (78)	58 A5
Leschères-sur-le-Blaiseron (52)	92 A4	Levoncourt (55)	64 C3
Lescherolles (77)	60 D5	Levoncourt (68)	97 B6
Lescheroux (01)	172 C5	Levroux (36)	147 J4
Lesches (77)	59 J3	Lewarde (59)	11 J2
Lesches-en-Diois (26)	241 J5	Lexy (54)	26 C2
Lescouët-Gouarec (22)	76 B4	Ley (57)	67 F4
Lescousse (09)	288 C6	Leychert (09)	307 K3
Lescout (81)	289 J1	Leyme (46)	234 C2
Lescun (64)	303 F3	Leymen (68)	97 D5
Lescuns (31)	287 H5	Leyment (01)	189 H5
Lescure (09)	306 E2	Leynes (71)	188 B1
Lescure-d'Albigeois (81)	270 E2	Leynhac (15)	235 G3
Lescure-Jaoul (12)	251 H4	Leyr (54)	66 B3
Lescurry (65)	285 J4	Leyrat (23)	166 E6
Lesdain (59)	11 K5	Leyrieu (38)	206 E2
Lesdins (02)	20 A2	Leyritz-Moncassin (47)	247 G3
Lesges (02)	40 A3	Leyssard (01)	189 J2
Lesgor (40)	264 C3	Leyvaux (15)	218 E2
Lésignac-Durand (16)	197 J1	Leyviller (57)	68 B4
Lésigny (77)	59 J5	Lez (31)	305 J3
Lésigny (86)	146 A6	Lez-Fontaine (59)	13 J4
le Leslay (22)	76 E1	Lézan (30)	274 D1
Lesme (71)	169 J2	Lézardrieux (22)	48 D2
Lesménils (54)	65 K2	Lézat (39)	174 A4
Lesmont (10)	90 D3	Lézat-sur-Lèze (09)	288 A5
Lesneven (29)	46 B4	Lezay (79)	178 E1
Lesparre-Médoc (33)	210 D2	Lezennes (59)	6 E4
Lesparrou (09)	308 B3	Lézéville (52)	92 D3
Lespéron (07)	238 C3	Lezey (57)	66 E4
Lesperon (40)	264 B1	Lézignan (65)	304 E1
Lespesses (62)	5 J5	Lézignan-Corbières (11)	291 F6
Lespielle (64)	285 F2	Lézignan-la-Cèbe (34)	292 C2
Lespignan (34)	291 K5	Lézigné (49)	125 K1
Lespinasse (31)	269 G5	Lézigneux (42)	204 D4
Lespinassière (11)	290 D3	Lézinnes (89)	114 B5
Lespinoy (62)	9 G1	Lezoux (63)	203 G1
Lespiteau (31)	305 K1	Lhéraule (60)	37 F1
Lespouey (65)	285 J5	Lherm (31)	287 K3
Lespourcy (64)	285 F3	Lherm (46)	233 F6
Lespugue (31)	286 C6	Lhéry (51)	40 C5
Lesquerde (66)	309 H5	Lhez (65)	285 J5
Lesquielles-Saint-Germain (02)	20 D1	Lhommaizé (86)	163 H5
Lesquin (59)	6 E4	Lhomme (72)	107 H6
Lessac (16)	180 B4	L'Hôpital (01)	190 C4
Lessard-en-Bresse (71)	172 B1	Lhor (57)	67 G2
Lessard-et-le-Chêne (14)	33 J6	L'Hospitalet (46)	249 K2
Lessard-le-National (71)	154 A5	Lhoumois (79)	162 A1
Lessay (50)	30 C2	Lhuis (01)	207 H2
Lesse (57)	66 D1	Lhuître (10)	90 C1
Lesseux (88)	95 K4	Lhuys (02)	40 A4
Lessy (57)	44 E5	Liac (65)	285 H3
Lestanville (76)	15 J4	Liancourt (60)	38 A3
Lestards (19)	200 B5	Liancourt-Fosse (80)	19 F4
Lestelle-Bétharram (64)	284 E6	Liancourt-Saint-Pierre (60)	37 F4
Lestelle-de-Saint-Martory (31)	306 B1	Liart (08)	21 K3
Lesterps (16)	180 C5	Lias (32)	287 J1
Lestiac-sur-Garonne (33)	229 K4	Lias-d'Armagnac (32)	266 B3
Lestiou (41)	109 H6	Liausson (34)	273 G6
Lestrade-et-Thouels (12)	252 C6	Libaros (65)	286 A5
Lestre (50)	29 F4	Libercourt (62)	6 D6
Lestrem (62)	6 A4	Libermont (60)	19 H4
Létanne (08)	23 G6	Libourne (33)	230 A1
Lételon (03)	167 H2	Licey-sur-Vingeanne (21)	136 D3
Léthuin (28)	85 K4	Lichans-Sunhar (64)	302 C1
Letia (2A)	320 C1	Lichères (16)	179 G6
Létra (69)	187 K5	Lichères-près-Aigremont (89)	113 J6
Létricourt (54)	66 B2	Lichères-sur-Yonne (89)	133 G3
Letteguives (27)	36 A2	Lichos (64)	283 H4
Lettret (05)	242 E6	Lichtenberg (67)	69 H5
Leubringhen (62)	2 B4	Licourt (80)	19 G3
Leuc (11)	290 B6	Licq-Athérey (64)	302 C1
Leucamp (15)	235 J4	Licques (62)	2 D4
Leucate (11)	310 D4	Licy-Clignon (02)	39 J6
Leuchey (52)	116 C6	Lidrezing (57)	67 F2
Leudeville (91)	86 E1	Liebenswiller (68)	97 D5
Leudon-en-Brie (77)	60 D5	Liebsdorf (68)	97 B6
Leuglay (21)	115 H5	Liebvillers (25)	109 H4
Leugny (86)	146 A4	Liederschiedt (57)	69 H2
Leugny (89)	132 E1	Lieffrans (70)	137 K2
Leuhan (29)	75 G5	le Liège (37)	146 E1
Leuilly-sous-Coucy (02)	39 J1	Liéhon (57)	66 B1
Leulinghem (62)	3 F5	Liencourt (62)	10 C3
Leulinghen-Bernes (62)	2 B4	Liépvre (68)	96 B1
Leurville (52)	92 D4	Liéramont (80)	11 H6
Leury (02)	39 J2	Liercourt (80)	9 G6
Leutenheim (67)	25 C3	Lières (62)	5 H5
Leuville-sur-Orge (91)	86 D1	Liergues (69)	188 B5
Leuvrigny (51)	40 C6	Liernais (21)	152 E1
le Leuy (40)	265 F3	Liernolles (03)	169 J6
Leuze (02)	21 H2	Lierval (02)	40 B1
Levainville (28)	85 J2	Lierville (60)	37 F5
Leval (59)	13 F4	Lies (65)	304 D1
Leval (90)	119 J5	Liesle (25)	155 K2
Levallois-Perret (92)	58 C3	Liesse-Notre-Dame (02)	20 C5
Levaré (53)	80 D3	Liessies (59)	13 J5
Levécourt (52)	93 F6	Liesville-sur-Douve (50)	29 F6
Levens (06)	281 G2	Liettres (62)	5 H4
Levergies (02)	20 A1	Lieu-Saint-Amand (59)	12 B3
Levernois (21)	154 A3	Lieuche (06)	261 G6
Lèves (28)	85 G2	Lieucourt (70)	137 G5

Lieudieu (38)	206 E5
Lieuran (09)	308 A3
Lieuran-Cabrières (34)	292 C1
Lieuran-lès-Béziers (34)	292 A3
Lieurey (27)	34 C4
Lieuron (35)	102 D1
Lieusaint (50)	28 E4
Lieusaint (77)	59 G6
Lieutadès (15)	236 C2
Lieuvillers (60)	38 B1
Liévans (70)	138 C1
Liévin (62)	10 E1
Liez (02)	20 A4
Liez (85)	160 E5
Liézey (88)	95 G6
Liffol-le-Grand (88)	93 F4
Liffol-le-Petit (52)	92 E4
Liffré (35)	79 H3
Ligardes (32)	248 A6
Ligescourt (80)	9 G3
Liginiac (19)	217 G1
Liglet (86)	164 C4
Lignac (36)	164 D5
Lignairolles (11)	308 C1
Lignan-de-Bazas (33)	246 C1
Lignan-de-Bordeaux (33)	229 J2
Lignan-sur-Orb (34)	291 K3
Lignareix (19)	201 F4
Ligné (16)	179 F6
Ligné (44)	123 J2
Lignères (61)	55 F5
Lignereuil (62)	10 C3
Lignerolles (03)	184 A1
Lignerolles (21)	115 J4
Lignerolles (27)	56 E3
Lignerolles (36)	166 C4
Lignerolles (61)	83 H1
Lignéville (88)	93 J6
Ligneyrac (19)	215 K5
Lignières (10)	113 K3
Lignières (18)	166 D1
Lignières (41)	108 D4
Lignières (80)	18 E5
Lignières-Châtelain (80)	17 G3
Lignières-de-Touraine (37)	127 F6
Lignières-en-Vimeu (80)	17 F2
Lignières-la-Carelle (72)	82 E3
Lignières-Orgères (53)	82 A1
Lignières-Sonneville (16)	196 A4
Lignières-sur-Aire (55)	64 D4
Lignol (56)	76 B6
Lignol-le-Château (10)	91 H5
Lignon (51)	91 F1
Lignorelles (89)	113 H4
Lignou (61)	53 K5
Ligny-en-Barrois (55)	64 C5
Ligny-en-Brionnais (71)	187 G2
Ligny-en-Cambrésis (59)	12 C5
Ligny-le-Châtel (89)	113 H4
Ligny-le-Ribault (45)	129 J1
Ligny-lès-Aire (62)	5 H5
Ligny-Saint-Flochel (62)	10 B2
Ligny-sur-Canche (62)	10 A3
Ligny-Thilloy (62)	11 F5
Ligré (37)	145 G2
Ligron (72)	106 C5
Ligsdorf (68)	97 C6
Ligueil (37)	146 B3
Ligueux (24)	214 B2
Ligueux (33)	231 F3
Ligugé (86)	163 F4
Lihons (80)	19 F3
les Lilas (93)	59 F3
Lilhac (31)	287 F4
Lille (59)	6 D4
Lillebonne (76)	14 E6
Lillemer (35)	50 E4
Lillers (62)	5 J5
Lilly (27)	36 C2
Limalonges (79)	179 G3
Limans (04)	278 A1
Limanton (58)	151 K4
Limas (69)	188 B5
Limay (78)	57 J2
Limbrassac (09)	308 B2
Limé (02)	40 A3
Limeil-Brévannes (94)	59 F5
Limendous (64)	284 E4
Limeray (37)	128 C4
Limersheim (67)	70 E5
Limerzel (56)	101 K6
Limésy (76)	15 J5
Limetz-Villez (78)	57 G1
Limeuil (24)	232 C2
Limeux (18)	148 D3
Limeux (80)	9 G6
Limey-Remenauville (54)	65 H2
Limeyrat (24)	214 D4
Limoges (87)	199 F1
Limoges-Fourches (77)	59 H6
Limogne-en-Quercy (46)	250 D2
Limoise (03)	168 B2
Limon (58)	151 G4
Limonest (69)	206 A1
Limons (63)	185 J5
Limont-Fontaine (59)	13 G3
Limony (07)	222 A1
Limours (91)	58 C6
Limousis (11)	290 B4
Limoux (11)	308 E2
la Limouzinière (44)	141 H3

Limpiville (76). 14 E4
Linac (46). 234 E4
Linard (23). 166 A6
Linards (87). 199 H3
Linars (16). 196 D3
Linas (91). 58 D6
Linazay (86). 179 G3
Lindebeuf (76). 15 H4
le Lindois (16). 197 J2
Lindre-Basse (57). 67 F3
Lindre-Haute (57). 67 F3
Lindry (89). 112 E5
Linexert (70). 118 C3
Lingé (36). 164 C1
Lingeard (50). 52 C4
Lingèvres (14). 32 B5
Linghem (62). 5 H4
Lingolsheim (67). 71 D1
Lingreville (50). 30 D5
Linguizzetta (2B). 319 J6
Linières-Bouton (49). 126 C3
Liniers (86). 163 H3
Liniez (36). 148 A3
Linsdorf (68). 97 D5
Linselles (59). 6 E3
Linthal (68). 96 A6
Linthelles (51). 61 J3
Linthes (51). 61 J5
Lintot (76). 14 E6
Lintot-les-Bois (76). 15 H3
Linxe (40). 262 D2
Linzeux (62). 9 K3
Liocourt (57). 66 C2
Liomer (80). 17 G2
le Lion-d'Angers (49). 125 F1
Lion-devant-Dun (55). 43 G2
Lion-en-Beauce (45). 110 A4
Lion-en-Sullias (45). 111 F6
Lion-sur-Mer (14). 32 E3
Liorac-sur-Louyre (24). 231 K1
Liouc (30). 274 D7
Liourdres (19). 234 B1
Lioux (84). 277 G1
Lioux-les-Monges (23). 183 J5
Liposthey (40). 245 G2
Lipsheim (67). 70 E4
Lirac (30). 256 D6
Liré (49). 124 A5
Lirey (10). 90 A6
Lironcourt (88). 117 J2
Lironville (54). 65 H3
Liry (08). 42 B3
Lisbourg (62). 5 G6
Lisieux (14). 33 K5
Lisle (24). 213 J2
Lisle (41). 108 C4
Lisle-en-Barrois (55). 64 A2
Lisle-en-Rigault (55). 63 K5
Lisle-sur-Tarn (81). 270 A3
Lislet (02). 21 G4
Lison (14). 31 H2
Lisores (14). 54 E2
Lisors (27). 36 B3
Lissac (09). 288 C5
Lissac (43). 220 B4
Lissac-et-Mouret (46). 234 D5
Lissac-sur-Couze (19). 215 H5
Lissay-Lochy (18). 149 G4
Lisse-en-Champagne (51). 63 G4
Lisses (91). 87 F1
Lisseuil (63). 184 D4
Lissey (55). 43 H2
Lissieu (69). 188 B6
Lissy (77). 59 H6
Listrac-de-Durèze (33). 230 D3
Listrac-Médoc (33). 211 F4
Lit-et-Mixe (40). 244 C6
Lithaire (50). 30 D1
Litteau (14). 31 K3
Littenheim (67). 70 C1
Litz (60). 37 K2
Livaie (61). 82 C2
Livarot (14). 54 E1
Liverdun (54). 65 K4
Liverdy-en-Brie (77). 59 J5
Livernon (46). 234 B5
Livers-Cazelles (81). 270 C1
Livet (53). 105 H1
Livet-en-Saosnois (72). 82 E4
Livet-et-Gavet (38). 224 C4
Livet-sur-Authou (27). 34 D4
Livilliers (95). 37 H6
Livinhac-le-Haut (12). 235 F3
la Livinière (34). 290 E4
Livré (53). 104 C4
Livré-sur-Changeon (35). 79 K3
Livron (64). 285 F5
Livron-sur-Drôme (26). 240 C3
Livry (14). 32 A5
Livry (58). 168 C1
Livry-Gargan (93). 59 G3
Livry-Louvercy (51). 41 H6
Livry-sur-Seine (77). 87 H2
Lixhausen (67). 69 D4
Lixheim (57). 67 K3
Lixing-lès-Rouhling (57). 68 C2
Lixing-lès-Saint-Avold (57). 68 A4
Lixy (89). 88 B5
Lizac (82). 249 H6
Lizant (86). 179 H4

Lizeray (36). 148 B4
Lizières (23). 182 A2
Lizine (25). 156 B2
Lizines (77). 88 C2
Lizio (56). 101 H3
Lizos (65). 285 J5
Lizy (02). 40 A1
Lizy-sur-Ourcq (77). 60 A1
la Llagonne (66). 313 J4
Llauro (66). 315 F4
Llo (66). 313 J5
Llupia (66). 315 F3
Lobsann (67). 25 B2
Loc-Brévalaire (29). 46 B4
Loc-Eguiner (29). 46 D5
Loc-Eguiner-Saint-Thégonnec (29) . .46 E6
Loc-Envel (22). 48 A5
Locarn (22). 75 K2
Loché-sur-Indrois (37). 147 F3
Loches (37). 146 D2
Loches-sur-Ource (10). 115 F2
le Locheur (14). 32 C6
Lochieu (01). 190 B5
Lochwiller (67). 70 C2
Locmalo (56). 76 B5
Locmaria (56). 120 C4
Locmaria-Berrien (29). 75 H2
Locmaria-Grand-Champ (56). 101 F4
Locmaria-Plouzané (29). 72 C4
Locmariaquer (56). 100 D6
Locmélar (29). 46 E6
Locminé (56). 101 F2
Locmiquélic (56). 100 A4
Locoal-Mendon (56). 100 C4
Locon (62). 6 A5
Loconville (60). 37 F4
Locqueltas (56). 101 F4
Locquénolé (29). 47 G4
Locquignol (59). 12 E4
Locquirec (29). 47 J3
Locronan (29). 74 C4
Loctudy (29). 98 C3
Locunolé (29). 99 J2
Loddes (03). 186 C1
Lodes (31). 286 D6
Lodève (34). 273 G5
Lods (25). 156 E2
Loeuilley (70). 136 D3
Loeuilly (80). 17 K3
Loffre (59). 11 J2
la Loge (62). 9 J1
la Loge-aux-Chèvres (10). 90 E5
Loge-Fougereuse (85). 161 F2
la Loge-Pomblin (10). 114 A2
Logelheim (68). 96 C4
les Loges (14). 32 A6
les Loges (52). 116 E5
les Loges (76). 14 C4
les Loges-en-Josas (78). 58 C5
les Loges-Marchis (50). 80 C1
les Loges-Margueron (10). 114 B1
les Loges-Saulces (14). 53 K3
les Loges-sur-Brécey (50). 52 B4
Lognes (77). 59 H4
Logny-Bogny (08). 22 A3
Logny-lès-Aubenton (02). 21 J2
Logonna-Daoulas (29). 74 B2
Logrian-Florian (30). 274 D2
Logron (28). 108 E1
Loguivy-Plougras (22). 47 K5
Lohéac (35). 102 E1
Lohitzun-Oyhercq (64). 283 G4
Lohr (67). 69 F6
Lohuec (22). 47 J6
Loigné-sur-Mayenne (53). 104 E4
Loigny-la-Bataille (28). 109 J1
Loiré (49). 124 C1
Loire-les-Marais (17). 177 F4
Loiré-sur-Nie (17). 178 C5
Loire-sur-Rhône (69). 206 A4
Loiron (53). 104 D1
Loisail (61). 83 H2
Loisey-Culey (55). 64 C4
Loisia (39). 173 F4
Loisieux (73). 207 K3
Loisin (74). 174 D6
Loison (55). 26 B5
Loison-sous-Lens (62). 11 F1
Loison-sur-Créquoise (62). 9 H1
Loisy (54). 65 K3
Loisy (71). 172 B3
Loisy-en-Brie (51). 61 J3
Loisy-sur-Marne (51). 63 F4
Loivre (51). 40 E3
Loix (17). 176 A1
Lolif (50). 51 K2
Lolme (24). 232 B4
Lombard (25). 156 A2
Lombard (39). 155 G6
Lombers (81). 270 E4
Lombez (32). 287 G2
Lombia (64). 285 F4
Lombrès (65). 305 G2
Lombreuil (45). 111 H3
Lombron (72). 107 G2
Lomme (59). 6 D4
Lommerange (57). 26 E4
Lommoye (78). 57 G2
Lomné (65). 304 E2
Lomont (70). 139 F1
Lomont-sur-Crête (25). 138 D4
Lompnas (01). 207 H1

Lompnieu (01). 190 A5
Lompret (59). 6 D4
Lonçon (64). 284 C2
la Londe (76). 35 G3
la Londe-les-Maures (83). 298 B6
Londigny (16). 179 G4
Londinières (76). 16 C3
Long (80). 9 H4
Longages (31). 287 K4
Longaulnay (35). 78 D1
Longavesnes (80). 19 H1
Longchamp (21). 136 D6
Longchamp (52). 92 D6
Longchamp (88). 94 E5
Longchamp-sous-Châtenois (88) . .93 H4
Longchamp-sur-Aujon (10). 91 J6
Longchamps (27). 36 C3
Longchamps-sur-Aire (55). 64 C2
Longchaumois (39). 174 A4
Longcochon (39). 156 C6
Longeau-Percey (52). 116 C5
Longeault (21). 136 C6
Longeaux (55). 64 C6
Longechaux (25). 157 F1
Longechenal (38). 207 F6
Longecourt-en-Plaine (21). 154 D1
Longecourt-lès-Culêtre (21). 153 H2
Longemaison (25). 157 F2
Longepierre (71). 154 E4
le Longeron (49). 142 D3
Longes (69). 205 K5
Longessaigne (69). 205 G2
Longevelle (70). 138 D1
Longevelle-lès-Russey (25). 139 G6
Longevelle-sur-Doubs (25). 139 F3
Longèves (17). 177 F1
Longèves (85). 160 D4
la Longeville (25). 157 G3
Longeville (25). 156 D3
Longeville-en-Barrois (55). 64 B4
Longeville-lès-Metz (57). 44 E5
Longeville-lès-Saint-Avold (57). . .45 K5
Longeville-sur-la-Laines (52). . . .91 G2
Longeville-sur-Mer (85). 159 H4
Longeville-sur-Mogne (10). 114 A1
Longevilles-Mont-d'Or (25). 156 E6
Longfossé (62). 2 C6
la Longine (70). 119 F3
Longjumeau (91). 58 E5
Longlaville (54). 26 D2
Longmesnil (76). 16 E5
Longnes (72). 106 B2
Longnes (78). 57 H3
Longny-au-Perche (61). 83 K2
Longperrier (77). 59 H1
Longpont (02). 39 H4
Longpont-sur-Orge (91). 58 E6
Longpré-le-Sec (10). 91 F6
Longpré-les-Corps-Saints (80) . . .9 H6
Longraye (14). 32 B5
Longré (16). 178 E5
Longroy (76). 8 D6
Longsols (10). 90 C3
Longué-Jumelles (49). 126 A4
Longueau (80). 18 B2
Longuefuye (53). 105 G4
Longueil (76). 15 J2
Longueil-Annel (60). 38 E1
Longueil-Sainte-Marie (60). 38 D3
Longuenesse (62). 3 G5
Longuenoë (61). 82 B2
Longuerue (76). 16 B6
Longues-sur-Mer (14). 32 B3
Longuesse (95). 58 A1
Longueval (80). 11 F6
Longueval-Barbonval (02). 40 B3
Longueville (14). 29 J4
Longueville (47). 247 H1
Longueville (50). 30 D6
la Longueville (59). 13 G2
Longueville (62). 2 D5
Longueville (77). 88 D2
Longueville-sur-Aube (10). 89 K1
Longueville-sur-Scie (76). 15 K3
Longuevillette (80). 10 A5
Longuyon (54). 26 B3
Longvic (21). 136 A5
Longvillers (14). 32 B6
Longvilliers (62). 4 B5
Longvilliers (78). 86 B1
Longwé (08). 42 C2
Longwy (54). 26 D2
Longwy-sur-le-Doubs (39). 155 F4
Lonlay-l'Abbaye (61). 53 F6
Lonlay-le-Tesson (61). 53 J6
Lonnes (16). 179 G5
Lonny (08). 22 C3
Lonrai (61). 82 C2
Lons (64). 284 C4
Lons-le-Saunier (39). 173 G2
Lonzac (17). 195 J4
le Lonzac (19). 199 K6
Looberghe (59). 3 G3
Loon-Plage (59). 3 G2
Loos (59). 6 D4
Loos-en-Gohelle (62). 6 B6
Looze (89). 112 E3
Lopérec (29). 74 D2
Loperhet (29). 74 B1
Lopigna (2A). 320 C3
Loqueffret (29). 75 F2
Lor (02). 21 H6

Loray (25). 157 G1
Lorcières (15). 237 G1
Lorcy (45). 111 G2
Lordat (09). 307 K5
Loré (61). 81 G2
Lorentzen (67). 67 K1
Loreto-di-Casinca (2B). 319 J3
Loreto-di-Tallano (2A). 322 E2
Lorette (42). 205 J5
le Loreur (50). 30 E6
Loreux (41). 129 K4
le Lorey (50). 31 F3
Lorey (54). 94 B1
Lorges (41). 109 G5
Lorgies (62). 6 B5
Lorgues (83). 298 C1
Lorient (56). 99 K5
Loriges (03). 185 H1
Lorignac (17). 195 F5
Lorigné (79). 179 F3
Loriol-du-Comtat (84). 257 G6
Loriol-sur-Drôme (26). 240 B3
Lorlanges (43). 219 F2
Lorleau (27). 36 B2
Lormaison (60). 37 H4
Lormaye (28). 57 G6
Lormes (58). 133 J6
Lormont (33). 229 H1
Lornay (74). 190 D5
Loromontzey (54). 94 C2
le Loroux (35). 80 C3
le Loroux-Bottereau (44). 123 J4
Lorp-Sentaraille (09). 306 D2
Lorquin (57). 67 J5
Lorrez-le-Bocage-Préaux (77). 87 K5
Lorris (45). 111 J4
Lorry-lès-Metz (57). 44 E5
Lorry-Mardigny (57). 65 K1
Lortet (65). 305 F2
Loscouët-sur-Meu (22). 78 B3
Los Masos (66). 314 C3
Losne (21). 154 E2
Losse (40). 246 E5
Lostanges (19). 216 A5
Lostroff (57). 67 G2
Lothey (29). 74 E3
le Lou-du-Lac (35). 78 D3
Louailles (72). 105 K5
Louan-Villegruis-Fontaine (77) . . .61 F6
Louannec (22). 48 A2
Louans (37). 146 A1
Louargat (22). 48 B5
Louâtre (02). 39 H4
Loubajac (65). 285 F6
Loubaresse (07). 238 E5
Loubaresse (15). 237 F1
Loubaut (09). 288 A6
Loubédat (32). 266 C4
Loubejac (24). 232 D5
Loubens (09). 307 H2
Loubens (33). 230 C5
Loubens-Lauragais (31). 289 F1
Loubers (81). 270 B1
Loubersan (32). 286 C2
Loubès-Bernac (47). 231 F3
Loubeyrat (63). 184 E6
Loubieng (64). 283 J2
la Loubière (12). 252 C2
Loubières (09). 307 J2
Loubigné (79). 178 D4
Loubillé (79). 178 E4
Loubressac (46). 234 B2
Loucé (61). 54 B5
Loucelles (14). 32 C4
Louchats (33). 229 H6
Louches (62). 2 E4
Louchy-Montfand (03). 185 G5
Loucrup (65). 285 H6
Loudéac (22). 77 G4
Loudenvielle (65). 305 F5
Loudervielle (65). 305 F5
Loudes (43). 220 A5
Loudet (31). 286 C6
Loudrefing (57). 67 G2
Loudun (86). 144 E3
Loué (72). 106 A2
Louer (40). 264 C4
Louerre (49). 125 J5
Louesme (21). 115 H4
Louestault (37). 127 J2
Loueuse (60). 17 G5
Louey (65). 285 G6
Lougé-sur-Maire (61). 54 A5
Lougratte (47). 231 K5
Lougres (25). 139 G3
Louhans (71). 172 D2
Louhossoa (64). 263 D2
Louignac (19). 215 F3
Louin (79). 144 B6
Louisfert (44). 103 J4
Louit (65). 285 J4
Loulans-Verchamp (70). 138 B3
Loulay (17). 177 K4
Loulle (39). 173 K1
la Loupe (28). 84 C2
Loupeigne (02). 40 A4
Loupershouse (57). 68 C3
Loupes (33). 229 J2
Loupfougères (53). 81 J4
Loupia (11). 308 D2
Loupiac (33). 229 K5

Loupiac (46). 233 H2
Loupiac (81). 270 A4
Loupiac-de-la-Réole (33). 230 C6
Loupian (34). 292 E2
Louplande (72). 106 C3
Loupmont (55). 65 F3
Louppy-le-Château (55). 64 A3
Louppy-sur-Loison (55). 43 H1
la Louptière-Thénard (10). 88 E3
Lourches (59). 12 B2
Lourde (31). 305 J2
Lourdes (65). 304 B1
Lourdios-Ichère (64). 302 E1
Lourdoueix-Saint-Michel (36). . . .165 J5
Lourdoueix-Saint-Pierre (23). . . .165 K5
Lourenties (64). 285 F4
Loures-Barousse (65). 305 H2
Louresse-Rochemenier (49). 125 J6
Lourmais (35). 51 G5
Lourmarin (84). 277 H4
Lournand (71). 171 H5
Lourouer-Saint-Laurent (36). . . .166 B3
le Louroux (37). 146 B2
le Louroux-Béconnais (49). 124 D2
Louroux-Bourbonnais (03). 167 K4
Louroux-de-Beaune (03). 184 D1
Louroux-de-Bouble (03). 184 E2
Louroux-Hodement (03). 167 J5
Lourquen (40). 264 D4
Lourties-Monbrun (32). 286 C2
Louslitges (32). 266 D6
Loussous-Débat (32). 266 C5
Loutehel (35). 78 C6
Loutzviller (57). 69 G2
Louvagny (14). 54 C2
Louvaines (49). 104 E6
Louvatange (39). 155 J1
Louvemont (52). 91 J1
Louvemont-Côte-du-Poivre (55) . . .43 H4
Louvencourt (80). 10 C5
Louvenne (39). 173 F5
Louvergny (08). 22 D6
Louverné (53). 105 F1
le Louverot (39). 173 G1
Louversey (27). 56 B2
Louvetot (76). 15 G6
Louvie-Juzon (64). 303 H1
Louvie-Soubiron (64). 303 H2
la Louvière-Lauragais (11). 288 E5
Louvières (14). 29 K6
Louvières (52). 116 C2
Louvières-en-Auge (61). 54 C3
Louviers (27). 35 J5
Louvigné (53). 105 G2
Louvigné-de-Bais (35). 79 K5
Louvigné-du-Désert (35). 80 B2
Louvignies-Quesnoy (59). 12 E3
Louvigny (14). 32 E5
Louvigny (57). 66 A1
Louvigny (64). 284 C1
Louvigny (72). 82 E4
Louvil (59). 7 F5
Louville-la-Chenard (28). 85 K4
Louvilliers-en-Drouais (28). 56 E5
Louvilliers-lès-Perche (28). 56 C6
Louvois (51). 41 F5
Louvrechy (80). 18 B4
Louvres (95). 59 F1
Louvroil (59). 13 H3
Louye (27). 56 E4
Louzac-Saint-André (16). 195 J2
Louze (52). 91 G3
Louzes (72). 83 F3
Louzignac (17). 196 A1
Louzouer (45). 111 K2
Louzy (79). 144 B3
Lovagny (74). 190 E5
Loyat (56). 101 K1
la Loye (39). 155 H3
Loye-sur-Arnon (18). 167 F2
la Loyère (71). 154 C3
Loyettes (01). 206 E2
Lozanne (69). 188 B6
Lozay (17). 177 K4
Loze (82). 250 D3
Lozinghem (62). 5 J5
Lozon (50). 31 F3
Lozzi (2B). 318 D5
Luant (36). 165 H1
le Luart (72). 107 H2
Lubbon (40). 246 E5
Lubécourt (57). 66 D3
Lubersac (19). 199 G6
Lubey (54). 26 E6
Lubilhac (43). 219 F3
Lubine (88). 96 A1
Lublé (37). 126 E3
Lubret-Saint-Luc (65). 285 K4
Luby-Betmont (65). 285 K4
Luc (12). 252 B3
Luc (48). 238 C4
Luc (65). 285 J6
le Luc (83). 298 C2
Luc-Armau (64). 285 G3
Luc-en-Diois (26). 241 J4
Luc-sur-Aude (11). 309 F3
Luc-sur-Mer (14). 32 E3
Luc-sur-Orbieu (11). 291 F6
Lucarré (64). 285 F3
Luçay-le-Libre (36). 148 B3

Luçay-le-Mâle (36) . . . 147 H2
Lucbardez-et-Bargues (40) . . . 265 H1
Lucciana (2B) . . . 319 H3
Lucé (28) . . . 85 G3
Lucé (61) . . . 81 G1
Lucé-sous-Ballon (72) . . . 82 E6
Luceau (72) . . . 107 F6
Lucelle (68) . . . 97 B6
Lucenay (69) . . . 188 B6
Lucenay-le-Duc (21) . . . 135 F2
Lucenay-lès-Aix (58) . . . 169 F2
Lucenay-l'Évêque (71) . . . 152 E3
Lucéram (06) . . . 281 H1
la Lucerne-d'Outremer (50) . . . 51 J1
Lucey (21) . . . 115 J4
Lucey (54) . . . 65 H4
Lucey (73) . . . 208 A2
Lucgarier (64) . . . 284 E5
Luchapt (86) . . . 180 C3
Luchat (17) . . . 195 F2
Luché-Pringé (72) . . . 106 C6
Luché-sur-Brioux (79) . . . 178 D3
Luché-Thouarsais (79) . . . 144 A5
Lucheux (80) . . . 10 B4
Luchy (60) . . . 17 K6
Lucinges (74) . . . 191 H2
Lucmau (33) . . . 246 C2
Luçon (85) . . . 160 A4
Lucq-de-Béarn (64) . . . 283 K4
Lucquy (08) . . . 22 B6
les Lucs-sur-Boulogne (85) . . . 141 J5
Lucy (57) . . . 66 D1
Lucy (76) . . . 16 D3
Lucy-le-Bocage (02) . . . 60 D1
Lucy-le-Bois (89) . . . 133 K2
Lucy-sur-Cure (89) . . . 133 H2
Lucy-sur-Yonne (89) . . . 133 G3
le Lude (72) . . . 126 D1
Ludes (51) . . . 41 F5
Ludesse (63) . . . 202 D4
Ludiès (09) . . . 307 K1
Ludon-Médoc (33) . . . 211 G6
Ludres (54) . . . 66 A6
Lüe (40) . . . 245 F4
Lué-en-Baugeois (49) . . . 125 K3
Luemschwiller (68) . . . 97 B3
Lugagnac (46) . . . 250 D2
Lugagnan (65) . . . 304 B1
Lugaignac (33) . . . 230 B2
Lugan (12) . . . 251 J1
Lugan (81) . . . 269 K5
Lugarde (15) . . . 218 D2
Lugasson (33) . . . 230 B3
Luglon (40) . . . 245 H5
Lugny (02) . . . 20 E3
Lugny (71) . . . 171 J4
Lugny-Bourbonnais (18) . . . 149 K5
Lugny-Champagne (18) . . . 150 A1
Lugny-lès-Charolles (71) . . . 170 D5
Lugo-di-Nazza (2B) . . . 321 H3
Lugon-et-l'Ile-du-Carnay (33) . . . 211 K6
Lugos (33) . . . 228 D6
Lugrin (74) . . . 175 H5
Lugy (62) . . . 5 F5
le Luhier (25) . . . 157 H1
Luigné (49) . . . 125 H6
Luigny (28) . . . 84 C5
Luisant (28) . . . 85 G3
Luisetaines (77) . . . 88 C3
Luitré (35) . . . 80 B4
Lullin (74) . . . 175 F6
Lully (74) . . . 174 E6
Lumbin (38) . . . 224 C1
Lumbres (62) . . . 3 H5
Lumeau (28) . . . 109 K1
Lumes (08) . . . 22 D4
Lumigny-Nesles-Ormeaux (77) . . . 60 A5
Lumio (2B) . . . 318 D3
Lunac (12) . . . 251 G4
Lunan (46) . . . 234 E5
Lunas (24) . . . 231 H1
Lunas (34) . . . 272 E5
Lunax (31) . . . 286 D4
Lunay (41) . . . 108 A5
Luneau (03) . . . 170 A6
Lunegarde (46) . . . 234 A4
Lunel (34) . . . 274 E5
Lunel-Viel (34) . . . 274 E5
Luneray (76) . . . 15 J3
Lunery (18) . . . 149 F5
Lunéville (54) . . . 66 D6
le Luot (50) . . . 52 A4
Lupcourt (54) . . . 66 B6
Lupé (42) . . . 222 A1
Lupersat (23) . . . 183 H5
Lupiac (32) . . . 266 D5
Luplanté (28) . . . 85 F5
Luppé-Violles (32) . . . 266 A4
Luppy (57) . . . 66 C1
Lupsault (16) . . . 178 E5
Lupstein (67) . . . 70 C1
Luquet (65) . . . 285 F4
Lurais (36) . . . 164 B2
Luray (28) . . . 57 F5
Lurbe-Saint-Christau (64) . . . 284 A6
Lurcy (42) . . . 188 C1
Lurcy-le-Bourg (58) . . . 151 G2
Lurcy-Lévis (03) . . . 168 A1
Luré (42) . . . 186 D6
Lure (70) . . . 118 E6
Lureuil (36) . . . 164 C1
Luri (2B) . . . 317 D3

Luriecq (42) . . . 204 D6
Lurs (04) . . . 278 C1
Lury-sur-Arnon (18) . . . 148 D2
Lus-la-Croix-Haute (26) . . . 242 A4
Lusanger (44) . . . 103 G4
Luscan (31) . . . 305 J2
Lusignac (24) . . . 213 G2
Lusignan (86) . . . 162 D5
Lusignan-Petit (47) . . . 248 A3
Lusigny (03) . . . 169 G3
Lusigny-sur-Barse (10) . . . 90 C5
Lusigny-sur-Ouche (21) . . . 153 J2
Lussac (16) . . . 197 H1
Lussac (17) . . . 195 H5
Lussac (33) . . . 212 C6
Lussac-les-Châteaux (86) . . . 163 J5
Lussac-les-Églises (87) . . . 164 D6
Lussagnet (40) . . . 265 K4
Lussagnet-Lusson (64) . . . 284 E2
Lussan (30) . . . 255 K5
Lussan (32) . . . 267 K6
Lussan-Adeilhac (31) . . . 287 G4
Lussant (17) . . . 177 G5
Lussas (07) . . . 239 J5
Lussas-et-Nontronneau (24) . . . 197 J5
Lussat (23) . . . 183 H3
Lussat (63) . . . 202 E1
Lussault-sur-Loire (37) . . . 128 A4
Lusse (88) . . . 95 K4
Lusseray (79) . . . 178 D3
Lustar (65) . . . 286 A5
Luthenay-Uxeloup (58) . . . 151 F6
Lutilhous (65) . . . 286 A6
Luttange (57) . . . 27 J5
Luttenbach-près-Munster (68) . . . 119 K1
Lutter (68) . . . 97 C6
Lutterbach (68) . . . 97 B2
Lutz-en-Dunois (28) . . . 109 F2
Lutzelbourg (57) . . . 70 A1
Lutzelhouse (67) . . . 70 B4
Luvigny (88) . . . 95 J1
Lux (21) . . . 136 C3
Lux (31) . . . 289 F3
Lux (71) . . . 171 K1
Luxé (16) . . . 179 F6
Luxe-Sumberraute (64) . . . 283 F3
Luxémont-et-Villotte (51) . . . 63 F5
Luxeuil-les-Bains (70) . . . 118 D4
Luxey (40) . . . 245 K3
Luxiol (25) . . . 138 D4
Luyères (10) . . . 90 C3
Luynes (37) . . . 127 H5
Luz-Saint-Sauveur (65) . . . 304 B4
Luzancy (77) . . . 60 C2
Luzarches (95) . . . 38 A6
Luzay (79) . . . 144 B4
Luzé (37) . . . 145 H3
Luze (70) . . . 139 G1
Luzech (46) . . . 249 J1
Luzenac (09) . . . 308 A5
Luzeret (36) . . . 165 F4
la Luzerne (50) . . . 31 H3
Luzillat (63) . . . 185 J5
Luzillé (37) . . . 128 C6
Luzinay (38) . . . 206 C4
Luzoir (02) . . . 21 G1
Luzy (58) . . . 152 C6
Luzy-Saint-Martin (55) . . . 23 H6
Luzy-sur-Marne (52) . . . 116 B2
Ly-Fontaine (02) . . . 20 A4
Lyas (07) . . . 239 K3
Lyaud (74) . . . 175 F5
Lye (36) . . . 147 H1
Lynde (59) . . . 3 H5
Lyoffans (70) . . . 119 F6
Lyon (69) . . . 206 A2
Lyons-la-Forêt (27) . . . 36 B2
Lys (58) . . . 133 G5
Lys (64) . . . 284 D6
Lys-lez-Lannoy (59) . . . 7 F3
Lys-Saint-Georges (36) . . . 165 K3

M

Maast-et-Violaine (02) . . . 39 K4
Maâtz (52) . . . 116 E6
Mably (42) . . . 186 E4
Macau (33) . . . 211 G5
Macaye (64) . . . 282 D3
Macé (61) . . . 54 D6
Macey (10) . . . 89 K5
Macey (50) . . . 51 J4
Machault (08) . . . 41 K3
Machault (77) . . . 87 J3
Maché (85) . . . 141 G6
Machecoul (44) . . . 141 F3
Mâchecourt (02) . . . 21 F5
Machemont (60) . . . 38 F1
Macheren (57) . . . 68 A3
Machézal (42) . . . 187 H6
Machiel (80) . . . 9 G3
Machilly (74) . . . 191 H1
la Machine (58) . . . 151 G5
Machy (10) . . . 114 A1
Machy (80) . . . 9 F3
Mackenheim (67) . . . 71 C6
Mackwiller (67) . . . 67 K1
Maclas (42) . . . 222 A1
Macogny (02) . . . 39 H5
Mâcon (71) . . . 188 C1

Maconcourt (88) . . . 93 J3
Maconge (21) . . . 153 H1
Macornay (39) . . . 173 G3
Mâcot-la-Plagne (73) . . . 209 J4
Macqueville (17) . . . 196 A1
Macquigny (02) . . . 20 C1
Madaillan (47) . . . 248 B3
Madecourt (88) . . . 94 A5
Madegney (88) . . . 94 B4
la Madelaine-sous-Montreuil (62) . . . 4 C6
la Madeleine (59) . . . 6 E4
la Madeleine-Bouvet (61) . . . 84 B2
la Madeleine-de-Nonancourt (27) . . . 56 D4
la Madeleine-sur-Loing (77) . . . 87 H6
la Madeleine-Villefrouin (41) . . . 109 F5
Madic (15) . . . 217 H1
Madière (09) . . . 307 H1
Madirac (33) . . . 229 J3
Madiran (65) . . . 285 G1
Madonne-et-Lamerey (88) . . . 94 B5
Madranges (19) . . . 200 A6
Madré (53) . . . 81 J2
Madriat (63) . . . 202 D6
Maël-Carhaix (22) . . . 75 K3
Maël-Pestivien (22) . . . 76 B1
Maennolsheim (67) . . . 70 C2
Maffliers (95) . . . 37 K6
Maffrécourt (51) . . . 42 C6
Magalas (34) . . . 292 A2
la Magdelaine-sur-Tarn (31) . . . 269 H4
la Magdeleine (16) . . . 179 F4
le Mage (61) . . . 83 K2
Magenta (51) . . . 61 K1
les Mages (30) . . . 255 H4
Magescq (40) . . . 262 D3
Magland (74) . . . 192 A4
Magnac-Bourg (87) . . . 199 G4
Magnac-Laval (87) . . . 181 G2
Magnac-Lavalette-Villars (16) . . . 197 F5
Magnac-sur-Touvre (16) . . . 196 E3
Magnan (32) . . . 266 A4
Magnant (10) . . . 90 E6
Magnanville (78) . . . 57 J2
Magnas (32) . . . 267 K2
Magnat-l'Étrange (23) . . . 201 F2
Magné (79) . . . 161 G6
Magné (86) . . . 163 F6
Magnet (03) . . . 185 K2
Magneux (51) . . . 40 C3
Magneux (52) . . . 91 K2
Magneux-Haute-Rive (42) . . . 204 E3
Magneville (50) . . . 28 D5
Magnicourt (10) . . . 90 D3
Magnicourt-en-Comte (62) . . . 10 C1
Magnicourt-sur-Canche (62) . . . 10 B1
Magnien (21) . . . 153 G2
Magnières (54) . . . 94 E2
Magnieu (01) . . . 207 K1
les Magnils-Reigniers (85) . . . 159 K4
Magnivray (70) . . . 118 E5
Magnoncourt (70) . . . 118 C3
le Magnoray (70) . . . 138 A3
Magny (28) . . . 84 E4
le Magny (36) . . . 166 B3
Magny (68) . . . 139 K1
les Magny (70) . . . 138 C2
le Magny (88) . . . 118 B2
Magny (89) . . . 134 A3
Magny-Châtelard (25) . . . 138 D6
Magny-Cours (58) . . . 150 E5
Magny-Danigon (70) . . . 119 H6
Magny en-Bessin (14) . . . 32 B4
Magny-en-Vexin (95) . . . 36 E5
Magny-Fouchard (10) . . . 91 F5
Magny-Jobert (70) . . . 119 F6
Magny-la-Campagne (14) . . . 54 B1
Magny-la-Fosse (02) . . . 19 K1
Magny-la-Ville (21) . . . 134 E3
Magny-Lambert (21) . . . 135 F1
Magny-le-Désert (61) . . . 81 K1
Magny-le-Freule (14) . . . 33 G6
Magny-le-Hongre (77) . . . 59 J3
Magny-lès-Aubigny (21) . . . 154 D2
Magny-les-Hameaux (78) . . . 58 B5
Magny-lès-Jussey (70) . . . 117 K4
Magny-lès-Villers (21) . . . 154 A2
Magny-Lormes (58) . . . 133 J6
Magny-Montarlot (21) . . . 136 D6
Magny-Saint-Médard (21) . . . 136 C4
Magny-sur-Tille (21) . . . 136 B6
Magny-Vernois (70) . . . 118 E6
Magoar (22) . . . 76 C1
Magrie (11) . . . 308 E2
Magrin (81) . . . 270 B6
Magstatt-le-Bas (68) . . . 97 D4
Magstatt-le-Haut (68) . . . 97 C4
Mahalon (29) . . . 73 D3
Mahéru (61) . . . 55 G6
Maîche (25) . . . 139 H5
Maidières (54) . . . 65 J2
Maignaut-Tauzia (32) . . . 267 G2
Maigné (72) . . . 106 B3
Maignelay-Montigny (60) . . . 18 D6
Mailhac (11) . . . 291 G4
Mailhac-sur-Benaize (87) . . . 181 H1
Mailhoc (81) . . . 270 D1
Mailholas (31) . . . 287 K5
Maillane (13) . . . 276 B3
Maillas (40) . . . 246 D4
Maillat (01) . . . 189 K3
Maillé (37) . . . 145 J3
Maillé (85) . . . 160 E6

Maillé (86) . . . 162 C2
Maillebois (28) . . . 56 D6
la Mailleraye-sur-Seine (76) . . . 34 E1
Maillères (40) . . . 246 A6
Mailleroncourt-Charette (70) . . . 118 C5
Mailleroncourt-Saint-Pancras (70) . . . 118 A3
Maillet (03) . . . 167 H5
Maillet (36) . . . 165 J3
Mailley-et-Chazelot (70) . . . 138 A2
Maillezais (85) . . . 160 E5
Maillot (89) . . . 88 D6
Mailly (71) . . . 187 F2
Mailly-Champagne (51) . . . 41 F5
Mailly-la-Ville (89) . . . 133 H2
Mailly-le-Camp (10) . . . 62 C6
Mailly-le-Château (89) . . . 133 G2
Mailly-Maillet (80) . . . 10 D5
Mailly-Raineval (80) . . . 18 C4
Mailly-sur-Seille (54) . . . 66 B2
les Maillys (21) . . . 155 F2
Maimbeville (60) . . . 38 B2
Maincy (77) . . . 87 H2
Maine-de-Boixe (16) . . . 196 E1
Mainfonds (16) . . . 196 C5
Maing (59) . . . 12 C2
Mainneville (27) . . . 36 D3
Mainsat (23) . . . 183 J4
Maintenay (62) . . . 9 G2
Maintenon (28) . . . 85 H1
Mainvillers (57) . . . 45 J6
Mainvilliers (28) . . . 85 G3
Mainvilliers (45) . . . 86 D5
Mainxe (16) . . . 196 A3
Mainzac (16) . . . 197 H5
Mairé (86) . . . 146 A5
Mairé-Levescault (79) . . . 179 F3
Mairieux (59) . . . 13 H2
Mairy (08) . . . 23 G5
Mairy-Mainville (54) . . . 26 E5
Mairy-sur-Marne (51) . . . 62 D3
Maisdon-sur-Sèvre (44) . . . 123 J5
Maisey-le-Duc (21) . . . 115 G4
Maisnières (80) . . . 8 E6
le Maisnil (59) . . . 6 C4
Maisnil (62) . . . 10 B2
Maisnil-lès-Ruitz (62) . . . 5 K6
Maisod (39) . . . 173 H4
Maison-des-Champs (10) . . . 91 F5
la Maison-Dieu (58) . . . 133 G4
Maison-Feyne (23) . . . 165 J6
Maison-Maugis (61) . . . 83 J3
Maison-Ponthieu (80) . . . 9 J4
Maison-Roland (80) . . . 9 H5
Maison-Rouge (77) . . . 88 C1
Maisoncelle (62) . . . 5 F6
Maisoncelle-et-Villers (08) . . . 23 F5
Maisoncelle-Saint-Pierre (60) . . . 37 H1
Maisoncelle-Tuilerie (60) . . . 18 A6
Maisoncelles (52) . . . 92 E6
Maisoncelles (72) . . . 107 H3
Maisoncelles-du-Maine (53) . . . 105 F3
Maisoncelles-en-Brie (77) . . . 60 A3
Maisoncelles-en-Gâtinais (77) . . . 87 H6
Maisoncelles-la-Jourdan (14) . . . 52 E4
Maisoncelles-Pelvey (14) . . . 32 B6
Maisoncelles-sur-Ajon (14) . . . 32 C6
Maisonnais (18) . . . 166 D3
Maisonnais-sur-Tardoire (87) . . . 197 K3
Maisonnay (79) . . . 178 E2
Maisonneuve (86) . . . 162 C1
Maisonnisses (23) . . . 182 D4
Maisons (11) . . . 309 K3
Maisons (14) . . . 32 A3
Maisons (28) . . . 85 K3
Maisons-Alfort (94) . . . 59 F4
Maisons-du-Bois-Lièvremont (25) . . . 157 F3
Maisons-en-Champagne (51) . . . 62 E4
Maisons-Laffitte (78) . . . 58 C2
Maisons-lès-Chaource (10) . . . 114 B2
Maisons-lès-Soulaines (10) . . . 91 H4
Maisonsgoutte (67) . . . 70 B6
Maisontiers (79) . . . 144 A6
Maisse (91) . . . 86 E3
Maissemy (02) . . . 19 J2
Maixe (54) . . . 66 D5
Maizeray (55) . . . 44 A5
Maizeroy (57) . . . 45 H5
Maizery (57) . . . 45 G5
Maizet (14) . . . 32 D6
Maizey (55) . . . 64 E2
Maizicourt (80) . . . 9 J4
Maizières (14) . . . 54 B1
Maizières (52) . . . 92 A2
Maizières (54) . . . 65 K6
Maizières (62) . . . 10 C2
Maizières (70) . . . 137 K3
Maizières-la-Grande-Paroisse (10) . . . 89 J2
Maizières-lès-Brienne (10) . . . 91 F3
Maizières-lès-Metz (57) . . . 27 G6
Maizières-lès-Vic (57) . . . 67 G4
Maizières-sur-Amance (52) . . . 117 F4
Maizilly (42) . . . 187 G2
Maizy (02) . . . 40 C2
Majastres (04) . . . 279 G2
Malabat (32) . . . 285 J2
la Malachère (70) . . . 138 A3
Malafretaz (01) . . . 172 C6
Mâlain (21) . . . 135 J5
Malaincourt (88) . . . 93 G5
Malaincourt-sur-Meuse (52) . . . 93 F6
Malakoff (92) . . . 58 E4
Malancourt (55) . . . 43 F4

Malandry (08) . . . 23 H5
Malange (39) . . . 155 H1
Malans (25) . . . 156 B2
Malans (70) . . . 137 F6
Malansac (56) . . . 102 A3
Malarce-sur-la-Thines (07) . . . 255 G1
Malataverne (26) . . . 240 B6
Malaucène (84) . . . 257 H4
Malaucourt-sur-Seille (57) . . . 66 C3
Malaunay (76) . . . 15 K6
Malause (82) . . . 249 F6
Malaussanne (64) . . . 284 C1
Malaussène (06) . . . 281 F1
Malauzat (63) . . . 202 D1
Malaville (16) . . . 196 B4
Malavillers (54) . . . 26 E4
Malay (71) . . . 171 H3
Malay-le-Grand (89) . . . 88 E6
Malay-le-Petit (89) . . . 88 E6
Malbo (15) . . . 218 A6
Malbosc (07) . . . 255 G3
Malbouhans (70) . . . 119 F5
Malbouzon (48) . . . 236 E4
Malbrans (25) . . . 156 C2
Malbuisson (25) . . . 156 E5
Mâle (61) . . . 83 K5
Malegoude (09) . . . 308 C1
Malemort-du-Comtat (84) . . . 257 H6
Malemort-sur-Corrèze (19) . . . 215 J4
la Malène (48) . . . 253 J2
Malesherbes (45) . . . 87 F5
Malestroit (56) . . . 101 K3
Malétable (61) . . . 83 J1
Maleville (12) . . . 251 G2
Malguénac (56) . . . 76 D5
la Malhoure (22) . . . 77 J2
Malicornay (36) . . . 165 H3
Malicorne (03) . . . 184 C1
Malicorne (89) . . . 112 B5
Malicorne-sur-Sarthe (72) . . . 106 B5
Maligny (21) . . . 153 H2
Maligny (89) . . . 113 H4
Malijai (04) . . . 259 G6
Malincourt (59) . . . 11 K6
Malintrat (63) . . . 202 E1
Malissard (26) . . . 240 D1
Mallefougasse-Augès (04) . . . 259 F5
Malleloy (54) . . . 66 A3
Mallemoisson (04) . . . 259 H6
Mallemort (13) . . . 277 F4
Malléon (09) . . . 307 K2
Malleret (23) . . . 201 F2
Malleret-Boussac (23) . . . 166 C6
Mallerey (39) . . . 173 F2
Malleval (38) . . . 223 H4
Malleval (42) . . . 222 A1
Malleville-les-Grès (76) . . . 15 F2
Malleville-sur-le-Bec (27) . . . 34 E4
Mallièvre (85) . . . 142 E4
Malling (57) . . . 27 H3
Malloué (14) . . . 31 J5
la Malmaison (02) . . . 40 E1
Malmerspach (68) . . . 119 K3
Malmy (51) . . . 42 C5
Malons-et-Elze (30) . . . 255 G2
Malouy (27) . . . 34 C6
Malpart (80) . . . 18 C4
Malpas (25) . . . 156 E5
Malras (11) . . . 308 E2
Malrevers (43) . . . 220 D5
Malroy (57) . . . 27 H6
Maltat (71) . . . 169 K2
Maltot (14) . . . 32 D5
Malval (23) . . . 166 A6
Malvalette (43) . . . 220 E1
Malvès-en-Minervois (11) . . . 290 C5
Malvezie (31) . . . 305 J2
Malvières (43) . . . 220 A2
Malviès (11) . . . 308 E1
Malville (44) . . . 122 D2
Malvillers (70) . . . 117 H5
Malzéville (54) . . . 66 A4
le Malzieu-Forain (48) . . . 237 G2
le Malzieu-Ville (48) . . . 237 G2
Malzy (02) . . . 20 E2
Mamers (72) . . . 83 F4
Mametz (62) . . . 3 H6
Mametz (80) . . . 10 E6
Mamey (54) . . . 65 J2
Mamirolle (25) . . . 138 B6
Manas (26) . . . 240 D5
Manas-Bastanous (32) . . . 286 A3
Manaurie (24) . . . 214 D6
Mance (54) . . . 26 E5
la Mancelière (28) . . . 56 B6
la Mancellière-sur-Vire (50) . . . 31 H4
Mancenans (25) . . . 138 E3
Mancenans-Lizerne (25) . . . 139 H5
Mancey (71) . . . 171 K3
Manchecourt (45) . . . 86 E5
Manciet (32) . . . 266 C4
Mancieulles (54) . . . 26 E5
Mancioux (31) . . . 287 G6
Mancy (51) . . . 61 K2
Mandagout (30) . . . 273 K1
Mandailles-Saint-Julien (15) . . . 217 K5
Mandelieu-la-Napoule (06) . . . 280 D6
Manderen (57) . . . 27 K3
Mandeure (25) . . . 139 H3
Mandeville (27) . . . 35 H4
Mandeville-en-Bessin (14) . . . 31 K1
Mandray (88) . . . 95 J5

Mandres (27) . . . 56 A5
Mandres-aux-Quatre-Tours (54) . . 65 G3
Mandres-en-Barrois (55) . . 92 D2
Mandres-la-Côte (52) . . 116 D1
Mandres-les-Roses (94) . . 59 G5
Mandres-sur-Vair (88) . . 93 J5
Mandrevillars (70) . . 139 G1
Manduel (30) . . 275 H3
Mane (04) . . 278 B1
Mane (31) . . 306 B1
Manéglise (76) . . 14 C6
Manéhouville (76) . . 15 K2
Manent-Montané (32) . . 286 D4
Manerbe (14) . . 33 K5
Mangiennes (55) . . 26 B4
Manglieu (63) . . 203 F4
Mangonville (54) . . 94 B2
Manhac (12) . . 252 A4
Manheulles (55) . . 43 K5
Manhoué (57) . . 66 C3
Manicamp (02) . . 19 J6
Manigod (74) . . 191 H6
Manin (62) . . 10 C2
Maninghem (62) . . 4 D5
Maninghen-Henne (62) . . 2 B1
Maniquerville (76) . . 14 C4
Manlay (21) . . 153 F2
Manneville-ès-Plains (76) . . 15 G2
Manneville-la-Goupil (76) . . 14 C5
Manneville-la-Pipard (14) . . 33 K4
Manneville-la-Raoult (27) . . 34 A2
Manneville-sur-Risle (27) . . 34 C3
Mannevillette (76) . . 14 B5
Mano (40) . . 245 J1
le Manoir (14) . . 32 C3
le Manoir (27) . . 35 J3
Manois (52) . . 92 D4
Manom (57) . . 27 G4
Manoncourt-en-Vermois (54) . . 66 B6
Manoncourt-en-Woëvre (54) . . 65 J4
Manonville (54) . . 65 H3
Manonviller (54) . . 67 F6
Manosque (04) . . 278 B3
Manot (16) . . 180 B5
Manou (28) . . 84 B2
Manre (08) . . 42 B4
le Mans (72) . . 106 E2
Mansac (19) . . 215 G4
Mansan (65) . . 285 J4
Mansat-la-Courrière (23) . . 182 C5
Mansempuy (32) . . 268 A4
Mansencôme (32) . . 267 F3
Manses (09) . . 308 A1
Mansigné (72) . . 106 D6
Mansle (16) . . 179 G6
Manso (2B) . . 316 E3
Mansonville (82) . . 268 A1
Manspach (68) . . 97 A4
Mant (40) . . 265 G6
Mantallot (22) . . 48 B3
Mantenay-Montlin (01) . . 172 B5
Mantes-la-Jolie (78) . . 57 J2
Mantes-la-Ville (78) . . 57 J2
Mantet (66) . . 314 A5
Manteyer (05) . . 242 D5
Manthelan (37) . . 146 B2
Manthelon (27) . . 56 C3
Manthes (26) . . 222 D2
Mantilly (61) . . 80 E1
Mantoche (70) . . 137 F4
Mantry (39) . . 155 H6
Manvieux (14) . . 32 B3
Many (57) . . 66 D1
Manzac-sur-Vern (24) . . 213 J5
Manzat (63) . . 184 D5
Manziat (01) . . 172 A6
Marac (52) . . 116 B3
Marainville-sur-Madon (88) . . 94 A3
Marainviller (54) . . 66 E6
le Marais-la-Chapelle (14) . . 54 C3
Marais-Vernier (27) . . 34 C2
Marambat (32) . . 267 F4
Marandeuil (21) . . 136 D5
Marange-Silvange (57) . . 27 G6
Marange-Zondrange (57) . . 45 J5
Marans (17) . . 160 C6
Marans (49) . . 124 D1
Maransin (33) . . 212 A5
Marant (62) . . 4 C6
Maranville (52) . . 115 J1
Maranwez (08) . . 21 K4
Marast (70) . . 138 D2
Marat (63) . . 203 K3
Maraussan (34) . . 291 K4
Maravat (32) . . 267 K4
Maray (41) . . 148 B1
Maraye-en-Othe (10) . . 89 J6
Marbache (54) . . 65 K3
Marbaix (59) . . 13 G4
Marbeuf (27) . . 35 G5
Marbéville (52) . . 91 K5
Marboué (28) . . 108 E1
Marboz (01) . . 172 D6
Marby (08) . . 22 A2
Marc-la-Tour (19) . . 216 B3
Marçais (18) . . 167 F2
Marçay (37) . . 145 F2
Marçay (86) . . 162 E5
Marcé (49) . . 125 J2
Marcé-sur-Esves (37) . . 145 K3
Marcei (61) . . 54 C6
Marcelcave (80) . . 18 D2

Marcellaz (74) . . 191 H2
Marcellaz-Albanais (74) . . 190 E6
Marcellois (21) . . 135 G5
Marcellus (47) . . 247 G1
Marcenais (33) . . 211 K5
Marcenat (03) . . 185 J2
Marcenat (15) . . 218 B2
Marcenay (21) . . 114 E4
Marcenod (42) . . 205 H4
Marcey-les-Grèves (50) . . 51 K3
Marchainville (61) . . 84 A1
Marchais (02) . . 20 E6
Marchais-Beton (89) . . 112 B5
Marchais-en-Brie (02) . . 61 F3
Marchamp (01) . . 207 H1
Marchampt (69) . . 187 K3
Marchastel (15) . . 218 A2
Marchastel (48) . . 236 E5
Marchaux (25) . . 138 B5
la Marche (58) . . 150 C2
Marché-Allouarde (80) . . 19 G4
Marchélepot (80) . . 19 G3
Marchemaisons (61) . . 83 F2
Marchémoret (77) . . 59 J1
Marchenoir (41) . . 109 F5
Marcheprime (33) . . 228 E4
Marches (26) . . 222 E6
les Marches (73) . . 208 C5
Marcheseuil (21) . . 153 F2
Marchésieux (50) . . 31 F2
Marcheville (28) . . 84 E4
Marchéville-en-Woëvre (55) . . 44 A6
Marchezais (28) . . 57 G4
Marchiennes (59) . . 11 K1
Marciac (32) . . 285 J1
Marcieu (38) . . 242 A1
Marcieux (73) . . 207 K3
Marcigny (71) . . 186 E1
Marcigny-sous-Thil (21) . . 134 E4
Marcilhac-sur-Célé (46) . . 234 B6
Marcillac (33) . . 211 H2
Marcillac-la-Croisille (19) . . 216 D3
Marcillac-la-Croze (19) . . 216 A5
Marcillac-Lanville (16) . . 196 C1
Marcillac-Saint-Quentin (24) . . 233 F1
Marcillac-Vallon (12) . . 252 A1
Marcillat (63) . . 184 E4
Marcillat-en-Combraille (03) . . 184 A3
Marcillé-la-Ville (53) . . 81 H4
Marcillé-Raoul (35) . . 79 H1
Marcillé-Robert (35) . . 79 K6
Marcilloles (38) . . 223 F1
Marcilly (50) . . 52 A5
Marcilly (77) . . 59 K1
Marcilly-d'Azergues (69) . . 188 B6
Marcilly-en-Bassigny (52) . . 116 E3
Marcilly-en-Beauce (41) . . 108 B6
Marcilly-en-Gault (41) . . 129 K4
Marcilly-en-Villette (45) . . 110 B6
Marcilly-la-Campagne (27) . . 56 D4
Marcilly-la-Gueurce (71) . . 170 E5
Marcilly-le-Châtel (42) . . 204 C3
Marcilly-le-Hayer (10) . . 89 G4
Marcilly-lès-Buxy (71) . . 171 G1
Marcilly-lès-Vitteaux (21) . . 135 F4
Marcilly-Ogny (21) . . 134 E6
Marcilly-sur-Eure (27) . . 57 F4
Marcilly-sur-Maulne (37) . . 126 E2
Marcilly-sur-Seine (51) . . 89 H1
Marcilly-sur-Tille (21) . . 136 B3
Marcilly-sur-Vienne (37) . . 145 J3
Marck (62) . . 2 D2
Marckolsheim (67) . . 71 C6
Marclopt (42) . . 204 E3
Marcoing (59) . . 11 J5
Marcolès (15) . . 235 G3
Marcollin (38) . . 222 E2
Marcols-les-Eaux (07) . . 239 H2
Marçon (72) . . 107 G6
Marconne (62) . . 9 J2
Marconnelle (62) . . 9 H2
Marcorignan (11) . . 291 H5
Marcoussis (91) . . 58 D6
Marcoux (04) . . 259 K5
Marcoux (42) . . 204 C3
Marcq (08) . . 42 D3
Marcq (78) . . 57 K3
Marcq-en-Barœul (59) . . 6 E3
Marcq-en-Ostrevent (59) . . 11 K3
Marcy (02) . . 20 B2
Marcy (58) . . 132 E2
Marcy (69) . . 188 B6
Marcy-l'Étoile (69) . . 205 K2
Marcy-sous-Marle (02) . . 20 E4
Mardeuil (51) . . 61 K1
Mardié (45) . . 110 B4
Mardilly (61) . . 55 F3
Mardor (52) . . 116 B4
Mardore (69) . . 187 H4
Mareau-aux-Bois (45) . . 110 D1
Mareau-aux-Prés (45) . . 109 K5
Mareil-en-Champagne (72) . . 106 A3
Mareil-en-France (95) . . 59 F1
Mareil-le-Guyon (78) . . 57 K4
Mareil-Marly (78) . . 58 C3
Mareil-sur-Loir (72) . . 106 C6
Mareil-sur-Mauldre (78) . . 58 A3
Mareilles (52) . . 92 C6
Marenla (62) . . 4 D6
Marennes (17) . . 194 B1
Marennes (69) . . 206 B4
Mareschi (72) . . 82 D5

Maresches (59) . . 12 D2
Maresquel-Ecquemicourt (62) . . 9 H1
Marest (62) . . 5 H6
Marest-Dampcourt (02) . . 19 J5
Marest-sur-Matz (60) . . 38 D1
Marestaing (32) . . 287 H1
Marestmontiers (80) . . 18 D4
Maresville (62) . . 4 C6
les Marêts (77) . . 60 D6
Maretz (59) . . 12 C6
Mareugheol (63) . . 202 E6
Mareuil (16) . . 196 B2
Mareuil (24) . . 197 G6
Mareuil-Caubert (80) . . 9 G5
Mareuil-en-Brie (51) . . 61 H2
Mareuil-en-Dôle (02) . . 40 A4
Mareuil-la-Motte (60) . . 19 F6
Mareuil-le-Port (51) . . 40 C6
Mareuil-lès-Meaux (77) . . 59 K2
Mareuil-sur-Arnon (18) . . 148 E5
Mareuil-sur-Ay (51) . . 62 A1
Mareuil-sur-Cher (41) . . 128 E6
Mareuil-sur-Lay-Dissais (85) . . 159 K3
Mareuil-sur-Ourcq (60) . . 39 G6
Marey (88) . . 117 J1
Marey-lès-Fussey (21) . . 154 A3
Marey-sur-Tille (21) . . 136 A2
Marfaux (51) . . 40 D5
Marfontaine (02) . . 20 E3
Margaux (33) . . 211 G5
Margencel (74) . . 174 E5
Margency (95) . . 58 E2
Margerides (19) . . 201 G6
Margerie-Chantagret (42) . . 204 D5
Margerie-Hancourt (51) . . 91 F1
Margès (26) . . 222 E4
le Margnès (81) . . 271 J6
Margny (08) . . 23 J5
Margny (51) . . 61 G2
Margny-aux-Cerises (60) . . 19 G5
Margny-lès-Compiègne (60) . . 38 D2
Margny-sur-Matz (60) . . 38 D1
Margon (28) . . 84 A4
Margon (34) . . 292 B2
Margouët-Meymes (32) . . 266 D3
Margueray (50) . . 31 G6
Marguerittes (30) . . 275 H3
Margueron (33) . . 231 F3
Marguestau (32) . . 266 B2
Margut (08) . . 23 J5
Mariac (07) . . 239 H1
Maricourt (80) . . 19 F1
Marie (06) . . 261 J5
Marieulles (57) . . 65 K1
Marieux (80) . . 10 B5
Marigna-sur-Valouse (39) . . 173 G4
Marignac (17) . . 195 H5
Marignac (31) . . 305 J3
Marignac (82) . . 268 B3
Marignac-en-Diois (26) . . 241 G2
Marignac-Lasclares (31) . . 287 J4
Marignac-Laspeyres (31) . . 287 G5
Marignana (2A) . . 316 E5
Marignane (13) . . 296 A2
Marigné (49) . . 105 G6
Marigné-Laillé (72) . . 107 F5
Marigné-Peuton (53) . . 104 E4
Marignier (74) . . 191 J3
Marignieu (01) . . 207 K1
Marigny (03) . . 168 D3
Marigny (39) . . 173 J1
Marigny (50) . . 31 G3
Marigny (51) . . 61 J2
Marigny (71) . . 171 F2
Marigny (79) . . 178 A2
Marigny-Brizay (86) . . 163 F1
Marigny-Chémereau (86) . . 162 D5
Marigny-en-Orxois (02) . . 60 C1
Marigny-le-Cahouët (21) . . 134 E3
Marigny-le-Châtel (10) . . 89 H3
Marigny-l'Église (58) . . 133 K5
Marigny-les-Reullée (21) . . 154 B3
Marigny-les-Usages (45) . . 110 B3
Marigny-Marmande (37) . . 145 J4
Marigny-Saint-Marcel (74) . . 190 E6
Marigny-sur-Yonne (58) . . 133 H6
Marillac-le-Franc (16) . . 197 G2
le Marillais (49) . . 124 B4
Marillet (85) . . 161 F3
Marimbault (33) . . 246 C2
Marimont-lès-Bénestroff (57) . . 67 G2
Marin (74) . . 175 F5
Marines (95) . . 37 G5
Maringes (42) . . 205 F3
Maringues (63) . . 185 H6
Mariol (03) . . 185 K5
Marions (33) . . 246 E2
Marizy (71) . . 171 F3
Marizy-Saint-Mard (02) . . 39 H5
Marizy-Sainte-Geneviève (02) . . 39 H5
Marle (02) . . 20 E4
Marlemont (08) . . 22 A3
Marlenheim (67) . . 70 D3
Marlens (74) . . 209 F3
Marlers (80) . . 17 G3
Marles-en-Brie (77) . . 59 K5
Marles-les-Mines (62) . . 5 J6
Marles-sur-Canche (62) . . 4 C5
Marlhes (42) . . 221 H2
Marliac (31) . . 288 C5
Marliens (21) . . 154 D1

Marlieux (01) . . 188 E4
Marlioz (74) . . 190 E4
Marly (57) . . 45 F6
Marly (59) . . 12 D2
Marly-Gomont (02) . . 20 E2
Marly-la-Ville (95) . . 38 B6
Marly-le-Roi (78) . . 58 C3
Marly-sous-Issy (71) . . 170 A1
Marly-sur-Arroux (71) . . 170 A3
Marmagne (18) . . 149 F3
Marmagne (21) . . 134 D1
Marmagne (71) . . 153 F6
Marmande (47) . . 230 E6
Marmanhac (15) . . 217 H6
Marmeaux (89) . . 134 B2
Marminiac (46) . . 233 F4
Marmont-Pachas (47) . . 248 B6
Marmouillé (61) . . 54 E5
Marmoutier (67) . . 70 B2
Marnac (24) . . 232 D2
Marnand (69) . . 187 H4
Marnans (38) . . 223 F2
Marnaves (81) . . 250 E6
Marnay (70) . . 137 H5
Marnay (71) . . 172 A1
Marnay (86) . . 163 F5
Marnay-sur-Marne (52) . . 116 C2
Marnay-sur-Seine (10) . . 89 F2
Marnaz (74) . . 191 K3
Marnefer (61) . . 55 H3
Marnes (79) . . 144 D5
Marnes-la-Coquette (92) . . 58 C4
Marnézia (39) . . 173 H3
Marnhagues-et-Latour (12) . . 272 D3
Marnoz (39) . . 156 A4
Maroeuil (62) . . 10 E2
Maroilles (59) . . 13 F4
la Marolle-en-Sologne (41) . . 129 J3
Marolles (14) . . 34 B5
Marolles (41) . . 128 E1
Marolles (51) . . 63 F5
Marolles (60) . . 39 G5
Marolles-en-Beauce (91) . . 86 D4
Marolles-en-Brie (77) . . 60 C4
Marolles-en-Brie (94) . . 59 G5
Marolles-en-Hurepoix (91) . . 86 E1
Marolles-lès-Bailly (10) . . 90 D6
Marolles-les-Braults (72) . . 83 F5
Marolles-les-Buis (28) . . 84 B4
Marolles-lès-Saint-Calais (72) . . 107 K4
Marolles-sous-Lignières (10) . . 113 K3
Marolles-sur-Seine (77) . . 88 B4
Marollette (72) . . 83 F4
Marols (42) . . 204 C6
Maromme (76) . . 35 H1
Mâron (36) . . 148 B6
Maron (54) . . 65 K5
Maroncourt (88) . . 94 A5
Marpaps (40) . . 264 E6
Marpent (59) . . 13 J2
Marpiré (35) . . 79 K4
Marquaix (80) . . 19 H1
Marquay (24) . . 232 E1
Marquay (62) . . 10 B1
Marquefave (31) . . 287 K4
Marquéglise (60) . . 38 D1
Marquein (11) . . 288 E4
Marquerie (65) . . 285 J5
Marques (76) . . 17 F3
Marquette-en-Ostrevant (59) . . 11 K3
Marquette-lez-Lille (59) . . 6 D3
Marquigny (08) . . 22 D6
Marquillies (59) . . 6 C5
Marquion (62) . . 11 H4
Marquise (62) . . 2 B4
Marquivillers (80) . . 18 E5
Marquixanes (66) . . 314 C3
Marray (37) . . 127 J2
la Marre (39) . . 173 H1
Marre (55) . . 43 G4
Mars (07) . . 221 G5
les Mars (23) . . 183 K5
Mars (30) . . 273 J1
Mars (42) . . 187 G3
Mars-la-Tour (54) . . 44 C5
Mars-sous-Bourcq (08) . . 42 A2
Mars-sur-Allier (58) . . 150 D6
Marsa (11) . . 308 E5
Marsac (16) . . 196 D2
Marsac (23) . . 182 A4
Marsac (65) . . 285 H4
Marsac (82) . . 268 A2
Marsac-en-Livradois (63) . . 203 K6
Marsac-sur-Don (44) . . 103 F5
Marsac-sur-l'Isle (24) . . 213 K3
Marsainvilliers (45) . . 86 D6
Marsais (17) . . 177 J3
Marsais-Sainte-Radégonde (85) . . 160 D3
Marsal (57) . . 66 E3
Marsal (81) . . 271 F2
Marsalès (24) . . 232 C4
Marsan (32) . . 267 K5
Marsaneix (24) . . 214 B5
Marsangis (51) . . 89 J1
Marsangy (89) . . 112 D1
Marsannay-la-Côte (21) . . 136 A6
Marsannay-le-Bois (21) . . 136 B4
Marsanne (26) . . 240 C4
Marsas (33) . . 211 K5
Marsas (65) . . 304 C2
Marsat (63) . . 202 D1

Marsaz (26) . . 222 C4
Marseillan (32) . . 286 A2
Marseillan (34) . . 292 D4
Marseillan (65) . . 285 J4
Marseille (13) . . 296 C4
Marseille-en-Beauvaisis (60) . . 17 H6
Marseilles-lès-Aubigny (18) . . 150 C3
Marseillette (11) . . 290 C6
Marsillargues (34) . . 275 F5
Marsilly (17) . . 176 D1
Marsilly (57) . . 45 G5
Marsolan (32) . . 267 H2
Marson (51) . . 62 C2
Marson-sur-Barboure (55) . . 64 D6
Marsonnas (01) . . 172 B6
Marsoulas (31) . . 306 C1
Marssac-sur-Tarn (81) . . 270 C2
Martagny (27) . . 36 D2
Martailly-lès-Brancion (71) . . 171 J4
Martainneville (80) . . 9 F6
Martainville (14) . . 53 K2
Martainville (27) . . 34 B3
Martainville-Épreville (76) . . 35 K1
Martaizé (86) . . 144 D5
Martel (46) . . 233 K1
Marthemont (54) . . 93 K1
Marthille (57) . . 66 D2
Marthod (73) . . 209 G2
Marthon (16) . . 197 G4
Martiel (12) . . 250 E2
Martigna (39) . . 173 H5
Martignargues (30) . . 255 H6
Martignas-sur-Jalle (33) . . 229 F2
Martignat (01) . . 190 A2
Martigné-Briand (49) . . 125 H6
Martigné-Ferchaud (35) . . 103 K2
Martigné-sur-Mayenne (53) . . 81 F5
Martigny (02) . . 21 H2
Martigny (50) . . 52 C6
Martigny (76) . . 16 A2
Martigny-Courpierre (02) . . 40 B1
Martigny-le-Comte (71) . . 170 E4
Martigny-les-Bains (88) . . 117 H1
Martigny-les-Gerbonvaux (88) . . 93 H2
Martigny-sur-l'Ante (14) . . 53 K3
Martigues (13) . . 295 J5
Martillac (33) . . 229 H3
Martin-Église (76) . . 16 A2
Martincourt (54) . . 65 J3
Martincourt (60) . . 37 F1
Martincourt-sur-Meuse (55) . . 23 H6
le Martinet (30) . . 255 G4
Martinet (85) . . 159 F1
Martinpuich (62) . . 10 E6
Martinvast (50) . . 28 C3
Martinvelle (88) . . 117 K2
Martisserre (31) . . 287 F3
Martizay (36) . . 146 D6
Martot (27) . . 35 H4
Martragny (14) . . 32 C4
la Martre (83) . . 279 K3
Martres (33) . . 230 B4
les Martres-d'Artière (63) . . 203 F1
Martres-de-Rivière (31) . . 305 J1
les Martres-de-Veyre (63) . . 202 E3
Martres-sur-Morge (63) . . 185 G6
Martres-Tolosane (31) . . 287 H6
Martrin (12) . . 271 J2
Martrois (21) . . 135 F5
la Martyre (29) . . 46 D6
les Martys (11) . . 290 A3
Maruéjols-lès-Gardon (30) . . 274 E1
Marval (87) . . 198 A4
Marvaux-Vieux (08) . . 42 B3
Marvejols (48) . . 237 G6
Marvelise (25) . . 139 F2
Marville (55) . . 26 A3
Marville-Moutiers-Brûlé (28) . . 57 F6
Mary (71) . . 171 F3
Mary-sur-Marne (77) . . 60 D1
Marzan (56) . . 121 K2
Marzens (81) . . 270 B6
Marzy (58) . . 150 D4
le Mas (06) . . 280 C2
Mas-Blanc-des-Alpilles (13) . . 276 B4
Mas-Cabardès (11) . . 290 B3
le Mas-d'Agenais (47) . . 247 H2
Mas-d'Artige (23) . . 200 E2
Mas-d'Auvignon (32) . . 267 H2
le Mas-d'Azil (09) . . 307 F1
Mas-de-Londres (34) . . 274 A4
le Mas-de-Tence (43) . . 221 G4
Mas-des-Cours (11) . . 309 G1
Mas-d'Orcières (48) . . 254 D1
Mas-Grenier (82) . . 268 C4
Mas-Saint-Chély (48) . . 253 K3
Mas-Saintes-Puelles (11) . . 289 G4
Masbaraud-Mérignat (23) . . 182 C5
Mascaraàs-Haron (64) . . 284 E1
Mascaras (32) . . 285 K1
Mascaras (65) . . 285 J5
Mascarville (31) . . 289 F1
Masclat (46) . . 233 H2
Masevaux (68) . . 119 J4
Maslacq (64) . . 283 K2
Masléon (87) . . 199 J2
Maslives (41) . . 129 G2
le Masnau-Massuguiès (81) . . 271 H4
Masnières (59) . . 11 J5
Masny (59) . . 11 J2
Masparraute (64) . . 283 F3
Maspie-Lalonquère-Juillacq (64) . . 285 F2

Commune	Page	Réf.
Masquières (47)	249	F2
Massabrac (31)	288	B5
Massac (11)	309	J3
Massac (17)	178	C6
Massac-Séran (81)	270	D0
Massaguel (81)	289	K2
Massais (79)	144	A3
Massals (81)	271	H3
Massanes (30)	274	E1
Massangis (89)	134	A2
Massat (09)	307	F4
Massay (18)	148	C2
le Massegros (48)	253	H2
Masseilles (33)	246	E2
Massels (47)	248	D3
Massérac (44)	102	D4
Masseret (19)	199	H5
Masseube (32)	286	C3
Massiac (15)	219	F3
Massieu (38)	207	J6
Massieux (01)	188	C6
Massiges (51)	42	C5
Massignac (16)	197	K2
Massignieu-de-Rives (01)	207	K2
Massillargues-Attuech (30)	274	D1
Massilly (71)	171	H4
Massingy (21)	115	F4
Massingy (74)	190	D6
Massingy-lès-Semur (21)	134	E3
Massingy-lès-Vitteaux (21)	135	G4
Massognes (86)	162	C1
Massoins (06)	281	F1
Massongy (74)	174	E6
Massoulès (47)	248	D5
Massugas (33)	230	D3
Massy (71)	171	G4
Massy (76)	16	C4
Massy (91)	58	D5
Mastaing (59)	11	K2
Matafelon-Granges (01)	189	K1
les Matelles (34)	274	B5
Matemale (66)	313	J3
Matha (17)	178	B6
Mathaux (10)	90	E4
Mathay (25)	139	H3
Mathenay (39)	155	J4
les Mathes (17)	194	B2
Mathieu (14)	32	E4
Mathons (52)	92	A3
Mathonville (76)	16	C5
Matignicourt-Goncourt (51)	63	G5
Matignon (22)	50	A3
Matigny (80)	19	H3
Matougues (51)	62	C1
Matour (71)	187	J1
Matra (2B)	319	H6
Matringhem (62)	5	F5
Mattaincourt (88)	94	A4
Mattexey (54)	94	D2
Matton-et-Clémency (08)	23	H4
Matzenheim (67)	70	E5
Maubec (38)	207	F4
Maubec (82)	268	B4
Maubec (84)	276	E3
Maubert-Fontaine (08)	22	A4
Maubeuge (59)	13	H3
Maubourguet (65)	285	H2
Mauchamps (91)	86	D2
Maucomble (76)	16	C4
Maucor (64)	284	D3
Maucourt (60)	19	H5
Maucourt (80)	19	H5
Maucourt-sur-Orne (55)	26	A6
Maudétour-en-Vexin (95)	36	E6
Mauguio (34)	274	D6
Maulan (55)	64	B5
Maulay (86)	145	F2
Maulde (59)	7	H6
Maule (78)	57	K3
Mauléon (79)	143	G4
Mauléon-Barousse (65)	305	H3
Mauléon-d'Armagnac (32)	266	A2
Mauléon-Licharre (64)	283	H5
Maulers (60)	17	K6
Maulette (78)	57	H4
Maulévrier (49)	143	G3
Maulévrier-Sainte-Gertrude (76)	15	G6
Maulichères (32)	266	B5
Maumusson (44)	124	D3
Maumusson (82)	268	B2
Maumusson-Laguian (32)	266	B6
Mauny (76)	35	F2
Maupas (10)	114	B1
Maupas (32)	266	A3
Mauperthuis (77)	60	B4
Maupertuis (50)	31	G5
Maupertus-sur-Mer (50)	28	C2
Mauprévoir (86)	179	K3
Mauquenchy (76)	16	D5
Mauran (31)	287	H6
Maure (64)	285	G3
Maure-de-Bretagne (35)	102	H1
Maurecourt (78)	58	B2
Mauregard (77)	59	G1
Mauregny-en-Haye (02)	20	C6
Maureilhan (34)	291	K4
Maureillas-las-Illas (66)	315	G4
Mauremont (31)	288	E2
Maurens (24)	231	H1
Maurens (31)	289	F2
Maurens (32)	268	B6
Maurens-Scopont (81)	289	F1
Maurepas (78)	58	A5
Maurepas (80)	11	F6
Mauressac (31)	288	B4
Mauressargues (30)	274	E2
Maureville (31)	288	E2
Mauriac (15)	217	G3
Mauriac (33)	230	C3
Mauries (40)	265	J6
Maurines (15)	236	E2
Maurois (59)	12	C5
Mauron (56)	78	A4
Mauroux (32)	268	A2
Mauroux (46)	249	F1
Maurrin (40)	265	J3
Maurs (15)	235	F4
Maurupt-le-Montois (51)	63	H4
Maury (66)	309	J5
Mausoléo (2B)	318	D3
Maussac (19)	200	D6
Maussane-les-Alpilles (13)	276	B4
Maussans (70)	138	C3
Mautes (23)	183	J6
Mauvages (55)	64	E6
Mauvaisin (31)	288	C4
Mauves (07)	222	B5
Mauves-sur-Huisne (61)	83	J3
Mauves-sur-Loire (44)	123	J3
Mauvezin (31)	287	G3
Mauvezin (32)	268	B5
Mauvezin (65)	304	E1
Mauvezin-d'Armagnac (40)	266	A2
Mauvezin-de-Prat (09)	306	C2
Mauvezin-de-Sainte-Croix (09)	306	E1
Mauvières (36)	164	C3
Mauvilly (21)	115	G6
Maux (58)	152	A3
Mauzac (31)	288	A3
Mauzac-et-Grand-Castang (24)	232	B2
Mauzé-sur-le-Mignon (79)	177	J2
Mauzé-Thouarsais (79)	144	A4
Mauzens-et-Miremont (24)	214	C6
Mauzun (63)	203	G3
Maves (41)	109	F6
Mavilly-Mandelot (21)	153	K3
la Maxe (57)	45	F4
Maxent (35)	78	C6
Maxéville (54)	66	A4
Maxey-sur-Meuse (88)	93	G2
Maxey-sur-Vaise (55)	93	F1
Maxilly-sur-Léman (74)	175	G5
Maxilly-sur-Saône (21)	136	E5
Maxou (46)	233	H6
Maxstadt (57)	68	B3
May-en-Multien (77)	60	A1
le May-sur-Èvre (49)	142	E2
May-sur-Orne (14)	32	E6
Mayac (24)	214	C2
Mayenne (53)	81	G4
Mayet (72)	106	E5
le Mayet-de-Montagne (03)	186	B4
le Mayet-d'École (03)	185	J6
Maylis (40)	264	E6
Maynal (39)	172	E3
les Mayons (83)	298	E3
Mayot (02)	20	B4
Mayrac (46)	233	J1
Mayran (12)	251	K2
Mayrègne (31)	305	H4
Mayres (07)	238	E4
Mayres (63)	220	A1
Mayres-Savel (38)	242	A1
Mayreville (11)	289	F5
Mayrinhac-Lentour (46)	234	B3
Mayronnes (11)	309	H2
Maysel (60)	37	K4
Mazamet (81)	290	B2
Mazan (84)	257	H6
Mazan-l'Abbaye (07)	238	E3
Mazangé (41)	108	B5
Mazaugues (83)	297	J3
Mazaye (63)	202	B2
Mazé (49)	125	K3
le Mazeau (85)	161	F6
Mazeirat (23)	182	E3
Mazeley (88)	94	C5
Mazerat-Aurouze (43)	219	J4
Mazeray (17)	177	K6
Mazères (09)	288	E5
Mazères (33)	230	A6
Mazères-de-Neste (65)	305	H1
Mazères-Lezons (64)	284	D4
Mazères-sur-Salat (31)	287	G6
Mazerier (03)	185	G3
Mazerny (08)	22	C5
Mazerolles (16)	197	H2
Mazerolles (17)	195	G4
Mazerolles (40)	265	H2
Mazerolles (64)	284	C2
Mazerolles (65)	285	K3
Mazerolles (86)	160	D3
Mazerolles-du-Razès (11)	308	D1
Mazerolles-le-Salin (25)	137	J6
Mazerulles (54)	66	C4
Mazet-Saint-Voy (43)	221	F5
Mazeuil (86)	144	E6
Mazeyrat-d'Allier (43)	219	J4
Mazeyrolles (24)	232	D4
la Mazière-aux-Bons-Hommes (23)	183	J6
Mazières (16)	197	J1
Mazières-de-Touraine (37)	127	F3
Mazières-en-Gâtine (79)	161	J4
Mazières-en-Mauges (49)	143	F3
Mazières-Naresse (47)	232	A4
Mazières-sur-Béronne (79)	178	D2
Mazille (71)	171	G5
Mazingarbe (62)	6	A6
Mazinghem (62)	5	H4
Mazinghien (59)	12	D5
Mazion (33)	211	G3
Mazirat (03)	183	K2
Mazirot (88)	94	A4
le Mazis (80)	17	G2
Mazoires (63)	218	D1
Mazouau (65)	305	F2
Mazuby (11)	308	C5
les Mazures (08)	22	C2
Mazzola (2B)	319	H6
Méailles (04)	260	D6
Méallet (15)	217	H3
Méasnes (23)	165	K5
Meaucé (28)	84	B1
Méaudre (38)	223	J4
la Méauffe (50)	31	H2
la Méaugon (22)	49	F6
Méaulne (03)	167	H3
Méaulte (80)	18	E1
Méautis (50)	31	F1
Meaux (77)	59	K2
Meaux-la-Montagne (69)	187	J4
Meauzac (82)	249	H6
Mecé (35)	79	K3
Méchmont (46)	233	H5
Mécleuves (57)	45	G6
Mecquignies (59)	13	F3
Mécrin (55)	64	E3
Mécringes (51)	61	F3
Médan (78)	58	B2
Médavy (61)	54	D5
Médeyrolles (63)	220	B1
Médière (25)	139	F3
Médillac (16)	212	D3
Médis (17)	194	D3
Médonville (88)	93	G5
Médréac (35)	78	C2
le Mée (28)	109	F3
le Mée (53)	104	D5
le Mée-sur-Seine (77)	87	H2
les Mées (04)	259	G6
Mées (40)	264	A4
les Mées (72)	82	E4
Mégange (57)	27	K6
Megève (74)	192	A6
Mégevette (74)	191	J1
Mégrit (22)	50	B6
Méharicourt (80)	18	E2
Méharin (64)	282	E3
Méhers (41)	129	F5
Méhoncourt (54)	94	C1
Méhoudin (61)	81	J2
Mehun-sur-Yèvre (18)	148	E2
la Meignanne (49)	125	F3
Meigné (49)	125	K6
Meigné-le-Vicomte (49)	126	D3
Meigneux (77)	88	B2
Meigneux (80)	17	H3
Meilars (29)	73	D3
Meilhac (87)	198	E3
Meilhan (32)	286	D3
Meilhan (40)	264	E2
Meilhan-sur-Garonne (47)	230	D6
Meilhards (19)	199	J5
Meilhaud (63)	202	E5
Meillac (35)	51	F6
Meillant (18)	167	G1
Meillard (03)	168	D6
le Meillard (80)	9	K4
la Meilleraie-Tillay (85)	160	D1
Meilleray (77)	60	E4
la Meilleraye-de-Bretagne (44)	103	J5
Meillerie (74)	175	H4
Meillers (03)	168	C4
Meillon (64)	284	D4
Meillonnas (01)	189	F4
Meilly-sur-Rouvres (21)	153	H1
Meisenthal (57)	69	G2
Meistratzheim (67)	70	D5
le Meix (21)	135	K2
le Meix-Saint-Epoing (51)	61	G5
le Meix-Tiercelin (51)	62	E6
Méjannes-le-Clap (30)	255	K5
Méjannes-lès-Alès (30)	255	H6
Mela (2A)	323	F2
Mélagues (12)	272	A3
Mélamare (76)	14	D4
Melay (49)	143	G1
Melay (52)	117	H3
Melay (71)	186	E2
le Mêle-sur-Sarthe (61)	83	F2
Mélecey (70)	138	C3
Melesse (35)	79	F2
Melgven (29)	99	F2
Mélicocq (60)	38	E1
Mélicourt (27)	55	H2
Méligny-le-Grand (55)	64	E5
Méligny-le-Petit (55)	64	D5
Melin (70)	117	H5
Melincourt (70)	118	A3
Mélisey (70)	119	F5
Mélisey (89)	114	B4
Meljac (12)	252	A5
Mellac (29)	99	H3
Mellé (35)	80	B2
Melle (79)	178	D2
Mellecey (71)	153	K6
Melleran (79)	178	E3
Melleray (72)	107	K1
Melleroy (45)	112	A4
Melles (31)	305	K4
Melleville (76)	16	D1
Mellionnec (22)	76	B4
Mello (60)	37	K4
Meloisey (21)	153	K3
Melrand (56)	100	C1
Melsheim (67)	70	D1
Melun (77)	87	H2
Melve (04)	259	G2
Melz-sur-Seine (77)	88	E2
Membrey (70)	137	H1
la Membrolle-sur-Choisille (37)	127	H4
la Membrolle-sur-Longuenée (49)	125	F2
Membrolles (41)	109	G3
Méménil (88)	94	E5
Memmelshoffen (67)	25	B2
le Mémont (25)	157	J1
Menades (89)	133	J4
Ménarmont (88)	95	F2
Menars (41)	129	F1
Menat (63)	184	D4
Menaucourt (55)	64	C5
Mencas (62)	5	F5
Menchhoffen (67)	69	H5
Mende (48)	237	J6
Mendionde (64)	282	D3
Menditte (64)	283	H5
Mendive (64)	282	E6
Ménéac (56)	77	J5
Ménerbes (84)	277	F3
Ménerval (76)	16	E6
Ménerville (78)	57	K4
Menesble (21)	115	J5
Méneslies (80)	8	D5
Ménesplet (24)	212	E5
Ménesqueville (27)	36	A3
Ménessaire (21)	152	D2
Menestreau (58)	132	D4
Ménestreau-en-Villette (45)	130	B1
Menet (15)	217	J2
Menetou-Couture (18)	150	B3
Menetou-Râtel (18)	131	J5
Menetou-Salon (18)	149	H1
Menetou-sur-Nahon (36)	147	K1
Ménétréol-sous-Sancerre (18)	131	K5
Ménétréol-sur-Sauldre (18)	130	E4
Ménétréols-sous-Vatan (36)	148	B4
Ménétreuil (71)	172	C3
Ménétreux-le-Pitois (21)	134	E2
Ménétrol (63)	202	D1
Ménévillers (60)	38	C1
Menglon (26)	241	J4
Menigoute (79)	162	B4
Ménil (53)	105	F5
le Ménil (88)	119	G3
Ménil-Annelles (08)	41	J2
Ménil-aux-Bois (55)	64	D4
le Ménil-Bérard (61)	55	H5
le Ménil-Broût (61)	82	E2
le Ménil-Ciboult (61)	53	F4
le Ménil-de-Briouze (61)	53	J5
Ménil-de-Senones (88)	95	J3
Ménil-en-Xaintois (88)	93	J4
Ménil-Erreux (61)	82	E2
Ménil-Froger (61)	55	F5
Ménil-Gondouin (61)	53	K4
le Ménil-Guyon (61)	83	F1
Ménil-Hermei (61)	53	K3
Ménil-Hubert-en-Exmes (61)	54	E4
Ménil-Hubert-sur-Orne (61)	53	J3
Ménil-Jean (61)	54	A5
Ménil-la-Horgne (55)	64	E5
Ménil-la-Tour (54)	65	H4
Ménil-Lépinois (08)	41	H2
le Ménil-Scelleur (61)	54	B6
Ménil-sur-Belvitte (88)	95	F3
Ménil-sur-Saulx (55)	64	B6
le Ménil-Vicomte (61)	55	F5
Ménil-Vin (61)	53	K3
Ménilles (27)	57	F1
la Ménitré (49)	125	K4
Mennecy (91)	87	F1
Mennessis (02)	19	K4
Mennetou-sur-Cher (41)	129	K6
Menneval (27)	34	D6
Menneville (02)	40	E2
Menneville (62)	2	C6
Mennevret (02)	12	D6
Mennouveaux (52)	116	D1
Ménoire (19)	216	B5
Menomblet (85)	160	E1
Menoncourt (90)	119	J6
Ménonval (76)	16	D4
Menotey (39)	155	G1
Menou (58)	132	D5
le Menoux (36)	165	H4
Menoux (70)	118	A4
Mens (38)	242	B2
Mensignac (24)	213	J3
Menskirch (57)	27	K4
Mentheville (76)	14	D4
Menthon-Saint-Bernard (74)	191	G6
Menthonnex-en-Bornes (74)	191	F3
Menthonnex-sous-Clermont (74)	190	D5
Mentières (15)	218	E5
Menton (06)	281	K3
Mentque-Nortbécourt (62)	2	E4
Menucourt (95)	58	B1
les Menus (61)	84	B2
Menville (31)	268	E5
Méobecq (36)	165	F1
Méolans-Revel (04)	260	B1
Méon (49)	126	D3
Méounes-lès-Montrieux (83)	297	J4
Mer (41)	129	G1
Méracq (64)	284	C1
Méral (53)	104	C3
Méras (09)	288	A6
Mercatel (62)	11	F3
Mercenac (09)	306	C2
Merceuil (21)	154	A4
Mercey (27)	36	A6
Mercey-le-Grand (25)	137	H6
Mercey-sur-Saône (70)	137	G2
Mercin-et-Vaux (02)	39	J3
Merck-Saint-Liévin (62)	5	F4
Merckeghem (59)	3	G3
Mercoeur (19)	216	C6
Mercoeur (43)	219	G3
Mercuer (07)	239	H5
Mercuès (46)	249	K1
Mercurey (71)	153	K5
Mercurol (26)	222	C5
Mercury (73)	209	F2
Mercus-Garrabet (09)	307	J4
Mercy (03)	169	G5
Mercy (89)	113	G2
Mercy-le-Bas (54)	26	D4
Mercy-le-Haut (54)	26	D4
Merdrignac (22)	77	K4
Méré (78)	57	K4
Méré (89)	113	J4
Méreau (18)	148	D2
Méréaucourt (80)	17	H4
Méréglise (28)	84	D5
Mérélessart (80)	17	G1
Mérens (32)	267	H4
Mérens-les-Vals (09)	313	F2
Mérenvielle (31)	268	D5
Méreuil (05)	258	D2
Méréville (54)	66	A6
Méréville (91)	86	C4
Merey (27)	57	F2
Mérey-sous-Montrond (25)	156	C1
Mérey-Vieilley (25)	138	A5
Merfy (51)	40	E3
Mergey (10)	90	A3
Meria (2B)	317	D2
Mérial (11)	308	C5
Méricourt (62)	11	F1
Méricourt (78)	57	H1
Méricourt-en-Vimeu (80)	17	H2
Méricourt-l'Abbé (80)	18	D1
Méricourt-sur-Somme (80)	18	E2
Mériel (95)	37	J6
Mérifons (34)	273	F6
Mérignac (16)	196	B3
Mérignac (17)	212	A2
Mérignac (33)	229	G2
Mérignas (33)	230	C3
Mérignat (01)	189	J3
Mérignies (59)	6	E6
Mérigny (36)	164	B3
Mérigon (09)	306	E1
Mérilheu (65)	304	D1
Mérillac (22)	77	K3
Mérinchal (23)	183	K6
Mérindol (84)	277	F4
Mérindol-les-Oliviers (26)	257	H3
Mérinville (45)	112	A2
le Mériot (10)	88	E2
Méritein (64)	283	J3
Merkwiller-Pechelbronn (67)	25	B2
Merlas (38)	207	J5
la Merlatière (85)	142	A6
Merlaut (51)	63	G4
Merle-Leignec (42)	220	D1
Merléac (22)	76	E3
le Merlerault (61)	55	F5
Merles (82)	249	F6
Merles-sur-Loison (55)	26	A4
Merlevenez (56)	100	B4
Merlieux-et-Fouquerolles (02)	40	A1
Merlimont (62)	4	A6
Merlines (19)	201	H4
Mernel (35)	102	D1
Mérobert (91)	86	B3
Mérona (39)	173	G3
Mérouville (28)	86	A5
Meroux (90)	139	J1
Merpins (16)	195	J3
Merrey (52)	117	F1
Merrey-sur-Arce (10)	114	E1
Merri (61)	54	C3
Merris (59)	6	A3
Merry-la-Vallée (89)	112	D5
Merry-Sec (89)	133	F1
Merry-sur-Yonne (89)	133	G2
Mers-les-Bains (80)	8	C5
Mers-sur-Indre (36)	166	A2
Merschweiller (57)	27	J3
Mersuay (70)	118	A5
Merten (57)	45	K3
Mertrud (52)	91	J3
Mertzen (68)	97	A4
Mertzwiller (67)	69	K5
Méru (60)	37	H4

380

Merval (02) 40 C3
Mervans (71) 154 D6
Mervent (85) 160 E4
Mervilla (31) 288 C2
Merville (31) 269 F5
Merville (59) 3 K6
Merville-Franceville-Plage (14) . . 33 F3
Merviller (54) 95 G1
Merxheim (68) 96 B6
Méry (73) 208 B3
Méry-Corbon (14) 33 G5
Méry-ès-Bois (18) 130 E6
Méry-la-Bataille (60) 18 D6
Méry-Prémecy (51) 40 D4
Méry-sur-Cher (18) 148 C1
Méry-sur-Marne (77) 60 C2
Méry-sur-Oise (95) 58 D1
Méry-sur-Seine (10) 89 J2
le Merzer (22) 48 D5
Mésandans (25) 138 D3
Mésanger (44) 124 A3
Mésangueville (76) 16 E6
Mesbrecourt-Richecourt (02) . . 20 C4
Meschers-sur-Gironde (17) . . 194 D4
Mescoules (24) 231 H3
le Mesge (80) 17 J1
Mesgrigny (10) 89 J2
Mésigny (74) 190 E4
Meslan (56) 75 K6
Mesland (41) 128 C3
Meslay (14) 53 J2
Meslay (41) 108 C5
Meslay-du-Maine (53) . . . 105 G3
Meslay-le-Grenet (28) 85 F4
Meslay-le-Vidame (28) 85 G5
Meslières (25) 139 J3
Meslin (22) 77 H1
Mesmay (25) 156 A2
Mesmont (08) 22 A5
Mesmont (21) 135 H5
Mesnac (16) 195 K2
Mesnard-la-Barotière (85) . . 142 C5
Mesnay (39) 155 K4
les Mesneux (51) 40 E4
la Mesnière (61) 83 G2
Mesnières-en-Bray (76) . . . 16 C3
le Mesnil (50) 28 C5
le Mesnil-Adelée (50) 52 C5
le Mesnil-Amand (50) 30 E6
le Mesnil-Amelot (77) 59 G1
le Mesnil-Amey (50) 31 G3
le Mesnil-Angot (50) 31 G2
le Mesnil-au-Grain (14) . . . 32 C6
le Mesnil-au-Val (50) 28 D3
le Mesnil-Aubert (50) 30 E5
le Mesnil-Aubry (95) 59 F1
le Mesnil-Auzouf (14) 53 F1
le Mesnil-Bacley (14) 54 D1
le Mesnil-Benoist (14) 31 J6
Mesnil-Bruntel (80) 19 G2
le Mesnil-Caussois (14) . . . 52 D3
Mesnil-Clinchamps (14) . . . 52 D3
le Mesnil-Conteville (60) . . . 17 J5
Mesnil-Domqueur (80) 9 J4
le Mesnil-Durand (14) 54 D1
le Mesnil-Durdent (76) 15 G3
Mesnil-en-Arrouaise (80) . . . 11 G6
le Mesnil-en-Thelle (60) . . . 37 J5
le Mesnil-en-Vallée (49) . . . 124 C4
le Mesnil-Esnard (76) 35 J2
le Mesnil-Eudes (14) 33 K6
le Mesnil-Eury (50) 31 G3
Mesnil-Follemprise (76) . . . 16 B3
le Mesnil-Fuguet (27) 35 H6
le Mesnil-Garnier (50) 31 F6
le Mesnil-Germain (14) 54 E1
le Mesnil-Gilbert (50) 52 C5
le Mesnil-Guillaume (14) . . . 34 A6
le Mesnil-Hardray (27) 56 B2
le Mesnil-Herman (50) 31 G4
le Mesnil-Jourdain (27) 35 H5
Mesnil-la-Comtesse (10) . . . 90 C2
le Mesnil-le-Roi (78) 58 C2
Mesnil-Lettre (10) 90 C3
le Mesnil-Lieubray (76) 36 B1
Mesnil-Martinsart (80) 10 D6
le Mesnil-Mauger (14) 33 H6
Mesnil-Mauger (76) 16 D5
le Mesnil-Opac (50) 31 H4
le Mesnil-Ozenne (50) 52 B5
Mesnil-Panneville (76) 15 H6
le Mesnil-Patry (14) 32 C4
le Mesnil-Rainfray (50) 52 C5
Mesnil-Raoul (76) 35 K2
le Mesnil-Raoult (50) 31 H4
le Mesnil-Réaume (76) 16 D1
le Mesnil-Robert (14) 31 J6
le Mesnil-Rogues (50) 30 E6
Mesnil-Rousset (27) 55 H3
le Mesnil-Rouxelin (50) 31 H3
le Mesnil-Saint-Denis (78) . . 58 B5
le Mesnil-Saint-Firmin (60) . . 18 C5
Mesnil-Saint-Georges (80) . . 18 D5
Mesnil-Saint-Laurent (02) . . . 20 A3
Mesnil-Saint-Loup (10) 89 H5
Mesnil-Saint-Nicaise (80) . . . 19 G5
Mesnil-Saint-Père (10) 90 D5
Mesnil-Sellières (10) 90 C4
le Mesnil-Simon (14) 33 J6
le Mesnil-Simon (28) 57 G3
le Mesnil-sous-Jumièges (76) . . 35 F2
Mesnil-sous-Vienne (27) . . . 36 D2

le Mesnil-sur-Blangy (14) . . . 34 A4
le Mesnil-sur-Bulles (60) . . . 37 K1
Mesnil-sur-l'Estrée (27) 56 E4
le Mesnil-sur-Oger (51) 62 A2
le Mesnil-Théribus (60) 37 G4
le Mesnil-Thomas (28) 84 C1
le Mesnil-Tôve (50) 52 C5
le Mesnil-Véneron (50) 31 G2
Mesnil-Verclives (27) 36 B3
le Mesnil-Vigot (50) 31 F3
le Mesnil-Villeman (50) 31 F6
le Mesnil-Villement (14) 53 J3
les Mesnils (50) 31 F3
le Mesnilbus (50) 31 F3
le Mesnillard (50) 52 C6
Mesnois (39) 173 H2
les Mesnuls (78) 57 K5
Mespaul (29) 46 E4
Mesplède (64) 284 A1
Mesples (03) 166 E5
Mespuits (91) 86 D4
Mesquer (44) 121 J3
Messac (17) 212 A1
Messac (35) 102 E2
Messanges (21) 154 A1
Messanges (40) 262 C3
Messas (45) 109 H5
Messé (79) 179 F1
Messei (61) 53 H5
Messein (54) 66 A6
Messeix (63) 201 H4
Messemé (86) 145 F3
Messery (74) 174 D5
Messey-sur-Grosne (71) . . . 171 J2
Messia-sur-Sorne (39) 173 F2
Messigny-et-Vantoux (21) . . 136 A4
Messimy (69) 205 J3
Messimy-sur-Saône (01) . . . 188 B4
Messincourt (08) 23 H4
Messon (10) 89 K5
Messy (77) 59 H2
Mesterrieux (33) 230 C4
Mestes (19) 201 F5
Mesves-sur-Loire (58) 150 C1
Mesvres (71) 152 E5
Métabief (25) 157 F6
les Métairies (16) 196 B2
Métairies-Saint-Quirin (57) . . 67 J5
Méteren (59) 6 A3
Méthamis (84) 277 F1
Métigny (80) 17 H1
Metting (57) 69 F6
Mettray (37) 127 J4
Metz (57) 45 F5
Metz-en-Couture (62) 11 H5
Metz-le-Comte (58) 133 G5
Metz-Robert (10) 114 B2
Metz-Tessy (74) 191 F5
Metzeral (68) 119 K1
Metzeresche (57) 27 J5
Metzervisse (57) 27 H5
Metzing (57) 68 C3
Meucon (56) 101 F4
Meudon (92) 58 D4
Meuilley (21) 154 A2
Meulan (78) 58 A2
Meulers (76) 16 B2
Meulles (14) 55 F2
Meulson (21) 115 G6
Meunet-Planches (36) 148 C6
Meunet-sur-Vatan (36) 148 B3
Meung-sur-Loire (45) 109 J5
Meurcé (72) 82 E5
Meurchin (62) 6 C6
Meurcourt (70) 118 B5
la Meurdraquière (50) 51 K1
Meures (52) 92 A6
Meurival (02) 40 C3
Meursac (17) 194 E3
Meursanges (21) 154 B4
Meursault (21) 153 K4
Meurville (10) 91 G6
Meusnes (41) 129 G6
Meussia (39) 173 H4
Meuvaines (14) 32 C3
Meux (17) 195 J6
le Meux (60) 38 D3
Meuzac (87) 199 G5
Mévoisins (28) 85 H1
Mévouillon (26) 258 B3
Meximieux (01) 189 G6
Mexy (54) 26 D2
Mey (57) 45 F5
Meyenheim (68) 96 C6
Meylan (38) 224 B3
Meymac (19) 200 D5
Meynes (30) 275 J3
Meyrals (24) 232 D1
Meyrannes (30) 255 H3
Meyrargues (13) 277 J5
Meyras (07) 239 G4
Meyreuil (13) 296 D1
Meyrié (38) 207 F4
Meyrieu-les-Étangs (38) . . . 206 E5
Meyrieux-Trouet (73) 208 A3
Meyrignac-l'Église (19) 216 B1
Meyronne (46) 233 J2
Meyronnes (04) 227 C4
Meyrueis (48) 254 A5
Meys (69) 205 G3
Meyssac (19) 215 K5
Meysse (07) 240 A5
Meyssiès (38) 206 D5

Meythet (74) 191 F5
la Meyze (87) 198 E4
Meyzieu (69) 206 C2
Mézangers (53) 81 J6
Mèze (34) 292 C3
Mézel (04) 259 J6
Mezel (63) 202 E2
Mézens (81) 269 K4
Mézeray (72) 106 C5
Mézères (43) 220 D4
Mézériat (01) 188 E2
Mézerolles (80) 9 K4
Mézidon-Canon (14) 33 G6
la Mézière (35) 79 F3
Mézières-au-Perche (28) . . . 84 E5
Mézières-en-Brenne (36) . . . 147 F6
Mézières-en-Drouais (28) . . . 57 H5
Mézières-en-Gâtinais (45) . . . 111 F2
Mézières-en-Santerre (80) . . . 18 D3
Mézières-en-Vexin (27) 36 B5
Mézières-lez-Cléry (45) 109 K5
Mézières-sous-Lavardin (72) . . 82 C6
Mézières-sur-Couesnon (35) . . 79 J2
Mézières-sur-Issoire (87) . . . 180 D3
Mézières-sur-Oise (02) 20 B3
Mézières-sur-Ponthouin (72) . . 83 F6
Mézières-sur-Seine (78) 57 K2
Mézilhac (07) 239 G2
Mézilles (89) 132 C1
Mézin (47) 247 H6
Méziré (90) 139 J2
Mézos (40) 244 D5
Mézy-Moulins (02) 61 F1
Mézy-sur-Seine (78) 58 A2
Mhère (58) 152 A1
Mialet (24) 198 D3
Mialet (30) 255 F5
Mialos (64) 284 C2
Miannay (80) 9 F5
Michaugues (58) 133 F6
Michelbach (68) 97 A2
Michelbach-le-Bas (68) 97 D4
Michelbach-le-Haut (68) 97 D4
Michery (89) 88 D4
Midrevaux (88) 93 F3
Mièges (39) 156 C6
Miélan (32) 286 A3
Miellin (70) 119 G4
Miermaigne (28) 84 B5
Miers (46) 234 A2
Miéry (39) 155 J6
Mietesheim (67) 69 J5
Mieussy (74) 191 K2
Mieuxcé (61) 82 C3
Migé (89) 133 F1
Migennes (89) 113 F2
Miglos (09) 307 J5
Mignaloux-Beauvoir (86) . . . 163 F4
Mignavillers (70) 138 E1
Migné (36) 164 E2
Migné-Auxances (86) 162 E3
Mignères (45) 111 H2
Mignerette (45) 111 G2
Mignéville (54) 95 G1
Mignières (28) 85 F4
Mignovillard (39) 156 D6
Migny (36) 148 D3
Migré (17) 177 K3
Migron (17) 195 J1
Mijanès (09) 308 D6
Mijoux (01) 174 A5
la Milesse (72) 106 D2
Milhac (46) 233 G3
Milhac-d'Auberoche (24) . . . 214 C4
Milhac-de-Nontron (24) 198 A6
Milhars (81) 250 E5
Milhas (31) 306 C2
Milhaud (30) 275 G4
Milhavet (81) 270 C1
Milizac (29) 72 C3
Millac (86) 180 A1
Millam (59) 3 G4
Millançay (41) 129 J4
Millas (66) 309 K6
Millau (12) 253 G6
Millay (58) 152 C6
Millebosc (76) 16 D1
Millemont (78) 57 J4
Millencourt (80) 10 D6
Millencourt-en-Ponthieu (80) . . 9 G4
Millery (21) 134 D2
Millery (54) 66 A3
Millery (69) 206 A3
Millevaches (19) 200 D3
Millières (50) 30 E2
Millières (52) 92 D6
Millonfosse (59) 12 C1
Milly (50) 52 C6
les Moëres (59) 3 J3
Milly-la-Forêt (91) 87 F3
Milly-Lamartine (71) 171 H6
Milly-sur-Bradon (55) 43 G2
Milly-sur-Thérain (60) 37 G1
Milon-la-Chapelle (78) 58 B5
Mimbaste (40) 264 C5
Mimet (13) 296 D2
Mimeure (21) 153 G2
Mimizan (40) 244 C4
Minaucourt-le-Mesnil-
  lès-Hurlus (51) 42 B5
Minerve (34) 291 F4
Mingot (65) 285 J3

Mingoval (62) 10 D2
Miniac-Morvan (35) 50 E5
Miniac-sous-Bécherel (35) . . . 78 E2
le Minihic-sur-Rance (35) . . . 50 D4
Minihy-Tréguier (22) 48 C2
Minorville (54) 65 H3
Minot (21) 135 J1
Minversheim (67) 69 J6
Minzac (24) 212 D6
Minzier (74) 190 E3
Miolles (81) 271 J3
Mionnay (01) 188 D6
Mions (69) 206 B3
Mios (33) 228 D5
Miossens-Lanusse (64) 284 D2
Mirabeau (04) 259 H5
Mirabeau (84) 278 A4
Mirabel (07) 239 J5
Mirabel (82) 249 K5
Mirabel-aux-Baronnies (26) . . 257 H3
Mirabel-et-Blacons (26) 240 E3
Miradoux (32) 267 K1
Miramas (13) 276 D6
Mirambeau (17) 211 H1
Mirambeau (31) 287 F3
Miramont-d'Astarac (32) . . . 286 B1
Miramont-de-Comminges (31) . 305 K1
Miramont-de-Guyenne (47) . . 231 H3
Miramont-de-Quercy (82) . . . 249 G4
Miramont-Latour (32) 267 J4
Miramont-Sensacq (40) 265 J6
Mirande (32) 286 B1
Mirandol-Bourgnounac (81) . . 251 H5
Mirannes (32) 267 F5
Miraumont (80) 10 E5
Miraval-Cabardès (11) 290 B3
Mirbel (52) 92 A4
Miré (49) 105 H5
Mirebeau (86) 145 F6
Mirebeau-sur-Bèze (21) 136 C3
Mirebel (39) 173 H1
Mirecourt (88) 94 A4
Mirefleurs (63) 202 E3
Miremont (31) 288 B3
Miremont (63) 184 B6
Mirepeisset (11) 291 G5
Mirepeix (64) 284 E5
Mirepoix (09) 308 B1
Mirepoix (32) 267 J4
Mirepoix-sur-Tarn (31) 269 J4
Mireval (34) 293 G2
Mireval-Lauragais (11) 289 H5
Miribel (01) 206 B1
Miribel (26) 222 E3
Miribel-Lanchâtre (38) 223 K6
Miribel-les-Échelles (38) . . . 207 K6
Mirmande (26) 240 C4
le Miroir (71) 172 E3
Mirvaux (80) 10 B6
Mirville (76) 14 D5
Miscon (26) 241 J4
Miserey (27) 56 E1
Miserey-Salines (25) 137 K5
Misérieux (01) 188 C5
Misery (80) 19 G2
Mison (04) 259 F3
Missé (79) 144 B4
Missècle (81) 270 C5
Missègre (11) 309 G2
Missery (21) 134 E5
Missillac (44) 102 B6
Missiriac (56) 101 K3
Misson (40) 264 C6
Missy (14) 32 C5
Missy-aux-Bois (02) 39 H3
Missy-lès-Pierrepont (02) . . . 20 E5
Missy-sur-Aisne (02) 39 K2
Misy-sur-Yonne (77) 88 B4
Mitry-Mory (77) 59 G2
Mittainville (78) 57 H6
Mittainvilliers (28) 84 E2
Mittelbergheim (67) 70 C5
Mittelbronn (57) 70 A1
Mittelhausbergen (67) 25 A6
Mittelhausen (67) 70 E1
Mittelschaeffolsheim (67) . . . 70 E2
Mittelwihr (68) 96 B3
Mittersheim (57) 67 H2
Mittlach (68) 119 J1
Mittois (14) 54 C1
Mitzach (68) 119 J3
Mizérieux (42) 204 E2
Mizoën (38) 224 E4
Moÿ-de-l'Aisne (02) 20 A4
Mobecq (50) 30 D1
Moca-Croce (2A) 320 E6
Modane (73) 226 A2
Modène (84) 257 H5
Moëlan-sur-Mer (29) 99 H4
les Moëres (59) 3 J3
Moëslains (52) 91 G6
Moeurs-Verdey (51) 61 G5
Moeuvres (59) 11 H4
Mœze (17) 176 E5
Moffans-et-Vacheresse (70) . . 138 E1
Mogeville (55) 26 B6
Mognard (73) 208 B2
Mogneneins (01) 188 C3
Mognéville (55) 63 K4
Mogneville (60) 38 A3
Mogues (08) 23 J4

Mohon (56) 77 J6
Moidieu-Détourbe (38) 206 C5
Moigny-sur-École (91) 87 F3
Moimay (70) 138 D2
Moineville (54) 26 E6
Moings (17) 195 J5
Moinville-la-Jeulin (28) 85 J4
Moirans (38) 223 J1
Moirans-en-Montagne (39) . . 173 H5
Moirax (47) 248 B5
Moiré (69) 188 A5
Moiremont (51) 42 D5
Moirey-Flabas-Crépion (55) . . 43 H3
Moiron (39) 173 G2
Moiry (08) 23 J5
Moisdon-la-Rivière (44) 103 J3
Moisenay (77) 87 J1
Moislains (80) 11 G6
Moissac (82) 249 G6
Moissac-Bellevue (83) 279 F5
Moissac-Vallée-Française (48) . 254 D5
Moissannes (87) 199 J1
Moissat (63) 203 F2
Moisselles (95) 58 E1
Moissey (39) 155 G1
Moissieu-sur-Dolon (38) . . . 222 E4
Moisson (78) 57 J1
Moissy-Cramayel (77) 59 G6
Moissy-Moulinot (58) 133 H5
Moisville (27) 56 D4
Moisy (41) 108 E4
Moïta (2B) 319 J6
les Moitiers-d'Allonne (50) . . . 28 B5
les Moitiers-en-Bauptois (50) . . 28 E6
Moitron (21) 135 J1
Moitron-sur-Sarthe (72) 82 C5
Moivre (51) 63 G2
Moivrons (54) 66 B3
Molac (56) 101 J4
Molagnies (76) 36 D1
Molain (02) 12 D6
Molain (39) 155 K5
Molamboz (39) 155 J4
Molandier (11) 288 E5
Molas (31) 286 E3
Molay (39) 155 F3
Molay (70) 117 G5
Môlay (89) 113 K6
le Molay-Littry (14) 31 K2
la Môle (83) 298 D5
Moléans (28) 109 F1
Molèdes (15) 218 D3
Molère (65) 304 C1
Molesme (21) 114 D3
Molesmes (89) 133 F2
Molezon (48) 254 C4
Moliens (60) 17 G5
Molières (24) 232 B2
Molières (46) 234 C3
Molières (82) 249 J5
les Molières (91) 58 C6
Molières-Cavaillac (30) 273 J2
Molières-Glandaz (26) 241 H3
Molières-sur-Cèze (30) 255 H4
Moliets-et-Maa (40) 262 C2
Molinchart (02) 20 C6
Molines-en-Queyras (05) . . . 227 C2
Molinet (03) 170 A5
Molineuf (41) 128 D2
Molinges (39) 173 J5
Molinons (89) 89 F5
Molinot (21) 153 H3
Molins-sur-Aube (10) 90 D3
Molitg-les-Bains (66) 314 B2
Mollans (70) 118 D6
Mollans-sur-Ouvèze (26) . . . 257 J4
Mollau (68) 119 J3
Mollégès (13) 276 C3
Molles (03) 185 K3
les Mollettes (73) 208 D5
Molleville (11) 289 F4
Molliens-au-Bois (80) 10 B6
Molliens-Dreuil (80) 17 J2
Mollkirch (67) 70 C4
Molompize (15) 218 D3
Molosmes (89) 114 A4
Moloy (21) 135 K2
Molphey (21) 134 C5
Molpré (39) 156 C6
Molring (57) 67 G2
Molsheim (67) 70 D4
Moltifao (2B) 318 E3
les Molunes (39) 173 K6
Momas (64) 284 C2
Mombrier (33) 211 H4
Momères (65) 285 H6
Momerstroff (57) 45 J4
Mommenheim (67) 70 E1
Momuy (40) 265 F6
Momy (64) 285 F3
Monacia-d'Aullène (2A) 322 E4
Monacia-d'Orezza (2B) 319 H5
Monampteuil (02) 40 B1
Monassut-Audiracq (64) . . . 284 D2
le Monastère (12) 252 B3
le Monastier-Pin-Moriès (48) . . 237 F6
le Monastier-sur-Gazeille (43) . 238 D1
Monay (39) 155 H5
Monbahus (47) 231 J6
Monbalen (47) 248 C3
Monbardon (32) 286 E3
Monbazillac (24) 231 H3

Monbéqui (82) 268 E3
Monblanc (32) 287 H2
Monbrun (32) 268 C5
Moncale (2B) 316 E1
Moncassin (32) 286 B2
Moncaup (31) 305 J3
Moncaup (64) 285 G2
Moncaut (47) 248 A5
Moncayolle-Larrory-Mendibieu (64) . . 283 H4
Moncé-en-Belin (72) 106 C4
Moncé-en-Saosnois (72) 83 F5
Monceau-le-Neuf-et-Faucouzy (02) . . 20 D3
Monceau-le-Waast (02) 20 E5
Monceau-lès-Leups (02) 20 C5
Monceau-Saint-Waast (59) 13 G4
Monceau-sur-Oise (02) 20 D2
les Monceaux (14) 33 J6
Monceaux (60) 38 B3
Monceaux-au-Perche (61) 83 J2
Monceaux-en-Bessin (14) 32 B4
Monceaux-l'Abbaye (60) 17 G5
Monceaux-le-Comte (58) 133 H5
Monceaux-sur-Dordogne (19) . . . 216 C5
Moncel-lès-Lunéville (54) 66 D6
Moncel-sur-Seille (54) 66 C4
Moncel-sur-Vair (88) 93 G3
la Moncelle (08) 23 F4
Moncetz-l'Abbaye (51) 63 G6
Moncetz-Longevas (51) 62 E3
Moncey (25) 138 B4
Monchaux-Soreng (76) 16 E1
Monchaux-sur-Écaillon (59) 12 C3
Moncheaux (59) 6 D6
Moncheaux-lès-Frévent (62) . . . 10 B2
Monchecourt (59) 11 J2
Monchel-sur-Canche (62) 9 K2
Moncheux (57) 66 B4
Monchiet (62) 10 D3
Monchy-au-Bois (62) 10 D4
Monchy-Breton (62) 10 B1
Monchy-Cayeux (62) 10 A1
Monchy-Humières (60) 38 D1
Monchy-Lagache (80) 19 H2
Monchy-le-Preux (62) 11 F3
Monchy-Saint-Éloi (60) 38 A4
Monchy-sur-Eu (76) 8 C6
Moncla (64) 265 K6
Monclar (32) 266 E2
Monclar (47) 248 A1
Monclar-de-Quercy (82) 269 J2
Monclar-sur-Losse (32) 286 A1
Moncley (25) 137 J5
Moncontour (22) 77 H2
Moncontour (86) 144 D5
Moncorneil-Grazan (32) 286 D2
Moncourt (57) 66 E4
Moncoutant (79) 161 G1
Moncrabeau (47) 267 H1
Moncy (61) 53 G3
Mondavezan (31) 287 H5
Mondelange (57) 27 G5
Mondement-Montgivroux (51) . . 61 H4
Mondescourt (60) 19 J5
Mondevert (35) 104 B1
Mondeville (14) 32 E5
Mondeville (91) 87 F2
Mondicourt (62) 10 C4
Mondigny (08) 22 C4
Mondilhan (31) 286 E4
Mondion (86) 145 H4
Mondon (25) 138 C3
Mondonville (31) 269 F5
Mondonville-Saint-Jean (28) . . . 85 K4
Mondorff (57) 27 H2
Mondoubleau (41) 108 A3
Mondouzil (31) 269 H6
Mondragon (84) 256 D4
Mondrainville (14) 32 C5
Mondrepuis (02) 21 G1
Mondreville (77) 111 G1
Mondreville (78) 57 H3
Monein (64) 284 A4
Monès (31) 287 H3
Monesple (09) 307 G1
Monestier (03) 185 F2
Monestier (07) 221 F2
Monestier (24) 231 G3
le Monestier (63) 203 J5
Monestier-d'Ambel (38) 242 C2
Monestier-de-Clermont (38) . . . 241 K1
le Monestier-du-Percy (38) 242 A2
Monestier-Merlines (19) 201 H3
Monestier-Port-Dieu (19) 201 H5
Monesiés (81) 251 G6
Monestrol (31) 288 E4
Monétay-sur-Allier (03) 168 E6
Monétay-sur-Loire (03) 169 K3
Monéteau (89) 113 G4
Monêtier-Allemont (05) 259 F1
le Monêtier-les-Bains (05) 225 J5
Monfaucon (24) 231 F1
Monfaucon (65) 285 H2
Monferran-Plavès (32) 286 D2
Monferran-Savès (32) 268 C6
Monflanquin (47) 232 K1
Monfort (32) 268 A4
Monfréville (14) 31 H1
Mongaillard (47) 247 J4
Mongausy (32) 287 F2
Mongauzy (33) 230 D5
Monget (40) 265 G6
Monguilhem (32) 266 A3

Monheurt (47) 247 J3
Monhoudou (72) 83 F5
Monieux (84) 258 A6
Monistrol-d'Allier (43) 219 K6
Monistrol-sur-Loire (43) 221 F2
Monlaur-Bernet (32) 286 C4
Monléon-Magnoac (65) 286 C5
Monlet (43) 220 A3
Monlezun (32) 285 J2
Monlezun-d'Armagnac (32) 266 A3
Monlong (65) 286 B5
Monmadalès (24) 231 K3
Monmarvès (24) 231 K4
Monnai (61) 55 G3
Monnaie (37) 127 K3
la Monnerie-le-Montel (63) 203 J1
Monnerville (91) 86 B4
Monnes (02) 39 H5
Monnet-la-Ville (39) 173 J1
Monnetay (39) 173 F4
Monnetier-Mornex (74) 191 G2
Monneville (60) 37 G5
Monnières (39) 155 G2
Monnières (44) 123 J5
Monoblet (30) 274 C1
Monpardiac (32) 285 K2
Monpazier (24) 232 C4
Monpezat (64) 285 G2
Monplaisant (24) 232 D3
Monprimblanc (33) 230 A4
Mons (16) 178 E6
Mons (17) 195 K1
Mons (30) 255 H5
Mons (31) 269 J6
Mons (34) 291 H1
Mons (63) 185 J5
Mons (83) 280 B4
Mons-Boubert (80) 8 E5
Mons-en-Baroeul (59) 6 E4
Mons-en-Laonnois (02) 20 C6
Mons-en-Montois (77) 88 C2
Mons-en-Pévèle (59) 6 E6
Monsac (24) 232 A3
Monsaguel (24) 231 J3
Monsec (24) 197 H6
Monségur (33) 230 D4
Monségur (40) 265 G6
Monségur (47) 248 E1
Monségur (64) 285 G2
la Monselie (15) 217 J2
Monsempron-Libos (47) 248 E1
Monsireigne (85) 160 C1
Monsols (69) 187 K2
Monsteroux-Milieu (38) 206 B6
Monsures (80) 17 K4
Monswiller (67) 70 B1
Mont (64) 284 A2
Mont (65) 305 G4
Mont (71) 169 K3
le Mont (88) 95 J2
Mont-Bernanchon (62) 5 K5
Mont-Bertrand (14) 31 H4
Mont-Bonvillers (54) 26 D5
Mont-Cauvaire (76) 15 K6
Mont-d'Astarac (32) 286 C4
Mont-Dauphin (05) 227 A3
Mont-de-Galié (31) 305 J2
Mont-de-Lans (38) 224 E5
Mont-de-Laval (25) 157 H1
Mont-de-l'If (76) 15 H6
Mont-de-Marrast (32) 286 A3
Mont-de-Marsan (40) 265 G2
Mont-de-Vougney (25) 139 G5
Mont-devant-Sassey (55) 43 F2
le Mont-Dieu (08) 22 E6
Mont-Disse (64) 285 F1
Mont-Dol (35) 51 F4
Mont Dore (63) 202 A4
Mont-d'Origny (02) 20 C2
Mont-et-Marré (58) 151 J3
Mont-Laurent (08) 41 K1
Mont-le-Vernois (70) 138 A1
Mont-le-Vignoble (54) 65 H6
Mont-lès-Lamarche (88) 117 H2
Mont-lès-Neufchâteau (88) 93 F3
Mont-lès-Seurre (71) 154 D4
Mont-l'Étroit (54) 93 G2
Mont-l'Évêque (60) 38 C5
Mont-Louis (66) 313 J4
Mont-Notre-Dame (02) 40 B4
Mont-Ormel (61) 54 E3
Mont-près-Chambord (41) 129 F2
Mont-Roc (81) 271 G4
le Mont-Saint-Adrien (60) 37 G2
Mont-Saint-Aignan (76) 35 H1
Mont-Saint-Éloi (62) 10 E2
Mont-Saint-Jean (02) 21 J4
Mont-Saint-Jean (21) 134 E6
Mont-Saint-Jean (72) 82 B5
Mont-Saint-Léger (70) 137 H1
Mont-Saint-Martin (02) 40 B4
Mont-Saint-Martin (08) 42 B3
Mont-Saint-Martin (38) 224 A6
Mont-Saint-Martin (54) 26 D2
le Mont-Saint-Michel (50) 51 J3
Mont-Saint-Père (02) 40 A6
Mont-Saint-Remy (08) 41 K2
Mont-Saint-Sulpice (89) 113 G2
Mont-Saint-Vincent (71) 171 F2
Mont-Saxonnex (74) 191 J4
Mont-sous-Vaudrey (39) 155 H3

Mont-sur-Courville (51) 40 C4
Mont-sur-Meurthe (54) 66 D6
Mont-sur-Monnet (39) 173 J1
Montabard (61) 54 B4
Montabon (72) 127 F1
Montabot (50) 31 G5
Montacher-Villegardin (89) 88 B6
Montadet (32) 287 G3
Montady (34) 291 K4
Montagagne (09) 307 G3
Montagna-le-Reconduit (39) . . . 172 E4
Montagna-le-Templier (39) 173 F6
Montagnac (30) 274 E2
Montagnac (34) 292 C2
Montagnac-d'Auberoche (24) . . . 214 C4
Montagnac-la-Crempse (24) . . . 213 J4
Montagnac-Montpezat (04) 278 E3
Montagnac-sur-Auvignon (47) . . 247 K5
Montagnac-sur-Lède (47) 232 B6
Montagnat (01) 189 G2
Montagne (33) 230 B1
Montagne (38) 223 F4
la Montagne (44) 123 F4
la Montagne (70) 119 F3
Montagne-Fayel (80) 17 H2
Montagney (70) 137 G5
Montagney-Servigney (25) 138 C3
Montagnieu (01) 207 G1
Montagnieu (38) 207 G5
Montagnol (12) 272 D3
Montagnole (73) 208 B4
Montagny (42) 187 G4
Montagny (69) 205 K3
Montagny (73) 209 J5
Montagny-en-Vexin (60) 36 C5
Montagny-lès-Beaune (21) 154 A4
Montagny-lès-Buxy (71) 171 H1
Montagny-les-Lanches (74) 190 E6
Montagny-lès-Seurre (21) 154 E3
Montagny-près-Louhans (71) . . . 172 D2
Montagny-Sainte-Félicité (60) . . 38 D6
Montagny-sur-Grosne (71) 171 G6
Montagoudin (33) 230 C5
Montagrier (24) 213 H2
Montagudet (82) 249 G4
Montagut (64) 284 B1
Montaignac-Saint-Hippolyte (19) . . 216 D2
Montaigu (02) 21 F6
Montaigu (39) 173 G2
Montaigu (85) 142 A3
Montaigu-de-Quercy (82) 249 F3
Montaigu-la-Brisette (50) 28 E3
Montaigu-le-Blin (03) 185 K1
Montaigu-les-Bois (50) 31 F6
Montaiguët-en-Forez (03) 186 C1
Montaigut (63) 184 C3
Montaigut-le-Blanc (23) 182 C3
Montaigut-le-Blanc (63) 202 D4
Montaigut-sur-Save (31) 268 E5
Montaillé (72) 107 J2
Montailleur (73) 209 F3
Montaillou (09) 308 B5
Montaimont (73) 209 F6
Montain (39) 173 G1
Montaïn (82) 268 D2
Montainville (28) 85 G5
Montainville (78) 57 K3
Montalba-le-Château (66) 309 J6
Montalembert (79) 179 G3
Montalet-le-Bois (78) 57 K1
Montalieu-Vercieu (38) 207 G1
Montalzat (82) 250 A4
Montamat (32) 287 F2
Montambert (58) 169 H1
Montamel (46) 233 H5
Montamisé (86) 163 F3
Montamy (14) 53 F1
Montanay (69) 188 D6
Montancy (25) 139 K4
Montandon (25) 139 H4
Montanel (50) 51 J5
Montaner (64) 285 G3
Montanges (01) 190 C2
Montans (81) 270 B3
Montapas (58) 151 J4
Montarcher (42) 204 C6
Montardit (09) 306 E1
Montardon (64) 284 E3
Montaren-et-Saint-Médiers (30) . . 275 G1
Montargis (45) 111 J3
Montarlot (77) 87 K4
Montarlot-lès-Rioz (70) 137 K4
Montarnaud (34) 274 A6
Montaron (58) 152 K5
Montastruc (47) 248 A1
Montastruc (65) 285 J2
Montastruc (82) 249 J6
Montastruc-de-Salies (31) 306 B2
Montastruc-la-Conseillère (31) . . 269 J5
Montastruc-Savès (31) 287 H4
le Montat (46) 250 A2
Montataire (60) 38 A4
Montauban (82) 269 F1
Montauban-de-Bretagne (35) . . . 78 C3
Montauban-de-Luchon (31) 305 H5
Montauban-de-Picardie (80) . . . 10 E6
Montauban-sur-l'Ouvèze (26) . . . 258 B3
Montaud (34) 274 C4
Montaud (38) 223 J4
Montaudin (53) 80 D3
Montaulieu (26) 257 J2
Montaulin (10) 90 C5

Montaure (27) 35 H4
Montauriol (11) 289 F5
Montauriol (47) 231 J5
Montauriol (66) 315 F3
Montauriol (81) 251 J6
Montauroux (83) 280 B5
Montaut (09) 288 D6
Montaut (24) 231 K3
Montaut (31) 288 A4
Montaut (32) 286 B3
Montaut (40) 265 F4
Montaut (47) 231 K5
Montaut (64) 284 E6
Montaut-les-Créneaux (32) 267 J5
Montautour (35) 80 B5
Montauville (54) 65 J2
Montay (59) 12 D5
Montayral (47) 249 F1
Montazeau (24) 230 E1
Montazels (11) 309 F3
Montbard (21) 134 D1
Montbarla (82) 249 G4
Montbarrey (39) 155 J3
Montbarrois (45) 111 F2
Montbartier (82) 269 F2
Montbavin (02) 40 A1
Montbazens (12) 251 H1
Montbazin (34) 293 F2
Montbazon (37) 127 J6
Montbel (09) 308 C2
Montbel (48) 238 A5
Montbéliard (25) 139 H2
Montbéliardot (25) 139 G6
Montbellet (71) 171 K4
Montbenoît (25) 157 G3
Montberaud (31) 287 J6
Montbernard (31) 286 E4
Montberon (31) 269 H5
Montbert (44) 123 H6
Montberthault (21) 134 C3
Montbeton (82) 269 F1
Montbeugny (03) 169 F4
Montbizot (72) 82 D6
Montblainville (55) 42 E4
Montblanc (34) 292 B3
Montboillon (70) 137 J4
Montboissier (28) 85 F6
Montbolo (66) 314 E5
Montbonnot-Saint-Martin (38) . . 224 B2
Montboucher (23) 182 B5
Montboucher-sur-Jabron (26) . . . 240 B5
Montboudif (15) 218 A1
Montbouton (90) 139 J2
Montbouy (45) 111 J4
Montboyer (16) 212 E2
Montbozon (70) 138 C3
Montbrand (05) 242 A5
Montbras (55) 93 G1
Montbray (50) 31 H6
Montbré (51) 41 F5
Montbrehain (02) 20 A1
Montbrison (26) 257 G1
Montbrison (42) 204 D4
Montbron (16) 197 H3
Montbronn (57) 69 F4
Montbrun (46) 250 E1
Montbrun (48) 254 B3
Montbrun-Bocage (31) 306 E1
Montbrun-des-Corbières (11) . . . 290 E6
Montbrun-Lauragais (31) 288 C2
Montbrun-les-Bains (26) 258 A4
Montcabrier (46) 232 D6
Montcabrier (81) 269 K6
Montcaret (24) 230 D2
Montcarra (38) 207 G3
Montcavrel (62) 4 C5
Montceau-et-Écharnant (21) . . . 153 J3
Montceau-les-Mines (71) 170 E2
Montceaux (01) 188 C3
Montceaux-lès-Meaux (77) 60 A2
Montceaux-lès-Provins (77) 60 E5
Montceaux-lès-Vaudes (10) 90 B6
Montceaux-l'Étoile (71) 170 B6
Montceaux-Ragny (71) 171 K2
Montcel (63) 185 F5
Montcel (73) 208 C2
Montcenis (71) 153 G6
Montcet (01) 189 F2
Montcey (70) 118 B6
Montchaboud (38) 224 B4
Montchal (42) 205 F1
Montchâlons (02) 40 C1
Montchamp (14) 53 F2
Montchamp (15) 219 F5
Montchanin (71) 171 F1
Montcharvot (52) 117 G3
Montchâton (50) 30 D4
Montchaude (16) 196 A6
Montchauvet (14) 53 F2
Montchauvet (78) 57 H3
Montchenu (26) 222 D3
Montcheutin (08) 42 C3
Montchevrel (61) 83 F1
Montchevrier (36) 165 J5
Montclar (04) 259 K1
Montclar (11) 309 F1
Montclar (12) 271 K2
Montclar-de-Comminges (31) . . . 287 H6
Montclar-Lauragais (31) 288 E4
Montclar-sur-Gervanne (26) . . . 241 F3
Montclard (43) 219 J3
Montcléra (46) 233 F5

Montclus (05) 258 D1
Montclus (30) 256 A4
Montcombroux-les-Mines (03) . . 169 H6
Montcony (71) 172 D1
Montcorbon (45) 112 B3
Montcornet (02) 21 G4
Montcornet (08) 22 C2
Montcourt (70) 117 J3
Montcourt-Fromonville (77) 87 H5
Montcoy (71) 154 C6
Montcresson (45) 111 J4
Montcuit (50) 31 F3
Montcuq (46) 249 H3
Montcusel (39) 173 H6
Montcy-Notre-Dame (08) 22 D4
Montdardier (30) 273 J2
Montdauphin (77) 60 E3
Montdidier (57) 67 G1
Montdidier (80) 18 D5
Montdoré (70) 118 A3
Montdoumerc (46) 250 A3
Montdragon (81) 270 D4
Montdurausse (81) 269 J2
Monte (2B) 319 H3
Monteaux (41) 128 C3
Montebourg (50) 29 F4
Montech (82) 268 E2
Montécheroux (25) 139 H4
Montegrosso (2B) 318 C3
Montégut (32) 267 J6
Montégut (40) 265 K3
Montégut (65) 305 G1
Montégut-Arros (32) 285 J3
Montégut-Bourjac (31) 287 G4
Montégut-en-Couserans (09) . . . 306 C3
Montégut-Lauragais (31) 289 G2
Montégut-Plantaurel (09) 307 H2
Montégut-Savès (32) 287 G2
Monteignet-sur-l'Andelot (03) . . . 185 G3
le Monteil (15) 217 J2
le Monteil (43) 220 C5
le Monteil-au-Vicomte (23) 182 D6
Monteille (14) 33 H6
Monteils (12) 251 F4
Monteils (30) 255 H6
Monteils (82) 250 B5
Montel-de-Gelat (63) 184 A6
Montéléger (26) 240 C2
Montélier (26) 222 D6
Montélimar (26) 240 B5
le Montellier (01) 188 E5
Montels (09) 307 G2
Montels (34) 291 J4
Montels (81) 270 B2
Montemboeuf (16) 197 J2
Montenach (57) 27 J3
Montenay (53) 80 D4
Montendre (17) 211 J2
Montendry (73) 208 E4
Montenescourt (62) 10 D3
Monteneuf (56) 102 B1
Montenils (77) 61 F4
Montenois (25) 139 G2
Montenoison (58) 151 G1
Montenoy (54) 66 B3
Montépilloy (60) 38 C5
Montéplain (39) 155 J1
Montépreux (51) 62 B5
Monterblanc (56) 101 G4
Montereau (45) 111 G4
Montereau-Fault-Yonne (77) . . . 88 A4
Montereau-sur-le-Jard (77) 87 H1
Monterfil (35) 78 D4
Montérolier (76) 16 C5
Monterrein (56) 101 K2
Montertelot (56) 101 J2
Montescot (66) 315 H3
Montescourt-Lizerolles (02) 19 K4
Montespan (31) 306 A1
Montesquieu (34) 292 A1
Montesquieu (47) 247 K4
Montesquieu (82) 249 G5
Montesquieu-Avantès (09) 306 E2
Montesquieu-des-Albères (66) . . 315 G4
Montesquieu-Guittaut (31) 286 E4
Montesquieu-Lauragais (31) . . . 288 D3
Montesquieu-Volvestre (31) 287 K5
Montesquiou (32) 286 A1
Montessaux (70) 118 E5
Montesson (78) 58 C3
Montestruc-sur-Gers (32) 267 J4
le Montet (03) 168 B5
Montet-et-Bouxal (46) 234 D3
Monteton (47) 231 F5
Monteux (84) 257 G6
Montévrain (77) 59 J3
Montézic (12) 235 K4
Montfa (09) 307 F1
Montfa (81) 271 F5
Montfalcon (38) 223 F2
Montfarville (50) 29 G2
Montfaucon (02) 60 E2
Montfaucon (25) 138 A6
Montfaucon (30) 256 D6
Montfaucon (46) 233 J4
Montfaucon (49) 142 C2
Montfaucon-d'Argonne (55) 43 F4
Montfaucon-en-Velay (43) 221 G3
Montfermeil (93) 59 G3
Montfermier (82) 249 K4
Montfermy (63) 184 C6

Montferrand (11). 289 F4
Montferrand-du-Périgord (24) 232 B3
Montferrand-la-Fare (26) 258 A2
Montferrand-le-Château (25) . . . 156 A1
Montferrat (38) 207 J5
Montferrat (83) 279 J5
Montferrer (66) 314 D5
Montferrier (09) 308 A4
Montferrier-sur-Lez (34) 274 B5
Montfey (10) 113 J2
Montfiquet (14) 31 K3
Montfleur (39) 173 F6
Montflours (53) 81 F6
Montflovin (25) 157 F3
Montfort (04) 259 G5
Montfort (25) 156 A2
Montfort (49) 144 B1
Montfort (64) 283 H3
Montfort-en-Chalosse (40) 264 D4
Montfort-l'Amaury (78) 57 K4
Montfort-le-Gesnois (72) 107 F2
Montfort-sur-Argens (83) 298 A1
Montfort-sur-Boulzane (11) 309 F6
Montfort-sur-Meu (35) 78 D4
Montfort-sur-Risle (27) 34 D3
Montfranc (12) 271 J3
Montfrin (30) 275 K3
Montfroc (26) 258 C4
Montfuron (04) 278 A3
Montgaillard (09) 307 J3
Montgaillard (11) 309 J4
Montgaillard (40) 265 G4
Montgaillard (65) 285 H6
Montgaillard (81) 269 J2
Montgaillard (82) 268 B2
Montgaillard-de-Salies (31) 306 B2
Montgaillard-Lauragais (31) 288 E3
Montgaillard-sur-Save (31) 286 E5
Montgardin (05) 243 G5
Montgardon (50) 30 D1
Montgaroult (61) 54 B4
Montgauch (09) 306 C2
Montgaudry (61) 83 G3
Montgazin (31) 288 A4
Montgé-en-Goële (77) 59 J1
Montgeard (31) 288 D4
Montgellafrey (73) 209 F6
Montgenèvre (05) 226 A6
Montgenost (51) 89 G1
Montgérain (60) 18 D6
Montgermont (35) 79 F3
Montgeron (91) 59 F5
Montgeroult (95) 37 G6
Montgesoye (25) 156 D2
Montgesty (46) 233 G5
Montgey (81) 289 G2
Montgibaud (19) 199 G5
Montgilbert (73) 209 F4
Montgirod (73) 209 J4
Montgiscard (31) 288 D2
Montgivray (36) 166 B3
Montgobert (02) 39 G3
Montgon (08) 42 B1
Montgradail (11) 308 C1
Montgras (31) 287 H2
Montgreleix (15) 218 C2
Montgru-Saint-Hilaire (02) 39 J5
Montguers (26) 258 B3
Montgueux (10) 89 K4
Montguillon (49) 104 E6
Montguyon (17) 212 B3
les Monthairons (55) 43 J6
Montharville (28) 84 E4
Monthault (35) 80 B1
Monthaut (11) 308 D1
Monthelie (21) 153 K4
Monthelon (51) 61 K2
Monthelon (71) 152 E4
Monthenault (02) 40 B1
Montheries (52) 91 J6
Montherlant (60) 37 G4
Monthermé (08) 22 D2
Monthiers (02) 39 J6
Monthieux (01) 188 D5
Monthion (73) 209 F4
Monthodon (37) 128 A1
Monthoiron (86) 163 H1
Monthois (08) 42 B3
Montholier (39) 155 J4
Monthou-sur-Bièvre (41) 128 C3
Monthou-sur-Cher (41) 128 E5
Monthuchon (50) 30 E3
Monthurel (02) 61 F1
Monthureux-le-Sec (88) 93 K6
Monthureux-sur-Saône (88) 117 J2
Monthyon (77) 59 J1
Monticello (2B) 318 D2
Montier-en-Der (52) 91 H2
Montier-en-l'Isle (10) 91 G5
Montiéramey (10) 90 D5
Montierchaume (36) 148 A5
Montiers (60) 38 B1
Montiers-sur-Saulx (55) 92 C1
Monties (32) 286 D3
Montignac (24) 214 E5
Montignac (33) 230 A3
Montignac (65) 285 J6
Montignac-Charente (16) 196 D2
Montignac-de-Lauzun (47) 231 H5
Montignac-le-Coq (16) 213 F1
Montignac-Toupinerie (47) 231 G6
Montignargues (30) 275 F2

Montigné (16) 196 B1
Montigné-le-Brillant (53) 104 E2
Montigné-lès-Rairies (49) 126 A1
Montigné-sur-Moine (49) 142 C2
Montigny (14) 32 C6
Montigny (18) 149 K1
Montigny (45) 110 C1
Montigny (54) 95 G1
Montigny (72) 82 E2
Montigny (76) 35 G1
Montigny-aux-Amognes (58) 151 F3
Montigny-devant-Sassey (55) 43 F1
Montigny-en-Arrouaise (02) 20 B2
Montigny-en-Cambrésis (59) 12 C5
Montigny-en-Gohelle (62) 11 G1
Montigny-en-Morvan (58) 152 A2
Montigny-en-Ostrevent (59) 11 J2
Montigny-la-Resle (89) 113 H4
Montigny-l'Allier (02) 39 G6
Montigny-le-Bretonneux (78) . . . 58 B4
Montigny-le-Chartif (28) 84 D5
Montigny-le-Franc (02) 21 F4
Montigny-le-Gannelon (28) 108 D2
Montigny-le-Guesdier (77) 88 D4
Montigny-Lencoup (77) 88 B3
Montigny-Lengrain (02) 39 G3
Montigny-lès-Arsures (39) 155 K4
Montigny-lès-Cherlieu (70) 117 H5
Montigny-lès-Condé (02) 61 F2
Montigny-lès-Cormeilles (95) . . . 58 D2
Montigny-les-Jongleurs (80) 9 J4
Montigny-lès-Metz (57) 45 F5
Montigny-lès-Monts (10) 113 K1
Montigny-lès-Vaucouleurs (55) . . . 65 F6
Montigny-lès-Vesoul (70) 138 A1
Montigny-Montfort (21) 134 D2
Montigny-Mornay-Villeneuve-
    sur-Vingeanne (21) 136 E2
Montigny-Saint-Barthélemy (21) . . 134 D4
Montigny-sous-Marle (02) 20 E4
Montigny-sur-Armançon (21) . . . 134 E4
Montigny-sur-Aube (21) 115 H3
Montigny-sur-Avre (28) 56 C5
Montigny-sur-Canne (58) 151 J5
Montigny-sur-Chiers (54) 26 C3
Montigny-sur-Crécy (02) 20 C4
Montigny-sur-l'Ain (39) 173 J1
Montigny-sur-l'Hallue (80) 18 C1
Montigny-sur-Loing (77) 87 J4
Montigny-sur-Meuse (08) 24 C2
Montigny-sur-Vence (08) 22 C5
Montigny-sur-Vesle (51) 40 D3
Montilliers (49) 143 J1
Montillot (89) 133 H3
Montilly (03) 168 D3
Montilly-sur-Noireau (61) 53 H3
Montils (17) 195 H3
les Montils (41) 128 E3
Montipouret (36) 166 A2
Montirat (11) 290 C6
Montirat (81) 251 G5
Montireau (28) 84 C3
Montiron (32) 287 F1
Montivernage (25) 138 D5
Montivilliers (76) 14 B6
Montjardin (11) 308 C3
Montjaux (12) 252 E6
Montjavoult (60) 36 E5
Montjay (05) 258 C2
Montjay (71) 155 F6
Montjean (16) 179 F3
Montjean (53) 104 D2
Montjean-sur-Loire (49) 124 D4
Montjoi (11) 309 H3
Montjoi (82) 248 E3
Montjoie-en-Couserans (09) 306 D2
Montjoie-le-Château (25) 139 J4
Montjoie-Saint-Martin (50) 80 A1
Montjoire (31) 269 H4
Montjoux (26) 240 E6
Montjoyer (26) 256 E1
Montjustin (04) 277 K3
Montjustin-et-Velotte (70) 138 D1
Montlandon (28) 84 C3
Montlaur (11) 309 J1
Montlaur (12) 272 B3
Montlaur (31) 288 D2
Montlaur-en-Diois (26) 241 H4
Montlaux (04) 259 F6
Montlauzun (46) 249 H3
Montlay-en-Auxois (21) 134 D5
Montlebon (25) 157 H2
Montlevicq (36) 166 C3
Montlevon (02) 61 F2
Montlhéry (91) 58 D6
Montliard (45) 111 F2
Montlieu-la-Garde (17) 212 A3
Montlignon (95) 58 D1
Montliot-et-Courcelles (21) 115 F4
Montlivault (41) 129 F1
Montlognon (60) 38 C5
Montloué (02) 21 H4
Montlouis (18) 149 F6
Montlouis-sur-Loire (37) 127 K5
Montluçon (03) 167 H6
Montluel (01) 188 E6
Montmachoux (77) 88 A4
Montmacq (60) 38 E1
Montmagny (95) 58 E2
Montmahoux (25) 156 C3
Montmain (21) 154 D3
Montmain (76) 35 K2

Montmançon (21) 136 D5
Montmarault (03) 184 E1
Montmarlon (39) 156 B5
Montmartin (60) 38 C1
Montmartin-en-Graignes (50) 31 G1
Montmartin-le-Haut (10) 91 F6
Montmartin-sur-Mer (50) 30 D5
Montmaur (05) 242 C5
Montmaur (11) 289 F3
Montmaur-en-Diois (26) 241 H4
Montmaurin (31) 286 D5
Montmédy (55) 23 K6
Montmeillant (08) 21 K4
Montmelard (71) 171 F6
Montmelas-Saint-Sorlin (69) 188 A4
Montmélian (73) 208 D5
Montmerle-sur-Saône (01) 188 B4
Montmerrei (61) 54 C6
Montmeyan (83) 278 E5
Montmeyran (26) 240 D2
Montmin (74) 208 E1
Montmirail (51) 61 F3
Montmirail (72) 107 K1
Montmiral (26) 222 E4
Montmirat (30) 274 E2
Montmirey-la-Ville (39) 137 F6
Montmirey-le-Château (39) 137 F6
Montmoreau-Saint-Cybard (16) . . . 212 E1
Montmorency (95) 58 E2
Montmorency-Beaufort (10) 91 F2
Montmorillon (86) 164 A5
Montmorin (05) 258 B3
Montmorin (63) 203 F3
Montmorot (39) 173 F2
Montmort (71) 170 B1
Montmort-Lucy (51) 61 J2
Montmotier (88) 118 B2
Montmoyen (21) 115 H6
Montmurat (15) 235 F5
Montner (66) 309 K6
Montoillot (21) 135 G6
Montoir-de-Bretagne (44) 122 B2
Montoire-sur-le-Loir (41) 108 A6
Montois-la-Montagne (57) 27 F6
Montoison (26) 240 D2
Montoldre (03) 169 F6
Montolieu (11) 289 K4
Montolivet (77) 60 E4
Montonvillers (80) 10 A6
Montord (03) 185 G1
Montory (64) 283 J6
Montot (21) 154 E2
Montot (70) 137 F2
Montot-sur-Rognon (52) 92 C4
Montouliers (34) 291 G4
Montoulieu (09) 307 J4
Montoulieu (34) 274 B2
Montoulieu-Saint-Bernard (31) . . . 287 G5
Montournais (85) 160 E1
Montours (35) 51 K6
Montourtier (53) 81 G5
Montoussé (65) 305 F1
Montoussin (31) 287 H5
Montoy-Flanville (57) 45 G5
Montpellier (34) 274 C6
Montpellier-de-Médillan (17) 195 F3
Montpensier (63) 185 G4
Montperreux (25) 157 F5
Montpeyroux (12) 236 B5
Montpeyroux (24) 230 D1
Montpeyroux (34) 273 J5
Montpeyroux (63) 202 E4
Montpezat (30) 274 E3
Montpezat (32) 287 G3
Montpezat (47) 248 A3
Montpezat-de-Quercy (82) 250 A4
Montpezat-sous-Bauzon (07) 239 F4
Montpinchon (50) 31 F4
Montpinier (81) 270 E5
Montpitol (31) 269 J5
Montplonne (55) 64 B5
Montpollin (49) 126 B2
Montpon-Ménestérol (24) 212 E6
Montpont-en-Bresse (71) 172 C3
Montpothier (10) 89 F1
Montpouillan (47) 247 G1
Montrabé (31) 269 H6
Montrabot (50) 31 K3
Montracol (01) 189 F2
Montravers (79) 143 G5
Montréal (07) 239 G6
Montréal (11) 289 J6
Montréal (32) 266 E2
Montréal (89) 134 A3
Montréal-la-Cluse (01) 189 K2
Montréal-les-Sources (26) 257 K2
Montrécourt (59) 12 C3
Montredon (46) 235 F5
Montredon-des-Corbières (11) . . . 291 H6
Montredon-Labessonnié (81) 271 F5
Montregard (43) 221 G4
Montréjeau (31) 305 H1
Montrelais (44) 124 C4
Montrem (24) 213 J4
Montrésor (37) 147 F2
Montret (71) 172 B2
Montreuil (28) 57 H4
Montreuil (62) 4 C6
Montreuil (85) 160 D5
Montreuil (93) 59 F3
Montreuil-au-Houlme (61) 53 K5
Montreuil-aux-Lions (02) 60 C1

Montreuil-Bellay (49) 144 C2
Montreuil-Bonnin (86) 162 D3
Montreuil-des-Landes (35) 80 A5
Montreuil-en-Auge (14) 33 J5
Montreuil-en-Caux (76) 16 A4
Montreuil-en-Touraine (37) 128 B3
Montreuil-Juigné (49) 125 G2
Montreuil-la-Cambe (61) 54 D3
Montreuil-l'Argillé (27) 55 G2
Montreuil-le-Chétif (72) 82 C5
Montreuil-le-Gast (35) 79 F2
Montreuil-le-Henri (72) 107 H4
Montreuil-Poulay (53) 81 H3
Montreuil-sous-Pérouse (35) 80 A6
Montreuil-sur-Barse (10) 90 D5
Montreuil-sur-Blaise (52) 91 K2
Montreuil-sur-Brêche (60) 37 J1
Montreuil-sur-Epte (95) 36 D5
Montreuil-sur-Ille (35) 79 G2
Montreuil-sur-Loir (49) 125 J1
Montreuil-sur-Lozon (50) 31 G3
Montreuil-sur-Maine (49) 125 F1
Montreuil-sur-Thérain (60) 37 H3
Montreuil-sur-Thonnance (52) 92 B2
Montreuillon (58) 152 A1
Montreux (54) 67 H6
Montreux-Château (90) 139 K1
Montreux-Jeune (68) 139 K1
Montreux-Vieux (68) 119 K6
Montrevault (49) 124 B6
Montrevel (38) 207 G5
Montrevel (39) 173 F5
Montrevel-en-Bresse (01) 172 C6
Montrichard (41) 128 D5
Montricher-Albanne (73) 225 H2
Montricoux (82) 250 B6
Montrieux-en-Sologne (41) 129 J3
Montrigaud (26) 222 E3
Montriond (74) 192 A1
Montrodat (48) 237 G6
Montrol-Sénard (87) 180 E4
Montrollet (16) 180 D5
Montromant (69) 205 H3
Montrond (05) 258 D2
Montrond (39) 156 A6
Montrond-le-Château (25) 156 C1
Montrond-les-Bains (42) 204 E3
Montrosier (81) 250 E5
Montrottier (69) 205 G2
Montroty (76) 36 D2
Montrouge (92) 58 E4
Montrouveau (41) 107 J6
Montroy (17) 176 E2
Montrozier (12) 252 C2
Montry (77) 59 J3
Monts (37) 127 H6
Monts (60) 37 G5
Monts-en-Bessin (14) 32 C5
Monts-en-Ternois (62) 10 B2
Monts-sur-Guesnes (86) 145 F5
les Monts-Verts (48) 237 F2
Montsalès (12) 251 F1
Montsalier (04) 258 C6
Montsalvy (15) 235 J4
Montsapey (73) 209 F4
Montsauche-les-Settons (58) 152 C1
Montsaugeon (52) 136 C1
Montsaunès (31) 306 B1
Montsec (55) 65 G2
Montsecret (61) 53 G4
Montségur (09) 308 A4
Montségur-sur-Lauzon (26) 256 E2
Montselgues (07) 238 D6
Montséret (11) 310 B1
Montsérié (65) 305 G2
Montseron (09) 307 F2
Montseveroux (38) 206 C6
Montsoreau (49) 144 E1
Montsoué (40) 265 G4
Montsoult (95) 58 E1
Montsûrs (53) 81 G6
Montsuzain (10) 90 B3
Montureux-et-Prantigny (70) 137 G3
Montureux-lès-Baulay (70) 117 K4
Montusclat (43) 220 E6
Montussaint (25) 138 C3
Montussan (33) 229 J1
Montvalen (81) 269 J3
Montvalent (46) 233 K2
Montvalezan (73) 193 B3
Montvendre (26) 240 D1
Montverdun (42) 204 D3
Montvernier (73) 225 G1
Montvert (15) 216 E6
Montvicq (03) 184 C1
Montviette (14) 54 D1
Montville (76) 15 K6
Montviron (50) 51 J2
Montzéville (55) 43 G4
Monviel (47) 231 J5
Monze (11) 290 C6
Moon-sur-Elle (50) 31 H2
Moosch (68) 119 K3
Mooslargue (68) 139 J5
Moraches (58) 133 G6
Moragne (17) 177 G5
Morainville (28) 85 K4
Morainville-Jouveaux (27) 34 B4
Morainvilliers (78) 58 A2
Morancé (69) 188 B6
Morancez (28) 85 G3

Morancourt (52) 91 K3
Morand (37) 128 B2
Morangis (51) 61 K2
Morangis (91) 58 E5
Morangles (60) 37 J5
Morannes (49) 105 H5
Moranville (55) 43 K5
Moras (38) 206 E3
Moras-en-Valloire (26) 222 D2
Morbecque (59) 3 J6
Morbier (39) 174 A3
Morcenx (40) 245 F6
Morchain (80) 19 G3
Morchies (62) 11 G4
Morcourt (02) 20 A2
Morcourt (80) 18 E2
Mordelles (35) 78 E4
Moréac (56) 101 F2
Morée (41) 108 D4
Moreilles (85) 160 B5
Morelmaison (88) 93 J4
Morembert (10) 90 D2
Morestel (38) 207 G3
Morette (38) 223 H2
Moreuil (80) 18 C3
Morey (71) 153 J6
Morey-Saint-Denis (21) 154 B1
Morez (39) 174 A3
Morfontaine (54) 26 D3
Morganx (40) 265 G6
Morgemoulin (55) 26 B6
Morgny (27) 36 C2
Morgny-en-Thiérache (02) 21 H3
Morgny-la-Pommeraye (76) 35 K1
Morhange (57) 66 E2
Moriat (63) 219 F1
Morienne (76) 17 F3
Morienval (60) 38 E4
Morières-lès-Avignon (84) 276 C2
Moriers (28) 85 F6
Morieux (22) 49 H6
Moriez (04) 279 J1
Morigny (50) 31 H6
Morigny-Champigny (91) 86 D3
Morillon (74) 192 A3
Moringhem (62) 3 F5
Morionvilliers (52) 92 D3
Morisel (80) 18 C3
Moriville (88) 94 D3
Moriviller (54) 94 D2
Morizécourt (88) 117 H1
Morizès (33) 230 C5
Morlaàs (64) 284 E3
Morlac (18) 166 E2
Morlaix (29) 47 G4
Morlancourt (80) 18 D1
Morlanne (64) 284 B1
Morlet (71) 153 H4
Morley (55) 92 B1
Morlhon-le-Haut (12) 251 G3
Morlincourt (60) 19 H6
Mormaison (85) 141 K4
Mormant (77) 87 K1
Mormant-sur-Vernisson (45) 111 J3
Mormès (32) 266 A3
Mormoiron (84) 257 J6
Mornac (16) 197 F3
Mornac-sur-Seudre (17) 194 C2
Mornand (42) 204 D3
Mornans (26) 240 E5
Mornant (69) 205 J4
Mornas (84) 256 D4
Mornay (71) 170 E4
Mornay-Berry (18) 150 B3
Mornay-sur-Allier (18) 150 C6
Moroges (71) 171 H1
Morogues (18) 149 J1
Morosaglia (2B) 319 G4
Morre (25) 138 A6
Morsain (02) 39 H2
Morsains (51) 61 F4
Morsalines (50) 29 F3
Morsan (27) 34 D5
Morsang-sur-Orge (91) 58 E6
Morsang-sur-Seine (91) 87 F1
Morsbach (57) 68 B2
Morsbronn-les-Bains (67) 25 A3
Morschwiller (67) 69 J6
Morschwiller-le-Bas (68) 97 B2
Morsiglia (2B) 317 C2
Mortagne (88) 95 G4
Mortagne-au-Perche (61) 83 H2
Mortagne-du-Nord (59) 7 H6
Mortagne-sur-Gironde (17) 194 C5
Mortagne-sur-Sèvre (85) 142 E3
Mortain (50) 52 D5
Mortcerf (77) 59 K4
la Morte (38) 224 C5
Morteau (25) 157 H2
Morteaux-Coulibœuf (14) 54 B2
Mortefontaine (02) 39 G3
Mortefontaine (60) 38 B6
Mortefontaine-en-Thelle (60) . . . 37 H4
Mortemart (87) 180 E4
Mortemer (60) 18 E6
Mortemer (76) 16 E4
Mortery (77) 88 D1
Morthomiers (18) 149 F3
Mortiers (02) 20 D4
Mortiers (17) 195 K6

Morton (86) 144 D2
Mortrée (61) 54 D6
Mortroux (23) 166 A6
Mortzwiller (68) 119 K5
Morval (62) 11 F6
Morvillars (90) 139 J2
Morville (50) 28 D4
Morville (88) 93 H5
Morville-en-Beauce (45) 86 C5
Morville-lès-Vic (57) 66 D3
Morville-sur-Andelle (76) 36 A3
Morville-sur-Nied (57) 66 C1
Morville-sur-Seille (54) 66 A2
Morvillers (60) 17 G6
Morvillers-Saint-Saturnin (80) . . 17 G3
Morvilliers (10) 91 H3
Morvilliers (28) 56 B6
Mory (62) 11 F4
Mory-Montcrux (60) 18 B6
Morzine (74) 192 B2
Mosles (14) 32 A3
Moslins (51) 61 K2
Mosnac (16) 196 C4
Mosnac (17) 195 H5
Mosnay (36) 165 H3
Mosnes (37) 128 C4
Mosset (66) 314 B2
Mosson (21) 115 G3
Mostuéjouls (12) 253 H4
Motey-Besuche (70) 137 G5
Motey-sur-Saône (70) 137 H2
la Mothe-Achard (85) 159 F2
la Mothe-Saint-Héray (79) . . . 162 A6
Mothern (67) 25 E2
Motreff (29) 75 J3
la Motte (22) 77 G4
la Motte (83) 298 E1
la Motte-Chalancon (26) 241 H6
la Motte d'Aigues (84) 277 J4
la Motte-d'Aveillans (38) 224 B6
la Motte-de-Galaure (26) 222 C3
la Motte-du-Caire (04) 259 G2
la Motte-en-Bauges (73) 208 D2
la Motte-en-Champsaur (05) . . 242 E3
la Motte-Fanjas (26) 223 G5
la Motte-Feuilly (36) 166 C4
la Motte-Fouquet (61) 81 K1
la Motte-Saint-Jean (71) 170 A4
la Motte-Saint-Martin (38) . . . 224 A6
la Motte-Servolex (73) 208 B3
la Motte-Ternant (21) 134 C5
la Motte-Tilly (10) 88 E2
Mottereau (28) 84 D5
Motteville (76) 15 H5
Mottier (38) 207 F6
Motz (73) 190 C5
Mouacourt (54) 66 C5
Mouais (44) 103 G4
Mouans-Sartoux (06) 280 D5
Mouaville (54) 26 C4
Mouazé (35) 79 G3
Mouchamps (85) 142 C6
Mouchan (32) 267 F2
Mouchard (39) 155 K3
la Mouche (50) 51 K1
Mouchès (32) 286 B1
Mouchin (59) 7 F5
Mouchy le-Châtel (60) 37 J3
Moudeyres (43) 220 E6
Mouen (14) 32 D5
Mouettes (27) 57 F3
Mouffy (89) 133 F1
Mouflaines (27) 36 C4
Mouflers (80) 9 J6
Mouflières (80) 17 F1
Mougins (06) 280 E5
Mougon (79) 178 C1
Mouguerre (64) 282 C1
Mouhers (36) 165 K3
Mouhet (36) 165 F6
Mouhous (64) 284 E2
Mouillac (33) 211 K5
Mouillac (82) 250 C4
la Mouille (39) 174 A4
Mouilleron (52) 116 B6
Mouilleron-en-Pareds (85) . . . 160 D2
Mouilleron-le-Captif (85) 159 H1
Mouilly (55) 43 K6
Moulainville (55) 43 H3
Moularès (81) 251 J6
Moulay (53) 81 G5
Moulayrès (81) 270 C6
Moulédous (65) 285 K5
Moulès-et-Baucels (34) 274 A2
Mouloydier (24) 231 J2
Moulézan (30) 274 E2
Moulhard (28) 84 C6
Moulicent (61) 83 K1
Moulidars (16) 196 C3
Mouliets-et-Villemartin (33) . . 230 C2
Mouliherne (49) 126 C3
Moulin-Mage (81) 272 B5
Moulin-Neuf (09) 308 C1
Moulin-Neuf (24) 212 D6
Moulin-sous-Touvent (60) . . . 39 G2
Moulineaux (76) 35 G3
Moulines (14) 53 K1
Moulines (50) 80 C1
Moulinet (06) 311 B4
Moulinet (47) 231 J6
le Moulinet-sur-Solin (45) . . . 111 H5
Moulins (02) 40 C2

Moulins (03) 168 E3
Moulins (35) 79 J6
Moulins-en-Tonnerrois (89) . . . 114 A6
Moulins-Engilbert (58) 152 A4
Moulins-la-Marche (61) 55 G6
Moulins-le-Carbonnel (72) . . . 82 C3
Moulins-lès-Metz (57) 44 E5
Moulins-Saint-Hubert (55) . . . 23 G5
Moulins-sur-Céphons (36) . . . 147 J4
Moulins-sur-Orne (61) 54 B4
Moulins-sur-Ouanne (89) . . . 112 E6
Moulins-sur-Yèvre (18) 149 H3
Moulis (09) 306 D3
Moulis-en-Médoc (33) 211 F5
Moulismes (86) 163 K6
Moulle (62) 3 F1
Moulon (33) 230 A2
Moulon (45) 111 G2
Moulotte (55) 44 B3
Moult (14) 33 G6
Moumoulous (65) 285 K3
Moumour (64) 283 K5
Mounes-Prohencoux (12) . . . 272 B4
Mourède (32) 267 F4
Mourens (33) 230 A4
Mourenx (64) 284 A3
Mouret (12) 235 J6
Moureuille (63) 184 D3
Mourèze (34) 273 G6
Mouriès (13) 276 C5
Mouriez (62) 9 H2
Mourioux-Vieilleville (23) . . . 182 B4
Mourjou (15) 235 G4
Mourmelon-le-Grand (51) . . . 41 J5
Mourmelon-le-Petit (51) 41 H5
Mournans-Charbonny (39) . . . 156 B6
Mouron (08) 42 C3
Mouron-sur-Yonne (58) 151 K1
Mouroux (77) 60 B4
Mours (95) 37 J6
Mours-Saint-Eusèbe (26) . . . 222 D5
Mourvilles-Basses (31) 288 C2
Mourvilles-Hautes (31) 289 F3
Mouscardès (40) 264 C6
Moussac (30) 275 F1
Moussac (86) 180 B1
Moussages (15) 217 H3
Moussan (11) 291 H6
Moussé (35) 104 A3
Mousseaux-lès-Bray (77) 88 C3
Mousseaux-Neuville (27) 57 F3
Mousseaux-sur-Seine (78) . . . 57 H1
Moussey (10) 90 B6
Moussey (57) 67 G5
Moussey (88) 95 J2
les Moussières (39) 173 K6
Mousson (54) 65 K2
Moussonvilliers (61) 55 K6
Moussoulens (11) 289 K5
Moussy (51) 61 K1
Moussy (58) 151 G1
Moussy (95) 37 F6
Moussy-le-Neuf (77) 59 G1
Moussy-le-Vieux (77) 59 H1
Moussy-Verneuil (02) 40 B2
Moustajon (31) 305 H5
Moustey (40) 245 H2
Moustier (47) 231 F5
Moustier-en-Fagne (59) 13 K5
Moustier-Ventadour (19) 216 E1
Moustiers-Sainte-Marie (04) . . 279 F2
le Moustoir (22) 75 J4
Moustoir-Ac (56) 101 F3
Moustoir-Remungol (56) 100 E1
la Moutade (63) 185 G5
le Moutaret (38) 208 D5
Mouterhouse (57) 69 H4
Mouterre-Silly (86) 144 D4
Mouterre-sur-Blourde (86) . . . 180 C2
Mouthe (25) 174 C1
le Moutherot (25) 137 H6
Mouthier-en-Bresse (71) 155 F5
Mouthier-Haute-Pierre (25) . . 156 E2
Mouthiers-sur-Boëme (16) . . . 196 D4
Mouthoumet (11) 309 H3
Moutier-d'Ahun (23) 183 F4
Moutier-Malcard (23) 166 B6
Moutier-Rozeille (23) 183 G6
Moutiers (28) 85 J5
Moutiers (35) 104 A2
Moutiers (54) 27 F6
Moûtiers (73) 209 H5
Moutiers-au-Perche (61) 84 A2
les Moutiers-en-Auge (14) . . . 54 C3
les Moutiers-en-Cinglais (14) . . 53 J1
Moutiers-en-Puisaye (89) . . . 132 C2
les Moutiers-en-Retz (44) . . . 122 C6
les Moutiers-Hubert (14) 55 F2
Moutiers-les-Mauxfaits (85) . . 159 H4
Moutiers-Saint-Jean (21) 134 C2
Moutiers-sous-Argenton (79) . . 143 K4
Moutiers-sous-Chantemerle (79) . . 161 F1
Moutiers-sur-le-Lay (85) 160 A3
Mouton (16) 179 H6
Moutonne (39) 173 G3
Moutonneau (16) 179 H6
Moutoux (39) 156 B6
Moutrot (54) 65 H6
Mouvaux (59) 6 E3
Moux (11) 290 E6
Moux-en-Morvan (58) 152 D1

Mouxy (73) 208 B2
Mouy (60) 37 K3
Mouy-sur-Seine (77) 88 D3
Mouzay (37) 146 C3
Mouzay (55) 43 G5
Mouzeil (44) 123 J1
Mouzens (24) 232 D2
Mouzens (81) 289 G1
Mouzeuil-Saint-Martin (85) . . 160 C4
Mouzieys-Panens (81) 250 E6
Mouzieys-Teulet (81) 271 F3
Mouzillon (44) 123 K5
Mouzon (08) 23 G5
Mouzon (16) 197 J1
Moval (90) 139 H1
Moyaux (14) 34 B5
Moydans (05) 258 B1
Moye (74) 190 D6
Moyemont (88) 94 E3
Moyen (54) 94 E1
Moyencourt (80) 19 G4
Moyencourt-lès-Poix (80) . . . 17 J3
Moyenmoutier (88) 95 H3
Moyenneville (60) 38 C1
Moyenneville (62) 10 E4
Moyenneville (80) 9 F5
Moyenvic (57) 66 E3
Moyeuvre-Grande (57) 27 F5
Moyeuvre-Petite (57) 27 F5
Moyon (50) 31 H5
Moyrazès (12) 252 A3
Moyvillers (60) 38 C2
Mozac (63) 185 F6
Mozé-sur-Louet (49) 125 G5
Muchedent (76) 16 A3
Mudaison (34) 274 D6
Muel (35) 78 B4
Muespach (68) 97 C5
Muespach-le-Haut (68) 97 D5
Mugron (40) 264 E4
Muhlbach-sur-Bruche (67) . . . 70 B4
Muhlbach-sur-Munster (68) . . 119 K1
Muides-sur-Loire (41) 129 G3
Muidorge (60) 37 H1
Muids (27) 35 K4
Muille-Villette (80) 19 H5
Muirancourt (60) 19 H5
Muizon (51) 40 D4
les Mujouls (06) 280 C2
la Mulatière (69) 206 A2
Mulcent (78) 57 H3
Mulcey (57) 67 F3
Mulhausen (67) 69 J5
Mulhouse (68) 97 C2
Mulsanne (72) 106 E4
Mulsans (41) 129 F1
Mun (65) 285 K4
Munchhausen (67) 25 D2
Munchhouse (68) 97 D1
Muncq-Nieurlet (62) 3 F1
Mundolsheim (67) 25 A6
Muneville-le-Bingard (50) . . . 30 D3
Muneville-sur-Mer (50) 30 D5
le Mung (17) 177 H6
Munster (57) 67 H2
Munster (68) 96 A4
Muntzenheim (68) 96 D3
Munwiller (68) 96 C3
Mur-de-Barrez (12) 235 K2
Mûr-de-Bretagne (22) 76 D4
Mur-de-Sologne (41) 129 H4
Muracciole (2B) 321 F2
Murasson (12) 272 A4
Murat (03) 168 A6
Murat (15) 218 C5
Murat-le-Quaire (63) 201 K4
Murat-sur-Vèbre (81) 272 B5
Murato (2B) 319 G2
la Muraz (74) 191 G2
Murbach (68) 96 A6
la Mure (38) 242 B1
la Mure-Argens (04) 260 C6
Mureaumont (60) 17 G5
les Mureaux (78) 58 A2
Mureils (26) 222 C3
Mûres (74) 208 C1
Muret (31) 288 C3
Muret-et-Crouttes (02) 39 K4
Muret-le-Château (12) 252 B1
la Murette (38) 207 H6
Murianette (38) 224 B3
Murinais (38) 223 H3
Murles (34) 274 A5
Murlin (58) 150 E1
Muro (2B) 318 C3
Murol (63) 202 C4
Murols (12) 235 J3
Muron (17) 177 G4
Murs (36) 146 E5
Murs (84) 277 F1
Mûrs-Érigné (49) 125 G4
Murs-et-Géligneux (01) 207 J3
Murtin-et-Bogny (08) 22 B3
Murvaux (55) 43 G2
Murviel-lès-Béziers (34) 291 K3
Murviel-lès-Montpellier (34) . . 274 A6
Murville (54) 26 D4
Murzo (2A) 320 C2
Mus (30) 275 F4
Muscourt (02) 40 C4
Musculdy (64) 283 G5
Musièges (74) 190 D4

Musigny (21) 153 H1
Mussey-sur-Marne (52) 92 B3
Mussidan (24) 213 G5
Mussig (67) 71 C5
Mussy-la-Fosse (21) 134 E3
Mussy-sous-Dun (71) 187 H2
Mussy-sur-Seine (10) 115 F3
Mutigney (39) 137 F5
Mutigny (51) 41 F6
Mutrécy (14) 32 D6
Muttersholtz (67) 71 C5
Mutzenhouse (67) 70 D1
Mutzig (67) 70 C4
le Muy (83) 298 E1
Muzeray (55) 26 B5
Muzillac (56) 121 J1
Muzy (27) 57 F4
Myans (73) 208 C4
Myennes (58) 132 A4
Myon (25) 156 B3

N

Nabas (64) 283 H3
Nabinaud (16) 213 F2
Nabirat (24) 233 G3
Nabringhen (62) 2 C5
Nachamps (17) 177 J4
Nadaillac (24) 215 H5
Nadaillac-de-Rouge (46) . . . 233 H2
Nades (03) 184 E3
Nadillac (46) 233 J6
Nagel-Séez-Mesnil (27) 56 H2
Nages (81) 272 A5
Nages-et-Solorgues (30) . . . 275 F4
Nahuja (66) 313 H5
Nailhac (24) 214 E3
Naillat (23) 182 B2
Nailloux (31) 288 D4
Nailly (89) 88 C6
Naintré (86) 163 G1
Nainville-les-Roches (91) . . . 87 F2
Naisey-lès-Granges (25) 138 C6
Naives-en-Blois (55) 64 E5
Naives-Rosières (55) 64 B4
Naix-aux-Forges (55) 64 D6
Naizin (56) 101 F1
Najac (12) 251 F6
Nalliers (85) 160 B4
Nalliers (86) 164 A3
Nalzen (09) 308 A3
Nambsheim (68) 96 E5
Nampcel (60) 39 G1
Nampcelles-la-Cour (02) 21 G3
Nampont (80) 9 F2
Namps-Maisnil (80) 17 J3
Nampteuil-sous-Muret (02) . . 39 K3
Nampty (80) 18 A3
Nan-sous-Thil (21) 134 D5
Nanc-lès-Saint-Amour (39) . . 172 E5
Nançay (18) 130 D5
Nance (39) 172 F1
Nances (73) 208 A4
Nanclars (16) 196 E1
Nançois-le-Grand (55) 64 D5
Nançois-sur-Ornain (55) 64 C5
Nancras (17) 194 D2
Nancray (25) 138 C6
Nancray-sur-Rimarde (45) . . . 110 E2
Nancuise (39) 173 G4
Nancy (54) 66 A5
Nancy-sur-Cluses (74) 191 K3
Nandax (42) 187 F3
Nandy (77) 87 G1
Nangeville (45) 86 E5
Nangis (77) 88 A1
Nangy (74) 191 G2
Nannay (58) 132 C6
Nans (25) 138 D3
les Nans (39) 156 B6
Nans-les-Pins (83) 297 G3
Nans-sous-Sainte-Anne (25) . . 156 B3
Nant (12) 273 F1
Nant-le-Grand (55) 64 B5
Nant-le-Petit (55) 64 B5
Nanteau-sur-Essonne (77) . . . 87 H4
Nanteau-sur-Lunain (77) 87 J5
Nanterre (92) 58 D3
Nantes (44) 123 G4
Nantes-en-Ratier (38) 224 B6
Nanteuil (79) 178 C1
Nanteuil-Auriac-de-Bourzac (24) . . 213 G1
Nanteuil-en-Vallée (16) 179 H5
Nanteuil-la-Forêt (51) 40 E6
Nanteuil-la-Fosse (02) 39 K2
Nanteuil-le-Haudouin (60) . . . 38 D6
Nanteuil-lès-Meaux (77) 59 K2
Nanteuil-Notre-Dame (02) . . . 39 K5
Nanteuil-sur-Aisne (08) 41 H1
Nanteuil-sur-Marne (77) 60 C2
Nantey (39) 172 E5
Nantheuil (24) 214 C1
Nanthiat (24) 214 D1
Nantiat (87) 181 G5
Nantillé (17) 178 A6
Nantillois (55) 43 F3
Nantilly (70) 137 F3
Nantoin (38) 207 F6
Nantois (55) 64 C6
Nanton (71) 171 J2

Nantouillet (77) 59 H2
Nantoux (21) 153 K3
Nantua (01) 190 A2
Naours (80) 10 A6
Narbéfontaine (57) 45 J5
Narbief (25) 157 J1
Narbonne (11) 291 H6
Narcastet (64) 284 D5
Narcy (52) 92 A1
Narcy (58) 150 D1
Nargis (45) 111 J1
Narnhac (15) 236 B1
Narp (64) 283 J3
Narrosse (40) 264 B4
Nasbinals (48) 236 D4
Nassandres (27) 34 E6
Nassiet (40) 264 E6
Nassigny (03) 167 H4
Nastringues (24) 230 E2
Nattages (01) 207 K2
Natzwiller (67) 70 B5
Naucelle (12) 251 K5
Naucelles (15) 235 H1
Naujac-sur-Mer (33) 210 C2
Naujan-et-Postiac (33) 230 B3
Nauroy (02) 19 K1
Naussac (12) 234 E6
Naussac (48) 238 B4
Naussannes (24) 232 A3
Nauvay (72) 83 F5
Nauviale (12) 235 H6
Navacelles (30) 255 J5
Navailles-Angos (64) 284 D3
Navarrenx (64) 283 J4
Naveil (41) 108 C5
Navenne (70) 138 B1
Naves (03) 185 F3
Naves (19) 216 B2
Naves (59) 11 K4
Navès (81) 289 K1
Nâves-Parmelan (74) 191 G5
Navilly (71) 154 D4
Nay (50) 30 E2
Nay (64) 284 D5
Nayemont-les-Fosses (88) . . . 95 J4
le Nayrac (12) 235 K5
Nazelles-Négron (37) 128 B4
Néac (33) 230 B1
Néant-sur-Yvel (56) 101 K1
Neau (53) 81 H6
Neaufles-Auvergny (27) 55 K3
Neaufles-Saint-Martin (27) . . 36 D4
Neauphe-sous-Essai (61) . . . 82 E1
Neauphe-sur-Dive (61) 54 D3
Neauphle-le-Château (78) . . . 58 A4
Neauphle-le-Vieux (78) 57 K4
Neauphlette (78) 57 G2
Neaux (42) 187 G5
Nébian (34) 273 H6
Nébias (11) 308 D4
Nébing (57) 67 G2
Nébouzat (63) 202 B3
Nécy (61) 54 B3
Nedde (87) 200 A3
Nédon (62) 5 H5
Nédonchel (62) 5 H5
Neewiller-près-Lauterbourg (67) . . 25 D2
Neffes (05) 242 E6
Neffiès (34) 292 B1
Néfiach (66) 309 K6
Nègrepelisse (82) 250 A6
Négreville (50) 28 D4
Négrondes (24) 214 B2
Néhou (50) 28 D5
Nelling (57) 67 G1
Nemours (77) 87 H5
Nempont-Saint-Firmin (62) . . . 9 F2
Nénigan (31) 286 E3
Néons-sur-Creuse (36) 164 B1
Néoules (83) 297 K3
Néoux (23) 183 H6
Nepvant (55) 23 H6
Nérac (47) 247 J5
Nerbis (40) 264 E4
Nercillac (16) 196 A2
Néré (17) 178 C5
Néret (36) 166 C3
Nérigean (33) 230 A2
Nérignac (86) 180 C1
Néris-les-Bains (03) 184 B1
Nernier (74) 174 D5
Néron (28) 85 G1
Néronde (42) 204 E1
Néronde-sur-Dore (63) 203 H2
Nérondes (18) 150 A4
Ners (30) 274 E1
Nersac (16) 196 D4
Nervieux (42) 204 D1
Nerville-la-Forêt (95) 37 J6
Néry (60) 38 D4
Neschers (63) 202 E4
Nescus (09) 307 G2
Neslette (80) 19 G4
Nesle (80) 19 H4
Nesle-et-Massoult (21) 114 E5
Nesle-Hodeng (76) 16 D4
Nesle-la-Reposte (51) 61 F6
Nesle-le-Repons (51) 61 H1
Nesle-l'Hôpital (80) 17 F2
Nesle-Normandeuse (76) . . . 17 F2
Nesles (62) 4 B4
Nesles-la-Montagne (02) 60 E1
Nesles-la-Vallée (95) 37 H6

383

384

Neslette (80) . . . 17 F1
Nesmy (85) . . . 159 J2
Nesploy (45) . . . 110 E3
Nespouls (19) . . . 215 J5
Nessa (2B) . . . 318 D3
Nestier (65) . . . 305 G1
Nettancourt (55) . . . 63 J3
Neublans-Abergement (39) . . . 155 F4
Neubois (67) . . . 71 A5
le Neubourg (27) . . . 35 G5
Neuchâtel-Urtière (25) . . . 139 G4
Neuf-Berquin (59) . . . 6 A4
Neuf-Brisach (68) . . . 96 D4
Neuf-Église (63) . . . 184 D4
Neuf-Marché (76) . . . 36 D2
Neuf-Mesnil (59) . . . 13 G3
Neufbosc (76) . . . 16 C5
le Neufbourg (50) . . . 52 D5
Neufchâteau (88) . . . 93 G3
Neufchâtel-en-Bray (76) . . . 16 D4
Neufchâtel-en-Saosnois (72) . . . 82 F3
Neufchâtel-Hardelot (62) . . . 4 B4
Neufchâtel-sur-Aisne (02) . . . 41 F2
Neufchef (57) . . . 27 F5
Neufchelles (60) . . . 39 G6
Neuffons (33) . . . 230 D4
Neuffontaines (58) . . . 133 H5
Neufgrange (57) . . . 68 D3
Neuflieux (02) . . . 19 J5
Neuflize (08) . . . 41 H2
Neufmaison (08) . . . 22 B3
Neufmaisons (54) . . . 95 G2
Neufmanil (08) . . . 22 D3
Neufmesnil (50) . . . 28 D6
Neufmoulin (80) . . . 9 G5
Neufmoulins (57) . . . 67 H4
Neufmoutiers-en-Brie (77) . . . 59 J4
le Neufour (55) . . . 42 E5
Neufvillage (57) . . . 67 F1
Neufvy-sur-Aronde (60) . . . 38 C1
Neugartheim-Ittlenheim (67) . . . 70 D2
Neuhaeusel (67) . . . 25 D3
Neuil (37) . . . 145 J1
Neuilh (65) . . . 304 C1
Neuillac (17) . . . 195 J5
Neuillay-les-Bois (36) . . . 165 G1
Neuillé (49) . . . 126 B5
Neuillé-le-Lierre (37) . . . 128 A3
Neuillé-Pont-Pierre (37) . . . 127 H2
Neuilly (27) . . . 57 F2
Neuilly (58) . . . 151 H1
Neuilly (89) . . . 112 E4
Neuilly-en-Donjon (03) . . . 169 K6
Neuilly-en-Dun (18) . . . 150 A6
Neuilly-en-Sancerre (18) . . . 131 H6
Neuilly-en-Thelle (60) . . . 37 J5
Neuilly-en-Vexin (95) . . . 37 G5
Neuilly-la-Forêt (14) . . . 31 H1
Neuilly-le-Bisson (61) . . . 82 E2
Neuilly-le-Brignon (37) . . . 146 B4
Neuilly-le-Dien (80) . . . 9 J3
Neuilly-le-Réal (03) . . . 169 F5
Neuilly-le-Vendin (53) . . . 81 K2
Neuilly-lès-Dijon (21) . . . 136 B6
Neuilly-l'Évêque (52) . . . 116 E3
Neuilly-l'Hôpital (80) . . . 9 G4
Neuilly-Plaisance (93) . . . 59 G3
Neuilly-Saint-Front (02) . . . 39 H5
Neuilly-sous-Clermont (60) . . . 38 A3
Neuilly-sur-Eure (61) . . . 84 B2
Neuilly-sur-Marne (93) . . . 59 G3
Neuilly-sur-Seine (92) . . . 58 D3
Neuilly-sur-Suize (52) . . . 116 B2
Neulette (62) . . . 9 K1
Neulise (42) . . . 187 G6
Neulles (17) . . . 195 J5
Neulliac (56) . . . 76 D5
Neung-sur-Beuvron (41) . . . 129 K3
Neunkirchen-lès-Bouzonville (57) . . . 45 J2
Neure (03) . . . 168 B1
Neurey-en-Vaux (70) . . . 118 B5
Neurey-lès-la-Demie (70) . . . 138 B2
Neussargues-Moissac (15) . . . 218 D4
Neuve-Chapelle (62) . . . 6 B5
Neuve-Église (67) . . . 71 A4
la Neuve-Grange (27) . . . 36 C3
la Neuve-Lyre (27) . . . 55 K3
Neuve-Maison (02) . . . 21 G1
Neuvecelle (74) . . . 175 G5
Neuvéglise (15) . . . 236 D1
Neuvelle-lès-Cromary (70) . . . 138 A4
Neuvelle-lès-la-Charité (70) . . . 137 K2
la Neuvelle-lès-Lure (70) . . . 118 E5
la Neuvelle-lès-Scey (70) . . . 117 J3
Neuvelle-lès-Voisey (70) . . . 117 H4
Neuves-Maisons (54) . . . 65 K6
la Neuveville-devant-
Lépanges (88) . . . 95 F5
la Neuveville-sous-Châtenois (88) . . . 93 H4
la Neuveville-sous-Montfort (88) . . . 93 K5
Neuvic (19) . . . 217 F1
Neuvic (24) . . . 213 H4
Neuvic-Entier (87) . . . 199 J3
Neuvicq (17) . . . 212 E3
Neuvicq-le-Château (17) . . . 196 B1
Neuvillalais (72) . . . 82 C6
Neuville (19) . . . 216 B5
la Neuville (59) . . . 6 D6
Neuville (63) . . . 203 G2
la Neuville-à-Maire (08) . . . 22 E5
Neuville-au-Bois (80) . . . 17 G1
Neuville-au-Cornet (62) . . . 10 B2

Neuville-au-Plain (50) . . . 29 F5
la Neuville-au-Pont (51) . . . 42 D5
Neuville-aux-Bois (45) . . . 110 B2
la Neuville-aux-Bois (51) . . . 63 J2
la Neuville-aux-Joûtes (08) . . . 21 J1
la Neuville-aux-Larris (51) . . . 40 D5
Neuville-Bosc (60) . . . 37 G5
la Neuville-Bosmont (02) . . . 21 F4
Neuville-Bourjonval (62) . . . 11 H5
la Neuville-Chant-d'Oisel (76) . . . 35 K3
Neuville-Coppegueule (80) . . . 17 F2
la Neuville-d'Aumont (60) . . . 37 H3
Neuville-Day (08) . . . 42 B1
Neuville-de-Poitou (86) . . . 162 E2
la Neuville-du-Bosc (27) . . . 35 F5
Neuville-en-Avesnois (59) . . . 12 D4
la Neuville-en-Beaumont (50) . . . 28 C6
la Neuville-en-Beine (02) . . . 19 J5
la Neuville-en-Ferrain (59) . . . 6 E3
la Neuville-en-Hez (60) . . . 37 K2
la Neuville-en-Tourne-à-Fuy (08) . . . 41 J3
Neuville-en-Verdunois (55) . . . 64 C2
la Neuville-Ferrières (76) . . . 16 D4
la Neuville-Garnier (60) . . . 37 G3
la Neuville-Housset (02) . . . 21 E3
la Neuville-lès-Bray (80) . . . 18 E1
Neuville-les-Dames (01) . . . 188 E2
la Neuville-lès-Decize (58) . . . 168 E1
la Neuville-lès-Dorengt (02) . . . 20 D1
Neuville-lès-Loeuilly (80) . . . 17 K3
la Neuville-lès-This (08) . . . 22 C3
la Neuville-lès-Vaucouleurs (55) . . . 65 F6
la Neuville-lès-Wasigny (08) . . . 21 K5
Neuville-lez-Beaulieu (08) . . . 21 K2
Neuville-près-Sées (61) . . . 54 E6
la Neuville-Saint-Amand (02) . . . 20 A3
la Neuville-Saint-Pierre (60) . . . 37 J1
la Neuville-Saint-Rémy (59) . . . 11 J4
la Neuville-Saint-Vaast (62) . . . 10 E2
la Neuville-Sire-Bernard (80) . . . 18 C4
Neuville-sous-Montreuil (62) . . . 4 C6
Neuville-sur-Ailette (02) . . . 40 C1
Neuville-sur-Ain (01) . . . 189 H3
Neuville-sur-Authou (27) . . . 34 D5
Neuville-sur-Brenne (37) . . . 128 A2
Neuville-sur-Escaut (59) . . . 12 B2
la Neuville-sur-Essonne (45) . . . 86 E5
Neuville-sur-Margival (02) . . . 39 K2
Neuville-sur-Oise (95) . . . 58 B1
Neuville-sur-Ornain (55) . . . 63 K3
la Neuville-sur-Oudeuil (60) . . . 17 J6
la Neuville-sur-Ressons (60) . . . 19 F6
Neuville-sur-Saône (69) . . . 188 C6
Neuville-sur-Sarthe (72) . . . 106 E1
Neuville-sur-Seine (10) . . . 114 E2
Neuville-sur-Touques (61) . . . 55 F3
Neuville-sur-Vannes (10) . . . 89 J5
la Neuville-Vault (60) . . . 37 F1
Neuville-Vitasse (62) . . . 11 F3
Neuviller-la-Roche (67) . . . 70 A5
Neuviller-lès-Badonviller (54) . . . 95 H1
Neuviller-sur-Moselle (54) . . . 94 B1
Neuvillers-sur-Fave (88) . . . 95 J4
Neuvillette (02) . . . 20 B2
Neuvillette (80) . . . 10 A4
Neuvillette-en-Charnie (72) . . . 106 A1
Neuvilley (39) . . . 155 H4
Neuvilly (59) . . . 12 D4
Neuvilly-en-Argonne (55) . . . 42 E5
Neuvireuil (62) . . . 11 G2
Neuvizy (08) . . . 22 B5
Neuvy (03) . . . 168 B2
Neuvy (41) . . . 129 H2
Neuvy (51) . . . 61 F5
Neuvy-au-Houlme (61) . . . 54 A4
Neuvy-Bouin (79) . . . 161 H2
Neuvy-Deux-Clochers (18) . . . 131 H6
Neuvy-en-Beauce (28) . . . 86 A5
Neuvy-en-Champagne (72) . . . 106 B1
Neuvy-en-Dunois (28) . . . 85 G6
Neuvy-en-Mauges (49) . . . 124 D6
Neuvy-en-Sullias (45) . . . 110 D5
Neuvy-Grandchamp (71) . . . 170 A3
Neuvy-le-Barrois (18) . . . 150 C5
Neuvy-le-Roi (37) . . . 127 H4
Neuvy-Pailloux (36) . . . 148 B5
Neuvy-Saint-Sépulchre (36) . . . 165 K4
Neuvy-Sautour (89) . . . 113 J2
Neuvy-sur-Barangeon (18) . . . 130 D6
Neuvy-sur-Loire (58) . . . 131 K3
Neuwiller (68) . . . 97 E5
Neuwiller-lès-Saverne (67) . . . 69 G6
Névache (05) . . . 225 K5
Nevers (58) . . . 150 E4
Névez (29) . . . 99 F4
Névian (11) . . . 291 G5
Néville (76) . . . 15 G3
Néville-sur-Mer (50) . . . 29 F2
Nevoy (45) . . . 111 G6
Nevy-lès-Dole (39) . . . 155 G3
Nevy-sur-Seille (39) . . . 173 G1
Nexon (87) . . . 198 E3
Ney (39) . . . 173 K1
Neydens (74) . . . 191 F3
les Neyrolles (01) . . . 190 A2
Neyron (01) . . . 206 B1
Nézel (78) . . . 57 K2
Nézignan-l'Évêque (34) . . . 292 C3
Niafles (53) . . . 104 C4
Niaux (09) . . . 307 J5
Nibas (80) . . . 8 E5
Nibelle (45) . . . 110 E2

Nibles (04) . . . 259 G3
Nice (06) . . . 281 G4
Nicey (21) . . . 114 D4
Nicey-sur-Aire (55) . . . 64 C3
Nicole (47) . . . 247 J3
Nicorps (50) . . . 30 E4
Niderhoff (57) . . . 67 J5
Niderviller (57) . . . 67 K4
Niederbronn-les-Bains (67) . . . 69 J4
Niederbruck (68) . . . 119 J4
Niederentzen (68) . . . 96 C5
Niederhaslach (67) . . . 70 B5
Niederhausbergen (67) . . . 25 A6
Niederhergheim (68) . . . 96 C5
Niederlauterbach (67) . . . 25 D2
Niedermodern (67) . . . 69 J5
Niedermorschwihr (68) . . . 96 B4
Niedernai (67) . . . 70 D5
Niederroedern (67) . . . 25 D2
Niederschaeffolsheim (67) . . . 25 A4
Niedersoultzbach (67) . . . 69 H6
Niedersteinbach (67) . . . 69 K3
Niederstinzel (57) . . . 67 J2
Niedervisse (57) . . . 45 J4
Nielles-lès-Ardres (62) . . . 2 E4
Nielles-lès-Bléquin (62) . . . 2 E6
Nielles-lès-Calais (62) . . . 2 C3
Nieppe (59) . . . 6 B3
Niergnies (59) . . . 11 K4
Nieudan (15) . . . 217 F6
Nieuil (16) . . . 179 K6
Nieuil-l'Espoir (86) . . . 163 G4
Nieul (87) . . . 181 G6
Nieul-le-Dolent (85) . . . 159 H3
Nieul-le-Virouil (17) . . . 195 H6
Nieul-lès-Saintes (17) . . . 195 F2
Nieul-sur-l'Autise (85) . . . 161 F5
Nieul-sur-Mer (17) . . . 176 D2
Nieulle-sur-Seudre (17) . . . 194 C2
Nieurlet (59) . . . 3 G4
Niévroz (01) . . . 206 C1
Niffer (68) . . . 97 D3
Niherne (36) . . . 147 J6
Nijon (52) . . . 93 F5
Nilvange (57) . . . 27 F4
Nîmes (30) . . . 275 G3
Ninville (52) . . . 116 D1
Niort (79) . . . 161 H6
Niort-de-Sault (11) . . . 308 C1
Niozelles (04) . . . 278 C1
Nissan-lez-Enserune (34) . . . 291 K4
Nistos (65) . . . 305 G2
Nitry (89) . . . 133 K1
Nitting (57) . . . 67 J5
Nivelle (59) . . . 7 H6
Nivillac (56) . . . 102 A5
Nivillers (60) . . . 37 H2
Nivolas-Vermelle (38) . . . 207 F4
Nivollet-Montgriffon (01) . . . 189 J4
Nixéville-Blercourt (55) . . . 43 G5
le Nizan (33) . . . 246 C1
Nizan-Gesse (31) . . . 286 D5
Nizas (32) . . . 287 H2
Nizas (34) . . . 292 C2
Nizerolles (03) . . . 186 A4
Nizy-le-Comte (02) . . . 21 H6
Noailhac (12) . . . 235 G6
Noailhac (19) . . . 215 K5
Noailhac (81) . . . 290 B1
Noaillac (33) . . . 230 C6
Noaillan (33) . . . 229 K6
Noailles (19) . . . 215 J5
Noailles (60) . . . 37 J3
Noailles (81) . . . 270 C1
Noailly (42) . . . 186 E3
Noalhac (48) . . . 236 E3
Noalhat (63) . . . 185 J6
Noards (27) . . . 34 C4
Nocario (2B) . . . 319 H4
Nocé (61) . . . 83 J4
Noceta (2B) . . . 321 G1
Nochize (71) . . . 170 C5
la Nocle-Maulaix (58) . . . 169 J1
Nod-sur-Seine (21) . . . 115 F5
Nods (25) . . . 156 E2
Noé (31) . . . 288 A4
Noé (89) . . . 88 E6
la Noë-Blanche (35) . . . 103 F2
Noë-les-Mallets (10) . . . 115 F1
la Noë-Poulain (27) . . . 34 C4
Noël-Cerneux (25) . . . 157 H1
Noëllet (49) . . . 104 B6
les Noës (42) . . . 186 C4
les Noës-près-Troyes (10) . . . 90 A4
Noeux-lès-Auxi (62) . . . 9 K3
Noeux-les-Mines (62) . . . 6 A6
Nogaret (31) . . . 289 G2
Nogaro (32) . . . 266 B4
Nogent (52) . . . 116 D2
Nogent-en-Othe (10) . . . 113 J1
Nogent-l'Abbesse (51) . . . 41 G4
Nogent-l'Artaud (02) . . . 60 D2
Nogent-le-Bernard (72) . . . 83 G5
Nogent-le-Phaye (28) . . . 85 H3
Nogent-le-Roi (28) . . . 57 G6
Nogent-le-Rotrou (28) . . . 84 A4
Nogent-le-Sec (27) . . . 56 C2
Nogent-lès-Montbard (21) . . . 134 D2
Nogent-sur-Aube (10) . . . 90 D2
Nogent-sur-Eure (28) . . . 85 F3
Nogent-sur-Loir (72) . . . 127 F1
Nogent-sur-Marne (94) . . . 59 F4

Nogent-sur-Oise (60) . . . 38 A4
Nogent-sur-Seine (10) . . . 89 F2
Nogent-sur-Vernisson (45) . . . 111 J5
Nogna (39) . . . 173 H2
Noguères (64) . . . 284 A2
Nohanent (63) . . . 202 D2
Nohant-en-Goût (18) . . . 149 J3
Nohant-en-Graçay (18) . . . 148 D5
Nohant-Vic (36) . . . 166 B3
Nohèdes (66) . . . 314 A3
Nohic (82) . . . 269 G3
Noidan (21) . . . 134 E5
Noidans-le-Ferroux (70) . . . 137 K2
Noidans-lès-Vesoul (70) . . . 138 A1
Noidant-Chatenoy (52) . . . 116 D5
Noidant-le-Rocheux (52) . . . 116 C5
Noilhan (32) . . . 287 G1
Nointel (60) . . . 38 A3
Nointel (95) . . . 37 J6
Nointot (76) . . . 14 E5
Noircourt (02) . . . 21 H4
Noirefontaine (25) . . . 139 H4
Noirémont (60) . . . 18 A6
Noirétable (42) . . . 204 A1
Noirlieu (51) . . . 63 H2
Noirmoutier-en-l'Île (85) . . . 140 B3
Noiron (70) . . . 137 G4
Noiron-sous-Gevrey (21) . . . 154 C1
Noiron-sur-Bèze (21) . . . 136 D4
Noiron-sur-Seine (21) . . . 114 E3
Noironte (25) . . . 137 J3
Noirval (08) . . . 42 C1
Noiseau (94) . . . 59 G4
Noisiel (77) . . . 59 H3
Noisseville (57) . . . 45 G5
Noisy-le-Grand (93) . . . 59 G4
Noisy-le-Roi (78) . . . 58 B4
Noisy-le-Sec (93) . . . 59 F3
Noisy-Rudignon (77) . . . 88 A4
Noisy-sur-École (77) . . . 87 G4
Noisy-sur-Oise (95) . . . 37 K6
Noizay (37) . . . 128 A4
Nojals-et-Clotte (24) . . . 232 A4
Nojeon-en-Vexin (27) . . . 36 C3
Nolay (21) . . . 153 G2
Nolay (58) . . . 151 F2
Nolléval (76) . . . 36 B1
Nollieux (42) . . . 204 C1
Nomain (59) . . . 7 F6
Nomdieu (47) . . . 248 A6
Nomécourt (52) . . . 92 A3
Nomeny (54) . . . 66 A2
Nomexy (88) . . . 94 C4
Nommay (25) . . . 139 H2
Nompatelize (88) . . . 95 H3
Nonac (16) . . . 196 D6
Nonancourt (27) . . . 56 D4
Nonant (14) . . . 32 B4
Nonant-le-Pin (61) . . . 54 E5
Nonards (19) . . . 216 B6
Nonaville (16) . . . 196 B5
Noncourt-sur-le-Rongeant (52) . . . 92 C3
Nonette (63) . . . 203 F6
Nonglard (74) . . . 190 E5
Nonhigny (54) . . . 67 H6
Nonières (07) . . . 239 J1
Nonsard-Lamarche (55) . . . 65 G2
Nontron (24) . . . 197 K5
Nonville (77) . . . 87 J5
Nonville (88) . . . 117 K1
Nonvilliers-Grandhoux (28) . . . 84 D1
Nonza (2B) . . . 317 C4
Nonzeville (88) . . . 95 F4
Noordpeene (59) . . . 3 H4
Nordausques (62) . . . 2 E4
Nordheim (67) . . . 70 D2
Nordhouse (67) . . . 71 D3
Noreuil (62) . . . 11 G4
Norges-la-Ville (21) . . . 136 A4
Normandel (61) . . . 55 K6
Normanville (27) . . . 35 J6
Normanville (76) . . . 15 F4
Normier (21) . . . 134 E5
Norolles (14) . . . 33 K5
Noron-la-Poterie (14) . . . 32 A4
Noron-l'Abbaye (14) . . . 54 A3
Noroy (60) . . . 38 B2
Noroy-le-Bourg (70) . . . 138 C1
Noroy-sur-Ourcq (02) . . . 39 H5
Norrent-Fontes (62) . . . 5 H5
Norrey-en-Auge (14) . . . 54 C2
Norrois (51) . . . 63 F5
Norroy (88) . . . 93 J5
Norroy-le-Sec (54) . . . 26 D5
Norroy-le-Veneur (57) . . . 27 G6
Norroy-lès-Pont-à-Mousson (54) . . . 65 J2
Nort-Leulinghem (62) . . . 2 E4
Nort-sur-Erdre (44) . . . 123 H1
Nortkerque (62) . . . 2 E3
Norville (76) . . . 34 D1
la Norville (91) . . . 86 D1
Nossage-et-Bénévent (05) . . . 258 D2
Nossoncourt (88) . . . 95 F2
Nostang (56) . . . 100 B4
Noth (23) . . . 182 A2
Nothalten (67) . . . 70 C6
Notre-Dame-d'Aliermont (76) . . . 16 B2
Notre-Dame-d'Allençon (49) . . . 125 H5
Notre-Dame-de-Bellecombe (73) . . . 191 K6
Notre-Dame-de-Bliquetuit (76) . . . 34 E1
Notre-Dame-de-Boisset (42) . . . 187 F5

Notre-Dame-de-Bondeville (76) . . . 35 H1
Notre-Dame-de-Cenilly (50) . . . 31 F5
Notre-Dame-de-Commiers (38) . . . 224 A5
Notre-Dame-de-Courson (14) . . . 55 F1
Notre-Dame-de-Gravenchon (76) . . . 34 D1
Notre-Dame-de-la-Rouvière (30) . . . 254 D6
Notre-Dame-de-l'Isle (27) . . . 36 B5
Notre-Dame-de-Livaye (14) . . . 33 H6
Notre-Dame-de-Livoye (50) . . . 52 B4
Notre-Dame-de-Londres (34) . . . 274 B3
Notre-Dame-de-l'Osier (38) . . . 223 H2
Notre-Dame-de-Mésage (38) . . . 224 B4
Notre-Dame-de-Monts (85) . . . 140 C5
Notre-Dame-de-Riez (85) . . . 140 C6
Notre-Dame-de-Sanilhac (24) . . . 214 A4
Notre-Dame-de-Vaux (38) . . . 224 B5
Notre-Dame-d'Elle (50) . . . 31 H1
Notre-Dame-d'Épine (27) . . . 34 D5
Notre-Dame-des-Landes (44) . . . 123 F2
Notre-Dame-des-Millières (73) . . . 209 F3
Notre-Dame-d'Estrées (14) . . . 33 H5
Notre-Dame-d'Oé (37) . . . 127 J4
Notre-Dame-du-Bec (76) . . . 14 B5
Notre-Dame-du-Cruet (73) . . . 209 F6
Notre-Dame-du-Hamel (27) . . . 55 H3
Notre-Dame-du-Parc (76) . . . 16 A4
Notre-Dame-du-Pé (72) . . . 105 J6
Notre-Dame-du-Pré (73) . . . 209 J4
Notre-Dame-du-Rocher (61) . . . 53 J4
Notre-Dame-du-Touchet (50) . . . 52 D6
Nottonville (28) . . . 109 G1
la Nouaille (23) . . . 200 D1
Nouaillé-Maupertuis (86) . . . 163 F4
Nouainville (50) . . . 28 C2
Nouan-le-Fuzelier (41) . . . 130 B3
Nouans (72) . . . 82 E5
Nouans-les-Fontaines (37) . . . 147 F2
Nouart (08) . . . 42 E1
Nouâtre (37) . . . 145 J3
la Nouaye (35) . . . 78 D3
la Noue (51) . . . 61 G5
Nouelles (31) . . . 288 C3
Nougaroulet (32) . . . 267 K5
Nouhant (23) . . . 183 J1
Nouic (87) . . . 180 D4
Nouilhan (65) . . . 285 H3
les Nouillers (17) . . . 177 J5
Nouillonpont (55) . . . 26 C4
Nouilly (57) . . . 45 F5
Noulens (32) . . . 266 D3
Nourard-le-Franc (60) . . . 37 K1
Nourray (41) . . . 108 C6
Nousse (40) . . . 264 D4
Noussevillers-lès-Bitche (57) . . . 69 G2
Noussevillers-Saint-Nabor (57) . . . 68 C2
Nousty (64) . . . 284 E4
Nouvelle-Église (62) . . . 2 E3
Nouvion (80) . . . 9 F4
le Nouvion-en-Thiérache (02) . . . 13 F6
Nouvion-et-Catillon (02) . . . 20 B4
Nouvion-le-Comte (02) . . . 20 B4
Nouvion-le-Vineux (02) . . . 40 B1
Nouvion-sur-Meuse (08) . . . 22 D4
Nouvoitou (35) . . . 79 H5
Nouvron-Vingré (02) . . . 39 H2
Nouzerines (23) . . . 166 C6
Nouzerolles (23) . . . 165 J6
Nouziers (23) . . . 166 B5
Nouzilly (37) . . . 127 J3
Nouzonville (08) . . . 22 D3
Novacelles (63) . . . 203 A6
Novalaise (73) . . . 208 A4
Novale (2B) . . . 319 J5
Novéant-sur-Moselle (57) . . . 44 E2
Novel (74) . . . 175 J5
Novella (2B) . . . 318 E2
Noves (13) . . . 276 C2
Noviant-aux-Prés (54) . . . 65 H3
Novillard (90) . . . 139 J1
Novillars (25) . . . 138 B5
Novillers (60) . . . 37 J4
Novion-Porcien (08) . . . 22 A5
Novy-Chevrières (08) . . . 22 A6
Noyal (22) . . . 77 J1
Noyal-Châtillon-sur-Seiche (35) . . . 79 G5
Noyal-Muzillac (56) . . . 101 J2
Noyal-Pontivy (56) . . . 76 E6
Noyal-sous-Bazouges (35) . . . 51 G6
Noyal-sur-Brutz (44) . . . 103 K3
Noyal-sur-Vilaine (35) . . . 79 H4
Noyales (02) . . . 20 C2
Noyalo (56) . . . 101 G6
Noyant (49) . . . 126 D3
Noyant-d'Allier (03) . . . 168 C5
Noyant-de-Touraine (37) . . . 145 J2
Noyant-et-Aconin (02) . . . 39 J3
Noyant-la-Gravoyère (49) . . . 104 C3
Noyant-la-Plaine (49) . . . 125 J6
Noyarey (38) . . . 223 K2
Noyers-Vion (62) . . . 10 C2
Noyelles-en-Chaussée (80) . . . 9 H4
Noyelles-Godault (62) . . . 11 G1
Noyelles-lès-Humières (62) . . . 9 K2
Noyelles-lès-Seclin (59) . . . 6 D5
Noyelles-lès-Vermelles (62) . . . 6 B6
Noyelles-sous-Bellonne (62) . . . 11 H2
Noyelles-sous-Lens (62) . . . 11 F1
Noyelles-sur-Escaut (59) . . . 11 J4
Noyelles-sur-Mer (80) . . . 9 F4
Noyelles-sur-Sambre (59) . . . 13 F4
Noyelles-sur-Selle (59) . . . 12 C3
Noyellette (62) . . . 10 D2

Noyen-sur-Sarthe (72) 106 B4
Noyen-sur-Seine (77) 88 E3
le Noyer (05) 242 D3
le Noyer (18) 131 H5
le Noyer (73) 208 C2
le Noyer-en-Ouche (27) 55 K1
Noyers (27) 36 D4
Noyers (45) 111 G4
Noyers (52) 116 E1
Noyers (89) 114 A6
Noyers-Auzécourt (55) 63 J3
Noyers-Bocage (14) 32 C5
Noyers-Pont-Maugis (08) 23 F4
Noyers-Saint-Martin (60) 18 A6
Noyers-sur-Cher (41) 129 F6
Noyers-sur-Jabron (04) 258 A4
Noyon (60) 19 H6
Nozay (10) 90 B2
Nozay (44) 103 G5
Nozay (91) 58 D6
Nozeroy (39) 156 C6
Nozières (07) 221 H5
Nozières (18) 167 F1
Nuaillé (49) 143 F2
Nuaillé-d'Aunis (17) 177 F1
Nuaillé-sur-Boutonne (17) 178 A4
Nuars (58) 133 H5
Nubécourt (55) 64 B1
Nucourt (95) 36 E5
Nueil-sous-Faye (86) 145 G4
Nueil-sur-Argent (79) 143 H4
Nueil-sur-Layon (49) 143 K2
Nuelles (69) 205 J1
Nuillé-le-Jalais (72) 107 G2
Nuillé-sur-Vicoin (53) 104 E2
Nuisement-sur-Coole (51) . . . 62 C3
Nuits (89) 114 C6
Nuits-Saint-Georges (21) . . . 154 B2
Nullemont (76) 16 E3
Nully-Trémilly (52) 91 H3
Nuncq-Hautecôte (62) 10 A2
Nuret-le-Ferron (36) 165 F2
Nurieux-Volognat (01) 189 K2
Nurlu (80) 11 H6
Nuzéjouls (46) 233 G6
Nyer (66) 314 A4
Nyoiseau (49) 104 D6
Nyons (26) 257 H2

O

Obenheim (67) 71 D4
Oberbronn (67) 69 J4
Oberbruck (68) 119 J4
Oberdorf (68) 97 C5
Oberdorf-Spachbach (67) 25 A4
Oberdorff (57) 45 J3
Oberentzen (68) 96 C5
Obergailbach (57) 68 E2
Oberhaslach (67) 70 B4
Oberhausbergen (67) 71 D1
Oberhergheim (68) 96 C5
Oberhoffen-lès-Wissembourg (67) . 25 B1
Oberhoffen-sur-Moder (67) . . . 25 B4
Oberlarg (68) 97 B6
Oberlauterbach (67) 25 D2
Obermodern-Zutzendorf (67) . . 69 J6
Obermorschwihr (68) 96 B5
Obermorschwiller (68) 97 C4
Obernai (67) 70 D5
Oberroedern (67) 25 C2
Obersaasheim (68) 96 E5
Oberschaeffolsheim (67) . . . 70 D4
Obersoultzbach (67) 69 H6
Obersteinbach (67) 69 K3
Oberstinzel (57) 67 J3
Obervisse (57) 45 J4
Obies (59) 13 F3
Objat (19) 215 H3
Oblinghem (62) 5 K5
Obrechies (59) 13 H3
Obreck (57) 66 E3
Obsonville (77) 87 G6
Obterre (36) 146 D5
Obtrée (21) 115 F3
Ocana (2A) 320 D5
Occagnes (61) 54 B4
Occey (52) 136 C1
Occhiatana (2B) 318 D2
Occoches (80) 10 A4
Ochancourt (80) 8 E5
Oches (08) 42 D1
Ochey (54) 93 J6
Ochtezeele (59) 3 H4
Ocquerre (77) 60 B1
Ocqueville (76) 15 G3
Octeville-l'Avenel (50) 29 F3
Octeville-sur-Mer (76) 14 A6
Octon (34) 273 F6
Odars (31) 288 D2
Odenas (69) 188 A3
Oderen (68) 119 J3
Odomez (59) 7 J6
Odos (65) 285 H5
Odratzheim (67) 70 C4
Oëlleville (88) 93 K3
Oermingen (67) 68 E4
Oeting (57) 68 C2
Oeuf-en-Ternois (62) 9 K2
Oeuilly (02) 40 C2

Oeuilly (51) 40 D6
Oeyregave (40) 283 F1
Oeyreluy (40) 264 A5
Offekerque (62) 2 E2
Offemont (90) 119 H6
Offendorf (67) 25 C5
Offignies (80) 17 G3
Offin (62) 4 D6
Offlanges (39) 137 F6
Offoy (60) 17 J4
Offoy (80) 19 H3
Offranville (76) 15 K2
Offrethun (62) 2 B4
Offroicourt (88) 93 K4
Offwiller (67) 69 J5
Ogenne-Camptort (64) 283 K4
Oger (51) 62 A2
Ogeu-les-Bains (64) 284 B6
Ogéviller (54) 67 F6
Ogliastro (2B) 317 C4
Ognes (02) 19 K5
Ognes (51) 61 K5
Ognes (60) 38 E6
Ognéville (54) 93 K2
Ognolles (60) 19 G4
Ognon (60) 38 C4
Ogy (57) 45 G5
Ohain (59) 13 J6
Oherville (76) 15 F4
Ohis (02) 21 J2
Ohlungen (67) 69 K6
Ohnenheim (67) 71 C6
l'Oie (85) 142 C6
Oigney (70) 117 H5
Oignies (62) 6 D6
Oigny (21) 135 H2
Oigny (41) 108 B2
Oigny-en-Valois (02) 39 G5
Oingt (69) 188 A5
Oinville-Saint-Liphard (28) . . 86 A5
Oinville-sous-Auneau (28) . . 85 J3
Oinville-sur-Montcient (78) . . 57 K1
Oiron (79) 144 C4
Oiry (51) 62 A1
Oiselay-et-Grachaux (70) . . . 137 J4
Oisemont (80) 17 F1
Oisilly (21) 136 D4
Oisly (41) 129 F6
Oison (45) 110 B1
Oisseau (53) 81 F4
Oisseau-le-Petit (72) 82 D4
Oissel (76) 35 H3
Oissery (77) 59 J1
Oissy (80) 17 J2
Oisy (02) 12 E6
Oisy (58) 133 F4
Oisy (59) 12 C2
Oisy-le-Verger (62) 11 H3
Oizé (72) 106 D5
Oizon (18) 131 G4
Olargues (34) 291 G1
Olby (63) 202 B2
Olcani (2B) 317 D4
Oléac-Debat (65) 285 J4
Oléac-Dessus (65) 285 J4
Olemps (12) 252 B3
Olendon (14) 54 B2
Oletta (2B) 317 D4
Olette (66) 314 A4
Olivese (2A) 321 F6
Olivet (45) 110 A4
Olivet (53) 80 D6
Olizy (51) 40 C5
Olizy-Primat (08) 42 C3
Olizy-sur-Chiers (55) 23 H6
Ollainville (88) 93 H4
Ollainville (91) 86 D1
Ollans (25) 138 C3
Ollé (28) 84 E3
Olley (54) 44 B5
Ollezy (02) 19 J4
les Ollières (74) 191 F4
Ollières (83) 297 H1
les Ollières-sur-Eyrieux (07) . 239 K2
Olliergues (63) 203 J3
Ollioules (83) 297 H6
Olloix (63) 202 D4
les Olmes (69) 187 K6
Olmet (63) 203 J3
Olmet-et-Villecun (34) 273 F5
Olmeta-di-Capocorso (2B) . . 317 D4
Olmeta-di-Tuda (2B) 317 D5
Olmeto (2A) 322 D2
Olmi-Cappella (2B) 318 D3
Olmiccia (2A) 323 F2
Olmo (2B) 319 H3
Olonne-sur-Mer (85) 158 C3
Olonzac (34) 291 F5
Oloron-Sainte-Marie (64) . . . 284 A5
Ols-et-Rinhodes (12) 251 F1
Oltingue (68) 97 D5
Olwisheim (67) 70 D4
Ombléze (26) 241 F6
Omécourt (60) 17 G5
Omelmont (54) 94 A1
les Omergues (04) 258 C4
Omerville (95) 36 D6
Omessa (2B) 319 H4
Omet (33) 230 A4
Omex (65) 304 B1
Omey (51) 62 E3
Omicourt (08) 22 E5

Omiécourt (80) 19 F3
Omissy (02) 20 A2
Omméel (61) 54 D4
Ommeray (57) 67 F4
Ommoy (61) 54 D3
Omont (08) 22 D5
Omonville (76) 15 K3
Omonville-la-Petite (50) . . . 28 A1
Omonville-la-Rogue (50) . . . 28 B1
Omps (15) 235 F2
Oms (66) 314 E4
Onans (25) 139 F2
Onard (40) 264 D3
Onay (70) 137 G4
Oncieu (01) 189 J5
Oncourt (88) 94 C4
Oncy-sur-École (91) 87 F4
Ondefontaine (14) 53 G1
Ondes (31) 269 F4
Ondres (40) 262 B6
Ondreville-sur-Essonne (45) . 87 F6
Onesse-et-Laharie (40) . . . 244 E6
Onet-le-Château (12) 252 B2
Oneux (80) 9 H4
Ongles (04) 258 D6
Onglières (39) 156 B6
Onjon (10) 90 C3
Onlay (58) 152 B4
Onnaing (59) 12 D1
Onnion (74) 191 J2
Onoz (39) 173 H4
Ons-en-Bray (60) 37 F2
Ontex (73) 208 A2
Onville (54) 65 J1
Onzain (41) 128 D3
Oô (31) 305 G2
Oost-Cappel (59) 3 K3
Opio (06) 280 D4
Opoul-Périllos (66) 310 B4
Oppède (84) 277 F3
Oppedette (04) 277 K2
Oppenans (70) 138 D1
Oppy (62) 11 F3
Optevoz (38) 207 F2
Oraàs (64) 283 G2
Oradour (15) 236 C1
Oradour (16) 178 E6
Oradour-Fanais (16) 180 C3
Oradour-Saint-Genest (87) . . 181 F4
Oradour-sur-Glane (87) . . . 180 E6
Oradour-sur-Vayres (87) . . . 198 B2
Orain (21) 136 E1
Orainville (02) 41 F2
Oraison (04) 278 C2
Orange (84) 256 E5
Orbagna (39) 173 F3
Orbais-l'Abbaye (51) 61 H2
Orban (81) 270 D3
Orbec (14) 55 G1
Orbeil (63) 203 F5
Orbessan (32) 286 D1
Orbey (68) 96 A3
Orbigny (37) 147 F1
Orbigny-au-Mont (52) 116 E4
Orbigny-au-Val (52) 116 E4
l'Orbrie (85) 160 E4
Orçay (41) 130 C6
Orcemont (78) 85 K1
Orcenais (18) 167 F2
Orcet (63) 202 E3
Orcevaux (52) 116 C5
Orchaise (41) 128 D2
Orchamps (39) 155 J1
Orchamps-Vennes (25) . . . 157 G1
Orches (86) 145 G5
Orchies (59) 7 F6
Orcier (74) 175 F6
Orcières (05) 243 J4
Orcinas (26) 241 F5
Orcines (63) 202 C2
Orcival (63) 202 B3
Orconte (51) 63 G5
Ordan-Larroque (32) 267 G5
Ordiarp (64) 283 G5
Ordizan (65) 304 D1
Ordonnac (33) 210 E2
Ordonnaz (01) 189 K6
Ore (31) 305 J3
Orègue (64) 283 F2
Oreilla (66) 314 A4
Orelle (73) 225 J2
Oresmaux (80) 18 A3
Organ (65) 286 B4
Orgeans-Blanchefontaine (25) . 139 G5
Orgedeuil (16) 197 H3
Orgeix (09) 308 B6
Orgelet (39) 173 G3
Orgères (35) 79 G5
Orgères (61) 55 F4
Orgères-en-Beauce (28) . . . 109 J1
Orgerus (78) 57 J4
Orges (52) 115 J1
Orgeux (21) 136 B5
Orgeval (02) 40 C1
Orgeval (78) 58 B3
Orgibet (09) 306 D3
Orglandes (50) 28 E5
Orgnac-l'Aven (07) 256 A3
Orgnac-sur-Vézère (19) . . . 215 H2
Orgon (13) 276 D4
Orgueil (82) 269 G2
Oricourt (70) 138 D1

Orieux (65) 285 K5
Orignac (65) 285 J6
Origne (33) 229 H6
Origné (53) 105 F3
Orignolles (17) 212 A3
Origny (21) 115 G6
Origny-en-Thiérache (02) . . . 21 G2
Origny-le-Butin (61) 83 G4
Origny-le-Roux (61) 83 G4
Origny-le-Sec (10) 89 H2
Origny-Sainte-Benoite (02) . . 20 B2
Orin (64) 283 K5
Orincles (65) 285 H6
Oriocourt (57) 66 C2
Oriol-en-Royans (26) 223 G5
Oriolles (16) 212 C1
Orion (64) 283 H2
Oris-en-Rattier (38) 224 C6
Orist (40) 262 C5
Orival (16) 212 D2
Orival (76) 35 G3
Orléans (45) 110 A4
Orléat (63) 203 G1
Orleix (65) 285 H4
Orliac (24) 232 D4
Orliac-de-Bar (19) 216 B1
Orliaguet (24) 233 G1
Orliénas (69) 205 K3
Orlu (09) 308 B6
Orlu (28) 86 A4
Orly (94) 58 E5
Orly-sur-Morin (77) 60 C3
Ormancey (52) 116 B3
Ormenans (70) 138 B3
Ormersviller (57) 69 F2
Ormes (10) 90 B1
Ormes (27) 56 B1
Ormes (45) 109 K3
Ormes (51) 40 E4
Ormes (71) 172 A2
les Ormes (86) 145 K4
les Ormes (89) 112 D5
Ormes-et-Ville (54) 94 B2
les Ormes-sur-Voulzie (77) . . 88 C3
Ormesson (77) 87 H5
Ormesson-sur-Marne (94) . . 59 G4
Ormoiche (70) 118 C4
Ormoy (28) 57 G6
Ormoy (70) 117 K3
Ormoy (89) 113 G3
Ormoy (91) 87 F1
Ormoy-la-Rivière (91) 86 C3
Ormoy-le-Davien (60) 39 F5
Ormoy-lès-Sexfontaines (52) . 92 A5
Ormoy-Villers (60) 38 E5
Ornacieux (38) 206 E6
Ornaisons (11) 291 G6
Ornans (25) 156 D2
Ornes (55) 26 A6
Ornex (01) 190 E1
Ornézan (32) 286 D2
Orniac (46) 233 K6
Ornolac-Ussat-les-Bains (09) . 307 J5
Ornon (38) 224 D5
Orny (57) 45 F6
Oroër (60) 37 H1
Oroix (65) 285 G4
Oron (57) 66 D2
Oroux (79) 162 B2
Orphin (78) 85 K1
Orpierre (05) 258 D2
Orquevaux (52) 92 D4
les Orres (05) 243 K5
Orret (21) 135 G2
Orriule (64) 283 H2
Orrouer (28) 84 E3
Orrouy (60) 38 E4
Orry-la-Ville (60) 38 B6
Ors (59) 12 E5
Orsan (30) 256 C5
Orsanco (64) 283 F4
Orsans (11) 289 H6
Orsans (25) 138 D5
Orsay (91) 58 D5
Orschwihr (68) 96 B6
Orschwiller (67) 71 A4
Orsennes (36) 165 J5
Orsinval (59) 12 E3
Orsonnette (63) 203 F6
Orsonville (78) 85 K2
Ortaffa (66) 315 H3
Ortale (2B) 319 J5
Orthevielle (40) 262 E6
Orthez (64) 283 J1
Orthoux-Sérignac-Quilhan (30) . 274 D3
Ortillon (10) 90 C2
Ortiporio (2B) 319 H4
Orto (2A) 320 D2
Ortoncourt (88) 94 D3
Orus (09) 307 H5
Orval (18) 167 G2
Orval (50) 30 D4
Orvault (44) 123 G3
Orvaux (27) 56 C2
Orve (25) 139 F4
Orveau (91) 86 E3
Orveau-Bellesauve (45) . . . 86 E5
Orville (21) 136 C2
Orville (36) 148 A2
Orville (45) 87 F5
Orville (61) 55 F3
Orville (62) 10 B5

Orvillers-Sorel (60) 18 E6
Orvilliers (78) 57 J3
Orvilliers-Saint-Julien (10) . . 89 J3
Orx (40) 262 C5
Os-Marsillon (64) 284 A3
Osani (2A) 316 C4
Osches (55) 43 G6
Osenbach (68) 96 B5
Oslon (71) 154 B6
Osly-Courtil (02) 39 H2
Osmanville (14) 29 H6
Osmery (18) 149 K5
Osmets (65) 285 K4
Osmoy (18) 149 H3
Osmoy (78) 57 J3
Osmoy-Saint-Valery (76) . . . 16 C3
Osne-le-Val (52) 92 B2
Osnes (08) 23 H4
Osny (95) 58 B1
Ossages (40) 264 C6
Ossas-Suhare (64) 283 H6
Osse (25) 138 B5
Ossé (35) 79 J5
Osse-en-Aspe (64) 303 F2
Osséja (66) 313 H5
Osselle (25) 156 A1
Ossen (64) 304 B1
Ossenx (64) 283 J3
Osserain-Rivareyte (64) . . . 283 G3
Ossès (64) 282 D4
Ossey-les-Trois-Maisons (10) . 89 H3
Ossun (65) 285 G5
Ossun-ez-Angles (65) 304 C1
Ostabat-Asme (64) 283 F4
Ostel (02) 40 B2
Ostheim (68) 96 C3
Osthoffen (67) 70 D3
Osthouse (67) 70 E5
Ostreville (62) 10 B1
Ostricourt (59) 6 D6
Ostwald (67) 71 D1
Ota (2A) 316 C4
Othe (54) 26 A3
Othis (77) 38 C6
Ottange (57) 27 F3
Ottersthal (67) 70 B1
Otterswiller (67) 70 B1
Ottmarsheim (68) 97 D2
Ottonville (57) 45 J4
Ottrott (67) 70 C5
Ottwiller (67) 69 F5
Ouagne (58) 133 F4
Ouainville (76) 15 F3
Ouanne (89) 132 E1
Ouarville (28) 85 J4
les Oubeaux (14) 31 H1
Ouchamps (41) 128 E4
Ouches (42) 186 E5
Oucques (41) 108 E5
Oudalle (76) 34 A3
Oudan (58) 132 E5
Oudeuil (60) 17 J6
Oudezeele (59) 3 J4
Oudincourt (52) 92 A5
l'Oudon (14) 54 C2
Oudon (44) 123 K2
Oudrenne (57) 27 J4
Oudry (71) 170 C3
Oueilloux (65) 285 J6
Ouerre (28) 57 G5
Ouessant (29) 72 A1
Ouffières (14) 53 H1
Ouge (70) 117 G5
Ouges (21) 136 B6
Ougney (39) 137 G6
Ougney-Douvot (25) 138 C5
Ougny (58) 151 K3
Ouhans (25) 156 E3
Ouides (43) 238 A1
Ouillon (64) 284 C4
Ouilly-du-Houley (14) 34 A5
Ouilly-le-Tesson (14) 54 A1
Ouilly-le-Vicomte (14) 33 K5
Ouistreham (14) 33 F3
Oulches (36) 164 D3
Oulches-la-Vallée-Foulon (02) . 40 C2
Oulchy-la-Ville (02) 39 J5
Oulchy-le-Château (02) . . . 39 J5
Oulins (28) 57 G3
Oulles (38) 224 D4
Oullins (69) 206 A2
Oulmes (85) 161 F5
Oulon (58) 151 G1
Ounans (39) 155 J3
Oupia (34) 291 F4
Our (39) 155 J2
Ourcel-Maison (60) 17 K6
Ourches (26) 240 D2
Ourches-sur-Meuse (55) . . . 65 G5
Ourde (65) 305 H3
Ourdis-Cotdoussan (65) . . . 304 C2
Ourdon (65) 304 B2
Ourouër (58) 151 F3
Ourouer-les-Bourdelins (18) . 150 A5
Ouroux (69) 188 B2
Ouroux-en-Morvan (58) . . . 152 B1
Ouroux-sous-le-Bois-
  Sainte-Marie (71) 170 E6
Ouroux-sur-Saône (71) . . . 172 A1
Oursbelille (65) 285 H4
Ourton (62) 5 J6
Ourville-en-Caux (76) 15 F4

Ousse-Suzan (40) 264 E1
Oussières (39) 155 H4
Ousson-sur-Loire (45) 131 J2
Oussoy-en-Gâtinais (45) 111 H4
Oust (09) 306 E4
Oust-Marest (80) 8 C6
Ousté (65) 304 B1
Outarville (45) 86 B6
Outines (51) 91 G1
Outreau (62) 2 A5
Outrebois (80) 10 A4
Outremécourt (52) 93 G5
Outrepont (51) 63 H4
Outriaz (01) 189 K3
Ouvans (25) 138 E5
Ouve-Wirquin (62) 3 F6
Ouveillan (11) 291 H4
Ouville (50) 30 E4
Ouville-la-Bien-Tournée (14) 54 C1
Ouville-la-Rivière (76) 15 J2
Ouville-l'Abbaye (76) 15 H4
Ouvrouer-les-Champs (45) 110 C5
Ouzilly (86) 163 F1
Ouzouer-des-Champs (45) 111 H4
Ouzouer-le-Doyen (41) 108 E3
Ouzouer-le-Marché (41) 109 G4
Ouzouer-sous-Bellegarde (45) 111 F3
Ouzouer-sur-Loire (45) 111 H6
Ouzouer-sur-Trézée (45) 131 J1
Ouzous (65) 304 A2
Ovanches (70) 137 J1
Ovillers-la-Boisselle (80) 10 E6
Oxelaëre (59) 3 H4
Oyé (71) 170 D6
Oye-et-Pallet (25) 156 E5
Oye-Plage (62) 2 E2
Oyes (51) 61 H4
Oyeu (38) 207 H6
Oyonnax (01) 190 A1
Oyré (86) 145 K5
Oyrières (70) 137 F2
Oysonville (28) 86 A3
Oytier-Saint-Oblas (38) 206 C4
Oz (38) 224 D3
Ozan (01) 172 A5
Oze (05) 242 B6
Ozenay (71) 171 K3
Ozenx-Montestrucq (64) 283 J2
Ozerailles (54) 26 D6
Ozeville (50) 29 F4
Ozières (52) 92 E6
Ozillac (17) 195 J6
Ozoir-la-Ferrière (77) 59 H4
Ozoir-le-Breuil (28) 109 G2
Ozolles (71) 170 E6
Ozon (07) 222 B4
Ozon (65) 285 K6
Ozouer-le-Voulgis (77) 59 J6
Ozourt (40) 264 C5

P

Paars (02) 40 B3
Pabu (22) 48 C5
la Pacaudière (42) 186 D3
Pacé (35) 79 F4
Pacé (61) 82 C3
Pact (38) 222 D1
Pacy-sur-Armançon (89) 114 B5
Pacy-sur-Eure (27) 57 F1
Padern (11) 309 K4
Padiès (81) 271 G1
Padirac (46) 234 A2
Padoux (88) 94 E4
Pageas (87) 198 C3
Pagney (39) 137 G6
Pagney-derrière-Barine (54) 65 H5
Pagnoz (39) 155 K4
Pagny-la-Blanche-Côte (55) 93 G1
Pagny-la-Ville (21) 154 D3
Pagny-le-Château (21) 154 D3
Pagny-lès-Goin (57) 66 A1
Pagny-sur-Meuse (55) 65 G5
Pagny-sur-Moselle (54) 65 J1
Pagolle (64) 283 G5
Pailhac (65) 305 F3
Pailharès (07) 221 J5
Pailherols (15) 236 A1
Pailhès (09) 307 G1
Pailhès (34) 291 K3
Paillart (60) 18 B5
Paillé (17) 178 B5
Paillencourt (59) 11 K3
Paillet (33) 229 K4
Pailloles (47) 248 B1
le Pailly (52) 116 D5
Pailly (89) 88 D4
Paimboeuf (44) 122 C3
Paimpol (22) 48 D2
Paimpont (35) 78 B5
Painblanc (21) 153 J2
Pair-et-Grandrupt (88) 95 J4
Paissy (02) 40 C2
Paisy-Cosdon (10) 89 H5
Paizay-le-Chapt (79) 178 D3
Paizay-le-Sec (86) 163 K3
Paizay-le-Tort (79) 178 D2
Paizay-Naudouin-Embourie (16) 178 K4
Pajay (38) 222 E1
Paladru (38) 207 H5

Palairac (11) 309 K3
le Palais (56) 120 B4
le Palais-sur-Vienne (87) 199 F1
Palaiseau (91) 58 D5
Palaiseul (52) 116 D5
Palaja (11) 290 B6
Palaminy (31) 287 H5
Palante (70) 119 F6
Palantine (25) 156 B2
Palasca (2B) 318 E2
Palau-de-Cerdagne (66) 313 H5
Palau-del-Vidre (66) 315 H3
Palavas-les-Flots (34) 293 H1
Palazinges (19) 216 A4
Paley (77) 87 K5
Palhers (48) 237 G6
Palinges (71) 170 D3
Palis (10) 89 H5
Palise (25) 138 A4
Palisse (19) 217 F1
Palladuc (63) 186 A6
Pallanne (32) 285 K2
Palleau (71) 154 C4
Pallegney (88) 94 D4
le Pallet (44) 123 J5
Palleville (81) 289 H2
la Pallu (53) 81 K2
Palluau (85) 141 H5
Palluau-sur-Indre (36) 147 G4
Palluaud (16) 213 F1
Pallud (73) 209 G2
Palluel (62) 11 H3
Palmas (12) 252 E2
la Palme (11) 310 C3
Palneca (2A) 321 G4
Palogneux (42) 204 B2
la Palud-sur-Verdon (04) 279 H3
Paluel (76) 15 F2
Pamfou (77) 87 K3
Pamiers (09) 307 J1
Pampelonne (81) 251 J5
Pamplie (79) 161 H3
Pamproux (79) 162 B5
Panassac (32) 286 C3
Panazol (87) 199 F1
Pancé (35) 103 G1
Pancey (52) 92 C2
Pancheraccia (2B) 321 H1
Pancy-Courtecon (02) 40 B1
Pandrignes (19) 216 B3
Pange (57) 45 G5
Panges (21) 135 J5
Panilleuse (27) 36 B5
Panissage (38) 207 G5
Panissières (42) 205 F2
Panjas (32) 266 B3
Pannecé (44) 124 A3
Pannecières (45) 86 C5
Pannes (45) 111 H2
Pannes (54) 65 G2
Pannessières (39) 173 G1
Panon (72) 83 F4
Panossas (38) 206 E3
la Panouse (48) 237 K4
Pantin (93) 59 F3
Panzoult (37) 145 H2
Papleux (02) 13 G6
Paradou (13) 276 B4
Parassy (18) 149 H1
Parata (2B) 319 J5
Paray-Douaville (78) 86 A3
Paray-le-Frésil (03) 169 H2
Paray-le-Monial (71) 170 C5
Paray-sous-Briailles (03) 185 H1
Paray-Vieille-Poste (91) 58 E5
Paraza (11) 291 G5
Parbayse (64) 284 B4
Parc-d'Anxtot (76) 14 D6
Parçay-les-Pins (49) 126 D4
Parçay-Meslay (37) 127 J4
Parçay-sur-Vienne (37) 145 H2
Parcé (35) 80 B4
Parcé-sur-Sarthe (72) 106 A4
Parcey (39) 155 G3
Parcieux (01) 188 C6
Parcoul (24) 212 D3
le Parcq (62) 9 J1
Parcy-et-Tigny (02) 39 J4
Pardailhan (34) 291 G2
Pardaillan (47) 231 F4
Pardies (64) 284 A3
Pardies-Piétat (64) 284 D5
Pardines (63) 202 E5
Paréac (65) 304 C1
Pareid (55) 44 B5
Parempuyre (33) 211 G6
Parennes (72) 106 A1
Parent (63) 202 E4
Parentignat (63) 203 F5
Parentis-en-Born (40) 244 E2
Parenty (62) 4 C5
Parey-Saint-Césaire (54) 93 K1
Parey-sous-Montfort (88) 93 J5
Parfondeval (02) 21 H4
Parfondeval (61) 83 H2
Parfondru (02) 20 E6
Parfondrupt (55) 44 B5
Parfouru-sur-Odon (14) 32 C6
Pargnan (02) 40 C2
Pargny (80) 19 G3
Pargny-Filain (02) 40 A1
Pargny-la-Dhuys (02) 61 F2

Pargny-les-Bois (02) 20 D4
Pargny-lès-Reims (51) 40 E4
Pargny-sous-Mureau (88) 93 F3
Pargny-sur-Saulx (51) 63 H4
Pargues (10) 114 C2
Parignargues (30) 275 F3
Parigné (35) 80 B2
Parigné-le-Pôlin (72) 106 D4
Parigné-l'Évêque (72) 107 F3
Parigné-sur-Braye (53) 81 G4
Parigny (42) 187 F5
Parigny (50) 52 C6
Parigny-la-Rose (58) 133 F5
Parigny-les-Vaux (58) 150 D3
Paris (75) 58 E3
Paris-l'Hôpital (71) 153 J5
Parisot (81) 270 A4
Parisot (82) 250 E4
Parlan (15) 234 E2
Parleboscq (40) 266 C2
Parly (89) 112 E6
Parmain (95) 37 J5
Parmilieu (38) 189 H6
Parnac (36) 165 F5
Parnac (46) 249 J1
Parnans (26) 222 E4
Parnay (18) 149 J6
Parnay (49) 126 C6
Parné-sur-Roc (53) 105 F2
Parnes (60) 36 D5
Parnoy-en-Bassigny (52) 117 F2
les Paroches (55) 64 E2
Paron (89) 88 D4
Paroy (25) 156 A3
Paroy (77) 88 C2
Paroy-sur-Saulx (52) 92 C2
Paroy-sur-Tholon (89) 112 E3
Parpeçay (36) 147 K1
Parpeville (02) 20 C3
Parranquet (47) 232 B4
Parroy (54) 66 E5
Pars-lès-Chavanges (10) 90 E2
Pars-lès-Romilly (10) 89 H2
Parsac (23) 183 G2
Parthenay (79) 161 K2
Parthenay-de-Bretagne (35) 78 E3
Partinello (2A) 316 D4
Parux (54) 67 H6
Parves (01) 207 K2
Parville (27) 56 C1
Parvillers-le-Quesnoy (80) 18 E4
Parzac (16) 179 J5
le Pas (53) 81 F3
Pas-de-Jeu (79) 144 D4
Pas-en-Artois (62) 10 C4
le Pas-Saint-l'Homer (61) 84 B2
Pasilly (89) 114 B6
Paslières (63) 185 K6
Pasly (02) 39 J2
Pasques (21) 135 J5
le Pasquier (39) 156 A6
Passa (66) 315 G3
le Passage (38) 207 H4
le Passage (47) 248 B4
Passais (61) 81 F1
Passavant (25) 138 D5
Passavant-en-Argonne (51) 63 K1
Passavant-la-Rochère (70) 117 K2
Passavant-sur-Layon (49) 143 K2
Passel (60) 19 G6
Passenans (39) 155 H6
Passins (38) 207 K3
Passirac (16) 212 C1
Passonfontaine (25) 157 F2
Passy (71) 171 G4
Passy (74) 192 B5
Passy (89) 112 D1
Passy-en-Valois (02) 39 H5
Passy-Grigny (51) 40 C6
Passy-sur-Marne (02) 61 F1
Passy-sur-Seine (77) 88 E3
Pastricciola (2A) 320 D2
Patay (45) 109 J2
Patornay (39) 173 H3
Patrimonio (2B) 320 E6
Paudy (36) 148 C3
Paucourt (45) 111 J2
Pauilhac (32) 267 J3
Pauillac (33) 211 F3
Paule (22) 75 K3
Paulhac (15) 218 C6
Paulhac (31) 269 H4
Paulhac (43) 219 G2
Paulhac-en-Margeride (48) 237 H1
Paulhaguet (43) 219 J3
Paulhan (34) 292 C1
Paulhe (12) 253 G5
Paulhenc (15) 236 B2
Paulhiac (47) 232 B6
Pauligne (11) 308 E2
Paulin (24) 215 G6
Paulinet (81) 271 G3
Paulmy (37) 146 B4
Paulnay (36) 146 E6
Paulx (44) 141 G4
Paunat (24) 232 B1
Paussac-et-Saint-Vivien (24) 213 J1
Pautaines-Augeville (52) 92 C4
Pauvres (08) 41 K2
Pavant (02) 60 D2
Pavezin (42) 205 K6

Pavie (32) 267 H6
le Pavillon-Sainte-Julie (10) 89 K4
les Pavillons-sous-Bois (93) 59 G3
Pavilly (76) 15 J6
Payns (51) 89 K3
Payra-sur-l'Hers (11) 289 G5
Payrac (46) 233 H3
Payré (86) 162 D6
Payrignac (46) 233 G3
Payrin-Augmontel (81) 290 B2
Payros-Cazautets (40) 265 H6
Payroux (86) 179 K2
Payssous (31) 305 J2
Payzac (07) 255 H1
Payzac (24) 215 F1
Pazayac (24) 215 G4
Paziols (11) 310 A3
Pazy (58) 151 J1
le Péage-de-Roussillon (38) 222 B1
Péas (51) 61 H5
Peaugres (07) 222 A2
Péaule (56) 101 K6
Péault (85) 159 K4
Pébées (32) 287 H2
Pébrac (43) 219 J5
Pech (09) 307 K5
Pech-Luna (11) 289 F5
Péchabou (31) 288 C2
Pécharic-et-le-Py (11) 289 F6
Péchaudier (81) 289 G1
Pechbonnieu (31) 269 H5
Pechbusque (31) 288 C1
le Pêchereau (36) 165 G3
Pécorade (40) 265 J5
le Pecq (78) 58 C3
Pecquencourt (59) 11 J1
Pecqueuse (91) 58 B6
Pécy (77) 60 B6
Pédernec (22) 48 B4
Pégairolles-de-Buèges (34) 273 J4
Pégairolles-de-l'Escalette (34) 273 G4
Pégomas (06) 280 D5
le Pègue (26) 257 G1
Péguilhan (31) 286 E4
Peigney (52) 116 D4
Peillac (56) 102 A3
Peille (06) 281 J2
Peillon (06) 281 H3
Peillonnex (74) 191 H2
Peintre (39) 155 G1
les Peintures (33) 212 C5
Peipin (04) 259 G5
Peisey-Nancroix (73) 193 A4
Pel-et-Der (10) 90 E3
Pélissanne (13) 277 F5
Pellafol (38) 242 C2
Pelleautier (05) 242 E6
Pellefigue (32) 287 F2
Pellegrue (33) 230 D3
Pelleport (31) 268 D5
Pellerey (21) 135 H3
le Pellerin (44) 122 E4
la Pellerine (49) 126 D3
la Pellerine (53) 80 C4
Pellevoisin (36) 147 H4
Pellouailles-les-Vignes (49) 125 H3
Pelonne (26) 258 A2
Pelouse (48) 237 K6
Pelousey (25) 137 J5
Peltre (57) 45 F6
Pélussin (42) 205 K6
Pelves (62) 11 G3
Pelvoux (05) 243 J1
Penchard (77) 59 K2
Pencran (29) 46 C6
Pendé (80) 8 E4
Pénestin (56) 121 J2
Penguily (22) 77 J2
Penin (62) 10 C2
Penly (76) 16 B1
Penmarch (29) 73 E6
Pennautier (11) 290 A5
la Penne (06) 280 D1
Penne (81) 250 C6
Penne-d'Agenais (47) 248 D2
la Penne-sur-Huveaune (13) 296 E4
la Penne-sur-l'Ouvèze (26) 257 J3
Pennedepie (14) 33 K2
Pennes-le-Sec (26) 241 G4
les Pennes-Mirabeau (13) 296 B2
Pennesières (70) 138 A3
Penol (38) 206 E6
Pensol (87) 198 A4
Penta-Acquatella (2B) 319 H4
Penta-di-Casinca (2B) 319 J3
Penvénan (22) 48 B2
Péone (06) 261 F4
Pépieux (11) 290 E4
Pérassay (36) 166 C5
Peray (72) 83 F5
Perceneige (89) 88 E4
Percey (89) 113 J3
Percey-le-Grand (70) 136 D1
le Perchay (95) 37 F6
la Perche (18) 167 G3
Perchède (32) 266 A4
Percy (38) 242 A2
Percy (50) 31 G6
Percy-en-Auge (14) 33 G6
Perdreauville (78) 57 H2
Péré (17) 177 G3
Péré (65) 285 K6

Péreille (09) 308 A3
Perelli (2B) 319 H5
Pérenchies (59) 6 D4
Péret (34) 292 C1
Péret-Bel-Air (19) 200 D6
Péreuil (16) 196 C5
Péreyres (07) 239 F3
Pergain-Taillac (32) 248 B6
Peri (2A) 320 D4
le Périer (38) 224 D6
Périers (50) 30 E2
Périers-en-Auge (14) 33 G4
Périers-sur-le-Dan (14) 32 E4
Pérignac (16) 196 H6
Pérignac (17) 195 H3
Pérignat-lès-Sarliève (63) 202 D2
Pérignat-sur-Allier (63) 202 E3
Périgné (79) 178 C2
Périgneux (42) 204 E6
Périgny (03) 185 K2
Périgny (14) 53 G2
Périgny (17) 176 E2
Périgny (41) 108 D6
Périgny (94) 59 G5
Périgny-la-Rose (10) 89 G1
Périgueux (24) 214 A3
Périssac (33) 211 K5
Perles (02) 40 B3
Perles-et-Castelet (09) 308 A6
Pern (46) 249 K3
Pernand-Vergelesses (21) 154 A2
Pernant (02) 39 H3
Pernay (37) 127 G4
la Pernelle (50) 29 F2
Pernes (62) 5 H6
Pernes-lès-Boulogne (62) 2 B5
Pernes-les-Fontaines (84) 276 D1
Pernois (80) 9 K6
Pero-Casevecchie (2B) 319 J4
Pérols (34) 293 H1
Pérols-sur-Vézère (19) 200 C4
Péron (01) 190 D2
Péronnas (01) 189 G2
Péronne (71) 171 J5
Péronne (80) 19 G1
Péronne-en-Mélantois (59) 6 E5
Péronville (28) 109 H2
Pérouges (01) 189 G6
la Pérouille (36) 165 G6
Pérouse (90) 119 J6
Péroy-les-Gombries (60) 38 E5
Perpezac-le-Blanc (19) 215 G3
Perpezac-le-Noir (19) 215 J2
Perpezat (63) 202 A3
Perpignan (66) 310 C6
les Perques (50) 28 C4
Perquie (40) 265 J2
Perrancey-les-Vieux-Moulins (52) 116 C4
le Perray-en-Yvelines (78) 57 K5
Perrecy-les-Forges (71) 170 D3
le Perréon (69) 188 A4
Perret (22) 76 C4
Perreuil (71) 153 H6
Perreux (42) 187 F4
Perreux (89) 112 C4
le Perreux-sur-Marne (94) 59 F4
Perrex (01) 188 D1
Perrier (63) 202 E5
le Perrier (85) 140 D5
la Perrière (61) 83 G3
la Perrière (73) 209 J5
Perrières (14) 54 B2
Perriers-en-Beauficel (50) 52 D4
Perriers-la-Campagne (27) 34 E5
Perriers-sur-Andelle (27) 36 A2
Perrignier (74) 175 F6
Perrigny (39) 173 G2
Perrigny (89) 113 F5
Perrigny-lès-Dijon (21) 136 A6
Perrigny-sur-Armançon (89) 134 C1
Perrigny-sur-l'Ognon (21) 136 E5
Perrigny-sur-Loire (71) 169 K4
Perrogney-les-Fontaines (52) 116 B5
le Perron (50) 31 K4
Perros-Guirec (22) 48 A2
Perrou (61) 81 H1
Perrouse (70) 138 A4
Perroy (58) 132 C4
Perruel (27) 36 A2
Perrusse (52) 116 E1
Perrusson (37) 146 D2
Pers (15) 235 F2
Pers (79) 179 F2
Pers-en-Gâtinais (45) 111 K1
Pers-Jussy (74) 191 G3
Persac (86) 163 J6
Persan (95) 37 J5
Persquen (56) 76 B6
Pertain (80) 19 G3
Perthes (08) 41 H1
Perthes (52) 63 H6
Perthes (77) 87 G2
Perthes-lès-Brienne (10) 91 H3
Pertheville-Ners (14) 54 B3
le Perthus (66) 315 G6
le Pertre (35) 104 C2
le Pertuis (43) 220 D5
Pertuis (84) 277 J5
la Péruse (16) 180 A6
Pervenchères (61) 83 G3
Perville (82) 248 E5
Pescadoires (46) 232 E4

Peschadoires (63) 203 H1
le Pescher (19) 216 A5
Péseux (25) 139 G5
Peseux (39) 155 F3
Peslières (63) 203 H6
Pesmes (70) 137 F5
Pessac (33) 229 G2
Pessac-sur-Dordogne (33) 230 D2
Pessan (32) 267 J6
Pessans (25) 156 A2
Pessat-Villeneuve (63) 185 F6
la Pesse (39) 173 K6
Pessines (17) 195 F2
Pessoulens (32) 268 B3
Petersbach (67) 69 F5
le Petit-Abergement (01) 190 A4
Petit-Bersac (24) 213 F2
le Petit-Bornand-les-Glières (74) . 191 H4
le Petit-Celland (50) 52 B5
Petit-Couronne (76) 35 H2
Petit-Croix (90) 139 J1
Petit-Failly (54) 26 A3
Petit-Fayt (59) 13 F5
le Petit-Fougeray (35) 103 G1
Petit-Landau (68) 97 E2
Petit-Mars (44) 123 H2
le Petit-Mercey (39) 155 J1
Petit-Mesnil (10) 91 F4
Petit-Noir (39) 155 F4
Petit-Palais-et-Cornemps (33) . . . 212 C6
le Petit-Pressigny (37) 146 C5
le Petit-Quevilly (76) 35 H2
Petit-Réderching (57) 69 F3
Petit-Tenquin (57) 67 G1
Petit-Verly (02) 20 C1
la Petite-Boissière (79) 143 G5
Petite-Chaux (25) 174 C1
Petite-Forêt (59) 12 C1
la Petite-Fosse (88) 95 J3
la Petite-Marche (03) 184 A2
la Petite-Pierre (67) 69 G5
la Petite-Raon (88) 95 J2
Petite-Rosselle (57) 68 B1
la Petite-Verrière (71) 152 D3
Petitefontaine (90) 119 K5
les Petites-Armoises (08) 42 C1
les Petites-Loges (51) 41 G5
Petitmagny (90) 119 J5
Petitmont (54) 67 H6
Petiville (14) 33 G4
Petiville (76) 34 D1
Petosse (85) 100 C4
Petreto-Bicchisano (2A) 322 C4
Pettoncourt (57) 66 C3
Pettonville (54) 95 F1
Peujard (33) 211 J4
Peumérit (29) 73 E4
Peumerit-Quintin (22) 76 B2
Peuplingues (62) 2 C3
Peuton (53) 104 E4
Peuvillers (55) 43 H2
Peux-et-Couffouleux (12) 272 B4
Pévange (57) 66 E2
Pévy (51) 40 D3
Pexiora (11) 289 H5
Pexonne (54) 95 H1
Pey (40) 262 D5
Peymeinade (06) 280 C5
Peynier (13) 297 F2
Peypin (13) 296 E3
Peypin-d'Aigues (84) 277 K3
Peyraboul (23) 182 D4
le Peyrat (09) 308 B3
Peyrat-de-Bellac (87) 181 F3
Peyrat-la-Nonière (23) 183 H4
Peyrat-le-Château (87) 200 A1
la Peyratte (79) 162 A2
Peyraube (65) 285 K5
Peyraud (07) 222 B2
Peyre (40) 265 G6
Peyrecave (32) 268 A1
Peyrefitte-du-Razès (11) 308 C2
Peyrefitte-sur-l'Hers (11) 289 F5
Peyregoux (81) 270 E5
Peyrehorade (40) 264 D5
Peyreleau (12) 253 H5
Peyrelevade (19) 200 D3
Peyrelongue-Abos (64) 285 F2
Peyremale (30) 255 G3
Peyrens (11) 289 H4
Peyrestortes (66) 310 B6
Peyret-Saint-André (65) 286 C4
Peyriac-de-Mer (11) 310 C1
Peyriac-Minervois (11) 290 D4
Peyriat (01) 189 K2
Peyrière (47) 231 G5
Peyrieu (01) 207 J3
Peyrignac (24) 215 F4
Peyriguère (65) 285 K5
Peyrilhac (87) 181 F5
Peyrillac-et-Millac (24) 233 H2
Peyrilles (46) 233 H5
Peyrins (26) 222 D4
Peyrissac (19) 199 K5
Peyrissas (31) 287 G4
Peyrole (81) 270 B4
Peyroles (30) 254 E6
Peyrolles (11) 309 G3
Peyrolles-en-Provence (13) 277 K5
Peyroules (04) 280 A3
Peyrouse (65) 304 A1

Peyrouzet (31) 287 F5
Peyruis (04) 259 F6
Peyrun (65) 285 J4
Peyrus (26) 240 E1
Peyrusse (15) 218 D3
Peyrusse-Grande (32) 266 E6
Peyrusse-le-Roc (12) 251 H1
Peyrusse-Massas (32) 267 H4
Peyrusse-Vieille (32) 266 D6
Peyssies (31) 287 J4
Peyzac-le-Moustier (24) 214 D6
Peyzieux-sur-Saône (01) 188 C3
Pézarches (77) 60 A5
Pezé-le-Robert (72) 82 B6
Pézenas (34) 292 C2
Pézènes-les-Mines (34) 292 A1
Pezens (11) 290 A5
Pézilla-de-Conflent (66) 309 H6
Pézilla-la-Rivière (66) 310 A6
Pezou (41) 108 D4
Pezuls (24) 232 B1
Pézy (28) 85 H1
Pfaffenheim (68) 96 B5
Pfaffenhoffen (67) 69 J6
Pfalzweyer (67) 69 F6
Pfastatt (68) 97 B2
Pfetterhouse (68) 97 A5
Pfettisheim (67) 70 E2
Pfulgriesheim (67) 70 E2
Phaffans (90) 119 J6
Phalempin (59) 6 D1
Phalsbourg (57) 70 A1
Philippsbourg (57) 69 J4
Philondenx (40) 265 H6
Phlin (54) 66 B2
Pia (66) 310 C6
Piacé (72) 82 D5
le Pian-Médoc (33) 211 G6
le Pian-sur-Garonne (33) 230 A5
Piana (2A) 316 C5
Pianello (2B) 319 H6
Piano (2B) 319 H4
Pianottoli-Caldarello (2A) 323 F5
les Piards (39) 173 J4
la Piarre (05) 242 A6
Piazzali (2B) 319 J5
Piazzole (2B) 319 H4
Piblange (57) 27 K5
Pibrac (31) 269 F6
Picarreau (39) 155 K6
Picauville (50) 28 E5
Pichanges (21) 136 B3
Picherande (63) 202 A6
Picquigny (80) 17 K1
Pie-d'Orezza (2B) 319 H5
Pied-de-Borne (48) 255 F1
Piedicorte-di-Gaggio (2B) 321 H1
Piedicroce (2B) 319 H5
Piedigriggio (2B) 319 F4
Piedipartino (2B) 319 H5
Piégon (26) 257 H3
Piégros-la-Clastre (26) 240 E4
Piégut (04) 243 F6
Piégut-Pluviers (24) 197 K4
Piencourt (27) 34 B5
Piennes (54) 26 D5
Piennes-Onvillers (80) 18 E5
Pierlas (06) 261 H5
la Pierre (38) 224 C2
Pierre-Bénite (69) 206 A3
Pierre-Buffière (87) 199 G3
Pierre-Châtel (38) 224 B6
Pierre-de-Bresse (71) 154 E5
Pierre-la-Treiche (54) 65 J5
Pierre-Levée (77) 60 B3
Pierre-Morains (51) 62 A4
Pierre-Percée (54) 95 H1
Pierre Perthuis (89) 133 J4
Pierreclos (71) 171 H6
Pierrecourt (70) 137 F1
Pierrecourt (76) 17 F2
Pierrefeu (06) 280 E2
Pierrefeu-du-Var (83) 298 A4
Pierrefiche (12) 253 F1
Pierrefiche (48) 238 A4
Pierrefiques (76) 14 B4
Pierrefitte (19) 199 J6
Pierrefitte (23) 183 G3
Pierrefitte (79) 144 A5
Pierrefitte (88) 94 B6
Pierrefitte-en-Auge (14) 00 H4
Pierrefitte-en-Beauvaisis (60) . . 37 G1
Pierrefitte-en-Cinglais (14) . . . 53 J2
Pierrefitte-ès-Bois (45) 131 H3
Pierrefitte-Nestalas (65) 304 B3
Pierrefitte-sur-Aire (55) 64 C2
Pierrefitte-sur-Loire (03) 169 K4
Pierrefitte-sur-Sauldre (41) . . . 130 C3
Pierrefitte-sur-Seine (93) 58 E2
Pierrefonds (60) 39 F3
Pierrefontaine-lès-Blamont (25) . . 139 H4
Pierrefontaine-les-Varans (25) . . 139 F6
Pierrefort (15) 236 B1
Pierregot (80) 10 B6
Pierrelatte (26) 256 D5
Pierrelaye (95) 58 C1
Pierrelongue (26) 257 J3
Pierremande (02) 19 K6
Pierremont (62) 10 A1
Pierremont-sur-Amance (52) 117 G5
Pierrepont (02) 20 E5
Pierrepont (14) 53 K3

Pierrepont (54) 26 C4
Pierrepont-sur-Avre (80) 18 D4
Pierrepont-sur-l'Arentèle (88) . . 95 F4
Pierrerue (04) 278 C1
Pierrerue (34) 291 H3
Pierres (14) 53 F3
Pierres (28) 85 H1
Pierreval (76) 16 B6
Pierrevert (04) 278 B3
Pierreville (50) 28 B4
Pierreville (54) 94 A1
Pierrevillers (57) 27 G6
Pierric (44) 103 F4
Pierry (51) 61 K1
Pietra-di-Verde (2B) 319 J6
Pietracorbara (2B) 317 D3
Pietralba (2B) 319 F3
Pietraserena (2B) 321 H1
Pietricaggio (2B) 319 H5
Pietrosella (2A) 320 C6
Pietroso (2B) 321 G2
Piets-Plasence-Moustrou (64) . . . 284 B1
Pieusse (11) 308 E1
les Pieux (50) 28 B4
Piève (2B) 319 G2
Piffonds (89) 112 C2
Pigna (2B) 318 C2
Pignan (34) 293 H1
Pignans (83) 298 B3
Pignicourt (02) 41 F2
Pignols (63) 203 F4
Pigny (18) 149 H2
Pihem (62) 3 G6
Pihen-lès-Guînes (62) 2 C3
Pila-Canale (2A) 322 D1
Pillac (16) 213 F2
Pillemoine (39) 173 K1
les Pilles (26) 257 J2
Pillon (55) 26 B4
Pimbo (40) 265 H6
Pimelles (89) 114 C5
Pimorin (39) 173 F4
Pimprez (60) 39 F1
le Pin (03) 170 A5
le Pin (14) 34 A4
le Pin (17) 212 A2
le Pin (30) 256 B6
le Pin (38) 207 H5
le Pin (39) 173 G1
le Pin (44) 124 B1
Pin (70) 137 J5
le Pin (77) 59 H3
le Pin (79) 143 G5
le Pin (82) 268 C1
le Pin-au-Haras (61) 54 D5
Pin-Balma (31) 269 H6
le Pin-en-Mauges (49) 124 D6
le Pin-la-Garenne (61) 83 H3
le Pin-Murelet (31) 287 H3
Pinas (65) 305 G1
Pinay (42) 187 F6
Pincé (72) 105 J5
Pindères (47) 247 F3
Pindray (86) 163 K4
les Pineaux (85) 160 A2
Pinel-Hauterive (47) 248 B1
Pinet (34) 292 D3
Pineuilh (33) 231 F2
Piney (10) 90 D4
Pino (2B) 317 C2
Pinols (43) 219 H5
Pinon (02) 39 K1
les Pins (16) 197 G1
Pins-Justaret (31) 288 B2
Pinsac (46) 233 J2
Pinsaguel (31) 288 B2
Pinsot (38) 224 E1
Pintac (65) 285 G4
Pinterville (27) 35 J5
Pintheville (55) 44 A5
les Pinthières (28) 57 H5
Piobetta (2B) 319 H5
Pioggiola (2B) 318 D3
Piolenc (84) 256 D4
Pionnat (23) 182 E3
Pionsat (63) 184 B3
Pioussay (79) 179 F4
Pipriac (35) 102 D2
Piquecos (82) 249 E5
Pirajoux (01) 172 D5
Piré-sur-Seiche (35) 79 J5
Pirey (25) 137 K5
Piriac-sur-Mer (44) 121 H3
Pirmil (72) 106 B3
Pirou (50) 30 D2
Pis (32) 267 K4
Pisany (17) 194 E2
Piscop (95) 58 E1
Piseux (27) 56 B4
Pisieu (38) 222 B1
Pisseleu (60) 17 J6
Pisseloup (52) 117 G4
la Pisseure (70) 118 B4
Pissos (40) 245 H3
Pissotte (85) 160 D4
Pissy (80) 17 J2
Pissy-Pôville (76) 15 J6
Pisy (89) 134 B2
Pitgam (59) 3 H3
Pithiviers (45) 86 D6
Pithiviers-le-Vieil (45) 110 D1
Pithon (02) 19 J4

Pîtres (27) 35 J3
Pittefaux (62) 2 B5
Pizay (01) 189 F6
le Pizou (24) 212 D5
Pizieux (72) 83 F4
Placé (53) 80 E5
les Places (27) 34 B5
Placey (25) 137 J6
Plachy-Buyon (80) 18 A3
Placy (14) 53 J1
Placy-Montaigu (50) 31 J4
Plagne (01) 190 B2
Plagne (31) 287 H6
Plagnole (31) 287 H3
Plaigne (11) 289 F6
Plailly (60) 38 B6
Plaimbœuf-du-Miroir (25) 139 G6
Plaimbois-Vennes (25) 139 F6
Plaimpied-Givaudins (18) 149 H4
la Plaine (49) 143 H4
Plaine (67) 95 K2
Plaine-de-Walsch (57) 67 K4
Plaine-Haute (22) 77 H5
la Plaine-sur-Mer (44) 122 A5
Plainemont (70) 118 B4
Plaines-Saint-Lange (10) 114 E3
Plainfaing (88) 95 J5
Plainoiseau (39) 173 G1
les Plains-et-Grands-Essarts (25) . 139 J5
Plaintel (22) 77 F1
Plainval (60) 38 A1
Plainville (27) 34 C6
Plainville (60) 18 C5
Plaisance (12) 271 J2
Plaisance (24) 231 J4
Plaisance (32) 266 C6
Plaisance (86) 164 A6
Plaisance-du-Touch (31) 288 A1
Plaisia (39) 173 G3
Plaisians (26) 257 K4
Plaisir (78) 58 A4
Plaissan (34) 292 D1
Plaizac (16) 196 B2
le Plan (31) 287 J6
Plan (38) 223 H2
Plan-d'Aups-Sainte-Baume (83) . . . 297 G3
Plan-de Baix (26) 241 F2
Plan-de-Cuques (13) 296 D3
Plan-de-la-Tour (83) 298 C3
Plan-d'Orgon (13) 276 D3
Planaise (73) 208 D5
Planay (21) 114 E6
Planay (73) 209 K5
la Planche (44) 141 K3
Plancher-Bas (70) 119 G5
Plancher-les-Mines (70) 119 G5
Plancherine (73) 209 F2
Planches (61) 55 F5
les Planches-en-Montagne (39) . . . 174 A2
les Planches-près-Arbois (39) . . . 155 K5
Planchez (58) 152 C2
Plancoët (22) 50 B4
Plancy-l'Abbaye (10) 89 K1
la Planée (25) 156 E5
Planès (66) 313 J4
Planèzes (66) 309 J5
Planfoy (42) 221 H1
Planguenoual (22) 49 H6
Planioles (46) 234 D5
le Planois (71) 155 F6
le Planquay (27) 34 B6
Planquery (14) 31 K3
Planques (62) 5 F6
Planrupt (52) 91 H2
les Plans (30) 255 J5
les Plans (34) 273 F4
le Plantay (01) 189 F4
les Plantiers (30) 254 D6
le Plantis (61) 83 F1
Planty (10) 89 G5
Planzolles (07) 255 H1
Plappeville (57) 44 E5
Plasne (39) 155 H6
Plasnes (27) 34 D5
Plassac (17) 195 G5
Plassac (33) 211 G4
Plassac-Rouffiac (16) 196 D5
Plassay (17) 195 F1
Plats (07) 222 B5
Plaudren (56) 101 G4
Plauzat (63) 202 D4
Plavilla (11) 289 G6
Plazac (24) 214 D5
Pleaux (15) 217 F4
Pléboulle (22) 50 A3
Pléchâtel (35) 103 F1
Plédéliac (22) 50 B4
Plédran (22) 77 H1
Pléguien (22) 48 E4
Pléhédel (22) 48 E3
Pleine-Fougères (35) 51 H5
Pleine-Selve (02) 20 C3
Pleine-Selve (33) 211 H5
Pleine-Sève (76) 15 G3
Plélan-le-Grand (35) 78 C5
Plélan-le-Petit (22) 50 B5
Plélauff (22) 76 B2
Plélo (22) 48 E5
Plémet (22) 77 H4

Plémy (22) 77 G2
Plénée-Jugon (22) 77 K2
Pléneuf-Val-André (22) 49 J5
Plénise (39) 156 C5
Plénisette (39) 156 C6
Plerguer (35) 50 E5
Plérin (22) 49 G5
Plerneuf (22) 49 F6
Plescop (56) 101 F4
Plesder (35) 50 E6
Plésidy (22) 76 C1
Pleslin-Trigavou (22) 50 D4
Plesnois (57) 44 E4
Plesnoy (52) 116 E4
Plessala (22) 77 H3
Plessé (44) 102 E5
le Plessier-Huleu (02) 39 J4
le Plessier-Rozainvillers (80) . . 18 D4
le Plessier-sur-Bulles (60) 37 K1
le Plessier-sur-Saint-Just (60) . . 38 A1
le Plessis-aux-Bois (77) 59 J2
Plessis-Barbuise (10) 89 G1
le Plessis-Belleville (60) 38 D6
le Plessis-Bouchard (95) 58 D2
le Plessis-Brion (60) 38 E1
Plessis-de-Roye (60) 19 F6
le Plessis-Dorin (41) 108 A1
le Plessis-Feu-Aussoux (77) 60 B5
le Plessis-Gassot (95) 59 F1
le Plessis-Grammoire (49) 125 H3
le Plessis-Grimoult (14) 53 G2
le Plessis-Grohan (27) 56 D2
le Plessis-Hébert (27) 57 F2
le Plessis-Lastelle (50) 30 E1
le Plessis-l'Échelle (41) 109 F5
le Plessis-l'Évêque (77) 59 J1
le Plessis-Luzarches (95) 38 A6
le Plessis-Macé (49) 125 F2
le Plessis-Pâté (91) 86 E1
le Plessis-Patte-d'Oie (60) 19 H4
le Plessis-Placy (77) 60 A1
le Plessis-Robinson (92) 58 D4
Plessis-Saint-Benoist (91) 86 B3
Plessis-Saint-Jean (89) 88 D4
le Plessis-Sainte-Opportune (27) . 35 F6
le Plessis-Trévise (94) 59 G4
Plessix-Balisson (22) 50 C4
Plestan (22) 77 K1
Plestin-les-Grèves (22) 47 J3
Pleubian (22) 48 D1
Pleucadeuc (56) 101 K4
Pleudaniel (22) 48 D2
Pleudihen-sur-Rance (22) 50 D5
Pleugriffet (56) 101 G1
Pleugueneuc (35) 50 E6
Pleumartin (86) 163 K1
Pleumeleuc (35) 78 E3
Pleumeur-Bodou (22) 47 K2
Pleumeur-Gautier (22) 48 C2
Pleure (39) 155 G4
Pleurs (51) 61 J5
Pleurtuit (35) 50 D4
Pleuven (29) 98 C2
Pleuvezain (88) 93 J3
Pleuville (16) 179 K4
Pléven (22) 50 A5
Plévin (22) 75 J3
Pleyben (29) 74 E3
Pleyber-Christ (29) 47 F5
Pliboux (79) 179 G2
Plichancourt (51) 63 G4
Plieux (32) 267 K2
Plivot (51) 62 A1
Plobannalec (29) 98 B3
Plobsheim (67) 71 D2
Ploemel (56) 100 C5
Ploemeur (56) 99 K5
Ploërdut (56) 76 B5
Ploeren (56) 100 E5
Ploërmel (56) 101 K2
Ploeuc-sur-Lié (22) 77 G2
Ploéven (29) 74 C4
Ploëzal (22) 48 C3
Plogastel-Saint-Germain (29) . . . 74 B6
Plogoff (29) 73 B3
Plogonnec (29) 74 C5
Ploisy (02) 39 J3
Plomb (50) 52 A4
Plombières-les-Bains (88) 118 D2
Plombières-lès-Dijon (21) 135 K5
Plomelin (29) 98 C2
Plomeur (29) 73 E6
Plomion (02) 21 G3
Plomodiern (29) 74 C3
Plonéis (29) 74 C5
Plonéour-Lanvern (29) 98 B2
Plonévez-du-Faou (29) 75 G3
Plonévez-Porzay (29) 74 C4
Plorec-sur-Arguenon (22) 50 A5
Plou (18) 148 E2
Plouagat (22) 48 E5
Plouaret (22) 47 K4
Plouarzel (29) 72 B3
Plouasne (22) 78 D2
Plouay (56) 100 A1
Ploubalay (22) 50 C4
Ploubazlanec (22) 48 E2
Ploubezre (22) 48 A3
Ploudalmézeau (29) 72 C2
Ploudaniel (29) 46 B5
Ploudiry (29) 46 D6
Plouëc-du-Trieux (22) 48 C4

387

Plouédern (29) 46 C5	Poilley (50) 52 A6	Pomport (24) 231 H3
Plouégat-Guérand (29) 47 H4	Poilly (51) 40 D4	Pomps (64) 284 B2
Plouégat-Moysan (29) 47 J5	Poilly-lez-Gien (45) 131 G1	Pomy (11) 308 D2
Plouénan (29) 46 E4	Poilly-sur-Serein (89) 113 K5	Poncé-sur-le-Loir (72) 107 J6
Plouër-sur-Rance (22) 50 D4	Poilly-sur-Tholon (89) 112 E4	Poncey-lès-Athée (21) 136 D5
Plouescat (29) 46 D3	Poinçon-lès-Larrey (21) 114 E4	Poncey-sur-l'Ignon (21) 135 H3
Plouézec (22) 48 E3	le Poinçonnet (36) 165 J1	le Ponchel (62) 9 J3
Plouézoch (29) 47 G4	Poincy (77) 60 A2	Ponches-Estruval (80) 9 G2
Ploufragan (22) 49 F6	Poinsenot (52) 115 K6	Ponchon (60) 37 J3
Plougar (29) 46 D4	Poinson-lès-Fayl (52) 117 F5	Poncin (01) 189 J3
Plougasnou (29) 47 G3	Poinson-lès-Grancey (52) 115 K6	Poncins (42) 204 E2
Plougastel-Daoulas (29) 72 E5	Poinson-lès-Nogent (52) 116 D2	Pondaurat (33) 230 C6
Plougonvelin (29) 72 B5	Pointel (61) 53 K5	le Pondy (18) 149 J6
Plougonven (29) 47 H5	Pointis-de-Rivière (31) 305 J1	Ponet-et-Saint-Auban (26) 241 G2
Plougonver (22) 48 A6	Pointis-Inard (31) 306 A1	Ponlat-Taillebourg (31) 305 H1
Plougoulm (29) 46 E3	Pointre (39) 137 F6	Pons (17) 195 H4
Plougoumelen (56) 100 E5	Pointvillers (25) 156 A2	Ponsampère (32) 286 A2
Plougourvest (29) 46 D4	Poinville (28) 86 A6	Ponsan-Soubiran (32) 286 B4
Plougras (29) 47 J5	le Poiré-sur-Velluire (85) 160 D5	Ponsas (26) 222 B4
Plougrescant (22) 48 C1	le Poiré-sur-Vie (85) 141 J6	Ponson-Debat-Pouts (64) 285 G4
Plouguenast (22) 77 G3	Poiroux (85) 159 G3	Ponson-Dessus (64) 285 G4
Plouguerneau (29) 46 A4	Poisat (38) 224 B1	Ponsonnas (38) 242 B1
Plouguernével (22) 76 B3	Poiseul (52) 116 E3	Pont (21) 154 E1
Plouguiel (22) 48 C2	Poiseul-la-Grange (21) 135 J2	Pont-à-Marcq (59) 6 E5
Plouguin (22) 72 C2	Poiseul-la-Ville-et-Laperrière (21) . . . 135 G2	Pont-à-Mousson (54) 65 K4
Plouha (22) 48 E4	Poiseul-lès-Saulx (21) 135 K2	Pont-à-Vendin (62) 6 C6
Plouharnel (56) 100 C6	Poiseux (58) 150 E2	Pont-Arcy (02) 40 B2
Plouhinec (29) 73 D3	Poisieux (18) 148 B3	Pont-Audemer (27) 34 C3
Plouhinec (56) 100 B4	le Poislay (41) 108 C2	Pont-Authou (27) 34 E4
Plouider (29) 46 C4	Poisson (71) 170 C6	Pont-Aven (29) 99 G3
Plouigneau (29) 47 H5	Poissons (52) 92 B3	Pont-Bellanger (14) 31 J5
Plouisy (22) 48 C5	Poissy (78) 58 B2	le Pont-Chrétien-Chabenet (36) . . . 165 G3
Ploulec'h (22) 47 K3	Poisvilliers (28) 85 G2	Pont-Croix (29) 73 D3
Ploumagoar (22) 48 C5	Poisy (74) 190 E5	Pont-d'Ain (01) 189 H4
Ploumilliau (22) 47 K3	la Poitevinière (49) 124 D6	Pont-de-Barret (26) 240 D5
Ploumoguer (29) 72 B4	Poitiers (86) 163 F3	le Pont-de-Beauvoisin (38) 207 J4
Plounéour-Ménez (29) 47 F6	Poivres (10) 62 C5	le Pont-de-Beauvoisin (73) 207 J4
Plounéour-Trez (29) 46 B3	Poix (51) 63 F2	Pont-de-Buis-lès-Quimerch (29) . . . 74 D2
Plounérin (22) 47 J5	Poix-de-Picardie (80) 17 H3	Pont-de-Chéruy (38) 206 E2
Plounéventer (29) 46 C5	Poix-du-Nord (59) 12 E4	le Pont-de-Claix (38) 224 A4
Plounévez-Lochrist (29) 46 C4	Poix-Terron (08) 22 C5	Pont-de-Labeaume (07) 239 G4
Plounévez-Moëdec (22) 47 K5	le Poizat (01) 190 B2	Pont-de-l'Arche (27) 35 J3
Plounévez-Quintin (22) 76 B3	Polaincourt-et-Clairefontaine (70) . . . 118 A3	Pont-de-Larn (81) 290 B2
Plounévézel (29) 75 J2	Polastron (31) 287 G4	Pont-de-l'Isère (26) 222 C6
Plourac'h (22) 75 J1	Polastron (32) 287 F1	Pont-de-Metz (80) 18 A2
Plouray (56) 76 A4	Poleymieux-au-Mont-d'Or (69) . . . 188 C6	le Pont-de-Montvert (48) 254 D2
Plourhan (22) 49 F4	Poliénas (38) 223 H2	Pont-de-Planches (70) 137 J2
Plourin (22) 72 B3	Polignac (17) 212 A2	Pont-de-Poitte (39) 173 H5
Plourin-lès-Morlaix (29) 47 G5	Polignac (43) 220 C5	Pont-de-Roide (25) 139 H4
Plourivo (22) 48 D3	Poligné (35) 103 F1	Pont-de-Ruan (37) 127 H6
Plouvain (62) 11 G2	Poligny (05) 242 E3	Pont-de-Salars (12) 252 D4
Plouvara (22) 48 E6	Poligny (10) 90 D6	Pont-de-Vaux (01) 172 A5
Plouvien (29) 46 A5	Poligny (39) 155 J5	Pont-de-Veyle (01) 188 D1
Plouvorn (29) 46 E4	Poligny (77) 87 J2	Pont-d'Héry (39) 156 A5
Plouyé (29) 75 G2	Polincove (62) 2 E4	Pont-d'Ouilly (14) 53 J3
Plouzané (29) 72 C4	Polisot (10) 114 D2	Pont-du-Bois (70) 118 A2
Plouzélambre (22) 47 J4	Polisy (10) 114 D2	Pont-du-Casse (47) 248 C4
Plouzévédé (29) 46 D4	Pollestres (66) 315 G3	Pont-du-Château (63) 202 E2
Plovan (29) 73 E5	Polliat (01) 189 F1	Pont-du-Navoy (39) 173 J1
Ployart-et-Vaurseine (02) 40 C1	Pollieu (01) 207 K1	Pont-en-Royans (38) 223 G5
le Ployron (60) 18 D6	Pollionnay (69) 205 J2	Pont-et-Massène (21) 134 D3
Plozévet (29) 73 D4	Polminhac (15) 235 J1	Pont-Évêque (38) 206 B5
Pludual (22) 48 E4	Polveroso (2B) 319 H4	Pont-Farcy (14) 31 H4
Pluduno (22) 50 B4	Pomacle (51) 41 G3	Pont-Hébert (50) 31 H3
Plufur (22) 47 J4	la Pomarède (11) 289 G3	Pont-la-Ville (52) 115 J1
Pluguffan (29) 74 C6	Pomarède (46) 232 E6	Pont-l'Abbé (29) 98 B3
Pluherlin (56) 101 K5	Pomarez (40) 264 D5	Pont-l'Abbé-d'Arnoult (17) 194 E1
Plumaudan (22) 78 C1	Pomas (11) 309 F1	Pont-lès-Bonfays (88) 94 A4
Plumaugat (22) 78 B2	Pomayrols (12) 253 G5	Pont-les-Moulins (25) 138 D5
Plumelec (56) 101 G3	Pomerol (33) 230 B1	Pont-l'Évêque (14) 33 K3
Pluméliau (56) 100 D1	Pomérols (34) 292 D3	Pont-l'Évêque (60) 19 H6
Plumelin (56) 100 E2	Pomeys (69) 205 G3	Pont-Melvez (22) 48 B6
Plumergat (56) 100 E4	Pommard (21) 153 K3	Pont-Noyelles (80) 18 C1
Plumetot (14) 32 E3	Pommera (62) 10 B4	Pont-Péan (35) 79 F5
Plumieux (22) 77 H5	la Pommeraie-sur-Sèvre (85) 143 F5	Pont-Remy (80) 9 G6
Plumont (39) 155 J2	la Pommeraye (14) 53 J2	Pont-Saint-Esprit (30) 256 C4
Pluneret (56) 100 D5	la Pommeraye (49) 124 D4	Pont-Saint-Mard (02) 39 J1
Plurien (22) 49 K5	Pommeret (22) 77 H1	Pont-Saint-Martin (44) 123 G5
Plusquellec (22) 75 K1	Pommereuil (59) 12 D5	Pont-Saint-Pierre (27) 35 K3
Plussulien (22) 76 D3	Pommereux (76) 16 E5	Pont-Saint-Vincent (54) 65 K6
Pluvault (21) 154 E1	Pommeréval (76) 16 B4	Pont-Sainte-Marie (10) 90 B4
Pluvet (21) 154 E1	Pommerieux (53) 104 D4	Pont-Sainte-Maxence (60) 38 C4
Pluvigner (56) 100 D3	Pommérieux (57) 66 A1	Pont-Salomon (43) 221 F2
Pluzunet (22) 48 A4	Pommerit-Jaudy (22) 48 C3	Pont-Scorff (56) 99 K4
Pocancy (51) 62 B2	Pommerit-le-Vicomte (22) 48 D4	Pont-sur-l'Ognon (70) 138 D2
Pocé-les-Bois (35) 80 A6	Pommerol (26) 258 A4	Pont-sur-Madon (88) 94 A3
Pocé-sur-Cisse (37) 128 B4	Pommeuse (77) 60 A4	Pont-sur-Meuse (55) 64 E4
Podensac (33) 229 K4	Pommevic (82) 248 E6	Pont-sur-Sambre (59) 13 G3
le Poët (05) 259 F3	Pommier (62) 10 D4	Pont-sur-Seine (10) 89 G2
le Poët-Célard (26) 240 E5	Pommier-de-Beaurepaire (38) . . . 206 D6	Pont-sur-Vanne (89) 88 E6
le Poët-en-Percip (26) 258 A3	Pommiers (02) 39 H2	Pont-sur-Yonne (89) 88 C5
le Poët-Laval (26) 240 D6	Pommiers (30) 273 J2	Pont-Trambouze (69) 187 H4
le Poët-Sigillat (26) 257 K2	Pommiers (36) 165 H4	Pontacq (64) 285 F5
Poeuilly (80) 19 J2	Pommiers (42) 204 D1	Pontailler-sur-Saône (21) 136 E5
Poey-de-Lescar (64) 284 C3	Pommiers (69) 188 B5	Pontaix (26) 241 G3
Poey-d'Oloron (64) 283 K5	Pommiers-la-Placette (38) 223 K1	Pontamafrey-Montpascal (73) . . . 225 G1
Poëzat (03) 185 G4	Pommiers-Moulons (17) 211 K1	Pontarion (23) 182 D5
Poggio-di-Nazza (2B) 321 H3	Pomoy (70) 118 D6	Pontarlier (25) 157 F4
Poggio-di-Venaco (2B) 319 F6	Pompaire (79) 161 K3	Pontarmé (60) 38 B5
Poggio-d'Oletta (2B) 317 D6	Pompéjac (33) 246 C2	Pontaubault (50) 51 K3
Poggio-Marinaccio (2B) 319 H4	Pompertuzat (31) 288 C2	Pontaubert (89) 133 J3
Poggio-Mezzana (2B) 319 J4	Pompey (54) 66 A4	Pontault-Combault (77) 59 G4
Poggiolo (2A) 320 D2	Pompiac (32) 287 H2	Pontaumur (63) 201 K1
Pogny (51) 62 E3	le Pompidou (48) 254 D4	Pontavert (02) 40 D2
Poids-de-Fiole (39) 173 G3	Pompierre (88) 93 G5	Pontcarré (77) 59 H4
Poigny (77) 88 D2	Pompierre-sur-Doubs (25) 138 E3	Pontcey (70) 137 K3
Poigny-la-Forêt (78) 57 J6	Pompiey (47) 247 H4	Pontchardon (61) 55 F2
Poil (58) 152 D5	Pompignac (33) 229 J2	Pontcharra (38) 208 C5
Poilcourt-Sydney (08) 41 F2	Pompignan (30) 274 B3	Pontcharra-sur-Turdine (69) . . . 187 K6
Poilhes (34) 291 J4	Pompignan (82) 269 F4	Pontcharraud (23) 201 F1
Poillé-sur-Vègre (72) 105 K3	Pompogne (47) 247 F2	Pontchâteau (44) 122 B1
Poilley (35) 80 A2	Pomponne (77) 59 H3	Pontcirq (46) 233 F6

Pontécoulant (14) 53 G3	la Poterie-Mathieu (27) 34 C4	
Ponteilla (66) 315 G3	Pothières (21) 115 F3	
Ponteils-et-Brésis (30) 255 F2	Potigny (14) 54 A2	
Pontenx-les-Forges (40) 244 D3	Potte (80) 19 G3	
le Pontet (73) 208 E5	Pouan-les-Vallées (10) 90 A1	
le Pontet (84) 276 C1	Pouançay (86) 144 C2	
les Pontets (25) 174 C1	Pouancé (49) 104 A5	
Pontevès (83) 278 E6	Pouant (86) 145 F3	
Ponteyraud (24) 213 F3	Poubeau (31) 305 G5	
Pontfaverger-Moronvilliers (51) . . . 41 H3	Poucharramet (31) 287 J3	
Pontgibaud (63) 202 B1	Poudenas (47) 247 H6	
Pontgouin (28) 84 D2	Poudenx (40) 265 F6	
Ponthévrard (78) 86 A1	Poudis (81) 289 H2	
Ponthion (51) 63 G3	Poueyferré (65) 285 F6	
Ponthoile (80) 9 F3	la Pouëze (49) 124 E2	
le Ponthou (29) 47 J5	Pouffonds (79) 178 D2	
Ponthoux (39) 173 J5	la Pouge (23) 182 E5	
Pontiacq-Viellepinte (64) 285 G3	le Pouget (34) 273 J6	
Pontigné (49) 126 B2	Pougnadoresse (30) 256 B2	
Pontigny (89) 113 H4	Pougne-Hérisson (79) 161 H2	
Pontis (04) 243 H6	Pougny (01) 190 D2	
Pontivy (56) 76 E5	Pougny (58) 132 A5	
Pontlevoy (41) 128 E5	Pougues-les-Eaux (58) 150 D3	
Pontmain (53) 80 C2	Pougy (10) 90 D3	
Pontoise (95) 58 C1	Pouillac (17) 212 A2	
Pontoise-lès-Noyon (60) 19 H6	Pouillat (01) 173 F6	
Pontonx-sur-l'Adour (40) 264 C3	Pouillé (41) 128 E5	
Pontorson (50) 51 J4	Pouillé (85) 160 C4	
Pontours (24) 232 A2	Pouillé (86) 163 H4	
Pontoux (71) 154 D4	Pouillé-les-Côteaux (44) 124 A3	
Pontoy (57) 45 G6	Pouillenay (21) 134 E3	
Pontpierre (57) 45 K6	Pouilley-Français (25) 137 J6	
Pontpoint (60) 38 C4	Pouilley-les-Vignes (25) 137 K6	
Pontrieux (22) 48 C3	Pouillon (40) 264 B6	
Pontru (02) 19 K2	Pouillon (51) 40 E3	
Pontruet (02) 19 K2	Pouilloux (71) 170 E3	
Ponts (50) 51 K3	Pouilly (57) 45 F6	
Ponts-et-Marais (76) 8 C3	Pouilly (60) 37 G4	
Pontvallain (72) 106 D6	Pouilly-en-Auxois (21) 135 F6	
Popian (34) 273 J6	Pouilly-le-Monial (69) 188 A5	
Popolasca (2B) 319 F4	Pouilly-lès-Feurs (42) 204 E1	
Porcaro (56) 78 B6	Pouilly-les-Nonains (42) 186 E4	
Porcelette (57) 45 K4	Pouilly-sous-Charlieu (42) 187 F3	
Porchères (33) 212 D5	Pouilly-sur-Loire (58) 132 A6	
la Porcherie (87) 199 H4	Pouilly-sur-Meuse (55) 23 G6	
Porcheux (60) 37 F3	Pouilly-sur-Saône (21) 154 D3	
Porcheville (78) 57 K2	Pouilly-sur-Serre (02) 20 C4	
Porcieu-Amblagnieu (38) 207 G1	Pouilly-sur-Vingeanne (21) 136 E2	
Pordic (22) 49 F5	le Poujol-sur-Orb (34) 291 J1	
le Porge (33) 228 C1	Poujols (34) 273 G4	
Pornic (44) 122 B5	Poulaines (36) 147 K2	
Pornichet (44) 121 K5	Poulainville (80) 18 B1	
Porquéricourt (60) 19 G6	Poulan-Pouzols (81) 270 D3	
Porri (2B) 319 J4	Poulangy (52) 116 C2	
Porspoder (29) 72 B3	Pouldergat (29) 73 E3	
Port (01) 189 K2	Pouldouran (22) 48 C2	
le Port (09) 307 F4	Pouldreuzic (29) 73 E4	
Port-Brillet (53) 104 D1	Poule-les-Écharmeaux (69) 187 J3	
Port-de-Bouc (13) 295 J5	Pouliacq (64) 284 D1	
Port-de-Lanne (40) 262 E6	les Poulières (88) 95 G5	
Port-de-Piles (86) 145 K4	Pouligney-Lusans (25) 138 B5	
Port-d'Envaux (17) 195 F1	Pouligny-Notre-Dame (36) 166 B5	
Port-des-Barques (17) 176 E5	Pouligny-Saint-Martin (36) 166 B4	
Port-en-Bessin-Huppain (14) . . . 32 A3	Pouligny-Saint-Pierre (36) 164 C2	
Port-la-Nouvelle (11) 310 D2	le Pouliguen (44) 121 J5	
Port-Launay (29) 74 D3	Poullan-sur-Mer (29) 73 D2	
Port-le-Grand (80) 9 F4	Poullaouen (29) 75 H2	
Port-Lesney (39) 155 K3	Poulligac (16) 196 C6	
Port-Louis (56) 99 K5	Poulx (30) 275 F2	
le Port-Marly (78) 58 C3	Poumarous (65) 285 J6	
Port-Mort (27) 36 A5	Poupas (82) 268 A2	
Port-Saint-Louis-du-Rhône (13) . . . 295 G5	Poupry (28) 109 K1	
Port-Saint-Père (44) 122 E5	Pouques-Lormes (58) 133 J5	
Port-Sainte-Foy-et-Ponchapt (24) . . . 231 F2	Pourcharesses (48) 255 F1	
Port-Sainte-Marie (47) 247 K4	Pourchères (07) 239 J3	
Port-sur-Saône (70) 117 K6	Pourcieux (83) 297 G2	
Port-sur-Seille (54) 66 A2	Pourcy (51) 40 E5	
Port-Vendres (66) 315 J4	Pourlans (71) 154 E4	
Port-Villez (78) 57 G1	Pournoy-la-Chétive (57) 45 F6	
la Porta (2B) 319 H4	Pournoy-la-Grasse (57) 45 F6	
Porta (66) 313 F4	Pourrain (89) 112 E6	
Portbail (50) 28 C6	Pourrières (83) 297 G1	
Porte-Joie (27) 35 K4	Poursac (16) 179 H5	
Porté-Puymorens (66) 313 F4	Poursay-Garnaud (17) 178 A5	
le Portel (62) 2 A4	Poursiugues-Boucoue (64) 284 D1	
Portel-des-Corbières (11) 310 C2	Pouru-aux-Bois (08) 23 G4	
Portes (27) 56 B1	Pouru-Saint-Remy (08) 23 G4	
Portes (30) 255 G3	Poussan (34) 292 E4	
les Portes-en-Ré (17) 176 A1	Poussanges (23) 200 E1	
Portes-en-Valdaine (26) 240 C6	Poussay (88) 94 A4	
Portes-lès-Valence (26) 240 C1	Pousseaux (58) 133 F3	
Portet (64) 265 K6	Poussignac (47) 247 F2	
Portet-d'Aspet (31) 306 A3	Poussy-la-Campagne (14) . . . 33 F6	
Portet-de-Luchon (31) 305 G5	Pousthomy (12) 271 J3	
Portet-sur-Garonne (31) 288 B2	le Pout (33) 229 K2	
Portets (33) 229 J4	Pouvrai (61) 83 H5	
Portieux (88) 94 C3	Pouxeux (88) 94 E6	
Portiragnes (34) 292 B4	Pouy (65) 286 C5	
Porto-Vecchio (2A) 323 H3	Pouy-de-Touges (31) 287 H4	
Ports (37) 145 J3	Pouy-Loubrin (32) 286 D2	
Posanges (21) 135 F4	Pouy-Roquelaure (32) 267 H1	
Poses (27) 35 K3	Pouy-sur-Vannes (10) 89 G3	
Possesse (51) 63 H3	Pouyastruc (65) 285 J5	
la Possonnière (49) 125 F4	Pouydesseaux (40) 265 J1	
la Postolle (89) 88 E5	Pouydraguin (32) 266 C3	
Postroff (57) 67 J2	Pouylebon (32) 285 K1	
Potangis (51) 89 G1	Pouzac (65) 304 D1	
Potelières (30) 255 J6	Pouzauges (85) 143 F6	
Potelle (59) 12 E3	Pouzay (37) 145 J2	
la Poterie-au-Perche (61) 55 K6	Pouze (31) 288 C3	
la Poterie-Cap-d'Antifer (76) 14 B4	Pouzilhac (30) 256 C6	
	le Pouzin (07) 240 B3	

388

Pouzol (63) . . . 184 E4
Pouzolles (34) . . . 292 A2
Pouzols (34) . . . 273 J6
Pouzols-Minervois (11) . . . 291 G5
Pouzy-Mésangy (03) . . . 168 B2
Poyanne (40) . . . 264 D4
Poyans (70) . . . 136 E3
Poyartin (40) . . . 264 D5
Poyols (26) . . . 241 H5
Pozières (80) . . . 10 E6
le Pradal (34) . . . 272 E6
les Pradeaux (63) . . . 203 F5
Pradelle (26) . . . 241 G5
Pradelles (43) . . . 238 C3
Pradelles (59) . . . 3 K5
Pradelles-Cabardès (11) . . . 290 C3
Pradelles-en-Val (11) . . . 290 C6
Pradère-les-Bourguets (31) . . . 268 E6
Prades (07) . . . 239 G5
Prades (09) . . . 308 B5
Prades (43) . . . 219 K6
Prades (66) . . . 314 C6
Prades (81) . . . 270 C6
Prades-d'Aubrac (12) . . . 236 C6
Prades-le-Lez (34) . . . 274 B5
Prades-Salars (12) . . . 252 D4
Prades-sur-Vernazobre (34) . . . 291 H3
le Pradet (83) . . . 297 K6
Pradettes (09) . . . 308 A3
Pradières (09) . . . 307 J3
Pradiers (15) . . . 218 C3
Pradinas (12) . . . 251 J4
Pradines (19) . . . 200 B5
Pradines (42) . . . 187 G5
Pradines (46) . . . 249 K1
Pradons (07) . . . 255 K1
Prads-Haute-Bléone (04) . . . 260 B3
Prahecq (79) . . . 178 B1
Prailles (79) . . . 161 K6
Pralognan-la-Vanoise (73) . . . 193 A6
Prâlon (21) . . . 135 H5
Pralong (42) . . . 204 C3
Pranles (07) . . . 239 K3
Pranzac (16) . . . 197 G3
Praslay (52) . . . 116 B6
Praslin (10) . . . 114 C2
Prasville (28) . . . 85 J5
Prat (22) . . . 48 B3
Prat-Bonrepaux (09) . . . 306 C2
Prato-di-Giovellina (2B) . . . 319 F4
Prats-de-Carlux (24) . . . 233 G1
Prats-de-Mollo-la-Preste (66) . . . 314 C6
Prats-de-Sournia (66) . . . 309 H6
Prats-du-Périgord (24) . . . 232 D4
Pratviel (81) . . . 270 B6
Pratz (39) . . . 173 J5
Prauthoy (52) . . . 116 C6
Pray (41) . . . 128 C1
Praye (54) . . . 94 A2
Prayols (09) . . . 307 J5
Prayssac (46) . . . 249 H1
Prayssas (47) . . . 248 A3
Praz-sur-Arly (74) . . . 191 K6
le Pré-d'Auge (14) . . . 33 J5
Pré-en-Pail (53) . . . 82 A2
Pré-Saint-Évroult (28) . . . 85 G6
le Pré-Saint-Gervais (93) . . . 59 F3
Pré-Saint-Martin (28) . . . 85 G6
Préaux (07) . . . 222 A4
les Préaux (27) . . . 34 C3
Préaux (36) . . . 147 F3
Préaux (53) . . . 105 H3
Préaux (76) . . . 35 J1
Préaux-Bocage (14) . . . 32 C6
Préaux-du-Perche (61) . . . 83 J4
Préaux-Saint-Sébastien (14) . . . 55 F2
Prébois (38) . . . 242 A4
Précey (50) . . . 51 K4
Préchac (32) . . . 267 H4
Préchac (33) . . . 246 B2
Préchac (65) . . . 304 B2
Préchac-sur-Adour (32) . . . 266 B6
Préchacq-Josbaig (64) . . . 283 K4
Préchacq-les-Bains (40) . . . 264 C4
Préchacq-Navarrenx (64) . . . 283 K4
Précieux (42) . . . 204 D4
Précigné (72) . . . 105 J5
Précilhon (64) . . . 284 A5
Précorbin (50) . . . 31 J4
Précy (18) . . . 150 B3
Précy-le-Sec (89) . . . 133 J2
Précy-Notre-Dame (10) . . . 90 E3
Précy-Saint-Martin (10) . . . 90 E3
Précy-sous-Thil (21) . . . 134 D2
Précy-sur-Marne (77) . . . 59 J2
Précy-sur-Oise (60) . . . 37 K5
Précy-sur-Vrin (89) . . . 112 D3
Prédefin (62) . . . 5 G6
Préfailles (44) . . . 122 A5
Préfontaines (45) . . . 111 H1
Prégilbert (89) . . . 133 H1
Préguillac (17) . . . 195 G3
Préhy (89) . . . 113 H6
Preignac (33) . . . 229 K5
Preignan (32) . . . 267 J5
Preigney (70) . . . 117 H5
Preixan (11) . . . 290 A6
Prémanon (39) . . . 174 B4
Premeaux-Prissey (21) . . . 154 C3
Prémery (58) . . . 151 F2
Prémesques (59) . . . 6 C4
Prémeyzel (01) . . . 207 J2

Prémian (34) . . . 291 G2
Premières (21) . . . 136 C6
Prémierfait (10) . . . 90 A2
Prémilhat (03) . . . 183 K1
Prémillieu (01) . . . 189 K6
Prémont (02) . . . 12 C6
Prémontré (02) . . . 20 B6
Prendeignes (46) . . . 234 E4
Préneron (32) . . . 266 E4
la Prénessaye (22) . . . 77 H4
Prenois (21) . . . 135 J4
Prénouvellon (41) . . . 109 G3
Prénovel (39) . . . 173 J3
Prény (54) . . . 65 J1
Préporché (58) . . . 152 A5
Prépotin (61) . . . 55 H6
les Prés (26) . . . 241 K6
Présailles (43) . . . 238 D1
Préseau (59) . . . 12 D2
Présentevillers (25) . . . 139 G2
Préserville (31) . . . 288 D2
Présilly (39) . . . 173 J3
Présilly (74) . . . 190 E3
Presle (73) . . . 208 D5
Presles (14) . . . 53 F3
Presles (38) . . . 223 H4
Presles (95) . . . 37 J6
Presles-en-Brie (77) . . . 59 J5
Presles-et-Boves (02) . . . 40 A2
Presles-et-Thierny (02) . . . 40 B1
Presly (18) . . . 130 E5
Presnoy (45) . . . 111 G3
Pressac (86) . . . 180 A3
Pressagny-l'Orgueilleux (27) . . . 36 B6
Pressiat (01) . . . 172 E6
Pressignac (16) . . . 198 A1
Pressignac-Vicq (24) . . . 232 A1
Pressigny (52) . . . 117 G5
Pressigny (79) . . . 162 B1
Pressigny-les-Pins (45) . . . 111 J4
Pressins (38) . . . 207 J4
Pressy (62) . . . 5 H4
Pressy-sous-Dondin (71) . . . 171 G4
la Prétière (25) . . . 139 F3
Pretin (39) . . . 156 A1
Prétot-Sainte-Suzanne (50) . . . 28 E6
Prétot-Vicquemare (76) . . . 15 H4
Prôtreville (14) . . . 33 K6
Préty (71) . . . 172 A3
Pretz-en-Argonne (55) . . . 64 A2
Preuilly (18) . . . 148 E3
Preuilly-la-Ville (36) . . . 164 B2
Preuilly-sur-Claise (37) . . . 146 C5
Preures (62) . . . 4 D5
Preuschdorf (67) . . . 25 J1
Preuseville (76) . . . 16 D2
Preutin-Higny (54) . . . 26 D4
Preux-au-Bois (59) . . . 12 E4
Preux-au-Sart (59) . . . 12 E3
Préval (72) . . . 83 J5
Prévelles (72) . . . 83 G6
Prévenchères (48) . . . 238 C6
Préveranges (18) . . . 166 D5
Prévessin-Moëns (01) . . . 190 E1
la Prévière (49) . . . 104 A6
Prévillers (60) . . . 17 J5
Prévinquières (12) . . . 251 H2
Prévocourt (57) . . . 66 C2
Prey (27) . . . 56 D2
Prey (88) . . . 95 F5
Preyssac-d'Excideuil (24) . . . 214 E2
Prez (08) . . . 21 K3
Prez-sous-Lafauche (52) . . . 92 E4
Priaires (79) . . . 177 J3
Priay (01) . . . 189 H4
Priez (02) . . . 39 H6
Prignac (17) . . . 195 J1
Prignac-en-Médoc (33) . . . 210 E1
Prignac-et-Marcamps (33) . . . 211 J5
Prigonrieux (24) . . . 231 H2
Primarette (38) . . . 206 C6
Primelin (29) . . . 73 B3
Primelles (18) . . . 148 E5
Prin-Deyrançon (79) . . . 177 J2
Prinçay (86) . . . 145 F4
Princé (35) . . . 80 C5
Pringy (51) . . . 62 E4
Pringy (74) . . . 191 F5
Pringy (77) . . . 87 G2
Prinquiau (44) . . . 122 C2
Prinsuéjols (48) . . . 237 F4
Printzheim (67) . . . 69 H6
Prisces (02) . . . 21 F3
Prisches (59) . . . 13 F5
Prissac (36) . . . 164 E4
Prissé (71) . . . 171 J6
Prissé-la-Charrière (79) . . . 178 A3
Privas (07) . . . 239 K3
Privezac (12) . . . 251 H2
Prix-lès-Mézières (08) . . . 22 C3
Priziac (56) . . . 75 K5
Prizy (71) . . . 170 D6
la Proiselière-et-Langle (70) . . . 118 C6
Proissans (24) . . . 233 F1
Proisy (02) . . . 20 E4
Proix (02) . . . 20 C2
Projan (32) . . . 265 K6
Promilhanes (46) . . . 250 D2
Prompsat (63) . . . 185 F5
Prondines (63) . . . 201 K2
Pronleroy (60) . . . 38 B1
Pronville (62) . . . 11 G4

Propiac (26) . . . 257 J3
Propières (69) . . . 187 J2
Propriano (2A) . . . 322 D2
Prosnes (51) . . . 41 H5
Prouilly (51) . . . 40 E5
Proupiary (31) . . . 287 F6
Proussy (14) . . . 53 H3
Prouvais (02) . . . 40 E5
Prouville (80) . . . 9 J4
Prouvy (59) . . . 12 C2
Prouzel (80) . . . 18 A3
Provenchère (25) . . . 139 F5
Provenchère (70) . . . 118 A5
Provenchères-lès-Darney (88) . . . 93 J6
Provenchères-sur-Fave (88) . . . 95 K3
Provency (89) . . . 133 K3
Proverville (10) . . . 91 G5
Proveysieux (38) . . . 224 A2
Proville (59) . . . 11 J4
Provin (59) . . . 6 C5
Provins (77) . . . 88 D1
Proviseux-et-Plesnoy (02) . . . 40 E1
Proyart (80) . . . 18 E2
Prudemanche (28) . . . 56 D5
Prudhomat (46) . . . 234 B1
Prugnanes (66) . . . 309 G5
Prugny (10) . . . 89 K5
Pruillé (49) . . . 125 F2
Pruillé-le-Chétif (72) . . . 106 D3
Pruillé-l'Éguillé (72) . . . 107 G5
Pruines (12) . . . 235 J6
Prunay (51) . . . 41 H4
Prunay-Belleville (10) . . . 89 H4
Prunay-Cassereau (41) . . . 128 A1
Prunay-en-Yvelines (78) . . . 85 K2
Prunay-le-Gillon (28) . . . 85 H4
Prunay-le-Temple (78) . . . 57 J3
Prunay-sur-Essonne (91) . . . 86 E4
Prunelli-di-Casacconi (2B) . . . 319 H4
Prunelli-di-Fiumorbo (2B) . . . 321 H4
Prunet (07) . . . 239 G6
Prunet (15) . . . 235 H2
Prunet (31) . . . 288 E1
Prunet-et-Belpuig (66) . . . 314 E4
Prunières (05) . . . 243 H5
Prunières (38) . . . 242 D1
Prunières (48) . . . 237 G2
Pruniers (36) . . . 166 C1
Pruniers-en-Sologne (41) . . . 129 H5
Pruno (2B) . . . 319 J4
Prunoy (89) . . . 112 C4
Prusly-sur-Ource (21) . . . 115 G4
Prusy (10) . . . 114 A3
Pruzilly (71) . . . 188 B1
Publier (74) . . . 175 G5
Publy (39) . . . 173 G2
Puceul (44) . . . 103 G6
le Puch (09) . . . 308 D6
Puch-d'Agenais (47) . . . 247 H3
Puchay (27) . . . 36 C3
Puchevillers (80) . . . 10 B6
le Puech (34) . . . 273 G5
Puéchabon (34) . . . 273 K5
Puéchoursi (81) . . . 289 G2
Puechredon (30) . . . 274 D2
Puellemontier (52) . . . 91 G2
Puessans (25) . . . 138 C3
Puget (84) . . . 277 G4
Puget-Rostang (06) . . . 261 G6
Puget-sur-Argens (83) . . . 299 G5
Puget-Théniers (06) . . . 280 C1
Puget-Ville (83) . . . 298 A4
Pugey (25) . . . 156 B1
Pugieu (01) . . . 207 J1
Puginier (11) . . . 289 G3
Pugnac (33) . . . 211 J4
Pugny (79) . . . 161 G1
Pugny-Chatenod (73) . . . 208 B2
Puichéric (11) . . . 290 E5
le Puid (88) . . . 95 J2
Puihardy (79) . . . 161 G4
Puilacher (34) . . . 292 D1
Puilaurens (11) . . . 309 F5
Puilboreau (17) . . . 176 D2
Puilly-et-Charbeaux (08) . . . 23 J4
Puimichel (04) . . . 278 D1
Puimisson (34) . . . 292 A3
Puimoisson (04) . . . 278 E2
la Puisaye (28) . . . 84 B1
Puiseaux (45) . . . 87 F6
Puiselet-le-Marais (91) . . . 86 D3
Puisenval (76) . . . 16 D2
le Puiset (28) . . . 85 K6
le Puiset-Doré (49) . . . 124 B6
Puiseux (08) . . . 22 B5
Puiseux (28) . . . 57 F6
Puiseux-en-Bray (60) . . . 36 E2
Puiseux-en-France (95) . . . 59 F1
Puiseux-en-Retz (02) . . . 39 G4
Puiseux-le-Hauberger (60) . . . 37 J5
Puiseux-Pontoise (95) . . . 58 B1
Puisieulx (51) . . . 41 H5
Puisieux (62) . . . 10 E5
Puisieux (77) . . . 59 K1
Puisieux-et-Clanlieu (02) . . . 20 D3
Puissalicon (34) . . . 292 A2
Puisseguin (33) . . . 230 C1
Puisserguier (34) . . . 291 J3
Puits (21) . . . 114 E6
Puits-et-Nuisement (10) . . . 90 E5
Puits-la-Vallée (60) . . . 17 K6

Puivert (11) . . . 308 D3
Pujaudran (32) . . . 287 J1
Pujaut (30) . . . 276 B1
Pujo (65) . . . 285 H3
Pujo-le-Plan (40) . . . 265 J3
les Pujols (09) . . . 307 K1
Pujols (33) . . . 230 C2
Pujols (47) . . . 248 C2
Pujols-sur-Ciron (33) . . . 229 K5
le Puley (71) . . . 171 G2
Puligny-Montrachet (21) . . . 153 K4
Pullay (27) . . . 56 A5
Pulligny (54) . . . 94 A1
Pulney (54) . . . 93 K3
Pulnoy (54) . . . 66 B5
Pulvérières (63) . . . 184 D6
Pulversheim (68) . . . 97 B1
Punchy (80) . . . 19 F3
Punerot (88) . . . 93 H2
Puntous (65) . . . 286 B4
Pupillin (39) . . . 155 K5
Pure (08) . . . 23 H4
Purgerot (70) . . . 117 K5
Pusey (70) . . . 118 A6
Pusignan (69) . . . 206 D2
Pussay (91) . . . 86 B4
Pussigny (37) . . . 145 J4
Pusy-et-Épenoux (70) . . . 118 B6
Putanges-Pont-Écrepin (61) . . . 54 A4
Puteaux (92) . . . 58 D3
Putot-en-Auge (14) . . . 33 G4
Putot-en-Bessin (14) . . . 32 C4
Puttelange-aux-Lacs (57) . . . 68 C3
Puttelange-lès-Thionville (57) . . . 27 H2
Puttigny (57) . . . 66 D3
Puxe (54) . . . 44 B5
Puxieux (54) . . . 44 C6
le Puy (25) . . . 138 C4
le Puy (33) . . . 230 D4
Puy-d'Arnac (19) . . . 216 B6
Puy-de-Serre (85) . . . 161 F3
Puy-du-Lac (17) . . . 177 H5
le Puy-en-Velay (43) . . . 220 C5
Puy-Guillaume (63) . . . 185 K5
Puy-l'Évêque (46) . . . 232 E6
Puy-Malsignat (23) . . . 183 G4
le Puy-Notre-Dame (49) . . . 144 B2
Puy-Saint-André (05) . . . 243 K1
Puy-Saint-Eusèbe (05) . . . 243 H5
Puy-Saint-Gulmier (63) . . . 201 J2
Puy-Saint-Martin (26) . . . 240 D4
Puy-Saint-Pierre (05) . . . 225 K6
Puy-Saint-Vincent (05) . . . 243 J1
le Puy-Sainte-Réparade (13) . . . 277 H5
Puy-Sanières (05) . . . 243 J5
Puybarban (33) . . . 230 C5
Puybegon (81) . . . 270 B4
Puybrun (46) . . . 234 B1
Puycalvel (81) . . . 270 D5
Puycasquier (32) . . . 267 K4
Puycelci (81) . . . 269 K1
Puycornet (82) . . . 249 J5
Puydaniel (31) . . . 288 B4
Puydarrieux (65) . . . 286 A1
la Puye (86) . . . 163 K2
Puygaillard-de-Lomagne (82) . . . 268 B2
Puygaillard-de-Quercy (82) . . . 269 J1
Puygiron (26) . . . 240 C6
Puygouzon (81) . . . 270 E3
Puygros (73) . . . 208 C4
Puyjourdes (46) . . . 250 E2
Puylagarde (82) . . . 250 E3
Puylaroque (82) . . . 250 B4
Puylaurens (81) . . . 289 H1
Puylausic (32) . . . 287 G2
Puyloubier (13) . . . 297 F1
Puymangou (24) . . . 212 D3
Puymaurin (31) . . . 286 E2
Puyméras (84) . . . 257 H3
Puymiclan (47) . . . 231 G6
Puymirol (47) . . . 248 D5
Puymoyen (16) . . . 196 E4
Puynormand (33) . . . 212 D6
Puyol-Cazalet (40) . . . 265 H6
Puyôo (64) . . . 283 H1
Puyravault (17) . . . 177 G3
Puyravault (85) . . . 160 B5
Puyréaux (16) . . . 179 G6
Puyrenier (24) . . . 197 H5
Puyrolland (17) . . . 177 J4
Puységur (32) . . . 267 J4
Puysségur (31) . . . 268 C4
Puysserampion (47) . . . 231 G5
Puyvalador (66) . . . 313 J3
Puyvert (84) . . . 277 G4
Puzeaux (80) . . . 19 F3
Puzieux (57) . . . 66 C3
Puzieux (88) . . . 94 A3
Py (66) . . . 314 B4
la Pyle (27) . . . 35 F5
Pys (80) . . . 10 E5

Q

Quaëdypre (59) . . . 3 J3
Quaix-en-Chartreuse (38) . . . 224 A2
Quantilly (18) . . . 149 H1
Quarante (34) . . . 291 H4
Quarouble (59) . . . 12 E1
Quarré-les-Tombes (89) . . . 134 A5

la Quarte (70) . . . 117 G5
le Quartier (63) . . . 184 C3
Quasquara (2A) . . . 320 E5
Quatre-Champs (08) . . . 42 C1
les Quatre-Routes-du-Lot (46) . . . 215 K6
Quatremare (27) . . . 35 H5
Quatzenheim (67) . . . 70 D3
Quéant (62) . . . 11 G4
Queaux (86) . . . 163 J6
Québriac (35) . . . 79 F1
Quédillac (35) . . . 78 C2
Queige (73) . . . 209 G2
Quelaines-Saint-Gault (53) . . . 104 E3
Quelmes (62) . . . 3 F5
Quelneuc (56) . . . 102 C2
Quéménéven (29) . . . 74 D4
Quemigny-Poisot (21) . . . 135 J6
Quemigny-sur-Seine (21) . . . 135 G1
Quemper-Guézennec (22) . . . 48 B3
Quemperven (22) . . . 48 B3
Quend (80) . . . 8 E2
Quenne (89) . . . 113 G5
Quenoche (70) . . . 138 A3
Quenza (2A) . . . 323 F1
Quercamps (62) . . . 2 E5
Quercitello (2B) . . . 319 H4
Quérénaing (59) . . . 12 D3
Quérigut (09) . . . 308 D6
Quernes (62) . . . 5 H4
Querqueville (50) . . . 28 C2
Querré (49) . . . 105 G6
Querrien (29) . . . 99 J2
Querrieu (80) . . . 18 C1
Quers (70) . . . 118 D5
Quesmy (60) . . . 19 H5
le Quesne (80) . . . 17 G2
le Quesnel (80) . . . 18 D3
le Quesnel-Aubry (60) . . . 37 K1
le Quesnoy (59) . . . 12 E3
le Quesnoy-en-Artois (62) . . . 9 J2
Quesnoy-le-Montant (80) . . . 8 E5
Quesnoy-sur-Airaines (80) . . . 17 H1
Quesnoy-sur-Deûle (59) . . . 6 D3
Quesques (62) . . . 2 D5
Quessigny (27) . . . 56 E2
Quessoy (22) . . . 77 H1
Questembert (56) . . . 101 J5
Questrecques (62) . . . 2 B6
Quet-en-Beaumont (38) . . . 242 C1
Quetigny (21) . . . 136 B5
Quettehou (50) . . . 29 F3
Quettetot (50) . . . 28 C4
Quetteville (14) . . . 34 A3
Quettreville-sur-Sienne (50) . . . 30 D5
Queudes (51) . . . 61 H6
la Queue-en-Brie (94) . . . 59 G4
la Queue-les-Yvelines (78) . . . 57 J4
Queuille (63) . . . 184 C5
Quevauvillers (80) . . . 17 J3
Quéven (56) . . . 99 K4
Quévert (22) . . . 50 C5
Quevillon (76) . . . 35 G2
Quévreville-la-Poterie (76) . . . 35 J3
Queyrac (33) . . . 210 D1
Queyrières (43) . . . 220 E5
Queyssac (24) . . . 231 J1
Queyssac-les-Vignes (19) . . . 216 B6
Quézac (15) . . . 235 F3
Quézac (48) . . . 254 B2
Quiberon (56) . . . 120 C2
Quiberville (76) . . . 15 J2
Quibou (50) . . . 31 G4
Quié (09) . . . 307 J4
Quiers (77) . . . 80 A1
Quiers-sur-Bézonde (45) . . . 111 F3
Quiéry-la-Motte (62) . . . 11 G2
Quierzy (02) . . . 19 J6
Quiestède (62) . . . 3 G6
Quiévelon (59) . . . 13 J3
Quièvrechain (59) . . . 12 E1
Quièvrecourt (76) . . . 16 C4
Quiévy (59) . . . 12 C4
Quilen (62) . . . 4 D5
Quillan (11) . . . 308 E4
Quillebeuf-sur-Seine (27) . . . 34 C1
le Quillio (22) . . . 76 F3
Quilly (08) . . . 42 A2
Quilly (44) . . . 102 C2
Quily (56) . . . 101 J2
Quimper (29) . . . 74 D6
Quimperlé (29) . . . 99 J3
Quincampoix (76) . . . 35 J1
Quincampoix-Fleuzy (60) . . . 17 G4
Quinçay (86) . . . 162 E3
Quincerot (21) . . . 134 D2
Quincerot (89) . . . 113 K4
Quincey (21) . . . 154 B2
Quincey (70) . . . 138 B1
Quincié-en-Beaujolais (69) . . . 188 A3
Quincieu (38) . . . 223 H2
Quincieux (69) . . . 188 C6
Quincy (18) . . . 148 E2
Quincy-Basse (02) . . . 39 J1
Quincy-Landzécourt (55) . . . 43 G1
Quincy-le-Vicomte (21) . . . 134 C2
Quincy-sous-le-Mont (02) . . . 40 A3
Quincy-sous-Sénart (91) . . . 59 G6
Quincy-Voisins (77) . . . 59 K3
Quinéville (50) . . . 29 F4
Quingey (25) . . . 156 A2
Quinquempoix (60) . . . 18 C6

Quins (12) 251 K4
Quinsac (24) 197 K6
Quinsac (33) 229 H3
Quinson (04) 278 E4
Quint-Fonsegrives (31) 288 C1
Quintal (74) 191 F6
la Quinte (72) 106 C2
Quintenas (07) 222 A3
Quintenic (22) 49 K6
Quintigny (39) 173 F1
Quintillan (11) 309 K3
Quintin (22) 76 E1
le Quiou (22) 78 D1
Quirbajou (11) 308 E5
Quiry-le-Sec (80) 18 B5
Quissac (30) 274 D2
Quissac (46) 234 A5
Quistinic (56) 100 C2
Quittebeuf (27) 35 G2
Quivières (80) 19 H3
Quœux-Haut-Maînil (62) 9 J2

R

Rabastens (81) 269 K4
Rabastens-de-Bigorre (65) 285 J3
Rabat-les-Trois-Seigneurs (09) 307 H4
la Rabatelière (85) 142 B5
Rablay-sur-Layon (49) 125 G5
Rabodanges (61) 53 K4
Rabou (05) 242 D5
Rabouillet (66) 309 G6
Racécourt (88) 94 B4
Rachecourt-sur-Marne (52) 92 A1
Rachecourt-Suzémont (52) 91 K2
Râches (59) 11 J1
Racines (10) 113 J2
la Racineuse (71) 154 D5
Racquinghem (62) 3 H6
Racrange (57) 67 F2
Raddon-et-Chapendu (70) 118 D4
Radenac (56) 101 G1
Radepont (27) 36 A3
Radinghem (62) 5 F5
Radinghem-en-Weppes (59) 6 C4
Radon (61) 82 D2
Radonvilliers (10) 90 E4
Raedersdorf (68) 97 C6
Raedersheim (68) 96 B6
Raffetot (76) 14 E5
Rageade (15) 219 G5
Rahart (41) 108 C4
Rahay (72) 108 A3
Rahling (57) 69 F4
Rahon (25) 139 F4
Rahon (39) 155 G3
Rai (61) 55 H5
Raids (50) 31 F2
Raillencourt-Sainte-Olle (59) 11 J4
Railleu (66) 313 K3
Raillicourt (08) 22 C5
Raillimont (02) 21 H4
Raimbeaucourt (59) 11 H1
Rainans (39) 155 G1
Raincheval (80) 10 B5
Raincourt (70) 117 J4
le Raincy (93) 59 G3
Rainfreville (76) 15 J3
Rainneville (80) 18 B1
Rainsars (59) 13 H5
Rainville (88) 93 H3
Rainvillers (60) 37 G2
les Rairies (49) 126 A1
Raismes (59) 12 C1
Raissac (09) 308 A3
Raissac-d'Aude (11) 291 G5
Raissac-sur-Lampy (11) 289 K5
Raival (55) 64 C3
Raix (16) 179 F5
Raizeux (78) 57 J6
Ramasse (01) 189 H2
Ramatuelle (83) 299 F4
Rambaud (05) 243 F5
Rambervillers (88) 95 F3
Rambluzin-et-Benoite-Vaux (55) . . . 64 C1
Rambouillet (78) 57 K6
Rambucourt (55) 65 G3
Ramburelles (80) 17 F1
Rambures (80) 17 F1
Ramecourt (62) 10 A2
Ramecourt (88) 94 A4
Ramerupt (10) 90 C2
Ramicourt (02) 20 A1
Ramillies (59) 11 K4
Rammersmatt (68) 119 K4
Ramonchamp (88) 119 G3
Ramonville-Saint-Agne (31) 288 C1
Ramoulu (45) 86 E6
Ramous (64) 283 H1
Ramousies (59) 13 H5
Ramouzens (32) 266 D3
Rampan (50) 31 H3
Rampieux (24) 232 B4
Rampillon (77) 88 B1
Rampoux (46) 233 G5
Rancé (01) 188 D5
Rancenay (25) 156 B1
Rancennes (08) 24 C1
Rances (10) 91 F2

Ranchal (69) 187 J3
Ranchot (39) 155 J1
Ranchy (14) 32 A4
Rancogne (16) 197 G3
Rançonnières (52) 117 F3
Rancourt (80) 11 G6
Rancourt (88) 94 A5
Rancourt-sur-Ornain (55) 63 J3
Rancy (71) 172 B3
Randan (63) 185 H5
Randens (73) 209 F4
Randevillers (25) 138 E5
Randonnai (61) 55 J6
Rânes (61) 54 A6
Rang (25) 139 F3
Rang-du-Fliers (62) 8 E1
Rangecourt (52) 116 E2
Rangen (67) 70 C2
Ranguevaux (57) 27 F5
Rannée (35) 104 A3
Ranrupt (67) 70 A6
Rans (39) 155 J1
Ransart (62) 10 E4
Ranspach (68) 119 J3
Ranspach-le-Bas (68) 97 D4
Ranspach-le-Haut (68) 97 D4
Rantechaux (25) 157 F1
Rantigny (60) 38 A3
Ranton (86) 144 D3
Rantzwiller (68) 97 C3
Ranville (14) 33 F4
Ranville-Breuillaud (16) 178 D6
Ranzevelle (70) 117 K3
Ranzières (55) 64 D1
Raon-aux-Bois (88) 118 E1
Raon-lès-Leau (54) 95 K1
Raon-l'Étape (88) 95 G2
Raon-sur-Plaine (88) 95 K1
Rapaggio (2B) 319 H5
Rapale (2B) 319 G2
Rapey (88) 94 B4
Rapilly (14) 53 K3
Rapsécourt (51) 63 H1
Raray (60) 38 D4
Rarécourt (55) 43 F6
Rasiguères (66) 309 J5
Raslay (86) 144 D2
Rasteau (84) 257 G4
Ratenelle (71) 172 B4
Ratières (26) 222 D3
Ratte (71) 172 D2
Ratzwiller (67) 69 F4
Raucoules (43) 221 G3
Raucourt (54) 66 A2
Raucourt-au-Bois (59) 12 E3
Raucourt-et-Flaba (08) 23 F5
Raulhac (15) 235 K1
Rauret (43) 238 B2
Rauville-la-Bigot (50) 28 C4
Rauville-la-Place (50) 28 D5
Rauwiller (67) 67 K3
Rauzan (33) 230 B3
Raveau (58) 150 D1
Ravel (63) 203 G2
Ravenel (60) 38 B1
Ravenoville (50) 29 H5
Raves (88) 95 J4
Ravières (89) 114 C6
Ravigny (53) 82 B3
Raville (57) 45 J5
Raville-sur-Sânon (54) 66 D5
Ravilloles (39) 173 J5
la Ravoire (73) 208 C4
Ray-sur-Saône (70) 137 H2
Raye-sur-Authie (62) 9 H2
Rayet (47) 232 A4
Raymond (18) 149 K4
Raynans (25) 139 G2
Rayol-Canadel-sur-Mer (83) 298 D5
Rayssac (81) 271 G4
Razac-de-Saussignac (24) 231 F4
Razac-d'Eymet (24) 231 H4
Razac-sur-l'Isle (24) 213 K4
Raze (70) 137 K1
Razecueillé (31) 305 K3
Razengues (32) 268 C6
Razès (87) 181 H3
Razimet (47) 247 H2
Razines (37) 145 G4
Réal (66) 313 J3
Réalcamp (76) 16 E2
Réallon (05) 243 H4
Réalmont (81) 270 E4
Réalville (82) 250 A6
Réans (32) 266 C3
Réau (77) 87 H1
Réaumont (38) 223 J1
Réaumur (85) 160 E1
Réaup-Lisse (47) 247 H6
Réauville (26) 256 E1
Réaux (17) 195 J5
Rebais (77) 60 C3
Rebecques (62) 3 G6
Rébénacq (64) 284 C6
Rebergues (62) 2 D5
Rebets (76) 36 A1
Rebeuville (88) 93 G4
Rebigue (31) 288 C2
Rebourguil (12) 272 A3
Reboursin (36) 148 B2
Rebréchien (45) 110 B3

Rebreuve-Ranchicourt (62) 10 C1
Rebreuve-sur-Canche (62) 10 B3
Rebreuviette (62) 10 B3
Recanoz (39) 155 G6
Recey-sur-Ource (21) 115 J5
Rechésy (90) 97 A5
Réchicourt-la-Petite (54) 66 E4
Réchicourt-le-Château (57) 67 G5
Récicourt (55) 43 F5
Réclainville (28) 85 J4
Reclesne (71) 152 E3
Reclinghem (62) 5 F5
Réclonville (54) 67 F6
Recloses (77) 87 H4
Recologne (25) 137 J5
Recologne (70) 137 H2
Recologne-lès-Rioz (70) 137 K3
Recoubeau-Jansac (26) 241 H4
Recoules-d'Aubrac (48) 236 D4
Recoules-de-Fumas (48) 237 G5
Recoules-Prévinquières (12) 253 F3
Récourt (62) 11 H3
Récourt-le-Creux (55) 64 D1
Recouvrance (90) 139 J1
le Recoux (48) 253 H3
Recques-sur-Course (62) 4 C5
Recques-sur-Hem (62) 2 E4
Recquignies (59) 13 H3
le Reculey (14) 31 K6
Reculfoz (25) 174 C1
Recurt (65) 286 B5
Recy (51) 62 C2
Rédange (57) 26 E2
Rédené (29) 99 J3
Redessan (30) 275 J3
Réding (57) 67 K4
Redon (35) 102 C4
la Redorte (11) 290 E5
Redortiers (04) 258 C5
Réez-Fosse-Martin (60) 38 E6
Reffannes (79) 162 A3
Reffroy (55) 64 D6
Reffuveille (50) 52 C5
Régades (31) 305 K2
Régat (09) 308 B3
Regnauville (62) 9 H2
Regnévelle (88) 117 J2
Regnéville-sur-Mer (50) 30 D4
Regnéville-sur-Meuse (55) 43 H4
Regney (88) 94 C4
Régnié-Durette (69) 188 A3
Regnière-Ecluse (80) 9 F3
Regniowez (08) 22 A1
Regny (02) 20 B3
Régny (42) 187 G5
la Regrippière (44) 142 C1
Réguiny (56) 101 F1
Réguisheim (68) 96 C6
Régusse (83) 279 F5
Rehaincourt (88) 94 D3
Rehainviller (54) 66 D6
Rehaupal (88) 95 G6
Reherrey (54) 95 G1
Réhon (54) 26 C2
Reichsfeld (67) 70 C6
Reichshoffen (67) 69 K4
Reichstett (67) 25 A6
Reignac (16) 196 A6
Reignac (33) 211 H3
Reignac-sur-Indre (37) 146 C1
Reignat (63) 203 F2
Reigneville-Bocage (50) 28 E5
Reignier (74) 191 G2
Reigny (18) 166 E3
Reilhac (15) 217 H6
Reilhac (46) 234 A4
Reilhaguet (46) 233 J3
Reilhanette (26) 258 A4
Reillanne (04) 278 A2
Reillon (54) 67 F6
Reilly (60) 36 E4
Reims (51) 41 F4
Reims-la-Brûlée (51) 63 G5
Reinhardsmunster (67) 70 B2
Reiningue (68) 97 B2
Reipertswiller (67) 69 H4
Reithouse (39) 173 G3
Réjaumont (32) 267 H3
Réjaumont (65) 286 B6
Rejet-de-Beaulieu (59) 12 E6
Relanges (88) 93 K6
Relans (39) 155 G6
le Relecq-Kerhuon (29) 46 A6
Relevant (01) 188 D3
Rely (62) 5 H5
Remaisnil (80) 10 A4
Rémalard (61) 83 K3
Remaucourt (02) 20 A2
Remaucourt (08) 21 J5
la Remaudière (44) 123 K4
Remaugies (80) 18 E5
Remauville (77) 87 J6
Rembercourt-Sommaisne (55) 64 B2
Rembercourt-sur-Mad (54) 65 H1
Rémécourt (60) 38 B2
Rémelfang (57) 45 J3
Rémelfing (57) 68 D3
Rémeling (57) 27 K3
Remennecourt (55) 63 J4
Remenoville (54) 94 D2
Rémérangles (60) 37 J2
Réméréville (54) 66 C4

Rémering (57) 45 K3
Rémering-lès-Puttelange (57) 68 C3
Remicourt (51) 63 J2
Remicourt (88) 93 K4
Remiencourt (80) 18 B3
Remies (02) 20 C4
Rémigny (02) 20 A4
Rémigny (71) 153 H5
Rémilly (57) 45 H6
Rémilly (58) 152 A6
Remilly-Aillicourt (08) 23 F4
Remilly-en-Montagne (21) 135 H6
Remilly-les-Pothées (08) 22 B3
Remilly-sur-Lozon (50) 31 F2
Remilly-sur-Tille (21) 136 C5
Remilly-Wirquin (62) 3 F6
Réminiac (56) 102 A1
Remiremont (88) 118 E2
Remoiville (55) 43 H1
Remollon (05) 243 F6
Remomeix (88) 95 J4
Remoncourt (54) 67 F5
Remoncourt (88) 93 K5
Rémondans-Vaivre (25) 139 G4
Remoray-Boujeons (25) 156 E6
Remouillé (44) 123 J6
Remoulins (30) 275 J2
Removille (88) 93 H3
Rempnat (87) 200 B3
la Remuée (76) 14 D6
Remungol (56) 100 E2
Rémuzat (26) 257 K1
Remy (60) 38 C2
Rémy (62) 11 G3
Renac (35) 102 D3
Renage (38) 223 J1
Renaison (42) 186 D4
Renansart (02) 20 B4
Renaucourt (70) 137 H1
la Renaudie (63) 203 K2
la Renaudière (49) 142 D2
Renauvoid (88) 94 C6
Renay (41) 108 D3
Renazé (53) 104 C5
Rencurel (38) 223 J4
René (72) 82 E5
Renédale (25) 156 E3
Renescure (59) 3 H5
Renève (21) 136 E4
Réning (57) 67 G1
Rennemoulin (78) 58 B4
Rennepont (52) 91 J2
Rennes (35) 79 G4
Rennes-en-Grenouilles (53) 81 H2
Rennes-le-Château (11) 309 G5
Rennes-les-Bains (11) 309 F3
Rennes-sur-Loue (25) 156 A3
Renneval (02) 21 G4
Renneville (08) 21 H5
Renneville (27) 35 K2
Renneville (31) 288 E3
Renno (2A) 320 C1
le Renouard (61) 54 D2
Rentières (63) 218 E1
Renty (62) 4 E5
Renung (40) 265 J4
Renwez (08) 22 C2
la Réole (33) 230 C5
la Réorthe (85) 160 B2
Réotier (05) 243 K3
Repaix (54) 67 G5
la Répara-Auriples (26) 240 D4
Réparsac (16) 196 A2
Repel (88) 93 J3
Repentigny (14) 33 H4
Replonges (01) 171 K6
le Reposoir (74) 191 K4
les Repôts (39) 172 E2
Reppe (90) 119 K6
Requeil (72) 106 D5
Requista (12) 271 H1
Résenlieu (61) 55 F4
la Résie-Saint-Martin (70) 137 F5
Résigny (02) 21 J4
Resson (55) 64 B4
Ressons-l'Abbaye (60) 37 H4
Ressons-le-Long (02) 39 G2
Ressons-sur-Matz (60) 19 F6
les Ressuintes (28) 84 B1
Restigné (37) 126 E6
Restinclières (34) 274 D5
le Retail (79) 161 H3
Rétaud (17) 195 F3
Reterre (23) 183 K4
Rethel (08) 41 J1
Retheuil (02) 39 F3
Rethondes (60) 39 F2
Rethonvillers (80) 19 G4
Réthoville (50) 29 F2
Retiers (35) 103 J1
Retjons (40) 246 C5
Retonfey (57) 45 G5
Rétonval (76) 16 E3
Retournac (43) 220 D3
Retschwiller (67) 25 B2
Rettel (57) 27 J3
Rety (62) 2 C4
Retzwiller (68) 97 A4
Reugney (25) 156 D3
Reugny (03) 167 H5
Reugny (37) 128 A3
Reuil (51) 40 D6

Reuil-en-Brie (77) 60 C2
Reuil-sur-Brêche (60) 37 J3
Reuilly (27) 35 J6
Reuilly (36) 148 D3
Reuilly-Sauvigny (02) 61 F1
Reulle-Vergy (21) 154 A1
Reumont (59) 12 C5
la Réunion (47) 247 G3
Reutenbourg (67) 70 C2
Reuves (51) 61 J4
Reuville (76) 15 H4
Reux (14) 33 J4
Réveillon (51) 60 E5
Réveillon (61) 83 H2
Revel (31) 289 H2
Revel (38) 224 C3
Revel-Tourdan (38) 222 D1
Revelles (80) 17 K2
Revens (30) 253 H2
Reventin-Vaugris (38) 206 A3
Revercourt (28) 56 C5
Revest-des-Brousses (04) 278 A1
Revest-du-Bion (04) 258 C5
le Revest-les-Eaux (83) 297 J5
Revest-les-Roches (06) 281 F1
Revest-Saint-Martin (04) 258 E6
Reviers (14) 32 D3
Revigny (39) 173 G2
Revigny-sur-Ornain (55) 63 K3
Réville (50) 29 G3
Réville-aux-Bois (55) 43 H2
Révillon (02) 40 C3
Revin (08) 22 C1
Revonnas (01) 189 H2
Rexingen (67) 67 K2
Rexpoëde (59) 3 J3
Reyersviller (57) 69 G3
Reygade (19) 216 C6
Reynel (52) 92 C4
Reynès (66) 314 E5
Reyniès (82) 269 G2
Reyrevignes (46) 234 C5
Reyrieux (01) 188 C5
Reyssouze (01) 172 A5
Reyvroz (74) 175 G6
Rezay (18) 166 D2
Rezé (44) 123 G4
Rézentières (15) 218 D4
Rezonville (57) 44 D5
Rezza (2A) 320 D2
Rhèges (10) 90 A1
le Rheu (35) 79 F4
Rhinau (67) 71 D4
Rhodes (57) 67 H4
Rhodon (41) 108 E6
Rhuis (60) 38 C3
Ri (61) 54 B4
Ria-Sirach (66) 314 B3
Riaillé (44) 103 K6
le Rialet (81) 290 C1
Rians (18) 149 J1
Rians (83) 278 B6
Riantec (56) 100 A4
Riaucourt (52) 92 B6
Riaville (55) 44 A5
Ribagnac (24) 231 H3
Ribarrouy (64) 284 E1
Ribaute (11) 309 K1
Ribaute-les-Tavernes (30) 274 D1
le Ribay (53) 81 J3
Ribeaucourt (55) 92 C1
Ribeaucourt (80) 9 J5
Ribeauville (02) 12 D6
Ribeauvillé (68) 71 A6
Ribécourt-Dreslincourt (60) 38 C1
Ribécourt-la-Tour (59) 11 J5
Ribemont (02) 20 B3
Ribemont-sur-Ancre (80) 18 D1
Ribennes (48) 237 H5
Ribérac (24) 213 G3
Ribes (07) 239 F6
Ribeyret (05) 258 B1
Ribiers (05) 259 F3
Ribouisse (11) 289 G6
Riboux (83) 297 G4
la Ricamarie (42) 221 G1
Ricarville (76) 15 F5
Ricarville-du-Val (76) 16 B3
Ricaud (11) 289 G4
Ricaud (65) 285 K6
les Riceys (10) 114 D3
la Richardais (35) 50 D3
Richardménil (54) 66 A6
Richarville (91) 86 B2
la Riche (37) 127 J4
Riche (57) 66 E2
Richebourg (52) 116 A2
Richebourg (62) 6 B3
Richebourg (78) 57 H4
Richecourt (55) 65 G2
Richelieu (37) 145 G3
Richeling (57) 68 C4
Richemont (57) 27 G5
Richemont (76) 16 E3
Richerenches (84) 257 F2
Richeval (57) 67 H5
Richeville (27) 36 C4
Richtolsheim (67) 71 C5
Richwiller (68) 97 B2
Ricourt (32) 285 J2
Ricquebourg (60) 19 F6
Riec-sur-Belon (29) 99 G3

Riedisheim (68) . . . 97 C2
Riedseltz (67) . . . 25 C1
Riedwihr (68) . . . 96 D3
Riel-les-Eaux (21) . . . 115 G3
Riencourt (80) . . . 17 J1
Riencourt-lès-Bapaume (62) . . . 11 F5
Riencourt-lès-Cagnicourt (62) . . . 11 G4
Riervescemont (90) . . . 119 H5
Riespach (68) . . . 97 C5
Rieucazé (31) . . . 305 K1
Rieucros (09) . . . 308 A1
Rieulay (59) . . . 11 K1
Rieumajou (31) . . . 289 F3
Rieumes (31) . . . 287 J3
Rieupeyroux (12) . . . 251 H3
Rieussec (34) . . . 291 F3
Rieutort-de-Randon (48) . . . 237 J5
Rieux (31) . . . 287 K5
Rieux (51) . . . 61 F3
Rieux (56) . . . 102 B5
Rieux (60) . . . 38 B4
Rieux (76) . . . 16 E1
Rieux-de-Pelleport (09) . . . 307 J2
Rieux-en-Cambrésis (59) . . . 12 B4
Rieux-en-Val (11) . . . 309 H1
Rieux-Minervois (11) . . . 290 D5
Riez (04) . . . 278 E3
Rigarda (66) . . . 314 D3
Rigaud (06) . . . 261 G6
Rignac (12) . . . 251 J2
Rignac (46) . . . 234 A3
Rigney (25) . . . 138 B4
Rignieux-le-Franc (01) . . . 189 G5
Rignosot (25) . . . 138 B4
Rignovelle (70) . . . 118 E5
Rigny (70) . . . 137 G3
Rigny-la-Nonneuse (10) . . . 89 G3
Rigny-la-Salle (55) . . . 65 G6
Rigny-le-Ferron (10) . . . 89 G6
Rigny-Saint-Martin (55) . . . 65 G6
Rigny-sur-Arroux (71) . . . 170 B4
Rigny-Ussé (37) . . . 126 E6
Riguepeu (32) . . . 267 F5
Rilhac-Lastours (87) . . . 198 D3
Rilhac-Rancon (87) . . . 181 H6
Rilhac-Treignac (19) . . . 199 K5
Rilhac-Xaintrie (19) . . . 217 F4
Rillans (25) . . . 138 D3
Rillé (37) . . . 126 E4
Rillieux-la-Pape (69) . . . 206 B1
Rilly-la-Montagne (51) . . . 41 F5
Rilly-Sainte-Syre (10) . . . 89 K3
Rilly-sur-Aisne (08) . . . 42 A1
Rilly-sur-Loire (41) . . . 128 C4
Rilly-sur-Vienne (37) . . . 145 J3
Rimaucourt (52) . . . 92 C5
Rimbach-près-Guebwiller (68) . . . 96 A6
Rimbach-près-Masevaux (68) . . . 119 J4
Rimbachzell (68) . . . 96 A6
Rimbez-et-Baudiets (40) . . . 247 F6
Rimboval (62) . . . 4 E6
Rimeize (48) . . . 237 G3
Rimling (57) . . . 69 F3
Rimogne (08) . . . 22 B2
Rimon-et-Savel (26) . . . 241 G4
Rimondeix (23) . . . 183 F2
Rimons (33) . . . 230 D4
Rimont (09) . . . 307 F2
Rimou (35) . . . 51 H6
Rimplas (06) . . . 261 J5
Rimsdorf (67) . . . 67 K1
Ringeldorf (67) . . . 69 J6
Ringendorf (67) . . . 69 J6
Rinxent (62) . . . 2 B4
Riocaud (33) . . . 231 F3
Riolas (31) . . . 287 G4
Riols (34) . . . 291 F2
le Riols (81) . . . 250 E5
Riom (63) . . . 185 H6
Riom-ès-Montagnes (15) . . . 217 K2
Rioms (26) . . . 258 B3
Rion-des-Landes (40) . . . 264 C2
Rions (33) . . . 229 K4
Riorges (42) . . . 186 E4
Riotord (43) . . . 221 H3
Rioux (17) . . . 195 F3
Rioux-Martin (16) . . . 212 D3
Rioz (70) . . . 138 A3
Riquewihr (68) . . . 96 B3
Ris (63) . . . 185 K5
Ris (65) . . . 305 F4
Ris-Orangis (91) . . . 59 F6
Riscle (32) . . . 266 B5
Risoul (05) . . . 227 A4
Ristolas (05) . . . 227 D2
Rittershoffen (67) . . . 25 C3
Ritzing (57) . . . 27 K3
Riupeyrous (64) . . . 284 E3
Rivarennes (36) . . . 165 F3
Rivarennes (37) . . . 127 F6
Rivas (42) . . . 204 E4
Rive-de-Gier (42) . . . 205 J3
Rivecourt (60) . . . 38 D3
Rivedoux-Plage (17) . . . 176 C2
Rivehaute (64) . . . 283 H3
Rivel (11) . . . 308 C3
Riventosa (2B) . . . 321 F1
Rivèrenert (09) . . . 306 E3
Riverie (69) . . . 205 J4
Rivery (80) . . . 18 B2
les Rives (34) . . . 273 F3
Rives (38) . . . 223 J1

Rives (47) . . . 232 A5
Rivesaltes (66) . . . 310 B5
la Rivière (33) . . . 229 K1
Rivière (37) . . . 145 G3
la Rivière (38) . . . 223 J2
Rivière (62) . . . 10 E3
la Rivière-de-Corps (10) . . . 90 A5
la Rivière-Drugeon (25) . . . 156 D5
la Rivière-Enverse (74) . . . 192 A3
Rivière-les-Fosses (52) . . . 136 C1
Rivière-Saas-et-Gourby (40) . . . 262 E5
la Rivière-Saint-Sauveur (14) . . . 34 A2
Rivière-sur-Tarn (12) . . . 253 H5
Rivières (16) . . . 197 G2
Rivières (30) . . . 255 J4
Rivières (81) . . . 270 C2
les Rivières-Henruel (51) . . . 63 F6
Rivières-le-Bois (52) . . . 116 E5
Riville (76) . . . 14 B4
Rivolet (69) . . . 188 A5
Rix (39) . . . 156 C6
Rix (58) . . . 133 F4
Rixheim (68) . . . 97 C2
la Rixouse (39) . . . 173 K4
Rizaucourt-Buchey (52) . . . 91 J5
Roaillan (33) . . . 230 A6
Roaix (84) . . . 257 G4
Roanne (42) . . . 187 F4
Roannes-Saint-Mary (15) . . . 235 H2
Robécourt (88) . . . 93 G6
Robecq (62) . . . 5 K4
Robersart (59) . . . 12 B4
Robert-Espagne (55) . . . 63 K4
Robert-Magny-Laneuville-à-Rémy (52) . . . 91 J2
Robertot (76) . . . 15 G4
Roberval (60) . . . 38 C4
Robiac-Rochessadoule (30) . . . 255 H3
la Robine-sur-Galabre (04) . . . 259 J4
Robion (84) . . . 276 E3
le Roc (46) . . . 233 H2
le Roc-Saint-André (56) . . . 101 J3
Rocamadour (46) . . . 233 K3
Rocbaron (83) . . . 298 A4
Rocé (41) . . . 108 D5
Roche (38) . . . 206 E4
Roche (42) . . . 204 B4
la Roche-Bernard (56) . . . 121 K2
la Roche-Blanche (44) . . . 124 B3
la Roche-Blanche (63) . . . 202 D3
la Roche-Canillac (19) . . . 216 C3
la Roche-Chalais (24) . . . 212 D4
Roche-Charles-la-Mayrand (63) . . . 202 C6
la Roche-Clermault (37) . . . 145 F2
la Roche-de-Glun (26) . . . 222 C5
la Roche-de-Rame (05) . . . 243 K2
la Roche-Derrien (22) . . . 48 B3
la Roche-des-Arnauds (05) . . . 242 D5
la Roche-en-Brenil (21) . . . 134 C5
la Roche-en-Régnier (43) . . . 220 C3
Roche-et-Raucourt (70) . . . 137 G1
la Roche-Guyon (95) . . . 36 C6
Roche-la-Molière (42) . . . 205 F6
la Roche-l'Abeille (87) . . . 198 E4
Roche-le-Peyroux (19) . . . 217 G1
Roche-lès-Clerval (25) . . . 138 E1
la Roche-lez-Beaupré (25) . . . 138 B5
la Roche-Mabile (61) . . . 82 B2
la Roche-Maurice (29) . . . 46 C5
la Roche-Morey (70) . . . 117 G6
la Roche-Noire (63) . . . 202 E3
la Roche-Posay (86) . . . 146 B6
la Roche-Rigault (86) . . . 145 F4
Roche-Saint-Secret-Béconne (26) . . . 257 G1
la Roche-sur-Foron (74) . . . 191 H3
la Roche-sur-Grane (26) . . . 240 D4
la Roche-sur-le-Buis (26) . . . 257 K3
Roche-sur-Linotte-et-Sorans-les-Cordiers (70) . . . 138 B3
la Roche-sur-Yon (85) . . . 159 H1
la Roche-Vanneau (21) . . . 135 F3
la Roche-Vineuse (71) . . . 171 J6
Rochebaudin (26) . . . 240 E5
la Rochebeaucourt-et-Argentine (24) . . . 197 G5
Rochebrune (05) . . . 243 F6
Rochebrune (26) . . . 257 J2
Rochechinard (26) . . . 223 F5
Rochechouart (87) . . . 198 A1
Rochecolombe (07) . . . 239 H6
Rochecorbon (37) . . . 127 K4
Rochefort (17) . . . 177 F5
Rochefort (21) . . . 115 H6
Rochefort (73) . . . 207 K4
Rochefort-du-Gard (30) . . . 276 A1
Rochefort-en-Terre (56) . . . 101 K5
Rochefort-en-Valdaine (26) . . . 240 C6
Rochefort-en-Yvelines (78) . . . 86 B1
Rochefort-Montagne (63) . . . 202 A3
Rochefort-Samson (26) . . . 222 E6
Rochefort-sur-la-Côte (52) . . . 92 B5
Rochefort-sur-Loire (49) . . . 125 F5
Rochefort-sur-Nenon (39) . . . 155 H2
la Rochefoucauld (16) . . . 197 G2
Rochefourchat (26) . . . 241 G5
la Rochegiron (04) . . . 258 D5
Rochegude (26) . . . 256 E4
Rochegude (30) . . . 255 J4
Rochejean (25) . . . 156 E6
la Rochelle (17) . . . 176 D2
la Rochelle (70) . . . 117 G5

la Rochelle-Normande (50) . . . 51 J2
Rochemaure (07) . . . 240 A5
la Rochénard (79) . . . 177 J2
Rochepaule (07) . . . 221 H5
la Rochepot (21) . . . 153 J4
Rocher (07) . . . 239 G5
le Rochereau (86) . . . 162 D1
Roches (23) . . . 182 E1
Roches (41) . . . 109 F5
Roches-Bettaincourt (52) . . . 92 C4
les Roches-de-Condrieu (38) . . . 206 A6
Roches-lès-Blamont (25) . . . 139 H3
les Roches-l'Évêque (41) . . . 108 A5
Roches-Prémarie-Andillé (86) . . . 163 F4
Roches-sur-Marne (52) . . . 63 K6
Rocheservière (85) . . . 141 J4
Rochessauve (07) . . . 239 K4
Rochesson (88) . . . 119 G1
Rochetaillée (52) . . . 116 B4
Rochetaillée-sur-Saône (69) . . . 206 A1
Rochetoirin (38) . . . 207 G4
Rochetrejoux (85) . . . 142 D6
la Rochette (04) . . . 280 C1
la Rochette (05) . . . 243 F4
la Rochette (07) . . . 239 F1
la Rochette (16) . . . 197 F1
la Rochette (73) . . . 208 D5
la Rochette (77) . . . 87 H2
la Rochette-du-Buis (26) . . . 258 A3
Rocheville (50) . . . 28 D4
Rochonvillers (57) . . . 27 F3
Rochy-Condé (60) . . . 37 H2
Rocles (03) . . . 168 B5
Rocles (07) . . . 239 F5
Rocles (48) . . . 238 B4
Roclincourt (62) . . . 10 E7
Rocourt (88) . . . 117 G1
Rocourt-Saint-Martin (02) . . . 39 K5
Rocquancourt (14) . . . 32 E6
la Rocque (14) . . . 53 G3
Rocquefort (76) . . . 15 G5
Rocquemont (60) . . . 38 D4
Rocquemont (76) . . . 16 B5
Rocquencourt (60) . . . 18 C5
Rocquencourt (78) . . . 58 C4
Rocques (14) . . . 33 K5
Rocquigny (02) . . . 13 H6
Rocquigny (08) . . . 21 J4
Rocquigny (62) . . . 11 G5
Rocroi (08) . . . 22 B1
Rodalbe (57) . . . 67 F2
Rodelinghem (62) . . . 2 D4
Rodelle (12) . . . 252 C1
Rodemack (57) . . . 27 H3
Roderen (68) . . . 119 K4
Rodern (68) . . . 71 A6
Rodès (66) . . . 314 D2
Rodez (12) . . . 252 B3
Rodilhan (30) . . . 275 H3
Rodome (11) . . . 308 D5
la Roë (53) . . . 104 B3
Roëllecourt (62) . . . 10 B2
Roeschwoog (67) . . . 25 D3
Roeulx (59) . . . 11 K2
Roeux (62) . . . 11 F2
Roézé-sur-Sarthe (72) . . . 106 C4
Roffey (89) . . . 113 K4
Roffiac (15) . . . 218 D5
Rogécourt (02) . . . 20 B5
Rogerville (76) . . . 34 A1
Rogéville (54) . . . 65 J3
Roggenhouse (68) . . . 96 D6
Rogliano (2B) . . . 317 D2
Rogna (39) . . . 173 J6
Rognac (13) . . . 296 B2
Rognaix (73) . . . 209 G3
Rognes (13) . . . 277 H5
Rognon (25) . . . 138 C4
Rognonas (13) . . . 276 B2
Rogny (02) . . . 20 D3
Rogny-les-Sept-Écluses (89) . . . 111 K6
Rogues (30) . . . 273 J3
Rogy (80) . . . 18 A4
Rohaire (28) . . . 56 A6
Rohan (56) . . . 77 F6
Rohr (67) . . . 70 D2
Rohrbach-lès-Bitche (57) . . . 69 F3
Rohrwiller (67) . . . 25 B4
Roiffé (86) . . . 144 D2
Roiffieux (07) . . . 221 K3
Roiglise (00) . . . 19 F4
Roilly (21) . . . 134 D4
Roinville (28) . . . 85 J3
Roinville (91) . . . 86 B2
Roinvilliers (91) . . . 86 D3
Roisel (80) . . . 19 J1
les Roises (55) . . . 93 F2
Roisey (42) . . . 221 K1
Roissard (38) . . . 241 K1
Roissy-en-Brie (77) . . . 59 H4
Roissy-en-France (95) . . . 59 G2
Roiville (61) . . . 54 E3
Roizy (08) . . . 41 G2
Rolampont (52) . . . 116 C3
Rolbing (57) . . . 69 G2
Rollainville (88) . . . 93 G3
Rolleboise (78) . . . 57 H2
Rolleville (76) . . . 14 B5
Rollot (80) . . . 18 E6
Rom (79) . . . 179 G1
Romagnat (63) . . . 202 D3

la Romagne (08) . . . 21 K4
Romagne (33) . . . 230 B3
Romagné (35) . . . 80 A3
la Romagne (49) . . . 142 D2
Romagne (86) . . . 179 H1
Romagne-sous-les-Côtes (55) . . . 26 A5
Romagne-sous-Montfaucon (55) . . . 42 E3
Romagnieu (38) . . . 207 J4
Romagny (50) . . . 52 D6
Romagny (68) . . . 139 K1
Romagny-sous-Rougemont (90) . . . 119 J5
Romain (25) . . . 138 D3
Romain (39) . . . 137 H6
Romain (51) . . . 40 C3
Romain (54) . . . 94 C1
Romain-aux-Bois (88) . . . 117 G1
Romain-sur-Meuse (52) . . . 92 E6
Romainville (93) . . . 59 F3
Roman (27) . . . 56 C3
Romanèche-Thorins (71) . . . 188 B2
Romange (39) . . . 155 H1
Romans (01) . . . 188 E3
Romans (79) . . . 161 K6
Romans-sur-Isère (26) . . . 222 D5
Romanswiller (67) . . . 70 C2
Romazières (17) . . . 178 D5
Romazy (35) . . . 79 J1
Rombach-le-Franc (68) . . . 96 B1
Rombas (57) . . . 27 G5
Rombies-et-Marchipont (59) . . . 12 E2
Rombly (62) . . . 5 H4
Romegoux (17) . . . 177 G6
Romelfing (57) . . . 67 J3
Romenay (71) . . . 172 B4
Romeny-sur-Marne (02) . . . 60 D2
Romeries (59) . . . 12 D4
Romery (02) . . . 20 E2
Romery (51) . . . 40 E6
Romescamps (60) . . . 17 G4
Romestaing (47) . . . 247 F2
Romeyer (26) . . . 241 H2
la Romieu (32) . . . 267 H1
Romigny (51) . . . 40 C5
Romiguières (34) . . . 273 F4
Romillé (35) . . . 78 E3
Romilly (41) . . . 108 C3
Romilly-la-Puthenaye (27) . . . 56 A1
Romilly-sur-Aigre (28) . . . 108 E3
Romilly-sur-Andelle (27) . . . 35 K3
Romilly-sur-Seine (10) . . . 89 H2
Romont (88) . . . 94 E3
Romorantin-Lanthenay (41) . . . 129 J5
Rompon (07) . . . 240 A3
Rônai (61) . . . 54 B4
Roncenay (10) . . . 90 A6
le Roncenay-Authenay (27) . . . 56 C3
Roncey (50) . . . 31 F5
Ronchamp (70) . . . 119 F5
Ronchaux (25) . . . 156 A2
Ronchères (02) . . . 40 B5
Ronchères (89) . . . 132 C1
Roncherolles-en-Bray (76) . . . 16 D5
Roncherolles-sur-le-Vivier (76) . . . 35 J1
Ronchin (59) . . . 6 E4
Ronchois (76) . . . 16 E4
Roncourt (57) . . . 27 F6
Roncq (59) . . . 6 E2
la Ronde (17) . . . 160 D6
la Ronde-Haye (50) . . . 30 E3
Rondefontaine (25) . . . 156 D6
Ronel (81) . . . 270 E4
Ronfeugerai (61) . . . 53 H4
Rongères (03) . . . 185 J1
Ronnet (03) . . . 184 B2
Ronno (69) . . . 187 J5
Ronquerolles (95) . . . 37 J5
Ronsenac (16) . . . 197 F5
Ronssoy (80) . . . 19 J1
Rontalon (69) . . . 205 J3
Rontignon (64) . . . 284 D4
Ronvaux (55) . . . 43 K5
Roost-Warendin (59) . . . 11 H1
Roppe (90) . . . 119 J6
Roppenheim (67) . . . 25 D3
Roppentzwiller (68) . . . 97 C5
Roppeviller (57) . . . 69 H2
la Roque-Alric (84) . . . 257 G5
la Roque-Baignard (14) . . . 33 J5
la Roque-d'Anthéron (13) . . . 277 G4
la Roque-Esclapon (83) . . . 280 A4
la Roque-Gageac (24) . . . 232 E2
la Roque-Sainte-Marguerite (12) . . . 253 J5
la Roque-sur-Cèze (30) . . . 256 B4
la Roque-sur-Pernes (84) . . . 276 E1
Roquebillière (06) . . . 311 A3
Roquebrun (34) . . . 291 J2
Roquebrune (32) . . . 267 F5
Roquebrune (33) . . . 230 D5
Roquebrune-Cap-Martin (06) . . . 281 J3
Roquebrune-sur-Argens (83) . . . 299 F2
la Roquebrussanne (83) . . . 297 J3
Roquecor (82) . . . 248 E3
Roquecourbe (81) . . . 271 F6
Roquecourbe-Minervois (11) . . . 290 E5
Roquedur (30) . . . 273 K2
Roquefère (11) . . . 290 B3
Roquefeuil (11) . . . 308 C5
Roquefixade (09) . . . 307 K3
Roquefort (32) . . . 267 J4
Roquefort (40) . . . 246 B6
Roquefort (47) . . . 248 B5
Roquefort-de-Sault (11) . . . 308 E6

Roquefort-des-Corbières (11) . . . 310 C3
Roquefort-la-Bédoule (13) . . . 296 E4
Roquefort-les-Cascades (09) . . . 307 K3
Roquefort-les-Pins (06) . . . 280 E4
Roquefort-sur-Garonne (31) . . . 287 G6
Roquefort-sur-Soulzon (12) . . . 272 C2
Roquelaure (32) . . . 267 H5
Roquelaure-Saint-Aubin (32) . . . 268 A3
Roquemaure (30) . . . 256 E6
Roquemaure (81) . . . 269 J4
Roquepine (32) . . . 267 G2
Roqueredonde (34) . . . 273 F4
Roques (31) . . . 288 B2
Roques (32) . . . 267 F4
Roquesérière (31) . . . 269 J5
Roquessels (34) . . . 292 A1
Roquesteron (06) . . . 280 E2
Roquestéron-Grasse (06) . . . 280 E2
Roquetaillade (11) . . . 308 E2
Roquetoire (62) . . . 3 H6
la Roquette (27) . . . 36 A4
la Roquette-sur-Siagne (06) . . . 280 D5
la Roquette-sur-Var (06) . . . 281 F2
Roquettes (31) . . . 288 B2
Roquevaire (13) . . . 296 E3
Roquevidal (81) . . . 270 B6
Roquiague (64) . . . 283 H5
la Roquille (33) . . . 231 G4
Rorbach-lès-Dieuze (57) . . . 67 G3
Rorschwihr (68) . . . 71 A6
Rosans (05) . . . 258 B2
Rosay (39) . . . 173 F3
Rosay (76) . . . 16 B4
Rosay (78) . . . 57 J3
Rosay-sur-Lieure (27) . . . 36 B3
Rosazia (2A) . . . 320 C2
Rosbruck (57) . . . 68 B2
Roscanvel (29) . . . 72 C5
Roscoff (29) . . . 47 F2
Rosel (14) . . . 32 D4
Rosenau (68) . . . 97 E3
Rosenwiller (67) . . . 70 C4
Roset-Fluans (25) . . . 155 K1
Rosey (70) . . . 137 K2
Rosey (71) . . . 171 H1
Rosheim (67) . . . 70 C4
la Rosière (70) . . . 119 F3
Rosières (07) . . . 255 J1
Rosières (43) . . . 220 D4
Rosières (60) . . . 38 D5
Rosières (81) . . . 270 E1
Rosières-aux-Salines (54) . . . 66 C6
Rosières-en-Haye (54) . . . 65 J3
Rosières-en-Santerre (80) . . . 18 E3
Rosières-près-Troyes (10) . . . 90 B5
Rosières-sur-Barbèche (25) . . . 139 G5
Rosières-sur-Mance (70) . . . 117 H4
Rosiers-de-Juillac (19) . . . 215 G2
Rosiers-d'Égletons (19) . . . 216 D1
les Rosiers-sur-Loire (49) . . . 125 K5
Rosis (34) . . . 272 D5
Rosnay (36) . . . 164 D2
Rosnay (51) . . . 40 D4
Rosnay (85) . . . 159 J3
Rosnay-l'Hôpital (10) . . . 90 E2
Rosnoën (29) . . . 74 C2
Rosny-sous-Bois (93) . . . 59 F3
Rosny-sur-Seine (78) . . . 57 H2
Rosoy (60) . . . 38 B3
Rosoy-en-Multien (60) . . . 39 F6
Rosoy-le-Vieil (45) . . . 112 A1
Rospez (22) . . . 48 A3
Rospigliani (2B) . . . 321 G1
Rosporden (29) . . . 75 F6
Rosselange (57) . . . 27 F5
Rossfeld (67) . . . 70 E6
Rossillon (01) . . . 207 J1
Rosteig (67) . . . 69 G5
Rostrenen (22) . . . 76 A3
Rosult (59) . . . 7 G2
Rosureux (25) . . . 139 G6
Rotalier (39) . . . 173 F3
Rotangy (60) . . . 17 J6
Rothau (67) . . . 70 A5
Rothbach (67) . . . 69 H5
Rotherens (73) . . . 208 D5
la Rothière (10) . . . 91 F4
Rothois (60) . . . 17 H6
Rothonay (39) . . . 173 G3
les Rotours (61) . . . 54 A4
Rots (14) . . . 32 D4
Rott (67) . . . 25 B1
Rottelsheim (67) . . . 25 A4
Rottier (26) . . . 241 H6
Rou-Marson (49) . . . 126 A6
Rouairoux (81) . . . 290 D2
Rouans (44) . . . 122 D4
la Rouaudière (53) . . . 104 A4
Roubaix (59) . . . 6 E3
Roubia (11) . . . 291 F5
Roubion (06) . . . 261 H5
Roucamps (14) . . . 53 G1
Roucourt (59) . . . 11 J2
Roucy (02) . . . 40 D3
Roudouallec (56) . . . 75 G4
Rouécourt (52) . . . 92 A4
Rouède (31) . . . 306 B2
Rouellé (61) . . . 53 F6
Rouelles (52) . . . 116 A5
Rouen (76) . . . 35 H2
Rouessé-Fontaine (72) . . . 82 D4
Rouessé-Vassé (72) . . . 82 A6

Rouet (34) . . . 274 B4
Rouez (72) . . . 82 B6
Rouffach (68) . . . 96 B5
Rouffange (39) . . . 137 G6
Rouffiac (15) . . . 216 E6
Rouffiac (16) . . . 212 E2
Rouffiac (17) . . . 195 H3
Rouffiac (81) . . . 270 D3
Rouffiac-d'Aude (11) . . . 309 F1
Rouffiac-des-Corbières (11) . . . 309 G4
Rouffiac-Tolosan (31) . . . 269 H5
Rouffignac (17) . . . 211 J1
Rouffignac-de-Sigoulès (24) . . . 231 H3
Rouffignac-Saint-Cernin-
  de-Reilhac (24) . . . 214 D5
Rouffigny (50) . . . 52 A3
Rouffilhac (46) . . . 233 H3
Rouffy (51) . . . 62 B2
Rougé (44) . . . 103 J3
la Rouge (61) . . . 83 J5
Rouge-Perriers (27) . . . 35 F5
Rougefay (62) . . . 9 K3
Rougegoutte (90) . . . 119 H5
Rougemont (21) . . . 134 C1
Rougemont (25) . . . 138 D3
Rougemont-le-Château (90) . . . 119 J5
Rougemontiers (27) . . . 34 E3
Rougemontot (25) . . . 138 C4
Rougeou (41) . . . 129 G5
Rougeries (02) . . . 20 E3
les Rouges-Eaux (88) . . . 95 G4
le Rouget (15) . . . 235 F2
Rougeux (52) . . . 117 F4
Rougiers (83) . . . 297 H3
Rougnac (16) . . . 197 G5
Rougnat (23) . . . 183 K4
Rougon (04) . . . 279 H3
Rouhe (25) . . . 156 B2
Rouhling (57) . . . 68 C2
Rouillac (16) . . . 196 C2
Rouillac (22) . . . 77 K3
Rouillé (86) . . . 162 C5
Rouillon (72) . . . 106 D2
Rouilly (77) . . . 88 D1
Rouilly-Sacey (10) . . . 90 C4
Rouilly-Saint-Loup (10) . . . 90 B5
Roujan (34) . . . 292 B2
Roulans (25) . . . 138 C5
le Roulier (88) . . . 95 F5
Roullée (72) . . . 83 F2
Roullens (11) . . . 290 A6
Roullet-Saint-Estèphe (16) . . . 196 D4
Roullours (14) . . . 52 E3
Roumagne (47) . . . 231 G5
Roumare (76) . . . 35 G1
Roumazières-Loubert (16) . . . 180 A6
Roumégoux (15) . . . 235 F2
Roumégoux (81) . . . 271 F4
Roumengoux (09) . . . 308 D2
Roumens (31) . . . 289 G2
Roumoules (04) . . . 279 F3
Rountzenheim (67) . . . 25 C4
Roupeldange (57) . . . 27 K6
Rouperroux (61) . . . 82 B1
Rouperroux-le-Coquet (72) . . . 83 G5
Roupy (02) . . . 19 J3
la Rouquette (12) . . . 251 F3
Roure (06) . . . 261 H5
le Rouret (06) . . . 280 E4
Rousies (59) . . . 13 H3
Roussac (87) . . . 181 G4
Roussas (26) . . . 256 E1
Roussay (49) . . . 142 D2
Roussayrolles (81) . . . 250 D6
Rousseloy (60) . . . 37 K4
Roussennac (12) . . . 251 J1
Roussent (62) . . . 9 F2
les Rousses (39) . . . 174 B4
Rousses (48) . . . 254 B4
Rousset (05) . . . 243 G6
Rousset (13) . . . 297 F1
le Rousset (71) . . . 171 F3
Rousset-les-Vignes (26) . . . 257 G1
la Roussière (27) . . . 55 H2
Roussieux (26) . . . 258 B2
Roussillon (38) . . . 222 B1
Roussillon (84) . . . 277 G2
Roussillon-en-Morvan (71) . . . 152 D3
Roussines (16) . . . 197 J2
Roussines (36) . . . 165 F5
Rousson (30) . . . 255 H5
Rousson (89) . . . 112 D1
Roussy-le-Village (57) . . . 27 G3
Routelle (25) . . . 156 A1
Routes (76) . . . 15 G4
Routier (11) . . . 308 D1
Routot (27) . . . 34 E2
Rouvenac (11) . . . 308 E3
Rouves (54) . . . 66 A2
la Rouvière (30) . . . 275 F2
Rouvignies (59) . . . 12 C2
Rouville (60) . . . 38 E5
Rouville (76) . . . 14 E5
Rouvillers (60) . . . 38 C2
Rouvray (21) . . . 134 B4
Rouvray (27) . . . 57 F1
Rouvray (89) . . . 113 H4
Rouvray-Catillon (76) . . . 16 D6
Rouvray-Saint-Denis (28) . . . 86 A5
Rouvray-Saint-Florentin (28) . . . 85 H5
Rouvray-Sainte-Croix (45) . . . 109 J2
Rouvrel (80) . . . 18 C3

Rouvres (14) . . . 54 B1
Rouvres (28) . . . 57 G4
Rouvres (77) . . . 59 H1
Rouvres-en-Multien (60) . . . 39 F6
Rouvres-en-Plaine (21) . . . 136 B6
Rouvres-en-Woëvre (55) . . . 26 C6
Rouvres-en-Xaintois (88) . . . 93 K4
Rouvres-la-Chétive (88) . . . 93 G4
Rouvres-les-Bois (36) . . . 147 K3
Rouvres-les-Vignes (10) . . . 91 H5
Rouvres-Saint-Jean (45) . . . 86 D4
Rouvres-sous-Meilly (21) . . . 153 H1
Rouvres-sur-Aube (52) . . . 115 K4
Rouvrois-sur-Meuse (55) . . . 64 E2
Rouvrois-sur-Othain (55) . . . 26 B4
Rouvroy (02) . . . 20 A2
Rouvroy (62) . . . 11 G1
Rouvroy-en-Santerre (80) . . . 18 E3
Rouvroy-les-Merles (60) . . . 18 B5
Rouvroy-Ripont (51) . . . 42 B4
Rouvroy-sur-Audry (08) . . . 22 B3
Rouvroy-sur-Marne (52) . . . 92 B4
Rouvroy-sur-Serre (02) . . . 21 J4
le Roux (07) . . . 238 E4
Rouxeville (50) . . . 31 J3
la Rouxière (44) . . . 124 B3
Rouxmesnil-Bouteilles (76) . . . 15 K2
Rouy (58) . . . 151 H3
Rouy-le-Grand (80) . . . 19 G3
Rouy-le-Petit (80) . . . 19 G3
Rouze (09) . . . 308 D6
Rouzède (16) . . . 197 J3
Rouziers (15) . . . 235 F3
Rouziers-de-Touraine (37) . . . 127 J3
le Rove (13) . . . 296 B3
Roville-aux-Chênes (88) . . . 94 E3
Roville-devant-Bayon (54) . . . 94 B2
Rovon (38) . . . 223 H3
Roy-Boissy (60) . . . 17 H6
Royan (17) . . . 194 C3
Royas (38) . . . 206 D5
Royat (63) . . . 202 D2
Royaucourt (60) . . . 18 D4
Royaucourt-et-Chailvet (02) . . . 40 A1
Royaumeix (54) . . . 65 H4
Roybon (38) . . . 223 F2
Roye (70) . . . 118 E6
Roye (80) . . . 19 F4
Roye-sur-Matz (60) . . . 19 F6
Royer (71) . . . 171 J3
Royère-de-Vassivière (23) . . . 200 B1
Royères (87) . . . 199 G1
Roynac (26) . . . 240 D4
Royon (62) . . . 4 E6
Royville (76) . . . 15 J4
Roz-Landrieux (35) . . . 51 H4
Roz-sur-Couesnon (35) . . . 51 H4
Rozay-en-Brie (77) . . . 60 A6
le Rozel (50) . . . 28 A4
Rozelieures (54) . . . 94 D2
Rozérieulles (57) . . . 44 E5
Rozerotte (88) . . . 93 K5
Rozès (32) . . . 267 F4
Rozet-Saint-Albin (02) . . . 39 J5
le Rozier (48) . . . 253 H5
Rozier-Côtes-d'Aurec (42) . . . 220 E1
Rozier-en-Donzy (42) . . . 205 F1
Rozières-en-Beauce (45) . . . 109 J3
Rozières-sur-Crise (02) . . . 39 J3
Rozières-sur-Mouzon (88) . . . 93 G6
Roziers-Saint-Georges (87) . . . 199 H2
Rozoy-Bellevalle (02) . . . 60 E3
Rozoy-sur-Serre (02) . . . 21 H4
Ruages (58) . . . 133 H5
Ruan (45) . . . 110 A1
Ruan-sur-Egvonne (41) . . . 108 D2
Ruaudin (72) . . . 106 E3
Rubécourt-et-Lamécourt (08) . . . 23 F4
Rubelles (77) . . . 87 H1
Rubempré (80) . . . 10 B6
Rubercy (14) . . . 31 K1
Rubescourt (80) . . . 18 D5
Rubigny (08) . . . 21 J4
Rubrouck (59) . . . 3 H4
Ruca (22) . . . 50 A4
Ruch (33) . . . 230 C3
Rucqueville (14) . . . 32 C4
Rudeau-Ladosse (24) . . . 197 H5
Rudelle (46) . . . 234 C4
Rue (80) . . . 8 E3
la Rue-Saint-Pierre (60) . . . 37 J2
la Rue-Saint-Pierre (76) . . . 16 B6
Ruederbach (68) . . . 97 B5
Rueil-la-Gadelière (28) . . . 56 B5
Rueil-Malmaison (92) . . . 58 D3
Ruelisheim (68) . . . 97 C1
Ruelle-sur-Touvre (16) . . . 196 E3
les Rues-des-Vignes (59) . . . 11 K5
Ruesnes (59) . . . 12 D3
Rueyres (46) . . . 234 B3
Ruffec (16) . . . 179 G4
Ruffec (36) . . . 164 D3
Ruffey-le-Château (25) . . . 137 H5
Ruffey-lès-Beaune (21) . . . 154 B3
Ruffey-lès-Echirey (21) . . . 136 B4
Ruffey-sur-Seille (39) . . . 173 F1
Ruffiac (56) . . . 102 A2
Ruffieu (01) . . . 190 A4
Ruffieux (73) . . . 190 C6
Ruffigné (44) . . . 103 H3
Rugles (27) . . . 55 K4
Rugney (88) . . . 94 B3

Rugny (89) . . . 114 B4
Ruhans (70) . . . 138 B3
Ruillé-en-Champagne (72) . . . 106 B2
Ruillé-Froid-Fonds (53) . . . 105 F3
Ruillé-le-Gravelais (53) . . . 104 D1
Ruillé-sur-Loir (72) . . . 107 H6
Ruisseauville (62) . . . 5 F5
Ruitz (62) . . . 5 K6
Rullac-Saint-Cirq (12) . . . 252 A5
Rully (14) . . . 53 F3
Rully (60) . . . 38 D4
Rully (71) . . . 153 K5
Rumaucourt (62) . . . 11 H3
Rumegies (59) . . . 7 G6
Rumersheim-le-Haut (68) . . . 97 D1
Rumesnil (14) . . . 33 H5
Rumigny (08) . . . 21 J3
Rumigny (80) . . . 18 A3
Rumilly (62) . . . 4 E5
Rumilly (74) . . . 190 D6
Rumilly-en-Cambrésis (59) . . . 11 J5
Rumilly-lès-Vaudes (10) . . . 114 C1
Ruminghem (62) . . . 3 F4
Rumont (55) . . . 64 C3
Rumont (77) . . . 87 F5
Runan (22) . . . 48 C3
Rungis (94) . . . 58 E5
Ruoms (07) . . . 255 K1
Rupéreux (77) . . . 60 D6
Ruppes (88) . . . 93 G2
Rupt (52) . . . 92 B3
Rupt-aux-Nonains (55) . . . 64 A5
Rupt-devant-Saint-Mihiel (55) . . . 64 D3
Rupt-en-Woëvre (55) . . . 43 J6
Rupt-sur-Moselle (88) . . . 119 F3
Rupt-sur-Othain (55) . . . 26 A4
Rupt-sur-Saône (70) . . . 137 J1
Rurange-lès-Thionville (57) . . . 27 H5
Rurey (25) . . . 156 B2
Russ (67) . . . 70 B4
Russange (57) . . . 26 E3
le Russey (25) . . . 157 J1
Russy (14) . . . 32 A3
Russy-Bémont (60) . . . 39 F4
Rustenhart (68) . . . 96 D5
Rustiques (11) . . . 290 C5
Rustrel (84) . . . 277 J2
Rustroff (57) . . . 27 J3
Rutali (2B) . . . 319 H2
Ruvigny (10) . . . 90 C5
Ruy (38) . . . 207 F4
Ruyaulcourt (62) . . . 11 H5
Ruynes-en-Margeride (15) . . . 219 F6
Ry (76) . . . 36 A1
Rye (39) . . . 155 G5
Ryes (14) . . . 32 C3

S

Saâcy-sur-Marne (77) . . . 60 C2
Saales (67) . . . 95 K3
Saâne-Saint-Just (76) . . . 15 J3
Saasenheim (67) . . . 71 D5
Sabadel-Latronquière (46) . . . 234 D4
Sabadel-Lauzès (46) . . . 233 K6
Sabaillan (32) . . . 287 F2
Sabalos (65) . . . 285 J4
Sabarat (09) . . . 307 G1
Sabarros (65) . . . 286 B5
Sabazan (32) . . . 266 C5
Sablé-sur-Sarthe (72) . . . 105 J4
les Sables-d'Olonne (85) . . . 158 E3
Sablet (84) . . . 257 G4
Sablières (07) . . . 238 E6
Sablonceaux (17) . . . 194 D2
Sablonnières (77) . . . 60 D3
Sablons (33) . . . 212 B5
Sablons (38) . . . 222 B2
Sabonnères (31) . . . 287 H2
Sabran (30) . . . 256 B5
Sabres (40) . . . 245 H4
Saccourvielle (31) . . . 305 H5
Sacé (53) . . . 81 F6
Sacey (50) . . . 51 J5
Saché (37) . . . 127 H6
Sachin (62) . . . 5 H6
Sachy (08) . . . 23 G4
Sacierges-Saint-Martin (36) . . . 165 F4
Saclas (91) . . . 86 C4
Saclay (91) . . . 58 C5
Saconin-et-Breuil (02) . . . 39 H3
Sacoué (65) . . . 305 H2
le Sacq (27) . . . 56 E3
Sacquenay (21) . . . 136 D2
Sacquenville (27) . . . 35 H6
Sacy (51) . . . 40 E5
Sacy (89) . . . 133 J1
Sacy-le-Grand (60) . . . 38 B3
Sacy-le-Petit (60) . . . 38 C3
Sadeillan (32) . . . 286 A3
Sadillac (24) . . . 231 H3
Sadirac (33) . . . 229 J3
Sadournin (65) . . . 286 B4
Sadroc (19) . . . 215 J2
Saessolsheim (67) . . . 70 D2
Saffais (54) . . . 66 C6
Saffloz (39) . . . 173 J2
Saffré (44) . . . 103 G6

Saffres (21) . . . 135 G5
Sagelat (24) . . . 232 D3
Sagnat (23) . . . 182 B1
Sagnes-et-Goudoulet (07) . . . 239 F3
Sagonne (18) . . . 150 A6
Sagy (71) . . . 172 D3
Sagy (95) . . . 58 A1
Sahorre (66) . . . 314 B4
Sahune (26) . . . 257 J1
Sahurs (76) . . . 35 G3
Sai (61) . . . 54 C5
Saignes (15) . . . 217 H2
Saignes (46) . . . 234 B3
Saigneville (80) . . . 9 F4
Saignon (84) . . . 277 H2
Sail-les-Bains (42) . . . 186 C2
Sail-sous-Couzan (42) . . . 204 C2
Sailhan (65) . . . 305 F4
Saillac (19) . . . 215 K5
Saillac (46) . . . 250 D3
Saillagouse (66) . . . 313 H5
Saillans (26) . . . 241 F4
Saillans (33) . . . 212 A6
Saillant (63) . . . 204 B6
Saillat-sur-Vienne (87) . . . 180 C6
Saillenard (71) . . . 172 E1
Sailly (08) . . . 23 H5
Sailly (52) . . . 92 C3
Sailly (71) . . . 171 G4
Sailly (78) . . . 57 K1
Sailly-Achâtel (57) . . . 66 B2
Sailly-au-Bois (62) . . . 10 D5
Sailly-en-Ostrevent (62) . . . 11 G3
Sailly-Flibeaucourt (80) . . . 9 F4
Sailly-Labourse (62) . . . 6 A6
Sailly-Laurette (80) . . . 18 D2
Sailly-le-Sec (80) . . . 18 D1
Sailly-lez-Cambrai (59) . . . 11 J4
Sailly-lez-Lannoy (59) . . . 7 F4
Sailly-Saillisel (80) . . . 11 G6
Sailly-sur-la-Lys (62) . . . 6 B4
Sain-Bel (69) . . . 205 J1
Saincaize-Meauce (58) . . . 150 D5
Sainghin-en-Mélantois (59) . . . 6 E5
Sainghin-en-Weppes (59) . . . 6 C5
Sainneville (76) . . . 14 C6
Sainpuits (89) . . . 132 D3
Sains (35) . . . 51 H4
Sains-du-Nord (59) . . . 13 H5
Sains-en-Amiénois (80) . . . 18 B3
Sains-en-Gohelle (62) . . . 6 A6
Sains-lès-Fressin (62) . . . 4 E6
Sains-lès-Marquion (62) . . . 11 H4
Sains-lès-Pernes (62) . . . 5 H6
Sains-Morainvillers (60) . . . 18 C6
Sains-Richaumont (02) . . . 20 D3
le Saint (56) . . . 75 J5
Saint-Abit (64) . . . 284 D5
Saint-Abraham (56) . . . 101 J3
Saint-Acheul (80) . . . 9 K4
Saint-Adjutory (16) . . . 197 H2
Saint-Adrien (22) . . . 48 C6
Saint-Affrique (12) . . . 272 B2
Saint-Affrique-les-Montagnes (81) . . . 289 K1
Saint-Agathon (22) . . . 48 D5
Saint-Agil (41) . . . 108 B2
Saint-Agnan (02) . . . 61 G1
Saint-Agnan (58) . . . 134 B5
Saint-Agnan (71) . . . 169 K4
Saint-Agnan (81) . . . 269 K5
Saint-Agnan (89) . . . 88 B5
Saint-Agnan-de-Cernières (27) . . . 55 H2
Saint-Agnan-de-Vercors (26) . . . 223 H6
Saint-Agnan-le-Malherbe (14) . . . 32 C6
Saint-Agnan-sur-Erre (61) . . . 83 K4
Saint-Agnan-sur-Sarthe (61) . . . 55 G6
Saint-Agnant (17) . . . 177 F6
Saint-Agnant-de-Versillat (23) . . . 181 K1
Saint-Agnant-près-Crocq (23) . . . 201 F2
Saint-Agne (24) . . . 231 K2
Saint-Agnet (40) . . . 265 J6
Saint-Agnin-sur-Bion (38) . . . 206 E4
Saint-Agoulin (63) . . . 185 F4
Saint-Agrève (07) . . . 221 H6
Saint-Aignan (08) . . . 22 E5
Saint-Aignan (33) . . . 212 A6
Saint-Aignan (41) . . . 129 F6
Saint-Aignan (56) . . . 76 D4
Saint-Aignan (72) . . . 83 F5
Saint-Aignan (82) . . . 268 D1
Saint-Aignan-de-Couptrain (53) . . . 81 K2
Saint-Aignan-de-Cramesnil (14) . . . 33 F6
Saint-Aignan-des-Gués (45) . . . 110 E5
Saint-Aignan-des-Noyers (18) . . . 167 K1
Saint-Aignan-Grandlieu (44) . . . 123 F5
Saint-Aignan-le-Jaillard (45) . . . 111 F6
Saint-Aignan-sur-Roë (53) . . . 104 B4
Saint-Aignan-sur-Ry (76) . . . 36 A1
Saint-Aigulin (17) . . . 212 D4
Saint-Ail (54) . . . 44 D4
Saint-Albain (71) . . . 171 K5
Saint-Alban (01) . . . 189 J3
Saint-Alban (22) . . . 49 J5
Saint-Alban (31) . . . 269 G5
Saint-Alban-Auriolles (07) . . . 255 J1
Saint-Alban-d'Ay (07) . . . 221 K3
Saint-Alban-de-Montbel (73) . . . 208 A4
Saint-Alban-de-Roche (38) . . . 206 E4
Saint-Alban-des-Hurtières (73) . . . 209 H1
Saint-Alban-des-Villards (73) . . . 225 F1

Saint-Alban-du-Rhône (38) . . . 206 A6
Saint-Alban-en-Montagne (07) . . . 238 C4
Saint-Alban-les-Eaux (42) . . . 186 D5
Saint-Alban-Leysse (73) . . . 208 C4
Saint-Alban-sur-Limagnole (48) . . . 237 H3
Saint-Albin-de-Vaulserre (38) . . . 207 K5
Saint-Alexandre (30) . . . 256 C4
Saint-Algis (02) . . . 20 E2
Saint-Allouestre (56) . . . 101 G2
Saint-Alpinien (23) . . . 183 G5
Saint-Alyre-d'Arlanc (63) . . . 219 K1
Saint-Alyre-ès-Montagne (63) . . . 218 D1
Saint-Amadou (09) . . . 307 K1
Saint-Amancet (81) . . . 289 J2
Saint-Amand (23) . . . 183 G5
Saint-Amand (50) . . . 31 J4
Saint-Amand (62) . . . 10 C4
Saint-Amand-de-Belvès (24) . . . 232 D3
Saint-Amand-de-Coly (24) . . . 215 F5
Saint-Amand-de-Vergt (24) . . . 214 A6
Saint-Amand-des-
  Hautes-Terres (27) . . . 35 G4
Saint-Amand-en-Puisaye (58) . . . 132 B3
Saint-Amand-Jartoudeix (23) . . . 182 B6
Saint-Amand-le-Petit (87) . . . 200 A2
Saint-Amand-les-Eaux (59) . . . 7 H6
Saint-Amand-Longpré (41) . . . 128 B1
Saint-Amand-Magnazeix (87) . . . 181 J3
Saint-Amand-Montrond (18) . . . 167 G2
Saint-Amand-sur-Fion (51) . . . 63 F4
Saint-Amand-sur-Ornain (55) . . . 64 D6
Saint-Amand-sur-Sèvre (79) . . . 143 F5
Saint-Amandin (15) . . . 218 A2
Saint-Amans (09) . . . 288 C6
Saint-Amans (11) . . . 289 G5
Saint-Amans (48) . . . 237 H4
Saint-Amans-de-Pellagal (82) . . . 249 G4
Saint-Amans-des-Cots (12) . . . 235 K4
Saint-Amans-du-Pech (82) . . . 248 E3
Saint-Amans-Soult (81) . . . 290 C2
Saint-Amans-Valtoret (81) . . . 290 C2
Saint-Amant (16) . . . 212 E1
Saint-Amant-de-Boixe (16) . . . 196 E1
Saint-Amant-de-Bonnieure (16) . . . 197 F1
Saint-Amant-de-Nouère (16) . . . 196 C2
Saint-Amant-Roche-Savine (63) . . . 203 J4
Saint-Amant-Tallende (63) . . . 202 D3
Saint-Amarin (68) . . . 119 K3
Saint-Ambreuil (71) . . . 171 K2
Saint-Ambroix (18) . . . 148 D5
Saint-Ambroix (30) . . . 255 H4
Saint-Amé (88) . . . 119 F1
Saint-Amour (39) . . . 172 E5
Saint-Amour-Bellevue (71) . . . 188 B1
Saint-Andelain (58) . . . 132 A6
Saint-Andéol (26) . . . 241 G2
Saint-Andéol (38) . . . 223 J6
Saint-Andéol-de-Berg (07) . . . 239 J6
Saint-Andéol-de-Clerguemort (48) . . . 255 F3
Saint-Andéol-de-Fourchades (07) . . . 239 G2
Saint-Andéol-de-Vals (07) . . . 239 H4
Saint-Andeux (21) . . . 134 B4
Saint-Andiol (13) . . . 276 C3
Saint-André (06) . . . 281 G3
Saint-André (31) . . . 287 F5
Saint-André (32) . . . 287 F1
Saint-André (66) . . . 315 H4
Saint-André (73) . . . 225 K2
Saint-André (81) . . . 271 H2
Saint-André-Capcèze (48) . . . 255 F2
Saint-André-d'Allas (24) . . . 232 E2
Saint-André-d'Apchon (42) . . . 186 D4
Saint-André-de-Bâgé (01) . . . 188 D1
Saint-André-de-Boëge (74) . . . 191 H2
Saint-André-de-Bohon (50) . . . 31 F2
Saint-André-de-Briouze (61) . . . 53 K5
Saint-André-de-Buèges (34) . . . 273 K3
Saint-André-de-Chalencon (43) . . . 220 D2
Saint-André-de-Corcy (01) . . . 188 D5
Saint-André-de-Cruzières (07) . . . 255 J3
Saint-André-de-Cubzac (33) . . . 211 J4
Saint-André-de-Double (24) . . . 213 G4
Saint-André-de-la-Marche (49) . . . 142 D2
Saint-André-de-Lancize (48) . . . 254 E4
Saint-André-de-l'Épine (50) . . . 31 J3
Saint-André-de-l'Eure (27) . . . 56 E3
Saint-André-de-Lidon (17) . . . 195 F4
Saint-André-de-Majencoules (30) . . . 273 K1
Saint-André-de-Messei (61) . . . 53 H5
Saint-André-de-Najac (12) . . . 251 G5
Saint-André-de-Roquelongue (11) . . . 310 B1
Saint-André-de-Roquepertuis (30) . . . 256 A4
Saint-André-de-Rosans (05) . . . 258 B2
Saint-André-de-Sangonis (34) . . . 273 H6
Saint-André-de-Seignanx (40) . . . 262 C6
Saint-André-de-Valborgne (30) . . . 254 C5
Saint-André-de-Vézines (12) . . . 253 J5
Saint-André-d'Embrun (05) . . . 243 K4
Saint-André-des-Eaux (22) . . . 78 D1
Saint-André-des-Eaux (44) . . . 121 K4
Saint-André-d'Hébertot (14) . . . 34 A3
Saint-André-d'Huiriat (01) . . . 188 D2
Saint-André-d'Olérargues (30) . . . 256 B5
Saint-André-du-Bois (33) . . . 230 B5
Saint-André-en-Barrois (55) . . . 64 B1
Saint-André-en-Bresse (71) . . . 172 B2
Saint-André-en-Morvan (58) . . . 133 J4
Saint-André-en-Royans (38) . . . 223 G4
Saint-André-en-Terre-Plaine (89) . . . 134 B3
Saint-André-en-Vivarais (07) . . . 221 H4
Saint-André-et-Appelles (33) . . . 230 E2

Saint-André-Farivillers (60)......18 A6
Saint-André-Goule-d'Oie (85)...142 B5
Saint-André-la Côte (69)......205 J3
Saint-André-Lachamp (07)......239 F6
Saint-André-le-Bouchoux (01)...188 E3
Saint-André-le-Coq (63)......185 H5
Saint-André-le-Désert (71)....171 G4
Saint-André-le-Gaz (38)......207 H4
Saint-André-le-Puy (42)......205 F3
Saint-André-les-Alpes (04)....279 J1
Saint-André-les-Vergers (10)....90 A5
Saint-André-lez-Lille (59)......6 D4
Saint-André-sur-Cailly (76)....16 B6
Saint-André-sur-Orne (14)......32 E5
Saint-André-sur-Sèvre (79)....143 G6
Saint-André-sur-Vieux-Jonc (01)...189 F2
Saint-André-Treize-Voies (85)...141 K4
Saint-Androny (33)......211 G3
Saint-Ange-et-Torçay (28)......56 D6
Saint-Ange-le-Viel (77)......87 K5
Saint-Angeau (16)......197 F1
Saint-Angel (03)......167 J6
Saint-Angel (19)......200 E5
Saint-Angel (63)......184 D5
Saint-Anthème (63)......204 B5
Saint-Anthot (21)......135 G5
Saint-Antoine (15)......235 G3
Saint-Antoine (25)......157 F6
Saint-Antoine (32)......268 A1
Saint-Antoine (33)......211 J5
Saint-Antoine-Cumond (24)....213 F2
Saint-Antoine-d'Auberoche (24)...214 C4
Saint-Antoine-de-Breuilh (24)...230 E2
Saint-Antoine-de-Ficalba (47)...248 C3
Saint-Antoine-du-Queyret (33)...230 D3
Saint-Antoine-du-Rocher (37)...127 H3
Saint-Antoine-la-Forêt (76)....14 E6
Saint-Antoine-l'Abbaye (38)...223 F3
Saint-Antoine-sur-l'Isle (33)...212 D5
Saint-Antonin (06)......280 D1
Saint-Antonin (32)......268 A5
Saint-Antonin-de-Lacalm (81)...271 F4
Saint-Antonin-de-Sommaire (27)...55 J4
Saint-Antonin-du-Var (83)......298 B1
Saint-Antonin-Noble-Val (82)...250 D5
Saint-Antonin-sur-Bayon (13)...296 E1
Saint-Aoustrille (36)......148 C5
Saint-Août (36)......166 B1
Saint-Apollinaire (05)......243 H5
Saint-Apollinaire (21)......136 B5
Saint-Apollinaire-de-Rias (07)...239 K1
Saint-Appolinaire (69)......187 J5
Saint-Appolinard (38)......223 F3
Saint-Appolinard (42)......221 K1
Saint-Aquilin (24)......213 J3
Saint-Aquilin-de-Corbion (61)...55 H6
Saint-Aquilin-de-Pacy (27)......57 F1
Saint-Araille (31)......287 H4
Saint-Arailles (32)......267 F6
Saint-Arcons-d'Allier (43)......219 J5
Saint-Arcons-de-Barges (43)...238 C2
Saint-Arey (38)......242 B1
Saint-Armel (35)......79 G5
Saint-Armel (56)......101 F6
Saint-Arnac (64)......284 D3
Saint-Arnac (66)......309 H5
Saint-Arnoult (14)......33 J3
Saint-Arnoult (41)......108 A6
Saint-Arnoult (60)......17 G5
Saint-Arnoult (76)......15 F6
Saint-Arnoult-des-Bois (28)....84 E2
Saint-Arnoult-en-Yvelines (78)...86 A1
Saint-Arroman (32)......286 C2
Saint-Arroman (65)......305 F2
Saint-Arroumex (82)......268 C1
Saint-Astier (24)......213 J4
Saint-Astier (47)......231 F4
Saint-Auban (06)......280 B2
Saint-Auban-d'Oze (05)......242 C6
Saint-Auban-sur-l'Ouvèze (26)...258 A3
Saint-Aubert (59)......12 C4
Saint-Aubert-sur-Orne (61)....53 K4
Saint-Aubin (02)......39 H1
Saint-Aubin (10)......89 F2
Saint-Aubin (21)......153 J4
Saint-Aubin (36)......148 D6
Saint-Aubin (39)......155 F3
Saint-Aubin (40)......264 E4
Saint-Aubin (47)......248 E1
Saint-Aubin (59)......13 G4
Saint-Aubin (62)......4 B6
Saint-Aubin (91)......58 C6
Saint-Aubin-Celloville (76)....35 J3
Saint-Aubin-Château-Neuf (89)...112 D5
Saint-Aubin-d'Appenai (61)....83 F1
Saint-Aubin-d'Arquenay (14)....33 F4
Saint-Aubin-d'Aubigné (35)......79 G2
Saint-Aubin-de-Blaye (33)......211 H2
Saint-Aubin-de-Bonneval (61)...55 G2
Saint-Aubin-de-Branne (33)....230 B2
Saint-Aubin-de-Cadelech (24)...231 H4
Saint-Aubin-de-Courteraie (61)...55 G6
Saint-Aubin-de-Crétot (76)....15 F6
Saint-Aubin-de-Lanquais (24)...231 J3
Saint-Aubin-de-Locquenay (72)...82 C5
Saint-Aubin-de-Luigné (49)...125 F5
Saint-Aubin-de-Médoc (33)......229 F1
Saint-Aubin-de-Nabirat (24)...233 F4
Saint-Aubin-de-Scellon (27)....34 C5
Saint-Aubin-de-Terregatte (50)...52 A6
Saint-Aubin-d'Écrosville (27)...35 G5
Saint-Aubin-des-Bois (14)......52 C3

Saint-Aubin-des-Bois (28)......85 F2
Saint-Aubin-des-Châteaux (44)...103 H3
Saint-Aubin-des-Chaumes (58)...133 H4
Saint-Aubin-des-Coudrais (72)...83 H6
Saint-Aubin-des-Grois (61)....83 J4
Saint-Aubin-des-Hayes (27)....55 J1
Saint-Aubin-des-Landes (35)...79 K4
Saint-Aubin-des-Ormeaux (85)...142 D3
Saint-Aubin-des-Préaux (50)....51 J1
Saint-Aubin-du-Cormier (35)...79 J2
Saint-Aubin-du-Désert (53)....82 A4
Saint-Aubin-du-Pavail (35)....79 J5
Saint-Aubin-du-Perron (50)....30 E3
Saint-Aubin-du-Plain (79)....143 J4
Saint-Aubin-du-Thenney (27)...55 H1
Saint-Aubin-en-Bray (60)......37 F2
Saint-Aubin-en-Charollais (71)...170 D4
Saint-Aubin-Épinay (76)......35 J2
Saint-Aubin-Fosse-Louvain (53)...80 E2
Saint-Aubin-la-Plaine (85)...160 B4
Saint-Aubin-le-Cauf (76)......16 A2
Saint-Aubin-le-Cloud (79)...161 J2
Saint-Aubin-le-Dépeint (37)...127 F1
Saint-Aubin-le-Guichard (27)...55 J1
Saint-Aubin-le-Monial (03)...168 B4
Saint-Aubin-le-Vertueux (27)...55 J1
Saint-Aubin-lès-Elbeuf (76)...35 H3
Saint-Aubin-les-Forges (58)...150 E2
Saint-Aubin-Montenoy (80)....17 J2
Saint-Aubin-Rivière (80)......17 G2
Saint-Aubin-Routot (76)......14 C6
Saint-Aubin-sous-Erquery (60)...38 A2
Saint-Aubin-sur-Aire (55)......64 D5
Saint-Aubin-sur-Gaillon (27)...36 A5
Saint-Aubin-sur-Loire (71)...169 J3
Saint-Aubin-sur-Mer (14)......32 E3
Saint-Aubin-sur-Mer (76)......15 H2
Saint-Aubin-sur-Quillebeuf (27)...34 C1
Saint-Aubin-sur-Scie (76)......15 K2
Saint-Aubin-sur-Yonne (89)...112 D3
Saint-Augustin (17)......194 B3
Saint-Augustin (19)......200 B6
Saint-Augustin (77)......60 B4
Saint-Augustin-des-Bois (49)...124 C3
Saint-Aulaire (19)......215 G3
Saint-Aulais-la-Chapelle (16)...196 C6
Saint-Aulaye (24)......212 E3
Saint-Aunès (34)......274 C6
Saint-Aunix-Lengros (32)......266 C6
Saint-Aupre (38)......207 K6
Saint-Austremoine (43)......219 G4
Saint-Auvent (87)......198 C1
Saint-Avaugourd-des-Landes (85)...159 H3
Saint-Avé (56)......101 F5
Saint-Aventin (31)......305 H5
Saint-Avertin (37)......127 A3
Saint-Avit (16)......212 D3
Saint-Avit (26)......222 D3
Saint-Avit (40)......265 H2
Saint-Avit (41)......108 B1
Saint-Avit (47)......231 F5
Saint-Avit (63)......201 H1
Saint-Avit (81)......289 J2
Saint-Avit-de-Soulège (33)...230 E2
Saint-Avit-de-Tardes (23)...183 H6
Saint-Avit-de-Vialard (24)...232 B1
Saint-Avit-Frandat (32)......267 J1
Saint-Avit-le-Pauvre (23)...183 F5
Saint-Avit-les-Guespières (28)...84 E5
Saint-Avit-Rivière (24)......232 C3
Saint-Avit-Saint-Nazaire (33)...231 F2
Saint-Avit-Sénieur (24)......232 B3
Saint-Avold (57)......68 A3
Saint-Avre (73)......225 G1
Saint-Ay (45)......109 J4
Saint-Aybert (59)......7 K6
Saint-Babel (63)......203 F4
Saint-Baldoph (73)......208 C4
Saint-Bandry (02)......39 H3
Saint-Baraing (39)......155 G3
Saint-Barbant (87)......180 D3
Saint-Bard (23)......183 J6
Saint-Bardoux (26)......222 D4
Saint-Barnabé (22)......77 G5
Saint-Barthélemy (38)......222 E1
Saint-Barthélemy (40)......282 D1
Saint-Barthélemy (50)......52 D5
Saint-Barthélemy (56)......100 D2
Saint-Barthélemy (70)......119 F5
Saint-Barthélemy (77)......60 E4
Saint-Barthélemy-d'Agenais (47)...231 G6
Saint-Barthélemy-d'Anjou (49)...125 H3
Saint-Barthélemy-de-Bellegarde (24)...213 F5
Saint-Barthélemy-de-Bussière (24)...198 A4
Saint-Barthélemy-de-Séchilienne (38)...224 B5
Saint-Barthélemy-de-Vals (26)...222 C3
Saint-Barthélemy-Grozon (07)...221 K6
Saint-Barthélemy-le-Meil (07)...239 J1
Saint-Barthélemy-le-Plain (07)...222 B5
Saint-Barthélemy-Lestra (42)...205 F2
Saint-Basile (07)......221 K6
Saint-Baslemont (88)......93 K6
Saint-Baudel (18)......148 E6
Saint-Baudelle (53)......81 G4
Saint-Baudille-de-la-Tour (38)...207 H4
Saint-Baudille-et-Pipet (38)...242 B2
Saint-Bauld (37)......146 B1
Saint-Baussant (54)......65 G2
Saint-Bauzeil (09)......307 H1
Saint-Bauzély (30)......275 F2

Saint-Bauzile (07)......240 A4
Saint-Bauzile (48)......254 B1
Saint-Bauzille-de-la-Sylve (34)...273 J6
Saint-Bauzille-de-Montmel (34)...274 C4
Saint-Bauzille-de-Putois (34)...274 A3
Saint-Bazile (87)......198 A2
Saint-Bazile-de-la-Roche (19)...216 C4
Saint-Bazile-de-Meyssac (19)...216 A5
Saint-Béat (31)......305 J3
Saint-Beaulize (12)......272 E1
Saint-Beauzeil (82)......248 E3
Saint-Beauzély (12)......253 F5
Saint-Beauzile (81)......270 A1
Saint-Beauzire (43)......219 F2
Saint-Beauzire (63)......202 E1
Saint-Bénézet (30)......274 E1
Saint-Bénigne (01)......172 A5
Saint-Benin (59)......12 D5
Saint-Benin-d'Azy (58)......151 G4
Saint-Benin-des-Bois (58)...151 G2
Saint-Benoist-sur-Mer (85)...159 J5
Saint-Benoist-sur-Vanne (10)...89 H5
Saint-Benoît (01)......207 J2
Saint-Benoît (04)......260 E6
Saint-Benoît (11)......308 D2
Saint-Benoît (86)......163 F3
Saint-Benoît-de-Carmaux (81)...270 D1
Saint-Benoît-des-Ombres (27)...34 D4
Saint-Benoît-des-Ondes (35)...50 E3
Saint-Benoît-d'Hébertot (14)...34 A3
Saint-Benoît-du-Sault (36)...165 F5
Saint-Benoît-en-Diois (26)...241 G4
Saint-Benoît-la-Chipotte (88)...95 G3
Saint-Benoît-la-Forêt (37)...145 G1
Saint-Benoît-sur-Loire (45)...110 E5
Saint-Benoît-sur-Seine (10)...90 A4
Saint-Bérain (43)......219 K5
Saint-Berain-sous-Sanvignes (71)...170 D2
Saint-Bérain-sur-Dheune (71)...153 J4
Saint-Bernard (01)......188 B5
Saint-Bernard (21)......154 C1
Saint-Bernard (38)......224 C1
Saint-Bernard (68)......97 B3
Saint-Béron (73)......207 K5
Saint-Berthevin (53)......105 J1
Saint-Berthevin-la-Tannière (53)...80 D3
Saint-Bertrand-de-Comminges (31)...305 H2
Saint-Biez-en-Belin (72)...106 E5
Saint-Bihy (22)......76 E2
Saint-Blaise (06)......281 G2
Saint-Blaise (74)......190 E3
Saint-Blaise-du-Buis (38)...223 J1
Saint-Blaise-la-Roche (67)...70 A4
Saint-Blancard (32)......286 D4
Saint-Blimont (80)......8 D5
Saint-Blin (52)......92 D5
Saint-Boès (64)......283 J1
Saint-Bohaire (41)......128 E1
Saint-Boil (71)......171 H2
Saint-Boingt (54)......94 D2
Saint-Bois (01)......207 J2
Saint-Bomer (28)......84 A6
Saint-Bômer-les-Forges (61)...53 G6
Saint-Bon (51)......61 F6
Saint-Bon-Tarentaise (73)...209 J5
Saint-Bonnet (16)......196 B5
Saint-Bonnet-Avalouze (19)...216 C4
Saint-Bonnet-Briance (87)...199 H3
Saint-Bonnet-de-Bellac (87)...180 E3
Saint-Bonnet-de-Chavagne (38)...223 F4
Saint-Bonnet-de-Chirac (48)...237 F2
Saint-Bonnet-de-Condat (15)...218 B2
Saint-Bonnet-de-Cray (71)...187 F2
Saint-Bonnet-de-Four (03)...184 D1
Saint-Bonnet-de-Joux (71)...171 F4
Saint-Bonnet-de-Montauroux (48)...238 A2
Saint-Bonnet-de-Mure (69)...206 C3
Saint-Bonnet-de-Rochefort (03)...185 F3
Saint-Bonnet-de-Salendrinque (30)...274 B1
Saint-Bonnet-de-Salers (15)...217 H4
Saint-Bonnet-de-Valclérieux (26)...222 E3
Saint-Bonnet-de-Vieille-Vigne (71)...170 D4
Saint-Bonnet-des-Bruyères (69)...187 J1
Saint-Bonnet-des-Quarts (42)...186 A2
Saint-Bonnet-du-Gard (30)...275 J2
Saint-Bonnet-Elvert (19)...216 C4
Saint-Bonnet-en-Bresse (71)...154 D5
Saint-Bonnet-en-Champsaur (05)...242 E3
Saint-Bonnet-la-Rivière (19)...215 G2
Saint-Bonnet-le-Bourg (63)...203 J6
Saint-Bonnet-le-Chastel (63)...203 J6
Saint-Bonnet-le-Château (42)...204 D6
Saint-Bonnet-le-Courreau (42)...204 B3
Saint-Bonnet-le-Froid (43)...221 H4
Saint-Bonnet-le-Troncy (69)...187 H4
Saint-Bonnet-l'Enfantier (19)...215 J2
Saint-Bonnet-lès-Allier (63)...202 E2
Saint-Bonnet-les-Oules (42)...205 F5
Saint-Bonnet-les-Tours-de-Merle (19)...216 D5
Saint-Bonnet-près-Bort (19)...201 G3
Saint-Bonnet-près-Orcival (63)...202 B3
Saint-Bonnet-près-Riom (63)...185 F6
Saint-Bonnet-sur-Gironde (17)...211 G1
Saint-Bonnet-Tronçais (03)...167 J2
Saint-Bonnot (58)......151 F1
Saint-Bouize (58)......150 D1
Saint-Brancher (89)......134 A4
Saint-Branchs (37)......146 B1
Saint-Brandan (22)......77 F2
Saint-Brès (30)......255 H3

Saint-Brès (32)......267 K4
Saint-Brès (34)......274 D5
Saint-Bresson (30)......273 K2
Saint-Bresson (70)......118 E3
Saint-Bressou (46)......234 D4
Saint-Brévin-les-Pins (44)...122 B3
Saint-Briac-sur-Mer (35)...50 C3
Saint-Brice (16)......195 K3
Saint-Brice (33)......230 B4
Saint-Brice (50)......52 A5
Saint-Brice (53)......105 H4
Saint-Brice (61)......81 G1
Saint-Brice (77)......88 D1
Saint-Brice-Courcelles (51)...40 E4
Saint-Brice-de-Landelles (50)...80 B1
Saint-Brice-en-Coglès (35)...51 K6
Saint-Brice-sous-Forêt (95)...58 E2
Saint-Brice-sous-Rânes (61)...54 A5
Saint-Brice-sur-Vienne (87)...180 E6
Saint-Brieuc (22)......49 G6
Saint-Brieuc-de-Mauron (56)...77 K6
Saint-Brieuc-des-Iffs (35)...78 E2
Saint-Bris-des-Bois (17)...195 H2
Saint-Bris-le-Vineux (89)...113 G6
Saint-Brisson (58)......134 B6
Saint-Brisson-sur-Loire (45)...131 H1
Saint-Broing (70)......137 G3
Saint-Broing-les-Moines (21)...115 J6
Saint-Broingt-le-Bois (52)...116 E6
Saint-Broingt-les-Fosses (52)...116 D6
Saint-Broladre (35)......51 G4
Saint-Bueil (38)......207 K5
Saint-Calais (72)......107 K4
Saint-Calais-du-Désert (53)...81 K2
Saint-Calez-en-Saosnois (72)...83 F4
Saint-Cannat (13)......277 G6
Saint-Caprais (03)......167 J4
Saint-Caprais (18)......149 F4
Saint-Caprais (32)......268 A6
Saint-Caprais (46)......232 E5
Saint-Caprais-de-Blaye (33)...211 H2
Saint-Caprais-de-Bordeaux (33)...229 J2
Saint-Caprais-de-Lerm (47)...248 C4
Saint-Capraise-de-Lalinde (24)...231 K2
Saint-Capraise-d'Eymet (24)...231 H4
Saint-Caradec (22)......77 F4
Saint-Caradec-Trégomel (56)...76 A6
Saint-Carné (22)......50 C6
Saint-Carreuc (22)......77 G2
Saint-Cassien (24)......232 B4
Saint-Cassien (38)......223 J1
Saint-Cassin (73)......208 B4
Saint-Cast-le-Guildo (22)...50 B3
Saint-Castin (64)......284 D3
Saint-Célerin (72)......107 J1
Saint-Céneré (53)......105 G1
Saint-Céneri-le-Gérei (61)...82 B3
Saint-Céols (18)......149 J1
Saint-Céré (46)......234 C2
Saint-Cergues (74)......191 H1
Saint-Cernin (15)......217 H5
Saint-Cernin (46)......233 J5
Saint-Cernin-de-Labarde (24)...231 J4
Saint-Cernin-de-Larche (19)...215 H5
Saint-Cernin-de-l'Herm (24)...232 D5
Saint-Césaire (17)......195 H2
Saint-Césaire-de-Gauzignan (30)...275 F1
Saint-Cézaire-sur-Siagne (06)...280 C5
Saint-Cézert (31)......268 E4
Saint-Chabrais (23)......183 G3
Saint-Chaffrey (05)......225 K6
Saint-Chamant (15)......217 H5
Saint-Chamant (19)......216 C4
Saint-Chamarand (46)......233 H4
Saint-Chamas (13)......295 J3
Saint-Chamond (42)......205 H5
Saint-Champ (01)......207 K1
Saint-Chaptes (30)......275 F1
Saint-Charles-de-Percy (14)...53 F2
Saint-Charles-la-Forêt (53)...105 G3
Saint-Chartier (36)......166 B2
Saint-Chef (38)......207 F3
Saint-Chels (46)......234 B6
Saint-Chély-d'Apcher (48)...237 G3
Saint-Chély-d'Aubrac (12)...236 C5
Saint-Chéron (51)......63 F6
Saint-Chéron (91)......86 C1
Saint-Chinian (34)......291 H3
Saint-Christ-Briost (80)...19 G2
Saint-Christaud (31)......287 J6
Saint-Christaud (32)......285 K1
Saint-Christo-en-Jarez (42)...205 H5
Saint-Christol (07)......239 H2
Saint-Christol (34)......274 E5
Saint-Christol (84)......258 B6
Saint-Christol-de-Rodières (30)...256 B3
Saint-Christol-lès-Alès (30)...255 G6
Saint-Christoly-de-Blaye (33)...211 H4
Saint-Christoly-Médoc (33)...210 E1
Saint-Christophe (03)......186 A3
Saint-Christophe (16)......180 D5
Saint-Christophe (17)......177 F2
Saint-Christophe (23)......182 D4
Saint-Christophe (28)......109 F1
Saint-Christophe (69)......187 K1
Saint-Christophe (73)......208 A5
Saint-Christophe (81)......251 G5
Saint-Christophe (86)......145 G5
Saint-Christophe-à-Berry (02)...39 G2
Saint-Christophe-d'Allier (43)...238 A2
Saint-Christophe-de-Chaulieu (61)...52 E4

Saint-Christophe-de-Double (33)...212 D5
Saint-Christophe-de-Valains (35)...79 J1
Saint-Christophe-des-Bardes (33)...230 B1
Saint-Christophe-des-Bois (35)...80 A5
Saint-Christophe-Dodinicourt (10)...90 E3
Saint-Christophe-du-Bois (49)...142 D3
Saint-Christophe-du-Foc (50)...28 B3
Saint-Christophe-du-Jambet (72)...82 C5
Saint-Christophe-du-Ligneron (85)...141 G5
Saint-Christophe-du-Luat (53)...81 H6
Saint-Christophe-en-Bazelle (36)...148 A1
Saint-Christophe-en-Boucherie (36)...166 C2
Saint-Christophe-en-Bresse (71)...172 A1
Saint-Christophe-en-Brionnais (71)...187 F1
Saint-Christophe-en-Champagne (72)...106 A3
Saint-Christophe-en-Oisans (38)...225 F6
Saint-Christophe-et-le-Laris (26)...222 E3
Saint-Christophe-le-Chaudry (18)...167 J4
Saint-Christophe-le-Jajolet (61)...54 C5
Saint-Christophe-sur-Avre (27)...56 A5
Saint-Christophe-sur-Condé (27)...34 D4
Saint-Christophe-sur-Dolaison (43)...220 B6
Saint-Christophe-sur-Guiers (38)...208 A6
Saint-Christophe-sur-le-Nais (37)...127 G2
Saint-Christophe-sur-Roc (79)...161 J5
Saint-Christophe-Vallon (12)...251 K1
Saint-Cibard (33)......230 C1
Saint-Cierge-la-Serre (07)...240 A3
Saint-Cierge-sous-le-Cheylard (07)...239 H1
Saint-Ciergues (52)......116 C4
Saint-Ciers-Champagne (17)...195 K6
Saint-Ciers-d'Abzac (33)...212 A5
Saint-Ciers-de-Canesse (33)...211 G4
Saint-Ciers-du-Taillon (17)...195 G6
Saint-Ciers-sur-Bonnieure (16)...197 F1
Saint-Ciers-sur-Gironde (33)...211 H2
Saint-Cirgue (81)......271 G2
Saint-Cirgues (43)......219 H4
Saint-Cirgues (46)......234 F4
Saint-Cirgues-de-Jordanne (15)...217 H5
Saint-Cirgues-de-Malbert (15)...217 G5
Saint-Cirgues-de-Prades (07)...230 G5
Saint-Cirgues-en-Montagne (07)...238 E3
Saint-Cirgues-la-Loutre (19)...216 E5
Saint-Cirgues-sur-Couze (63)...202 D5
Saint-Cirice (82)......248 D6
Saint-Cirq (24)......232 C1
Saint-Cirq (82)......250 B5
Saint-Cirq-Lapopie (46)......250 C1
Saint-Cirq-Madelon (46)...233 G3
Saint-Cirq-Souillaguet (46)...233 H4
Saint-Civran (36)......165 F4
Saint-Clair (07)......222 A2
Saint-Clair (46)......233 H4
Saint-Clair (82)......248 E5
Saint-Clair (86)......144 D5
Saint-Clair-d'Arcey (27)...34 D6
Saint-Clair-de-Halouze (61)...53 G5
Saint-Clair-de-la-Tour (38)...207 H4
Saint-Clair-du-Rhône (38)...206 A6
Saint-Clair-sur-Epte (95)...36 D4
Saint-Clair-sur-Galaure (38)...222 E2
Saint-Clair-sur-l'Elle (50)...31 H2
Saint-Clair-sur-les-Monts (76)...15 G4
Saint-Clar (32)......267 K3
Saint-Clar-de-Rivière (31)...287 K2
Saint-Claud (16)......179 K6
Saint-Claude (39)......173 K5
Saint-Claude-de-Diray (41)...129 F2
Saint-Clément (02)......21 H3
Saint-Clément (03)......186 B4
Saint-Clément (07)......221 G6
Saint-Clément (15)......217 K6
Saint-Clément (19)......216 A2
Saint-Clément (30)......274 D3
Saint-Clément (54)......94 E1
Saint-Clément (89)......88 D6
Saint-Clément-à-Arnes (08)...41 J3
Saint-Clément-de-la-Place (49)...124 E2
Saint-Clément-de-Régnat (63)...185 H5
Saint-Clément-de-Rivière (34)...274 B5
Saint-Clément-de-Valorgue (63)...204 B5
Saint-Clément-de-Vers (69)...187 J2
Saint-Clément-des-Baleines (17)...158 B5
Saint-Clément-des-Levées (49)...126 A5
Saint-Clément-les-Places (69)...205 G2
Saint-Clément-Rancoudray (50)...52 E5
Saint-Clément-sur-Durance (05)...243 K4
Saint-Clément-sur-Guye (71)...171 G3
Saint-Clément-sur-Valsonne (69)...187 J6
Saint-Clémentin (79)......143 J4
Saint-Clet (22)......48 D4
Saint-Cloud (92)......58 D4
Saint-Cloud-en-Dunois (28)...109 G2
Saint-Colomb-de-Lauzun (47)...231 H5
Saint-Colomban (44)......141 H3
Saint-Colomban-des-Villards (73)...225 F1
Saint-Côme (33)......246 D1
Saint-Côme-de-Fresné (14)...32 C3
Saint-Côme-d'Olt (12)......236 B6
Saint-Côme-du-Mont (50)...29 H6
Saint-Côme-et-Maruéjols (30)...275 F3
Saint-Congard (56)......101 K4
Saint-Connan (22)......76 D1
Saint-Connec (22)......76 E4
Saint-Constant (15)......235 F4
Saint-Contest (14)......32 C4
Saint-Corneille (72)......107 F2
Saint-Cornier-des-Landes (61)...53 F5
Saint-Cosme (68)......119 K5

Saint-Cosme-en-Vairais (72) 83 G5
Saint-Couat-d'Aude (11) 290 E6
Saint-Couat-du-Razès (11) 308 D2
Saint-Coulitz (29) 74 D3
Saint-Coulomb (35) 50 E3
Saint-Coutant (16) 179 K5
Saint-Coutant (79) 178 E2
Saint-Coutant-le-Grand (17) 177 H5
Saint-Créac (32) 268 A2
Saint-Créac (65) 304 B1
Saint-Crépin (05) 243 H3
Saint-Crépin (17) 177 H4
Saint-Crépin-aux-Bois (60) 39 F2
Saint-Crépin-d'Auberoche (24) 214 C4
Saint-Crépin-de-Richemont (24) 197 J6
Saint-Crépin-et-Carlucet (24) 215 F6
Saint-Crépin-Ibouvillers (60) 37 G4
Saint-Crespin (76) 15 K3
Saint-Crespin-sur-Moine (49) 142 C2
Saint-Cricq (32) 268 C5
Saint-Cricq-Chalosse (40) 264 E6
Saint-Cricq-du-Gave (40) 283 G1
Saint-Cricq-Villeneuve (40) 265 J2
Saint-Cybardeaux (16) 196 C2
Saint-Cybranet (24) 232 E3
Saint-Cyprien (19) 215 G3
Saint-Cyprien (24) 232 C2
Saint-Cyprien (42) 204 E5
Saint-Cyprien (46) 249 J3
Saint-Cyprien (66) 315 H5
Saint-Cyprien-sur-Dourdou (12) 235 H6
Saint-Cyr (07) 222 A2
Saint-Cyr (50) 28 E4
Saint-Cyr (71) 171 K2
Saint-Cyr (86) 163 G1
Saint-Cyr (87) 198 C2
Saint-Cyr-au-Mont-d'Or (69) 206 A1
Saint-Cyr-de-Favières (42) 187 F5
Saint-Cyr-de-Salerne (27) 34 D5
Saint-Cyr-de-Valorges (42) 187 H6
Saint-Cyr-des-Gâts (85) 160 D3
Saint-Cyr-du-Bailleul (50) 80 E1
Saint-Cyr-du-Doret (17) 177 H5
Saint-Cyr-du-Gault (41) 128 B2
Saint-Cyr-du-Ronceray (14) 55 F1
Saint-Cyr-en-Arthies (95) 57 J1
Saint-Cyr-en-Bourg (49) 144 C1
Saint-Cyr-en-Pail (53) 82 A3
Saint-Cyr-en-Talmondais (85) 159 J4
Saint-Cyr-en-Val (45) 110 B5
Saint-Cyr-la-Campagne (27) 35 H4
Saint-Cyr-la-Lande (79) 144 C3
Saint-Cyr-la-Rivière (91) 86 C4
Saint-Cyr-la-Roche (19) 215 H3
Saint-Cyr-la-Rosière (61) 83 J4
Saint-Cyr-le-Chatoux (69) 187 K4
Saint-Cyr-le-Gravelais (53) 104 C2
Saint-Cyr-l'École (78) 58 B4
Saint-Cyr-les-Champagnes (24) 215 G1
Saint-Cyr-les-Colons (89) 113 H6
Saint-Cyr-les-Vignes (42) 205 F3
Saint-Cyr-Montmalin (39) 155 J4
Saint-Cyr-sous-Dourdan (91) 86 B1
Saint-Cyr-sur-le-Rhône (69) 206 B5
Saint-Cyr-sur-Loire (37) 127 J4
Saint-Cyr-sur-Menthon (01) 188 D1
Saint-Cyr-sur-Mer (83) 297 G5
Saint-Cyr-sur-Morin (77) 60 C3
Saint-Cyran-du-Jambot (36) 146 E2
Saint-Dalmas-le-Selvage (06) 261 F2
Saint-Daunès (46) 249 H3
Saint-Denis (11) 289 K4
Saint-Denis (30) 255 J4
Saint-Denis (89) 88 D5
Saint-Denis (93) 58 E2
Saint-Denis-Catus (46) 233 G6
Saint-Denis-Combarnazat (63) 185 H5
Saint-Denis-d'Aclon (76) 15 J2
Saint-Denis-d'Anjou (53) 105 H5
Saint-Denis-d'Augerons (27) 55 G2
Saint-Denis-d'Authou (28) 84 B4
Saint-Denis-de-Cabanne (42) 187 G2
Saint-Denis-de-Gastines (53) 80 E4
Saint-Denis-de-Jouhet (36) 166 A4
Saint-Denis-de-l'Hôtel (45) 110 C4
Saint-Denis-de-Mailloc (14) 34 A6
Saint-Denis-de-Méré (14) 53 H3
Saint-Denis-de-Palin (61) 149 H5
Saint-Denis-de-Pile (33) 212 B6
Saint-Denis-de-Vaux (71) 153 J6
Saint-Denis-de-Villenette (61) 81 H2
Saint-Denis-des-Coudrais (72) 83 G4
Saint-Denis-des-Monts (27) 35 F4
Saint-Denis-des-Murs (87) 199 H2
Saint-Denis-des-Puits (28) 84 D3
Saint-Denis-d'Oléron (17) 176 B4
Saint-Denis-d'Orques (72) 105 K2
Saint-Denis-du-Béhélan (27) 56 D2
Saint-Denis-du-Maine (53) 105 H3
Saint-Denis-du-Payré (85) 159 K5
Saint-Denis-du-Pin (17) 177 K5
Saint-Denis-en-Bugey (01) 189 H5
Saint-Denis-en-Margeride (48) 237 J3
Saint-Denis-en-Val (45) 110 A4
Saint-Denis-la-Chevasse (85) 142 A5
Saint-Denis-le-Ferment (27) 36 D3
Saint-Denis-le-Gast (50) 31 F5
Saint-Denis-le-Thiboult (76) 36 A2
Saint-Denis-le-Vêtu (50) 30 E5
Saint-Denis-lès-Bourg (01) 189 G2
Saint-Denis-lès-Martel (46) 233 K1
Saint-Denis-les-Ponts (28) 108 E2

Saint-Denis-lès-Rebais (77) 60 C4
Saint-Denis-Maisoncelles (14) 31 K5
Saint-Denis-sur-Coise (42) 205 G4
Saint-Denis-sur-Huisne (61) 83 H2
Saint-Denis-sur-Loire (41) 129 F2
Saint-Denis-sur-Ouanne (89) 112 C5
Saint-Denis-sur-Sarthon (61) 82 B2
Saint-Denis-sur-Scie (76) 15 K4
Saint-Deniscourt (60) 17 G5
Saint-Denoeux (62) 4 D6
Saint-Denoual (22) 49 K6
Saint-Derrien (29) 46 D4
Saint-Désert (71) 171 H1
Saint-Désir (14) 33 K5
Saint-Désirat (07) 222 B2
Saint-Désiré (03) 167 F4
Saint-Dézéry (30) 275 F1
Saint-Didier (21) 134 C5
Saint-Didier (35) 79 K4
Saint-Didier (39) 173 F1
Saint-Didier (58) 133 G5
Saint-Didier (84) 276 E1
Saint-Didier-au-Mont-d'Or (69) 206 A1
Saint-Didier-d'Allier (43) 220 A6
Saint-Didier-d'Aussiat (01) 172 B6
Saint-Didier-de-Bizonnes (38) 207 F5
Saint-Didier-de-Formans (01) 188 C5
Saint-Didier-de-la-Tour (38) 207 H4
Saint-Didier-des-Bois (27) 35 H4
Saint-Didier-en-Bresse (71) 154 C5
Saint-Didier-en-Brionnais (71) 170 C6
Saint-Didier-en-Donjon (03) 169 K6
Saint-Didier-en-Velay (43) 221 G2
Saint-Didier-la-Forêt (03) 185 H2
Saint-Didier-sous-Aubenas (07) 239 H5
Saint-Didier-sous-Écouves (61) 82 C1
Saint-Didier-sous-Riverie (69) 205 J4
Saint-Didier-sur-Arroux (71) 152 D6
Saint-Didier-sur-Beaujeu (69) 187 K3
Saint-Didier-sur-Chalaronne (01) 188 C3
Saint-Didier-sur-Doulon (43) 219 J2
Saint-Didier-sur-Rochefort (42) 204 A2
Saint-Dié (88) 95 J4
Saint-Dier-d'Auvergne (63) 203 H3
Saint-Diéry (63) 202 C5
Saint-Dionizy (30) 275 F4
Saint-Disdier (05) 242 C3
Saint-Dizant-du-Bois (17) 195 G6
Saint-Dizant-du-Gua (17) 195 F6
Saint-Dizier (52) 63 J6
Saint-Dizier-en-Diois (26) 241 J6
Saint-Dizier-la-Tour (23) 183 G3
Saint-Dizier-les-Domaines (23) 182 E1
Saint-Dizier-l'Évêque (90) 139 J2
Saint-Dizier-Leyrenne (23) 182 B4
Saint-Dolay (56) 102 B5
Saint-Domet (23) 183 H4
Saint-Domineuc (35) 78 E1
Saint-Donan (22) 49 F6
Saint-Donat (63) 201 K6
Saint-Donat-sur-l'Herbasse (26) 222 D4
Saint-Dos (64) 283 G2
Saint-Doulchard (18) 149 G2
Saint-Drézéry (34) 274 D5
Saint-Dyé-sur-Loire (41) 129 G1
Saint-Ebremond-de-Bonfossé (50) 31 G4
Saint-Edmond (71) 187 G2
Saint-Égrève (38) 224 A2
Saint-Elier (27) 56 B2
Saint-Éliph (28) 84 C3
Saint-Élix (32) 286 E2
Saint-Élix-le-Château (31) 287 J5
Saint-Élix-Séglan (31) 287 F6
Saint-Élix-Theux (32) 286 B3
Saint-Ellier-du-Maine (53) 80 C3
Saint-Ellier-les-Bois (61) 82 B2
Saint-Éloi (01) 189 F5
Saint-Éloi (23) 182 C4
Saint-Éloi (58) 150 E4
Saint-Éloi-de-Fourques (27) 35 F4
Saint-Éloy (29) 74 D1
Saint-Éloy-d'Allier (03) 166 E4
Saint-Éloy-de-Gy (18) 149 G2
Saint-Éloy-la-Glacière (63) 203 J5
Saint-Éloy-les-Mines (63) 184 C5
Saint-Éloy-les-Tuileries (19) 199 F6
Saint-Éman (28) 84 D4
Saint-Émiland (71) 153 G5
Saint-Émilion (33) 230 B1
Saint-Ennemond (03) 169 F2
Saint-Épain (37) 145 J2
Saint-Epvre (57) 66 C1
Saint-Erblon (35) 79 G5
Saint-Erblon (53) 104 B5
Saint-Erme-Outre-
et-Ramecourt (02) 40 D1
Saint-Escobille (91) 86 B3
Saint-Esteben (64) 282 E3
Saint-Estèphe (24) 197 K4
Saint-Estèphe (33) 211 F2
Saint-Estève (66) 310 B6
Saint-Estève-Janson (13) 277 H5
Saint-Étienne (42) 205 G6
Saint-Étienne-à-Arnes (08) 41 K3
Saint-Étienne-au-Mont (62) 2 A6
Saint-Étienne-au-Temple (51) 62 D1
Saint-Étienne-aux-Clos (19) 201 H5
Saint-Étienne-Cantalès (15) 235 F1
Saint-Étienne-d'Albagnan (34) 291 G1
Saint-Étienne-de-Baïgorry (64) 263 E4
Saint-Étienne-de-Boulogne (07) 239 J4

Saint-Étienne-de-Brillouet (85) 160 C3
Saint-Étienne-de-Carlat (15) 235 J1
Saint-Étienne-de-Chigny (37) 127 G5
Saint-Étienne-de-Chomeil (15) 217 K2
Saint-Étienne-de-Crossey (38) 207 J6
Saint-Étienne-de-Cuines (73) 225 G1
Saint-Étienne-de-Fontbellon (07) 239 H5
Saint-Étienne-de-Fougères (47) 248 B2
Saint-Étienne-de-Fursac (23) 181 K3
Saint-Étienne-de-Gourgas (34) 273 G4
Saint-Étienne-de-Lisse (33) 230 C1
Saint-Étienne-de-l'Olm (30) 255 H6
Saint-Étienne-de-Lugdarès (07) 238 D4
Saint-Étienne-de-Maurs (15) 235 F4
Saint-Étienne-de-Mer-Morte (44) 141 G4
Saint-Étienne-de-Montluc (44) 122 E3
Saint-Étienne-de-Puycorbier (24) 213 G5
Saint-Étienne-de-Saint-Geoirs (38) 223 G1
Saint-Étienne-de-Serre (07) 239 J2
Saint-Étienne-de-Tinée (06) 261 F3
Saint-Étienne-de-Tulmont (82) 269 H1
Saint-Étienne-de-Valoux (07) 222 B3
Saint-Étienne-de-Vicq (03) 185 K3
Saint-Étienne-de-Villeréal (47) 232 A5
Saint-Étienne-des-Champs (63) 201 J1
Saint-Étienne-des-Guérets (41) 128 C2
Saint-Étienne-des-Oullières (69) 188 A4
Saint-Étienne-des-Sorts (30) 256 D4
Saint-Étienne-d'Orthe (40) 262 E6
Saint-Étienne-du-Bois (01) 189 G1
Saint-Étienne-du-Bois (85) 141 H5
Saint-Étienne-du-Grès (13) 276 A4
Saint-Étienne-du-Gué-de-l'Isle (22) 77 G5
Saint-Étienne-du-Rouvray (76) 35 H3
Saint-Étienne-du-Valdonnez (48) 254 B1
Saint-Étienne-du-Vauvray (27) 35 J4
Saint-Étienne-du-Vigan (43) 238 B3
Saint-Étienne-en-Bresse (71) 172 B1
Saint-Étienne-en-Coglès (35) 51 K6
Saint-Étienne-en-Dévoluy (05) 242 D3
Saint-Étienne-Estréchoux (34) 272 D5
Saint-Étienne-la-Cigogne (79) 178 A3
Saint-Étienne-la-Geneste (19) 201 F6
Saint-Étienne-la-Thillaye (14) 33 J3
Saint-Étienne-la-Varenne (69) 188 A4
Saint-Étienne-l'Allier (27) 34 C4
Saint-Étienne-Lardeyrol (43) 220 D5
Saint-Étienne-le-Laus (05) 243 F6
Saint-Étienne-le-Molard (42) 204 D2
Saint-Étienne-les-Orgues (04) 258 E6
Saint-Étienne-lès-Remiremont (88) 119 F1
Saint-Étienne-Roilaye (60) 39 F3
Saint-Étienne-sous-Bailleul (27) 36 A6
Saint-Étienne-sous-Barbuise (10) 90 A2
Saint-Étienne-sur-Blesle (43) 218 E2
Saint-Étienne-sur-Chalaronne (01) 188 C3
Saint-Étienne-sur-Reyssouze (01) 172 B5
Saint-Étienne-sur-Suippe (51) 41 F2
Saint-Étienne-sur-Usson (63) 203 G5
Saint-Étienne-Vallée-
Française (48) 254 E5
Saint-Eugène (02) 61 F1
Saint-Eugène (17) 195 K5
Saint-Eugène (71) 170 C1
Saint-Eulien (51) 63 J5
Saint-Euphraise-et-Clairizet (51) 40 D5
Saint-Euphrône (21) 134 E3
Saint-Eusèbe (71) 171 F1
Saint-Eusèbe (74) 190 D5
Saint-Eusèbe-en-Champsaur (05) 242 E3
Saint-Eustache (74) 208 D1
Saint-Eustache-la-Forêt (76) 14 D6
Saint-Eutrope (16) 196 D6
Saint-Eutrope-de-Born (47) 231 K5
Saint-Evarzec (29) 98 D2
Saint-Évroult-de-Montfort (61) 55 F4
Saint-Évroult-Notre-
Dame-du-Bois (61) 55 G4
Saint-Exupéry (33) 230 B5
Saint-Exupéry-les-Roches (19) 201 G5
Saint-Fargeau (89) 132 B1
Saint-Fargeau-Ponthierry (77) 87 G2
Saint-Fargeol (03) 184 A3
Saint-Faust (64) 284 C4
Saint-Félicien (07) 221 K5
Saint-Féliu-d'Amont (66) 310 A6
Saint-Féliu-d'Avall (66) 315 F2
Saint-Félix (03) 185 K2
Saint-Félix (16) 212 D1
Saint-Félix (17) 177 J3
Saint-Félix (46) 234 E5
Saint-Félix (60) 37 J3
Saint-Félix (74) 208 C1
Saint-Félix-de-Bourdeilles (24) 197 J6
Saint-Félix-de-Foncaude (33) 230 C4
Saint-Félix-de-l'Héras (34) 273 F3
Saint-Félix-de-Lodez (34) 273 H5
Saint-Félix-de-Lunel (12) 235 J6
Saint-Félix-de-Pallières (30) 274 C1
Saint-Félix-de-Reillac-
et-Mortemart (24) 214 C6
Saint-Félix-de-Rieutord (09) 307 J2
Saint-Félix-de-Sorgues (12) 272 C5
Saint-Félix-de-Tournegat (09) 307 K1
Saint-Félix-de-Villadeix (24) 231 K1
Saint-Félix-Lauragais (31) 289 G3
Saint-Fergeux (08) 21 J6
Saint-Ferjeux (70) 138 E2
Saint-Ferme (33) 230 D4
Saint-Ferréol (31) 286 E1
Saint-Ferréol (74) 209 F1
Saint-Ferréol-d'Auroure (43) 221 F1

Saint-Ferréol-des-Côtes (63) 203 K5
Saint-Ferréol-Trente-Pas (26) 257 J1
Saint-Ferriol (11) 308 E4
Saint-Fiacre (22) 48 D6
Saint-Fiacre (77) 60 A3
Saint-Fiacre-sur-Maine (44) 123 H5
Saint-Fiel (23) 182 D2
Saint-Firmin (05) 242 D2
Saint-Firmin (54) 94 A2
Saint-Firmin (58) 151 G3
Saint-Firmin (71) 153 G6
Saint-Firmin-des-Bois (45) 111 K3
Saint-Firmin-des-Prés (41) 108 C5
Saint-Firmin-sur-Loire (45) 131 J2
Saint-Flavy (10) 89 H3
Saint-Florent (2B) 317 C5
Saint-Florent (45) 131 F1
Saint-Florent-des-Bois (85) 159 J2
Saint-Florent-le-Vieil (49) 124 C4
Saint-Florent-sur-Auzonnet (30) 255 H4
Saint-Florent-sur-Cher (18) 149 F4
Saint-Florentin (36) 148 B3
Saint-Florentin (89) 113 H3
Saint-Floret (63) 202 D5
Saint-Floris (62) 5 K4
Saint-Flour (15) 218 E5
Saint-Flour (63) 203 H3
Saint-Flour-de-Mercoire (48) 238 B4
Saint-Flovier (37) 146 D4
Saint-Floxel (50) 29 F4
Saint-Folquin (62) 3 F2
Saint-Fons (69) 206 B2
Saint-Forgeot (71) 153 F4
Saint-Forget (78) 58 B5
Saint-Forgeux (69) 205 G1
Saint-Forgeux-Lespinasse (42) 186 D3
Saint-Fort (53) 105 F5
Saint-Fort-sur-Gironde (17) 195 F5
Saint-Fort-sur-le-Né (16) 195 K4
Saint-Fortunat-sur-Eyrieux (07) 240 A2
Saint-Fraigne (16) 178 E5
Saint-Fraimbault (61) 81 F2
Saint-Fraimbault-de-Prières (53) 81 G4
Saint-Frajou (31) 287 F2
Saint-Franc (73) 207 K5
Saint-Franchy (58) 151 G2
Saint-François-de-Sales (73) 208 C2
Saint-François-Lacroix (57) 27 K4
Saint-François-Longchamp (73) 209 F6
Saint-Frégant (29) 46 B4
Saint-Fréjoux (19) 201 G5
Saint-Frézal-d'Albuges (48) 238 B6
Saint-Frézal-de-Ventalon (48) 254 E3
Saint-Frichoux (11) 290 D5
Saint-Frion (23) 200 E1
Saint-Fromond (50) 31 H2
Saint-Front (16) 179 H6
Saint-Front (43) 220 E6
Saint-Front-d'Alemps (24) 214 B2
Saint-Front-de-Pradoux (24) 213 G5
Saint-Front-la-Rivière (24) 197 K6
Saint-Front-sur-Lémance (47) 232 C5
Saint-Front-sur-Nizonne (24) 197 J5
Saint-Froult (17) 176 E5
Saint-Fulgent (85) 142 B5
Saint-Fulgent-des-Ormes (61) 83 G4
Saint-Fuscien (80) 18 B3
Saint-Gabriel-Brécy (14) 32 C3
Saint-Gal (48) 237 H4
Saint-Gal-sur-Sioule (63) 184 E3
Saint-Galmier (42) 205 F4
Saint-Gand (70) 137 J2
Saint-Ganton (35) 102 E3
Saint-Gatien-des-Bois (14) 33 K3
Saint-Gaudens (31) 305 K1
Saint-Gaudent (86) 179 H3
Saint-Gaudéric (11) 308 C3
Saint-Gauzens (81) 270 B4
Saint-Gein (40) 265 J3
Saint-Gelais (79) 161 H5
Saint-Gelven (22) 76 C3
Saint-Gély-du-Fesc (34) 274 B5
Saint-Génard (79) 178 D2
Saint-Gence (87) 181 F6
Saint-Généroux (79) 144 C5
Saint-Genès-Champanelle (63) 202 C3
Saint-Genès-Champespe (63) 218 A1
Saint-Genès-de-Blaye (33) 211 G3
Saint-Genès-de-Castillon (33) 230 C1
Saint-Genès-de-Fronsac (33) 211 K5
Saint-Genès-de-Lombaud (33) 229 J3
Saint-Genès-du-Retz (63) 185 G4
Saint-Genès-la-Tourette (63) 203 H5
Saint-Genest (03) 184 A2
Saint-Genest (88) 94 E3
Saint-Genest-d'Ambière (86) 145 G6
Saint-Genest-de-Beauzon (07) 255 H1
Saint-Genest-de-Contest (81) 270 E4
Saint-Genest-Lachamp (07) 239 H2
Saint-Genest-Lerpt (42) 205 F6
Saint-Genest-Malifaux (42) 221 H1
Saint-Genest-sur-Roselle (87) 199 G3
Saint-Geneys-près-
Saint-Paulien (43) 220 B4
Saint-Gengoulph (02) 39 H6
Saint-Gengoux-de-Scissé (71) 171 J4
Saint-Gengoux-le-National (71) 171 H3
Saint-Geniès (24) 215 G6
Saint-Geniès-Bellevue (31) 269 H5
Saint-Geniès-de-Comolas (30) 256 D6
Saint-Geniès-de-Fontedit (34) 291 K2

Saint-Geniès-de-Malgoirès (30) 275 F2
Saint-Geniès-de-Varensal (34) 272 C5
Saint-Geniès-des-Mourgues (34) 274 D5
Saint-Geniez (04) 259 G3
Saint-Geniez-d'Olt (12) 253 F1
Saint-Geniez-ô-Merle (19) 216 D5
Saint-Génis (05) 258 E2
Saint-Génis-de-Saintonge (17) 195 G5
Saint-Génis-des-Fontaines (66) 315 H4
Saint-Génis-d'Hiersac (16) 196 C2
Saint-Genis-du-Bois (33) 230 B4
Saint-Genis-l'Argentière (69) 205 H3
Saint-Genis-Laval (69) 206 A3
Saint-Genis-les-Ollières (69) 205 K2
Saint-Genis-Pouilly (01) 190 E1
Saint-Genis-sur-Menthon (01) 188 E1
Saint-Genix-sur-Guiers (73) 207 J4
Saint-Genou (36) 147 G5
Saint-Genouph (37) 127 H5
Saint-Geoire-en-Valdaine (38) 207 J5
Saint-Geoirs (38) 223 G1
Saint-Georges (15) 218 E6
Saint-Georges (16) 179 H5
Saint-Georges (32) 268 B5
Saint-Georges (47) 248 E1
Saint-Georges (57) 67 H5
Saint-Georges (62) 9 J2
Saint-Georges (82) 250 C4
Saint-Georges-Antignac (17) 195 H5
Saint-Georges-Armont (25) 139 F4
Saint-Georges-Blancaneix (24) 231 G1
Saint-Georges-Buttavent (53) 81 F4
Saint-Georges-d'Annebecq (61) 53 K6
Saint-Georges-d'Aunay (14) 53 G1
Saint-Georges-d'Aurac (43) 219 J4
Saint-Georges-de-Baroille (42) 204 D1
Saint-Georges-de-Bohon (50) 31 F1
Saint-Georges-de-Chesné (35) 80 A4
Saint-Georges-de-Commiers (38) 224 A5
Saint-Georges-de-Didonne (17) 194 C3
Saint-Georges-de-Gréhaigne (35) 51 H4
Saint-Georges-de-la-Couée (72) 107 H5
Saint-Georges-de-la-Rivière (50) 28 B6
Saint-Georges-de-Lévéjac (48) 253 J3
Saint-Georges-de-Livoye (50) 52 B4
Saint-Georges-de-
Longuepierre (17) 178 B4
Saint-Georges-de-Luzençon (12) 253 F6
Saint-Georges-de-Mons (63) 184 C6
Saint-Georges-de-Montaigu (85) 142 A4
Saint-Georges-de-Montclard (24) 231 K1
Saint-Georges-de-Noisné (79) 161 K4
Saint-Georges-de-Pointindoux (85) 159 G2
Saint-Georges-de-Poisieux (18) 167 G2
Saint-Georges-de-
Reintembault (35) 80 A1
Saint-Georges-de-Reneins (69) 188 B4
Saint-Georges-de-Rex (79) 177 J1
Saint-Georges-de-Rouelley (50) 53 F6
Saint-Georges-d'Elle (50) 31 J3
Saint-Georges-des-Agoûts (17) 211 G1
Saint-Georges-des-Coteaux (17) 195 F2
Saint-Georges-des-Gardes (49) 143 G1
Saint-Georges-des-
Groseillers (61) 53 H4
Saint-Georges-des-Hurtières (73) 209 F5
Saint-Georges-des-Sept-Voies (49) 125 J5
Saint-Georges-d'Espéranche (38) 206 B6
Saint-Georges-d'Orques (34) 274 B6
Saint-Georges-du-Bois (17) 177 H3
Saint-Georges-du-Bois (49) 125 K3
Saint-Georges-du-Bois (72) 106 D3
Saint-Georges-du-Mesnil (27) 34 C4
Saint-Georges-du-Rosay (72) 83 G6
Saint-Georges-du-Vièvre (27) 34 D4
Saint-Georges-en-Auge (14) 54 D1
Saint-Georges-en-Couzan (42) 204 B3
Saint-Georges-Haute-Ville (42) 204 D5
Saint-Georges-la-Pouge (23) 182 E5
Saint-Georges-Lagricol (43) 220 C2
Saint-Georges-le-Fléchard (53) 105 H2
Saint-Georges-le-Gaultier (72) 82 B4
Saint-Georges-lès-
Baillargeaux (86) 163 F2
Saint-Georges-les-Bains (07) 240 B2
Saint-Georges-les-Landes (87) 164 E6
Saint-Georges-Montcocq (50) 31 H5
Saint-Georges-Motel (27) 57 F4
Saint-Georges-Nigremont (23) 201 F1
Saint-Georges-sur-Allier (63) 202 E3
Saint-Georges-sur-Arnon (36) 148 D4
Saint-Georges-sur-Baulche (89) 113 F5
Saint-Georges-sur-Cher (41) 128 C5
Saint-Georges-sur-Erve (53) 81 K6
Saint-Georges-sur-Eure (28) 85 F3
Saint-Georges-sur-Fontaine (76) 16 A6
Saint-Georges-sur-la-Prée (18) 148 C1
Saint-Georges-sur-l'Aa (59) 3 F2
Saint-Georges-sur-Layon (49) 143 K1
Saint-Georges-sur-Loire (49) 124 E4
Saint-Georges-sur-Moulon (18) 149 G1
Saint-Georges-sur-Renon (01) 188 E3
Saint-Geours-d'Auribat (40) 264 D4
Saint-Geours-de-Maremne (40) 262 D5
Saint-Gérand (56) 76 E5
Saint-Gérand-de-Vaux (03) 169 F6
Saint-Gérand-le-Puy (03) 185 K2
Saint-Géraud (47) 230 E5
Saint-Géraud-de-Corps (24) 213 F6
Saint-Géréon (44) 124 A4
Saint-Germain (07) 239 H6

Saint-Germain (10)........... 90 A5
Saint-Germain (54)........... 94 C2
Saint-Germain (70).......... 118 E5
Saint-Germain (86).......... 164 A3
Saint-Germain-au-Mont-d'Or (69) .. 188 C6
Saint-Germain-Beaupré (23)..... 182 A1
Saint-Germain-Chassenay (58) .. 169 F1
Saint-Germain-d'Anxure (53) 81 F5
Saint-Germain-d'Arcé (72)..... 126 E1
Saint-Germain-d'Aunay (61)..... 55 G2
Saint-Germain-de-Belvès (24) ... 232 D3
Saint-Germain-de-Calberte (48) .. 254 E4
Saint-Germain-de-Clairefeuille (61) .. 54 E5
Saint-Germain-de-Confolens (16) .. 180 B4
Saint-Germain-de-Coulamer (53) .. 82 A5
Saint-Germain-de-Fresney (27) ... 56 E2
Saint-Germain-de-Grave (33).... 230 A5
Saint-Germain-de-Joux (01)..... 190 B2
Saint-Germain-de-la-Coudre (61) .. 83 H5
Saint-Germain-de-la-Grange (78) .. 58 A4
Saint-Germain-de-la-Rivière (33) .. 211 K6
Saint-Germain-de-Livet (14) 33 K6
Saint-Germain-de-Longue-Chaume (79) 161 J1
Saint-Germain-de-Lusignan (17) .. 195 K6
Saint-Germain-de-Marencennes (17) 177 G3
Saint-Germain-de-Martigny (61) .. 83 G1
Saint-Germain-de-Modéon (21) .. 134 B5
Saint-Germain-de-Montbron (16) . 197 G4
Saint-Germain-de-Montgommery (14)........... 54 E2
Saint-Germain-de-Pasquier (27) .. 35 G4
Saint-Germain-de-Prinçay (85) .. 160 C1
Saint-Germain-de-Salles (03) 185 G3
Saint-Germain-de-Tallevende-la-Lande-Vaumont (14)..... 52 E4
Saint-Germain-de-Tournebut (50) .. 28 E4
Saint-Germain-de-Varreville (50) .. 29 G5
Saint-Germain-de-Vibrac (17)... 195 K6
Saint-Germain-d'Ectot (14)..... 32 B5
Saint-Germain-d'Elle (50)...... 31 J3
Saint-Germain-des-Angles (27) ... 35 J6
Saint-Germain-des-Bois (18) ... 149 H5
Saint-Germain-des-Bois (58) ... 133 F5
Saint-Germain-des-Champs (89) .. 133 K1
Saint-Germain-des-Essourts (76) .. 16 B6
Saint-Germain-des-Fossés (03) .. 185 J2
Saint-Germain-des-Grois (61).... 84 A3
Saint-Germain-des-Prés (24) 214 D2
Saint-Germain-des-Prés (45) 111 K3
Saint-Germain-des-Prés (49) 124 D4
Saint-Germain-des-Prés (81) 289 J1
Saint-Germain-des-Vaux (50).... 28 A1
Saint-Germain-d'Esteuil (33)..... 210 E2
Saint-Germain-d'Étables (76) 16 A2
Saint-Germain-du-Bel-Air (46) ... 233 H5
Saint-Germain-du-Bois (71) 172 D1
Saint-Germain-du-Corbéis (61).... 82 C3
Saint-Germain-du-Crioult (14).... 53 G3
Saint-Germain-du-Pert (14) 29 H6
Saint-Germain-du-Pinel (35)..... 104 B2
Saint-Germain-du-Plain (71) 172 A1
Saint-Germain-du-Puch (33)..... 229 K2
Saint-Germain-du-Puy (18)..... 149 H3
Saint-Germain-du-Salembre (24) .. 213 H4
Saint-Germain-du-Seudre (17) .. 195 F5
Saint-Germain-du-Teil (48) 253 H1
Saint-Germain-en-Brionnais (71) .. 170 D6
Saint-Germain-en-Coglès (35) ... 80 A3
Saint-Germain-en-Laye (78) 58 C3
Saint-Germain-en-Montagne (39) .. 156 B6
Saint-Germain-et-Mons (24) 231 J2
Saint-Germain-la-Blanche-Herbe (14) 32 D5
Saint-Germain-la-Campagne (27) .. 55 G1
Saint-Germain-la-Chambotte (73) .. 208 B1
Saint-Germain-la-Montagne (42) .. 187 H2
Saint-Germain-la-Poterie (60).... 37 G2
Saint-Germain-la-Ville (51)..... 62 E3
Saint-Germain-l'Aiguiller (85) ... 160 D1
Saint-Germain-Langot (14)...... 53 K2
Saint-Germain-Laprade (43)..... 220 D5
Saint-Germain-Laval (42)...... 204 C1
Saint-Germain-Laval (77)...... 88 A3
Saint-Germain-Lavolps (19) 200 E4
Saint-Germain-Laxis (77) 87 H1
Saint-Germain-le-Châtelet (90)... 119 J3
Saint-Germain-le-Fouilloux (53)... 80 E6
Saint-Germain-le-Gaillard (28) ... 84 E3
Saint-Germain-le-Gaillard (50) ... 28 B4
Saint-Germain-le-Guillaume (50) .. 80 E5
Saint-Germain-le-Rocheux (21) .. 115 G6
Saint-Germain-le-Vasson (14).... 53 K1
Saint-Germain-le-Vieux (61)..... 55 F6
Saint-Germain-Lembron (63) 202 E6
Saint-Germain-lès-Arlay (39) 155 H6
Saint-Germain-lès-Arpajon (91)... 86 D1
Saint-Germain-lès-Belles (87) ... 199 H4
Saint-Germain-lès-Buxy (71) 171 J1
Saint-Germain-lès-Corbeil (91)... 59 F6
Saint-Germain-lès-Paroisses (01) .. 207 J1
Saint-Germain-lès-Senailly (21) .. 134 D2
Saint-Germain-lès-Vergnes (19) .. 215 K2
Saint-Germain-Lespinasse (42) .. 186 D3
Saint-Germain-l'Herm (63) 203 H6
Saint-Germain-près-Herment (63) .. 201 H3
Saint-Germain-Source-Seine (21) .. 135 H2
Saint-Germain-sous-Cailly (76) ... 16 A6
Saint-Germain-sous-Doue (77).... 60 C3
Saint-Germain-sur-Avre (27)..... 56 E4
Saint-Germain-sur-Ay (50) 30 C1

Saint-Germain-sur-Bresle (80) 17 F3
Saint-Germain-sur-Éaulne (76)... 16 D3
Saint-Germain-sur-École (77).... 87 G2
Saint-Germain-sur-Ille (35)..... 79 G3
Saint-Germain-sur-l'Arbresle (69) . 205 J1
Saint-Germain-sur-Meuse (55)... 65 F5
Saint-Germain-sur-Moine (49) ... 142 C2
Saint-Germain-sur-Morin (77)..... 59 K3
Saint-Germain-sur-Renon (01)... 188 E3
Saint-Germain-sur-Rhône (74)... 190 C3
Saint-Germain-sur-Sarthe (72)... 82 D5
Saint-Germain-sur-Sèves (50)... 30 E2
Saint-Germain-sur-Vienne (37)... 144 E1
Saint-Germain-Village (27)...... 34 C3
Saint-Germainmont (08)........ 41 G1
Saint-Germé (32)........... 266 A5
Saint-Germer-de-Fly (60)....... 36 F3
Saint-Germier (31).......... 288 E3
Saint-Germier (32).......... 268 B5
Saint-Germier (79).......... 162 B4
Saint-Germier (81).......... 270 E5
Saint-Géron (43)........... 219 G2
Saint-Gérons (15).......... 235 F1
Saint-Gervais (30).......... 256 C4
Saint-Gervais (33).......... 211 J5
Saint-Gervais (38).......... 223 J3
Saint-Gervais (85).......... 140 D4
Saint-Gervais (95)........... 36 E5
Saint-Gervais-d'Auvergne (63)... 184 C4
Saint-Gervais-de-Vic (72)...... 107 K4
Saint-Gervais-des-Sablons (61) ... 54 D3
Saint-Gervais-du-Perron (61) 82 D1
Saint-Gervais-en-Belin (72) 106 E4
Saint-Gervais-en-Vallière (71)... 154 B4
Saint-Gervais-la-Forêt (41)...... 129 F2
Saint-Gervais-les-Bains (74)... 192 B5
Saint-Gervais-les-Trois-Clochers (86) 145 H5
Saint-Gervais-sous-Meymont (63) .. 203 J3
Saint-Gervais-sur-Couches (71) .. 153 H4
Saint-Gervais-sur-Mare (34) ... 272 D6
Saint-Gervais-sur-Roubion (26) .. 240 C5
Saint-Gervasy (30).......... 275 H3
Saint-Gervazy (63).......... 219 F1
Saint-Géry (24)........... 213 G6
Saint-Géry (46)........... 250 B1
Saint-Geyrac (24).......... 214 C5
Saint-Gibrien (51)........... 62 C2
Saint-Gildas (22)........... 76 E1
Saint-Gildas-de-Rhuys (56) 120 E2
Saint-Gildas-des-Bois (44) 102 C6
Saint-Gilles (30).......... 275 H5
Saint-Gilles (35)........... 78 C3
Saint-Gilles (36).......... 165 F4
Saint-Gilles (50)........... 31 G3
Saint-Gilles (51)........... 40 B4
Saint-Gilles (71).......... 153 J5
Saint-Gilles-Croix-de-Vie (85) .. 158 D1
Saint-Gilles-de-Crétot (76)..... 15 F6
Saint-Gilles-de-la-Neuville (76) ... 14 D6
Saint-Gilles-des-Marais (61)..... 53 F6
Saint-Gilles-du-Mené (22)...... 77 J3
Saint-Gilles-les-Bois (22)...... 48 D4
Saint-Gilles-les-Forêts (87) 199 K4
Saint-Gilles-Pligeaux (22)...... 76 D2
Saint-Gilles-Vieux-Marché (22)... 76 E3
Saint-Gineis-en-Coiron (07) 239 J5
Saint-Gingolph (74)......... 175 J5
Saint-Girod (73).......... 208 C1
Saint-Girons (09).......... 306 D3
Saint-Girons (40).......... 264 D6
Saint-Girons-d'Aiguevives (33) .. 211 H4
Saint-Gladie-Arrive-Munein (64) .. 283 H3
Saint-Glen (22)............ 77 J2
Saint-Goazec (29)........... 75 G4
Saint-Gobain (02)........... 20 A5
Saint-Gobert (02)........... 20 B1
Saint-Goin (64).......... 283 K5
Saint-Gondon (45)......... 131 G1
Saint-Gondran (35).......... 78 E2
Saint-Gonlay (35)........... 78 C4
Saint-Gonnery (56).......... 77 H5
Saint-Gor (40)........... 246 C6
Saint-Gorgon (56)......... 102 A4
Saint-Gorgon (88).......... 95 F3
Saint-Gorgon-Main (25)...... 156 E3
Saint-Gourgon (41)......... 128 B1
Saint-Gourson (16)......... 180 H5
Saint-Goussaud (23)........ 182 A4
Saint-Gratien (80).......... 18 C1
Saint-Gratien (95).......... 58 D2
Saint-Gratien-Savigny (58).... 151 J5
Saint-Gravé (56).......... 102 A3
Saint-Grégoire (35).......... 79 G4
Saint-Grégoire (81)......... 271 G2
Saint-Grégoire-d'Ardennes (17) .. 195 H5
Saint-Grégoire-du-Vièvre (27)... 34 D4
Saint-Griède (32).......... 266 B4
Saint-Groux (16).......... 179 G6
Saint-Guen (22)........... 76 E4
Saint-Guilhem-le-Désert (34) ... 273 J5
Saint-Guillaume (38)......... 223 K6
Saint-Guinoux (35).......... 50 E4
Saint-Guiraud (34)......... 273 H5
Saint-Guyomard (56)........ 101 H4
Saint-Haon (43).......... 238 B2
Saint-Haon-le-Châtel (42).... 186 D4
Saint-Haon-le-Vieux (42) 186 D4
Saint-Héand (42).......... 205 H3
Saint-Hélen (22)........... 50 D5
Saint-Hélier (21).......... 135 G4

Saint-Hellier (76).......... 16 A4
Saint-Herblain (44)......... 123 F4
Saint-Herblon (44)......... 124 B4
Saint-Hérent (63)......... 202 E6
Saint-Hernin (29)........... 75 H3
Saint-Hervé (22)........... 77 F3
Saint-Hilaire (03)......... 168 D4
Saint-Hilaire (11).......... 309 F1
Saint-Hilaire (25).......... 138 C4
Saint-Hilaire (31).......... 288 A3
Saint-Hilaire (38).......... 224 C1
Saint-Hilaire (43).......... 219 H1
Saint-Hilaire (46).......... 234 E3
Saint-Hilaire (63).......... 184 A4
Saint-Hilaire (91)........... 86 C3
Saint-Hilaire-au-Temple (51).... 62 D1
Saint-Hilaire-Bonneval (87) ... 199 G3
Saint-Hilaire-Cottes (62)....... 5 H5
Saint-Hilaire-Cusson-la-Valmitte (42)....... 220 D1
Saint-Hilaire-de-Beauvoir (34) .. 274 D4
Saint-Hilaire-de-Brens (38) 207 F3
Saint-Hilaire-de-Brethmas (30) .. 255 H6
Saint-Hilaire-de-Briouze (61) 53 K5
Saint-Hilaire-de-Chaléons (44) .. 122 D5
Saint-Hilaire-de-Clisson (44).... 123 J6
Saint-Hilaire-de-Court (18) 148 D1
Saint-Hilaire-de-Gondilly (18) .. 150 B3
Saint-Hilaire-de-la-Côte (38) ... 207 F6
Saint-Hilaire-de-la-Noaille (33) .. 230 D5
Saint-Hilaire-de-Lavit (48) 254 E4
Saint-Hilaire-de-Loulay (85) ... 142 A3
Saint-Hilaire-de-Lusignan (47) .. 248 A4
Saint-Hilaire-de-Riez (85) 140 E6
Saint-Hilaire-de-Villefranche (17) . 177 K6
Saint-Hilaire-de-Voust (85) 161 F3
Saint-Hilaire-des-Landes (35)... 79 K1
Saint-Hilaire-des-Loges (85) ... 161 F4
Saint-Hilaire-d'Estissac (24) 213 J6
Saint-Hilaire-d'Ozilhan (30) 275 K1
Saint-Hilaire-du-Bois (17) 195 H6
Saint-Hilaire-du-Bois (33) 230 C4
Saint-Hilaire-du-Harcouët (50) .. 52 C6
Saint-Hilaire-du-Maine (53) 80 D5
Saint-Hilaire-du-Rosier (38) ... 223 F4
Saint-Hilaire-en-Lignières (18) .. 166 D1
Saint-Hilaire-en-Morvan (58)... 152 B3
Saint-Hilaire-en-Woëvre (55) 44 B6
Saint-Hilaire-Foissac (19) 216 E2
Saint-Hilaire-Fontaine (58) 169 H1
Saint-Hilaire-la-Croix (63) 184 E4
Saint-Hilaire-la-Forêt (85) 159 G4
Saint-Hilaire-la-Gravelle (41) .. 108 D4
Saint-Hilaire-la-Palud (79) 177 H1
Saint-Hilaire-la-Plaine (23) 182 E3
Saint-Hilaire-la-Treille (87) 181 H2
Saint-Hilaire-le-Château (23)... 182 D5
Saint-Hilaire-le-Châtel (61) 83 H1
Saint-Hilaire-le-Grand (51) 41 K5
Saint-Hilaire-le-Lierru (72) 107 H1
Saint-Hilaire-le-Petit (51)...... 41 J4
Saint-Hilaire-le-Vouhis (85) ... 160 B1
Saint-Hilaire-les-Andrésis (45) .. 112 B2
Saint-Hilaire-les-Courbes (19) .. 200 A4
Saint-Hilaire-les-Monges (63) .. 201 J1
Saint-Hilaire-les-Places (87) ... 198 E4
Saint-Hilaire-lez-Cambrai (59)... 12 C4
Saint-Hilaire-Luc (19)....... 217 F1
Saint-Hilaire-Petitville (50) 31 G1
Saint-Hilaire-Peyroux (19) 215 K3
Saint-Hilaire-Saint-Mesmin (45) . 109 K4
Saint-Hilaire-sous-Charlieu (42) .. 187 G3
Saint-Hilaire-sous-Romilly (10) .. 89 G2
Saint-Hilaire-sur-Benaize (36) .. 164 C3
Saint-Hilaire-sur-Erre (61)..... 83 K4
Saint-Hilaire-sur-Helpe (59) 13 G4
Saint-Hilaire-sur-Puiseaux (45) .. 111 H4
Saint-Hilaire-sur-Risle (61) 55 H5
Saint-Hilaire-sur-Yerre (28) 108 E2
Saint-Hilaire-Taurieux (19) 216 B5
Saint-Hilarion (78).......... 57 J6
Saint-Hilliers (77).......... 60 D6
Saint-Hippolyte (12)........ 235 K4
Saint-Hippolyte (15)........ 218 A3
Saint-Hippolyte (17)........ 177 F5
Saint-Hippolyte (25)........ 139 H4
Saint-Hippolyte (33)........ 230 B2
Saint-Hippolyte (37)........ 146 E3
Saint-Hippolyte (66)........ 310 C5
Saint-Hippolyte (68)......... 71 A6
Saint-Hippolyte-de-Caton (30) .. 255 J6
Saint-Hippolyte-de-Montaigu (30) . 275 J1
Saint-Hippolyte-du-Fort (30) ... 274 B2
Saint-Hippolyte-le-Graveyron (84) . 257 H5
Saint-Honoré (38)......... 224 B6
Saint-Honoré (76).......... 16 A3
Saint-Honoré-les-Bains (58)... 152 A5
Saint-Hostien (43)......... 220 B5
Saint-Hubert (57)........... 27 J6
Saint-Huruge (71)......... 171 G3
Saint-Hymer (14)........... 33 K4
Saint-Hymetière (39)....... 173 G6
Saint-Igeaux (22).......... 76 C3
Saint-Igest (12)........... 251 G2
Saint-Ignan (31).......... 286 D6
Saint-Ignat (63).......... 185 H6
Saint-Igny-de-Roche (71).... 187 H2
Saint-Igny-de-Vers (69)..... 187 J2
Saint-Illide (15).......... 217 G5
Saint-Illiers-la-Ville (78)...... 57 G2
Saint-Illiers-le-Bois (78)...... 57 G2

Saint-Ilpize (43).......... 219 H3
Saint-Imoges (51)........... 40 E6
Saint-Ismier (38).......... 224 B2
Saint-Izaire (12).......... 271 K2
Saint-Jacques (04)......... 279 H1
Saint-Jacques-d'Aliermont (76)... 16 B2
Saint-Jacques-d'Ambur (63) ... 184 C6
Saint-Jacques-d'Atticieux (07) .. 221 K1
Saint-Jacques-de-la-Lande (35) .. 79 F5
Saint-Jacques-de-Néhou (50) 28 C5
Saint-Jacques-de-Thouars (79) .. 144 B4
Saint-Jacques-des-Arrêts (69) .. 188 A1
Saint-Jacques-des-Blats (15) ... 218 A5
Saint-Jacques-des-Guérets (41) .. 107 K5
Saint-Jacques-en-Valgodemard (05) 242 E2
Saint-Jacut-de-la-Mer (22) 50 B3
Saint-Jacut-du-Mené (22) 77 J3
Saint-Jacut-les-Pins (56) 102 A3
Saint-Jal (19)........... 215 K1
Saint-James (50).......... 51 K5
Saint-Jammes (64)......... 284 E3
Saint-Jans-Cappel (59)........ 6 A2
Saint-Jean (31).......... 269 H5
Saint-Jean-aux-Amognes (58) .. 151 F4
Saint-Jean-aux-Bois (08)...... 21 K4
Saint-Jean-aux-Bois (60)...... 38 E3
Saint-Jean-Bonnefonds (42) ... 205 G6
Saint-Jean-Brévelay (56) 101 G3
Saint-Jean-Cap-Ferrat (06) 281 H4
Saint-Jean-Chambre (07) 239 J1
Saint-Jean-d'Aigues-Vives (09) .. 308 B3
Saint-Jean-d'Alcapiès (12) 272 C2
Saint-Jean-d'Angély (17) 177 K5
Saint-Jean-d'Angle (17) 194 D1
Saint-Jean-d'Ardières (69) 188 B3
Saint-Jean-d'Arves (73) 225 G2
Saint-Jean-d'Arvey (73) 208 C4
Saint-Jean-d'Assé (72) 82 D6
Saint-Jean-d'Ataux (24) 213 H4
Saint-Jean-d'Aubrigoux (43) .. 220 B1
Saint-Jean-d'Aulps (74) 192 A1
Saint-Jean-d'Avelanne (38) ... 207 K5
Saint-Jean-de-Barrou (11) 310 D3
Saint-Jean-de-Bassel (57) 67 H3
Saint-Jean-de-Beauregard (91) .. 58 C6
Saint-Jean-de-Belleville (73) ... 209 H5
Saint-Jean-de-Beugné (85) ... 160 B3
Saint-Jean-de-Blaignac (33) ... 230 B4
Saint-Jean-de-Boeuf (21) 153 K1
Saint-Jean-de-Boiseau (44) ... 123 F4
Saint-Jean-de-Bonneval (10) ... 90 A6
Saint-Jean-de-Bournay (38) ... 206 D5
Saint-Jean-de-Braye (45) 110 B4
Saint-Jean-de-Buèges (34) ... 273 K3
Saint-Jean-de-Ceyrargues (30) .. 255 J6
Saint-Jean-de-Chevelu (73) ... 208 A2
Saint-Jean-de-Côle (24) 198 B6
Saint-Jean-de-Cornies (34) ... 274 D4
Saint-Jean-de-Couz (73) 208 A5
Saint-Jean-de-Crieulon (30) ... 274 D2
Saint-Jean-de-Cuculles (34) ... 274 B4
Saint-Jean-de-Daye (50) 31 H2
Saint-Jean-de-Duras (47) 231 F4
Saint-Jean-de-Folleville (76) 14 E6
Saint-Jean-de-Fos (34) 273 J5
Saint-Jean-de-Gonville (01) ... 190 D1
Saint-Jean-de-la-Blaquière (34) . 273 H5
Saint-Jean-de-la-Croix (49) ... 125 G4
Saint-Jean-de-la-Forêt (61)..... 83 J4
Saint-Jean-de-la-Haize (50) 51 K2
Saint-Jean-de-la-Léqueraye (27) . 34 C2
Saint-Jean-de-la-Motte (72) ... 106 C6
Saint-Jean-de-la-Neuville (76) ... 14 D6
Saint-Jean-de-la-Porte (73) ... 208 D4
Saint-Jean-de-la-Rivière (50) ... 28 B5
Saint-Jean-de-la-Ruelle (45) ... 110 A4
Saint-Jean-de-Laur (46) 250 D3
Saint-Jean-de-Lier (40) 264 D3
Saint-Jean-de-Linières (49) ... 125 F3
Saint-Jean-de-Liversay (17) ... 177 G1
Saint-Jean-de-Livet (14) 33 K6
Saint-Jean-de-Losne (21) 154 E2
Saint-Jean-de-Luz (64) 263 B1
Saint-Jean-de-Marcel (81) 251 J6
Saint-Jean-de-Marsacq (40) ... 262 D5
Saint-Jean-de-Maruéjols-et-Avéjan (30) 255 J4
Saint-Jean-de-Maurienne (73) .. 225 G2
Saint-Jean-de-Minervois (34) .. 291 G3
Saint-Jean-de-Moirans (38) ... 223 J1
Saint-Jean-de-Monts (85) 140 D5
Saint-Jean-de-Muzols (07) 222 B5
Saint-Jean-de-Nay (43) 220 A5
Saint-Jean-de-Niost (01) 206 E1
Saint-Jean-de-Paracol (11) ... 308 D4
Saint-Jean-de-Rebervilliers (28) . 84 E1
Saint-Jean-de-Rives (81) 270 A5
Saint-Jean-de-Sauves (86) ... 144 E5
Saint-Jean-de-Savigny (50) 31 J2
Saint-Jean-de-Serres (30) 274 D1
Saint-Jean-de-Sixt (74) 191 J5
Saint-Jean-de-Soudain (38) ... 207 G4
Saint-Jean-de-Tholome (74) ... 191 H3
Saint-Jean-de-Thouars (79) ... 144 B4
Saint-Jean-de-Thurac (47) 248 C5
Saint-Jean-de-Thurigneux (01) .. 188 D3
Saint-Jean-de-Touslas (69) ... 205 J4
Saint-Jean-de-Trézy (71) 153 H6
Saint-Jean-de-Valériscle (30) .. 255 H4

Saint-Jean-de-Vals (81) 271 F5
Saint-Jean-de-Vaulx (38) 224 B5
Saint-Jean-de-Vaux (71) 153 J6
Saint-Jean-de-Védas (34) 293 G1
Saint-Jean-de-Verges (09) 307 J2
Saint-Jean-Delnous (12) 271 H1
Saint-Jean-des-Baisants (50) ... 31 J3
Saint-Jean-des-Bois (61)...... 53 F5
Saint-Jean-des-Champs (50) ... 51 J1
Saint-Jean-des-Échelles (72) ... 107 J1
Saint-Jean-des-Essartiers (14) .. 31 K4
Saint-Jean-des-Mauvrets (49) .. 125 H4
Saint-Jean-des-Ollières (63) ... 203 G4
Saint-Jean-des-Vignes (69) ... 188 B6
Saint-Jean-d'Estissac (24) 213 J5
Saint-Jean-d'Étreux (39) 172 E5
Saint-Jean-devant-Possesse (51) . 63 H3
Saint-Jean-d'Eyraud (24) 213 H6
Saint-Jean-d'Hérans (38) 242 B1
Saint-Jean-d'Heurs (63) 203 G1
Saint-Jean-d'Illac (33) 229 F2
Saint-Jean-d'Ormont (88) 95 J3
Saint-Jean-du-Bois (72) 106 B4
Saint-Jean-du-Bouzet (82) ... 268 B1
Saint-Jean-du-Bruel (12) 273 G1
Saint-Jean-du-Cardonnay (76) .. 35 H1
Saint-Jean-du-Castillonnais (09) . 306 B3
Saint-Jean-du-Corail (50) 52 D6
Saint-Jean-du-Corail-des-Bois (50) . 52 B4
Saint-Jean-du-Doigt (29) 47 G3
Saint-Jean-du-Falga (09) 307 J1
Saint-Jean-du-Gard (30) 254 G6
Saint-Jean-du-Pin (30) 255 G5
Saint-Jean-du-Thenney (27) 55 G1
Saint-Jean-en-Royans (26) ... 223 G5
Saint-Jean-en-Val (63) 203 F5
Saint-Jean-et-Saint-Paul (12) .. 272 C2
Saint-Jean-Froidmentel (41) ... 108 D3
Saint-Jean-Kerdaniel (22) 48 D5
Saint-Jean-Kourtzerode (57) ... 70 A1
Saint-Jean-la-Bussière (69) ... 187 H5
Saint-Jean-la-Fouillouse (48) .. 238 A4
Saint-Jean-la-Poterie (56) 102 B4
Saint-Jean-la-Vêtre (42) 204 A2
Saint-Jean-Lachalm (43) 238 A1
Saint-Jean-Lagineste (46) 234 B2
Saint-Jean-Lasseille (66) 315 G3
Saint-Jean-le-Blanc (14) 53 G2
Saint-Jean-le-Blanc (45) 110 A4
Saint-Jean-le-Centenier (07) ... 239 J5
Saint-Jean-le-Comtal (32) 286 C1
Saint-Jean-le-Thomas (50) 51 J2
Saint-Jean-le-Vieux (01) 109 H4
Saint-Jean-le-Vieux (38) 224 C3
Saint-Jean-le-Vieux (64) 282 E5
Saint-Jean-les-Deux-Jumeaux (77) . 60 A2
Saint-Jean-lès-Longuyon (54) ... 26 A3
Saint-Jean-Lespinasse (46) ... 234 B2
Saint-Jean-Lherm (31) 269 J5
Saint-Jean-Ligoure (87) 199 F3
Saint-Jean-Mirabel (46) 234 E5
Saint-Jean-Pied-de-Port (64) .. 282 D5
Saint-Jean-Pierre-Fixte (28) 84 A5
Saint-Jean-Pla-de-Corts (66) .. 315 F4
Saint-Jean-Poudge (64) 284 E1
Saint-Jean-Poutge (32) 267 F5
Saint-Jean-Rohrbach (57) 68 B4
Saint-Jean-Roure (07) 239 H1
Saint-Jean-Saint-Germain (37) .. 146 D3
Saint-Jean-Saint-Gervais (63) .. 219 G1
Saint-Jean-Saint-Maurice-sur-Loire (42) 186 D5
Saint-Jean-Saint-Nicolas (05) .. 243 G4
Saint-Jean-Saverne (67) 70 B1
Saint-Jean-Soleymieux (42) ... 204 C5
Saint-Jean-sur-Couesnon (35) .. 79 K2
Saint-Jean-sur-Erve (53) 105 J2
Saint-Jean-sur-Mayenne (53) ... 81 F6
Saint-Jean-sur-Moivre (51) 63 F3
Saint-Jean-sur-Reyssouze (01) .. 172 B5
Saint-Jean-sur-Tourbe (51) 42 B5
Saint-Jean-sur-Veyle (01) 188 D1
Saint-Jean-sur-Vilaine (35) 79 K4
Saint-Jean-Trolimon (29) 98 B3
Saint-Jeannet (04) 278 E1
Saint-Jeannet (06) 281 F3
Saint-Jeanvrin (18) 166 D3
Saint-Jeoire (74) 191 J2
Saint-Jeoire-Prieuré (73) 208 C4
Saint-Jeure-d'Andaure (07) ... 221 H5
Saint-Jeure-d'Ay (07) 222 A4
Saint-Jeures (43) 221 H5
Saint-Joachim (44) 122 A2
Saint-Jodard (42) 187 H6
Saint-Joire (55) 64 D6
Saint-Jores (50) 30 E1
Saint-Jorioz (74) 191 F6
Saint-Jory (31) 269 G4
Saint-Jory-de-Chalais (24) ... 198 B5
Saint-Jory-las-Bloux (24) 214 C1
Saint-Joseph (42) 205 J4
Saint-Joseph (50) 28 D3
Saint-Joseph-de-Rivière (38) .. 207 K6
Saint-Joseph-des-Bancs (07) .. 239 H3
Saint-Josse (62) 4 B6
Saint-Jouan-des-Guérets (35) .. 50 D4
Saint-Jouan-de-l'Isle (22) 78 B2
Saint-Jouin (14) 33 H4
Saint-Jouin-Bruneval (76) 14 B5
Saint-Jouin-de-Blavou (61) 83 G3
Saint-Jouin-de-Marnes (79) ... 144 C5

Saint-Jouin-de-Milly (79) 161 F1
Saint-Jouvent (87) 181 G5
Saint-Juan (25) 138 D5
Saint-Judoce (22) 78 D1
Saint-Juéry (12) 271 K2
Saint-Juéry (48) 236 E2
Saint-Juéry (81) 270 E2
Saint-Juire-Champgillon (85) 160 B3
Saint-Julia (31) 289 G2
Saint-Julia-de-Bec (11) 309 H4
Saint-Julien (21) 136 B4
Saint-Julien (22) 77 F1
Saint-Julien (31) 287 J5
Saint-Julien (34) 291 H1
Saint-Julien (39) 173 F5
Saint-Julien (69) 188 A4
Saint-Julien (83) 278 C4
Saint-Julien (88) 117 J2
Saint-Julien-aux-Bois (19) 216 E4
Saint-Julien-Beychevelle (33) 211 F3
Saint-Julien-Boutières (07) 221 G6
Saint-Julien-Chapteuil (43) 220 E5
Saint-Julien-d'Ance (43) 220 C2
Saint-Julien-d'Armagnac (40) 266 A1
Saint-Julien-d'Arpaon (48) 254 C3
Saint-Julien-d'Asse (04) 278 E2
Saint-Julien-de-Bourdeilles (24) . . . 213 J1
Saint-Julien-de-Briola (11) 289 G6
Saint-Julien-de-Cassagnas (30) . . . 255 H4
Saint-Julien-de-Chédon (41) 128 D5
Saint-Julien-de-Civry (71) 170 D6
Saint-Julien-de-Concelles (44) . . . 123 J3
Saint-Julien-de-Coppel (63) 203 F3
Saint-Julien-de-Crempse (24) 231 J1
Saint-Julien-de-Gras-Capou (09) . . . 308 A3
Saint-Julien-de-Jonzy (71) 187 F2
Saint-Julien-de-la-Liègue (27) 35 K6
Saint-Julien-de-la-Nef (30) 273 K2
Saint-Julien-de-Lampon (24) 233 G2
Saint-Julien-de-l'Escap (17) 177 K5
Saint-Julien-de-l'Herms (38) 206 D6
Saint-Julien-de-Mailloc (14) 34 A6
Saint-Julien-de-Peyrolas (30) 256 B3
Saint-Julien-de-Raz (38) 223 K1
Saint-Julien-de-Toursac (15) 235 H4
Saint-Julien-de-Vouvantes (44) . . . 124 A1
Saint-Julien-des-Chazes (43) 219 K5
Saint-Julien-des-Landes (85) 159 H4
Saint-Julien-des-Points (48) 255 F4
Saint-Julien-d'Eymet (24) 231 H3
Saint-Julien-d'Oddes (42) 204 C1
Saint-Julien-du-Gua (07) 239 H3
Saint-Julien-du-Pinet (43) 220 D4
Saint-Julien-du-Puy (81) 270 D4
Saint-Julien-du-Sault (89) 112 D2
Saint-Julien-du-Serre (07) 239 H4
Saint-Julien-du-Terroux (53) 81 J2
Saint-Julien-du-Tournel (48) 254 C1
Saint-Julien-du-Verdon (04) 279 K1
Saint-Julien-en-Beauchêne (05) . . . 242 A4
Saint-Julien-en-Born (40) 244 C6
Saint-Julien-en-Champsaur (05) . . . 243 F4
Saint-Julien-en-Genevois (74) 190 E2
Saint-Julien-en-Quint (26) 241 G2
Saint-Julien-en-Saint-Alban (07) . . . 240 A3
Saint-Julien-en-Vercors (26) 223 H5
Saint-Julien-Gaulène (81) 271 G1
Saint-Julien-la-Geneste (63) 184 B4
Saint-Julien-la-Genête (23) 183 K3
Saint-Julien-la-Vêtre (42) 204 A1
Saint-Julien-Labrousse (07) 239 J1
Saint-Julien-l'Ars (86) 163 G3
Saint-Julien-le-Châtel (23) 183 H3
Saint-Julien-le-Faucon (14) 33 J6
Saint-Julien-le-Pèlerin (19) 216 E6
Saint-Julien-le-Petit (87) 199 K1
Saint-Julien-le-Roux (07) 240 A2
Saint-Julien-le-Vendômois (19) . . . 199 F6
Saint-Julien-les-Gorze (54) 65 H1
Saint-Julien-lès-Metz (57) 45 F5
Saint-Julien-lès-Montbéliard (25) . . 139 G2
Saint-Julien-les-Rosiers (30) 255 H5
Saint-Julien-lès-Russey (25) 139 G6
Saint-Julien-les-Villas (10) 90 B5
Saint-Julien-Maumont (19) 216 A6
Saint-Julien-Molhesabate (43) 221 H3
Saint-Julien-Molin-Molette (42) . . . 221 K2
Saint-Julien-Mont-Denis (73) 225 H2
Saint-Julien-près-Bort (19) 217 H1
Saint-Julien-Puy-Lavèze (63) 201 K3
Saint-Julien-sous-les-Côtes (55) . . . 65 F3
Saint-Julien-sur-Bibost (69) 205 H1
Saint-Julien-sur-Calonne (14) 33 K3
Saint-Julien-sur-Cher (41) 129 J6
Saint-Julien-sur-Dheune (71) 153 H6
Saint-Julien-sur-Reyssouze (01) . . . 172 C5
Saint-Julien-sur-Sarthe (61) 83 F2
Saint-Julien-sur-Veyle (01) 188 D2
Saint-Julien-Vocance (07) 221 J3
Saint-Junien (87) 180 D6
Saint-Junien-la-Bregère (23) 182 C6
Saint-Junien-les-Combes (87) 181 F4
Saint-Jure (57) 66 A2
Saint-Jurs (04) 279 F2
Saint-Just (01) 189 G2
Saint-Just (07) 256 C3
Saint-Just (15) 237 F2
Saint-Just (18) 149 H4
Saint-Just (24) 213 J2
Saint-Just (27) 36 B6
Saint-Just (34) 274 E5
Saint-Just (35) 102 D3

Saint-Just (63) 204 A6
Saint-Just-Chaleyssin (38) 206 C4
Saint-Just-d'Avray (69) 187 J5
Saint-Just-de-Claix (38) 223 G5
Saint-Just-en-Bas (42) 204 B2
Saint-Just-en-Brie (77) 88 B1
Saint-Just-en-Chaussée (60) 38 A1
Saint-Just-en-Chevalet (42) 186 C6
Saint-Just-et-le-Bézu (11) 309 F4
Saint-Just-et-Vacquières (30) 255 J5
Saint-Just-Ibarre (64) 283 F5
Saint-Just-la-Pendue (42) 187 G6
Saint-Just-le-Martel (87) 199 G1
Saint-Just-Luzac (17) 194 C1
Saint-Just-Malmont (43) 221 G1
Saint-Just-près-Brioude (43) 219 G3
Saint-Just-Saint-Rambert (42) 204 E5
Saint-Just-Sauvage (51) 89 H1
Saint-Just-sur-Dive (49) 144 C1
Saint-Just-sur-Viaur (12) 251 K5
Saint-Justin (32) 285 J2
Saint-Justin (40) 265 K1
Saint-Juvat (22) 78 D1
Saint-Juvin (08) 42 D3
Saint-Lactencin (36) 147 H5
Saint-Lager (69) 188 B3
Saint-Lager-Bressac (07) 240 A4
Saint-Lamain (39) 155 H6
Saint-Lambert (14) 53 H2
Saint-Lambert (78) 58 B5
Saint-Lambert-du-Lattay (49) 125 F5
Saint-Lambert-et-
  Mont-de-Jeux (08) 42 A1
Saint-Lambert-la-Potherie (49) . . . 125 F3
Saint-Lambert-sur-Dive (61) 54 D1
Saint-Langis-lès-Mortagne (61) . . . 83 H2
Saint-Lanne (65) 266 B6
Saint-Laon (86) 144 D4
Saint-Lary (09) 306 B3
Saint-Lary (32) 267 H5
Saint-Lary-Boujean (31) 286 E5
Saint-Lary-Soulan (65) 304 E4
Saint-Lattier (38) 223 F4
Saint-Launeuc (22) 77 K4
Saint-Laure (63) 185 H6
Saint-Laurent (08) 22 D3
Saint-Laurent (18) 148 E1
Saint-Laurent (22) 48 C4
Saint-Laurent (23) 182 E3
Saint-Laurent (31) 287 F4
Saint-Laurent (47) 247 K4
Saint-Laurent (58) 132 A5
Saint-Laurent (74) 191 H3
Saint-Laurent-Blangy (62) 11 F2
Saint-Laurent-Bretagne (64) 284 E3
Saint-Laurent-Chabreuges (43) . . . 219 G2
Saint-Laurent-d'Agny (69) 205 K3
Saint-Laurent-d'Aigouze (30) 275 F6
Saint-Laurent-d'Andenay (71) 171 F1
Saint-Laurent-d'Arce (33) 211 J5
Saint-Laurent-de-Belzagot (16) . . . 212 E1
Saint-Laurent-de-Brèvedent (76) . . . 14 C6
Saint-Laurent-de-Carnols (30) 256 B4
Saint-Laurent-de-Cerdans (66) 314 E6
Saint-Laurent-de-Céris (16) 179 K5
Saint-Laurent-de-Chamousset (69) . . 205 G2
Saint-Laurent-de-Cognac (16) 195 J3
Saint-Laurent-de-Condel (14) 53 J1
Saint-Laurent-de-Cuves (50) 52 C4
Saint-Laurent-de-Gosse (40) 282 D1
Saint-Laurent-de-Jourdes (86) 163 H5
Saint-Laurent-de-la-Barrière (17) . . . 177 H4
Saint-Laurent-de-
  la-Cabrerisse (11) 309 K1
Saint-Laurent-de-la-Plaine (49) . . . 124 E5
Saint-Laurent-de-la-Prée (17) 176 E4
Saint-Laurent-de-la-Salanque (66) . . 310 C5
Saint-Laurent-de-la-Salle (85) 160 C3
Saint-Laurent-de-Lévézou (12) 253 F4
Saint-Laurent-de-Lin (37) 126 E3
Saint-Laurent-de-Mure (69) 206 C2
Saint-Laurent-de-Muret (48) 237 F5
Saint-Laurent-de-Neste (65) 305 G1
Saint-Laurent-de-Terregatte (50) . . . 52 A6
Saint-Laurent-de-Trèves (48) 254 C4
Saint-Laurent-de-Vaux (69) 205 J2
Saint-Laurent-de-Veyrès (48) 236 E3
Saint-Laurent-des-Arbres (30) 256 D6
Saint-Laurent-des-Autels (49) 124 A5
Saint-Laurent-des-Bâtons (24) 214 A6
Saint-Laurent-des-Bois (27) 56 E3
Saint-Laurent-des-Bois (41) 109 F5
Saint-Laurent-des-Combes (16) . . . 212 D1
Saint-Laurent-des-Combes (33) . . . 230 B1
Saint-Laurent-des-Hommes (24) . . . 213 F5
Saint-Laurent-des-Mortiers (53) . . . 105 G5
Saint-Laurent-des-Vignes (24) 231 H2
Saint-Laurent-d'Oingt (69) 187 K5
Saint-Laurent-d'Olt (12) 253 G1
Saint-Laurent-d'Onay (26) 222 E3
Saint-Laurent-du-Bois (33) 230 B4
Saint-Laurent-du-Cros (05) 242 E4
Saint-Laurent-du-Mont (14) 33 H5
Saint-Laurent-du-Mottay (49) 124 C5
Saint-Laurent-du-Pape (07) 240 B2
Saint-Laurent-du-Plan (33) 230 B5
Saint-Laurent-du-Pont (38) 207 H6
Saint-Laurent-du-Tencement (27) . . . 55 G3
Saint-Laurent-du-Var (06) 281 G4
Saint-Laurent-du-Verdon (04) 278 E4
Saint-Laurent-en-Beaumont (38) . . . 242 C1
Saint-Laurent-en-Brionnais (71) . . . 187 G1

Saint-Laurent-en-Caux (76) 15 H4
Saint-Laurent-en-Gâtines (37) 127 K2
Saint-Laurent-en-Grandvaux (39) . . 174 A3
Saint-Laurent-en-Royans (26) 223 G5
Saint-Laurent-la-Conche (42) 204 E3
Saint-Laurent-la-Gâtine (28) 57 G5
Saint-Laurent-la-Roche (39) 173 F3
Saint-Laurent-la-Vallée (24) 232 E3
Saint-Laurent-la-Vernède (30) 256 A5
Saint-Laurent-le-Minier (30) 273 K2
Saint-Laurent-les-Églises (87) 181 K5
Saint-Laurent-les-Bains (07) 238 D5
Saint-Laurent-les-Tours (46) 234 C2
Saint-Laurent-Lolmie (46) 249 H3
Saint-Laurent-Médoc (33) 210 E4
Saint-Laurent-Nouan (41) 109 H6
Saint-Laurent-Rochefort (42) 204 B2
Saint-Laurent-sous-Coiron (07) . . . 239 J5
Saint-Laurent-sur-Gorre (87) 198 C2
Saint-Laurent-sur-Manoire (24) . . . 214 B4
Saint-Laurent-sur-Mer (14) 29 K6
Saint-Laurent-sur-Othain (55) 26 A4
Saint-Laurent-sur-Oust (56) 101 K4
Saint-Laurent-sur-Saône (01) 188 C1
Saint-Laurent-sur-Sèvre (85) 142 E4
Saint-Laurs (79) 161 G4
Saint-Léger (06) 261 F6
Saint-Léger (16) 196 D6
Saint-Léger (17) 195 G3
Saint-Léger (47) 247 J3
Saint-Léger (53) 105 H1
Saint-Léger (62) 11 F4
Saint-Léger (73) 209 F5
Saint-Léger (77) 60 D4
Saint-Léger-aux-Bois (60) 39 F1
Saint-Léger-aux-Bois (76) 16 E3
Saint-Léger-Bridereix (23) 182 A1
Saint-Léger-de-Balson (33) 246 A1
Saint-Léger-de-Fougeret (58) 152 B3
Saint-Léger-de-la-Martinière (79) . . 178 D2
Saint-Léger-de-Montbrillais (86) . . . 144 D3
Saint-Léger-de-Montbrun (79) 144 C4
Saint-Léger-de-Peyre (48) 237 G5
Saint-Léger-de-Rôtes (27) 34 D6
Saint-Léger-des-Aubées (28) 85 J3
Saint-Léger-des-Bois (49) 125 F3
Saint-Léger-des-Prés (35) 51 G6
Saint-Léger-des-Vignes (58) 151 G6
Saint-Léger-du-Bois (71) 153 G3
Saint-Léger-du-Bourg-Denis (76) . . . 35 J2
Saint-Léger-du-Gennetey (27) 34 E4
Saint-Léger-du-Malzieu (48) 237 G2
Saint-Léger-du-Ventoux (84) 257 J4
Saint-Léger-Dubosq (14) 33 H4
Saint-Léger-en-Bray (60) 37 G2
Saint-Léger-en-Yvelines (78) 57 J5
Saint-Léger-la-Montagne (87) 181 J4
Saint-Léger-le-Guérétois (23) 182 C3
Saint-Léger-le-Petit (18) 150 C2
Saint-Léger-lès-Authie (80) 10 C5
Saint-Léger-lès-Domart (80) 9 J6
Saint-Léger-les-Mélèzes (05) 243 F4
Saint-Léger-lès-Paray (71) 170 C4
Saint-Léger-les-Vignes (44) 123 F5
Saint-Léger-Magnazeix (87) 181 H1
Saint-Léger-près-Troyes (10) 90 B5
Saint-Léger-sous-Beuvray (71) 152 D5
Saint-Léger-sous-Brienne (10) 90 E3
Saint-Léger-sous-Cholet (49) 142 E2
Saint-Léger-sous-Bussière (71) 187 K1
Saint-Léger-sous-Margerie (10) . . . 90 E2
Saint-Léger-sur-Bresle (80) 17 F2
Saint-Léger-sur-Dheune (71) 153 J5
Saint-Léger-sur-Roanne (42) 186 E4
Saint-Léger-sur-Sarthe (61) 83 F2
Saint-Léger-sur-Vouzance (03) 170 A5
Saint-Léger-Triey (21) 136 D5
Saint-Léger-Vauban (89) 134 A4
Saint-Léomer (86) 164 B5
Saint-Léon (03) 169 H5
Saint-Léon (31) 288 D3
Saint-Léon (33) 230 A3
Saint-Léon (47) 247 H3
Saint-Léon-d'Issigeac (24) 231 K4
Saint-Léon-sur-l'Isle (24) 213 J4
Saint-Léon-sur-Vézère (24) 214 E6
Saint-Léonard (32) 267 K3
Saint-Léonard (51) 41 F4
Saint-Léonard (62) 2 A6
Saint-Léonard (76) 14 D4
Saint-Léonard (88) 95 J5
Saint-Léonard-de-Noblat (87) 199 H1
Saint-Léonard-des-Bois (72) 82 B4
Saint-Léonard-des-Parcs (61) 55 F6
Saint-Léonard-en-Beauce (41) 109 F5
Saint-Léons (12) 253 F4
Saint-Léopardin-d'Augy (03) 168 C2
Saint-Léry (56) 78 A4
Saint-Leu-d'Esserent (60) 38 A5
Saint-Leu-la-Forêt (95) 58 D1
Saint-Lézer (65) 285 H3
Saint-Lézin (49) 124 E6
Saint-Lieux-Lafenasse (81) 270 E6
Saint-Lieux-lès-Lavaur (81) 270 A4
Saint-Lin (79) 161 K6
Saint-Lions (04) 260 A6
Saint-Lizier (09) 306 D2
Saint-Lizier-du-Planté (32) 287 G3
Saint-Lô (50) 31 H3
Saint-Lô-d'Ourville (50) 28 C6
Saint-Lon-les-Mines (40) 262 E5
Saint-Longis (72) 83 F4

Saint-Lormel (22) 50 B4
Saint-Lothain (39) 155 J5
Saint-Loube (32) 287 H3
Saint-Loubert (33) 230 B5
Saint-Loubès (33) 229 J1
Saint-Loubouer (40) 265 H5
Saint-Louet-sur-Seulles (14) 32 B6
Saint-Louet-sur-Vire (50) 31 J5
Saint-Louis (57) 70 A2
Saint-Louis (68) 97 J6
Saint-Louis-de-Montferrand (33) . . . 211 H6
Saint-Louis-en-l'Isle (24) 213 G5
Saint-Louis-et-Parahou (11) 309 F4
Saint-Louis-lès-Bitche (57) 69 G4
Saint-Loup (03) 168 E6
Saint-Loup (17) 177 J4
Saint-Loup (23) 183 J5
Saint-Loup (39) 154 E3
Saint-Loup (41) 129 K6
Saint-Loup (50) 52 A5
Saint-Loup (51) 61 J5
Saint-Loup (58) 132 A4
Saint-Loup (69) 187 K6
Saint-Loup (82) 248 D6
Saint-Loup-Cammas (31) 269 H5
Saint-Loup-Champagne (08) 41 G1
Saint-Loup-de-Buffigny (10) 89 G3
Saint-Loup-de-Fribois (14) 33 H6
Saint-Loup-de-Gonois (45) 111 K2
Saint-Loup-de-Naud (77) 88 C2
Saint-Loup-de-Varennes (71) 171 K1
Saint-Loup-des-Chaumes (18) 149 G6
Saint-Loup-des-Vignes (45) 111 F2
Saint-Loup-d'Ordon (89) 112 C2
Saint-Loup-du-Dorat (53) 105 J4
Saint-Loup-du-Gast (53) 81 G3
Saint-Loup-en-Comminges (31) . . . 286 C5
Saint-Loup-Hors (14) 32 B4
Saint-Loup-Lamairé (79) 144 B6
Saint-Loup-Nantouard (70) 137 G4
Saint-Loup-sur-Aujon (52) 116 A4
Saint-Loup-sur-Semouse (70) 118 C3
Saint-Loup-Terrier (08) 22 C6
Saint-Loyer-des-Champs (61) 54 C5
Saint-Lubin-de-Cravant (28) 56 C5
Saint-Lubin-de-la-Haye (28) 57 H4
Saint-Lubin-des-Joncherets (28) . . . 56 D4
Saint-Lubin-en-Vergonnois (41) . . . 128 D2
Saint-Luc (27) 56 E2
Saint-Lucien (28) 57 H6
Saint-Lumier-en-Champagne (51) . . . 63 F4
Saint-Lumier-la-Populeuse (51) . . . 63 H5
Saint-Lumine-de-Clisson (44) 123 J6
Saint-Lumine-de-Coutais (44) 123 F6
Saint-Lunaire (35) 50 C3
Saint-Luperce (28) 84 E3
Saint-Lupicin (39) 173 J5
Saint-Lupien (10) 89 H4
Saint-Lyé (10) 90 A4
Saint-Lyé-la-Forêt (45) 110 B2
Saint-Lyphard (44) 121 K3
Saint-Lys (31) 287 J2
Saint-Macaire (33) 230 A5
Saint-Macaire-du-Bois (49) 144 A2
Saint-Macaire-en-Mauges (49) 142 D2
Saint-Maclou (27) 34 B3
Saint-Maclou-de-Folleville (76) . . . 15 K4
Saint-Maclou-la-Brière (76) 14 E5
Saint-Macoux (86) 179 H3
Saint-Maden (22) 78 C1
Saint-Magne (33) 229 G6
Saint-Magne-de-Castillon (33) 230 C2
Saint-Maigner (63) 184 B4
Saint-Maigrin (17) 195 K6
Saint-Maime (04) 278 B2
Saint-Maime-de-Péreyrol (24) 213 K6
Saint-Maixant (23) 183 G5
Saint-Maixant (33) 230 A5
Saint-Maixent (72) 107 J1
Saint-Maixent-de-Beugné (79) 161 F4
Saint-Maixent-l'École (79) 161 K5
Saint-Maixent-sur-Vie (85) 141 F6
Saint-Maixme-Hauterive (28) 84 D1
Saint-Malo (35) 50 D3
Saint-Malo-de-Beignon (56) 78 B6
Saint-Malo-de-Guersac (44) 122 B2
Saint-Malo-de-la-Lande (50) 30 D4
Saint-Malo-de-Phily (35) 103 F1
Saint-Malo-des-
  Trois-Fontaines (56) 101 K1
Saint-Malô-du-Bois (85) 142 E4
Saint-Malo-en-Donziois (58) 132 D6
Saint-Malon-sur-Mel (35) 78 C4
Saint-Mamert (69) 188 A1
Saint-Mamert-du-Gard (30) 275 F3
Saint-Mamet (31) 305 H5
Saint-Mamet-la-Salvetat (15) 235 G2
Saint-Mammès (77) 87 J4
Saint-Mandé (94) 59 F4
Saint-Mandé-sur-Brédoire (17) 178 B4
Saint-Mandrier-sur-Mer (83) 300 C5
Saint-Manvieu-Bocage (14) 52 D3
Saint-Manvieu-Norrey (14) 32 D5
Saint-Marc (31) 237 F1
Saint-Marc-à-Frongier (23) 183 F6
Saint-Marc-à-Loubaud (23) 200 C1
Saint-Marc-du-Cor (41) 108 B3
Saint-Marc-Jaumegarde (13) 296 E1
Saint-Marc-la-Lande (79) 161 J4
Saint-Marc-le-Blanc (35) 79 J1
Saint-Marc-sur-Couesnon (35) 79 K2

Saint-Marc-sur-Seine (21) 115 G6
Saint-Marcan (35) 51 G4
Saint-Marceau (08) 22 D4
Saint-Marceau (72) 82 D6
Saint-Marcel (01) 188 C5
Saint-Marcel (08) 22 B3
Saint-Marcel (27) 36 B6
Saint-Marcel (36) 165 G3
Saint-Marcel (54) 44 D5
Saint-Marcel (56) 101 J3
Saint-Marcel (70) 117 H4
Saint-Marcel (71) 154 B6
Saint-Marcel (73) 209 H4
Saint-Marcel-Bel-Accueil (38) 206 E3
Saint-Marcel-Campes (81) 251 F6
Saint-Marcel-d'Ardèche (07) 256 C5
Saint-Marcel-de-Careiret (30) 256 B5
Saint-Marcel-de-Félines (42) 187 G6
Saint-Marcel-du-Périgord (24) 232 A1
Saint-Marcel-d'Urfé (42) 186 D6
Saint-Marcel-en-Marcillat (03) 184 A3
Saint-Marcel-en-Murat (03) 184 E1
Saint-Marcel-l'Éclairé (69) 187 J6
Saint-Marcel-lès-Annonay (07) 221 K2
Saint-Marcel-lès-Sauzet (26) 240 B5
Saint-Marcel-lès-Valence (26) 222 D6
Saint-Marcel-Paulel (31) 269 J6
Saint-Marcel-sur-Aude (11) 291 H5
Saint-Marcelin-de-Cray (71) 171 G3
Saint-Marcellin (38) 223 G4
Saint-Marcellin-en-Forez (42) 204 E5
Saint-Marcellin-lès-Vaison (84) . . . 257 H4
Saint-Marcet (31) 286 E6
Saint-Marcory (24) 232 C4
Saint-Marcouf (14) 31 J1
Saint-Marcouf (50) 29 F4
Saint-Mard (02) 40 B2
Saint-Mard (17) 177 H3
Saint-Mard (54) 94 B1
Saint-Mard (77) 59 H1
Saint-Mard (80) 19 F4
Saint-Mard-de-Réno (61) 83 J2
Saint-Mard-de-Vaux (71) 153 J6
Saint-Mard-lès-Rouffy (51) 62 B2
Saint-Mard-sur-Auve (51) 63 G1
Saint-Mard-sur-le-Mont (51) 63 H2
Saint-Mards (76) 15 J3
Saint-Mards-de-Blacarville (27) . . . 34 C2
Saint-Mards-de-Fresne (27) 34 C6
Saint-Mards-en-Othe (10) 89 J6
Saint-Marien (23) 166 D5
Saint-Mariens (33) 211 J4
Saint-Mars-de-Coutais (44) 122 E5
Saint-Mars-de-Locquenay (72) 107 G3
Saint-Mars-d'Égrenne (61) 81 F1
Saint-Mars-d'Outillé (72) 107 F4
Saint-Mars-du-Désert (44) 123 J2
Saint-Mars-du-Désert (53) 82 A4
Saint-Mars-la-Brière (72) 107 F2
Saint-Mars-la-Jaille (44) 124 A2
Saint-Mars-la-Réorthe (85) 142 E5
Saint-Mars-sous-Ballon (72) 82 E6
Saint-Mars-sur-Colmont (53) 81 F3
Saint-Mars-sur-la-Futaie (53) 80 C2
Saint-Mars-Vieux-Maisons (77) . . . 60 D5
Saint-Marsal (66) 314 E4
Saint-Martial (07) 239 G2
Saint-Martial (15) 236 D2
Saint-Martial (16) 212 D1
Saint-Martial (17) 178 A4
Saint-Martial (30) 274 A1
Saint-Martial (33) 230 B4
Saint-Martial-d'Albarède (24) 214 D2
Saint-Martial-d'Artenset (24) 213 F5
Saint-Martial-de-Gimel (19) 216 C3
Saint-Martial-de-Mirambeau (17) . . 211 H1
Saint-Martial-de-Nabirat (24) 233 F3
Saint-Martial-de-Valette (24) 197 J5
Saint-Martial-de-Vitaterne (17) . . . 195 J5
Saint-Martial-Entraygues (19) 216 D4
Saint-Martial-le-Mont (23) 183 F4
Saint-Martial-le-Vieux (23) 201 F3
Saint-Martial-sur-Isop (87) 180 D3
Saint-Martial-sur-Né (17) 195 J4
Saint-Martial-Viveyrol (24) 213 G1
Saint-Martin (32) 286 A2
Saint-Martin (54) 67 G6
Saint-Martin (65) 102 A3
Saint-Martin (65) 285 H6
Saint-Martin (66) 309 H5
Saint-Martin (67) 70 B6
Saint-Martin (83) 278 C6
Saint-Martin-au-Bosc (76) 17 F3
Saint-Martin-au-Laërt (62) 3 G5
Saint-Martin-aux-Arbres (76) 15 H5
Saint-Martin-aux-Bois (60) 38 B1
Saint-Martin-aux-Buneaux (76) . . . 14 E3
Saint-Martin-aux-Champs (51) 62 E4
Saint-Martin-aux-Chartrains (14) . . . 33 K3
Saint-Martin-Belle-Roche (71) 171 K5
Saint-Martin-Bellevue (74) 191 F5
Saint-Martin-Boulogne (62) 2 A5
Saint-Martin-Cantalès (15) 217 G5
Saint-Martin-Château (23) 200 A1
Saint-Martin-Choquel (62) 2 D6
Saint-Martin-Curton (47) 247 F2
Saint-Martin-d'Abbat (45) 110 D4
Saint-Martin-d'Ablois (51) 61 J1
Saint-Martin-d'Août (26) 222 D3
Saint-Martin-d'Arberoue (64) 282 E3
Saint-Martin-d'Arc (73) 225 H2
Saint-Martin-d'Arcé (49) 126 B2

396

Saint-Martin-d'Ardèche (07) 256 B3
Saint-Martin-d'Armagnac (32) 266 B5
Saint-Martin-d'Arrossa (64) 282 D4
Saint-Martin-d'Ary (17) 212 B3
Saint-Martin-d'Aubigny (50) 31 F2
Saint-Martin-d'Audouville (50) 29 F4
Saint-Martin-d'Auxigny (18) 149 G1
Saint-Martin-d'Auxy (71) 171 G1
Saint-Martin-de-Bavel (01) 190 B6
Saint-Martin-de-Beauville (47) 248 D4
Saint-Martin-de-Belleville (73) 209 H6
Saint-Martin-de-Bernegoue (79) . . . 178 B2
Saint-Martin-de-
  Blentaite-la-Cressonnière (14) . . 55 F1
Saint-Martin-de-Blagny (14) 31 J2
Saint-Martin-de-Bonfossé (50) 31 G4
Saint-Martin-de-Boscherville (76) 35 G2
Saint-Martin-de-Bossenay (10) . . . 89 H3
Saint-Martin-de-Boubaux (48) 255 F4
Saint-Martin-de-Bréthencourt (78) . . 86 A2
Saint-Martin-de-Brômes (04) 278 D3
Saint-Martin-de-Caralp (09) 307 H3
Saint-Martin-de-Castillon (84) 277 J3
Saint-Martin-de-Cenilly (50) 31 F5
Saint-Martin-de-Clelles (38) 241 K2
Saint-Martin-de-Commune (71) . . . 153 H5
Saint-Martin-de-Connée (53) 82 A5
Saint-Martin-de-Coux (17) 212 C4
Saint-Martin-de-Crau (13) 276 B5
Saint-Martin-de-Fontenay (14) . . . 32 E5
Saint-Martin-de-Fraigneau (85) . . . 160 E5
Saint-Martin-de-Fressengeas (24) . . 198 B6
Saint-Martin-de-Fugères (43) 238 C1
Saint-Martin-de-Goyne (32) 267 H1
Saint-Martin-de-Gurson (24) 212 E6
Saint-Martin-de-Hinx (40) 262 D6
Saint-Martin-de-Juillers (17) 178 B5
Saint-Martin-de-Jussac (87) 180 E6
Saint-Martin-de-la-Brasque (84) . . . 277 J4
Saint-Martin-de-la-Cluze (38) 224 A6
Saint-Martin-de-la-Lieue (14) 33 K6
Saint-Martin-de-la-Mer (21) 134 C6
Saint-Martin-de-la-Place (49) 126 A5
Saint-Martin-de-la-Porte (73) 225 H2
Saint-Martin-de-Lamps (36) 147 J4
Saint-Martin-de-Landelles (50) 80 B1
Saint-Martin-de-Lansuscle (48) . . . 254 D4
Saint-Martin-de-l'Arçon (34) 291 H1
Saint-Martin-de-Laye (33) 212 A5
Saint-Martin-de-Lenne (12) 253 F2
Saint-Martin-de-Lerm (33) 230 C4
Saint-Martin-de-Lixy (71) 187 G2
Saint-Martin-de-Londres (34) 274 A4
Saint-Martin-de-Mâcon (79) 144 C3
Saint-Martin-de-Mailloc (14) 34 A6
Saint-Martin-de-Mieux (14) 54 A3
Saint-Martin-de-Nigelles (28) 85 H1
Saint-Martin-de-Queyrières (05) . . . 243 K1
Saint-Martin-de-Ré (17) 176 B2
Saint-Martin-de-Ribérac (24) 213 G3
Saint-Martin-de-Saint-Maixent (79) . . 161 K5
Saint-Martin-de-Salencey (71) . . . 171 F4
Saint-Martin-de-Sallen (14) 53 H2
Saint-Martin-de-Sanzay (79) 144 B2
Saint-Martin-de-Seignanx (40) . . . 262 B6
Saint-Martin-de-Sescas (33) 230 B5
Saint-Martin-de-Valamas (07) 239 H1
Saint-Martin-de-Valgalgues (30) . . . 255 G5
Saint-Martin-de-Varreville (50) 29 G5
Saint-Martin-de-Vaulserre (38) . . . 207 K5
Saint-Martin-de-Vers (46) 233 J5
Saint-Martin-de-Villeréal (47) 232 B5
Saint-Martin-de-Villereglan (11) . . . 308 E1
Saint-Martin-d'Écublei (61) 55 J4
Saint-Martin-d'Entraunes (06) 260 E4
Saint-Martin-des-Besaces (14) 31 K5
Saint-Martin-des-Bois (41) 107 K0
Saint-Martin-des-Champs (18) . . . 150 B2
Saint-Martin-des-Champs (29) 47 G4
Saint-Martin-des-Champs (50) 51 K3
Saint-Martin-des-Champs (77) 60 D4
Saint-Martin-des-Champs (78) 57 J3
Saint-Martin-des-Champs (89) . . . 132 B1
Saint-Martin-des-Combes (24) . . . 213 K6
Saint-Martin-des-Entrées (14) 32 B3
Saint-Martin-des-Fontaines (85) . . . 160 D3
Saint-Martin-des-Lais (03) 169 H2
Saint-Martin-des-Landes (61) 82 B1
Saint-Martin-des-Monts (72) 107 H1
Saint-Martin-des-Noyers (85) 160 A1
Saint-Martin-des-Olmes (63) 204 A5
Saint-Martin-des-Pézerits (61) 55 G6
Saint-Martin-des-Plains (63) 203 F5
Saint-Martin-des-Prés (22) 76 E3
Saint-Martin-des-Puits (11) 309 J2
Saint-Martin-des-Tilleuls (85) . . . 142 D3
Saint-Martin-d'Estréaux (42) 186 C2
Saint-Martin-d'Hardinghem (62) . . . 5 F4
Saint-Martin-d'Hères (38) 224 B3
Saint-Martin-d'Heuille (58) 150 E3
Saint-Martin-d'Ollières (63) 203 G6
Saint-Martin-Don (14) 31 J4
Saint-Martin-d'Oney (40) 265 F2
Saint-Martin-d'Ordon (89) 112 C2
Saint-Martin-d'Oydes (09) 288 C6
Saint-Martin-du-Bec (76) 14 B5
Saint-Martin-du-Bois (33) 212 A5
Saint-Martin-du-Bois (49) 104 E1
Saint-Martin-du-Boschet (77) 60 E5
Saint-Martin-du-Clocher (16) 179 G4
Saint-Martin-du-Fouilloux (49) . . . 125 F4
Saint-Martin-du-Fouilloux (79) . . . 162 A3

Saint-Martin-du-Frêne (01) 189 K3
Saint-Martin-du-Lac (71) 186 E2
Saint-Martin-du-Limet (53) 104 C4
Saint-Martin-du-Manoir (76) 14 B6
Saint-Martin-du-Mesnil-Oury (14) . . 54 D1
Saint-Martin-du-Mont (01) 189 H3
Saint-Martin-du-Mont (21) 135 H1
Saint-Martin-du-Mont (71) 172 D2
Saint-Martin-du-Puy (33) 230 C4
Saint-Martin-du-Puy (58) 133 K5
Saint-Martin-du-Tartre (71) 171 G4
Saint-Martin-du-Tertre (89) 88 D6
Saint-Martin-du-Tertre (95) 37 K6
Saint-Martin-du-Tilleul (27) 34 C6
Saint-Martin-du-Var (06) 281 F2
Saint-Martin-du-Vieux-Bellême (61) . . 83 H3
Saint-Martin-du-Vivier (76) 35 J1
Saint-Martin-d'Uriage (38) 224 B3
Saint-Martin-en-Bière (77) 87 G3
Saint-Martin-en-Bresse (71) 154 C6
Saint-Martin-en-Campagne (76) . . . 16 B1
Saint-Martin-en-Gâtinois (71) 154 C4
Saint-Martin-en-Haut (69) 205 H3
Saint-Martin-en-Vercors (26) 223 H5
Saint-Martin-Gimois (32) 287 F2
Saint-Martin-la-Campagne (27) . . . 56 C1
Saint-Martin-la-Garenne (78) 57 J1
Saint-Martin-la-Méanne (19) 216 D4
Saint-Martin-la-Patrouille (71) 171 G3
Saint-Martin-la-Plaine (42) 205 J5
Saint-Martin-la-Sauveté (42) 204 B3
Saint-Martin-Labouval (46) 250 B1
Saint-Martin-Lacaussade (33) 211 G4
Saint-Martin-Laguépie (81) 251 F5
Saint-Martin-l'Aiguillon (61) 54 A6
Saint-Martin Lalande (11) 289 H4
Saint-Martin-l'Ars (86) 180 A3
Saint-Martin-Lars-en-
  Sainte-Hermine (85) 160 C3
Saint-Martin-l'Astier (24) 213 G5
Saint-Martin-le-Beau (37) 128 A5
Saint-Martin-le-Bouillant (50) 52 B4
Saint-Martin-le-Châtel (01) 189 F1
Saint-Martin-le-Colonel (26) 223 G6
Saint-Martin-le-Gaillard (76) 16 C1
Saint-Martin-le-Gréard (50) 28 C3
Saint-Martin-le-Hébert (50) 28 C4
Saint-Martin-le-Mault (87) 164 D6
Saint-Martin-le-Noeud (60) 37 G2
Saint-Martin-le-Pin (24) 197 J5
Saint-Martin-le-Redon (46) 232 D6
Saint-Martin-le-Vieil (11) 289 J4
Saint-Martin-le-Vieux (87) 198 D2
Saint-Martin-le-Vinoux (38) 224 A3
Saint-Martin-les-Eaux (04) 278 B2
Saint-Martin-lès-Langres (52) 116 C4
Saint-Martin-lès-Melle (79) 178 D2
Saint-Martin-lès-Seyne (04) 259 J1
Saint-Martin-Lestra (42) 205 F2
Saint-Martin-l'Heureux (51) 41 J4
Saint-Martin-l'Hortier (76) 16 C4
Saint-Martin-Longueau (60) 38 C3
Saint-Martin-Lys (11) 308 E5
Saint-Martin-Osmonville (76) 16 B5
Saint-Martin-Petit (47) 230 D5
Saint-Martin-Rivière (02) 12 D6
Saint-Martin-Saint-Firmin (27) 34 C4
Saint-Martin-Sainte-Catherine (23) . . 182 A5
Saint-Martin-Sepert (19) 199 H6
Saint-Martin-sous-Montaigu (71) . . . 153 H6
Saint-Martin-sous-Vigouroux (15) . . 236 B1
Saint-Martin-sur-Armançon (89) . . . 114 B4
Saint-Martin-sur-Cojeul (62) 11 F3
Saint-Martin-sur-Écaillon (59) 12 D3
Saint-Martin-sur-la-Chambre (73) . . 209 F6
Saint-Martin-sur-Lavezon (07) . . . 240 A4
Saint-Martin-sur-le-Pré (51) 62 D2
Saint-Martin-sur-Nohain (58) 132 A5
Saint-Martin-sur-Ocre (45) 131 H1
Saint-Martin-sur-Ocre (89) 112 D5
Saint-Martin-sur-Ouanne (89) 112 B5
Saint-Martin-Terressus (87) 181 J6
Saint-Martin-Valmeroux (15) 217 H4
Saint-Martin-Vésubie (06) 261 K5
Saint-Martinien (03) 183 K1
Saint-Martory (31) 287 G6
Saint-Mary (16) 197 G1
Saint-Mary-le-Plain (15) 218 E4
Saint-Masmes (51) 41 H3
Saint-Mathieu (87) 198 A3
Saint-Mathieu-de-Tréviers (34) . . . 274 B4
Saint-Mathurin (85) 159 F3
Saint-Mathurin-sur-Loire (49) 125 J4
Saint-Matré (46) 249 G2
Saint-Maudan (22) 77 F5
Saint-Maudez (22) 50 B5
Saint-Maugan (35) 78 C4
Saint-Maulvis (80) 17 G2
Saint-Maur (18) 166 E3
Saint-Maur (32) 286 A2
Saint-Maur (36) 147 K6
Saint-Maur (39) 173 G2
Saint-Maur (60) 17 H5
Saint-Maur-des-Bois (50) 52 B3
Saint-Maur-des-Fossés (94) 59 F4
Saint-Maur-sur-le-Loir (28) 109 F1
Saint-Maurice (52) 116 D4
Saint-Maurice (58) 151 H1
Saint-Maurice (63) 202 E3
Saint-Maurice (67) 71 A4
Saint-Maurice (94) 59 F4
Saint-Maurice-aux-Forges (54) 95 G1

Saint-Maurice-aux-
  Riches-Hommes (89) 89 F4
Saint-Maurice-Colombier (25) 139 F3
Saint-Maurice-Crillat (39) 173 J3
Saint-Maurice-d'Ardèche (07) 239 H6
Saint-Maurice-de-Beynost (01) . . . 206 C1
Saint-Maurice-de-Cazevieille (30) . . 275 F1
Saint-Maurice-de-Gourdans (01) . . . 206 E1
Saint-Maurice-de-Lestapel (47) . . . 231 J5
Saint-Maurice-de-Lignon (43) 221 F3
Saint-Maurice-de-Rémens (01) . . . 189 G5
Saint-Maurice-de-Satonnay (71) . . . 171 J5
Saint-Maurice-de-Tavernole (17) . . . 195 J5
Saint-Maurice-de-Ventalon (48) . . . 254 E3
Saint-Maurice-des-Champs (71) . . . 171 G2
Saint-Maurice-des-Lions (16) 180 B5
Saint-Maurice-des-Noues (85) 160 E3
Saint-Maurice-d'Ételan (76) 34 D1
Saint-Maurice-d'Ibie (07) 239 J6
Saint-Maurice-du-Désert (61) 53 J6
Saint-Maurice-en-Chalencon (07) . . 239 K2
Saint-Maurice-en-Cotentin (50) . . . 28 C5
Saint-Maurice-en-Gourgois (42) . . . 221 F1
Saint-Maurice-en-Quercy (46) 234 C3
Saint-Maurice-en-Rivière (71) 154 C5
Saint-Maurice-en-Trièves (38) 242 A3
Saint-Maurice-
  en-Valgodemard (05) 242 E2
Saint-Maurice-la-Clouère (86) 163 F6
Saint-Maurice-la-Fougereuse (79) . . 143 J3
Saint-Maurice-la-Souterraine (23) . . 181 J2
Saint-Maurice-le-Girard (85) 160 E2
Saint-Maurice-le-Vieil (89) 112 E5
Saint-Maurice-les-Brousses (87) . . . 108 C3
Saint-Maurice-lès-Charencey (61) . . 55 K6
Saint-Maurice-
  lès-Châteauneuf (71) 187 G2
Saint-Maurice-lès-Couches (71) . . . 153 H5
Saint-Maurice-l'Exil (38) 222 B1
Saint-Maurice-Montcouronne (91) . . 86 C1
Saint-Maurice-Navacelles (34) 273 J3
Saint-Maurice-près-Crocq (23) 201 F1
Saint-Maurice-près-Pionsat (63) . . . 184 A1
Saint-Maurice-Saint-Germain (28) . . 84 C2
Saint-Maurice-sous-les-Côtes (55) . . 65 F1
Saint-Maurice-sur-Adour (40) 265 H4
Saint-Maurice-sur-Aveyron (45) . . . 112 A5
Saint-Maurice-sur-Dargoire (69) . . . 205 J4
Saint-Maurice-sur-Eygues (26) . . . 257 G3
Saint-Maurice-sur-Fessard (45) . . . 111 H3
Saint-Maurice-sur-Huisne (61) 83 J1
Saint-Maurice-sur-Mortagne (88) . . 94 E3
Saint-Maurice-sur-Moselle (88) . . . 119 H3
Saint-Maurice-sur-Vingeanne (21) . . 136 D2
Saint-Maurice-Thizouaille (89) 112 E5
Saint-Maurin (47) 248 E4
Saint-Max (54) 66 A5
Saint-Maxent (80) 17 F5
Saint-Maximin (30) 275 H1
Saint-Maximin (38) 208 C6
Saint-Maximin (60) 38 A5
Saint-Maximin-la-
  Sainte-Baume (83) 297 H2
Saint-Maxire (79) 161 H5
Saint-May (26) 257 K1
Saint-Mayeux (22) 76 D3
Saint-Méard (87) 199 H3
Saint-Méard-de-Drône (24) 213 H3
Saint-Méard-de-Gurçon (24) 230 E1
Saint-Médard (16) 196 B5
Saint-Médard (17) 195 J6
Saint-Médard (31) 306 A1
Saint-Médard (32) 286 B2
Saint-Médard (36) 147 F4
Saint-Médard (46) 233 G6
Saint-Médard (57) 66 E3
Saint-Médard (64) 284 A1
Saint-Médard (79) 178 C2
Saint-Médard-d'Aunis (17) 177 F2
Saint-Médard-de-Guizières (33) . . . 212 C5
Saint-Médard-de-Mussidan (24) . . . 213 G5
Saint-Médard-de-Presque (46) 234 B2
Saint-Médard-d'Excideuil (24) 214 D2
Saint-Médard-d'Eyrans (33) 229 H3
Saint-Médard-en-Forez (42) 205 H4
Saint-Médard-en-Jalles (33) 229 F1
Saint-Médard-la-Rochette (23) 183 F4
Saint-Médard-Nicourby (46) 234 D3
Saint-Médard-sur-Ille (35) 79 G2
Saint-Méen (29) 46 C4
Saint-Méen-le-Grand (35) 78 B3
Saint-Mélaine-sur-Aubance (49) . . . 125 H4
Saint-Mélany (07) 238 E6
Saint-Méloir-des-Bois (22) 50 B5
Saint-Méloir-des-Ondes (35) 50 C2
Saint-Même-le-Tenu (44) 122 E6
Saint-Même-les-Carrières (16) 196 B3
Saint-Memmie (51) 62 D2
Saint-Menge (88) 93 J4
Saint-Menges (08) 23 F3
Saint-Menoux (03) 168 C3
Saint-Merd-de-Lapleau (19) 216 E3
Saint-Merd-la-Breuille (23) 201 G4
Saint-Merd-les-Oussines (19) 200 C4
Saint-Méry (77) 87 J1
Saint-Meslin-du-Bosc (27) 35 F5
Saint-Mesmes (77) 59 H2
Saint-Mesmin (10) 89 K3
Saint-Mesmin (21) 135 G5
Saint-Mesmin (24) 215 F1
Saint-Mesmin (85) 143 G6

Saint-Mexant (19) 215 K2
Saint-Mézard (32) 267 H1
Saint-M'Hervé (35) 80 B6
Saint-M'Hervon (35) 78 C2
Saint-Micaud (71) 171 G2
Saint-Michel (02) 21 H1
Saint-Michel (09) 307 H1
Saint-Michel (16) 196 D3
Saint-Michel (31) 287 H6
Saint-Michel (32) 286 B3
Saint-Michel (34) 273 G3
Saint-Michel (45) 110 E2
Saint-Michel (64) 282 E6
Saint-Michel (82) 268 B1
Saint-Michel-Chef-Chef (44) 122 B4
Saint-Michel-d'Aurance (07) 239 H1
Saint-Michel-de-Bannières (46) . . . 216 A6
Saint-Michel-de-Boulogne (07) . . . 239 H4
Saint-Michel-de-Castelnau (33) . . . 246 E3
Saint-Michel-de-Chabrillanoux (07) . . 239 K2
Saint-Michel-de-Chaillol (05) 243 F3
Saint-Michel-de-Chavaignes (72) . . 107 H2
Saint-Michel-de-Dèze (48) 255 F4
Saint-Michel-de-Double (24) 213 F5
Saint-Michel-de-Feins (53) 105 G5
Saint-Michel-de-Fronsac (33) 230 A1
Saint-Michel-de-la-Roë (53) 104 B4
Saint-Michel-de-Lanès (11) 289 F4
Saint-Michel-de-Lapujade (33) 230 D5
Saint-Michel-de-Livet (14) 54 D1
Saint-Michel-de-Llotes (66) 314 E2
Saint-Michel-de-Maurienne (73) . . . 225 J2
Saint-Michel-de-Montaigne (24) . . . 230 D2
Saint-Michel-de-Montjoie (50) 52 C4
Saint-Michel-de-Plélan (22) 50 B5
Saint-Michel-de-Rieufret (33) 229 J5
Saint-Michel-de-Saint-Geoirs (38) . . 223 G2
Saint-Michel-de-Vax (81) 250 D6
Saint-Michel-de-Veisse (23) 183 F5
Saint-Michel-de-Villadeix (24) 214 A6
Saint-Michel-de-Volangis (18) 149 H2
Saint-Michel-des-Andaines (61) . . . 81 J1
Saint-Michel-d'Euzet (30) 256 B4
Saint-Michel-d'Halescourt (76) 17 F5
Saint-Michel-en-Beaumont (38) . . . 242 C1
Saint-Michel-en-Brenne (36) 146 E6
Saint-Michel-en-Grève (22) 47 H3
Saint-Michel-en-l'Herm (85) 159 K5
Saint-Michel-Escalus (40) 262 D2
Saint-Michel-et-Chanveaux (49) . . . 104 B6
Saint-Michel-Labadié (81) 271 G1
Saint-Michel-le-Cloucq (85) 160 E4
Saint-Michel-les-Portes (38) 241 K1
Saint-Michel-l'Observatoire (04) . . . 278 A2
Saint-Michel-Loubéjou (46) 234 B2
Saint-Michel-Mont-Mercure (85) . . . 142 E5
Saint-Michel-sous-Bois (62) 4 D5
Saint-Michel-sur-Loire (37) 127 F5
Saint-Michel-sur-Meurthe (88) 95 H3
Saint-Michel-sur-Orge (91) 58 E6
Saint-Michel-sur-Rhône (42) 205 K6
Saint-Michel-sur-Savasse (26) 222 E4
Saint-Michel-sur-Ternoise (62) 10 B2
Saint-Michel-Tuboeuf (61) 55 J5
Saint-Mihiel (55) 64 E2
Saint-Mitre-les-Remparts (13) 295 J4
Saint-Molf (44) 121 J3
Saint-Momelin (59) 3 G4
Saint-Mont (32) 266 A5
Saint-Montant (07) 256 C6
Saint-Moré (89) 133 J2
Saint-Moreil (23) 199 K1
Saint-Morel (08) 42 B3
Saint-Morillon (33) 229 H4
Saint-Mury-Monteymond (38) 224 C2
Saint-Myon (63) 185 F5
Saint-Nabor (67) 70 C5
Saint-Nabord (88) 118 E1
Saint-Nabord-sur-Aube (10) 90 C2
Saint-Nauphary (82) 269 G2
Saint-Nazaire (30) 256 C4
Saint-Nazaire (44) 122 A3
Saint-Nazaire (66) 315 H2
Saint-Nazaire-d'Aude (11) 291 G5
Saint-Nazaire-de-Ladarez (34) 291 J2
Saint-Nazaire-de-Pézan (34) 274 E6
Saint-Nazaire-de-Valentane (82) . . . 267 K1
Saint-Nazaire-des-Gardies (30) . . . 274 D1
Saint-Nazaire-en-Royans (26) 223 F5
Saint-Nazaire-le-Désert (26) 241 G5
Saint-Nazaire-les-Eymes (38) 224 B2
Saint-Nazaire-sur-Charente (17) . . . 176 E5
Saint-Nectaire (63) 202 C4
Saint-Nexans (24) 231 J2
Saint-Nic (29) 74 B3
Saint-Nicodème (22) 76 A2
Saint-Nicolas (62) 10 E2
Saint-Nicolas-aux-Bois (02) 20 B6
Saint-Nicolas-d'Aliermont (76) 16 B2
Saint-Nicolas-d'Attez (27) 56 B4
Saint-Nicolas-de-Bliquetuit (76) . . . 34 E1
Saint-Nicolas-de-Bourgueil (37) . . . 126 D6
Saint-Nicolas-de-la-Balerme (47) . . 248 D5
Saint-Nicolas-de-la-Grave (82) . . . 249 F6
Saint-Nicolas-de-la-Haie (76) 15 F6
Saint-Nicolas-de-la-Taille (76) 34 C1
Saint-Nicolas-de-Macherin (38) . . . 207 H6
Saint-Nicolas-de-Pierrepont (50) . . . 28 D6
Saint-Nicolas-de-Port (54) 66 B5
Saint-Nicolas-de-Redon (44) 102 C4
Saint-Nicolas-de-Sommaire (61) . . . 55 J4

Saint-Nicolas-des-Biefs (03) 186 C4
Saint-Nicolas-des-Bois (50) 52 B4
Saint-Nicolas-des-Bois (61) 82 C2
Saint-Nicolas-des-Laitiers (61) 55 G3
Saint-Nicolas-des-Motets (37) 128 C2
Saint-Nicolas-du-Bosc (27) 35 F5
Saint-Nicolas-du-Pélem (22) 76 C2
Saint-Nicolas-du-Tertre (56) 102 A3
Saint-Nicolas-la-Chapelle (10) 89 F2
Saint-Nicolas-la-Chapelle (73) 191 K6
Saint-Nicolas-lès-Cîteaux (21) 154 C2
Saint-Nizier-d'Azergues (69) 187 J4
Saint-Nizier-de-Fornas (42) 220 E5
Saint-Nizier-du-Moucherotte (38) . . 223 K3
Saint-Nizier-le-Bouchoux (01) 172 C4
Saint-Nizier-le-Désert (01) 189 F4
Saint-Nizier-sous-Charlieu (42) . . . 187 F3
Saint-Nizier-sur-Arroux (71) 152 D6
Saint-Nolff (56) 101 G5
Saint-Nom-la-Bretèche (78) 58 B3
Saint-Offenge-Dessous (73) 208 C2
Saint-Offenge-Dessus (73) 208 C2
Saint-Omer (14) 53 J2
Saint-Omer (62) 3 G5
Saint-Omer-Capelle (62) 3 F3
Saint-Omer-en-Chaussée (60) 17 J6
Saint-Ondras (38) 207 H5
Saint-Onen-la-Chapelle (35) 78 B3
Saint-Oradoux-de-Chirouze (23) . . . 201 F2
Saint-Oradoux-près-Crocq (23) . . . 201 G4
Saint-Orens (32) 268 B5
Saint-Orens-de-Gameville (31) 288 C1
Saint-Orens-Pouy-Petit (32) 267 G2
Saint-Ost (32) 286 B3
Saint-Ouen (17) 178 D6
Saint-Ouen (41) 108 C3
Saint-Ouen (80) 9 J6
Saint-Ouen (93) 58 E3
Saint-Ouen-d'Attez (27) 56 B4
Saint-Ouen-d'Aunis (17) 176 E1
Saint-Ouen-de-la-Cour (61) 83 H3
Saint-Ouen-de-Mimbré (72) 82 B4
Saint-Ouen-de-Pontcheuil (27) 35 G4
Saint-Ouen-de-Sécherouve (61) . . . 83 G1
Saint-Ouen-de-Thouberville (27) . . . 35 G4
Saint-Ouen-des-Alleux (35) 79 J1
Saint-Ouen-des-Besaces (14) 31 K4
Saint-Ouen-des-Champs (27) 34 C2
Saint-Ouën-des-Toits (53) 80 D6
Saint-Ouen-des-Vallons (53) 81 G6
Saint-Ouen-Domprot (51) 62 D6
Saint-Ouen-du-Breuil (76) 15 J5
Saint-Ouen-du-Mesnil-Oger (14) . . . 33 G5
Saint-Ouen-du-Tilleul (27) 35 G4
Saint-Ouen-en-Belin (72) 106 E5
Saint-Ouen-en-Brie (77) 87 K1
Saint-Ouen-en-Champagne (72) . . . 106 A3
Saint-Ouen-la-Rouërie (35) 51 J5
Saint-Ouen-l'Aumône (95) 58 C1
Saint-Ouen-le-Brisoult (61) 81 K2
Saint-Ouen-le-Houx (14) 54 E2
Saint-Ouen-le-Mauger (76) 15 J3
Saint-Ouen-le-Pin (14) 33 J4
Saint-Ouen-lès-Parey (88) 93 G5
Saint-Ouen-les-Vignes (37) 128 B4
Saint-Ouen-Marchefroy (28) 57 G3
Saint-Ouen-sous-Bailly (76) 16 B2
Saint-Ouen-sur-Gartempe (87) . . . 181 G2
Saint-Ouen-sur-Iton (61) 55 J5
Saint-Ouen-sur-Loire (58) 151 F5
Saint-Ouen-sur-Maire (61) 54 A5
Saint-Ouen-sur-Morin (77) 60 C3
Saint-Oulph (10) 89 J2
Saint-Ours (63) 202 B2
Saint-Ours (73) 208 C1
Saint-Outrille (18) 148 B2
Saint-Ovin (50) 52 A5
Saint-Oyen (73) 209 H4
Saint-Pabu (29) 72 C2
Saint-Paër (76) 35 F3
Saint-Pair (14) 33 F5
Saint-Pair-sur-Mer (50) 51 H1
Saint-Pal-de-Chalencon (43) 220 C1
Saint-Pal-de-Mons (43) 221 G3
Saint-Pal-de-Senouire (43) 219 K3
Saint-Palais (03) 166 E5
Saint-Palais (18) 149 G1
Saint-Palais (33) 211 H2
Saint-Palais (64) 283 G2
Saint-Palais-de-Négrignac (17) . . . 212 B2
Saint-Palais-de-Phiolin (17) 195 G5
Saint-Palais-du-Né (16) 195 K4
Saint-Palais-sur-Mer (17) 194 B3
Saint-Pancrace (24) 197 K6
Saint-Pancrace (73) 225 G2
Saint-Pancrasse (38) 224 C2
Saint-Pancré (54) 26 A2
Saint-Pandelon (40) 264 B5
Saint-Pantaléon (46) 249 J2
Saint-Pantaléon (84) 277 F2
Saint-Pantaléon-de-Lapleau (19) . . . 217 G2
Saint-Pantaléon-de-Larche (19) . . . 215 H4
Saint-Pantaléon-les-Vignes (26) . . . 257 G2
Saint-Pantaly-d'Ans (24) 214 D3
Saint-Pantaly-d'Excideuil (24) 214 D2
Saint-Papoul (11) 289 H4
Saint-Pardon-de-Conques (33) 230 B5
Saint-Pardoult (17) 178 A4
Saint-Pardoux (63) 184 E4
Saint-Pardoux (79) 161 J3
Saint-Pardoux (87) 181 H4
Saint-Pardoux-Corbier (19) 199 G6

Saint-Pardoux-d'Arnet (23) 201 F1
Saint-Pardoux-de-Drône (24) . . . 213 H3
Saint-Pardoux-du-Breuil (47) . . . 247 H1
Saint-Pardoux-et-Vielvic (24) . . . 232 D3
Saint-Pardoux-Isaac (47) 231 G5
Saint-Pardoux-la-Croisille (19) . . 216 D3
Saint-Pardoux-la-Rivière (24) . . . 197 K5
Saint-Pardoux-le-Neuf (19) 201 F4
Saint-Pardoux-le-Neuf (23) 183 G6
Saint-Pardoux-le-Vieux (19) 201 F4
Saint-Pardoux-les-Cards (23) . . . 183 F4
Saint-Pardoux-l'Ortigier (19) . . . 215 J2
Saint-Pardoux-Morterolles (23) . . 182 C6
Saint-Pargoire (34) 292 D1
Saint-Parize-en-Viry (58) 168 E1
Saint-Parize-le-Châtel (58) 150 E6
Saint-Parres-aux-Tertres (10) 90 B4
Saint-Parres-lès-Vaudes (10) 90 C6
Saint-Parthem (12) 235 G5
Saint-Pastour (47) 248 B1
Saint-Pastous (65) 304 B2
Saint-Paterne (72) 82 D3
Saint-Paterne-Racan (37) 127 G2
Saint-Pathus (77) 59 J1
Saint-Patrice (37) 126 E6
Saint-Patrice-de-Claids (50) 30 E2
Saint-Patrice-du-Désert (61) 81 K1
Saint-Paul (06) 281 F4
Saint-Paul (19) 216 C3
Saint-Paul (33) 211 H4
Saint-Paul (60) 37 G2
Saint-Paul (61) 53 G4
Saint-Paul (65) 305 G1
Saint-Paul (73) 208 A3
Saint-Paul (87) 199 G2
Saint-Paul (88) 93 H4
Saint-Paul-aux-Bois (02) 19 K6
Saint-Paul-Cap-de-Joux (81) . . . 270 C6
Saint-Paul-de-Baïse (32) 267 F4
Saint-Paul-de-Fenouillet (66) . . . 309 H5
Saint-Paul-de-Fourques (27) 35 F4
Saint-Paul-de-Jarrat (09) 307 J3
Saint-Paul-de-Loubressac (46) . . 250 A3
Saint-Paul-de-Salers (15) 217 J4
Saint-Paul-de-Serre (24) 213 K5
Saint-Paul-de-Tartas (43) 238 C3
Saint-Paul-de-Varax (01) 189 F3
Saint-Paul-de-Varces (38) 223 K4
Saint-Paul-de-Vern (46) 234 C2
Saint-Paul-de-Vézelin (42) 187 F6
Saint-Paul-des-Landes (15) 235 G1
Saint-Paul-d'Espis (82) 249 F5
Saint-Paul-d'Izeaux (38) 223 H1
Saint-Paul-d'Oueil (31) 305 H4
Saint-Paul-du-Bois (49) 143 J2
Saint-Paul-du-Vernay (14) 32 A4
Saint-Paul-d'Uzore (42) 204 D3
Saint-Paul-en-Born (40) 244 D4
Saint-Paul-en-Chablais (74) 175 G5
Saint-Paul-en-Cornillon (42) . . . 221 F1
Saint-Paul-en-Forêt (83) 280 B6
Saint-Paul-en-Gâtine (79) 161 F2
Saint-Paul-en-Jarez (42) 205 J5
Saint-Paul-en-Pareds (85) 142 D5
Saint-Paul-et-Valmalle (34) 273 K6
Saint-Paul-la-Coste (30) 255 F5
Saint-Paul-la-Roche (24) 198 C6
Saint-Paul-le-Froid (48) 237 J3
Saint-Paul-le-Gaultier (72) 82 B4
Saint-Paul-le-Jeune (07) 255 H3
Saint-Paul-lès-Dax (40) 264 B4
Saint-Paul-lès-Durance (13) 278 A5
Saint-Paul-les-Fonts (30) 256 C6
Saint-Paul-lès-Monestier (38) . . . 223 K6
Saint-Paul-lès-Romans (26) 222 E5
Saint-Paul-Lizonne (24) 213 G2
Saint-Paul-Mont-Penit (85) 141 H5
Saint-Paul-sur-Isère (73) 209 G3
Saint-Paul-sur-Save (31) 268 C5
Saint-Paul-sur-Ubaye (04) 227 B5
Saint-Paul-Trois-Châteaux (26) . . 256 D2
Saint-Paulet (11) 289 G3
Saint-Paulet-de-Caisson (30) . . . 256 C6
Saint-Paulien (43) 220 B4
Saint-Pavace (72) 106 D2
Saint-Pé-d'Ardet (31) 305 J2
Saint-Pé-de-Bigorre (65) 304 A1
Saint-Pé-de-Léren (64) 283 G1
Saint-Pé-Delbosc (31) 286 E5
Saint-Pé-Saint-Simon (47) 266 D1
Saint-Pée-sur-Nivelle (64) 263 C2
Saint-Pellerin (28) 108 D2
Saint-Pellerin (50) 31 G1
Saint-Péran (35) 78 C5
Saint-Péravy-la-Colombe (45) . . . 109 J3
Saint-Péray (07) 222 C6
Saint-Perdon (40) 265 F2
Saint-Perdoux (24) 231 H4
Saint-Perdoux (46) 234 D4
Saint-Père (35) 50 E4
Saint-Père (58) 132 A4
Saint-Père (89) 133 J4
Saint-Père-en-Retz (44) 122 C4
Saint-Père-sur-Loire (45) 110 E6
Saint-Péreuse (58) 152 A3
Saint-Pern (35) 78 D2
Saint-Perreux (56) 102 A3
Saint-Péver (22) 48 D6
Saint-Pey-d'Armens (33) 230 B2
Saint-Pey-de-Castets (33) 230 C2
Saint-Phal (10) 114 A1
Saint-Philbert-de-Bouaine (85) . . 141 J3

Saint-Philbert-de-Grand-Lieu (44) . . 123 F6
Saint-Philbert-des-Champs (14) . . . 34 A4
Saint-Philbert-du-Peuple (49) . . . 126 B4
Saint-Philbert-en-Mauges (49) . . . 142 D1
Saint-Philbert-sur-Boissey (27) . . . 34 E4
Saint-Philbert-sur-Orne (61) 53 J3
Saint-Philbert-sur-Risle (27) 34 D3
Saint-Philibert (21) 154 C1
Saint-Philibert (56) 100 D6
Saint-Philippe-d'Aiguille (33) . . . 230 C1
Saint-Philippe-du-Seignal (33) . . 231 F2
Saint-Piat (28) 85 H2
Saint-Pierre (04) 280 D1
Saint-Pierre (15) 217 H1
Saint-Pierre (31) 269 G5
Saint-Pierre (39) 173 K3
Saint-Pierre (51) 62 C2
Saint-Pierre (67) 70 D6
Saint-Pierre-à-Arnes (08) 41 J3
Saint-Pierre-Aigle (02) 39 H3
Saint-Pierre-Avez (05) 258 E3
Saint-Pierre-Azif (14) 33 H3
Saint-Pierre-Bellevue (23) 182 D6
Saint-Pierre-Bénouville (76) 15 J4
Saint-Pierre-Bois (67) 70 C6
Saint-Pierre-Brouck (59) 3 F3
Saint-Pierre-Canivet (14) 54 A2
Saint-Pierre-Chérignat (23) 182 A5
Saint-Pierre-Colamine (63) 202 C5
Saint-Pierre-d'Albigny (73) 208 D4
Saint-Pierre-d'Allevard (38) 208 D6
Saint-Pierre-d'Alvey (73) 207 K3
Saint-Pierre-d'Amilly (17) 177 H2
Saint-Pierre-d'Argençon (05) . . . 242 A6
Saint-Pierre-d'Arthéglise (50) . . . 28 C5
Saint-Pierre-d'Aubézies (32) . . . 266 D6
Saint-Pierre-d'Aurillac (33) 230 B5
Saint-Pierre-d'Autils (27) 36 B6
Saint-Pierre-de-Bailleul (27) 36 A6
Saint-Pierre-de-Bat (33) 230 A4
Saint-Pierre-de-Belleville (73) . . . 209 F5
Saint-Pierre-de-Boeuf (42) 222 A1
Saint-Pierre-de-Bressieux (38) . . 223 G2
Saint-Pierre-de-Buzet (47) 247 H4
Saint-Pierre-de-Cernières (27) . . . 55 H2
Saint-Pierre-de-Chandieu (69) . . 206 C3
Saint-Pierre-de-Chartreuse (38) . . 224 B1
Saint-Pierre-de-Chérennes (38) . . 223 G4
Saint-Pierre-de-Chevillé (72) . . . 127 G1
Saint-Pierre-de-Chignac (24) . . . 214 B4
Saint-Pierre-de-Clairac (47) 248 D5
Saint-Pierre-de-Côle (24) 214 B1
Saint-Pierre-de-Colombier (07) . . 239 G4
Saint-Pierre-de-Cormeilles (27) . . 34 B4
Saint-Pierre-de-Coutances (50) . . 30 E4
Saint-Pierre-de-Curtille (73) . . . 208 A1
Saint-Pierre-de-Frugie (24) 198 C4
Saint-Pierre-de-Fursac (23) 181 K3
Saint-Pierre-de-Genebroz (73) . . 207 K5
Saint-Pierre-de-Jards (36) 148 C3
Saint-Pierre-de-Juillers (17) 178 B5
Saint-Pierre-de-la-Fage (34) 273 H4
Saint-Pierre-de-Lages (31) 288 D1
Saint-Pierre-de-Lamps (36) 147 H4
Saint-Pierre-de-l'Île (17) 178 A4
Saint-Pierre-de-Maillé (86) 164 A2
Saint-Pierre-de-Mailloc (14) 34 A6
Saint-Pierre-de-Manneville (76) . . 35 G2
Saint-Pierre-de-Méaroz (38) . . . 242 B1
Saint-Pierre-de-Mésage (38) . . . 224 B5
Saint-Pierre-de-Mézoargues (13) . . 275 K3
Saint-Pierre-de-Mons (33) 230 A5
Saint-Pierre-de-Nogaret (48) . . . 253 H1
Saint-Pierre-de-Plesguen (35) . . . 50 E5
Saint-Pierre-de-Rivière (09) 307 H3
Saint-Pierre-de-Salerne (27) 34 D5
Saint-Pierre-de-Semilly (50) 31 J3
Saint-Pierre-de-Soucy (73) 208 D5
Saint-Pierre-de-Trivisy (81) 271 G4
Saint-Pierre-de-Varengeville (76) . . 35 G1
Saint-Pierre-de-Varennes (71) . . . 153 H5
Saint-Pierre-de-Vassols (84) 257 H5
Saint-Pierre-dels-Forcats (66) . . . 313 J4
Saint-Pierre-d'Entremont (38) . . . 208 B6
Saint-Pierre-d'Entremont (61) . . . 53 G4
Saint-Pierre-d'Entremont (73) . . . 208 B6
Saint-Pierre-des-Bois (72) 106 A3
Saint-Pierre-des-Champs (11) . . . 309 J2
Saint-Pierre-des-Corps (37) 127 J4
Saint-Pierre-des-
  Échaubrognes (79) 143 G3
Saint-Pierre-des-Fleurs (27) 35 G4
Saint-Pierre-des-Ifs (14) 33 J6
Saint-Pierre-des-Ifs (27) 34 D4
Saint-Pierre-des-Jonquières (76) . . 16 D2
Saint-Pierre-des-Landes (53) 80 C4
Saint-Pierre-des-Loges (61) 55 G5
Saint-Pierre-des-Nids (53) 82 B3
Saint-Pierre-des-Ormes (72) 83 G4
Saint-Pierre-des-Tripiers (48) . . . 253 J4
Saint-Pierre-d'Exideuil (86) 179 H3
Saint-Pierre-d'Eyraud (24) 231 G2
Saint-Pierre-d'Irube (64) 282 B1
Saint-Pierre-d'Oléron (17) 176 B5
Saint-Pierre-du-Bosguérard (27) . . 35 F4
Saint-Pierre-du-Bû (14) 54 A3
Saint-Pierre-du-Champ (43) 220 C3
Saint-Pierre-du-Chemin (85) . . . 161 F1
Saint-Pierre-du-Fresne (14) 53 F1
Saint-Pierre-du-Jonquet (14) 33 G5
Saint-Pierre-du-Lorouër (72) . . . 107 H5
Saint-Pierre-du-Mesnil (27) 55 H2

Saint-Pierre-du-Mont (14) 29 J6
Saint-Pierre-du-Mont (40) 265 G2
Saint-Pierre-du-Mont (58) 133 F5
Saint-Pierre-du-Palais (17) 212 B4
Saint-Pierre-du-Perray (91) 87 F1
Saint-Pierre-du-Regard (61) 53 H3
Saint-Pierre-du-Val (27) 34 B2
Saint-Pierre-du-Vauvray (27) 35 J4
Saint-Pierre-Église (50) 28 E2
Saint-Pierre-en-Faucigny (74) . . . 191 H3
Saint-Pierre-en-Port (76) 14 E3
Saint-Pierre-en-Val (76) 8 C6
Saint-Pierre-en-Vaux (21) 153 H3
Saint-Pierre-es-Champs (60) 36 D2
Saint-Pierre-Eynac (43) 220 D5
Saint-Pierre-la-Bourlhonne (63) . . 203 K4
Saint-Pierre-la-Bruyère (61) 83 K4
Saint-Pierre-la-Cour (53) 104 C1
Saint-Pierre-la-Garenne (27) 36 A5
Saint-Pierre-la-Noaille (42) 187 F2
Saint-Pierre-la-Palud (69) 205 J1
Saint-Pierre-la-Rivière (61) 54 E4
Saint-Pierre-la-Roche (07) 239 K4
Saint-Pierre-la-Vieille (14) 53 H2
Saint-Pierre-Lafeuille (46) 233 H6
Saint-Pierre-Langers (50) 51 J1
Saint-Pierre-Laval (03) 186 C2
Saint-Pierre-Lavis (76) 15 F5
Saint-Pierre-le-Bost (23) 166 E6
Saint-Pierre-le-Chastel (63) 202 B2
Saint-Pierre-le-Moûtier (58) 168 C1
Saint-Pierre-le-Vieux (48) 237 G2
Saint-Pierre-le-Vieux (71) 187 K1
Saint-Pierre-le-Vieux (76) 15 H3
Saint-Pierre-le-Vieux (85) 160 E5
Saint-Pierre-le-Viger (76) 15 H3
Saint-Pierre-lès-Bitry (60) 39 G2
Saint-Pierre-les-Bois (18) 166 E2
Saint-Pierre-lès-Elbeuf (76) 35 H4
Saint-Pierre-lès-Étieux (18) 167 H1
Saint-Pierre-lès-Franqueville (02) . . 20 E3
Saint-Pierre-lès-Nemours (77) . . . 87 H5
Saint-Pierre-Montlimart (49) . . . 124 C5
Saint-Pierre-Quiberon (56) 120 B1
Saint-Pierre-Roche (63) 202 B2
Saint-Pierre-Saint-Jean (07) 255 H1
Saint-Pierre-sur-Dives (14) 54 C1
Saint-Pierre-sur-Doux (07) 221 H4
Saint-Pierre-sur-Dropt (47) 230 E4
Saint-Pierre-sur-Erve (53) 105 J2
Saint-Pierre-sur-Orthe (53) 82 A5
Saint-Pierre-sur-Vence (08) 22 C4
Saint-Pierre-Tarentaine (14) 53 F2
Saint-Pierre-Toirac (46) 234 C6
Saint-Pierremont (02) 21 F4
Saint-Pierremont (08) 42 D1
Saint-Pierremont (88) 94 E2
Saint-Pierreville (07) 239 J2
Saint-Pierrevillers (55) 26 C4
Saint-Plaisir (03) 168 B3
Saint-Plancard (31) 286 C6
Saint-Planchers (50) 51 J1
Saint-Plantaire (36) 165 J5
Saint-Point (71) 171 H6
Saint-Point-Lac (25) 156 E5
Saint-Pois (50) 52 C4
Saint-Poix (53) 104 C3
Saint-Pol-de-Léon (29) 47 F3
Saint-Pol-sur-Mer (59) 3 H1
Saint-Pol-sur-Ternoise (62) 10 B1
Saint-Polgues (42) 186 E6
Saint-Polycarpe (11) 309 F2
Saint-Pompain (79) 161 F5
Saint-Pompont (24) 232 E4
Saint-Poncy (15) 219 F4
Saint-Pons (04) 260 C1
Saint-Pons (07) 239 K5
Saint-Pons-de-Mauchiens (34) . . 292 D2
Saint-Pons-de-Thomières (34) . . 291 F2
Saint-Pons-la-Calm (30) 256 B5
Saint-Pont (03) 185 H3
Saint-Porchaire (17) 194 E1
Saint-Porquier (82) 268 E1
Saint-Pôtan (22) 50 A4
Saint-Pouange (10) 90 A5
Saint-Pourçain-sur-Besbre (03) . . 169 H5
Saint-Pourçain-sur-Sioule (03) . . 185 H1
Saint-Prancher (88) 93 J3
Saint-Préjet-Armandon (43) 219 J3
Saint-Préjet-d'Allier (43) 237 K1
Saint-Prest (28) 85 G2
Saint-Preuil (16) 196 A4
Saint-Priest (07) 239 J4
Saint-Priest (23) 183 H4
Saint-Priest (69) 206 B3
Saint-Priest-Bramefant (63) 185 J4
Saint-Priest-d'Andelot (03) 185 G4
Saint-Priest-de-Gimel (19) 216 C2
Saint-Priest-des-Champs (63) . . . 184 C5
Saint-Priest-en-Jarez (42) 205 G5
Saint-Priest-en-Murat (03) 168 A6
Saint-Priest-la-Feuille (23) 181 K2
Saint-Priest-la-Marche (18) 166 D5
Saint-Priest-la-Plaine (23) 182 B2
Saint-Priest-la-Prugne (42) 186 B5
Saint-Priest-la-Roche (42) 187 F6
Saint-Priest-la-Vêtre (42) 204 A1
Saint-Priest-les-Fougères (24) . . 198 C5
Saint-Priest-Ligoure (87) 199 F3
Saint-Priest-Palus (23) 182 B6
Saint-Priest-sous-Aixe (87) 198 D1
Saint-Priest-Taurion (87) 181 J6

Saint-Prim (38) 206 A6
Saint-Privat (07) 239 H5
Saint-Privat (19) 216 E4
Saint-Privat (34) 273 H4
Saint-Privat-d'Allier (43) 220 A6
Saint-Privat-de-Champclos (30) . . 255 K3
Saint-Privat-de-Vallongue (48) . . 254 E3
Saint-Privat-des-Prés (24) 213 F3
Saint-Privat-des-Vieux (30) 255 H5
Saint-Privat-du-Dragon (43) . . . 219 H4
Saint-Privat-du-Fau (48) 237 G1
Saint-Privat-la-Montagne (57) . . . 27 F6
Saint-Privé (71) 171 G1
Saint-Privé (89) 132 A1
Saint-Prix (03) 186 A2
Saint-Prix (07) 239 J1
Saint-Prix (71) 152 C4
Saint-Prix (95) 58 D1
Saint-Prix-lès-Arnay (21) 153 F2
Saint-Projet (46) 233 H3
Saint-Projet (82) 250 D3
Saint-Projet-de-Salers (15) 217 J5
Saint-Projet-Saint-Constant (16) . . 197 G2
Saint-Prouant (85) 142 D6
Saint-Pryvé-Saint-Mesmin (45) . . 109 K4
Saint-Puy (32) 267 G3
Saint-Python (59) 12 E4
Saint-Quantin-de-Rançanne (17) . . 195 G5
Saint-Quay-Perros (22) 48 A2
Saint-Quay-Portrieux (22) 49 F4
Saint-Quentin (02) 19 K2
Saint-Quentin-au-Bosc (76) 16 C1
Saint-Quentin-de-Baron (33) . . . 230 A2
Saint-Quentin-de-Blavou (61) . . . 83 H2
Saint-Quentin-de-Caplong (33) . . 230 E3
Saint-Quentin-de-Chalais (16) . . 212 D2
Saint-Quentin-des-Isles (27) 55 H1
Saint-Quentin-des-Prés (60) 36 E1
Saint-Quentin-du-Dropt (47) . . . 231 J4
Saint-Quentin-en-Mauges (49) . . 124 D5
Saint-Quentin-en-Tourmont (80) . . 8 E3
Saint-Quentin-Fallavier (38) 206 D3
Saint-Quentin-la-Chabanne (23) . . 200 E1
Saint-Quentin-la-Motte-
  Croix-au-Bailly (80) 8 C5
Saint-Quentin-la-Poterie (30) . . . 256 A6
Saint-Quentin-la-Tour (09) 308 E2
Saint-Quentin-le-Petit (08) 21 H2
Saint-Quentin-le-Verger (51) 61 H6
Saint-Quentin-les-Anges (53) . . . 104 D5
Saint-Quentin-lès-
  Beaurepaire (49) 126 B1
Saint-Quentin-les-
  Chardonnets (61) 53 F4
Saint-Quentin-les-Marais (51) . . . 63 G4
Saint-Quentin-sur-Charente (16) . . 197 K1
Saint-Quentin-sur-Cher (41) . . . 129 F5
Saint-Quentin-sur-Coole (51) . . . 62 D3
Saint-Quentin-sur-Indrois (37) . . 146 D1
Saint-Quentin-sur-Isère (38) . . . 223 J2
Saint-Quentin-sur-le-Homme (50) . . 52 A5
Saint-Quentin-sur-Nohain (58) . . 132 B5
Saint-Quentin-sur-
  Sauxillanges (63) 203 G5
Saint-Quintin-sur-Sioule (63) . . . 185 F4
Saint-Quirc (09) 288 C5
Saint-Quirin (57) 67 J5
Saint-Rabier (24) 214 E4
Saint-Racho (71) 187 H1
Saint-Rambert-d'Albon (26) 222 B2
Saint-Rambert-en-Bugey (01) . . . 189 J5
Saint-Raphaël (24) 214 E2
Saint-Raphaël (83) 299 G2
Saint-Régis-du-Coin (42) 221 H2
Saint-Règle (37) 128 C4
Saint-Remèze (07) 256 B2
Saint-Remimont (54) 94 B1
Saint-Remimont (88) 93 J5
Saint-Rémy (01) 189 F2
Saint-Rémy (12) 251 G2
Saint-Rémy (14) 53 H2
Saint-Rémy (19) 201 F3
Saint-Rémy (21) 134 D1
Saint-Rémy (21) 230 E1
Saint-Remy (70) 118 A4
Saint-Rémy (71) 171 J1
Saint-Rémy (79) 161 G5
Saint-Remy (88) 95 G3
Saint-Rémy-au-Bois (62) 9 G2
Saint-Rémy-aux-Bois (54) 94 C2
Saint-Rémy-Blanzy (02) 39 J4
Saint-Rémy-Boscrocourt (76) 8 C6
Saint-Remy-Chaussée (59) 13 G4
Saint-Rémy-de-Blot (63) 184 D4
Saint-Rémy-de-Chargnat (63) . . . 203 F5
Saint-Rémy-de-Chaudes-
  Aigues (15) 236 D3
Saint-Rémy-de-Maurienne (73) . . 209 F6
Saint-Rémy-de-Provence (13) . . . 276 B4
Saint-Rémy-de-Sillé (72) 82 B6
Saint-Rémy-des-Landes (50) 28 C6
Saint-Rémy-des-Monts (72) 83 G4
Saint-Remy-du-Nord (59) 13 G3
Saint-Rémy-du-Plain (35) 79 H1
Saint-Rémy-du-Val (72) 82 E4
Saint-Rémy-en-Bouzemont-
  Saint-Genest-et-Isson (51) . . . 63 G6
Saint-Remy-en-l'Eau (60) 38 A1
Saint-Rémy-en-Mauges (49) 124 B5
Saint-Rémy-en-Rollat (03) 185 J3
Saint-Rémy-la-Calonne (55) 43 K6
Saint-Rémy-la-Vanne (77) 60 C4
Saint-Rémy-la-Varenne (49) 125 J4

Saint-Remy-le-Petit (08) 41 H2
Saint-Rémy-lès-Chevreuse (78) . . . 58 C5
Saint-Rémy-l'Honoré (78) 58 A5
Saint-Remy-sous-Barbuise (10) . . . 90 B2
Saint-Remy-sous-Broyes (51) 61 H5
Saint-Rémy-sur-Avre (28) 56 E5
Saint-Rémy-sur-Bussy (51) 42 A4
Saint-Rémy-sur-Creuse (86) 146 A4
Saint-Rémy-sur-Durolle (63) 186 A6
Saint-Renan (29) 72 C4
Saint-Restitut (26) 256 D2
Saint-Révérend (85) 158 E1
Saint-Révérien (58) 151 H1
Saint-Rieul (22) 77 K1
Saint-Rigomer-des-Bois (72) 82 D3
Saint-Rimay (41) 108 B6
Saint-Riquier (80) 9 H5
Saint-Riquier-en-Rivière (76) 16 E2
Saint-Riquier-ès-Plains (76) 15 F3
Saint-Rirand (42) 186 C4
Saint-Rivoal (29) 74 E1
Saint-Robert (19) 215 G3
Saint-Robert (47) 248 D4
Saint-Roch (37) 127 H4
Saint-Roch-sur-Égrenne (61) 81 F1
Saint-Rogatien (17) 176 E2
Saint-Romain (16) 212 E2
Saint-Romain (21) 153 J3
Saint-Romain (63) 204 B5
Saint-Romain (86) 179 J2
Saint-Romain-au-Mont-d'Or (69) . . 206 A1
Saint-Romain-d'Ay (07) 222 A4
Saint-Romain-de-Benet (17) 194 E2
Saint-Romain-de-Colbosc (76) . . . 14 D6
Saint-Romain-de-Jalionas (38) . . 206 E2
Saint-Romain-de-Lerps (07) 222 B6
Saint-Romain-de-Monpazier (24) . . 232 B4
Saint-Romain-de-Popey (69) . . . 205 H1
Saint-Romain-de-Surieu (38) . . . 222 C1
Saint-Romain-d'Urfé (42) 186 C6
Saint-Romain-en-Gal (69) 206 B5
Saint-Romain-en-Gier (69) 205 K4
Saint-Romain-en-Jarez (42) 205 H4
Saint-Romain-en-Viennois (84) . . 257 H3
Saint-Romain-et-
  Saint-Clément (24) 198 B6
Saint-Romain-la-Motte (42) 186 E4
Saint-Romain-la-Virvée (33) 211 J6
Saint-Romain-Lachalm (43) 221 G2
Saint-Romain-le-Noble (47) 248 D5
Saint-Romain-le-Preux (89) 112 D3
Saint-Romain-le-Puy (42) 204 D5
Saint-Romain-les-Atheux (42) . . . 221 G1
Saint-Romain-sous-Gourdon (71) . . 170 E3
Saint-Romain-sous-Versigny (71) . . 170 C2
Saint-Romain-sur-Cher (41) 129 F5
Saint-Romain-sur-Gironde (17) . . 194 E5
Saint-Roman (26) 241 H4
Saint-Roman-de-Codières (30) . . 274 A1
Saint-Roman-de-Malegarde (84) . . 257 F3
Saint-Romans (38) 223 G4
Saint-Romans-des-Champs (79) . . 178 B2
Saint-Romans-lès-Melle (79) . . . 178 D2
Saint-Rome (31) 288 E3
Saint-Rome-de-Cernon (12) 272 C1
Saint-Rome-de-Dolan (48) 253 H4
Saint-Rome-de-Tarn (12) 272 B1
Saint-Romphaire (50) 31 H4
Saint-Rustice (31) 269 F4
Saint-Saëns (76) 16 B5
Saint-Saire (76) 16 D4
Saint-Salvadou (12) 251 G4
Saint-Salvadour (19) 216 B1
Saint-Salvi-de-Carcavès (81) . . . 271 J4
Saint-Salvy (47) 247 K3
Saint-Salvy-de-la-Balme (81) . . . 271 G6
Saint-Samson (14) 33 G5
Saint-Samson (53) 82 A2
Saint-Samson-de-Bonfossé (50) . . . 31 G4
Saint-Samson-de-la-Roque (27) . . . 34 B2
Saint-Samson-la-Poterie (60) 17 F6
Saint-Samson-sur-Rance (22) 50 D5
Saint-Sandoux (63) 202 D4
Saint-Santin (12) 235 F5
Saint-Santin-Cantalès (15) 217 F6
Saint-Santin-de-Maurs (15) 235 F5
Saint-Sardos (47) 248 A3
Saint-Sardos (82) 268 D2
Saint-Satur (18) 131 K5
Saint-Saturnin (15) 218 B3
Saint-Saturnin (16) 196 D3
Saint-Saturnin (18) 166 D4
Saint-Saturnin (48) 253 H2
Saint-Saturnin (51) 61 K6
Saint-Saturnin (63) 202 D3
Saint-Saturnin (72) 106 D2
Saint-Saturnin-de-Lenne (12) . . . 253 F2
Saint-Saturnin-de-Lucian (34) . . . 273 H5
Saint-Saturnin-du-Bois (17) 177 H3
Saint-Saturnin-du-Limet (53) . . . 104 B4
Saint-Saturnin-lès-Apt (84) 277 H1
Saint-Saturnin-lès-Avignon (84) . . 276 C1
Saint-Saturnin-sur-Loire (49) . . . 125 H4
Saint-Saud-Lacoussière (24) . . . 198 A5
Saint-Saulge (58) 151 H2
Saint-Saulve (59) 12 D1
Saint-Saury (15) 234 E2
Saint-Sauvant (17) 195 H2
Saint-Sauvant (86) 162 C6
Saint-Sauves-d'Auvergne (63) . . . 201 K4
Saint-Sauveur (05) 243 J5

Saint-Sauveur (21) 136 E4
Saint-Sauveur (24) 201 J4
Saint-Sauveur (29) 46 E6
Saint-Sauveur (31) 269 G4
Saint-Sauveur (33) 210 A3
Saint-Sauveur (38) 223 G4
Saint-Sauveur (54) 67 J6
Saint-Sauveur (60) 38 D3
Saint-Sauveur (70) 118 D4
Saint-Sauveur (80) 18 A1
Saint-Sauveur (86) 145 K6
Saint-Sauveur-Camprieu (30) 254 A6
Saint-Sauveur-d'Aunis (17) 177 G2
Saint-Sauveur-de-Carrouges (61) . . 82 B1
Saint-Sauveur-de-Cruzières (07) . . 255 J3
Saint-Sauveur-de-Flée (49) 104 E5
Saint-Sauveur-de-Ginestoux (48) . . 237 K4
Saint-Sauveur-de-Landemont (49) . 123 K3
Saint-Sauveur-de-Meilhan (47) . . . 247 F1
Saint-Sauveur-de-Montagut (07) . . 239 K2
Saint-Sauveur-de-Peyre (48) 237 G4
Saint-Sauveur-de-Pierrepont (50) . . 28 C6
Saint-Sauveur-de-Puynormand (33) 212 C6
Saint-Sauveur-d'Émalleville (76) . . 14 C5
Saint-Sauveur-des-Landes (35) . . 79 K1
Saint-Sauveur-en-Diois (26) . . . 241 F4
Saint-Sauveur-en-Puisaye (89) . . 132 C2
Saint-Sauveur-en-Rue (42) 221 J2
Saint-Sauveur-Gouvernet (26) . . . 257 K2
Saint-Sauveur-la-Pommeraye (50) . 51 J1
Saint-Sauveur-la-Sagne (63) . . . 219 K1
Saint-Sauveur-la-Vallée (46) . . . 233 J5
Saint-Sauveur-Lalande (24) 213 F6
Saint-Sauveur-le-Vicomte (50) . . . 28 D5
Saint-Sauveur-Lendelin (50) . . . 30 E3
Saint-Sauveur-lès-Bray (77) 88 C3
Saint-Sauveur-Marville (28) 84 E1
Saint-Sauveur-sur-École (77) . . . 87 G2
Saint-Sauveur-sur-Tinée (06) . . . 261 H5
Saint-Sauvier (03) 166 E6
Saint-Sauvy (32) 268 A5
Saint-Savin (33) 211 J4
Saint-Savin (38) 207 F3
Saint-Savin (65) 304 A4
Saint-Savin (86) 164 A3
Saint-Savinien (17) 177 H6
Saint-Saviol (86) 179 H3
Saint-Savournin (13) 296 E2
Saint-Sébastien (23) 165 G6
Saint-Sébastien (38) 242 B1
Saint-Sébastien-d'Aigrefeuille (30) . 255 G6
Saint-Sébastien-de-Morsent (27) . . 56 C1
Saint-Sébastien-de-Raids (50) . . 30 E2
Saint-Sébastien-sur-Loire (44) . . 123 H4
Saint-Secondin (86) 163 G6
Saint-Ségal (29) 74 D3
Saint-Séglin (35) 102 D1
Saint-Seine (58) 169 K1
Saint-Seine-en-Bâche (21) . . . 155 F2
Saint-Seine-l'Abbaye (21) 135 H4
Saint-Seine-sur-Vingeanne (21) . . 136 E2
Saint-Selve (33) 229 H4
Saint-Senier-de-Beuvron (50) . . 52 A6
Saint-Senier-sous-Avranches (50) . 51 K3
Saint-Senoch (37) 146 C3
Saint-Senoux (35) 103 F1
Saint-Sériès (34) 274 E4
Saint-Sernin (07) 239 H5
Saint-Sernin (11) 289 F5
Saint-Sernin (47) 231 F4
Saint-Sernin-du-Bois (71) . . . 153 G6
Saint-Sernin-du-Plain (71) . . . 153 J5
Saint-Sernin-lès-Lavaur (81) . . . 289 H1
Saint-Sernin-sur-Rance (12) . . . 271 J3
Saint-Sérotin (89) 88 C5
Saint-Servais (22) 76 A1
Saint-Servais (29) 46 D5
Saint-Servant (56) 101 J2
Saint-Setiers (19) 200 D3
Saint-Seurin-de-Bourg (33) . . . 211 H5
Saint-Seurin-de-Cadourne (33) . . 211 F2
Saint-Seurin-de-Cursac (33) . . . 211 G3
Saint-Seurin-de-Palenne (17) . . . 195 H3
Saint-Seurin-de-Prats (24) 230 D2
Saint-Seurin-sur-l'Isle (33) 212 D5
Saint-Sève (33) 230 C5
Saint-Sever (40) 265 G4
Saint-Sever-Calvados (14) 52 C3
Saint-Sever-de-Rustan (65) 285 K3
Saint-Sever-de-Saintonge (17) . . 195 H3
Saint-Sever-du-Moustier (12) . . . 271 K4
Saint-Séverin (16) 213 F2
Saint-Séverin-d'Estissac (24) . . . 213 H5
Saint-Séverin-sur-Boutonne (17) . . 178 A3
Saint-Siffret (30) 275 H1
Saint-Sigismond (45) 109 J3
Saint-Sigismond (49) 124 C3
Saint-Sigismond (74) 192 A3
Saint-Sigismond (85) 160 E6
Saint-Sigismond-de-Clermont (17) . 195 H6
Saint-Silvain-Bas-le-Roc (23) . . . 183 G1
Saint-Silvain-Bellegarde (23) . . . 183 H1
Saint-Silvain-Montaigut (23) . . . 182 C3
Saint-Silvain-sous-Toulx (23) . . . 183 G1
Saint-Siméon (27) 34 C4
Saint-Siméon (61) 81 F2
Saint-Siméon (77) 60 C4
Saint-Siméon-de-Bressieux (38) . . 223 F1
Saint-Simeux (16) 196 C3
Saint-Simon (02) 19 J4
Saint-Simon (15) 235 J1

Saint-Simon (16) 196 B3
Saint-Simon (46) 234 B4
Saint-Simon-de-Bordes (17) . . . 195 H6
Saint-Simon-de-Pellouaille (17) . . 195 F3
Saint-Sixt (74) 191 H3
Saint-Sixte (42) 204 C2
Saint-Sixte (47) 248 D5
Saint-Solve (19) 215 H2
Saint-Sorlin (69) 205 J4
Saint-Sorlin-d'Arves (73) . . . 225 F2
Saint-Sorlin-de-Conac (17) . . . 211 G1
Saint-Sorlin-de-Morestel (38) . . 207 H3
Saint-Sorlin-de-Vienne (38) . . . 206 B5
Saint-Sorlin-en-Bugey (01) . . . 189 H6
Saint-Sorlin-en-Valloire (26) . . . 222 C2
Saint-Sornin (03) 168 B5
Saint-Sornin (16) 197 G3
Saint-Sornin (17) 194 C1
Saint-Sornin-la-Marche (87) . . . 180 E2
Saint-Sornin-Lavolps (19) . . . 215 H1
Saint-Sornin-Leulac (87) . . . 181 H2
Saint-Soulan (32) 287 F2
Saint-Souplet (59) 12 D5
Saint-Souplet-sur-Py (51) 41 K4
Saint-Soupplets (77) 59 J1
Saint-Sozy (46) 233 J2
Saint-Stail (88) 95 K3
Saint-Suliac (35) 50 D4
Saint-Sulpice (01) 172 B6
Saint-Sulpice (41) 128 C2
Saint-Sulpice (46) 234 B6
Saint-Sulpice (49) 125 H4
Saint-Sulpice (53) 105 F3
Saint-Sulpice (58) 151 F3
Saint-Sulpice (60) 37 H3
Saint-Sulpice (63) 201 J4
Saint-Sulpice (70) 138 D2
Saint-Sulpice (73) 208 A4
Saint-Sulpice (81) 269 K4
Saint-Sulpice-d'Arnoult (17) . . . 194 E1
Saint-Sulpice-de-Cognac (16) . . . 195 J2
Saint-Sulpice-de-Faleyrens (33) . . 230 B1
Saint-Sulpice-de-Favières (91) . . 86 D2
Saint-Sulpice-de-Grimbouville (27) . 34 B2
Saint-Sulpice-de-Guilleragues (33) . 230 D5
Saint-Sulpice-de-Mareuil (24) . . . 197 H6
Saint-Sulpice-de-Pommiers (33) . . 230 B1
Saint-Sulpice-de-Roumagnac (24) . 213 H3
Saint-Sulpice-de-Royan (17) . . . 194 C3
Saint-Sulpice-de-Ruffec (16) . . . 179 H5
Saint-Sulpice-des-Landes (35) . . 103 G3
Saint-Sulpice-des-Landes (44) . . 124 A2
Saint-Sulpice-des-Rivoires (38) . . 207 J5
Saint-Sulpice-d'Excideuil (24) . . 214 D1
Saint-Sulpice-en-Pareds (85) . . . 160 D2
Saint-Sulpice-et-Cameyrac (33) . . 229 J1
Saint-Sulpice-la-Forêt (35) . . . 79 H3
Saint-Sulpice-Laurière (87) . . . 181 K4
Saint-Sulpice-le-Dunois (23) . . . 182 C1
Saint-Sulpice-le-Guérétois (23) . . 182 C2
Saint-Sulpice-le-Verdon (85) . . . 141 K4
Saint-Sulpice-les-Bois (19) . . . 200 D4
Saint-Sulpice-les-Champs (23) . . 182 E5
Saint-Sulpice-les-Feuilles (87) . . 181 J1
Saint-Sulpice-sur-Lèze (31) . . . 288 K4
Saint-Sulpice-sur-Risle (61) . . . 55 J4
Saint-Supplet (54) 26 C4
Saint-Sylvain (14) 33 F4
Saint-Sylvain (19) 216 C4
Saint-Sylvain (76) 15 F2
Saint-Sylvain-d'Anjou (49) . . . 125 H3
Saint-Sylvestre (07) 222 B6
Saint-Sylvestre (74) 190 E6
Saint-Sylvestre (87) 181 J5
Saint-Sylvestre-Cappel (59) . . . 3 K5
Saint-Sylvestre-de-Cormeilles (27) . 34 B4
Saint-Sylvestre-Pragoulin (63) . . 105 J4
Saint-Sylvestre-sur-Lot (47) . . . 248 D2
Saint-Symphorien (18) 149 F6
Saint-Symphorien (27) 34 C3
Saint-Symphorien (33) 246 A1
Saint-Symphorien (48) 237 K2
Saint-Symphorien (72) 106 B1
Saint-Symphorien (79) 178 A1
Saint-Symphorien-d'Ancelles (71) . 188 B2
Saint-Symphorien-de-Lay (42) . . 187 G5
Saint-Symphorien-de-Mahun (07) . 221 J4
Saint-Symphorien-de-Marmagne (71) . . . 153 F6
Saint-Symphorien-de-Thénières (12) . . . 236 A4
Saint-Symphorien-des-Bois (71) . . 170 D6
Saint-Symphorien-des-Bruyères (61) . . . 55 H4
Saint-Symphorien-des-Monts (50) . 80 D1
Saint-Symphorien-d'Ozon (69) . . 206 B3
Saint-Symphorien-le-Château (28) . 85 J2
Saint-Symphorien-le-Valois (50) . . 30 D1
Saint-Symphorien-sous-Chomérac (07) . . . 240 A3
Saint-Symphorien-sur-Coise (69) . . 205 G3
Saint-Symphorien-sur-Couze (87) . 181 G4
Saint-Symphorien-sur-Saône (21) . . 154 E2
Saint-Thégonnec (29) 47 F5
Saint-Thélo (22) 77 F4
Saint-Théodorit (30) 274 E2
Saint-Théoffrey (38) 224 B5
Saint-Thibaud-de-Couz (73) . . . 208 A5
Saint-Thibault (10) 90 B6
Saint-Thibault (21) 135 F5
Saint-Thibault (60) 17 G4
Saint-Thibault-des-Vignes (77) . . 59 H3

Saint-Thibaut (02) 40 B3
Saint-Thibéry (34) 292 C3
Saint-Thiébaud (39) 156 A3
Saint-Thiébault (52) 93 F5
Saint-Thierry (51) 40 E3
Saint-Thois (29) 75 F4
Saint-Thomas (02) 40 D1
Saint-Thomas (31) 287 H2
Saint-Thomas-de-Conac (17) . . . 195 F6
Saint-Thomas-de-Courceriers (53) . 81 K5
Saint-Thomas-en-Argonne (51) . . 42 D5
Saint-Thomas-en-Royans (26) . . . 223 G5
Saint-Thomas-la-Garde (42) . . . 204 D4
Saint-Thomé (07) 239 K6
Saint-Thonan (29) 46 B5
Saint-Thual (35) 78 E1
Saint-Thurial (35) 78 D5
Saint-Thuriau (56) 76 E6
Saint-Thurien (27) 34 C2
Saint-Thurien (29) 99 H2
Saint-Thurin (42) 204 B1
Saint-Tricat (62) 2 C3
Saint-Trimoël (22) 77 J2
Saint-Trinit (84) 258 B5
Saint-Trivier-de-Courtes (01) . . . 172 B4
Saint-Trivier-sur-Moignans (01) . . 188 D4
Saint-Trojan (33) 211 H4
Saint-Trojan-les-Bains (17) . . . 176 C6
Saint-Tropez (83) 299 F4
Saint-Tugdual (56) 76 A5
Saint-Ulphace (72) 83 K6
Saint-Ulrich (68) 97 A4
Saint-Uniac (35) 78 D3
Saint-Urbain (29) 46 C6
Saint-Urbain (85) 140 D4
Saint-Urbain-Maconcourt (52) . . 92 B3
Saint-Urcisse (47) 248 D5
Saint-Urcisse (81) 269 J2
Saint-Urcize (15) 236 D4
Saint-Usage (10) 115 G1
Saint-Usage (21) 154 E2
Saint-Usuge (71) 172 D2
Saint-Utin (51) 90 E1
Saint-Uze (26) 222 C3
Saint-Vaast-de-Longmont (60) . . 38 D4
Saint-Vaast-d'Équiqueville (76) . . 16 R3
Saint-Vaast-Dieppedalle (76) . . . 15 G3
Saint-Vaast-du-Val (76) . . . 15 J4
Saint-Vaast-en-Auge (14) . . . 33 H3
Saint-Vaast-en-Cambrésis (59) . . 12 C4
Saint-Vaast-en-Chaussée (80) . . 18 A1
Saint-Vaast-la-Hougue (50) . . . 29 G3
Saint-Vaast-lès-Mello (60) . . . 37 K4
Saint-Vaast-sur-Seulles (14) . . . 32 B5
Saint-Vaize (17) 195 G1
Saint-Valbert (70) 118 D4
Saint-Valentin (36) 148 B4
Saint-Valérien (85) 160 C3
Saint-Valérien (89) 88 B6
Saint-Valery (60) 17 F4
Saint-Valery-en-Caux (76) . . . 15 G2
Saint-Valery-sur-Somme (80) . . 8 E4
Saint-Vallerin (71) 171 H2
Saint-Vallier (16) 212 C4
Saint-Vallier (26) 222 B3
Saint-Vallier (71) 170 E2
Saint-Vallier (88) 94 C4
Saint-Vallier-de-Thiey (06) . . . 280 C4
Saint-Vallier-sur-Marne (52) . . . 116 D4
Saint-Varent (79) 144 B5
Saint-Vaury (23) 182 C2
Saint-Venant (62) 5 K4
Saint-Vénérand (43) 238 A2
Saint-Véran (05) 227 C3
Saint-Vérand (38) 223 G3
Saint-Vérand (69) 187 K6
Saint-Vérand (71) 188 B1
Saint-Vert (43) 219 J1
Saint-Viance (19) 215 H3
Saint-Viâtre (41) 130 A3
Saint-Viaud (44) 122 C3
Saint-Victeur (72) 82 C4
Saint-Victor (03) 167 H6
Saint-Victor (07) 222 A4
Saint-Victor (15) 217 G6
Saint-Victor (24) 213 H2
Saint-Victor-de-Buthon (28) . . . 84 B3
Saint-Victor-de-Cessieu (38) . . . 207 G4
Saint-Victor-de-Chrétienville (27) . 34 C6
Saint-Victor-de-Malcap (30) . . . 255 J4
Saint-Victor-de-Morestel (38) . . . 207 H2
Saint-Victor-de-Réno (61) . . . 83 J2
Saint-Victor-d'Épine (27) . . . 34 C5
Saint-Victor-des-Oules (30) . . . 256 B6
Saint-Victor-en-Marche (23) . . . 182 C3
Saint-Victor-et-Melvieu (12) . . . 272 B1
Saint-Victor-la-Coste (30) . . . 256 C6
Saint-Victor-la-Rivière (63) . . . 202 B5
Saint-Victor-l'Abbaye (76) . . . 16 A4
Saint-Victor-Malescours (43) . . . 221 G2
Saint-Victor-Montvianeix (63) . . . 186 A6
Saint-Victor-Rouzaud (09) . . . 307 H1
Saint-Victor-sur-Arlanc (43) . . . 220 B2
Saint-Victor-sur-Avre (27) . . . 56 A5
Saint-Victor-sur-Ouche (21) . . . 135 H6
Saint-Victor-sur-Rhins (42) . . . 187 H5
Saint-Victoret (13) 296 B2
Saint-Victour (19) 201 G6
Saint-Victurnien (87) 180 E6
Saint-Vidal (43) 220 B5
Saint-Vigor (27) 35 K6

Saint-Vigor-des-Mézerets (14) . . . 53 G2
Saint-Vigor-des-Monts (50) . . . 31 H6
Saint-Vigor-d'Ymonville (76) . . . 34 B1
Saint-Vigor-le-Grand (14) . . . 32 B3
Saint-Vincent (31) 289 F3
Saint-Vincent (43) 220 C4
Saint-Vincent (63) 202 D5
Saint-Vincent (64) 285 F6
Saint-Vincent (82) 250 A5
Saint-Vincent-Bragny (71) . . . 170 C4
Saint-Vincent-Cramesnil (76) . . . 34 B1
Saint-Vincent-de-Barbeyrargues (34) . . . 274 C5
Saint-Vincent-de-Barrès (07) . . . 240 A4
Saint-Vincent-de-Boisset (42) . . . 187 F5
Saint-Vincent-de-Connezac (24) . . 213 H4
Saint-Vincent-de-Cosse (24) . . . 232 C2
Saint-Vincent-de-Durfort (07) . . . 239 K2
Saint-Vincent-de-Lamontjoie (47) . . 248 A6
Saint-Vincent-de-Mercuze (38) . . 208 C6
Saint-Vincent-de-Paul (33) . . . 211 J6
Saint-Vincent-de-Paul (40) . . . 264 B4
Saint-Vincent-de-Pertignas (33) . . 230 B2
Saint-Vincent-de-Reins (69) . . . 187 J4
Saint-Vincent-de-Salers (15) . . . 217 J3
Saint-Vincent-de-Tyrosse (40) . . . 262 C5
Saint-Vincent-des-Bois (27) . . . 57 F1
Saint-Vincent-des-Landes (44) . . 103 H4
Saint-Vincent-des-Prés (71) . . . 171 G4
Saint-Vincent-des-Prés (72) . . . 83 F4
Saint-Vincent-d'Olargues (34) . . . 291 G1
Saint-Vincent-du-Boulay (27) . . . 34 C6
Saint-Vincent-du-Lorouër (72) . . . 107 G5
Saint-Vincent-du-Pendit (46) . . . 234 C2
Saint-Vincent-en-Bresse (71) . . . 172 B2
Saint-Vincent-Jalmoutiers (24) . . . 213 F3
Saint-Vincent-la-Châtre (79) . . . 178 E2
Saint-Vincent-la-Commanderie (26) . . . 222 E6
Saint-Vincent-le-Paluel (24) . . . 233 F2
Saint-Vincent-les-Forts (04) . . . 243 H6
Saint-Vincent-Lespinasse (82) . . . 248 E5
Saint-Vincent-Rive-d'Olt (46) . . . 249 J1
Saint-Vincent-Sterlanges (85) . . . 160 B1
Saint-Vincent-sur-Jabron (04) . . . 258 D4
Saint-Vincent-sur-Jard (85) . . . 159 G5
Saint-Vincent-sur-l'Isle (24) . . . 214 C3
Saint-Vincent-sur-Oust (56) . . . 102 B3
Saint-Vit (25) 155 K1
Saint-Vital (73) 209 F4
Saint-Vite (47) 248 E1
Saint-Vitte (03) 167 G4
Saint-Vitte-sur-Briance (87) . . . 199 H4
Saint-Vivien (17) 176 E3
Saint-Vivien (24) 230 E1
Saint-Vivien-de-Blaye (33) . . . 211 H4
Saint-Vivien-de-Médoc (33) . . . 194 C6
Saint-Vivien-de-Monségur (33) . . 230 E5
Saint-Voir (03) 169 G5
Saint-Vougay (29) 46 D4
Saint-Vrain (51) 63 H5
Saint-Vrain (91) 86 E2
Saint-Vran (22) 77 J4
Saint-Vulbas (01) 207 F1
Saint-Waast (59) 13 F2
Saint-Wandrille-Rançon (76) . . . 15 G6
Saint-Witz (95) 38 B6
Saint-Xandre (17) 176 E2
Saint-Yaguen (40) 264 E2
Saint-Yan (71) 170 B5
Saint-Ybard (19) 199 H6
Saint-Ybars (09) 288 B5
Saint-Yon (91) 86 D1
Saint-Yorre (03) 185 J4
Saint-Yrieix-la-Montagne (23) . . . 182 E6
Saint-Yrieix-la-Perche (87) . . . 198 E5
Saint-Yrieix-le-Déjalat (19) . . . 200 C6
Saint-Yrieix-les-Bois (23) . . . 182 D4
Saint-Yrieix-sous-Aixe (87) . . . 198 D1
Saint-Yrieix-sur-Charente (16) . . . 196 D2
Saint-Ythaire (71) 171 G3
Saint-Yvoine (63) 202 E4
Saint-Yvy (29) 74 E6
Saint-Yzan-de-Soudiac (33) . . . 211 J4
Saint-Yzans-de-Médoc (33) . . . 211 F1
Saint-Zacharie (83) 297 F3
Sainte-Adresse (76) 33 J1
Sainte-Agathe (63) 203 J1
Sainte-Agathe-d'Aliermont (76) . . 16 C3
Sainte-Agathe-en-Donzy (42) . . . 205 F1
Sainte-Agathe-la-Bouteresse (42) . 204 D2
Sainte-Agnès (06) 281 J2
Sainte-Agnès (38) 224 C3
Sainte-Agnès (39) 173 F2
Sainte-Alauzie (46) 249 J3
Sainte-Alvère (24) 232 B1
Sainte-Anastasie (15) 218 D4
Sainte-Anastasie-sur-Issole (83) . . 298 A3
Sainte-Anne (25) 156 B4
Sainte-Anne (32) 268 C4
Sainte-Anne (41) 108 C6
Sainte-Anne-d'Auray (56) . . . 100 D4
Sainte-Anne-Saint-Priest (87) . . . 199 K3
Sainte-Anne-sur-Brivet (44) . . . 102 C4
Sainte-Anne-sur-Gervonde (38) . . 206 E5
Sainte-Anne-sur-Vilaine (35) . . . 102 E3
Sainte-Aulde (77) 60 C2
Sainte-Aurence-Cazaux (32) . . . 286 B3
Sainte-Austreberthe (62) . . . 9 J2
Sainte-Austreberthe (76) . . . 15 J5

Sainte-Barbe (57) 45 G4
Sainte-Barbe (88) 95 F2
Sainte-Barbe-sur-Gaillon (27) . . . 35 K5
Sainte-Bazeille (47) 230 D6
Sainte-Beuve-en-Rivière (76) . . . 16 D3
Sainte-Blandine (38) 207 G4
Sainte-Blandine (79) 178 C1
Sainte-Brigitte (56) 76 A7
Sainte-Camelle (11) 289 F5
Sainte-Catherine (62) 10 E2
Sainte-Catherine (63) 203 H6
Sainte-Catherine (69) 205 H4
Sainte-Catherine-de-Fierbois (37) . 145 K2
Sainte-Cécile (36) 147 K1
Sainte-Cécile (50) 52 B3
Sainte-Cécile (71) 171 H5
Sainte-Cécile (85) 142 C6
Sainte-Cécile-d'Andorge (30) . . . 255 F4
Sainte-Cécile-du-Cayrou (81) . . . 270 A1
Sainte-Cécile-les-Vignes (84) . . . 257 F4
Sainte-Céronne-lès-Mortagne (61) . 83 H1
Sainte-Cérotte (72) 107 J4
Sainte-Christie (32) 267 J4
Sainte-Christie-d'Armagnac (32) . . 266 C4
Sainte-Christine (49) 124 D5
Sainte-Christine (63) 184 C4
Sainte-Colombe (16) 197 F1
Sainte-Colombe (17) 212 A2
Sainte-Colombe (21) 134 E4
Sainte-Colombe (25) 156 E4
Sainte-Colombe (33) 230 C1
Sainte-Colombe (35) 103 J1
Sainte-Colombe (40) 265 G5
Sainte-Colombe (46) 234 D4
Sainte-Colombe (50) 28 D5
Sainte-Colombe (69) 206 B5
Sainte-Colombe (76) 15 G3
Sainte-Colombe (77) 88 D2
Sainte-Colombe (89) 134 A2
Sainte-Colombe-de-Duras (47) . . . 230 E4
Sainte-Colombe-de-la-Commanderie (66) . . . 315 F3
Sainte-Colombe-de-Peyre (48) . . . 237 F4
Sainte-Colombe-de-Villeneuve (47) . . . 248 C2
Sainte-Colombe-des-Bois (58) . . . 132 C5
Sainte-Colombe-en-Bruilhois (47) . . 248 A5
Sainte-Colombe-la-Commanderie (27) . . . 35 G6
Sainte-Colombe-près-Vernon (27) . . 36 A6
Sainte-Colombe-sur-Gand (42) . . . 187 H6
Sainte-Colombe-sur-Guette (11) . . 308 E6
Sainte-Colombe-sur-l'Hers (11) . . . 308 C3
Sainte-Colombe-sur-Loing (89) . . . 132 D2
Sainte-Colombe-sur-Seine (21) . . . 115 F4
Sainte-Colome (64) 303 H1
Sainte-Consorce (69) 205 K2
Sainte-Croix (01) 188 E6
Sainte-Croix (02) 40 C1
Sainte-Croix (12) 251 F2
Sainte-Croix (24) 232 B3
Sainte-Croix (26) 241 G3
Sainte-Croix (46) 249 H3
Sainte-Croix (71) 172 D3
Sainte-Croix (81) 270 D2
Sainte-Croix-à-Lauze (04) . . . 277 K2
Sainte-Croix-aux-Mines (68) . . . 96 A2
Sainte-Croix-de-Caderle (30) . . . 254 E6
Sainte-Croix-de-Mareuil (24) . . . 197 G6
Sainte-Croix-de-Quintillargues (34) . 274 C4
Sainte-Croix-de-Verdon (04) . . . 279 F4
Sainte-Croix-du-Mont (33) . . . 230 A5
Sainte-Croix-en-Jarez (42) . . . 205 J5
Sainte-Croix-en-Plaine (68) . . . 96 C5
Sainte-Croix-Grand-Tonne (14) . . 32 C4
Sainte-Croix-Hague (50) . . . 28 B2
Sainte-Croix-sur-Aizier (27) . . . 34 D2
Sainte-Croix-sur-Buchy (76) . . . 16 C6
Sainte-Croix-sur-Mer (14) . . . 32 D3
Sainte-Croix-sur-Orne (61) . . . 53 K4
Sainte-Croix-Vallée-Française (48) . 254 D5
Sainte-Croix-Volvestre (09) . . . 306 D1
Sainte-Dode (32) 286 A3
Sainte-Eanne (79) 162 A5
Sainte-Engrâce (64) 302 C2
Sainte-Énimie (48) 254 A2
Sainte-Eugénie-de-Villeneuve (43) . 219 K4
Sainte-Eulalie (07) 239 F2
Sainte-Eulalie (11) 289 K5
Sainte-Eulalie (15) 217 G4
Sainte-Eulalie (33) 229 J1
Sainte-Eulalie (48) 237 H3
Sainte-Eulalie-d'Ans (24) . . . 214 D3
Sainte-Eulalie-de-Cernon (12) . . . 272 E2
Sainte-Eulalie-d'Eymet (24) . . . 231 G4
Sainte-Eulalie-d'Olt (12) . . . 253 F1
Sainte-Eulalie-en-Born (40) . . . 244 D3
Sainte-Eulalie-en-Royans (26) . . . 223 G5
Sainte-Euphémie (01) 188 C5
Sainte-Euphémie-sur-Ouvèze (26) . 258 A3
Sainte-Eusoye (60) 18 A6
Sainte-Fauste (36) 148 B6
Sainte-Féréole (19) 215 J3
Sainte-Feyre (23) 182 D3
Sainte-Feyre-la-Montagne (23) . . 183 G6
Sainte-Flaive-des-Loups (85) . . . 159 G2
Sainte-Florence (33) 230 C2
Sainte-Florence (85) 142 C6
Sainte-Florine (43) 219 G1
Sainte-Foi (09) 308 B1
Sainte-Fortunade (19) 216 B3

Sainte-Foy (40) ... 265 J2
Sainte-Foy (71) ... 187 F1
Sainte-Foy (76) ... 16 A3
Sainte-Foy (85) ... 159 F3
Sainte-Foy-d'Aigrefeuille (31) ... 288 D1
Sainte-Foy-de-Belvès (24) ... 232 D3
Sainte-Foy-de-Longas (24) ... 232 A1
Sainte-Foy-de-Montgommery (14) ... 54 E2
Sainte-Foy-de-Peyrolières (31) ... 287 J2
Sainte-Foy-la-Grande (33) ... 231 F2
Sainte-Foy-la-Longue (33) ... 230 B5
Sainte-Foy-l'Argentière (69) ... 205 H3
Sainte-Foy-lès-Lyon (69) ... 206 A2
Sainte-Foy-Saint-Sulpice (42) ... 204 D2
Sainte-Foy-Tarentaise (73) ... 193 B3
Sainte-Gauburge-
Sainte-Colombe (61) ... 55 G5
Sainte-Gemme (17) ... 194 D1
Sainte-Gemme (32) ... 268 A4
Sainte-Gemme (33) ... 230 D5
Sainte-Gemme (36) ... 147 G6
Sainte-Gemme (51) ... 40 B5
Sainte-Gemme (79) ... 144 A5
Sainte-Gemme (81) ... 251 H6
Sainte-Gemme-en-Sancerrois (18). 131 J5
Sainte-Gemme-la-Plaine (85) ... 160 B4
Sainte-Gemme-Martaillac (47) ... 247 G2
Sainte-Gemme-Moronval (28) ... 57 F5
Sainte-Gemmes (41) ... 108 E5
Sainte-Gemmes-d'Andigné (49) ... 104 D6
Sainte-Gemmes-le-Robert (53) ... 81 J6
Sainte-Gemmes-sur-Loire (49) ... 125 G4
Sainte-Geneviève (02) ... 21 H4
Sainte-Geneviève (50) ... 29 F2
Sainte-Geneviève (54) ... 65 K2
Sainte-Geneviève (60) ... 37 J4
Sainte-Geneviève (76) ... 16 C5
Sainte-Geneviève-des-Bois (45) ... 111 J5
Sainte-Geneviève-des-Bois (91) ... 58 E6
Sainte-Geneviève-lès-Gasny (27) .. 36 C6
Sainte-Geneviève-
sur-Argence (12) ... 236 B3
Sainte-Hélène (33) ... 210 E6
Sainte-Hélène (48) ... 237 K6
Sainte-Hélène (56) ... 100 B4
Sainte-Hélène (71) ... 171 H1
Sainte-Hélène (88) ... 95 H4
Sainte-Hélène-Bondeville (76) ... 14 D3
Sainte-Hélène-du-Lac (73) ... 208 D5
Sainte-Hélène-sur-Isère (73) ... 209 F3
Sainte-Hermine (85) ... 160 B3
Sainte-Honorine-de-Ducy (14) ... 32 A5
Sainte-Honorine-des-Pertes (14) ... 32 A2
Sainte-Honorine-du-Fay (14) ... 32 D6
Sainte-Honorine-
la-Chardonne (61) ... 53 H3
Sainte-Honorine-la-Guillaume (61) . 53 J4
Sainte-Innocence (24) ... 231 H3
Sainte-Jalle (26) ... 257 J2
Sainte-Jamme-sur-Sarthe (72) ... 106 D1
Sainte-Julie (01) ... 189 G6
Sainte-Juliette (82) ... 249 H3
Sainte-Juliette-sur-Viaur (12) ... 252 B4
Sainte-Léocadie (66) ... 313 H5
Sainte-Lheurine (17) ... 195 J5
Sainte-Livrade (31) ... 268 D6
Sainte-Livrade-sur-Lot (47) ... 248 B2
Sainte-Lizaigne (36) ... 148 D4
Sainte-Luce (38) ... 242 C1
Sainte-Luce-sur-Loire (44) ... 123 H3
Sainte-Lucie-de-Tallano (2A) ... 323 F2
Sainte-Lunaise (18) ... 149 G5
Sainte-Magnance (89) ... 134 B4
Sainte-Marguerite (43) ... 219 K3
Sainte-Marguerite (88) ... 95 H4
Sainte-Marguerite-
de-Carrouges (61) ... 82 B1
Sainte-Marguerite-de-l'Autel (27) ... 56 A3
Sainte-Marguerite-de-Viette (14) ... 54 D1
Sainte-Marguerite-d'Elle (14) ... 31 J2
Sainte-Marguerite-des-Loges (14) ... 54 E1
Sainte-Marguerite-en-Ouche (27) ... 55 J1
Sainte-Marguerite-Lafigère (07) ... 255 F1
Sainte-Marguerite-sur-Duclair (76) . 35 F1
Sainte-Marguerite-sur-Fauville (76). 15 F4
Sainte-Marguerite-sur-Mer (76) ... 15 J2
Sainte-Marie (05) ... 258 B1
Sainte-Marie (08) ... 42 B2
Sainte-Marie (15) ... 236 C2
Sainte-Marie (25) ... 139 G2
Sainte-Marie (32) ... 268 B5
Sainte-Marie (35) ... 102 C3
Sainte-Marie (58) ... 151 G2
Sainte-Marie (65) ... 305 J3
Sainte-Marie (66) ... 310 D6
Sainte-Marie-à-Py (51) ... 41 K4
Sainte-Marie-au-Bosc (76) ... 14 B4
Sainte-Marie-aux-Chênes (57) ... 27 F6
Sainte-Marie-aux-Mines (68) ... 96 A2
Sainte-Marie-Cappel (59) ... 3 J4
Sainte-Marie-d'Alloix (38) ... 208 C6
Sainte-Marie-d'Alvey (73) ... 207 K4
Sainte-Marie-de-Chignac (24) ... 214 B4
Sainte-Marie-de-Cuines (73). ... 225 G1
Sainte-Marie-de-Gosse (40) ... 262 D6
Sainte-Marie-de-Ré (17) ... 176 C2
Sainte-Marie-de-Vatimesnil (27) ... 36 C4
Sainte-Marie-de-Vaux (87) ... 198 D1
Sainte-Marie-des-Champs (76) ... 15 G5
Sainte-Marie-du-Bois (50) ... 80 E1
Sainte-Marie-du-Bois (53) ... 81 H2
Sainte-Marie-du-

Lac-Nuisement (51) ... 63 H6
Sainte-Marie-du-Mont (38) ... 208 C6
Sainte-Marie-du-Mont (50) ... 29 G6
Sainte-Marie-en-Chanois (70) ... 118 C4
Sainte-Marie-en-Chaux (70) ... 118 C4
Sainte-Marie-Kerque (62) ... 3 F3
Sainte-Marie-la-Blanche (21) ... 154 B4
Sainte-Marie-la-Robert (61) ... 54 B6
Sainte-Marie-Lapanouze (19) ... 201 F6
Sainte-Marie-Laumont (14) ... 31 J6
Sainte-Marie-Outre-l'Eau (14) ... 31 H5
Sainte-Marie-sur-Ouche (21) ... 135 J6
Sainte-Marthe (27) ... 56 A2
Sainte-Marthe (47) ... 247 G2
Sainte-Maure (10) ... 90 A4
Sainte-Maure-de-Peyriac (47) ... 266 D1
Sainte-Maure-de-Touraine (37) ... 145 K2
Sainte-Maxime (83) ... 299 F3
Sainte-Même (17) ... 178 A6
Sainte-Menehould (51) ... 42 D6
Sainte-Mère (32) ... 267 J1
Sainte-Mère-Église (50) ... 29 F5
Sainte-Mesme (78) ... 86 A2
Sainte-Mondane (24) ... 233 G2
Sainte-Montaine (18) ... 130 E3
Sainte-Nathalène (24) ... 233 F1
Sainte-Néomaye (79) ... 161 K6
Sainte-Olive (01) ... 188 D4
Sainte-Opportune (61) ... 53 J4
Sainte-Opportune-du-Bosc (27) ... 35 F5
Sainte-Opportune-la-Mare (27) ... 34 C2
Sainte-Orse (24) ... 214 E3
Sainte-Osmane (72) ... 107 H4
Sainte-Ouenne (79) ... 161 H5
Sainte-Pallaye (89) ... 133 H1
Sainte-Paule (69) ... 187 K5
Sainte-Pazanne (44) ... 122 E5
Sainte-Pexine (85) ... 160 A3
Sainte-Pience (50) ... 52 A4
Sainte-Pôle (54) ... 95 G1
Sainte-Preuve (02) ... 21 F5
Sainte-Radegonde (12) ... 252 C3
Sainte-Radegonde (17) ... 177 G6
Sainte-Radegonde (24) ... 231 K4
Sainte-Radegonde (32) ... 267 H3
Sainte-Radegonde (33) ... 230 D2
Sainte-Radegonde (71) ... 170 B2
Sainte-Radegonde (79) ... 144 B4
Sainte-Radégonde (86) ... 163 J2
Sainte-Radégonde-
des-Noyers (85) ... 160 B5
Sainte-Ramée (17) ... 195 F6
Sainte-Reine (70) ... 137 H3
Sainte-Reine (73) ... 208 D3
Sainte-Reine-de-Bretagne (44) ... 122 A1
Sainte-Ruffine (57) ... 44 E5
Sainte-Sabine (21) ... 153 J1
Sainte-Sabine-Born (24) ... 232 A4
Sainte-Sabine-sur-Longève (72) ... 106 D1
Sainte-Savine (10) ... 90 A5
Sainte-Scolasse-sur-Sarthe (61). ... 83 G1
Sainte-Segrée (80) ... 17 H4
Sainte-Sève (29) ... 47 F5
Sainte-Sévère (16) ... 196 A2
Sainte-Sévère-sur-Indre (36) ... 166 C4
Sainte-Sigolène (43) ... 221 F3
Sainte-Solange (18) ... 149 J2
Sainte-Soline (79) ... 179 F1
Sainte-Souline (16) ... 212 D1
Sainte-Soulle (17) ... 176 E2
Sainte-Suzanne (09) ... 288 B5
Sainte-Suzanne (25) ... 139 H2
Sainte-Suzanne (53) ... 105 J1
Sainte-Suzanne-sur-Vire (50) ... 31 H4
Sainte-Terre (33) ... 230 B2
Sainte-Thérence (03) ... 184 A2
Sainte-Thorette (18) ... 148 E3
Sainte-Tréphine (22) ... 76 C3
Sainte-Trie (24) ... 215 F2
Sainte-Tulle (04) ... 278 B3
Sainte-Valière (11) ... 291 G5
Sainte-Vaubourg (08) ... 42 A1
Sainte-Verge (79) ... 144 B3
Sainte-Vertu (89) ... 113 K6
Sainteny (50) ... 31 F2
Saintes (17) ... 195 G2
Saintes-Maries-de-la-Mer (13) ... 294 C5
Saintines (60) ... 38 D3
Saintry-sur-Seine (91) ... 87 F1
Saints (77) ... 60 B5
Saints (89) ... 132 D2
Saints-Geosmes (52) ... 116 D4
Sainville (28) ... 86 A3
Saires (86) ... 145 F5
Saires-la-Verrerie (61) ... 53 H5
Saissac (11) ... 289 K4
Saisseval (80) ... 17 K2
Saisy (71) ... 153 H4
Saivres (79) ... 161 K5
le Saix (05) ... 242 C6
Saïx (81) ... 289 K1
Saix (86) ... 144 D2
Saizenay (39) ... 156 A4
Saizerais (54) ... 65 K3
Saizy (58) ... 133 H5
Sajas (31) ... 287 H3
Salagnac (24) ... 215 F2
Salagnon (38) ... 207 F3
Salaise-sur-Sanne (38) ... 222 B1
Salans (39) ... 155 K1
Salasc (34) ... 273 G6
Salaunes (33) ... 210 E6

Salavas (07) ... 255 K2
Salavre (01) ... 172 E6
Salazac (30) ... 256 B4
Salbris (41) ... 130 B4
les Salces (48) ... 237 F6
Saléchan (65) ... 305 J3
Saleich (31) ... 306 B2
Saleignes (17) ... 178 D4
Saleilles (66) ... 315 H2
les Salelles (07) ... 255 G5
les Salelles (48) ... 253 J1
Salency (60) ... 19 H6
Salenthal (67) ... 70 B2
Saléon (05) ... 258 E2
Salérans (05) ... 258 D3
Salerm (31) ... 287 F4
Salernes (83) ... 279 G6
Salers (15) ... 217 J4
Sales (74) ... 190 D6
Salesches (59) ... 12 D4
la Salette-Fallavaux (38) ... 242 D1
Salettes (26) ... 240 D5
Salettes (43) ... 238 D2
Saleux (80) ... 18 A2
Salice (2A) ... 320 D3
Saliceto (2B) ... 319 G4
Saliès (81) ... 270 D3
Salies-de-Béarn (64) ... 283 H2
Salies-du-Salat (31) ... 306 B1
Salignac (04) ... 259 G4
Salignac (33) ... 211 K5
Salignac-de-Mirambeau (17) ... 211 J1
Salignac-Eyvignes (24) ... 215 G6
Salignac-sur-Charente (17) ... 195 J3
Saligney (39) ... 137 G6
Saligny (85) ... 141 K5
Saligny (89) ... 88 E6
Saligny-le-Vif (18) ... 150 A3
Saligny-sur-Roudon (03) ... 169 J5
Saligos (65) ... 304 B3
Salindres (30) ... 255 H5
Salinelles (30) ... 274 D4
Salins (15) ... 217 H4
Salins (77) ... 88 B3
Salins-les-Bains (39) ... 156 A4
Salins-les-Thermes (73) ... 209 H5
Salives (21) ... 135 K1
Sallagriffon (06) ... 280 C2
Sallanches (74) ... 192 A5
Sallaumines (62) ... 11 F1
la Salle (71) ... 171 K5
la Salle (88) ... 95 G3
la Salle-de-Vihiers (49) ... 143 H1
la Salle-en-Beaumont (38) ... 242 C1
la Salle-et-Chapelle-Aubry (49) ... 124 C6
la Salle-Prunet (48) ... 254 C3
Salleboeuf (33) ... 229 J2
Sallèdes (63) ... 203 F3
Sallèles-Cabardès (11) ... 290 C4
Sallèles-d'Aude (11) ... 291 H5
la Salle les Alpes (05) ... 225 K6
Sallen (14) ... 31 K3
Sallenelles (14) ... 33 F4
Sallenôves (74) ... 190 E4
Sallertaine (85) ... 140 E5
Salles (33) ... 228 E5
les Salles (42) ... 204 A1
Salles (47) ... 232 B6
Salles (65) ... 304 A2
Salles (79) ... 162 A5
Salles (81) ... 251 F6
Salles-Adour (65) ... 285 H6
Salles-Arbuissonnas-
en-Beaujolais (69) ... 188 A4
Salles-Courbatiès (12) ... 251 G1
Salles-Curan (12) ... 252 D5
Salles-d'Angles (16) ... 195 K4
Salles-d'Armagnac (32) ... 266 D5
Salles-d'Aude (11) ... 291 K5
Salles-de-Barbezieux (16) ... 196 B6
Salles-de-Belvès (24) ... 232 D4
les Salles-de-Castillon (33) ... 230 D1
Salles-de-Villefagnan (16) ... 179 G5
les Salles-du-Gardon (30) ... 255 G4
Salles-et-Pratviel (31) ... 305 H4
Salles-la-Source (12) ... 252 B2
Salles-Lavalette (16) ... 213 F1
les Salles-Lavauguyon (87) ... 197 K2
Salles-Mongiscard (64) ... 283 J1
Salles-sous-Bois (26) ... 257 F1
Salles-sur-Garonne (31) ... 287 J5
Salles-sur-l'Hers (11) ... 289 F4
Salles-sur-Mer (17) ... 176 E3
les Salles-sur-Verdon (83) ... 279 F3
Sallespisse (64) ... 283 K1
Salmagne (55) ... 64 C4
Salmaise (21) ... 135 G3
Salmbach (67) ... 25 D2
Salmiech (12) ... 252 B5
Salomé (59) ... 6 C5
Salon (10) ... 62 A6
Salon (24) ... 214 B6
Salon-de-Provence (13) ... 276 E5
Salon-la-Tour (19) ... 199 H5
Salonnes (57) ... 66 D3
Salornay-sur-Guye (71) ... 171 G4
Salouël (80) ... 18 A2
Salperwick (62) ... 3 G5
Salsein (09) ... 306 C3
Salses-le-Château (66) ... 310 C4
Salsigne (11) ... 290 B4
Salt-en-Donzy (42) ... 205 F2

Salvagnac (81) ... 269 K2
Salvagnac-Cajarc (12) ... 250 E1
la Salvetat-Belmontet (82) ... 269 H2
la Salvetat-Lauragais (31) ... 289 F1
la Salvetat-Peyralès (12) ... 251 H4
la Salvetat-Saint-Gilles (31) ... 288 A1
la Salvetat-sur-Agout (34) ... 271 K6
Salvezines (11) ... 309 H5
Salviac (46) ... 233 F4
Salvizinet (42) ... 205 F2
Salza (11) ... 309 H3
Salzuit (43) ... 219 J3
Samadet (40) ... 265 G6
Saman (31) ... 286 E5
Samaran (32) ... 286 C3
Samatan (32) ... 287 G2
Samazan (47) ... 247 G1
Sambin (41) ... 128 E4
Sambourg (89) ... 114 A5
Saméon (59) ... 7 G6
Samer (62) ... 2 B6
Samerey (21) ... 155 F2
Sames (64) ... 282 E1
Sammarçolles (86) ... 144 E3
Sammeron (77) ... 60 B2
Samoëns (74) ... 192 B3
Samognat (01) ... 189 K1
Samogneux (55) ... 43 H4
Samois-sur-Seine (77) ... 87 J3
Samonac (33) ... 211 H5
Samoreau (77) ... 87 J3
Samouillan (31) ... 287 G5
Samoussy (02) ... 20 E6
Sampans (39) ... 155 G2
Sampigny (55) ... 64 E3
Sampigny-lès-Maranges (71) ... 153 J5
Sampolo (2A) ... 321 F5
Sampzon (07) ... 255 K1
Samson (25) ... 156 A2
Samsons-Lion (64) ... 285 F2
Samuran (65) ... 305 H2
San-Damiano (2B) ... 319 H4
San-Gavino-d'Ampugnani (2B) ... 319 J4
San-Gavino-di-Carbini (2A) ... 323 G2
San-Gavino-di-Fiumorbo (2B) ... 321 H4
San-Gavino-di-Tenda (2B) ... 317 C6
San-Giovanni-di-Moriani (2B) ... 319 J5
San-Giuliano (2B) ... 319 J5
San-Lorenzo (2B) ... 319 G5
San-Martino-di-Lota (2B) ... 317 E5
San-Nicolao (2B) ... 319 K5
Sana (31) ... 287 H5
Sanary-sur-Mer (83) ... 297 H6
Sancé (71) ... 171 K6
Sancergues (18) ... 150 B2
Sancerre (18) ... 131 K5
Sancey-le-Grand (25) ... 139 F5
Sancey-le-Long (25) ... 139 F5
Sancheville (28) ... 85 H6
Sanchey (88) ... 94 C5
Sancoins (18) ... 150 B6
Sancourt (27) ... 36 D3
Sancourt (59) ... 11 J3
Sancourt (80) ... 19 H3
Sancy (54) ... 26 E4
Sancy (77) ... 60 A3
Sancy-les-Cheminots (02) ... 39 K2
Sancy-lès-Provins (77) ... 60 E5
Sand (67) ... 70 E6
Sandarville (28) ... 85 F4
Sandaucourt (88) ... 93 H4
Sandillon (45) ... 110 B5
Sandouville (76) ... 34 A1
Sandrans (01) ... 188 E4
Sangatte (62) ... 2 C2
Sanghen (62) ... 2 D5
Sanguinet (40) ... 228 C6
Sanilhac (07) ... 239 G6
Sanilhac-Sagriès (30) ... 275 H2
Sannat (23) ... 183 J3
Sannerville (14) ... 33 F5
Sannes (84) ... 277 J4
Sannois (95) ... 58 D2
Sanous (65) ... 285 G3
Sanry-lès-Vigy (57) ... 27 H6
Sanry-sur-Nied (57) ... 45 G6
Sans-Vallois (88) ... 94 A6
Sansa (66) ... 313 K3
Sansac-de-Marmiesse (15) ... 235 H3
Sansac-Veinazès (15) ... 235 H3
Sansais (79) ... 177 K1
Sansan (32) ... 286 D1
Sanssac-l'Église (43) ... 220 B5
Sanssat (03) ... 185 J2
Santa-Lucia-di-Mercurio (2B) ... 319 G5
Santa-Lucia-di-Moriani (2B) ... 319 K4
Santa-Maria-di-Lota (2B) ... 317 D4
Santa-Maria-Figaniella (2A) ... 322 E2
Santa-Maria-Poggio (2B) ... 319 J5
Santa-Maria-Siché (2A) ... 317 D5
Santa-Reparata-di-Balagna (2B) ... 318 C2
Santa-Reparata-di-Moriani (2B) ... 319 J5
Sant'Andréa-di-Bozio (2B) ... 319 H6
Sant'Andréa-di-Cotone (2B) ... 319 J5
Sant'Andréa-d'Orcino (2A) ... 320 C4
Santans (39) ... 155 J3
Sant'Antonino (2B) ... 318 C2
Santeau (45) ... 110 C1
Santec (29) ... 46 E2
Santenay (21) ... 153 J5
Santenay (41) ... 128 C2
Santeny (94) ... 59 G5

Santes (59) ... 6 D4
Santeuil (28) ... 85 J4
Santeuil (95) ... 37 F6
Santigny (89) ... 134 B2
Santilly (28) ... 110 A1
Santilly (71) ... 171 H3
Santo-Pietro-di-Tenda (2B) ... 317 C6
Santo-Pietro-di-Venaco (2B) ... 321 F1
Santoche (25) ... 138 E3
Santosse (21) ... 153 J3
Santranges (18) ... 131 J3
Sanvensa (12) ... 251 G3
Sanvignes-les-Mines (71) ... 170 D2
Sanxay (86) ... 162 B4
Sanzay (79) ... 143 J4
Sanzey (54) ... 65 H4
Saon (14) ... 31 K1
Saône (25) ... 138 B6
Saonnet (14) ... 31 K1
Saorge (06) ... 311 D3
Saosnes (72) ... 82 E4
Saou (26) ... 240 E4
le Sap (61) ... 55 F3
le Sap-André (61) ... 55 G4
Sapignicourt (51) ... 63 H6
Sapignies (62) ... 11 F5
Sapogne-et-Feuchères (08) ... 22 D4
Sapogne-sur-Marche (08) ... 23 J5
Sapois (39) ... 156 B6
Sapois (88) ... 119 G1
Saponay (02) ... 40 A5
Saponcourt (70) ... 117 K4
le Sappey (74) ... 191 F3
le Sappey-en-Chartreuse (38) ... 224 B2
Saramon (32) ... 286 E1
Saran (45) ... 110 A3
Saraz (25) ... 156 B3
Sarbazan (40) ... 265 J1
Sarcé (72) ... 106 E6
Sarceaux (61) ... 54 C5
Sarcelles (95) ... 58 E2
Sarcenas (38) ... 224 B2
Sarcey (52) ... 116 C2
Sarcey (69) ... 187 K6
Sarcos (32) ... 286 D3
Sarcus (60) ... 17 G4
Sarcy (51) ... 40 D5
Sardan (30) ... 274 D3
Sardent (23) ... 182 D4
Sardieu (38) ... 223 F1
Sardon (63) ... 185 G5
Sardy-lès-Épiry (58) ... 151 K1
Sare (64) ... 263 C2
Sargé-lès-le-Mans (72) ... 106 E2
Sargé-sur-Braye (41) ... 108 A4
Sari-d'Orcino (2A) ... 320 C3
Sari-Solenzara (2A) ... 321 H6
Sariac-Magnoac (65) ... 286 C4
Sarlabous (65) ... 304 E1
Sarlande (24) ... 198 D6
Sarlat-la-Canéda (24) ... 233 F2
Sarliac-sur-l'Isle (24) ... 214 C3
Sarniguet (65) ... 285 H4
Sarnois (60) ... 17 H5
Saron-sur-Aube (51) ... 89 H1
Sarp (65) ... 305 H2
Sarpourenx (64) ... 283 K2
Sarragachies (32) ... 266 B5
Sarrageois (25) ... 174 C1
Sarraguzan (32) ... 286 A3
Sarralbe (57) ... 68 D4
Sarraltroff (57) ... 67 J3
Sarran (19) ... 216 C1
Sarrance (64) ... 303 F1
Sarrancolin (65) ... 305 F3
Sarrant (32) ... 268 B4
Sarras (07) ... 222 B3
Sarrazac (24) ... 198 C6
Sarrazac (46) ... 215 J6
Sarraziet (40) ... 265 G5
Sarre-Union (67) ... 67 J1
Sarrebourg (57) ... 67 J4
Sarrecave (31) ... 286 D5
Sarreguemines (57) ... 68 D2
Sarreinsming (57) ... 68 D3
Sarremezan (31) ... 286 D5
Sarrewerden (67) ... 67 J1
Sarrey (52) ... 116 D2
Sarriac-Bigorre (65) ... 285 J3
Sarrians (84) ... 257 G6
Sarrigné (49) ... 125 J3
Sarrogna (39) ... 173 G4
Sarrola-Carcopino (2A) ... 320 C4
Sarron (40) ... 265 J6
Sarrouilles (65) ... 285 H6
Sarroux (19) ... 217 H1
Sarry (51) ... 62 D2
Sarry (71) ... 187 F1
Sarry (89) ... 134 G2
le Sars (62) ... 10 E5
Sars-et-Rosières (59) ... 7 G6
Sars-le-Bois (62) ... 10 B3
Sars-Poteries (59) ... 13 H4
Sartène (2A) ... 322 E3
Sartes (88) ... 93 G5
Sartilly (50) ... 51 J2
Sartrouville (78) ... 58 C2
Sarzay (36) ... 166 A3
Sarzeau (56) ... 121 F1
Sasnières (41) ... 108 B3
Sassangy (71) ... 171 H1

Sassay (41) 129 F5
Sassegnies (59) 13 F4
Sassenage (38) 224 A3
Sassenay (71) 154 B4
Sassetot-le-Malgardé (76) 15 H3
Sassetot-le-Mauconduit (76) 14 E3
Sasseville (76) 15 F3
Sassey (27) 56 E1
Sassey-sur-Meuse (55) 43 F2
Sassierges-Saint-Germain (36) 166 A1
Sassis (65) 304 B4
Sassy (14) 54 B1
Sathonay-Camp (69) 206 B1
Sathonay-Village (69) 206 B1
Satillieu (07) 221 K4
Satolas-et-Bonce (38) 206 D3
Saturargues (34) 274 E5
Saubens (31) 288 A2
Saubion (40) 262 C6
Saubole (64) 285 F4
Saubrigues (40) 262 C5
Saubusse (40) 262 E5
Saucats (33) 229 G4
Saucède (64) 283 K4
la Saucelle (28) 56 C6
Sauchay (76) 16 A1
Sauchy-Cauchy (62) 11 H3
Sauchy-Lestrée (62) 11 H3
Sauclières (12) 273 G2
Saudemont (62) 11 H3
Saudoy (51) 61 H5
Saudron (52) 92 C2
Saudrupt (55) 64 A5
Saugeot (39) 173 J2
Saugnac-et-Cambran (40) 264 B5
Saugnacq-et-Muret (40) 245 G1
Saugon (33) 211 J3
Saugues (43) 237 J1
Sauguis-Saint-Étienne (64) 283 H6
Saugy (18) 148 D4
Saujac (12) 250 E1
Saujon (17) 194 D3
la Saulce (05) 259 G1
Saulce-sur-Rhône (26) 240 B4
Saulces-Champenoises (08) 41 K1
Saulces-Monclin (08) 22 B6
Saulcet (03) 185 G1
Saulchery (02) 60 D2
le Saulchoy (60) 17 K5
Saulchoy (62) 9 F2
Saulchoy-sous-Poix (80) 17 H4
Saulcy (10) 91 H5
le Saulcy (88) 95 J2
Saulcy-sur-Meurthe (88) 95 J4
Saules (25) 156 D1
Saules (71) 171 H2
Saulge (86) 164 A6
Saulgé-l'Hôpital (49) 125 J5
Saulges (53) 105 J3
Saulgond (16) 180 C5
Sauliac-sur-Célé (46) 234 A6
Saulieu (21) 134 C6
Saulles (52) 116 E6
Saulmory-et-Villefranche (55) 43 F1
Saulnay (36) 147 F5
Saulnes (54) 26 D2
Saulnières (28) 56 E6
Saulnières (35) 103 G1
Saulnot (70) 139 F1
Saulny (57) 44 E5
Saulon-la-Chapelle (21) 154 C1
Saulon-la-Rue (21) 136 A6
la Saulsotte (10) 89 F2
Sault (84) 258 A5
Sault-Brénaz (01) 189 J6
Sault-de-Navailles (64) 283 K1
Sault-lès-Rethel (08) 41 J1
Sault-Saint-Remy (08) 41 G2
Saultain (59) 12 D2
Saulty (62) 10 C4
Saulvaux (55) 64 D5
Saulx (70) 118 C6
Saulx-le-Duc (21) 136 A2
Saulx-lès-Champlon (55) 44 A6
Saulx-les-Chartreux (91) 58 D5
Saulx-Marchais (78) 57 K4
Saulxerotte (54) 93 J2
Saulxures (67) 95 K2
Saulxures-lès-Bulgnéville (88) 93 H5
Saulxures-lès-Nancy (54) 66 B5
Saulxures-lès-Vannes (54) 93 H1
Saulxures-sur-Moselotte (88) 119 G2
Saulzais-le-Potier (18) 167 G3
Saulzet (03) 185 G3
Saulzet-le-Froid (63) 202 B4
Saulzoir (59) 12 C3
Saumane (04) 258 D5
Saumane (30) 254 D5
Saumane-de-Vaucluse (84) 276 E2
Sauméjan (47) 247 F4
Saumeray (28) 84 E5
Saumont (47) 247 K5
Saumont-la-Poterie (76) 16 E6
Saumos (33) 210 D6
Saumur (49) 126 B6
Saunay (37) 128 B2
la Saunière (23) 182 D3
Saunières (71) 154 C5
Sauqueville (76) 15 K2
Saurais (79) 162 A2
Saurat (09) 307 H4
Sauret-Besserve (63) 184 C5

Saurier (63) 202 C5
Sausheim (68) 97 C2
Saussan (34) 293 F1
Saussay (28) 57 F3
Saussay (76) 15 J5
Saussay-la-Campagne (27) 36 B3
la Saussaye (27) 35 G4
Saussemesnil (50) 28 E3
Saussenac (81) 271 F1
Saussens (31) 288 E1
Sausses (04) 260 E6
Sausset-les-Pins (13) 295 K6
Sausseuzemare-en-Caux (76) 14 C4
Saussey (21) 153 H3
Saussey (50) 30 E4
Saussignac (24) 231 G3
Saussines (34) 274 D4
Saussy (21) 135 K3
Sautel (09) 308 A3
Sauternes (33) 229 K6
Sauteyrargues (34) 274 C3
Sauto (66) 313 J4
Sautron (44) 123 F3
la Sauvagère (61) 53 J6
les Sauvages (69) 187 H6
Sauvagnac (16) 197 J2
Sauvagnas (47) 248 C4
Sauvagnat (63) 201 J2
Sauvagnat-Sainte-Marthe (63) 202 E4
Sauvagney (25) 137 J5
Sauvagnon (64) 284 C3
Sauvagny (03) 167 K5
Sauvain (42) 204 B3
Sauvat (15) 217 H2
Sauve (30) 274 C2
la Sauve (33) 229 K3
Sauvelade (64) 283 K3
Sauverny (01) 174 B6
Sauvessanges (63) 220 C1
la Sauvetat (32) 267 H3
la Sauvetat (63) 202 E4
la Sauvetat-de-Savères (47) 248 D4
la Sauvetat-du-Dropt (47) 231 G4
la Sauvetat-sur-Lède (47) 248 C1
Sauveterre (30) 270 D1
Sauveterre (32) 287 F2
Sauveterre (65) 285 G1
Sauveterre (81) 290 D2
Sauveterre (82) 249 J4
Sauveterre-de-Béarn (64) 283 H3
Sauveterre-de-Comminges (31) 305 J2
Sauveterre-de-Guyenne (33) 230 C4
Sauveterre-de-Rouergue (12) 251 J4
Sauveterre-la-Lémance (47) 232 D5
Sauveterre-Saint-Denis (47) 248 C5
Sauviac (32) 286 B3
Sauviac (33) 246 D2
Sauvian (34) 292 A4
Sauviat (63) 203 H3
Sauviat-sur-Vige (87) 182 A6
Sauvignac (16) 212 C2
Sauvigney-lès-Gray (70) 137 H3
Sauvigney-lès-Pesmes (70) 137 F5
Sauvigny (55) 93 G2
Sauvigny-le-Beuréal (89) 134 B3
Sauvigny-le-Bois (89) 133 K3
Sauvigny-les-Bois (58) 151 F4
Sauville (08) 22 E6
Sauville (88) 93 G6
Sauvillers-Mongival (80) 18 C4
Sauvimont (32) 287 G2
Sauvoy (55) 65 F6
Saux (46) 249 G2
Saux-et-Pomarède (31) 286 E6
Sauxillanges (63) 203 G5
Sauze (06) 261 F5
le Sauze-du-Lac (05) 243 G6
Sauzé-Vaussais (79) 179 F3
Sauzelles (36) 164 B2
Sauzet (26) 240 B5
Sauzet (30) 275 F2
Sauzet (46) 249 H2
la Sauzière-Saint-Jean (81) 269 J2
Sauzon (56) 120 A3
Savarthès (31) 306 A1
Savas (07) 222 A4
Savas-Mépin (38) 206 D5
Savasse (26) 240 B5
Savenay (44) 122 D2
Savenès (82) 268 E3
Savennes (23) 182 D4
Savennes (63) 201 H4
Savennières (49) 125 F4
Saverdun (09) 288 D5
Savères (31) 287 J3
Saverne (67) 70 B1
Saveuse (80) 18 A2
Savianges (71) 171 G2
Savières (10) 89 K3
Savigna (39) 173 G4
Savignac (12) 251 F3
Savignac (33) 230 B6
Savignac-de-Duras (47) 230 E4
Savignac-de-l'Isle (33) 212 A6
Savignac-de-Miremont (24) 214 C6
Savignac-de-Nontron (24) 197 K5
Savignac-Lédrier (24) 215 F1
Savignac-les-Églises (24) 214 C2
Savignac-les-Ormeaux (09) 308 A6
Savignac-Mona (32) 287 H2
Savignac-sur-Leyze (47) 248 D1
Savignargues (30) 274 E2

Savigné (86) 179 H3
Savigné-l'Évêque (72) 107 F2
Savigné-sous-le-Lude (72) 126 C1
Savigné-sur-Lathan (37) 127 F4
Savigneux (01) 188 C4
Savigneux (42) 204 D4
Savignies (60) 37 H1
Savigny (50) 31 H4
Savigny (52) 117 G6
Savigny (69) 205 H1
Savigny (74) 190 D3
Savigny (88) 94 B3
Savigny-en-Revermont (71) 172 E2
Savigny-en-Sancerre (18) 131 J4
Savigny-en-Septaine (18) 149 H3
Savigny-en-Terre-Plaine (89) 134 B3
Savigny-en-Véron (37) 144 E1
Savigny-le-Sec (21) 136 A4
Savigny-le-Temple (77) 87 G1
Savigny-le-Vieux (50) 80 C1
Savigny-lès-Beaune (21) 154 A3
Savigny-Lévescault (86) 163 G4
Savigny-Poil-Fol (58) 169 K1
Savigny-sous-Faye (86) 145 G5
Savigny-sous-Mâlain (21) 135 H5
Savigny-sur-Aisne (08) 42 B3
Savigny-sur-Ardres (51) 40 C4
Savigny-sur-Braye (41) 107 K4
Savigny-sur-Clairis (89) 112 B2
Savigny-sur-Grosne (71) 171 H3
Savigny-sur-Orge (91) 58 E6
Savigny-sur-Seille (71) 172 B2
Savilly (21) 152 E2
Savines-le-Lac (05) 243 H5
Savins (77) 88 C2
Savoillan (84) 258 A4
Savoisy (21) 114 E6
Savolles (21) 136 C4
Savonnières (37) 127 H5
Savonnières-devant-Bar (55) 64 B4
Savonnières-en-Perthois (55) 64 A6
Savouges (21) 154 C1
Savournon (05) 258 E1
Savoyeux (70) 137 H2
Savy (02) 19 J3
Savy-Berlette (62) 10 D2
Saxel (74) 191 H1
Saxi-Bourdon (58) 151 H3
Saxon-Sion (54) 93 K2
Sayat (63) 202 D1
Saze (30) 276 A2
Sazeray (36) 166 C5
Sazeret (03) 168 A6
Sazilly (37) 145 G2
Sazos (65) 304 B4
Scaër (29) 75 G6
Scata (2B) 319 H4
Sceau-Saint-Angel (24) 197 K5
Sceautres (07) 239 K5
Sceaux (89) 134 A3
Sceaux (92) 58 E4
Sceaux-d'Anjou (49) 125 G1
Sceaux-du-Gâtinais (45) 111 G1
Sceaux-sur-Huisne (72) 107 H1
Scey-Maisières (25) 156 C2
Scey-sur-Saône-et-Saint-Albin (70) 117 K6
Schaeffersheim (67) 70 E5
Schaffhouse-près-Seltz (67) 25 D2
Schaffhouse-sur-Zorn (67) 70 D1
Schalbach (57) 69 J2
Schalkendorf (67) 69 J6
Scharrachbergheim-Irmstett (67) 70 D2
Scheibenhard (67) 25 D1
Scherlenheim (67) 70 D1
Scherwiller (67) 71 B5
Schillersdorf (67) 69 H5
Schiltigheim (67) 25 A6
Schirmeck (67) 70 A5
Schirrhein (67) 25 B4
Schirrhoffen (67) 25 C4
Schleithal (67) 25 C1
Schlierbach (68) 97 D3
Schmittviller (57) 68 E4
Schneckenbusch (57) 67 J4
Schnersheim (67) 70 D2
Schoenau (67) 71 D5
Schoenbourg (67) 69 F6
Schoeneck (57) 68 C1
Schoenenbourg (67) 25 B2
Schopperten (67) 67 J1
Schorbach (57) 69 G3
Schweighouse-sur-Moder (67) 25 A4
Schweighouse-Thann (68) 97 A2
Schwenheim (67) 70 C2
Schwerdorff (57) 45 J2
Schweyen (57) 69 G2
Schwindratzheim (67) 70 D1
Schwoben (68) 97 C4
Schwobsheim (67) 71 D5
Sciecq (79) 161 H5
Scientrier (74) 191 H3
Scieurac-et-Flourès (32) 285 J1
Sciez (74) 174 E6
Scillé (79) 161 G3
Scionzier (74) 191 K3
Scolca (2B) 319 H3
Scorbé-Clairvaux (86) 145 H6
Scrignac (29) 74 E4
Scrupt (51) 63 H5
Scy-Chazelles (57) 44 E5
Scye (70) 118 A6
Séailles (32) 266 D4

la Séauve-sur-Semène (43) 221 F2
Sébazac-Concourès (12) 252 B2
Sébécourt (27) 56 A2
Sébeville (50) 29 F5
Seboncourt (02) 20 B1
Sebourg (59) 12 E2
Sébrazac (12) 235 K6
Sementron (89) 132 E2
Séméries (59) 13 H5
Semerville (41) 109 F3
Semezanges (21) 154 A1
Sémézies-Cachan (32) 286 E2
Semide (08) 42 A3
Semillac (17) 195 G6
Semilly (52) 92 E5
Semmadon (70) 117 J5
Semoine (10) 62 B5
Semond (21) 115 G6
Semondans (25) 139 G2
Semons (38) 206 E6
Semousies (59) 13 H4
Semoussac (17) 195 G6
Semoutiers-Montsaon (52) 116 A2
Semoy (45) 110 A4
Sempesserre (32) 267 J1
Sempigny (60) 19 H6
Sempy (62) 4 D6
Semur-en-Auxois (21) 134 D3
Semur-en-Brionnais (71) 187 F1
Semur-en-Vallon (72) 107 J2
Sémussac (17) 194 D4
Semuy (08) 42 B1
le Sen (40) 246 A5
Sénac (65) 285 J3
Senaide (88) 117 H2
Sénaillac-Latronquière (46) 234 D2
Sénaillac-Lauzès (46) 233 K5
Senailly (21) 134 D2
Senan (89) 112 E4
Senantes (28) 57 H6
Senantes (60) 36 E1
Sénarens (31) 287 G4
Senargent-Mignafans (70) 138 E1
Senarpont (80) 17 F2
Sénas (13) 276 E4
Senaud (39) 172 E5
Senaux (81) 271 J4
Sencenac-Puy-de-Fourches (24) 213 K2
Senconac (09) 307 K5
Sendets (33) 246 E1
Sendets (64) 285 F2
Séné (56) 101 F6
Sénéchas (30) 255 G3
Sénergues (12) 235 J5
Sénestis (47) 247 H2
Séneujols (43) 220 B6
Senez (04) 279 H1
Sénezergues (15) 235 H4
Sengouagnet (31) 305 K2
Séniergues (46) 233 J4
Senillé (86) 163 H1
Seningham (62) 2 E5
Senlecques (62) 2 D6
Senlis (60) 38 B5
Senlis (62) 5 F5
Senlis-le-Sec (80) 10 D6
Senlisse (78) 58 B6
Sennecey (21) 149 G4
Sennecey-le-Grand (71) 171 K2
Sennecey-lès-Dijon (21) 136 B5
Sennely (45) 130 C1
Sennevières (37) 146 E2
Senneville-sur-Fécamp (76) 14 D3
Sennevoy-le-Bas (89) 114 D5
Sennevoy-le-Haut (89) 114 D5
Senon (55) 26 C5
Senonches (28) 84 C1
Senoncourt (70) 118 A4
Senoncourt-les-Maujouy (55) 43 H6
Senones (88) 95 J2
Senonges (88) 93 K6
Senonnes (53) 104 A5
Senots (60) 37 G4
Senouillac (81) 270 C2
Sénoville (50) 28 B5
Senozan (71) 171 K5
Sens (89) 88 D6
Sens-Beaujeu (18) 131 H5
Sens-de-Bretagne (35) 79 H1
Sens-sur-Seille (71) 172 D1
Sentein (09) 306 B4
Sentelie (80) 17 J4
Sentenac-de-Sérou (09) 307 G3
Sentenac-d'Oust (09) 306 D4
Sentheim (68) 119 K5
Sentilly (61) 54 B4
la Sentinelle (59) 12 C2
Sentous (65) 286 A2
Senuc (08) 42 C3
Senven-Léhart (22) 76 D1
Sépeaux (89) 112 D3
Sepmeries (59) 12 D3
Sepmes (37) 145 K3
Seppois-le-Bas (68) 97 A5
Seppois-le-Haut (68) 97 B5
Sept-Forges (61) 81 H2
Sept-Meules (76) 16 C1
Sept-Frères (14) 31 H6
Sept-Saulx (51) 41 H5
Sept-Sorts (77) 60 B2
Sept-Vents (14) 31 K4
Septème (38) 206 C4
Septèmes-les-Vallons (13) 296 C3
Septeuil (78) 57 J3
Septfonds (82) 250 B5
Septfontaines (25) 156 D3

Septmoncel (39) . . . 173 K5	Serreslous-et-Arribans (40) . . . 265 F5	Sickert (68) . . . 119 J4	Six-Fours-les-Plages (83) . . . 297 H6	Songieu (01) . . . 190 B5
Septmonts (02) . . . 39 J3	Serriera (2A) . . . 316 D4	Sideville (50) . . . 28 C3	Sixt-Fer-à-Cheval (74) . . . 192 B3	Songy (51) . . . 62 E4
Septsarges (55) . . . 43 F3	Serrières (07) . . . 222 B2	Sidiailles (18) . . . 166 E4	Sixt-sur-Aff (35) . . . 102 C2	Sonnac (12) . . . 234 E6
Septvaux (02) . . . 20 B6	Serrières (71) . . . 188 B1	Siecq (17) . . . 196 A1	Sizun (29) . . . 46 D6	Sonnac (17) . . . 195 K1
Sepvigny (55) . . . 93 F1	Serrières-de-Briord (01) . . . 207 G1	Siegen (67) . . . 25 D2	Smarves (86) . . . 163 F4	Sonnac-sur-l'Hers (11) . . . 308 D2
Sepvret (79) . . . 178 E1	Serrières-en-Chautagne (73) . . . 190 C6	les Sièges (89) . . . 89 F6	Smermesnil (76) . . . 16 D2	Sonnay (38) . . . 222 C1
Sepx (31) . . . 287 F6	Serrières-sur-Ain (01) . . . 189 J2	Sierck-les-Bains (57) . . . 27 A1	Soccia (2A) . . . 320 D2	Sonnaz (73) . . . 208 B3
Sequedin (59) . . . 6 D4	Serrigny (89) . . . 113 K5	Sierentz (68) . . . 97 D3	Sochaux (25) . . . 139 H2	Sonneville (16) . . . 196 B1
Sequehart (02) . . . 20 A1	Serrigny-en-Bresse (71) . . . 154 D6	Siersthal (57) . . . 69 G3	Socourt (88) . . . 94 B3	Sons-et-Ronchères (02) . . . 20 D3
le Sequestre (81) . . . 270 D2	Serris (77) . . . 59 J4	Sierville (76) . . . 15 K6	Socx (59) . . . 3 H3	Sonthonnax-la-Montagne (01) . . . 189 K1
Serain (02) . . . 12 B6	Serrouville (54) . . . 26 E4	Siest (40) . . . 262 E5	Sode (31) . . . 305 H5	Sonzay (37) . . . 127 G3
Seraincourt (08) . . . 21 J5	Serruelles (18) . . . 149 G5	Sieurac (81) . . . 270 D4	Soeurdres (49) . . . 105 G6	Soorts-Hossegor (40) . . . 262 B5
Seraincourt (95) . . . 58 A1	Sers (16) . . . 197 F4	Sieuras (09) . . . 288 A6	Sognolles-en-Montois (77) . . . 88 C2	Soppe-le-Bas (68) . . . 119 K5
Sérandon (19) . . . 217 G1	Sers (65) . . . 304 C4	Siévoz (38) . . . 242 C1	Sogny-aux-Moulins (51) . . . 62 D3	Soppe-le-Haut (68) . . . 119 K5
Séranon (06) . . . 280 B3	Servais (02) . . . 20 A5	Siewiller (67) . . . 69 F6	Sogny-en-l'Angle (51) . . . 63 H4	Sor (09) . . . 306 C3
Serans (60) . . . 36 E5	Serval (02) . . . 40 C3	Sigale (06) . . . 280 D2	Soignolles (14) . . . 54 A1	Sorans-lès-Breurey (70) . . . 138 A4
Serans (61) . . . 54 B5	Servance (70) . . . 119 F4	Sigalens (33) . . . 246 E1	Soignolles-en-Brie (77) . . . 59 H6	Sorbais (02) . . . 21 F2
Seranville (54) . . . 94 D2	Servanches (24) . . . 212 E4	Sigean (11) . . . 310 C2	Soindres (78) . . . 57 J2	Sorbets (32) . . . 266 B4
Séranvillers-Forenville (59) . . . 11 K5	Servant (63) . . . 184 D3	Sigloy (45) . . . 110 D5	Soing-Cubry-Charentenay (70) . . . 137 J2	Sorbets (40) . . . 265 J5
Seraucourt-le-Grand (02) . . . 19 K3	Servas (01) . . . 189 F3	Signac (31) . . . 305 J3	Soings-en-Sologne (41) . . . 129 G4	Sorbey (55) . . . 26 B4
Seraumont (88) . . . 93 F2	Servas (30) . . . 255 H5	Signes (83) . . . 297 H4	Soirans (21) . . . 154 E1	Sorbey (57) . . . 45 G6
Serazereux (28) . . . 85 F1	Servaville-Salmonville (76) . . . 35 K1	Signéville (52) . . . 92 C5	Soissons (02) . . . 39 J2	Sorbier (03) . . . 169 H6
Serbannes (03) . . . 185 H4	Serverette (48) . . . 237 H4	Signy-l'Abbaye (08) . . . 22 A4	Soissons-sur-Nacey (21) . . . 136 E6	Sorbiers (05) . . . 258 C2
Serbonnes (89) . . . 88 C4	Serves-sur-Rhône (26) . . . 222 B4	Signy-le-Petit (08) . . . 21 J2	Soisy-Bouy (77) . . . 88 D2	Sorbiers (42) . . . 205 G5
Serches (02) . . . 39 J4	Servian (34) . . . 292 B3	Signy-Montlibert (08) . . . 23 J5	Soisy-sous-Montmorency (95) . . . 58 E2	Sorbo-Ocagnano (2B) . . . 319 J3
Sercoeur (88) . . . 94 E4	Servières (48) . . . 237 H5	Signy-Signets (77) . . . 60 B2	Soisy-sur-École (91) . . . 87 F2	Sorbollano (2A) . . . 323 F1
Sercus (59) . . . 3 J4	Servières-le-Château (19) . . . 216 D4	Sigogne (16) . . . 196 B2	Soisy-sur-Seine (91) . . . 59 F6	Sorbon (08) . . . 21 K6
Sercy (71) . . . 171 H3	Serviers-et-Labaume (30) . . . 255 K6	Sigolsheim (68) . . . 96 B3	Soize (02) . . . 21 H4	Sorbs (34) . . . 273 G3
Serdinya (66) . . . 314 B3	Serviès (81) . . . 270 C6	Sigonce (04) . . . 278 C1	Soizé (28) . . . 84 A6	Sorcy-Bauthémont (08) . . . 22 B6
Sère (32) . . . 286 D3	Serviès-en-Val (11) . . . 309 H1	Sigottier (05) . . . 258 D1	Soizy-aux-Bois (51) . . . 61 H4	Sorcy-Saint-Martin (55) . . . 65 F5
Sère-en-Lavedan (65) . . . 304 A2	Servignat (01) . . . 172 B5	Sigoulès (24) . . . 231 H3	Solaize (69) . . . 206 A3	Sorde-l'Abbaye (40) . . . 283 F1
Sère-Lanso (65) . . . 304 B1	Servigney (70) . . . 118 C5	Sigournais (85) . . . 160 C1	Solaro (2B) . . . 321 H5	Sore (40) . . . 245 K3
Sère-Rustaing (65) . . . 285 K5	Servigny (50) . . . 30 D3	Sigoyer (04) . . . 259 F2	Solbach (67) . . . 70 A5	Soréac (65) . . . 285 J4
Serécourt (88) . . . 117 H1	Servigny-lès-Raville (57) . . . 45 H5	Sigoyer (05) . . . 242 D6	Soleilhas (04) . . . 280 A2	Sorède (66) . . . 315 H4
Sérilhac (87) . . . 198 D2	Servigny-lès-Sainte-Barbe (57) . . . 45 G5	Siguer (09) . . . 307 H5	Solemont (25) . . . 139 G4	Sorel (80) . . . 11 H6
Serémange-Erzange (57) . . . 27 G5	Serville (28) . . . 57 G4	Sigy (77) . . . 88 C2	Solente (60) . . . 19 G4	Sorel-en-Vimeu (80) . . . 9 G6
Sérempuy (32) . . . 268 A4	Servilly (03) . . . 186 A1	Sigy-en-Bray (76) . . . 16 C3	le Soler (66) . . . 315 F2	Sorel-Moussel (28) . . . 57 F4
Sérénac (81) . . . 271 F2	Servin (25) . . . 138 E5	Sigy-le-Châtel (71) . . . 171 G3	Solérieux (26) . . . 256 E2	Sorèze (81) . . . 289 J2
Sérent (56) . . . 101 J3	Servins (62) . . . 10 D1	Silfiac (56) . . . 76 C4	Solers (77) . . . 59 H6	Sorgeat (09) . . . 308 B6
Sérévillers (60) . . . 18 C5	Servon (50) . . . 51 J4	Silhac (07) . . . 239 K1	Solesmes (59) . . . 12 D4	Sorges (24) . . . 214 C2
Serez (27) . . . 57 F2	Servon (77) . . . 59 G5	Sillans (38) . . . 223 H1	Solesmes (72) . . . 105 K4	Sorgues (84) . . . 276 C1
Sérézin-de-la-Tour (38) . . . 207 F4	Servon-Melzicourt (51) . . . 42 C4	Sillans-la-Cascade (83) . . . 279 F6	Soleymieu (38) . . . 207 F2	Sorigny (37) . . . 127 J6
Sérézin-du-Rhône (69) . . . 206 A3	Servon-sur-Vilaine (35) . . . 79 J4	Sillars (86) . . . 163 K5	Soleymieux (42) . . . 204 C5	les Sorinières (44) . . . 123 G5
Sergeac (24) . . . 214 E6	Servoz (74) . . . 192 B5	Sillas (33) . . . 246 E2	Solférino (40) . . . 245 F5	Sorio (2B) . . . 319 G2
Sergenaux (39) . . . 155 G5	Sery (08) . . . 21 K5	Sillé-le-Guillaume (72) . . . 82 B6	Solgne (57) . . . 66 B1	Sormery (89) . . . 113 H1
Sergenon (39) . . . 155 G4	Sery (89) . . . 133 H2	Sillé-le-Philippe (72) . . . 107 F1	Soliers (14) . . . 32 E5	Sormonne (08) . . . 22 B3
Sergines (89) . . . 88 D4	Séry-lès-Mézières (02) . . . 20 B3	Sillegny (57) . . . 66 A1	Solignac (87) . . . 199 F2	Sornac (19) . . . 200 E3
Sergy (01) . . . 190 D1	Séry-Magneval (60) . . . 38 E4	Sillery (51) . . . 41 G5	Solignac-sous-Roche (43) . . . 220 D3	Sornay (70) . . . 137 G5
Sergy (02) . . . 40 B5	Serzy-et-Prin (51) . . . 40 C4	Silley-Amancey (25) . . . 156 D3	Solignac-sur-Loire (43) . . . 220 C6	Sornay (71) . . . 172 C2
Séricourt (62) . . . 10 A3	Sessenheim (67) . . . 25 C4	Silley-Bléfond (25) . . . 138 C5	Solignat (63) . . . 202 E5	Sornéville (54) . . . 66 C4
Sériers (15) . . . 218 D6	Sète (34) . . . 293 F3	Sillingy (74) . . . 190 E5	Soligny-la-Trappe (61) . . . 55 H6	Sorquainville (76) . . . 14 E4
Sérifontaine (60) . . . 36 E3	Setques (62) . . . 3 F5	Silly-en-Gouffern (61) . . . 54 D4	Soligny-les-Étangs (10) . . . 89 F3	Sorrus (62) . . . 4 B6
Sérignac (46) . . . 249 G2	Seugy (95) . . . 37 K6	Silly-en-Saulnois (57) . . . 66 B1	Sollacaro (2A) . . . 322 D2	Sort-en-Chalosse (40) . . . 264 C5
Sérignac (82) . . . 268 C2	Seuil (08) . . . 41 J1	Silly-la-Poterie (02) . . . 39 G5	Sollières-Sardières (73) . . . 226 B2	Sortosville (50) . . . 28 E4
Sérignac-Péboudou (47) . . . 231 J5	Seuil-d'Argonne (55) . . . 63 K1	Silly-le-Long (60) . . . 38 D6	Solliès-Pont (83) . . . 297 K5	Sortosville-en-Beaumont (50) . . . 28 B5
Sérignac-sur-Garonne (47) . . . 248 A4	Seuillet (03) . . . 185 J2	Silly-sur-Nied (57) . . . 45 G5	Solliès-Toucas (83) . . . 297 K5	Sos (47) . . . 247 G6
Sérignan (34) . . . 292 A5	Seuilly (37) . . . 145 F2	Silly-Tillard (60) . . . 37 H3	Solliès-Ville (83) . . . 297 K5	Sospel (06) . . . 281 J1
Sérignan-du-Comtat (84) . . . 256 E4	Seur (41) . . . 128 E3	Silmont (55) . . . 64 B4	Sologny (71) . . . 171 H6	Sossais (86) . . . 145 G5
Sérigné (85) . . . 160 D4	le Seure (17) . . . 195 J1	Siltzheim (67) . . . 68 D3	Solomiac (32) . . . 268 B4	Sost (65) . . . 305 H3
Sérigny (61) . . . 83 H4	Seurre (21) . . . 154 D3	Silvareccio (2B) . . . 319 H4	Solre-le-Château (59) . . . 13 J4	Sotta (2A) . . . 323 G4
Sérigny (86) . . . 145 G5	Seux (80) . . . 17 K2	Silvarouvres (52) . . . 115 H2	Solrinnes (59) . . . 13 J3	Sottevast (50) . . . 28 D4
Sérilhac (19) . . . 216 A5	Seuzey (55) . . . 64 E1	Simacourbe (64) . . . 285 F2	Solterre (45) . . . 111 J4	Sotteville (50) . . . 28 B3
Seringes-et-Nesles (02) . . . 40 A5	Sevelinges (42) . . . 187 H3	Simandre (71) . . . 172 A2	Solutré-Pouilly (71) . . . 188 B1	Sotteville-lès-Rouen (76) . . . 35 H2
Séris (41) . . . 109 G6	Sevenans (90) . . . 139 H1	Simandre-sur-Suran (01) . . . 189 J2	Somain (59) . . . 11 K2	Sotteville-sous-le-Val (76) . . . 35 J3
Serley (71) . . . 154 E6	Sévérac (44) . . . 102 C5	Simandres (69) . . . 206 B4	Sombacour (25) . . . 156 E4	Sotteville-sur-Mer (76) . . . 15 H2
Sermages (58) . . . 152 A3	Sévérac-le-Château (12) . . . 253 G3	Simard (71) . . . 172 C1	Sombernon (21) . . . 135 H5	Soturac (46) . . . 249 F1
Sermaise (49) . . . 125 K3	Sévérac-l'Église (12) . . . 252 E2	Simencourt (62) . . . 10 D3	Sombrin (62) . . . 10 C3	Sotzeling (57) . . . 66 E2
Sermaise (91) . . . 86 C2	Seveux (70) . . . 137 H2	Simeyrols (24) . . . 233 G1	Sombrun (65) . . . 285 G2	Souain-Perthes-lès-Hurlus (51) . . . 41 K5
Sermaises (45) . . . 86 D5	Sévignac (22) . . . 78 A1	Simiane-Collongue (13) . . . 296 D4	Somloire (49) . . . 143 H3	Soual (81) . . . 289 J1
Sermaize (60) . . . 19 G5	Sévignacq (64) . . . 284 E2	Simiane-la-Rotonde (04) . . . 277 J1	Sommaing (59) . . . 12 D3	Souancé-au-Perche (28) . . . 84 A5
Sermaize-les-Bains (51) . . . 63 J4	Sévignacq-Meyracq (64) . . . 284 C6	Simorre (32) . . . 286 E2	Sommancourt (52) . . . 91 K2	Souanyas (66) . . . 314 A4
Sermamagny (90) . . . 119 H5	Sévigny (61) . . . 54 C4	Simplé (53) . . . 104 E4	Sommant (71) . . . 152 E3	Souastre (62) . . . 10 D4
Sermange (39) . . . 155 J1	Sévigny-la-Forêt (08) . . . 22 B2	Sin-le-Noble (59) . . . 11 H2	Sommauthe (08) . . . 42 D1	Soubès (34) . . . 273 G4
Sermano (2B) . . . 319 G6	Sévigny-Waleppe (08) . . . 21 H5	Sinard (38) . . . 224 A6	Somme-Bionne (51) . . . 42 B6	Soubise (17) . . . 176 E5
Sermentizon (63) . . . 203 H2	Sévis (76) . . . 16 A4	Sinceny (02) . . . 19 K6	Somme-Suippe (51) . . . 42 A6	Soublecause (65) . . . 285 G1
Sermérieu (38) . . . 207 G3	Sevrai (61) . . . 54 B5	Sincey-lès-Rouvray (21) . . . 134 B4	Somme-Tourbe (51) . . . 42 B6	Soubran (17) . . . 211 H1
Sermersheim (67) . . . 70 D6	Sevran (93) . . . 59 G2	Sindères (40) . . . 245 F6	Somme-Vesle (51) . . . 63 F2	Soubrebost (23) . . . 182 D5
Sermesse (71) . . . 154 C5	Sèvres (92) . . . 58 D4	Singles (63) . . . 201 H5	Somme-Yèvre (51) . . . 63 H2	Soucé (53) . . . 81 G2
Sermiers (51) . . . 40 E5	Sèvres-Anxaumont (86) . . . 163 G3	Singleyrac (24) . . . 231 H3	Sommecaise (89) . . . 112 D5	Soucelles (49) . . . 125 H2
Sermizelles (89) . . . 133 J3	Sevrey (71) . . . 171 K1	Singly (08) . . . 22 D5	Sommedieue (55) . . . 43 J6	la Souche (07) . . . 239 F5
Sermoise (02) . . . 39 K3	Sévrier (74) . . . 191 F6	Singrist (67) . . . 70 C2	Sommeilles (55) . . . 63 J2	Souchez (62) . . . 10 E1
Sermoise-sur-Loire (58) . . . 150 E4	Sévry (18) . . . 150 A2	Sinsat (09) . . . 307 J5	Sommelans (02) . . . 39 J6	Soucht (57) . . . 69 G4
Sermoyer (01) . . . 172 A4	Sewen (68) . . . 119 J4	Sinzos (65) . . . 285 J5	Sommelonne (55) . . . 63 K5	Soucia (39) . . . 173 J3
Sermur (23) . . . 183 J5	Sexcles (19) . . . 216 D5	Sion (32) . . . 266 C4	Sommepy-Tahure (51) . . . 42 A4	Soucieu-en-Jarrest (69) . . . 205 K3
Sernhac (30) . . . 275 J2	Sexey-aux-Forges (54) . . . 65 K6	Sion-les-Mines (44) . . . 103 G3	Sommerance (08) . . . 42 E3	Soucirac (46) . . . 233 J4
Serocourt (88) . . . 117 J1	Sexey-les-Bois (54) . . . 65 J4	Sioniac (19) . . . 216 B6	Sommerécourt (52) . . . 93 F5	Souclin (01) . . . 189 J6
Séron (65) . . . 285 F4	Sexfontaines (52) . . . 92 A5	Sionne (88) . . . 93 F3	Sommereux (60) . . . 17 H5	Soucy (02) . . . 39 G3
Serpaize (38) . . . 206 B4	Seychalles (63) . . . 203 F2	Sionviller (54) . . . 66 D5	Sommeron (02) . . . 21 F1	Soucy (89) . . . 88 D3
la Serpent (11) . . . 308 E3	Seyches (47) . . . 231 F6	Siorac-de-Ribérac (24) . . . 213 G3	Sommervieu (14) . . . 32 B3	Soudaine-Lavinadière (19) . . . 199 K5
Serques (62) . . . 3 F4	Seyne (04) . . . 260 A2	Siorac-en-Périgord (24) . . . 232 D2	Sommerviller (54) . . . 66 C5	Soudan (44) . . . 103 K3
Serqueux (52) . . . 117 G2	la Seyne-sur-Mer (83) . . . 297 H6	Siouville-Hague (50) . . . 28 A3	Sommery (76) . . . 16 D5	Soudan (79) . . . 162 A5
Serqueux (76) . . . 16 D5	Seynes (30) . . . 255 J5	Sirac (32) . . . 268 B5	Sommesnil (76) . . . 15 F4	Soudat (24) . . . 197 J4
Serquigny (27) . . . 34 E6	Seynod (74) . . . 191 F5	Siracourt (62) . . . 10 A2	Sommesous (51) . . . 62 C5	Souday (41) . . . 108 A2
Serra-di-Ferro (2A) . . . 322 C2	Seyre (31) . . . 288 E4	Siradan (65) . . . 305 H3	la Sommette (25) . . . 138 E6	Soudé (51) . . . 62 D5
Serra-di-Fiumorbo (2B) . . . 321 H4	Seyresse (40) . . . 264 B5	Siran (15) . . . 234 E1	Sommette-Eaucourt (02) . . . 19 J4	Soudeilles (19) . . . 200 D6
Serra-di-Scopamène (2A) . . . 323 F1	Seyssel (01) . . . 190 C5	Siran (34) . . . 290 E4	Sommeval (10) . . . 89 K6	Soudorgues (30) . . . 254 E6
Serralongue (66) . . . 314 D6	Seyssel (74) . . . 190 C5	Sireix (65) . . . 304 A2	Sommevoire (52) . . . 91 J3	Soudron (51) . . . 62 C3
Serraval (74) . . . 209 F1	Seysses (31) . . . 288 A2	Sireuil (16) . . . 196 C4	Sommières (30) . . . 274 E4	Soueich (31) . . . 305 K2
la Serre (12) . . . 271 K3	Seysses-Savès (32) . . . 287 H2	Sirod (39) . . . 174 A1	Sommières-du-Clain (86) . . . 179 J1	Soueix-Rogalle (09) . . . 306 E4
la Serre-Bussière-Vieille (23) . . . 183 H4	Seyssinet-Pariset (38) . . . 224 A3	Siros (64) . . . 284 B3	Sompt (79) . . . 178 D3	Souel (81) . . . 270 C1
Serre-les-Moulières (39) . . . 137 G6	Seyssins (38) . . . 224 A3	Sisco (2B) . . . 317 D3	Sompuis (51) . . . 62 D5	Soues (65) . . . 285 H5
Serre-les-Sapins (25) . . . 137 K6	Seyssuel (38) . . . 206 B4	Sissonne (02) . . . 21 F4	Somsois (51) . . . 90 A1	Soues (80) . . . 17 J1
Serre-Nerpol (38) . . . 223 H2	Seythenex (74) . . . 209 F2	Sissy (02) . . . 20 B3	Son (08) . . . 21 K6	Souesmes (41) . . . 130 C4
Serres (05) . . . 258 D1	Seytroux (74) . . . 192 A1	Sistels (82) . . . 248 D6	Sonac (46) . . . 234 B4	Souffelweyersheim (67) . . . 25 A6
Serres (11) . . . 309 F3	Sézanne (51) . . . 61 H5	Sisteron (04) . . . 259 F4	Sonchamp (78) . . . 86 A1	Soufflenheim (67) . . . 25 C3
Serres (54) . . . 66 D5	Siarrouy (65) . . . 285 H4	Sivergues (84) . . . 277 H3	Soncourt (88) . . . 93 J3	Souffrignac (16) . . . 197 H4
Serres-Castet (64) . . . 284 D3	Siaugues-Sainte-Marie (43) . . . 219 K5	Sivignon (71) . . . 171 F5	Soncourt-sur-Marne (52) . . . 92 A5	Sougé (36) . . . 147 H4
Serres-et-Montguyard (24) . . . 231 J4	Sibiril (29) . . . 46 E3	Sivry (54) . . . 66 A3	Sondernach (68) . . . 119 K2	Sougé (41) . . . 107 J3
Serres-Gaston (40) . . . 265 G5	Sibiville (62) . . . 10 A2	Sivry-Ante (51) . . . 63 H1	Sondersdorf (68) . . . 97 C6	Sougé-le-Ganelon (72) . . . 82 C4
Serres-Morlaàs (64) . . . 284 E4	Siccieu-Saint-Julien-et-Carisieu (38) . . . 207 F2	Sivry-Courtry (77) . . . 87 J2	la Sône (38) . . . 223 G4	Sougéal (35) . . . 51 H5
Serres-Sainte-Marie (64) . . . 284 B2	Sichamps (58) . . . 151 F2	Sivry-la-Perche (55) . . . 43 G5	Songeons (60) . . . 17 G6	Sougères-en-Puisaye (89) . . . 132 D2
Serres-sur-Arget (09) . . . 307 H3		Sivry-sur-Meuse (55) . . . 43 G3	Songeson (39) . . . 173 J2	Sougraigne (11) . . . 309 G4

Sougy (45) . . . 109 K2
Sougy-sur-Loire (58) . . . 151 G6
les Souhesmes-Rampont (55) . . . 43 G6
Souhey (21) . . . 134 E3
le Souich (62) . . . 10 B3
Souilhanels (11) . . . 289 G4
Souilhe (11) . . . 289 G4
Souillac (46) . . . 233 H1
Souillé (72) . . . 106 D1
Souilly (55) . . . 64 C1
Soula (09) . . . 307 K3
Soulac-sur-Mer (33) . . . 194 B5
Soulages (15) . . . 219 G5
Soulages-Bonneval (12) . . . 236 B4
Soulaines-Dhuys (10) . . . 91 H3
Soulaines-sur-Aubance (49) . . . 125 G4
Soulaire-et-Bourg (49) . . . 125 G2
Soulaires (28) . . . 85 H2
Soulan (09) . . . 306 E3
Soulanges (51) . . . 63 F4
Soulangis (18) . . . 149 H1
Soulangy (14) . . . 54 A2
Soulatgé (11) . . . 309 H4
Soulaucourt-sur-Mouzon (52) . . . 93 G5
Soulaures (24) . . . 232 C4
Soulce-Cernay (25) . . . 139 H4
Soulgé-sur-Ouette (53) . . . 105 G1
le Soulié (34) . . . 290 E1
Soulières (51) . . . 61 K3
Soulignac (33) . . . 230 A4
Souligné-Flacé (72) . . . 106 C3
Souligné-sous-Ballon (72) . . . 106 E1
Soulignonne (17) . . . 194 E1
Souligny (10) . . . 90 A6
Soulitré (72) . . . 107 G2
Soullans (85) . . . 140 E5
Soulles (50) . . . 31 G4
Soulom (65) . . . 304 B3
Soulomès (46) . . . 233 H2
Soulosse-sous-Saint-Élophe (88) . . 93 G3
Soultz-Haut-Rhin (68) . . . 96 B6
Soultz-les-Bains (67) . . . 70 D3
Soultz-sous-Forêts (67) . . . 25 B2
Soultzbach-les-Bains (68) . . . 96 A4
Soultzeren (68) . . . 119 K1
Soultzmatt (68) . . . 96 B5
Soulvache (44) . . . 103 H2
Soumaintrain (89) . . . 113 J2
Soumans (23) . . . 183 H1
Soumensac (47) . . . 231 G4
Souméras (17) . . . 211 J2
Soumont (34) . . . 273 G5
Soumont-Saint-Quentin (14) . . . 54 A2
Soumoulou (64) . . . 284 E4
Soupex (11) . . . 289 G3
Soupir (02) . . . 40 B2
Souppes-sur-Loing (77) . . . 87 J6
Souprosse (40) . . . 264 E3
Souraïde (64) . . . 263 D2
Sourans (25) . . . 139 F3
Sourcieux-les-Mines (69) . . . 205 J1
le Sourd (02) . . . 20 E2
Sourdeval (50) . . . 52 D4
Sourdeval-les-Bois (50) . . . 31 F6
Sourdon (80) . . . 18 B4
Sourdun (77) . . . 88 E2
le Sourn (56) . . . 76 D6
Sournia (66) . . . 309 H6
Sourniac (15) . . . 217 G2
Sourribes (04) . . . 259 G4
Sours (28) . . . 85 H3
Soursac (19) . . . 217 F3
Sourzac (24) . . . 213 H5
Sous-Parsat (23) . . . 182 E4
Sousceyrac (46) . . . 234 D2
Sousmoulins (17) . . . 211 K2
Souspierre (26) . . . 240 D6
Soussac (33) . . . 230 D3
Soussans (33) . . . 211 G5
Soussey-sur-Brionne (21) . . . 135 F5
Soustelle (30) . . . 255 G5
Soustons (40) . . . 262 C4
Sousville (38) . . . 224 B6
Souternon (42) . . . 186 E6
la Souterraine (23) . . . 181 K2
Soutiers (79) . . . 161 K3
Souvans (39) . . . 155 H3
Souvignargues (30) . . . 274 E3
Souvigné (16) . . . 179 F5
Souvigné (37) . . . 127 F3
Souvigné (79) . . . 161 KC
Souvigné-sur-Même (72) . . . 83 J5
Souvigné-sur-Sarthe (72) . . . 105 J4
Souvigny (03) . . . 168 D4
Souvigny-de-Touraine (37) . . . 128 C4
Souvigny-en-Sologne (41) . . . 130 C1
Souyeaux (65) . . . 285 J5
Souzay-Champigny (49) . . . 126 B6
Souzy (69) . . . 205 G3
Souzy-la-Briche (91) . . . 86 C2
Soveria (2B) . . . 319 F5
Soyans (26) . . . 240 D4
Soyaux (16) . . . 196 E3
Soye (25) . . . 138 E3
Soye-en-Septaine (18) . . . 149 H3
Soyécourt (80) . . . 19 F2
Soyers (52) . . . 117 G4
Soyons (07) . . . 240 C1
Sparsbach (67) . . . 69 G5
Spay (72) . . . 106 D3
Spechbach-le-Bas (68) . . . 97 B3
Spechbach-le-Haut (68) . . . 97 B3

Speloncato (2B) . . . 318 D3
Spéracèdes (06) . . . 280 C5
Spézet (29) . . . 75 G4
Spicheren (57) . . . 68 C2
Spincourt (55) . . . 26 C5
Sponville (54) . . . 44 C6
Spoy (10) . . . 91 H4
Spoy (21) . . . 136 C3
Spycker (59) . . . 3 G2
Squiffiec (22) . . . 48 C4
Staffelfelden (68) . . . 97 B1
Stains (93) . . . 58 E2
Stainville (55) . . . 64 B6
Staple (59) . . . 3 J5
Stattmatten (67) . . . 25 C4
Stazzona (2B) . . . 319 H5
Steenbecque (59) . . . 3 J6
Steene (59) . . . 3 H2
Steenvoorde (59) . . . 3 K4
Steenwerck (59) . . . 6 B3
Steige (67) . . . 70 A6
Steinbach (68) . . . 97 A1
Steinbourg (67) . . . 70 C1
Steinbrunn-le-Bas (68) . . . 97 C3
Steinbrunn-le-Haut (68) . . . 97 C3
Steinseltz (67) . . . 25 B1
Steinsoultz (68) . . . 97 C5
Stenay (55) . . . 43 F1
Sternenberg (68) . . . 97 A3
Stetten (68) . . . 97 D4
Stigny (89) . . . 114 C5
Still (67) . . . 70 C4
Stiring-Wendel (57) . . . 68 C1
Stonne (08) . . . 23 F6
Storckensohn (68) . . . 119 J3
Stosswihr (68) . . . 119 K1
Stotzheim (67) . . . 70 D6
Strasbourg (67) . . . 71 D1
Strazeele (59) . . . 3 K5
Strenquels (46) . . . 215 K6
Strueth (68) . . . 97 A4
Struth (67) . . . 69 F5
Stuckange (57) . . . 27 H4
Stundwiller (67) . . . 25 C2
Sturzelbronn (57) . . . 69 J3
Stutzheim-Offenheim (67) . . . 70 E2
Suarce (90) . . . 139 K1
Suaux (16) . . . 197 H1
le Subdray (18) . . . 149 F4
Sublaines (37) . . . 128 B6
Subles (14) . . . 32 A4
Subligny (18) . . . 131 J4
Subligny (50) . . . 51 K2
Subligny (89) . . . 88 C6
Suc-et-Sentenac (09) . . . 307 G5
Succieu (38) . . . 207 F5
Sucé-sur-Erdre (44) . . . 123 H2
Sucy-en-Brie (94) . . . 59 G4
Suèvres (41) . . . 129 F1
Sugères (63) . . . 203 G4
Sugny (08) . . . 42 B3
Suhescun (64) . . . 282 E4
Suilly-la-Tour (58) . . . 132 B5
Suin (71) . . . 171 F5
Suippes (51) . . . 41 K5
Suizy-le-Franc (51) . . . 61 H2
Sulignat (01) . . . 188 D2
Sully (14) . . . 32 A3
Sully (60) . . . 17 G6
Sully (71) . . . 171 H4
Sully-la-Chapelle (45) . . . 110 D3
Sully-sur-Loire (45) . . . 110 E6
Sulniac (56) . . . 101 H5
Sumène (30) . . . 274 A1
Sundhoffen (68) . . . 96 C4
Sundhouse (67) . . . 71 C5
Supt (39) . . . 156 B5
Surat (63) . . . 185 G6
Surba (09) . . . 307 H4
Surbourg (67) . . . 25 B3
Surcamps (80) . . . 9 J5
Surdoux (87) . . . 199 J4
Suré (61) . . . 83 G4
Suresnes (92) . . . 58 D3
Surfonds (72) . . . 107 G3
Surfontaine (02) . . . 20 B4
Surgères (17) . . . 177 H3
Surgy (58) . . . 133 F3
Suriauville (88) . . . 93 H6
Surin (79) . . . 161 H4
Surin (86) . . . 179 J4
Suris (16) . . . 197 J1
Surjoux (01) . . . 190 C4
Surmont (25) . . . 139 F5
Surques (62) . . . 2 D5
Surrain (14) . . . 29 K6
Surtainville (50) . . . 28 B4
Surtauville (27) . . . 35 H5
Survie (61) . . . 54 E3
Surville (14) . . . 33 K3
Surville (27) . . . 35 H5
Surville (50) . . . 30 C1
Survilliers (95) . . . 38 B6
Sury (08) . . . 22 C3
Sury-aux-Bois (45) . . . 110 E3
Sury-en-Vaux (18) . . . 131 J5
Sury-ès-Bois (18) . . . 131 H4
Sury-le-Comtal (42) . . . 204 E5
Sury-près-Léré (18) . . . 131 K3
Surzur (56) . . . 101 G6
Sus (64) . . . 283 J4

Sus-Saint-Léger (62) . . . 10 B3
Susmiou (64) . . . 283 J4
Sussac (87) . . . 199 J3
Sussargues (34) . . . 274 D5
Sussat (03) . . . 185 F3
Sussey (21) . . . 153 F1
Susville (38) . . . 224 B6
Sutrieu (01) . . . 190 A5
Suzan (09) . . . 307 G2
Suzanne (08) . . . 22 C6
Suzanne (80) . . . 19 F1
Suzannecourt (52) . . . 92 B2
Suzay (27) . . . 36 B4
Suze (26) . . . 240 E3
Suze-la-Rousse (26) . . . 256 E3
la Suze-sur-Sarthe (72) . . . 106 C4
Suzette (84) . . . 257 G5
Suzoy (60) . . . 19 G6
Suzy (02) . . . 20 B6
Sy (08) . . . 22 E6
Sylvains-les-Moulins (27) . . . 56 C3
Sylvanès (12) . . . 272 C3
le Syndicat (88) . . . 119 F1

T

Tabaille-Usquain (64) . . . 283 H3
Tabanac (33) . . . 229 J3
la Table (73) . . . 208 E5
le Tablier (85) . . . 159 J3
Tabre (09) . . . 308 B3
la Tâche (16) . . . 179 J6
Tachoires (32) . . . 286 D2
Tacoignières (78) . . . 57 J4
Taconnay (58) . . . 133 F6
Taden (22) . . . 50 D5
Tadousse-Ussau (64) . . . 284 E1
Taglio-Isolaccio (2B) . . . 319 J4
la Tagnière (71) . . . 152 E6
Tagnon (08) . . . 41 H2
Tagolsheim (68) . . . 97 B3
Tagsdorf (68) . . . 97 C4
Tailhac (43) . . . 219 H5
Taillades (84) . . . 276 E3
le Taillan-Médoc (33) . . . 229 G1
Taillancourt (55) . . . 93 G1
Taillant (17) . . . 177 J6
Taillebois (61) . . . 53 J4
Taillebourg (17) . . . 195 G1
Taillebourg (47) . . . 247 H1
Taillecavat (33) . . . 230 E4
Taillecourt (25) . . . 139 H2
la Taillée (85) . . . 160 C5
Taillefontaine (02) . . . 39 F3
Taillepied (50) . . . 28 D5
Taillet (66) . . . 314 C6
Taillette (08) . . . 22 B1
Taillis (35) . . . 80 A5
Tailly (08) . . . 42 E1
Tailly (21) . . . 154 A4
Tailly (80) . . . 17 H1
Tain-l'Hermitage (26) . . . 222 B5
Taingy (89) . . . 132 E2
Taintrux (88) . . . 95 H4
Taisnières-en-Thiérache (59) . . . 13 F4
Taisnières-sur-Hon (59) . . . 13 G2
Taissy (51) . . . 41 F4
Taïx (81) . . . 270 D1
Taizé (71) . . . 171 H4
Taizé (79) . . . 144 C4
Taizé-Aizie (16) . . . 179 H4
Taizy (08) . . . 21 J6
Tajan (65) . . . 286 B6
Talairan (11) . . . 309 K2
Talais (33) . . . 194 C5
Talange (57) . . . 27 G6
Talant (21) . . . 136 A5
Talasani (2B) . . . 319 J4
la Talaudière (42) . . . 205 G5
Talazac (65) . . . 285 H4
Talcy (41) . . . 109 H6
Talcy (89) . . . 134 B2
Talence (33) . . . 229 G2
Talencieux (07) . . . 222 B3
Talensac (35) . . . 78 D4
Talissieu (01) . . . 190 B6
Talizat (15) . . . 218 D4
Tallans (25) . . . 138 C3
Tallard (05) . . . 242 E6
Tallenay (25) . . . 138 A5
Tallende (63) . . . 202 D3
Taller (40) . . . 264 B2
Talloires (74) . . . 191 G6
Tallone (2B) . . . 321 J1
le Tallud (79) . . . 161 J2
Tallud-Sainte-Gemme (85) . . . 160 D1
Talmas (80) . . . 10 A6
Talmay (21) . . . 136 E5
Talmont-Saint-Hilaire (85) . . . 159 F4
Talmont-sur-Gironde (17) . . . 194 D4
Talmontiers (60) . . . 36 D2
Talon (58) . . . 133 G5
Talus-Saint-Prix (51) . . . 61 H4
Taluyers (69) . . . 205 K3
Tamerville (50) . . . 28 E4
Tamnay-en-Bazois (58) . . . 151 K3
Tamniès (24) . . . 214 E6
Tanavelle (15) . . . 218 D6
Tanay (21) . . . 136 C4

Tancarville (76) . . . 34 C1
Tancoigné (49) . . . 143 K1
Tancon (71) . . . 187 G2
Tanconville (54) . . . 67 H5
Tancrou (77) . . . 60 B2
Tancua (39) . . . 174 A3
Tangry (62) . . . 5 H6
Taninges (74) . . . 191 K3
Tanis (50) . . . 51 J4
Tanlay (89) . . . 114 B4
Tannay (08) . . . 22 E6
Tannay (58) . . . 133 G5
Tanneron (83) . . . 280 C5
Tannerre-en-Puisaye (89) . . . 112 C6
Tannières (02) . . . 40 A4
Tannois (55) . . . 64 B5
Tanques (61) . . . 54 B5
Tantonville (54) . . . 94 A2
le Tanu (50) . . . 51 K1
Tanus (81) . . . 251 J6
Tanville (61) . . . 82 C1
Tanzac (17) . . . 195 G4
Taponas (69) . . . 188 B3
Taponnat-Fleurignac (16) . . . 197 G2
Tarabel (31) . . . 288 E2
Taradeau (83) . . . 298 D1
Tarare (69) . . . 187 J6
Tarascon (13) . . . 275 K3
Tarascon-sur-Ariège (09) . . . 307 J4
Tarasteix (65) . . . 285 G4
Tarbes (65) . . . 285 H5
Tarcenay (25) . . . 156 C1
Tardes (23) . . . 183 H3
Tardets-Sorholus (64) . . . 283 H6
la Tardière (85) . . . 160 E2
Tardinghen (62) . . . 2 A3
Tarentaise (42) . . . 221 J1
Tarerach (66) . . . 309 H6
Targassonne (66) . . . 313 H4
Target (03) . . . 185 F1
Targon (33) . . . 230 A3
Tarnac (19) . . . 200 C3
Tarnès (33) . . . 211 K6
Tarnos (40) . . . 262 B6
Taron-Sadirac-Viellenave (64) . . . 284 E1
Tarquimpol (57) . . . 67 F3
Tarrano (2B) . . . 319 H5
Tarsac (32) . . . 266 A5
Tarsacq (64) . . . 284 B3
Tarsul (21) . . . 135 K2
Tart-l'Abbaye (21) . . . 154 E1
Tart-le-Bas (21) . . . 154 E1
Tart-le-Haut (21) . . . 154 D1
Tartaras (42) . . . 205 J4
Tartas (40) . . . 264 D3
Tartécourt (70) . . . 117 K4
Tartiers (02) . . . 39 H2
Tartigny (60) . . . 18 B5
Tartonne (04) . . . 260 A5
le Tartre (71) . . . 172 E1
le Tartre-Gaudran (78) . . . 57 H5
Tarzy (08) . . . 21 K2
Tasque (32) . . . 266 C6
Tassé (72) . . . 106 A4
Tassenières (39) . . . 155 G4
Tassillé (72) . . . 106 B2
Tassin-la-Demi-Lune (69) . . . 206 A2
Tasso (2A) . . . 321 F5
Tatinghem (62) . . . 3 F5
le Tâtre (16) . . . 196 A6
Taugon (17) . . . 160 D6
Taulé (29) . . . 47 F4
Taulignan (26) . . . 257 F1
Taulis (66) . . . 314 E4
Taupont (56) . . . 101 J1
Tauriac (33) . . . 211 H5
Tauriac (46) . . . 234 B1
Tauriac (81) . . . 269 J3
Tauriac-de-Camarès (12) . . . 272 D4
Tauriac-de-Naucelle (12) . . . 251 J5
Tauriers (07) . . . 239 G6
Taurignan-Castet (09) . . . 306 D2
Taurignan-Vieux (09) . . . 306 D2
Taurinya (66) . . . 314 C3
Taurize (11) . . . 309 H1
Taussac (12) . . . 235 K2
Taussac-la-Billière (34) . . . 272 D6
Tautavel (66) . . . 310 A5
Tauves (03) . . . 201 J5
Tauxières-Mutry (51) . . . 41 F6
Tauxigny (37) . . . 146 B1
Tavaco (2A) . . . 320 D4
Tavant (37) . . . 145 H2
Tavaux (39) . . . 155 F3
Tavaux-et-Pontséricourt (02) . . . 21 F1
Tavel (30) . . . 276 A1
Tavera (2A) . . . 320 E3
Tavernay (71) . . . 152 E3
Tavernes (83) . . . 278 E6
Taverny (95) . . . 58 C1
Tavers (45) . . . 109 H6
Tavey (70) . . . 139 G1
Taxat-Senat (03) . . . 185 F2
Taxenne (39) . . . 137 G6
Tayac (33) . . . 212 D6
Taybosc (32) . . . 267 K4
Tayrac (12) . . . 251 H4
Tayrac (47) . . . 248 D4
Tazilly (58) . . . 170 A1
le Tech (66) . . . 314 D5
Têche (38) . . . 223 H3
Técou (81) . . . 270 C3

le Teich (33) . . . 228 C4
Teigny (58) . . . 133 H5
le Teil (07) . . . 240 A6
Teilhède (63) . . . 185 F5
Teilhet (09) . . . 308 A1
Teilhet (63) . . . 184 C4
Teillay (35) . . . 103 H2
Teillé (44) . . . 123 K1
Teillé (72) . . . 82 E6
Teillet (81) . . . 271 G3
Teillet-Argenty (03) . . . 183 K2
le Teilleul (50) . . . 80 E1
Teillots (24) . . . 215 F3
Teissières-de-Cornet (15) . . . 217 G6
Teissières-lès-Bouliès (15) . . . 235 J2
Telgruc-sur-Mer (29) . . . 72 E6
Tellancourt (54) . . . 26 B2
Tellecey (21) . . . 136 C5
Tellières-le-Plessis (61) . . . 55 G6
Teloché (72) . . . 106 E4
le Temple (33) . . . 228 B3
le Temple (41) . . . 108 B3
le Temple-de-Bretagne (44) . . . 122 E2
Temple-Laguyon (24) . . . 214 B3
le Temple-sur-Lot (47) . . . 248 A2
Templemars (59) . . . 6 D5
Templeuve (59) . . . 6 E5
Templeux-la-Fosse (80) . . . 19 H1
Templeux-le-Guérard (80) . . . 19 J1
Tenay (01) . . . 189 K5
Tence (43) . . . 221 G4
Tencin (38) . . . 224 C1
Tende (06) . . . 311 D2
Tendon (88) . . . 95 F6
Tendron (18) . . . 150 A4
Tendu (36) . . . 165 H2
Teneur (62) . . . 5 G6
Tennie (72) . . . 106 B1
Tenteling (57) . . . 68 C2
Tercé (86) . . . 163 H4
Tercillat (23) . . . 166 C5
Tercis-les-Bains (40) . . . 204 A5
Terdeghem (59) . . . 3 J4
Tergnier (02) . . . 20 A6
Terjat (03) . . . 184 A2
Termes (08) . . . 42 C3
Termes (11) . . . 309 J2
Termes (48) . . . 237 F3
Termes-d'Armagnac (32) . . . 266 B5
Termignon (73) . . . 226 B1
Terminiers (28) . . . 109 J2
Ternand (69) . . . 187 K5
Ternant (17) . . . 177 J5
Ternant (21) . . . 154 A1
Ternant (58) . . . 169 K1
Ternant-les-Eaux (63) . . . 202 D6
Ternas (62) . . . 10 B3
Ternat (52) . . . 116 B3
Ternay (41) . . . 107 K6
Ternay (69) . . . 206 A4
Ternay (86) . . . 144 C3
les Ternes (15) . . . 218 D6
Ternuay-Melay-et-Saint-Hilaire (70) . . . 119 F4
Terny-Sorny (02) . . . 39 J2
Terramesnil (80) . . . 10 B5
la Terrasse (38) . . . 224 C1
la Terrasse-sur-Dorlay (42) . . . 205 J6
Terrasson-Lavilledieu (24) . . . 215 G4
Terrats (66) . . . 315 C3
Terraube (32) . . . 267 H2
Terre-Clapier (81) . . . 271 F3
Torre-Natale (52) . . . 117 F3
Terrebasse (31) . . . 287 G5
Terrefondrée (21) . . . 115 J6
Terrehault (72) . . . 83 G6
les Terres-de-Chaux (25) . . . 139 G4
la Terrisse (12) . . . 236 B3
Terroles (11) . . . 309 G3
Terron-sur-Aisne (08) . . . 42 B1
Terrou (46) . . . 234 D3
Tersanne (26) . . . 222 D4
Tersannes (87) . . . 181 F1
Terssac (81) . . . 270 D2
le Tertre-Saint-Denis (78) . . . 57 H2
Tertry (80) . . . 19 H2
Terville (57) . . . 27 G4
Tessancourt-sur-Aubette (78) . . . 58 A1
Tessé-Froulay (61) . . . 81 J1
Tessé-la-Madeleine (61) . . . 81 J1
Tessel (14) . . . 32 C5
Tesson (17) . . . 195 G3
Tessonnière (79) . . . 144 B6
la Tessoualle (49) . . . 143 F3
Tessy-sur-Vire (50) . . . 31 H5
la Teste-de-Buch (33) . . . 228 B3
Tétaigne (08) . . . 23 G4
Téterchen (57) . . . 3 J2
Téthieu (40) . . . 45 K6
Teting-sur-Nied (57) . . . 45 K6
Teuillac (33) . . . 211 H4
Teulat (81) . . . 269 K6
Teurthéville-Bocage (50) . . . 28 E4
Teurthéville-Hague (50) . . . 28 B3
Teyjat (24) . . . 197 J4
Teyran (34) . . . 274 C5
Teyssières (26) . . . 257 H1
Teyssieu (46) . . . 234 C1
Teyssode (81) . . . 270 C6
Thaas (51) . . . 61 J6
Thaims (17) . . . 194 E3
Thairé (17) . . . 176 E3

Thaix (58)	151	K6
Thal-Drulingen (67)	67	K2
Thal-Marmoutier (67)	70	B2
Thalamy (19)	201	H5
Thann (68)	97	A2
Thannenkirch (68)	96	B2
Thanvillé (67)	71	A4
Thaon (14)	32	D4
Thaon-les-Vosges (88)	94	D4
Tharaux (30)	255	K4
Tharoiseau (89)	133	J4
Tharot (89)	133	J3
Thaumiers (18)	149	K6
Thauron (23)	182	C5
Thauvenay (18)	131	K6
Thèbe (65)	305	H3
Théding (57)	68	C2
Thédirac (46)	233	G5
Thégra (46)	234	A2
Théhillac (56)	102	B5
le Theil (03)	168	C6
le Theil (50)	28	E3
le Theil (61)	83	J5
le Theil-Bocage (14)	53	F3
le Theil-de-Bretagne (35)	103	J1
le Theil-en-Auge (14)	34	A3
le Theil-Nolent (27)	34	C5
Theil-Rabier (16)	179	F4
Theil-sur-Vanne (89)	88	E6
Theillay (41)	130	B6
Theillement (27)	35	F4
Theix (56)	101	G5
Theizé (69)	188	A5
Thel (69)	187	H3
Théligny (72)	83	K6
Thélis-la-Combe (42)	221	J2
Thélod (54)	93	K1
Thelonne (08)	23	F5
Thélus (62)	11	F2
Théméricourt (95)	37	F6
Thémines (46)	234	B3
Théminettes (46)	234	B4
Thénac (17)	195	G3
Thénac (24)	231	G3
Thenailles (02)	21	J3
Thenay (36)	165	F3
Thenay (41)	128	E5
Thenelles (02)	20	B3
Thénésol (73)	209	G2
Theneuil (37)	145	K1
Theneuille (03)	167	K3
Thénezay (79)	162	B1
Thénioux (18)	130	A6
Thenissey (21)	135	G3
Thénisy (77)	88	C2
Thennelières (10)	90	B5
Thennes (80)	18	C3
Thenon (24)	214	D4
Thénorgues (08)	42	D2
Théoule-sur-Mer (06)	280	D6
Therdonne (60)	37	H2
Thérines (60)	17	H5
Thermes-Magnoac (65)	286	D4
Thérondels (12)	236	B2
Thérouanne (62)	3	G6
Thérouldeville (76)	14	E3
Thervay (39)	137	G6
Thésée (41)	128	E5
Thésy (39)	156	B4
Theuley (70)	137	H1
Théus (05)	243	F6
Theuville (28)	85	H4
Theuville (95)	37	G5
Theuville-aux-Maillots (76)	14	E3
Thevet-Saint-Julien (36)	166	C3
Théville (50)	28	E4
Thevray (27)	55	K2
They-sous-Montfort (88)	93	J5
They-sous-Vaudemont (54)	93	K3
Theys (38)	224	D1
Théza (66)	315	H3
Thézac (17)	194	E3
Thézac (47)	249	F2
Thézan-des-Corbières (11)	310	A1
Thézan-lès-Béziers (34)	291	K3
Thèze (04)	259	F2
Thèze (64)	284	D2
Thézey-Saint-Martin (54)	66	B2
Théziers (30)	275	K2
Thézillieu (01)	190	A6
Thézy-Glimont (80)	18	C3
Thiais (94)	58	E5
Thiancourt (90)	139	K2
Thianges (58)	151	H5
Thiant (59)	12	C2
Thiat (87)	180	E1
Thiaucourt-Regniéville (54)	65	H2
Thiaville-sur-Meurthe (54)	95	G2
Thiberville (27)	34	B3
Thibie (51)	62	C2
Thibivillers (60)	37	F4
Thibouville (27)	35	F5
Thicourt (57)	66	D1
Thiébauménil (54)	66	E6
Thiéblemont-Farémont (51)	63	G5
Thiébouhans (25)	139	H5
Thieffrain (10)	90	E6
Thieffrans (70)	138	C2
Thiéfosse (88)	119	G2
Thiel-sur-Acolin (03)	169	G4
Thiembronne (62)	4	E4
Thiénans (70)	138	C3
Thiennes (59)	3	J6
Thiepval (80)	10	E6
Thiergeville (76)	14	E4
Thiernu (02)	20	E3
Thiers (63)	203	H1
Thiers-sur-Thève (60)	38	B5
Thierville (27)	34	E4
Thierville-sur-Meuse (55)	43	H5
Thiéry (06)	261	H6
Thiescourt (60)	19	G6
Thiétreville (76)	14	E4
le Thieulin (28)	84	D3
Thieulloy-la-Ville (80)	17	H4
Thieulloy-l'Abbaye (80)	17	H3
la Thieuloye (62)	10	B1
Thieux (60)	18	B5
Thieux (77)	59	H1
Thiéville (14)	54	C1
Thièvres (62)	10	C5
Thièvres (80)	10	C5
Thiézac (15)	217	K6
Thignonville (45)	86	C5
Thil (01)	206	C1
Thil (10)	91	H4
le Thil (27)	36	C3
Thil (31)	268	D5
Thil (51)	40	C3
Thil (54)	26	E3
le Thil-Manneville (76)	15	J2
le Thil-Riberpré (76)	16	E5
Thil-sur-Arroux (71)	152	D6
Thilay (08)	22	D2
le Thillay (95)	59	F2
Thilleux (52)	91	H3
les Thilliers-en-Vexin (27)	36	C4
Thillois (51)	40	E4
Thillombois (55)	64	D2
Thillot (55)	65	F1
le Thillot (88)	119	G3
Thilouze (37)	145	J1
Thimert-Gâtelles (28)	84	E1
Thimonville (57)	66	C1
Thimory (45)	111	G4
Thin-le-Moutier (08)	22	B4
Thiolières (63)	203	H4
Thionne (03)	169	G5
Thionville (57)	27	G4
Thiouville (76)	15	F4
Thiraucourt (88)	93	K4
Thiré (85)	160	C3
Thiron Gardais (28)	84	D3
This (08)	22	C3
Thise (25)	138	A5
Thivars (28)	85	G4
Thivencelle (59)	7	K6
Thiverny (60)	38	A4
Thiverval-Grignon (78)	58	A3
Thivet (52)	116	C2
Thiviers (24)	198	B6
Thiville (28)	109	F2
Thizay (36)	148	C5
Thizay (37)	144	E1
Thizy (69)	187	H4
Thizy (89)	134	B2
Thoard (04)	259	H4
Thodure (38)	222	E2
Thoigné (72)	82	E5
Thoiras (30)	255	F6
Thoiré-sous-Contensor (72)	82	E4
Thoiré-sur-Dinan (72)	107	G6
Thoires (21)	115	G3
Thoirette (39)	189	K1
Thoiria (39)	173	H3
Thoiry (01)	190	D1
Thoiry (73)	208	C4
Thoiry (78)	57	K3
Thoissey (01)	188	C2
Thoissia (39)	172	E5
Thoisy-la-Berchère (21)	134	D6
Thoisy-le-Désert (21)	135	F2
Thoix (80)	17	J4
Thol-lès-Millières (52)	92	E6
Thollet (86)	164	C5
Thollon-les-Mémises (74)	175	H5
le Tholonet (13)	296	D1
le Tholy (88)	95	G6
Thomer-la-Sôgne (27)	56	D3
Thomery (77)	87	J3
Thomirey (21)	153	H2
Thonac (24)	214	E6
Thônes (74)	191	H5
Thonnance-lès-Joinville (52)	92	B2
Thonnance-les-Moulins (52)	92	C3
Thonne-la-Long (55)	23	K5
Thonne-le-Thil (55)	23	J5
Thonne-les-Près (55)	23	K6
Thonnelle (55)	23	K6
Thonon-les-Bains (74)	175	F5
les Thons (88)	117	J2
Thonville (57)	66	D1
le Thor (84)	276	D2
Thorailles (45)	111	K2
Thoraise (25)	156	A1
Thorame-Basse (04)	260	B5
Thorame-Haute (04)	260	C5
Thoras (43)	237	J2
Thoré-la-Rochette (41)	108	B5
Thorée-les-Pins (72)	106	D3
Thorens-Glières (74)	191	G4
Thorey (89)	114	B4
Thorey-en-Plaine (21)	154	D1
Thorey-Lyautey (54)	93	K2
Thorey-sous-Charny (21)	134	E5
Thorey-sur-Ouche (21)	153	J2
Thorigné (79)	178	C1
Thorigné-d'Anjou (49)	125	F1
Thorigné-en-Charnie (53)	105	J2
Thorigné-Fouillard (35)	79	H4
Thorigné-sur-Dué (72)	107	H2
Thorigny (79)	177	K2
Thorigny (85)	159	K2
Thorigny-sur-Marne (77)	59	H3
Thorigny-sur-Oreuse (89)	88	E5
le Thoronet (83)	298	C2
Thorrenc (07)	222	B3
Thors (10)	91	H4
Thors (17)	195	K1
Thory (80)	18	C4
Thory (89)	133	K2
Thoste (21)	134	C4
le Thou (17)	177	F3
Thou (18)	131	H4
Thou (45)	131	K2
Thouarcé (49)	125	G6
Thouaré-sur-Loire (44)	123	H4
Thouars (79)	144	B4
Thouars-sur-Arize (09)	287	K6
Thouars-sur-Garonne (47)	247	J4
Thouarsais-Bouildroux (85)	160	D2
le Thoult-Trosnay (51)	61	H3
le Thour (08)	21	H6
le Thoureil (49)	125	K4
Thourie (35)	103	H2
Thouron (87)	181	G5
Thourotte (60)	38	E1
Thoury (41)	129	H2
Thoury-Férottes (77)	88	A5
Thoux (32)	268	C5
Thuboeuf (53)	81	J2
le Thuel (02)	21	H5
Thuès-Entre-Valls (66)	313	K4
Thueyts (07)	239	F4
Thugny-Trugny (08)	41	J3
la Thuile (73)	208	D4
les Thuiles (04)	260	C1
Thuilley-aux-Groseilles (54)	65	J6
Thuillières (88)	93	K6
Thuir (66)	315	F3
le Thuit (27)	36	A4
le Thuit-Anger (27)	35	F3
Thuit-Hébert (27)	35	F3
le Thuit-Signol (27)	35	G4
le Thuit-Simer (27)	35	G4
Thulay (25)	139	H3
Thumeréville (54)	26	D6
Thumeries (59)	6	D6
Thun-l'Évêque (59)	11	K3
Thun-Saint-Amand (59)	7	H6
Thun-Saint-Martin (59)	11	K3
Thurageau (86)	162	E1
Thuré (86)	145	H6
Thuret (63)	185	G5
Thurey (71)	172	C1
Thurey-le-Mont (25)	138	B4
Thurins (69)	205	J3
Thury (21)	153	H3
Thury (89)	132	D2
Thury-en-Valois (60)	39	F5
Thury-Harcourt (14)	53	J1
Thury-sous-Clermont (60)	37	K3
Thusy (74)	190	D5
Thuy (65)	285	K5
Thyez (74)	191	K3
Tibiran-Jaunac (65)	305	H2
Ticheville (61)	55	F3
Tichey (21)	154	E3
Tieffenbach (67)	69	F5
Tiercé (49)	125	H1
Tierceville (14)	32	C3
le Tiercent (35)	79	J1
Tieste-Uragnoux (32)	285	H1
la Tieule (48)	253	H2
Tiffauges (85)	142	C3
Tigeaux (77)	59	K4
Tigery (91)	59	G6
Tignac (09)	308	A4
Tigné (49)	143	K1
Tignécourt (88)	117	J1
Tignes (73)	193	G2
le Tignet (06)	280	C5
Tignieu-Jameyzieu (38)	206	E2
Tigny-Noyelle (62)	9	F2
Tigy (45)	110	D5
Til-Châtel (21)	136	B3
Tilh (40)	264	D6
Tilhouse (65)	304	E1
Tillac (32)	285	K2
Tillay-le-Péneux (28)	109	J1
Tillé (60)	37	H2
Tillenay (21)	155	F1
le Tilleul (76)	14	B4
Tilleul-Dame-Agnès (27)	56	B1
le Tilleul-Lambert (27)	35	G6
le Tilleul-Othon (27)	35	F6
Tilleux (88)	93	G4
Tillières (49)	142	C1
Tillières-sur-Avre (27)	56	C5
Tilloloy (80)	19	F5
Tillou (79)	178	D3
Tilloy-et-Bellay (51)	63	F1
Tilloy-Floriville (80)	8	E6
Tilloy-lès-Conty (80)	17	K4
Tilloy-lès-Hermaville (62)	10	C2
Tilloy-lès-Mofflaines (62)	11	F3
Tilloy-lez-Cambrai (59)	11	J4
Tilloy-lez-Marchiennes (59)	11	K5
Tilly (27)	36	B5
Tilly (36)	164	D5
Tilly (78)	57	H3
Tilly-Capelle (62)	5	G6
Tilly-la-Campagne (14)	32	E6
Tilly-sur-Meuse (55)	64	D1
Tilly-sur-Seulles (14)	32	B5
Tilques (62)	3	F5
Tincebray (61)	53	F4
Tincey-et-Pontrebeau (70)	137	H1
Tincourt-Boucly (80)	19	H1
Tincques (62)	10	C2
Tincry (57)	66	C2
Tingry (62)	4	B4
Tinqueux (51)	40	E4
Tinténiac (35)	78	E1
Tintry (71)	153	G4
Tintury (58)	151	J4
Tiranges (43)	220	D2
Tirent-Pontéjac (32)	287	F1
Tirepied (50)	52	A5
Tissey (89)	113	K4
le Titre (80)	9	F4
Tivernon (45)	110	A1
Tiviers (15)	218	E5
Tizac-de-Curton (33)	230	A2
Tizac-de-Lapouyade (33)	212	A5
Tocane-Saint-Apre (24)	213	J3
Tocqueville (50)	29	F2
Tocqueville (27)	34	C2
Tocqueville-en-Caux (76)	15	H3
Tocqueville-les-Murs (76)	14	E5
Tocqueville-sur-Eu (76)	8	B6
Toeufles (80)	9	F5
Toges (08)	42	C2
Togny-aux-Boeufs (51)	62	E3
Tolla (2A)	320	E4
Tollaincourt (88)	117	G1
Tollent (62)	9	H3
Tollevast (50)	28	C3
la Tombe (77)	88	B4
Tombeboeuf (47)	231	H6
Tomblaine (54)	66	B5
Tomino (2B)	317	D2
les Tonils (26)	241	F5
Tonnac (81)	250	E6
Tonnay-Boutonne (17)	177	H5
Tonnay-Charente (17)	177	F5
Tonneins (47)	247	J2
Tonnerre (89)	114	A4
Tonneville (50)	28	C2
Tonnoy (54)	94	B1
Tonquédec (22)	48	A3
Torcé (35)	104	A1
Torcé-en-Vallée (72)	107	F1
Torcé-Viviers-en-Charnie (53)	105	K1
Torcenay (52)	116	E4
Torchamp (61)	81	F1
Torchefelon (38)	207	G5
Torcheville (57)	67	G2
Torcieu (01)	189	J5
Torcy (62)	4	E6
Torcy (71)	153	G6
Torcy (77)	59	H3
Torcy-en-Valois (02)	39	J6
Torcy-et-Pouligny (21)	134	C3
Torcy-le-Grand (10)	90	B2
Torcy-le-Grand (76)	16	A3
Torcy-le-Petit (10)	90	C2
Torcy-le-Petit (76)	16	A3
Tordères (66)	315	F4
Tordouet (14)	55	F1
Torfou (49)	142	C3
Torfou (91)	86	D2
Torigni-sur-Vire (50)	31	J4
Tornac (30)	274	D1
Tornay (52)	117	F6
le Torp-Mesnil (76)	15	H4
Torpes (25)	156	A1
Torpes (71)	155	F5
le Torpt (27)	34	B3
le Torquesne (14)	33	K4
Torreilles (66)	310	D5
Torsac (16)	196	E4
Torsiac (43)	219	F2
Tortebesse (63)	201	J3
Tortefontaine (62)	9	H2
Tortequesne (62)	11	H3
Torteron (18)	150	C3
Torteval-Quesnay (14)	32	A5
Tortezais (03)	167	K5
Tortisambert (14)	54	D2
Torvilliers (10)	89	K5
Torxé (17)	177	J5
Tosny (27)	36	A5
Tossiat (01)	189	H3
Tostat (65)	285	H4
Tostes (27)	35	H4
Totainville (88)	93	J4
Tôtes (76)	15	K4
Touchay (18)	166	D2
la Touche (26)	240	C6
les Touches (44)	123	J1
les Touches-de-Périgny (17)	178	C6
Toucy (89)	112	D6
Toudon (06)	281	F1
Touët-de-l'Escarène (06)	281	H2
Touët-sur-Var (06)	280	D1
Touffailles (82)	249	F4
Toufflers (59)	7	F4
Touffréville (14)	33	F5
Touffreville (27)	36	B3
Touffreville-la-Cable (76)	15	F6
Touffreville-la-Corbeline (76)	15	G6
Touffreville-sur-Eu (76)	8	B6
Touget (32)	268	B5
Touille (31)	306	E2
Touillon (21)	134	E1
Touillon-et-Loutelet (25)	157	F5
Toujouse (32)	266	A3
Toul (54)	65	H5
Toulaud (07)	240	B1
Toulenne (33)	230	A5
Touligny (08)	22	C4
Toulis-et-Attencourt (02)	20	E4
Toulon (83)	297	J6
Toulon-sur-Allier (03)	168	E4
Toulon-sur-Arroux (71)	170	C2
Toulonjac (12)	251	F2
Toulouges (66)	315	G2
Toulouse (31)	269	G6
Toulouse-le-Château (39)	155	H5
Toulouzette (40)	264	C5
Toulx-Sainte-Croix (23)	183	G1
Touques (14)	33	J3
le Touquet-Paris-Plage (62)	4	A5
Touquettes (61)	55	G4
Touquin (77)	60	A5
la Tour (06)	261	J6
la Tour (74)	191	J2
la Tour-Blanche (24)	213	H1
la Tour-d'Aigues (84)	277	J4
la Tour-d'Auvergne (63)	201	K5
Tour-de-Faure (46)	250	C1
la Tour-de-Salvagny (69)	205	K1
la Tour-de-Sçay (25)	138	C4
la Tour-du-Crieu (09)	307	J1
la Tour-du-Meix (39)	173	H3
le Tour-du-Parc (56)	121	G2
la Tour-du-Pin (38)	207	G4
Tour-en-Bessin (14)	32	A3
la Tour-en-Jarez (42)	205	G5
Tour-en-Sologne (41)	129	G3
la Tour-Saint-Gelin (37)	145	H3
la Tour-sur-Orb (34)	272	E6
Tourailles (41)	128	D1
les Tourailles (61)	53	J4
Tourbes (34)	292	B2
Tourcelles-Chaumont (08)	42	A2
Tourch (29)	75	F2
Tourcoing (59)	6	E3
Tourdun (32)	285	J1
la Tourette (42)	204	E6
la Tourette-Cabardès (11)	290	B3
Tourette-du-Château (06)	281	F1
Tourgéville (14)	33	J3
la Tourlandry (49)	143	G1
Tourlaville (50)	28	D2
Tourliac (47)	232	B4
Tourly (60)	37	F4
Tourmignies (59)	6	E6
Tourmont (39)	155	J5
Tournai-sur-Dive (61)	54	D4
Tournan (32)	286	E1
Tournan-en-Brie (77)	59	J5
Tournans (25)	138	C3
Tournavaux (08)	22	D2
Tournay (65)	285	K6
Tournay-sur-Odon (14)	32	C6
le Tourne (33)	229	J3
Tournebu (14)	53	K2
Tournecoupe (32)	268	A3
Tournedos-Bois-Hubert (27)	35	G6
Tournedos-sur-Seine (27)	35	K4
Tournefeuille (31)	288	A1
Tournefort (06)	281	F1
Tournehem-sur-la-Hem (62)	2	E4
Tournemire (12)	272	D2
Tournemire (15)	217	H5
Tournes (08)	22	C3
le Tourneur (14)	31	K5
Tourneville (27)	35	H6
Tournières (14)	31	J2
Tournissan (11)	309	K1
Tournoisis (45)	109	H3
Tournon (73)	209	F3
Tournon-d'Agenais (47)	249	F2
Tournon-Saint-Martin (36)	164	B1
Tournon-Saint-Pierre (37)	164	B1
Tournon-sur-Rhône (07)	222	B5
Tournous-Darré (65)	286	A4
Tournous-Devant (65)	286	B5
Tournus (71)	171	K3
Tourny (27)	36	C5
Tourouvre (61)	83	J1
Tourouzelle (11)	291	F5
Tourreilles (11)	308	E2
les Tourreilles (31)	305	H1
Tourrenquets (32)	267	J4
Tourrette-Levens (06)	281	G3
les Tourrettes (26)	240	B4
Tourrettes-sur-Loup (06)	280	E4
Tourriers (16)	196	E1
Tours (37)	127	J4
Tours-en-Savoie (73)	209	G3
Tours-en-Vimeu (80)	8	E6
Tours-sur-Marne (51)	62	B1
Tours-sur-Meymont (63)	203	J3

404

Tourtenay (79) 144 C3
Tourteron (08) 22 C6
Tourtoirac (24) 214 D2
Tourtour (83) 279 G6
Tourtouse (09) 306 D1
Tourtrès (47) 231 H6
Tourtrol (09) 308 A2
Tourves (83) 297 F3
Tourville-en-Auge (14) 33 K3
Tourville-la-Campagne (27) 35 G4
Tourville-la-Chapelle (76) 16 B1
Tourville-la-Rivière (76) 35 H3
Tourville-les-Ifs (76) 14 D1
Tourville-sur-Arques (76) 15 K2
Tourville-sur-Odon (14) 32 D5
Tourville-sur-Pont-Audemer (27) . . 34 C3
Tourville-sur-Sienne (50) 30 D4
Toury (28) 86 A6
Toury-Lurcy (58) 169 F1
Toury-sur-Jour (58) 168 D1
Tourzel-Ronzières (63) 202 D5
Toussaint (76) 14 D1
Toussieu (69) 206 C3
Toussieux (01) 188 C5
Tousson (77) 87 F4
Toussus-le-Noble (78) 58 C5
Toutainville (27) 34 C3
Toutenant (71) 154 D5
Toutencourt (80) 10 C6
Toutens (31) 288 E2
Toutlemonde (49) 143 F3
Toutry (21) 134 B3
Touvérac (16) 212 B1
le Touvet (38) 224 C1
Touville (27) 34 E3
Touvois (44) 141 G4
Touvre (16) 197 H5
Touzac (16) 196 B4
Touzac (46) 249 G1
Tox (2B) 319 J6
Toy-Viam (19) 200 B4
Tracy-Bocage (14) 32 B6
Tracy-le-Mont (60) 39 F1
Tracy-le-Val (60) 39 F1
Tracy-sur-Loire (58) 131 K5
Tracy-sur-Mer (14) 32 B3
Trades (69) 187 K1
Traenheim (67) 70 C4
Tragny (57) 66 C1
Traînel (10) 88 E3
Traînou (45) 110 C3
le Trait (76) 35 F1
Traitiéfontaine (70) 138 A4
Traize (73) 207 K3
Tralaigues (63) 184 A6
Tralonca (2B) 319 F5
Tramain (22) 77 K2
Tramayes (71) 188 A1
Trambly (71) 171 G6
Tramecourt (62) 5 F6
Tramery (51) 40 D4
Tramezaïgues (65) 304 E5
Tramolé (38) 207 F5
Tramont-Émy (54) 93 J3
Tramont-Lassus (54) 93 J3
Tramont-Saint-André (54) 93 J3
Tramoyes (01) 188 D6
Trampot (88) 92 D3
la Tranche-sur-Mer (85) 159 H5
la Tranclière (01) 189 G3
Trancrainville (28) 85 K5
Trangé (72) 106 D2
le Tranger (36) 147 F4
Trannes (10) 91 H4
Tranqueville-Graux (88) 93 H2
Trans (53) 81 K5
Trans-en-Provence (83) 298 D1
Trans-la-Forêt (35) 51 H5
Trans-sur-Erdre (44) 123 J1
le Translay (80) 17 F1
le Transloy (62) 11 F5
Tranzault (36) 165 K3
Trappes (78) 58 B4
Trassanel (11) 290 C4
Traubach-le-Bas (68) 97 A3
Traubach-le-Haut (68) 97 A3
Trausse (11) 290 D4
Travaillan (84) 257 F4
Travecy (02) 20 A4
Traversères (32) 286 D1
Traves (70) 137 K1
le Travet (81) 271 F4
Trayes (79) 161 H2
Tréal (56) 102 A2
Tréauville (50) 28 B3
Trébabu (29) 72 B4
Treban (03) 168 D5
Tréban (81) 251 K6
Trébas (81) 271 H2
Trébédan (22) 50 B6
Trèbes (11) 290 C5
Trébeurden (22) 47 J2
Trébons (65) 304 D1
Trébons-de-Luchon (31) 305 H5
Trébons-sur-la-Grasse (31) 288 E2
Trébrivan (22) 75 K2
Trébry (22) 77 J2
Tréclun (21) 154 E1
Trécon (51) 62 A3
Trédaniel (22) 77 H2
Trédarzec (22) 48 C2
Trédias (22) 78 B1

Trédion (56) 101 H3
Trédrez-Locquémeau (22) 47 J3
Tréduder (22) 47 J4
Trefcon (02) 19 J2
Treffendel (35) 78 D5
Treffiagat (29) 98 B3
Treffieux (44) 103 H5
Treffléan (56) 101 G5
Treffort (38) 242 A1
Treffort-Cuisiat (01) 189 H1
Treffrin (22) 75 J2
Tréflaouénan (29) 46 D4
Tréflévénez (29) 46 D5
Tréflez (29) 46 C3
Tréfols (51) 61 F4
Tréfumel (22) 78 D1
Trégarantec (29) 46 C4
Trégarvan (29) 74 C2
Trégastel (22) 47 K2
Tréglamus (22) 48 B5
Tréglonou (29) 72 D2
Trégomeur (22) 49 F5
Trégon (22) 50 B4
Trégonneau (22) 48 C4
Trégourez (29) 75 F4
Trégrom (22) 48 A4
Tréguennec (29) 73 E5
Trégueux (22) 49 G6
Tréguidel (22) 48 E5
Tréguier (22) 48 C2
Trégunc (29) 99 F3
Tréhet (41) 107 H6
Tréhorenteuc (56) 78 A5
le Tréhou (29) 74 D1
Treignac (19) 200 A5
Treignat (03) 166 E6
Treigny (89) 132 C3
Treilles (11) 310 C3
Treilles-en-Gâtinais (45) 111 H2
Treillières (44) 123 G2
Treix (52) 92 B6
Treize-Septiers (85) 142 B3
Treize-Vents (85) 143 F4
Tréjouls (82) 249 H4
Trélans (48) 253 G1
Trélazé (49) 126 H3
Trélévern (22) 48 B2
Trelins (42) 204 C2
Trélissac (24) 214 B3
Trélivan (22) 50 C6
Trelly (50) 30 E5
Trélon (59) 13 J5
Trélou-sur-Marne (02) 40 B6
Trémaouézan (29) 46 C5
Trémargat (22) 76 B2
Trémauville (76) 14 E5
la Tremblade (17) 194 B1
Tremblay (35) 51 J6
le Tremblay (49) 104 C6
Tremblay-en-France (93) 59 G2
Tremblay-les-Villages (28) 85 F1
le Tremblay-Omonville (27) 35 G6
le Tremblay-sur-Mauldre (78) 58 A4
Tremblecourt (54) 65 J3
le Tremblois (70) 137 F4
Tremblois-lès-Carignan (08) 23 J4
Tremblois-lès-Rocroi (08) 22 B2
Trémeheuc (35) 51 G6
Trémel (22) 47 J4
Trémentines (49) 143 F2
Tréméoc (29) 98 C2
Tréméreuc (22) 50 D4
Trémery (57) 27 H4
Trémeur (22) 78 B1
Tréméven (22) 48 E4
Tréméven (29) 99 J3
Tréminis (38) 242 B3
Trémoins (70) 139 G1
Trémolat (24) 232 B2
Trémons (47) 248 E2
Trémont (49) 143 J1
Trémont (61) 82 E1
Trémont-sur-Saulx (55) 63 K4
Trémonzey (88) 118 B2
Trémorel (22) 78 A3
Trémouille (15) 218 A1
Trémouille-Saint-Loup (63) 201 H6
Trémouilles (12) 252 C4
Trémoulet (09) 288 E6
Trémuson (22) 49 F6
Trenal (39) 173 F2
Trensacq (40) 245 H4
Trentels (47) 248 E1
Tréogan (22) 75 J4
Tréogat (29) 73 F4
Tréon (28) 56 E6
Tréouergat (29) 72 C3
Trépail (51) 41 G6
le Tréport (76) 8 C5
Tréprel (14) 53 K3
Trept (38) 207 F3
Trésauvaux (55) 43 K6
Tresboeuf (35) 103 H1
Trescault (62) 11 H5
Treschenu-Creyers (26) 241 J3
Trescléoux (05) 258 D2
Trésilley (70) 137 K3
Treslon (51) 40 D4
Tresnay (58) 168 D2
Trespoux-Rassiels (46) 249 K2

Tresques (30) 256 C5
Tressan (34) 292 D1
Tressandans (25) 138 C2
Tressange (57) 27 F4
Tressé (35) 50 E5
Tresserre (66) 315 G4
Tresserve (73) 208 B3
Tresses (33) 229 J2
Tressignaux (22) 48 E4
Tressin (59) 7 F1
Tresson (72) 107 H4
Treteau (03) 169 G6
la Trétoire (77) 60 D3
Trets (13) 297 F2
Treux (80) 18 D1
Treuzy-Levelay (77) 87 J5
Trévé (22) 77 F4
Trévenans (90) 139 H1
Tréveneuc (22) 49 F4
Tréveray (55) 64 D6
Trévérec (22) 48 D4
Trévérien (35) 78 E1
Trèves (30) 253 K6
Trèves (69) 205 K5
Trévien (81) 251 G6
Trévières (14) 31 K1
Trévignin (73) 208 B2
Trévillach (66) 309 H6
Tréville (11) 289 G3
Trévillers (25) 139 J5
Trévilly (89) 134 B3
Trévol (03) 168 E3
Trévou-Tréguignec (22) 48 B2
Trévoux (01) 188 C5
le Trévoux (29) 99 H3
Trévron (22) 50 C6
Trézelles (03) 186 A1
Tréziers (11) 308 C2
Trézilidé (29) 46 D4
Trézioux (63) 203 H3
Triac-Lautrait (16) 196 B3
le Triadou (34) 274 R4
Triaize (85) 160 A5
Tribehou (50) 31 F3
Trichey (89) 114 B3
Tricot (60) 18 D6
Trie-Château (60) 36 E4
Trie-la-Ville (60) 36 E4
Trie-sur-Baïse (65) 286 A4
Triel-sur-Seine (78) 58 B2
Triembach-au-Val (67) 70 B6
Trieux (54) 26 E5
Trigance (83) 279 J3
Trignac (44) 122 A2
Trigny (51) 40 D3
Triguères (45) 112 A3
Trilbardou (77) 59 J2
Trilla (66) 309 H6
Trilport (77) 60 A2
Trimbach (67) 25 C2
Trimer (35) 78 E1
la Trimouille (86) 164 C5
Trinay (45) 110 A2
la Trinitat (15) 236 C3
la Trinité (06) 281 H3
la Trinité (27) 56 E2
la Trinité (50) 52 B4
la Trinité (73) 208 D5
la Trinité-de-Réville (27) 55 H2
la Trinité-de-Thouberville (27) . . . 35 F3
la Trinité-des-Laitiers (61) 55 G4
la Trinité-du-Mont (76) 14 E6
la Trinité-Porhoët (56) 77 H5
la Trinité-sur-Mer (56) 100 E4
la Trinité-Surzur (56) 101 H6
Triors (26) 222 E4
le Trioulou (15) 235 F4
Tripleville (41) 109 G3
Triqueville (76) 34 D1
Triqueville (27) 34 B3
Trith-Saint-Léger (59) 12 C2
Tritteling (57) 45 K5
Trivy (71) 171 F5
Trizac (15) 217 J3
Trizay (17) 194 E1
Trizay-Coutretot-Saint-Serge (28) . 84 A5
Trizay-lès-Bonneval (28) 84 E6
Troarn (14) 33 F4
Troche (19) 215 H1
Trochères (21) 136 D5
Trocy-en-Multien (77) 60 A1
Troësnes (02) 39 H5
Troguéry (22) 48 C3
Trogues (37) 145 J2
les Trois-Domaines (55) 64 C2
Trois-Fonds (23) 183 G2
Trois-Fontaines-l'Abbaye (51) . . . 63 J5
Trois-Monts (14) 32 D6
les Trois-Moutiers (86) 144 D5
Trois-Palis (16) 196 D3
les Trois-Pierres (76) 14 D5
Trois-Puits (51) 41 F5
Trois-Vèvres (58) 151 G5
Trois-Villes (64) 283 H6
Troisfontaines (57) 67 K5
Troisfontaines-la-Ville (52) 91 K1
Troisgots (50) 31 H4
Troissereux (60) 37 G1
Troissy (51) 40 C6
Troisvaux (62) 10 B1
Troisvilles (59) 12 C5

Tromarey (70) 137 G5
Tromborn (57) 45 J3
Troncens (32) 285 J2
la Tronche (38) 224 A3
le Tronchet (35) 51 F5
le Tronchet (72) 82 D6
Tronchoy (89) 113 K4
Tronchy (71) 172 B1
le Troncq (27) 35 G5
Trondes (54) 65 G5
Tronget (03) 168 C5
le Tronquay (14) 32 A4
le Tronquay (27) 36 B2
Tronsanges (58) 150 D2
Tronville (54) 44 C6
Tronville-en-Barrois (55) 64 C5
Troo (41) 107 K5
Trosly-Breuil (60) 39 F2
Trosly-Loire (02) 39 H1
Trouans (10) 62 D4
Troubat (65) 305 H3
Trouhans (21) 154 E1
Trouhaut (21) 135 H4
Trouillas (66) 315 F3
Trouley-Labarthe (65) 285 K4
Troussencourt (60) 18 A5
Troussey (55) 65 G5
Troussures (60) 37 G2
Trouvans (25) 138 D3
Trouville (76) 15 F6
Trouville-la-Haule (27) 34 D2
Trouville-sur-Mer (14) 33 J2
Trouy (18) 149 G4
Troye-d'Ariège (09) 308 B2
Troyes (10) 90 B4
Troyon (55) 64 D1
la Truchère (71) 172 A4
Truchtersheim (67) 70 E2
Trucy (02) 40 B1
Trucy-l'Orgueilleux (58) 132 E4
Trucy-sur-Yonne (89) 133 H2
le Truel (12) 272 A1
Trugny (21) 154 D4
Truinas (26) 240 E5
Trumilly (60) 38 D4
Trun (61) 54 D1
Trungy (14) 32 B4
Truttemer-le-Grand (14) 52 E4
Truttemer-le-Petit (14) 52 E4
Truyes (37) 128 A6
Tubersent (62) 4 B5
Tuchan (11) 310 A4
Tucquegnieux (54) 26 E5
Tudeils (19) 216 B5
Tudelle (32) 266 E5
Tuffé (72) 107 H1
Tugéras-Saint-Maurice (17) 211 K1
Tugny-et-Pont (02) 19 J2
la Tuilière (42) 186 C5
Tulette (26) 257 F3
Tulle (19) 216 B3
Tullins (38) 223 J2
Tully (80) 8 D5
Tupigny (02) 20 C1
Tupin-et-Semons (69) 206 A5
la Turballe (44) 121 H4
la Turbie (06) 281 J3
Turcey (21) 135 H4
Turckheim (68) 96 B4
Turenne (19) 215 J5
Turgon (16) 179 J5
Turgy (10) 114 A2
Turny (89) 113 H2
Turquant (49) 144 D1
Turquestein-Blancrupt (57) 67 K6
Turqueville (50) 29 F5
Turretot (76) 14 B5
Turriers (04) 259 H1
Tursac (24) 214 D6
Tusson (16) 179 F5
Tuzaguet (65) 305 G1
le Tuzan (33) 245 K1
Tuzie (16) 179 G5

U

Uberach (67) 69 J5
Ubexy (88) 94 B3
Ubraye (04) 280 A1
Ucciani (2A) 320 E3
Ucel (07) 239 H5
Uchacq-et-Parentis (40) 265 G2
Uchaud (30) 275 F4
Uchaux (84) 256 E6
Uchentein (09) 306 C4
Uchizy (71) 171 K4
Uchon (71) 152 E6
Uckange (57) 27 G5
Ueberstrass (68) 97 A5
Uffheim (68) 97 D3
Uffholtz (68) 97 A1
Ugine (73) 209 G1
Uglas (65) 286 B5
Ugnouas (65) 285 H4
Ugny (54) 26 C3
Ugny-le-Gay (02) 19 J5
Ugny-l'Équipée (80) 19 H3
Ugny-sur-Meuse (55) 65 G6
Uhart-Cize (64) 282 D5
Uhart-Mixe (64) 283 G4

Uhlwiller (67) 69 K6
Uhrwiller (67) 69 J5
Ulcot (79) 143 K3
les Ulis (91) 58 C6
Ully-Saint-Georges (60) 37 J4
les Ulmes (49) 144 B1
Umpeau (28) 85 J2
Unac (09) 308 A5
Uncey-le-Franc (21) 135 F5
Unchair (51) 40 C4
Ungersheim (68) 96 B6
Unias (42) 204 E4
Unienville (10) 91 H4
Unieux (42) 221 F1
l'Union (31) 269 H6
Unverre (28) 84 C6
Unzent (09) 288 C6
Upaix (05) 259 F2
Upie (26) 240 D2
Ur (66) 313 G5
Urau (31) 306 B2
Urbalacone (2A) 320 D6
Urbanya (66) 314 A3
Urbeis (67) 96 A1
Urbès (68) 119 J3
Urbise (42) 186 D2
Urçay (03) 167 H3
Urcel (02) 40 A1
Urcerey (90) 139 H1
Urciers (36) 166 C4
Urcuit (64) 282 D1
Urcy (21) 135 J2
Urdens (32) 267 K3
Urdès (64) 284 C2
Urdos (64) 303 F4
Urepel (64) 263 D5
Urgons (40) 265 H5
Urgosse (32) 266 B4
Uriménil (88) 94 D6
Urmatt (67) 70 B4
Urost (64) 285 F4
Urou-et-Crennes (61) 54 C4
Urrugne (64) 263 B2
Urs (09) 307 K5
Urschenheim (68) 96 D4
Urt (64) 282 D1
Urtaca (2B) 319 F2
Urtière (25) 139 J5
Uruffe (54) 93 G1
Urval (24) 232 C2
Urville (10) 91 G6
Urville (14) 53 K1
Urville (50) 28 E5
Urville (88) 93 G5
Urville-Nacqueville (50) 28 B2
Urvillers (02) 20 A3
Ury (77) 87 G4
Urzy (58) 150 E3
Us (95) 37 F6
Usclades-et-Rieutord (07) 239 F3
Usclas-d'Hérault (34) 292 C2
Usclas-du-Bosc (34) 273 G5
Usinens (74) 190 C4
Ussac (19) 215 J3
Ussat (09) 307 J5
Usseau (79) 177 K2
Usseau (86) 145 J5
Ussel (15) 218 C5
Ussel (19) 201 F5
Ussel (46) 233 J5
Ussel-d'Allier (03) 185 G2
Usson (63) 203 F3
Usson-du-Poitou (86) 180 A1
Usson-en-Forez (42) 220 C1
Ussy (14) 53 K2
Ussy-sur-Marne (77) 60 B2
Ustaritz (64) 263 D1
Ustou (09) 306 E5
Utelle (06) 281 G1
Uttenheim (67) 70 C5
Uttenhoffen (67) 69 K5
Uttwiller (67) 69 H6
Uvernet-Fours (04) 260 C1
Uxeau (71) 170 B2
Uxegney (88) 94 C5
Uxelles (39) 173 J2
Uxem (59) 3 J1
Uz (65) 304 A2
Uza (40) 244 C6
Uzan (64) 284 B2
Uzay-le-Venon (18) 149 H6
Uzech (46) 233 H5
Uzein (64) 284 C3
Uzel (62) 77 D3
Uzelle (25) 138 D3
Uzemain (88) 118 C1
Uzer (07) 239 G6
Uzer (65) 304 D1
Uzerche (19) 199 J6
Uzès (30) 275 H1
Uzeste (33) 246 C1
Uzos (64) 284 D4

V

Vaas (72) 127 F1
Vabre (81) 271 G5
Vabre-Tizac (12) 251 H4
Vabres (15) 219 F5
Vabres (30) 274 C1

Vabres-l'Abbaye (12) 272 B2
Vacherauville (55) 43 H4
Vachères (04) 277 K2
Vachères-en-Quint (26) 241 G2
Vacheresse (74) 175 H5
la Vacheresse-et-la-Rouillie (88) . . . 93 H6
la Vacherie (27) 35 J6
Vacognes-Neuilly (14) 32 C6
la Vacquerie (14) 31 K4
la Vacquerie-et-Saint-Martin-de-Castries (34) 273 H4
Vacquerie-le-Boucq (62) 9 K3
Vacqueriette-Erquières (62) 9 J2
Vacqueville (54) 95 G1
Vacqueyras (84) 257 G5
Vacquières (34) 274 C3
Vacquiers (31) 269 H4
Vadans (39) 155 J4
Vadans (70) 137 F5
Vadelaincourt (55) 43 G6
Vadenay (51) 41 J6
Vadencourt (02) 20 C1
Vadencourt (80) 10 C6
Vadonville (55) 64 E4
Vagnas (07) 255 K2
Vagney (88) 119 G2
Vahl-Ebersing (57) 68 A3
Vahl-lès-Bénestroff (57) 67 G2
Vahl-lès-Faulquemont (57) 45 K6
Vaiges (53) 105 H2
Vailhan (34) 292 B1
Vailhauquès (34) 274 A5
Vailhourles (12) 250 E3
Vaillac (46) 233 J4
Vaillant (52) 116 B6
Vailly (10) 90 B4
Vailly (74) 175 G6
Vailly-sur-Aisne (02) 40 A2
Vailly-sur-Sauldre (18) 131 H4
Vains (50) 51 K3
Vairé (85) 158 E2
Vaire-Arcier (25) 138 B5
Vaire-le-Petit (25) 138 B5
Vaire-sous-Corbie (80) 18 D2
Vaires-sur-Marne (77) 59 H3
Vaison-la-Romaine (84) 257 G4
Vaïssac (82) 269 J1
Vaite (70) 137 G1
la Vaivre (70) 118 C3
Vaivre-et-Montoille (70) 138 A1
le Val (83) 297 K2
le Val-d'Ajol (88) 118 E3
Val-d'Auzon (10) 90 D3
le Val-David (57) 56 E2
Val-de-Bride (57) 67 F3
Val-de-Chalvagne (04) 280 C1
Val-de-Fier (74) 190 D5
le Val-de-Gouhenans (70) 138 E1
le Val-de-Guéblange (57) 67 H1
Val-de-la-Haye (76) 35 G2
Val-de-Mercy (89) 133 G1
Val-de-Meuse (52) 116 E2
Val-de-Reuil (27) 35 J4
Val-de-Roulans (25) 138 C4
Val-de-Saâne (76) 15 J4
Val-de-Vesle (51) 41 G5
Val-de-Vière (51) 63 G4
Val-d'Épy (39) 172 E5
Val-des-Marais (51) 61 K3
Val-des-Prés (05) 226 A6
le Val-d'Esnoms (52) 116 C6
Val-d'Isère (73) 193 C5
Val-d'Izé (35) 79 K3
Val-d'Ornain (55) 64 A4
Val-d'Orvin (10) 89 G4
Val-et-Châtillon (54) 67 H6
Val-Maravel (26) 241 K5
le Val-Saint-Éloi (70) 118 B5
le Val-Saint-Germain (91) 86 B1
le Val-Saint-Père (50) 51 K3
Val-Suzon (21) 135 J4
Valady (12) 251 K1
Valailles (27) 34 C4
Valaire (41) 128 E4
Valanjou (49) 125 G6
Valaurie (26) 256 E1
Valavoire (04) 259 H3
Valay (70) 137 G5
Valbeleix (63) 202 C6
Valbelle (04) 259 F4
Valbois (55) 65 F2
Valbonnais (38) 242 C1
Valbonne (06) 280 E5
Valcabrère (31) 305 H2
Valcanville (50) 29 F2
Valcebollère (66) 313 H6
Valcivières (63) 204 A4
Valcourt (52) 63 J6
Valdahon (25) 156 E1
Valdampierre (60) 37 G4
Valdeblore (06) 261 J5
le Valdécie (50) 28 C5
Valderiès (81) 270 E1
Valderoure (06) 280 B3
Valdieu-Lutran (68) 119 K6
Valdivienne (86) 163 H4
Valdoie (90) 119 H6
Valdrôme (26) 241 K6
Valdurenque (81) 290 A1
Valeille (42) 205 F3
Valeilles (82) 248 E2
Valeins (01) 188 C3

Valempoulières (39) 156 A5
Valençay (36) 147 J2
Valence (16) 179 H6
Valence (26) 240 C1
Valence (82) 248 E6
Valence-d'Albigeois (81) 271 G1
Valence-en-Brie (77) 87 K3
Valence-sur-Baïse (32) 267 F3
Valenciennes (59) 12 D2
Valencin (38) 206 C4
Valencogne (38) 207 H5
Valennes (72) 107 K3
Valensole (04) 278 D3
Valentigney (25) 139 H3
Valentine (31) 305 J1
Valenton (94) 59 F5
Valergues (34) 274 D5
Valernes (04) 259 G3
Valescourt (60) 38 A1
Valette (15) 217 K3
la Valette (38) 224 C6
la Valette-du-Var (83) 297 K5
Valeuil (24) 213 K2
Valeyrac (33) 194 D6
Valezan (73) 209 K3
Valff (67) 70 D5
Valfin-sur-Valouse (39) 173 F5
Valflaunès (34) 274 B4
Valfleury (42) 205 H5
Valframbert (61) 82 D2
Valfroicourt (88) 94 A5
Valgorge (07) 238 E5
Valhey (54) 66 D5
Valhuon (62) 10 B1
Valiergues (19) 201 F6
Valignat (03) 185 F3
Valigny (03) 167 K2
Valines (80) 8 E5
Valjouffrey (38) 242 D1
Valjouze (15) 218 D4
la Valla (42) 204 B2
la Valla-en-Gier (42) 205 H6
Vallabrègues (30) 275 K3
Vallabrix (30) 256 B6
Vallan (89) 113 F6
Vallangoujard (95) 37 H6
Vallans (79) 177 K2
Vallant-Saint-Georges (10) 89 K2
Vallauris (06) 280 E5
Valle-d'Alesani (2B) 319 J5
Valle-di-Campoloro (2B) 319 J5
Valle-di-Mezzana (2A) 320 C4
Valle-di-Rostino (2B) 319 G4
Valle-d'Orezza (2B) 319 H5
Vallecalle (2B) 317 D6
la Vallée (17) 177 G6
la Vallée-au-Blé (02) 20 E2
la Vallée-Mulâtre (02) 12 D6
Vallègue (31) 289 F3
Valleiry (74) 190 D3
Vallenay (18) 149 G6
Vallentigny (10) 91 F3
Vallerange (57) 67 F1
Vallérargues (30) 255 K5
Valleraugue (30) 254 C6
Vallères (37) 127 G5
Valleret (52) 91 K2
Vallereuil (24) 213 J5
Vallerois-le-Bois (70) 138 C2
Vallerois-Lorioz (70) 138 B2
Valleroy (25) 138 B4
Valleroy (52) 117 G6
Valleroy (54) 26 E6
Valleroy-aux-Saules (88) 94 A5
Valleroy-le-Sec (88) 93 K5
Vallery (89) 88 B5
Vallesvilles (31) 288 D1
Vallet (44) 123 K5
Valletot (27) 34 D3
Vallica (2B) 318 E3
Vallière (23) 182 E6
Vallières (10) 114 A3
Vallières (74) 190 D5
Vallières-les-Grandes (41) 128 D4
Valliguières (30) 275 J1
Valliquerville (76) 15 F5
Valloire (73) 225 H3
Vallois (54) 94 E2
les Vallois (88) 94 A6
Vallon-en-Sully (03) 167 H4
Vallon-Pont-d'Arc (07) 256 A2
Vallon-sur-Gée (72) 106 B3
Vallorcine (74) 192 D3
Vallouise (05) 243 J1
Valmanya (66) 314 D4
Valmascle (34) 273 F6
Valmeinier (73) 225 J3
Valmestroff (57) 27 H4
Valmigère (11) 309 G3
Valmondois (95) 37 H6
Valmont (57) 68 A3
Valmont (76) 14 E4
Valmunster (57) 45 J3
Valmy (51) 42 C6
Valognes (50) 28 E4
Valojoulx (24) 214 E6
Valonne (25) 139 G4
Valoreille (25) 139 G5
Valouse (26) 257 J1
Valprionde (46) 249 G3
Valprivas (43) 220 D2
Valpuiseaux (91) 86 D3

Valras-Plage (34) 292 B5
Valréas (84) 257 G2
Valros (34) 292 B3
Valroufié (46) 233 H6
Vals (09) 308 A1
Vals-des-Tilles (52) 116 A6
Vals-le-Chastel (43) 219 J2
Vals-les-Bains (07) 239 H4
Vals-près-le-Puy (43) 220 C5
Valsemé (14) 33 J4
Valserres (05) 243 F5
Valsonne (69) 187 J5
le Valtin (88) 95 J6
Valuéjols (15) 218 C5
Valvignères (07) 239 K6
Valz-sous-Châteauneuf (63) 203 G6
Valzergues (12) 251 H1
Vanault-le-Châtel (51) 63 G3
Vanault-les-Dames (51) 63 H3
Vançais (79) 179 F1
Vancé (72) 107 J5
la Vancelle (67) 96 B1
Vanclans (25) 157 F2
Vandeins (01) 188 E2
Vandelainville (54) 65 J1
Vandelans (70) 138 B4
Vandeléville (54) 93 J2
Vandélicourt (60) 38 D1
Vandenesse (58) 151 K5
Vandenesse-en-Auxois (21) 153 H1
Vandeuil (51) 40 D4
Vandières (51) 40 C6
Vandières (54) 65 J1
Vandoeuvre-lès-Nancy (54) 66 A5
Vandoncourt (25) 139 J3
Vandré (17) 177 H4
Vandrimare (27) 36 A3
Vandy (08) 42 B2
Vanlay (10) 114 A2
Vannaire (21) 115 F4
Vanne (70) 137 H1
le Vanneau (79) 177 J1
Vannecourt (57) 66 D2
Vannecrocq (27) 34 B3
Vannes (56) 101 F5
Vannes-le-Châtel (54) 93 J1
Vannes-sur-Cosson (45) 110 D6
Vannoz (39) 156 B6
Vanosc (07) 221 J3
les Vans (07) 255 H2
Vantoux (57) 45 F5
Vantoux-et-Longevelle (70) 137 J3
Vanves (92) 58 E4
Vanvey (21) 115 H4
Vanvillé (77) 88 B1
Vanxains (24) 213 G3
Vany (57) 45 F5
Vanzac (17) 212 A1
Vanzay (79) 179 F2
Vanzy (74) 190 D4
Vaour (81) 250 D6
Varacieux (38) 223 G3
Varades (44) 124 C4
Varages (83) 278 D6
Varaignes (24) 197 H4
Varaire (46) 250 C3
Varaize (17) 178 A5
Varambon (01) 189 H4
Varanges (21) 136 C6
Varangéville (54) 66 B5
Varaville (14) 33 G4
Varces-Allières-et-Risset (38) 224 A4
Vareilles (23) 181 K1
Vareilles (71) 187 G1
Vareilles (89) 89 F6
Varen (82) 250 E5
Varengeville-sur-Mer (76) 15 J2
Varenguebec (50) 28 D6
la Varenne (49) 123 J3
Varenne-l'Arconce (71) 170 C6
Varenne-Saint-Germain (71) 170 B5
Varennes (24) 231 K2
Varennes (31) 288 E2
Varennes (37) 146 C3
Varennes (80) 10 C6
Varennes (82) 269 H3
Varennes (86) 162 D1
Varennes (89) 113 J4
Varennes-Changy (45) 111 H4
Varennes-en-Argonne (55) 42 E4
Varennes-Jarcy (91) 59 G6
Varennes-le-Grand (71) 171 K1
Varennes-lès-Mâcon (71) 188 C1
Varennes-lès-Narcy (58) 150 D1
Varennes-Saint-Honorat (43) 219 K4
Varennes-Saint-Sauveur (71) 172 D4
Varennes-sous-Dun (71) 187 H1
Varennes-sur-Allier (03) 185 J1
Varennes-sur-Fouzon (36) 147 J1
Varennes-sur-Loire (49) 126 C6
Varennes-sur-Morge (63) 185 G6
Varennes-sur-Seine (77) 87 K4
Varennes-sur-Tèche (03) 186 A1
Varennes-sur-Usson (63) 203 F5
Varennes-Vauzelles (58) 150 D4
Varès (47) 247 J1
Varesnes (60) 19 H4
Varessia (39) 173 G3
Varetz (19) 215 H3
Varilhes (09) 307 J2
Varinfroy (60) 39 F6
Variscourt (02) 40 E2

Varize (28) 109 G1
Varize (57) 45 H5
Varmonzey (88) 94 B4
Varneville (55) 65 F3
Varneville-Bretteville (76) 15 K5
Varogne (70) 118 B5
Varois-et-Chaignot (21) 136 B5
Varouville (50) 29 F2
Varrains (49) 144 C1
Varreddes (77) 59 K2
Vars (05) 227 A4
Vars (16) 196 D2
Vars (70) 137 F2
Vars-sur-Roseix (19) 215 G3
Varsberg (57) 45 K4
Varzay (17) 195 F2
Varzy (58) 132 E5
Vascoeuil (27) 36 A2
Vasles (79) 162 B3
Vasperviller (57) 67 J5
Vassel (63) 203 F2
Vasselay (18) 149 G2
Vasselin (38) 207 G3
Vassens (02) 39 G1
Vasseny (02) 40 A3
Vassieux-en-Vercors (26) 241 H1
Vassimont-et-Chapelaine (51) 62 B4
Vassincourt (55) 63 K4
Vassogne (02) 40 C2
Vassonville (76) 15 K4
Vassy (14) 53 G3
Vassy (89) 134 C2
le Vast (50) 29 F2
Vasteville (50) 28 B3
les Vastres (43) 221 F6
Vatan (36) 148 B3
Vathiménil (54) 94 E1
Vatierville (76) 16 D3
Vatilieu (38) 223 H2
Vatimont (57) 66 D1
Vatry (51) 62 C4
Vattetot-sous-Beaumont (76) 14 D5
Vattetot-sur-Mer (76) 14 C4
Vatteville (27) 35 K4
Vatteville-la-Rue (76) 34 E1
Vaubadon (14) 31 K2
Vauban (71) 187 G1
Vaubecourt (55) 64 A2
Vaubexy (88) 94 B4
Vaucelles (14) 32 A3
Vaucelles-et-Beffecourt (02) 20 C6
Vauchamps (25) 138 C5
Vauchamps (51) 61 G3
Vauchassis (10) 89 K5
Vauchelles (60) 19 G6
Vauchelles-lès-Authie (80) 10 C5
Vauchelles-lès-Domart (80) 9 J1
Vauchelles-lès-Quesnoy (80) 9 G5
Vauchignon (21) 153 J4
Vauchonvilliers (10) 91 F5
Vauchoux (70) 117 K6
Vauchrétien (49) 125 H5
Vauciennes (51) 61 J1
Vauciennes (60) 39 F4
Vauclaix (58) 152 A1
Vauclerc (51) 63 G5
Vaucluse (25) 139 G5
Vauclusotte (25) 139 G5
Vaucogne (10) 90 D2
Vauconcourt-Nervezain (70) 117 H6
Vaucouleurs (55) 65 F6
Vaucourt (54) 67 F5
Vaucourtois (77) 60 A3
Vaucresson (92) 58 C4
Vaudancourt (60) 36 E4
Vaudebarrier (71) 170 E5
Vaudelnay (49) 144 B2
Vaudeloges (14) 54 C2
Vaudemanges (51) 41 G6
Vaudémont (54) 93 K2
Vaudes (10) 90 C6
Vaudesincourt (51) 41 J4
Vaudesson (02) 40 A1
Vaudeurs (89) 113 F1
Vaudevant (07) 221 K4
Vaudeville (54) 94 B2
Vaudéville (88) 94 E5
Vaudeville-le-Haut (55) 93 F2
Vaudherland (95) 59 F2
Vaudigny (54) 94 B2
le Vaudioux (39) 173 K1
Vaudoncourt (55) 26 C5
Vaudoncourt (88) 93 H5
le Vaudoué (77) 87 G4
Vaudoy-en-Brie (77) 60 B5
Vaudreching (57) 45 J3
Vaudrecourt (52) 93 F5
Vaudrémont (52) 115 J1
le Vaudreuil (27) 35 J4
Vaudreuille (31) 289 H3
Vaudreville (50) 29 F4
Vaudrey (39) 155 H3
Vaudricourt (62) 5 H5
Vaudricourt (80) 8 D5
Vaudrimesnil (50) 30 E3
Vaudringhem (62) 2 E6
Vaudrivillers (25) 138 D5
Vaudry (14) 52 E3
Vaufrey (25) 139 J2
Vaugines (84) 277 H4
Vaugneray (69) 205 J2
Vaugrigneuse (91) 86 C1

Vauhallan (91) 58 D5
Vaujany (38) 224 E3
Vaujours (93) 59 G2
Vaulandry (49) 126 B2
le Vaulmier (15) 217 J4
Vaulnaveys-le-Bas (38) 224 B4
Vaulnaveys-le-Haut (38) 224 B4
Vaulry (87) 181 F4
Vault-de-Lugny (89) 133 J3
Vaulx (62) 9 J3
Vaulx (74) 190 E5
Vaulx-en-Velin (69) 206 B1
Vaulx-Milieu (38) 206 E4
Vaulx-Vraucourt (62) 11 G4
le Vaumain (60) 37 F3
Vaumas (03) 169 H5
Vaumeilh (04) 259 F3
Vaumoise (60) 39 F4
Vaumort (89) 112 E1
Vaunac (24) 214 B1
Vaunaveys-la-Rochette (26) 240 D3
Vaunoise (61) 83 G4
la Vaupalière (76) 35 G1
Vaupillon (28) 84 B3
Vaupoisson (10) 90 C2
Vauquois (55) 42 E4
Vauréal (95) 58 B1
Vaureilles (12) 251 H1
le Vauroux (60) 37 F3
Vausseroux (79) 162 A3
Vautebis (79) 162 A4
Vauthiermont (90) 119 K5
Vautorte (53) 80 E4
Vauvenargues (13) 277 K6
Vauvert (30) 275 G5
Vauville (14) 33 J4
Vauville (50) 28 A2
Vauvillers (70) 118 A3
Vauvillers (80) 18 E2
Vaux (03) 167 H5
Vaux (31) 289 F2
Vaux (57) 44 E5
Vaux (86) 179 H1
Vaux-Andigny (02) 12 D6
Vaux-Champagne (08) 41 K2
Vaux-devant-Damloup (55) 26 A6
Vaux-en-Amiénois (80) 18 A1
Vaux-en-Beaujolais (69) 188 A4
Vaux-en-Bugey (01) 189 H5
Vaux-en-Dieulet (08) 42 E1
Vaux-en-Pré (71) 171 G2
Vaux-en-Vermandois (02) 19 J3
Vaux-et-Chantegrue (25) 156 E5
Vaux-Lavalette (16) 196 E6
Vaux-le-Moncelot (70) 137 J3
Vaux-le-Pénil (77) 87 H2
Vaux-lès-Mouron (08) 42 C3
Vaux-lès-Mouzon (08) 23 G5
Vaux-lès-Palameix (55) 64 E1
Vaux-lès-Prés (25) 137 J6
Vaux-lès-Rubigny (08) 21 J4
Vaux-lès-Saint-Claude (39) 173 J5
Vaux-Marquenneville (80) 17 G1
Vaux-Montreuil (08) 22 B6
Vaux-Rouillac (16) 196 B2
Vaux-Saules (21) 135 J3
Vaux-sous-Aubigny (52) 136 C1
Vaux-sur-Aure (14) 32 B3
Vaux-sur-Blaise (52) 91 K2
Vaux-sur-Eure (27) 57 F1
Vaux-sur-Lunain (77) 88 A2
Vaux-sur-Mer (17) 194 C3
Vaux-sur-Poligny (39) 155 J5
Vaux-sur-Saint-Urbain (52) 92 B3
Vaux-sur-Seine (78) 58 B1
Vaux-sur-Seulles (14) 32 B4
Vaux-sur-Somme (80) 18 D1
Vaux-sur-Vienne (86) 145 J5
Vaux-Villaine (08) 22 B3
Vauxaillon (02) 39 K1
Vauxbons (52) 116 B4
Vauxbuin (02) 39 J3
Vauxcéré (02) 40 B3
Vauxrenard (69) 188 A2
Vauxrezis (02) 39 J2
Vauxtin (02) 40 B3
Vavincourt (55) 64 B3
Vavray-le-Grand (51) 63 G4
Vavray-le-Petit (51) 63 G4
Vaxainville (54) 95 G1
Vaxoncourt (88) 94 D4
Vaxy (57) 66 D2
Vay (44) 103 F5
Vaychis (09) 308 A6
Vaylats (46) 250 C3
Vayrac (46) 234 A1
Vayres (33) 229 K1
Vayres (87) 198 A2
Vayres-sur-Essonne (91) 86 E3
Vazeilles-Limandre (43) 220 A4
Vazeilles-près-Saugues (43) 237 K1
Vazerac (82) 249 J5
Veauce (03) 184 E3
Veauche (42) 205 F4
Veauchette (42) 205 F4
Veaugues (18) 131 J4
Veaunes (26) 222 C5
Veauville-lès-Baons (76) 15 G5
Veauville-lès-Quelles (76) 15 G4
Vèbre (09) 307 K5
Vebret (15) 217 J2
Vebron (48) 254 B4

Veckersviller (57) . . . . 67　K2
Veckring (57) . . . . 27　J4
Vecoux (88) . . . . 119　F2
Vecquemont (80) . . . . 18　C2
Vecqueville (52) . . . . 92　B2
Vedène (84) . . . . 276　C1
Védrines-Saint-Loup (15) . . . . . 219　G5
Végennes (19) . . . . 216　A6
Vého (54) . . . . 67　F6
Veigné (37) . . . . 127　J6
Veigy-Foncenex (74) . . . . 174　D6
Veilhes (81) . . . . 270　A6
Veilleins (41) . . . . 129　H4
Veilly (21) . . . . 153　H2
Veix (19) . . . . 200　A5
Velaine-en-Haye (54) . . . . 65　J5
Velaine-sous-Amance (54) . . . . . 66　B4
Velaines (55) . . . . 64　C5
Velanne (38) . . . . 207　J5
Velars-sur-Ouche (21) . . . . . . 135　K5
Velaux (13) . . . . 296　B1
Velennes (60) . . . . 37　H1
Velennes (80) . . . . 17　J3
Velesmes-Echevanne (70) . . . . 137　G3
Velesmes-Essarts (25) . . . . . . 156　A1
Velet (70) . . . . 137　F4
Vélieux (34) . . . . 291　H4
Vélines (24) . . . . 230　E2
Vélizy-Villacoublay (78) . . . . . . 58　D4
Velle-le-Châtel (70) . . . . 138　A1
Velle-sur-Moselle (54) . . . . 94　B1
Vellèches (86) . . . . 145　J4
Vellechevreux-et-Courbenans (70) . . 138　E2
Velleclaire (70) . . . . 137　J3
Vellefaux (70) . . . . 138　B2
Vellefrey-et-Vellefrange (70) . . . 137　H3
Vellefrie (70) . . . . 118　B6
Velleguindry-et-Levrecey (70) . . 138　A2
Velleminfroy (70) . . . . 118　C6
Vellemoz (70) . . . . 137　H3
Velleron (84) . . . . 276　D1
Vellerot-lès-Belvoir (25) . . . . . 139　F4
Vellerot-lès-Vercel (25) . . . . . 138　E6
Velles (36) . . . . 165　H2
Velles (52) . . . . 117　G1
Vellescot (90) . . . . 139　K1
Vellevans (25) . . . . 138　F5
Vellexon-Queutrey-et-Vaudey (70) . . 137　H2
Velloreille-lès-Choye (70) . . . . 137　H4
Velluire (85) . . . . 160　D5
Velogny (21) . . . . 134　E4
Velone-Orneto (2B) . . . . 319　J4
Velorcey (70) . . . . 118　B5
Velosnes (55) . . . . 26　A2
Velotte-et-Tatignécourt (88) . . . . 94　A4
Vélu (62) . . . . 11　G3
Velving (57) . . . . 45　J3
Vélye (51) . . . . 62　B3
Velzic (15) . . . . 217　K6
Vémars (95) . . . . 59　G1
Venables (27) . . . . 35　K5
Venaco (2B) . . . . 321　H1
Venansault (85) . . . . 159　H1
Venanson (06) . . . . 261　K5
Venarey-les-Laumes (21) . . . . 134　E2
Venarsal (19) . . . . 215　K3
Venas (03) . . . . 167　J5
Venasque (84) . . . . 276　E1
Vence (06) . . . . 281　F3
Vendargues (34) . . . . 274　C5
Vendat (03) . . . . 185　H3
Vendays-Montalivet (33) . . . . . 210　C1
Vendegies-au-Bois (59) . . . . . . 12　D4
Vendegies-sur-Écaillon (59) . . . 12　D3
Vendel (35) . . . . 79　K2
la Vendelée (50) . . . . 30　E3
Vendelles (02) . . . . 19　J2
Vendémian (34) . . . . 292　D1
Vendenesse-lès-Charolles (71) . 170　E5
Vendenesse-sur-Arroux (71) . . 170　B3
Vendenheim (67) . . . . 25　A6
Vendes (14) . . . . 32　C5
Vendeuil (02) . . . . 20　A4
Vendeuil-Caply (60) . . . . 18　A5
Vendeuvre (14) . . . . 54　B1
Vendeuvre-du-Poitou (86) . . . . 162　E1
Vendeuvre-sur-Barse (10) . . . . 90　E5
Vendeville (59) . . . . 6　E5
Vendhuile (02) . . . . 11　J6
Vendières (02) . . . . 60　E3
Vendin-le-Vieil (62) . . . . 6　C6
Vendin-lès-Béthune (62) . . . . . . 5　K5
Vendine (31) . . . . 289　F1
Vendœuvres (36) . . . . 147　G6
Vendoire (24) . . . . 197　F6
Vendôme (41) . . . . 108　C5
Vendranges (42) . . . . 187　F5
Vendrennes (85) . . . . 142　C5
Vendres (34) . . . . 292　A5
Vendresse (08) . . . . 22　D6
Vendresse-Beaulne (02) . . . . . 40　B2
Vendrest (77) . . . . 60　B1
la Vendue-Mignot (10) . . . . . . 90　B6
Vénéjan (30) . . . . 256　C4
Venelles (13) . . . . 277　K6
Vénérand (17) . . . . 195　H1
Venère (70) . . . . 137　G4
Vénérieu (38) . . . . 207　F3
Vénérolles (02) . . . . 12　E6
Venerque (31) . . . . 288　B3
Vénès (81) . . . . 270　E5
Venesmes (18) . . . . 149　F6

Vénestanville (76) . . . . 15　H3
Venette (60) . . . . 38　D2
Veneux-les-Sablons (77) . . . . . 87　J4
Veney (54) . . . . 95　G2
Vengeons (50) . . . . 52　D4
le Verguier (02) . . . . 19　J1
Venise (25) . . . . 138　A4
Venisey (70) . . . . 117　K4
Vénissieux (69) . . . . 206　B3
Venizel (02) . . . . 39　K3
Venizy (89) . . . . 113　H4
Vennans (25) . . . . 138　C5
Vennecy (45) . . . . 110　B3
Vennes (25) . . . . 157　G1
Vennezey (54) . . . . 94　D2
Venon (27) . . . . 35　H5
Venon (38) . . . . 224　B3
Vénosc (38) . . . . 224　E5
Venouse (89) . . . . 113　H4
Venoy (89) . . . . 113　G5
Vensac (33) . . . . 194　C6
Vensat (63) . . . . 185　G4
Ventabren (13) . . . . 296　B1
Ventavon (05) . . . . 259　F2
Ventelay (51) . . . . 40　D3
Ventenac (09) . . . . 307　K2
Ventenac-Cabardès (11) . . . . . 290　A5
Ventenac-en-Minervois (11) . . . 291　G5
Venterol (04) . . . . 259　H1
Venterol (26) . . . . 257　H2
les Ventes (27) . . . . 56　C2
les Ventes-de-Bourse (61) . . . . 82　E2
Ventes-Saint-Rémy (76) . . . . . 16　B4
Venteuges (43) . . . . 219　J6
Venteuil (51) . . . . 40　D6
Venthon (73) . . . . 209　G2
Ventiseri (2B) . . . . 321　H4
Ventouse (16) . . . . 179　H6
Ventron (88) . . . . 119　H2
la Ventrouze (61) . . . . 55　J4
Venzolasca (2B) . . . . 319　J3
Ver (50) . . . . 30　E6
Ver-lès-Chartres (28) . . . . 85　G4
Ver-sur-Launette (60) . . . . 38　C6
Ver-sur-Mer (14) . . . . 32　C3
Vérac (33) . . . . 211　K6
Véranne (42) . . . . 221　K1
Vérargues (34) . . . . 274　E5
Véraza (11) . . . . 309　F3
Verberie (60) . . . . 38　D3
Verbiesles (52) . . . . 116　B1
Vercel-Villedieu-le-Camp (25) . . 138　D6
Verchain-Maugré (59) . . . . 12　C3
Verchaix (74) . . . . 192　A3
Vercheny (26) . . . . 241　G3
les Verchers-sur-Layon (49) . . 144　A1
Verchin (62) . . . . 5　F6
Verchocq (62) . . . . 4　E5
Vercia (39) . . . . 173　F3
Verclause (26) . . . . 258　A2
Vercoiran (26) . . . . 257　K3
Vercourt (80) . . . . 9　F2
Verdaches (04) . . . . 259　K3
Verdalle (81) . . . . 289　K2
Verdelais (33) . . . . 230　A5
Verdelot (77) . . . . 60　E3
Verdenal (54) . . . . 67　G6
Verderel-lès-Sauqueuse (60) . . 37　H1
Verderonne (60) . . . . 38　B3
Verdes (41) . . . . 109　F3
Verdèse (2B) . . . . 319　H4
Verdets (64) . . . . 284　A5
le Verdier (81) . . . . 270　B1
la Verdière (83) . . . . 278　D5
Verdigny (18) . . . . 131　J5
Verdille (16) . . . . 178　D6
Verdilly (02) . . . . 39　K6
Verdon (24) . . . . 231　K2
Verdon (51) . . . . 61　G2
le Verdon-sur-Mer (33) . . . . . 194　C4
Verdonnet (21) . . . . 114　D6
Verdun (09) . . . . 307　K5
Verdun (55) . . . . 43　H5
Verdun-en-Lauragais (11) . . . . 289　J4
Verdun-sur-Garonne (82) . . . . 268　E3
Verdun-sur-le-Doubs (71) . . . . 154　C5
Vereaux (18) . . . . 150　B5
Verel-de-Montbel (73) . . . . . . 207　K4
Verel-Pragondran (73) . . . . . . 208　D3
Véretz (37) . . . . 127　K5
Vereux (70) . . . . 137　G2
Verfeil (31) . . . . 289　J6
Verfeil (82) . . . . 250　E6
Verfeuil (30) . . . . 256　A5
Vergaville (57) . . . . 67　F3
Vergéal (35) . . . . 104　A2
la Vergenne (70) . . . . 138　E1
le Verger (35) . . . . 78　D4
Vergeroux (17) . . . . 177　F5
Verges (39) . . . . 173　H2
Vergetot (76) . . . . 14　C5
Vergezac (43) . . . . 220　A5
Vergèze (30) . . . . 275　F4
Vergheas (63) . . . . 184　A4
Vergies (80) . . . . 17　G1
Vergigny (89) . . . . 113　H3
Vergisson (71) . . . . 188　B1
Vergné (17) . . . . 177　K3
la Vergne (17) . . . . 177　K5
Vergoignan (32) . . . . 265　K4
Vergoncey (50) . . . . 51　K4
Vergongheon (43) . . . . 219　G1
Vergonnes (49) . . . . 104　B5

Vergons (04) . . . . 279　K1
Vergranne (25) . . . . 138　D3
Vergt (24) . . . . 214　A5
Vergt-de-Biron (24) . . . . 232　B5
le Verguier (02) . . . . 19　J1
Véria (39) . . . . 173　F4
Vérignon (83) . . . . 279　G5
Vérigny (28) . . . . 84　E2
Vérin (42) . . . . 205　K6
Vérines (17) . . . . 177　F2
Vérissey (71) . . . . 172　C1
Verjon (01) . . . . 172　E6
Verjux (71) . . . . 154　B5
Verlans (70) . . . . 139　G1
Verlhac-Tescou (82) . . . . 269　H2
Verlin (89) . . . . 112　D2
Verlincthun (62) . . . . 4　B4
Verlinghem (59) . . . . 6　D3
Verlus (32) . . . . 265　K6
Vermand (02) . . . . 19　J2
Vermandovillers (80) . . . . 19　F2
Vermelles (62) . . . . 6　B6
Vermenton (89) . . . . 133　H1
le Vermont (88) . . . . 95　J2
Vern-d'Anjou (49) . . . . 124　E1
Vern-sur-Seiche (35) . . . . 79　G5
Vernais (18) . . . . 167　J1
Vernaison (69) . . . . 206　A3
Vernajoul (09) . . . . 307　J3
Vernancourt (51) . . . . 63　H3
Vernantes (49) . . . . 126　C4
Vernantois (39) . . . . 173　G2
la Vernarède (30) . . . . 255　G3
Vernas (38) . . . . 207　F1
Vernassal (43) . . . . 220　A4
Vernaux (09) . . . . 307　K5
Vernay (69) . . . . 187　K3
la Vernaz (74) . . . . 175　G6
Verne (25) . . . . 138　D4
Vernègues (13) . . . . 277　F5
Verneiges (23) . . . . 183　H2
le Verneil (73) . . . . 208　E5
Verneil-le-Chétif (72) . . . . 106　E6
Vornoix (03) . . . . 167　H6
la Vernelle (36) . . . . 148　G6
le Vernet (03) . . . . 185　J3
le Vernet (04) . . . . 260　A3
le Vernet (09) . . . . 288　D6
Vernet (31) . . . . 288　B3
le Vernet (43) . . . . 220　A5
Vernet-la-Varenne (63) . . . . . 203　G6
Vernet-les-Bains (66) . . . . . . 314　B4
le Vernet-Sainte-Marguerite (63) . . 202　C4
Verneugheol (63) . . . . 201　H2
Verneuil (16) . . . . 197　K2
Verneuil (18) . . . . 149　J6
Verneuil (51) . . . . 40　B6
Verneuil (58) . . . . 151　H5
Verneuil-en-Bourbonnais (03) . . 168　D6
Verneuil-en-Halatte (60) . . . . . 38　B4
Verneuil-Grand (55) . . . . 23　K6
Verneuil-le-Château (37) . . . . 145　H3
Verneuil-l'Étang (77) . . . . 59　J6
Verneuil-Moustiers (87) . . . . . 164　C6
Verneuil-Petit (55) . . . . 23　K6
Verneuil-sous-Coucy (02) . . . . 20　A6
Verneuil-sur-Avre (27) . . . . . . 56　B5
Verneuil-sur-Igneraie (36) . . . 166　B2
Verneuil-sur-Indre (37) . . . . . 146　D3
Verneuil-sur-Seine (78) . . . . . 58　B2
Verneuil-sur-Serre (02) . . . . . . 20　D5
Verneuil-sur-Vienne (87) . . . . 198　D1
Verneusses (27) . . . . 55　G3
Vernéville (57) . . . . 44　D5
Vernie (72) . . . . 82　C6
Vernierfontaine (25) . . . . 156　E2
Vernines (63) . . . . 202　B3
Verniolle (09) . . . . 307　J1
Vernioz (38) . . . . 206　B6
Vernix (50) . . . . 52　B4
Vernoil (49) . . . . 126　C4
le Vernois (39) . . . . 173　G1
Vernois-lès-Belvoir (25) . . . . . 139　F4
Vernois-lès-Vesvres (21) . . . . 136　B1
Vernois-sur-Mance (70) . . . . . 117　H4
Vernols (15) . . . . 218　C3
Vernon (07) . . . . 239　F6
Vernon (27) . . . . 36　B6
Vernon (86) . . . . 163　G5
Vernonvilliers (10) . . . . 91　G4
Vernosc-lès-Annonay (07) . . . 222　A3
Vernot (21) . . . . 135　K3
la Vernotte (70) . . . . 137　J2
Vernou-en-Sologne (41) . . . . . 129　J3
Vernou-la-Celle-sur-Seine (77) . . 87　K4
Vernou-sur-Brenne (37) . . . . . 128　A4
Vernouillet (28) . . . . 57　F5
Vernouillet (78) . . . . 58　B2
Vernoux (01) . . . . 172　C4
Vernoux-en-Gâtine (79) . . . . . 161　G2
Vernoux-en-Vivarais (07) . . . . 239　K1
Vernoux-sur-Boutonne (79) . . 178　C2
le Vernoy (25) . . . . 139　G1
Vernoy (89) . . . . 112　C1
Vernusse (03) . . . . 184　E1
Verny (57) . . . . 66　A1
Vero (2A) . . . . 320　D3
Véron (89) . . . . 112　D1
Véronne (26) . . . . 241　G3
Véronnes (21) . . . . 136　C2
Verosvres (71) . . . . 171　F5
Verpel (08) . . . . 42　D2

la Verpillière (38) . . . . 206　D3
Verpillières (80) . . . . 19　F5
Verpillières-sur-Ource (10) . . . 115　F2
Verquières (13) . . . . 276　C3
Verquin (62) . . . . 6　A6
Verrens-Arvey (73) . . . . 209　F3
Verreries-de-Moussans (34) . . 290　E3
Verrey-sous-Drée (21) . . . . . . 135　H5
Verrey-sous-Salmaise (21) . . . 135　G4
Verricourt (10) . . . . 90　D3
Verrie (49) . . . . 126　A6
la Verrie (85) . . . . 142　D4
la Verrière (78) . . . . 58　B5
Verrières (08) . . . . 42　C1
Verrières (10) . . . . 90　B5
Verrières (12) . . . . 253　G4
Verrières (16) . . . . 195　K4
Verrières (51) . . . . 42　D6
Verrières (61) . . . . 83　K3
Verrières (63) . . . . 202　C4
Verrières (86) . . . . 163　H5
Verrières-de-Joux (25) . . . . . 157　G4
Verrières-du-Grosbois (25) . . . 138　C5
Verrières-en-Forez (42) . . . . . 204　C4
Verrières-le-Buisson (91) . . . . 58　D5
Verrue (86) . . . . 144　E5
Verruyes (79) . . . . 161　J4
Vers (46) . . . . 250　B1
Vers (71) . . . . 171　K3
Vers (74) . . . . 190　E3
Vers-en-Montagne (39) . . . . . 156　B5
Vers-Pont-du-Gard (30) . . . . . 275　J1
Vers-sous-Sellières (39) . . . . 155　H5
Vers-sur-Méouge (26) . . . . . . 258　C4
Vers-sur-Selles (80) . . . . 18　A2
Versailles (78) . . . . 58　C4
Versailleux (01) . . . . 189　F5
Versainville (14) . . . . 54　B2
la Versanne (42) . . . . 221　J2
Versaugues (71) . . . . 170　B6
Verseilles-le-Bas (52) . . . . . . 116　C5
Verseilles-le-Haut (52) . . . . . 116　C5
Versigny (02) . . . . 20　B5
Versigny (60) . . . . 38　D5
Versols-et-Lapeyre (12) . . . . . 272　C3
Verson (14) . . . . 32　C4
Versonnex (01) . . . . 174　B6
Versonnex (74) . . . . 190　D5
le Versoud (38) . . . . 224　C3
Vert (40) . . . . 245　K5
Vert (78) . . . . 57　J2
Vert-en-Drouais (28) . . . . 56　E5
Vert-le-Grand (91) . . . . 86　E1
Vert-le-Petit (91) . . . . 86　E1
Vert-Saint-Denis (77) . . . . 87　H1
Vert-Toulon (51) . . . . 61　K3
Vertain (59) . . . . 12　D3
Vertaizon (63) . . . . 203　F2
Vertamboz (39) . . . . 173　H2
Vertault (21) . . . . 114　D4
Verteillac (24) . . . . 213　G1
Verteuil-d'Agenais (47) . . . . . 247　K1
Verteuil-sur-Charente (16) . . . 179　G5
Verthemex (73) . . . . 208　A3
Vertheuil (33) . . . . 210　E3
Vertolaye (63) . . . . 203　K3
Verton (62) . . . . 8　E1
Vertou (44) . . . . 123　H6
Vertrieu (38) . . . . 189　H6
Vertus (51) . . . . 62　A3
Vervant (16) . . . . 196　D1
Vervant (17) . . . . 178　A5
Vervezelle (88) . . . . 95　G5
Vervins (02) . . . . 21　F2
Véry (55) . . . . 42　E4
Verzé (71) . . . . 171　J6
Verzeille (11) . . . . 309　F1
Verzenay (51) . . . . 41　G5
Verzy (51) . . . . 41　G5
Vesaignes-sous-Lafauche (52) . . 92　D4
Vesaignes-sur-Marne (52) . . . 116　C2
Vesancy (01) . . . . 174　B5
Vesc (26) . . . . 241　F4
Vescemont (90) . . . . 119　H5
Vescheim (57) . . . . 69　F6
Vescles (39) . . . . 173　G5
Vescours (01) . . . . 172　R4
Vescovato (2B) . . . . 319　J3
Vesdun (18) . . . . 167　F4
Vésigneul-sur-Marne (51) . . . . 62　E3
Vésines (01) . . . . 171　K6
le Vésinet (78) . . . . 58　C3
Vesles-et-Caumont (02) . . . . . 20　E5
Veslud (02) . . . . 20　E6
Vesly (27) . . . . 36　D4
Vesly (50) . . . . 30　D1
Vesoul (70) . . . . 138　B1
la Vespière (14) . . . . 55　G1
Vesseaux (07) . . . . 239　H4
Vessey (50) . . . . 51　J5
Vestric-et-Candiac (30) . . . . . 275　F4
Vesvres (21) . . . . 135　F4
Vesvres-sous-Chalancey (52) . . 116　B6
Vétheuil (95) . . . . 57　J1
Vétraz-Monthoux (74) . . . . . . 191　G2
Vétrigne (90) . . . . 119　J6
Veuil (36) . . . . 147　J2
Veuilly-la-Poterie (02) . . . . . . 39　H6
Veules-les-Roses (76) . . . . . . 15　H2
Veulettes-sur-Mer (76) . . . . . 15　F2
le Veurdre (03) . . . . 168　B1

Veurey-Voroize (38) . . . . 223　K2
la Veuve (51) . . . . 62　D1
Veuves (41) . . . . 128　C4
Veuvey-sur-Ouche (21) . . . . . 153　J1
Veuxhaulles-sur-Aube (21) . . . 115　H3
Vevy (39) . . . . 173　H2
Vexaincourt (88) . . . . 95　J1
le Vey (14) . . . . 53　J2
Veynes (05) . . . . 242　C5
Veyrac (87) . . . . 181　F6
Veyras (07) . . . . 239　J3
Veyre-Monton (63) . . . . 202　E3
Veyreau (12) . . . . 253　J5
Veyrier-du-Lac (74) . . . . 191　F6
Veyrières (15) . . . . 217　G2
Veyrières (19) . . . . 201　G6
Veyrignac (24) . . . . 233　G2
Veyrines-de-Domme (24) . . . . 232　E5
Veyrines-de-Vergt (24) . . . . . 214　A6
Veyrins-Thuellin (38) . . . . . . 207　H3
les Veys (50) . . . . 29　G6
Veyssilieu (38) . . . . 206　E3
Veyziat (38) . . . . 206　E3
Vez (60) . . . . 39　F4
Vézac (15) . . . . 235　J2
Vézac (24) . . . . 232　E2
Vézannes (89) . . . . 113　J4
Vézaponin (02) . . . . 39　H2
Vèze (15) . . . . 218　D3
la Vèze (25) . . . . 138　A6
Vézelay (89) . . . . 133　H4
Vézelise (54) . . . . 93　K2
Vézelois (90) . . . . 139　J1
Vezels-Roussy (15) . . . . 236　J3
Vézénobres (30) . . . . 255　H6
Vézeronce-Curtin (38) . . . . . . 207　G3
Vezet (70) . . . . 137　J2
Vézézoux (43) . . . . 219　G1
le Vézier (51) . . . . 60　E4
Vézières (86) . . . . 144　E2
Vézillon (27) . . . . 36　A4
Vézilly (02) . . . . 40　C5
Vezin-le-Coquet (35) . . . . . . 79　H4
Vézinnes (89) . . . . 113　K4
Vezins (49) . . . . 143　G2
Vézins-de-Lévézou (12) . . . . . 253　F4
Vezot (72) . . . . 83　F4
Vezzani (2B) . . . . 321　G2
Viabon (28) . . . . 85　J6
Viala-du-Pas-de-Jaux (12) . . . 272　D2
Viala-du-Tarn (12) . . . . 252　E6
Vialas (48) . . . . 254　E3
Vialer (64) . . . . 285　F1
Viam (19) . . . . 200　B4
Viane (81) . . . . 271　J5
Vianges (21) . . . . 153　F2
Vianne (47) . . . . 247　J4
Viâpres-le-Petit (10) . . . . 90　A1
Viarmes (95) . . . . 37　K6
Vias (34) . . . . 292　C4
Viazac (46) . . . . 234　E6
le Vibal (12) . . . . 252　D3
Vibersviller (57) . . . . 67　H2
Vibeuf (76) . . . . 15　H4
Vibrac (16) . . . . 196　C3
Vibrac (17) . . . . 211　K1
Vibraye (72) . . . . 107　K2
Vic-de-Chassenay (21) . . . . . 134　D3
Vic-des-Prés (21) . . . . 153　J2
Vic-en-Bigorre (65) . . . . 285　H3
Vic-Fezensac (32) . . . . 267　F4
Vic-la-Gardiole (34) . . . . 293　G2
Vic-le-Comte (63) . . . . 202　E4
Vic-le-Fesq (30) . . . . 274　E3
Vic-sous-Thil (21) . . . . 134　D5
Vic-sur-Aisne (02) . . . . 39　G2
Vic-sur-Cère (15) . . . . 217　K6
Vic-sur-Seille (57) . . . . 66　D3
Vicdessos (09) . . . . 307　H5
le Vicel (50) . . . . 29　F2
Vichel (63) . . . . 202　E6
Vichel-Nanteuil (02) . . . . 39　J5
Vichères (28) . . . . 84　B5
Vicherey (88) . . . . 93　J3
Vichy (03) . . . . 185　J3
Vico (2A) . . . . 316　E5
la Vicogne (80) . . . . 10　A6
la Vicomté-sur-Rance (22) . . . 50　D5
Vicq (03) . . . . 185　F3
Vicq (52) . . . . 117　F3
Vicq (59) . . . . 12　D1
Vicq (78) . . . . 57　K4
Vicq-d'Auribat (40) . . . . 264　D3
Vicq-Exemplet (36) . . . . 166　C3
Vicq-sur-Breuilh (87) . . . . . . 199　C4
Vicq-sur-Gartempe (86) . . . . . 164　A1
Vicq-sur-Nahon (36) . . . . 147　J2
Vicques (14) . . . . 54　B2
Victot-Pontfol (14) . . . . 33　H5
Vidai (61) . . . . 83　F2
Vidaillac (46) . . . . 250　D3
Vidaillat (23) . . . . 182　D5
Vidauban (83) . . . . 298　D2
Videcosville (50) . . . . 29　F3
Videix (87) . . . . 197　K2
Videlles (91) . . . . 87　F3
Vidou (65) . . . . 286　A4
Vidouville (50) . . . . 31　K3
Vidouze (65) . . . . 285　G2
Viefvillers (60) . . . . 17　K5
le Vieil-Baugé (49) . . . . 126　A3
le Vieil-Dampierre (51) . . . . . 63　J1
le Vieil-Évreux (27) . . . . 56　E1

Vieil-Hesdin (62) 9 J2
Vieil-Moutier (62) 2 D6
Vieille-Brioude (43) 219 H3
Vieille-Chapelle (62) 6 A4
Vieille-Église (62) 2 E3
Vieille-Église-en-Yvelines (78) . . . 58 A6
la Vieille-Loye (39) 155 H3
la Vieille-Lyre (27) 55 K2
Vieille-Toulouse (31) 288 B2
Vieilles-Maisons-sur-Joudry (45) . . 111 F4
Vieillespesse (15) 218 E4
Vieillevie (15) 235 H5
Vieillevigne (31) 288 E3
Vieillevigne (44) 141 K3
Vieilley (25) 138 A5
Vieilmoulin (21) 135 G5
Viel-Arcy (02) 40 B4
Viel-Saint-Remy (08) 22 B5
Viella (32) 266 A4
Viella (65) 304 B4
Vielle-Adour (65) 285 H6
Vielle-Aure (65) 305 F4
Vielle-Louron (65) 305 F4
Vielle-Saint-Girons (40) 262 D1
Vielle-Soubiran (40) 246 D6
Vielle-Tursan (40) 265 H5
Viellenave-d'Arthez (64) 284 B3
Viellenave-de-Navarrenx (64) 283 J3
Vielleségure (64) 283 K3
Vielmanay (58) 132 C6
Vielmur-sur-Agout (81) 270 D6
Vielprat (43) 238 D2
Viels-Maisons (02) 60 E3
Vielverge (21) 136 K5
Viennay (79) 161 K2
Vienne (38) 206 B5
Vienne-en-Arthies (95) 57 J1
Vienne-en-Bessin (14) 32 C3
Vienne-en-Val (45) 110 C5
Vienne-la-Ville (51) 42 D5
Vienne-le-Château (51) 42 D5
Viens (84) 277 K2
Vienville (88) 95 H5
Vier-Bordes (65) 304 B2
Viersat (23) 183 J1
Vierville (28) 86 A4
Vierville (50) 29 G6
Vierville-sur-Mer (14) 29 K6
Vierzon (18) 148 D1
Vierzy (02) 39 J4
Viesly (59) 12 C4
Viessoix (14) 53 F3
Viéthorey (25) 138 D3
Vieu (01) 190 B6
Vieu-d'Izenave (01) 189 K3
Vieure (03) 168 A4
Vieussan (34) 291 H1
Vieuvicq (28) 84 D5
Vieuvy (53) 80 E2
Vieux (14) 32 D6
Vieux (81) 270 B1
Vieux-Berquin (59) 3 K6
Vieux-Boucau-les-Bains (40) 262 B3
Vieux-Bourg (14) 34 A3
le Vieux-Bourg (22) 76 E1
le Vieux-Cérier (16) 179 K5
Vieux-Champagne (77) 88 C1
Vieux-Charmont (25) 139 H2
Vieux-Château (21) 134 B3
Vieux-Condé (59) 7 J6
Vieux-Ferrette (68) 97 C5
Vieux-Fumé (14) 33 G6
Vieux-lès-Asfeld (08) 41 F1
Vieux-Lixheim (57) 67 K3
Vieux-Manoir (76) 16 B4
le Vieux-Marché (22) 47 K4
Vieux-Mareuil (24) 197 H6
Vieux-Mesnil (59) 13 H3
Vieux-Moulin (60) 38 E2
Vieux-Moulin (88) 95 J4
Vieux-Pont (14) 54 D1
Vieux-Pont (61) 54 B6
Vieux-Port (27) 34 D2
Vieux-Reng (59) 13 H2
Vieux-Rouen-sur-Bresle (76) 17 F3
la Vieux-Rue (76) 35 K1
Vieux-Ruffec (16) 179 J5
Vieux-Thann (68) 97 A2
Vieux-Viel (35) 51 H1
Vieux-Villez (27) 35 K5
Vieux-Vy-sur-Couesnon (35) 79 J1
Vieuzos (65) 286 B5
Viévigne (21) 136 C4
Viéville (52) 92 B5
Viéville-en-Haye (54) 65 H2
Viévy (21) 153 G3
Vievy-le-Rayé (41) 108 E4
Viey (65) 304 B4
Vif (38) 224 A5
Viffort (02) 60 E2
le Vigan (30) 273 J1
le Vigan (46) 233 H3
le Vigean (15) 217 G3
le Vigeant (86) 180 B2
le Vigen (87) 199 F2
Vigeois (19) 215 J1
Viger (65) 304 B1
Vigeville (23) 183 F3
Viggianello (2A) 322 E2
Viglain (45) 110 E6
Vignacourt (80) 9 K6
Vignale (2B) 319 H3

Vignats (14) 54 B3
le Vignau (40) 265 J4
Vignaux (31) 268 D5
les Vigneaux (05) 243 J1
Vignec (65) 304 E4
Vignely (77) 59 J2
Vignemont (60) 38 D1
les Vignes (48) 253 J4
Vignes (64) 284 C1
Vignes (89) 134 B3
Vignes-la-Côte (52) 92 C5
Vigneul-sous-Montmédy (55) 23 J6
Vigneulles (54) 66 C6
Vigneulles-lès-Hattonchâtel (55) . . 65 F1
Vigneux-de-Bretagne (44) 123 F2
Vigneux-Hocquet (02) 21 G4
Vigneux-sur-Seine (91) 59 F5
Vignevieille (11) 309 H2
Vignieu (38) 207 G3
Vignol (58) 133 H5
Vignoc (35) 79 H4
Vignoles (21) 154 A3
Vignolles (16) 196 B5
Vignols (19) 215 H2
Vignonet (33) 230 B2
Vignory (52) 92 A5
Vignot (55) 65 F4
Vignoux-sous-les-Aix (18) 149 H1
Vignoux-sur-Barangeon (18) 148 E1
Vigny (57) 66 B1
Vigny (95) 37 F6
Vigoulant (36) 166 C5
Vigoulet-Auzil (31) 288 C2
Vigoux (36) 165 G4
Vigueron (82) 268 C5
Vigy (57) 27 J6
Vihiers (49) 143 J2
Vijon (36) 166 C5
Vilcey-sur-Trey (54) 65 J2
Vildé-Guingalan (22) 50 C5
le Vilhain (03) 167 K4
Vilhonneur (16) 197 G3
Villabé (91) 87 F1
Villabon (18) 149 K3
Villac (24) 215 F4
Villacerf (10) 90 A3
Villadin (10) 89 H4
Villafans (70) 138 E1
Village-Neuf (68) 97 E4
Villaines-en-Duesmois (21) 135 F1
Villaines-la-Carelle (72) 83 F3
Villaines-la-Gonais (72) 107 H1
Villaines-la-Juhel (53) 81 K4
Villaines-les-Prévôtes (21) 134 D2
Villaines-les-Rochers (37) 145 J1
Villaines-sous-Bois (95) 37 K6
Villaines-sous-Lucé (72) 107 J2
Villaines-sous-Malicorne (72) 106 B5
Villainville (76) 14 C5
Villalet (27) 56 C2
Villalier (11) 290 B5
Villamblain (45) 109 G3
Villamblard (24) 213 J5
Villamée (35) 80 A2
Villampuy (28) 109 G2
Villandraut (33) 246 B1
Villandry (37) 127 G5
Villanière (11) 290 B4
Villanova (2A) 320 A5
Villapourçon (58) 152 B4
Villar-d'Arène (05) 225 G5
Villar-en-Val (11) 309 H1
Villar-Loubière (05) 243 F2
Villar-Saint-Anselme (11) 309 F2
Villar-Saint-Pancrace (05) 227 A1
Villard (23) 182 B1
Villard (74) 191 J1
Villard-Bonnot (38) 224 C2
Villard-de-Lans (38) 223 J4
Villard-d'Héry (73) 208 D4
Villard-Léger (73) 208 E4
Villard-Notre-Dame (38) 224 D5
Villard-Reculas (38) 224 D4
Villard-Reymond (38) 224 D5
Villard-Saint-Christophe (38) 224 B6
Villard-Saint-Sauveur (39) 173 K5
Villard-Sallet (73) 208 D5
Villard-sur-Bienne (39) 173 K4
Villard-sur-Doron (73) 209 H2
Villardebelle (11) 309 G2
Villardonnel (11) 290 A4
Villards-d'Héria (39) 173 H5
les Villards-sur-Thônes (74) 191 H5
Villarembert (73) 225 G2
Villargent (70) 138 E2
Villargoix (21) 134 D6
Villargondran (73) 225 H2
Villariès (31) 269 H4
Villarlurin (73) 209 H5
Villarodin-Bourget (73) 226 A2
Villaroger (73) 193 B3
Villaroux (73) 208 D5
Villars (24) 198 A6
Villars (28) 85 G5
Villars (42) 205 F4
le Villars (71) 172 A4
Villars (84) 277 H2
Villars-Colmars (04) 260 C4
Villars-en-Azois (52) 115 H2
Villars-en-Pons (17) 195 G4
Villars-et-Villenotte (21) 134 E3

Villars-Fontaine (21) 154 A2
Villars-le-Pautel (70) 117 J3
Villars-le-Sec (90) 139 K3
Villars-lès-Blamont (25) 139 J4
Villars-les-Bois (17) 195 J1
Villars-les-Dombes (01) 188 E4
Villars-Saint-Georges (25) 155 K2
Villars-Santenoge (52) 115 K5
Villars-sous-Dampjoux (25) 139 J4
Villars-sous-Écot (25) 139 G3
Villarzel-Cabardès (11) 290 C5
Villarzel-du-Razès (11) 308 E1
Villasavary (11) 289 H5
Villate (31) 288 B2
Villaudric (31) 269 G3
Villautou (11) 289 F6
Villavard (41) 108 A6
Villaz (74) 191 H5
Ville (60) 19 G6
Villé (67) 70 B6
Ville-au-Montois (54) 26 D4
Ville-au-Val (54) 65 K3
la Ville-aux-Bois (10) 91 G3
la Ville-aux-Bois-lès-Dizy (02) 21 G5
la Ville-aux-Bois-lès-Pontavert (02) . . 40 D2
la Ville-aux-Clercs (41) 108 C4
la Ville-aux-Dames (37) 127 K4
Ville-d'Avray (92) 58 D4
Ville-devant-Belrain (55) 64 C3
Ville-devant-Chaumont (55) 43 J3
Ville-di-Paraso (2B) 318 D3
Ville-di-Pietrabugno (2B) 317 D5
la Ville-Dieu-du-Temple (82) 268 E1
Ville-Dommange (51) 40 E5
la Ville-du-Bois (91) 58 D6
Ville-du-Pont (25) 157 G3
Ville-en-Blaisois (52) 91 K3
Ville-en-Sallaz (74) 191 J2
Ville-en-Selve (51) 41 F6
Ville-en-Tardenois (51) 40 D5
Ville-en-Vermois (54) 66 B6
Ville-en-Woëvre (55) 44 A5
la Ville-ès-Nonais (35) 50 E4
Ville-Houdlémont (54) 26 B2
la Ville-la-Grand (74) 191 G1
Ville-Langy (58) 151 H4
Ville-le-Marclet (80) 9 J6
Ville-Saint-Jacques (77) 87 K4
Ville-Savoye (02) 40 B4
Ville-sous-Anjou (38) 222 I1
Ville-sous-la-Ferté (10) 115 H1
la Ville-sous-Orbais (51) 61 G2
Ville-sur-Ancre (80) 18 D1
Ville-sur-Arce (10) 114 E1
Ville-sur-Cousances (55) 43 F6
Ville-sur-Illon (88) 94 B5
Ville-sur-Jarnioux (69) 188 A5
Ville-sur-Lumes (08) 22 D3
Ville-sur-Retourne (08) 41 J2
Ville-sur-Saulx (55) 64 A5
Ville-sur-Terre (10) 91 H4
Ville-sur-Tourbe (51) 42 C5
Ville-sur-Yron (54) 44 D5
Villeau (28) 85 H5
Villebadin (61) 54 D4
Villebarou (41) 128 E2
Villebaudon (50) 31 G5
Villebazy (11) 309 F2
Villebéon (77) 88 A6
Villebernier (49) 126 B6
Villeberny (21) 135 G4
Villebichot (21) 154 C2
Villeblevin (89) 88 B4
Villebois (01) 189 J6
Villebois-Lavalette (16) 197 F5
Villebois-les-Pins (26) 258 C2
Villebon (28) 84 D3
Villebon-sur-Yvette (91) 58 D5
Villebougis (89) 88 C6
Villebourg (37) 127 H1
Villebout (41) 108 D3
Villebramar (47) 231 H6
Villebret (03) 184 D4
Villebrumier (82) 269 G2
Villecelin (18) 148 E6
Villecerf (77) 87 K4
Villecey-sur-Mad (54) 65 J1
Villechantria (39) 173 F5
Villechauve (41) 128 B1
Villechenève (69) 205 G1
Villechétif (10) 90 B4
Villechétive (89) 113 F1
Villechien (50) 52 D6
Villecien (89) 112 D3
Villécloye (55) 23 K6
Villecomtal (12) 235 J6
Villecomtal-sur-Arros (32) 285 J3
Villecomte (21) 136 A3
Villeconin (91) 86 C2
Villecourt (80) 19 H3
Villecresnes (94) 59 G5
Villecroze (83) 279 G6
Villedaigne (11) 291 G6
Villedieu (15) 218 D6
la Villedieu (17) 178 B4
Villedieu (21) 114 C2
la Villedieu (23) 200 B4
les Villedieu (25) 156 E6
la Villedieu (48) 237 J4
Villedieu (84) 257 G3
la Villedieu-du-Clain (86) 163 F5

la Villedieu-en-Fontenette (70) 118 B5
Villedieu-la-Blouère (49) 142 D1
Villedieu-le-Château (41) 107 J6
Villedieu-lès-Bailleul (61) 54 C4
Villedieu-les-Poêles (50) 52 B3
Villedieu-sur-Indre (36) 147 J6
Villedômain (37) 147 F3
Villedômer (37) 128 A3
Villedoux (17) 176 E1
Villedubert (11) 290 C5
Villefagnan (16) 179 F4
Villefargeau (89) 113 F5
Villefavard (87) 181 G3
Villeferry (21) 135 F4
Villefloure (11) 309 G1
Villefollet (79) 178 C3
Villefontaine (38) 206 D4
Villefort (11) 308 C3
Villefort (48) 255 F1
Villefranche (32) 286 E3
Villefranche (89) 112 C3
Villefranche-d'Albigeois (81) 271 F3
Villefranche-d'Allier (03) 167 K6
Villefranche-de-Conflent (66) 314 B3
Villefranche-de-Lauragais (31) 288 C3
Villefranche-de-Lonchat (24) 212 D6
Villefranche-de-Panat (12) 252 C6
Villefranche-de-Rouergue (12) 251 F3
Villefranche-du-Périgord (24) 232 D5
Villefranche-du-Queyran (47) 247 H3
Villefranche-le-Château (26) 258 B4
Villefranche-sur-Cher (41) 129 J6
Villefranche-sur-Mer (06) 281 H4
Villefranche-sur-Saône (69) 188 B5
Villefrancoeur (41) 128 D1
Villefrancon (70) 137 H4
Villefranque (64) 263 G2
Villefranque (65) 285 G2
Villegailhenc (11) 290 B5
Villegats (16) 179 G5
Villegats (27) 57 G2
Villegaudin (71) 154 D6
Villegenon (18) 131 G4
Villegly (11) 290 C5
Villegongis (36) 147 J5
Villegouge (33) 211 K6
Villegouin (36) 147 G4
Villegusien-le-Lac (52) 116 D6
Villeherviers (41) 129 K5
Villejésus (16) 179 F6
Villejoubert (16) 196 E1
Villejuif (94) 58 E4
Villejust (91) 58 D6
Villelaure (84) 277 H4
Villeloin-Coulangé (37) 147 F2
Villelongue (65) 304 B3
Villelongue-d'Aude (11) 308 D2
Villelongue-de-la-Salanque (66) 310 C6
Villelongue-dels-Monts (66) 315 G4
Villeloup (10) 89 J4
Villemade (82) 249 J6
Villemagne (11) 289 J4
Villemagne-l'Argentière (34) 272 E6
Villemain (79) 178 D4
Villemandeur (45) 111 H3
Villemanoche (89) 88 C5
Villemardy (41) 108 D6
Villemaréchal (77) 87 K5
Villemareuil (77) 60 A3
Villematier (31) 269 H3
Villemaur-sur-Vanne (10) 89 H5
Villembits (65) 286 A4
Villembray (60) 37 F1
Villemer (77) 87 J5
Villemer (89) 113 F4
Villemereuil (10) 90 B6
Villemeux-sur-Eure (28) 57 G6
Villemoirieu (38) 206 E2
Villemoiron-en-Othe (10) 89 J6
Villemoisan (49) 124 D3
Villemoisson-sur-Orge (91) 58 E6
Villemolaque (66) 315 G3
Villemomble (93) 59 G3
Villemontais (42) 186 D5
Villemontoire (02) 39 J4
Villemorien (10) 114 D1
Villemorin (17) 178 B4
Villemort (86) 164 B4
Villemotier (01) 172 E6
Villemoustaussou (11) 290 B5
Villemoutiers (45) 111 G3
Villemoyenne (10) 90 C6
Villemur (65) 286 C5
Villemur-sur-Tarn (31) 269 H3
Villemurlin (45) 130 E1
Villemus (04) 278 A2
Villenauxe-la-Grande (10) 89 F1
Villenauxe-la-Petite (77) 88 D3
Villenave (40) 264 D1
Villenave-d'Ornon (33) 229 H3
Villenave-près-Béarn (65) 285 F3
Villenave-près-Marsac (65) 285 H4
Villenavotte (89) 88 D5
Villeneuve (01) 188 C4
Villeneuve (04) 278 C2
Villeneuve (09) 306 C3
Villeneuve (12) 251 F2
la Villeneuve (23) 183 J6
Villeneuve (33) 211 G4
Villeneuve (63) 202 E6
la Villeneuve (71) 154 D4

la Villeneuve-au-Châtelot (10) 89 G1
Villeneuve-au-Chemin (10) 113 J1
la Villeneuve-au-Chêne (10) 90 D5
la Villeneuve-Bellenoye-
et-la-Maize (70) 118 C6
Villeneuve-d'Allier (43) 219 H3
Villeneuve-d'Amont (25) 156 C4
Villeneuve-d'Ascq (59) 6 E4
Villeneuve-d'Aval (39) 155 K4
Villeneuve-de-Berg (07) 239 J6
Villeneuve-de-Duras (47) 231 F3
Villeneuve-de-la-Raho (66) 315 H3
Villeneuve-de-Marc (38) 206 D5
Villeneuve-de-Marsan (40) 265 J2
Villeneuve-de-Rivière (31) 305 J1
Villeneuve-d'Olmes (09) 308 A4
Villeneuve-du-Latou (09) 288 B6
Villeneuve-du-Paréage (09) 288 D6
la Villeneuve-en-Chevrie (78) 57 G1
Villeneuve-en-Montagne (71) 171 G1
Villeneuve-Frouville (41) 108 E5
Villeneuve-la-Comptal (11) 289 G5
Villeneuve-la-Comtesse (17) 177 K3
Villeneuve-la-Dondagre (89) 112 C1
Villeneuve-la-Garenne (92) 58 E2
Villeneuve-la-Guyard (89) 88 B4
Villeneuve-la-Lionne (51) 60 E4
Villeneuve-la-Rivière (66) 310 B6
Villeneuve-l'Archevêque (89) 89 F5
Villeneuve-le-Comte (77) 59 J4
Villeneuve-le-Roi (94) 59 F5
Villeneuve-Lécussan (31) 286 C6
Villeneuve-lès-Avignon (30) 276 B1
Villeneuve-lès-Béziers (34) 292 A4
Villeneuve-lès-Bordes (77) 88 B2
Villeneuve-lès-Bouloc (31) 269 G4
Villeneuve-les-Cerfs (63) 185 H5
la Villeneuve-lès-Charleville (51) 61 H4
Villeneuve-lès-Charnod (39) 173 F6
la Villeneuve-lès-Convers (21) 135 F2
Villeneuve-lès-Corbières (11) 310 A3
Villeneuve-lès-Genêts (89) 112 B6
Villeneuve-lès-Lavaur (81) 270 A6
Villeneuve-lès-Maguelone (34) 293 G1
Villeneuve-lès-Montréal (11) 289 J6
Villeneuve-les-Sablons (60) 37 G4
Villeneuve-Loubet (06) 281 F4
Villeneuve-Minervois (11) 290 C4
Villeneuve-Renneville-
Chevigny (51) 62 A2
Villeneuve-Saint-Denis (77) 59 J4
Villeneuve-Saint-Georges (94) 59 F5
Villeneuve-Saint-Germain (02) 39 J3
Villeneuve-Saint-Nicolas (28) 85 H5
Villeneuve-Saint-Salves (89) 113 G4
Villeneuve-Saint-Vistre-
et-Villevotte (51) 61 H6
Villeneuve-sous-Charigny (21) 134 E4
Villeneuve-sous-Dammartin (77) 59 H1
Villeneuve-sous-Pymont (39) 173 G1
la Villeneuve-sous-Thury (60) 39 G5
Villeneuve-sur-Allier (03) 168 D2
Villeneuve-sur-Auvers (91) 86 D2
Villeneuve-sur-Bellot (77) 60 D3
Villeneuve-sur-Cher (18) 148 E3
Villeneuve-sur-Conie (45) 109 H2
Villeneuve-sur-Fère (02) 40 A3
Villeneuve-sur-Lot (47) 248 C2
Villeneuve-sur-Verberie (60) 38 C4
Villeneuve-sur-Vère (81) 270 C1
Villeneuve-sur-Yonne (89) 112 D2
Villeneuve-Tolosane (31) 288 A2
Villeneuvette (34) 273 G6
Villennes-sur-Seine (78) 58 B2
Villenouvelle (31) 288 E3
Villenoy (77) 59 K2
Villentrois (36) 147 H1
Villeny (41) 129 J2
Villepail (53) 81 K3
Villeparisis (77) 59 G2
Villeparois (70) 118 B6
Villeperdrix (26) 257 J1
Villeperdue (37) 145 K1
Villeperrot (89) 88 C5
Villepinte (11) 289 J5
Villepinte (93) 59 G2
Villeporcher (41) 128 B1
Villepot (41) 103 K3
Villepreux (78) 58 B4
Villequier (76) 34 E1
Villequier-Aumont (02) 19 K5
Villequiers (18) 150 A3
Viller (57) 66 E1
Villerable (41) 108 C6
Villeréal (47) 232 A5
Villereau (45) 110 B2
Villereau (59) 12 E3
Villereversure (01) 189 H2
Villermain (41) 109 G4
Villeromain (41) 108 D6
Villeron (95) 59 G1
Villerouge-Termenès (11) 309 J2
Villeroy (77) 59 J2
Villeroy (80) 17 F1
Villeroy (89) 88 C6
Villeroy-sur-Méholle (55) 64 E6
Villers (42) 187 B4

Villers (88) . . . 94 A4
Villers-Agron-Aiguizy (02) . . . 40 C5
Villers-Allerand (51) . . . 41 F5
Villers-au-Bois (62) . . . 10 D2
Villers-au-Flos (62) . . . 11 G5
Villers-au-Tertre (59) . . . 11 J2
Villers-aux-Bois (51) . . . 61 K2
Villers-aux-Érables (80) . . . 18 D3
Villers-aux-Noeuds (51) . . . 40 E5
Villers-aux-Vents (55) . . . 63 K3
Villers-Bocage (14) . . . 32 A6
Villers-Bocage (80) . . . 10 A6
Villers-Bouton (70) . . . 137 K3
Villers-Bretonneux (80) . . . 18 D3
Villers-Brûlin (62) . . . 10 C2
Villers-Buzon (25) . . . 137 J6
Villers-Campsart (80) . . . 17 G2
Villers-Canivet (14) . . . 54 A2
Villers-Carbonnel (80) . . . 19 G2
Villers-Cernay (08) . . . 23 G4
Villers-Châtel (62) . . . 10 D1
Villers-Chemin-et-Mont-
  lès-Etrelles (70) . . . 137 J3
Villers-Chief (25) . . . 138 E6
Villers-Cotterêts (02) . . . 39 G4
Villers-devant-Dun (55) . . . 43 F2
Villers-devant-le-Thour (08) . . . 41 F1
Villers-devant-Mouzon (08) . . . 23 G4
Villers-Écalles (76) . . . 15 J6
Villers-en-Argonne (51) . . . 63 J1
Villers-en-Arthies (95) . . . 36 D6
Villers-en-Cauchies (59) . . . 12 C3
Villers-en-Haye (54) . . . 65 J3
Villers-en-Ouche (61) . . . 55 G3
Villers-en-Prayères (02) . . . 40 B2
Villers-en-Vexin (27) . . . 36 C4
Villers-Farlay (39) . . . 155 K3
Villers-Faucon (80) . . . 19 J1
Villers-Franqueux (51) . . . 40 E3
Villers-Grélot (25) . . . 138 C4
Villers-Guislain (59) . . . 11 J6
Villers-Hélon (02) . . . 39 H4
Villers-la-Chèvre (54) . . . 26 C2
Villers-la-Combe (25) . . . 138 E6
Villers-la-Faye (21) . . . 154 A2
Villers-la-Montagne (54) . . . 26 D3
Villers-la-Ville (70) . . . 138 E2
Villers-le-Château (51) . . . 62 C2
Villers-le-Lac (25) . . . 157 H2
Villers-le-Rond (54) . . . 26 A3
Villers-le-Sec (02) . . . 20 C3
Villers-le-Sec (51) . . . 63 H4
Villers-le-Sec (55) . . . 64 C6
Villers-le-Sec (70) . . . 138 E1
Villers-le-Tilleul (08) . . . 22 D5
Villers-le-Tourneur (08) . . . 22 B5
Villers-les-Bois (39) . . . 155 H4
Villers-lès-Cagnicourt (62) . . . 11 G3
Villers-lès-Guise (02) . . . 20 D1
Villers-lès-Luxeuil (70) . . . 118 C5
Villers-lès-Mangiennes (55) . . . 26 A4
Villers-lès-Moivrons (54) . . . 66 B3
Villers-lès-Nancy (54) . . . 66 A5
Villers-les-Ormes (36) . . . 147 K5
Villers-lès-Pots (21) . . . 155 F1
Villers-lès-Roye (80) . . . 18 E4
Villers-l'Hôpital (62) . . . 9 K3
Villers-Marmery (51) . . . 41 G5
Villers-Outréaux (59) . . . 11 K6
Villers-Pater (70) . . . 138 B3
Villers-Patras (21) . . . 115 F2
Villers-Plouich (59) . . . 11 J5
Villers-Pol (59) . . . 12 E3
Villers-Robert (39) . . . 155 G4
Villers-Rotin (21) . . . 155 F1
Villers-Saint-Barthélemy (60) . . . 37 F2
Villers-Saint-Christophe (02) . . . 19 J3
Villers-Saint-Frambourg (60) . . . 38 C4
Villers-Saint-Genest (60) . . . 38 E6
Villers-Saint-Martin (25) . . . 138 D4
Villers-Saint-Paul (60) . . . 38 A4
Villers-Saint-Sépulcre (60) . . . 37 J3
Villers-Semeuse (08) . . . 22 D3
Villers-Sir-Simon (62) . . . 10 C2
Villers-Sire-Nicole (59) . . . 13 H2
Villers-sous-Ailly (80) . . . 9 H5
Villers-sous-Chalamont (25) . . . 156 C1
Villers-sous-Châtillon (51) . . . 40 E4
Villers-sous-Foucaucourt (76) . . . 16 E2
Villers-sous-Montrond (25) . . . 156 C1
Villers-sous-Pareid (55) . . . 44 B5
Villers-sous-Prény (54) . . . 65 J2
Villers-sous-Saint-Leu (60) . . . 37 K5
Villers-Stoncourt (57) . . . 45 H6
Villers-sur-Auchy (60) . . . 36 E1
Villers-sur-Authie (80) . . . 9 F2
Villers-sur-Bar (08) . . . 22 E4
Villers-sur-Bonnières (60) . . . 17 H6
Villers-sur-Coudun (60) . . . 38 D1
Villers-sur-Fère (02) . . . 40 A5
Villers-sur-le-Mont (08) . . . 22 C4
Villers-sur-le-Roule (27) . . . 36 A5
Villers-sur-Mer (14) . . . 33 H5
Villers-sur-Meuse (55) . . . 64 D1
Villers-sur-Nied (57) . . . 66 D2
Villers-sur-Port (70) . . . 118 A6
Villers-sur-Saulnot (70) . . . 139 F2
Villers-sur-Trie (60) . . . 36 E3
Villers-Tournelle (80) . . . 18 C5
Villers-Vaudey (70) . . . 117 H6
Villers-Vermont (60) . . . 17 F6
Villers-Vicomte (60) . . . 18 A5

Villerserine (39) . . . 155 J5
Villersexel (70) . . . 138 D2
Villerupt (54) . . . 26 E3
Villerville (14) . . . 33 J2
Villery (10) . . . 90 A4
Villes (01) . . . 190 C3
Villes-sur-Auzon (84) . . . 257 J6
Villeselve (60) . . . 19 J4
Villeseneux (51) . . . 62 B3
Villesèque (46) . . . 249 J2
Villesèque-des-Corbières (11) . . . 310 D3
Villesèquelande (11) . . . 289 K5
Villesiscle (11) . . . 289 J5
Villespassans (34) . . . 291 G3
Villespy (11) . . . 289 J4
Villetaneuse (93) . . . 58 G2
la Villetelle (23) . . . 183 H6
Villetelle (34) . . . 274 E4
Villethierry (89) . . . 88 B5
Villeton (47) . . . 247 H2
Villetoureix (24) . . . 213 G2
Villetritouls (11) . . . 309 H1
Villetrun (41) . . . 108 D5
la Villette (14) . . . 53 H2
Villette (54) . . . 26 B3
Villette (78) . . . 57 J2
Villette-d'Anthon (38) . . . 206 D1
Villette-de-Vienne (38) . . . 206 B4
Villette-lès-Arbois (39) . . . 155 K4
Villette-lès-Dole (39) . . . 155 G3
Villette-sur-Ain (01) . . . 189 G5
Villette-sur-Aube (10) . . . 90 B2
Villettes (27) . . . 35 H5
les Villettes (43) . . . 221 F3
Villeurbanne (69) . . . 206 B2
Villevallier (89) . . . 112 D2
Villevaudé (77) . . . 59 H3
Villevenard (51) . . . 61 J4
Villevêque (49) . . . 125 H2
Villeveyrac (34) . . . 292 E2
Villevieille (30) . . . 274 E4
Villevieux (39) . . . 173 F1
Villevocance (07) . . . 221 K3
Villevoques (45) . . . 111 H2
Villexanton (41) . . . 109 F6
Villexavier (17) . . . 211 J1
le Villey (39) . . . 155 G5
Villey-le-Sec (54) . . . 65 J5
Villey-Saint-Étienne (54) . . . 65 J4
Villey-sur-Tille (21) . . . 136 B2
Villez-sous-Bailleul (27) . . . 36 A6
Villez-sur-le-Neubourg (27) . . . 35 F5
Villié-Morgon (69) . . . 188 B3
Villiers (36) . . . 146 E5
Villiers (86) . . . 162 D2
Villiers-Adam (95) . . . 58 D1
Villiers-au-Bouin (37) . . . 126 E2
Villiers-aux-Corneilles (51) . . . 89 H1
Villiers-Charlemagne (53) . . . 105 F3
Villiers-Couture (17) . . . 178 D5
Villiers-en-Bière (77) . . . 87 G2
Villiers-en-Bois (79) . . . 178 A3
Villiers-en-Désoeuvre (27) . . . 57 G2
Villiers-en-Lieu (52) . . . 63 J5
Villiers-en-Morvan (21) . . . 152 E2
Villiers-en-Plaine (79) . . . 161 G5
Villiers-Fossard (50) . . . 31 H3
Villiers-Herbisse (10) . . . 62 B6
Villiers-le-Bâcle (91) . . . 58 C5
Villiers-le-Bel (95) . . . 58 E1
Villiers-le-Bois (10) . . . 114 C3
Villiers-le-Duc (21) . . . 115 H5
Villiers-le-Mahieu (78) . . . 57 J3
Villiers-le-Morhier (28) . . . 57 H6
Villiers-le-Pré (50) . . . 51 K5
Villiers-le-Roux (16) . . . 179 F4
Villiers-le-Sec (14) . . . 32 C3
Villiers-le-Sec (52) . . . 116 A1
Villiers-le-Sec (58) . . . 132 E5
Villiers-le-Sec (95) . . . 58 E1
Villiers-lès-Aprey (52) . . . 116 C5
Villiers-les-Hauts (89) . . . 114 B6
Villiers-Louis (89) . . . 88 E6
Villiers-Saint-Benoît (89) . . . 112 C5
Villiers-Saint-Denis (02) . . . 60 D2
Villiers-Saint-Frédéric (78) . . . 58 A4
Villiers-Saint-Georges (77) . . . 60 E6
Villiers-Saint-Orien (28) . . . 109 G1
Villiers-sous-Grez (77) . . . 87 H4
Villiers-sous-Mortagne (61) . . . 83 H2
Villiers-sous-Praslin (10) . . . 114 C2
Villiers-sur-Chizé (79) . . . 178 B3
Villiers-sur-Loir (41) . . . 108 B5
Villiers-sur-Marne (94) . . . 59 G4
Villiers-sur-Morin (77) . . . 59 K3
Villiers-sur-Orge (91) . . . 58 E6
Villiers-sur-Seine (77) . . . 88 E3
Villiers-sur-Suize (52) . . . 116 B3
Villiers-sur-Tholon (89) . . . 112 E4
Villiers-sur-Yonne (58) . . . 133 G4
Villiersfaux (41) . . . 108 B6
Villieu-Loyes-Mollon (01) . . . 189 G5
Villing (57) . . . 45 K3
Villognon (16) . . . 179 F6
Villon (89) . . . 114 C4
Villoncourt (88) . . . 94 E4
Villons-les-Buissons (14) . . . 32 D4
Villorceau (45) . . . 109 H5
Villosanges (63) . . . 184 B6
Villotran (60) . . . 37 G3
Villotte (88) . . . 117 H1

Villotte-devant-Louppy (55) . . . 64 A3
Villotte-Saint-Seine (21) . . . 135 H4
Villotte-sur-Aire (55) . . . 64 C3
Villotte-sur-Ource (21) . . . 115 G4
Villouxel (88) . . . 93 F4
Villuis (77) . . . 88 E3
Villy (08) . . . 23 H5
Villy (89) . . . 113 H4
Villy-Bocage (14) . . . 32 B6
Villy-en-Auxois (21) . . . 135 G4
Villy-en-Trodes (10) . . . 90 D6
Villy-le-Bois (10) . . . 90 B6
Villy-le-Bouveret (74) . . . 191 F4
Villy-le-Maréchal (10) . . . 90 B6
Villy-le-Moutier (21) . . . 154 B3
Villy-le-Pelloux (74) . . . 191 F4
Villy-lez-Falaise (14) . . . 54 B3
Villy-sur-Yères (76) . . . 16 D1
Vilory (70) . . . 118 B5
Vilosnes-Haraumont (55) . . . 43 G3
Vilsberg (57) . . . 70 A1
Vimarcé (53) . . . 82 A6
Vimenet (12) . . . 253 F2
Viménil (88) . . . 95 F5
Vimines (73) . . . 208 B4
Vimont (14) . . . 33 F5
Vimory (45) . . . 111 H3
Vimoutiers (61) . . . 54 E2
Vimpelles (77) . . . 88 C3
Vimy (62) . . . 11 F2
Vinantes (77) . . . 59 J1
Vinassan (11) . . . 291 J6
Vinax (17) . . . 178 C5
Vinay (38) . . . 223 H3
Vinay (51) . . . 61 J1
Vinça (66) . . . 314 D3
Vincelles (39) . . . 173 F3
Vincelles (51) . . . 40 B6
Vincelles (71) . . . 172 D1
Vincelles (89) . . . 113 G6
Vincelottes (89) . . . 113 G6
Vincennes (94) . . . 59 F4
Vincent (39) . . . 155 H6
Vincey (88) . . . 94 C3
Vincly (62) . . . 5 F3
Vincy-Manoeuvre (77) . . . 39 F6
Vincy-Reuil-et-Magny (02) . . . 21 H4
Vindecy (71) . . . 170 B6
Vindefontaine (50) . . . 28 E6
Vindelle (16) . . . 196 D2
Vindey (51) . . . 61 H5
Vindrac-Alayrac (81) . . . 250 E6
Vinets (10) . . . 90 C2
Vineuil (36) . . . 147 K5
Vineuil (41) . . . 129 F2
Vineuil-Saint-Firmin (60) . . . 38 B5
la Vineuse (71) . . . 171 G4
Vinezac (07) . . . 239 G6
Vingrau (66) . . . 310 A4
Vingt-Hanaps (61) . . . 82 D2
Vinnemerville (76) . . . 14 E3
Vinneuf (89) . . . 88 C4
Vinon (18) . . . 131 K6
Vinon-sur-Verdon (83) . . . 278 B4
Vins-sur-Caramy (83) . . . 298 A2
Vinsobres (26) . . . 257 G2
le Vintrou (81) . . . 290 C2
Vinzelles (63) . . . 185 J6
Vinzelles (71) . . . 188 B1
Vinzier (74) . . . 175 J3
Vinzieux (07) . . . 222 A2
Viocourt (88) . . . 93 H4
Viodos-Abense-de-Bas (64) . . . 283 H5
Violaines (62) . . . 6 B5
Violay (42) . . . 205 F1
Violès (84) . . . 257 F5
Violot (21) . . . 116 C5
Viols-en-Laval (34) . . . 274 A4
Viols-le-Fort (34) . . . 274 A4
Vioménil (88) . . . 118 B1
Vion (07) . . . 222 A4
Vion (72) . . . 105 K5
Vions (73) . . . 208 A1
Vionville (57) . . . 44 D5
Viozan (32) . . . 286 B3
Viplaix (03) . . . 167 F5
Vira (09) . . . 308 A2
Vira (66) . . . 309 G5
Virac (81) . . . 270 D1
Virandeville (50) . . . 28 B3
Virargues (15) . . . 218 C4
Virazeil (47) . . . 231 F6
Vire (14) . . . 52 E3
Viré (71) . . . 171 K5
Viré-en-Champagne (72) . . . 105 K3
Vire-sur-Lot (46) . . . 249 G1
Vireaux (89) . . . 114 A5
Virecourt (54) . . . 94 C2
Virelade (33) . . . 229 J4
Vireux-Molhain (08) . . . 24 C2
Vireux-Wallerand (08) . . . 24 C2
Virey (50) . . . 52 B6
Virey-le-Grand (71) . . . 154 B3
Virey-sous-Bar (10) . . . 114 D1
Virginy (51) . . . 42 C5
Viriat (01) . . . 189 G1
Viricelles (42) . . . 205 G3
Virieu (38) . . . 207 H5
Virieu-le-Grand (01) . . . 190 A4
Virieu-le-Petit (01) . . . 190 B5
Virigneux (42) . . . 205 F3
Virignin (01) . . . 207 K2

Viriville (38) . . . 223 F2
Virlet (63) . . . 184 B3
Virming (57) . . . 67 F1
Viroflay (78) . . . 58 C4
Virollet (17) . . . 195 F4
Vironchaux (80) . . . 9 G3
Vironvay (27) . . . 35 J5
Virsac (33) . . . 211 G5
Virson (17) . . . 177 F3
Viry (39) . . . 173 G6
Viry (71) . . . 170 E4
Viry (74) . . . 190 E3
Viry-Châtillon (91) . . . 58 E6
Viry-Noureuil (02) . . . 19 K5
Vis-en-Artois (62) . . . 11 G3
Visan (84) . . . 257 F3
Viscomtat (63) . . . 203 K1
Viscos (65) . . . 304 B3
Viserny (21) . . . 134 D2
Visker (65) . . . 285 H6
Vismes (80) . . . 8 E6
Visoncourt (70) . . . 118 C5
Vissac-Auteyrac (43) . . . 219 K4
Vissec (30) . . . 273 H3
Visseiche (35) . . . 79 K6
Viterbe (81) . . . 270 B5
Viterne (54) . . . 65 K6
Vitot (27) . . . 35 G5
Vitrac (15) . . . 235 G3
Vitrac (24) . . . 233 F2
Vitrac (63) . . . 184 D5
Vitrac-en-Viadène (12) . . . 236 B3
Vitrac-Saint-Vincent (16) . . . 197 H2
Vitrac-sur-Montane (19) . . . 216 C1
Vitrai-sous-Laigle (61) . . . 55 J5
Vitray (03) . . . 167 H3
Vitray-en-Beauce (28) . . . 85 F5
Vitré (35) . . . 80 A6
Vitré (79) . . . 178 D1
Vitreux (39) . . . 137 G6
Vitrey (54) . . . 93 K2
Vitrey-sur-Mance (70) . . . 117 H4
Vitrimont (54) . . . 66 D6
Vitrolles (05) . . . 259 F1
Vitrolles (13) . . . 296 B2
Vitrolles-en-Lubéron (84) . . . 277 K3
Vitry-aux-Loges (45) . . . 110 D3
Vitry-en-Artois (62) . . . 11 G2
Vitry-en-Charollais (71) . . . 170 B5
Vitry-en-Montagne (52) . . . 116 A4
Vitry-en-Perthois (51) . . . 63 F4
Vitry-la-Ville (51) . . . 62 E3
Vitry-Laché (58) . . . 151 H1
Vitry-le-Croisé (10) . . . 91 F6
Vitry-le-François (51) . . . 63 H5
Vitry-lès-Cluny (71) . . . 171 G4
Vitry-lès-Nogent (52) . . . 116 D2
Vitry-sur-Loire (71) . . . 169 J2
Vitry-sur-Orne (57) . . . 27 G5
Vitry-sur-Seine (94) . . . 58 E4
Vittarville (55) . . . 43 H2
Vitteaux (21) . . . 135 F4
Vittefleur (76) . . . 15 F3
Vittel (88) . . . 93 J5
Vittersbourg (57) . . . 67 H1
Vittoncourt (57) . . . 45 H6
Vittonville (54) . . . 65 K1
Vitz-sur-Authie (80) . . . 9 J3
Viuz-en-Sallaz (74) . . . 191 H2
Viuz-la-Chiésaz (74) . . . 208 C1
Vivaise (02) . . . 20 C5
Vivans (42) . . . 186 D2
Vivario (2B) . . . 321 F2
Viven (64) . . . 284 D2
Viverols (63) . . . 204 B6
Vivès (66) . . . 315 F4
Vivey (52) . . . 116 A6
le Vivier (66) . . . 309 H5
Vivier-au-Court (08) . . . 22 E4
le Vivier-sur-Mer (35) . . . 51 F4
Vivières (02) . . . 39 G4
Viviers (07) . . . 256 D1
Viviers (57) . . . 66 C2
Viviers (89) . . . 113 K5
Viviers-du-Lac (73) . . . 208 B3
Viviers-le-Gras (88) . . . 93 J6
Viviers-lès-Lavaur (81) . . . 270 A6
Viviers-lès-Montagnes (81) . . . 289 K1
Viviers-lès-Offroicourt (88) . . . 93 K4
Viviers-sur-Artaut (10) . . . 114 E1
Viviers-sur-Chiers (54) . . . 26 B3
Viviès (09) . . . 308 A2
Viviez (12) . . . 235 F6
Viville (16) . . . 196 B5
Vivoin (72) . . . 82 D5
Vivonne (86) . . . 162 E5
Vivy (49) . . . 126 B5
Vix (21) . . . 115 F4
Vix (85) . . . 160 D5
Vizille (38) . . . 224 B4
Vizos (65) . . . 304 B3
Vocance (07) . . . 221 J3
Vodable (63) . . . 202 D5
Voegtlinshoffen (68) . . . 96 B5
Voelfling-lès-Bouzonville (57) . . . 45 J3
Voellerdingen (67) . . . 67 K1
Voeuil-et-Giget (16) . . . 196 E4
Vogelgrun (68) . . . 96 E5
Voglans (73) . . . 208 B3
Vogüé (07) . . . 239 H6
Voharies (02) . . . 20 E3

Void-Vacon (55) . . . 65 F5
Voigny (10) . . . 91 H5
Voilemont (51) . . . 63 H1
Voillans (25) . . . 138 D4
Voilleconte (52) . . . 91 J2
Voimhaut (57) . . . 45 H6
Voinémont (54) . . . 94 A1
Voingt (63) . . . 201 H2
Voinsles (77) . . . 60 A5
Voipreux (51) . . . 62 A3
Voires (25) . . . 156 D2
Voiron (38) . . . 223 K1
Voiscreville (27) . . . 34 E4
Voise (28) . . . 85 J3
Voisenon (77) . . . 87 H1
Voisey (52) . . . 117 H3
Voisines (52) . . . 116 B4
Voisines (89) . . . 88 E5
Voisins-le-Bretonneux (78) . . . 58 B5
Voissant (38) . . . 207 K5
Voissay (17) . . . 177 J5
Voiteur (39) . . . 155 H6
la Voivre (70) . . . 118 E4
la Voivre (88) . . . 95 H3
les Voivres (88) . . . 118 C1
Voivres-lès-le-Mans (72) . . . 106 C3
Volckerinckhove (59) . . . 3 G4
Volesvres (71) . . . 170 C4
Volgelsheim (68) . . . 96 E4
Volgré (89) . . . 112 D4
Volksberg (67) . . . 69 F4
Vollore-Montagne (63) . . . 203 J2
Vollore-Ville (63) . . . 203 J2
Volmerange-lès-Boulay (57) . . . 27 K6
Volmerange-les-Mines (57) . . . 27 F3
Volmunster (57) . . . 69 G2
Volnay (21) . . . 153 K3
Volnay (72) . . . 107 G3
Volon (70) . . . 137 G1
Volonne (04) . . . 259 G5
Volpajola (2B) . . . 319 H3
Volstroff (57) . . . 27 H5
Volvent (26) . . . 241 H5
Volvic (63) . . . 202 C1
Volx (04) . . . 278 C2
Vomécourt (88) . . . 94 E4
Vomécourt-sur-Madon (88) . . . 94 A3
Voncourt (52) . . . 117 G6
Voncq (08) . . . 42 B1
Vonges (21) . . . 136 E5
Vongnes (01) . . . 207 K1
Vonnas (01) . . . 188 E2
Voray-sur-l'Ognon (70) . . . 137 K5
Voreppe (38) . . . 223 K2
Vorey (43) . . . 220 C3
Vorges (02) . . . 40 B1
Vorges-les-Pins (25) . . . 156 A1
Vorly (18) . . . 149 H4
Vornay (18) . . . 149 J4
Vosbles (39) . . . 173 G6
Vosne-Romanée (21) . . . 154 B1
Vosnon (10) . . . 113 J1
Vou (37) . . . 146 B3
Vouarces (51) . . . 89 J1
Voudenay (21) . . . 153 F2
Voué (10) . . . 90 B3
Vouécourt (52) . . . 92 B5
Vougécourt (70) . . . 117 K3
Vougeot (21) . . . 154 B1
Vougrey (10) . . . 114 C1
Vougy (42) . . . 187 F3
Vougy (74) . . . 191 J3
Vouharte (16) . . . 196 D1
Vouhé (17) . . . 177 G2
Vouhé (79) . . . 161 K3
Vouhenans (70) . . . 118 E6
Vouillé (79) . . . 161 J6
Vouillé (86) . . . 162 D2
Vouillé-les-Marais (85) . . . 160 C5
Vouillers (51) . . . 63 H5
Vouillon (36) . . . 148 C6
Vouilly (14) . . . 31 H1
Voujeaucourt (25) . . . 139 H2
Voulaines-les-Templiers (21) . . . 115 H5
Voulangis (77) . . . 59 K3
Voulême (86) . . . 179 H3
Voulgézac (16) . . . 196 D5
Voulon (86) . . . 162 E6
Voulpaix (02) . . . 20 E2
la Voulte-sur-Rhône (07) . . . 240 B2
Voultegon (79) . . . 143 J4
Voulton (77) . . . 60 D6
Voulx (77) . . . 88 A5
Vouneuil-sous-Biard (86) . . . 162 E3
Vouneuil-sur-Vienne (86) . . . 163 H1
Vourey (38) . . . 223 J3
Vourles (69) . . . 206 A3
Voussac (03) . . . 185 F1
Voutenay-sur-Cure (89) . . . 133 J2
Voutezac (19) . . . 215 H2
Vouthon (16) . . . 197 H3
Vouthon-Bas (55) . . . 93 F2
Vouthon-Haut (55) . . . 93 F2
Voutré (53) . . . 81 K6
Vouvant (85) . . . 160 E3
Vouvray (37) . . . 127 K4
Vouvray-sur-Huisne (72) . . . 107 H1
Vouvray-sur-Loir (72) . . . 107 G6
Vouxey (88) . . . 93 H3
Vouzailles (86) . . . 162 C1
Vouzan (16) . . . 197 G4
Vouzeron (18) . . . 130 D6

Vouziers (08) 42 B2
Vouzon (41) 130 B1
Vouzy (51) 62 B2
Voves (28) 85 H5
Vovray-en-Bornes (74) 191 F3
Voyenne (02) 20 E4
Voyennes (80) 19 H3
Voyer (67) 67 J5
la Vraie-Croix (56) 101 H5
Vraignes-en-Vermandois (80) . . . 19 H2
Vraignes-lès-Hornoy (80) 17 H3
Vraincourt (52) 92 B5
Vraiville (27) 35 H4
Vraux (51) 62 C1
Vrécourt (88) 93 G6
Vred (59) 11 J1
Vregille (70) 137 J5
Vregny (02) 39 K2
Vrély (80) 18 E3
le Vrétot (50) 28 C4
Vriange (39) 155 H1
Vrigne-aux-Bois (08) 22 E3
Vrigne-Meuse (08) 22 E4
Vrigny (45) 110 D2
Vrigny (51) 40 E4
Vrigny (61) 54 C5
Vritz (44) 124 B2
Vrizy (08) 42 B2
Vrocourt (60) 37 F1
Vroil (51) 63 J3
Vron (80) 9 F2
Vroncourt (54) 93 K2
Vroncourt-la-Côte (52) 92 E6
Vroville (88) 94 A4
Vry (57) 27 J6
Vue (44) 122 D4
Vuillafans (25) 156 D2
Vuillecin (25) 156 E4
Vuillery (02) 39 K2
Vulaines (10) 89 G5
Vulaines-lès-Provins (77) 88 C1
Vulaines-sur-Seine (77) 87 J3
Vulbens (74) 190 D3
Vulmont (57) 66 B2
Vulvoz (39) 173 J6
Vy-le-Ferroux (70) 137 K1
Vy-lès-Filain (70) 138 B2
Vy-lès-Lure (70) 118 D6
Vy-lès-Rupt (70) 137 J1
Vyans-le-Val (70) 139 G2
Vyt-lès-Belvoir (25) 139 F4

W

Waben (62) 8 E1
Wacquemoulin (60) 38 C1
Wacquinghen (62) 2 B4
Wadelincourt (08) 23 F4
Wagnon (08) 22 A5
Wahagnies (59) 6 D6
Wahlbach (68) 97 C4
Wahlenheim (67) 70 E1
Wail (62) 9 J2
Wailly (62) 10 E3
Wailly-Beaucamp (62) 9 F1
Walbach (68) 96 B4
Walbourg (67) 25 A3
la Walck (67) 69 J5
Waldersbach (67) 70 A5
Waldhambach (67) 69 F5
Waldhouse (57) 69 H2
Waldighofen (68) 97 C5
Waldolwisheim (67) 70 C1
Waldweistroff (57) 27 K4
Waldwisse (57) 45 J1
Walheim (68) 97 B4
Walincourt-Selvigny (59) 12 B5
Wallers (59) 12 C1
Wallers-Trélon (59) 13 K5
Wallon-Cappel (59) 3 J5
Walschbronn (57) 69 H2
Walscheid (57) 67 K5
Waltembourg (57) 70 A1
Waltenheim (68) 97 D3
Waltenheim-sur-Zorn (67) 70 E1
Waly (55) 64 A1
Wambaix (59) 11 K5
Wambercourt (62) 9 H1
Wambez (60) 36 E1
Wambrechies (59) 6 D3
Wamin (62) 9 J1
Wanchy-Capval (76) 16 C2
Wancourt (62) 11 F3
Wandignies-Hamage (59) 11 K1
Wangen (67) 70 C3
Wangenbourg-Engenthal (67) . . 70 B3
Wannehain (59) 7 F5
Wanquetin (62) 10 D3
la Wantzenau (67) 25 B6
Warcq (08) 22 C3
Warcq (55) 26 C6
Wardrecques (62) 3 H5
Wargemoulin-Hurlus (51) 42 B5
Wargnies (80) 10 A6
Wargnies-le-Grand (59) 12 E2
Wargnies-le-Petit (59) 12 E2
Warhem (59) 3 J2
Warlaing (59) 11 K1
Warlencourt-Eaucourt (62) 11 F5
Warlincourt-lès-Pas (62) 10 C4
Warloy-Baillon (80) 10 C6

Warluis (60) 37 H2
Warlus (62) 10 D3
Warlus (80) 17 H1
Warluzel (62) 10 C3
Warmeriville (51) 41 G3
Warnécourt (08) 22 C4
Warneton (59) 6 C3
Warsy (80) 18 E4
Warvillers (80) 18 E3
Wasigny (08) 21 K5
Wasnes-au-Bac (59) 11 K3
Wasquehal (59) 6 E3
Wasselonne (67) 70 C2
Wasserbourg (68) 96 A5
Wassigny (02) 12 D6
Wassy (52) 91 J2
le Wast (62) 2 C5
Watigny (02) 21 J2
Watronville (55) 43 K5
Watten (59) 3 G4
Wattignies (59) 6 D5
Wattignies-la-Victoire (59) 13 H4
Wattrelos (59) 7 F3
Wattwiller (68) 97 A1
Wavignies (60) 18 B6
Waville (54) 65 J1
Wavrans-sur-l'Aa (62) 3 F6
Wavrans-sur-Ternoise (62) 10 A1
Wavrechain-sous-Denain (59) . . 12 C2
Wavrechain-sous-Faulx (59) . . . 11 K3
Wavrille (55) 43 H3
Wavrin (59) 6 C5
Waziers (59) 11 H1
Weckolsheim (68) 96 D5
Wegscheid (68) 119 J4
Weinbourg (67) 69 H5
Weislingen (67) 69 F5
Weitbruch (67) 25 A4
Weiterswiller (67) 69 G6
Welles-Pérennes (60) 18 C5
Wemaers-Cappel (59) 3 J4
Wentzwiller (68) 97 D5
Werentzhouse (68) 97 C5
Wervicq-Sud (59) 6 D2
West-Cappel (59) 3 J3
Westhalten (68) 96 B5
Westhoffen (67) 70 C3
Westhouse (67) 70 E5
Westhouse-Marmoutier (67) . . . 70 C2
Westrehem (62) 5 H5
Wettolsheim (68) 96 B4
Weyer (67) 67 K2
Weyersheim (67) 25 B5
Wickerschwihr (68) 96 C3
Wickersheim-Wilshausen (67) . . 69 J6
Wicquinghem (62) 4 D5
Wicres (59) 6 C5
Widehem (62) 4 B5
Widensolen (68) 96 D4
Wiège-Faty (02) 20 D2
Wiencourt-l'Équipée (80) 18 D2
Wierre-au-Bois (62) 2 C6
Wierre-Effroy (62) 2 B5
Wiesviller (57) 68 E3
Wignehies (59) 13 H6
Wignicourt (08) 22 C6
Wihr-au-Val (68) 96 A4
Wildenstein (68) 119 J2
Wildersbach (67) 70 A5
Willeman (62) 9 K2
Willems (59) 7 F4
Willencourt (62) 9 J3
Willer (68) 97 C4
Willer-sur-Thur (68) 119 K3
Willeroncourt (55) 64 C5
Willerval (62) 11 F2
Willerwald (57) 68 D4
Willgottheim (67) 70 D2
Williers (08) 23 J4
Willies (59) 13 J5
Wilwisheim (67) 70 D1
Wimereux (62) 2 A5
Wimille (62) 2 A5
Wimmenau (67) 69 G5
Wimy (02) 21 G1
Windstein (67) 69 K4
Wingen (67) 25 A1
Wingen-sur-Moder (67) 69 G5
Wingersheim (67) 70 E1
Wingles (62) 6 C6
Winkel (68) 97 B6
Winnezeele (59) 3 J4
Wintersbourg (57) 67 K3
Wintershouse (67) 69 K6
Wintzenbach (67) 25 D2
Wintzenheim (68) 96 B4
Wintzenheim-Kochersberg (67) . . 70 D2
Wirwignes (62) 2 C6
Wiry-au-Mont (80) 17 G1
Wisches (67) 70 B4
Wisembach (88) 95 K4
Wiseppe (55) 43 F1
Wismes (62) 2 E6
Wisques (62) 3 F5
Wissant (62) 2 B3
Wissembourg (67) 25 C1
Wissignicourt (02) 39 K1
Wissous (91) 58 E5
Witry-lès-Reims (51) 41 F3
Wittelsheim (68) 97 B2
Wittenheim (68) 97 C1
Witternesse (62) 5 H4

Witternheim (67) 71 C4
Wittersdorf (68) 97 B4
Wittersheim (67) 69 K6
Wittes (62) 3 H6
Wittisheim (67) 71 C5
Wittring (57) 68 E3
Wiwersheim (67) 70 E2
Wizernes (62) 3 G5
Woël (55) 44 B6
Woelfling-lès-Sarreguemines (57) . 68 E3
Woerth (67) 25 A2
Woignarue (80) 8 D5
Woimbey (55) 64 D1
Woincourt (80) 8 D5
Woippy (57) 44 E5
Woirel (80) 17 G1
Wolfersdorf (68) 97 A4
Wolfgantzen (68) 96 D4
Wolfisheim (67) 70 E3
Wolfskirchen (67) 67 J2
Wolschheim (67) 70 C2
Wolschwiller (68) 97 D6
Wolxheim (67) 70 D3
Wormhout (59) 3 J3
Woustviller (57) 68 D3
Wuenheim (68) 97 B1
Wuisse (57) 66 E2
Wulverdinghe (59) 3 G4
Wy-dit-Joli-Village (95) 36 E6
Wylder (59) 3 J3

X

Xaffévillers (88) 94 E2
Xaintrailles (47) 247 H4
Xaintray (79) 161 H4
Xambes (16) 196 D1
Xammes (54) 65 H1
Xamontarupt (88) 95 F6
Xanrey (57) 66 E4
Xanton-Chassenon (85) 160 E4
Xaronval (88) 94 A3
Xermaménil (54) 94 D1
Xertigny (88) 118 D7
Xeuilley (54) 65 K6
Xirocourt (54) 94 A2
Xivray-et-Marvoisin (55) 65 G3
Xivry-Circourt (54) 26 D4
Xocourt (57) 66 C2
Xonrupt-Longemer (88) 95 H6
Xonville (54) 44 C6
Xouaxange (57) 67 J4
Xousse (54) 67 F5
Xures (54) 67 F4

Y

Y (80) 19 H3
Yainville (76) 35 F2
Yaucourt-Bussus (80) 9 H5
Ychoux (40) 245 F2
Ydes (15) 217 H2
Yébleron (76) 14 E5
Yèbles (77) 59 J6
Yenne (73) 207 K2
Yermenonville (28) 85 H1
Yerres (91) 59 F5
Yerville (76) 15 H5
Yèvre-la-Ville (45) 110 E1
Yèvres (28) 84 D6
Yèvres-le-Petit (10) 90 E2
Yffiniac (22) 49 H6
Ygos-Saint-Saturnin (40) 264 E1
Ygrande (03) 168 A4
Ymare (76) 35 J3
Ymeray (28) 85 J2
Ymonville (28) 85 J5
Yolet (15) 235 J1
Yoncq (08) 23 F6
Yonval (80) 9 F5
Youx (63) 184 C3
Yport (76) 14 C4
Ypreville-Biville (76) 14 E4
Yquebeuf (76) 16 B5
Yquelon (50) 30 D6
Yronde-et-Buron (63) 202 E4
Yrouerre (89) 113 K5
Yssac-la-Tourette (63) 185 F6
Yssandon (19) 215 G3
Yssingeaux (43) 220 E4
Ytrac (15) 235 G1
Ytres (62) 11 G5
Yutz (57) 27 G4
Yvecrique (76) 15 H4
Yvernaumont (08) 22 C4
Yversay (86) 162 E2
Yves (17) 176 E4
les Yveteaux (61) 53 K5
Yvetot (76) 15 G5
Yvetot-Bocage (50) 28 D4
Yvias (22) 48 D3
Yviers (16) 212 D2
Yvignac (22) 78 B1
Yville-sur-Seine (76) 35 F2
Yvoire (74) 174 D5
Yvoy-le-Marron (41) 129 K2
Yvrac (33) 229 J1
Yvrac-et-Malleyrand (16) 197 H2
Yvrandes (61) 53 F5
Yvré-le-Pôlin (72) 106 D5

Yvré-l'Évêque (72) 106 E2
Yvrench (80) 9 H4
Yvrencheux (80) 9 H4
Yzengremer (80) 8 D5
Yzernay (49) 143 G3
Yzeron (69) 205 J3
Yzeure (03) 168 E3
Yzeures-sur-Creuse (37) 146 B6
Yzeux (80) 17 K1
Yzosse (40) 264 B4

Z

Zaessingue (68) 97 C4
Zalana (2B) 319 H6
Zarbeling (57) 67 F2
Zegerscappel (59) 3 H3
Zehnacker (67) 70 C2
Zeinheim (67) 70 C2
Zellenberg (68) 71 A6
Zellwiller (67) 70 D5
Zermezeele (59) 3 J4
Zérubia (2A) 323 F1
Zetting (57) 68 E3
Zévaco (2A) 320 E5
Zicavo (2A) 321 F5
Zigliara (2A) 320 E6
Zilia (2B) 318 C3
Zilling (57) 70 A1
Zillisheim (68) 97 B3
Zimmerbach (68) 96 B4
Zimmersheim (68) 97 C3
Zimming (57) 45 J5
Zincourt (88) 94 D4
Zinswiller (67) 69 J5
Zittersheim (67) 69 G5
Zoebersdorf (67) 69 H6
Zommange (57) 67 G3
Zonza (2A) 323 G1
Zoteux (62) 4 D4
Zouafques (62) 2 E4
Zoufftgen (57) 27 G3
Zoza (2A) 323 F2
Zuani (2B) 319 H6
Zudausques (62) 3 F5
Zutkerque (62) 2 E4
Zuydcoote (59) 3 J1
Zuytpeene (59) 3 H4

410